FRENCH PAINTING IN THE TIME OF JEAN DE BERRY

THE LIMBOURGS AND THEIR CONTEMPORARIES

The Franklin Jasper Walls Lectures

Franklin Jasper Walls, who died in 1963, bequeathed his residuary estate to The Pierpont Morgan Library to establish a lecture series in the fine arts, iconography, and archaeology, with the provision that the lectures be ultimately published in book form.

Throughout his life, Mr. Walls was interested in the fine arts and in the study of art history. When the Association of Fellows of The Pierpont Morgan Library was organized in 1949, he became one of the founding members. He was particularly concerned with the Library's lecture program, and served on the Association's Lecture Committee. Without ever revealing his testamentary plans, he followed with keen attention the design and construction of the Library's new Lecture Hall, completed a few months before his death.

Professor Millard Meiss's five illustrated lectures here printed in revised and expanded form are the second series of the Franklin Jasper Walls Lectures to be published.

FRENCH PAINTING IN THE TIME OF JEAN DE BERRY

THE LIMBOURGS AND THEIR CONTEMPORARIES

BY MILLARD MEISS

WITH THE ASSISTANCE OF

SHARON OFF DUNLAP SMITH

AND ELIZABETH HOME BEATSON

TEXT VOLUME

THAMES AND HUDSON · LONDON

THE PIERPONT MORGAN LIBRARY

First published in Great Britain in 1974 by Thames & Hudson Ltd, London

Originally published in the United States by George Braziller Inc., New York in 1974

Typeset by The Stinehour Press, Lunenburg, Vermont

Printed in the USA by The Murray Printing Company, Forge Village, Massachusetts

Bound by Haddon Craftsmen, Scranton, Pennsylvania

ISBN 0 500 23201 6

Contents

Preface

LIKE most titles the one borne by these books is inexact. The Rohan Master, studied in an epilogue, produced his most famous paintings in the decade *after* the Duke of Berry's death. The greatest contemporary of the Limbourgs among illuminators, the Boucicaut Master, often appears in these pages, but he is closely studied only in the preceding volume of the series, which is entirely devoted to him. I think the reader will agree that the present volumes are quite large enough without him. They conclude this history of an extraordinary half-century of French painting and illumination. What had taken shape as a single book during the days when I taught at Harvard grew to its present dimensions, despite other interests, at the Institute for Advanced Study in Princeton. In few other positions would I have attempted—or if attempted, completed—a work of this scope.

Portions of this book were written for the Franklin Jasper Walls Lectures, which I delivered at the Pierpont Morgan Library in March, 1972. For the occasion the Library held a memorable exhibition of French illumination, directed by the Research Fellow for Art, John Plummer, with whom I had the pleasure of working. No scholar could hope to speak in a more sympathetic house, and I feel deeply grateful to its director, Charles Ryskamp, as well as to Dr. Plummer. Dr. Ryskamp and his staff have facilitated in every respect the publication of this book, including the provision of many excellent photographs by Charles Pasella, the photographer of the Library. Dr. Plummer kindly communicated to me, and added to the Catalogue, some interesting observations on the make-up of the *Belles Heures*.

The Library's generous grant in aid of publication has been increased by contributions from the Institute for Advanced Study, arranged by its director, Carl Kaysen, and from Miss Helen Frick, who has thus kindly continued to support to its final stage the progress of this work.

The problem of providing the reader with good reproductions of the hundreds of extant miniatures by the Limbourgs has been met in two ways. This volume includes reproductions of all their miniatures in the *Bible moralisée*, almost all their work in the *Très Riches Heures*, and much of the *Belles Heures*. These illustrations may now be supplemented by two color facsimiles, to which I contributed part of the text. The *Très Riches Heures* was published in 1969 and the *Belles Heures* will appear a few months after the present volume. Both facsimiles reproduce the entire folios in actual size, and the one devoted to the *Très Riches Heures* is especially useful because it gives the visual effect of the full area of *unpainted* vellum that constitutes the borders of many miniatures. This effect cannot be achieved well in a black and white plate, and in fact no black and white photographs were available that included all of these borders. The reader will find the exact dimensions of all the miniatures and borders in a table in the Catalogue of Single Manuscripts.

This study could not have been completed without the continued interest and hospitality of the directors and keepers of many museums and libraries. I acknowledge gratefully the help of Marcel Thomas and François Avril of the Bibliothèque nationale, Raymond Cazelles of the Musée Condé, Chantilly, Jacques Guignard of the Bibliothèque de l'Arsenal, Thomas Hoving and Harvey Stahl of the Metropolitan Museum, Julien Cain of the Musée Jacquemart-André, H.

Hickl-Szabo of the Royal Ontario Museum, Toronto, Michel Laclotte of the Louvre, William Wixom of the Cleveland Museum, William Bond of the Houghton Library, Harvard University, (now, alas, the late) Dorothy Miner of the Walters Art Gallery, and Janet Backhouse of the British Museum.

I wish to thank Gilbert Ouy and two of his colleagues in the study of French humanism, Carla Bozzolo and Gianni Mombello, for helpful conversations. With unfailing generosity Jean-Yves Ribault, director of the Archives du Cher at Bourges, contributed to the clarification of the documents on the Limbourgs and Jean de Berry. M. Jean-Bernard de Vaivre, of the Institut d'histoire des textes, helped to solve two problems of heraldry. The book has benefited especially from the knowledge and judgment of François Avril.

For valuable facts or suggestions I wish to thank André Chastel, Maureen Curnow, Marthe Dulong, Patricia Gathercole, Marie-Madeleine Gauthier, Gerhard Schmidt, Reiner Haussherr, G. I. Lieftinck, James Marrow, Florentine Mütherich, Willibald Sauerländer, Charles Sterling, Charity Willard, Rosalie Green of the Index of Christian Art and her colleagues Adelaide Bennett, Virginia W. Egbert, and Isa Ragusa. I have acknowledged my large indebtedness to two research assistants by including their names on the title page.

I am grateful to the publisher, George Braziller, and to his staff, especially Julianne J. deVere. I thank the house of Joh. Enschedé en Zonen for the care it has given to the production of the plates. It has been a delight to work with Mr. C. Freeman Keith and his colleagues at The Stinehour Press. Finally I express a special word of thanks to Johanna M. Cornelissen for preparing and editing the typescript with her usual great skill.

M. M.

Princeton
December 28, 1972

FRENCH PAINTING IN THE TIME OF JEAN DE BERRY

I

Introduction

WHEN in 1935 I looked over the slide collection at Columbia University after having received an invitation to teach there I found for late medieval manuscripts only the calendar pictures of the *Très Riches Heures*. They were labeled: "Early fifteenth century. Decadent Style." Such an estimate was not uncommon at the time. Many medievalists believed that in the North the centuries after the glorious thirteenth brought only a steady decline. Some historians of the Italian Renaissance, on the other hand, regarded Northern art of the fourteenth and fifteenth centuries as backward and benighted. Indeed, in the grand design of the course of European painting the fifteenth century in the North proved, until recently, an embarrassment; it was caught in the medieval-Renaissance syndrome. In the late nineteenth century Louis Courajod tried to rescue French art around 1400 by identifying realism rather than a revival of antique form as the essential accomplishment of the Renaissance and by claiming, therefore, that this movement began in France.[1]

Even though in the twentieth century Northern art became increasingly attractive, a problem of periodization remained—inevitably, because it was the Italians who formulated our historical categories, and they were ambivalent about the *ultramontani*. The critical tradition was so exclusively peninsular that even Jan van Eyck was at first remembered because some of his panels went to Italy and were praised in the later fifteenth century by a Neapolitan, Fazio, and in the sixteenth century by Vasari. Centuries of silence would not have engulfed the *Très Riches Heures* if, say, the Medici had acquired it.

As it was, when the largest of extant early French panels, the altarpiece by Bellechose from the Chartreuse at Dijon, appeared in Paris in 1849, it was sold as a work of none other than Vasari's nonexistent Simone Memmi (Fig. 608).[2] The awakening of interest in medieval art that had, however, begun earlier with respect to architecture is exemplified by the emergence from oblivion of the *Très Riches Heures*. The Duc d'Aumale, who had been collecting manuscripts, found it in Genoa in 1855, six years after the sale of the "Simone Memmi" in Paris. Two years later the first printed notice and assessment of the manuscript was published by Gustav Waagen, director of the Royal Gallery in Berlin.[3] Waagen, an eminent art historian, indefatigable traveler and recorder of works of art in Great Britain where for a time the Duc d'Aumale resided, had just expounded what with good reason he claimed to be a new idea: "The importance of manuscripts with miniatures in the history of art."[4] He proposed to "illuminate the total night of the arts, from which Johann van Eyck suddenly emerged as a star of the first rank."[5]

About thirty years later, in 1884, the incomparable Léopold Delisle, who had been studying inventories and the history of manuscript collections in France, identified the Duc d'Aumale's Book of Hours with an unfinished manuscript by "Pol et ses freres" inventoried after the death of Jean de Berry. Thus the Limbourgs came upon the stage of the history of art.[6] In 1904 Paul

Durrieu, a convert from political history to medieval illumination, published his fundamental monograph on the manuscript, and in the same year the first exhibition of "primitifs français" ever held opened in Paris, stimulated by the example of the equally novel exhibition of Netherlandish panel paintings held in Belgium two years earlier. The decade immediately following the great Paris show witnessed the publication of an astonishingly large number of studies of the painting, the illumination, and the iconography of the period. These articles and books by Delisle, Durrieu, Laborde, Couderc and Mâle have remained the greatest contribution to the field.[7] After this burst of activity interest in illuminated manuscripts began to lag until after the Second World War.

The poster of the Paris exhibition shows that the new enthusiasm was aroused partly by contemporary trends in the arts (Fig. 17). The elegance and the sinuous linearity of *art nouveau* resemble those tendencies in the early fifteenth century that are commonly indicated by the terms courtly style and "weiche Stil." Looking at the poster of 1904 one understands that Hulin de Loo, the keenest of the critics around 1900, should have preferred, among all the miniatures in the *Très Riches Heures*, the *Coronation of the Virgin* (Fig. 574).[8] The stylistic aspect of the manuscript exemplified by this miniature—in our opinion actually the work of brother Jean—has in fact remained until today the one with which the book as a whole has been identified—so deeply embedded are the categories of the "courtly" and the "weich," and so durable the concept of what may best be called "gothick."[9]

The exhibition of 1904, divided between the Louvre and the Bibliothèque nationale, contained 105 manuscripts of the thirteenth century to *ca.* 1450; of these a remarkably high proportion, 41, were of the period of Jean de Berry.[10] This number rose to 84 in the larger exhibition of 1955, including 24 manuscripts that originally belonged to the Duke.[11] The artists named on the poster of 1904, however, were exclusively painters of panels or perhaps murals, many of them not identifiable with surviving works; none of the important artists around 1400 represented by extant miniatures—Jacquemart, Beauneveu, the Limbourgs, all identified by Delisle—are included, though their manuscripts (or photographs of them) were visible in the exhibition.[12] It was assumed that at this period painting on panels was inherently superior to painting in books. The two kinds of painting, moreover, began to be studied by different groups of scholars, so that there appeared already the professional division which, with one or two exceptions, prevailed until recently. Specialization has had, as always, advantages, but the division of the objects fails to correspond with the circumstances of pictorial production in France at the time. From 1380 to 1420 illumination was deeply affected by more monumental arts; sculptors as well as panel or mural painters, furthermore, undertook illumination and, by so doing, helped to revolutionize it.

As the study of French art of this time was carried forward during the late nineteenth and early twentieth century two synoptic views were advanced that attempted to fill the general critical vacuum. They still influence our estimates today. Louis Courajod, who as we have mentioned asserted that Renaissance style originated in France (especially in sculpture) in the late fourteenth century rather than in Florence in the fifteenth, observed also what seemed an exceptional stylistic uniformity in European art about 1400 and he proposed the now famous term, The International Style.[13] Its wide acceptance demonstrates its relevance, but my study of the period has not diminished my suspicion that the uniformity has seemed greater than it really was because of our ignorance; the study of regional distinctiveness was undertaken relatively late. In other words, to a Westerner all Chinese tend to look alike.

At the end of the First World War the Dutch historian Johan Huizinga published a dramatic and somewhat sentimental book, *The Waning of the Middle Ages*, that presented a very different estimate of the period.[14] Whereas Courajod had pointed to a new art developing in a bourgeois civilization, Huizinga concentrated on what he considered a dying court culture—particularly in Burgundy, but also earlier in France. Though he was not an art historian, and the bibliography in *The Waning* contains few books on art, he set out to elucidate the work of Jan van Eyck by characterizing his cultural environment. In the painting of van Eyck Huizinga saw mostly reflections of feudal extravagance and frivolity. The *Rolin Madonna* has far too much detail, he felt; it is "decadent rather than primitive."[15] Similarly he found the *Adoration of the Magi* in the *Très Riches Heures* "affected and bizarre."[16] As a Dutch republican Huizinga was hostile to all aspects of courtly life, but he failed to recognize that much of the "simple, pure" Italian art he admired was produced at or for courts also. His book, modeled on Burckhardt's *Civilization of the Renaissance* and applying Burckhardt's low estimate of "medieval" art to the fifteenth century in the North, was written to condemn rather than to celebrate Northern culture. Huizinga's text, however, is so learned and so colorful that it continues to be widely read and enjoyed, so that his judgments remain more influential than they deserve to be. His long shadow still fell in 1935 on Columbia University.

Even before the publication of Huizinga's book, however, other scholars, regularly cited in preceding volumes of this publication, undertook the intensive study of early Netherlandish painting and of its origins, especially in metropolitan France. They found some stars in Dr. Waagen's "total night."

Although monographs have been written on the principal painters in the Netherlands, not to mention such contemporary Italian masters as Olivuccio di Cicarello, the Limbourgs have never been comprehensively studied. Instead of appearing by themselves in a separate volume, in accordance with my original intention, they are presented here together with their contemporaries, who provide the stylistic and intellectual context within which they worked and who help us to recognize more fully their exceptional individuality.

As in preceding volumes of this series the principal manuscripts discussed in the text are included in a Catalogue of Manuscripts, which presents information of various kinds often assumed by the text. In the instance of the *Belles Heures* and, still more, the *Très Riches Heures* this information, formidable in its mass, is essential to some of my major conclusions about the chronology and authorship of the manuscripts. The few surviving panels of the period 1400–1420, far more closely studied in the past than the miniatures and lacking an equally intricate context, compose a briefer Catalogue of Panels. Mural painting, of which we possess only sorry remains, adds nothing significant, as far as we can see, to the leading edge of painting in metropolitan France. The same seems true of stained glass. The Catalogue of Workshops in this volume is exceptional because it is cumulative. It is also much fuller than its predecessors in the two preceding volumes.

In this final section of the series we shall continue to confront less the international than the local or regional qualities of French painting, which seem to us far more interesting and historically of much greater importance. Of course the styles created in France were in a sense international; Paris was then the greatest and most cosmopolitan center in Europe. Most, indeed, of the major painters and illuminators who settled there, or in Bourges or Dijon, were born in the Low Countries. To the large group of other foreign artists there we now add a Bohemian. We shall, furthermore, continue to be less concerned with what in French painting is "weich" than "streng." We propose to bring together for the first time illustrations of ancient history, literature, and mythology, a few of them in manuscripts virtually unknown. It is time now to devote more attention to the religious, intellectual and literary environment of the French courts than to their cutlery, dazzling though that undoubtedly was.

II

The Illustration of Secular Literature

DURING the first two decades of the fifteenth century illuminators in Paris produced an unprecedented number of extensively illustrated secular manuscripts; indeed, the renown of the French book of this period derives in significant measure from works of this kind. As comparable manuscripts Italy could not show much more than the Lombard herbals and *tacuina* or the Neapolitan and Venetian versions of ancient history and the Trojan legend.[1] The French secular manuscripts established a tradition that lasted during the fifteenth century and sometimes passed, as we shall see, into the printed book.[2] In preceding volumes of this publication we have considered most of these texts, many of which were new or had not previously been accompanied by large cycles of illustrations. The subjects fall into four main categories: accounts of foreign travels, allegories, histories of the ancient world, and stories of eminent persons, chiefly of antiquity. The first group reflects a greatly increased curiosity about distant lands. The collectors of manuscripts wanted to see what strange people and animals, described by the travelers, looked like, although they knew that the painters themselves had never set foot outside France.[3] For some impressions, to be sure, the painters did not in fact need to move; they could see in Paris many exotic people and things. The zoos, furthermore, contained strange animals, such as Jean de Berry's monkeys, ostrich and camel.[4] Both the reality of the larger world and fantasy about it affected deeply the representation of sacred events in manuscripts such as the *Très Riches Heures.*

Curiosity about the distant in place was accompanied by fascination with the remote in time. The ancient world in particular was the principal subject of a series of texts and illustrations. It had already enjoyed a certain popularity in the thirteenth century, and then about 1340 a new version of the *Histoire ancienne*, based in part on Orosius, was extensively illustrated by a Neapolitan workshop (Fig. 275).[5] Shortly before 1402 the Duke of Berry acquired this manuscript and also a copy of it illustrated in Paris *ca.* 1400 by the Orosius Master and associates (Figs. 274, 275).[6] A few years later another copy was illuminated by a master trained, no doubt, in the southern Netherlands, probably Bruges (Fig. 276).[7] King Charles V had made ancient history and literature more accessible by commissioning numerous translations from Latin into French. Livy and Valerius Maximus proved especially interesting to the early fifteenth century (Fig. 272).[8]

In illustrations at this time of the French translation of St. Augustine's *City of God* the references to the pagan world were often stressed. Both of Boccaccio's historical treatises were translated and, though no Italian precedent existed, extensively illustrated. In the *Cleres femmes* and in the *Cas des nobles hommes et femmes* Boccaccio presented pithy accounts of the destinies of famous men and women, most of them from the ancient world but ranging from Adam and Eve to his own day.[9] Their fate usually exemplifies a moral issue. Morality is less important to the *Cleres femmes* and to the *Decameron*, which, too, was translated and, again without Italian precedent, fully illustrated towards 1415 (Figs. 3, 8, 9, 73, 689).[10]

The vogue of the writings of Boccaccio, of travel books and of histories of the ancient world was accompanied by a declining interest in the great medieval romances and allegories, the Arthurian cycle and the *Roman de la rose*. Two good illuminated manuscripts of Lancelot were produced, but not one of the great allegorical poem.[11] This exclusion is interesting in the light of the fact that *ca.* 1400 the *Roman* became the center of a sharp controversy for its supposed defamation of women. Christine de Pisan, who launched the attack, was an admirer of Boccaccio and of his *Cleres femmes*, just then becoming enormously popular in France. Soon after 1400 she herself wrote an allegory, the *Cité des Dames*, devoted to correcting the prevalent low estimate of her sex. Although she was not a great poet the *Cité des Dames* together with the earlier *Epître d'Othéa* aroused wide interest in France and throughout Europe. She was the one writer of her time, furthermore, who regularly commissioned illustrated copies of her works, so that she occupies a special place in the history of illumination.

1 · CHRISTINE DE PISAN: *LA MUTACION DE FORTUNE*

Christine de Pisan was the child of Italian parents, born in Venice in 1364 and brought to Paris at the age of four by her father, an astrologer, who was called to serve professionally at the court of Charles V.[12] Married at fifteen and soon the mother of three children, Christine was suddenly deprived of a livelihood in the late 'eighties by the death in quick succession of her father and her husband. To support her family she turned, as she tells us in her *Vision*, to letters.[13] She soon became a professional writer, the first of her sex in France and probably in Europe. Beginning with ballads and poems of love, she began to prepare herself for works of larger scope and weightier content by reading the Latin poets as well as more recent authors, above all Boccaccio. To adopt the title of one of her earlier works, she took "le chemin de longue estude."

Christine established herself as a writer in an era when females were universally regarded as inferior to males.[14] The objects of a persistent ambivalence in Christian thought, women were often idealized in religion and in chivalric or poetic sentiment, as Laura by Petrarch, but they were at the same time reviled even by learned men, including Petrarch, and especially by the clergy. They were judged to be unreliable, impure creatures, menacing agents of the devil, from whom they obtained a fearful power that could readily undo a man, just as Delilah undid Samson and Phyllis Aristotle (Fig. 10). They were often considered dull-witted and not even worth instructing in reading and writing. Until the fifteenth century the Church itself held that only men, and not women, were made in the image of God. There was of course no difference of opinion about the indispensability of women for domestic life.

Christine set out, during the early part of her career, to revise these misogynist ideas, which she regarded as unjust masculine myths. She insisted, for instance, that woman too was fashioned in God's image, and in the *Epître d'Othéa* she pointed out that whereas God made man merely from dust, Eve was created from Adam's bone. She defended ardently the dignity and worth of her sex, heaping scorn on its detractors, and around 1400 she attacked as such the *Roman de la rose*, embroiling in the issue all the intellectual circles of Paris, including the humanists Gontier Col and Jean de Montreuil as well as the formidable chancellor of the university, Jean Gerson, who spoke of her as "virilis femina."[15] Though Christine labored passionately for the rights of women she complained bitterly in two of her major works, *La mutacion de Fortune* and *La Cité des Dames*, that she had not been born a man.[16] And of course her concern with the obligations of women to their spouses would not qualify her for the pantheon of her modern feminist descendants.

In the first three years of the century, when Christine began to prepare illustrated copies of her texts for the princes, she seems to have employed illuminators who worked in grisaille. The manuscript of *Le livre de long estude* that she gave to the Duke of Berry on March 20, 1403, was, as the inventory states, "historié de blanc et de noir."[17] What appears to be, as we shall see, the earliest illustrated *Epître d'Othéa* has tinted drawings. For these manuscripts Christine did not employ any of the great Parisian workshops but more modest illuminators, probably because of her limited financial resources. Late in 1403, however, immediately after completing a long poem, the *Mutacion de Fortune*, she engaged a master who not only worked in color but was one of the original and imaginative illuminators in cosmopolitan France. Because of his principal work, which will be discussed shortly, we have called him the Master of the Epître d'Othéa, or briefly the Epître Master.[18] At the end of 1403 Christine asked him to work rapidly on not one but four manuscripts of the poem for presentation to the great princes who were, or might become, her patrons. Though she completed the poem only on November 18, 1403, she was able to offer a well-written copy with six miniatures by the Epître atelier to Philippe le Hardi two months later, in January 1404 (Figs. 12, 21, 25, 29, 33).[19]

The *Mutacion* describes the caprices of Fortune in history, especially in ancient history and in mythology. Ideas of Boethius and of Isidore of Seville are combined with stories from the *Histoire ancienne* and with imagery from the *Ovide moralisé*. Though Christine's fabrication is not a poetical masterpiece the Duke of Burgundy was pleased and forthwith commissioned her to write the well-known life of his brother, King Charles V. The Duke of Berry, who in March 1403 was the recipient of a copy of Christine's account of, as it were, her classical education—*Le livre de long estude*—received his *Mutacion* in March 1404, two months later than Philippe le Hardi (Figs. 14, 19, 23). Two other extant copies (Chantilly 494 and Pierre Berès) were likewise illuminated by the Epître workshop, presumably for other princes or the king. All these manuscripts have the same cycle of miniatures and similar iconography as well as a related redaction of the poem,[20] and they were probably produced within a period of a year or two. There are, nevertheless, signs of a stylistic development within them, as we shall see.

A few years after the first four copies of the *Mutacion* were illuminated by the Epître atelier the workshop of the Cité des Dames Master illustrated two more manuscripts, fr. 603 and Munich gall. 11 (Figs. 11, 13, 15, 16, 27, 28, 31). In fr. 603 the *Mutacion* is combined with another text, the *Livre des fais d'armes et de chevallerie*, which Christine wrote in 1410[21] and which was likewise illustrated by the Cité des Dames workshop (Fig. 11). This workshop probably illuminated the entire manuscript shortly after 1410.[22] Both fr. 603 and the Munich manuscript derive from a revised version of the text of the *Mutacion*,[23] and the Cité des Dames workshop departed somewhat from the compositions and the subjects of the earlier manuscripts, though not clearly at the request of the poet herself.

In the first miniature in all the manuscripts Christine is shown writing her poem (Figs. 12, 13). In the Duke of Burgundy's copy the Epître Master shows both the writer's house, opened in front, and the buildings that rise beyond it, all in the manner of the late fourteenth century, whereas six or seven years afterward the Cité des Dames Master projects an interior alone behind an entrance arch (Figs. 12, 13). Christine, accompanied by her little dog, now works in a more cozy interior, provided even with a plant in the window. This iconographic innovation is bound up with a new conception of light and the continuity of space; through the bars the poetess has a view of sky and landscape.

In her text, which is in part an allegorical autobiography, Christine says she was born in Lombardy; her father was a philosopher, her mother Nature. Nature put her in the service of Fortune, that power which can grant

> choses qui semblent impossibles
> et anientir les possibles. (I, 79–80)

Fortune leads Christine to Hymen, who gives her a husband, children, and ten years of happy family life. When she loses her husband in a storm at sea Fortune transforms her into a man, so that he (she) can steer the ship—of her life and of her career, of course. The ship sails on the sea known as "Grant Péril" to the castle of Fortune, which appears in the second miniature of the manuscripts (Fig. 1).

The earliest manuscripts show the principal portal of the castle of Fortune, where the younger sister of Fortune, Richesse, presides (Figs. 1, 14). She is accompanied by Eur, one of the brothers in this family. Dressed in green, a laurel chaplet on his head, Eur demonstrates his innate affability by extending a hand to the newcomers who arrive by boat. An assistant of the Epître Master, employing the free, rapid brush-stroke so characteristic of the atelier, painted the scene in the Duke of Berry's copy (Fig. 14). We should note in passing that in this manuscript the title of the chapter and the miniature were fitted, very awkwardly, into the space left after the text was written. Since the later manuscripts contain normal titles Berry's text was apparently written before the pattern was established. In the miniature in Chantilly 494 the illuminator arranged essentially the same elements in a more plausible space (Fig. 1). He surrounded Fortune, crowned and dressed in white and gold, with cool, rich colors. His beautiful combination of maroon, blue, blue-green, and yellow-brown, exceptional in the art of the time, recurs in the paintings of the workshop.

The Cité des Dames workshop, undertaking the illustration of the *Mutacion* several years later in fr. 603, selected a different aspect of the text. Though capable of projecting more consistent volumes and space the illuminator attempted paradoxically to represent the more unreal aspects of the vision, which the earlier miniaturists avoided (Fig. 15). The massive building is, according to the text, sustained by four chains. Christine says also that Fortune's castle, to convey the idea of *Mutacion*, revolves constantly, and the illuminator, though unable to portray motion, especially when confronted also with great chains, alluded to it by putting the building on a flat disk of earth. Despite the suspension of the castle above the water it is still accessible to visitors, but in the later miniature in Munich by another illuminator in the workshop the castle hovers above a flame-like crag in fantastic isolation (Fig. 16).[24] Here we may probably observe the consequences of the painter's fascination with landscape and wide space, unrestrained by Christine or by difficulties it creates for the story.

After presenting Fortune's castle all four manuscripts illuminated by the Epître workshop show Fortune herself accompanied by her two brothers, Eur, whom we have already met at the gate, and the far less agreeable Meseur (Figs. 19–22).[25] In accordance with a tradition as old as Boethius and Fulgentius, Fortune is a composite figure, bright and refined on one side, dark and coarse on the other. With one hand she proffers a golden crown, in the other she wields a huge arrow.[26] Her "good" foot is in water, her "bad" one in fire—both unstable elements. Underneath is a large wheel, which Eur spins in one direction, then Meseur in the opposite. Eur, favored by Fortune's crown, holds out a branch of laurel. He is an elegant young nobleman, whereas Meseur is older and ugly, more simply dressed, and provided with a forbidding club.

Christine's text states quite explicitly that Fortune's *right* hand holds a crown, and her *right* foot is in water. By one of the fundamental principles of medieval iconography her "good" side should indeed be her right. When she appears in illustrations in manuscripts of Boethius Fortune's bright side is her right, her dark side is her left.[27] This convention is preserved in two manuscripts—the Duke of Berry's in the Hague and Chantilly 494 (Figs. 19, 20). Surprisingly enough the miniatures in the three other early manuscripts, including Burgundy's, are entirely reversed (Figs. 21, 22). Two of these three manuscripts lack also a symbolical detail present in the other two: on Fortune's ugly side her golden crown turns into a spear-head and a knife.[28] Berry's manuscript and Chantilly 494 are therefore much closer to Christine's imagery, and we can safely conclude that the other four were not made under her close supervision. It is surprising that one of these was destined for Burgundy, to whom she gave it in January 1404, two months after she had completed the text. Apparently Berry's copy, which reached him only in March, was nevertheless illustrated first, or at the very least followed correctly a faithful model.[29] There is another small indication of the early date of Berry's copy. The title, "ci devise la figure de fortune," which appears in the line below the miniature in Chantilly 494 and Burgundy's copy, in Berry's manuscript is (as in the preceding miniature) crowded into the right margin after the writing of the text.

Within the castle of Fortune the throne of St. Peter, "le plus hault siege" as Christine describes it, is occupied by two men (Figs. 23–26). These two tenants, alike in their desire for power though distinguished by red and blue colors, are the pope and anti-pope during the Schism, which Christine bitterly condemns. Below them the thrones formerly occupied by the apostles now have been usurped by evil councillors of all kinds. Once again the miniature in Berry's copy is much more freely painted, and the title was added in the margin at the right. Only in it is the ground plane, rather anomalously, of grass; all the other scenes show a more consistent tile floor. Together with Chantilly 494, as usual neater and duller, the architecture of Berry's manuscript is relatively simple (Figs. 23, 24). The greater complexity of the structure in Burgundy's copy, and the beautiful, elaborate canopy in the Berès manuscript suggest a slightly later date and a somewhat different taste (Figs. 25, 26). The Cité des Dames Master, guided by his Italianate predilections, eliminated entirely this lively, fanciful superstructure (Fig. 27). He emphasized the figures and their orderly arrangement in space; in the Munich manuscript, as in Trecento compositions, there is a front row in which the lay and clerical persons are seen from the back (Fig. 28).

The walls of the hall high in the *donjon* of the castle are covered with paintings, "pourtraictures" as they are called, of the exploits of rulers, good and bad, of the Arts and Sciences and of the worthies of the Old Testament (Figs. 2, 29, 30).[30] The Cité des Dames workshop, striving for a more telling illustration of the episode, elected to show Christine in the hall looking at the pictorial friezes (Fig. 31). The figures, mostly warriors, are large in scale, and the scenes have visible *tituli*. The miniatures, painted in the second decade of the century when the workshop was studying the compositions of the Boucicaut Master, show the hall extending back into space, perpendicular to the picture plane.

The Epître Master, contemplating this text late in 1403, saw in it very different possibilities (Figs. 2, 29, 30). The mural paintings enabled him to distribute freely many small forms of various colors. He gave figures, horses, and buildings simplified, geometric shapes, and he wove these units together into a superb mosaic of color. Indeed below the friezes a dazzling mosaic of geometric shapes composes the tiled floor. In two miniatures the tiles fall into large wheels that seem to spin—a symbolism that may not have been conscious. In any event Christine chose for her *Mutacion* the Parisian artist most capable of conveying transiency.

The Epître Master was able to transmute the subject of the next illustration into similar patterns of shape and color (Figs. 32–34). Rulers, Christine says, have an insatiable thirst for power. History, from ancient times to the present, proves it. To represent armed aggression the Epître Master showed a city besieged—perhaps Babylon attacked by the army of Ninus. The invaders are all mounted knights and the illuminator demonstrates again his remarkable virtuosity in catching horses in every possible position. Again the design attains its greatest complexity in the Berès manuscript (Fig. 34). The scene is full of flashing light and color, and the countless small forms seem to shift before the eye like the varicolored pieces in a kaleidoscope. It is not insignificant that the Cité des Dames workshop avoided this scene entirely, showing instead less numerous and larger figures close by, without much of a setting.

2 · CHRISTINE DE PISAN: *LA CITE DES DAMES*

About a year after finding the Epître Master Christine de Pisan demonstrated a consistency of taste by engaging a second illuminator who had studied Italian painting, though not so closely. She asked him and his assistants to illustrate four manuscripts of her *Cité des Dames*, finished by Easter 1405.[31] This master, taking his name from these commissions, is the one who about 1410 directed the illustration of Christine's collected works for the Queen, including the *Cité des Dames*, which we have discussed in the preceding chapter. A third illuminator, the Egerton Master, who had collaborated with the Epître Master on the illustration of the earlier copy of Christine's writings, received from her *ca.* 1410 the commission to paint a miniature at the beginning of three manuscripts of the *Sept psaumes allegorisées.*[32]

In the *Cité des Dames* Christine set out to extol the contributions of women to civilization, inspired by Boccaccio's *De mulieribus claris*, illustrated French translations of which had just entered the collections of Philippe le Hardi and Jean de Berry (Figs. 3, 6). Christine tells how one night she was tearfully reproaching God for making her a woman rather than a man when suddenly three ladies of "souveraine reverence" appeared before her: *Raison* bearing a mirror, *Droiture* (Rectitude) with a rule, and *Justice* with a measuring vessel (Figs. 35–38). They invite Christine to build a city—a city inspired perhaps by St. Augustine's but with occupancy limited to the virtuous who are also feminine. Christine eagerly joins the enterprise, and the right half of the miniature shows her laying a bed of mortar while *Raison* carefully lowers a stone onto it. Each of the stones represents a heroic feminine deed recounted later in the text. *Raison* wears a dress with a white bodice in the miniature of this scene in all the manuscripts. *Droiture* and *Justice*, when they take the lead in subsequent miniatures, are similarly dressed. Curiously *Raison* wears the same dress in her initial appearance before Christine only in Burgundy's copy (Fig. 37). In Berry's manuscript *Justice* wears it (Fig. 36), and in other more or less early manuscripts, including Harley 4431, the dress of *Raison* as mason does not correspond to any of the Virtues (Fig. 38).[33] She is correctly dressed, therefore, only in Burgundy's copy. These details give us no clear clues for the priority of the manuscripts, and they imply that Christine did not supervise these aspects of even the first illustrations of her text. Queen Isabeau's manuscript, which we know was illuminated after 1410, betrays this later date in its more advanced landscape, but curiously it does not show the dappled sky of Berry's copy but the diapered ground of Burgundy's.

When the city was nearly completed *Droiture* welcomes to it Christine and its foremost inhabitants, the Queen and the Valois duchesses, great ladies of France and her patronesses (Figs. 39–42). In a second ceremony of welcome, royal in a sense also, and illustrated in the third and last miniature in the manuscripts, Christine and *Justice* kneel before a crowned Virgin Mary, Catherine of Alexandria, and other saints (Figs. 43–45). The presence of a host of saints is indicated by a sequence of overlapping haloes, arranged as in the Italian Trecento, particularly in the painting of Ambrogio Lorenzetti.[34] Of the more distant saints only golden arcs are visible, whereas the similarly terraced ladies opposite, though haloless, have the advantage of exhibiting faces, or at least eyes and foreheads.

In the *Cité des Dames* Christine, like Italian humanists, hoped to advance a cause dear to her heart by adducing ancient precedents. In the dialogue in Book I she persuades *Raison* to recount the contribution of women to the culture of antiquity. *Raison* cites wise princesses and ladies accomplished in the arts and crafts; many of them—Ceres, Isis, Minerva and others—had already been praised in the *Epître d'Othéa*. *Raison* adds to this group three ancient female painters. Christine replies sadly that long ago such people were much more highly esteemed than now, but she quickly adds:

> With regard to painting at the present time I know a woman called Anastaise, who is so skillful and experienced in painting the borders of manuscripts and the backgrounds of miniatures (champaignes

> d'ystoires) that no one can cite a craftsman (modern: craftsperson) in the city of Paris, the center of the best illuminators on earth, who in these endeavors surpasses her in any way. . . . And this I know by my own experience, for she has produced some things for me which are held to be outstanding among the ornamental borders of the great masters.[35]

Though Christine's phrase "champaignes d'ystoires" has been read as "landscapes in painted scenes" by an eminent French specialist the scanty evidence that can be educed indicates rather "backgrounds of miniatures," so that Anastaise would have been skilled in these subordinate specialties rather than in the painting of "histoires" themselves.[36]

Christine apparently did not know that the daughter of an outstanding illuminator, Jean le Noir, perhaps identifiable with the Passion Master, was active as "enlumineresse" during the third quarter of the century.[37] Christine was well aware, however, of three painters of her sex who had lived a milennium and a half earlier, in Greece and Rome. She had learned of these ladies—Thamar, Marcia, and Irene—from Boccaccio's treatise on famous women. Boccaccio in turn had read about these three women in a passage in Pliny's *Natural History* that is devoted to female painters. In the manuscript of the French translation of Boccaccio's *Famous Women* received by Philippe le Hardi in January 1403 we see Marcia engaged in painting her own portrait, working with what Boccaccio aptly calls the *consiglio* of a small oval mirror (Fig. 3).

Boccaccio's final words about Marcia reveal the profound changes, mentioned in the preceding chapter, which were taking place in the attitude toward the naked and the nude. Pliny had presented Marcia simply as a painteress, but in Boccaccio's text she becomes notable for a second commitment, as you can see from the text, "vierge perpetuelle." Not wishing anyone to infer, however, that a chaste life was a boon to an artist (an idea that Cennino Cennini, in fact, came close to asserting),[38] Boccaccio immediately referred to a serious limitation it imposed upon the painter. Marcia, he states, often portrayed women but never men. "Modesty was the cause of this, because the ancients mostly figured people nude, so that Marcia would either have had to render men imperfect, or if perfect, she would have been obliged to abandon the modesty of a virgin." Laurent de Premierfait, the French translator, skipped this entire passage. Even in the late fifteenth century in Germany the professional activity of Marcia was rendered less dubious by transforming her into a nun.[39]

Though Petrarch had earlier written a treatise on eminent men, Boccaccio's *De mulieribus claris* was the very first devoted to women, and he speaks of his innovation proudly. He did not abandon the ideal of the modest, submissive and uneducated woman, but he introduced representatives of the sex who were memorable for very different qualities—learned writers, inventors and warriors. Around this time in the North the *neuf preuses* appeared more frequently alongside their male counterparts, and sometimes they were even represented quite alone.[40] We may see the two groups on successive pages of a manuscript of the *Chevalier errant*, a little-known allegorical romance written in French by Thomas de Saluces (Saluzzo) while he was imprisoned near Turin in 1395 (Figs. 47, 48).[41] The Cité des Dames Master and associates, who painted the illustrations about 1404, may have used a tapestry or mural painting as a model, because the Worthies appear in serried array, without the thrones that are described in the text. The Wandering Knight of the romance saw them in a palace near that of Fortune. The illuminator gave the *Preuses* an appearance no less martial than that of the *Preux*, but instinctively he has contrasted the massive building of the men with the light, airy structure of the ladies.[42] The members of the two groups vary somewhat in contemporary art and literature. Every one of the women of Thomas de Saluces, unlike Boccaccio's more modern conception, belong to the ancient world, whereas the nine men are composed of the characteristic triads of three ancient Worthies (Hector, Julius Caesar, Alexander), three Old Testament (Joshua, David, Judas Maccabaeus), and three Christian (Arthur, Charlemagne, and Godefroy de Bouillon).

De mulieribus claris, completed towards 1375, corresponded to, but also promoted, a change in contemporary society. The book enjoyed an immediate success and was followed in the fifteenth century in Italy by two similar works. In 1401 it was translated into French. By 1500 it had not only been printed three times in Italy but also, in translation, in France, Spain, and Germany. Christine's own literary life was certainly facilitated by Boccaccio's treatise. Among the career women included in it were the Sibyls and several writers, including Sappho, lucky in poetry, according to Boccaccio, but unlucky in love. Their example sanctioned Christine's unprecedented career. We will not underestimate the novelty of her life and her work if we recall that in 1521 Pepwell, the English translator of her *Cité des Dames*, said in his prologue that he liked the book but hesitated to print it because of its unconventional estimates of women.[43] Though professional writers like Christine continued to be very rare, in Italy towards 1500 cultivated women such as Isabella d'Este began to play, quite normally, an important role in the intellectual and artistic life of their age.[44] Much has been claimed for the effect of the ancient world (real or fictitious) upon the new forms of life and art at the beginning of modern times, but perhaps not enough has been said about the liberation of the minds—and the hands—of women.

3 · FORTUNA

When Christine de Pisan ascribed the vicissitudes of her life to the intervention of a power called Fortune she associated herself with an interpretation of human destiny that was formulated in antiquity and that, despite challenge and modification, persisted in the Christian era. Indeed Fortuna, the Roman personification of chance in life, is the only ancient goddess who has a long Christian history (Figs. 53, 54).[45] Roman writers such as Seneca sought to limit her vast power by reliance on reason or virtue, and the Church Fathers, above all Augustine, denied her influence and indeed her existence while insisting upon the will of God and of man. In the famous fifth book of the *City of God*, which Augustine devotes to fate, astrology, God and free will, the stoic Hippocrates claims that the similarity of twins must be ascribed to the accident of their birth under one constellation. In an illustration of this book by the Virgil Master about 1410–12, we see Hippocrates laying his hands on a pair of twins and then, at the right, looking up at the stars (Fig. 50). Nigidius the potter disproves his astrological theory by a physical test that simulates successive births under a moving heaven. He made two marks in rapid succession on a spinning wheel, and when the wheel stopped turning the two marks proved to be not close together but far apart. The illuminator could not refrain from adding to the scene the enormously popular image of Fortune and her wheel, though it is not mentioned in the text.[46] In the scene below, the noble figure of the Lord, the ultimate source even of chance events, is contrasted with Fortuna, who rests uneasily upon her globe. In an illustration for the same book by the Master of Berry's Apocalypse about 1408–10, it is the Lord, visible in the upper right corner, who has foreknowledge of the fall of kings, though the ignorant believe that Fortuna with her wheel is in control (Fig. 51). At the sides two men, probably a pre-Christian and a Christian philosopher, discuss the event.

In his *Consolation of Philosophy* Boethius gave Fortuna a new life by making her merely an agent of divine providence. The frontispieces of many manuscripts of his book show Fortune, blindfolded as a sign of impartiality or indifference, turning a large wheel. In a hitherto unidentified miniature by the Boucicaut workshop in Douai the usual four kings are arranged around the wheel, bearing finely curled scrolls inscribed "I rule, I ruled, I am without a kingdom, I will rule" (Fig. 53).[47] As usual the Boucicaut Master has given a traditional composition an exceptional monumentality, based on clear geometric forms and bold rhythms that course from the scrolls through the beautifully disposed figure of the fallen King. Boethius, composing while lying in bed, receives the enviable aid of the three poetical Muses and of Philosophy, who arrives toting the seven books of the liberal arts.[48]

Partly because of the enormous influence of Boethius the wheel of Fortune became one of the most widely diffused images in the fourteenth and fifteenth centuries, appearing in manuscripts of Valerius Maximus (Fig. 52), the *Roman de la rose*,[49] and many other texts.

In the twelfth century Alanus de Insulis, and after him other writers, passed from discussions of Fortune to descriptions of her dwelling, and it was from these predecessors that Christine de Pisan took her conception of the castle of Fortune rising on an island of rock (Figs. 15, 16).[50] In the *Chevalier errant*, illuminated *ca.* 1404, Thomas de Saluces increased the elevation of the dwelling to a height from which the entire world is visible.[51] In the illustrated manuscript of this text to which we have referred above[52] the Cité des Dames Master failed to achieve a suggestive elevation but otherwise he translated the image into paint in a full-page miniature that is more remarkable for its scale and monumentality than its fidelity to the text (Fig. 49). The composition anticipates several by this workshop in the *Dialogues de Pierre Salmon* of 1409.[53] Fortune, winged and bearing the symbols of universal authority including a tiara, is seated on three lions. Below her, on successive stages of the mountain, sit representatives of ecclesiastical and secular power. Most of humanity, excluded from the mountain, seeks Fortune's aid, though not very actively, it must be said, in the miniature. She finally relents and casts down persons from high positions, saying:

> Qui plus hault monte qu'il ne doit
> de plus hault chiet qu'il ne croit.

Envious and "unfortunate" persons below then hack the fallen to pieces.

The description of Fortune's home by Alanus de Insulis was adopted by Jean de Meun in the *Roman de la rose* for Reason's vivid portrait of the realm of the "unstable, changeable, vagabond" lady.[54] An impressive illustration of this passage appears in a remarkable cycle of illustrations of the poem in Valencia datable towards 1425 (Fig. 55).[55] The two aspects of Fortune, which we have seen symbolized as light and dark in Christine's *Mutacion* (Fig. 19), now inform her entire domain. The right side of her house, in which she stands holding a winged wheel, is bright and solid, the left half flimsy and decrepit. Entering it she herself stumbles and ends up seated on the floor. Small birds chitter in the trees at the right; owls, "prophets of evil and messengers of grief," screech at the left, perching in the sparse trees that grow from barren rocks. Two streams flow around the island. Into one, clear and honeylike, people plunge headlong and "shout how much at ease they are." The dark waters of the other, "smelly as a smoking chimney," terrify its bathers. In the foreground, not mentioned by the poem, winged Cupid accompanies the momentarily fortunate while a brutal soldier demonstrates all too clearly the fate of the condemned.

The significance of caprice in human affairs, the source of much reflection in antiquity and the Middle Ages, became a special concern of the early humanists. Petrarch dealt with worldly vicissitudes in his *De remediis utriusque Fortunae* and *De viris illustribus*. When in 1361 he went to Paris as ambassador of the Visconti to King Jean le Bon, who had recently been freed from an English prison, his address at the court ascribed the King's troubles to Fortuna. His remarks disturbed the learned men in the audience, who challenged him afterward at dinner and then in his bedroom.[56] Petrarch's book on the rise and fall of illustrious men inspired Boccaccio to undertake a similar account, *De casibus virorum illustrium*, the last chapter of which deals with King Jean le Bon and his capture by the English.[57] Less philosophical, more dramatic and even more visual than Petrarch's, Boccaccio's book found a wider audience, and Laurent de Premierfait translated it into French in 1409.[58] At the very beginning of his text Boccaccio refers to Fortune,[59] and a manuscript of the *Cas des nobles hommes et femmes* illustrated *ca.* 1415 by the Cité des Dames workshop contains a frontispiece that represents a winged Fortune with her customary symbol (Fig. 54). At the top of the wheel in this instance is an unusual figure. The temporal ruler normal in this place wears a tiara, perhaps an anticlerical sign that refers to the papal events described by Boccaccio in Book IX, chapters 6, 7, and 20.

Whereas much of Boccaccio's treatise bears witness to the power of Fortune, he demonstrates how that may be limited by telling a simple but vivid story.[60] One day Fortune, coming upon a skinny, sallow-faced, bedraggled Poverty, laughed condescendingly at her. Poverty, provoked by this scorn, challenged Fortune to a test of strength. The first illustrator of this contest, the Luçon Master, in the manuscript given to the Duke of Berry in 1411, shows the two figures locked in struggle, much like traditional biblical illustrations of Jacob wrestling with an angel (Figs. 69, 70). Conforming to the elegant canons of the Luçon Master, Poverty shows comparatively little evidence of his state. The illuminator, while designing an attractive miniature, has not followed the text, which characterizes Poverty as a woman, and thus he committed an error that is corrected in all subsequent illustrations.

Before engaging in the struggle Poverty, according to Boccaccio, agreed to be bound in chains if she lost whereas if she won she would ask the supremely confident Fortune to meet one request. To Fortune's surprise and dismay Poverty succeeded in throwing her to the ground and pinning her down with one knee, as we see in illustrations by the Cité des Dames workshop between about 1415 and 1420 (Figs. 71, 72). There Poverty held her until she agreed to keep her word. "I think I would enjoy breaking your wheel," Poverty says, "and returning you to a private life. . . . I wish on my own to remove the means of your power from you, and I command that you fasten Misfortune to a stake in public. . . . You can send *Good* Fortune where you want. . . ."[61]

Thus Poverty became a *mulier clara.* Only she could assure good fortune, or at least freedom from bad fortune and the certainty of worldly losses. A view of this kind had recently been reinforced for Boccaccio by the bankruptcy of his father's business, the Black Death, and the social and political upheaval in his native Tuscany in the years preceding the writing of *De casibus.* He now aligned himself with the original Franciscans, whose patron saint had taken Poverty as his bride.

Despite the vividness of Boccaccio's story, the painters who illustrated it were guided also, naturally enough, by their own inclinations and by the conventions of the art of their time. The Cité des Dames Master envisaged the contestants as equally noble, perhaps because he grasped Boccaccio's point and also because of his Italianate predilection for idealized figures. For the Rohan workshop, with its usual dour outlook, Poverty, though a heroine, is emaciated and bedraggled, and her victory is not implied, although her antagonist scarcely enjoys a much more robust physique (Fig. 65). Both Poverty and Misfortune wear tattered clothes, and the grim face of the latter peers out between a mass of unkempt hair. What in these early fifteenth-century miniatures had been a wrestling match became in 1494 a polite encounter between a well-dressed lady out for a stroll with her friends and a slightly disrespectful beggar (Fig. 68).[62] Indications of a surprising victory and of its consequences have disappeared altogether.

Visual images could not readily convey the subtle distinctions in Christian thought between chance, free will and divine foreknowledge. The early Fathers had, in fact, argued that Fortune is only a convenient fiction, that she does not really exist, or that she is at most the lever of God's intentions. Coluccio Salutati, a friend as we shall see of Jean de Montreuil, distinguished between the "essential character" of divine providence and "the winding and turning of mundane affairs."[63] In this period the image of Fortuna and her wheel became enormously popular, in part no doubt just because of the ambiguity of its significance. While Ripa included Fortuna in his iconological manual, he referred to the extravagant claims of her power advanced by the ignorant and he insisted that, as Thomas Aquinas said, it is Divine Providence that arranges everything.

The goddess, who has so large a role in Boccaccio's *De casibus*, suddenly appeared before him as he approached the end of his work (Fig. 66).[64] "The horrible monster, administrator of all mortal affairs," he writes, "had a hundred hands and arms, a dress of many colors, a voice like rough iron." She tells him that the story of her defeat by Poverty that he had written earlier was untrue, only a joke. "You think," she continues, "Fortune is inexorable, indiscreet, and blind. This is the way you paint me on the walls of your buildings." Then Boccaccio's visitor proves that she can recognize literary accomplishment by promising him that, if he completes his text, he will be numbered among the "nobles hommes."

In the end, then, a humanized Fortune became for Boccaccio less of a menace than she had seemed at the beginning, and certainly less of a frightening force than she had been throughout the Middle Ages. Personifications of her in the Renaissance reflect this change (Fig. 67). Fortuna reacquires the noble humanity of the ancient goddess. In one notable respect, however, she became different. She was basically transformed by the Renaissance conviction that gods and goddesses wore no clothes.

III

Antiquity in Early Fifteenth-Century Paris

1 · FRENCH HUMANISM

In our account of secular illumination and of the circle of Christine de Pisan we have mentioned several scholars who were discussed in a preceding volume on the patronage of Jean de Berry.[1] Some of them, like Nicolas de Clamanges, Jean de Montreuil, and Gontier Col, were humanists in the same sense as their Italian colleagues; others, like Jean Courtecuisse and Jean Gerson, were theologians with strong humanist interests. Nicolas de Gonesse was professor at the University of Paris. They all admired and studied the writing of their Italian predecessors, especially Petrarch and Boccaccio, and they shared with them an enthusiasm for ancient literature. Half a century ago Sabbadini pointed to their importance, and in 1949 Franco Simone devoted some valuable chapters to them,[2] but they have been studied even less closely than the illuminators of their time. During the last decade, however, a group of younger scholars, inspired initially by Professor Simone, has been preparing editions of their work, tracing their public life, examining their influence, and reconstructing their libraries.[3] Many new letters and writings have been discovered, including a paraphrase by Nicolas de Clamanges of Virgil's *Georgics*.[4]

As imaginative writers the French humanists of the first two decades of the fifteenth century lack distinction, and as Latin stylists they did not equal their great Italian contemporary, Coluccio Salutati. Nevertheless, Salutati admired Nicolas de Clamanges and he bestowed high praise on Jean de Montreuil, considering him a man of outstanding eloquence. He sent him copies of his work and even invited him to correct it.

The French humanists composed a group that was unique in Europe outside of Italy, and the significance of their work for the collectors of manuscripts and for illumination has not been adequately recognized. They themselves did not launch the humanist movement in France; in a sense it had begun earlier with the presence of Petrarch at Avignon and of a few minor Italian followers at the curia.[5] Petrarch visited Paris in 1360, where he was welcomed by Bersuire, translator of Livy and author of the *Ovidius moralizatus*.[6] Present also was another friend of Petrarch, Philippe de Vitry, who in a treatise of *ca.* 1320 became the first musician to characterize the music of his time as "modern"—*ars nova*, he called it.[7]

In Paris the *studia humaniora* were centered in the Collège de Navarre. Almost all the humanists studied or taught there; one of its great professors, Pierre d'Ailly, taught both Gerson and Clamanges. Most of these men, like their Italian colleagues, held ecclesiastical positions. One, Jean de Montreuil, was provost of Lille. Jean Muret and Nicolas de Clamanges worked at the papal court.[8] Jean Gerson was chancellor of the University of Paris. Several of the humanists served at the same time, or even exclusively, as secretaries of the king and the princes, so that their rhetoric had, as in Florence, political significance. Gontier Col, Jean Lebègue, and Jean de Montreuil were secretaries of Charles VI and also, at various times, of Jean de Berry. Ambrogio de' Migli, a

Lombard friend of Valentina Visconti, wife of Louis d'Orléans, became the secretary of this duke.[9] Writing to Gontier Col, Jean de Montreuil congratulated him on his position with Jean de Berry, the most indulgent of princes, he said, who would give him the freedom he needed for his studies.[10] When Laurent de Premierfait was translating the *Decameron* he described himself as secretary of the same prince.[11]

The theme of political liberty that had concerned and united the Florentine humanists as chancellors of a republic held little interest for the French humanists. They were professionally occupied with the relations of their kingdom to the Papacy and the Empire, and they developed a national rather than a municipal sense of identity. Although they admired Petrarch beyond every other modern writer they bitterly condemned his view that orators and poets were not to be found outside Italy. They vigorously maintained the reality of a *translatio studii* from Rome to Paris. They asserted that the transfer to the North began when Charlemagne launched his revival in the ninth century.[12] Charles V had greatly intensified the cult of this French king and founder of the Holy Roman Empire,[13] and Jean de Montreuil included a detailed account of Charlemagne's life in two letters.[14] The Emperor is prominent in the art and illumination of our period (Fig. 407). The French humanists of the early fifteenth century pointed with pride to the continuous interest of their scholarly predecessors in the great ancient writers—an interest that was, in fact, greater in France than in Italy. Though the past thus seemed to them respectable the future appeared decidedly bright. Jean de Montreuil spoke of a return of the *saecula aurea*, and Nicolas de Clamanges became the first humanist in Europe to apply to the movement not the similes of night to day or dark to light employed by the Italians but the idea of a rebirth—*eloquentia renata*.[15] Since Philippe de Vitry had already used the concept of *ars nova* for the new polyphony in French music of his time, the group of French followers of Petrarch and Boccaccio not only assimilated their self-consciousness about innovations in the arts but they made new contributions to the growth of historiography.

The incomparable model for the new eloquence was, as in Italy, Cicero, whom Jean Lebègue, another Parisian humanist, considered almost sacred.[16] Clamanges studied the famous manuscript of Cicero at Cluny before Poggio, during the Council of Constance, sent it to Italy—perhaps Poggio found the manuscript in the hands of Clamanges.[17] The French scholar collected hundreds of variants of Cicero in the hope of establishing a more authentic text, and he extensively annotated Virgil.[18] Under Virgilian influence Gerson had *ca.* 1382 written a *pastorium carmen*, and in 1394 Clamanges composed a true eclogue, in hexameters and arcadian in subject and mood.[19]

Gontier Col visited Florence in 1396. Jean de Montreuil, who had been at Arezzo in 1384, corresponded regularly with Salutati, employing the latter's correct classical form of address, "tu" instead of the medieval "voi."[20] Like Clamanges, he constantly sought the works of ancient authors, and he wrote with great excitement of manuscripts he received from Italy of Vitruvius, Cato, and Varro. Addressing an unnamed patron he promised to have these texts copied, and it can now be said that the copy exists, in the Biblioteca Laurenziana, with a frontispiece by the Virgil Master—the earliest known illuminated copy of Vitruvius (Fig. 58).[21] In his eagerness to read new texts Montreuil accused Gontier Col of selfishly keeping too long a letter of Cicero.[22] He corresponded with Ambrogio dei Migli, claiming that Virgil was superior to Ovid, and he discussed with Laurent de Premierfait the poetry of Clamanges.[23] During the second decade of the century both Clamanges and Jean de Montreuil learned the new humanist script.[24]

In 1403 Jean de Montreuil addressed a letter on papal policy to Benedict XIII in which he cited Roman authors, especially Terence, more frequently than Christian. This practice stirred objections, especially in the royal chancellery.[25] Around this time the relationship between pagan and Christian authors seemed more problematic, as it had earlier in Italy. Even in his sermons Gerson normally quoted a long series of Roman writers, including Terence, Virgil, and Ovid.[26] He pointed to the fact that all great Christian writers—Jerome, Augustine, Bernard—read the ancient texts. About 1405 another humanist theologian, Nicolas de Gonesse, confronted the issue in a defense of poetry, inspired by the writing of Petrarch and Boccaccio, and similar to the latter's essay in his *Genealogia*.[27] Jean de Montreuil was criticized by a certain Laurentius, probably Laurent de Premierfait, for having displayed the Laws of Lycurgus on the façade of his house.[28] Montreuil, in turn, accused Ambrogio dei Migli of atheism. Ambrogio, frightened by the violent written attack and concerned lest it should trouble Louis d'Orléans, whom he was serving as secretary, suddenly underwent "conversion."[29] These polemics are symptoms of the new fascination with Greco-Roman antiquity rather than evidence of any real atheistic convictions.

The humanists communicated their enthusiasm for ancient literature to their patrons. Scholars who worked in the chancelleries of the king and the princes, and who often accompanied their patrons on political missions, had ample opportunity to exhort them to study the classics, demonstrating that ancient rulers normally had this kind of intellectual and moral preparation.[30] Gerson, writing to the Dauphin's tutor, recommended a series of ancient writers, including Valerius Maximus, Sallust, Livy, and Suetonius.[31] The scholars built small libraries, which are only today being reconstructed. Gontier Col, Jean de Berry's secretary, possessed some volumes that were closely related to contemporary illumination. He owned one of the very few copies then in France of Boccaccio's *Genealogia deorum*, a text which Christine de Pisan, as we shall see, apparently knew and which influenced the iconography of illustrations of her *Epître*.[32] Col possessed also Boccaccio's *De casibus* and a well-known copy of Laurent de Premierfait's French translation, illuminated by the Cité des Dames workshop.[33]

The Roman authors were more accessible to the king and the princes in the vernacular. For Jean le Bon Bersuire turned Livy into French, and Charles V continued with a long series of translations. Nicolas de Gonesse completed the translation of Valerius Maximus for Jean de Berry,[34] and the first of numerous illustrated copies went to the Duke (Fig. 414).[35] For Louis II Duke of Bourbon Laurent de Premierfait translated Cicero's *De senectute* in 1405; the frontispiece of an early copy of the text shows Laurent presenting his book to the Duke (Fig. 57).[36] Premierfait then turned from the Roman orator to a Florentine humanist, and completed in 1409 a translation of Boccaccio's *De casibus virorum illustrium*, which he dedicated to Jean de Berry, whose secretary he then was. The *Cas des nobles hommes et femmes* enjoyed immediately and for many years an unparalleled success (Figs. 66, 69, 159).[37] Premierfait then undertook the *Decameron*, which he completed in June, 1414 (Figs. 8, 9, 689).[38]

Although none of the French humanists attained the stature of Petrarch, Boccaccio or Salutati in philological and historical study, not to mention poetry and imaginative writing, they launched a serious movement for the recovery of antiquity—the only one at the time outside Italy. They lived much farther from the center of the ancient Roman world but they recognized it as a period in time and, like their Italian colleagues, felt a nostalgia for it.[39] "Redeant saecula quae aurea vocabantur," wrote Jean de Montreuil.[40] The impetus these scholars gave to classical studies was destined to diminish abruptly, however, as a consequence of the upheaval in France. Three humanists, Gontier Col, Jean de Montreuil and Laurent de Premierfait, were killed by Burgundian partisans during the seizure of Paris in 1418. Pierre d'Ailly died in 1420, Jean Courtecuisse in 1423, and Jean Gerson in 1429. Only Nicolas de Clamanges lived on—not, it seems, very active—until 1437.[41] The threads were picked up again in the second half of the century, but it is symptomatic that after the eclogue of Clamanges none was written until the period of Francis I.[42]

Though the French humanists of the early fifteenth century studied and sought to emulate the Latin style of Cicero, Virgil, and Terence they seem to have had little understanding of the formal—as distinct from the historical and symbolical—aspects of ancient art. In this respect they did not, however, differ essentially from their Italian colleagues.[43] The French said virtually nothing about ancient objects,[44] although we shall quote below the remarks of Raoul de Praelles about Roman amphitheaters.[45] Jean de Montreuil praised a statue of the Madonna at the abbey of Chaalis, writing that one might have thought it had been made by Praxiteles or Lysippus—an observation that reveals both the prestige accorded ancient art and the distance of the writer from it.[46]

Jean de Montreuil and his fellow humanists were nevertheless ultimately responsible for an unprecedented wave of illustration of ancient history and mythology. Although the *Histoire ancienne* and the *Ovide moralisé* had been illuminated in the fourteenth century, for many subjects the modern tradition of pictorial representation began in early fifteenth-century France. It has been said that these images were merely "mirrors" of contemporary chivalry,[47] and that they were entirely unrelated both to ancient models and to the representations derived from them in the second half of the Quattrocento.[48] Antiquity was, of course, always understood to some degree in terms of contemporary civilization. The gods and goddesses wore contemporary dress not only in French illumination of 1400 to 1415 but in Italian painting past the middle of the fifteenth century—indeed the dress there was often French in origin (Fig. 158).[49] More important, French painters, before their Italian successors, occasionally endowed ancient myth and history with an appropriate emotional depth, transferring to these subjects the qualities of contemporary religious art (Figs. 62, 91, 122, 270).

The chapters that follow, moreover, reveal that some continuity can be observed between the new French mythological representations and the subsequent ones in Italy—a continuity not clearly based on the transmission of the image but upon the use of the same literary sources. Some of the French cycles, too, imply an awareness of the special, non-medieval character of ancient subjects, and the illuminators chosen to represent them were often close to Italian Trecento painting. The art of the Italian "proto-Renaissance," in other words, was quite rightly felt to be closer to antiquity than was Northern Gothic. One French cycle proves even to have adopted some of the fundamental peculiarities of a much earlier—and ultimately ancient—model. These more venturesome trends in France have remained much less well known than examples of the "International Style." Historians have not differentiated, furthermore, between artistic events in Paris before its fall to the English and those of Burgundy after the court moved north to Bruges and to Lille. The significance of these and the preceding observations will, we hope, become clear in the consideration of the illustration of specific texts that follows.

2 · L'EPITRE D'OTHEA

The *Epître d'Othéa* was Christine's first major work, and it proved to be her most popular. Over forty manuscripts of the fifteenth century alone have been identified.[50] The text was printed in Paris in 1499–1500, and by 1550 it was translated into English no less than three times.[51] Some part of this exceptional interest must be ascribed to the illustrations. More than any other text by Christine the *Epître* was designed for miniatures. There is one for each of the hundred chapters, and in the two most important early manuscripts several miniatures near the beginning of the text follow special rubrics that describe the representations. When planning an illustrated manuscript of this kind Christine probably had in mind the related *De mulieribus claris* of Boccaccio, which during the same period, *ca.* 1400–1403, was being translated into French; copies presented in 1403 and 1404 to the Dukes of Burgundy and Berry contain a similar cycle of miniatures, one for each chapter (Figs. 3, 6, 73, 74).[52]

In the *Epître d'Othéa* a goddess bearing this strange name undertakes to instruct the youthful Hector of Troy, whom Christine may have identified with her own young son. Morality was the primary purpose of the education, and the first division or "texte" of each of the hundred chapters offers a precept. It is striking that these precepts were drawn not from religious texts but from ancient mythology or the story of Troy. Thus Christine gave her readers a large, succinct compendium of classical history and legend, based primarily on the *Histoire ancienne*, which we have discussed above, and the *Ovide moralisé*, which will concern us shortly.[53] The Trojan legend occupies a prominent place in the *Epître*, and indeed the first printed edition of 1499 was entitled "Les cent histoires de Troye." This story, popular everywhere since antiquity, had a special meaning for those peoples who, like the French, claimed descent from Trojan leaders. Indeed in the dedication of the principal manuscripts of the *Epître* Christine described Louis d'Orléans as "d'estoc troyan ancianne noblece."

The moral precept given in the first part of each chapter of the *Epître* is developed in the second part or *Glose*, and the third or *Allegorie* reveals the Christian meaning of the ancient figure or story.[54] Ancient myth and history are fulfilled in the Era of Grace. Some of the interpretations seem consistent with the inherent character of the myth. A mild Jupiter dispensing balm instead of thunderbolts readily becomes God giving grace (Fig. 76), and the eloquence of Mercury resembles that of Christ (Fig. 146). Other subjects, however, such as Apollo surprising the sleeping lovers Mars and Venus, present greater difficulties. The pious knight, the text says, should not overstay his time. On the other hand Perseus, according to the *Glose*, is the good knight who rescues a woman in distress (Fig. 91). The *Allegorie* identifies Andromeda as his soul, delivered from the devil, and Pegasus as his angel, who will intercede for him at the Judgment. Interpretations of this kind, which appear strange to us, are not peculiar to Christine and her time. They continued to be offered, though less frequently, in the concordances of the Renaissance.

The miniatures of the *Epître* illustrate the quatrain that constitutes the *texte* or first part of each chapter, and in these quatrains near the beginning of the book the ancient gods play a prominent part (Figs. 75, 76, 146). Each of the gods contributes a virtue. Saturn, for instance, who is "slow and heavy," teaches Hector to reflect and to form judgments cautiously (Fig. 75). In the earliest surviving manuscripts that contain the full cycle of illustrations, Bibl. nat. fr. 606 acquired *ca.* 1408 by the Duke of Berry and the somewhat later Harley 4431 made for Queen Isabeau de Bavière, seven miniatures devoted to the planetary gods are preceded by special rubrics that describe the representation. No one can doubt that Christine herself composed these rubrics. About Saturn she said:

> Saturnus est planette tardive et pesant et se peut segnefier en aucun cas a sagesse . . . et pour ce est il pourtrait comme un ancien homme . . . il est figure assis sur sept cercles, et a terre dessoubz lui avocas et sages hommes qui parlent de sagesse ensemble. Il tient une faucille pour ce que celle planette fu nommee d'un sage roy qui ot nom Saturnus qui trouva la maniere de soyer les blez des faucilles. (Harley 4431, fol. 100)

Now part of this description, like many of Christine's on the ancient deities, was taken from the moralized Ovid. This popular text characterizes Saturn as wise, the discoverer of the sickle, and it even adds that paintings show him holding it:

> Est il en ces paintures poins
> Tenans la faucille en deux poins. (Bk. I, 699)

The *Ovide moralisé*, to which Christine referred simply as "la fable," is a long French poem of the early fourteenth century. It represented a late phase of the medieval endeavor to discover behind the literal sense of Ovid's ever-magnetic *Metamorphoses* an allegorical and Christian meaning.[55] As Panofsky said, the poem and similar texts transform the *Transformations*.[56] In a copy of the *Ovide moralisé* datable about 1385 that belonged to the Duke of Berry[57] a highly unclassical Saturn appears between stands of grain, weighed down by two enormous sickles (Fig. 78). In a second copy of the text that was in the library of Jean de Berry by 1402 and that may have been painted a very few years before this date[58] the figure of Saturn seems scarcely more classical, but he is now, as Ovid and antiquity conceived him, the ruler of the universe in the Golden Age (Fig. 80). He holds a scythe entwined by the dragon of Time, and in his other hand he grasps one of his children, whom he prepares to devour. At his sides stand four of his children, Juno, Jupiter, Neptune, and Pluto. Jupiter, who succeeded Saturn as universal ruler, cut off the genitals of his father and threw them into the sea. From them, as we see in the miniature, Venus is born. This representation of Saturn conforms less with the French verse Ovid that accompanies the miniature, where the dragon biting its tail is not mentioned, than with the description in a Latin prose version written *ca.* 1340 by Pierre Bersuire, a French friend of Petrarch as we have seen, upon whose knowledge of the pagan gods he drew.[59]

Though Berry's second copy of the moralized Ovid was painted hardly fifteen years later than the first, the great stylistic difference between the two measures the rapid change that occurred in France in the last twenty years of the fourteenth century (Figs. 78, 80). The miniature in Lyon reflects the Boqueteaux style that spread from Paris over much of northern France. Though the second copy has attracted little attention, it represents a new, much more pictorial style that, I believe, originated in the Netherlands (Fig. 5).[60] The forms are rendered in washes of pale yellow, green, rose, violet and gray, heightened by extensive touches of opaque white. A closely related painter illuminated in the early fifteenth century the beautiful *Histoire ancienne* in the British Museum (Fig. 84).[61] The style, mingled with Rhenish elements, is carried into the second decade of the century in a *Grandes Chroniques*, Sloane 2433 in the British Museum (Fig. 83).[62]

Though Saturn in Berry's later Ovid has become more substantial and more effective than in the Lyon miniature he has a childlike simplicity characteristic of this group of Netherlandish paintings. Despite his larger size he shows little of that "prerogative d'aucune grace" that Christine, following the euhemerist interpretation, ascribed to the gods.[63] Saturn in the *Epître d'Othéa*, however, has clearly become a commanding figure (Fig. 75). Seated erect, his large beard divided formally into two parts, he points forcefully to the wise men below. He grips the sickle firmly and holds it quite vertical. His gestures are echoed by broad movements in his great cloak; at its left edge it forms a sort of sickle to balance the higher one on the right.

Of course Saturn lacks the antique attribute of nudity,[64] but he is a powerful, imposing ruler. Does he fit the conception of "Gothic" exemplified by the miniature in Lyon or in fr. 373? Is he a representative of the "Courtly Style"? Often our accepted terminology fails to illuminate, or even distorts, what is before us. In some basic respects Christine's Saturn is less like the god as we see him in manuscripts of the *Ovide moralisé* or in a manuscript of the *Epître* made for Duke Philip of Burgundy in 1461 (Fig. 81)[65] than in early Renaissance representations, where he is also clothed (Figs. 82, 88).[66] This fact may be explained by Christine's familiarity with Italian and French humanism, and by the painter's familiarity with Trecento painting. To these relationships we shall return later.

One large aspect of the miniature of Saturn in the *Epître* does not, however, derive from Trecento art—no model at least exists. Below the god, according to Christine's rubric, "avocas et sages hommes" talk. The planets thus "influence" men, as Christine said in her first rubric in which she describes them. Mercury, she said, grants "beau lengage," the eloquence so highly prized by the humanists. Since rhetoric and good style bring riches, Mercury has a full purse (Fig. 146).[67] Christine naturally hoped to be one of his "children." In the miniature the god holds the flower of eloquence.

The very old belief in the power of the planets was an essential tenet of the profession of her father, who was one of the numerous astrologers responsible for the revival of this pseudo-science in the fourteenth century. The first known representations of the planets and their so-called children belong to that period.[68] In these compositions the different effects of the seven planets, or rather their different kinds of children, are shown in single compartments, as in an Arabic manuscript of the fourteenth century (Fig. 77). The early Quattrocento frescoes in the Salone in Padua still preserve this scheme.[69] What is novel in the *Epître d'Othéa*, as Panofsky and Saxl pointed out many years ago,[70] is the reduction in the number and variety of the children and the grouping of them in a single space below the god who reigns in heaven. The elevation of the god on a sort of rainbow was, to be sure, undertaken in a slightly earlier miniature of Jupiter in the Duke of Berry's moralized Ovid (Fig. 79).[71] The general design in the *Epître*, however, seems to reflect earlier Christian representations, such as Pentecost, or Boethius as the source of music (Fig. 90).[72] Whatever its antecedents, the *Epître d'Othéa* is the earliest known example of a design for the *Planetenkinderbild* that became standard in the fifteenth century in the North and in the early Renaissance (Fig. 88).

In Christine's comprehensive rubric for the seven planets she says that since they revolve around the circles that are called zodiacs they sit on circles and are portrayed in the starry heaven above the clouds.[73] In the charming miniature for Venus the elegant goddess in the sky affects lovers, who offer her their hearts (Fig. 87). Though slender-waisted she has an ample lap for them, and it already contains a sizeable collection.

This miniature, or a copy of it, was perhaps the source of a unique representation painted on the lid of an Italian cake-box dated 1421 and preserved in the Louvre (Fig. 89). Around the rim runs an inscription that reads: "Let him who wishes to live happily behold this person to whom Cupid ("amore") and the other gods are subject 1421"—ample testimony of the power of an image![74] If Venus has power over the gods, how much greater is her effect on mere men! On the clouds sits the goddess, perfectly frontal as in the *Epître*, dressed "alla franzese" and holding out on opposite sides a bow and an arrow, which are clasped by two symmetrically arranged cupids. In a flowery meadow below, instead of the planet's children, three young women sing and make music. Their number suggests they represent the Three Graces.[75] Many years ago I published this painting as the earliest work of the Sienese master Giovanni di Paolo, preceding by five years his first dated work. In subsequent monographs Pope-Hennessy and Brandi, observing that the style varies from that of Giovanni's *Madonna* dated 1426, deeply influenced by Taddeo di Bartolo, tentatively ascribed the cake-box to Lombardy or to Florence.[76] They cited, however, no very similar works and the painting still suggests to me, if not Giovanni di Paolo, a Sienese work by a follower of Paolo di Giovanni Fei. In any event the cake-box, like the later fifteenth-century Italian representations of the Planets' Children (Fig. 88), bears witness to the diffusion of French pictorial forms in Italy. In Italy, too, figures from ancient history and mythology, like Christine's Venus, were dressed in the height of contemporary fashion (Fig. 158).

The non-planetary gods and goddesses in the *Epître*, lacking "children," instead perform the actions for which mankind venerates them. Isis, displaying a technique she learned in Egypt, grafts a scion to the trunk of an old tree (Fig. 85). Deeper in the space a completed graft is visible, and three trunks, already prepared, await their turn. The text refers only briefly to grafting; the illuminator, on his own or under Christine's direction, devised this full demonstration. Philip of Burgundy's copy of the *Epître* shows Isis as a Flemish lady in her garden, identifiable as a goddess only by her wings and by the huge size of the trees she plants (Fig. 86).

The new technique introduced by Ceres is demonstrated in fr. 606 with equal care and vividness (Fig. 85). The goddess, who taught the Greeks to plow, hovers conveniently above the field and sows seed into the newly turned furrows. The plow stands nearby, in the shadow of a stand of magnificent grain, far superior, as the story tells, to the produce of untilled ground. The field in the miniature, prolonged by perspective and variation of value, is impressively deep. It resembles the tessellated floors introduced just about the same time by the Boucicaut Master.[77]

The uniformity of style maintained in all the miniatures in the *Epître d'Othéa* implies supervision by one illuminator, but he himself executed, I believe, only about a dozen miniatures. He designed and partly painted some others, including *Ceres* and *Isis* (Figs. 85, 122), and he left the rest to four assistants, to whom we shall refer below. The first miniature in the manuscript that seems to me entirely by the Epître Master is the scene of Perseus battling the sea-monster to free Andromeda (Fig. 91). Only fifteen or twenty years earlier the struggle had been depicted in the Duke of Berry's Ovid now in Lyon (Fig. 92). The two representations seem a world apart. In the *Epître* the beautiful Andromeda pleads, the monster has become huge and truly frightening, while Perseus flies in over the water on Pegasus, soaring on two splendid and remarkably functional wings. The horse rears as it draws close, Perseus balances his sword for the blow, and the fine coordination of the two explains and makes possible the impending victory. Though there are conspicuous un-antique elements, such as the chain armor on both warrior and horse, the scene captures some of the excitement and drama of the ancient myth. The Epître Master, taking a significant step, has infused it with the emotion of contemporary religious painting.

This representation by the Epître Master is historically important not only for its novel drama but also for its iconography. It holds, indeed, a significant place in the tradition of the representation of the subject—a tradition that has not, despite its interest, been closely studied. In the *Metamorphoses* Ovid gave the story much the same form as other ancient writers.[78] Perseus, son of Danaë and Jove, flew to Ethiopia on miraculous wings fixed to his feet. There he saw a beautiful maiden, Andromeda, bound by her arms to a cliff. When she overcame her shyness she explained to him that she was doomed to pay the penalty of her mother's pride. "While she was yet speaking there came a loud sound from the sea, and there, advancing over the broad expanse, a monstrous creature loomed up, breasting the wide waves." Perseus flew high, plunged on the monster from above, and after a tremendous battle stabbed it to death.

In ancient art the rescue of Andromeda was represented in two different ways, both lacking the drama of Ovid's story. One, exemplified by a splendid relief in the Capitoline Museum, is a scene of ceremonial release in which Andromeda, assisted by her liberator, gracefully steps down from the cliff (Fig. 95).[79] The other type, favored in Campanian murals, shows Andromeda bound to the cliff while Perseus, brandishing Medusa's head, flies down to attack the monster as it looms up below (Fig. 94).[80] In accordance with almost all ancient descriptions the maiden wears bridal robes, a transparent chiton covering the upper part of her body.[81]

Christine's main source for the *Epître*, the verse *Ovide moralisé*, in general follows Ovid's account, telling how Perseus tied his two wings to his feet ("En ses piez lia ses deus cles") and flew to the maiden bound to the rocks. Here, however, the poem departs curiously from ancient models by referring, three times, to Andromeda's nudity.[82] The reason for this surprising change is not clear; perhaps the poet took Ovid's description of her as looking like "a marble statue" to refer to a *nude* statue. It seems possible also that the author of the *Ovide* was familiar with Andromeda as she appeared in astrological representations, where the illustrators, not understanding the transparent chiton, painted her nude with at most some ringlets on her arms (Fig. 100).[83]

The miniature by the Epître Master departs from the *Ovide moralisé* not only by dressing Andromeda but by putting Perseus on Pegasus. The former conforms with the ancient tradition but the latter decidedly does not.[84] In the French poem, in Ovid's *Metamorphoses* as well as in all other ancient sources Perseus is carried aloft by the wings bound to his feet. In the illustration in the late fourteenth-century French manuscript of the verse *Ovide moralisé*, Perseus descends on the monster without benefit of Mercury's winged feet but without Pegasus either (Fig. 92). When clothing Andromeda the Epître Master may have followed Christine's verbal instructions but not her text, which is silent on the maiden's appearance. The text does state, however, that Perseus flew to the rescue on Pegasus: ". . . . chevaucha par lair en volant." What induced Christine to abandon her usual source? Probably the *Ovidius moralizatus*, written from about 1330 to 1350 by Pierre Bersuire, who says that Perseus flew to Ethiopia on Pegasus and there encountered Andromeda.[85] About the same time in Italy Boccaccio, in his *De genealogiis deorum*, allows the reader to understand that Perseus went to the aid of Andromeda in the same way.[86] The mounted Perseus appeared in France not only in Bersuire's Latin text[87] but in the prose version of the *Ovide moralisé* written in the third quarter of the fifteenth century.[88]

The image of Perseus on Pegasus, which had attracted Christine and her painter, appealed equally to Renaissance artists, in France as well as in Italy. It was widely disseminated especially by woodcuts used and reused as illustrations of printed versions of the Latin *Metamorphoses* (Fig. 93).[89] Though it had no ancient sanction whatever it survived long after the "rediscovery" of the ancient world, appearing even in the painting by Annibale Carracci and Domenichino in the Palazzo Farnese (Fig. 97).[90] In this representation as in many others there is a conspicuous redundancy: Perseus as well as Pegasus is winged. In his fresco of 1500 in Orvieto Signorelli gave wings to the helmet and sandals of Perseus but, amazingly enough, withheld them from Pegasus (Fig. 99).

In its conception of the figures and the intensity of their confrontation the miniature by the Epître Master is far closer to Signorelli's fresco of 1500 (Fig. 99) or even to Bernard Salomon's engraving of 1557 (Fig. 93) than to the miniature in the late fourteenth-century Ovid (Fig. 92). This advanced character is not maintained in the Netherlands half a century later in Philip the Good's copy of the *Epître* (Fig. 101). The Epître Master very probably lacked a pictorial model—no related medieval representation of the myth is known to exist. The mode of his scene, the space, and the articulation of the figures certainly derive from Trecento painting.

The illuminator was probably guided by a portrayal of the corresponding Christian legend, St. George freeing the princess, as in the miniature by the Master of the Codex of St. George (Fig. 96). Figures in other miniatures in the *Epître*, such as the imposing Cupid receiving a heart from a pair of lovers (Fig. 106), and *Atropos*, which we shall consider shortly, likewise imply Trecento canons, and they all resemble later Italian imagery more closely than earlier Northern.

In the sixteenth century some artists returned to the ancient tradition of Perseus flying with winged feet (Fig. 98), but many of them, Titian included, departed from that tradition in one significant respect.[91] Andromeda does not wear bridal clothes but is quite nude (Fig. 97).[92] Whereas in the Middle Ages and even well into the Quattrocento nudity signified evil or at least vulgarity, thereafter it became a symbol of the Greco-Roman ideal of beauty, as we have seen in the representation of Fortuna (Fig. 67). The nude Andromeda is thus more Roman than the Romans.

In the *Epître d'Othéa* the gods and goddesses naturally wear clothes, and they doff them only when demanded by the story, as Diana bathing, surprised by Actaeon (Fig. 102). The goddess is not immersed in a "pool girt with grassy banks," as Ovid describes it (III, 161), but in a tub that continued to be represented in the early Renaissance (Fig. 103). In the Duke of Berry's *Ovide moralisé* of *ca.* 1400 horned Pan can be nude (Fig. 104), and in the *Epître* four men bathing in a pond (Fig. 105). These men are rustics, however, and wicked to boot, because they are the remnants of the men who tried to keep poor Latona from drinking clean water. This desperate Titaness, soon to give birth to Jupiter's children, Apollo and Diana, had been driven by jealous Juno to Lycia. Arriving exhausted and seeking to quench her thirst, she was forced to change the hostile Lycians into frogs. Whereas in his miniature the Epître Master showed that Latona's magical power was giving her clean water Tintoretto, painting this rare subject, concentrated on the transformation of one rustic into a huge, rather pathetic frog (Fig. 107). He took the liberty of adding the infant Apollo and Diana as a means of increasing contrast in his condensed and dramatic composition. The emotional content of ancient myths, adumbrated in a few miniatures in the *Epître* such as *Perseus and Andromeda* and *Tisiphone* (Figs. 91, 122), was communicated more powerfully in Italian art of the later fifteenth century. In Tintoretto the pathos is greater than in ancient representations themselves.

Christine described Daphne, the personification of the laurel, only as a "demoiselle" (Fig. 108). Depictions of her transformation in manuscripts of the verse *Ovide moralisé* of the fourteenth century show a human head set into an otherwise quite normal tree.[93] For the nymph the Epître Master, perhaps at Christine's suggestion, made a fascinating choice. He probably employed, as Stechow showed,[94] a figure of Mandragora in those illustrations of Rhabanus Maurus which preserve the nudity of ancient mythological figures (Fig. 109). The Epître Master's figure seems to be the first nude Daphne in post-classical art, and one of the first to capture the idea of metamorphosis. The change proceeds, in fact, in unprecedented manner, involving the head as well as the arms. The human body was more fully preserved in a North Italian representation a few years earlier where only the arms of the clothed nymph have changed (Fig. 110). In the later Renaissance, as in antiquity, the integrity of the human form was more completely preserved by limiting the transformation to peripheral members—fingers, toes, or hair.

The unprecedented illustration by the Epître Master is strangely impressive. The dense, waving branches with their over-size leaves attached to the soft, smooth, white body create a mysterious, pathetic effect. The red-faced sun-god breaks off some leaves. This action derives from the medieval reading of the myth. Essential was the preservation of Daphne's chastity, and therefore Diana's transformation of her into a tree was a great victory. Christine, familiar with laurel crowns, says that Apollo plucks laurel leaves as signs of his triumph. In Ovid, however, the god adopted the laurel tree as a symbol of his love, undying despite his loss.

The composition created by the Epître Master, probably at the suggestion of Christine, persisted in the North for a century, though not, I believe we can agree, in improved versions (Fig. 111).[95] Greater realism of detail makes the unnatural combination appear merely preposterous. The illustration of 1461 by the workshop of Loyset Liédet for Duke Philip the Good[96] demonstrates that Burgundian culture of the second half of the century liked its mythology thoroughly domesticated, with scarcely a hint of an utterly different, admirable, long-lost civilization (Fig. 112).

A mythological figure who plies her craft more constantly then Ceres and Isis is Atropos (Fig. 62). The Epître Master himself certainly painted the memorable figure in the sky, but perhaps not her victims below. Christine's description, written next to the miniature, is brief:

> Ayes a toute heure regard
> A Atropos et a son dart
> Qui fiert et nespargne nul ame . . .
> Les poetes appellerent la mort Atropos. . . .

In the miniature a swarthy woman in a dun dress brandishes large arrows, her unkempt brown hair falling over her bare shoulder. Her décolletage exposes a bony frame and a sagging breast. Atropos soars on a soft yet dark cloud, which spreads in a menacing way over the beautiful limpid blue sky. Beneath her blows a bishop and a king are laid low, two noblemen tumble, and a pope is about to fall. The action unfolds from left to right in a regular, rational, Italianate manner. The rhythmical movement is accompanied by a flow of beautiful pale colors, culminating in the white and clear scarlet of the pope—Death's largest and most important victim.

With vigor and skill the cloud-borne woman exercises her fateful power. Her action as well as her attributes associate her more with the traditional representation of Death than of Atropos. In Roman art Atropos, an idealized personification, often reads her fateful words from a rotulus. In conformity with ideas held in antiquity and in the Middle Ages about death, Christine's Atropos strikes, not the weak and the aged, but the young and the powerful, especially kings, bishops, popes.[97] The painter has given to these victims, despite their high station, little of the strength with which he has endowed the embodiment of their fate. Atropos may be unkempt but she is determined, and she aims one arrow at the pope while keeping three others in reserve in her left hand. She moves indeed within an extraordinary geometric design. The lowering cloud sustains her and introduces a balancing diagonal. The bundle of darts provides an orderly focus of force as well as a promise of continued effective action. The pendant breast is one of the most conspicuous verticals in a mobile field, seeming to acquire, therefore, a special though uncertain significance.

The idea of Death's preference for the strong rather than the weak had been dramatically represented during the preceding century in the fresco of the *Triumph of Death* in the Camposanto in Pisa, painted by Francesco Traini,[98] and it was communicated in 1361 by a relief, little known, in the Museo di S. Martino in Naples (Fig. 115). In the relief the victim tries, like a good burgher, to buy his freedom. The personification of death here assumes the skeletal form that had become conventional in the Trecento and that persisted in the art of later centuries.[99] *Mors* is a skeleton in the Giottesque allegory of chastity in the lower church at Assisi and in several representations of the "Triumph of Death."[100] Similarly, it is a skeleton that hurls a lance at a nobleman in a French miniature that entered the Duke of Berry's collection shortly after the *Epître d'Othéa*.[101]

Very few personifications of death in the late Middle Ages depart from this skeletal image, which communicates the Christian insistence upon the corruptibility of the body. One is the famous old woman in black who, wielding a scythe, flies to the attack in Traini's fresco in the

Camposanto (Fig. 113). Her finger- and toe-nails have grown to the size of predacious talons.[102] Death is conceived as an old woman also by Guillaume de Deguilleville in his *Pèlerinage de vie humaine*, composed in 1330–1331 and revised in 1355.[103] The menacing figure comes to the bedside of the pilgrim, bearing a scythe and a coffin.[104] Illustrations of this passage conform with the text, except that the woman is not tall (Fig. 121). Like Atropos, she is entirely human, without even the avian talons of the flying figure in Pisa. There, however, the similarity ends, for "la vieille," her head bound in a kerchief, looks like a crabbed ancient grave-keeper.

Atropos on the other hand is neither very old nor bent. On the contrary, with her high forehead and regular features, she has a spirited and even noble bearing. Indeed, the drawing, the structure, the pattern of drapery folds, and the large geometric design all suggest a Trecento model, though I cannot point to it. The personification of death as a dignified human being rather than a grinning skeleton seems to reflect ancient ideas, ideas that were studied by the early Italian humanists and their followers in the circle of Christine de Pisan in Paris. Though the skeleton was sometimes represented in antiquity as a *memento mori*,[105] in personifications the Greeks and Romans affirmed the value of life even in—indeed, especially in—death. Thanatos was a handsome, winged young man (Fig. 116), and the Fates were rendered no less ideal than other women.

Among the Romans *Mors* assumed a female form. Horace said she flies on black wings.[106] According to Cicero, Boccaccio wrote, she was the daughter of Night. Boccaccio described the terrible figure in his *De genealogiis deorum*, on which he worked during the third quarter of the fourteenth century. Mors, he said, is given other names, the first of which is Atropos.[107] When Christine referred to the "poets" who stated this fact, she probably had Boccaccio in mind; copies of his treatise were in fact owned by two French scholars whom Christine knew.[108] Petrarch's *Trionfi*, written at approximately the same time as the *Genealogiae*, singles out "pontefici, regnanti, e 'mperadori" as the victims of Death, who is a furious woman wrapped in a black dress:

> ed una donna involta in veste negra.
> Con un furor, qual io non so se mai
> al tempo de' giganti fosse a Flegra,
> si mosse. . . .[109]

The two pictorial representations of Death that approximate these ancient conceptions revived by Boccaccio and Petrarch are the fresco in Pisa and the miniature in the *Epître d'Othéa*. Traini's *Morte*, probably painted somewhat earlier than the composition of the two relevant texts,[110] corresponds with Petrarch's image of a woman in black, whereas the Epître Master's Atropos conforms with the literary tradition more closely insofar as she is completely a woman.

The figure of Atropos, so unusual and so compelling, is distinguished by one attribute that appears to be unique. A common connotation of a bared breast—mercy—can scarcely be intended here. Does the pendant shape, together with the rather prominent ribs, indicate age? Remembering Death's *furor*, emphasized especially by Petrarch, and keeping in mind the long, disheveled hair of our figure, we may ask whether to Atropos-Mors are added attributes of a Fury. In antiquity the Furies were in fact represented with a bared breast and long, wild hair (Fig. 117),[111] and they were given these attributes by Orosius (I, 15), whose history formed the basis of the *Histoire ancienne*. Though the Furies have little place in medieval art they appear, nude and tearing their breasts, in illustrations of Canto IX of Dante's *Commedia.*[112] It is interesting that the Fury Tisiphone is represented in fr. 606, seven folios before Atropos (Fig. 122). The miniature tells a story that Christine had in large part taken from the *Ovide moralisé.* Standing possessively at the gate of the palace of King Athamas, the forceful and dramatic Fury releases a pair of serpents that drive him mad. His wife Ino already lies dead, and he kills his two children. The Epître Master's Tisiphone is a kind of sister of his Atropos, a more furious sister, we might say, darker and wilder. Her brown dress, however, seems to show no sign of a similar décolleté though we are left uncertain because of her averted position.

The proximity of Tisiphone in the manuscript of the *Epître* would of course not be relevant if the Trecento model of Atropos that we have tentatively inferred showed all the attributes of the figure by the Epître Master. In such circumstances another image would not be relevant either, though it appears in a poem that Christine knew very well. In a gruesome passage in the *Roman de la rose* devoted to the Three Fates, Atropos, who cuts the thread of life, throws corpses to Cerberus and, to satisfy his insatiable appetite, suckles him also (Fig. 118).[113] She offers him three breasts, one for each of his heads. The feeding is thus perfectly economical, but only as a consequence of a gross anatomical anomaly.

The miniature by the Epître Master, together with the entire cycle in fr. 606, was copied shortly afterward in a manuscript illuminated for the Queen of France by the Cité des Dames workshop (Fig. 114).[114] One would have expected that these two miniatures, the earliest illustrations of Christine's chapter on Atropos, would have established a pictorial tradition. On the contrary, it was abandoned in some of the best illustrations in the later fifteenth century. They regressed, so to speak, from the mythological figure to the widely diffused Christian image of the skeleton (Figs. 120, 123).[115] A similar abandonment of the classical personification occurred even in the illustration of Petrarch's *Triumphus mortis*, one of the probable sources, we have seen, of Christine's figure. This part of Petrarch's poem, like the cycle as a whole, began to be illustrated in Italy about the middle of the fifteenth century. The representations appeared in manuscripts of the text as well as in paintings independent of it. Some depictions of the *Triumph of Death*, especially the earliest (Fig. 126), do show a woman in a dark dress, her hair streaming out behind her. She is not entirely, however, a living woman; her head is hollow-eyed and skeletal. Petrarch's "donna involta in veste negra" was not, to be sure, forgotten in later art, and in his *Iconologia* Ripa described Morte as a "donna pallida . . . vestita di nero, secondo il parlar dei Poeti. . . ." After the figures by Traini and the Epître Master, however, this personification yielded to the image of the body partly decayed or reduced entirely to bones.[116] Even followers of the great antiquarian, Mantegna, preferred the skeleton (Fig. 125).[117]

In the *Roman de la rose*, too, the ubiquitous skeleton sometimes supplanted the three-breasted Atropos described in the poem (Fig. 119). Brandishing spears above a victim, the skeleton accompanies the verses devoted to the Three Fates, but it is more closely related to the rubric above it:

O chascun le deffende fort
Contre Atropos ce est la mort.[118]

The skeleton took precedence over images of Atropos or Death as a woman in other contexts as well. In the seventeenth century Bernini established it firmly in the history of the tomb.[119] In the early sixteenth century in France and the Netherlands, however, there was one peculiar and interesting innovation, which Müntz and d'Essling noticed long ago.[120] In cycles of Triumphs derived from Petrarch and accompanied by inscriptions taken from various sources, the Three Fates replaced the skeleton. The Sisters or Atropos alone sometimes ride in the usual chariot drawn by bulls or they may, in accordance with the sequence of Petrarch's poem, conquer Chastity (*Mors vincit pudicitiam*). Chastity even may, in medieval fashion, lie underfoot (Fig. 124).[121]

The *Epître d'Othéa* was published in Paris in 1499, shortly before the appearance of this series of representations, but the woodcut for the chapter on Atropos showed no figure of Fate. She has been replaced by a skeleton (Fig. 120), in conformity with the general preference of the time and the later fifteenth-century illustration of this chapter (Fig. 123). Such "regressions" only highlight the little triumph of restoration brought about by early French humanism, Christine, and the Epître Master. Recognition of this restoration of the classical tradition is due whether she or her painter invented the image of Mors-Atropos or whether they found it in the new repertory of late Trecento painting.

Whereas most of the miniatures in the *Epître* reflect ancient images and stories transmitted by Trecento painting or Italian and French mythographic texts, one illustration displays an entirely untraditional conception. It is the first miniature illustrating the main body of the text, and it shows Temperance as a sort of soaring goddess, like her "sister" Othéa or Prudence in the preceding miniature (Fig. 127). Temperance puts her hands on the wheels of a large clock. Five women seated below probably symbolize various aspects of the virtue, as in late fifteenth-century representations,[122] and in position they resemble the groups of people influenced by the planets in the following miniatures. As Lynn White has shown,[123] during the late thirteenth and fourteenth centuries Temperance steadily ascended, so to speak, the ladder of the virtues, until she reached the level of Sapientia, the highest of moral and intellectual qualities. In the earlier Middle Ages the moderation of Temperance had been visualized by the pouring of water into wine, but just after the middle of the fourteenth century in Italy measure rather than moderation began to be stressed. In Orcagna's relief in Or San Michele Temperance holds a pair of compasses.[124] In the *Allegory of Good Government* in the Town Hall, Siena, she measures again, not space but time, by displaying a sandglass.[125]

Meanwhile a new instrument for temporal measurement had appeared: the marvelous mechanical clock. This device, which counted the passing hours and described the turning of the celestial bodies, "suddenly, towards the middle of the fourteenth century, seized the imagination of our ancestors."[126] It excited not only burghers and capitalists, to whom time meant money, but princes and royalty as well. King Charles V introduced monumental clocks to Paris and Jean de Berry to Bourges. The most elaborate and the most famous instrument of this kind in the fourteenth century was a celestial sphere or *astrarium* completed in 1364 by Giovanni Dondi in Padua. Its fame reached Paris; indeed it was first described in detail in 1393 by Philippe de Mezières in his *Songe du vieil pelerin*.[127] Its builder was the same Giovanni Dondi who wrote so enthusiastically about ancient art and architecture after a visit to Rome.

> Few of the works of art produced by the ancient geniuses have been preserved; but those which have survived somewhere are eagerly looked for and inspected by sensitive persons and command high prices. And if you compare to them what is produced nowadays, it will be evident that their authors were superior in natural genius and more knowing in the application of their art. When carefully observing ancient buildings, statues, reliefs, and the like, the artists of our time are amazed. . . .[128]

It is interesting to observe that whereas Dondi felt certain of the superiority of the ancients over the moderns in art, a good friend of his, after revisiting Dondi's clock, thought the reverse was true in technology.

> I saw again the globe-clock . . . to me it is a magnificent work, a work of divine speculation, a work unattainable by human genius and never produced in generations past; although Cicero tells how Posidonius had constructed a sphere which revolved, showing, through the sun, moon and five planets, what happens in the heavens at night and during the day. I do not believe that there was such competency in art at that time, nor was there such mastery of skill as is shown in this.[129]

Human artifacts as well as natural phenomena can become symbols of religious or cosmic ideas. Just as the stained glass window, once devised, served to convey the idea of the Incarnation,[130] the marvelous new mechanical clock became a metaphor of the universe. According to Oresme, the great physicist at the court of Charles V, the cosmic clock was created and set running by God so that "all the wheels move as harmoniously as possible."[131] Thomas de Pisan, the astrologer, was professionally concerned with timepieces, especially with those intricate mechanisms that measured the movements of heavenly bodies. It is therefore not surprising that in a text written by his daughter, which furthermore expounds the effects of the planets upon men, there should appear some of the earliest known representations of mechanical clocks. An example is depicted in fr. 848, a copy of the *Epître* that, on textual and palaeographical grounds, has been dated before fr. 606 (Fig. 129).[132] Here Temperance stands on the floor, touching a clock set on a corbel. The illuminator, though working in a conservative linear style, has described the wheels, weights, and escapement with considerable care and precision.

It is a very interesting fact that the text of this manuscript contains no reference whatever to a clock. That may be found only in the somewhat later manuscripts of the *Epître* such as fr. 606 that embody Christine's revisions—in other words the second redaction of the text.[133] There, in the rubric preceding the miniature of Temperance, Christine says that the human body, which is composed of diverse parts, needs to be regulated by reason, and it can therefore be represented by a clock, which has several wheels and controls.[134] This rubric gave the illuminator his subject. What, however, brought the clock into fr. 848? Certainly explicit instructions of Christine, who perhaps wrote this manuscript herself and certainly supervised its illustration.[135] She formulated the analogy, in other words, after writing the text of fr. 848 but before she gave instructions to the illuminator. She incorporated the explanation of the new iconography in her text when, shortly afterward, she revised the *Epître* and added the long descriptive rubrics before several miniatures of which we have spoken above.

Earlier in the fourteenth century the clock caught the imagination of a great German mystic. About 1334 Heinrich Suso wrote a popular devotional treatise under the title *Horologium sapientiae*.

Christ demonstrated the nature of this book, Suso wrote, when he showed to its author a beautiful clock, with excellent wheels and bells sweetly ringing.

> . . . a pleu a la doulceur et pitie de nostre sauveur Jhesucrist demonstrer par raison espirituelle la façon et la valeur de cest livre a cellui qui le compassa quant il lui monstra un reloge ou orloge de tres noble et tres belle fourme, dont les roez estoient excellentes, les cloches doulcement sonnans. Et par la diverse et soubtive façon de lui tout cuer humain se merveilloit et s'esjoissoit en regardant y cellui.[136]

Suso did not press the analogy, and probably for this reason as well as the general lack of excitement about the clock until the later fourteenth century the early illustrations of the text do not appear to include the new instrument.[137]

Suso's text was translated into French in 1389, and whereas one early fifteenth-century copy of this *Horologe de sapience* has a large frontispiece that does not show a clock (Fig. 130)[138] a timepiece is prominent in another copy that forms part of a manuscript given to Marie, daughter of Jean de Berry, by her confessor in 1406 (Fig. 131). Here Sapience-Attrempance, descending from the Trinity and from heaven, demonstrates a large golden clock to Suso, a Dominican friar. The Franciscan translator stands apart at the right. Though the illuminator, the Luçon Master, has shown the face of the clock and the Epître Master in fr. 606 the back (Fig. 127), the two machines are remarkably similar. They have similar bases and proportions and a prominent bell and clapper above the works. The two miniatures were painted at just about the same time, and one illuminator may have seen the work of the other, or they both may have had in mind the same actual timepiece. In one respect the illustrations conform more fully with Suso's text than with Christine's, because he alone speaks of the sweet sounds of bells. It is true, however, that the bells and clappers prominent in the miniatures crown many, though not all, early representations of clocks (Figs. 128, 132).

Most miniatures in the *Epître* that we have hitherto considered contain only a few figures; they celebrate a god, a goddess, or a virtue, who is accompanied by smaller persons affected by them. There are many scenes, however, of a very different kind, illustrating an episode in the struggle for Troy. Now I must confess to an ineradicable allergy to pictures of battles. The study of the illustrations of Bibles, chronicles and histories is highly irritating because of the innumerable and utterly boring scenes of armies on the move or, worse still, tangled in mortal combat. Still, a few painters at certain moments in history made something exciting and even noble of such unpromising subjects: Paolo Uccello, for instance, Piero della Francesca, Leonardo, Rubens, and Poussin. The Epître Master, working on a far smaller scale, succeeded in his own way.

The six battle miniatures in fr. 606 that I believe the Epître Master painted himself even anticipate, in some respects, Paolo Uccello—Uccello on the scale of the Urbino predella or the Ashmolean *Hunt* (Fig. 696) rather than the very large battle panels. In the scene of the burning of the fortress of Ilion and the capture of the city of Thune (Tunis or Carthage?) a unified perspective and consistent diminution are of course lacking, and the event at the left is rendered in smaller scale than the one at the right, probably to differentiate two historical episodes that are represented within one frame (Fig. 61). The painter has, however, effectively created two streams of parallel movement into space. All the forms are simplified and raised to an astonishing level of abstraction. The geometricity of most forms is emphasized by contrast with a few free, irregular ones. Fixed shapes give way here and there to mobile ones, such as the brown flag and the legs of the black and gray horses. Color too is reduced to a limited number of hues: white, black, light red and blue, deep clear red and, as in Piero della Francesca, buffers of gray and brown. Whereas the color at the right appears in repeated geometric units, at the left the red flames flow rapidly and freely over the dimly seen fortress of Ilion.

In episodes where there is no confrontation the scene is scarcely less spirited and dashing. King Laomedon of Troy comes out of the city with his troops to oppose Hercules and his men, who had sailed in to the attack, only to find the ships empty (Fig. 133). Meanwhile Greeks under Telamon, who had been hiding nearby, move upon the unprotected city. The moral of the story, certainly well exemplified, is: Don't be too trustful, especially of your enemies. Greeks had been concealed behind bushes with the long palm-like leaves the illuminator favors, and the two armies are effectively contrasted in color and value despite some confusion at the left in direction. Characteristically the Epître Master, seeking geometric uniformities, has given Telamon's ladder a form very similar to the roofs above, and the ships bulge and curl like the horses on the shore near them.

These miniatures of the Trojan story resemble in the excellence of their design and execution the miniatures of Perseus and Andromeda, Latona, and Atropos, which seem entirely from the brush of the chief illuminator. Other paintings in the manuscript appear to have been designed by him but largely executed by assistants who were thoroughly trained in his style. We have seen several collaborative efforts of this kind: *Saturn* (Fig. 75), *Venus* (Fig. 87), *Jupiter* (Fig. 76), and *Diana and Actaeon* (Fig. 102). This large category contains also such miniatures as *Fortune*, in which the "deesse," though gigantic, sways from the effort of spinning the wheel and its comparatively light cargo (Fig. 149). The turning planes of her face continue below the tight bandage, creating an unusual effect of unseeing eyes. In another miniature Queen Ino orders that seed-corn be boiled before it is planted; a peasant then sows it, uselessly of course (Fig. 134). The moral of this unusual representation is that rationality is lost on those who cannot understand it.[139]

In addition to the miniatures by assistants of the Epître Master, two of whom are identifiable,[140] there are paintings by two other illuminators working in quite different styles. One, the Egerton Master, painted the last, or one-hundredth miniature, the *Aracoeli* (Fig. 400).[141] A second illuminator may be called the Saffron Master because of the abundance of a yellow of this kind in his work. His style, though weaker, resembles that of an assistant of the Master of Berry's *Cleres femmes* who worked on the Duke's Bible in the Arsenal.[142] The Saffron Master, who was responsible for more than ten miniatures, painted the charming scene of dawn on a farm, the cock crowing, birds beginning to feed, and a peasant coming out of his house to welcome the rising sun (Fig. 138). The rural scene anticipates, in a modest way, the calendar pictures in the *Très Riches Heures*.

In this miniature Aurora brings the golden orb into view, though both are partly dimmed by the clouds that streak across the sky.[143] Christine retells the touching myth in modified form. Aurora lost her son "Cycnus" (Memnon in antiquity) to the spear of Achilles, and she transformed him into the first of all swans. Two white birds, presumably swans, fly up at the center of the miniature. When Aurora's time comes to move into the sky—when the morning star shines, according to her main source, the *Ovide moralisé*[144]—she gives light to the world while within herself she weeps over her great loss.

> En signe de sa grant tristesce
> Fu li cieulz couvers de nublesce.[145]

The miniatures of the Duke of Berry's copy of the *Epître d'Othéa* constitute an important cycle in the history of Western iconography. Christine designed it to include many more illustrations of ancient myths than the *Ovide moralisé*, one of her chief models. Even in the instance of those illustrations that depend in part on Trecento models, the combination of the attentive, learned authoress and the imaginative painter produced an exceptional result. No comparable text was written elsewhere in Europe, and in Italy the related treatises, such as Boccaccio's, to which we shall turn shortly, were given only frontispieces or no illustrations at all. The *Epître* thus frequently led the illuminators to represent subjects that painters in Italy did not touch until the late fifteenth century. No early manuscript of the *Epître*, such as fr. 606, is known to have gone to Italy. The miniatures in this manuscript, however, are in fundamental respects much closer to late Quattrocentro mythological paintings than to the illustrations of this same text executed at that time in the Netherlands. No wonder that studies of the heritage of classical history and myth commonly give a prominent place to the miniatures in Christine's text.

In the nineteenth century several students of manuscripts, including Léopold Delisle, commented on the close relationship of four manuscripts in the Bibliothèque nationale that contain the earlier writings of Christine—fr. 835, 606, 836, and 605 (unillustrated). In 1886 Maurice Roy argued that these manuscripts composed a collected edition, which was acquired by Jean de Berry and described in his inventory of 1413.[146] The texts are numbered consecutively from 1 to 25 in the four manuscripts, in the order given above. Size, layout, script, and initials are quite similar, so that the thesis of Roy has recently been regarded as very probable. The remaining clouds of doubt can, I think, be dissipated entirely by two facts. First, the dedication of some texts to Louis d'Orléans rather than to Jean de Berry poses no problem whatever in the light of our recent demonstration that Berry acquired the collection in 1408 or early 1409, after the assassination of Orléans in 1407.[147] Berry thus proved once again that he would forego flattering dedications for an outstanding cycle of miniatures. Since the latest text in the collection is of October, 1405,[148] the manuscript was illuminated between that date and its receipt by Jean de Berry in 1408–1409. The second important reason for the conclusion that the manuscripts were planned as a series is the fact, in our opinion absolutely clear, that the masters who illuminated fr. 606 also produced 835 and 836.[149]

The Epître Master supervised the work, designed many miniatures and himself painted a few. More were executed by the assistant thoroughly trained in his style. The fact that the single known instance of the collaboration of the Epître Master with the Egerton workshop occurs in fr. 835, 606, 836 links them tightly together. They are no doubt the product of one campaign that might have extended over two or even three years.[150]

The nature of the intervention of the Egerton workshop is interesting. The master painted the last miniature of six in fr. 835, the last of one hundred in fr. 606, and, with an assistant, the last eight of eighteen in fr. 836. Apparently the agreement with the Epître Master gave this workshop a definite but secondary share. Some of the Egerton miniatures show the strong color characteristic of this workshop; to this group belongs the scene of Christine riding out with companions to visit her daughter in the royal abbey at Poissy (Fig. 139)[151]—the abbey in which a great-niece of Jean de Berry was also a nun and to which he gave an imposing Italian altarpiece of bone now in the Louvre (Fig. 383).[152] In other miniatures the Egerton workshop adopted the very blond colors of the Epître Master (Fig. 140).[153]

Fr. 835 and 836 contain less work by the Epître Master himself. Perhaps the most interesting miniature in 835 is the illustration for the *Epistre au dieu damours*, in which a young man hands a letter to Cupid (Fig. 145).[154] The god of love, seated before a rose-trellis, holds two huge arrows and wears large, substantial blue wings which, like those of Pegasus (Fig. 91), seem to be quite capable of rendering him air-worthy. Four white doves, the birds of Venus, fly and turn overhead. One of the illustrations of the *Chemin de longue estude*, in fr. 836, is devoted to the infrequently represented myth of the creation of the spring Hippocrene by a blow of the hoof of Pegasus, who is about to take off from the slope of Mount Helicon (Fig. 144). In a manuscript of Christine's chief source, the *Ovide moralisé*, illuminated about ten years earlier, the muses bathe in a pond formed by the spring while Apollo sounds his lyre (Fig. 143).[155] Pallas, a witness of the scene, has been replaced in the *Epître d'Othéa* by a sibyl who, performing the usual late medieval function of guide, shows the spectacle of the "fontaine de sapience" to Christine. The nine muses, unclothed except for their fifteenth-century bonnets, do not bathe in a natural pond but in a tub. This kind of outdoor pool survives in early Renaissance art, as in a Florentine panel of Diana and Actaeon (Fig. 103). The smooth textures and pale, powdery colors of the miniature give the mountainous setting a sort of boudoir character. The painting of the Epître workshop brings to mind the French rococo.

In the miniature of Christine's prayer to the Virgin and Child:

O vierge pure incomparable
pleine de grace inextimable

the pure, transparent colors and the simple yet strong design disclose the hand of the Epître Master himself (Fig. 147). The curling movement of the Virgin's drapery is echoed by the curvatures of the extraordinary, indeed unique palm fronds behind. The tabernacle opens to the diminutive worshipper; the Virgin gazes toward her and seems to acknowledge her presence by extending a hand that at the same time holds the mantle. Christine, though small, is painted in an unusual gray that counts within the narrow range of color: beige, olive-green, blue, and a bright, joyous red. The white mantle and tunic of the Virgin ("Notre-Dame-la-blanche") shaded in pale blue and lined in a deeper shade of this color associate her with the sky. These beautiful harmonies prove that the French, who today use blue far more subtly than any other people, understood it already around 1400. Indeed, already in the thirteenth century they employed it superbly, and it is true that the blues and reds of the Epître Master, though in another key, sing with the harmonies of stained glass.

Christine prepared a second richly illuminated collection of her writings for the Queen of France, Isabeau de Bavière, for whom she wrote a dedication and who appears in a frontispiece, the largest miniature in the manuscript (Fig. 151).[156] Like her husband Charles VI when receiving in 1412 the princes and his counsellor Pierre Salmon,[157] the Queen reposes on a couch while Christine, kneeling, extends the very sizeable manuscript to her. Six ladies-in-waiting, seated on cushions, watch the presentation. Two dogs, as it were, frame the gathering; one small white creature next to his mistress resembles the omnipresent pets of Jean de Berry which appear even on the Duke's dining table (Fig. 539). The walls of the large room are covered with hangings bearing the arms of France and Bavaria, and as an elaborate scene of presentation the miniature is rivalled only by the Boucicaut Master's composition of Pierre Salmon presenting his *Dialogues* to Charles VI.[158] The Cité des Dames Master certainly knew this miniature of 1409 very well because he collaborated with the Boucicaut Master on the illustration of the manuscript.

The scene of presentation in Harley 4431, like most of the 130 miniatures in the manuscript, was painted by the Master of Christine's *Cité des Dames* and his workshop.[159] This allegorical treatise, composed before Easter, 1405, is included in the Harley manuscript, along with other texts written as late as 1410.[160] Philologists and palaeographers, observing that the manuscript is composed of parts written by several scribes, have suggested it may have been put together over a considerable span of time, but the illumination, largely by one workshop and rather uniform in character, implies that it, at least, was completed in one campaign. Though the miniatures in Harley 4431 have been judged to be the models for the corresponding miniatures in the Duke of Berry's manuscript[161] the reverse is true, at least for much of the cycle. In a few miniatures the distinctive color of the Epître Master has even displaced the normal palette of the Cité des Dames workshop.[162] In the representation of Atropos the Queen's manuscript is clearly inferior to Berry's with regard to spacing, the articulation of the main figure, and the use of a rather coarse diaper background instead of a modulated sky (Figs. 62, 114). The Cité des Dames workshop has lost the impressive vitality of the laurel sprouting from Daphne (Figs. 108, 148). Similarly small changes in the design of Pegasus and his wings have robbed him of the buoyancy so striking in fr. 606 (Figs. 91, 154). Raising the horizon above the head of Andromeda has not improved the design either. Some miniatures in the Queen's manuscript betray lack of comprehension of the myth. The hoof of Pegasus, for instance, unlike its model in the Duke of Berry's manuscript, fails to strike Mt. Helicon to produce a spring.[163] The white swan in the Duke of Berry's *Aurora*, very important to Christine's story, has disappeared in the Queen's copy (Figs. 137, 138).[164]

Although the illuminator of the story of Aurora in Harley 4431 ignored the bird into which her son had been transformed he did not remain unaware that he was depicting dawn, and he gave it a new note by showing the peasant still hitching up his trousers (Fig. 137). There are, indeed, a few instances in which the Cité des Dames workshop told the story more clearly. Most of them are miniatures that correspond to those in fr. 836, many of which had been executed by the Egerton workshop. Thus in *Le duc des vrais amans* the lady for whom the knight jousts is not easily distinguished in the miniature by the Egerton workshop in fr. 836 but has become an imposing, uniquely frontal woman in the Queen's copy—perhaps a compliment to her (Figs. 140, 155).

The relationship between illustrations of the *Epître d'Othéa* executed by rather mediocre assistants in the two workshops suggests the existence of a lost model, probably a series of drawings executed by the Epître Master. Thus the curled fingers of the racing Atalanta quite sensibly hoist her skirt in Harley 4431 while in fr. 606 they are empty (Figs. 141, 142).[165] We should recall that even the special rubrics for the planetary gods do not describe the illustrations fully, and normally Christine's text says little about the event to be depicted. Hippomenes and his golden apples, for instance, are not even mentioned, so that when the large cycle was first undertaken Christine—for it was no doubt she—must have given verbal instructions to the Epître Master, who transformed them into visual models.

In those rare instances in the cycle where the text called for a familiar subject the Cité des Dames workshop felt far less dependent, of course, on a model, and one example of independence is instructive about the historical orientation of the style. The prayer to Christ in Berry's manuscript is illustrated in the Egerton style by a Man of Sorrows supported by an angel (Fig. 135). This is a French version of the theme, created twenty-five years earlier, whereas the Cité des Dames illuminator represented Christ alone in the tomb (Fig. 136). This reversion to the Italian type in a miniature painted after 1410 shows the persistent Italian predilections of the workshop, which we have discussed elsewhere.[166]

After the execution of the small cycles in the manuscripts of the *Mutacion* from late 1403 to, let us say, about 1405, and the large cycle in Jean de Berry's manuscript of the collected works from 1406 to 1408, the Epître Master worked on no other books, as far as we know, and there are only a very few miniatures in his style. Apart from two or three single miniatures of Christine at her desk in manuscripts of her writings,[167] about 1410–1415 an assistant who had worked on the *Epître* painted four miniatures in a *Chroniques de St. Denis* (Fig. 152); most of the cycle was perfunctorily executed by the second workshop Christine employed, that of the Cité des Dames Master (Fig. 153).[168] The Epître style, as we see it at this later date in a scene such as King Clothaire II remitting to three Lombards the tribute due him (Fig. 152), is more fluent and mannered, in other words more "international" than in the earlier manuscripts.

The style of the Epître Master is so original and so distinctive that the identification of his work presents no problems, but the same cannot be said of the nature of his known career. Unless additional manuscripts of a different date still lie hidden in libraries, he devoted himself to books less than a decade, and then only in the service of Christine de Pisan. Though he was surely active in Paris, he left almost no trace on illumination in the capital nor indeed anywhere else. These facts together with certain peculiarities of his style indicate that he may have worked in another pictorial medium. The problem of his origins, on the other hand, is less obscure. Jean Porcher believed he was a Lombard master,[169] and though this seems to me doubtful the Epître Master does seem to have studied Lombard illumination of the last fifteen years of the fourteenth century. The manuscripts of the *Tacuinum sanitatis*, especially one style related to the De Veris brothers in the Vienna copy (Figs. 156, 157),[170] seem closer than any other earlier paintings to the color and the open brushwork of the Epître Master. In these Milanese miniatures, too, white is used extensively, together with blue and red, though the hues are not as clear and bright as in the work of the Epître Master. Here also may be found naturalistic plants that anticipate the palms at the sides of the *Madonna* in fr. 836 (Figs. 147, 157). The *Tacuinum* now in Paris could have provided models for some of the drapery-patterns and the fanciful architecture of the French master (Fig. 150).[171] So deep are the relationships that the northern painter must have been in Lombardy when he was young and still forming his style. It is not clear, however, that he would have found in this region of Italy adequate sources for all aspects of his style. His geometric forms are more likely to have been inspired by Tuscan or perhaps Paduan paintings. Enriched by his Italian experience the Epître Master created one of the gayest, most colorful and original styles at the beginning of the fifteenth century in the whole of Europe.

3 · TERENCE

The Manuscripts

One of the most striking instances of the revival of the illustration of a Roman text was the illumination of three copies of the *Comedies* of Terence. One of them, the so-called *Térence des ducs*, is justly famous as the most elegant and, within its limits, the most perfect illumination in a period of extraordinary accomplishment in this art (Figs. 63, 160, 161, 164, 176, 178, 182, 188, 193, 194, 199, 203, 204, 210, 230). Almost all of its 133 miniatures are bright and clear, and an exceptionally fine parchment has made possible a rare smoothness of color. Small wonder that all the paintings were reproduced as early as 1907.[172] Though the identity of the original owner remains uncertain, the manuscript was in the quite notable collection of the young dauphin, Louis duc de Guyenne.[173] From the beginning of 1415 until his death in December Martin Gouge, donor of an earlier Terence, served as his chancellor. When the Dauphin died at the age of eighteen his confessor gave the manuscript to the duc de Berry, then aged but no less fascinated than earlier by illuminated books.

Historically the most important copy of the *Comedies*, however, and very probably, as we shall see, the earliest is the manuscript given at New Year 1408 to Jean de Berry by his treasurer, Martin Gouge (Figs. 64, 163, 174, 177, 180, 183, 185, 189, 191, 195, 197, 202, 209). This learned man, who just at this time was nominated by the Duke as bishop of Chartres, gave his patron a distinctive series of interrelated humanist manuscripts, as we have seen.[174] Though the third copy of the *Comedies*, lat. 8193, is no less impressive it has attracted very little attention (Figs. 7, 59, 181, 187, 190, 192, 196, 198, 205).[175] It bears no indication of its original destination, and indeed the illustration was abandoned after the excellent master and an assistant had painted 14 miniatures, leaving 7 of his splendid preliminary sketches without any color.

Those historians who have studied the miniatures in the *Térence des ducs* and in Berry's copy of the same text have not succeeded in placing them in French illumination of the period. No agreement has been reached, furthermore, about the relationship of the two manuscripts and their chronological sequence, although some years ago Marcel Thomas proposed, rightly we think, that the *Térence des ducs* depended upon lat. 7907 A.[176] The difficulty has been in large part due to the conception of the Arsenal manuscript as stylistically uniform. The illustration of one play, to be sure, the *Adelphoe* or *Brothers*, is strikingly different and has long been associated with that movement in Paris we prefer to call simply the Bedford trend. The strongest miniature in this sequence, the first one for the play (Fig. 204), was painted by an illuminator who worked on the famous

Livre de la chasse and numerous other manuscripts of the first fifteen years of the century (Fig. 255). His setting in another miniature in the *Adelphoe* is the same as the one employed by a closely related illuminator who painted a few miniatures in the *Cas des nobles hommes et femmes* of Jean sans Peur, produced about 1410–1412 (Figs. 159, 160).[177] The linear perspective is superior in the Terence, especially in the half-timbered wing of the building, but the space and the relation of the figures to it seem more effective in the scene in the Boccaccio of Hannibal drinking poison and dying (Fig. 159). Whether the two miniatures are connected directly or through a workshop model, they were not painted at widely different times, and we thus have our first clue to the date of the *Térence des ducs*.

The painter of the *Adelphoe* in the Arsenal manuscript appears in only one miniature outside this play, the first in the Phormio, but a closely related master, somewhat more delicate, was asked to paint the borders of the frontispiece (Fig. 210). He embellished the miniature with swirling acanthus that at intervals forms a medallion inhabited by an angel holding a banner decorated with *France ancien*, puttos holding a scroll with the motto (so far unidentified) of the same member of the court, and a woman entertaining a young man with music on the lyre. Since a putto holding a scroll and an angel holding a banner both point to this youth he probably alludes to the original owner—more likely than not the Dauphin.

The fact that the miniature of the Roman theater was copied, as we shall see, from the frontispiece of Berry's Terence does not altogether mask the signs of the authorship of the Luçon Master. He seems to have exercised supervision over the illumination of the entire manuscript. His workshop painted about half the miniatures, but they were influenced in composition and style by Berry's Terence (Figs. 189, 193). Furthermore, one of the illuminators of the earlier Terence, the Orosius Master, whom we have encountered in the *Histoire ancienne* of *ca.* 1400, painted miniatures in the *Hecyra* in the *Térence des ducs*. In the scene of the Athenian, Laches, accusing his wife Sostrata of offending their daughter-in-law we recognize the smooth, rounded surfaces of the *Destruction of Troy* (Figs. 63, 274). The juxtaposition of bright and deep or warm and cool tones reappears in the Terence.

Often in collaborative enterprises the styles of the workshops tend to merge. There may be spontaneous exchanges, or the directing illuminator may impose a certain uniformity. Thus the deep blues and reds in the miniatures in the Terence painted by the Cité des Dames workshop, which are not characteristic of that style around 1412, must be ascribed to the wish to conform with the color of the rest of the cycle. In the first play in the Terence, the *Andria*, illuminated by the Luçon workshop, some miniatures show characteristic Luçon figures embedded in the deep circumambient color of the Orosius Master (Fig. 161). A similar influence may be observed in the deep blues, bluish pink, and gray green of the Adelphoe Master (Fig. 204).

The splendid clothes of the characters in the Arsenal Terence differentiate it decisively from the other two copies of the plays. The fanciful turbans and escalloped mantles and collars give it the appearance of fashion plates, establishing the taste of the second decade of the century. Thus the courtesan Philotis in the *Hecyra* sports a much fancier hat than the corresponding figure in Berry's Terence, which is, furthermore, in the same Orosius style though by a less strong master (Figs. 163, 164). The author of this miniature in the *Térence des ducs* is, indeed, the best painter in the manuscript. His house is proportionately larger, his perspective improved, his space deeper. The somewhat sentimental courtesan and the procuress Syra, who is trying to give her hard-headed advice, are arranged essentially parallel to the picture plane in Berry's Terence but oblique to it in the Arsenal manuscript. This turned compositional axis was introduced chiefly by the Boucicaut Master and it became common in the second decade of the century.[178]

We have given some of the evidence for dating Arsenal 664 well after Berry's Terence, which was executed a year or two before 1408. The third copy, lat. 8193, also depends on Berry's Terence, and it was probably illuminated around the same time or just afterwards. There are indications of this dependence in the miniature of Syra and Philotis (Figs. 59, 163, 164). To be sure, both women are seated in lat. 8193 as in the *Térence des ducs*; Syra is stout in both miniatures and a purse hangs from her girdle. Berry's Terence, however, is reflected in the lined neck of Syra and in the nearly identical red hat of Philotis. Was it a misunderstanding of the artist or a satirical joke that Syra the procuress carries a rosary?

Some of the trees painted by the Luçon workshop in the *Térence des ducs* might seem to imply a knowledge of lat. 8193 (Figs. 59, 230). The Luçon workshop, however, had earlier adopted this tree when, as we shall see, it copied a cycle of miniatures in a Virgil by the illuminators of lat. 8193.

The frame of the miniature in lat. 8193 remains unpainted (Fig. 59); the bands were left untouched to the end so that they would cover any color that lapped over in the narrow spaces, as we can see here and there it has actually done. No colored or gilded background, however, was ever intended; the completion of the unusual yellow trees assures us of that. The painter, employing pale washes deftly laid in spots and *taches*, let the bare parchment act as light. He achieved an exceptional luminosity.

The chief illuminator of lat. 8193 is a very impressive master, superior to the illuminators of the corresponding scenes in the other manuscripts. Since, in addition to this Terence, the only other miniatures in his style illustrate a manuscript of the *Eclogues* and *Georgics* of Virgil, he may not inappropriately be named the Master of the Roman Texts. The rarity of his style and the fact that it resembles Jacquemart de Hesdin suggest that he did not normally work in the book but on panel or on the wall. Like Jacquemart in the *Brussels Hours* he collaborated in the Terence and in the Virgil at Lyon with an Italian calligrapher, who embellished many of the initials and borders with fine penwork.[179]

In style the Duke of Berry's Terence is not as uniform as lat. 8193 nor as complex as Arsenal 664. There are two major groups of miniatures, one best represented by the painter of the frontispiece (Fig. 209). He influenced the entire cycle, but most strongly the miniatures of the first play, the *Andria*, whose miniatures were all executed by his assistant (Figs. 64, 177, 180, 189). A closely related illuminator painted the miniatures of the next play, the *Eunuch*, up through folio 42 (Fig. 195); but this master was responsive to the work of the Orosius Master, who took over on folio 42v and continued through the following four plays to the end of the manuscript (Figs. 163, 183, 191, 197, 202). As he proceeded he tended to abandon the relatively pale colors of the frontispiece and the *Andria* for his own brighter and deeper hues.

The painter of the frontispiece, who apparently served in 1406–1407 as the entrepreneur of the cycle, was, as far as we can see, a newcomer to French illumination (Fig. 209). He thus resembles the Roman Texts Master, and like that master he owed much to Jacquemart de Hesdin (Figs. 342, 369, 456). He employed a similar range of pastel colors and he constructed his figures in accordance with Italian principles. Many of them show the high foreheads and straight noses that Jacquemart introduced, following Trecento models, in the early *Petites Heures* (Fig. 162). Indeed, a head in the frontispiece such as the white-haired one emerging from the portal of the Roman theater, with its large features, its impersonality, its bulk and bearing, suggests in this context not only the Trecento but, in a vague way, antiquity itself.

This remarkable painter was apparently trained in the circle of Jacquemart in the late nineties. We have not identified any miniature by him before the Terence of 1406–1407. He appeared rarely, as we have said, in manuscripts. Five miniatures in a Book of Hours in the British Museum, towards 1415, are extremely close in style, and one or two by his hand (Figs. 165, 166).[180] At about the same time the author of the frontispiece surely painted two large miniatures in a text concerned, once again, with the remote Mediterranean past. The manuscript represents one more attempt in Paris in the early fifteenth century to recover the ancient world visually.

The *History of the Jews* by Josephus was translated into French during the reign of Charles VI,[181] and the Duke of Berry acquired a manuscript illustrated by the Cité des Dames workshop towards 1410 (fr. 6446—Fig. 169). About 1415 the Duke commissioned a more splendid copy (Figs. 167, 170). His *ex libris* was inscribed in the second volume, although it was not illuminated during his lifetime. A note written in the manuscript at the end of the fifteenth century by the secretary of Pierre de Bourbon, who then owned it, said that of the twelve miniatures nine were painted by Fouquet (as indeed they were) whereas the first three were executed by "l'enlumineur du duc Jehan de Berry." This statement, not long after the event, has misled many historians because it is not quite correct. Stylistic evidence clearly shows, it seems to us, that the first miniature in the manuscript was not painted for the Duke of Berry and not by his illuminator (Fig. 167). The telling fact is that the figures in the right border bearing the armorials of the Armagnac family are, like the miniature itself, the work of the Harvard Hannibal Master.[182] This illuminator, who first appeared as an associate and follower of the Boucicaut Master *ca.* 1412,[183] adopted that painter's composition of Adam and Eve in the garden enclosed by a hexagonal wall (Fig. 168). However, the Hannibal Master, a very garrulous artist, multiplied the animals and he filled with fish the river that waters the garden and, according to the text, encircles the earth. Like his contemporary, the Rohan Master, he chose for expressive purposes to abandon naturalistic proportions in the scale of his figures. God the Father gives Eve to Adam in what seems to be a ceremony of marriage. They are joined in a *junctio dextrarum*, while angels hold around them the mantle of God. The Harvard Hannibal Master no doubt found a model for this subject in the initial miniature of the copy of the *Antiquités* that Jean de Berry had acquired about 1410 (Fig. 169).[184] The miniature in fr. 247, but not the armorials of Jacques d'Armagnac added below the text after 1455, was probably painted for his father Bernard VIII, the son of the Duke of Berry's daughter, Bonne.

It is the second and third miniatures in this manuscript, both manifestly by the same painter, that concern us now. They were undoubtedly painted for Jean de Berry, as the inscription states, because his arms decorate the banners flying from the tents of the Israelites in the desert of Sinai after their departure from Egypt (Fig. 170). Not far from the shore of the Red Sea the Israelites dig a well, while below they kneel before a tabernacle and an altar bearing the tablets of the Law, or they negotiate with Amalekite kings and soldiers who have arrived on camels.[185] These animals contribute to the exotic effect otherwise created, as in the approximately contemporary *Très Riches Heures* (Fig. 572), by the scimitars, the turbans, and other strange headgear.[186] The turban and the sharp profile of a squatting, bearded man before a tent suggest that the painter had seen a Near-Eastern painting. In the preceding miniature, devoted to the story of Joseph, the youth is sent out by Rachel to join his brothers, who soon cast him into a dry well. Then the Ishmaelites on their camels, as the text says, carry him off to Egypt.

The illuminator has left no doubt about the color of the Red Sea, and to contain this bright orange area he has reddened the faces and distributed spots of yellowish red on the costumes, while giving his hills an unusually saturated yellow- or blue-green. He uses gilt for reflections on the trunks and leaves of trees, whose peculiar gnarled trunks and crowns resemble those we have seen in lat. 8193 (Fig. 59). Thus we have another indication of the relationship of the illustrators of the texts of Terence and of Josephus. The boldness of the pattern of color in the *Antiquités* is matched by strong rhythms, which sweep through the composition as they do in the miniatures of the Holy Ghost Master, painted about ten years earlier and also for Berry.[187] Even the sky is animated by soaring cranes and wheeling ravens. These powerful linear movements and garish colors sharply differentiate the two miniatures from the frontispiece of the Terence, but there are, nevertheless, such deep and pervasive relationships that the miniatures in the text of Josephus were very probably painted by the same master eight or nine years later, in other words shortly before the death of Jean de Berry in June 1416. We may thus designate him the Josephus Master.

The Plays

After this lengthy, and yet in a sense too brief, digression on the identity of the illuminators of the three manuscripts of the *Comedies*, we shall now return to the place of these manuscripts in the history of the illustration of Terence and to the most interesting, and what we must still prove to be the earliest, copy received by the Duke of Berry at New Year 1408. Though the plays of Terence were illustrated in antiquity, no ancient manuscript survives, and our knowledge of the nature of the early illustration derives from later copies, especially those of the Carolingian period. Of the two extant ninth-century manuscripts, one illustrated at Reims and now in Paris, the other further northeast and now in the Vatican, the latter reflects far more of the style of the early model (Figs. 171–173, 184, 186). The *Comedies* continued to be read throughout the Middle Ages, and the excellence of their Latin gave them a place in the schools.[188] Illustrated copies survive from the ninth through the twelfth centuries, and in the early fifteenth century some of them were in France. The manuscript illuminated at Reims now in Paris (lat. 7899) was at St. Denis until 1595; the Vatican manuscript (Vat. lat. 3868) was in France from the tenth through the twelfth century, and perhaps until its appearance in the library of Sixtus IV in 1475. A tenth-century manuscript now in Paris (lat. 7900) was at Fleury,[189] so that models were available for any later Parisian illuminators who might be interested in them. The tradition of illustration, interrupted at the end of the twelfth century, was revived only in the early fifteenth century in Paris by the three manuscripts we are considering.

Historians have hitherto denied any similarity between the miniatures in these manuscripts and those in the Carolingian and Romanesque cycles,[190] but a closer study of the Duke of Berry's copy shows, we believe, that a relationship definitely exists. In Berry's manuscript, as in the Carolingian copy of the ancient model, the scenes compose rectangular strips set within, above, or below the column of the text (Figs. 173, 174). The strips are, to be sure, framed in Berry's manuscript, but the main events or confrontations represented are, with only a few exceptions, similar, and the total number of them is the same. The absence of spectators or secondary figures, who commonly appear in religious and historical scenes of the time, is striking. The designer of Berry's Terence was clearly aware of the special nature of his task.

He placed his figures, furthermore, on a ground plane that is shallower than normal for the early fifteenth century (Fig. 174). They are rather regularly aligned and the heads adhere to one or two levels. The servants Byrria and Davus, like some servants in Carolingian manuscripts (Fig. 173), are shorter than their masters. The name of each actor is written over or near his head—in gold in Berry's copy. Identifying inscriptions of this kind belong to the tradition of illustration of the *Comedies* and not to early fifteenth-century painting. In the early manuscripts, furthermore, the actors are arranged from left to right in the order of their initial speech,[191] and the same sequence is often visible in the Duke of Berry's manuscript. The inscriptions above many figures in the Carolingian and early medieval manuscripts give not only their names but also their social rank or principal character, as *senex*, *servus*, or *adulescens* (Fig. 171). Fuller inscriptions of this kind are rare in Berry's manuscript, but it is a striking fact that they do occur (Fig. 180).

In Berry's Terence buildings often flank the figures. To judge from the Carolingian copies the late antique manuscript contained only simple, symbolic stage properties (Fig. 184), of the kind that are familiar from the *Vienna Genesis*. Already in tenth-century copies the architectural setting becomes more specific and realistic, so that in this respect the illuminators of Berry's manuscript conform with medieval rather than ancient conventions (Fig. 175). Naturally, they conform in other fundamental aspects also. The gestures, for one thing, do not resemble those of the Carolingian manuscripts; the movement of the hand to indicate speech, with curled fourth and fifth fingers, had of course become a Christian gesture of blessing. In Berry's Terence the parts of the figures—head, torso, limbs—tend to be described in a plane, parallel to the picture plane. The figures do not possess full roundness nor the kind of easy, flowing movement that the Vatican copy still retains, reflecting ancient norms for the articulation of the body. True, Pamphilus in the Andria Master's scene (Fig. 174) is revolving from his servant Davus to his father Simo—who is properly shown as an older man. Alert French painters at this time were just re-learning from Italian Trecento examples how to create such spiral movements in space. The body, however, lacks the center of gravity that inheres in the ancient figure; its silhouette is more important, and it belongs more completely to a pictorial field.

These qualities are not new; they emerged already in the copy of the same antique model made at Reims in the ninth century (Fig. 172). Here, in the same scene we have been considering, a powerful rhythmical impulse surges through the actors and unites them in a new way. The Reims illuminator introduced principles that, though recessive at times, persist in later Western art.

The concept of the unified field is accompanied in Berry's manuscript by a wish for a more specific environment (Fig. 174). The illuminator replaced the nondescript parchment background with a graduated blue sky, and around the composition he introduced a frame, which appears here for the first time in the tradition of Terence illustrations. This is of course a momentous change, and what it can come to mean for the enclosed area we may readily recognize by turning to the same episode in the *Térence des ducs* (Fig. 176). The frame has become more decisively a window giving onto a perspective view of a deeper space. Though the traditional four figures exist within it, both in sequence and arrangement in depth they no longer conform with the long-established canons of Terence illustration.

The departures of the early fifteenth-century illuminators from their models are not, however, entirely consistent. While they sought a more defined, perspective space, which might imply a unity of time, their interest in the progression of events led them often to represent immediately successive episodes within one miniature. Thus two figures in conversation may be repeated in a cinematic way, the difference between the two groups being only an exchange of the roles of speaker and listener (Fig. 177). The illuminators of the *Térence des ducs* recapture more of a unity of time by allocating to each group of this kind a distinct spatial compartment (Fig. 178).[192] Occasionally the Carolingian illuminators and their copyists repeated a figure (Fig. 179), but the practice is much more common in the early fifteenth century. The narrative impulses of the painters at that time led them, furthermore, to develop the story in another way. At the beginning of the *Eunuch*, as we see it in Berry's manuscript, Parmeno advises his master Phaedria (Fig. 180). In the miniature in lat. 8193, by an assistant of the Roman Texts Master, Phaedria leaves the house of Laches and then turns to speak to Parmeno, who is only partly on stage (Fig. 181). In the *Térence des ducs* the two watch the approach of the courtesan Thais, who is due to come out of her house in the next scene (Fig. 182). The introduction of a figure from the subsequent or even the preceding scene, frequent in the *Térence des ducs*, may be seen earlier, in tenth-century and Romanesque manuscripts (Fig. 175). Although this similarity may indicate that the illuminators of the Arsenal manuscript utilized a model of this kind in addition to the Duke of Berry's copy, it seems more probable that they independently hit upon the same narrative device.

The illustrators of the Duke of Berry's manuscript faced an unusual task, because the subjects were new to them and exceptional in character. Unlike most religious, historical or mythological subjects they entailed little action and very much talk. In almost all scenes the painters were constrained to limit movement to gestures. In those few scenes calling for action of a different kind we detect more readily the influence of the earlier model. In a scene in the *Adelphoe* or *Brothers*, painted by the Orosius Master, the servant Syrus boldly gives an order in the presence of one of the brothers, the Athenian gentleman Demea (Fig. 183).

> *Syrus* Gut these fish, Dromo, except the biggest conger, let that play in the water for a bit; when I come back it shall be filleted, not before, mind.
>
> *Demea* Perfectly scandalous!
>
> *Syrus* (turning round) It doesn't satisfy me either, Sir: I often protest. (Turning again to the door) Those salt fish. Stephanio, see they're properly soaked.[193]

It can scarcely be an accident that the same scene in the ninth-century illumination of Reims, though in reverse order, should be so similar (Fig. 184). It is true that Stephanio is missing, so that the Orosius Master would in that respect have followed the text. But is not the one error in his miniature revealing? Instead of putting in the water a large eel, as the text requires, he has put a fish. But doesn't the fish wriggle rather like an eel?

Another scene in the *Adelphoe* represented by the Orosius workshop seems at first quite different from the corresponding scene in the Reims manuscript (Figs. 185, 186). Given the many pictorial possibilities offered by the encounter between Aeschinus, an Athenian gentleman, his servant Parmeno, and the slave-dealer Sannio, the choice of the moment of physical struggle over the slave-girl owned by Sannio is probably not accidental.[194] The Orosius Master has again reversed the group, putting Sannio at the right, but he departs from the early tradition and the text by giving the servant Parmeno the dress of Ctesipho, half-brother of Aeschinus. This group is repeated in the miniature in the *Térence des ducs*, where even the slave-dealer has become a dandy (Fig. 188). Parmeno, present in the early model, is restored in the miniature by the assistant of the Roman Texts Master in lat. 8193 (Fig. 187). Here master and servant act together, and the clarification of the story discloses the relative independence of this remarkable Terence cycle. Still, the Roman Texts Master either saw the miniature in Berry's manuscript or painted his at the same time, because he introduced unusual details such as the scalloped hood of the slave-dealer. He even adopted its green color.

Our study of the three manuscripts of Terence illuminated in the early fifteenth century has shown that the Duke of Berry's copy was illuminated first, followed almost immediately by lat. 8193, and a few years later by the *Térence des ducs*. Since lat. 8193 has not been studied, and all scholars but Marcel Thomas have held that the other two manuscripts were contemporary or even that the *Térence des ducs* held priority,[195] it is probably useful to point to a few more of the countless signs of the true interrelationship of these manuscripts.

Berry's Terence and lat. 8193 share one feature which is uncommon in the illumination of this period. In both manuscripts the artists in charge wrote brief directions above the figures, which in lat. 7907A are legible under ultraviolet light. These words—"la mere," "le frere," "ladvocat," "le paisant," "valet"—identify the figures by their roles. Our surmise, presented above, that the illuminators of Berry's Terence depended upon a pictorial model for some aspects of their cycle is strengthened by the certainty of such a model for the miniatures in lat. 8193. How else could one explain the fact that in some miniatures with two figures (folios 109v, 114) the Roman Texts Master identified one by his function but the other only as "lautre"? That the model may have been Berry's Terence may be inferred from the correspondence of one of the more complete preparatory drawings, folio 112v, with the same scene in lat. 7907A, fol. 86v.[196]

Near the beginning of the *Andria* Simo, an Athenian gentleman, speaks to his steward Sosia, while his two slaves bring provisions for his son's wedding (Figs. 189, 193). Though there are obvious differences in the groups of figures in Berry's manuscript and the *Térence des ducs*—the slaves have been exchanged—the similarities extend to details of costume, and the associate of the Luçon Master has even adopted the technique of stippling hair and other forms that was employed by the Josephus and Andria Masters. As usual, the *Térence des ducs* shows greater depth and scale. In the corresponding scene in lat. 8193 the Roman Texts Master reversed the positions of

Simo and Sosia but he retained other elements of the composition in Berry's Terence such as the slave bearing a basket on his head, the shelf, and the cooking equipment (Fig. 190).

At the beginning of the *Self-Tormentor* the owner of a large farm in Attica, Chremes, chides his neighbor, Menedemus.

> It seems to me you are working too hard for your time of life, harder than your circumstances demand. Heaven and earth, man, what's your meaning? what's your object? You are sixty years old, if not more, at least I guess so. As for estate there is no one hereabouts has a better or one worth more. You have plenty of men to work it, yet, just as if you hadn't a single one, there you are, straining yourself to do *their* work.[197]

The Orosius Master dressed the two landowners similarly (Fig. 191), whereas the Roman Texts Master represented Menedemus as a peasant, probably wishing to emphasize his devotion to agriculture (Figs. 7, 192). Certainly he works more energetically, although the tines of his rake are less effectively set. Since this impressive miniature by the Roman Texts Master lacks a painted background and a setting or even a deep ground plane, the painter may have wished to recall the early tradition, although this scene in the Carolingian manuscripts shows vegetation. However that may be, his principal point of departure was the miniature in Berry's Terence, which provided the model for the posture of Menedemus. The order of the speakers, which conforms with the text in Berry's Terence, is reversed in lat. 8193. A dependence of lat. 8193 upon Berry's manuscript is indicated also by forms such as a strangely thin wall (Fig. 196). A related wall in Berry's Terence, used again as a stage-prop and divider, has a more normal substantiality (Fig. 195).

The illuminator in the Cité des Dames workshop who painted the corresponding scene in the *Térence des ducs* seems to have been familiar with the two earlier miniatures (Fig. 194). Although Chremes clearly derives from Berry's Terence, certain aspects of Menedemus, such as the loose stockings, the pouch, and the face turned outward, indicate a knowledge of lat. 8193. The extra tools were apparently suggested by Berry's manuscript. The addition of a second, later episode—Chremes at the door of a house—is characteristic of the more elaborate narrative of the *Térence des ducs*.

In one of the scenes of the *Brothers* an Athenian lady, Sostrata, expresses to her servant Canthara her concern about her daughter Pamphila, who lies on a bed in labor (Figs. 197, 198). In Berry's manuscript Sostrata is curiously averted, and Pamphila is discreetly concealed except for her head and shoulders. Only the interior of the room appears in the sophisticated composition of lat. 8193, and the Roman Texts workshop has portrayed a more effective movement, particularly the torsion of Canthara. For the immediately subsequent episode, when Sostrata steps outside, the illuminator, in cinematic fashion, repeated only a corner of the room and merely the feet of Pamphila (Fig. 198).

In the miniature in the *Térence des ducs* poor Pamphila distracts herself by pulling on a cloth rope tied to a bedpost (Fig. 199)—a contemporary practice of women in labor, as we may see in a miniature of their patron Juno in the manuscript of the *Cleres femmes* painted by the Coronation Master just before 1403 (Fig. 200). In the Arsenal miniature, however, Pamphila has another patron. Over her bed hangs a roundel with an image of the Madonna and Child.

The *Brothers* opens with the Athenian gentleman Micio on the stage, calling out for his servant Storax, who, being absent, fails to respond. In medieval art the subject or content of thought can be given physical shape, and Storax, though absent in the Carolingian Terences, stands near Micio in manuscripts of the Romanesque period (Fig. 201).[198] The Orosius Master has shown him in a doorway, turning around as if to listen (Fig. 202). The Roman Texts Master devised a most unusual composition, averting Micio and representing Storax in an extraordinarily well executed twist (Fig. 205). It seems doubtful that this figure could be matched at the time anywhere north of Italy. Once again there are no buildings and no background.

The illuminator of the corresponding miniature in the *Térence des ducs* gave to the figures the conventionalized vivacity of the Bedford trend to which he belongs, regardless of the anomalous result that Micio and Storax seem to converse (Fig. 204). Even this animated exchange did not seem sufficient, so the painter, preceded to be sure by much earlier illustrations (Fig. 201), added Micio's brother Demea, who enters the room in a rage. The illuminator effectively contrasted his fiery temperament with that of his kind, patient brother.

These comparisons of corresponding scenes not only disclose the unique qualities of the three cycles but they demonstrate beyond any doubt the relative lateness of the *Térence des ducs*. Its illuminators certainly knew Berry's manuscript and possibly lat. 8193.[199] Lat. 8193 resembles Berry's manuscript, painted before 1408, in many ways (Figs. 59, 163, 189–192). Berry's manuscript was indubitably begun first and it is closest to the early tradition. Lat. 8193 would not seem to have been executed significantly later, and the *Térence des ducs* followed probably about 1412.

The Roman Theater and the Mask

One conspicuous difference between the early fifteenth-century illustrations and those in the ancient prototype or its more faithful later copies is the complete absence of masks. These essential accouterments of ancient drama were still partially understood in illustrations of the twelfth century (Fig. 179), but not one scene in the fifteenth-century manuscripts shows them. The Josephus Master painted them, however, in his portrayal of a Roman theater in the Duke of Berry's Terence (Fig. 209), and they reappear, of course, in the copy of this miniature in the *Térence des ducs* (Fig. 210). They are worn by four prancing men labelled *gesticulatores* in Berry's manuscript and *joculatores* (the more common term) in the Arsenal manuscript. As in antiquity the masks are varicolored: light yellow, gray, red and brown in Berry's manuscript and intense hues, including green, in the *Térence des ducs*. Only Berry's manuscript includes one functional detail—a string or thong that fastens the mask to the head.

These two miniatures are our most important visual records of the late medieval or early Renaissance conception of the ancient theater. The late antique illustrated Terence, reflected in the Carolingian copies, showed at the beginning, as a sort of frontispiece, a bust of the author in a medallion. In our miniatures he appears in a city full of gabled houses inscribed, in Berry's copy, CIVITAS ROMANA. In an open house the poet, a manumitted slave, presents a copy of his plays to two men, the more elaborately dressed of whom may be his patron, the senator Terentius Lucanus, who educated and freed him. The presumed senator wears a splendid hat similar to those on the heads of the ancient Hebrews and Ishmaelites in the *Antiquités judaïques*. The poet's hair is covered with a simple black skull cap.

The space behind is filled by a large, open circular building inscribed THEATRUM. Within it spectators are seated on two levels. Of those nearest us we see only the upper part of the averted heads; the faces of the spectators opposite are in shade. Near these groups are inscriptions in gold: ROMANI and POPULUS ROMANUS. The curtains of the house at the center, inscribed SCENA, are opened to disclose Calliopius, the fourth- or fifth-century editor of Terence, reading a copy of the plays. His name appears just below him. Towards the right an actor emerges from the *scena*.

What is the source of this remarkable reconstruction of a Roman theater? An unusual frontispiece of a late tenth- or early eleventh-century Terence in the Vatican Library may be regarded as an iconographic precedent (Fig. 211). At the center of an *aedicula* Calliopius, outranking Terence in size and position, turns the page of an open book with one hand while pointing with his other at the poet, who is seated at the left. The adversaries or competitors of Terence are at the right, and the ROMANI appear above a wavy ribbon probably intended to signify the wall of the theater. In the register below there are scenes from the first play, the *Andria*.

The illuminator of the Duke of Berry's Terence or his adviser would not, however, have been dependent on an earlier miniature of this kind when designing the frontispiece. Roman semicircular theaters, or amphitheaters used as theaters, were not only still visible in France but used for performances of mystery plays.[200] Chapter 8 of the *Mirabilia urbis Romae* gave a sizeable list of the extant theaters in the city. Since the time of Augustine, furthermore, Christian scholars had written accounts of the ancient stage and the plays performed on it. In the great compendium of knowledge about the ancient world, the *Etymologiae* compiled by Isidore of Seville in the early seventh century, the theater is described as follows:

> The 'scene' was the place below the theatre built in the form of a house, with a platform which was called the orchestra. On it the comic and tragic actors sang, and the *histriones* and *mimi* danced. There the comic and tragic poets ascended for their contests, while the others (the *histriones*) provided suitable gestures for the words they chanted.[201]

Isidore here sets forth the idea, which persisted for centuries, that the poet or his representative read the play aloud while the actors provided an appropriate pantomime. In our miniatures Calliopius serves as the expositor. The *scena* was described by others as a sort of curtained pulpit from which the masked characters (*personae larvatae*) might come onto the stage.[202] It thus resembles the curtained *maison* of the mystery play, devoted to a *tableau vivant*, as we see it in Fouquet's miniature of the Martyrdom of St. Apollonia (Fig. 207). Constructions similar to these *maisons* and curtains as backdrops signifying an interior appeared on the ancient stage, as we may see in a Roman relief representing a comic setting (Fig. 215).

In his commentary on *Hercules furens* by Seneca, Nicolas Treveth (1260–1330) described the ancient theater in much the same way as Isidore of Seville.

> The theatre was a semi-circular building in the midst of which was a small house [*parva domuncula*] which was called the "scene." In it was a platform on which the poet stood to recite his poems. Outside it were the mimes, who accompanied the reciting of the poems by physical action, adapting their gestures to whatsoever character the poet was interpreting.[203]

Much closer in time to our miniatures are the references to the "anciens theatres" in the commentary by Raoul de Praelles on the *Cité de Dieu*, completed in 1375. In these descriptions, which have not hitherto been cited in discussions of the miniatures or of the history of the theater, Raoul de Praelles referred to the usual authority, Isidore of Seville, but he specifically said that the seats were arranged in mounting tiers as "they still appear in the ancient theaters."

> For in those times theaters were constructed with seats mounting in tiers so that everyone had an unobstructed view, just as one can still see from the arrangement of ancient theaters. And because these theatrical plays originated in Greece, they are known as Greek prodigalities or extravagances. Now, since we have spoken of tragedy and comedy you must know that, as Isidore says in the eighteenth book of his *Etymologia*, tragedy consists of the extraordinary deeds of great kings and powerful princes and of their cruelty and wickedness. Comedy is made up of the actions of ordinary people, of the intrigues of women and men and of the deceptions they practice in such ribaldries. . . . And, moreover, you must take note of the difference between a theater and an amphitheater; for an amphitheater was completely round and the entire space was used for spectacles of armed and unarmed men, and the prize was awarded to the one who comported himself best. A theater was made in the form of a half of an amphitheater, and it was used for theatrical plays, gallanteries, dancing and the characters of tragedies and comedies (Bk. 1, Ch. 31). . . . the *asena* is a small house in the middle of a theater, with a lectern which was used for reading the tragedies and comedies of the poets, and there people in disguises comported themselves in accordance with the subjects of these songs and diversions, just as you may see one does today, in plays and charivaris. And there were players of various instruments, and others who disguised themselves and imitated the characters of whom the tragedy or comedy spoke. Titus Livius says that these performances were of little profit and did much harm because they corrupted the morals of the Romans. And he says, moreover, that when they were first organized they were quite moderate and of small cost, but later on there were so many excesses, such expenditure and great display that it was scarcely possible for great princes or kings to afford or bear them.[204]

The building in the miniatures is full-round, reflecting no doubt the use of existing ancient amphitheaters for plays. The existence of a similar practice in Italy led Francesco di Giorgio also to present, as a "theatrum," a circular structure, resembling in this instance a colosseum.[205] The building in the miniatures thus conforms with Raoul's circular amphitheater and not with his half-round theater. On the other hand the miniatures do conform with Raoul's description of the *scena*, of the masked mimes and of the players of musical instruments. Within the *scena* the comedy is being read but outside it Raoul seems to mention two different activities without clearly distinguishing them: the masked mimes who enact the play as it is read, and the players who perform more or less extemporaneously in the manner of the *jongleurs* as "you see them still today."

In the miniatures of the theater the four actors near Calliopius, inscribed *gesticulatores* or *joculatores*, are quite unlike the *personae* in the miniatures illustrating the plays. For one thing, they wear masks. Furthermore, they do not converse, the normal behavior of the actors in the *Comedies* of Terence which Calliopius is reading. They scamper about as if in burlesque, and the most that one dares say about this lack of coherence is that they may be involved in a prelude or interlude to the *Comedies*.

It is a fascinating fact that the *jongleurs*, the creators of gay, popular entertainment, sometimes wore masks[206] whereas the actors in our manuscripts of the *Comedies* do not, even though the illuminators and their adviser knew an early manuscript in which they did. We can begin to understand this differentiation and this apparent rejection of an established convention by considering the re-interpretation of the ancient mask in the Christian era. In antiquity masks were employed in the theater and in the religious rites of the mystery cults.[207] They appeared as symbols in art, especially in funerary monuments. The early Christian Fathers, however, violently condemned theatrical plays—"those spectacles of uncleanness, those licentious vanities," Augustine called them[208]—and the mask suffered the same fate. The Church maintained this strong opposition throughout the Middle Ages.[209] Raoul de Praelles echoed it in the passage quoted above, and cited the opposition to the plays even of the Roman historian Livy.

The demoralizing effects of which Raoul de Praelles spoke in his commentary are vividly conveyed in a miniature that accompanies it in a *Cité de Dieu* in the Bibliothèque de l'Arsenal, illuminated *ca.* 1425 by the Valerius Maximus Master (Fig. 208).[210] This miniature, which has not been given a place in accounts of the history of the theater, shows two authors holding scrolls inscribed with their plays; one or perhaps both read aloud, supervised by the two Roman censors whom Raoul mentioned, Cassius and Messala. All around couples embrace, to the din of trumpets (*buysines*) and makeshift drums. In the foreground a mask, held before a woman by a man who may also be an actor, has so intoxicating an effect that she immediately begins to undress. The three gilt figures at the center are not simply statues of pagan gods on an altar, as Laborde said. Though damage has made the illuminator's intention less clear the figure at the left and probably also the one at the center wear rectangular cloth masks like the one held below. Apparently the artist compounded the evil of pagan idols by giving them pagan masks.[211]

The mask has a strong magical power, radiating evil like the face of Medusa. Christian opposition to it was rooted, we may infer, in its capacity to conceal the moral, rational person, permitting under its cover the expression of otherwise unacceptable wishes and wants. Given such a function, it was naturally the devil and the irresponsible characters who were given masks in the mystery plays.[212] At the moment when our miniatures in the Terence manuscripts were painted the Bishop of Nantes prohibited even mimes from using "grotesque masks" (*monstra larvarum*).[213]

Thus we can understand why the *jongleurs* in our Roman theater might wear masks whereas the *personae* in an ancient comedy of manners, widely admired for its Latin style, would not. There was no change in this respect even in the period of more intensive study of Roman literature, nor when, in the late fifteenth century, the *Comedies* began to be performed, in Latin and in vernacular translation, first in Italy and then elsewhere.[214] The faces of the actors in illustrations of the printed editions of Terence in the late fifteenth and sixteenth centuries remain uncovered (Fig. 206). Although this period began to value the mask as the product of antiquity and restored to it its ancient expressive function, medieval values persisted, and the mask was introduced into paintings of this period as a symbol of deceit, fraud, and the emptiness of sensual pleasure (Fig. 220).[215]

When the Orosius Master, who had collaborated on the *Térence des ducs*, undertook a few years later the illustration of Augustine's chapter on the *jeux sceniques* he naturally remembered the frontispiece painted by his colleague in the Terence of 1407 (Figs. 209, 218). The result, showing an octagonal theater, is scarcely an improvement on the model, and the *jongleur* with the large nose proves that the illuminator no longer had a clear notion of a mask. About 1410, that is in the interval between Berry's Terence and the *Térence des ducs*, another illuminator, the Virgil Master, contrived a very different picture of the ancient theater in a *Cité de Dieu* (Fig. 212).[216] The composition shares with the earlier miniatures and with the description of Raoul de Praelles the roundness of the structure, the poet reading, and the trumpeters. Otherwise the conception is entirely different. Actors are not visible, and the audience sits far below the entertainers, not above them. The structure looks like a kind of freestanding pulpit, though such a form is otherwise unknown. It is probably the ultimate source of a no less strange image of the ancient theater in the Latin edition of Terence printed by Grüninger at Strasbourg in 1496 (Fig. 213). Here, however, the audience occupies the balconies around the theater and seemingly also the rooms on the ground floor.[217] The picture of the theater in the edition printed in Paris in 1500 by Vérard is similar. The structure in the earliest edition of all the plays, printed at Lyon in 1493,[218] incorporates Renaissance architectural forms and returns to some semblance of the ancient design (Fig. 214).

It was Albrecht Dürer, however, who first approximated the true Roman theater in his woodcuts of 1492 for an edition of Terence in Basel, not printed at the time because of the appearance of the Lyon volume the following year (Fig. 216).[219] Though his plumed German *Landsknechte* seem much more remote from the ancient tradition than the actors in Berry's manuscript (Figs. 174, 221) his semicircular design for the theater—the very first one—followed not only existing Roman monuments but also—and here lay the full impact of humanism—the descriptions of Vitruvius. The hemisphere introduced by Dürer was then covered with a dome in the first Venetian illustrated Terence of 1497 (Fig. 217).

Consideration of the representation of the Roman theater in illustrations of the fifteenth century discloses that the illuminator of the Duke of Berry's Terence, the Josephus Master, came closer than the authors of some of the fantastic later woodcuts to basic elements of its design. Of course the same information or misinformation recorded from the time of Isidore on was presumably available to all these artists and their scholarly advisers, who then chose among the various possibilities. The fact, in any event, remains that later fifteenth-century images of the theater, like later fifteenth-century representations of ancient mythology, drew further away from the antique tradition.[220] The Josephus Master and his adviser were guided by a description and perhaps also by their own personal experience of an existing amphitheater—Raoul de Praelles tells us he knew them. Scholars and humanists in early fifteenth-century France, however, had clearly not associated with this problem the text of Vitruvius.[221] That remained to be done by the stronger and more experienced humanist movement at the end of the century.

The remarkable revival of the illustrated Terence that led to the production of three manuscripts within about five to seven years was, like French humanism and all related movements in French painting of this period, cut short. Only one manuscript of any significance survives from the next eighty years, and it has merely six miniatures (Fig. 219).[222] Then, under the stimulus of a revived humanist movement, a more secularized culture, and a new medium and technique, the *Comedies* of Terence illustrated with woodcuts began to flow from the printing presses of Lyon, Strasbourg and Paris.[223]

4 · VIRGIL

About five years before the execution of the first illustrated Terence a parallel initiative involving another great Roman writer was undertaken in Paris. Three manuscripts of Virgil have come down to us, one illuminated by 1403, the others soon afterwards. The poetry of Virgil was illustrated in antiquity; indeed by good fortune two illustrated manuscripts of the fifth and sixth centuries have survived (Figs. 224, 252).[224] Virgil, like Terence, continued to be read in subsequent centuries, but the illustrated Terence manuscripts of the ninth to the twelfth century that are more or less close to a classical model have no parallel in the case of Virgil. During the Middle Ages the *Eclogues* and/or the *Aeneid* were rarely illustrated; of three illuminated manuscripts, all from the period of the tenth through the thirteenth century, only one has an extensive (though artistically not very important) cycle, and it is entirely unrelated to the ancient manuscripts.[225] We know that around 1400 Virgil was one of the Roman writers who were especially admired by the humanists for their style.[226] As we have seen, Nicolas de Clamanges even wrote *Eclogues* in the Virgilian manner. Among the princes Jean de Berry, as usual exceptional, possessed not only two illustrated copies of Terence but a manuscript of Virgil's *Eclogues*.[227] No illustrated manuscript of either of these authors existed in the great Burgundian or Visconti libraries.[228]

The first post-antique painting that can be described as Virgilian in atmosphere is a miniature painted for a humanist in a codex of the principal works of the Mantuan poet. The famous picture executed by Simone Martini about 1340 for Petrarch's manuscript of Virgil represents the Roman poet seated on the ground under a tree, gazing upward while his quill is poised in one hand and the book in which he had been working lies open on his lap (Fig. 222).[229] The poet's position is unusual; in the later Middle Ages authors normally wrote indoors and some, such as Boethius, in bed. There are, to be sure, exceptions, the most notable being St. John on the island of Patmos. Still, Simone, counseled by Petrarch, introduced a new conception of Virgil, which influenced the later images of this poet and of other writers as well. Dürer's woodcut of Terence composing made for the Basel edition belongs to the new type (Fig. 231), though its specific source was Schongauer's engraving of *St. John on Patmos*. It is perhaps worth remarking that Simone, who represented Virgil seated on the ground, was the first artist who gave a similar position to the Virgin (Madonna of Humility), although for different reasons.

In Simone's miniature the commentator Servius, drawing back a transparent veil, points out the poet to a soldier, who alludes no doubt to Aeneas. Two farmers look up at Virgil. One, pruning a vine, represents the *Georgics*, and another, milking goats, refers to the *Eclogues*. The lower inscription speaks of these three figures.

> Servius uncovers the secrets of Virgil . . . so that they may be plain to knights, shepherds and husbandmen.

Virgil reclines in a meadow within the shade of soft, feathery trees, as though he were one of the shepherds in the *Eclogues*, enjoying the *locus amoenus*. Simone has communicated more of the pastoral sentiment than any artist since antiquity, and he was, of course, aware of a novel task. Did he not for this reason abandon his normal palette and render the entire scene in a very narrow range of color? The figures, the curtain and the animals are white delicately shaded in blue or violet, and they appear before blue vegetation and a deep blue sky.

In July 1403 Pierre de l'Ormel, licensed bookdealer of the University of Paris, as he tells us in a colophon (Fig. 264), finished writing a beautiful text of Virgil, complete, like the *Térence des ducs* and part of the Terence lat. 8193, with exegetical notes or *scholia*. He prepared the book for Jacques Courau, an officer of Jean de Berry, who gave him illustrated manuscripts of Valerius Maximus and of the *City of God* (Figs. 271, 413, 414).[230] The frontispiece, no doubt connected with the *Eclogues*, has been cut from the manuscript, but the miniature for the *Georgics* (Fig. 223) and the more routine miniature for the *Aeneid* survive.[231] For the *Georgics* the illuminator represented four main agricultural activities: ploughing, sowing, beekeeping, and pruning. Oddly, the pruner is not working on the usual object of his attention in Italy—the vine or the olive—but on a sizeable, large-leaved tree. In 1956 I referred to the illuminator, head of a large but not outstanding workshop in Paris, as the Virgil Master. To be consistent I have retained the name, though since then I have become aware of a much more interesting cycle of Virgil illustrations.

The illumination of the remarkable manuscript of Virgil's *Eclogues*, *Georgics*, and *Aeneid* now in the Bibliothèque municipale at Lyon, was begun in an unusual way (Fig. 226).[232] The simple rectangular frames of the miniatures and the initials were completed but no conventional vines were painted in the borders, and indeed none were ever intended. As a result the column of text and the miniature, which is of approximately the same width, are surrounded by large areas of bare parchment. The folio, with its wide, white borders, looks less like contemporary French examples than Italian early Renaissance manuscripts (Fig. 225). And the miniatures in many of these manuscripts, as in the famous Riccardiana Virgil of *ca.* 1460, with its figures in contemporary dress and its encyclopaedic realism, do not seem more antique than the Lyon Virgil (Figs. 225, 226).

The manuscript, or at least the section up to the *Aeneid* (which was completed later), exhibits other qualities that we may characterize as non-Gothic. The miniatures, which were painted by the Roman Texts Master and an assistant, have, like his miniatures in the Terence lat. 8193, unpainted backgrounds (Fig. 234). The bare vellum becomes the symbol of a limitless space both within the frame and inevitably, to a degree, outside it. In the miniatures exposed vellum serves also for lighted areas, and the colors alongside such areas are pale and limited in number, as in the Terence: apple and olive green, straw yellow, brown, gray, blue, rose, and violet. To these washes are added touches of yellow-orange on the flesh and white for the highest lights. The strokes of the illuminator's brush remain quite visible; the paint is laid in streaks or spots that create the kind of vibration we have seen in the Terence.

The initials at the beginning of the *Eclogues* and the *Aeneid* have a conventional Gothic character, but the other initials are executed in a fine penwork, no doubt by the same Italian calligrapher who collaborated with the Roman Texts Master on the Terence (Fig. 232). The immediate precedent for such Italian initials was provided by the *Brussels Hours* shortly before 1402.[233] In the first miniature the prominent tree—the spreading beech described in the first line of the poem—resembles closely the peculiar tree we have seen in lat. 8193 (Figs. 59, 226).[234] It is, however, less luminous and more stylized than in the Terence, and all the forms in the Virgil tend to differ in the same way. The painter of the Lyon Virgil renders details such as the nose and eye with a more sophisticated shorthand of a few rapid strokes.

The painters of the two groups of miniatures certainly were closely associated, but it is not easy to determine whether the variations imply a difference of time or of hand. The Lyon miniatures, however, are less consistently strong. The legs of Alexis on folio 3v (Fig. 228) or the folded arms on folio 11 (Fig. 236), for instance, are not well constructed. The position in space of Cybele's lions is not clear (Fig. 245). Probably the miniatures were executed by an associate and follower of the painter of lat. 8193, possibly after drawings or a lost manuscript of Virgil illustrated by him. Painter rather than illuminator the chief artist may well have been, because so few miniatures by him and his assistants survive, and because there seems to be no trace of his influence on subsequent painting in the book.

The *Eclogues* reflect Virgil's life in the country a few miles north of Mantua. His farm and many others around that city and Cremona were confiscated by Augustus and given to his soldiers when he became emperor. Virgil recovered his land only through the intervention of a patron in Rome, Maecenas. The first *Eclogue*, written in gratitude, is a dialogue between an elderly land-owner, Tityrus, and one of his less fortunate neighbors (Fig. 226). The verses at the beginning read, in Dryden's translation:

Meliboeus Beneath the shade which beechen boughs diffuse,
You, Tityrus, entertain your sylvan muse.
Round the wide world in banishment we roam,
Forced from our pleasing fields and native home;
While, stretched at ease, you sing your happy loves,
And Amaryllis fills the shady groves.
Tityrus These blessings, friend, a deity bestowed:
For never can I deem him less than god.
The tender firstlings of my woolly breed
Shall on his holy altar often bleed.[235]

In posture and position Tityrus recalls Virgil in Simone's miniature (Fig. 222), though Tityrus holds a rustic pipe and Simone's figure is of course artistically superior. The similarity may not be entirely accidental, because Tityrus was believed to represent Virgil, and indeed, despite the obvious discomfort it entails, the illuminator has given the recumbent Tityrus the high hat Virgil and other poets wear in following miniatures of the cycle (Figs. 233, 245). In the centuries after his death Virgil came to be regarded not only as a poet but a magician and sometimes a prophet.[236] In images he wore a high hat, often (even as late as Botticelli) resembling a tiara.[237] It was Simone Martini, counselled by Petrarch, who turned away from this iconography and gave the poet a crown of laurel and a white, toga-like mantle (Fig. 222).[238]

At this point we should introduce a second illustrated manuscript of the *Eclogues* and *Georgics*, preserved in the library of the Earl of Leicester at Holkham Hall. Scarcely better known than the manuscript in Lyon, it has never been connected with it, though the miniatures are for the most part copies. Curiously the Holkham manuscript can even be traced back to Lyon, where Thomas Coke, the builder of Holkham Hall, acquired it in 1713.[239] It seems highly doubtful, however, that either manuscript was produced there rather than in Paris. In 1908 Dorez, the author of the catalogue of the Holkham manuscripts, ascribed the miniatures in the Virgil to the workshop of the illuminator of the *Térence des ducs*,[240] and they were indeed, it seems to us, painted by a rather mediocre assistant of *one* of the illuminators of that manuscript, the Luçon Master (Fig. 227). Neither the miniatures nor the script equals the manuscript in Lyon, but the existence of a second illustrated copy of this text is an interesting and important historical fact.

The miniatures in Holkham were copied, with small changes, from the Lyon cycle. They substitute, however, a blue sky for the parchment background, and, with certain exceptions, they restore the color pattern characteristic of the Luçon style, which includes bright red, blue, and green. In the first miniature Tityrus has lost his high hat and the gesture of Meliboeus is different, but the odd tree, characteristic of the Roman Texts Master and not the Luçon Master, has been clumsily adopted. Perhaps the Luçon workshop became familiar with this tree when employing the Lyon manuscript as a model. Certain it is, in any event, that more able Luçon illuminators adopted the unusual form in a Boccaccio received by Berry on New Year's, 1411 (Fig. 507) and later in the *Térence des ducs* (Fig. 230).[241]

In the miniature of the second *Eclogue* in both manuscripts the old shepherd Corydon woos the young Alexis, offering him his prized seven-chambered pipe (Figs. 228, 229). In the Lyon miniature Alexis turns about like figures by the Roman Texts Master in the Terence (Fig. 205), though the bodily implications are less well understood. In both manuscripts the figure of Tityrus in the first miniature is repeated for Corydon. Perhaps this puzzling repetition may be explained by the rubric in Lyon, "Poeta. Coridon," which appears immediately below the miniature. In this *Eclogue* the dialogue is preceded by five verses clearly ascribed, in the Lyon manuscript but not in the Holkham copy, to Virgil. Thus the illuminator might well have thought the poet was offering his pipe to Corydon, rather than Corydon to Alexis. In the representation of Alexis as a dandy the Luçon assistant has worked a typical transformation.

The title for *Eclogue III* in the Lyon manuscript is again misleading. Menalcas and Damoetas, engaged in a musical contest, invite their neighbor Palaemon to act as judge (Fig. 232). Palaemon enters on the scene later than the other two, and his name should have appeared last. The complex posture of the third figure in the miniature, in any event, brilliantly suggests listening as well as appraising. The figure of Menalcas is no less impressive, his weight supported by the crook so that his arms are free for the lute. Naturally the illuminator of the Holkham manuscript did not even try to copy it.

Near the beginning of the fourth *Eclogue* occurs the famous passage that was read in the Middle Ages as a prophecy of the birth of Christ.

> Now is come the last age of the song of Cumae; the great line of the centuries begins anew. Now the Virgin returns, the reign of Saturn returns; now a new generation descends from heaven on high.[242]

The miniature is surprisingly prosaic. Virgil sits on a grassy knoll, facing a chamber; within it a woman lies in bed, holding her child in her arms. The poet records his "vision" on a tablet, whether by writing or drawing it is difficult to say (Fig. 233).

In *Eclogue V* two shepherds, Mopsus and Menalcas, lament in song the death of Daphnis, who alludes to Julius Caesar (Figs. 235, 237).

Since on the downs our flocks together feed,
And since my voice can match your tuneful reed,
Why sit we not beneath the grateful shade,
Which hazels, intermixed with elms, have made?[243]

In the poem Menalcas sings but in both miniatures he has an instrument. Though the posture of each of the shepherds in the Lyon miniature is attractive, and though they compose an interesting group, the Luçon assistant basically altered that of Mopsus.[244] The suspicion that the illuminator followed suggestions of an adviser or possibly the indications of another cycle is greatly reinforced by the illustration of the next *Eclogue*, the sixth. In it the Holkham miniature includes the garland omitted in Lyon (Figs. 236, 238).

> The lads Chromis and Mnasyllos saw Silenus lying asleep in a cave, his veins swollen, as ever, with the wine of yesterday. Hard by lay the garlands, just fallen from his head, and his heavy tankard was hanging by its well-worn handle.[245]

In the illustrations for *Eclogue VII* Meliboeus or Daphnis judges a musical contest between Corydon and Thyrsis (Figs. 239, 240). The judge, accompanied by his sheep, sits under a tree designated an ilex by Virgil and rendered in the characteristic manner of the Roman Texts Master.

The illustrations of the eighth *Eclogue* portray the lament of the pastoral poet Damon, "at whose song lynxes stood spell-bound, and rivers . . . changed . . . their course" (Figs. 241, 242). The illuminator of the Lyon miniature gave Damon the high hat of the poet. He bewails the loss of his mistress, Nysa, who disappears behind a ridge with his rival Mopsus. At the right a witch, described by another poet, Alphesiboeus, lights a fire on an altar (*altaria*):

> Bring out water, and wreathe these shrines with soft wool; and burn rich herbs and male frankincense, that I may try with magic rites to turn to fire my lover's coldness of mood. Naught is lacking here save songs.[246]

In the tenth and last *Eclogue* Virgil sings the love of his fellow poet Gallus, whose mistress, Cytheris, departs with another man (Figs. 243, 244). Here the illuminator of the Lyon manuscript did not give the poets high hats but crowns of laurel. The painter of the Holkham miniature mistakenly put the laurel around a poet's high hat. The error suggests again that the Luçon illuminator, who knew the Lyon manuscript, was influenced also by another source.

In both manuscripts the text of the *Eclogues* is followed by the *Georgics*. In this poem Virgil "sings," as he says, of agriculture: tillage, planting, the rearing of cattle, and beekeeping. At the beginning of Book I he praises the gods of the fields, particularly "bounteous Ceres, if by your grace Earth changed Chaonia's acorn for the rich corn-ear." Then the poet invokes Augustus. In the foreground of both miniatures Virgil, wearing a hat like a Jewish priest's (Lyon) or a mitre (Holkham), bows before a man whose frontal position and sword leave little doubt that he represents, however oddly in our eyes, the Emperor (Figs. 245, 246). Across the meadow behind rolls a large wagon that bears a nude female balancing a tower on her head. She is not Ceres but another earth-goddess not mentioned in the poem, Cybele or Berecynthia. The bell in her hand and those on the wagon refer to the cymbals associated with her, and the tower is a characteristic attribute, as St. Augustine makes clear in his reference to the goddess in the *City of God*.[247] Indeed, in contemporary illustrations of this text by the Virgil Master Berecynthia and her tower appear in a wagon drawn by lions (Fig. 248), and a miniature of this kind may have been the model for the earth-goddess in the *Georgics*. There is one notable difference: Berecynthia, clothed in the *City of God*, is nude in the miniature by the Roman Texts Master and his imitator.

As in other miniatures (Figs. 181, 198) the Roman Texts workshop has designed the composition so that part of an important figure (the foremost lion) lies beyond the frame. This device, which clearly implies an extension of the pictorial space behind and beyond the frame, was soon to be more consistently exploited by the Limbourgs in the *Très Riches Heures* (Figs. 548, 586).

The second book of the *Georgics* begins:

> ... now thee, Bacchus, will I sing, and with thee the forest saplings, and the offspring of the slow-growing olive ... for thee blossoms the field teeming with the harvest of the vine. ...

Or, as Dryden rephrases it:

> Great father Bacchus! to my song repair;
> For clust'ring grapes are thy peculiar care:

The god in the miniature who presides over planting and pruning is, in accordance with an old tradition, bisexual (Fig. 247). This conception of Bacchus can be traced back to the encyclopedia of Isidore of Seville, written in the early seventh century. The figure painted by the Roman Texts workshop conforms perfectly with Isidore's description: "The god has a delicate body, like a woman's ... his brow is wreathed with vine tendrils and he has a crown of vine leaves and a horn."[248] The horn, to be sure, has grown greatly, to the dimension of a unicorn's. Isidore's description was transmitted by Hrabanus Maurus of the ninth century and by other medieval mythographers to the versions of Ovid in the fourteenth century. Berchorius, in the *Ovidius moralizatus*, speaks of Bacchus "cum capite cornuto" riding on a tiger.[249] Thus, after a fashion, we see him (with two horns) in the Duke of Berry's *Ovide moralisé*, mounted on what looks like a Chinese dragon (Fig. 249).

Book III of the *Georgics*, like other divisions of the poem, offers various possibilities to the illustrator. After brief references to some rural gods Virgil honors Caesar and his shrine, and then turns to animal husbandry. The Roman Texts workshop has designed animals as lively as those of the Boucicaut Master, though not quite as well constructed (Fig. 251).[250] Some of the cows are, in characteristic manner, overlapped by the frame. Perhaps it is not accidental that the miniature resembles the one for the same book in the late antique *Vergilius Romanus*, with the animals distributed over a steeply rising meadow in much the same way (Figs. 251, 252).

The Roman Texts Master probably knew the early fifteenth-century illustrations of the *Livre de la chasse*. Three closely related Parisian copies have come down to us. Ms. fr. 616 in the Bibliothèque nationale is famous (Fig. 253),[251] but two related copies, one in the collection of Miss Clara Peck in New York (Fig. 258),[252] and another, fr. 619 in the Bibliothèque nationale (Fig. 254), are much less well-known. For several reasons fr. 619 would seem to be the earliest copy. It is the only one that bears the arms of the family of the author of the text, Gaston Phébus, the Count of Foix.[253] Its portrait of him shows a younger man than the corresponding miniature in fr. 616 (Figs. 255, 256), and its style looks earlier, or at least much more traditional (Figs. 259, 260). There are signs that the miniatures of fr. 619, too, followed a model. In the scene of the rural banquet the illuminator has clearly misunderstood the structure of two tables and omitted the benches alongside them (Figs. 257, 258). In the upper right section of the frontispiece a dog lies in the air above the ground (Fig. 256).

In the miniature by the Roman Texts workshop for Virgil's fourth book, devoted to bees, the keeper sounds his gong (Fig. 250)—"the Mighty Mother's cymbal," the poet says,[254] referring to Cybele, who had actually been introduced, with bells, in the miniature for the first book (Fig. 245). In the illustration of beekeeping one of the gigantic insects, whom the keeper wishes to coax into the hives, has settled on his face, and the event is made more alarming by the transparency of the keeper's veil, through which his features, in a very sophisticated rendering, appear only too clearly.

The execution of two illustrated copies of the *Eclogues* and *Georgics* in rapid succession constitutes an event unprecedented since antiquity. It implies, of course, a devotion to Virgil's poems as models of Latin literature. There was, too, a new interest in the content of the particular poems, their concern with agriculture and their praise of rural life. The calendar of the *Très Riches Heures*, to which we shall turn shortly, provides additional evidence of that (Figs. 539–549). At this time literature as well as art turned with delight to the natural world. Christine de Pisan wrote a *Dit de la pastoure*, and already in the time of Charles V Jean de Brie had composed *L'art de bergerie*. The ballades of Eustache Deschamps and Charles d'Orléans, like the miniatures of the Limbourgs, celebrated the beauty of the changing seasons and the serenity of country life.[255] The scenes of sowing and harvest in the *Très Riches Heures* suggest less the difficulty of the task than the bounteousness of nature. A cloudless blue sky arches over the tranquil earth and its rich produce (Figs. 544, 545, 547, 548). The painters present a kind of earthly paradise, the praises of which can be sung, in the age of early humanism, by pagan as well as Christian poets.

In Books of Hours the shepherds, who were the first to learn of the birth of Christ, gained equal prominence with the Three Kings from the East (Fig. 263). Though inferior in dress and stature, their home was an inviting pasture strewn with flowers and watered by a spring or a stream (Fig. 262). Less committed now to labor, they enjoy what has become a pleasance—in Virgilian terms a *locus amoenus*.[256] When not responding to the angelic message one of them may recline blissfully in the lap of his mistress, her head crowned with flowers (Fig. 261).

Of course the aristocracy, too, move out to quiet, untroubled meadows. Not even their tight, elaborate dresses prevent them from bending to pluck flowers (Fig. 542). One remarkable monument, lost and half forgotten, showed Philippe le Hardi and Marguerite of Burgundy seated like shepherds below an elm and surrounded by sheep. This pastoral scene was carved during the 'nineties by none other than Claus Sluter on a large stone that was placed on a wall of the Burgundian chateau of Germolles.[257] This subject was not inspired, to be sure, only by a wish for a rural idyll. It is true that Marguerite resided principally at Germolles, where she supervised a large working farm which had large flocks of sheep, but it is also true that her name-saint, Margaret, had tended sheep as a young girl.[258] Sheep were represented—great numbers of them—in mural paintings and tapestries in Marguerite's chateau,[259] along with daisies, roses and various rustic scenes of the kind that were favored in other chateaux.[260] Although Sluter's relief of the Duke and Duchess reflected to a degree a religious association, it was one more—and a fascinating—sign of current pastoral inclinations.

5 · JEAN DE BERRY AND ANTIQUITY

A remarkably high proportion of the illustrated texts concerning antiquity that we have discussed in preceding chapters belonged to the Duke of Berry. To him went the first Terence and the first translation of Boccaccio's *De casibus* (Figs. 69, 507, 509, 512). He received from his brother Philippe le Hardi one of the first copies of Boccaccio's *Cleres femmes* (Figs. 6, 73). He possessed two manuscripts of the *Ovide moralisé* (Figs. 78–80, 92, 104, 249), and several of Livy (Fig. 272). He acquired the first and best cycle of illustrations of ancient history and mythology in Christine's *Epître d'Othéa* (Figs. 76, 87, 91, 122, 146). Under his patronage the translation of Valerius Maximus, begun under Charles V, was completed by Nicholas de Gonesse. The Duke's treasurer, Jacques Coureau, gave him the first copy, illuminated by the Virgil Master, as a New Year's present in 1402 (Figs. 271, 413, 414). The illustrations of this *Fais et dis de la cité de Romme*, like those of Boccaccio's *De casibus* which it influenced (Figs. 66, 69, 159), are often *exempla*. Thus the miniature at the beginning of Book IX exemplifies "luxure" and "cruaute" (Fig. 271).[261]

To this unique group of manuscripts may now be added, thanks to identification by François Avril, two outstanding manuscripts of a medieval compilation of ancient history and mythology.[262] The text, the "Histoire ancienne" based primarily on the work of the first Christian historian, Orosius,[263] had been illustrated earlier, and indeed the Duke acquired both a manuscript now in the British Museum illuminated by a Neapolitan workshop *ca.* 1340 for the Anjou and a copy of it, fr. 301, made in Paris about 1400 (Figs. 274, 275).[264] The Neapolitan manuscript served as a model again a few years later for a Netherlandish illuminator who was working in Paris (Fig. 276).

The illuminator of the best miniatures in fr. 301 takes his name, the Orosius Master, from this work. In one of the full-page miniatures, which represents the rather unbelievable equine ruse of the Greeks and the capture of Troy, the Orosius Master took his general design, as usual, from the corresponding scene in the Angevin manuscript now in the British Museum (Figs. 274, 275). The Neapolitan illuminator employed his tectonic capacities to give to some fifteen separate episodes in the taking of the city a certain unity of space and architectural plausibility. The Orosius Master has, in turn, recognized and restored the Giottesque principles inherent in this intricate structure. He simplified it and he reduced the movement in the framing members to enhance that of the figures. To give each episode a greater unity and discreteness he varied his hues and he widened and deepened the spaces. Very significantly, he limited the open buildings to the upper part of the composition, giving the lower part a more impressive architectural bulk. The master used rare hues of burnt orange and raspberry red, pale yellow, blue, which can drop to a very deep tone, blue-green and violet.

It is evident that the Orosius Master highly valued order. He preferred regular, geometric shapes, simple cubes, and smoothly turning planes. He managed to make even so intricate a design and so turbulent a series of events seem almost neat. He changed one episode in a highly significant way. In the Neapolitan miniature the victim of the Greek soldier who climbs a ladder in the lower right corner of Troy is a woman in a window, facing her destroyer. The Orosius Master, the creator of remarkably still figures, replaced her with a couple lying quietly asleep in bed. Most of the other "acts" in the play are the same in the two manuscripts, from the decapitation of Priam in the upper right to the Greeks issuing from the gates carrying their booty.

A Netherlandish illuminator, whom we have already encountered at an earlier stage of his career in the Duke of Berry's Ovid, fr. 373 (Fig. 80), simplified the composition when introducing it into his illustrations of Stowe 54 (Fig. 276), which also depend upon Royal 20 D 1 (Fig. 275). He preferred lighter, pale hues, and a pattern of juxtaposed warm and cool colors. His color is more fluid and less bound to volume and mass.

Raoul de Praelles, who accompanied his translation of the *City of God* (completed in 1375) with a long commentary, was particularly interested in the ancient historical and mythological content of Augustine's great work. When therefore the Orosius Master, undertaking *ca.* 1408–10 the illumination of one of the many manuscripts of the *Cité de Dieu*, devoted the miniature for book III to a novel subject, Troy, he was quite consistent with the concern of de Praelles and his period (Fig. 277). Since there are many reasons to date the illumination of this manuscript in Philadelphia about 1408–10, the illuminator could draw upon his recollection of the Trojan pictures in his *Histoire ancienne* (Fig. 274). The miniature in the *Cité de Dieu* exemplifies the *mutacion de fortune*, or more precisely the destructiveness of time. At the left Ilion is built, at the right it burns and collapses under the watchful eyes of the Greeks, gathered offshore in their ships.

Within the same decade as the illustrations of the *Histoire ancienne* and the depiction of Troy in the *Cité de Dieu* the *Thebaid* of Statius was given one of its unusual cycles, although not, as far as we know, for the Duke of Berry.[265] The manuscript, now in the British Museum, was undoubtedly illuminated in Paris, because of a collaboration of workshops that could only have occurred in the capital. Though most of the cycle seems remote from the tragic history of ancient Thebes, a few miniatures show that in early fifteenth-century France it was quite possible to communicate in paint some of the anguish and terror of the poem. In these miniatures the ancient stories are charged with the emotional depth of contemporary religious painting. In one of them Oedipus, as Statius described him, "with avenging hand probed deep his sinning eyes and sunk his guilty shame in eternal night . . ." (Fig. 270).[266] Jocasta gestures in dismay while her two sons talk excitedly. They bear crowns of the kind that has fallen from the head of their father. "Raised to royalty . . . they mock the blindness (of Oedipus) and abhor his groans."[267]

The Duke of Berry's collection of writings on antiquity is related to one aspect of the famous picture for January in the *Très Riches Heures* (Fig. 539). Behind the Duke, who sits at table, a large tapestry covers the rear wall. Its subject—two armies in combat—seems surprising for the least martial of princes. Though as a young man Jean de Berry took to the field against the English his performance failed to satisfy his brother, King Charles V. Later in life the Duke was far less notable for victories than for the avoidance of military enterprises, and he became in fact a major moderator between the warring factions in France.[268] Why, then, should he be depicted in front of a battle picture? The militant display might have had a topical reference that now eludes us. However that may be, part at least of the significance of the tapestry lies in the *kind* of battle it represents. This is no recent struggle, as the verses on the tapestry tell us. They are carefully written and will some day be identified in their entirety. To the right of the canopy M. Jean Longnon has read, quite correctly we believe, the phrase "de tro(?)yes le grant."[269] A battle fought long ago, in other words, by the great and revered Trojans, their own ancestors, as the French believed. Though the inventories do not record a tapestry devoted to Trojan exploits, Jean de Berry possessed no less than six manuscripts of the history of "Troye la grant," as one of them is entitled.[270] One of these manuscripts was given to him in 1403 by the very man who might sit at his table, his counselor, the learned Bishop Martin Gouge.[271]

This ancient battle, like most of the other ancient subjects in the ducal collection, is realized in an Italianate mode. The distinctive forms of ancient art had not yet come into clear focus. The recurring phrase in the inventories, "d'ancienne façon," still lacked a precise historical significance.[272] Jean de Berry's obvious enthusiasm for antiquity, compounded of genealogical, moral, historical, and religious motives, was normally satisfied by the theme and the Trecento manner. It is essential to recall, however, that he acquired many authentic examples of ancient art—all described in some detail in a preceding volume.[273] He possessed a remarkable collection of coins and cameos; some of the latter can be definitely identified today (Fig. 266). When a medal *all'antica* was produced for Francesco da Carrara, Jean de Berry almost immediately acquired a copy of it (Fig. 265). His collection included a large antique silver plate representing a mythological scene and the Emperor Constantine.

The Duke felt a special affinity for the Roman emperors. He became the chief sponsor, as we demonstrated in a preceding volume, of the image of Aracoeli (Figs. 397, 399, 557). In the fifteenth century he took to wearing an imposing hat nearly identical with that given to the Emperor Augustus (Figs. 404, 405, 557), and it is fascinating that the idea for this headgear probably was provided by the sojourn in Paris from 1400 to 1402 of the Emperor Manuel Paleologus and his retinue. We recognize the hat in Pisanello's drawings of Manuel's son, Emperor John VIII, during his visit to Italy in 1438 (Fig. 273). The notion that these men from Greek Byzantium somehow preserved elements of the ancient world was not, after all, entirely wrong. The Duke probably knew that the medals representing emperors he acquired about 1402 had been made recently, probably in Paris and expressly for him, but since they represented ancient persons and contained Early Christian or Byzantine symbols (not to mention Greek inscriptions) they presumably seemed to him "antique" (Figs. 267, 268, 482, 483). We know that in Renaissance Italy itself they were judged ancient until the late sixteenth century.

The famous medals of Constantine and Heraclius have been discussed in a preceding volume[274] and because of their relation to the Limbourgs they reappear frequently in the following pages. There remain to be added here some observations about the reverse of the medal of Constantine that have not, to our knowledge, been made in the very extensive literature on this problematic representation (Fig. 268). Around the rim of this face of the medal runs an inscription that, with slight variations in different copies, reads:

MIHI ABSIT GLORIARI NISI IN CRUCE DOMINI NOSTRI JESU CHRISTI

God forbid that I should glory, save in the cross of our Lord Jesus Christ. . . .

It has not been noticed that this passage, from Paul's Epistle to the Galatians (6, 14), recurs four times for the feast of the Invention of the Cross in the Breviary, appearing in exactly the above form in the capitulum for Sext.[275]

The text of this Office is connected with the medal not only by its principal symbol, the cross, and by the inscription but by other details as well. Its references to baptism and rebirth are related to the *fons vitae*, the water spouting from the top of the cross and falling into a sort of font. The description of the cross—"nulla silva talem profert, fronde, flore, germine . . ."—seems to be embodied in the flowers springing from the cone-like plant. Most interesting of all is the relation of another section of the Office to the two beautiful and puzzling figures on the medal. The contrast between them is striking. The older woman, clothed and wearing a wimple, responds to the cross while the younger, half nude, turns away. She places her foot on a small animal, probably a weasel, identified by the bestiaries with worldly pleasure. Everyone agrees that these two women symbolize a dualism—of Christianity and Paganism, or the Church and the Synagogue, or as I tended to agree in my preceding volume, Grace and Nature.

The fourth lesson of Matins, second Nocturn, of the Office of the Invention of the Cross reads as follows:

> Post insignem victoriam, quam Constantinus imperator, divinitus accepto signo Dominicae Crucis, ex Maxentio reportavit, Helena Constantini mater, in somnis admonita, conquirendae Crucis studio Jerosolymam venit; ubi marmoream Veneris statuam, in Crucis loco a Gentibus collocatam ad tollendam Christi Domini passionis memoriam, post centum circiter octoginta annos evertendam curavit . . . The Response: Nos autem gloriari oportet in Cruce Domini nostri Jesu Christi . . .[276]

Does not the old woman at the left embody allusions not only to grace or the Church but also to the elderly Helena, who normally wears a wimple? As for her youthful companion, probably few if any Parisians of the early fifteenth century knew what a Roman statue of Venus looked like. Artists and their primary audience were aware, however, that ancient statues normally were not seated but stood. Nevertheless, should we not suggest that the idea of the goddess of love contributed to the creation of what was surely the most sensuous female nude since antiquity? She is well conceived to distract attention from the cross and, like the marble Venus, "ad tollendam Christi Domini passionis memoriam." When the time is right religious texts, too, can contribute to the beginning of an understanding of the ancient world.

IV

The Limbourgs: Introduction

HISTORIANS have written about the art of the Limbourg brothers since the discovery of the *Très Riches Heures* in 1856. The literature is full of perceptive observations of all kinds, but no one has hitherto undertaken, as we have remarked, a comprehensive study. In considerable measure this rather extraordinary failure must be ascribed to difficulties of access to the major works. Paul Durrieu, to be sure, published a valuable monograph on the *Très Riches Heures* in 1904, though many of the smaller miniatures by the Limbourgs were reproduced for the first time only in the color facsimile of 1969. The *Belles Heures* remained only partially reproduced and virtually inaccessible—I can testify to this point—until Jean Porcher's monograph of 1953 and the acquisition of the manuscript by the Metropolitan Museum in 1954. Serious as these obstacles were, they represented only part of the problem, because other manuscripts ascribed to the Limbourgs by eminent specialists, such as the first gatherings of the *Bible moralisée* and the Breviary of Jean sans Peur, were not closely studied despite their presence in the Bibliothèque nationale and the British Museum. Thus even the Limbourgs suffered from the general inattention to the illumination of this period.

Many historians were rightly put off, too, by the formidable stylistic problems that the Limbourgs present, more complex even than those that surround the still controversial Van Eycks. There are, after all, not two brothers but three. Their careers, furthermore, were short—a span of only about sixteen years for all three. We have, however, from their brush 158 miniatures in the *Belles Heures* and 129 in the *Très Riches Heures*, plus 384 small ones in the *Bible moralisée*, which I am convinced they painted also. 671 miniatures, then, presumably by three illuminators, many of them painted in the first years of their career when they were changing most rapidly. And to make matters worse I shall propose that they engaged collaborators for the *Très Riches Heures*.

A historian of style, faced with the task of sorting these paintings and dating them within narrow limits, examines with special eagerness the judgments of his predecessors. They are often, alas, contradictory, and their validity is limited, except in the special instances of Durrieu and Porcher, by brief exposure to the originals. A deeper difficulty lies in the practice of forming conclusions about one manuscript or another, rather than about the surviving oeuvre as a whole.

In so complex a problem the historian turns with more than usual hope for clues in other realms. Luckily, the Limbourgs are by far the best-documented illuminators and painters in France in the fourteenth and early fifteenth centuries. The entire series of documents, matched by few records even of Italian artists of the time, is given in an appendix to this chapter (pp. 71–81). The significance of some facts contained in them has not, it seems to me, hitherto been grasped. Even after exploiting all of them, however, I am well aware that I leave problems for younger, or at least better, eyes.

1 · THE RECORDS OF THE PAINTERS

The Limbourgs first appear in recorded history because of one of those trivial episodes that, paradoxically, so often give us fundamental facts about important figures of the past. Because of an epidemic in Paris the goldsmith Alebret de Bolure decided to send two young apprentices, "Hermant Maleuel" and "Jacquemin Malauel," back to their native country, Guelders.[1] On the way these boys, "jonnes enfans," were imprisoned and held for ransom in Brussels because of a conflict between Brabant and Guelders. Their expenses in prison had to be paid by their mother, a very poor woman, the record says, and in this very year she had in fact lost her husband, a sculptor of Nijmegen and the father of the boys.[2] She was, however, the sister of the painter Jean Maleuel (Malouel), *valet de chambre* of Duke Philippe le Hardi of Burgundy. The document, indeed, calls the boys his nephews, and out of respect for their colleague Malouel the goldsmiths and painters of Brussels agreed to pay the ransom. On May 2, 1400, by an order given at Conflans near Paris, the Duke himself advanced the sum to free the boys after they had been in prison for about six months—since the end, in other words, of 1399.

The document refers on one occasion to Jacquemin and on another to Gillequin, clearly interchangeable diminutives. In later records the same boy, whose name follows Herman and who might be the younger, is called Janequin, Jannechin, Hennequin, etc. The form Herman remained comparatively invariable. The third and most famous of the illuminators, Paul, not mentioned by the document, is later sometimes called Polequin.

Thus we know that two of the Limbourg brothers, the sons of a sculptor, had been apprenticed by Jean Malouel to a Parisian goldsmith from early 1399, at least. At that time an apprenticeship in this guild lasted eight years,[3] but we have no reason to believe that the Limbourgs, who apparently lacked financial means, had served very long. The phrase "jonnes enfans" and the use of the diminutive form of their names indicates Herman and Jean were youthful, probably teen-agers, but one still might be called an *enfant* in one's twenties.[4] Jean Malouel had himself been active in Paris in 1396 and perhaps earlier, though as a painter; and after his appointment as the painter of Philippe le Hardi in 1397 he worked chiefly in Dijon.[5] The document of 1400 about the Limbourgs gives the boys his family name, Maelwael ("paint well"), whereas their father employed the name of Limburg, probably reflecting the name of the small duchy (today in Holland) along the Meuse River near Aachen, from which the family had come.

What the boys did after regaining their freedom in May 1400 we do not know. In early 1402, however, we hear of two of them again, in an extraordinary document that is in many ways unique among surviving records of this period. It concerns, as we shall later prove, the *Bible moralisée*, fr. 166 in the Bibliothèque nationale. By a series of orders given in Paris from February to May Philippe le Hardi engaged Paul and Jean to illuminate a "très belle et notable Bible" that the Duke had recently commissioned. The scribe, indeed, had not yet completed his work. The "enlumineurs," as they are described, were charged with the completion of the manuscript and particularly the miniatures ("ystoires") as soon as possible, or at least in four years, and during that period they were not to accept employment from anyone else, nor to undertake any other work.

Paul and Jean were each to receive 10 sous a day, whether workday or holiday ("jour ouvrable et non ouvrable"). Because of this provision their salary was comparatively high, especially for beginners.[6] The Duke at this time resided mostly in Paris, and he gave supervision of the work to his physician, Jean Durant, resident likewise in the capital and indeed within the cloister of Notre-Dame. For the writing and illumination of the Bible Durant, who was to disburse to the boys, received a first payment of 600 francs. It is significant that in January 1402, just before the commission to the Limbourgs, their uncle Jean Malouel had been in Paris.[7] He probably was the catalyst.

A few months later, in July, Jean Durant was repaid for 6 ounces of "fin asur," probably lapis lazuli, purchased for the illumination of "certain books" that he was having made for the Duke. Some of this ultramarine might have gone also to Jacques Coene, Imbert Stanier, and Haincelin de Haguenau, who were illuminating another Bible, in Latin and French, for the Duke.[8] Jean and Paul were clearly getting on with their work, because early in the following year the Duke made a special gift to each of the boys for clothing while they worked in Durant's house. In January 1404, nearly two years after the first payment to Jean Durant, chiefly for Paul and Jean, the Duke gave him an equal sum of 600 francs for the "perfeccion des histoires et enlumineure de certaine bible." Whereas Paul and Jean had earlier been called "enlumineurs" as well as "peintres," and though they were clearly required to execute the decoration of the folios as well as the miniatures, they are here called "paintres et historieurs." The latter is an unusual but perfectly logical term for the makers of "histoires." Philippe le Hardi died shortly thereafter, on April 27, and that is all we hear of the Limbourgs' Bible. It does not appear in the inventory of the Duke's manuscripts in Paris after his death, nor in his wife's, who died in 1405.

The death of Philippe le Hardi moved his brother, Jean de Berry, to complete and to consecrate his own mortuary chapel in Bourges, and one copy of the charter, dated April 18, 1405, bore a miniature that is clearly in the style of the Limbourgs. The original manuscript, to be sure, was burned in 1858, but the copy made earlier by Bastard, which we shall consider presently, leaves no room for doubt about the original painter (Fig. 387). One at least of the Limbourgs entered the service of Jean de Berry not long after the death of their first major patron in 1404. The fact that Paul and Jean completed only three gatherings of a Bible we shall presently consider probably indicates that they did not remain in Burgundian service after the death of Philippe le Hardi, who commissioned the work.

This conclusion is proved by evidence we have recently offered for the date of the *Belles Heures*. This richly illuminated manuscript was completed and accessioned in the Duke's inventory in 1408–9. The accession in 1408–9, though five years earlier than preceding historians had maintained, now seems to us established by its place in the chronological order of entries in Robinet's inventory.[9] The manuscript described in item 960 of the inventory conforms so completely with the manuscript now in the Cloisters that the identification has not been, and cannot be, questioned, and though Robinet d'Estampes says only that the *Belles Heures* was executed by the "ouvriers" of the Duke, no one has ever challenged the attribution to the Limbourgs. Indeed, Robinet's failure to name the illuminators is probably explained by the early date of the manuscript. The young brothers had not attained the exceptional eminence of a few years later.

The fact that the Limbourgs—which ones, if not all, we shall discuss later—were working on the *Belles Heures* from 1405 or 1406 increases the interest of a reference to a "German painter" ("ung paintre alemant") who in 1408 was working for the Duke of Berry at Bicêtre, his *hôtel* on the periphery of Paris that was famous for its works of art, which were largely destroyed in the sack of 1411.[10] Since the time of Champeaux and Gauchery this painter has been tentatively associated with Paul, or at least one of the Limbourgs,[11] and indeed an order of King Charles VII of 1434 describes "Pol" as a painter of the Duke who was "natif dallemagne." This same document greatly strengthens the identification, because it concerns a house in Bourges that the Duke gave to Paul after the discharge of his treasurer Christophe de la Mer on June 22, 1411 and the recovery of his house.[12]

The house was described as one of the largest in Bourges, suitable for a nobleman, and by giving it to Paul Jean de Berry showed quite clearly his exceptionally high esteem. It was not unusual for a painter or sculptor of one of the great patrons of the time to receive a house; Philippe le Hardi, for example, lent one to Sluter.[13] Paul's, however, previously occupied by the Duke's treasurer and described as "une des plus grans et plus spacieuse et notable de . . . Bourges . . . bien seant et propre pour logier l'un des seigneurs de nostre sang et lignage . . ." was entirely unusual. No earlier painter, and very few since, ever lived in such style.

After Paul's death in 1416 his wife continued to live in the house, together with her second husband. This woman, Gillette la Mercière, was the cause of the petition of 1408.[14] At the age of eight years she was being held, against her mother's wishes, in the Château d'Etampes, near Paris, by the Duke of Berry. She was the daughter of a wealthy merchant of Bourges, Gillet Mercier. Several years after his death in 1402 Gillette's mother married Audebert de Catin, a Parisian money-changer and purveyor of gold and silver plate to Jean de Berry. The Duke, apparently recognizing that Gillette was a good catch, wished to marry her to the "paintre alemant" who in 1408 was working in Bicêtre. His forceful methods, however, were not approved by the Parlement. Within a year, which saw the intervention of King Charles VI, an accommodation seems to have been worked out. Gillette became twelve years old in 1411 and therefore eligible for marriage according to canon law, so that then or shortly afterward she married Paul, who at about the same time received the large house from the Duke.

In the summer of 1410 we hear of the other two brothers. Herman and Jean then transferred all their property in Nijmegen to their mother, who was, we recall, described in 1400 as a very poor woman. The first, and most famous, of the gifts exchanged by the Duke and the brothers is recorded for January 1, 1411. "Pol de Limbourc et ses deux freres" gave their patron an extraordinary New Year's gift: a piece of wood painted to simulate a book. It lacked, Robinet added somewhat wryly, folios and script, but it was covered in white velour, and had two gilt silver clasps enameled with the Duke's arms. This gift is quite rightly taken as a sign of unusual intimacy between the painters, then in their twenties, and their patron. Artisans, furthermore, normally gave patrons gifts of other crafts rather than their own, which they were paid to produce. For New Year 1415 Paul thus offered Jean de Berry an agate and gold salt cellar. To give the most discerning and passionate collector of illuminated manuscripts in history a *fake* book shows the wit and understanding of the donors.

The one gift of all three brothers to their patron, and Paul's later present of a salt cellar, were of course more than matched by the Duke's gifts to them. Special gifts there certainly were, even though no records survive of regular payments to the three painters for their work for the Duke. We cannot be certain precisely when the gifts began, for we have a series of *post quem* dates beginning 1404–1405. Sometime after this date Jean de Berry gave "Pol et ses freres"—this is the usual phrase—nine gold coins, then twelve more. Around the same time he gave Paul alone a diamond ring, and it was upon this brother that the Duke lavished gifts. After 1408 Paul received a gold ring with an emerald carved in the shape of a bear—the Duke's emblem and a favored animal in his "zoo."[15] Probably in 1411 Paul received the large house in Bourges. In 1413 he was the recipient of three large sums of money.[16] The Duke did not, however, entirely forget the other two brothers, for at New Year 1414 he gave them diamonds. In the final year of his life there occurred the mysterious transaction in which the Duke gave Paul and his brothers a precious gold ring set with a ruby as security for the very large sum of 1000 *escus*, which the Duke owed the painters.

Only two records indicate where one of the brothers worked. In 1408 Paul was apparently at Bicêtre, where he might have painted on the wall or on panel as well as on parchment. The receipt of a house in Bourges sometime after June 1411 suggests he then resided there, but how long or how uninterruptedly he remained we do not know.[17] Many signs, as we shall see, point to his frequent presence in Paris, the principal residence of his patron from 1402 on.

As far as existing documents show, the Limbourgs bore the title of *valet de chambre* only after some seven or eight years' service with the Duke. Paul is so described for the first time on November 9, 1413, and all three brothers in 1415. They enjoyed this position only a very short time. Like Masaccio, who lived 26 years, they disappeared early. News of the death of Jean had reached Nijmegen by March 9, 1416, and Paul and Herman were reported dead by September or October. Their patron, Jean de Berry, breathed his last on June 15. Thus the rare team was destroyed all at once.

A younger brother and an heir, Arnold, became an apprentice to a goldsmith in Nijmegen in 1417.[18] Perhaps he may be identified with an artist I have called the Master of St. Jerome.[19] Another brother, Roger, was a canon of the Sainte-Chapelle in Bourges from 1414.[20]

In later years we hear of Jean de Berry's three painters only once, in a description of Paris (not Bourges!) written in 1434 by Guillebert de Metz. The writer names eminent musicians in the city, harpists and flautists, as well as a scribe, such as Flamel, and among the painters only "les trois freres enlumineurs."[21]

This review of the documents on the Limbourgs leads us to reconsider one problem. In 1967 I had inferred from the language and arrangement of the post-mortem inventory that the *Très Riches Heures* had been found in Paris at the Duke's death, together with other important manuscripts such as the *Grandes Heures*, *Heures de Pucelle*, and the Duke's early Terence.[22] I observed that the larger part of the library had been "trouvez et inventoriez a Mehun,"[23] and since no such statement precedes the lists containing the *Heures de Pucelle*, the *Très Riches Heures*, and other manuscripts I inferred that they probably were found in Paris. It is true that half a dozen manuscripts were explicitly said to have been found and inventoried in Paris, but they are apparently not important and not a single Book of Hours was among them.[24] The outstanding manuscripts mentioned above are in lists that give no hint of the place in which they had been found at the Duke's death, nor why these particular books had been chosen.[25] The books used at the end of the Duke's life in the chapel of the Hôtel de Nesle by the chaplain Pierre Belon were more or less ordinary liturgical books, and not the Duke's beautifully illustrated manuscripts.[26]

The documents, therefore, show that most of the Duke's manuscripts were kept at Mehun. They do not clearly indicate that he had more than a half-dozen comparatively unimportant books in Paris. The sojourns of the Duke in Bourges and in the Berry began to become shorter and less frequent in 1389, and he spent proportionately more of his time in Paris. After 1404 he resided in the metropolis, with only occasional visits to his *châteaux*, and he never even visited the Berry after 1412.[27] In the intensifying conflict between the Burgundians and the Armagnacs, of whom Jean de Berry was a leader, the Parisians tended to favor the former. In 1411 a mob looted the Hôtel de Nesle and severely damaged the Duke's chateau of Bicêtre and its rich collections.[28]

The Duke had good reason, therefore, to keep the larger part of his collections in the comparative safety of Bourges and Mehun. There they were appropriately placed, in his own domain, part of his *apanage*. Can we, however, imagine this remarkable man living for years in Paris in a large hotel, a veritable stronghold, without representative examples of the objects he had so passionately collected? He had no sons, and the risks of the metropolis were surely not considerable enough to force him to forego the enjoyment of some of his most prized *joyaux*, manuscripts, and tapestries. And apart from the pleasure these possessions would have given the aging collector they served as attributes of his position and they gave collectors clear signs of his special enthusiasm and discernment.

For similar reasons we may suppose that although Paul and his wife occupied a large house in Bourges he as well as his brothers visited Paris frequently, no doubt carrying forward in the Hôtel de Nesle some of the work on the *Très Riches Heures*. This understanding of the circumstances is supported by the exchange of gifts between the painters and their patron and the familiarity that the character of some of the gifts (or debts) clearly implies. Still more indicative is the exchange of artistic ideas between the illuminators of the Duke and those definitely resident in Paris. In preceding volumes of this publication we have had occasion to observe the relation of Jacquemart de Hesdin to painting in Paris, and of the Boucicaut Master, resident in the capital, to the Limbourgs. Or vice versa. Much more will be said on this subject in the chapters that follow.

DOCUMENTS ON THE LIMBOURG BROTHERS

Most of the documents were collected by Champeaux and Gauchery (*Travaux*, 1894) and by Gorissen (1954). Gorissen added important records about the family in Nijmegen; he overlooked, however, some documents published by Champeaux and Gauchery. Because both these collections contain a few errors, even in the dates of the documents, the text that follows differs accordingly. It adds one previously unpublished, though relatively unimportant, record (1413, October 1).

1400 May 2. Conflans-les-Paris

Philippe le Hardi ransoms Herman and Jean de Limbourg, "jonnes enfans," from prison in Brussels, where they had been held about six months because of a conflict between Guelders, their native country, and Brabant. Because of an epidemic in Paris the goldsmith to whom they were apprenticed had sent them home. Because they were nephews of Jean Malouel, the painter of Philippe le Hardi, some painters and goldsmiths of Brussels decided to pay the ransom, and then the Duke of Burgundy paid it.

A Hermant Maleuel et Jacquemin Malauel freres, jonnes enfans, et nepveus de Jehan Maleuel, paintre et varlet de chambre de mondit seigneur, auxquelz mondit seigneur, pour cause de la mortalite estant nagaires a Paris et pour eulx faire tenir et aprenre leur mestier d'orfaverie de Alebret de Bolure (?) orfevre demourant a Paris, leur maistre eust fait mener les diz enfans ou pais de Ghelre dont ils etoient nez; et il soit ainsi que, en alant oudit pais, le varlet qui conduisoit yceulx enfans, fist passer par Brouxelles ou ilz furent detenuz prisonniers et pris pour marque pour occasion du debat estans lors entre ceulx de Brabant et ceulx de Ghelres, ou ilz demouroient en grieve prison par l'espace de environ demi an aux despens de leur mere qui estoit une très povre femme, de laquelle prison ilz n'ont peu eschapper, se non que, pour pittié et en faveur dudit Maleuel, aucuns orfevres et painctres de la dicte ville de Bruxelles composerent et traictierent pour yceulx enfans et se obligièrent de paier pour eulx dedens la Pentecouste prochain enssuivant la somme de LV escuz ou de rendre yceulx esffans prisonniers audit Bruxelles comme devant, pour laquelle chose yceulx enfans n'avoient de quoy paier et par ce conviendroit qu'ilz retournassent prisonniers, comme dit est, a leur tres grant dommaige et retardement de tout leur bien, mondit seigneur, aians consideration a ce que dit est, et aux bons et agreables services que icellui Maleuel, oncle d'iceulx enfans, avoit faiz le temps passé a mondit seigneur, fait chascun jour et espere que face ou temps avenir et yceulx Herman Maluel et Gillequin Maluel enfans, a donné de grace especial la dicte somme de LV escuz pour eulx acquicter de leur raençon, si qu'il appert plus a plain par lettres patentes données a Conflans le second jour de May l'an mil CCCC . . .

LV escuz

Archives Dép. Côte-d'Or, B 1519, fol. 158v. This document was apparently first published by Dehaisnes, *Documents et extraits*, 1886, II, p. 790 f. Dehaisnes was copied, but with an error in the date, by Champeaux and Gauchery, *Travaux*, 1894, p. 139. Monget, *Chartreuse*, I, 1898, p. 286 f., returning to the document itself, read "Bonne" instead of "Bolure." See also Gorissen, 1954, p. 201.

1402 February 9 – May 8. Paris

Philippe le Hardi engages Paul and Jean to illuminate a Bible. They are ordered to do the work as quickly as possible within a period of four years, and during this time they may not accept any other commissions. Jean Durant, physician of the Duke, is asked to supervise the work, and he receives a first payment of 600 francs.

A Polequin Manuel et Jehanequin Manuel, enlumineurs, lesquelz mon dit seigneur par ses lettres donnees a Paris le IXe jour de fevrier mil CCCC et ung collacionnees par l'un de ses secretaires le derrenier jour d'avril ensivant, si comme il appert par la copie d'icelle cy rendue, eust retenuz pour parfaire les histoires d'une tres belle et notable Bible que avoit nagaires fait encommencier ledit seigneur, que pour l'acomplissement d'icelles et des ystoires qui y devront estre faictes, iceulx Polequin et Jehannequin ne se povoient louer a autre que a mon dit seigneur mais entendre et besongner seulement en l'ouvraige d'icelle, icellui seigneur desirant acertes ledit ouvraige estre fait et parfait le mieulx et si brief que faire se pourroit, ordena et tauxa que aus dessus diz Polequin et Jehannequin tant pour leur peine et vivre comme pour avoir leurs autres necessitéz, la somme de XX s. p. pour chascun jour ouvrable et non ouvrable jusques a quatre ans prouchains [-venans] ensivant IIII^{c} et cinq. C'est assavoir pour chascun d'iceulx Polequin et Jehannequin X s. p. pour chascun jour durans lesdiz quatre ans, si comme tout ce puet plus a plain apparoir par la dicte copie, pour laquelle Bible faire et historier a esté paié, baillié et delivré par ledit commis du commandement et ordonnance de mon dit seigneur a maistre Jehan Durant, son phisicien la somme de VI^c frans pour iceulz emploier es escriptures et perfection d'icelle Bible et aussi es gaiges desdiz Polequin et Jehannequin desdiz XX s. p. par jour, par vertu d'un mandement de mon dit seigneur donné a Paris le VIe jour de mars l'an mil IIII^c et I, laquelle somme mon dit seigneur veult qu'elle soit allouee es comptes d'icellui commis. Pour ce, par vertu d'icellui mandement avec quittance dudit maistre Jehan Durant, escripte le VIIIe jour de may mil IIII^c et deux, tout rendu a court VI^c frans

Dijon, Archives Dép. Côte d'Or, B 1526, fols. 292v–293 = 298v–299 old foliation. Rec. gén. des Finances, 22–3–1401 to 21–3–1402. From Cockshaw, 1969, p. 133 f. Published earlier by Prost, 1891, p. 342; Champeaux and Gauchery, *Travaux*, 1894, p. 137 f.; Durrieu, 1895, p. 115; Gorissen, 1954, p. 203 no. 76.

1402 July 10. Paris

Jean Durant bought 6 ounces of "fin asur" (ultramarine?) in Paris for the illumination of certain books—probably the Bible on which the two Limbourgs were working in his house and another being illuminated by Coene, Stanier, and Haincelin de Haguenau.

Audit commis qu'il a paié du commandement et ordonnance de mon dit seigneur la somme de XLII escuz d'or pour les choses qui s'ensuivent: C'est assavoir pour six onces de fin asur que mon dit seigneur fist achater pour enluminer certainz livres que faisoit faire ledit seigneur, chascune once du pris de VII escuz. Montent ycelles VI onces a la dicte somme de XLII escuz si comme il appert plus a plain par les letres patentes dudit seigneur sur ce faictes, donnees a Paris le Xe jour de juillet l'an mil CCCC et deux cy rendues avec certifficacion de maistre Jehan Durant phisicien dudit seigneur sur le pris, achat et delivrance dudit azur. Pour ce XLII escuz

Dijon, Archives Dép. Côte d'Or, B 1532, fols. 322v–323. Rec. gén. des Finances, 22–3–1402 to 30–9–1403. From Cockshaw, 1969, p. 136.

1403 January 12. St. Germain en Laye

Jean and Paul each receive from Philippe le Hardi a special gift of 10 ecus of gold for clothing while working in Durant's house.

A Jehannequin et Paulequin, paintres, pour don a euls fait par mon dit seigneur de grace especial, la somme de XX escus d'or. C'est assavoir a chascun X escuz pour avoir de la robe pour ce qu'ilz besoignoient pour mon dit seigneur chascun jour en l'ostel de maistre Jehan Durant son phisicien si comme il appert plus a plain par les lettres patentes dudit seigneur sur ce faictes, donnees a Saint Germain en Laye le XIIe jour de janvier l'an mil CCCC et deux cy rendu avec quictance. Pour ce XX escuz

Dijon, Archives Dép. Côte d'Or, B 1532, fols. 194v–195. Rec. gén. des Finances, 22–3–1402 to 30–9–1403. From Cockshaw, 1969, p. 135. See also Gorissen, 1954, p. 203 no. 75.

1404 January 17. Paris

About two years after the first payment of 600 francs for the Bible of Paul and Jean, Durant receives a second, in equal amount.

A Paulequin Maluel et Jehannequin, paintres et historieurs, ausquelz mon dit seigneur a ordonnéz prendre et avoir chascun jour XX s. p. jusques a quatre ans, tant pour leur vivre comme pour la perfeccion des histoires et enlumineure de certaine Bible que mon dit seigneur a ordonnee faire, enluminer et historier par les dessus diz, si comme il appert plus a plain par ung vidimus des letres de mon dit seigneur auquel est attaché ung mandement dudit seigneur donné le XVIe jour de mars l'an mil CCCC et ung, yceuls renduz par le premier compte dudit commis ou chappitre de despense commune folio II^{c} IIII^{xx} XIXe sur la partie desdiz Paulequin et Jehnequin, sur laquelle pour la premiere annee a esté baillé a maistre Jehan Durant phisicien dudit seigneur auquel mon dit seigneur a commis ladicte besongne, pour bailler aux dessus diz, la somme de VI^{c} frans. Pour ce cy, par vertu desdictes letres rendues comme dit est pour la IIe, IIIe annee baillé audit maistre Jehan Durant et par sa recongnoissance faicte le XVIIe jour de janvier l'an mil quatrecens et trois cy rendue. Pour ce VI^{c} frans

Dijon, Archives Dép. Côte d'Or, B 1532, fol. 323^{rv}. Rec. gén. des Finances, 22–3–1402 to 30–9–1403. From Cockshaw, *op. cit.*, p. 136.

After 1401. *Ca.* 1405?

Jean de Berry gave Paul and his two brothers, illuminators, 9 gold coins. Then 12.

122. Item, quarente-sept pièces de monnoie d'or, de diverses manières.

De dictis peciis Dominus dedit novem Paulo et II^{bus} fratribus suis, illuminatoribus, ut apparet per compotum dicti Robineti. Item, plus XII pecias.

From Guiffrey, *Inventaires*, II, 1896, p. 26.

The phrases in Latin are marginal notes added in brown ink (see Bibl. nat. fr. 11496, fol. 15v). They were added after the inventory was drawn in December, 1401. Other similar Latin notes refer to gifts to the Sainte-Chapelle in 1405 or even later events. Porcher's opinion that the notes about the gold coins were added in 1408–9, at the earliest, is based only on his assumption that the Duke first engaged the Limbourgs at that time.

1406 September 1. Paris

Agents of Jean de Berry broke into the *hôtel* of the Bishop of Le Puy and stole a Bible, a Breviary, a silver belt, and a young girl who was lodged there. They left a Bible because it was "de trop menue lettre." Champeaux and Gauchery, *Travaux*, 1894, p. 203, suggested that this girl might be the one who is the subject of the following documents. If so, however, she would have been only six years old, as we shall see, and she would have been detained more than two years.

Mercredi, premier jour de septembre.

Cedit jour, fu ordonné que xij ou xiij de messeigneurs avec les procureur et advocas du Roy iroient à S. Victor, où se doit tenir le Grant Conseil où doivent estre les ducs de Berry, d'Orleans et de Bourgoigne et de Bourbon, sur ce que hier le duc de Berri, duquel aucuns des gens puiz ij ou iij jour avoient esté miz ou Chastellet, pour ce qu'il estoient alez à minuit en l'ostel de la Banniere, en la rue des Lombars, où estoit logez l'evesque du Puy, et avoient rompu l'uiz et avoient prinz une bible, breviaire, ceincture et autres chosettes, et une fillette que l'en disoit que ledit evesque avoit. . . . .

From Tuetey, *Journal*, 1885, pp. 168–170.

After January 1, 1408.

Jean de Berry gave Paul de Limbourg a gold ring bearing an emerald in the shape of a bear on a patch of greensward. The Duke had received the ring from the Florentine merchant Baude de Guy.

415. Item, un annel d'or, où il a un ours d'esmeraude sur une terrace de mesmes; ladicte esmeraude que Baude de Guy donna à mondit Seigneur aux estrainnes mil CCCC et VII. Ainsi declairée en la IIIIe partie dudit III^{c} XIIIe fueillet.

K.—Datus fuit Paulo de Limbourc per mandatum super ultima parte CLXIIII^{ti} folii hujus compoti redditum; virtute cujus dictus Robinetus acquittatur hic de eodem.

From Guiffrey, *Inventaires*, I, 1894, p. 125 f.

1408 November 21. Paris

The Parlement attempts to obtain the release of a girl (Gillette la Mercière) about 8 years old of Bourges whom Jean de Berry was holding in his chateau at Etampes near Paris. Against the wishes of her mother and friends the Duke wanted to marry the child to a "peintre alemant" who was working for him in his château de Bicêtre. (In a document of 1434 Paul de Limbourg was described as "natif d'Alemaigne.")

Mardi XXIe jour, assez tost après IX heures au matin, firent les seigneurs de la court partir les advocas, procureurs et autres estans aux plaidoiries, et tindrent conseil sur certeinnes lectres envoyées depar le duc de Berry à monseigneur Henry de Marle, premier président, sur ce que la court avoit eu plainte d'une juesne fille, d'environ VIII ans, née de Bourges, de bourgoisie, que voloit marier icellui duc à un peintre alemant qui besoignoit pour lui en son hostel de Wincestre lez Paris; contredisant la mère et autres amis, si comme l'en disoit. Et de fait avoit fait détenir icelle fille, le duc, en son chastel d'Estampes, où il estoit alé un huissier de parlement, par justice, quérir ladicte fille, que l'en lui avoit refusée. Pour quoy avoit adjorné les désobeyssans céans. Sur quoy avoit en présent [*supp.* le duc de Berry], envoyé lesd. lectres aud. président, contenans en effect qu'il se pranroit à sa personne et à ses biens se la chose prenoit autre conclusion qu'il n'eust ordonnée. Sur quoy fu délibéré que aucun, ou aucuns des seigneurs de céans alassent audit duc le desmouvoir, combien que ledit président se présentast d'y aler en personne.

From Douët d'Arcq, *Pièces inédites*, 1863, p. 313; Tuetey, *op. cit.*, p. 248; Champeaux and Gauchery, *Travaux*, 1894, p. 140.

1409 January 7. Paris

King Charles VI orders the *Court au Conseil* to release to his *Grand Maître de l'hôtel* Gillette la Mercière of Bourges, now about 9 years old.

Ceditjour, à heure de x heures, s'est retraicte la Court au Conseil pour certeinnes lettres que le grant maistre d'ostel a monstrées à la Court, par lesquelles le Roy lui mandoit qu'il feist commandement à la Court qu'elle ly delivrast Gilette la Merciere, fille de IX ans environ, qui estoit en la main de la Court, et en cas de refus que la preist et baillast au duc de Berri, qui s'en disoit avoir la garde en son chastel d'Estampes paravant, et laquelle il voloit marier à un peintre qui ly faisoit besoigne, comme l'en dit, contredisant la mere et justice requerant.

From Tuetey, *op. cit.*, p. 253. See Champeaux and Gauchery, *op. cit.*, p. 203.

1409 February 11. Paris

With the consent of her mother Gillette has been released to the *Grand Maître*.

Gillette, fille de feu Giles Le Mercier, qui à la requeste de Marie du Brueil, nagueres femme dudit feu Gillet, et mere de ladicte Gilette, avoit esté mise en la main du Roy et depuiz en garde de par la Court à maistre Guillaume Le Clerc, conseiller du Roy nostre Sire, du consentement de ladicte Marie a esté baillée et delivrée au Grant maistre d'ostel du Roy, comme en la main de monseigneur le duc de Berry, par ce que ledit Grant maistre a promiz à ladicte Marie, si comme il dit, en bonne foy et par sa loyauté et conscience, que il fera tout son povoir et diligence à ce que ladicte fille ne soit mise.

From Tuetey, *op. cit.*, p. 257. See Champeaux and Gauchery, *op. cit.*, p. 203.

1408–9. Accounts of Robinet d'Estampes

The *Belles Heures*, ascribed to the "ouvriers" of the Duke of Berry, is inventoried.

960. Item, unes belles *Heures*, très bien et richement historiées; et au commancement est le kalendrier, bien richement escript et historié; et après est historiée la Vie et Passion de Saincte Katherine; et ensuivant sont escriptes les quatre Euvangiles et deux oroisons de Nostre Dame; et après commancent

les Heures de Nostre Dame, et s'ensuivent pluseurs autres heures et oroisons; et au commancement du second fueillet desdictes Heures de Nostre Dame, a escript: *audieritis*; couvertes de veluiau vermeil, à deux fermouers d'or, esquielx sont les armes de Monseigneur de haulte taille; et par dessus lesdictes Heures a une chemise de veluiau vermeil, doublé de satin rouge; lesquelles Heures Monseigneur a fait faire par ses ouvriers.

From Guiffrey, *Inventaires*, I, 1894, p. 253. See Appendix A. Also Meiss, with Sharon Off, 1971, pp. 228, 233, 235.

1410 June 29. Nijmegen

Herman and Jean de Limbourg consign all their property in Nijmegen to their mother and her heirs.

(subiudex, Heze, Th. Theoderici) Hermannus et Johannes de Lymborch fratres, filii quondam Arnoldi de Aquis beldesniders, vendicione eorum legitima omnia eorum bona mobilia et immobilia in scabinatu Novimagensi sita ad usus Mechteldis eorum matris eiusque heredum efestucando resignaverunt.

From Gorissen, 1954, p. 206 no. 92.

(Subjudge, Heze, Th. Theodericus) Herman and Jean de Limbourg, brothers, sons of the late sculptor Arnold de Aquis (Aachen), by a lawful transaction consigned all their goods, movable and immovable (real estate), situated in Nijmegen to the use of Mechteld their mother and of her heirs.

1411 January 1.

Paul de Limbourg and his two brothers gave the Duke, as a New Year's gift, a simulated book. It consisted of a piece of wood painted "en semblance d'un livre," though without any folios or any script. It was covered in white velvet and had two gilded silver clasps enamelled with the arms of the Duke. This fake book was inventoried with the actual ones.

994. Item, un livre contrefait d'une pièce de bois paincte en semblance d'un livre, où il n'a nuls fueillets ne riens escript; couvert de veluiau blanc, à deux fermouers d'argent dorez, esmaillez aux armes de Monseigneur; lequel livre Pol de Limbourc et ses deux freres donnerent à mondit Seigneur ausdictes estrainnes mil CCCC et X.

From Guiffrey, *Inventaires*, I, 1894, p. 265.

After February 1, 1412 (beginning of Robinet's Fourth Account).

Jean de Berry gave Paul a diamond ring he had bought in February, 1402.

421. Item, un dyament à pluseurs poinctez, assis en un annel d'or plat, lequel Monseigneur achata à Paris, ou mois de fevrier l'an mil CCCC et un, de Hermant Rince, orfevre demourant à Paris, pour le pris et somme de XXX escus d'or. Ainsi declaré en la VIIe partie du CLXVII^{e} fueillet dudit livre.

K.—Datus fuit per dominum Paulo de Limbourc per mandatum suum super II^{da} parte C^{mi} primi folii hujus compoti traditum; virtute cujus dictus Robinetus acquittatur hic de eodem.

From Guiffrey, *Inventaires*, I, 1894, p. 128.

After January 1, 1413.

Jean de Berry gave Paul de Limbourg a diamond ring he had received from the Count of Nevers January 1, 1413.

457. Item, un diament fait en lozange, assis en un annel d'or, que monseigneur de Nevers donna à Monseigneur ausdictes estrainnes.

K.—Datus fuit per dictum mandatum Paulo de Limbourc. Et quittus hic dictus Robinetus de eodem.

From Guiffrey, *op. cit.*, I, 1894, p. 135 f.

1413 October 1 – 1414 March 31.

List of recipients of sums, not further specified, from Jean de Berry.

Paoul, Jehannequin, et Harmant, freres. . . .

Arch. nat. KK 250 *Trésorerie du duc de Berry*, fol. 36v (not previously published).

1413 October 24.

Item paye a Paul de Limbourg ledit jour VI escuz.

(Champeaux and Gauchery, *Travaux*, 1894, p. 136.)

1413 November 7.

Item au Paoul le VII jour dudit mois X escus.

(Champeaux and Gauchery, *ibid.*)

1413 November 9.

The Duke, very pleased with the work of Paul de Limbourg, gave him a special gift of 100 *écus*.

A Pol de Lumbourc, varlet de chambre de monseigneur, pour don a luy fait par monseigneur pour consideracion des bons et agreables services quil luy a faiz, fait chascun jour et espere que fasce ou temps a venir, et pour soy vestir et estre plus honnestement en son service, non obstant autres dons a luy faits par ledit seigneur par mandement donné le 9e jour de novembre lan 1413, cy rendu avec quictance dudit Pol faicte cedit jour et oudit an 100 escuz, vallent 112 livres 10 sol. t.

Arch. nat. KK 250, fol. 25v. (Champeaux and Gauchery, and Gorissen have incorrectly given the number of *escuz* as 50.)

To Paul de Limbourg, *valet de chambre*, in consideration of the good and welcome services he has rendered, renders each day and, it is hoped, will render in the future, and also to clothe himself and to be more honorably in the Duke's service, notwithstanding other gifts given him by the Duke. . . . 9 November 1413 . . . 100 *escus* (worth 112 *livres* 10 *sous tournaisiens*).

1413 December 5. Nijmegen

Johannes dictus Jenneken Maelwael filius quondam magistri Arnoldi confitetur, quod infra hinc et diem beati Joannis nativitatis veniet in iudicio Novimagensi faciendo Ade de Stockhem solucionem . . . super impeticionem dicto Jenneken per dictum Adam proponendam, si non, se cecidisse in penam 14 br. kr. den. pandando.

From Gorissen, 1954, p. 210 no. 118.

1414 or 1415? January 1.

At New Year Jean de Berry gave diamonds to Herman and Jean, brothers, to his scribe Jean Flamel, to the wife of his painter Michelet Saumon, and to others.

Item pour neuf dyamans que mondit seign. donna c'est assavoir a Hermant et Hannequin freres, Maistre Jean Flamel, aux femmes du maistre de la chambre, Jehan du Pre, Estienne de Bonpuis, Pierre de Serizy, Michelet Saumon et Pierre Castellain a chacun ung pour ce au pris de X escuz la piece valent CI.l.V.s.t.

Arch. nat. KK 250, fol. 45. (See also Guiffrey, *Inventaires*, II, 1896, p. 333, apparently incorrectly as Jan. 1, 1415. On fol. 45v, however, a payment on March 14, 1414 [n.s.] is recorded, and on fol. 91 begin the accounts from April 1, 1414 [n.s.] to September 30 of the same year.)

1414 July 9. Nijmegen

(Johannes Heze, Duven) subiudex pandavit Adam de Stockem in omnibus bonis mobilibus et immobilibus Johannis dicti Jenneken Maelwael filii quondam magistri Arnoldi in scabinatu Novimagensi sitis pro 14 veteribus currentibus et pro iure; et subiudex percussit postem in ianua domus in qua Mechteldis mater dicti Joannis morabatur in der Borchstraten ex parte Ade . . .

From Gorissen, 1954, p. 210 no. 122.

1415 January 1.

Paul de Limbourg gave Jean de Berry a little agate and gold salt cellar.

1211. Item, une petite sallière de gathe, garnie d'or, dont le couvercle est d'or, et au dessus a ung fertelet garny d'un saphir et quatre perles, laquelle sallière Pol de Limbourg donna à mondit Seigneur ausdictes estrainnes mil quatre cens et quatourze.

From Guiffrey, *Inventaires*, I, 1894, p. 323 f.

1415 March 6. Nijmegen

Paul and Jean de Limbourg, acting also for their brothers Herman, Roger, and Arnold, and for their sister Greta, turn over half of a house in Nijmegen and its contents to the priest Segerus of Weelderen and his heirs.

(subiudex, Herwen, Boye) Paulus et Johannes de Lymborch vendicione legitima medietatem domus et aree com medietate pertinentium integraliter quondam domus domini Johannis Maelwael presbiteri in qua diem clausit extremum sitam iuxta cymeterium nostre civitatis . . . ad usus domini Segeri de Weelderen presbiteri et heredum efestucando resignaverunt. Itaque warandizare pro Hermanno, Rutgero et Arnoldo eorum fratribus et Greta sorore eorum.

From Gorissen, 1954, p. 211 no. 126.

Paul and Jean de Limbourg consigned by legal deed the half of a house and of its area with half the things belonging to it as integral parts, [that is to say] the house formerly of master John Maelwael, priest, in which he breathed his last, situated next to the churchyard of our town. . . . to the use of master Segerus of Weelderen, priest, and of his heirs. Consequently they warrant for Herman, Roger, and Arnold, their brothers, and Greta their sister.

1415 March 6. Nijmegen

(Herwen, Boye) Paulus et Johannes de Lymborch fratres Marsilio de Oesterholt 45 cronen vel pagamentum aureum Assumpcionis Marie, pena quartalis Renensis.

From Gorissen, 1954, p. 211 no. 127.

1415 March 15. Nijmegen

Jean and Paul de Limbourg make a payment to Arnold de Drueten.

(Galen, Colleken) Johannes et Paulus de Lymborch fratres Arnoldo de Drueten filio Nycolai iuniori 36 overl. R. vel pagamentum die Jacobi proxime, pena 10 sol.

From Gorissen, 1954, p. 211 no. 130.

1415 March 15. Nijmegen

Jean de Limbourg deeded all his possessions in Nijmegen to his brother Paul.

(subiudex, Galen, Colleken) Johannes de Lymborch voluntate libera omnia mobilia et immobilia in scabinatu sita ad usus Pauli sui fratris efestucando, itaque et warandizare promittit.

From Gorissen, 1954, p. 211 no. 131.

Jean de Limbourg of his own free will deeded all his movable possessions and real estate in the municipality to the use of Paul his brother.

1415 March 16. Nijmegen

Paul and Jean de Limbourg (called Maelwael) must pay 170 Rhenish gulden to a certain Peter Lauwert.

(Adam, Colleken) Paulus et Johannes (Maelwael dicti) de Lymborch fratres Petro Lauwert filio Rudolphi 170 overl. R. gulden vel pagamentum Joannis baptiste proxime vel infra mensem, deinde pena ½ Renensis.

From Gorissen, 1954, p. 211 no. 132.

Paul and Jean (called Maelwael) de Limbourg, brothers, [owe?] to Peter Lauwert son of Rudolph 170 good Rhenish *gulden*, to be paid at the next Feast of John the Baptist or within a month; afterwards the penalty will be ½ a Rhenish [gulden?].

1415 August 22.

The Duke gave to Paul de Limbourg and to his brothers Herman and Jean, *valets de chambre*, a gold ring with a fine small ruby. The Duke gave the ring, which he had bought from a Venetian merchant in 1412, as security for the very large sum of 1000 *escus*, which the Duke owed the painters.

349. Item, un petit ruby fin, fait en façon d'un grain d'orge, assis en un annel d'or, que mondit Seigneur achata dudit Loys Gradenigo, le XVIIIe jour de novembre, l'an que dessus, pour le pris et somme de III[m] escuz d'or, et est apellé le *Grain d'orge*. Et n'est point rendu en recepte ou compte precedent.

Dictus dominus Dux, per suas patentes litteras datas XXII[da] augusti M CCCC XV, hic redditas, fatetur habuisse et recepisse a dicto Robineto istum parvum ruby et eundem tradidisse Paulo de Limbourc et Hermando et Jehannequino, ipsius fratribus et varletis camere dicti domini Ducis, per modum pignoris et securitatis somme M scutorum auri, de quo quidem ruby idem dominus Dux voluit et mandavit per easdem litteras ipsum Robinetum, reapportando predictas litteras una cum recognicione ipsorum camere varletorum, exonerari; a quo Paulo dumtaxat attulit litteras recognicionis, que videantur si sufficiant.

From Guiffrey, *Inventaires*, I, 1894, p. 102 f.

The said lord duke, by his letters patent dated August the 22nd 1415, here produced, agrees that he has had and received from the said Robinet this small ruby, and that he has given it to Paul de Limbourg and Herman and Jean his brothers, valets of the bedchamber of the said lord duke, as a form of pledge and security against a sum of 1000 *escus* of gold. About this ruby the same lord duke desired and instructed by the same letters that the same Robinet be relieved of responsibility for it, by producing the above-mentioned letters along with the receipt of the said valets of the bedchamber; from whom, at least from Paul, he brought letters of receipt; let it be seen if they suffice.

1416 March 9. Nijmegen

Jean de Limbourg (Jenneken Maelwael, son of the late Master Arnold) is dead, leaving property in Nijmegen.

(Sander, Baers) subiudex pandavit Adam de Stockem concivem in omnibus bonis mobilibus et immobilibus quondam Johannis dicti Jenneken Maelwael filii quondam magistri Arnoldi per obitum eiusdem Jenneken relictis in scabinatu sitis pro 14 Vrancr. cronen et pro iudice . . .

From Gorissen, 1954, p. 214 no. 139.

1416 September – October. Nijmegen

All three Limbourg brothers are dead. Their brother Arnold and sister Margaret appoint an executor for the identification and collection of all their goods and property in France and in the Berry. Subsequent proceedings imply these possessions were considerable.

(borchgravius, Joannes de Ubbergen et Sanderus de Redinchaven) coram nobis Aernoldus de Limborch et Margareta eius sorer nostri concives voluntate eorum libera omnia bona mobilia et immobilia prefatis Arnoldo et Grete per obitum quondam Hermanni, Pauli et Johannis de Lymborch pie memorie fratrum devoluta ubicumque locorum in partibus Francie vel Biturie sita ad usus Theoderici Neven nostri concivis et heredum efestucando recognoverunt, itaque quod dictus Theodericus prefata bona percipere et recipere poterit sine contradiccione.

From Gorissen, 1954, p. 214 no. 142.

(Burgrave, John of Ubbergen and Sanderus of Redinchaven) before us Arnold of Limburg and Margaret his sister, our fellow-citizens, voluntarily agreed by solemn deed that all the goods, movable and immovable, which pass to the above said Arnold and Grete through the death of the late Herman, Paul and Jean de Limbourg of blessed memory, their brothers, wherever these goods may be in France or Berry, should go to the use of Theoderic Neven (brother-in-law of Arnold), our fellow-citizen, and his heirs, so that the said Theoderic might perceive and receive the said goods without contradiction.

For subsequent documents about the property of the brothers see Gorissen, 1954, pp. 214 no. 143, 215 no. 149, 216 no. 155.

1416 – April 29, 1417.

Yolande d'Aragon, wife of Duke Louis II of Anjou, asked the executors of the estate of Jean de Berry for permission to examine the *Belles Heures*. The manuscript was sent to her and after she had looked at it for a considerable time she decided to keep it, but to pay only 300 *livres tournois* instead of the 875 at which it had been appraised. She paid for the manuscript before the death of her husband on April 29, 1417, because he was alive when the note about the payment was written.

Pour diminucion et dechiet de la somme de 700 liv. par. qui font 875 liv. t. que ont esté prisées unes belles Heures très bien et richement historiées, au commencement desquelles est le kalendrier, etc.;[1] lesquelles Heures très haulte et puissant dame la royne de Secille a envoyé quérir et demander par maistre Pierre Franchomme, chantre de l'esglise de Paris, à messeigneurs les exécuteurs, et lesquelles mesditz seigneurs lui ont envoiées par ledit chantre pour icelles veoir et retenir s'il lui plaisoit en payant ladicte somme de 700 liv. par., ou telle autre somme d'argent, comme bon lui sembleroit, affin qu'elle eust envers le roy de Secille, son seigneur et mari, principal executeur du testament dudit feu Seigneur, le fait de ladite exécution pour recommandé; laquelle dicte Royne, après ce qu'elle ot longuement veues et advisées icelles Heures, a retenu ycelles par devers elle et paié à ladite execution seulement la somme de 300 liv. t. Et ainsi est ladite somme de 875 liv. t. diminuée de 575 liv. t.

[1] The description of the manuscript was copied from the item in the inventory of Robinet, given above.

From Guiffrey, *Inventaires*, II, 1896, p. 299 f.

Ca. 1418.

A section added to the inventory of the Duke's possessions compiled after his death on June 15, 1416, includes numerous gatherings of a splendid Book of Hours, very rich in miniatures and illumination. These gatherings, preserved in a box, were painted by Paul and his brothers.

1164. Item, en une layette plusieurs cayers d'unes très riches Heures, que faisoient Pol et ses frères, très richement historiez et enluminez; prisez V^{c} liv. t.

From Guiffrey, *Inventaires*, II, 1896, p. 280.

For a discussion of this item and its context in the inventory see the preceding chapter and the Catalogue of Manuscripts, Observations on the History of the *Très Riches Heures*.

1434 February 1. Bourges

An order of King Charles VII concerning a house in Bourges which Jean de Berry, who acquired it from his architect Guy de Dammartin, had given to his treasurer Christophe de la Mer, and then to his painter

Paul, a native of "Alemaigne." Paul died (in 1416) without an heir, but his wife continued to live in the house, soon with her second husband, André Le Roy, who remained in it after her death. The house is described as one of the largest and most spacious and impressive houses of Bourges, worth in 1434 about 2000–3000 *escus*, and suitable for a nobleman of royal blood.

> Charles, par la grâce de Dieu, roy de France, à tous ceulx qui ces présentes lectres verront salut. Comme feu nostre très chier et très amé oncle le duc de Berry, que Dieux absoille, eust en son vivant acquis de feu maistre Guy de Dampmartin, ou autrement, ung hostel assis en nostre ville de Bourges, devant l'église de Nostre-Dame de l'Affichault, d'une part, et de l'autre part en une rue devant l'ostel Jehan Harpin, lequel hostel ycellui feu nostre oncle donna dès lors à Xristofle de La Mer, son tresorier, et deppuis pour certains grant reste dargent en quoy luy estoit ledit de La Mer tenu et obligié, retourna et mist en sa main ledit hostel, lequel nostre dit feu oncle bailla depuis à ung sien paintre, nommé Pol, natif du païs d'Alemaigne, qui est alé de vie à trespassement sans hoir de son corps ne autre qui se soit monstré ni porté son heritier, par quoy ycelluy hostel nous est advenu et escheu comme bien vacant. Ce non obstant ung nommé Andry le Roy, que l'en dit avoir espousée la femme dudit Pol, a longuement tenu et occupé ledit hostel et depuis, après ce que sadite femme a esté trespassée, pour vouloir attribuer à luy ledit hostel se tira devers le sire de Sainte Severe, en son vivant mareschal de France, et, moyennant la somme de cent escuz d'or ou environ, ou autre petite somme qu'il lui donna, comme l'en dit, traicta et appointa avecques ledit mareschal qu'i nous requeroit que lui donnissions ledit hostel, lequel, comme non adverty de ce que dit est, ne de la valeur dudit hostel, luy eussions donné, lequel depuis le transporta audit Andry par le moyen que dessuz, comme l'en dit, et à ce tiltre, ou aultre non vallable, en a ycellui Andry tousjours joy et encore joyst, et pour ce que nagaires avons esté advisiez de ce que dit est, et que ladicte maison est une des plus grans et plus spacieuse et notable de nostre dite ville de Bourges, et peut bien valoir de deux à trois mil escuz d'or ou environ à vendre à une foiz, et qu'elle seroit bien séant et propre pour logier l'un des seigneurs de nostre sang et lignage . . .
>
> From H. Bréholles, "Paul, natif d'Allemaigne," in *Archives de l'art français*, Paris, VI, 1858–1860, p. 216 f. See also Champeaux and Gauchery, *Travaux*, 1894, p. 140 f.; Gorissen, 1954, p. 218 f.

According to documents to be published by M. Ribault, the Duke actually bought the house in 1401 from his former sénéchal, Thibault Portier. Gillette la Mercière, Paul's wife, married André Le Roy after Paul's death and before July, 1422.

2 · BEGINNINGS: THE *BIBLE MORALISEE*

After the publication in the nineteenth century of records of payment by Philippe le Hardi to Paul and Jean de Limbourg for the illumination of a Bible, historians began to speculate about their relevance to a *Bible moralisée*, ms. fr. 166 in the Bibliothèque nationale (Figs. 278–332). No one failed to recognize that the earliest miniatures in this manuscript are somehow related in style to the *Belles Heures* and the *Très Riches Heures*, and a "très belle et très notable Bible," as the commission describes it, might very well be a *Bible moralisée*. A Bible of this kind would, furthermore, be very "notable," for it requires more than 5000 miniatures. Created in France between 1220 and 1240, the *Bible moralisée* met a wish for scholastic interpretation and extensive illustration.

Sorrows.[33] In fr. 166, however, Adam is already assuming his responsibilities (Fig. 284). God gives him the two instruments of his mission, the keys for the gate and—though the manuscript was made for a great prince at the height of the so-called courtly style—a very large spade with which to dig. Earlier instances of Adam in this scene with a spade are extremely rare, and the key is unprecedented.[34]

Here and elsewhere in the Bible the Limbourgs manifest the absorbing concern with instruments and techniques that is so striking a feature of their later work. As in *Hell* in the *Très Riches Heures* the devils in the Bible produce a hotter fire by the use of bellows (Fig. 279). There is no precedent in fr. 167 for most of the spades, pickaxes, hoes, axes and carpentry tools that are prominent in many miniatures of fr. 166 (Figs. 281, 282, 286, 287, 290, 296).[35] Novel also are the lantern on folio 4 (Fig. 286), the winch above the well on 11v (Fig. 301), and the astronomical instruments on 5v (Fig. 289). It is quite clear that the alert artisans from Nijmegen, like many of their contemporaries, were enthusiastic about technology and its rapid development in their time. Just during their first years in Paris an important new instrument, the mechanical clock, became, as we saw in the *Epître d'Othéa*, the symbol of a major virtue, Temperance (Fig. 127).

Instead of the symbolism of Christ with the Church and the Synagogue in fr. 167 the Limbourgs on folio 9 preferred to represent two workmen with their tools (Fig. 296). One kneels before Ecclesia while the other gives alms to a beggar. This miniature is one of many by the Limbourgs that contain an obvious social estimate. The nobility are more often connected with vices, leaving to the other estates, particularly simple people, association with virtue. Pride is personified as a nobleman wearing a splendid *escharpe*, and Luxury drives two courtiers to amorous embrace (Fig. 304). Occasionally, as on folio 1v, the text provides the theme (Fig. 281). "The great whales devour the little ones" is illustrated by a workman with a spade turned from his digging by a soldier who points to an enthroned ruler—clearly "a great whale." "Les grans balainnes," says the text, "sont les grans seigneurs." On the other hand the pilgrims at the Holy Sepulchre are modestly dressed (Fig. 307).[36]

These estimates suggest what we shall encounter frequently in the course of our study: that in the thought of the time the "lower classes" were not regarded simply with condescension and what has been described as "artificial fondness."[37] Religious writings in particular disclose a very different and far more complex view. The greatest theologian of the time, Jean Gerson, was preoccupied with the religious growth of simple people. For this purpose just before and after 1400 he wrote a series of texts in the vernacular, including "l'A.B.C. des simples gens."[38] Gerson was patronized by Philippe le Hardi, he was prominent in the chapter of Notre-Dame in Paris, and therefore the most likely adviser for the illustration of the *Bible moralisée*. In his treatises and sermons Gerson argued that penitential mysticism, which he advocated, was more perfect than scholasticism because it permitted even a simpleton (and women!)—not only scholars—to know God.[39] Partly for this reason Gerson promoted the cult of St. Joseph, and in a long letter he urged Jean de Berry to help him in this cause.[40] The prominence of workmen and their tools in the *Bible moralisée* foreshadows striking innovations in the *Belles Heures* and especially in the calendar of the *Très Riches Heures*. All these developments lie behind the much-discussed prominence of St. Joseph as a carpenter in the *Annunciation* by the Master of Flémalle.

Since fr. 166 was painted nearly half a century after 167 its miniatures naturally reflect the new naturalism; the Limbourgs were, in fact, among the chief pioneers. They demonstrate in no. 3 on 22v that, unlike their predecessors, they know what locusts are and how to depict them (Fig. 279). On this folio atmospheric phenomena, such as hail (no. 1) or fog (no. 5) as well as fire (no. 2), attain an unprecedented vividness. The painters gave actuality to the corpse suspended from a gibbet in no. 5 on 13 by adding two large, fluttering black birds which peck at the flesh (Fig. 304). With such interests the Limbourgs naturally did not fail to make the most of the story of Noah's raven (Fig. 287). The accompanying text said that the master of the ark sent out a raven, and since it did not return he sent out a dove. The dove, failing to find a place on which to alight, flew back to the ark. In the miniature there is no sign of the dove. In the watery foreground the raven perches on a dead animal, probably a horse, and eats its flesh. The Limbourgs might have seen one of the few earlier representations of this episode in thirteenth-century manuscripts of the *Bible moralisée*; here the raven justifies its classification in the Bible and later literature as an unclean bird.[41]

In no. 8 on 13 the Limbourgs, departing entirely from their model, turn the contrast between the seven Virtues and the seven Deadly Sins into a violent conflict (Fig. 304). The Virtues, all female, wield sticks as they turn on the Sins, all male. The miniatures in the Bible anticipate the delight of the Limbourgs, well known from later work, in the portrayal of nudes, especially female (Figs. 439, 558). Though Thamar, for instance, is fully clothed in fr. 167 at the moment of giving birth she appears nude in 166, her hair falling loose on her shoulder (Fig. 302). On the other hand, when Adam and Eve are expelled from Paradise and the text says that God clothed them in skins (fol. 3v) Jean de Limbourg elected to follow it instead of the fig leaf visible in fr. 167.

Though there is no record of the early ownership of fr. 166 its dependence upon fr. 167 indicates that it was made for Philippe le Hardi, or at least that the Duke lent his manuscript as a model. Thus the case for the identification of fr. 166 with the Bible for which the two Limbourg boys were paid from 1402 to 1404 would seem to be strong, but contrary opinions have been expressed for a century, up to the present time.[42] Although the objections have not been explicitly stated they must be of two kinds. The first is that though the commission called for completion of the illumination in four years or less, in two years on fr. 166 the Limbourgs had painted far less than half the 5152 miniatures. They completed, in fact, only 384 miniatures in the first three gatherings. They also painted, however—though this fact has seldom been recognized—most of the surfaces except for the heads and hands in the 128 miniatures in the fourth gathering (Fig. 332).[43] These unfinished flesh areas were executed later by a mediocre imitator. Thus, calculating roughly, the two boys painted nearly 500 small miniatures in about 760 days, from early March 1402 to the Duke's death in April 1404. Working constantly they would have painted a miniature in 1½ days; with time out for holidays a miniature would have been executed in about a day. It would have taken *each* illuminator, then, about two days to paint a miniature. This pace seems reasonable certainly for young and comparatively inexperienced men who were obviously trying to do something new.

The second objection to the identification was much more serious—indeed, it was the source of my own uncertainty for many years. The style of the miniatures in fr. 166, and especially those in the third gathering, resembles rather closely the miniatures in the *Belles Heures*. When the *Belles Heures* seemed datable from 1410 to 1413, how could the miniatures by the Limbourgs in the

Bible be as early as 1402–1404? This difficulty began to seem to me less severe only as I recognized that the *Belles Heures* was probably painted before 1410,[44] a hypothesis that was subsequently confirmed by showing, as will be seen shortly, that Jean de Berry received the completed manuscript in 1408 or the earlier part of 1409. The interval between the last work on the Bible and the first on the *Belles Heures* was therefore narrowed to a couple of years—an entirely acceptable period, as the study of the relationship will prove.

The final problem, and by far the most difficult, is presented by the variety of styles in the first three gatherings of the Bible. The third gathering (folios 17–24v) is the most homogeneous, and obviously the work of the outstanding artist. We may provisionally identify him with Paul, who became the Duke's favorite illuminator. His work in the Bible is closest to the best miniatures in the *Belles Heures.* The reader will be better able to cope with the intricacies of the Bible if the discussion centers at the beginning on this third gathering and its relationship to the *Belles Heures* as well as the *Très Riches Heures*. Thereafter we shall confront the difficulties of the first two gatherings.

The pictorial field of the single miniatures is very small. In order to achieve a clear narrative within these limits and even, if we may say so, a monumental effect, the chief illuminator of the third gathering restricted the number of figures, the depth of the space, and the range of color (Fig. 278). The massive figures, indeed, are for the most part white, modeled in pale gray, rose, or blue, and often they wear hats or garments of the same colors. They appear before an olive-green landscape or they are enclosed in a white building. The bare parchment serves for many areas of high value. The gradation of tone is so delicate and yet so comprehensive that the voluminous figures are decisively evoked by light before a luminous sky.

In the *Way to Calvary* on folio 19 Christ looks back toward his mother, a stalwart woman wrapped in a remarkably ample mantle (Fig. 278). In accordance with a tradition established in the late fourteenth century in France and exemplified by the paintings of the Parement Master, Mary attempts to lighten his burden by grasping a bar of the cross.[45] The painter, wishing to leave undisturbed the sorrowful exchange between Mary and Christ, has represented to the right only an averted soldier—a figure that he might have seen, in fact, in the miniature of the same scene in the *Brussels Hours* (Fig. 340), a manuscript that Jean de Berry gave to his brother Philippe le Hardi while the Limbourgs were at work on the Bible. Whereas the garb of the soldier in the *Brussels Hours* reflects its model—the *Way to Calvary* by Simone Martini, already in France at that time—Paul de Limbourg gave his figure a curious high pink bonnet and other oddments of dress that disclose, even at this early date, his enthusiasm for exotic and fantastic costume.

The *Way to Calvary* in the *Belles Heures* employs the identical figure of Christ, but the turn of the head is not as effective nor as meaningful because Mary is not within the range of his glance (Fig. 341). The scene, painted in full color, is in every respect more complex but at the same time less unified. This is not one of the strong miniatures in the *Belles Heures*, and it seems artistically inferior to the little *Way to Calvary* in the Bible. A second representation of the same subject in the Bible, however, is very different from the one we have considered (Fig. 293). This miniature, on folio 7v, was, to be sure, painted some months earlier than the one on folio 19, but it is radically different in character and undeniably weaker. It nevertheless provided certain patterns for the miniature in the *Belles Heures*, chiefly the soldier who strains to drag Christ forward. The painter of the miniature in the Bible favors figures of this kind, and also forms like curling rocks and repeated lances which produce a more agitated design.

On folio 19 in the Bible (Fig. 278), near the miniature of the *Way to Calvary*, the illuminator whom we may tentatively call Paul de Limbourg chose a remarkable composition to illustrate the idea of compassion with the impoverished infancy of Christ. The idea is, according to the text, the Christian counterpart of the compassion felt for the infant Moses by Pharaoh's daughter, represented immediately above. "Ceste fille (daughter of Pharaoh) segnefie devote persone (in earlier texts the Church) qui a compassion et devotion p(our) la doulce et povre enfance de Jesus Crist." Mary's grief in the *Way to Calvary* was similarly prefigured by the preceding episode in the story of Moses, in *Exodus* II, the sorrow of his sister as she contemplates her infant brother afloat in the river. Paul de Limbourg, incidentally, gave Moses' sister the diadem of the princess, and quite clearly confused the two.

As an illustration of the idea of devotion to the infant Christ Paul saw in his model, fr. 167, a priest holding the Child above an altar, while a queen and two companions kneel in adoration. This representation, however, he abandoned entirely in favor of a composition showing the Virgin on her knees worshipping her son who lies at her feet, while Joseph stands nearby (Fig. 327). The painter might have found a similar scene in the description of the Nativity in a version of the *Meditationes vitae Christi* that was freely rendered into French for the Duke of Berry in 1380.[46]

> Adonc le benoit fils de dieu pardurable issist soubdainme[n]t du ve[n]tre de sa mere. . . . et en un moment fut s[ur] le foi[n] q[ue] ioseph avoit mis sus les piez de n[ot]re dame et i[n]contina[n]t elle sagenoulla et ladoura. . . .[47]

The Virgin's adoration of the Child immediately after his birth, not described in the earlier Latin or Italian versions of the *Meditationes*, resembles also a composition of diverse origin that had been introduced into France by the Parement Master in the *Très Belles Heures de Notre-Dame* (Fig. 330). This was a new form of the Nativity in which, inside a cave, Mary kneels before the newborn Infant while Joseph stands nearby. Historians recognized some years ago that this particular form of the Nativity, distinguished by the cave, the kneeling Virgin, the Christ Child on the ground, and other elements to be mentioned shortly, derived from St. Bridget's famous Roman vision of 1360–1370 and/or the Italian paintings that represented it shortly after.[48] In a panel by Niccolò di Tommaso of about 1380 Bridget herself is shown kneeling outside the cave (Fig. 336). The saint's *Revelations*, which contain this vision, were well known in France. Indeed the text was translated into French in 1397 for Louis d'Orléans, who immediately gave his uncle, Jean de Berry, a copy.[49]

The miniature in the *Très Belles Heures de Notre-Dame*, which was begun by the Parement workshop *ca.* 1383 and completed *ca.* 1404 by the Baptist Master, does not include the doffed mantle and shoes of the Virgin described by St. Bridget. It is interesting that Joseph, instead of crossing his arms on his breast, raises his hands, expressing, it seems, surprise as well as veneration. This is precisely the gesture the Parement Master employed again in the *Très Belles Heures de Notre-Dame* for the surprised Virgin Mary when the angel Gabriel arrives with his momentous message and when she finds her young son among the doctors in the temple.[50] This gesture had appeared earlier in Bohemian painting,[51] and, with some differences, in the problematic *Annunciation* in the Cleveland Museum.[52] The Cleveland panel, though it perhaps bears the arms of Hainaut and may have been painted there, shows in my opinion relationships with Bohemia, so that the raised hands may be one more form the Parement Master owes to the art of that region.[53]

In the Limbourg miniature in the Bible Joseph raises one hand, suggesting to us that Paul de Limbourg had seen this very painting in the *Très Belles Heures de Notre-Dame*, which was in the collection of their patron's brother and close friend, Jean de Berry. By this means Paul maintained the different kinds of response to the miraculous event, Joseph's that of a witness, the Virgin's full of understanding and deep feeling. Paul restored, however, the symmetry of the two large figures constant in the Italian representations of Bridget's vision. As in these Italian panels and Bridget's text Paul's Virgin prays in her tunic. A telling vestige of the cave remains, hardly explicable without knowledge of the Brigittine models.

Though the composition was introduced as an illustration of compassion, Paul did not hesitate to add two figures he had seen in Tuscan Trecento Nativities who do not clearly develop his theme. A shepherd stands behind the rock nearby, his eyes turned away, however, from the miraculous event just before him. This is perhaps the very first instance in French art of the close proximity of a shepherd to the scene of Christ's birth. Parisian art of the early fifteenth century manifested a special interest in these inhabitants of the meadows, as we have observed above,[54] though once again the particular iconographic innovation must be ascribed to the early Tuscan Trecento, where it appears in, for instance, a *Nativity* by Taddeo Gaddi.[55] In the miniature a second shepherd appears amidst his flock, and far from meditating, he has fallen tight asleep.

In his Italian Brigittine model Paul might have seen golden rays issuing from God the Father, Christ, and the Virgin (Fig. 336), but he showed no interest in the solid golden aureoles, preferring, as in all his work, widely spaced, vibrant rays of gold or red. Rays emanated from the Child in North Italian Trecento paintings of the Nativity, such as Giusto's in London (Fig. 335) or Giovannino's in the *Uffiziolo visconteo*.[56]

The rays in the Bible have become more prominent in a very similar miniature in the *Belles Heures*, which illustrates the Mass of the Nativity (Fig. 329). It reproduces not only the three main figures, but also Mary in her white tunic, the gesture of Joseph, and even the shepherd (now two) in the cleft. The vestigial cave, however, has disappeared in favor of a shed, traditional in Western representations of the scene, as are the ox, the ass, and the crib.[57] Iconographic history points strongly to the priority of the miniature in the Bible, which retains more links with the Brigittine model, and thus we have one more indication of its early date. The miniature in the Bible seems not only earlier but stronger than the one in the *Belles Heures*; the latter, indeed, is very probably not by Paul. The main elements of its composition were adopted about 1409–1410 by a Parisian illuminator, the Egerton Master, who was very attentive to innovations by the Limbourgs (Fig. 334).[58]

In the last miniature on the preceding folio in the Bible Paul introduced a rather less impressive Nativity of the traditional type; here Jesus in the crib is related to the finding of Moses in the basket (Fig. 328). The birth of Moses, no. 5 on the folio, is accompanied by a similar Nativity, except that the crib, the ox and the ass are missing, a midwife (signifying faith) receives the child, and a shepherd sits on a hill behind (Fig. 315). Paul employed the traditional composition again at the office of Prime in the Hours of the Virgin in the *Belles Heures* (Fig. 333). Here too the shepherds are prominent, and as in the Bible Paul added a little warmth to the usually bare Tuscan landscape by including a pot and a fire.[59]

This group of early representations of the Nativity helps us to understand the genesis of the composition in the *Très Riches Heures* (Fig. 569). Here the divine radiance, already more important in the *Belles Heures*, has become the central phenomenon, surrounding the Child and covering the hills with incandescent gold. Now the shepherds at the shed even receive a special beam from God. It is perhaps not accidental that Joseph, here seated on the ground, recalls the figure in the *Nativity* in the *Très Belles Heures de Notre-Dame*, especially because he wears a sort of oriental hat (Fig. 330). His unusual dramatic gesture, indeed, so unlike that of the traditional detached old husband, remains that of the *Très Belles Heures de Notre-Dame* and the miniatures in the Bible and the *Belles Heures* (Figs. 327, 329). We suspect the influence of Gerson's cult of the saint.

Many elements of Paul's *Nativity* were adopted by a follower who, when painting a Book of Hours now in the Spitz Collection about 1420, drew from both the *Belles Heures* and the *Très Riches Heures* (Fig. 634). The illuminator showed, however, an interesting thoughtfulness and independence. The golden idol on a column, visible through the radiance in the *Très Riches Heures*, is now adored by two shepherds who are unaware of the miracle. The illuminator introduced behind the Virgin a woman remarkably similar in posture and dress. Like the Virgin she adores the newborn Child but her praying hands have disappeared from her wrists; a blue cherub behind her holds them. She is surely St. Bridget, who appeared in Italian representations of the Nativity influenced by her vision, as we have seen (Fig. 336), but not in the principal French examples (Figs. 327, 329, 330). The miracle of the passage of her praying hands to an angel was, however, portrayed once, and in a more vivid manner, in the miniature of the saint in the *Boucicaut Hours*.[60] The *Nativity* by the Spitz Master thus confirms the interest in St. Bridget manifested by French piety and religious art. In the late fourteenth century a North Italian illuminator, the Brussels Initials Master, brought to Paris a kind of Nativity embodying another aspect of her vision: St. Joseph holding a candle—an image that soon was widely diffused in Flemish and German painting.[61]

In his miniature of the Entombment on folio 17v Paul grouped the sacred figures on the far side of the tomb, packing them closely together and arranging the tiered sequence of haloes to give the impression of a multitude of mourners (Fig. 337). What this dense crowd lacks in animation is supplied by the diagonal placement, the characteristic flamboyant crags, and the twisting movement of the sole figure—Nicodemus?—on the near side of the tomb.[62] Comparison with one of the few surviving panels of the time from metropolitan France, which happens to represent the same subject, impresses us with the remarkable spatial ambitions of Paul at the beginning of his career (Fig. 338). Though he differentiated the sorrow of the three foremost figures he seems more concerned with the collective mood and action—an interest that proved absorbing in the panoramic scenes of later moments of his career. The panel, painted towards 1405 probably in Paris or in Dijon,[63] maintains in the background the steep ascent of the ground in front of the tomb, so that the figures beyond it, unlike those in the miniature, rise to the top of the pictorial field. To show the entire body of Christ and to preserve one uninterrupted pictorial plane the man on the nearer side of the tomb drops to his knees. The spatial position of Christ is highly ambiguous because Joseph of Arimathea seems to hold the upper part of the body of Christ *over* the tomb but Nicodemus, who holds the feet, stands in front of it.

In its planarity this *Entombment* resembles the other surviving French panels of the time; in this respect as in others they are much more conservative than the best illumination. These panel painters were of course profoundly influenced by Simone Martini; even the description of sorrow in the *Entombment* reflects the expressive range of his art, if not its passion. The preference, however, of the French panel painters for a rhythmical design essentially in one plane cannot be ascribed entirely to their Simonesque enthusiasms. Simone, after all, gave his *Entombment* three clearly differentiated planes (Fig. 344).

The *Entombment* in the *Belles Heures* shares with the miniature in the Bible the active man in the foreground and the unusual flexibility of the body of Christ, the torso of which bends upward as it is held by the Virgin or, in the *Belles Heures*, by Joseph of Arimathea (Fig. 343). In the later miniature, whose larger size gave Paul greater opportunity for individualized behavior, he separated the Virgin and a woman—probably the Magdalene—from the group. The latter tears her hair precisely as one of the women in Simone's panel (Fig. 344).[64] Indeed, it is panels, French as well as Italian, that most closely resemble Paul's miniature in the *Belles Heures* (Fig. 343). The panel in the Louvre shows not only iconographic likenesses, such as the woman holding the crown of thorns and a man a prominent jar, but also a series of similarly conceived figures (Fig. 338).

Identity of the Brothers

If we may assume that the evidence adduced in the preceding paragraphs builds a strong case for the relationship of fr. 166 with Philippe le Hardi and with the Limbourgs in the period before about 1405–1406, when the *Belles Heures* was begun, we may turn to the final, and infinitely difficult, problem. Are the miniatures in the first three gatherings comprehensible as the work of Paul with one brother, as the documents state about the Duke's Bible? Part of the reply can be made readily. The identity of the painter of the third gathering with the strongest painter of the *Belles Heures*, probably Paul, is, we hope, already demonstrated. But what of the rest? Only two hypotheses have hitherto been advanced, and neither one was argued. In 1895 Paul Durrieu divided the miniatures in the three gatherings between two painters, and he made this division even though he refused to connect fr. 166 definitely with the Bible commissioned to the Limbourgs![65] His division, to be sure, was somewhat different from the one we have already suggested. He believed that the illuminator of the third gathering also painted the second, whereas his colleague painted the first. Jean Porcher, the only scholar in recent years who studied this question, found that each gathering was the work of a distinctive illuminator, and since this conclusion involved all three brothers Porcher recognized no connection between Philippe le Hardi's Bible and fr. 166—indeed, he inclined to date fr. 166 toward 1410.[66]

The sequence of styles on successive folios of the first two gatherings is at first utterly baffling.

There is no simple connection between styles and the opposite faces of folios, or between folios that compose a single sheet. Even problems of reworking by a later artist arise. Black ink is employed in the miniatures on folio 1, then again to a diminishing degree on 2v and the subsequent folios up to 7v.[67] Because the two distinctive and very strong folios 1v and 2 show almost no ink shall we conclude that this technique was employed originally by a second, inferior artist? A similar problem is raised by the more or less crude, flat layer of pink on the flesh surfaces on folios 1, 3–8v, and 10. On folios 14v and 16 this pasty color has become brownish. In some instances, as 7v no. 1, the pink has the appearance of hastily applied make-up, which leaves the outer edges of the flesh white, without cosmetic. If a later painter had added this color he would surely have "improved" folios 1v and 2 also (Figs. 281, 282). Here, however, there are only a few deft touches of red. Once again these folios emerge as the work of a distinctive and superior artist. They are readily intelligible as earlier accomplishments of the great painter who was largely responsible for the third gathering. He made additional contributions to the first two gatherings, as we shall see.

A strong artist is always more easily recognized than a lesser one, and the difficulty of identifying the lesser styles in the first two gatherings is compounded by the fact that they were presumably produced by brothers who had been, and continued to be, closely associated and who were active at a very early moment in their careers, when their styles would naturally grow and change rapidly. Working in the same house, furthermore—that of the Duke's physician—and perhaps in the same room, exchanges were inevitable. In addition to sharing conceptions the stronger master not infrequently, it seems to us, provided designs for his brother. Folios 4, 10v, 11, 12, 15, 15v, 16v, and perhaps also 2v seem to have been produced in this way. That there was collaboration in execution is proved by the third gathering itself, for despite the general high level of accomplishment some miniatures, such as no. 8 on 22v and several on 23 and 23v, were finished by a weaker hand.

The miniatures in the first two gatherings present, I am convinced, the kind of problem that would be insoluble without some extra-stylistic facts. In this dilemma the documents, fortunately, provide important clues. They tell us that a couple of years before the Bible was begun one of the illuminators, Jean, had been serving an apprenticeship in another art. He and presumably Paul also were very young in 1402. The payments for the Bible over two years refer, furthermore, to two illuminators, not three. Herman, the third of the famous brothers, is not mentioned at all.

The excellence of the miniatures on 1v and 2 implies that their author had been trained as a painter, not a goldsmith, and even that he had intently studied Italian paintings, probably in France but conceivably already in Italy (Figs. 281, 282). Since only Paul is not known to have served as a goldsmith's apprentice, there is all the more reason to connect him with the major artist of the Bible. To come closer, now, to the problem of his colleague, or colleagues, in the Bible let us turn to the folio that is most unlike the third gathering—the first folio in the manuscript (Fig. 280).

Despite the general resemblances in composition, in figure types and drapery patterns, God is, in comparison with the powerful men on folios 1v, 2, not to mention gathering 3 (Figs. 281, 282, 312, 313), almost a gnome—short, large-headed, and comparatively feeble. The scenes lack luminous transparency; they look pasty and muddy. To a considerable extent this murkiness is produced by the web of lines of black ink. These lines, intended to give greater volume and definition, may be seen on the frames as well. The painter's perspective is so uncertain that he shows *all* the outer faces of the three-dimensional quatrefoils.

The quatrefoils on folio 1v show the same perspective, but they as well as the architectural frames are rendered without any ink in soft tones, and the scenes, except no. 4, likewise have very few black lines (Fig. 281). They are, indeed, so luminous and transparent that the few visible lines of ink, as on the drapery folds of the Creator in no. 1, are highly destructive. In stature and effectiveness the Creator is conspicuously different from the rather puny figure on folio 1 (Fig. 280). The friars and their audience in no. 8 differ similarly from the groups of the good and the bad in the corresponding miniature on folio 1. The water, beautifully evoked by strokes of gray and blue—metal was employed in the manuscript only for haloes and ornament—has a silver transparency. In no. 3 the waves swirl around a mauve rock. Below filmy trees the garden in no. 7 consists of fluid, opalescent tans and blues.

Folio 2 shows a further development of many of the qualities visible on 1v (Fig. 282). God assumes imposing proportions, and the painter's command of the structure of figures and of animals, such as the bull in no. 5, has improved remarkably. The few strokes of black ink, as on the Creator in no. 1, are even more disturbing than on fol. 1v.

If we assume, provisionally, that these first folios were painted in their sequence in the manuscript, we might at this point ask whether from folio 1 through 2 we are witnessing the very rapid growth of only one painter. To this hypothesis folio 2v provides a powerful jolt (Fig. 283). The figures do, to be sure, resemble those on fol. 2, and Paul probably drew them. They are not, however, comparably executed. The painting is dry, and black ink covers many of the forms. On the other hand the posture of Adam created by the Trinity (in no. 1) is truly extraordinary. We must, then, suppose not simply the influence of Paul but some sort of contribution by him. Perhaps he undertook the drawings, whereas the ink enthusiast undertook the execution. We should add immediately that Paul took no similar role on either side of the conjoint half of this sheet, folio 7 recto and verso (Figs. 292, 293). Although his influence is felt there he was, as we shall see, directly concerned with only one other folio in this gathering.

Folios 3, which we have already discussed, and 3v show much less connection with Paul than 2v (Figs. 284, 285). 3v is in fact more closely related to folio 1, and it seems to have been executed by the same illuminator at a somewhat later moment, after he had begun to abandon, under the inspiration of his companion, the comparative opacity of the ink technique for luminous tones of color. The pasty red flesh tones, however, are even more prominent.

Folios 4–5v are more problematic (Figs. 286–289). The scale of the figures is increased and in other aspects as well they suggest drawings by Paul. His conceptions are especially clear in nos. 2 and 6 on 4v, in no. 5 on 5, and no. 1 on 5v. Again Jean seems to have been responsible for the execution of most of the miniatures on these folios. On folio 4 the scenes of Cain leading Abel out to the fields and then killing him are outstanding for the succinctness of the narrative and the simple, bold patterns of volume and space. The city gate has the solidity and even much of the architectural character of a Trecento monument; indeed we encounter here, apparently for the first time in the work of the Limbourgs, a combination of gate and moat that recurs frequently in their later paintings (Fig. 286, 405). Similar combinations were employed in Trecento painting, particularly Paduan (Fig. 345), and such relationships pose the question of a study, even at this early date, of Italian models. In the Christian scene which the story of Cain and Abel prefigures, the *Betrayal*, the comparative darkness of the blue sky suggests a nocturnal setting. To develop this suggestion a lantern falls forward over the lower frame. This folio appears to have been designed by Paul and largely executed by his colleague.

The subsequent folios with the story of Noah and Abraham contain nothing equally impressive. 6 and 6v revert to the style of the conjoint folio, 3 and 3v. At this time Paul was interested in massive figures, and his spaces therefore are rather shallow, whereas 6 and 6v show some ventures into deep landscape, especially in the scenes of the parting of Abraham and Lot and of Sarah and Hagar (Figs. 290, 291). Similarly, on folio 7 houses on a street of Sodom are visible through a gate of the city (Fig. 292). The doll-like feminine faces of 6 and 6v reappear on 7 and 7v, but the latter are cruder in execution and show an unusual brown-violet range of color (Figs. 292, 293). At one time I tentatively ascribed these differences to the intervention of another illuminator, and I entertained the hypothesis that Herman, though not paid by the Duke, lent a hand on these folios as well as on 14v and 16. I am now more inclined to see in them the youthful Jean captivated for a time by a different model.

The same style, slowly gaining in strength, continues through 8v, the last folio of the gathering (Fig. 295). There Jacob dreaming of the ladder to heaven anticipates completely David dreaming of the Resurrection in the *Très Riches Heures* (Figs. 427, 568). Jean's work appears again, including the pink faces, on 9, the first folio of the second gathering (Fig. 296). This folio, to be sure, was undoubtedly painted at a different moment, and—such are the vagaries of this manuscript—in some respects it seems less advanced than 8v. The scene of Christ and the apostles, however, is striking; the fluid surfaces and rippling drapery, especially of the averted apostle, suggest an excellent model. This is, indeed, to be found in Paul's second miniature on folio 11v (Fig. 301). Perhaps we may understand this relationship to mean that Paul drew on 9 or that folio 11v was executed before 9, and that Paul, who painted the smaller share of the first gathering, was getting on ahead of Jean in the second. Similar forms, though less beautiful, appear in Jean's miniatures on fol. 16, which is the other half of fol. 9 and the last sheet in the second gathering (Fig. 310).

Folio 9v glows with transparent, luminous colors that recall those on fols. 1v and 2 (Figs. 281, 282, 297). The illuminator, no doubt Paul, is somewhat less intent now on *valeurs* than on color, movement and space. The church in no. 2 has an unprecedented scale, and the structure of no. 8 is uncommonly elaborate and realized masterfully. Laban's vision of the Lord (no. 5) has a striking immediacy. Even the frames on this folio reflect the greater artist. For the first time the spandrels of the quatrefoils become diaphanous through the use of a dark grid over a light ground. The quatrefoils themselves no longer are three-dimensional and seen from both sides, but flat gold. Gold frames reappear on certain following folios—10v, 11, 11v, 12—all of which I had singled out as designed by Paul before observing the similarity of the frames. Jean, on the other hand, adopted the gold frame only on fol. 13. Thereafter he as well as Paul employed it consistently, Jean on his miniatures to the end of this gathering, Paul through the third gathering.

Folio 11, clearly by Paul, shows another innovation in the frames (Fig. 300). The front of the structure is splayed and is projected toward us from the plane of the folio, in which the outer piers seem to lie. The tessellated floor provides the most spectacular perspective yet seen in the Bible, stretching away, it seems, to a distant range of hills. Within this structure hovers the incarnate Christ, enclosed in an aureole. His assumption of human form is prefigured, as the text states, by Jacob's gift to Joseph of a many-colored robe, which in miniature no. 7, however, is rendered only in the usual grisaille. Tabernacles of the kind we see here were already foreshadowed in the Limbourgs' model, fr. 167,[68] and around 1400 Jacquemart de Hesdin employed one for an enthroned Madonna.[69] About 1406–1408 they were introduced as canopies or shrines for saints in the *Boucicaut Hours*.[70]

Another kind of similarity with the *Boucicaut Hours* appears in two of Paul's miniatures on fol. 11v (Fig. 301). The lowest scene at the left represents the Jews who, like the sons of Jacob with Joseph, immersed Christ in the "well of the world." In the miniature at the right the three Marys grieve at the empty tomb just as Reuben lamented Joseph. Neither text refers to light, but in both scenes Paul has put large golden orbs in the sky, the source of rays which shine on the world. In the scene at the left they mingle with the similar rays that issue from Christ's halo. In a complex allegory on the next folio a similar heavenly disk sends out red, white, and gold rays, while a group of Franciscans makes useless astronomical calculations (Fig. 302).

This next folio, 12, exhibits the same kind of collaboration between Paul and Jean, but almost all the painting must be ascribed to the latter (Fig. 302). The architectural structures in scenes 1 and 3 are impressive; the latter indeed repeat Paul's in no. 8 on folio 9v (Fig. 297). On the other hand the tiled floor in nos. 2 and 5 inclines upward steeply. The compositions are interesting and the story effectively told, particularly in the scene showing the first wife of Judas, son of Jacob, standing with her three children while he courts a second woman.

Paul's large, complex architectural settings on folios 9v and 12, with their colonnaded corridors flanked by a higher building, resemble structures by Jacquemart in the *Brussels Hours* (Figs. 297, 302, 342). Even the mountain that rises above Jacquemart's cloister reappears in Paul's miniature on fol. 9v. Another resemblance with the *Brussels Hours* is no less striking. In the scene on fol. 12 of Christ whipped before some horrified Franciscans the victim's tunic lies near his feet on the floor. No such form was included in the Limbourgs' model, fr. 167, fol. 12. One representation of the discarded tunic in the Flagellation appears in a Florentine triptych of the third quarter of the fourteenth century (Fig. 372), where it is preceded by the scene of Christ removing it. In her vision of the Flagellation, of about 1370, St. Bridget clearly implies that Christ's garment was lying nearby.[71] The earliest example of such a representation in French and indeed perhaps all Northern painting is the *Flagellation* in the *Brussels Hours* (Fig. 369).[72] In both instances the tunic is white, or in the *Brussels Hours* a filmy light gray. It would seem to represent, then, not the seamless blue tunic woven by the Virgin in which Christ usually appears, nor the purple mantle thrown over him at the Mockery, but the white garment in which Herod, in their immediately preceding encounter, had dressed him, as the *Meditationes vitae Christi* and other texts inform us.[73]

There are other signs around 1400 of a greater interest in the garments of Christ. The three principal ones, white, purple or rose, and blue, are displayed near the sarcophagus in miniatures of the Man of Sorrows (Fig. 375).[74] A *Flagellation* represented in a French enamel in the Louvre, *ca.*

1410, shows the tunic of Christ at the foot of the column (Fig. 370).[75] This garment, emblem of suffering, is removed by soldiers prior to the crucifixion in a miniature by Pseudo-Jacquemart in the *Grandes Heures*, painted 1407–1409.[76] By 1402 the Duke of Berry owned a gilt silver tabernacle that showed "des vestemens de Nostre Seigneur."[77]

The apparent dependence of the *Flagellation* in the Bible upon the *Brussels Hours* might seem to be complicated by the fact that the former illustrates the deeper meaning of the grief of Jacob when his sons hold before him Joseph's blood-stained coat.[78] The analogous Christian form, however, is not Christ's tunic but his bloody flesh, upon which in fact the illuminator dwelt. "La cote Joseph," the text says, "segnefie la precieuse cher Ihesu touillie en sanc." There is no reference to Christ's garment, and if the illuminator had chosen to show it because of an unconscious association, he would surely have painted it pink, like Joseph's coat. We may suppose, then, that his reason for including the white tunic was familiarity with the splendid manuscript, full of Trecento motifs, which had just come into his patron's collection.

There is no tunic in the *Flagellation* in the *Belles Heures*, but the scene in the *Très Riches Heures* restores it (Figs. 371, 584). Unlike the white garment in the symbolic Flagellation it is clear blue, and Christ's flesh, bloody in the Bible, is unmarked—miraculously preserved despite a brutal beating to which the spiked thongs described by St. Bridget and the broken and discarded sticks give vivid testimony. In representations of the Flagellation in the later fifteenth century, particularly in Netherlandish painting, Christ's garment frequently appears on the floor.[79]

When inferring that the Limbourgs studied the *Brussels Hours* late in 1402 or early in 1403 we have kept in mind its accessibility to them. The manuscript, described in Jean de Berry's inventory of manuscripts compiled in the summer of 1402, was given, after this time, according to a note alongside the item, to the Duke of Burgundy at an unspecified date. The connections of its miniatures with the *Bible moralisée*, during 1402–1404 in the hands of the Limbourgs in the house of the physician of Philippe le Hardi, and the intimacy during these years between Jean de Berry and Philippe le Hardi, indicate that Berry offered the manuscript shortly after the summer of 1402.[80] The gift was, indeed, of a most unusual kind—a richly illuminated Book of Hours containing two portraits of Jean de Berry and displaying everywhere his arms and emblems.[81] Occasionally a modern historian insists that the Duke would not have given away a manuscript like the *Brussels Hours*, and scholars normally envisage the book leaving Bourges for Arras, Lille or some other remote Burgundian seat.

No image could be more false. From about 1400 both Jean de Berry and Philippe le Hardi resided mostly in Paris, as I have previously stressed.[82] Not only that, they saw each other regularly, dining in each other's houses. Even more, Philippe le Hardi lived for long periods in the principal Parisian house of Jean de Berry, the Hôtel de Nesles. Most of the time from June 25—August 29, 1402, the two brothers were in this *hôtel* together. Philippe was a guest again from December 10 through Christmas as well as during the second half of January, 1403.[83] This close relationship with Jean de Berry greatly quickened Philippe's interest in illuminated manuscripts; from then on, as we shall see, he became a major patron. The two men exchanged gifts. In March 1403, when both Dukes were in Paris, Philippe gave Jean a fine copy of the *Fleur des histoires*.[84] Around this time Jean decided to make an exceptionally personal gift. When he did so the *Brussels Hours* probably went only from one room in the Hôtel de Nesles to another!

These realities of daily life touch also the story of the Limbourgs and of the *Bible moralisée*. Three days after Philippe le Hardi gave the commission to the Limbourgs on February 9, 1402, Jean de Berry dined with him. Then for more than a month beginning February 25 Philippe le Hardi lived almost continuously in the *hôtel* of his physician, where the Limbourgs were working. Twice during this period Jean de Berry came to dinner. No stretch of the imagination is required to envisage meetings between the boys and this passionate lover of books. Jean de Berry and his brother were clearly great friends; otherwise Jean might then have entertained dark thoughts of poison, the sooner to bring the exceptionally gifted youths into his service.

We have left the Bible at folio 12. The following folios, through 14v, show less inventiveness. To be sure, we find one curious means of meeting the problem of supernatural travel posed by scenes covered by vaulted tabernacles. In the *Resurrection* on folio 13v God the Father comes down through an opening in the keystone, and on folio 14 Christ ascends to heaven through the same aperture (Figs. 346, 348). The Limbourgs continue in the *Belles Heures* to remove the keystone for supernatural emanations: on folios 41, 84, and 155 golden rays descend through it from heaven (Fig. 406).

Jean seems to have been entirely responsible for folios 12v–14v, whereas Paul again supplied drawings for 15, 15v and 16v. The next to the last folio, however, 16, is a throwback. It shows the palette and facial types of 6v and 7 (Fig. 310). The figures, to be sure, have become much more imposing. To recognize how much one need only compare God the Father in no. 5 of folio 1 and Christ in no. 8 of folio 16 (Figs. 280, 310). In the Bible and in their later work the Limbourgs frequently employ figures of this kind, achieving breadth, volume, and rhythmical sweep by the device of an ample mantle held high over one raised hand.

When we turn to the third gathering we leave behind the intricacies of the first two (Fig. 312). It is beyond doubt the robust artist of folio 11, for instance, who reappears on 17, the first folio of the new gathering, but he reappears after a short interval (Fig. 300). Christ, addressing the apostles about things to come, is monumentalized by a long fold of his mantle that sweeps from his shoulder to the ground. The turning of planes in the light areas is now achieved by a much narrower range of gray.[85] We have already observed these subtleties of color and of light on the subsequent folio 19 (Fig. 278). The ground becomes for the first time a very light yellow-green. The richness and delicacy of tones in the *Death of Jacob* on folio 17 surpass anything visible in the preceding gatherings, and so do the clear spatial relations between the twelve sons of Jacob, who listen to their father's prophecy of the future. We have seen a similar, though less impressive, diagonal arrangement in the *Entombment* on 17v (Fig. 337). In general Paul experimented much more in this gathering with figures and their interrelationship than with very deep space, which virtually disappears. Many figures have become so tall they extend from the lower frame almost to the upper. Whereas Paul designed all the miniatures in the third gathering he did not himself paint every one. 19v is somewhat inferior in execution; witness the tree in no. 5 in comparison with the one on 20 (Figs. 316, 317). 21, 23v, and 24 are relatively weak, and they show a more opaque color (Figs. 319, 323, 324).

The miniatures throughout the gathering are full of forms that recur in the *Belles Heures* or even the *Très Riches Heures*. In addition to those we have cited above we might refer to *Darkness in Egypt* in no. 5 on 22v (Fig. 279) as a first step toward the nocturnes in the *Belles Heures* and *Très*

Riches Heures (Figs. 497, 587). The kind of radical foreshortening of foreground figures favored by Paul in the *Belles Heures* (Figs. 444, 641) appears in no. 2 of folio 14, painted by Jean (Fig. 306). Joseph pushed into prison on folio 12v anticipates Catherine's incarceration in the *Belles Heures* (Figs. 303, 435). The man on folio 21v in the Bible who whispers words of flattery into the ear of a king while holding his hat in his hand is repeated by a figure alongside Nero on folio 215v of the *Belles Heures* (Figs. 320, 799). Both texts imply his presence, but not in this specific posture. In the *Agony in the Garden* in the *Belles Heures* a cross extends from God the Father to Christ precisely as in the representation of this subject on folio 21 of the Bible (Figs. 319, 496). The flagellants on folio 23 announce those in the *Belles Heures* (Figs. 322, 463), and the street scenes with their long array of houses, exceptional in this gathering, predict the *Belles Heures* (Fig. 488) and the *Très Riches Heures* (Fig. 556). When we compare figures on folio 18 with those in corresponding subjects in the *Belles Heures* we recognize the comparative strength of the best miniatures of this gathering. Thus Pharaoh, who sits cross-legged on folio 18 as he orders Egyptian midwives to kill masculine Hebrew infants, is superior to the very similar Herod in the *Massacre of the Innocents* in the *Belles Heures* (Figs. 314, 363). The seduction on this folio that illustrates one of the three great vices, luxury, pride, and avarice, is more single-minded and vigorous than the similar one in the story of St. Paul (Figs. 314, 409).

The first three gatherings of the Bible show the kind of relation with the *Belles Heures* and the *Très Riches Heures*, not to mention the *Brussels Hours*, that one might expect of a manuscript painted by the Limbourgs in the very first years of the century. Its miniatures offer us a very exceptional insight into the emergence and early growth of a great painter and his less gifted brother. If our distinctions are correct this growth was not exactly steady, but in spurts (as at the beginning of the third gathering), and accompanied by lapses and diversions. Jean on the other hand was caught by more diverse interests, and the lesser style in the manuscript, in fact, veers so considerably that it suggests a third collaborator. Faced with these complexities, we must trust that the documents really conform with the facts, and that Paul and Jean alone began the Bible in early 1402 and continued without significant assistance to work on it through March 1404.

Stylistic Origins

What Paul de Limbourg did before 1402 we do not know. When in 1399 Jean was working with a Parisian goldsmith he would certainly have seen scintillating objects such as the *Madonna* at Altötting, which King Charles VI received from the Queen as a New Year's gift in January 1404 (Fig. 374). He was no doubt much impressed by the fluctuating light, the reflection, and the beautifully varied pale colors, displayed in depth, of these extraordinary Parisian *joyaux*. Paul surely had studied objects of this kind also. Indeed his first miniatures, on 1v–2, approximate more closely than those of Jean the luminary qualities of enamels.

Since the father of the Limbourg boys was a sculptor they became familiar with the arts at a very early age. It is next to impossible to envisage what they saw in Nijmegen because no significant sculptures or paintings remain.[86] A large colored drawing of the Emperor Charles IV and seven Electors in the *Gelre Wapenboek* has sometimes been presented as a work executed before 1378 and therefore a unique example in Europe at this date of the "new realism."[87] It seems to us, however, unintelligible at this early date; it was probably executed after the Limbourgs went to France. The only other important objects that can even hypothetically be ascribed to Guelders around 1400 are a set of panels divided between the Walters Art Gallery and the Mayer van den Bergh Collection in Antwerp (Fig. 359). In the *Nativity* Joseph slits his stocking to provide the swaddling cloth of Christ, and indeed a famous relic of Joseph's hose is preserved in the Cathedral at Aachen, which is near Nijmegen.[88] The miniatures of the Limbourgs, however, seem less related to these panels than to the *Madonna* at Altötting.

Illumination in the region of Utrecht, then a growing center of the art, shares with the miniatures in the *Bible moralisée* a primary interest in pale color and in the evocation of form by differences of value rather than by line. We may see, however, from the meek Alexander in a Bible written there in 1403,[89] or from an *Animation of Adam* in a treatise written by Dirk van Delft by 1404 (Fig. 349) that the figures are expressive but quite unstructured.[90] It was only about 1410 that Dutch pantomime, which had been very limited, began to acquire southern—that is to say French—eloquence. That we may observe in an enchanting little Book of Hours from Utrecht,[91] where the angel Gabriel, rushing toward the Virgin, eagerly points to heaven in the French manner,[92] and where the *Vesperbild* or *Lamentation* derives from a composition first known in the *Très Belles Heures de Notre-Dame* (Figs. 351, 352, 355).[93] Perhaps the spirited angels playing an organ were inspired by angels making music in the *bas-de-page* of the *Annunciation*, as we see them in a Book of Hours from the circle of Jacquemart.[94] The collaborator of this excellent Dutch illuminator looked to France as well, but particularly to the Boucicaut Master; he is the master responsible for much of the well-known prayer book of Mary of Guelders, dated 1415.[95] The Passion scenes in another Book of Hours from the same region, again small, show the same touching pathos; and the imposing volumes created by loosely wrapped mantles recall the *Bible moralisée* or even the sculpture of Sluter (Figs. 350, 353, 354). This beautiful and important but little-known manuscript, now in the Gulbenkian Foundation, belonged to Margaret of Cleves, who died in 1411.[96]

The kind of painting in the southern Netherlands that the youthful Limbourgs might have known perhaps included works in the style of the Apocalypse now in the Bibliothèque nationale (Fig. 358).[97] The graphic power of this rather over-touted illuminator might have had some influence on their later work, but its dry surface and obvious linearity would have captured their attention less than the beautiful chiaroscuro of the best illuminator of a Book of Hours made towards 1400, probably in Tournai (Fig. 347). An astrological manuscript in the Morgan Library is a capital document of Flemish painting of this period, the most vigorous work of its time and the only one that is firmly placed and dated. The learned abbot of the monastery of Eeckhout near Bruges, who concerned himself with astrology and who was close to the painters of Bruges, gave the manuscript to Jean de Berry in June, 1403.[98] It was presumably painted there shortly before this date. The planets, as boneless as their Dutch counterparts, are beautifully rendered in washes of violet, rose, and green. In conformity with local pictorial conventions, female figures, whether they be midwives or planets such as *Venus* (Fig. 362), are remarkably demure, girlish and innocent, whereas the men, such as *Mercury* or the *Sun*, have correspondingly coarse features and somewhat malicious psyches (Fig. 361). In Flanders wide mouths, thick lips, and large noses are obviously signs of masculine vitality. Two excellent Flemish illuminators, whom I have called the Coronation Master and the Cleres Femmes Master, revised such notions when, about the same time as the Limbourgs, they went down to Paris (Figs. 73, 74).[99]

We have no way of knowing whether on the way to or from Paris one of the Limbourgs visited Hesdin in Artois or Ypres in Flanders, where they would have found the greatest of pre-Eyckian panel painters. In any event the boys would surely have seen specimens of Broederlam's art, because no doubt Philippe le Hardi kept in his Parisian residences at least a small panel by his *valet de chambre* (1387) and *peintre* (1391). Two altar-wings of a sculptured retable for Champmol, which Broederlam had begun in the early 'nineties, were installed and generally visible from 1399 (Figs. 377, 378). There is no need here to discuss at length either the style or the iconography of these justly famous paintings, especially after the brilliant investigations of Erwin Panofsky.[100] We must, however, refer here and later to those aspects of his art that impressed the Limbourgs.

Broederlam loved color. He clearly cared for nothing quite so much as finding, for instance, just the right green for the mantle of Elizabeth. This was to be displayed alongside her white scarf and scarlet tunic as well as the blue of the Virgin, all conventional colors which he could modify only slightly. What gives the green its exceptional richness is its relation to the exact tone of buff and dark olive-green of the terrain, which is like a pale emanation from her mantle. Where in the *Flight* he must put the heavier blue of the Virgin before the landscape he painted the latter in a stronger, less transparent green. In the *Presentation* he dwelled on exquisite modulations of white, rose and cool blue; in this context the violet of Simeon and the gray-green of the altar and the floor become especially precious.

For Broederlam color attained its greatest fascination when light played upon it and made it seem to move. Few of his shapes, indeed, are fixed and contained. The colors in the landscape run like lava. The Virgin's blue, especially in the *Presentation* and the *Flight*, spills out unpredictably. In the *Flight* Joseph's red has a strong thrust, and the rose mantle of Gabriel thrashes bewilderingly back and forth. The flutter of the angel, to be sure, is in part the consequence of his sudden arrival. But no supernatural journey can be ascribed to the prophet on the building above, whose drapery is also agitated. Similar swirling planes, with powerful reversals, appear in the drapery of the *Madonna* of his colleague Claus Sluter, carved at the same time for the portal of Champmol (Fig. 379).

Broederlam wanted to maintain the traditional prominence of his figures while at the same time giving them a place inside the new and highly differentiated environment he created for them. Thus he invariably set them further back from the lower frame than his precedessors. The terrain in both panels, however, inclines steeply upwards in a very traditional way. Perhaps Broederlam increased the inclination in these particular compositions because of a desire to diminish the apparent depth of forms in the upper triangles. These spaces, determined by the shape of the sculptured center of the triptych for which he was asked to supply the wings, had become awkward for his new art. Into them the painter fitted objects that would be overlapped very little, if at all, by the frames and thus would seem to lie in the same plane with them.

While Broederlam sought and obtained this kind of planar conformity in the upper zone he seems to have cared less about the spatial and coloristic interrelationship of the two parts of each wing. The temple in the *Presentation* tends to detach itself because of its prevalent light white, even though the mountain at the right is brought up to a rather high value. The gray and rose of the structures in the *Annunciation* fit somewhat better into the pictorial field, but in depth and complexity the buildings are unique in the panels. Broederlam's conception perhaps had its origin in the diagonal of the angel and the Virgin—the angel outside the portico in the Trecento manner. Behind the portico of the Virgin, placed obliquely also, he introduced an unprecedented form: a circular tower, domed, it seems, as a symbol of the Synagogue and the world before Grace. In its darkened interior stands an altar. Attached to it is a curious open hall, crowned by a three-lighted gable that might refer to the Trinity.[101] This hall, with its dark ceiling and declamatory black and white floor recedes to an exceptional depth. While its stridency emphasizes the head of the Virgin nearby, the effect is generally distracting. Broederlam put a conical mountain alongside the domed tower, but the meandering hall at the left still seems to have got out of control.

Whereas the Limbourgs probably knew Broederlam's great panels and later, as we shall see, drew ideas from them, their own conception of the figure, already at the beginning of the Bible, seems quite different. They wanted a structure that is best described historically as Trecento, and their figures therefore resemble far more the corresponding forms of those masters who combined a taste developed in the North with the vocabulary and syntax of the Tuscan innovators. Thus Paul's Christ on the cross is articulated in a manner unprecedented in the Netherlands (Fig. 367). The painter describes the parts of the body, the flesh lying over the bone, and the particular muscular tension of the moment. Much of all this, which derives ultimately from Simone Martini and his Sienese followers (Fig. 494), Paul could have studied in Paris or in Dijon, in paintings by Jean de Beaumetz and his workshop (Fig. 368), and probably even to a certain extent in the work of the earlier Burgundian court painter, Jean d'Arbois, who was in Italy in 1378.[102] Paul might well have been in Dijon with his uncle Jean Malouel, who became court painter there in 1397.

Beaumetz, a native of the region of Arras or Cambrai, went down to Paris before 1375, when he departed for Dijon and service under Philippe le Hardi.[103] There he received so many commissions that he employed numerous assistants, and in 1388 he was directing two workshops, each of three or more painters.[104] The two extant panels of the Crucifixion in Cleveland and the Louvre, from a series he and his atelier painted between 1390 and 1395, show in fact signs of collaboration (Figs. 360, 368).[105] The group of the three Marys is similarly conceived in the two paintings but Christ in the panel in Paris is far less Sienese and indeed less impressive. Even within the Cleveland panel the canon of the figure varies somewhat, from the slender Christ to the very broad and bulky Carthusian, but these variations seem to have been effected by the artist himself. They may, indeed, be seen again in the three Madonnas in an excellent drawing in Basel which I have attributed to him, especially in the relation of the two slender Madonnas to the husky Child (Fig. 356).[106] The figure of Christ in the panel in Cleveland is inconceivable without knowledge of the Sienese tradition (Figs. 368, 494), and Simone's *Crucifixion* now in Antwerp may well have been in Dijon at the time. Beaumetz's Virgin, like Simone's, has swooned; she shows a pallid face, closed lids, and parted lips at a similar ¾ angle. Her right hand resembles Simone's, and the mantle of both figures (as well as of others) is bordered by the same kind of double gold line.

Paul's fainting Virgin has two long limp arms, like those of the Virgin in the panel by the atelier of Beaumetz in the Louvre (Figs. 360, 367). She is supported, however, by St. John rather than by one of the Marys, whereas in both Beaumetz panels John stands on the other side of the cross, wringing one hand in another. This gesture of grief, though uncommon, was occasionally employed earlier, in for example the sculpture of Strasbourg Cathedral, in Ducciesque painting, and in a Missal by a fascinating follower of Pucelle who may have worked in the very region where Beaumetz grew up.[107] All the figures in Paul's miniature show the concern with texture, especially of the flesh, that so sharply differentiates Beaumetz from his Sienese models. Paul gave his heads the full lips, heavy lids, and sensuous cheeks favored by his predecessors at the Burgundian court, Beaumetz and, as we shall see, his uncle Malouel.

A Virgin reminiscent of Paul's figure in the Bible, with bowed head and one extended arm, appears in a *Crucifixion* in a manuscript dated 1406 and made for Marie, daughter of Jean de Berry (Fig. 366). The illuminator, mysteriously close to the Limbourgs, painted a Virgin who in other respects is even more closely related to the figure in the *Belles Heures* (Fig. 364). The important *Crucifixion* of 1406 tends to confirm the prior date of the miniature in the Bible. It also indicates that the Limbourgs were then working in the circle of Jean de Berry, and that by 1406 they had developed the style of the *Belles Heures*. The seraphim who, instead of the more usual angels, appear at the sides of the cross become favorite forms of the Limbourgs.

The Limbourgs would surely have seen examples of the decisive modification of the Sienese tradition by Northern taste not only in the painting of Beaumetz but in the work of their uncle and sponsor, Jean Malouel, likewise a native of Nijmegen.[108] Malouel appeared in Paris in 1396, working for Queen Isabeau, and in the following year, upon the death of Beaumetz, he was appointed painter of Philippe le Hardi. Thereafter, apart from trips to Arras and especially Paris, he worked in Dijon until his death in 1415. Two extant paintings have with good reason been associated with his name.

The exquisite tondo in the Louvre bears on the reverse the arms of Burgundy (Fig. 380). The representation joins the theme of the Man of Sorrows with that of the Trinity by substituting God the Father for the angel who in the French type supports Christ (Figs. 375, 882).[109] The entire group appears above the clouds, in heaven. The style resembles Beaumetz in its combination of Simonesque qualities with sensuousness and realism of texture. Astonishing elegance does not exclude blatant signs of bodily injury and death. Christ in the tondo is especially close to the earlier figure in the Cleveland panel, though surpassing it in its searching description of flesh and bone. The hands dangle in the same way as the Virgin's in the Cleveland panel, but they are more beautifully painted. The enamel of the tondo is smoother, and the nuances of light and shade, as in the red mantle of St. John or the marvelous transparent loincloth of Christ, cannot be matched in the earlier panel. Nor can they be seen in another very good, earlier panel at Troyes, which is related iconographically to the Louvre tondo in many respects (Fig. 373). The emotional coolness of this painting and the less searching articulation of Christ throw into relief the deep relationship of the tondo and Beaumetz.

The *Trinity*, painted *ca.* 1400 for Philippe le Hardi by a master younger than Beaumetz yet much indebted to him, thus conforms with the historical place of Malouel as disclosed by the documents. The tondo implies a renewed study of Simone Martini; in color too it approximates Simone much more closely. The style of the Limbourgs, clearly related to the *Trinity*, approaches it still more closely later, when they were painting the *Très Riches Heures*. By this time Malouel's own style had changed considerably, if a *Madonna with Angels* on loan to the museum in Berlin-Dahlem is really his (Fig. 642). The attribution to the author of the tondo and the identification with Malouel, first tentatively proposed by Colin Eisler and the writer, have been generally regarded as probable.[110] The *Madonna* may have composed, as we suggested, a diptych with a portrait of Jean sans Peur in prayer, known only in copies, all of which do, however, show the figure reversed (Fig. 376). The relative openness of the composition of the Berlin canvas on the left side, and the lunging movement of the Child, not fully explained by the cherry held behind his hand by an angel, seem to suggest a pendant at the left.

Judgment of the stylistic relationship with the tondo is complicated by the fact that in the *Madonna*, unlike the *Man of Sorrows*, there appear to be variations of style; the six lower angels look like the work of a collaborator. The *Madonna*, furthermore, is painted in tempera on cloth—a unique surviving example of this technique in French or indeed in all North European painting of the time.[111] Instead of a smooth brilliant enamel the surface is matte; the brush strokes are more visible, and the contrasts sharper—partly, to be sure, because of abrasion. The two paintings share certain significant conventions. A few angels wear crosses on their diadems but none have haloes. There is in both works, in fact, a hierarchy of haloes. Christ's head is surrounded by rays alone—in the Berlin canvas they are large *jeux d'artifice*—whereas the head of the Virgin and of God the Father have disks as well as rays, and John only a disk. God the Father, a monumental and un-Simonesque figure, anticipates the gloriously majestic and powerful *Madonna* in Berlin. In this respect as well as in the very ample drapery, with its large tubular folds and dancing borders, the Madonna recalls the sculpture of Sluter. Malouel was, in fact, coloring it in 1402.[112]

There is very little reflection of Sluter in the tondo, and the Berlin *Madonna* was painted about 1410, so that the Limbourgs may have derived certain Sluteresque forms in their miniatures of 1402–1404 from studying his statuary themselves. The loose, abundant drapery in their miniatures, unprecedented in painting, was probably inspired by the work of the great sculptor (Figs. 379, 381), and it serves, as in his statues, to give the figures greater power and rhythmical force. The motif of drapery cascading from a raised hand, which we have seen in the miniatures in the Bible, was probably introduced in the nineties by Sluter, though we know it only in a magnificent *pleureur* of 1404–1405 (Fig. 382).

To a degree the miniatures by the Limbourgs in the Bible may be regarded as a mirror of lost Burgundian art. Precise sources, however, for some aspects of Jean's style as we first meet it have eluded us. Paul's earliest work arouses speculation about the extent and place of his study of Trecento painting. The majestic bearing of his figures, as of God the Father in no. 1 on folio 2, and the knowledge of bodily structure (Fig. 282), suggest an understanding of the principles of Giottesque art, gained conceivably by a prior trip to Italy. We actually know nothing whatever about him before February, 1402.

V

The *Belles Heures*

1 · THE CHARTER OF 1405

WHEREAS we have no written records of the activity of Paul and Jean de Limbourg for a few years after the death of Philippe le Hardi in April 1404, one important visual record is extant. It is a copy of the initial at the beginning of the Duke of Berry's charter of the Sainte-Chapelle in Bourges, dated April 18, 1405 (Fig. 387). The miniature represents the Duke in his robe of state investing a canon of his new chapel; an attendant holding the hood stands nearby. The original document, described as such in 1858, was destroyed by fire that year in the archives in Bourges, but copies had been made earlier by the Comte de Bastard for his precious collection of reproductions of medieval and Renaissance illumination.[113] These copies attracted little attention, and indeed the writer reproduced the initial for the first time in 1963.[114] In earlier discussions of this copy I accepted the date of the document as the date of the miniature, but M. Jean-Yves Ribault has kindly pointed out to me two paleographical differences from other extant manuscripts or copies of the charter that suggest it might have been completed afterwards.[115] If there was in fact a delay it may have been, for reasons that follow, a matter of months and hardly more than a couple of years.

Bastard's copies leave no doubt about the authorship, and even the approximate date seems to us not difficult to determine.[116] *France moderne* (three fleurs-de-lys), employed here for Berry's shield, appeared on the seal of the Treasurer of the Chapelle that was designed a few months later.[117] The novel form of the acanthus, peculiar to the Limbourgs, is common in the *Belles Heures*, and a version of it was introduced in 1406 by the Master of the Breviary of Jean sans Peur (Fig. 366). The Duke wears the cloak with ermine lining and collar in which he appeared in portraits prior to 1405 and in the *Belles Heures* soon afterwards (Fig. 386), but not from 1409 on.[118] The collar does not rise as high as in the *Belles Heures*, and the Duke is distinctly younger than in all definitely later representations of him except in that book (Fig. 386).

If we may trust the copy, the composition too implies an early date. The tiled floor, though similar in design to pavements in the *Belles Heures* (fol. 67v), inclines more steeply than pavements in that manuscript (Figs. 426, 427). The orthogonals, furthermore, do not converge to the same degree. It is true, however, that ceiling and floor are more coordinated than in the portrait in the *Belles Heures* (Fig. 386), but at this rather early date—1405–1408 as we shall see—the practice of the Limbourgs varies considerably. The oblique placement of the throne is another instance of the kind of composition the Limbourgs favored in the Bible (Fig. 313). The design of the Duke's drapery in the initial resembles that of Pilate and similar enthroned figures in the *Belles Heures* (Fig. 418). The flat plaits of the canon's drapery on the floor are similar to those of the Duchess of Berry in the *Belles Heures* (Fig. 385), and the colors of the miniature—yellow, pale orange, violet, light green—reappear in the *Belles Heures*, particularly in the *Preaching* and *Procession* of St. Gregory (Figs. 451, 641).

2 · THE DATE, THE BORDERS AND THE FRAMES

Even those historians who assume that Robinet d'Estampes was so good a registrar that he regularly equaled their own conception of completeness have not doubted that the Book of Hours which is now one of the glories of the Cloisters in New York is identical with the manuscript Robinet, in his Fourth Account, calls "une belles Heures."[119] The remarkably full description fits exactly, and the manuscript bears ample signs of the Duke's ownership. His arms and emblems appear on five folios (Fig. 410).[120] There are also two portraits as well as one of the Duchess (Figs. 385, 386, 403). Jean Flamel, his secretary and calligrapher, filled folio 1 with a superb inscription stating that Jean de Berry had commissioned the book (Fig. 402). Flamel's flamboyant capitals, of the kind then aptly called *cadeaux*, burst into marvelous serifs, freer in their flow than the related vines of the borders. Even the minuscules shoot out astonishing appendages, and indeed the size of a letter, as of the last "de," is partly determined by its place in the stream.

Though the manuscript was generally dated between 1410 and 1413 I proposed an earlier date, *ca.* 1408–1410, several years ago. Our demonstration that entries falling into specific groups in Robinet's accounts were recorded in chronological order proves that the *Belles Heures* was completed even a year or two earlier (see Appendix A). The entry describing it falls just before the *Grandes Heures*, which we know was completed in 1409, and just after manuscripts acquired after the death of Louis d'Orléans in November 1407. This position definitely fixes the completion of the *Belles Heures* in 1408 or early in 1409.[121] This date conforms with another fact not hitherto observed. At least one, and probably three figures in the calendar of the *Grandes Heures* copy corresponding figures in the *Belles Heures*. Although in both these manuscripts the representations of the months and the zodiacal signs belong in general to the tradition established by Jean Pucelle, the complex, backhand stroke of the man about to strike the boar in December is characteristic of Paul de Limbourg (see the *Decapitation of St. Catherine*, Fig. 445), and it, as well as the tubular folds and other details of the massive figure were copied in the *Grandes Heures* by an illuminator working in the Egerton style (fol. 6v). The colors, too, are quite similar. Sagittarius in November of the *Grandes Heures* reflects equally the corresponding figure in the *Belles Heures*, which is a type of centaur used by the Limbourgs in the cycle of St. Anthony and St. Paul (Fig. 479). In both instances Sagittarius wears the same kind of pink hat. For his Libra in September Pseudo-Jacquemart used, in reverse, the fashionable lady of the *Belles Heures*. The *Belles Heures* and the *Grandes Heures* are undeniably related in another way—if the *Way to Calvary* in the Louvre actually belonged to the latter manuscript. Until the early date of the *Belles Heures* was established the miniature in the Louvre appeared to be the first representation of the subject which included the suicide of Judas. The *Way to Calvary* in the *Belles Heures*, painted about the same time, includes the suicide also, although the posture of the figure and the position of the ladder are different (Fig. 341). Although a priority is difficult to establish, the representation in the *Belles Heures* would seem to be the earlier.

Precisely when the *Belles Heures* was begun is not quite clear. We may employ the pace of work in the *Bible moralisée* as a measure but it can only be approximate, especially because all three brothers definitely worked on the *Belles Heures*, as we shall see. We may estimate roughly that the execution of the *Belles Heures* required about three years, and that it was therefore begun *ca.* 1405.

The great significance of this earlier date for the understanding of the *Bible moralisée* has already been demonstrated. The accession in 1408–1409 together with the analysis of the inventory to which we have just referred also help us to understand one aspect of Robinet's notice that I had long found puzzling. The Limbourgs are not named; the Duke had the manuscript made, Robinet said, by his craftsmen—"ses ouvriers." This surprising anonymity becomes much more intelligible when we recall that though the surviving description of the manuscript appears in Robinet's Fourth Account, written during 1412, this description is an unaltered copy of his original notice of 1408–1409, as it appeared in his Second Account.[122] At this date the Limbourgs were very young and in the Duke's employ only three to five years. They had not yet attained the position and reputation of Jacquemart, named as the principal painter of the *Brussels Hours* and the *Grandes Heures* after service under the Duke beginning just before 1384.[123] Similarly André Beauneveu, to whom Robinet in 1402 ascribed some miniatures in the Duke's Psalter, had begun to work for him by 1386.[124]

Another problem that the early date of the *Belles Heures* clarifies is the similarity of its borders to those in manuscripts dated 1401 and 1402. The motif of small jugs threaded along a stem, which is employed on folios 84, 191, 209 and 215, appears, together with similar vines, in a manuscript of a French translation of Valerius Maximus completed by the Virgil workshop for Jean de Berry in 1401 (Figs. 409, 414). In both manuscripts the design of the borders is enlivened by varying the color of the jugs, or rendering them half light and half dark. The two manuscripts have in common also at least two other border patterns: a vibrant kind of meander in which bunches of pointed ivy leaves wave regularly back and forth along a stem (Figs. 411, 413), and a rather broad band covered with similar kinds of interlace (Fig. 492).[125] Two of these designs recur in a fine little Book of Hours in the Morgan Library which was completed in 1402 (Fig. 412). We are informed of this fact by the colophon of an ambitious scribe, Yves Luce, who liked, by repeated signatures, to assure the reader he had produced the text.[126] He tells us that the Horae or "matines," as he describes it, was written and illuminated in Nantes.[127] The illuminators, however, are clearly Parisian, out in Brittany, if Monsieur Luce is right, only briefly, or at least very recently. One of them probably is the great Coronation Master, who in the same year painted the beautiful *Coronation of the Virgin* at the beginning of a *Légende dorée*.[128]

The resemblance of the borders of the *Belles Heures* with these manuscripts reminds us also that all of them are filled with the traditional ivy, albeit in new, more dense patterns, and that the broad-leaved form of the future, the so-called acanthus, as yet appears rarely. We may find it, too, in the corners of the first folio of the Valerius Maximus, and in a splendid display around the *Annunciation* in the *Belles Heures* (Fig. 410). This latter border, painted or at least designed by Paul himself, shows, along with the borders of a Book of Hours in the Bodleian Library dated 1407 (Fig. 419), the first abundant use of the acanthus as a major element in the design.[129] These illuminators had become familiar with the form in Italian Trecento manuscripts, and particularly in the work of the North Italian illuminator who collaborated on the *Brussels Hours* of Jean de Berry and several other Books of Hours produced in Paris in the first years of the new century.[130] Comparing, however, these freely swirling leaves and scrambling figures with Paul de Limbourg's more regular design and enclosed medallions one recalls the proposal of Friedrich Winkler that the borders of the *Annunciation* reflect the recently carved frieze of the Porta della Mandorla of the Cathedral of Florence (Fig. 408).[131] The resemblance extends to the predilection for half-length figures within a medallion sufficiently large to leave open space around them, and to the use of leaves or vegetable forms to provide for these figures the semblance of a real support. Whether or not Paul had already seen this sculpture he certainly evinced a very similar taste for the structure and design of ornament.

We have maintained that Paul was responsible for at least the design of the border of the *Annunciation* and we must therefore consider the relationship of the Limbourgs to the rest of the borders in the manuscript.[132] In important respects they resemble, as we have seen, the borders in early fifteenth-century Parisian manuscripts, and the Limbourgs may in fact have employed collaborators for this work, as they were to do, we shall see, in the *Très Riches Heures*. In that case the brothers must, however, have been in close touch with their assistants. The miniatures up to folio 74 are simple rectangles. Then on that folio Paul—for he surely painted this superb depiction of death and burial during the plague—wanted to give greater scale to Castel Sant'Angelo and to show Michael near it sheathing his sword, so he cut away the ivy in the upper border to provide space for a superimposed rectangle (Fig. 452). Such projections to fill spaces around the text and to accommodate buildings or mountains had been employed earlier, especially in Italian Trecento illumination,[133] and the Limbourgs had seen altarpieces, such as the one by Jacques de Baerze and Broederlam, which have a rectangular projection at the center (Figs. 377, 378).

Folio 74 on which Paul made this change of format belongs to a cycle that, as we shall see, was painted somewhat later than the miniatures in the Psalter and the Hours of the Virgin preceding it. On folio 84, however, which apparently belongs to the initial design of the book, Paul again extended the usual rectangle by adding, once again for a relatively large building, a central projection, this time circular (Fig. 406). Four of the five other special frames appear in the last section of the book: on folio 157 the upper ivy was again erased, and circular projections, apparently planned before the painting of the border, appear on 161, 174, 211v, and 215. The entire upper frame of Paul's *All Saints* on folio 218 consists of an arch (Fig. 389).[134] Most of these miniatures were painted by Paul (136, 157, 174 and 215 are exceptions), and we may thus recognize in the *Belles Heures*, particularly in what we may take to be its later phase, the growth of a mode that leads to such remarkable forms in the *Très Riches Heures*.

3 · THE *BELLES HEURES* AS A BOOK OF HOURS

Our renewed study of the Fourth Account of Robinet d'Estampes has disclosed that he accessioned the *Très Belles Heures de Notre-Dame* in 1405–1406, presumably after the completion of the second campaign of illustration.[135] This second campaign, in which the miniatures were inserted in spaces established by the initial work on the manuscript in the early eighties, involved two illuminators, the Holy Ghost Master, and the Baptist Master, who was Flemish by training.[136] These painters, too, left the manuscript far from complete, and about New Year 1412 the Duke gave it to Robinet. The jeweled clasp and bookmark that had earlier—1405–1406—been attached to the manuscript was transferred to the *Belles Heures*.[137] Robinet accessioned the *Belles Heures* just before the *Grandes Heures*, which was completed in 1409. The *Belles Heures* was begun, as we have seen, about the time the second campaign on the *Très Belles Heures de Notre-Dame* ended, and the Duke must have commissioned the *Grandes Heures* not long afterwards. Even for the Duke of Berry these projects constitute an extraordinary moment.

During the years before 1409 Jean de Berry thus had in preparation two new, extensively illustrated Books of Hours. These manuscripts, though contemporaneous, are very different in character, and it is perfectly clear that Jean de Berry was no single-minded patron. Though he and his counselors determined, to a degree, the contents of the books, their principal decision was the selection of the painters, who were then free to contribute fundamentally to the design and illustration of the manuscript. Thus it can scarcely be an accident that Pseudo-Jacquemart repeated in the calendar of the *Grandes Heures* the principal elements of his calendar in the *Petites Heures*.[138] Nor is it more accidental that Jacquemart de Hesdin was the *chef d'équipe* for a Book of Hours of so enormous a format as the *Grandes Heures*, and no doubt the author of many of the major illustrations.[139] One of these illustrations probably survives, the *Way to Calvary* in the Louvre, which has been much discussed in recent years.[140] A huge miniature, approximately 37.9 x 27.8 cm. within its gold frame, it would very nearly fill a folio in the *Grandes Heures* (39.5 x 30 cm.), leaving little space for a border, if indeed one was intended. Such enormous miniatures of course required a book of extraordinary size, and when considering how this format, unique for a Book of Hours, was selected we must bear in mind that Jacquemart was probably a painter of panels and murals as well as an illuminator.[141]

Certainly the miniatures of Jacquemart in the *Brussels Hours* look very much like paintings of larger scale, and their blue backgrounds even remind us of murals. Their frames, furthermore, unlike the frames in many contemporary manuscripts, are regular and formal. Jacquemart's miniatures have, too, a new degree of independence from the text because they are all full-page, they are all on versos facing the beginning of an Office or Hour, and the backs of most of them are blank.[142] About six years later, when planning the *Grandes Heures*, Jacquemart took the next step. Here *every one* of the seventeen full-page miniatures, again on the versos, had a blank back, and he or his colleagues painted almost all of them on a single folio independent of the book. Then each of these pictures, upon completion, was inserted into the manuscript and held by a stub.[143]

The practice of Jacquemart and his collaborators in the *Grandes Heures* was adopted by the Limbourgs, particularly Paul, for a series of miniatures in the *Très Riches Heures*, as we shall see.[144] The *Belles Heures*, however, shows few of these innovations. There are no miniatures without text below them. The large miniatures always have four lines of script, either part of the text of an Office or, in seven unusual cycles which we shall consider shortly, rather long titles. Most of the miniatures are on normal folios in the gatherings. Most of them have text or another miniature on their opposite faces, and they thus are more traditional than the *Brussels Hours*.

In other respects, however, the *Belles Heures* is quite novel. For each hour of the Office of the

Passion there is not one miniature but two, and for Matins three. It is true that the plan of illustration of the Book of Hours varied during the course of the fourteenth century, particularly in specimens made for its greatest patrons, the Valois. Thus Pucelle's superb *Heures de Jeanne d'Evreux*, which lacks an Office of the Passion, adds a full-page scene from this cycle to each of the usual illustrations of the Hours of the Virgin. (Later in Holland, indeed, the Hours of the Virgin normally shows only a Passion cycle.) In the earliest Book of Hours acquired by Jean de Berry, the *Très Belles Heures de Notre-Dame*, each of the principal miniatures in the several offices is accompanied by one or more related events in the frieze in the lower border.[145] In the Duke's *Petites Heures*, illuminated shortly afterward (*ca.* 1387), this plan was adopted and then the marginal scenes were abandoned,[146] so that the number of subjects in the main offices was greatly reduced. In the *Brussels Hours*, planned about ten years later, the miniatures have become, as we said, full-page, and the *bas-de-page* has disappeared entirely.

This change in the *Petites Heures* and the *Brussels Hours* was due in large part to the transformation of pictorial style, to the development of more voluminous forms in deeper spaces, and to the exercise of the exquisite, peculiarly French sense of a proper accommodation of this new art to the pages of a book and to the columns of script on them. Compensation for the loss in the *Brussels Hours* of the *bas-de-page* was made, however, by adding to the full-page miniatures for the Hours of the Virgin and of the Cross small scenes of related episodes in the initials opposite. This plan was adopted and developed in the *Grandes Heures*, where the initials opposite the huge paintings became miniatures at the beginning of the first column of text.

Whereas the arms and emblems of the Duke are displayed on many borders in the *Brussels Hours* and the *Grandes Heures* they appear on only a few in the *Belles Heures*. Indeed, alongside the lavish exhibition of armorials in the *Grandes Heures* the *Belles Heures* seems positively reticent. The *Grandes Heures* includes, too, the extraordinary scene, apparently unprecedented, of St. Peter giving a person still very much alive—Jean de Berry—a personal welcome into heaven.[147] Other seemingly comparable representations show an admittance *after death*.[148] In the miniature in the *Grandes Heures* the prince of apostles brandishes his keys while the Duke, looking him straight in the eye, lifts his large pendant sapphire—a stone with a celestial connotation and also a collector's prize.[149] In the initial Jean de Berry, still down below on earth, prays with exceptional vigor, quite naturally entranced with this glimpse into the future and its promise of eternal connoisseurship in heaven.

There is only one other sizeable representation of Jean de Berry in the *Grandes Heures*: in prayer outside an initial of the Madonna at Matins in the Hours of the Virgin.[150] In the *Belles Heures* he appears at prayer in a miniature accompanying a text of the Fifteenth Joy of the Virgin, the Assumption (Fig. 386).[151] For the first time in all his religious books he is here represented alone in a miniature (except for a kind of guardian mace-bearer), without Christ, the Madonna or a saint. He kneels in the sort of private oratory he had in the choir of the Sainte-Chapelle in Bourges and no doubt also in his other chapels, and in which we see Philippe le Bon of Burgundy in a miniature painted about 1460 (Fig. 384). Though the context of the miniature of Jean de Berry is religious, the portrait—for it can be called that—is given a political emphasis by the surprisingly large mace and by the coronet.[152] Pentimenti show, in fact, that originally he had another object on his head.[153] Most puzzling of all is his youth. Jean de Berry was then about 66 years old, and what we see goes beyond the usual limits of flattery. The evidence for the identity of the sitter, however, is compelling,[154] and the lack of correspondence with actuality seems most plausibly explained by the youth of the painter and his belief that his patron should be idealized in this way. The woman portrayed on the verso of this folio must be the Duchess—the first and only instance of the representation of either of the two wives of Jean de Berry in a manuscript (Fig. 385). Her youthful appearance presents no problem because Jeanne de Boulogne, the Duke's second wife, was only thirty years old in 1406. Her crown is royal rather than ducal, and, though there are no signs of an alteration, it might conceivably have been added when the Duchess of Anjou, who was Queen of Sicily and Aragon, acquired the manuscript after the death of Jean de Berry.[155]

Curiously, neither of these portraits seems to have been painted by Paul. Indeed, the attenuated figures, the discrepancies in scale in the miniature of the Duke, and the confusing spatial position of the curtain, which hangs from a rod in the foreground and is pulled back deep into space, point to Jean rather than to his brother. A second representation of the Duke in the last miniature in the manuscript is not much stronger (Fig. 403). It illustrates a prayer for a safe journey which is either extremely rare or unprecedented in earlier Books of Hours.[156] The Duke introduced it into three of his manuscripts. In the *Belles Heures* it is painted on a single leaf in a small gathering at the end of the manuscript, and since the borders differ somewhat from preceding ones the gathering was probably added at the end of the work.

We know the second example of the Itinerary only from a lithograph of Bastard, which reproduced an entire folio, including the first lines of the prayer (Fig. 404). Even in this copy the style of the Limbourgs is clearly recognizable in the miniature, whereas the border must be of an earlier date. Durrieu concluded years ago that this folio belonged to the *Très Belles Heures de Notre-Dame*, to which the brothers did in fact add two other miniatures that survive and which we shall consider shortly (Figs. 500, 501).[157] Durrieu's hypothesis seems very probable, because the folio conforms better with this manuscript than with any other of the Duke's Books of Hours. Neither the script nor the borders fit completely, however,[158] and what one can judge of the style of the Limbourgs in a copy suggests a date somewhat later than that of their other two additions to this manuscript. It was the Limbourgs again who added the miniature of the Itinerary to the *Petites Heures* (Fig. 405).

I had earlier estimated on grounds of style that, of the three representations of this prayer by the brothers, the miniature in the *Belles Heures* was the first; this estimate is now strongly supported by the knowledge that the manuscript was completed in 1408 or early 1409.[159] The early date adds more substance also to my suggestion that the Duke became interested in this prayer because of an event that shook him deeply, the murder of one of his nephews, Louis d'Orléans, by another, Jean sans Peur, Duke of Burgundy. In the years after this dreadful and momentous act, when these miniatures were painted, the struggle between the Burgundian party and their opponents, the Armagnacs, became extremely bitter, and no one in France could feel safe, least of all a leading Armagnac such as Jean de Berry. Some relationship to these grim events the miniature in the *Belles Heures* certainly has, because the banners on the chateau to which the Duke is riding bear the blue and gold bands of Burgundy. The peace and even existence of the realm depended upon the relationship between the two political parties, and Jean de Berry was a principal mediator. He may therefore be represented here on a symbolic or even an actual journey. Hoping in fact in January 1408 to negotiate an arrangement with Jean sans Peur that would prevent a major civil war, Jean de Berry and Louis II d'Anjou went to meet him at Ypres.[160]

In the *Belles Heures* Paul has given the chateau a powerful volume that foreshadows his famous portrayal of the Louvre in the *Très Riches Heures* (Fig. 548). He placed the building in the foreground and he clearly wanted to show it from top to bottom, perhaps because it represents a specific Burgundian possession. As a result it is proportionately small for the figures and not directly accessible, though the drawbridge across the moat is down. To give the impression of movement and a sudden arrival Paul has boldly shown the figures emerging from the space behind the right frame, and even the Duke is not yet entirely visible. The foremost riders are just reining up, and the horses twist to one side or another as they do at that moment, swaying in a beautiful rhythmical pattern. The white horse of Jean de Berry is a sign of his eminence; when King Charles VI met the Byzantine Emperor Manuel II near Paris he deferred to him by offering him his horse of this color.[161] Three of the Duke's companions turn to look at him inquiringly as he sits quietly, apparently thoughtful just before the arrival at the gate. He looks older than in the portrait earlier in the book, and now wears a brown moustache and beard. All the figures lack luminosity and there are scarcely any spatial intervals between them, so that once again the Duke, and here also his companions, seem to have been painted by Jean.

The miniature preserved in the lithograph of Bastard shows a very different scene (Fig. 404). The Duke and his entourage move in from the right, coming perhaps from the castle with a large round donjon that resembles somewhat the Duke's own Dourdan shown in April of the *Très Riches Heures* (Fig. 542). The party encounters a monastic procession coming out of the gate. The friars, bearing reliquary tablets, sing, their banners flutter, and the Duke seems moved as he lowers his head and puts his hand on his breast, his fingers touching a gorgeous golden *escharpe* that may be an Armagnac emblem (Figs. 543, 604).[162] His mace-bearer holds open his purse while looking intently at the Duke, apparently to learn his decision about a contribution to the friars.[163] Perhaps this miniature commemorates a donation made after a safe return from a risky journey. The composition, which elaborates that of *Jerome leaving Constantinople* in the *Belles Heures* (Fig. 473), is focussed and symmetrical, though the Duke and his courtiers are larger than the friars, partly because they lack architectural aggrandizement. The miniature still shows an ornamented background but the space is deeper than in the scene in the *Belles Heures*, and the slender, verticalized architecture of the gate recalls the *Très Riches Heures* (Fig. 586). The Duke looks much older than in the *Belles Heures*, and the iconography of the image, especially the moustache and beard, point to a date towards 1410.[164]

In the miniature added to the *Petites Heures* the Duke has grown heavier and perhaps older and he is clean-shaven, as in all portraits after about 1410 (Figs. 405, 539). The painting, weaker than the other two representations of the Itinerary we have considered, is not the work of Paul but perhaps Jean. It does, however, illustrate more exactly the prayer "ad accipiendam viam" because it shows the Duke setting out on a trip. He points the way and the mace-bearer repeats the gesture, his fingers extending into the unrepresented space to suggest the difficulties of the venture.

A lively, elegant guardian angel flies above, pointing in the same direction.[165] As in the lithograph the Duke is attended by a cleric, probably his confessor.

The three unique miniatures of the Itinerary compose a fascinating series among the numerous, remarkably varied, and no less unique representations of Jean de Berry. These portraits extend from the enjoyment of a winter's banquet (Fig. 539) to absorption in one of his prize acquisitions. We have even seen his projected arrival before St. Peter, preserving undiminished his collector's passion. One of the travel pictures was, as we have proposed, designed and partly painted by Paul (Fig. 403), and one clearly not (Fig. 405). The author of the miniature reproduced by the lithograph must remain undetermined (Fig. 404). These attributions presuppose, of course, distinctions that will be made in the course of this section of the book and the one devoted to the *Très Riches Heures*.

4 · INTRODUCTION TO THE THREE PAINTERS

With the help of documents we have been able to ascribe most of the miniatures in the Bible to either Paul or Jean, or to Jean working on a drawing by Paul. In the discussion so far of the *Belles Heures* we have named with assurance the outstanding artist alone. He is identifiable beyond doubt with the greater artist of the Bible. That much is absolutely clear. Less definite, but very probable, is the identification of this master with Paul. Bearing in mind the nature of the Duke of Berry's patronage, it seems far more likely than not that the brother to whom he gave such exceptional gifts was the best artist. This conclusion is strongly supported by the fact that only Paul is not known to have served an apprenticeship with a goldsmith, and the miniatures in the Bible we connect with him show such a high level of accomplishment that their author was probably trained as a painter or illuminator, not in another art. What, however, are we to make of the lesser paintings in the *Belles Heures*? We lack external evidence. The inventory notice is mute; it does not mention the Limbourgs at all. The first certain records of all three in the service of the Duke are of 1411, two or three years after the manuscript was completed. It is only then that we really know that Herman had joined his brothers. His presence later alongside Paul and Jean is proved also by the notice of the *Très Riches Heures* in the inventory of 1416. The authors, we are told, were "Pol et ses frères."

For the 156 miniatures in the *Belles Heures* the one important fact we have is their early date. We would therefore expect a close relationship with the Bible and, since the painters were still very young, considerable stylistic change. The manuscript conforms with both these requirements. Jean, however, was so variable in the Bible that he does not emerge with an entirely clear profile, and it seemed to me hazardous to connect his miniatures with the lesser ones in the *Belles Heures* without knowing whether he alone, or with Herman, worked alongside Paul. Were differences to be understood, in other words, as signs of the growth of one artist or the presence of two?

Similar problems confront the student of the miniatures in the *Très Riches Heures*. The manuscript was begun, we shall propose, in 1411 or 1412 and left incomplete in 1416. In addition to the axis of personal growth and experimentation we must allow for constant exchanges between the collaborators. Ideas did not *always* originate with the strongest master. We cannot quite agree with the view that, though collective execution can and does occur frequently, collective invention is impossible. Art is in this respect not entirely different from science, and the Nobel Commission, which frequently divides its awards for a single achievement, is not likely to be wrong.

I recently compounded the difficulties surrounding the three brothers by demonstrating that still another important illuminator may definitely be distinguished in the *Très Riches Heures*. Together with associates he painted most of the borders and the initials, and since he was also responsible for the illumination of the *Breviary of Jean sans Peur* I called him the Master of this Breviary.[166] He was intimate with the Limbourgs from 1406 on, and for a time I therefore thought he might possibly be Herman.

Years ago I had resolved it would not be profitable to search for the three brothers. The job, to be sure, like Mark Twain's ceasing to smoke, had been done before. Indeed, no sooner had the *Très Riches Heures* emerged from obscurity in 1856 than the indefatigable Dr. Waagen divided the miniatures among several artists. Similar proposals for some miniatures have not been lacking since. The soundest of them, by Hulin de Loo and Panofsky, have succeeded in distinguishing one or more groups that, with qualifications, seem homogeneous.[167] How on the other hand the four groups that have been proposed by Hulin are to be connected with three brothers is not equally clear.

For all these reasons I decided to limit my attempts to disentangle individual styles to Paul alone. He was a great painter, and therefore far more readily distinguishable. His full range, however, remained unclear as long as the contributions of one or more collaborators were undefined. I nevertheless felt unwilling to undertake a more extensive stylistic fission.

Then I began to receive some new signals, as physicists did recently when, with an interferometer, they detected the quasars. My instruments were good color films of many of the miniatures. At the very least these films greatly reduced the time required for a solution of the problem, and they may have been absolutely necessary, even though I enjoyed the privilege of repeated examination of all the manuscripts. They gave me, I readily acknowledge, an advantage possessed by none of my predecessors. The color films permitted a direct comparison of three manuscripts preserved in Paris, New York, and Chantilly. Equally significant for the final result was the attempt to resolve the problems of the entire "field." Earlier endeavors had been limited to one manuscript or another, chiefly the *Très Riches Heures*.

None of my remarks about techniques and methods are intended to imply that I exclude errors in the conclusions. In so delicate and intricate a task mistakes are inevitable; the full truth, indeed, will always remain unobtainable. Where I feel less confident of a proposal about a particular miniature I shall employ the usual device of a question mark. For numerous miniatures, usually inferior artistically, I have been able to offer no solution worth recording.

After the identification of the Breviary Master and the provisional identification of Paul in the Bible and the *Belles Heures* the next advance in the maze was provided, surprisingly enough, by the least accomplished miniatures in the *Belles Heures*. I refer primarily to the scenes in the Passion cycle from the *Mockery* through the *Way to Calvary* (Figs. 341, 371, 418, 498). The surfaces in this cycle are pasty and lack transparency, the figures weakly structured. Movement tends to be generated more by the design as a whole than by the action of single figures. Since the work of this illuminator seemed comparatively modest and his role in the book limited, for some time I thought of him, uneasily, as a collaborator whom the Limbourgs engaged expressly for the task.

I recognized with astonishment that this style reappears in the *Très Riches Heures*, chiefly in a group of miniatures illustrating Masses near the end of the book (Figs. 590–594, 596). There we meet the same warm color and strong contrasts of warm and cool as well as of light and dark. The figures, though much more skillfully articulated than in the *Belles Heures*, still bear signs of the earlier incapacity. The men have the same severe, dramatic countenances. The illuminator, to be sure, has made great strides since working on the *Belles Heures*, where he was certainly the least experienced painter of the three. This pattern of a career fits very well what we know of Herman. He was apprenticed to a goldsmith and he is not mentioned in the documents on the Bible. During that period he may well have continued primarily as a goldsmith, even if, as we have *most* tentatively suggested, he assisted his brothers on a few folios. As it happened, Paul painted one miniature in Herman's Passion cycle, a *Lamentation* (Fig. 455), which measures perfectly the difference between the work of these two brothers. In the discussion that follows we shall assign the miniatures in the *Belles Heures* and (when they are mentioned) in the *Très Riches Heures* to the three brothers, making only more or less brief comments. We hope that the individuality of each will gradually become clear, not only in matters of form but of iconography and even in the choice of the miniatures each was to paint. As an initial guide we may add to what has already been said that Paul was the most perceptive, the most thoughtful, and the most deeply ambitious. Jean was the most lyrical, the most elegant, and the greatest opportunist. Herman was the most demonstrative; he can even be melodramatic.

5 · NOVEL CYCLES

We have hitherto considered several single miniatures in the *Belles Heures* that are unusual in iconography and design or unprecedented in a Book of Hours. We shall now turn to the novel cycles. The fact that there are no less than seven of these, and that at the same time the Duke's saint, John the Baptist, has only four miniatures and a Mass but no Office, demonstrates again the constantly changing conception of a personal prayer book in the Duke of Berry's circle.

The miniatures for the Penitential Psalms, exceptional themselves, may be briefly considered first, though they come after one of the novel cycles. These Psalms are usually illustrated only by a depiction of David in prayer before the Lord (Figs. 506, 517). In the *Belles Heures*, for the first time in a Book of Hours so far as we know, each of the seven Psalms has a miniature (Figs. 420,

421). The iconography of the miniatures is largely unprecedented, though usually explicable by part, if not all, of the Psalms they illustrate. Thus the first miniature in the cycle (Psalm 6), which in Psalters usually shows David in prayer, represents the Lord's answer to his prayer for salvation from his enemies: a pirouetting angel slays them with a lance.

The miniature is different in character from the paintings in the manuscript by Paul that we have seen, and not nearly as strong (Figs. 333, 343). The figures, while solid, tend to be curiously limp, but an impressive movement courses through them, flipping the peak of the king's hat down and his tunic up. The prominence of vermilion against saturated blue and in combination with raspberry red and blue-green confirms the presence of Herman. He surely painted the last miniature of the cycle on folio 72 (Fig. 421), and the others are more or less close to his style. In Psalm 38 David, stuck with arrows as the text says, seeks to appease an angry Lord, who remains aloof from him. The Psalmist, looking as though he had been struck by the thunderbolts of Jove, lies on a tiled floor that stretches into the distance very much like Paul's floor in a miniature in the Bible (Fig. 420). The tiles diminish proportionately and the orthogonals vanish toward a region, very much as in the approximately contemporary miniatures of the *Boucicaut Hours*.[168] When on folio 68v Nathan rebukes David for his adultery with Bathsheba he points to the kind of disk in heaven, golden with red rays, that we have seen in the Bible.

St. Catherine, St. Jerome and Pious Scholarship

The first special cycle in the *Belles Heures*, introduced immediately after the calendar and before even the readings from the Gospels, not to mention the Hours of the Virgin, consists of eleven scenes from the legend of St. Catherine (Figs. 422, 434–436, 438, 439, 441, 442, 444, 445, 448). In every one of these cycles the miniatures are of the same size and format as those in the Offices, Masses, and prayers, and they are likewise accompanied by four lines of text. In the special cycles, however, the script is not brown but in alternate lines of red and blue. These lines compose long explanatory titles.

The cycle of Catherine is not only the first but one of the longest in the manuscript, and we naturally wonder why she was given such prominence—a prominence, furthermore, that is maintained in the miniature of All Saints (Fig. 389). One explanation has the advantage of accounting for two altogether exceptional representations: Jeanne de Boulogne is depicted for the first and only time in a manuscript (Fig. 385) and Catherine was one of her saints. She stands behind the Duchess, as the Baptist stands behind the Duke, on the seal of 1405 of the treasurer of the Sainte-Chapelle.[169] On the large altarpiece now in the Louvre commissioned by Jean de Berry for Poissy she again accompanies the Duchess, along with John the Evangelist, Jeanne's name-saint (Fig. 383). The Duke's name-saint, John the Baptist, is as we have said less extensively present in the *Belles Heures* (Figs. 430, 431). A full Office of the Duke's patron appears, however, only in the *Petites Heures*.[170] The hypothesis that Jean de Berry ordered the manuscript for his wife gains no support, however, from the fact that after the marriage in 1389 their relationship deteriorated, and when the Duke settled in Paris she remained at Mehun, so that the two rarely met.[171] The inscription by Flamel at the beginning of the *Belles Heures*, moreover, remains utterly silent about such a gift and the contents of the rest of the manuscript do not suggest it.[172] Catherine was, on the other hand, one of the saints especially venerated by the Valois, and the Duke owned several relics.[173] Perhaps most significant of all, as a learned woman she was a patron of the University of Paris.[174]

Illustrations of the legend of Catherine are not rare in earlier manuscripts, and a few Italian Trecento mural cycles survive. There is nothing, however, so extensive as the legend in the *Belles Heures*, and the selection as well as the omission of subjects is very interesting. Thus though the later fourteenth century had witnessed an exceptionally intense development of religious mysticism, especially in the Rhineland, no room was found in a cycle of eleven scenes for Catherine's vision of the Madonna nor for her mystical marriage to Christ—an event in her life that from the late fourteenth century evoked the greatest interest.[175] The story begins, on the other hand, with a scene that is unprecedented and may, indeed, be unique (Fig. 422). In translation the title reads:

> Catherine, daughter of King Costus, versed in all including the liberal arts [and] of incredible beauty, the admiration of all eyes in Alexandria, a city of Egypt, lived in the time of the Emperor Maxentius. (fol. 15)

The beautiful daughter of the King of Egypt, probably painted by Jean, sits quietly reading, devoting herself to the "liberal arts."[176] The stand near her contains two circular tiers of books. On top of it appears a horned Moses, partly because as the recipient of the Ten Commandments, and so to speak the publisher of them, he represents learning and the written word. Every cultivated person then knew, furthermore, that he received the Law on a peak of Sinai right next to the one on which angels buried St. Catherine (Fig. 450). To insist upon the relationship between the two, Moses appears once again on the altar in the chapel behind, this time without the horns but still bearing the tablets. The "statue" of Moses is represented again in the *Annunciation*, where he stands on the Virgin's lectern as a symbol of the world under Law but before Grace (Fig. 410). In conformity with such ideas Paul, following Pseudo-Matthew, has shown the Virgin as a student of the Law, with an open book before her and two others in a cabinet below. Moses was generally revered then as later in the Renaissance for another reason also: as the leader of his people in times of trouble he was upheld as a model for rulers. Philippe de Mézières presented him thus to his pupil, King Charles VI.[177]

The picture that inaugurates the story of St. Catherine is one of a group of representations in the manuscript devoted to study and teaching. The second such scene seems likewise to be unprecedented (Fig. 423). It is centered on a Parisian professor of Holy Writ, "*circa* the year 1084," as the title says. This scholar, praised by St. Bruno and later identified as Raymond Diocrès, sits in a large academic *cathedra*. Monks and scholars have gathered around him, three of them on a bench below, for discussion or transcription. Diocrès is so buried in his work that only the top of his head rises above the large lectern, a very bold perspective device at this period; it greatly enhances, at the same time, the informality suggested by the casual asymmetry of the disciples. The impressive recession of a series of planes all parallel to the picture plane was no doubt devised by Paul, though the execution seems not his. Diocrès and the writing monk served as models for two of the Evangelists in the beautiful Book of Hours by a close follower of the Limbourgs in the collection of Count Seilern (Figs. 424, 425).[178] A tracing of the miniature in the *Belles Heures* or possibly of preparatory drawings for it was used because both Evangelists are reversed, with the result that the penholder and inkwell of Luke, not very conveniently placed in the model, have come out on the left side.

The miniature of Jerome and other students listening to a lecture on Plato may be less impressive as a composition, but its content is fascinating (Fig. 426). Again a subject not previously represented, though drawn from the *Golden Legend*, it illustrates how the great scholar, familiar with Greek, Hebrew and Latin literature, grew discontented with the plain, unadorned language of the Prophets and turned to an intensive study of pagan writers, Cicero by day and Plato by night.[179] The expounder of Plato, like Diocrès, is well installed in a large throne before a fine lectern, though here they are seen from the side. The audience, however, like other audiences represented in late medieval art, sits on the floor.[180]

Jerome soon felt guilty about his enthusiasm for pagan texts, tormented by the same problem that became so trying to the early humanists such as Petrarch, Boccaccio, Ambrogio de' Migli, and Jean de Montreuil. The resolution of his conflict, however, is far less like that of these scholars than of their clerical antagonists, such as Giovanni Dominici, the influential Dominican in Florence in the early fifteenth century.[181] In a vision represented in the next miniature, Jerome saw himself before the Lord (Fig. 427). Like David in similar circumstances (Fig. 420) Jerome lies on a deep tiled floor that is intended to give scope to the composition. When he asserted he was a Christian the Lord replied "Thou liest, thou art a Ciceronian." Forthwith he was severely beaten by angels. For obvious reasons this story was represented by conservative ecclesiastical groups during the Renaissance.[182]

Jerome then vowed to devote himself to Christian literature, but the dilemma, so profound for the later humanists, remained with him, too. Twenty-five years later when Rufinus, who had once been his friend, ridiculed him for his constant classical quotations, he was not unduly troubled. "No water will wash clean wool dyed with purple," he said. "If I am to be blamed for the poems I once knew I must drink of the waters of Lethe. . . . Besides, if I am not mistaken you too read Cicero in secret!" As for his vision of punishment by the Lord he wrote: "Can dreams be used in evidence? . . . How often I have dreamt that I was dead and in the grave. . . . How often have I flown over mountains and crossed the seas! Does that mean that I am dead or that I have wings growing from my sides?" (*Pat. lat.*, XXII, col. 441 f.)

Soon after his famous dream Jerome returned to the birthplace of Christ in Bethlehem where, as the title (from the *Golden Legend* as usual) tells us, he and the disciples who gathered around him spent fifty-five years and six months translating the Bible and Holy Scripture (Fig. 428). Jerome himself now occupies the *cathedra* of the scholar, and there are prie-dieus for the disciples, all of whom, however, are curiously absent. The saint is accompanied only by his loyal and ever grateful lion. Three prophets, sources of Jerome's inspiration, are accommodated in an attic made by lowering the arcaded wall that completely fills the picture-plane in the related compositions we have just seen.

This picture of St. Jerome in his study reflects a cult of the saint as a scholar that was promoted in the first half of the fourteenth century by an influential professor of canon law at the University of Bologna, Johannes Andreae.[183] Soon thereafter painters in North Italy began to produce images of Jerome that made vivid his life of study by showing him, as Tommaso da Modena did *ca.* 1360, in a well-stocked cubicle conveniently served by a bilateral arrangement of lecterns and bookshelves (Fig. 432). Since this fresco is painted on a column the lion, who sits at the left, is diminished in the reproduction by the perspective. Tommaso's remarkable painting, so rich in detail and so suggestive of scholarly seclusion, anticipates the Eyckian and later Renaissance conceptions of the scene. Representations of this type, although undoubtedly simpler than Tommaso's, appeared in France in the circle of Charles V. Records describe a splendid enameled *joyau* this learned King possessed of Jerome between a lectern and the lion, which must have resembled a Lombard miniature of about 1380 (Fig. 433).[184]

The miniature in the *Belles Heures* represents perhaps the earliest composition of this subject by the Limbourgs. The prophets may be novel in the history of the theme, and their presence here in a miniature painted in 1407–1408 strengthens my proposal advanced earlier that a lost model by the Limbourgs, datable, because of its Gothic architecture and other details, about 1411, lies behind the best known of all these pictures of St. Jerome in his study.[185] It is the large drawing, mentioned above, which was added to the *Bible moralisée* (Fig. 357). Though generally regarded as an important work by Paul himself, it is, as I hope to have demonstrated, only a copy made after their death by an inferior and later artist whom I have called the Master of St. Jerome. He may be identical with the youngest brother Arnold, who was apprenticed to a goldsmith.[186] The incisiveness of the drawing seems proper for a practitioner of that craft, and he probably inherited the artistic property of his brothers. The drawing shows not only a series of prophets, now on pinnacles or in baldachins, but a remarkably similar design of the lion as well as an eagle on the lectern, flapping its wings. Both the Synagogue and Moses on the pinnacles resemble these figures as we have seen them in the Bible and the *Belles Heures* (Figs. 303, 410), and counterparts of the music-making angels appear in the border of the *Annunciation* in the latter manuscript (Fig. 410).

The shelf with books on the far wall may be seen in another miniature by the Limbourgs, or rather I should say probably by Jean, now in the Vatican (Fig. 429). In it Valerius Maximus sits at his desk writing the famous compendium of Roman history, the translation of which into French was completed in 1402 for Jean de Berry (Figs. 413, 414).[187] This text, however, is Latin and, more interesting, the script is Italian rather than French. The miniature might therefore have been executed during an Italian journey, but precisely when it is difficult to know. In spatial composition the miniature resembles the more advanced designs of the *Belles Heures* but the style of the border is earlier.[188]

To return to the story of St. Catherine, the second miniature, in part by Jean on Paul's design represents, without notable imagination, the beginning of her tragedy, when she refuses the command of Emperor Maxentius to worship a pagan idol (Fig. 434). When about 1380 Altichiero painted this and other representations of the subject he depicted great public spectacles, which attracted people even to second-story windows (Fig. 443). This kind of scene became common in the *Très Riches Heures* (Figs. 573, 585); the miniature in the *Belles Heures*, however, includes less than a dozen persons, more like Masolino's fresco in S. Clemente, Rome, though here the setting, lacking in the *Belles Heures*, is a temple that resembles the Pantheon.

Catherine proved so unswerving in her faith and so influential in Alexandria that Maxentius decided to convene fifty of the most learned men from all parts of his Empire. When to his horror she succeeded in converting all of them to Christianity the Emperor decided, as we see in the next scene, to burn them and their writings at the stake (Fig. 436). Flames rise from their bodies and scrolls at the left while the angry Emperor, holding high a menacing Eastern scimitar, looks towards Catherine, who sits on a throne above some of the scholars. Dressed in blue, the one rich color among pale yellows, gray, rose and green, she is the central, dominant person. The miniature is to our knowledge the only representation of this event in which she is enthroned while the Emperor stands—indeed, the reverse is normal.[189]

A still more interesting departure from tradition is the use of a close and low point of sight. Though the perspective is not systematic the benches overlapped by the lower frame and the decline of the orthogonals create the strong impression that we view the scene from below the frame and look up, even more than do the scholars, to the high throne of the saint. Though a composition of this kind has some antecedents in Trecento painting, particularly in the work of Ambrogio Lorenzetti,[190] it is novel in the North. Jacquemart de Hesdin introduced, but did not nearly equal, the location of the ground plane below the frame in his *Annunciation to the Shepherds* in the *Brussels Hours*, and the Boucicaut Master began to employ it, though in less radical form, in the *Merveilles du monde*, painted just before 1413.[191] The epoch-making conception in the *Belles Heures* is no doubt Paul's, and he executed the miniature also.

Maxentius, abandoning hope of shaking Catherine's convictions, supervises her imprisonment (Fig. 435). A soldier dressed only in a simple tunic of a beautiful pale yellow—a favorite shade in the *Belles Heures*—forcibly pushes the saint into her chamber. The opening is proportionately so small that she can enter only doubled up. Possibly this arrangement resulted in part from the fact that Paul—for it was no doubt he who designed this powerful miniature—wanted to maintain his usual large scale for the figures and yet he preferred to show the entire building, in the medieval tradition. Perhaps, too, he constricted the opening deliberately to convey the impression of the saint's confinement.

The *Golden Legend* tells that Catherine was beaten severely *before* being thrown into prison. That episode follows, however, in the *Belles Heures* (Fig. 438). In Italian painting, as in a fresco by the workshop of Spinello Aretino, the scene resembles the Flagellation of Christ (Fig. 440). Paul's unique design for the *Belles Heures* avoids the whipping entirely and shows her only being tied to the column—albeit very forcefully. Each of the soldiers raises a knee to brace himself in a posture which is adumbrated in the Bible (Fig. 303). Catherine exhibits that curious Northern ideal of the female body, best known in Jan van Eyck's *Eve*, that suggests pregnancy or at least fertility as a normal state, though the bodily structure surely has no such precise implication here.

Once within the prison, angels salve Catherine's wounds, watched by the Empress Faustina, her staunch supporter (Fig. 439).[192] Faustina has just been admitted by a jailer who holds a key of enormous size like the one the Lord gave to Adam in a miniature in the Bible (Fig. 284). For this intimate scene in the prison, rarely represented, the illuminator has once again chosen a close point of sight, and the entire lower part of the building passes below the frame. The usual blond hues have become even lighter. Catherine's beautiful nude body is surrounded by the pale pink of one angel and the whites of the other two and of her drapery. These tones are intended, perhaps, to suggest her purity. Together, however, with the elegance and femininity of the figures they compose a group that is unlike anything in earlier Italian or Northern painting. The miniature suggests Renaissance pictures of the toilet of Venus.

For her devotion to Catherine Empress Faustina pays with her life (Fig. 442).[193] Then comes the saint's turn, in the famous episode that gave her her usual attribute (Fig. 441). The fearsome wheel, of the double type that appeared frequently in Trecento painting (Fig. 443),[194] is in the *Belles Heures* beautifully carpentered and rich in its texture of wood and metal. The same concern with technique led the Limbourgs to depart from iconographic tradition in one notable respect. The *Golden Legend* says that the Lord sent angels to shake and to shatter the instrument of torture. Traditionally they appear waving swords (Fig. 443). In the *Belles Heures* all three of them apply well-constructed claw-hammers. This innovation speaks eloquently to us of one passionate concern of the artist.

Catherine is untouched by the wheels but three men are torn and bleeding. One of them is tossed into a posture that is extraordinary in the art of this time. Doubled up, he lies foreshortened, head foremost—the first of many figures of this kind designed by Paul in the *Belles Heures*. What source inspired such a remarkable innovation we cannot say, but it was surely similar to the soldier in Altichiero's fresco, whose one arm is likewise stretched out alongside his head (Fig. 443).

Paul designed more figures of this kind for the composition of the decapitation of the converted soldier, Porphyry, and his companions (Fig. 444). Corpses placed and foreshortened in this way, lacking in Trecento representations of the scene (Fig. 447), have a special impact, especially when they spout blood toward the beholder. The carnage continues with Catherine herself. Her abundant golden hair falls behind her clasped hands as a youthful executioner prepares a mighty backhanded blow (Fig. 445). What fresh observations of the world Paul embodied in his designs is proved by comparison with representations of the same subject by Altichiero (Fig. 446) or even Masolino (Fig. 449). In both the saint's hair remains neatly arranged on her head even at this final moment.[195]

Altichiero, a leading exponent of North Italian naturalism, was the first painter who sought to convey something of the height of the mountain at Sinai on which angels buried St. Catherine (Fig. 446). With a greater understanding of linear perspective Masolino, toward 1430, increased the size of the peak (Fig. 449). The Limbourgs allotted to Sinai a separate scene, in which three angels—one pale green, one deep blue, one part white and pink—fly with the body of the saint to the proportionately diminutive mountainous region (Fig. 448). Relatively diminutive this landscape may be, but it is unique among the paintings of the time. Four utterly barren peaks, greenish gray or reddish yellow, rise before a vibrant light blue sky. One of the peaks is the mountain of Moses. At the left pilgrims move upward through a defile. Near the center, at the end of a road, there is an exceptionally plain rectangular building. It is built of large gray stones and marked only by a couple of string courses. It has a small rectangular addition behind, and a monk or a hermit all in brown sits by the door.

The *Golden Legend* mentions no building on the mountain on which Catherine was buried, and none appears in the two Italian paintings we have considered (Figs. 446, 449). The structure represented by the Limbourgs, unique among their architectural representations, can only be the monastery of St. Catherine which, surrounded by its high stone walls, looks like the building in the miniature (Fig. 450).[196] This proposal is not as whimsical as it at first sounds. French pilgrims constantly visited the monastery, and some of the most distinguished among them were soldiers such as the Maréchal de Boucicaut, for St. Catherine was a patron of freed prisoners.[197] The

French court felt close to the monastery and patronized it; Charles VI gave it a chalice.[198] The travel books of Guillaume de Boldensele, Jean de Cor, and Mandeville all speak of its importance,[199] and in the *Merveilles du monde* the Boucicaut workshop represented the monument as a Gothic church.[200] A French official, Ghillebert de Lannoy, visited Sinai in 1422, and described it as "a maniere d'un chastel, forte et quarree."[201] An earlier French visitor of 1395, Ogier d'Anglure, spoke of "l'abbaye close de haulx murs a maniere d'une fort (*sic*) maison."[202] The Limbourgs, who showed in addition the large stones in the rectangular walls, were familiar with a more precise description, perhaps a drawing. In any event they have given us the earliest depiction of the monastery, and perhaps the first portrait in art of a remote pilgrimage site. They have captured the color, the wild emptiness, and some of the awesome natural beauty of the mountains. This little miniature clearly foretells the calendar pictures of the *Très Riches Heures*.

The Great Litany

The second special cycle in the *Belles Heures* is not only, like the first, novel in a Book of Hours but for the most part novel in the history of art. To judge from surviving monuments, only one of its four scenes—St. Michael over Castel Sant'Angelo sheathing his sword (Fig. 452)—had ever been represented before, and even then only recently. The four miniatures with their titles on folios 73–74v follow upon the Penitential Psalms and they immediately precede the Litanies, both normal texts in Books of Hours. The four miniatures of the Great Litany, painted on a bifolio at the center of a gathering, as our diagram in the Catalogue of Manuscripts shows, are thus very probably not part of the original plan of the manuscript. The rubric for the Litanies was written on the preceding folio (72v) and the normal text for them begins only on 75.

The miniatures provide the first full illustrations of the institution of the Great Litany by Pope Gregory the Great in 590. The title below the first miniature reads:

> In the time of Pope Gregory the Great the litanies were instituted. Whereas the Romans lived temperately during Lent and after that relaxed all restraints, God, provoked, sent them the bubonic plague. Wherefore Gregory instituted the litanies.

Naturally the supplication of Gregory gained a special meaning for Europeans struck by repeated attacks of this dread disease after the catastrophic Black Death of 1348. Two of the Limbourg boys, indeed, fled from a recurrence of the plague from 1399 to 1402. What they saw in Paris or in neighboring regions was described by a witness, a contemporary chronicler:

> An epidemic and a pestilence that manifested itself in pustules struck Burgundy, Champagne, Brie, the whole area around Meaux and Paris. . . . So great was the number of dead . . . that in Paris it was forbidden to publish their names. . . . Bishops, clergy and people bore holy objects from church to church followed by a crowd of bare-footed men and women, prostrating themselves before God with tears and groans and praying with contrite hearts. . . . And so the deaths continued for three years, ceasing in one place only to begin in another.[203]

One of the fullest accounts of the events in the time of Pope Gregory is given by Jacobus de Voragine in the *Golden Legend*, which as we have seen in the discussion of St. Catherine the Limbourgs and the author of the titles certainly knew. The Tiber, this text says, flooded Rome, and

> then, when the flood subsided, a swarm of serpents, a great dragon, and other monsters were borne down and left by the waters and their bodies began to rot and poisoned the air with their fetidness; and this produced a pestilence so deadly that men saw arrows falling from Heaven and killing the Romans. The first victim of the plague was Pope Pelagius; and thereafter it carried off so many people that many of the houses in Rome stood empty. . . .[204]

After Pope Pelagius was smitten Gregory was chosen to succeed him by the entire populace, and he

> exhorted the faithful to besiege God with more fervent prayer. And while the folk were gathered about him in prayer, the plague in less than an hour laid low eighty persons among the assistants: but Gregory continued to preach nonetheless, urging the people not to desist from prayer until the pestilence had vanished.

The first miniature illustrates this moment, when Gregory, wearing a tiara and a halo that came to him only later, exhorts the Romans to prayer (Fig. 451). Laymen, friars, and cardinals, seated on the ground, respond to him by lifting their eyes to heaven or contemplating a book. People continue to be struck down. In the foreground one man with a pallid face, wearing a torn, pale green tunic, falls to the ground; another lies dead, while two bystanders flee.

The mortality continues in the scene on the verso, though chanting ecclesiastics have joined in procession (Fig. 641). They move out of a gate much as the similar figures in the *Itinerary* in the *Très Belles Heures de Notre-Dame* (Fig. 404), for which this miniature may have served as a model. Gregory—now only a bishop without a halo—raises his hands in supplication. Two mysterious shrouded figures in white bend to the ground. The title reads:

> It is said that that plague was so violent that people, suddenly sneezing in the road, at table, at the games, died. Whenever one heard someone sneezing there was hardly time to aid him with 'God help you' before he expired.

The scampering man in yellow with a violet peaked hat may be an actor or jester who has come from the "games." He begins to bless the man who has already died. One seems to see from a different angle the same prostrate man in blue who appeared in the preceding miniature. He lies foreshortened, his head toward the picture plane, like prone figures in the Catherine cycle (Figs. 441, 444).

These experiments in dramatic perspective were made by Paul, to whom this entire cycle must definitely be ascribed. It shows innovations in color as fresh and sensitive as those in form. The blue and to a lesser extent the red of the titles are repeated in the miniatures; indeed, one has the impression that the painter asked the scribe for his blue pigment. The *Preaching* shows rare combinations of chocolate, lemon, blue, pale green, scarlet, pink, and violet. Violet lies also in the shadows on scarlet. In the *Procession* the exquisitely modulated white becomes as prominent as in *St. Catherine tended by angels* (Figs. 439, 641). Together with yellow shaded in brown it frames the unusual taupe on the bishop's cope.

The culminating event in this entire story, the only one that we know had been represented earlier and that remained the most popular, normally brings together St. Gregory and the Archangel Michael (Fig. 457). When the procession arrived at the huge building that was to be called, after the impending miracle, Castel Sant'Angelo, Michael appeared over it and sheathed his bloody sword. The archangel thus gave the sign that God's anger had been appeased by Gregory's prayer. This is the moment represented in a fresco by Spinello Aretino in S. Francesco, Arezzo, in another *ca.* 1410 in the Cappella degli Arliqui of the Sacristy of Siena Cathedral, in a panel from the circle of Agnolo Gaddi in the Vatican (Fig. 457), and in another by Giovanni di Paolo in the Louvre.[205] The two Sienese paintings include St. Luke's painting of the Virgin Mary, patron of their city, which according to the *Golden Legend* was carried in the procession.[206]

The title for the corresponding miniature in the *Belles Heures* describes the event, without however placing Gregory at Castel Sant'Angelo (Fig. 452).

> At last after a great carnage of people, mourning, fasts, weighty penances, while the Pope was going through Rome with the entire populace and clergy, an angel appeared on the great palace sheathing his drawn, blood-stained sword.

Paul followed the title by representing the carnage and Michael sheathing his sword above the "palacium magnum." His Northern structure, which is much less like the Castello than were contemporary Italian representations (Fig. 457), has however a more imposing scale and mass, which predicts the extraordinary buildings of the calendar in the *Très Riches Heures* (Figs. 545, 547, 548). To achieve this scale he extended the miniature, as we have observed above, into the area of the border, but he became so fascinated with the description—novel in his time—of plumes of smoke rising from the chimneys that he disregarded their great distance behind the frame and carried them across it onto the white vellum.

Below Castel Sant'Angelo Paul omitted the usual papal procession, which is mentioned too in the title, in favor of a scene of burial not explicitly described by it. Two men lower a corpse into a freshly dug grave, which is strikingly brown against the light greensward. Two powerful men hold another large corpse in an even more daring position than comparable figures in the preceding miniatures. The body, face up, is oblique to the picture plane while the head and arms fall toward us. Only the damned in certain scenes of the Last Judgment would have shown Paul figures in a similar condition. There are hints in the Bible and in the Catherine cycle that he had already been in Padua and he would then have taken note of Giotto's *Judgment* (Fig. 453). We can be certain the Limbourgs visited this city before painting the *Très Riches Heures*.

It is in a novel scene of this kind and not in the traditional Christian subjects that Paul felt free to experiment most with perspective, foreshortening, and bodily posture. The boldness of this picture of death and burial cannot be matched elsewhere in the *Belles Heures*. His design for the illustration of the Office of the Dead, showing anonymous corpses, comes closest, but it is much more original in iconography than in form (Fig. 454). It is, indeed, much more original than I had believed before discovering the early date of the *Belles Heures*, for we now recognize that in this miniature Paul was the first painter to abandon the convention of illustrating the Office by a service around a bier. His scene in a cemetery, which inspired the *Boucicaut Master* and other Parisian illuminators to introduce similar representations, initiated a new tradition.

Paul probably did not himself contribute to the scene of St. Anthony burying St. Paul with the aid of two lions, who do for the venerable hermit what they never do in nature—dig holes (Fig.

466). The *Lamentation*, the strongest scene in the Passion cycle and the only one clearly executed as well as designed by him, is magnificent in several respects but more traditional in conception (Fig. 455). Even into this compact, comparatively two-dimensional composition, however, Paul introduced the averted, foreshortened Magdalene, developing a form he had no doubt seen in the *Entombment* by Jacquemart de Hesdin in the Book of Hours which, we have argued, the Limbourgs first saw when it was received by their patron, Philippe le Hardi (Fig. 456).

The death of Christ, of course, evokes far stronger emotion than the nameless victims of the bubonic plague (Figs. 452, 455). There the living go about their ghastly business calmly if grimly, and only the man in blue seems to contemplate sadly the loss of his fellows. Paul has not a trace of the morbidity (sometimes confused with "realism") that led some artists of the time to conceive of every event as an immediate precursor of total doom. On the contrary, he transforms the impact of death by the purity of his colors, the smoothness of his textures, and his unshakeable sense of order.

The title of the fourth and final miniature in the cycle is, unlike the others, not drawn from the *Golden Legend* (Fig. 463).

> And this custom is observed until the present day. Men go nude in some places, beating themselves and tormenting the flesh in fasting and prayer and lamentation, invoking the protection of all the saints in procession.

Though self-flagellation had long been practiced periodically by large groups of Christians this form of penance attracted enormous numbers of frightened and guilt-ridden people after the Black Death of 1348. Subsequent outbreaks of the plague in 1363, 1374, and 1400 were followed by similar waves of penitents.[207] Many cities attempted, however, to repulse them, and in France the pope and the king rather successfully blocked their entry.[208] Permanent societies of *battuti* flourished during this period in Italy, and we are familiar with their appearance from the numerous paintings they commissioned (Fig. 464). Similarly garbed flagellants, all in white with openings in their smocks only for their eyes and their shoulders, march ahead of St. Gregory in an illustration of the end of the plague in a Lombard Missal and Book of Hours of about 1380 (Fig. 462).[209]

Flagellants were much less frequently represented in Northern art of the fourteenth century. A South Netherlandish miniature in a chronicle written by an abbot of Tournai, Gilles le Muisit, shows a procession of them in 1349 (Fig. 465). Like most of the figures in the *Belles Heures*, they are, except for a collar, bare to the waist.[210] They wear, too, dark hats, though of a different shape than Paul's. The beautiful brown hats in the *Belles Heures* may be felt, the material that Froissart said the flagellants employed for their hats in 1349.[211] Three of Paul's flagellants wear the dress (except for their bare arms) of the Italian *battuti* (Fig. 464). The fire-breathing dragon, extremely vicious yet impaled on a pole, is probably an animated version of a curious object described by the *Golden Legend*. It is mentioned in the chapter on the Minor Litany, or Rogations:

> In certain churches, and especially in the churches of Gaul, there is the custom of carrying a dragon with a long tail stuffed with straw; the first two days it is so borne before the cross, but on the third day, it is carried behind the cross with the straw removed from the tail. By this is signified that in the first day, before the Law, and in the second day, under the Law, the Devil ruled in this world, but in the third day, namely the day of grace, he was driven from his kingdom by the Passion of Christ.[212]

In the miniature in the *Belles Heures* two men drop out of the procession and fall to the ground, apparently for a more vigorous whipping. The painter masterfully combines their fixed postures with the movement of the group by extending their arms to create a forward flow. The color of the miniature is as beautiful as it is exceptional, all white and flesh, except for the pale yellow-green grass and the brown of the hats and the hair—a simple yet subtle pattern that anticipates, if one dares say it, Piero della Francesca. There are, in addition, touches of bright blood on the backs of the flagellants. The red serves to maintain the relationship with the title below, though on this folio it is the white of the vellum, the blue of the script and the gold of the ivy that reappear most prominently in the miniature and its background.

The Great Litany is the most beautiful cycle in the manuscript, designed and painted by Paul at an especially fertile moment. His exploration of color resulted in new hues and combinations of hues that are not quite matched elsewhere in the *Belles Heures*, nor indeed in the *Très Riches Heures*. This venture was probably inspired by the light, soft color of Jean de Beaumetz, notable especially in his panel in the Louvre. Paul's range, however, is far greater, and the subtlety of his pattern anticipates the great Italians of the second quarter of the fifteenth century. In this respect as well as with regard to the varied and daring figural postures these miniatures seem more advanced than all but one of those Paul painted in the preceding Hours of the Virgin. Since the scenes of the Great Litany are all contained within one bifolio at the center of a gathering they are not an integral part of the manuscript and very probably were inserted at a late moment in the campaign of illustration. To the problem of the make-up of the manuscript we shall return below.

In the *Très Riches Heures* the Limbourgs devoted only one scene to the Great Litany, but they planned an extraordinary one (Figs. 575, 576). Planned must be said because they executed the miniature, which extends across two facing pages, only in part. They drew the entire composition, including the figures, and partially painted it. The only visible surface that seems theirs, however, is the upper part of Castel Sant'Angelo. Jean Colombe seems to us to have worked over all the rest, painting a lighter film over the architecture and a heavier one over the figures.[213] The faces are all his; the Limbourgs as usual left them for the last, and then, as in the fourth gathering of the *Bible moralisée* (Fig. 332), failed to paint them. As Durrieu observed[214] they nearly completed the bodies of a group of figures from the pope to the man in blue just outside the gate.

Probably influenced by the Italian convention the Limbourgs with their advisers decided to show Pope Gregory below the Archangel, who appears as usual on Castel Sant'Angelo. A desire for actuality of scale, which had led the Limbourgs to invade the upper margin in the *Belles Heures*, induced them here to begin in the lower margin and extend the castle, gate, and towers of Rome up alongside the text, which on this folio was limited to one column. The preceding part of the procession occupies the margins of the facing page. These are the only instances in the *Très Riches Heures* of the use of the lower margin by the Limbourgs, and the effect on both folios is of a continuation of the city behind the script. An illusion of this kind was attempted occasionally in Trecento illumination, especially Lombard,[215] and in the second decade of the fifteenth century the Boucicaut Master occasionally exploited it in his Books of Hours (Fig. 506). Paul himself had approximated the effect on a folio he painted in the *Très Belles Heures de Notre-Dame* (Fig. 500). French illuminators, however, were usually loathe to disturb the unity of the folio and the sense of its thinness by spatial extensions of this kind, and the design became most popular in North Italian illumination of the second half of the century.[216]

In the Florentine predella Gregory and his companions have dropped to their knees between the Castello and the church of St. Peter's (Fig. 457). In the *Très Riches Heures* the procession emerges from one gate—traditionally the Porta Flaminia—and moves outside the walls to another, the Porta near the Vatican—both shown on the plan of Rome in this manuscript (Fig. 721). It is proper to name these gates because by this time the Limbourgs had become far more concerned with what we might call local color in all its ramifications. While their city is no portrait of Rome, a possible Italian *campanile* rises near a purely French Gothic tower, and Castel Sant'Angelo has acquired its rectangular base and round drum. The variety of persons in the procession is much greater than in the *Belles Heures*, and now ecclesiastics rather than laymen fall stricken to the ground. The view of Rome is more fanciful than Ambrogio Lorenzetti's *Siena* painted nearly a century earlier, but it has Ambrogio's depth, scale, and monumentality.

The Limbourgs avoided a stale repetition of the design of folio 71v on 72, preferring instead a lively, unexpected differentiation and balance. The space is nevertheless clearly continuous, and the two miniatures were designed together also with regard to the source of the light and a partially centralized point of sight. We are not therefore surprised to discover that the two folios compose one folded sheet of parchment, on which the illuminators could work by laying it flat on their table. Then it was inserted at the center of a gathering by pasting to a stub.

The procession of St. Gregory was represented once again as an illustration of the Litanies in a Book of Hours. Following to a degree the example of the *Très Riches Heures* the artist drew the scenes in the margins, adding them *ca.* 1420 to a manuscript that had been illuminated in 1407 (Figs. 458–461).[217] The painter, who distributed the scenes over four folios between 105 and 110, is that curious imitator of the Limbourgs, the Master of St. Jerome, to whom we have already referred (Fig. 357).[218] In the first drawing he adopted the central theme of the *Très Riches Heures*, which shows Sts. Gregory and Michael together, but many of the figures on the ground as well as the entire group at the right are copied from the *Belles Heures* (Figs. 452, 458). The *Belles Heures* was then in the possession of Yolande, Duchess of Anjou, but the Master of St. Jerome, who drew constantly from the Limbourgs, may have had drawings or copies of some of the miniatures, and for this reason he may have been, as I have suggested, their younger brother Arnold, who inherited part at least of their artistic property and who in 1417 began his career, as they had theirs, by serving as an apprentice to a goldsmith.[219]

The second drawing shows a procession, part lay but mostly of friars, proceeding from a church and, as in the *Très Riches Heures*, bearing a large reliquary (Fig. 459). In the third drawing, which is on a facing folio, the same procession continues into a second church (Fig. 460). The figure on the banner seems to be St. Francis receiving the Stigmata, so that most of the friars must be Franciscan. The architecture in all these drawings is French Gothic and therefore resembles the *Très Riches Heures* much more than the *Belles Heures*. The final drawing, however, returns to the procession of flagellants represented in the *Belles Heures* but not in the *Très Riches Heures* (Fig. 461). The bodies of the flagellants, like some in the *Belles Heures*, are all covered, including their arms. The Master of St. Jerome has added, however, a curious lappet that hangs down from the mask and looks like a proboscis. The *Belles Heures* provided the design of the flagellant with lowered lash, but we do not know a model for the rest of the procession nor indeed for the pseudo-palm trees.

Diocrès and the Carthusian Order

The third exceptional cycle of miniatures in the *Belles Heures* tells the story of a theologian of the eleventh century, Raymond Diocrès, and of the foundation of the Carthusian order by his pupil St. Bruno (Figs. 423, 470).[220] No earlier representations of Diocrès are known and of St. Bruno we have only four single scenes,[221] although there are unverifiable reports of stories from his life painted in the fourteenth century in the Chartreuse in Paris.[222] Among the Valois princes it was Philippe le Hardi, builder of Champmol, who was most deeply attached to the Carthusian Order. Probably this was one of the many interests that Jean de Berry shared with his brother.[223] In any event the Duke of Berry, along with many of his contemporaries, bourgeois as well as noble, would have respected the strict monastic, nearly eremitic life of the members of this Order,[224] and we know that he patronized, so to speak, a holy man who was known as "hermite de monseigneur le duc de Berry."[225]

In a miniature probably designed but not executed by Paul we have already seen Diocrès teaching, according to the text, near the end of his life (Fig. 423). The next miniature, on folio 94v, represents the repetition of an astonishing event that occurred shortly afterward, when Diocrès died (Fig. 467). It is not mentioned by the title below it, which describes an initial episode that is not represented, but curiously by the title on the facing miniature (Fig. 468):

> The following day, while the obsequies were being celebrated, the defunct again cried out: I have been justly accused in the judgment of God. Then [the witnesses], greatly astonished, deliberated whether the judgment pronounced could be for good or for evil and reserved it to the next day. (fol. 95)

For this amazing occurrence the painter chose a diagonal design and a fast recession in the church, with its deep blue vaults over a floor of violet and olive-green tiles. The beholder, though nearby, is held at a distance from the event by an entrance arch. The rich cloth, black over tan, slips off the coffin as Diocrès pushes open the lid and opens his mouth to cry out, the words moving into space like the uninscribed scroll that emerges from his hand. The decisiveness and unity of the composition as well as the varied agitation of the friars imply a design by Paul.

This composition, which belongs to a cycle in the *Belles Heures* that immediately precedes the Office of the Dead, was adopted by the Seilern Master for the illustration of that Office (Fig. 469).[226] The subject recurs within the same Office in the *Très Riches Heures* (Fig. 578). The borders on this folio were painted by the workshop of the Master of the Breviary of Jean sans Peur, of whose role in the *Très Riches Heures* we shall speak later. The main miniature was laid out, as has been observed, by the Limbourgs, but no one seems to have noticed the dependence of the architecture upon the buildings of *St. Jerome in Prayer* in the *Belles Heures* (Fig. 474). This is a puzzling repetition, because the architecture has been adapted, not very happily, to a different scene, and the original design is itself not very impressive.

As his coffin was being lowered into the grave Diocrès made his final and most severe assertion (Fig. 468).[227]

> On the morrow, all being assembled for the burial of the deceased, again the corpse cried out: Justly I am judged by God and I am damned. Whereupon everyone was terrified that a man of such accomplishments could be lost. A certain [man] among them, Bruno, addressed his students. (fol. 95v)

The friars continue to chant, the ceremonial mourners in a beautiful dark gray are imperturbable, and at the right Bruno, in pink, blesses the corpse. Paul, who probably painted the miniature, showed his usual concern with materials and techniques, in this instance the wood coffin, the ropes and the postures of the men working them, the tools used to dig the grave and the exhumed bones of a predecessor in this cemetery. Whereas a Baroque painter, such as Eustache Le Sueur, portrayed an unnatural event of this kind in darkness relieved by radiances and beams,[228] Paul gave it concreteness by showing everything in the bright light of day. The black mourners, serving as a foil for the colors, appear before the light greensward of the cemetery, over which the varicolored tombslabs are scattered like fresh spring flowers.

In the next miniature Bruno and his companions leave Paris (Fig. 470). Jean probably executed this miniature, and presumably through carelessness Bruno's features differ from those in Paul's *Burial of Diocrès* and *Entry into the Chartreuse* (Figs. 468, 416).[229] Shaken by the condemnation of Diocrès Bruno says "What hope is there for us, miserable as we are? Let us flee and live in a solitary place." Standing at the gate of the city, Bruno points the way, and the magical power of his words has evoked in the distance clear symbols of the future. A hermit in a cave foretells the life of solitude, the large portal the institution of a monastic order. Indeed, through that very portal (after events represented in two comparatively uninteresting miniatures) the companions enter the monastic church (Fig. 416). One monk, already dressed like the others in a Carthusian habit, is inside. Bruno follows, bending forward and clasping his hands to express both eagerness and reverence. Behind him a companion slips on his tunic.

Paul—for it was surely he who painted this magnificent miniature—has contrived to combine exceptionally large, heavy, monumental figures with a superb rhythmical movement into the building. To accomplish this he has been willing to sacrifice a little more of the structure and plastic independence of his figures than would have seemed desirable to major Italian painters, for they insisted on an individual axis in each of them. Paul had, however, perfect models in sculptures by Sluter that he certainly knew; Bruno is remarkably similar to St. Catherine in the portal of Champmol (Fig. 379).

No painter of the period could have equaled the splendor of Paul's modulation of white, although it is true that such delicate luminosity would have been largely lost over the centuries in panel and mural paintings, which are exposed to surface abrasion and to light. Paul's decision to represent one man just pulling on his white tunic and behind him a companion still without it tells us much about his logical way of composing a scene. This companion, already tonsured, is addressed by a member of the Order. He must, therefore, be a novice. Paul has given him a color probably not worn by Carthusian novices at that time but which repeats the beautiful blue of the script.[230]

The last miniature in the cycle, on folio 97v, shows the monastery that Bruno and his companions founded (Fig. 472). Though the inability of the painter to coordinate this perspective and his insistence upon an enormous church shatter the unity of the miniature, the vista is in several respects very interesting.

> This house, called in truth the Charterhouse, is situated among the serried mountains of Burgundy; according to Jerome: the city is a prison, the desert paradise. In the cell is peace; strife and war threaten without.

The site for the Grande Chartreuse, which had been revealed to the Bishop of Grenoble in a vision, is not far from that city;[231] and it is not very far either from Vienne, where the most important relics of St. Anthony, one of Bruno's models, were held. A disastrous fire of 1371 swept away the buildings, and the king as well as the princes of the blood and the 550 Carthusian houses contributed to the reconstruction of this central monastery of the Order.[232] Though the mountainous terrain in the miniature suggests Grenoble, and the chapel on the hill probably is the one built above the monastery by Bruno, the main buildings may depict not so much the Grande Chartreuse as a typical Carthusian house with its cell for each monk. Brown eagles high on the peaks reinforce the wildness and solitude of the place. A large white bird rests on the steeple. The only visible men, lay brothers or *Donates*, are on or near the water. Three of them fish. This is not an idle occupation, because total abstinence from meat is a distinctive mark of the Order; but the Rule permits fish, even to the degree that it may be bought, if necessary, for a monk who is ill.[233]

The prominence of the monastic and eremitic life in the *Belles Heures* is unique in the personal books of Jean de Berry. Nothing that we know about him—and we know a good deal—leads us to suspect that he himself felt a strong inclination to adopt such a life. On the other hand he could not have been entirely immune, particularly at his advanced age (about 65 when the *Belles Heures* was planned), to the ever-growing and often-voiced desire for a more tranquil life. This desire was intensified by the growth of large cities, especially Paris, and by the wars and plagues that became disastrous in the second half of the fourteenth century. Humanists sought at least the solitude of the hermits, and, like Petrarch, wavered between the intellectual excitement of the court or the city and the retreat, such as Vaucluse, which he acclaimed as "transalpina solitudo mea iocundissima." Images of the simple, contemplative life were spread on the walls of Trecento buildings, in the Camposanto in Pisa and in the Castellani Chapel of S. Croce in Florence. Comparable representations in France, mostly smaller in scale, have all been lost.[234]

St. Jerome

To sanction the foundation of the *Grande Chartreuse* the title, as we have observed, quotes words of St. Jerome: "The city is a prison, the desert paradise" (Fig. 472). This conception the great man did not, however, maintain without qualification, and indeed some titles that accompany twelve unprecedented miniatures devoted to his life refer rather to his frightful suffering in the wilderness (Figs. 417, 474).[235] The paintings themselves, however, show nothing of the blackened skin and painful, twisted limbs stressed in the titles. He is, to be sure, whipped in the second miniature (Fig. 427), and although the seventh does show the kind of temptation to which the devil subjected him, the holy hermit is separated from the languid girls by a wall and he has the protection of an ecclesiastical building (Fig. 417). Surely Jean de Limbourg, who seems to have painted almost the entire cycle, came nowhere near Jerome's own depiction of his travail:

> Daily I wept, daily I groaned, and when, overcome by the sleep I resisted, my bones, scarce holding together, were bruised by the ground. Although my only companions were scorpions I often imagined I was surrounded by dancing girls, who kindled the fires of lust. (fol. 186)

Whereas the miniature accompanying this title does represent a temptation (Fig. 417), the preceding painting, on folio 185v, shows nothing whatever of the desert that is the sole subject of its title (Fig. 474).

> How often as I dwelt in that waste, in that vast solitude burnt by the heat of the sun, which provides a terrible abode for monks, I imagined myself among the delights of Rome. My twisted limbs shuddered in a garment of sack cloth. (fol. 185v)

What the illuminator represented instead, probably at the suggestion of an adviser, is neither clear nor very impressive. Jerome, praying within a church, seems absorbed by a vision of the Lord's sepulchre.[236] The tabernacle and to some degree the entire building resemble a structure in a fresco by a follower of Altichiero in the Santo, Padua (Fig. 475)—in other words the same style and the same place with which the Limbourgs otherwise prove their familiarity.

Instead of Jerome's tremendous trials the cycle stresses his scholarship, as we have seen (Figs. 426, 428), and his ecclesiastical career. In one miniature the pope ordains him priest and cardinal and in another he bids farewell to Gregory of Nazianzus as he leaves Constantinople—the latter giving Jean an opportunity for a remarkably deep marine view (Fig. 473). Jerome's monastic triumphs are exemplified by two miniatures from the famous and irresistible story of the lion[237] as well as the grief of the monks at his death and his obsequies (Fig. 476). These choices of subject disclose the values of Jean de Limbourg and of his adviser, but we should not infer too much from them because the story of Anthony and Paul, which follows immediately, has a rather different, sterner, character.

Before turning to St. Anthony, however, we wish to consider briefly the last miniature in the cycle of St. Jerome, which is in some respects the most interesting (Fig. 891). It does not illustrate the title, which describes the lowering of the body, clad only in a tunic, into the grave; and the *Golden Legend* says nothing whatever about the obsequies. Jean has combined around the corpse of the saint four diverse events. In the distance three hermits emerge from caves to express their reverence, and at the right chanting ecclesiastics dressed in white and buff move forth in procession from a pink church. Jerome's fellow monks, all in brown, have assembled behind the bier. Below, the deaf, blind and lame have come to be healed by touching the corpse, as they were said to do in Domenico Cavalca's popular *Lives of the Fathers*, of which Jean de Berry apparently owned French translations.[238] The struggles of these poor creatures in the foreground constitute the most impressive part of the miniature. The looseness of the composition seems to echo the threshing of the crippled. The yellows, browns, green-browns, whites, black and pink are not unified as they often were in Jean's painting at this time. The palette reflects Paul's in the Catherine cycle and the Litany. In the miniatures that follow those of St. Jerome Jean utilized solid, dense and quite different colors.

Paul and Anthony

St. Jerome wrote the lives of the hermits Paul and Anthony, who are the subjects of the next cycle. In a miniature the Limbourgs added to the *Très Belles Heures de Notre-Dame* Jerome appears in the initial above the representations of the two hermits (Fig. 500). Unlike most other cycles in the *Belles Heures* the miniatures of Paul and Anthony tell stories that were popular throughout the Middle Ages. The two saints were the outstanding representatives of the eremitic life, and Anthony was especially venerated because of the conviction that he could cure a disease of the skin, erysipelas, that was endemic in Europe until the nineteenth century. The Hospital Brothers of St. Anthony, in their black habit with a blue tau, were a familiar and welcome sight from the twelfth century on as they cared everywhere for the sick. Thousands of people, including kings and princes, tormented by or fearful of the infection that was universally called St. Anthony's Fire, visited his principal shrine at St. Antoine-le-viennois, founded when the crusaders in the late eleventh century brought relics to this small town in the Dauphiné, near the *Grande Chartreuse*.[239] In this church his life was depicted in several media, including the existing mural cycle dated in the early fifteenth century but entirely repainted.[240] Copies of these lost works, however, seem unrelated to the miniatures in the *Belles Heures*.

The eight scenes of Paul and Anthony, like the miniatures of Jerome that precede them, received little attention from the greatest of the Limbourg brothers. The first miniature, by Jean, is devoted to an episode that is described in the life of St. Paul in the *Golden Legend* and summarized in the title, but rarely illustrated (Fig. 409).

> Saint Paul, the first hermit, during the persecution of Decius, fled from Rome after seeing a Christian (who was bound in a place of delights and caressed by a lewd woman) bite off his tongue and spit it in her face, so that the pain put to flight the temptation. (fol. 191)

In the garden the young Christian, his one arm clearly fixed behind his back, spits a bloody fragment of his tongue at his temptress. Beyond, near a fine violet fountain, the terrified St. Paul slips away.

Fleeing from Rome Paul settled in the desert near the Red Sea, where we find him in the next miniature reading beside his cell (Fig. 478). A dweller in the region, Anthony, learns in a vision of Paul's arrival, and sets out to find him. Jean de Limbourg, little concerned with the concept of a wilderness, cannot refrain from putting boats on the water—a very red sea, as it was again a few years later in the Duke of Berry's *Antiquités judaïques* (Fig. 170). And Anthony, far from being an emaciated hermit, is so robust that the dragon attempting to bar the way is very decidedly the underdog. Probably Jean decided to introduce at this point, inappropriately, a copy of some massive figure by Paul. The miniature does, however, successfully suggest the scale of the desert, which is seen from a very high point of sight and stretches to—and presumably beyond—the upper frame, so that, unusually enough, the sky is not visible. The haloes, consisting only of golden rays, belong to that new type that had been introduced earlier in the manuscript (Fig. 638). This manner of suggesting a more vibrant light around the head began to be employed in late fourteenth-century painting in France, in panels (Figs. 368, 380) as well as in books. Paul had surrounded the Christ Child in the *Nativity* in the Bible with rays (Fig. 327), and in that manuscript he had distinguished Christ's halo by combining rays with a disk (Figs. 303, 322).[241] In the more luminous mode of the *Très Riches Heures* rays play a larger role, and haloes consisting of combinations or of rays alone, as the Virgin's in the *Deposition*, become common (Fig. 588).

Anthony, searching through the forests, as the title of the next miniature says, meets a centaur, who tells him how to go to Paul (Fig. 479). This episode, though not apparently significant in the lives of the two holy men, captured the medieval imagination, probably because of fascination with the centaur or *hippocentaurus*, as he was called, and with the helpfulness of this wild mythical pagan creature to a Christian saint. In the miniature in the *Belles Heures* the figure is not, as in some earlier paintings, a man with antlers (Fig. 481)[242] but a true, if not entirely functional, composite creature of the antique type. The Italian representations of the encounter in the decade or two preceding the *Belles Heures* show only the saint and the centaur in a constricted, rocky setting (Fig. 481). The illumination in the *Belles Heures*—weaker than the preceding miniature—opens a wide landscape, populated by lions, a giant lizard, even a giraffe, and of course St. Paul.

In the next to the last miniature in the cycle two of these species of animals, the lion and the crocodile, joined by the devil wielding a club, attack St. Anthony in his tomb (Fig. 477).[243] The lizards, olive-green modeled in yellow or rose, resemble somewhat the products of a goldsmith, but their sinuous approach is terrifying, and in the legend the saint was almost killed. In Jean's miniature he extends his arms as if in prayer, and the graceful loops of his rich, deep gray-black mantle are only slightly disturbed. Indeed the legend tells that he was soon healed. The beautiful little pool of water nearby is entirely still.

The eight miniatures of Paul and Anthony are painted on a gathering of four leaves. They are independent of the rest of the manuscript and they probably were inserted during a later phase of the work, as we shall point out below. The style of these scenes, however, is in most respects not very advanced. Jean's color at the end of the cycle of St. Jerome and on the immediately following folios (195–202) is much more luminous.

Heraclius and the Cross

One of the special cycles in the *Belles Heures* discloses sympathies of the Duke of Berry that are more immediately intelligible to us than those connected with stories of hermits. In 1401–03 the Duke purchased medals of Augustus and of three other emperors, Tiberius, Constantine, and Heraclius.[244] These rulers, connected respectively with the birth of Christ, his death, the establishment of the Church, and the recovery of the cross, all surely appeared in the Duke's series of portraits of historic figures—emperors, popes, and kings of France—in his castle at Bicêtre.[245]

Of all these works only copies of two of the medals have survived (Figs. 267, 268, 482, 483). Famous from their first appearance, they gave a strong impulse to the beginning in Renaissance Italy of a medallic art, and in the sixteenth century there they were still believed to be antique. A recent observation about the inscriptions strengthens the attribution of the medals to a Parisian goldsmith and to the years 1400–1402, when the Byzantine Emperor Manuel II was in that city seeking Western aid to protect the remnant of his empire from the Turks.[246] If the medals were indeed cast in the French capital some Parisians, among them Jean de Berry as well as Herman and Jean de Limbourg, who were then apprenticed to a goldsmith, probably knew that they were newly made but in the ancient manner: "d'ancienne façon," as the Duke's inventory sometimes states.

It is well known that the medals of Constantine and Heraclius made a deep impression on the Limbourgs. To the instances of their influence upon the illuminators we would like to add the young woman on the reverse of the medal of Constantine (Fig. 268). Paul probably had in mind this figure, the most sensuous female nude since antiquity, when he designed St. Catherine in prison, whom he endowed with similar qualities (Fig. 439). The relationships of the miniatures of the Limbourgs with the only two medals that happen to survive suggest how many of their sources have disappeared with the loss of practically all the *orfèvrerie* of the time. On the other hand, the illuminators clearly felt such a deep sympathy for the medals that we wonder whether they could have been produced by the goldsmith, Albert de Bolure, with whom Jean and Herman worked.[247]

In the *Belles Heures* the suffrage of the cross is expanded in an exceptional way. The usual prayer, to begin with, is accompanied by an illustration that is remarkable only for the great size of the golden cross and the cultural differentiation of the worshippers (Fig. 485). Fascinated as usual by such differences, Paul, who probably designed but did not paint this miniature, gave each of the four men strikingly diverse headgear, and they wear long hair and beards, quite contrary to prevailing French or indeed Italian fashion. Around the cross a dozen lamps burn, symbolizing perhaps the twelve apostles. Lamps of almost identical design appear on the reverse of the medal of Heraclius (Fig. 267). There they seem, curiously enough, less relevant, because the composition shows Heraclius bearing the cross as he rides in his imperial wagon. Perhaps they continue the idea of divine illumination expressed on the obverse by the rays moving toward Heraclius and by the inscription: ILLUMINA VULTUM TUUM DEUS (Fig. 483). The Greek inscription on the background below the three lamps refers to the emperor's rescue of the cross and to Christ's breaking open the gates of Hell.[248] Whether Heraclius is shown to be equally capable of opening the gate of Jerusalem is a question we shall consider very shortly.

A similar representation appears in the first of the two scenes in the *Belles Heures* that precede the *Exaltation of the Cross* and that, like the other special cycles, have titles in red and blue (Fig. 487). Much of the composition, apparently painted by Jean with the help of Herman, is nearly identical with the medal, but now Heraclius is on the road just outside Jerusalem. The gates swing closed, one horse rears, and the driver turns for help to the emperor, who lifts his face to heaven. This event is described very briefly in the titles below the two miniatures:

> In about A.D. 600 Chosroes, King of the Persians, set fire to the holy places and carried off the wood of the Holy Cross into Persia. The Emperor Heraclius proceeded against him and, having defeated Chosroes, he led the Christians with the Holy Cross back to Jerusalem. (fol. 156)
>
> When, arrayed in regal attire, he wanted to enter the city-gate through which Christ went out bearing his Cross the gate miraculously closed; on the other hand it opened to him when he humbled himself. Hence the solemnity of the Exaltation of the Cross was established. (fol. 156v)

These titles, like so many in the *Belles Heures*, are taken from the *Golden Legend*, but there is one small though significant difference. The title says that Heraclius is "arrayed in regal attire," but the *Golden Legend* adds "riding upon his royal charger." The passage reads:

> When he descended the Mount of Olives, riding upon his royal charger and arrayed in imperial splendour, and was about to enter by the gate through which Christ had gone to His Passion, suddenly the stones of the gate fell down and formed an unbroken wall against him. Then, to the astonishment of all, an

angel of the Lord appeared over the gate, holding a cross in his hands, and said: 'When the King of Heaven, coming up to His Passion, entered in by this gate, He came not in royal state, but riding upon a lowly ass.'

The medal and the miniature are the only early representations that depart from the *Golden Legend* and show the Emperor driving his covered wagon, which resembles strikingly late Roman vehicles (Fig. 269).[249] In all the Italian representations of the story of the cross, however, including Agnolo Gaddi's prominent frescoes in the choir of Sta. Croce in Florence—painted about 1390 and therefore one of the earliest (Fig. 491)—Heraclius is mounted on a horse, looking up at the angel.[250] His upward glance in the miniature despite the absence of the angel arouses our suspicion that the Limbourgs knew such paintings or, more likely, the *Golden Legend* itself. This suspicion is proved by the second miniature, which illustrates the passage that immediately follows.

Then the king burst into tears, took off his shoes, and stripped himself to his shirt, took up the Cross of the Lord and humbly carried it to the gate. Instantly the hardness of the stones felt the power of God go through them, and the gate lifted itself aloft, and left free passage to those who sought to enter.

Whereas the first miniature, like the *Golden Legend*, contrasts the entry in "royal state" with the one upon a "lowly ass" the second miniature, following the same text as well as the title, stresses the likeness with Christ bearing the cross as he went to his Passion (Fig. 488). A contemporary Sienese painter, probably Benedetto di Bindo, did the same thing in 1412–1413, taking a cue from the words on the scroll of the angel in the preceding panel: CHRISTUS HIC A PASSIONE EGRESSUS EST (Figs. 489, 490).[251] The emperor in the *Belles Heures* still wears his crown, as in Agnolo's fresco (Fig. 491), but he is bowed down by the weight of a greatly enlarged cross. Though the illuminator, here Herman probably employing for Heraclius a figure by Paul, has fallen back in the second miniature on the Limbourg convention of water and a bridge outside a gate, the two compositions tell the story clearly.

Can we say as much of the medal (Fig. 267)? Does the leading horse turn around only to conform with the circular edge of the medal? Probably not, because the driver, as in the first miniature, turns around also, appealing to the emperor for counsel. These actions are clearly explained in the miniature by the closed gate. Even though the Greek inscription on the medal, however, refers to the opening of the gates of Limbo by Christ, they are not shown. "Glory to Christ the Deity who has shattered the gates of Hell and recovered the Holy Cross in the reign of Heraclius."[252] The medal represents the triumphal return of the cross to Jerusalem, but not clearly the rebuke to the proud Emperor which is prominent in the miniature in the *Belles Heures*. Thus the later representation expands the content of the earlier one. Is its relation to the medal one of dependence, as has always been assumed? We are loathe thus to ask still one more question about this very problematic object, but perhaps here once again a newly perceived difficulty will later prove to be the way out of a dilemma.

Though Jean de Berry possessed medals and portraits in several media of Heraclius, Constantine, and other emperors it was Augustus for whom he felt a special sympathy. Apart from his medal of this Emperor he sponsored with special interest representations of the Emperor's vision of the birth of Christ in the Aracoeli. The event was first introduced into a Book of Hours in an initial before 1402 in the Duke's *Brussels Hours* (Fig. 399), and it was chosen for the first time to illustrate the usual prayer to the Virgin, *O Intemerata*, in the *Belles Heures* (Fig. 397). We shall return to this subject shortly.

Hours of the Passion

In our discussion of the *Belles Heures* we have concentrated on six cycles of miniatures that were entirely unprecedented in a Book of Hours, and we have considered only a few of the miniatures in the normal series, particularly in the Hours of the Virgin. The remaining miniatures in this cycle, normally the principal one, will be discussed later, some in connection with the *Très Riches Heures*. The cycle of the Hours of the Passion, usually of equal importance, is in fact much longer in the *Belles Heures*, containing no less than seventeen miniatures. Thirteen of these are in that very distinctive style, rather uncommon in the rest of the manuscript, that we connected above with Herman. It appears in these miniatures in its clearest, most individual form (Figs. 341, 364, 371, 418, 497, 498). Indeed, even a couple of the miniatures in this cycle not painted by him veer toward his color. Elsewhere in the manuscript, on the contrary, Herman's color and sometimes his form reflect the taste of his brothers.

It seems clear, then, that when painting the Passion cycle Herman felt an exceptional independence and authoritativeness. He gave full rein to his love of vermilion, pink, deep blue, and a kind of gold tone made by yellow light over a red-brown ground. His flesh is much warmer than that of his brothers. What he lacked in subtlety he tried to achieve by variety, giving us a coat of many colors. His fantastic hats open and curl like exotic flowers. His men are provided with jutting, rather aggressive beards. Their mouths, curving down, scowl with unrestrained zeal. Even Paul was unsuccessful with lost profiles (Fig. 415), but Herman had trouble with all views and postures—he clearly lacked experience in putting figures together. He tended to compose in one plane; he filled it completely, or even overcharged it, either with soft figures or with prominent ornament that competes equally for our attention. In all his compositions he created a swaying movement across the surface into which the figures, with little structure, are absorbed.

Herman's miniatures contain one important pictorial innovation. The miniature of the Death of Christ is painted entirely in tones of greenish-gray except for touches here and there of rust red or of light gray (Fig. 497). Into the gloom streaks an orange and yellow bolt of lightning. The illuminator has transformed the technique of grisaille to produce a nocturne.[253] His tonal painting has far less local color than the earlier night scenes by Taddeo Gaddi in S. Croce, Florence, either the fresco of the Annunciation to the Shepherds or the panel of the Vision of the Fiery Chariot now in the Accademia (Fig. 480), which one at least of the Limbourgs no doubt saw. In a miniature in the Bible Paul painted a kind of fog that to a degree anticipates this *Crucifixion* in the *Belles Heures* (Fig. 279). He may have been responsible for the conception of the latter, but Herman did the painting.

The first miniature in the Passion cycle, the *Agony in the Garden*, is different in style and exceptionally beautiful even in this splendid manuscript (Fig. 496). The slumbering apostles have slumped into highly informal positions but the hill with which they are so closely associated restores to them a certain majesty and importance. Though they sleep deeply their drapery glides actively across their bodies, and this movement is echoed by the flamboyant hill and the ripples of the encircling green and gold river. John, in a pale yellow mantle with brown shadows, huddles up against Peter in a complex and impressive movement. Alongside Peter lies his sword—a curved one—which he will employ in the following scene. Clothed in violet Christ returns from his prayer. Though looking at Peter he gently touches James.[254] In the distance when Christ, again in his pale purple tunic, prays, a cross extends from God to him, as in the *Bible moralisée* (Fig. 319). The miniature is extremely polished and sophisticated, and while as usual some of the ideas and postures came from Paul, it would seem to represent Jean at his best.

The same painter was probably responsible for the elegant and touching *Deposition*, though the more saturated color must reflect the preceding miniatures by Herman (Fig. 493). The scene is more intimate and less grand than the one in the *Brussels Hours* (Fig. 495), partly because, as usual in the *Belles Heures*, the foreground figures are almost two-thirds as high as the pictorial field. Nothing reveals the new interests of the Limbourgs in the *Très Riches Heures* better than the altered format of the miniature and the abandonment of the low rectangle of the *Belles Heures* for a much higher one (Fig. 588).

In one conspicuous way Jean's miniature is a naturalistic criticism of Jacquemart's *Deposition* and of famous earlier examples, such as Simone Martini's, which the French painters knew (Fig. 494). The man bearing most of Christ's weight sustains it by holding fast with his other arm to the cross, showing once again the concern of the Limbourgs with the way in which things are actually done. This is only one of the forms in the *Belles Heures* that, despite all differences, reappear in the miniature in the *Très Riches Heures* (Fig. 588).

A very similar scene appears on a preceding folio (80) of the *Belles Heures*, as an exceptional illustration of the Hours of the Cross (Fig. 492). The miniature represents not the normal lowering of the body but a moment of halted action when Christ is mourned and, as it seems, displayed. The composition, strange but imposing, is thus a real precursor of the famous *Lamentation* by Roger van der Weyden in the Prado.[255] The design defies the naturalistic premises that governed part at least of the *Deposition* (Fig. 493). The large corpse cannot easily be held upright in this way, although the figures press against it as buttresses. The man at the right (Nicodemus?) tries hard, but Joseph of Arimathea is deliberately not much involved, and perhaps that is why in the end the painter, confused about his role, made him a disturbingly mannered figure. The painter was well aware of the unreal aspects of this scene, for he enhanced them by introducing two symmetrical angels, quite substantial but nevertheless floating. These figures, lacking lower limbs, end below in streams of drapery, and the spear or pole that each holds, wedged in, so to speak, between the cross and the ground, provides the fiction of support. This design is very ingenious, and when a conception of this kind is joined to powerful volumes and unusual colors we may conclude that Paul was responsible for the work.[256]

An immediately subsequent moment in the earthly history of Christ, the lamentation over the corpse after it has been laid on the shroud, is represented within the Passion cycle after the *Deposition* (Fig. 455). Once again Paul, who was surely the author of this superb miniature, has massed monumental figures in geometric groups. Though his knowledge and experience were limited, he boldly foreshortened figures such as the woman who bends forward, tearing her hair, and the averted Magdalene who throws herself on Christ's feet. The cross is seen from the right, that is, near the center of the book. Once again a collaborator of Herman in this cycle has approached somewhat his demonstrative color.

6 · STRUCTURE OF THE MANUSCRIPT AND THE THREE STYLES

In the preceding discussion of the *Belles Heures* we have observed that certain cycles, such as those of Catherine and the Great Litany, seem more advanced than miniatures that follow them, but we have not considered whether such differences might originate in the make-up of the manuscript. Apart from a lost folio containing part of the reading from St. John and a miniature of this Evangelist the *Belles Heures* has come down to us substantially intact. Originally the Office of the Passion may have followed the Litany, as John Plummer observes in the Catalogue. There he has added to the facts we had recorded valuable observations on the make-up and borders of the manuscript. In the Catalogue the reader will find a list of the authors of the miniatures, or at least all those I have been able to identify.

The five major pictorial cycles in the manuscript—Catherine, the Litany, Diocrès and Bruno, Jerome, Paul and Anthony—are all self-contained, in the sense that they are painted on folios that were no doubt inserted into a pre-existing book.[257] Only one of them, the cycle of St. Jerome, is preceded by a rubric that refers to them. This rubric, on 182v, states that the Masses follow, the first devoted to the Birth of Christ, but before them is placed the "vita beati ieronomi tota ystoriata." This unique rubric is not written, however, in the minium normally used by the scribe for this purpose, as John Plummer has quite rightly emphasized, but in a bluish red—precisely the red used for alternate lines of the script in all the titles in the special cycles. The rubric, therefore, was entered at a second stage when the addition of the series of St. Jerome was planned. It does not even then, however, mention the cycle of Saints Paul and Anthony that follows that of Jerome and that likewise *precedes* the Masses. This puzzling omission seems to imply a still later insertion of Paul and Anthony. We shall presently cite some evidence to show that the story of St. Jerome was, in fact, painted after miniatures on the last folios of the manuscript, the style of which is late.

The four scenes of the Great Litany, apparently very advanced in style, are painted on the four sides of a bifolio, 73 and 74 (Figs. 451, 452, 463, 641). They are preceded (on 72v) by a rubric in the usual minium announcing the Litanies, the text of which begins, however, only on 75, after the last of the miniatures. The structure of this gathering, furthermore, is very unusual. It consists of ten folios rather than the normal eight and at its center there are two bifolios, 73–74 and 75–76. The gathering would have been normal without the pictures, which evidently were not planned when the manuscript was designed and written. If the scribe had had them in mind, and merely wished to give a bifolio to the illuminator for independent work, he could have chosen 75–76 and continued his text on the last folios (78–79) of what would then have been a normal gathering of eight leaves (see the diagram in the Catalogue). 78–79 are, however, quite blank—a clear proof that the Great Litany was added later. Thus the composition of the book proves the inference drawn from style that these miniatures are comparatively late. The style of Paul in the Catherine cycle is clearly later than in the Hours of the Virgin (except *The Flight*) which it precedes, so that it too belongs to a subsequent moment.

The *Belles Heures*, then, became much more of a picture book than was originally intended, although the exceptionally numerous miniatures in the Hours of the Passion reveal this inclination at a relatively early stage. Two of the picture cycles in the second half of the book are, furthermore, incorporated in regular gatherings. The story of the Cross, with its red and blue titles, was painted on a folio in gathering 21, and the four scenes of the Baptist on folios 211–212 form part of the normal gathering 29. These two cycles are very short, but they were clearly planned when the gathering was designed and written.

There is evidence to show that the execution of the special cycles was not greatly delayed during the course of the work. Jean's *Decapitation of St. Lucy* on folio 179v is essentially a copy of Paul's *Decapitation of St. Catherine* on folio 19v (Fig. 445).[258] Jean altered some forms and some colors but the most plausible interpretation of this relationship is his knowledge of his brother's painting. In his *Martyrdom of St. Agatha* on folio 179 Jean took his soldier with raised knee and to a degree his saint from *St. Catherine bound to a column* on folio 17 (Fig. 438). His other soldier recalls his own figure on folio 15v (Fig. 434). His Magdalene on 176v, like Lucy on 179v, is based on St. Catherine on 19v (Fig. 445). His priest on folio 202 recalls *St. Bruno entering the Chartreuse* on folio 97 (Fig. 416). We may conclude that two of the inserted cycles that seem comparatively late in style were painted before the illustrations of the suffrages and some miniatures in the last gatherings of the book. On the other hand a miniature in the cycle of St. Jerome seems to reflect one of Paul's latest compositions. The monks and the church on folio 184v follow closely Paul's *Funeral Service* on folio 221 with regard to design as well as the use of silvery metal in the windows, otherwise unknown in the manuscript (Fig. 499).

An independent study of motifs in the borders of the *Belles Heures* which John Plummer summarizes in the Catalogue supports the conclusions I had previously reached by consideration of the style of the miniatures, the make-up of the manuscript, and the relationships of compositions. One decorative motif appears only in the cycle of St. Jerome, another in the cycle of St. Anthony. A third was used only in the calendar, the style of which is clearly late. A fourth is limited to the calendar, the Great Litany, the Suffrages, and the Masses. This suggestion of the relatively late date of the Suffrages is an especially interesting addition to the evidence we have just offered above.

In many instances our reconstructed authors coincide with gatherings. Paul designed and painted most of the scenes of the months in the calendar. He designed almost all miniatures, and painted most of them, in gatherings 3, 5, 6, and 7. He was entirely responsible for all the large miniatures in gathering 10 (the bifolio 73–74) and, with assistance, for the subsequent gathering 11. He designed and partly painted much of gathering 13. Jean took on most of gatherings 21, 22, 24, 25, 26, and 27. Paul painted over half of the nine miniatures in the last three gatherings, 29–31. Herman, occasionally using a drawing by Paul, painted all the numerous miniatures in gatherings 18 and 19, and two out of three in 17.

One can readily understand the convenience and economy of allocating the work by gatherings. A division of this kind may commonly be observed in extensively illustrated manuscripts such as Bibles, which were often undertaken by illuminators from different workshops. Sometimes, as in the *Térence des ducs*, one illuminator drew his collaborators toward a certain uniformity. Manuscripts from the Boucicaut workshop all reflect the images, and occasionally also disclose the presence, of one great master. Often assistants apparently worked with a *chef* for a decade or more, so that the association resembles that of the Limbourgs.

The Limbourgs, however, represent a special case because they were brothers, and presumably friends. One of them, whom we have identified with Paul, was judged by the others to be a decisively superior artist. They worked on his drawings and they borrowed his forms. No doubt they in turn influenced him to some extent also, but since they are less strong their effect is more difficult to recognize. We have seen, however, that in the Passion cycle, largely executed by Herman, both Paul and Jean tended to approximate his color. We believe, furthermore, that there were more intricate forms of collaboration. Did Jean paint the figure of Christ in Paul's *Lamentation* (Fig. 455)? Did Herman execute Nicodemus and the man behind him in Paul's *Entombment* (Fig. 343)? Did not Paul supply the drawings and perhaps paint the Virgin and St. John in Herman's first scene of the Crucifixion (Fig. 364)? Did he also design Peter and Malchus for Herman's *Betrayal*? Paul similarly would seem to have provided the model for Heraclius in Herman's miniature on folio 156v (Fig. 488), and perhaps for the apostles in Jean's *Agony in the Garden* (Fig. 496). Jean and Herman appear to have worked together on folio 156 (Fig. 487). Many miniatures designed by Paul and in part painted by him seem to contain secondary figures executed by Jean: 15v (Fig. 434), 16v (Fig. 435), 18 (all but St. Catherine—Fig. 442), 19 (the king and his companions—Fig. 444). We have already seen that Jean probably painted the figures, including the Duke of Berry, in Paul's *Itinerary* (Fig. 403).

It is no surprise that the leading artist painted what was traditionally the most important miniature in a Book of Hours, the *Annunciation* at Matins of the Hours of the Virgin (Fig. 410), and that he proceeded to execute most of this cycle. We should expect him also, in the normal course of events, to paint the first series of pictures in the manuscript, those of St. Catherine. The choices and allotments, however, do not always meet our expectations, and they are often not simple. Thus Jean probably had a hand—forgive the pun—in the first miniature of the Catherine cycle, and he painted, too, the first of the scenes of the Passion. Most of the rest of this important series was, unexpectedly, taken by Herman, at that time the least accomplished of the brothers. Such allocations should restrain us from making very firm predictions about the *Très Riches Heures*, and that, in the light of what actually happened, is a big step forward.

We have assumed that the illumination of a manuscript as rich as the *Belles Heures* occupied the Limbourgs for about three years and that during this period they grew and changed. Jean's work, as we see it, exhibits a series of minor and rather unpredictable phases similar to those that occur in his miniatures in the Bible. Paul's style changed significantly, as we have seen, from the comparatively early miniatures in the Hours of the Virgin to the later ones in the special cycles, especially of Catherine, the Litany, and Bruno. He increased the height of the pictorial field in the interest of greater scale, and he experimented boldly with color and foreshortening. Paul's development in the original part of the book, as distinct from the special cycles, is less evident. Indeed at least one miniature in the first plan of the book seems conspicuously advanced, no doubt because its execution was delayed. The *Flight into Egypt* on folio 63 shows a luminous color, plastic power and rhythmical force that Paul equaled but did not surpass in his miniatures further on in the Passion cycle (Figs. 415, 455, 343).

In the *Flight*, as in all of Paul's miniatures, we find innovations, such as the prints of feet and hoofs in the dust on the road. The illuminator was quick to adopt and develop magnificently an averted position of the Virgin on the ass, which appeared first, as far as we know, in an otherwise conservative French miniature of *ca.* 1393 (Fig. 502), and then again in a Flemish panel of *ca.* 1400 in Antwerp and in a miniature by the Cité des Dames workshop *ca.* 1402 (Fig. 504).[259] Only the last-named, influenced by Italian precedents, followed the logical consequences of the new posture by shifting Mary's halo to the back of her head even though it is now "in front." With regard to the depiction of texture and light Paul's miniature resembles most, as we would expect, the Flemish panel. He increased the movement of the Virgin, so that she revolves towards the Child, while Joseph rotates in the opposite sense towards her. She is a broad, massive figure in strong blue, and Paul, feeling she needed more support than the little gray ass could give her, extended her mantle below it to serve as a vertical buttress.

In largeness of conception and control of color and shape this miniature approximates even those in the last section of the manuscript, which were apparently painted at a relatively late date. The *Baptism* on folio 211v has, like the *Flight*, a masterful simplicity and a similar harmony of tan, gold, pale green, violet, and blue (Fig. 431). Novel in this scene is the transparent water that spills over Christ's head and body, ending finally in the marvelously limpid blue of the kind of natural font—not the Jordan!—in which he stands.

This improvisation with water is like the play with smoke in Paul's *Castel Sant'Angelo* and other miniatures in the book (Fig. 452). Still, in his last folios in the manuscript there are a few forms that go beyond anything in the preceding pages. The large windows in the chapel in the *Funeral Service* for All Souls (Fig. 499) are a golden silver, as translucent as the similar windows created by the Boucicaut Master at just about the same time (Fig. 505). Paul did not here adopt that painter's scheme of the diaphragm arch which opens onto a partially visible interior, but he transformed the "doll's-house type" in which the building, while seen from outside, opens up to permit a view inside. The figures are proportionately small, the church is overlapped by the frame, below as well as above, and by emphasizing the extension of the structure into the invisible space Paul has created an extraordinary effect of scale.

The splendid illustration of All Saints a few folios before the *Funeral Service* is painted on the same sheet as the *Baptism* (Figs. 389, 431). Despite its beauty it might at first challenge our conception of Paul and of his originality, because an almost identical composition of the Madonna surrounded by the heavenly host may be seen on a folio of fr. 414 in the Bibliothèque nationale (Fig. 388). The painting appears at the beginning of a French version of the *Golden Legend* that, according to the colophon, was completed in September, 1404.[260] Jean Porcher, who first published the manuscript, and other scholars who followed him, accepted the date of the completion of the text as the date of this particular manuscript. Since the frontispiece contains forms characteristic of the Limbourgs, Porcher and others considered it an early work by them.[261] The miniature was really painted, however, by the Virgil Master, whose workshop, including the impressive Medallion Master, was responsible for the miniatures in the text.[262] The frontispiece shows his curiously elastic forms as well as his facial types and colors, both of which were much influenced by Jacquemart de Hesdin. The slate blue, orange-red, yellow-green derive from Jacquemart in the phase of the *Brussels Hours*.

The *Cour celeste* by the Virgil Master is unique in his work, and, apart from color, it corresponds in such detail to the same subject in the *Belles Heures* that one must conclude it derives from this very miniature; the hypothesis of another, identical, lost composition by the Limbourgs would seem implausible. The date in the colophon in the *Légende dorée* does not clearly contradict this conclusion; it could provide the date of the completion of a version of the text rather than of the particular manuscript. Even small details prove beyond any doubt that the Virgil Master was imitating Paul's design rather than the opposite. The upper edge of the coif of his St. Margaret, for instance, ends in an impossible manner at the roots of her hair—an inattentive imitation of the beautiful coif in Paul's miniature. The Virgil Master, furthermore, gave God the Father an imperial crown with five arches whereas the Limbourgs correctly used four, in *All Saints* and again for *Charlemagne* (Fig. 407). The two uppermost saints, moreover, are the Baptist, Jean de Berry's saint, and John the Evangelist, whose name he likewise bore. Absolute confirmation of the dependence of fr. 414 upon the *Belles Heures* has come only recently with my recognition that *St. Catherine refuting the Wise Men* on folio 386 derives in part from Paul's miniature of the same subject in the *Belles Heures* (Figs. 436, 437). The men again sit below the saint, their bench boldly extending below the lower frame.

In *All Saints* Paul applied more effectively than in any earlier miniature the perspective and drastic overlapping that he learned from the study of Trecento painting. Striving to suggest the vastness of the heavenly host he has violated medieval principles to the extent of obliterating the faces of most of the saints, leaving only a rim of hair or of the halo. The Virgil Master opened Paul's compact design both vertically and laterally.

Paul's *Madonna in the Sun*, though very substantial, is also unreal because there is no sign of the lower part of her body.[263] The swirls of her mantle mask it, and allow the impression that somehow it disappears in the brilliant light. As a special kind of abbreviated figure, she is contained by the two circles of the aureole. On a folio nearby (209) Paul painted a similar Madonna, equally strong and beautiful (Fig. 398). Here, accompanied by two angels, she is suspended before the background without an encircling radiance, so that her drapery, given a stronger masking function, falls more freely in three sections. Her suspension is aided by the rays that move upward from the golden disk, presumably of the sun, that is partly visible at the lower frame. Though this disk and the one in the same place in *All Saints* (Fig. 389) resemble the celestial orbs employed by the Boucicaut Master, it was Paul who used them to provide a radiance below.

Another half-length Madonna, which illustrates the prayer *O Intemerata* near the beginning of the *Belles Heures*, gives a similar impression of self-sufficiency (Fig. 397).[264] This folio was probably painted by two brothers, the *Madonna* by Jean and the miniature below by Herman. Two loops of the Madonna's mantle fall over the sickle moon above which she hovers. Actually the use of the moon, even though golden, departs from tradition, since in the legend of Aracoeli, which is represented here, it is the sun that encircles the Madonna whom the Sibyl reveals to Augustus. In a contemporary miniature in the *Boucicaut Hours* the mantle of the Virgin and the white cloth of the Child both fall over the moon (Fig. 401). Here the figure of the Virgin, though firmly bounded by the moon, is more traditional and it is terminated, so to speak, at its lower edge in the same way as the Virgin in the *Belles Heures*.

The Madonna in the *Boucicaut Hours*, which illustrates the Seven Heavenly Joys of the Virgin,[265] is clearly identified with the Woman in the twelfth chapter of the Apocalypse, who is clothed with the sun while the moon appears at her feet. Similar large, rapidly tapering rays issue from the Virgin in a miniature of the Aracoeli by the Egerton Master in a manuscript of Christine de Pisan which, we have recently proved, the Duke of Berry acquired in 1408 (Fig. 400).[266] Whatever the nature of the relationship between these two approximately contemporary paintings, it is clear that in design the Boucicaut miniature strikingly resembles illustrations of Aracoeli. Though in representations of this event the Sibyl often stands while the Emperor kneels, in a golden plaque that Jean de Berry gave to the Sainte-Chapelle, Bourges, in 1405, both figures kneel.[267] There is no reason to believe that the Marshal, whose helmet in the miniature is held by an angel, would have been annoyed or even embarrassed by identification with the Emperor Augustus. The Duke of Berry, after all, greatly enjoyed it.[268]

The vision of Aracoeli began to be represented in France in the late fourteenth century. It appeared in reliefs carved on two keystones of a vault in the church of the Celestins in Metz (Figs. 395, 396).[269] The unusual Madonna in the sun, full-length and seated, is identified with the Madonna of Humility, who often has a moon at her feet because of her association with the Woman of the twelfth chapter of the Apocalypse. Since the Madonna in the relief holds a nude, suckling Child the image conforms fully with that type of the Madonna of Humility that was favored in the illumination of Metz in the third quarter of the fourteenth century.[270]

The earliest extant image of the Aracoeli in French painting appears in an initial in the Duke's *Brussels Hours*, executed about 1400 or a few years earlier by Jacquemart's Italian collaborator, the Master of the Brussels Initials (Fig. 399).[271] This is the manuscript the Limbourgs saw, as we have shown above, when the Duke gave it to his brother Philippe le Hardi.[272] The Madonna in the Brussels initial differs from the usual earlier half-length figure in the sun, as we see it still in a slightly later, unpublished fresco in the sacristy of Siena Cathedral painted about 1410 (Figs. 392–394),[273] insofar as the illuminator has rounded the mantle of his Virgin to make her seem self-contained on the gold disk. The Egerton Master moved in the same direction (Fig. 400), perhaps already influenced by a miniature of the Limbourgs in the *Belles Heures*.

In the *Très Riches Heures* the Limbourgs corrected the iconographic blunder they had committed in the miniature of Aracoeli in the *Belles Heures*: the crescent is retained but the sun, so central to the story, has been restored (Fig. 557). Indeed the scene includes an unusual action not previously represented but described in the French translation of the *Golden Legend* of 1402 (Bibl. nat., fr. 242, fol. 14v): the Emperor is censing. The lambent rays issuing from the Madonna resemble those used by the Boucicaut and Egerton Masters. The Virgin regresses, however, to the earlier conception; far from seeming self-sufficient, she is shown nearly down to the knees and appears to continue behind the moon into the clouds below. The reason for this change must be the different nature of the pictorial field. Here the Madonna is alone in a separate medallion with its stronger framing, whereas in the miniatures in the *Belles Heures* she floats in a larger space. Thus we discover why the Limbourgs developed the new form in the first place.

By the same token, artists with a different bent might adopt the figure but disregard its novel character. Thus the workshop of the Rohan Master painted a verticalized and linear version of Paul's design for the prayer *Obsecro Te* in the *Grandes Heures de Rohan*, in which the spatial significance of the abbreviated Madonna has been lost (Fig. 390).[274]

Before the *Belles Heures* the legend of Aracoeli had not been employed as an illustration of the prayer O *Intemerata*. Perhaps, as I have observed, the phrase "ianua regni celorum" near the beginning of the prayer suggested the introduction of it. A stronger impulse, however, may have been the wish of Jean de Berry to associate himself, as the reader of the prayer, with the emperor, particularly at so momentous an occasion.

Paul's *All Saints* and miniatures like it, painted *ca.* 1408, suggest the kind of scale and luminosity that we might expect in his next paintings. They are, in fact, to be found in his additions to another Book of Hours of Jean de Berry, the *Très Belles Heures de Notre-Dame*.

7 · ADDITIONS TO THE *TRES BELLES HEURES DE NOTRE-DAME*

It has long been agreed that the Limbourgs worked on two, or probably three, of the incomplete folios in that most complex of Jean de Berry's manuscripts, the *Très Belles Heures de Notre-Dame*. One, the illustration of the Itinerary which probably belonged to the manuscript, we have already discussed (Fig. 404). On two other folios the Limbourgs painted the miniature, the initial, and the *bas-de-page*, working mostly within the limits of the framework executed in the Parement workshop *ca.* 1382 (Figs. 500, 501).[275] They added seraphs in the borders, and they enlarged both miniatures at the top by cutting into the original border, just as Paul had begun to do early in the *Belles Heures* (Fig. 452). One miniature, on page 225, illustrates a prayer to the Trinity (Fig. 501), the other on page 240 a prayer to the heavenly hierarchies (Fig. 500).[276] The devotion of the Duke to the Trinity was exemplified by one exceptionally splendid representation, a golden relief which he gave to the Sainte-Chapelle in Bourges in 1405.[277] Below the image of the Trinity there appeared the Aracoeli, and the two kneeling figures at the left in the miniature might reflect the Sibyl and Augustus in the now lost panel of gold.

In the *bas-de-page* of the magnificent prayer to the saints St. Anthony, on his way to St. Paul, encounters a centaur—the very same episode that is depicted by Jean in the *Belles Heures* (Fig. 479). Though there are similarities even with regard to the unusual iconographic feature of the centaur's staff, the composition in the *Très Belles Heures de Notre-Dame* is quite different. Probably because of the shape of the frieze all the figures are held near the picture plane. The ground stretches out with very little rise to some hills and trees. When compared with the miniature by Jean the articulation of these figures, though they are tiny, and their rich counterpoint with the landscape, give us a vivid impression of the qualitative range in the series of paintings classified hitherto only as the work of "the Limbourgs." The regular arcs of the angels in the main miniature are repeated by the hills and the figures below, giving the composition a geometric order, simplicity, and grandeur that are characteristic of Paul's best work. There is a steady crescendo of color. Tan, brown and olive-green predominate in the *bas-de-page*. In the miniature blue and olive-green figures against buff and gray hills are surmounted by rays, stars, and the bright colors of the angels and of God, who appears before a delicious pink cloth of honor.

Several figures on the other folio are likewise related to the *Belles Heures*. The worshipper wearing a cap resembles very closely the man to the right of the altar in the *Exaltation of the Cross*, perhaps designed by Paul but painted by Jean (Fig. 485). Here again the figure in the *Très Belles Heures de Notre-Dame* is superior, though not so markedly. The painter had difficulty with foreshortening, and this miniature as a whole seems less strong than the *Prayer to the Saints*. It looks like an aggregation of Paul's figures, hills, and architectural motifs, assembled by Jean in a cursory way. The Trinity closely resembles the Trinity on folio 204 of the *Belles Heures* (Fig. 503), but Jean transformed that group, which he painted, into the idiom of Paul.

In the beautiful initial, as Eve emerges from Adam's side, his arm crosses his face to create a far more interesting posture than that of Jean's figure in the Bible (Fig. 284). Similarly God swinging about to create the firmament is greatly superior to Jean's more traditional conception of the same moment in the Bible (Fig. 280). On the other hand the difference between the creation of the sun and the moon here and in the Bible, in this instance by Paul, is not so much qualitative as developmental (Fig. 282). It seems probable, therefore, that Paul himself painted both the frieze and the initial on this folio in the *Très Belles Heures de Notre-Dame*.

Though the billowy figures in the *Très Belles Heures de Notre-Dame* closely resemble Paul's in the *Belles Heures*, the best of them are more powerful and they are enveloped in a light that pervades the entire space. This radical increase in luminosity constitutes, indeed, a major change. The two folios must have been painted a year or two after the completion of the *Belles Heures* and shortly before the beginning of the *Très Riches Heures*. They were certainly executed before the Duke gave the manuscript to Robinet d'Estampes, very probably, as we have shown, for New Year 1412.[278] As the only surviving paintings by the Limbourgs from this period, except for the *Itinerary* in the *Petites Heures* (Fig. 405), they have a very special importance.

VI

The *Très Riches Heures*

1 · THE MANUSCRIPT AND THE INVENTORY

IN 1881 Léopold Delisle proposed to identify the glorious Book of Hours at Chantilly with the brief item in the post-mortem inventory of Jean de Berry that we have included among the documents (p. 80).[279] "A number of gatherings," the notice states, "of a very splendid Book of Hours that Paul and his brothers made." Since the time of Delisle's proposal only one voice has been raised against it.[280] Delisle based his opinion on three factors. This item is the only Book of Hours in the Duke's inventories described as incomplete—and the *Très Riches Heures* was indeed left only half complete in 1416. In the second place the appraisal—500 pounds—was very high for an unfinished Book of Hours that lacked a cover and precious stones or metals. Among all the Duke's manuscripts only the *Belles Heures* and the *Grandes Heures* were appraised at a higher figure, and they both had jeweled covers and bookmarks. Finally—and this is the least important—the *Très Riches Heures* did in fact seem to him to have been illuminated by three painters.

Delisle was not troubled by the vagueness of one aspect of the brief description, which was not written by Robinet because the manuscript was incomplete and not accessioned during the Duke's life. "A number of gatherings," the item says; actually there were 29! With their extensive knowledge of the inventories Delisle and Durrieu took into account broad relationships that a few modern historians ignore.[281] Fundamental to the identifications is the fact that there exist six Books of Hours of exceptional quality embellished with the armorials and portraits of Jean de Berry, and his inventories in turn single out six Books of Hours of exceptional richness. If we disregard so general but fundamental a conformity the *Très Riches Heures* as well as the *Brussels Hours* and the *Très Belles Heures de Notre-Dame* are still Manuscripts in Search of An Inventory Notice. In view of the completeness of the inventories such a situation is impossible—unless the Duke gave away a prayer book made especially for him immediately upon its completion and before it was accessioned by his extraordinary registrar—a quite unlikely event. The *Brussels Hours* was, to be sure, given to Philippe le Hardi, but only after it had been inventoried and after the Duke had enjoyed it for a short period of time.[282]

When the description of a manuscript in the inventory is brief, as it is for various reasons of the *Très Belles Heures de Notre-Dame* and the *Très Riches Heures*, confirmation should come from a variety of facts.[283] The case for the *Très Riches Heures* presented by Delisle and Durrieu was strong enough, and it is absolutely confirmed by the fact that the painters who illuminated the manuscript also produced the *Belles Heures*, a major book of Jean de Berry executed, the inventory states, by his illuminators, and the *Bible moralisée*, which can be connected with a documented work of the Limbourgs.

2 · THE PAINTERS AND THE ALTERED PLAN

At very first glance the *Très Riches Heures* creates a different effect than the *Belles Heures*—or indeed most earlier illuminated manuscripts. Many of its miniatures are exceptionally large, over eight inches high, and thus almost twice the size of the miniatures in the *Belles Heures*.[284] Many of them appear alone on the folio, without any text or border. These paintings in series give the impression of a collection of little pictures. Indeed, Jan van Eyck's *Madonna of the Fountain* is less large. But the *Très Riches Heures*, with its sixty-three large and sixty-six small miniatures, resembles less a picture gallery than a mural cycle—a diminutive Arena chapel—in which the single paintings exist in their original context.

Or almost. The manuscript is far more complex even than the *Belles Heures*. The masterpiece of the Limbourgs is so well known from Durrieu's great monograph and from countless reproductions that we inevitably think of the miniatures in their present sequence. However, many of the original folios, or even entire gatherings, are missing,[285] and we cannot take for granted where some existing miniatures were intended to fall. The Limbourgs only half completed the task, and although Jean Colombe greatly respected their work, we cannot simply assume he put back all the single folios into the places in which he found them. We shall, in short, want to ask, and try to answer, numerous questions not raised by Paul Durrieu, whose description of the manuscript in his monograph of 1904 remains, however, the foundation of all future studies.

As a Book of Hours the *Très Riches Heures* is no less original than the *Belles Heures*, but in different ways. The astronomical schemes in the calendar would alone distinguish it from all other manuscripts of its kind. They indicate at once that learned men participated in the decisions about the text and the illustration.[286] A small sign of a collaboration of this nature may be the words written at the middle of the blank folio 109: "nihil hic"—clearly a note for the illuminator and perhaps also for the scribe written in Latin rather than the vernacular.[287] Paul and his brothers certainly took part in the planning, and a folio like *Aracoeli* (Fig. 557) or 37v (Fig. 579), with their odd departures from the normal design of two equal columns of text, show that the illuminators must have advised the scribe.

In general the text of the *Très Riches Heures* resembles that of the *Belles Heures* and the much earlier *Très Belles Heures de Notre-Dame*. As in those manuscripts the normal Offices and prayers of a Book of Hours are followed by a series of special Masses. In the *Très Riches Heures*, however, the usual Suffrages as well as the Itinerary, an innovation in the Duke's Books of Hours beginning with the *Belles Heures*, were not written, or they have been completely lost. In the general plan of its illustration, too, the *Très Riches Heures* resembles the *Belles Heures*, although the special cycles in the earlier manuscript are entirely lacking. This resemblance we must keep in mind when we face some of the problems the *Très Riches Heures* raises.

The plan in the *Belles Heures* of giving each of the Penitential Psalms a miniature is expanded in the *Très Riches Heures* to the illustration of the Psalms in all the principal Offices. The design allows for miniatures the width of a single column of text, and a space was left blank either above or below for the addition of *tituli*. The Limbourgs executed only twenty-two of these miniatures, all in gatherings 6 through 8, for Matins through Terce of the Hours of the Virgin (Figs. 554, 555, 560, 561, 563–566, 568). This cycle shows some resemblances with Greek Psalters, and may derive from a manuscript of this kind that remains to be identified. Only the miniatures in gathering 6 are provided with the special titles originally envisaged (Figs. 554, 560, 563, 564). They are written in gold and blue. For their content we have found no precedent. Thereafter, in gatherings 7 and 8, the spaces left for them by the scribe are blank, even though the Limbourgs painted the miniatures (Figs. 555, 561, 565, 566, 568). Apparently the titles were to be inscribed *after* the illuminators had painted the miniatures. They returned only the sixth gathering to the scribe before death put an end to the work.[288]

Although the illustration of the *Très Riches Heures* resembles the *Belles Heures* with regard to subject, in form and format many of the miniatures are unique. This complete novelty appears on the very first folios, where for the first time in illuminated manuscripts a full-page miniature faces the text of each month in the calendar (Figs. 539–549, 562).[289] The calendrical text is thus written on the back of each of the miniatures (Figs. 536–538). At the end of the cycle of the months appears another miniature that is practically full-page (Fig. 550). Its subject, the influence of the zodiac upon man, is related to the calendar, in which these same signs appear, but this kind of zodiacal man, which had a long history in medical and astrological treatises, had never before been introduced into a Book of Hours, and indeed the *Très Riches Heures* did not set an example.[290] The same may be said of the unprecedented astronomical scheme in the calendar. The Zodiacal Man provided indications for, among other things, times that were favorable or unfavorable for bleeding,[291] just as the calendar marked days on which new enterprises should be avoided. The Duke, like other well-tended men of his time, was bled periodically. We learn from one of his contemporaries that only after blood-letting did he play dice.[292] In his essay on all this astronomical and calendaric compilation, however, Professor Neugebauer argues that since some of the indications vary in the calendars of the Duke's Books of Hours they were probably not intended as normal guides to practice. The various tables imply an ambitious intellectuality, a desire to be fully up to date. The table giving the length of daylight throughout the year—*la quantite des jours*—corresponds to Paris better than to Bourges; it thus seems suitable for a resident of the great city, which the Duke then was, and it may suggest that the compilation was undertaken there also. Within the Duke's circle, however, the most likely source for calendaric and astronomical information was his friend, Abbot Lubert Hautschild of Eeckhout, near Bruges, who devoted himself enthusiastically to such matters.

The calendar was often the last section of a Book of Hours to be completed, especially in manuscripts produced for the trade, and though the *Très Riches Heures*, like the *Belles Heures*, was designed from the beginning for a specific patron, its calendar, too, appears, as we shall see, to have been painted relatively late. After the calendar and the *Zodiacal Man* come the readings from the gospels, beginning with the miniature for St. John (Fig. 551). This miniature maintains in its way the entirely novel character of the manuscript demonstrated by the calendar. Earlier Books of Hours, and the *Belles Heures* too in John Plummer's reconstruction, show a close-up of the Evangelist writing, whereas Paul, who designed this miniature and painted much of it, shows an ecstatic saint beholding in the heavens a large Christ accompanied by the twenty-four Elders, while three angels sound trumpets that wave close to his ears. The recession of the celestial walls, which diminishes the farthest Elder to about half the size of the nearest one—not quite enough for our later eyes—is more than matched by the deep marine view below. This seascape shows a much lower horizon and more liquid water than comparable ones in the *Belles Heures*, such as *St. Nicholas saving seafarers* (Fig. 693). No Italian painter of this time or earlier (Fig. 650) wanted, as Paul clearly did, to show boundless space and the vastness of the sea.

St. John's isolation on the island of Patmos becomes vivid because of the departure of the row-boat, no doubt the craft that brought him there after Domitian's order of banishment.[293] A conspicuous gallows on the distant shore serves as a reminder of strife and evil in the world. John's contraposto resembles that of Adam in the Bible (Fig. 655) and of an old man below the cross in the *Death of Christ* in the *Belles Heures* (Fig. 497). This miniature in the *Belles Heures* was painted by Herman, but what an extraordinary advance, nevertheless, in Paul's articulation of the complex posture! He has now described the tense tendons and muscles of John's neck, and no figure in the *Belles Heures* shows an equal realization of the cheekbones or the jaw, or of the inter-play between flesh and bone. All of this implies a renewed and more penetrating study of Trecento painting, of which the gray-green underpainting, left quite visible in the shaded areas, is a symptom.

By an astonishing stroke of luck we may, in fact, possess the Trecento model for a part of the composition. It is an extraordinary and in some respects puzzling Sienese painting of the Fall of the Rebel Angels that came to light a few years ago in a private collection in, of all places, Bourges (Fig. 666). In a masterful study Michel Laclotte has placed this beautiful painting in the circle of Barna about 1340, correctly I believe, although the exceptionally deep perspective of the thrones and the searching analysis of the planes of the two heads on the reverse of the panel are troubling at this date (Fig. 667).[294] The miniature of St. John and the Sienese painting even share the use of a red oil glaze over the gold, on the mantle of Christ in the miniature and on the angels in the panel.

The *St. John*, the first illustration in the text of the *Très Riches Heures*, shows an entirely new approach to the relation between miniature and folio. Like the miniatures in the *Belles Heures* at the beginning of Offices or in the special cycles, *St. John* appears above a few—here three—lines of text. The miniature is proportionately higher and contains a crowning arch but the borders are proportionately much larger, and, more important, extraordinarily broad areas are entirely free of decoration. The yellow-white parchment surrounding the receding planes of the miniature becomes the symbol of space. Into it, indeed, the sprays of leaves and flowers move. Coming out from the initials and the text they remain generally parallel to it, but they evolve in three dimen-sions far more completely than any earlier forms of the kind. The violets are freer, too, of schemes, and they look as though they were painted, if not *al vif* then after fresh inspection.[295]

Columbine frequently refers to Christ, and violets, which appear in the border of *St. Mark* also (Fig. 556), often signify humility,[296] but a consistency of symbolic content of the flowers in the borders of the manuscript is difficult to determine. Perhaps columbine was chosen for the border of St. John because its Latin name, *aquilegia*, was derived from *aquila*, St. John's symbol.[297] The eagle adds to the scene a magnificent, fiery presence. The little brown and black fly may also have religious meanings,[298] but it certainly has illusionistic ones, playing upon the theme of the am-bivalence of the parchment as a flat plane or receding space.

The fly belongs also to that group of small, nimble, and exquisite creatures that populate the borders of late medieval manuscripts. Most common were birds—"les dieux de l'air," Eustache Deschamps called them.[299] Indeed in France small birds and flying insects are the only creatures commonly admitted into the marginal space. In Jean de Berry's manuscripts there appear also small bears, his emblem, and snails which, as we have suggested, may refer to his motto. Although French illuminators of the great period up to 1420 surely knew Italian manuscripts they did not find acceptable for their borders the large, weighty, terrestrial animals often selected by their Lombard contemporaries.

In all earlier or contemporary illumination the folios that most resemble this one in the *Très Riches Heures* are not Northern but Italian, or more precisely Lombard. The flowers in the borders of Michelino's superb little Book of Hours recently acquired by the Morgan Library are more formal in design and arrangement but the particular value of the unfilled space and its relation to the flowers and the miniature are similar (Fig. 681). The comparison is not, however, between Michelino and the Limbourgs in the normal sense of the term, because this border in the *Très Riches Heures*, like almost all the others, was not, as I observed a few years ago, painted by the author of any of the miniatures in the manuscript.[300] The art of this illuminator is so distinctive that we may speak not simply of a different hand but of a different mode and stylistic trend. Paul and his brothers were steeped in the traditions of Trecento painting, which they had been studying for a decade, and although, as we have seen in the Bible and the *Belles Heures*, they turned Italian conventions to their own ends, they cared much more than the painter of the border for generalized forms and for effects of mass and weight. The painter of the leaves and flowers had a lighter touch, and with his very fluid colors imparted a more delicate kind of life. He is the illuminator who, in the *Crucifixion* of 1406, proved to be close to, but quite independent of, Paul and Jean (Fig. 366). He maintained this fascinating relationship until the end of his known career, when he and his assistants illuminated the Breviary of Jean sans Peur, after which I have given him his name (Figs. 610, 611, 618–622, 648, 893).

It seems quite possible that collaboration on the folio of St. John did not end with the contributions of the Breviary Master and with Paul. Although the small size makes judgment difficult, the Elders seem to be painted in an inferior and less advanced style, and Paul was probably assisted by Herman.

The Breviary Master did not paint a single miniature in the *Très Riches Heures*, but with an assistant he tooled the gold haloes, the initials and certain other forms not only in *St. John on Patmos* but in most miniatures through 46v.[301] Similarly he tooled the initials through folio 49 and on several later folios, as the description in the Catalogue of Manuscripts shows. Seeking to enliven the gold he had already in the *Crucifixion* of 1406 broken its flat surface with small punches (Fig. 366). In the haloes of the miniature of *St. John* countless tiny circular punches transform the smooth sheen of burnished gold into an area of flashing lights (Fig. 551). To produce even stronger reflections in the initials he employed a larger punch at wider intervals. The conformity of these glistening spots with his own luminous borders is greater than that of his tooling in the miniature with Paul's painted surface. Probably the Breviary Master was responsible also for the gold glazed with red in the mantle of Christ. We should add that all the tooled haloes in the *Très Riches Heures* appear in miniatures that are accompanied by initials or borders by this master. The reverse, however, is not true, because Paul soon decided, as we shall see, that the reflections were too strong for his painted surface.

The folio of the *Martyrdom of St. Mark* is the consequence of a similar collaboration (Fig. 556). The Breviary Master again painted violets in the border; here they are accompanied by two of their own leaves, and the petals of each fall in an entirely different way. A hoopoe standing on the arabesque turns around to look in their direction. Within the miniature the Breviary Master gave St. Mark not only his scintillating halo but a gorgeous blue and gold chasuble, which glistens like a contemporary gold-enamel (Fig. 616). The bulky soldier who drags the saint from the altar implies, like *St. John*, the renewed study of Giottesque painting, but his dark skin represents a particular predilection of the Limbourgs. He is the first of a remarkably large group of colored people in the *Très Riches Heures*. Their presence adds to the miniatures the kind of deep brown that the illuminators favored, and which they employed in the *Belles Heures* for monastic habits and other forms. These brown and black figures were also introduced, of course, for various iconographic reasons. In the miniature of the martyrdom of Mark in Alexandria—a unique subject for the pericope in a Book of Hours—they diversify the inhabitants of that city, and they may also refer to the passage from St. Mark written nearby in the Gospel reading: "Go ye into all the world and preach the gospel to every creature."[302]

The receding façades of houses, which parallel the receding church, increase the sense of sudden action and excitement. The view down a street, a motif that the Limbourgs introduced first in the Bible (Fig. 322), is not excellently painted. Even the smoke fails to equal what Paul achieved in, for instance, *Castel Sant'Angelo* (Fig. 452). The soldiers also have the dry surface and the sheer bulk of Herman's figures, whereas St. Mark comes much closer to what we have seen of Jean in the *Belles Heures*. We have suspected that Herman worked also on the conjoint folio of *Aracoeli* (Fig. 557).

The *Annunciation* (Fig. 559), at Matins in the Hours of the Virgin, continues the sumptuousness of the preceding miniatures of *Aracoeli* (Fig. 557) and the Evangelists (Figs. 551–553, 556).[303] The two haloes as well as the mantle and the wings of the angel sparkle with the exquisite tooling of the Breviary Master. Indeed Gabriel far outshines the Virgin, even though his green contrasts less than her deep blue with the limpid light green of the church. His magnetism as well as the arabesques and strong blue of the background—a common feature of the *Belles Heures*—create some imbalance in the design. This, as well as the fine, linear, rather thin character of the forms, indicate that Jean was responsible for the execution, although usually the miniature at the beginning of the Hours of the Virgin was assumed by the leading partner in a collaborative enterprise. Paul probably, in fact, had a share in the work, for the bold scale of the church, its oblique position and its extension below the lower frame recall his late designs in the *Belles Heures*, particularly the *Funeral Mass* (Fig. 499).[304]

On this folio the Breviary Master seems to have been more influential than at any other moment. Even the head of the Virgin reflects his taste. He tooled the gold in the initials and the tiny crowns in the tiara of God the Father as well as the golden sickle around the yellow radiance.

The close collaboration between the Breviary Master and the painter of the miniature is maintained in the border. The Breviary Master executed the initials, the line-ending, and the two shields supported by bears and swans, whereas the rest of the border, like the miniature, is Jean's. As in the *Belles Heures* the musical angels are borne by cloud-like fluff that emerges from basket capitals, and below, a large book again serves as an airship. The angels rise above swirling leaves of exquisite colors, punctuated here and there by the little brown bears, which cling to them like acrobats. These short, free, rhythmical phrases introduced at perfect intervals in the wide borders make the folio one of the most beautiful in the manuscript.

Although since the painting of the *Belles Heures* the Limbourgs had revised radically their conception of both the border and the miniature, the *Annunciation* in the *Très Riches Heures* preserves much of the iconography of the corresponding miniature in the earlier manuscript, while dividing and distinguishing its several categories in a new way (Fig. 410). The shields are still there, though now floating buoyantly at an angle—one consequence among many of the new triumph over, and therefore play with, gravitation. Greater mastery of perspective and light has enabled the painter to put God the Father in a special zone of radiant yellow framed by blue clouds, a golden sickle, and the flashing red and blue wings of cherubs and seraphs. The loggia may therefore be reserved entirely for the musical angels, as it was in the miniature of the *Annunciation* by Jean Pucelle in which they first occupied the upper story of a building.[305] The Limbourgs undoubtedly knew this epoch-making manuscript because Jean de Berry not only owned it but probably kept it close by. The Old Testament heroes, present in the *Belles Heures* in the borders and on the lectern, have in the *Très Riches Heures* all become statues on the façade of the church.

The representation of the Annunciation in a church, not yet introduced in the *Belles Heures*, was begun tentatively in French painting in the 'eighties,[306] suggested perhaps by apocryphal texts and by the reports of travelers that the event had occurred in such a setting.[307] The miniature in the *Très Riches Heures* was surely inspired by paintings of the Boucicaut Master, who about 1406 painted the first large ecclesiastical structure (Fig. 639). Paul, however, the designer of the composition in the *Très Riches Heures*, set his building obliquely and ran the ground plane below the lower frame.

From the Boucicaut Master Paul and Jean probably took also the conception of metallic windows that simulate glass. All but one of the windows are silver splattered with a little gold, but the one opposite the Virgin is entirely gold. The rays from God the Father pass through it on their way to her. Jean has thus given more prominence to a symbol of the Incarnation familiar to theologians from the ninth century on, but first introduced into art, it seems, at the end of the fourteenth century by Melchior Broederlam (Figs. 377, 378). It appeared in his panel as one of the numerous kinds of light with religious connotations that the painters of this period, fascinated by luminary phenomena, found in traditional Christian literature and introduced into art.[308] Thus painters from the late fourteenth century on, first in the North and then in Italy, took pleasure in giving visible form to symbolic images of light such as burning candles, fire, and sunlight. St. Bridget, in her vision of the Nativity to which we have referred, followed earlier mystics such as Bernard of Clairvaux when she compared the miraculous Incarnation with the passage of light through glass.[309] "As the sun, penetrating a glass window, does not damage it, the virginity of the Virgin is not spoiled by Christ's assumption of human form." Or, in the words of a medieval Nativity hymn:

As the sunbeam through the glass
Passeth but not staineth
Thus the Virgin, as she was,
Virgin still remaineth.

This metaphor of the Virgin birth employs an image drawn from medieval art. Although it was current in religious writing of the twelfth and thirteenth centuries it was introduced into painting only by the first masters concerned with the depiction of natural light: Broederlam, the Limbourgs, and after them the Master of Flémalle and Jan van Eyck.

The miniature in the *Très Riches Heures* shares with Broederlam's panel not only the symbolism of the glass and the ray but the exterior-interior relation of the two principal figures, the attitude and gesture of the Virgin, and the prophets on the façade. Though Broederlam's prophets hold only scrolls they probably represent, as Panofsky proposed, Moses at the left and Isaiah at the right.[310] In the *Très Riches Heures*, however, the prophet at the upper left holds a staff and may undoubtedly be identified as Aaron. His rod, which suddenly flowered, was often compared with the "flowering" of a Virgin, particularly in the French version of the *Meditationes Vitae Christi* translated for Jean de Berry in 1380.[311] The prophet above the Virgin, holding a small attribute difficult to identify, might be Isaiah or Moses, who stood with his tablets on the lectern in the *Belles Heures* (Fig. 410). The statue of a soldier above Gabriel almost certainly is Gideon, whose fleece was a common symbol of the Incarnation.[312]

The *Visitation* in the *Très Riches Heures*, though similar in many respects to the one in the *Belles Heures* (Fig. 638), has been modernized by study of the same source as the *Annunciation*, the *Boucicaut Hours* (Figs. 567, 640). Only in the painting of the Boucicaut Master could Paul, who painted the *Visitation*, have seen a shower of gold like the one he introduced into his scene, giving it greater concentration and prominence than it had in his model. To match it Paul abandoned the kind of halo that had been tooled by the Breviary Master in the preceding miniatures, though that master continued to execute the initial with the wounded swan. He employed instead relatively dull gold disks across which rays move out from the heads.[313] For all these forms Paul used gold in emulsion, and he applied touches of the same metal to the hair of the Virgin and the leaves of the trees.

This miniature is therefore almost as sumptuous as the *Annunciation*, and the curling gold border of the Virgin's mantle certainly enhances this effect; but it is also simpler, stronger and more unified. The figures are three-fourths the height of the rectangular frame, much larger than the Virgin and Elizabeth in the *Boucicaut Hours* (Fig. 640), and their columnar or conical volumes are repeated by the mountains behind. Mary and Elizabeth are equated not only with mountains but with a building, which does not rise much higher than the Virgin. Paul's search for monumentality has here led him into unusual incongruity, and there is some confusion with regard to the Virgin's position. From his study of Italian painting he has learned more about the structure of the figure than the Boucicaut Master knew earlier, though the legs of Elizabeth function imperfectly. If Paul's figures seem more advanced than those of his great contemporary, the landscape, with fantastic forms and only the first signs of aerial perspective, is more old-fashioned.

Although Paul's figures, standing near the lower frame, are less embedded in the landscape than those of the Boucicaut Master, they are much more affected by the light. It plays over the smooth surfaces with an astonishing subtlety. In the preceding miniatures and still more in the *Belles Heures* the brushwork was open. The strokes remained clearly visible, whereas Paul has here merged them in the finely graduated tones of his turning planes.

The border, bolder but less exquisite in color than the border of the *Annunciation*, is witty. Armed and even armored men tilt at butterflies, a snail, or even a leaf, and one of these immensely courageous knights strikes out from a battlemented tower. In a wheelbarrow a golden bear sounds a bagpipe. Placed alongside the wounded swan, he is clearly an emblem of the Duke, and we therefore learn that fanciful treatment of these creatures was quite permissible. In the lower border an elderly man dressed as a scholar—and here there may be a parody too—tries to catch one of the birds that wheel and dive, while an owl, which he does not see, sits unconcernedly on a stick. A rabbit jumps from the acanthus out into the empty space.

The *Nativity* shows the kind of unification in color and design that, as in the *Visitation*, implies the authorship of Paul (Fig. 569). It shares with the *Visitation* also imposing figures, here however quite free of structural problems; and the contrast between the response to the Child of the delicate Virgin and the unusually powerful Joseph is a major theme of the design. In the *Nativity* of the Hours of the Virgin in the *Belles Heures* Paul, striving for voluminous figures in the Italian sense, did not care for refinements of this kind (Fig. 333). They are anticipated, however, in the Bible, painted before his major objective became the conquest of Trecento accomplishments (Fig. 327), and again in the *Nativity* illustrating a Mass in the *Belles Heures* (Fig. 329).[314] We have already noticed that both of these earlier representations stressed the centrality of the Child and the supernatural nature of the moment by surrounding him with rays.[315] To the rays in the *Très Riches Heures* are added four blue cherubim, similar to the seraphim which had already surrounded the Child in a French *Nativity* of 1407 (Fig. 419).[316]

This supernatural splendor in the *Très Riches Heures* outshines, but does not eliminate, earthly phenomena, which indeed are much more prominent than in the earlier miniatures. The bare tree, like the ones in the *Brussels Hours*,[317] refers to the wintry season. The ox, which had looked up to the heavens in the *Belles Heures* (Fig. 333), now joins the ass at the hay. Shepherds, well bundled up, are more numerous than before—near the animals, receiving the message on the hill, and in the defile as in the earlier miniatures, though indistinctly visible through the beam of light. Their sheep graze all over the hills. The heavenly radiance almost entirely obfuscates a golden idol standing on a column.

In the *Nativity* Paul brought the shepherds closer to the miraculous event than they had ever been in Northern painting. When giving them an unprecedented prominence here and again in the *Adoration of the Magi* (Fig. 572) the painter's personal inclinations were surely stimulated by the concern, discussed above, with peasants and simple people that developed in France at this time under the influence of religious as well as secular trends. An indication of this special interest may be found in the French version of the *Meditationes Vitae Christi* made for Jean de Berry in 1380, which contains a passage that, though preceded by pictorial imagery, is lacking in the earlier Italian texts. "... ils se merveillerent bie(n) grandement que pourroit estre et mectoient la main sur le front deuant les yeulx en regarda(n)t vers le ciel tous esbahis. ..."[318]

Although in the scene of the Nativity the shepherds have already learned of the miraculous birth the next miniature in the *Très Riches Heures* (Fig. 570) is devoted to a special annunciation to them, in accordance with a tradition established for French Books of Hours in the fourteenth century.[319] Once again the representation conforms with an aspect of the French version of the *Meditations* which is lacking in the original.

> Personne deuote reguarde lumilite de ton createur qui aux si[m]ples gens pastoureaux donna clere cognoyssance de sa natiuite Et les grands princes qui estoient en bethleem et les gros borgois et marchans se dormoint et nouyre[n]t riens de ceste glorieuse nativite . . . (*Vie de nostre sauveur*, p. 23).

The Creator decided, in other words, to reveal the Nativity to the shepherds while the great burghers and merchants, sleeping, learned nothing at all. Small wonder that Paul gave them special beams of light.

What a sea-change in Paul's art in the approximately six years since painting the same scene in the *Belles Heures* (Fig. 411)! The two miniatures are clearly related in design and even in such details as the dark felt hats, but the process of rational differentiation that we observed in the *Annunciation* (Fig. 559) has been carried a step further here. The miracle occurs in the foreground, which is rich in naturalistic detail: the water tumbling down the hill, the panting dog, and the tattered stocking as well as the unbuttoned tunic of the oldest shepherd, revealing his paunch. The boots of the young shepherd have gaping holes.[320] As in the *Nativity* (Fig. 569), bare trees establish the season. These entirely fresh observations do not, however, conceal the deeply Italianate character of the figures and of the multilayered, corkscrew hill. Although open brushwork is employed to suggest the swarthy, weathered skin of the shepherds, this area is generally rendered in the smooth, luminous enamel of the *Nativity* and the *Visitation* (Figs. 567, 569). Furthermore, Paul has again employed a narrow range of colors. Green, blue, brown, black, are mixed in various ways, so that even the sheep, which in the *Belles Heures* were as usual white, show brown patches on their tawny wool.

The angels, no longer limited to the three symbolizing the Trinity in the *Belles Heures*, occupy their usual supernatural zone of the arch as well as the nearer sky. They are painted in bright, warm colors quite different from the cool, somber hues of the "simples gens" below. All this foreground, however, despite its rich detail and succulent color, seems traditional compared to the panorama that opens between the hills. Two small shepherds in that space respond, it is true, to the miracle, but the swelling hills stretch out far behind them. These hills are utterly different from the twisting peak in the foreground, the type visible in Paul's two preceding miniatures and traditional in Trecento painting. The very active peak here, as well as in the *Visitation* and the *Nativity*, involves nature in the surprising, unnatural event. The hills behind show us the plotted and well-tended farms of France, some of them momentarily struck by a brighter light. The city at the horizon looks like a French city; Paul Durrieu tentatively, but not convincingly, proposed Poitiers.[321]

Thus this miniature represents a major new phase in the development that began in the early Trecento of a naturalistic context for supernatural events. An entire world lies beyond the celestial apparition, largely untouched by it; and it is the familiar world of the audience. This area is rendered in a somewhat different mode than the foreground; it is more sketchy, and, at the horizon, bluish like the sky. Indeed some of the forms are painted thinly over the clouds, and in a few instances the blue clouds pass across the buildings and trees.

In all of Europe only the Boucicaut Master envisaged landscapes of similar scope and naturalness. This bold illuminator had taken great strides as early as 1405–1408, in the *Boucicaut Hours* (Fig. 677). It is, however, the miniatures he painted in 1413–1414[322] that resemble most closely the *Annunciation to the Shepherds* in the *Très Riches Heures*, executed at just about the same time (Figs. 60, 507). He cared more than Paul for reflections and shimmering atmosphere, utilizing metallic paint to obtain the desired sparkle. Paul, who was less of a luminary radical, strove for the portrayal of wide, deep space and of the rolling masses of the earth. Similar conceptions may be found again, significantly, only in Italian painting beginning in the 'forties, in the works of Domenico Veneziano, Piero, and Castagno (Fig. 761).

Usually after a miniature was painted a narrow band of color was added at its edges to provide a regular transition to the gold. Though the miniature of the *Annunciation* and its border are complete, Jean left the space for the band empty, and the color of the miniature runs irregularly into it (Fig. 559). Paul added the very narrow band to both his *Visitation* and *Nativity* (Figs. 567, 569), but the latter, while possessing of course an initial, lacks decoration in the border. In the *Annunciation to the Shepherds* Paul was careful about his color at the gold frame; it just comes to the gold and only occasionally runs over. Apparently he decided to abandon the strip of color he had used in the two preceding miniatures. This small change is significant because it is accompanied by a far more important one.

The first two miniatures in the Hours of the Virgin, the *Annunciation* and the *Visitation*, have painted borders as well as initials (Figs. 559, 567), whereas the *Nativity* and the *Annunciation to the Shepherds* have initials only—painted, as usual, by the Breviary Master (Figs. 569, 570). Did Paul plan to add borders later, either himself or with assistance? Did he intend to continue the collaboration of the Breviary Master, who painted part of the border of the *Annunciation*? It has always, so far as we know, been inferred that painted borders were intended but not executed by the time work stopped in 1416.[323] But is this far-reaching assumption really correct?

For one thing, the execution of borders after miniatures would be most unconventional. Such a procedure would be especially improbable in the instance of miniatures so highly developed as the ones we are considering. In the second place the Breviary Master always executed the initials and in one instance part of the border, so that if he had intended to work in the border one might have expected him to do so when he had the folios on his table. Indeed, he *did* paint the borders on the conjoint folios of both the *Nativity* and the *Annunciation to the Shepherds*, as well as almost all the folios of this gathering. He would therefore have had deliberately to skip the two folios bearing the large miniatures. Equally important, we have observed that Paul's conceptions of the miniature were changing as he proceeded. To understand the present state of the folios of the *Nativity* and the *Annunciation to the Shepherds*, therefore, we must see what he decided to do in the next miniature which is surely his, and on subsequent folios in the manuscript.

Paul designed the *Adoration of the Magi* to continue some aspects of the design of his preceding miniatures (Figs. 572, 643). The arch above again serves as a supernatural zone. It provides space for the angels, who are marvelously evoked in gold and pale rose. From a dazzling star in their midst light descends to the Virgin and Child. The hills move away from the figures without most of the obstructions we have hitherto seen. They sweep even farther than in the preceding miniatures to a city that lies along the horizon. The three hills vary unpredictably in value and color, but all their tops are marked by fields of brighter green. On the rising slopes the greatly diminished shepherds vividly measure the distance. In the sky the wispy, irregularly lighted clouds below the supernatural figures, part gilt and part silver, merge with the clouds that float over the city and behind the towers.

In the heavens and on earth Paul demonstrates an unprecedented mastery of light and of perspective. He has applied his newly won principles to a far greater number of figures; we seem to see, indeed, only the vanguard of a vast throng that extends behind the frame. He conceived of Epiphany as a great spectacle, inspired no doubt by mystery plays and by the special affinity felt by contemporary princes such as Jean de Berry for the Eastern kings.[324] To maintain the visibility of many members of the crowd Paul put them on an inclining slope and chose a high point of sight, near the center of the riders and just below the level of their heads. Thus a great many people could not only be depicted but highly individualized with regard both to physiognomy and dress. Most of them, including one negro, wear turbans, and, in accordance with an oriental custom described by John of Hildesheim, the second king pays his respects by kissing the earth.[325] Leopards groom themselves nearby. Paul's reconstruction of a gorgeous Eastern pageant influenced the conception of the event throughout the rest of the century in all of Europe (Fig. 761).

Another aspect of the painter's mastery is his ability to cope with a figure such as the Virgin, who is seen from above and to the right, and who turns at the waist to present the Child to the kneeling king. The three figures compose a complex pyramid, in which the beautiful cascade of her mantle from well defined knees plays an important part. This stuff and other materials show an unprecedented richness of texture. The flesh, too, is soft and full, and differentiated in a new way from the lips and the hair. In these respects Paul discloses his continued relations with his uncle Jean Malouel, whose *Madonna* in Berlin, probably painted about 1412, looks like the work of, shall we say, a close relative (Fig. 642). The *Adoration* is so novel and so advanced that we may without hesitation conclude that it represents a new phase of Paul's art. The miniature must have been painted many months after the three he had already executed in the Hours of the Virgin.

All these new ideas led Paul to make a fundamental change in the illustration of the manuscript. To represent many people in a proportionately large setting he had to reduce their size, and in order to preserve their individuality he needed to avoid minuteness. For this reason, and also to increase the impact of the miniature, he wanted to double its size. No such increase would be possible above the four lines of text he found written by the scribe for the beginning of Sext, as at the beginning of all the Offices in the manuscript. Erasing the text would roughen the surface of the exquisitely prepared parchment. Therefore Paul had no alternative but to remove the original folio and paint his miniature on a new one, which afterward could be set in. This rather drastic approach did not dismay him; on the contrary, for several reasons he seems to have welcomed it.

There is no doubt that the folio of the *Adoration* was not a part of the book as originally planned; it is glued to a stub that bends around other folios to hold it fast. Durrieu observed that it was one of eight folios that he succinctly characterized as "hors texte."[326] Since then this group has been regarded as an addition or "afterthought." Durrieu believed that the model for this group was the Zodiacal Man, because it is painted on half a sheet of parchment (all the other three "faces" are blank) that was folded and inserted into a gathering.[327] This is no doubt a neater and perhaps more durable mode of insertion than was used for the *Adoration of the Magi* and all the other "added" sheets, but we do not believe that most of them, nevertheless, were ever designed to go into the manuscript along with another half-sheet or folio.

Durrieu and subsequent scholars did not correlate the observation about the miniatures "hors texte" with a conception of the manufacture of the *Très Riches Heures*, or with, in short, the story of its production. If these miniatures were not planned for the manuscript why were they included, as they surely were, in the "layette" at the Duke's death?[328] Do their present places in the book reflect only a decision of Jean Colombe in 1485? What was their original purpose?

We might as well begin by referring to a fact that has been completely disregarded. Jacquemart de Hesdin, a colleague of the Limbourgs in the service of Jean de Berry, somewhat earlier showed a predilection for very large miniatures, partly perhaps because he may have practiced also as a painter of panels or even murals. Almost all the miniatures at the beginning of the Offices in the *Grandes Heures*, painted by him and his associates before 1409, were single folios possessing, or attached to, stubs.[329] The Limbourgs, therefore, were thoroughly familiar with the practice we suppose Paul adopted for the *Adoration of the Magi*.[330]

There is evidence to prove beyond any doubt that the folio of the *Adoration* did not belong originally to the book, and that it was made to replace a folio that did.[331] It consists of somewhat heavier vellum and it bears no trace of the ruling in red ink that, on all original folios, measures the outer limits of the two text columns or, at the beginning of an Office, a miniature plus four lines of text, the two patterns being equal. This ruling defines a rectangle with which all the miniatures in the *Très Riches Heures* we have hitherto considered, up to the *Adoration of the Magi*, conform. We distinguish this format as the First Plan. Its dimensions, along with those of all the miniatures, are given in the table in the Catalogue. There too the reader will find the full description of the manuscript and the diagrams of the gatherings that are needed for the discussion that follows.

The verso of the *Adoration* (52v), furthermore, is not blank. On it is written the beginning of the Office of Sext, which continues, properly, on folio 53. The text on 52v, however, was not written in the time of Jean de Berry but in 1485, when the manuscript was being completed by Jean Colombe for the Duke of Savoy. The script is entirely different, and the ink not black but light brown. The text removed by Paul had, in other words, not been rewritten before the first campaign ended in 1416. By making contractions the later scribe included on 52v the four lines of text that were on the original 52, below the space for the miniature.

Unlike other full-page miniatures the outer margin of the new *Adoration* is narrower than the inner. This suggests that Paul first intended to use the sheet as a verso facing the beginning of Sext. The rubric for Sext is at the end of folio 50v, immediately preceding the folio originally intended for the miniature of the *Adoration*.[332] The new miniature therefore fell perfectly into place, but Paul and his colleagues decided, for some of the same reasons that led to the substitution of a new miniature, that this particular Office should be still more splendidly illustrated. Another folio or half-sheet was inserted for a facing miniature, attached likewise to a stub that in this instance is pasted onto a subsequent folio (Fig. 571).[333] Since the subject chosen represented an earlier moment in the story Paul's *Adoration*, probably not yet painted, was shifted from verso to recto. The new miniature, the *Meeting of the Magi*, was likewise given a wider margin on the inner edge to match the *Adoration*.

The *Meeting* was not represented before the end of the fourteenth century. The *Historia trium regum*, written by John of Hildesheim about 1370, tells that the Magi, coming from different Eastern countries, met outside Jerusalem, at a crossroads below Calvary, before proceeding together to Bethlehem.[334]

In the miniature the city behind the crag that refers to Calvary is a "new" Jerusalem, the capital of France. In the distance the Sainte-Chapelle, Notre Dame, and other buildings rise above the rolling hills, and beyond them we see a very steep Montmartre. At just about the same moment the Boucicaut Master, in two marvelous miniatures, painted a view of Paris with the same two ecclesiastical buildings, but the locale was fixed by the text he was illustrating (Fig. 60). The representations are far more accurate and detailed in the *Très Riches Heures*.

Since the city in the *Meeting* is clearly symbolic the kings in the foreground may denote living persons and a recent event. The youngest Magus, wearing an unusual large golden collar decorated with what seem to be fleurs-de-lys, might refer to King Charles VI.[335] The oldest Magus with eastern scimitar, flowing white beard, and imperial crown, might refer to the Emperor Manuel II. When Charles VI rode out toward St. Denis in 1400 to meet him he gave him, as a sign of respect, his white steed.[336] The hat of this Magus with an upturned brim of fur is very similar to the one worn by his son John VIII during his Italian sojourn, as we know from the drawings of Pisanello (Fig. 273). This is precisely the kind of hat Jean de Berry wore in the years after he became a friend of Manuel in Paris (Figs. 404, 405, 539).[337] The Duke must have been pleased to see it on the head of the Emperor Augustus in the *Très Riches Heures* (Fig. 557).[338]

According to tradition the Magi met near a pagan shrine, and the place was later marked by a monument.[339] In the miniature in the *Très Riches Heures* the statues, semi-nude females below and warriors above, are golden, and therefore, according to an almost invariable principle in the *Très Riches Heures*, pagan or at least pre-Christian. The fine Gothic monument is an example of the kind of *montjoie*, as it was called, that rose at intervals along major routes.[340]

Like the Duke of Berry's party in the Itinerary of the *Belles Heures* (Fig. 403), each of the three groups moves onto the scene from the space beyond the frame. Though the monument serves as a symbol of meeting, the parallel movement of the kings does not suggest that they will ever come together. The pageantry, nevertheless, is so splendid—this miniature is famous for it— that no one seems to have recognized the relative weakness of the single forms. Although the illuminator knew very well the style of the *Adoration of the Magi*, and was probably guided by Paul, he was quite unable to attain an equal luminosity, voluminousness, and articulation of the figures. Even the Magus who is a copy of Constantine on the famous medal (Fig. 482) remains comparatively flat and spindly, and the hills behind him are rather dull and shapeless. And one need only compare a detail such as the superb portrait of the camel in the *Adoration*—based on an animal in the Duke's possession[341]—with the uncertain, fudged creatures in the *Meeting* to become fully aware of the difference between Paul and his follower. The style of the miniature seems to be Herman's, but weaker, in fact, than any large miniature by Herman in the *Très Riches Heures.*

We shall return later to some interesting problems presented by this miniature, but we wish now to consider it and the *Adoration* together, since it was clearly planned as a facing miniature. The two are nearly identical in size; the lower margins are exactly the same, the others very similar. The lobes above both miniatures contain the star, with descending rays; but whereas the lobe in the *Meeting* appears where it usually does in earlier miniatures in this and other manuscripts, that is, on center (Figs. 570, 571), the one in the *Adoration* is placed at the left frame. The two lobes thus crown the focal areas of the two miniatures, and they emphasize the normal direction of movement from the miniature on the left to the one on the right.

Neither illuminator, however, seems to have sought a more subtle and pervasive relationship between the two paintings overall, either in their outer shape or in their internal composition. Large, related facing miniatures were not common in Books of Hours or in other manuscripts, although that great originator, Jean Pucelle, set opposite the usual illustration in the Hours of the Virgin a large Passion scene unaccompanied by any text. In the *Hours of Jeanne d'Evreux* the *Crucifixion*, facing the *Adoration of the Magi*, fills almost the entire folio.[342] In the early fifteenth century the Cité des Dames Master, illustrating the *Chevalier errant*, allowed portrayals of tournaments or fairs to run across an opening, to compose two miniatures of nearly equal size (Figs. 18, 56). In the *Belles Heures*, where most miniatures have the same rectangular shape, Paul and Jean strove in openings for a certain unity within variety, especially in color. Thus on 15v Maxentius wears an olive-green mantle over a rose tunic (Fig. 434). On the facing folio 16 Paul, adopting a principle of reverse relationships employed by Italian painters, especially Piero della Francesca,[343] exchanged the king's colors to rose over olive-green (Fig. 436).

The colors in the *Meeting of the Magi* and in the *Adoration* are quite similar—so similar, in fact, that they tend to mask the difference of authorship. The two miniatures differ, however, even with respect to their underpainting: pale gray-green in the *Adoration* and deeper blue-green in the *Meeting*. The attributes of the three principal figures vary. Details of the dress of the second king are different in the two miniatures, and none of the crowns are repeated exactly. The imperial symbol in the hat of the oldest king in the *Meeting* is lacking in the *Adoration*, leaving only a fur hat of the kind favored by Jean de Berry (Fig. 539); and the gold or silver blades in the crowns of the younger kings (echoes of the Roman solar rays) become green in Paul's miniature.[344] Paul made a more significant change in his miniature by removing shoes from the visible feet of the Magi to signify the sacred nature of their obeisance. Interesting is Paul's readiness to accept alongside his superbly painted miniature an inferior work by Herman.

The miniature at the beginning of the next Hour, None, is the famous copy of the fresco of the Presentation of the Virgin in the Temple by Taddeo Gaddi in S. Croce, Florence. Since one at least of the Limbourgs copied another fresco in Florence, as we shall see, he or they probably drew Taddeo's fresco on the spot (Figs. 573, 668). They may, however, have known a drawing of the composition like the one now in the Louvre, which Taddeo made before painting the fresco and which was then changed to conform with his alterations.[345]

The Limbourgs thus chose as a model the most spectacular of all early Trecento paintings. In Taddeo's fresco the youthful Mary ascends a great flight of fifteen steps, the temple looming high above. The priest and his companions as well as people on all sides watch her: there are her parents, of course, some children, the virgins in a loggia, and even a girl in the window of a neighboring house. It was clearly the spectacle in this composition that interested Herman de Limbourg, because he adapted it, not without considerable strain, for quite another subject, which Paul had represented simply but dramatically in the *Belles Heures* (Fig. 637).

The central figure in the miniature remains the girl on the steps, but she is now only a handmaiden carrying the sacrificial doves and a candle for the ceremony of the Virgin's purification and her presentation of the infant Christ in the Temple.[346] The Holy Family appears at the foot of the stairs, Joseph recognizable by his cane and his peaked Hebrew hat, as in the *Nativity* (Fig. 569). A hat with an even longer peak and a tassel, borrowed probably from Altichiero (Fig. 443), is worn by one of the Jews at the right, undoubtedly a priest. In conformity with Jewish tradition men and women are divided—one more instance of the enthusiasm of the Limbourgs for local color and historical reconstruction. Indeed, most of the spectators look up at the priest and none at the Virgin and Christ. They are not yet aware of the special nature of the ceremony which we of course recognize immediately. The concentration of glances on the priest is more complete in the miniature than in the fresco, and his significance is further enhanced by the prominent acolytes and the golden tablets of the Law displayed on the altar. Two statues of prophets characterize the scene still more as an Old Testament ritual of the fulfillment of the Law.

The painter of this miniature is Herman, the author of a series of miniatures illustrating Masses at the end of the book (Figs. 590–594, 596) and, in an earlier and much less skillful phase, of most of the Passion cycle in the *Belles Heures* (Figs. 341, 364, 371, 418, 497, 498). There are in the *Presentation* areas of his favorite deep colors—the blue of the Virgin, the dark green of the trees, and the red of the vaults. The flesh, especially of the men, is ruddy. Herman is more concerned than either Paul or Jean with the solidity of form. At the same time he envisages spatial intervals less clearly than they. The triangular groups of women at the left and men at the right are very tightly packed. Herman on the other hand expanded a scene that was already notable for its scale. He set the building at the left still farther away, and separated it from the temple by introducing a soft spreading tree. Behind the airy temple there is a luminous sky, brightened by matte gold and silver clouds. If in some respects Herman's composition seems more like Altichiero than Taddeo Gaddi, the impression is not incorrect, because, as we shall see, the Limbourgs were also in Padua and studied his frescoes (Fig. 443).

The *Presentation in the Temple*, like the *Adoration of the Magi*, is on a single folio (54v) that is glued into the gathering. Like the *Adoration* also it lacks any text, and the script on its back was written *ca.* 1485, again in light brown so that it would not show through—another sign of the scribe's and the patron's respect for the work of the Limbourgs. The text in this instance is the end of the Office of Sext, concluding with the rubric "ad nonam." The folio, exactly like the *Adoration*, replaces an original one. Whereas in the case of the *Adoration*, however, the scribe of Colombe and of the Duke of Savoy included the four lines of text that were written below the frame of the miniature on the original folio and thus provided a continuous text, None lacks at the beginning on folio 55 (which faces the *Presentation*) approximately what would have been written on the original folio that was removed. As it stands now the text of None begins in the middle of a sentence.

Like the *Meeting* and the *Adoration of the Magi* the *Presentation* is much larger than the miniatures in the first plan. Its projection is rectangular, and like Herman's *Pilate and Barabbas* (?) in the *Belles Heures* (Fig. 498) it accommodates a large building. Though the trimming of the top of some of Colombe's folios (see 75) probably affected the folios of the Limbourgs also, the *Presentation* seems uncomfortably high on the page (see the Table of Measurements). The upper margin, too, is exceptionally narrow, especially in relation to the facing text. It is tempting to connect this stilted position of the miniature with a wish to make the stairs and the temple seem still higher, but corroborating evidence for an adjustment of this kind is lacking.

It is conceivable that this miniature was not made for the Hours of the Virgin but to face the Mass of the Purification of the Virgin, which begins on folio 203.[347] Such a position would support in another way the authorship of Herman because he had the major responsibility for this section of the manuscript. It would account for the greater emphasis in the miniature on the Purification of the Virgin than on the Presentation of Christ. If this were the original position of the painting it would be, however, the only full-width miniature illustrating a Mass without four lines of text below. It is consequently very much larger than the other miniatures in that cycle and it would presumably have been painted somewhat later.

With the *Coronation of the Virgin* at Compline we return to the original design of the manuscript (Fig. 574). There are signs, however, that the miniature was painted a little later than the series of the *Annunciation* through the *Annunciation to the Shepherds* (Figs. 559, 567, 569, 570). Though in most respects the miniature, text, initial and border conform with the first plan, the addition of lobes at the sides—a design favored by Jean—is an innovation. Occasionally an illuminator in the early fifteenth century, such as the Cité des Dames Master, was moved by the nature of his composition to create an unconventional frame, as for *Fortuna* in the *Chevalier errant* (Fig. 49). The trefle of the *Coronation*, which is a rare form for miniatures, permits the inclusion of a greater number of saints who, in conformity with a general trend in the *Très Riches Heures*, are smaller in proportion to the field than corresponding figures in the *Belles Heures* (Fig. 389).

In the *Coronation* Jean painted again a subject he had represented in the Bible (Fig. 287). For the *Très Riches Heures* he created a more formal and less intimate ceremony, in which Christ merely blesses while angels lower the crown. As in paintings of the Coronation by the Boucicaut Master they also hold the splendid, fantastically long mantle of the Virgin.[348] She clasps her hands and bows before Christ as in the Bible.

The *Coronation* in the *Très Riches Heures* is in certain respects a modernized version of Paul's *All Saints* (Fig. 389), and the saint in the lower right corner is a copy of the corresponding figure in the earlier miniature. The celestial symbols of *All Saints*, the golden disks and arcs of seraphim, are now, so to speak, naturalized, because in the *Coronation* all figures repose on clouds. Unlike the clouds in a few earlier Italian representations,[349] however, they are not quite normal, but of gold and silver. There is, indeed, proportionately more golden surface in this scene of celestial splendor than in any other miniature in the manuscript. Above Christ's crowned head golden cherubim hold three additional crowns, alluding, in a most unusual way, to the Trinity.

The *Coronation* has always been singled out for its exceptional beauty.[350] It is, indeed, perfect in its rhythmical pattern, in its long, exquisitely cadenced flow of lines and the echoing curves of the frame. The repeated movements, however, particularly in the wings of the angels, seem a little tame, and the design as a whole is perhaps wanting in accent. It shows us Jean at an excellent moment, somewhat later than the *Annunciation* (Fig. 559).

We have watched the development of Paul's conceptions from the *Visitation* to the *Adoration of the Magi*, in other words through gatherings 7–9, so that a change in the work of Jean from the *Annunciation* in gathering 6 to the *Coronation* in gathering 10 should not prove surprising. Gathering 10 differs, furthermore, from all preceding gatherings in the Hours of the Virgin with respect to its borders and initials. In the gatherings after the calendar, in other words 4 through 8, all the original initials and borders were painted by the Master of the Breviary of Jean sans Peur and a close assistant. Gathering 9, which includes the three inserted miniatures we have just discussed, contains some different script and an unusually compressed text. It was left undecorated (except for line-endings) at the death of Jean de Berry, and Colombe's workshop painted the initials and what borders there are. The intricate problems presented by the text of this gathering will be discussed below and in the Catalogue of Manuscripts.

Gathering 10, including the *Coronation*, was not decorated in the style of the Breviary Master but in a quite distinctive and less attractive manner. This second master or his assistant substituted for the luminous and delicate saffron, rose, rust, and clear blue of the Breviary Master dull dry colors on stocky leaves. Nor did he usually enliven the gold by tooling, and, unlike the Breviary Master, he was not asked to prepare haloes or other surfaces in the main miniatures. His style, which I call that of the Dry Master, appears again in the initials and borders in gatherings 17, 18, 23, and 24—the last two containing the Hours of the Passion. Here the color is clearer and the design bolder than in gathering 10, either because of the painter's greater experience and resolution or because 10 was executed by an assistant. The initials in all these five gatherings recall in design the tradition of Pucelle, and particularly that late example of it, the Duke's own *Grandes Heures*. The youth playing a psaltery below the *Coronation* (Fig. 574) is virtually identical with an initial on folio 13v of the *Grandes Heures*. In style, too, the painting of the Dry Master closely resembles many initials in the Duke's gigantic prayer book; he may indeed have worked on it, though the color lacks the clarity of the *Très Riches Heures*. His leaves in the *Très Riches Heures* curling out from the initials are rather like those beginning on folio 53 in the *Grandes Heures*.

Except for these four gatherings in the latter part of the manuscript and a few unusual folios that we shall discuss presently, all the remaining folios from 49, where the Breviary Master stopped, to 158 were decorated by Colombe. It is therefore striking that the Breviary Master and his assistant should reappear near the end, on folio 153 in gathering 24, in gatherings 25 and 26 or folios 158–173, as well as on folios 182, 182v, 189v, 192–195v, and 198v. We must naturally surmise that this last part of the manuscript was produced not much later than the first.

Before turning to the latter part of the manuscript let us consider the decoration of the exceptional folios that appear soon after the Hours of the Virgin. The first is the initial on folio 72 at the beginning of the Litany, prettily decorated with flowers (Fig. 576). The second is the bifolio 86/89, all four faces of which were decorated by an assistant of the Breviary Master (Fig. 578), although the rest of this gathering 13 (apart from line-endings) was illuminated by Colombe. This bifolio was clearly decorated before the remainder of the gathering because one face (folio 86v) was to contain a miniature. This is one of the bifolios—158/165 is another—that show the decoration complete before the miniature was begun. Then, on folios 86v and 158, the Limbourgs began, as we shall see, the miniature, although they did not finish either one (Figs. 578, 589).

Folio 86v with its miniature, representing a subject we have seen in the *Belles Heures*, the miraculous outcry of Diocrès during his funeral service (Fig. 467), belongs to the first plan of the *Très Riches Heures*. The arabesques in the border, however, are introduced into the *Très Riches Heures* for the first time. This kind of border design, developing since the early years of the century, was employed by the Boucicaut Master *ca.* 1415 in the *Mazarine Hours*,[351] and we may infer that, as in this manuscript, the Limbourgs intended to fill the roundels with related episodes of the story. Colombe, in any event, did just that.

We meet this style again only in the decoration of the latter part of the manuscript. It appears first in the border of folio 158 at the beginning of the *Christmas Mass* (Fig. 589). The violets with their leaves are less skillful versions of those on folio 19v (Fig. 556). Here again the folio follows the first design, and the Limbourgs began but did not complete the miniature. Colombe finished it as well as the initial, and he inserted the figures in the border. The large vines, however, recall those on folio 86v, which we have just considered, and they appear once more near the end of the manuscript, on folio 182 (Fig. 595). They represent a conception of the folio that is quite different from the dominant one in the Hours of the Virgin. Should we infer that Paul was not directing these two parts of the book? We might suspect that the folios were decorated at a relatively early date—a hypothesis that is supported by the character of the miniature on 86v and also in the last part of the manuscript, as we shall see. The roundels defined by the arabesques on folio 86v, unlike those on the other two folios, provide spaces for a story that seems an important complement to the main miniature. On the other hand the Limbourgs did not execute much of the miniatures (and on folio 182 they may not even have designed it). Were the borders then painted late also? Since the miniatures on 86v and 158 contain the only two large interiors in the manuscript that were, as we shall see, planned by the Limbourgs one might be tempted to connect the arabesques with a representation of this kind. It seems possible also that though the Limbourgs commissioned borders of this kind from an assistant of the Breviary Master (Spindly Master) they came to dislike them and failed to proceed with the large paintings they were to contain.

The *Christmas Mass* is followed by seven more masses illustrated in the time of Jean de Berry. These folios all conform with the first design. There are in each instance four lines of text and a miniature which, with the exceptions to be noted, fall within the basic rectangle. These folios together with their conjoint leaves were decorated by the Breviary Master and his assistants. The master himself painted the one superb border and all but two of the initials. The design of most of the folios, which have only an initial, resembles that of the *Nativity* and *Annunciation to the Shepherds* in the Hours of the Virgin (Figs. 569, 570).

Within the centralized upper lobe of the miniature of the Temptation Christ stands on a high peak, looking down on "the kingdoms of the world" with which the devil tries to tempt him (Fig. 590). Before him the painter has depicted the greatest imaginable temptation, the favorite chateau of Jean de Berry, Mehun-sur-Yèvre. Froissart described it as "une des plus belles maisons du monde," and in 1393 Philippe le Hardi sent his painter Jean de Beaumetz and his sculptor Claus Sluter on a famous trip to see what "nouvelles ymages" had been created in the chateau under the direction of André Beauneveu.[352] The impressive portrait of the building, which corresponds very closely with other early records of it,[353] shows even such details as the sculpture at the entrance and on the pinnacles, the arms of the Duke, and of course striking features such as the large chapel near the entrance. The perspective, it is true, leaves something to be desired, because the low point of sight for the chateau varies from the high point for the landscape, even the small part of it in the immediate foreground. Within the landscape the many different elements do not compose the kind of broad, unified design we have seen in Paul's backgrounds, and the author of this miniature—not easy to determine—was probably Herman who, as we shall see, worked in the following gathering. The painter was in any event familiar with Paul's depiction of rolling farmland, as in the *Annunciation to the Shepherds* (Fig. 570).

The painter clothed Christ entirely in gold, for strong contrast with the black devil and also because, high within the upper lobe, he seems to be in heaven. The devil extends to him what may well be a stone, the object which in his first challenge he asked Christ to change into bread.[354] The central temptation represented in the miniature is certainly the third, when the devil, leading Christ to a high mountain, offers him the glories of the world; but the second temptation, too, may have been in the painter's mind because in it the devil leads Christ to the pinnacle of the temple, and the miniature shows Christ remarkably close to the tower of Mehun.[355] For this reason representations of the second temptation, such as Botticelli's in the Sistine Chapel (Fig. 675),[356] resemble the miniature. Botticelli, and before him the Sienese Master of the Pietà[357] as well as other painters, represented all three temptations side by side, and Herman (?) de Limbourg seems to have telescoped them into one image.

In 1414 Jean de Berry gave Mehun to the dauphin, Louis duc de Guyenne,[358] but the miniature presents it quite unmistakably as the Duke's. His arms are quite visible on it and his emblems are nearby, the swans swimming, and the bear sitting in a tree. Perhaps, then, this miniature was painted before 1414; if afterward, the scene may refer to the Duke's renunciation of his most beloved possession. The bear remains calm though he seems to be treed by a lion. Possibly Burgundy, in other words, besieges Berry, as indeed happened at Bourges in 1412; and of course since 1407 Jean de Berry and Jean sans Peur were leaders of the two warring French parties.[359]

The first folio of the gospel for the next Sunday in Lent, the third, is illustrated by the Healing of the Possessed (Fig. 591). The page resembles the *Temptation* in all basic respects. It has a miniature as wide as the text, a fine initial by the Breviary Master, and nothing in the borders. The lack of decoration in the margins is offset by a new decorativeness in the shape of the frame—a development that began, we observed, late in the Hours of the Virgin (Fig. 574). The projection above rises, however, not at the center but over the right part of the miniature, and at the left it has a small diagonal base that runs almost—but deliberately not quite—parallel to the porch of the building. Once again the projection permits a building to attain a larger size.

The miracle, in which Christ restores speech to a dumb youth, is apparently enacted in the porch of the temple.[360] Statues of prophets stand above the roof on capitals which, like the others in this building, shine with heavily gilded knobs and leaves. These capitals are small elements in an array of colors that is far more dense and solid than we have seen elsewhere in the manuscript. The imposing mass of the figures seems due to the weight of the color as well as to the modeling, and in every respect the miniature appears more Italian. The demoniac, a dramatic figure, is well articulated and expressive "de la façon italienne;" the painter rendered with special interest the prominent, exposed leg. It is even an ashen gray, approximating the dark gray of the devil who is just emerging from him. In contrast to the open, expressive posture of the possessed the bodily movements of Christ and the man behind him are muffled in elaborate drapery. Christ looks, in fact, as if he had his arm in a sling.

We have observed this kind of drapery in the Passion cycle in the *Belles Heures* (Figs. 418, 498). It is one aspect of designs that are showy and assertive in both mass and color. These qualities are intensified in the *Très Riches Heures*: the blue arabesque, for example, is much stronger, echoing vigorously in the background the brusque activity of the figures. The blue-violet and white tiles are more declamatory than the pale orange and green ones in the *Flagellation* in the *Belles Heures* (Fig. 371). This kind of changeable color, which was admired by the painter in the *Belles Heures*, reappears in the pale green shaded in purple of the boy in the temple. We recognize once again in the men the pointed, drooping nose, the overhanging brow, the tousled hair and wig-like beards, which create a not quite credible masculine fierceness. The florid faces, conspicuous in the Passion cycle in the *Belles Heures*, are accompanied again in the *Très Riches Heures* by a predilection for red, as in the striking, and spatially confusing, bright orange-red deep in the interior of the temple. Herman has progressed astonishingly under Paul's tutelage, but he remains very much the same old blustering fellow.

He is more difficult to recognize at first in the *Feeding of the Five Thousand* because his miniature is surrounded by the most beautiful border in the manuscript—indeed the greatest work of its kind in the entire early fifteenth century (Fig. 592). It is clearly the masterpiece of the Breviary Master, and we shall discuss it at greater length later. Once we succeed in turning our eyes from it to the miniature we find the familiar swarthy flesh, the sharp profiles and fancy curving headgear of Herman (Fig. 498). Though he has learned very rapidly since his inexperienced efforts in the *Belles Heures*, the figure in blue along the right frame proves that he does not yet know enough about the "lost profile" of a head turned inward (Fig. 592). The serious defects of Christ's left arm tend to be submerged in the fine flow of his violet mantle. Every head in the *Feeding*, even in the distance, claims equal attention, and they all press upon us without any intervals between them. They mount in two very similar triangles, leaving visible between them a dark green meadow entirely without the light that evokes the larkspur in the border. The far edge of the meadow closes the triangle with a remarkably straight line; above it some trees and light gray hills rise before an insistent deep blue patterned ground. In the lobe, on center as in miniatures of the first plan, a radiant God the Father presides over the scene.

The miniature of the miraculous multiplication of the five loaves and two fishes illustrates one of the Lenten Masses. They appear only rarely in Books of Hours, so that the subjects in this cycle, from the Temptation through the Entry into Jerusalem, are uncommon.[361] Among his relics the Duke of Berry possessed a stone that, according to the inventory, Christ "ou desert" changed into bread, although shortly after the inventory of 1401–1403 he mounted it in gold and gave it to

Wenceslas, Emperor of the Holy Roman Empire and King of Bohemia.[362] Whether this miniature and the restoration of speech in the preceding one embody a personal or topical reference is difficult to say, but we should not forget that King Charles VI periodically spent weeks mumbling, unwashed, and in torn clothing.

The miniature that follows the *Feeding*, the *Raising of Lazarus*, contains a large, ruined temple that makes the iconography one of the most interesting in the manuscript, as we shall see (Figs. 593, 647). The composition, like the *Feeding*, is triangular, and it shows the same tightly packed groups of figures. Lazarus, however, now appears at the apex while Christ stands at the side. The miniature shows, too, the deep, sonorous tones characteristic of Herman, more unified now than in his preceding miniatures. The blues, blue-greens and blue-grays reach a kind of culmination in the velvety, deep blue background with its large mauve, blue and gold arabesque.[363] The range of color creates a crepuscular effect. Herman has greatly reduced his favorite warm reds, although the masculine faces and the halo of Christ as well as his hair are tinged with this color. A cool gray-blue renders the surfaces in shade, and as a consequence of this brusque modeling even the small features of the women become slightly coarse. Herman has learned, however, from his collaborators how to produce a smooth enamel and a soft, richly textured surface.

In his miniature Herman has followed the Northern tradition of the Raising in which Lazarus begins to emerge from a horizontal sarcophagus. There are, too, Northern representations in which two men remove the lid to facilitate, in a naturalistic sense, the miracle.[364] Though the miniature in the *Très Riches Heures* thus differs from the Italian and Byzantine *iconography* of the scene, in which an erect, swaddled Lazarus comes forth from a vertical tomb, in *design* it shows a profound resemblance to Giottesque representations of the event. Its geometry, its voluminous figures, sometimes impressively foreshortened, and its gestures bring it within the formal tradition of Giotto and his followers (Fig. 670). Herman has learned even the expressive value of Giotto's extended hand with open fingers turned palm outward to the beholder. His work here resembles Paul's at an earlier date in the *Belles Heures*, when he was most Italianate (Fig. 333). After that time Paul became increasingly concerned with light and space and texture. We observed the development of these interests in his miniatures in the *Très Belles Heures de Notre-Dame* (Figs. 500, 501) and then in his first contributions to the *Très Riches Heures* (Figs. 551, 567, 569, 570). Herman, on the other hand, deepened his dependence on Trecento painting; his first miniatures in the *Très Riches Heures* are the most Italianate in the manuscript. His capacity for growth is surprising and not, we think, predictable from his miniatures in the *Belles Heures*. The *Raising of Lazarus* is perhaps his best painting.

The miniature for Palm Sunday, the *Entry into Jerusalem*, continues the triangulation and the deep colors of the preceding scenes by Herman (Fig. 594). The decorated background is now replaced by an equivalent sky of intense ultramarine filled with golden clouds. Since the borders consist of unpainted parchment the frame again assumes an individual and, as it were, decorative shape, accommodating the large city-gate and the high towers while dropping down closely over the lower ones. Precisely as in the *Temptation of Christ* (Fig. 590), a relatively low point of sight governs the foreground and a high point the distance. Behind the large gate, with its three golden idols,[365] a hill-town stretches along a ridge, extending much further into space than comparable representations in Trecento painting (Fig. 676) or in the miniatures of Jacquemart de Hesdin.[366] Far from observing the recently discovered principles of aerial perspective, Herman painted the most distant roofs the brightest red. Many of the buildings look more Italian than French; indeed there are *campanili* and *torri* in the town.

The citizens of Jerusalem, three of them shown in the perfect profile that Herman liked, come forth to greet Christ, their lips parted as they cry "Hosanna." Among them is a man distinguished as Hebrew by his cap and lappets, and this figure together with the gold idols on the gate may allude to the voluntary surrender of Christ to the religious and secular authorities. A boy lodged in a tree throws down branches, as usual; but unusual are the flowers amidst the leaves. It is probably not accidental that the passage on the Entry in the Duke of Berry's version of the *Meditations* (but not the original text) describes people in the trees throwing "les fleurs et les rameaux de la verdure sur les chemins."[367] The same *Vie de nostre sauveur* interprets the ass on which Christ rides as the Old Testament, and the foal, which is not commonly represented, as the New.[368] The text also develops at this point, as it does in the account of the Annunciation to the Shepherds, the contrast already implicit in the Gospels between the rich and the poor. Unlike Christ, we are told, the "seigneurs" ride on large steeds richly caparisoned. The *Très Riches Heures* offers ample, and to a degree embarrassing, proof of this observation in the *Meeting of the Magi*, *May*, and *August* (Figs. 543, 546, 571). The conspicuously bare tree behind the apostles can only be the fig tree which withered at Christ's command the morning after his entry into Jerusalem. In the fourteenth century and later, travelers wrote of the place of the tree outside the gate through which Christ entered the city.[369]

The miniatures by Herman that we have considered are all in gatherings 25 and 26. Apart from the puzzling *Christmas Mass*, he alone of the brothers worked in these gatherings, and in gathering 29 (27 and 28 contain no miniatures by the Limbourgs) he executed one more miniature. The *Exaltation of the Cross* belongs to the first plan but, as we should expect at this point, it has a more complex, two-stage projection (Fig. 596). The border contains a few leaves, but far fewer than on adjoining folios that contain text without any large miniature, so that the page of the *Exaltation* gives us no reason to doubt that it was the altered conception of the miniature itself that led to the reduction or elimination of the painted border. The quiet symmetry of the design might not suggest the authorship of Herman, but the checkered background and the deep colors, especially the red of the priest's mantle, remind us of his taste. The flesh is, as usual, rather pasty. The fascinating iconography of this miniature, never hitherto explored, will be discussed below.

It was not the Breviary Master himself but an assistant who painted the initial and vine on this folio. The same illuminator executed the initial below the next and last miniature in the manuscript by the Limbourgs, likewise in gathering 29 (Fig. 597). The rest of the border as well as the miniature were painted by Jean, whom we therefore encounter only two folios after the *Exaltation of the Cross*, though on a different sheet of parchment. Rather like the cusps of his *Coronation* (Fig. 574) the frame is surrounded by roundels, one partially invisible. Jean differentiates himself immediately from Herman also by his less insistent plasticity and his quieter range of color. Instead of a patterned background Jean has painted a transparent blue sky. For him Michael is gentle and graceful even in mortal combat, and he cannot imagine a dragon without elegance. The attendant angels watch or pray demurely, with touching sentiment.[370] Mont-Saint-Michel, marvelous as it is, lacks the luminosity that Paul would have given it. We shall return to this representation later.

The miniature falls within the rectangle of the initial design, except for a rectangular projection at the lower right, an innovation in this series of miniatures. The small busts of angels, unique in the manuscript, appear within gold medallions. Silver clouds support and surround these medallions, transforming them into frames through which the angels are visible in part. The clouds provide, thus, a kind of naturalistic setting for a perfectly geometric oculus. The slightly irregular, rhythmically beautiful distribution of the seven angels indicates that they belong to an order of reality more like St. Michael than the voluminous, stable masses of Mont-Saint-Michel. Neither the clouds, the golden rays emanating from them, nor the angels themselves may overlap the miniature or the text or even the initial, but they freely pass behind them. Along the inner border, always the narrowest, and just opposite the main mass of the architecture—where it might prove too distracting—an angel is half overlapped by the miniature. The arrangement is surprising and attractive at first glance. Though it is consistent with the other medallions, the overlapping of as much as half the figure more insistently challenges the spatial logic of the folio. The ambiguity is probably playful, a sort of spatial conceit. Paul would probably have avoided an idea of this kind.

Hitherto only a few scholars have attempted to distinguish the contributions of Paul and his brothers to the *Très Riches Heures*. Durrieu, who enjoyed free access to the manuscript, seems to have remained undecided. After limited periods of study Hulin de Loo and Panofsky grouped a certain number of the miniatures. Hulin's proposals of 1903 are the more comprehensive.[371] He believed that occasionally the brothers collaborated on one miniature,[372] and to one hand he ascribed the buildings in *September*, *October*, *December*, and (here we differ) *St. Michael*. Another painter was responsible for the buildings in *April*, *May*, *August*, and probably (but we differ) *July*. It is interesting that Hulin remained uncertain about *June*. In the lower parts of these compositions and in the other miniatures he identified four (sic!) painters. The first, who he identified as Paul, executed *January* (which we ascribe to him and Jean), the *Meeting of the Magi* and the *Possessed* (both in our opinion Herman's), and the *Presentation in the Temple*, which is probably Herman's also. A second master, according to Hulin, painted the most suave, decorative, and harmonious miniatures in the manuscript, including what was for him the supreme miniature, the *Coronation* (Fig. 574). He was responsible for *April*, *May*, *August*, and perhaps *February*, as well as the *Zodiacal Man*, and the *Fall of the Rebel Angels*. Except for the *Zodiacal Man*, *February* and the *Fall*, this group belongs, we believe, among the works of Jean. The third master, he judged, painted *June* and probably *July* and *March*. The final group consisted of *October* and *December*, which are the most realistic, and possibly *Hell*, *Ego Sum* and *St. Gregory*. Therefore they or the preceding group are probably by the youngest and therefore "most advanced" brother, Herman.

The criteria that Hulin presented for these distinctions in his short paper are rather different from ours, but we agree with many of his observations. Similarly, Panofsky, pointing many years later to the fact that *January*, *April*, *May*, and *August* were painted on two sheets, ascribed them all, as we do, to the same painter.[373] We cannot, however, accept the opinion that he also painted the original of the portrait of Jean sans Peur in the Louvre, which is extremely mannered, flat, and stringy.[374] The degree of conformity in these views is significant because of the extreme difficulty of the problem. No one can hope for a complete and final solution, but historians of art have been offered an important new instrument in recent years, the color photograph, which should enable them to refine to unprecedented levels their stylistic distinctions. Though of course nothing replaces prolonged study of the objects themselves—and in the case of the Limbourg manuscripts I have fortunately been granted this privilege—good color films maintain the memory of the originals far better than black and white photographs, and they permit much more valid comparisons. Without them I would not have been able, I believe, to identify the styles and make the proposals that are presented in this book.

3 · THE PASSION CYCLE

Our discussion of the work of the Limbourgs and their associates in the *Très Riches Heures* has concentrated hitherto on two parts of the manuscript: a first section including the readings from the Gospels and the Hours of the Virgin, and the Masses near the end of the book. Both these parts conform in general with the first design of the folios, and all the initials from the time of Jean de Berry were executed by the Breviary Master and his assistants or, in gathering 10, by the Dry Master or his assistant. They painted what borders there are, except the three executed by the Limbourgs; we recall that we have observed a tendency, led by Paul, to reduce or eliminate them. Apart from the bifolios of the *Great Litany* and *Diocrès* near the Hours of the Virgin, the Breviary Master and his close assistants worked only in these gatherings at the beginning and end of the book.

Since these gatherings are also the only ones that preserve the first design, we may conclude that they were illuminated in the early stages of the enterprise. Jean and Paul started with the large miniatures in the Hours of the Virgin, while Herman painted many of the small ones. Then he turned to the illustration of the Masses. The more individualized frames in this section suggest a moment shortly after the Hours of the Virgin. It is significant, too, that the tooled haloes of the Breviary Master, which sparkle in the first section of the book, were not continued in the Masses, even though the specialist who had produced them was decorating the folios. The haloes in these miniatures, like those of the Boucicaut Master, bear shadows, presumably cast by the heads.

Three groups of miniatures in the *Très Riches Heures* remain to be inserted into our reconstruction of the history of the manuscript: the calendar pictures, the five remaining inserted miniatures, and the illustrations of the Passion. The last tell us most about the making of the book, and we shall therefore turn to them first. The cycle begins, or rather has been believed to begin, with two facing miniatures that represent Ego Sum and Christ led to the praetorium of Pilate (Figs. 582, 583). The first, we shall argue, was painted by Paul, the second by Jean. More important at the moment is the fact that they are utterly unlike in size, tone, and overall shape. We must therefore immediately press the question of their original relationship, which is fundamental for an understanding of the art of the Limbourgs. The two pages that, we concluded above, must have composed an opening—the *Meeting of the Magi* and the *Adoration* (Figs. 571, 572)—resemble each other considerably. After contemplating these two miniatures, and noting also that they tell successive moments of the story, do we not begin to doubt that *Gethsemane* and the *Procession to the Praetorium* were really intended to be set side by side?

Long ago Paul Durrieu observed that the gatherings of the Hours of the Passion are very incomplete.[375] All the text for Matins, Lauds, and Compline is missing, other Hours are fragmentary, and some miniatures seem to be lacking also. Durrieu supposed there probably were two miniatures for each Hour, and that they faced one another. Since, however, we have no rubrics and no text for Matins and Lauds to indicate where *Gethsemane* and the *Procession* were, and since they are single leaves pasted to stubs, we are free to distribute them over these *two* Hours. A rearrangement must take account of the fact that the inner margin was normally narrower than the outer (see table in Catalogue), so that *Gethsemane* was always a verso and the *Procession* a recto unless it was subjected to unusual changes.[376]

Durrieu did not include these two miniatures, or indeed any others in the Hours of the Passion, in his group of eight added or inserted miniatures—"hors texte," as he said.[377] The two miniatures resemble that group, however, in several fundamental respects. They are inserted on stubs, their backs are blank, the vellum is heavier, they lack four lines of text with an initial and marginal decoration, and they are therefore much larger than the miniatures in the original plan. The first two miniatures, indeed, exceed even the original rectangle for both text and miniature, the *Procession* more than *Gethsemane*. This basic rectangle, moreover, is not ruled on either of the folios; they lack ruling of any kind. The two miniatures clearly belong, therefore, to the revised plan of the manuscript that we encountered in the *Meeting* and the *Adoration*. This is true of all the existing miniatures in the Hours of the Passion. Not all of them, however, possess all of the characteristics of the first two miniatures, and the differences may tell us more about the making of the book.

The next surviving miniature, the *Flagellation* (fol. 144), appears at the beginning of gathering 23, although like other miniatures of the Passion it is pasted onto a stub (fol. 149) and in fact in this entire cycle the normal concept of a gathering must be qualified because of the independence of many sheets (Fig. 584). We can, however, be certain that the *Flagellation* was intended for the place it now occupies because the text of Prime begins on its back, and this text was written and illuminated in the time of Jean de Berry. Thus we encounter our first fixed miniature, but it raises many important questions. Although the folio, first of all, was ruled in the original manner to provide the basic rectangle and the widths of two short columns of text that were presumably to go, in the usual way, below the miniature, the *Flagellation* occupies and indeed slightly exceeds all of the rectangle, while the four lines of text beginning the Office were shifted to the verso.

This is the first instance we have encountered of a shift of this kind completed in the time of Jean de Berry. In the Hours of the Virgin the text displaced by the miniatures of the "second plan," the *Adoration of the Magi* and the *Presentation in the Temple*, was either written in the time of Colombe or is still lacking. The character of the script of Prime on the verso of the *Flagellation* indicates, however, that the text was written before Paul painted the miniature. Whether we are confronted here with the same scribe (or scribes?) who wrote the original text of the entire manuscript we cannot say. We are unable to choose with confidence, either here or elsewhere, between the style of one scribe at a somewhat later moment or of an associate writing in a very similar manner. That the text here and in other parts of the book was indeed rewritten or redesigned because Paul and his brothers wanted to introduce a new plan is clear from numerous signs. Because these signs are varied and the evidence intricate the details of our observations on the text are presented separately, in the Catalogue. We must, however, mention here an important confirmation of our inference of a relatively late date for the Passion cycle. The initials and borders are all in the style of the Dry Master, who supplanted the Breviary Master late in the execution of the Hours of the Virgin (Fig. 574). Thus the character of the decoration and of the script of the *Très Riches Heures* frequently confirms the estimates of its history we have drawn from the evidence of the miniatures. In no instance is there a contradiction.

All four following miniatures by the Limbourgs in the Passion cycle resemble the *Flagellation*. They belong to the second plan but were ruled in the usual way. The versos of three of them (*Way to Calvary*, 147; *Death of Christ*, 153; *Deposition*, 156v) bear text of the period, and the reverse of a fourth (*Christ leaving the Praetorium*, 146v) has an early rubric "ad terciam" (Figs. 585–588). All the evidence points to the fact that Paul's *Flagellation* and indeed all the miniatures in the Hours of the Passion are later than those in the Hours of the Virgin except for the two that were inserted afterwards, the *Meeting* and the *Adoration* (Figs. 571, 572). The frames alone show new and largely unprecedented forms; we shall see more of them shortly. The text folios in these gatherings, we recall, were illuminated by the Dry Master apparently after the departure of the Breviary Master, who probably left for another important task. This might well have been the Breviary of Jean sans Peur (Figs. 610, 611, 618–622, 648).

The next two miniatures in the Hours of the Passion are especially interesting because, like the *Flagellation*, their position is established. The rubric of Terce appears on the back of *Christ leaving* (Fig. 585) and the beginning of the Office is on the back of the *Way to Calvary* (Fig. 586). We thus have a definite example of miniatures designed to face one another. They are of exactly the same height and nearly identical width. Their dimensions approximate very closely those of the inserted miniatures in the Hours of the Virgin, the *Meeting* and the *Adoration of the Magi* (Figs. 571, 572). Here, however, the miniatures were designed, we believe, by the same painter, Paul. He himself, furthermore, painted all of the miniature on the right and most of the one on the left. The latter is a superb miniature, clear in its narrative and bold in spatial design. The rich observations include even the flexing of the big toe of Christ over the edge of the step. Three or four spectators in the foreground, however, are flatter, more linear, and more attenuated than any member of the throng in the *Way to Calvary*. These qualities, together with the profusion of ornament, indicate the participation of Jean. Even his cobbles are flatter and less lapidary than Paul's.

Partly perhaps because these two scenes, unlike the pair in the Hours of the Virgin, involve no supernatural symbols, they have no projections at the top. Projections do occur, however, in more unconventional fashion at the sides. Their place and design are clearly related to the processional character of both compositions. In the miniature at the left Paul introduced lateral lobes at the level of Christ's head, concentrating our attention upon him and to a degree upon the beautiful nude thief coming out of the praetorium. At the same time the lobes increase the number of visible heads and they greatly strengthen the impression of a crowd and of a space existing beyond and behind the frames. The effect of movement downward from the building to the street is enhanced by the subtle refinement of expanding the space between the lateral frames below the lobes.

In the other miniature Paul is both simpler and bolder. The long descending line of the heads creates a powerful lateral movement, and this is increased by the projecting rectangle at the right. In this *Way to Calvary*, unlike the *Adoration of the Magi*, he did not simply focus his composition near the inner frame, so as to lead the eye back toward the middle of the book and the facing miniature. The *Way to Calvary* is both more complex and more dynamic. In various ways Paul countered the flow of the procession. The large arch establishes a strong anchor at the left. A long vertical spear blocks the movement along the frame at the right, and, more important, Christ looks back towards his mother. He turns his sorrowing countenance to her more fully than in the miniatures of this subject in the Bible and the *Belles Heures* (Figs. 293, 341). Indeed, in depth of feeling Paul's miniature comes closer to Simone Martini's *Way to Calvary* than any other French painting inspired by it.[378] Nevertheless, Paul's Virgin Mary does not quite equal the passion of his Sienese model. Paul is also less sure, even after his long study of Italian painting, of the movement of the body and the placement of feet. His great strength lies elsewhere, in his light, texture and clear color, and in his ability, related to Giusto's and Altichiero's but matched only by the later Venetians, to depict collective action and splendid spectacles.

The isolation of Christ's head from the soldiers around it makes his glance a major theme of the design, almost equal in compositional significance to the opposing surge of the crowd. The silver mace of the soldier in the foreground bridges the space between him and the Virgin and St. John. The lower bar of the cross moves backward in the same general direction while the upper bar points straight at the angle in the frame. The cross thus becomes part of a larger geometric design, and the shape of the frame in turn is an essential part of the composition. This reciprocity is common to Gothic and Renaissance painting. What distinguishes the frames of Paul and his brothers is their multiformity, their assumption of unique shapes as they are evolved in relation to the composition. They are, so to speak, custom-made.

The text of Terce, like that of Prime, is complete, beginning on the back of the *Way to Calvary* (147) and ending on 149v. The new gathering (24) that follows immediately with folio 150 contains the beginning of Sext. This is the only text for an Hour in the Office of the Passion that begins on a recto. If, in conformity with other Hours, two facing miniatures (none survive) were planned at this point, the blank verso of the second would have been opposite the beginning of the text—an exceptional and rather unattractive arrangement. Perhaps, however, the two were not intended to face, as occasionally in the Hours of the Passion in the *Belles Heures*.

The Hour of None requires no such speculation, because the facing miniatures that precede it, like those for Terce, appear between the rubric and the beginning of the Office on the back of the second miniature (Fig. 587). Colombe painted the first of the pair as a complement to the *Crucifixion* by Jean, representing a similar subject and adding his version of a Limbourg arabesque, based upon the partly original one on folio 158, although in this later part of the manuscript his predecessors had abandoned such decoration around their miniatures. It is true, however, that Jean did employ a multi-lobed frame. The three detached medallions close to it seem, like satellites, to have broken away from it. When introducing these roundels Jean returned to a form he had used earlier in *St. Michael* (Fig. 597). He permitted a return also to acanthus leaves, which curl out from the gold frame of his miniature—a unique kind of embellishment in the late work of the Limbourgs. This seems not only a regression but an inappropriate occasion for it; the bright, lively little leaves are petty around the nocturne of the death of Christ. The presence of the decoration must be ascribed to Jean—and it is consistent with his taste—even though he did not himself execute it. The folio was prepared for him by one of the last of the assistants of the Breviary Master who worked on the *Très Riches Heures*—the Spindly Master, who painted the very pretty initials of five folios of the text of the calendar and eleven elsewhere.

In his miniature Jean follows, but far surpasses, the night scene painted by Herman for the same moment in the *Belles Heures* (Fig. 497). Though he eliminated the beam of light, a pale orange sun and a silver moon hang in the sky. Envisaging more vividly the effect of sudden darkness, Jean introduced youths who, with extended arms, cautiously grope their way. The dim light reduces all forms to tones of gray tinged with red or with blue. The whole is more monochromatic than Paul's *Ego Sum*, which Jean probably had studied (Fig. 582). The gray ground and blue-gray sky are less distinct from the figures. The curvatures of Jean's frame echo the fluent pattern of his composition.

The throng, far larger than in the *Crucifixion* in the *Belles Heures*, is not struck with terror. Most men stand quietly, contemplating the death, and those who raise their arms may respond to the brilliant radiance above the cross. There God the Father with uplifted hand affirms the universal significance of the event. He appears similarly, though less impressively, over the crucified Christ in the altarpiece for Champmol by Henri Bellechose, finished in 1416 (Fig. 608)—another indication of the continued relationship of the Limbourgs with Burgundian painting.

In the most beautiful version of a theme developed by Sienese Trecento painters, especially by Simone Martini, Jean's Virgin has fallen limply but gracefully into the lap of one of the Marys. Another woman holds her from behind and John approaches protectively. In the foreground there are piles of the rocks that, according to the Gospel, were rent at this moment—less vividly cleft, to be sure, than in Herman's representation (Fig. 497). The dead rise in the lowest medallion, the veil of the temple is rent at the right, and the astronomer above observes the disturbance of the stars.

The other nocturne in the Passion cycle, the first of the extant miniatures, is a revelation (Fig. 582). It depicts an event described only by St. John, and seldom represented.[379] When Judas and the soldiers approached their victim in the garden Christ asked them whom they sought. To their reply "Jesus of Nazareth" Christ said "I am he." They then "went backward, and fell to the ground." Whereas earlier representations of this moment usually showed the band falling, or, if fallen, looking at Christ, in the *Très Riches Heures* the action is completed. The soldiers have obviously collapsed suddenly, some of them falling head-foremost into positions Paul already favored, we have seen, in the *Belles Heures* (Figs. 452, 641). Their bodies compose a carefully studied, rhythmically fascinating tangle. They lie still, seemingly unconscious; the eyes of only one soldier are open and stare blindly. Near us a fallen lantern and torch throw a little light into the gloom.

The lantern sends a golden beam across a soldier's skirt. Near the torch a soldier's armor reflects pale yellow light but, close to the flame, it becomes reddish—a beautiful refinement worthy of Jan van Eyck. Only one face in the scene is clearly visible, pointedly lighted by a torch. This bearded man has fallen pell-mell away from Christ. He lacks both armor and a weapon, so that he can be none other than the traitor, Judas.

Out of this ordered confusion rise the bowed figure of St. Peter and, at the center, quite erect, Christ. Peter, similar in his pale tone to the fallen soldiers, wears a dim silver halo. The mantle of Christ is deep brown. With eyes lowered, he stands still, as quiet as the night. His right hand rests on his side, where the wound will come. The disk and rays of his halo gleam in the darkness with unheard-of brilliance. His head and shoulders, rising above the rim of the hill, appear before the sky. The twinkling stars seem distant signs of his mysterious radiance.[380] Like the rays of the halo, a few of them shoot through the space.

The miraculous event occurs quite clearly, however, in the world. A hill separates Christ from heaven. Along it runs a secondary barrier, a fence; two tall, motionless trees rise from the further slope. The hill interposes a broad, sweeping, asymmetrical form between the jumble below and the sky sparkling with minute lights. Only Paul could have imagined a painting of this kind, combining unrivaled subtlety in the analysis of light with a strong design in the picture plane and in space. It is difficult to know what to admire most in this superb and historic painting, the astonishing mastery of tone or the unforgettable poetic mood.

Vespers, like Terce and None, has two facing miniatures between the rubric on folio 156 and the beginning of the text (the only extant part) on folio 157v. Again the Limbourgs executed only one of the two, the *Deposition* (Fig. 588). Colombe painted the facing *Entombment*, and he duplicated the lobed rectangle of Jean's *Deposition*—a surprisingly simple shape at this late moment. Colombe even imitated the refinement of placing the lobe somewhat nearer the inner margin, but he was unable to resist the temptation to enlarge the size of the miniature.

Among the three brothers Jean delighted most in rendering the patterns and textures of rich materials. He gave Mary Magdalen not only a superb flowered tunic and a mantle bordered with filigree but hair gleaming with gold. His gorgeous raiment owes much to Simone Martini (Fig. 494). In the work of the same painter he found examples of bright, clear color, of exquisite modeling and refined linearity. Simone's *Deposition* may even have taught him to give Christ's arm a certain pathetic limpness. Comparison with Simone's passionate composition once again reveals Jean's relative coolness.

Of course Jean emerged from a pictorial tradition much later than Simone. At the tops of the ladders both Joseph of Arimathea and his companion hold fast with one arm while lowering the body of Christ. Such elements of the composition as the high hill and the averted Magdalen embracing the cross had already appeared in the *Bible moralisée* by a Neapolitan painter that was then in France in the collection of the Anjou (Fig. 652).[381] For one conspicuous figure with a gesture that was novel in French painting he used a specific Italian model. The Virgin Mary who, with clasped hands, looks up at her son is a copy of the Virgin in—significantly, a great panoramic scene—the *Crucifixion* by Andrea da Firenze in the Spanish Chapel (Fig. 649).[382]

Jean must have painted the *Deposition* soon after he completed the *Crucifixion* (Fig. 587). Despite their great difference of tone the two miniatures are closely related stylistically; they share the curling line of a hill at the horizon and such exceptional iconography as one averted thief, tied to the more distant face of his cross.

Both the text and the miniatures of Compline are entirely missing. We may suppose that, like the other Hours, the Office was intended to begin with two facing miniatures. In the *Belles Heures* it is illustrated by the Entombment and the soldiers sleeping at the tomb (Fig. 343). In the *Très Riches Heures* Colombe added the Entombment to None, but we do not know that this subject had been chosen by the Limbourgs; they may, indeed, have intended to paint the Lamentation at this point, as they had in the *Belles Heures* (Fig. 455). The Hours of the Passion in the earlier manuscript cannot, however, be considered an exact model for the *Très Riches Heures*, because there the Flagellation appears at Lauds instead of Prime, and the first miniature at Terce represents Pilate washing his hands rather than Christ leaving the praetorium.

Although the subjects of the cycle of the Passion in the *Très Riches Heures* do not consistently conform with those in the *Belles Heures*, as our table in the Catalogue clearly shows, the number of miniatures for each Hour seems again normally to have been two, as Durrieu proposed. In the *Belles Heures*, however, Matins as the first Office has three miniatures, and this fact may explain a miniature in the *Très Riches Heures* that is unique in Books of Hours. It is a beautiful and famous map of Rome within two golden circles that extend almost the full width of the folio (Fig. 580). The space between the circles looks unfinished, and surely the small circles at the four points of the compass—north in this kind of map is below—were intended to be filled, possibly with personifications of winds. The bare parchment shows likewise where two ancient statues were to be represented, the Dioscurides and the equestrian Marcus Aurelius.

The Panorama of Rome is another of the miniatures that has a blank back and is painted on a single sheet held by a stub. But why does a miniature of this subject appear in the manuscript at all? Durrieu suggested that it reflects the widespread wish, shared by the Duke of Berry, that the papacy be re-established in Rome.[383] Whether or not this hypothesis is right, it does not account for the specific place of the map within the manuscript. That place is after the short weekday Offices and immediately before the illustrations of Matins of the Hours of the Passion. In accordance with the normal relationship between miniatures and text it should therefore be connected with the Hours of the Passion. Was it not one of three miniatures that, as in the *Belles Heures*, preceded Matins? *Ego Sum* (Fig. 582), as we have observed, was surely intended for the verso of an opening that would have shown, at the right, a miniature that might have represented the Betrayal and Peter cutting off the ear of Malchus.[384] If *Rome* belongs to Matins, as its present place indicates, it would have initiated the illustrations on a verso and they would have continued, as they do now, on the following verso. Though the intervening blank folio (the back of *Ego Sum*) does not constitute an altogether attractive arrangement, the small size of the buildings differentiates the map so basically from historical episodes that the Limbourgs would quite understandably have wanted to avoid a juxtaposition.

The reason for the appearance of a map of Rome at the very beginning of the Hours of the Passion may probably be discovered, we believe, in the fact that it includes approximately forty-three buildings which can be identified as churches (Fig. 580). This was the number of Station

Churches, in which, one after the other, the Pope celebrated Mass during Lent and on certain designated feasts. Of the five greater basilicas which it was necessary to visit to gain the Jubilee indulgence only S. Lorenzo, outside the walls of the city and therefore marginal, is missing. It is true that the Papal Masses could not be said in the Station Churches at Avignon, but there was no break in the tradition of granting important indulgences for visits to the churches on the specified days.[385] The map in the *Très Riches Heures* is so important as one of the early representations of the chief buildings and monuments of the Holy City that we shall discuss it at greater length below.

Before turning to the calendar, the only cycle of miniatures by the Limbourgs not yet discussed, it seems best to consider the remaining three miniatures that lack all text and that were inserted—or planned to be inserted—in the manuscript by a stub. All three are unruled. One appears on folio 64v at the end of Compline, a few folios past the *Coronation of the Virgin* (Fig. 574), which it far surpasses in size (Fig. 577). It now immediately precedes, and very probably was intended to illustrate, the Penitential Psalms; it represents the first great sin, the revolt and fall of the angels.[386] The subject had not previously been chosen to illustrate these prayers, and indeed it had not, to our knowledge, appeared earlier at any place in Books of Hours. Perhaps the small miniature at the beginning of the Psalms on the next folio (65) was the only illustration originally planned.[387]

Though the revolt and the fall did not appear in earlier Books of Hours it was of course represented in Bibles, in Apocalypses, where the event is described, and occasionally in other contexts. An impressive miniature in a *Bible historiale* purchased in 1415 by Jean sans Peur shows the Trinity commanding the Fall (Fig. 664).[388] Three angels remain seated while two tumble, and one of them undergoes before our eyes a metamorphosis into a devil, like Daphne into a tree (Fig. 108). Within the maw of Hell one figure is part angel, part devil, while the transformation of the others is complete.[389] The illuminator who copied this miniature soon afterwards rejected, probably as unnecessary or complicated, the idea of metamorphosis (Fig. 663), but it appeared earlier as an illustration of the fate of the proud in a manuscript given to the Duke of Berry in 1410 and so presumably known to the Limbourgs (Fig. 671).[390] The more common tradition of representing two distinct groups, perfect angels and no less perfect devils, is exemplified by a miniature of about 1410 at the beginning of a *Cité de Dieu* (Fig. 665). Even here, however, the hands of the two uppermost fallen angels have become devilish. The scene, painted by the Orosius Master, is divided into two compartments that parallel the Heavenly and the Earthly City, the one showing buildings with large glass windows and Gothic spires, the other designated as pagan by its onion domes and heavy masonry. God, again active, raises his right hand and holds a staff in his left, of the kind that the angels, too, employ to drive the devils down.

In the *Très Riches Heures* these staffs become a long lance with which an armored angel jabs at one of the rebels. Christ holds no weapon; on the contrary he sits impassively above the fray, his powerful transcendence symbolized by the white globe in his hand, the redness of his flesh, hair, and mandorla, and the golden rays that emanate on all sides from him. The red light warms the golden armor of his warrior angels, who stand below on a deep platform of clouds. The angels tumble from the great ellipse of thrones around him, undergoing a special kind of transformation as they fall. All the seated angels, the good and loyal ones, wear green or green and white wings, like the archangels. The rebellious angels have all lost the green; their wings are gold and white—probably a sign of their pretensions and their pride. Until they reach the clouds the falling angels retain the blue tunics lighted with gold common to all of them. Below the clouds—that is, in the more transparent atmosphere of the world—they lose the gold, their tunics now displaying only various beautiful shades of blue.[391]

Further than this the transformation does not go. The angels, unlike those in many of the representations we have seen, remain human beings.[392] Among contemporary painters only the like-minded Boucicaut Master, equally sympathetic to Italian art, also avoided devils almost entirely in his representation of the angels plunging into the mouth of a bestial Hell.[393] In the *Très Riches Heures* Satan himself, with his golden crown, is a very comely, though to be sure inverted, prince. Apparently Paul de Limbourg, rather like Giotto himself, believed evil could be most vividly and significantly conveyed by the portrayal of human beings who have lost control of themselves. In this respect Paul's painting differs also from those representations which, like his, show the devils plunging into the orb of the earth rather than into the mouth of a monster. In a painting of 1379 by Meister Bertram Lucifer and three of his fellows fall toward a floating globe (Fig. 651),[394] while in the extraordinary Sienese painting of about 1340 that has recently come to light the globe is partially visible above the lower frame (Fig. 666). Only in the *Très Riches Heures*, however, does Satan alone crash into the world, and only there do two companions sink into a silver sea at the sides.[395]

We have already seen that Paul adopted the thrones of the choir of angels in the Sienese *Fall* for the Elders in his miniature of St. John, although he tilted the orthogonals upward to reduce the impact of the recession, which is indeed unparalleled in Sienese Trecento painting itself (Figs. 551, 666). Paul borrowed the archangels for the *Fall* (Fig. 577), though he once again lowered the headgear deeply over the eyes in the curious manner visible already in his earlier miniatures in the *Bible moralisée* and the *Belles Heures* (Figs. 286, 463). Jean, in turn, profited from a study of the flying angels in the panel when he painted the battle in the air over *Mont-Saint-Michel* (Fig. 597).

The Sienese painting measures vividly the greatness of the miniature because it is an extraordinary work itself. Paul has given his composition both far greater scale and greater clarity and impact. By various means he has united all the zones. Whereas his model presented, in the usual medieval fashion, a neat opposition between the good angels and the empty stalls of the bad, Paul carried the excitement and confusion of the lower area into heaven by emptying his thrones—all three tiers of them—unpredictably.[396] Furthermore, he arranged the falling angels in an all-encompassing, inverted triangle that begins in the highest of the three rows of thrones and has its apex in the head of Satan. There, in the world near the entrance to Hell, Paul has located his point of sight. All the figures from Satan upward, though increasingly *good* angels, are regularly diminished by the perspective. Only God remains comparatively free of the inflexible application of the law of vision, but even he, in this very worldly representation, does not loom as large as his greatest enemy. Of course Paul's geometry and perspective have diminished the effect of scattered fall so prominent in his Sienese model, but he has compensated for this loss by a marvelous agitation *within* his two streams. The angels have tumbled into endlessly varied positions. They are often boldly foreshortened, and here, as well as in the imposing unity of the design and the superb luminosity, even of the tiny silver helmets shaded in transparent blue, we recognize clear signs of Paul's mastery.

Another miniature painted on a single unruled sheet and representing *Hell* resembles in design and content the *Fall of the Angels* (Fig. 581). It is inserted at a puzzling place (fol. 108), after the end of the Office of the Dead and before Colombe's full-page miniature of the Baptism at the beginning of the Office of the Trinity.[397] The subject, uncommon in French Books of Hours, was introduced regularly at the beginning of the Penitential Psalms by the North Italian illuminator, the Master of the Brussels Initials, who worked for the Duke of Berry and in France towards the end of the fourteenth century and in the first years of the fifteenth.[398]

The composition of *Hell* in the *Très Riches Heures* reverses in many respects the *Fall of the Angels*. As Longnon and Cazelles have observed, "In the latter we see heaven, the kingdom of the Lord, here we see hell, the realm of Satan; there blue and glittering gold predominate, here grayish black and flaming red stand out; there the rebel angels are hurled by God from the heights of heaven, here the damned are spewed up from the bowels of the earth by Leviathan's burning breath."[399] The unusual stream of the damned, which extends into the lobe at the top, reflects the most widely diffused of several visions of hell, written by a thirteenth-century Irish monk named Tundal.[400] Satan, according to Tundal, lies on an iron grate above burning coals. His powerful breath spews forth bodies of the damned. This terrifying sight had been witnessed by a friend of Jean de Berry, Ramon Viscount of Perelhos, of Roussillon. In 1397 he had gone to Ireland to see the mouth of hell, which was famous as the Purgatory of St. Patrick. He saw a sight similar to the one described by Tundal. ". . . una flama nera e pudert, ayssi coma de solpre. Aquela flama montava, a mon semblan, que me semblava que y avia homes e femnas de diversses statz tatz ardens, que volavan en l'ayre ayssi coma las belugas del fuoc. . . ."[401]

No painter before the *Très Riches Heures* had ever depicted such a wild exhalation of fire, sparks, smoke, and human beings, though the damned were rather similarly tossed about by Giotto in the descending river of fire in his *Last Judgment*, which the Limbourgs, who were certainly in Padua, knew (Fig. 453). The higher the bodies in the *Très Riches Heures* the smaller they appear, and indeed as in the *Fall of the Angels* the point of sight for the entire composition is low.

Just as in the *Fall* the banished angels remain human, so in *Hell* the damned suffer decorously. The devils, to be sure, though largely anthropomorphic, are relatively huge and menacing. Two of them work enormous bellows, the mechanics of which, in true Limbourg fashion, are described carefully. A large stone placed on each bellows facilitates its compression.[402] The conflagration, too, is awesome, and even the dark mountains assume ominous, flame-like shapes. They appear, however, before a clear blue sky, which delimits the terror.[403] The flames, furthermore, and even the devils are rendered in gold, a color normally associated with divinity. *Hell* has become, in fact, peculiarly ornamental. Despite the flames the miniature is less luminous than the *Fall*, and it is certainly flatter and more linear. It resembles less, therefore, the robust compositions by Paul than a later work of the painter of the elegant *Coronation*, in other words, Jean.

That the exquisite designs of miniatures such as the *Coronation* and *Hell* could be still further refined—a proposition that would seem highly dubious—is proved by the miniature of the Temptation of Adam and the Expulsion from the Garden on folio 25v (Fig. 558). This is the last of the inserted single folios to be considered. Though the miniature is so wide that it extends to both lateral margins, the forms and the movement come closer to the right margin. It was therefore clearly designed as a verso, and undoubtedly to face the *Annunciation*, where it now is (Fig. 559).

It clearly differs, however, from the *Annunciation* and the other miniatures in this and nearby gatherings. The modeling of the Limbourgs, always subtler than that of any other tempera painter except Simone Martini, is here carried to breath-taking delicacy. Almost imperceptible variations of value produce sure and effective undulations of plane. Eve, similar to but more sensuous than Paul's nude St. Catherine in the *Belles Heures* (Fig. 439), has such supple limbs that they seem all flesh and no bone.

This miniature, long greatly admired, presents the last phase of one of the Limbourg styles. The paintings closest to it are Jean's miniatures in the calendar, especially *April* (Fig. 542) and *May* (Fig. 543). The figures in *April* are woven into a similar, though not equally beautiful pattern, likewise disclosed against a steeply inclined ground plane. The design of both the miniatures presupposes three or more points of sight, which were determined primarily by the requirements of the linear and rhythmical design. Jean chose a relatively low point of sight for the gate in *Paradise* so that the descending orthogonals would join, so to speak, in the departure of Adam and Eve. The perspective of the upper part of the fountain tends to conform with the gate, whereas the base approximates the inclined plane of the garden. These differences, more conspicuous than usual even in the work of Jean, are probably related to other deliberately fictional qualities of the representation.

Large figures and a golden baldachin that resembles a huge reliquary[404] appear in a diminutive landscape. The lush garden, sprinkled with flowers and enclosed by a golden wall, is surrounded by an even smaller ring of mountains, unprecedented as far as we know in representations of Paradise. The contrast between these bleak brown or gray hills and the perfect world of the garden, finished down to the last leaf and flower, is extraordinary and telling. The somewhat enigmatic forms in cool blue outside the hills, probably representing the seas, maintain the difference. Ever more sketchily rendered, they move out over the parchment, which serves once again as a symbol of space. The miniature thus invades the entire folio.

Perhaps unconsciously the illuminator gave to the circular garden joined to the gate a shape quite like that of a Gothic capital letter, such as appears, in reverse, on the facing folio. In earlier manuscripts forms and figures occasionally move out from or into the initials to create a sort of overflow from the main composition (Fig. 672), but the flight of Adam and Eve is unusual and bold. Looking back wistfully to the perfect security of the closed garden, they step reluctantly into the rugged unframed space, like astronauts walking into the void. The round garden of course resembles in plan the miniature of Rome (Fig. 580), and it is interesting that at just about the same time as the painting of Paradise in the *Très Riches Heures* the Boucicaut workshop enclosed the Garden of Eden within a circular fence.[405] Since this workshop was established in Paris we recognize one of the many relationships between the *Très Riches Heures* and the painting of the illuminators active in the capital. A few years earlier the Boucicaut workshop had designed a hexagonal garden, enclosed by a high and very substantial wall that enhances the meaning of the rather violent expulsion.[406]

In the *Très Riches Heures* God comes into the garden, addressing primarily Eve, to whom Adam points. He begins, as the Bible states, by saying "I will multiply thy sorrow," and then counts out the other dire consequences on his golden fingers—a literal gesture that seems to reduce the import of his commands. He is, however, a powerful figure, based no doubt upon models by Paul, and rays dart toward Eve from his golden face. In an exceptional action she hides behind her back the hand that received and gave the apple to Adam. With her left hand she, like her partner, covers her genitals, not yet concealed by the leaves described in the Bible. Though Adam normally witnesses Eve's capitulation to the serpent, here his back is turned to the scene.

The serpent is made more seductive by bearing not only the head but part of the body of a woman, and indeed with her beautiful streaming hair, touched with gold, she seems an alter ego of Eve herself. Jean has introduced other significant subtleties, such as eliminating from the hair of Eve once she is expelled from the garden the gold that glistens brightly in it while she is within its walls.[407] Outside the gate she and Adam wear large, beautifully rendered fig leaves. The gold of the gate through which the figures go is laid over gray and therefore slightly darker than the gold of the fountain, which Jean painted over white. A more striking and far more familiar novelty of this miniature is the elaborate posture of Adam, based, we believe, upon an antique model. This we shall discuss later.

4 · THE CALENDAR PICTURES AND THEIR BORDERS

For a long time the twelve pictures for the calendar of the *Très Riches Heures* have been regarded as the greatest pictorial accomplishment of the early fifteenth century (Figs. 539–549, 562). As such they have stimulated many penetrating accounts, but important problems remain unsolved and some intriguing questions have not been asked. The picture for each month, always painted on a verso, faces the text on the recto. Pictures and text (except December) are contained in two gatherings, the first a normal one of eight folios from January through August, the second a small gathering of four folios from September through December.[408] These physical facts are not without real interest because, if the attributions we shall propose are correct, the same painter always proves to have executed both the miniatures that were to appear on the two halves, or folios, of one sheet. The Limbourgs completed all but one miniature (*March*) in the first gathering. In the second gathering they painted only the upper part of *September* and presumably little or nothing for *November* (except the astronomical lobe) because on ordinary inspection no traces of their work can be seen below the miniature executed by Colombe (Fig. 562).[409] Like the make-up of the gatherings the pattern of incompleteness will prove to be informative. The astronomical data in the arches, furthermore, is entered in all the months but four. These four are halves of two folded sheets (*January* and *August* as well as *April* and *May*), and, if we may already assert what style had taught us before observing the codicological details, the miniatures were painted by one master, Jean.[410] All the calendar pictures with completed astronomical scenes (except *November*) were, on the other hand, painted by Paul.

In these first two gatherings the initials and the arabesques that extend from them are, with two exceptions, in the style of the Breviary Master. The work was done by two assistants, presumably after the Breviary Master himself had left. One of these illuminators, whom we call the Spindly Master, worked in the first gathering (Fig. 536), the other, a rather velvety painter whom we may call the Plush Master, painted all the initials and arabesques in the second gathering and folio 13 in gathering 3 (Fig. 538). Within the first gathering two folios or one sheet—the texts for March and April—were illuminated by the Dry Master, who likewise was active after the Breviary Master's departure (Fig. 537).

The folios allocated to the miniatures, like the original folios in the rest of the book, were laid out in red ink, which defines, however, a much larger rectangle than the first plan.[411] All the calendar miniatures consist of a rectangle, slightly higher than wide, crowned by an arch which springs from points at or just inside the vertical frames. Only in *January*, the uniquely large miniature, is the rectangle somewhat wider than the arch. The lobe contains celestial phenomena, as in the religious scenes, and also astronomical information, the days of the week, the phases of the moon, the zodiacal signs, the length of daylight, and the passage of the sun through the ecliptic. In the innermost lobe Apollo, holding the blazing sun, rides in his wagon drawn by horses above the golden clouds. Many of these forms, like the divine beings in the lobes of the religious scenes, are rendered in gold or, less commonly, silver.

Each of the folded sheets of which the calendar is composed (except folios 1 and 8) contains two miniatures and the calendrical texts for two months. Text and picture, similar in size, were intended to match and since they are ruled in the same red they were probably laid out at the same time. After the scribe had written the text the illuminators painted the initials and the arabesques projecting from them. The illuminators completed their work in these gatherings; they apparently did not touch the parchment around the miniatures for the simple reason that no decoration was planned there. Because of the risk of damage no miniaturist would have wanted an illuminator to return and work around a miniature he had completed—especially around such incredibly detailed and finished surfaces as those of the *Très Riches Heures*.[412]

Thus the calendar pictures resemble the miniatures of the second plan in the rest of the book, which also lack text as well as all decoration. Even on the folios of the first plan, which contain four lines of text, the Limbourgs, led by Paul, decided at a certain point, as we have seen, to eliminate the arabesques and confine ornament to the initial. To our knowledge no one has previously claimed that the bare parchment around the miniatures is precisely what the painters intended. Our conclusions on these important matters are, furthermore, just the opposite of what has occasionally been stated by eminent specialists and more often implied: that the borders of the Limbourgs in the *Très Riches Heures* are empty because the book is unfinished.[413] Such an interpretation is naturally suggested by the rarity of empty borders at this time, especially in Books of Hours.

The vine that winds out into the margins is, of course, a Gothic invention. In pre-Gothic periods framed miniatures—unframed ones concern us less here—were normally surrounded by bare parchment. In late antiquity the frames were simple bands (Fig. 252). In later illumination—Byzantine, Carolingian, Ottonian, and Romanesque—the frames often become wide and elaborate. Within the Gothic period some framed miniatures, even when alone on a folio as in the

Très Riches Heures, lack decorated borders. They are more numerous in less deeply Gothic Italy: the Lombard manuscripts of the *Tacuinum sanitatis*, for example (Figs. 150, 156, 157), or, among religious books, the Canon pages of the Missal.[414] In these instances the borders of bare parchment are much narrower all around than in the *Très Riches Heures*, which, furthermore, were certainly trimmed a little at the top.[415] Relatively quite narrow, too, were the borders of the huge full-page miniatures in the *Grandes Heures*—if, indeed, the *Way to Calvary* in the Louvre did originally belong to this book.[416] Closer to the *Très Riches Heures* are the borders in the Virgil illuminated by the Roman Texts workshop (Fig. 232). Though the paintings appear in a column of text they are framed simply, the initials have no appendages or at most some airy penwork, and the bare parchment around both miniature and text is exceptionally wide. In the proportion of unfilled to filled surface, and in the general impression of clarity and spaciousness, these folios anticipate later Italian humanist manuscripts (Fig. 225). Indeed the Virgil was surely produced under the eye of a *French* humanist, and many folios of another ancient text, the *Comedies* of Terence, given to Jean de Berry by the scholar Martin Gouge, are similar in character (Fig. 177).

The folios of the calendar and of the second phase of the *Très Riches Heures* are, in fact, un-Gothic. No forms trail from the pictures. Nothing mediates, in the usual manner of Gothic painting or architecture, between the created object and the surrounding space. There is nothing resembling spires, crockets, or, as on letters, jutting points and serifs. The pictorial space ends abruptly at the frames, and they are much simpler than the normal frames of Gothic panels and of many Gothic miniatures. Beyond the frames the Limbourgs abolished the Gothic thicket. The broad expanse of yellow-white parchment is ambivalent: it serves as a symbol of space and at the same time it reasserts the flatness of the page and thus joins it to the facing page of text. It sacrifices, on the other hand, a unity with the script comparable to that apparent in earlier Gothic manuscripts.

The deep similarity between miniature, *vigneture*, and script in earlier Gothic illumination had been generally diminished in the early fifteenth century by the bold new pictorial style.[417] The linear principle they shared earlier no longer remained fundamental to the solids and space of the miniature. Largely for this reason Flemish miniatures of the second half of the fifteenth century, although essentially more linear than Paul's, not infrequently are surrounded by wide borders of undecorated vellum.[418] The picture had changed far more than the script. Surely this is one reason why the Limbourgs abandoned the first design of the manuscript in favor of large miniatures on folios without any text. They concluded also that decorative borders, which had, to be sure, developed in conformity with the changing character of the miniatures, now had to be fundamentally transformed or even abandoned entirely.

Already in the initial design of the *Très Riches Heures* the Limbourgs dispensed with the filigree border they had employed in the *Belles Heures*. They decided to limit, too, the size and the range of the acanthus leaf, tri-dimensional yet formalized, which had become increasingly popular from the first years of the century and was still extensively used, along with more naturalistic leaves and flowers, by the Boucicaut Master at the end of his career.[419] Only three folios of the *Très Riches Heures*, as we have remarked, show large swirls of acanthus that form medallions, within which Colombe, who executed the miniatures, painted figures (Figs. 578, 589, 595).[420] Arabesques defining historiated roundels of this kind became popular in the Boucicaut workshop about this time,[421] but in the *Très Riches Heures* only an assistant of the Breviary Master employed them.

Instead of using conventional schematized forms the Limbourgs concentrated—or they persuaded the Breviary Master to concentrate—upon leaves and flowers that were rendered with a kind of naturalism not visible even within the miniatures. We have seen the beautiful studies of columbine and violets by the Breviary Master on folios 17 and 19v (Figs. 551, 556). These little still-lifes culminated in the same illuminator's superb border around the *Miracle of the Loaves and Fishes* (Fig. 592). It consists of snails, which rest partly on the frame or parchment but principally on sprays of annual larkspur (*delphinium consolida*), upon which they feed.[422] The snail, a popular creature in medieval art, conveyed a variety of meanings. It might signify resurrection, cowardice, or false courage.[423] In the border of the *Visitation* in the *Très Riches Heures* a knight, safely ensconced in a tower, hurls a lance at one of these engaging little molluscs (Fig. 567). Sometimes earlier, as in the *Breviaire de Belleville* by the workshop of Pucelle, the snail, gliding along a wild pea, seems to be present primarily as one of those delicate creatures that were judged appropriate in character to the vines of a Gothic border.[424] The Limbourgs first painted it in the borders of the *Annunciation* of the *Belles Heures*, where it appears, on a very small scale, on the acanthus leaves (Fig. 410). Since the border contains shields of Jean de Berry, swans, and numerous brown bears we may wonder whether the snail served as an emblem of the Duke also.[425] Three snail-shells, two simulated in mother-of-pearl or another material, were inventoried in the Duke's collections.[426] More cogent is the content of a charming ballade by the contemporary poet Eustache Deschamps.

Moult se vantoit li cerfs d'estre legiers
Et de courir dix lieues d'une alaine,
Et li cengliers se vantoit d'estre fiers,
Et la brebiz se louoit pour sa laine,
Et li chevriaux de sauter en la plaine
Se vantoit fort, li chevaux estre biaux,
Et de force se vantoit li toreaux,
L'ermine aussi d'avoir biau peliçon;
Adonc respont en sa coquille a ciaulx:
"Aussi tost vient a Pasques limeçon."

Les lions voy, ours et lieppars premiers,
Loups et tigres, courir par la champaigne,
Estre chaciez de mastins et levriers
A cris de gens, et s'il est qu'om les praingne
Tant sont hais que chascun les mehaingne
Pour ce qu'ilz font destruction de piaulx;
Ravissables sont, fel et desloyaulx
Sanz espargner, et pour ce les het on.
Courent ilz bien, sont ilz fors et isneaulx?
Aussi tost vient a Pasques limeçon.

Cellui voient pluseurs par les sentiers:
Enclos se tient en la cruise qu'il maine,

Sanz faire mal le laiss' on voluntiers,
Tousjours s'en va de sepmaine en sepmaine;
Si font pluseurs en leur povre demaine
Qui vivent bien soubz leurs povres drapeaulx,
Et s'ilz ne font au monde leurs aveaulx,
Si courent ilz par gracieus renon
Quant desliez sont aux champs buefs et veaulx:
Aussi tost vient a Pasques limaçon.

L'ENVOY

Prince, les gens fors, grans, riches, entr'eaulx
Ne tiennent pas toudis une leçon;
Pour eulx haster n'approuche temps nouveaulx:
Aussi tost vient a Pasques limaçon.[427]

"The stag took great pride in his swiftness and in being able to run ten leagues without stopping for breath, and the wild boar was proud of his ferocity, and the sheep extolled her wool, and the roebuck was very proud of his ability to bound over the plain; the horse took pride in his beauty and the bull in his strength, and the ermine in the beauty of its fur; then to all these replied he from his shell: 'The snail will get to Easter just as soon.'

"I see first lions, bears, and leopards, then wolves and tigers running through the countryside, pursued by mastiffs and hounds, and by the shouts of men; and if they are caught, they are so much detested that everyone maims them because of the harm they cause among the fleeces. They are wicked and treacherous thieves, and merciless, and so they are hated. Do they run well? Are they both strong and swift? The snail will get to Easter just as soon.

"Many people see him on the path, housed in the shell he carries with him; they do not harm him, but gladly let him be, and on he goes from week to week; thus many men go on in their own poor sphere, who live their lives well under their poor attire; and if they do not get all they want from the world, yet they go on their way with men's good will. When oxen and calves run free in the field, the snail will get to Easter just as soon.

"Prince, among the strong, the great, the rich, there is one thing that is not always kept in mind; not all their haste can bring spring any nearer. The snail will get to Easter just as soon."[428]

This poem bears a tribute to the simple and the poor that is characteristic of Deschamps and, as we have observed above, of the *Vie de nostre sauveur* as well as the painting of the time.[429] Its central thought, that speed and haste, even by stags or princes, will not help, that steadiness tells, and that Easter will come when it is due, strikingly resembles the motto of Jean de Berry. "Aussi tost vient a Pasques limaçon" provides specific assurance that "le temps venra."

In the thirteenth century sculptors and painters in France began to portray flowers and plants "al vif," and the iris by Pucelle or his workshop in the *Bréviaire de Belleville* is a landmark in the history of still-life.[430] The impetus to incorporate more of the appearance of natural forms led Jacquemart de Hesdin about 1390 to paint extraordinary portraits of birds.[431] Somewhat earlier, painters in North Italy and especially in Lombardy undertook close studies of plants, animals, landscapes, and even seasons, as Otto Pächt has shown.[432] One drawing of hounds attacking a boar—incorrectly, we believe, ascribed to Giovannino de' Grassi—is, as everyone knows, nearly identical with a part of the calendar picture of *December*, and it will be discussed below (Figs. 714, 549). Inspired no doubt by the intellectual tradition of the University of Padua and the recently founded University of Pavia, North Italy became a center for the illustration of herbals and medical books, just as Bologna was for canon law. One of the illustrators of the Carrara herbal *ca.* 1400 certainly painted his morning glory from a specimen lying alongside him (Fig. 679). About 1390 the illuminator of a Book of Hours in Parma filled his borders with rose-like flowers (Fig. 680),[433] and there are daisies of approximately the same date in the *Visconti Hours* by Giovannino de' Grassi and his associates.[434] In the borders of the Hours of Isabelle of Castille, about 1400, roses bloom on a vine.[435] This Lombard tradition was carried on by Michelino da Besozzo, especially in the beautiful borders of his Book of Hours in the Morgan Library (Fig. 681).

Michelino's flowers, painted a few years later than the larkspurs of the *Très Riches Heures*, are more luminous than those of his Lombard predecessors, but they retain the traditional Italian concern with generalized volume and substance. By comparison the larkspurs seem all color and light, and they are far less formally conceived (Fig. 592). The sprays, to be sure, have been arranged to create a kind of filigree on the page. To maintain a semblance of a frame the seedpods lie parallel to the page, and acute foreshortening of the flowers is avoided. Beyond this, however, each spray is unique, and the soft petals fall freely and unpredictably in the space.

This border is the masterpiece of the Breviary Master. His keen eye and deft brush have managed to capture even the ever-changing, amorphous flesh of the snails. The great Flemish panel painters from Jan van Eyck to Hugo van der Goes refined further the portraiture of flowers, but within the book the larkspurs remained unrivaled until the appearance of the impressive specialist in still-life in the late fifteenth century, the Master of Mary of Burgundy (Fig. 678).[436] His flowers, however, appear to be specimens on display; the larkspurs are seen more informally, as wild flowers.

Whether or not larkspurs and snails have a symbolic relationship to the subject of the *Loaves and Fishes* they surely have a naturalistic one, because the miracle is enacted on a deep meadow filled with blue, red, and yellow flowers. The plants in the miniature are minute compared to those in the borders. This difference in size cannot of course be ascribed to a difference of value and to the painter's application of the medieval principle of the equivalence of size and importance. Already in the early stages of the Gothic border the stylized leaves were larger than similar forms within the miniature. After the development of a tri-dimensional style, however, and the implication that everything on the page was seen from approximately one point of sight, the differences of scale became problematic. In the *Très Riches Heures* there is a large and abrupt change of size between the otherwise similar kinds of forms just in front of and just behind the frame. If we were new to the convention we might suppose that we were looking at the forms in the border under a magnifying glass while those in the miniature appear in a telescope. The combination of these two modes persists in later fifteenth-century illumination. The amazing Master of Catherine of Cleves employs them for effects that appear to us—though not necessarily to him—bizarre.[437] The discrepancy in scale becomes still greater on the folios of the Master of Mary of Burgundy, where the scene drops further away into space (Fig. 678).

The border around the *Feeding of the Five Thousand* is unique in the *Très Riches Heures*. There are no signs that the Breviary Master began anything else like it. On the contrary, the folios in this gathering (26) and in gathering 25 on which he himself worked show his usual beautiful initials entirely completed, after which Herman took over and executed the miniatures (Figs. 590–594). While it is conceivable that Herman then intended to give the sheet back to the Breviary Master for the painting of a border, such a procedure would be exceptional and for practical reasons very odd. Nor does it seem probable that the Limbourgs themselves would have added borders after painting the miniatures. Except for the folio of the *Annunciation* (Fig. 410) the borders of the *Belles Heures* are conventional and surely executed by an assistant engaged especially for the job. The three brothers painted only three borders around large miniatures in the *Très Riches Heures*—around the *Annunciation* (Fig. 559), the *Visitation* (Fig. 567), and *St. Michael* (Fig. 597). They were described on one occasion as "historieurs" or painters of miniatures,[438] and it is clear that in the *Très Riches Heures* as well as the *Belles Heures* they intended to work as such, allocating the borders to the Breviary Master and the Dry Master. If we compare the *Feeding of the Five Thousand* with a somewhat similar miniature that appears alone on the folio (Fig. 544) we recognize that, freed of forms outside the frame, the illusory space of the miniature is much more vivid. Despite the extraordinary beauty of the snails and larkspur, the Limbourgs decided not to continue with decoration of that kind.

5 · THE CALENDAR AND ITS PAINTERS

The twelve scenes illustrating the calendar of the *Très Riches Heures* comprise a cycle that, as everyone knows, is novel in several respects. No full-page pictures had adorned the calendar of any earlier Book of Hours,[439] or indeed any other kind of medieval illuminated manuscript. No calendar cycle before the *Très Riches Heures*, furthermore, gave comparable prominence to a patron and his properties. Exceptional also is the wealth of calendrical and astronomical information included in all but four of the arches over each miniature;[440] it is discussed in an appendix by Professor Neugebauer. Although in Pucelle's calendar and its imitations the sun travels through the ecliptic (Fig. 683) the representations of this theme in the *Très Riches Heures* are so developed as to constitute an innovation. The band of starry sky in the middle of the arches contains two signs of the zodiac, each against a sky of a slightly different blue. The inner lobe, separated from the picture below by dense golden—and therefore not quite natural—clouds, is largely blue, and though deeper in tone it belongs to, and completes, the space below. Its importance in this respect can readily be proved by covering it; the picture then looks cramped.

Above the center of the lobe appears the sun, a gold disk filled with a pinwheel motif which emits a multitude of rays. It is sustained by a bearded man wearing a peaked crown with solar rays that look like feathers, and historians have long been aware that this figure and his covered wagon are based on the image of the Emperor Heraclius in his *carpentum* that appears on the reverse of the famous medal bought by Jean de Berry *ca.* 1403 and then in the *Belles Heures* (Figs. 267, 487).[441] The Limbourgs demonstrated their imaginativeness by transforming the prancing horses that pull the cart into winged, Pegasus-like creatures that extend their legs forward and back so that they seem to be flying through the clouds. The charioteer in the calendar is no longer Heraclius but Sol-Apollo, who sometimes appears in astrological manuscripts. In a North Italian one about 1400 he rises in his chariot from the river of paradise (Fig. 653).[442] It must have been an image like this that served as a catalyst for the change of Heraclius into the god of the sun. Relevant also, no doubt, is the fact that the obverse of one copy of the Heraclius medal bears alongside the Emperor the word ΑΠΟΛΙΝΙϹ, that is, Apollo.[443]

The numerals and symbols in the arches impose an abstract, rational order on the varied world in the main miniatures below. Behind the scenes of the cycle lie two long traditions. Representations of the seasons began in antiquity with personifications—a convention that survived into the fourteenth century in Ambrogio Lorenzetti's representation in the Palazzo Pubblico, Siena, of Winter as a man in a snowstorm (Fig. 690). On the other hand Winter or "Hiemps" is illustrated in the Lombard *Tacuinum* of about 1390 in Vienna by showing activities characteristic of the season, including a girl before a fire warming her body more effectively by raising one of her skirts (Fig. 691).[444] The method of representing a season by depiction of a typical activity relates this miniature to the cycles of the months, and indeed the theme of a better exposure to the fire reappears in, if we may pun, more advanced form in *February* in the *Très Riches Heures* (Fig. 540).

Many of the subjects chosen centuries earlier to characterize the months tended to persist in the art of the period before the painting of the *Très Riches Heures*, though with regional variations.[445] Thus the miniature for January in *Queen Mary's Psalter*, painted in England in the early fourteenth century, shows not only a banquet, as in the *Très Riches Heures*, but a king and queen as the principal participants (Fig. 684). In *June* in this Psalter three peasants cut hay (Fig. 686), so that in this manuscript as well as in others of the period, long before the *Très Riches Heures*, specific pastimes and labors are associated with different classes, the pastimes and pleasures of course with the nobility, the labors with the peasants.[446] The nobility were included as the principal owners of Psalters and Books of Hours, whereas the changing labors of the peasants conveyed most vividly the cycle of the seasons. Neither of these two requirements was met by the burghers or the artisans, and they were therefore not included. In the calendar of the *Belles Heures*, which contains the nucleus of most of the scenes in the *Très Riches Heures*, a nobleman appears only in *April* and *May* whereas a peasant represents each of the other ten months (Figs. 687, 861).

About 1325 the remarkable innovator Jean Pucelle, working in Paris, introduced a new kind of calendar. He seems to have designed it first in the *Bréviaire de Belleville*, a manuscript that *ca.* 1407 entered the collection of Jean de Berry, a great admirer of this illuminator.[447] Though only one of the calendar pictures survives we possess a series of reliable replicas by followers of Pucelle.[448] Except in *December* no human being appears in the cycle; the procession of the seasons is shown by bare trees in January, a rainstorm in February, budding trees in March (Fig. 683), flowers in May, ripe corn in July, and so forth. In the Psalter illuminated before 1349 probably by Pucelle's greatest follower, the Passion Master, for Bonne de Luxembourg, Jean de Berry's mother, rain falls on the fishing scene introduced for the zodiacal Pisces or "poissons," as the text says, in *February* (Fig. 682).[449] "Diagrammatic though they are," wrote Panofsky,[450] "these rudimentary little landscapes—all surmounted by arches on which the sun travels from left to right in the course of the year—announce a truly revolutionary shift of interest from the life of man to the life of nature. They are the humble ancestors of the famous Calendar pictures in the '*Très Riches Heures du Duc de Berry*'. . . ." The cycle of seasonal variations, including rain in February, had already been adopted in two of the Duke's *Books of Hours*, the *Petites Heures* and the *Grandes Heures*, completed in 1409.[451]

Toward the end of the century, in the Lombard *Tacuinum*, the same meteorological event is more vividly portrayed as an illustration of the East Wind (Fig. 692). As a woman and her child scramble for shelter rain beats upon them and a high wind nearly uproots the trees. That such depictions of the seasons and the weather were in the air, as it were, in Europe at the time is demonstrated by the combination of leafless trees and snowy mountain peaks in the *Annunciation to the Shepherds* by Jacquemart in the *Brussels Hours*,[452] and by the remarkable character of a large mural cycle of the months in the Torre dell'Aquila in Trent.[453] These paintings, now damaged and somewhat repainted, were apparently made for Bishop George of Liechtenstein not long before 1407, when he had to flee Trent. A local painter in his entourage, a certain Wenzel, may have been their author. The painting for January in the Trent cycle is the earliest landscape covered with snow that has come down to us (Fig. 695). In the foreground two parties of nobles, including ladies decolleté despite the low temperature, throw snowballs at each other. To the right of the castle two men with dogs, perhaps hunting, move more than ankle-deep in the snow. The castle itself, however, has inexplicably escaped the fall, and it is clear that, despite his fresh observations of many phenomena, the painter still adhered to ideograms. The vegetation within the walls of the castle is in full leaf. As in the Pucellesque calendars the sun shines above, and the zodiacal sign is named.

In *April* the countryside is more hospitable and the activities more varied: plowing in the foreground, harrowing and sowing in the background (Fig. 694). Two noblewomen stroll along a path so that this cycle combines in one landscape the same two classes as the *Très Riches Heures*. Partly in order to present numerous occupations clearly the painter has tilted his ground-plane steeply upward, bringing the horizon near the upper frame. In perspective and in the very limited understanding of a spatial continuum the Trent murals are archaic compared with the great panorama by Ambrogio Lorenzetti of 1338–1339, which affected the entire course of landscape painting in Europe for more than half a century (Fig. 669). The Limbourgs understood Ambrogio's epoch-making fresco far better than did the comparatively limited master in Trent, and indeed it must have been the mural in Siena that provided the basic conception and structure for landscapes such as *February* in the *Très Riches Heures* (Fig. 540). None of the Limbourg compositions, to be sure, adopt Ambrogio's foreground plateau; of all Northern painters only Jacquemart de Hesdin, in his miniature of the Entombment in the *Brussels Hours*, introduced it (Fig. 456), and then Jan van Eyck exploited it extensively.[454] Miniatures such as *February*, on the contrary, follow the older and simpler "high-rise" convention in accordance with which the sequence of forms in the pictorial field from the lower frame to the upper generally coincides with the altitude of forms in the illusory space. Of the numerous Italian examples of this type that the Limbourgs undoubtedly saw, a fresco by a follower of Altichiero in the Santo in Padua offers also a man, as in *February*, driving his donkey up the hill (Fig. 345).

What is unprecedented in *February* and in a remarkably similar landscape we have already seen in the *Adoration of the Magi* (Fig. 572) is the depth of the vista. This has been achieved by a superb control of diminution, so that one has the vivid and quite novel impression of traveling to a very distant hill, from which one can look off to the horizon. Though the landscapes in *February* and the *Adoration of the Magi* differ, so to speak, in their dress their fundamental structure is the same. Even the sheds and the chief persons in them are related. *February*, to be sure, lacking supernatural figures and the gold and the light associated with them, is a more unified, or at least less complex, painting. The two miniatures must, however, be the work of one painter. We have already ascribed the *Adoration of the Magi*, which is painted on an inserted sheet, to Paul in his latest panoramic phase in the main part of the book, and *February* was no doubt executed about the same time. To measure the astonishing development of his use of light and color it is useful to look back to a similar "high-rise" landscape he painted in the *Annunciation to the Shepherds* in his first or Italianate phase in the manuscript (Fig. 570).

February contains numerous additional signs of Paul's authorship. His exquisite portrayal of the Carthusians in the *Belles Heures* (Fig. 416) anticipated the mastery of white in the winter landscape. As in his much earlier miniature of the *End of the Plague* in the *Belles Heures* (Fig. 452) smoke swirls up from the chimney,[455] but the painter has added another kind of vapor, never before depicted in art: the breath of the man in the courtyard condensing in the frosty air. Footprints in the snow, likewise a new phenomenon in the visual arts, lead from the house through the gate and then down the path that passes below the lower frame. The verb "leads" is precise, because Paul has consistently pointed the feet, sole before heel, in this direction. These extraordinary observations are anticipated by the prints of feet and hoofs in the dust of the road in Paul's *Flight into Egypt* (Fig. 415).

The snow has settled in the crotches of the trees and, irregularly as indeed it would, into the haystack and the beehives. The feet of the peasants and the ass and even of the birds sink into it. All life is controlled by the cold. In February the main goal is survival. The sheep huddle together in the fold. The birds are kept alive by grain scattered in the dooryard. The man who has ventured out for a chore blows on his hands to keep warm. A youth, partly bare-legged, swings an axe against a tree, and another man drives an ass laden with wood up the hill to the distant hamlet.

The painter of this miniature was clearly testing what he had learned from French and Italian models against what he had come to see with his own eyes; and he did not hesitate to make the necessary modifications. Even at the stage of painting he altered slightly, to increase the impression of movement, the outlines of the ass and his driver, as well as the right foot of the man in the yard. On the other hand in his first strokes he caught to his satisfaction the lively little flock of birds. Most of them peck while a few quietly await a place at the feast, their gray and black feathers brilliant against the snow. The sheep seem to jostle each other, and in the house the fire flares, sending smoke and golden sparks up the chimney while the three figures—perhaps a mother and her children—toast themselves in various ways. Apart from all this the world is muffled and still. Even the dull gray sky seems frozen.

The color in the landscape is unusually limited. Except for small areas of blue, pink, and black, there are only gray and buff. Within this narrow range every slight variation in white becomes telling, producing a change in texture or in plane. The pigment is laid more or less thinly on the yellowish parchment, which sometimes remains entirely exposed. The fluctuation of the light on the snow is perhaps the painter's greatest achievement; it suggests a mode of reality that renders artificial the old convention of the house lacking a wall to reveal the interior.

Two approximately contemporary snow-scenes throw into relief the subtlety of Paul's painting. Both were painted by the Cité des Dames workshop, and both illustrate events that occurred in snow. One, in the *Miroir historial* of Vincent of Beauvais, shows the Emperor Henry III at night watching an unusual sight from his palace window (Fig. 688).[456] During a snowstorm—the first ever represented in art—a nun carries a cleric across a square. The miniature, difficult to date precisely, might even have been executed a year or two before Paul's *February*. The other miniature, which illustrates *novella 77* of the French translation of the *Decameron*, shows Régnier visiting his beloved Hélène in heavy snow on Christmas night (Fig. 689). The story tells that Hélène's maid locked him in the courtyard, but in the miniature the opening remains unbarred, and the snow through it and beyond the ardent lover is marked with footsteps—not mentioned, of course, by the text.[457] Since Laurent de Premierfait completed his translation of the *Decameron* on June 15, 1414, the manuscript, made for Jean sans Peur, could scarcely have been illuminated before 1415,[458] and it therefore seems possible that the miniaturist had seen Paul's miniature. He might, too, have heard about it from the Breviary Master, who as we shall see apparently abandoned his work on the *Très Riches Heures* to enter the service of Jean sans Peur. This derivation of the Decameron miniature might then support the date of 1414–1415 that, on grounds of style, seems to us correct for *February*, one of Paul's earliest miniatures in the calendar.

When confronting so difficult a problem as the contribution of each of the three brothers to the *Très Riches Heures* one naturally clutches at every straw of evidence. Thus I began my study of the illumination with the hypothesis, advanced earlier by Hulin de Loo,[459] that the leading painter, Paul according to all the records, painted *January* (Fig. 539). In this first miniature of the calendar the Duke himself is the principal figure, placed in his familiar environment, and who but Paul would have assumed responsibility for such an important and exceptional representation?

The scene of *January* is a complement to *February*. Though some historians seem unaware of the fact, the nobility as well as the peasants were affected by the cold. They were, to be sure, more protected from it by larger fires, woolen tapestries on the walls, mats on the floor, heavy clothing, and better food and drink (Fig. 539). Still, the prominence of hand-warming in *January* as well as the Duke's proximity to the fire, prove that low temperatures in the huge rooms of the castles were a cardinal fact of existence. In a somewhat earlier ballade Eustache Deschamps says that everyone appointed to the King's household, as he was to the court of Charles VI, had to serve four months but that he always avoided the period November through February because of the great discomfort and the likelihood of catching cold.

> Si comme on dit, chascuns sert quatre mois
> Des serviteurs qui sont en ordonnance,
> Entre lesquels en a quatre trop frais,
> Où je ne sers nul temps à court de France,

Car il m'ont trop refroidi dès m'enfance:
Novembre y est, puis Decembre et Janvier,
Fevrier après qui tous reumes avance:
En ce froit temps s'en fait bon estrangier.

Car adonc sont et gelees et nois,
Pluies et vens, en grant desordonnance;
Lors aux sengliers s'en va chassier li rois,
Et officiers qui sont sur la despence
Soufflent leurs mains; chascun gare sa pance,
Batent leurs corps pour eux du froit vengier,
Page à cheval font nice contenance.
En ce froit temps s'en fait bon estrangier.

"They say that every one of the king's servants who is attached to the Household is on duty for four months every year; but there are four very chilly ones when I never serve at the Court of France, for they have been too cold for me ever since my childhood: November is one of them, then December and January, and after that February, the great promoter of colds. In this cold weather it is best to keep away.

"For then come frosts and snows and rains and winds in great confusion; then the king goes off to hunt the boar, and the officers in attendance blow on their hands; each one keeps his belly well wrapped up, and they swing their arms to drive out the cold. Pages on horseback cut a sorry figure. In this cold weather it is best to keep away."[460]

January temperatures were surely not higher in the rooms of Jean de Berry than in those of Charles VI, and there are signs of the cold in the Duke's banquet hall. To absorb the heat of the fire courtiers near it, unlike the peasants, do not raise their clothes but only their hands. The prince, though seated right in front of the chimney, is bundled up in a heavy *houppelande* and a fur hat. He and his clerical companion at table are seated on a platform that elevates them a little above the floor, still cold though it is covered with a wall-to-wall mat. The illuminator has not, of course, dwelt on the chill but on the festivity. The Duke—without his Duchess, from whom he was estranged—sits at a well-stocked table, accompanied only by an elderly cleric, perhaps his friend and treasurer Bishop Martin Gouge. Attendants, two of them spurred and therefore knights, wield carving knives or, at the left, decant wine. Two tiny dogs have the freedom of the table, and one licks a plate near an enormous golden *nef* crowned by the ducal emblems, the bear and the swan.[461] Similar splendid golden vessels stand in three rows on a sideboard, near which one man drinks from a dish while another puts a morsel in his mouth.[462] Amidst all this elaborate service there is not one of the dazzling knives and forks described in the ducal inventories, so that for both the Duke and the bishop nothing will impede the passage of food from the fingers to the mouth.

Behind the Duke's bench a steward, holding a staff, calls out "aproche! aproche!" But precisely who is to approach? The waiters with the next course?[463] Do we witness a more important ceremony, connected with the presentation of the book, with New Year, or a similar event? The fact that varied hypotheses have been offered suggests that in the tangle of men in the steward's line of vision the candidates do not emerge with any clarity. The most likely are the two noblemen wearing red turbans. Their path forward may possibly be indicated by the position of the hands of the men in front of them. There is, however, no apprehensible space through which they might walk, and the difficulty is compounded by complete uncertainty as to how they, or anyone else, came into this congested hall. Worse still, near the place where one would expect a door there is a gate through which soldiers on horseback enter, but all this of course occurs in the tapestry behind. The illuminator has depicted with great subtlety the method by which this tapestry is hung on the wall and folded back over the fireplace, but he has carried into it the same reds, greens and blues he employed for the figures below, so that the two kinds of reality tend to merge. The tangle of the battle—an episode, as we have seen, from the Trojan war[464]—adds to the confusion in the room.

None of the figures around the Duke has been convincingly identified. A number wear emblems—the letter *m* or *r* or *tv*, leaves, crowns with rays—which have remained obscure. Durrieu suggested, without specific reasons, that the man wearing a gray cap might be a self-portrait of the painter, whom he believed to be Paul.[465] What the repeated letter on his collar signifies he did not say. The profile position of the head is not characteristic of the early known self-portraits, which show the sitter looking out into the mirror that was normally employed for this purpose. The identification with one of the Limbourgs might be more tenable if all three were present, in a new version of the scene in which an author or scribe presents a book to a patron.[466] No group of three, however, seems sufficiently conspicuous.

Our attempt to describe *January* has disclosed qualities of design that are quite foreign to Paul. One might suppose that the miniature was a much earlier work than *February*, but it is not more like *St. John* or the *Visitation* and the *Nativity*, which are the earliest paintings by Paul in the manuscript (Figs. 551, 567, 569). Part of the deep difference from *February* might seem due to the dissimilar subject. The richness of planar design, however, and the comparative indifference to volume and space as well as the rhythmical linearity and the great elegance are all fundamental qualities of the art of Jean rather than Paul. Probably Jean painted it soon after the *Deposition* (Fig. 588). As a contribution to this peculiarly important miniature by the Duke's favorite illuminator we are left, then, only with the portrait of the prince. Signs of Paul's intervention are, however, not really stronger here. The Duke has the loose, somewhat protruding lips characteristic of Jean. On the other hand it was probably Paul who imagined the structure of an interior in which no part of the room coincides with the frame—an entirely novel conception that we shall discuss below.

Illuminators had introduced portraits of the Duke of Berry in earlier manuscripts, but always within a religious context—except perhaps in representations of the prayer of the Itinerary. In prayer books of the later fourteenth century portraits of the owners occasionally appeared in a secular setting, as Giangaleazzo Visconti, Count of Milan, between deer and his hounds.[467] *January* in the *Très Riches Heures* is, however, the first instance in the long history of the illustrated calendar of a specific person represented in his own environment.

The basic artistic principles of *January* reappear in *April* (Fig. 542), but elegance and rhythmical interplay have been sought so single-mindedly and so passionately that the park has become a green carpet and the figures are almost disembodied. They scarcely possess the substance and the structure to enact even the limited roles assigned to them: to pluck flowers or to give and receive the ring, not to mention sustaining their gorgeous robes and hats. Not only these puppets but buildings and nature too must bend to the requirements of the pattern. Thus the wall, following the outline of the lady in pink, moves up and back at an irrationally steep angle. We gain thereby, to be sure, a fuller view of the garden it encloses and of the white and rose bloom of the fruit-trees. The silver water behind, probably the River Orge, in which two men in rowboats drag a net, assumes the shape of a teardrop that repeats, in reverse and on a smaller scale, the outline of the figures. The Duke's Château de Dourdan and the adjoining houses flow along the knoll in a curve parallel to the water.

This miniature represents the extreme stage of one stylistic trend in the *Très Riches Heures*. It has the most effete figures, the most linear design, and the least luminosity. Even the sky is a dense blue.[468] Only Jean would have been capable of this courtly mannerism, but it is also true—and puzzling—that the miniature is weaker than other paintings by him and it remains unique in his oeuvre. Whether or not it represents a specific event remains uncertain. The suggestion that we witness the betrothal of Charles d'Orléans and Bonne d'Armagnac is plausible but not proved.

In style *May* (Fig. 543) resembles *April*. The greensward and the wood look like studio properties, and there is little daylight on the buildings, which probably represent the Palais de la Cité.[469] In many respects the miniature seems closer to *January* (Fig. 539). Among the figures there is the same lack of defined spatial intervals, although the Palais appears at a very considerable distance. The rhythmical design now seems more complex yet more unified. Though the procession moves to the left, two principal figures, turning, look backward, and the combination of movement and counter-movement among the trumpeters is very subtle.[470] Since *May*, like *January*, was clearly painted by Jean it supports the attribution to him of *April*, because these two months are on the same sheet of parchment. *April* and *May* share other peculiarities, as we have observed above. The reverse of each was decorated by the Dry Master whereas the backs of all the other calendar paintings were illuminated by assistants of the Breviary Master. Furthermore, the arcs for astronomical data above these two miniatures as well as above *January* and *August* have remained empty. *January* and *August* are on the same sheet, and in our opinion Jean painted *August*, too. These are his only contributions to the calendar, and for whatever reason, the astronomical data was withheld on these two sheets, or four folios. It is curious that these four scenes are the only ones in the cycle that include specific contemporary people, but their presence would not affect the lunar cycles, which are predetermined and invariable.

The nobility in *May* enact the traditional rite of the first of the month, when they stream out into the country to celebrate the changing season. Green is the color of the event, and most of the figures are adorned with branches bearing the delicate new leaves of spring. Three women wear green dresses, and documents tell us that for the occasion King Charles VI normally gave new *houppelandes*, or mantles, often "vert gay," to his courtiers.[471] One new observation seems to support the suggestion, often advanced, that the two principal persons are the Duke's daughter, Marie, and her third husband, Jean de Bourbon.[472] Marie would be the foremost lady mounted on a white horse, sign of the highest rank. Her marriage to Jean, celebrated in the Palais royal in Paris on June 24, 1400—the feast of the Duke's name-saint, the Baptist[473]—was for Jean de Berry a major event, and to arrange it he persuaded the King to allow her to inherit the Duchy of Auvergne. In 1410 Jean de Bourbon succeeded his father as Duke of Bourbon. It has not been observed that the harnesses of all four visible horses bear ornaments that are identical with the badge of Bourbon:

a roundel filled with seven small disks, one at the center and the others around it (Fig. 779).[474] The only man whose horse wears this badge is seen from the back, though he turns towards the presumed Marie. By iconographical convention, we would expect to find Jean in the most richly dressed man who looks rather sentimentally at "Marie." He bears no Bourbon emblem, however, and his colors are royal—black, white and red.[475]

August, painted on the same sheet as *January* (Fig. 539) and likewise lacking calendrical facts, is the fourth miniature in this cycle painted by Jean and also, we believe, the latest (Fig. 546). The nobility, now setting out to hunt with falcons, seem more completely out of doors.[476] This new effect is achieved in part by greatly reducing the size of the figures, setting them a little deeper in space, and devoting half the pictorial field to the landscape and to the Duke's castle at Etampes, not far from Paris. For the first time in a miniature by Jean peasants appear on the land, cutting, stacking, and carting grain. Seeking relief from the heat of late summer, they swim in the River Juine. The ground plane does not show the regular, steep ascent of *April* but rises unevenly, ending in the hill on which the castle is placed. Furthermore, though the river and the road as well as the wall of the castle echo the flowing curves of the procession—and the painter uses so linear a device as a very long pole to unify and animate his group—the interrelationship of forms is looser and subtler, so that the space opens out more impressively.

Most remarkable in this late painting by Jean is the light. It brightens the curling straw hat of the falconer, the distant hill at the right, the horses before the wagon and the golden grain in the field. On the nearer animal high white pigment is scumbled over a gray ground tone. In the foreground small areas of intense red combined with white and wonderfully graduated blues add to the impression of a gay summer outing. In the procession there is a delicious sequence of pink, emerald green, and luminous brown. The grays or gray-blues in this group are repeated in the river, which consists of green, blue or gray thinly and irregularly spread over silver. The bodies of the swimmers, parts of which seem to be visible *through* the water, are actually painted *on* the silver. Only the castle is rather uniformly lighted, recessive, and dull. This is the best of Jean's paintings in the calendar. It is also closest to the miniatures by Paul, to which it owes much of its strength.

Up to now we have encountered Paul in the calendar only in *February* (Fig. 540). Perhaps it is best to turn next to the miniature on the other half of the sheet, *July* (Fig. 545). This miniature happens also to be the one that most influenced Jean's *August* (Fig. 546).

In *July* we look down on the valley of the River Clain and the Duke's chateau at Poitiers, flanked as it actually was by two hills. As in *February* there are no nobles, so that Paul was again free of the necessity of depicting figures on a large scale in the foreground. The two peasants he chose to place there (shearing, and iconographically unusual) are seated, so that they present no barriers to the free opening of the space.[477] Perhaps even more than in *February* the landscape itself is the principal subject. In structure it is less like the high-rise type of *February* than the tilted flat landscape that was common in earlier Parisian illumination,[478] and which the Limbourgs employed for marine views in the *Belles Heures* or in *St. John* in the *Très Riches Heures* (Figs. 473, 551, 693). The ground plane in *July*, however, rises much less steeply and it creates a far more vivid impression of depth. Its design, moreover, is less rhythmical and more geometric. Instead of meandering across the valley a stream flows straight inward along a diagonal and then makes almost a right-angle turn. The opposite diagonal is marked by the line of freshly cut grain and by the peasants. The reaper in gray dress who appears at the crossing of these major lines becomes a central figure despite his distance—an altogether novel conception of design. The diagonals that reach into the lower corners are repeated deeper in space by the row of pruned trees at the left and the bridge together with the road approaching it. The composition creates a stronger illusion of space beyond the frames at the sides than any earlier painting by the Limbourgs.

The triangle of the Duke's Château de Poitiers probably suggested to the painter the double triangle or rhombus of the field of grain. The successon of two such large, similar geometric spaces is unprecedented in the history of tri-dimensional composition, and though geometric plans abound in the paintings of Uccello, Domenico Veneziano, and Piero there is nothing quite like this. Paul's arrangement of his figures and other forms parallel to the main lines of the composition anticipates paintings such as Uccello's *Hunt* in Oxford (Fig. 696).

The beauty of *July* derives not so much from the bare frame we have described, fundamental though it be, as from the slight variations the painter introduced and the glorious mantle he threw over it. The apex of the field does not quite coincide with that of the castle, and the bridge is not parallel to the river-bank and the field. Countless such dissimilarities within likenesses give proof of Paul's sensitiveness and inexhaustible vitality. We recognize these qualities also in the color and the light, which are no less extraordinary than the shapes. The higher values are in the distance. The blue of the lower sky is more luminous than the blue of the roofs. The sun beats on the grain and the castle, giving each of its walls a slightly distinctive tone. Once again Paul has demonstrated his rare skill with white. This color is carried forward in the space, trickling so to speak through the river into the sheep. Transparent rose and green glaze the silver water, especially near the swans. The blue and rose of the peasants who shear the sheep are scattered in the field, as it were, in small drops. Here they are poppies and cornflowers, which have grown amidst the grain and become visible when it is cut.

Paul delights in observations of this kind. With a touching affection he paints the rushes in the water, the strands of wool on the grass, the gnarled trunks of the trees and the new shoots that have sprouted from them. His eye has caught the planks in the wood of the bridge, the finials and crockets over the windows, and even a statue on a turret at the extreme right end of the castle. Nowhere, however, do these astonishing particulars clog the broader aspects of the forms and the space. The balance achieved by Paul in this respect is one of the rarest accomplishments of his genius.

June appears on the same sheet as *March*, which Paul began but did not quite finish (Fig. 544). As we shall soon see *March* is, in fact, one of the latest of Paul's paintings—certainly the latest miniature in the first gathering of the calendar. Physical facts indicate, then, that *June* is a late work also. It does indeed show a low point of sight and a flat landscape, both late phenomena, as we shall see, but when we compare it with *July* we recognize that the problem has quite another dimension (Fig. 545).

The scene is captivating. Hay has ripened on a small island in the Seine, probably the Ile de Buci, which was later joined to the Ile de la Cité by filling in the branch of the river that in the miniature divides them. Three peasants mow in tandem, turning the field below their scythes from the deep green of the lush grass to the yellow-green of the stubble. Their women rake and stack. Behind the walls that protect the Ile de la Cité rise the old royal palace and the Sainte-Chapelle.

In the extremely clear air the buildings have an almost startling mass and crispness of detail. The roofs and the projecting wings throw sharp shadows onto the walls. The sky, flecked with small clouds, is a cool blue. It becomes lighter and more transparent near the horizon, but it lacks the contrasts of the sky in *July*. Indeed the entire scene is cooler and less luminous. This might reflect a deliberate intention to differentiate the months, but the landscape does not attain the great beauty of *July*. Many of the same forms are present, but the cattails lack comparable organic life, the silver water does not bear green and rose glazes (though the little boat casts a shadow on its surface), and the tree-trunks lack decisive individuality. Compared to the branches of the trees in the foreground of *July*, which move out into space, those in *June* seem uncertain and blurred.

The two miniatures are as dissimilar in their broader aspects as they have appeared in the touch of the brush. Each of the two areas of the field in *June*, the uncut and the cut, remains rather uniform in color, without the modulation from yellow-green to blue-green that is so telling in *July*. The flesh of the three reapers is even in tone and unusually swarthy. The light does not strike the limbs or the shoulders and reveal their volume, as it does in *July*. Although one of the two men wielding sickles in *July* is not entirely firm on his feet the legs of two of the peasants in *June* are spread so wide that they seem quite unsteady.

As a group the three mowers strengthen the movement that courses through the landscape. The Seine and its banks compose a long curve from the lower left frame to the upper right. The pruned trees follow this curve and even the row of haystacks bends in conformity. All this movement, taken together with the fact that the architecture is seen from the right, suggests that the painter wished to emphasize the choice of a point of sight at the center of the book. The landscape, in any event, lacks the dynamic equilibrium of *July*. Its curvatures relate it more closely to *February* but it is inferior to that miniature also. The trees, given luminosity by very open brushwork, seem to indicate a relatively late date.

The blue-greens in the landscape and the brown flesh of the mowers provide some reason to believe that Herman painted this part of the miniature, although we have not encountered him in the calendar or in this stylistic phase. On the other hand, the buildings and the vegetation in the garden of the king seem more beautifully painted than the island, inducing us to suspect that Paul painted the upper part of the miniature. Both these proposals must, in the nature of the case, remain quite tentative.

We have not even now, however, exhausted the riddle of this miniature. The two women in the foreground represent the most difficult problem of all. For many years I have been puzzled by them, by the strange, fussy pattern of folds in their sleeves and the thick, crude white paint employed on them and in their kerchiefs. Their faces, painted with a more open brushwork than the Limbourgs normally employ, are peculiarly vacuous. The eyes of the woman who rakes turn away from her work and roll up to heaven. The one visible eye of her companion is likewise averted and improperly foreshortened. In this eye as well as in the nearer one of the woman opposite there is a conspicuous highlight, formed of a sizeable spot of white paint. Observing this phenomenon we are less surprised to see that the raker's skirt casts a shadow on her left leg. In the late miniatures by Paul, to be sure, we shall encounter cast shadows, but primarily on the ground, and highlights in the eyes occur more decisively in animals than in people.

The legs of both women have a whitish cast like the faces, and closer inspection shows that whereas the blue in the dress of the woman who pitches hay has the purity and smoothness of a Limbourg color her white skirt is thickly painted and looks starched. The black neckline of the raker was surely not painted by one of the Limbourgs, nor were the prominent—too prominent—lines of white on the rake and the pitchfork. Who reworked these figures? For practical reasons the most likely candidate is the painter who completed the book, Jean Colombe, but the style does not seem to be clearly his and we must leave the question open.

6 · PAUL'S NEW VISION

On the other half of the sheet that bears *June* is *March*, and it too has been retouched later (Fig. 541). As in *June* the buildings, the plow, and the oxen are seen from the right, from a point in other words near the center of the book (Fig. 544). In other respects the miniature resembles *February*, which it follows (Fig. 540). *March* too is a high-rise landscape, and roads wind into the distance as the principal guides to the space. Its depth, however, is greater than *February*, and the Duke's chateau at Lusignan that crowns the hill is the most imposing picture of a building that painters had yet conceived. The effect of the whole has been spoiled by the heavy-handed retouching of the small figures, the white walls around the vineyards, and the *montjoie* at the crossroads.[479] These additions, probably by the workshop of Jean Colombe, were no doubt provoked by the fact that the miniature was not quite complete. The edges of the roads, for instance, still seem unfinished. The condition of the sky in the upper left corner is puzzling. Some damage and repair are visible here, but the painter may have intended to represent a storm. Two men and a dog seem to run away from it. The vertical dark blue streaks before the clouds perhaps indicate rain, but the brown streaks over the green field just below are often not vertical and cannot confidently be explained. The Limbourgs had, however, carried the execution of the landscape quite far. With their usual interest in tools and mechanisms they had rendered in silver the tiny pruner, the sickle, and the cutting edge of the plow.[480]

The foreground, including the plowman, has remained largely free of retouching, and it is the most extraordinary part of the picture. Though March is usually, as in the *Belles Heures*, illustrated by pruning, the plowman with his implement and his oxen was a common representative of rural life, from the time of Ambrogio Lorenzetti's fresco in the Palazzo Pubblico through the April and September calendar pictures at the Torre dell'Aquila (Fig. 694).[481] He had never, however, looked this way. He is an old man with a white beard who leans heavily on his plow. Exposure to the elements has reddened and roughened his face and his hands. He needs to be protected against the cold by a brown hat and a red scarf as well as a somewhat tattered gray coat over a blue tunic. The red area near his belt is perhaps a handkerchief. His gray stockings have been worn through at the knees.

The only elderly man in the calendar of the *Belles Heures*, far from working the fields in *March*, sits indoors in *February*, warming himself before a fire.[482] In his earlier miniatures Paul and his brothers distinguished peasants from nobles by dress as well as by occupation. One of the shepherds receiving the angels' message (Fig. 411) and the peasant shearing in *July* (Fig. 545) wear torn clothing; they are, however, well formed and physically vigorous, despite age. In the stiff, ungainly old man in *March* with an abnormally large head and worn clothes the painter wished to communicate something radically different. It is surely significant that this startling new conception is accompanied by other major visual innovations. Highlights sparkle on smooth, polished surfaces: on the plow, and on the eye and the horns of the ox. The oxen, the plow, and the plowman, furthermore, all cast shadows on the furrows of gray earth, and they fall rather consistently in accordance with a source of light in front of the picture and to the left. These, together with similar phenomena in *October* and *December* (Figs. 548, 549), are the earliest post-antique shadows consistently cast by figures onto the ground.

These shadows have often been regarded as the first cast shadows of whatever kind. Contrary to the usual belief, however, Italian painters from the end of the thirteenth century began to find new meaning in the strips of shade in medieval, especially Byzantine painting that survived as residual forms from antiquity.[483] Cavallini, the painters of the life of St. Francis in Assisi, and Giotto represented shadows cast by one part of a building upon another.[484] In the frescoes of the Passion cycle in Assisi by Pietro Lorenzetti and associates the shadows reflect precisely the architectural forms that cast them, and in the *Last Supper* a cat and a dog cast accurate shadows on the floor.[485] *March*, however, is the first painting in which the principal figures and forms in the foreground throw shadows on the ground. These shadows are more effective because they are exactly the same color as the shadows in the furrows, which, appearing behind clods of earth, are quite irregular and give the entire field a novel depth and a new kind of reality.

The highlights, which have escaped attention because of their small size, are even more unusual. Here Paul was not anticipated by the Trecento painters.[486] It seems clear, then, that the foreground of this miniature is the consequence of an altered purpose and intensified vision. More penetrating observation has produced not only highlights and cast shadows but in part also the new kind of plowman. Of course the depiction of worn clothing and a worn, declining man—of striking imperfection, in other words—reflects also an interest that was manifested by French secular and religious literature of the late fourteenth century, as we have seen. The art of the Netherlands had taken the lead in representing the contingent and the ugly (Fig. 121), and in the Duke's astrological manuscript that had come to him in 1403 from Bruges even the planetary divinities have become poor, crabbed creatures that perhaps seemed to him—as they do at first to us—mockeries of their traditional prototypes (Fig. 361). Certain aspects of *March*, therefore, demonstrate Paul's much closer approach to Netherlandish values and his corresponding disenchantment with those Italian canons of ideal form which had guided him for years.

In the first miniature, *September*, of the second gathering of the calendar only the upper part was painted by one of the Limbourgs (Fig. 547). He had apparently laid some preliminary color in the lower zone; the tan of the roads and the light green over it are the same pigments that are used above. Jean Colombe then completed the vineyard and the harvest of grapes.[487] He also retouched the sky and possibly the castle. The white clouds at the lower right are surely his handiwork, and he probably deepened the blue above. The chateau, Saumur in Anjou, is an imposing structure, set as usual oblique to the picture-plane with nearly horizontal orthogonals.[488] Though the perspective of the right face is faulty the building is powerful as a mass and captivating for its incredibly fine detail. Two chimneys cast shadows on the blue roof.

The only human being painted by the Limbourgs, a woman walking with a large basket on her head, throws a shadow on the road. She supports the basket with one arm and steadies herself with a staff in the other. No one but Paul could have caught her gait and her volume so perfectly. The luminous hills and the sure, fluid painting of the animals confirm his authorship of this part of the miniature. It is notable that apart from the castle the main lines of his composition, which may be deduced also in the lower zone, are not oblique as in his earlier work but parallel or perpendicular to the picture plane.

December is on the same sheet as *September*, and in style it is related to it as well as to *March* (Figs. 541, 547, 549, 646). The usual subject for December is the slaughtering of a pig, and the choice of a moment in a hunt, the *Hallali*, just before the death of the animal, is unprecedented.[489] For Paul, too, it represents a departure because it is the only scene he painted in the calendar that does not show exclusively peasants. On the other hand, though hunting is an avocation of noblemen, they are present in the miniature only by proxy. The slightly risky work we contemplate is done by employees, one of whom seems to wear his master's black and white colors. In the line of duty he has torn his fine green hose.

The geometric design of the composition is simpler but no less salient than that of *July* (Fig. 545). The near edge of the wood repeats the semicircular perimeter of the hunters and hounds. The Château de Vincennes seems to be almost, but not quite, parallel to the picture plane. The lack of full accord apparent in *March* between the scene of plowing and the landscape has become more conspicuous here. Into a wintry countryside that is all gray and stale brown the painter has inserted the bright and warm colors of the hunt. All these men and animals are seen in greater detail, as though closer to us, than the ground and the trees, even the trees or bushes that are actually nearer us in the space. The boar hunt is more brightly lighted, too, and although the blues and whites reappear in the sky and in the towers of the royal chateau of Vincennes, where Jean de Berry was born, no reds even remotely similar appear elsewhere in the composition. The painter wished to present the *Hallali* as a brilliant spectacle, but it seems too large and too minutely described for its setting. If Paul utilized an Italian model for the animals, as seems probable, that too augmented the difference from the landscape. Of course the difference was increased by the painter's insistence upon the depiction of a dull winter woodland.

This woodland is marvelously observed and rendered. Winter has come, but brown leaves, though dead, still cling to the branches. In the nearer trees we see single leaves, then only masses. Rhythmically spaced openings in these masses permit a view into the depth of the forest comparable to that obtainable through the tree-trunks below. The trunks, like the forms in the hunt, cast shadows. The ground is littered with fallen leaves and branches. The towers of Vincennes rise above the trees at an impressive distance. Seen from the right, like the buildings painted on versos in all the late Limbourg calendar miniatures, they are greatly diminished. The large windows have become minute, the forest seems to stretch back across the intervening space. Nothing like this deep, dense yet penetrable wood had ever been envisaged. Inevitably we are reminded of later paintings, the Ghent altarpiece perhaps but still more—and this is significant—Paolo Uccello's *Hunt* (Fig. 696).

Nearer the lower frame a few stones glisten in the light. The eyes of the hunters are intensely white. Altogether novel are the descriptions of the rippling skin of the hounds, the projection of the bones through it, their pointing tongues and even salivary flow. The face of the hunter leaning over the pack is largely evoked by the light; it consists of contrasting patches of light and dark nearly as broad and strong as in paintings by Masaccio. As in *March*, there are conspicuous and unmistakable highlights: on the glossy horns and in the eyes of the hounds, where their incidence shifts in accordance with the changing relation of the hounds to the observer. The spot of pure white in the eye of the huntsman blowing a horn might be due to reflection also, but the similar though larger white in the eye of the opposite man seems to represent the entire cornea. This head, though more traditionally modeled, is ugly to an extraordinary degree. The features are coarse and a horrible sadistic passion deforms them.

October and *November* are on one sheet. Since *November* was designed and painted in its entirety by Colombe we may assume that the Limbourgs, or more precisely Paul, had done little or nothing on it. This is therefore a unique miniature in the calendar, and it argues for the lateness of *October* (Figs. 548, 644). That is absolutely confirmed by its style. Sowing is commonly represented for this month, and the *Belles Heures* already shows the harrow, the sower holding seed in his apron, and a supply nearby in a bag (Fig. 687). Probably a little earlier than Paul Michelino da Besozzo painted a blackbird perspicaciously following the sower (Fig. 685).

For Paul these are only small forms in a broad landscape. Autumnal farming proceeds in a quite specific and not insignificant place: a field across the Seine from the new royal palace of the Louvre. Eloquent indeed is the contrast between the remarkably massive yet grimly protected dwelling of the king and the simple yet necessary activities of the peasants, who work in the bright light of the open spaces nearby. This is the view from the windows of the Duke of Berry's Hôtel de Nesle just a few hundred feet upstream. From there, now the site of the Institut de France, one looks at the south and east facades of the Louvre, as in the painting.

As the culmination of a development we have seen in Paul's preceding miniatures the flat plane of the ground extends steadily inward with only small variations of level from the lower frame to the castle. It begins, to be precise, somewhat below the lower frame, where there is a marvelously painted ribbon of vegetation—a sort of hedgerow serving also as a *repoussoir*. Of the older, conventional divisions into foreground, middleground, and distance there remains only the river and the slight elevation of its bank. No sinuous lines lead the eye across the fields; all the large forms are parallel to the picture-plane. Those forms that are not—the hedgerow at the left and the furrows in the second field—are perpendicular to it and more or less inconspicuous to boot. The powerful illusion of recession is accomplished by the perspective, designed from a comparatively low point of sight, and by the variations of color, value, and texture from strip to strip. The highest values and the smoothest planes appear in the river and the castle, farthest in the space.

The peasants are part of the landscape to a much greater degree than the hunters in *December*. This is particularly true of the glorious man and his horse, in which Paul has partially resisted his passion for total reconstruction. Since the horse appears at a certain distance the cloth would obviously maintain the illusion better if it were not too white, and Paul has been willing to show it dirty! The horse, furthermore, with unkempt, tangled mane and weak, sloping hindquarters is a far cry from the fine animals of the nobility. The sower in my opinion tells us only partly what Paul had in mind because his face and hands seem to have been painted by the illuminator who retouched the two women in *June* (Fig. 544).[490] We encounter here the same open, heavy brushwork and the eye rolled upward, quite expressionless. It may be puzzling that once again parts of a figure in the foreground should have been reworked until we recall that the flesh areas were normally the last to be painted. Paul, furthermore, was too fascinated by the way in which things are put together and people behave—look at the intent rider cracking his whip!—to have conceived such a stupid, moon-struck sower. Though the empty stare is due to a later hand the open purse and torn socks are surely Paul's.

This miniature has an extraordinary informality. The two principal figures appear near the lateral frames, their backs are turned to each other, and they proceed out of the represented space. Never before had a painting given so strong an impression of casualness and transience. Through the frame, which is now truly an Albertian window-frame, we view a scene that will be different in a moment. It is, moreover, clearly only a small part of a larger world whose presence is strongly felt. The vivid sense of the continuity of space beyond the frames is unprecedented—a culmination of Paul's first steps in some small miniatures in the calendar of the *Belles Heures* (Fig. 861). Horse and rider face the adjoining field, from which a magpie flies into view. On the river behind only a small part of a boat is visible. Beyond the sower the branches of a tree curve out behind the frame. All movement, indeed, is lateral; even the scarecrow aims his arrow directly off to the left.

All this, however, is only part of the story. The miniature has a firm, geometric structure like paintings by Masaccio or Piero. As in the compositions of these early Renaissance masters the space is still; only the figures move. They are similarly differentiated from their environment; the rhythmical context of the figure in earlier "Gothic" painting, including Paul's, is fundamentally diminished. Although Paul has departed from tradition by leaving the center of the composition wide open he has nevertheless discreetly established an axis. It is marked first by an inanimate but anthropomorphic object, the scarecrow, and then by the turret in the wall of the castle. Three trees rise at each side of the scarecrow, but in the nearer space the bilateral design is more complex and dynamic. The horse and rider are artistically "heavier" than the sower, so that the harrow lies to the right of the axis, the smaller bag and the canteen to the left. The sower is supported also by the tree and by the larger tower in the wall. The sprightly birds correspond to the swing of the sower. The nearest corner of the castle falls just to the right of the axis, whereas the larger part of the structure lies to the left. In view of the rationality of the composition and the exquisite interrelation of all the parts it is no accident that the plan of the harrow, corner towards us, resembles the plan of the Louvre.

For the first time in post-antique painting the design in space is almost as rich and significant as the vertical design. The two aspects of the composition are synthesized, anticipating the work of Uccello and above all Piero. Paul was less concerned, however, with interrelations of volumes than of color, light and texture. He gave to each object or creature a much higher degree of individuality. He attempted what we may designate a full and accurate reconstruction of forms seen from nearby, while not neglecting their function in the composition as a whole. Thus the walls of the Louvre bear statues and gargoyles, the roofs have spires with fleurs-de-lys and banners showing the royal arms, yet the volume and mass of the building remain powerful and imposing.[491] The detail does, however, disturb the illusion of distance.

The description of the magpies and blackbirds is astonishing. They cluster in the furrows where, as the footprints tell us, the sower has just scattered his seed. The magpie near the harrow has not remained aloof for no reason. It approaches the fresh droppings of the horse. Almost every bird is in a different position, and each casts a correct shadow. One can see, accurately rendered, all the wing and tail feathers, even sometimes the eye. The free, varied curvatures resemble the moving lappets of the horse's cloth and the dancing pieces of white paper tied to strings that are intended to frighten the birds. On the opposite side of the central axis there are the lively gray footprints of the sower—in soft earth rather than in February's snow—and his black hose, spotted so to speak by the rents in them.

Each surface strikes us as possessing all the qualities that are visible on close inspection: the hide, hair, and metal bit of the horse, the cloth seed-bag and the wooden canteen alongside it. Shadows are cast by all the vertical forms, from the birds to the scarecrow and the sticks that hold the strings. They all fall in the same direction, even in the distance, where one man's shadow is cast on the wall, anticipating the famous similar form in Uccello's *Flood*. All the patches of shadow in *October* are luminous, created by lines repeated at significant intervals.

In this miraculous painting Paul has described other visual phenomena with equal perceptiveness. Small stones in the turned soil glisten in the light. There are telling highlights on the eye of the horse and the nose of the scarecrow. The little water-barrel, though in the shade of the bag, is so highly polished that several lines of reflected light shine on it. The river, composed of silver glazed in green and gray, contains reflections of the boats and the people on the bank. Even the minute woman who has gone down the steps to do washing, or the man nearby repairing his boat, are accurately reflected upside down in the water. The point of sight for all these reflections is directly opposite, on the near bank of the Seine.

In *October* and in all his last miniatures Paul comes close to Campin and to Jan van Eyck (Figs. 697, 758–760). With Campin there may even have been some kind of exchange. These late miniatures also exhibit the geometric order of the Italian tradition; indeed, as we have suggested, they anticipate later Quattrocento developments of geometric design and of planar-spatial synthesis. Thus in Paul's last work qualities of the two great European centers, which might have seemed contradictory, are held in a remarkable equilibrium. Although a related blend of North and South was achieved in France by Jean Pucelle, Jacquemart, and the Boucicaut Master, the combination was much more complex and complete in Paul's latest paintings.

These paintings exhibit a degree of stylistic change that is a novel and un-medieval phenomenon. It was conditioned by the artist's new conception of himself and of the value of originality and individuality. The admiration of an extraordinary patron certainly quickened the development of these ideas. The gifts the two men exchanged, including the simulated book, suggest an unusual familiarity between prince and painter. The Duke transferred to Paul, as we have seen, one of the great houses of Bourges, previously occupied by his treasurer and judged suitable for a nobleman. Paul and his brothers no doubt had the money and the time that enabled them to travel to Italy—twice?—with the explicit purpose of developing their art.

The Duke's patronage provided both security and challenge. The enormously gifted Boucicaut Master, who never won such a position, failed—and here I differ from Panofsky[492]—to grow equally. Of course Paul's development needs to be seen in relation to the change in the status of the artist and the estimation of his product that had begun in the early years of the fourteenth century in Italy. His amazing trajectory over a period of only fourteen years resembles the stylistic evolution of the similarly shortlived Masaccio, who moved even faster within fewer years.

Since Paul was greatly preferred by his patron to his brothers they probably regarded him as the leader of the little *équipe*. He no doubt decided, among other things, what miniatures he wished to paint, and, if our hypotheses are correct, his choices, especially in the calendar, reveal an uncommon awareness of his gifts and of his artistic purposes. For important reasons which we now understand he consistently avoided scenes that were to include the nobility and he chose only peasants or, in *December*, their counterparts in the hunt. Surprisingly enough he even avoided the execution of the first scene, which is devoted to his patron. Similarly, the four miniatures in the calendar painted by Jean offered equal opportunities for that painter's particular gifts. This extraordinary self-awareness is implicit also, though to a lesser degree, in the allocation of subjects in the other sections of the *Très Riches Heures*.

7 · THE PORTRAITS OF BUILDINGS

The subjects of the calendar cycle in the *Très Riches Heures* are unprecedented in their references to a single person. Jean de Berry presides at table in *January* and eight of the other scenes contain "portraits" of contemporary castles. Three of these were royal—the Louvre, Palais de la Cité, and Vincennes. The Duke owned four, and a nephew, Louis II d'Anjou, another, but Jean de Berry possessed other important chateaux that are not represented. Evidently this particular kind of iconographic innovation could have been inspired by only a few of the most powerful princes in Europe. The calendar cycle was apparently judged secular in every respect, because none of the chapels the Duke owned nor either of those he built—the very large ones at Riom and Bourges—were included. Possibly, as we shall see, the Limbourgs intended an allusion to the Sainte-Chapelle, Bourges, in the *Christmas Mass* (Fig. 589). The evocation of the chateaux surely aroused nostalgia in the Duke, because he had not seen much of them since he settled in Paris *ca.* 1402, and almost nothing after his return to the capital at the end of the siege of Bourges in 1412.

It seems droll that the Duke's manuscripts should have had a far better rate of survival than his castles, but it is true that of all eight buildings depicted in the calendar only one, the castle of Saumur not far from Angers, exists (Fig. 699). It is no less odd that a few details of the buildings as we see it today are derived from the miniature (Fig. 547), for the latter was used as a model by restorers of the castle about 1932. They assumed that it reflected the original building more reliably than the existing castle, which had been altered (Fig. 698).[493] Their reconstruction affected primarily the superstructure, because the spires, chimneys and roofs had been largely lost. The pyramidal bonnets put on the towers no doubt protect them but do not contribute to their beauty. Large elements of the building that have not been changed are so similar in the miniature that the Limbourgs clearly intended a detailed and accurate representation. So strong, however, was their concern for a certain artistic effect that, like Botticelli copying ancient reliefs, they attenuated the entire structure, giving it stronger vertical accents and a less imposing mass. There is, furthermore, one minor difference, either deliberate or the result of an inadequate record. The towers, which in actuality are polygonal above (the northeast one was altered later), become circular in the miniature.

This is, however, no image of a building recalled sometime after a visit, and then recorded. It was surely based on a drawing made at the site, probably by Paul, and the character of the other buildings in the *Très Riches Heures* confirms this inference. One can even define the point of sight as the place towards the southeast from which the photograph here reproduced was taken (Fig. 699). The orthogonals of the two facades in the miniature do not, however, vanish correctly, and the spectator seems to be above the sloping terrain and the base of the building.

One detail measures vividly the commitment of the Limbourgs to the accurate depiction of a specific building and its environment. The Château de Saumur has a commanding site over the Loire (Fig. 700), and above the wall at the left in the miniature appears the top of a distant tower! Constructed in the thirteenth century, the chateau was remodeled by Louis I d'Anjou and his son, who was advised by the architect of Jean de Berry, Guy de Dammartin.[494] His presence provides one link between Jean de Berry and the castle of his nephew, Duke Louis II, or more precisely of his wife Yolande, to whom he had given it. The quality of the wine produced near it may have led to its selection for September in the calendar, but there probably were more compelling reasons, so far not detected. So exceptional is its appearance here that until about 1900—and occasionally since then—the building was identified as Jean de Berry's own Château de Bicêtre.[495] The engraving of this building, famous in its time, by Claude Chastillon in the seventeenth century shows, however, a building quite different from the one in *September* (Fig. 708). Despite the care that the Duke lavished on Bicêtre and the richness and variety of its collections he would probably not have wished to be reminded of it in 1415 because four years earlier a Parisian mob had set fire to it, gutting it completely.[496]

The miniature of *September* preserves for us accessory buildings of Saumur that were not included in early engravings and that are entirely lost. We see the gate-house and the drawbridge and its ropes, depicted with the usual attention of the Limbourgs to techniques. To the left is the large chimney of an oven and kitchen, very much like the one that still exists at the nearby abbey of Fontevrault.[497]

Since the other eight buildings, or clusters of buildings, in the calendar have been entirely or in large part destroyed since the eighteenth century, they can be identified only by comparison with early representations. An engraving of 1699 shows the chateau at Poitiers standing, already in ruins, below the town at the confluence of the rivers Clain and Boivre (Fig. 674). In an engraving published by Claude Chastillon half a century earlier the castle is largely intact (Fig. 701), and the two structures certainly represent the same building.[498] The three beautiful towers were built for Jean de Berry in the 'eighties.[499] The engraving by Chastillon shows the hills that rise at both sides of the building. The roofs, except over the towers, have disappeared, and of the building at the left, replete with spires in the miniature, only the gables remain. If we assume, as we probably should, that Paul produced as exact a likeness here as in *September*, the large windows in the wall and the towers were introduced later, and this alteration would conform with architectural development in general.

The first palace of the Louvre, constructed by Philippe Auguste and Charles V, which we see in *October* (Fig. 548), was entirely replaced by the present structure. Two later paintings of it attest to the precision of Paul's representation. One appears in the distance in a *Crucifixion* with saints painted about 1450 by a Flemish master active in Paris (Fig. 705).[500] The building is seen from approximately the same place, but it is overlapped toward the east by the Hôtel du Petit-Bourbon and towards the west by the structure on the nearer side of the Seine, the Tour de Nesles.

A full south view of the Louvre was introduced into a representation of the *Lamentation* about 1500 by a German painter working in Paris (Fig. 706).[501] On the nearer bank rises the church of Saint-Germain-des-Prés, for which the panel was made, and in the distance the hill of Montmartre. This painter included the surrounding wall with its towers, though he omitted the central one that would have concealed an important part of the castle itself. As in the *Très Riches Heures* people stroll along the bank below the wall and one has entered the gate, but they are generally less correct in scale. The northwest tower of the castle, hidden by the great donjon in *October*, is just visible here. It is the place to which Charles V, the real founder of the royal library, moved it about 1368.[502] He brought it there from the older royal palace, the Palais de la Cité.

This earlier palace of the kings is, as we have seen, the main building portrayed in *June* (Fig. 544).[503] All that remains of the large structure are towers. Two of the round ones are embedded in the Renaissance reconstruction along the Seine (Fig. 709). Behind the wall in the miniature one sees the royal garden, to which an exterior staircase, full of people, descends. The building with arched windows towards the right is the thirteenth-century palace of St. Louis. Though the representation of the Sainte-Chapelle is only about an inch high the accuracy of most of the details is striking, but the painter has rendered the stone less warm than it actually is.

The old conviction, which still persists, that the interests of Jean de Berry continued throughout his life to be centered in the Berry and his other possessions but not in Paris, influenced the identification of the architecture in the miniatures of the *Très Riches Heures*. Thus the buildings behind the wood in *May* were believed to be in the Duke's city of Riom in the Auvergne (Fig. 543).[504] This identification was based on a fifteenth-century drawing of Riom by Revel in an armorial of Auvergne (Fig. 710). This drawing tells us clearly how much Jean de Berry contributed to the skyline of this town, for the palace he reconstructed and the chapel he built are very conspicuous near the walls at the left. The buildings do not, however, resemble the complex in *May*; the absence of the donjon of the ducal palace is especially notable. What we really see, as M. G. Papertiant pointed out in 1952,[505] is once again the Palais de la Cité, beginning at the left with the projecting wing or *tourelle*, the towers of the Conciergerie, and the great Tour de l'Horloge (larger than in *June*). The view is to the left of the one in *June* (Fig. 544), so that the towers of other buildings are visible at the left and the Sainte-Chapelle does not appear on the right. The palace in *May* has tan or brown walls and it lacks the luminosity of Paul's building in *June*. *May* was painted by Jean, but the figures are struck by a light that does not seem to reach the dun buildings.

The chateau in Jean's miniature of *April* seems similarly rendered in accordance with a principle rather than painted as seen in daylight (Fig. 542). It can be identified with the Duke's Château de Dourdan, on the River Orge not far from Paris. The great donjon and the towers of this chateau, now in ruins, may still be seen in the engraving by Chastillon (Fig. 673). A reconstruction of the plan confirms the identification.[506] The building in the latest miniature by Jean, *August*, still preserves much of the studio appearance (Fig. 546). Its very unusual four-lobed donjon, part of which still survives, identifies it as another of the Duke's chateaux in the Parisian region, Etampes (Fig. 702).[507] The great wall on the side of the river Juine seems oddly broken along its upper edge. The castle was besieged and taken by the king in 1411, but one wonders whether the usual siege "engins" described by the chronicler Monstrelet would have effected damage at such an altitude.[508]

At first sight the great castle in *March* may seem as dull in color as those in *April*, *May*, and *August* (Fig. 541). It is painted, however, with much greater sensitiveness and subtlety; each part has a distinctive tone and its own range of value. The great structure acquires an impressive volume, or more precisely, series of volumes that develop rhythmically in the space. The color is maintained at a relatively low key because of the adjacent landscape and Paul's wish to suggest a rather dull March day, though this is not evident in the sky.

There can be no doubt that the castle is Lusignan, which was razed in the late sixteenth century.[509] Because it was held by the Protestants the royal army attacked it in 1574, and a rather schematic drawing made at the time to illustrate the cannonade shows us a structure similar to the one in *March* (Fig. 707). The draughtsman did not attempt to represent such embellishments as the large windows in the residential quarters on the upper part of the great tower that Jean de Berry himself added to his older building (Fig. 541). A golden dragon hovers over the castle, and its image appears at the tip of the tower at the left. This is the fairy Mélusine, protectress of the chateau, whose love for a mortal was shattered when he violated her wish not to be seen on Saturday, when she normally became a dragon. The tale was recorded by the Duke's secretary, Jean d'Arras.[510]

The magnificent towers of the royal palace of Vincennes, in which Jean de Berry was born, and which he occasionally visited, rise in the sunlight in the background of *December* (Fig. 549). The kings began the donjon, the only part that still exists, early in the fourteenth century. The vast enclosure with its nine towers, eight of which the Limbourgs represented, was built by the Duke's brother, Charles V, and we see it in a fine engraving by Androuet du Cerceau of 1576 (Fig. 711).[511] The difference in the appearance of the donjon suggests that the Limbourgs viewed the castle from the opposite side, where in fact the main part of the forest lay. Fouquet painted the tower from the same side in his miniature of Job in the *Hours of Etienne Chevalier* (Fig. 704).

The calendar of the *Très Riches Heures* offered special opportunities for the representation of specific buildings. So great was the interest of the painters and their patron in portraiture of this kind that famous contemporary architectural monuments such as Notre-Dame, the Sainte-Chapelle, and the chateau of Mehun emerged, as we have seen, in scenes of religious history. In his miniature for the Mass of St. Michael Jean seized the opportunity to represent as his main subject the great Breton shrine of this saint (Fig. 597). He showed the entire island and its exceptional surroundings, portraying vividly the peculiarities of the site. Boats lie stranded on the flat tidal plain while the water recedes or advances behind. The painting is full of perfectly rendered small forms that nevertheless do not impede the sense of a clear view of a nearby hill-town. There are even tiny yet precise portrayals of sea birds, two perched on a turret, others on a gargoyle and a buttress, while three are flying. The light flows consistently from the left, but it strikes the three main masses of the buildings with unequal intensity. The miniature far surpasses all earlier attempts to represent a town in perspective; it constitutes, in fact, a milestone in the tradition that passes from Ambrogio Lorenzetti's view of Siena to Jan van Eyck's city in the *Rolin Madonna*.

Mont-Saint-Michel is portrayed from the south. It lacks the ramparts that were begun after the battle of Agincourt in 1421; they appear in a later fifteenth-century representation, which is, however, by comparison with the miniature in the *Très Riches Heures*, utterly fantastic (Fig. 703). It has been asserted that Jean's remarkable portrait, like others in the book, was achieved in recollection only, without a drawing made on the spot.[512] Its *seeming* fidelity has recently been proved by archaeological excavation. The Romanesque choir of the church we see in the miniature, which collapsed in 1421, had, in fact, a deambulatory without chapels, and it did rise higher than the nave, just as Jean showed it.[513]

Whereas it is entirely appropriate that St. Michael should defeat the devil over Mont-Saint-Michel, the connection of the Sainte-Chapelle, Notre-Dame, and the city of Paris with the Meeting of the Magi is not so obvious (Fig. 571). The miniature is, as we have seen, a symbolic re-enactment, in which one king has taken the form of Constantine and Paris is Jerusalem.[514] The *montjoie* marks the spot, as the Crusaders learned, from which the Holy City first became visible.[515]

The boldest of these introductions of contemporary buildings in religious histories is in the *Temptation* (Fig. 590). There the Duke's chateau at Mehun-sur-Yèvre, described in detail, occupies most of the pictorial space. It serves to represent the riches of the world with which the devil seeks to corrupt Christ.[516]

The Château de Mehun in this miniature, the chateau at Poitiers in *July*, and the castle of Lusignan in *March* are the only buildings represented in the *Très Riches Heures* that stood in the territories of Jean de Berry. Mehun, in fact, had been given by the Duke in 1414 to his nephew, Louis duc de Guyenne.[517] We do not know what the Limbourgs had planned for *November*. We are struck by the absence of his two large religious constructions, the Sainte-Chapelle in Bourges and in Riom. His great palaces in Bourges and Poitiers are notable omissions also; perhaps they were omitted from the calendar cycle because they were urban. As against the three buildings in the Berry and Poitou that the Limbourgs represented they painted seven in Paris or in the Parisian region. There the Duke had lived almost continuously since 1401, and the *Très Riches Heures* clearly reflects his deep ties with the metropolis.

The buildings in the *Très Riches Heures* that we have been considering constitute an unprecedented cycle. In their prominence within the pictorial field and their fidelity to the monuments they are true architectural portraits. It is not surprising that they appear around the same time as the portraits of persons. Like all innovations they were, of course, anticipated in certain respects. From the late thirteenth or early fourteenth century Italian painters occasionally introduced specific buildings into their scenes. A recognizable, though much transformed version of the Roman temple in the piazza at Assisi was painted as such in an episode of the life of St. Francis that actually occurred there.[518] The Palazzo Vecchio symbolizes Florence in the fresco of the Expulsion of the Duke of Athens from the city in 1343.[519] A detailed description, on a large scale, of the model of the projected Cathedral of Florence serves as an image of the Church in the famous fresco by Andrea da Firenze *ca.* 1367 in the Spanish Chapel, Florence.[520]

In France municipal seals commonly contained images of an important local building. The building was represented on early seals by the aggregation of certain striking features, such as the huge, round (in actuality polygonal), arcaded tower of St. Sernin on the seal of Toulouse of 1242 (Fig. 729).[521] Later the proportions and structure of the image began to correspond much more closely with the actual building, as the cathedral on the seal of Bayonne of 1351 (Fig. 728). The closest predecessors of the calendar pictures in the *Très Riches Heures*, however, seem to be in this respect, too, the mural paintings in the Torre dell'Aquila. In *January* the painter described carefully the nearby castle of Stenico, both its original structure of the thirteenth century and its recent addition (Fig. 695).[522] The existence of such a representation in the work of a provincial painter indicates that originally others were to be seen in some of the countless examples of secular mural painting of the period that have been lost.

The portraits of buildings in the calendar pictures of the *Très Riches Heures* reflect a patron so exceptionally rich in possessions that they did not establish a real tradition in Books of Hours. Chateaux and palaces appear in the few calendar cycles inspired by the paintings of the Limbourgs, in the Book of Hours of *ca.* 1420 formerly in the Beatty collection (Fig. 524) and in the manuscripts illuminated in Bruges in the early sixteenth century (Figs. 756, 757). The buildings are not, however, individualized. On the other hand in Italy in the mid-sixteenth century the villas and parks of a great patron were frequently portrayed in murals in one of his buildings, but such cycles, perhaps distantly echoing the *Très Riches Heures*, were unconnected with the calendar (Fig. 712).[523] It was in France, so far as we know—but the question seems not to have been explored—that the principal elements were again combined, so that in *December*, one of a series of months designed for tapestries by Charles Le Brun, a boar is beset by hounds in front of the royal Château de Monceaux (Fig. 713).[524]

The calendar pictures in the *Très Riches Heures* are especially significant in the oeuvre of the Limbourgs because they are the only secular works by them that we have. The inventories do not, furthermore, refer to any paintings of this kind by them except for the famous fake book, and we would not, in fact, expect them to do so, because the favorite artists of the Duke, beginning with Beauneveu and Jacquemart de Hesdin, were asked to illustrate religious texts, a Psalter and Books of Hours—the latter clearly the kind of book he valued most. On the other hand the Duke acquired secular works of all kinds. The calendar may be said to represent the further penetration of the religious realm by worldly interests, although evidently so beautiful a world cannot be disengaged from divine order.

8 · INTERIOR SPACE

When designing the miniatures of the *Très Riches Heures* the Limbourgs showed a striking preference for exterior settings and landscapes. In a few compositions, as in the *Annunciation* and the *Healing of the Possessed*, the action moves into a portico (Figs. 559, 591), but most of the events occur outdoors. Of the twelve calendar pictures only *January* is represented within a building. The conception of this interior, to be sure, is strikingly advanced, for reasons that we shall discuss shortly. On the other hand, even though leading French illuminators from about 1373 had represented the Annunciation in a church or a building that resembled one, and Paul de Limbourg had himself manifested this preference in the *Belles Heures*, in the *Très Riches Heures* the Virgin alone kneels within an ecclesiastical portico whereas Gabriel remains largely outside (Figs. 410, 559).

This difference from the *Belles Heures* is all the more notable because that earlier manuscript contains numerous interiors. In several of them the space is seen through an architectural frame in the picture plane which constitutes the front face of the building, and which may therefore be designated an "entrance arch" (Fig. 410).[525] In only one composition—*St. Catherine in her study* (Fig. 422)—does the arcade in the picture plane seem much smaller in scale than the building behind it, and thus become the kind of diaphragm that the Boucicaut Master introduced in the *Boucicaut Hours* at the same time.[526] In the miniature of St. Catherine the color of the arcade is the same as that of the room behind, but even the Boucicaut Master himself only occasionally differentiated these hues.[527]

Scarce though interior scenes are in the *Très Riches Heures*, two do exist, insufficiently regarded because they are masked, so to speak, by the sumptuous prolixity of Colombe. Following the usual keen observations of Durrieu, part of the architecture in both miniatures has already been referred to the Limbourgs,[528] but there is evidence to prove that they designed the entire compositions. The more surprising of these two miniatures—indeed the most unexpected composition in the entire manuscript—is the *Funeral of Diocrès*, at Matins in the Office of the Dead (Fig. 578). This subject had already appeared in the *Belles Heures* (Fig. 467), but in the *Très Riches Heures* the Limbourgs disregarded the earlier setting and chose instead a composite structure utilized in another enigmatic miniature in their earlier manuscript, representing St. Jerome in prayer in a church (Fig. 474). The circular tabernacle over a sarcophagus alongside the church probably symbolizes, as we have said, the Holy Sepulchre, which the saint contemplates. The derivative form in the *Très Riches Heures*, however, clearly has no such meaning.

We must, nevertheless, accept this strange architectural conglomeration as a work of the Limbourgs for several reasons. Its surfaces suggest that they began to paint it. The folio was prepared for them by an assistant of the Breviary Master.[529] Finally, and conclusively, the buildings were copied in the 'twenties by the Master of St. Jerome, that puzzling artist—perhaps the youngest Limbourg brother Arnold—who borrowed, as we have seen, from the *Belles Heures* and other works of Paul, Jean and Herman (Fig. 600).[530] We now recognize his familiarity with the *Très Riches Heures* also, although we cannot be certain that he knew the miniature in its unfinished state rather than a drawing by the Limbourgs for it. In some details probably his copy in the *Psalter of Henry VI* comes closer than Colombe's painting to the original composition.

The Limbourgs created a far more impressive interior for the *Christmas Mass* (Fig. 589). The rite is celebrated beneath the soaring vaults of a church, which has the scale if not the spatial vividness of such late paintings by the Boucicaut Master as the *Mass for the Dead* in the Horae in London, painted a couple of years later (Fig. 598). The responsibility of the Limbourgs for the upper reaches of the architecture of the miniature in the *Très Riches Heures* was recognized by Durrieu,[531] and indeed the gray arches below the upper frame seem to have been painted by them and only lightly retouched by Colombe. Once again their authorship of the entire design can be proved by early copies. Around 1420 the Harvard Hannibal Master employed the composition twice for a funeral service illustrating the Office of the Dead (Figs. 599, 601). To conform with the new context he introduced not only a coffin but three averted mourners who are very similar to those in the foreground of the *Mass for the Dead* by the Boucicaut Master to which we have just referred.

As in the instance of the *Funeral of Diocrès* these early copies again preserve some details of the Limbourg design more faithfully than the version by Colombe in the *Très Riches Heures* itself.[532] Thus the large acanthus leaves of the kind favored by the Limbourgs that appear in the lateral spandrels of both copies by the Harvard Hannibal Master have been mostly eliminated by Colombe. The scale of the church, however, has been so reduced in the copies that Colombe's building must be closer to the original design. It is certainly possible that the Limbourgs, who described carefully the exteriors of specific churches and secular buildings, chose here to allude to the Duke of Berry's Sainte-Chapelle, with its large windows of stained glass and its statues of apostles and evangelists standing on the piers between them.[533] Possibly in their design the Duke of Berry appeared within the private oratory to the right of the altar, similar to the curtained structure occupied by Philippe le Bon at Mass (Fig. 384). Hovering high above the celebrant three angels bear ritual objects for the Mass. Perhaps their presence was inspired by the references to angels as ministers in Hebrews 1, which is the epistle in the accompanying Mass.

Like the borders around the *Funeral of Diocrès* the arabesques and the acanthus leaves at the initial on the folio of the *Christmas Mass* were painted by a follower of the Breviary Master. Colombe, however, inserted all the figures.[534] The presence of similar arabesques in the same style on the folio (182) of the *Resurrection* suggests that this miniature too may have been at least drawn in by the Limbourgs (Fig. 595).[535] Perhaps copies will soon be found to prove this hypothesis. The soldiers around the tomb, so fearful, St. Matthew said, they seemed to be dead, resemble those in *Ego sum* (Fig. 582).

The imposing scale of the interior in the *Christmas Mass* was matched in all of European painting only by such late paintings of the Boucicaut Master as the *Mass* in London (Fig. 598). Both miniatures employ the architectural diaphragm that these painters had devised a decade earlier. In *January* in the *Très Riches Heures*, however, Paul and Jean took the important step of eliminating any kind of entrance arch, whether a true diaphragm or the near face of a building just behind the picture plane (Fig. 539). The floor and perhaps the vault of the ducal dining hall extend forward to the frames above and below, whereas at the sides neither the building nor any other large forms coincide with the frames. Here the space opens freely and informally. Paul thus moved beyond established conceptions, giving to interior space the kind of continuity behind the frame that was developing in outdoor scenes—most vividly in his landscapes in the calendar of the *Très Riches*

Heures (Figs. 545, 548). Thus he created an interior that closely approximated the major innovations of the mid-twenties, Jan van Eyck's *Madonna in the Church* and Donatello's *Salome before Herod.* Donatello's relief is remarkably similar (Fig. 769).[536]

9 · THE MAP OF ROME

The *Très Riches Heures* is not only the first Book of Hours with a full-page cycle of calendar pictures, it is the first surviving example of this kind of prayer book that contains a map or, more precisely, a panorama of the principal monuments of a city (Fig. 580). The view of Rome is full of individualized buildings, and in this respect it resembles the architectural portraits in the rest of the manuscript. Where, however, the latter were portrayed *al vif*, the monuments of Rome were merely taken from a painted model. This model as well as the miniature in the *Très Riches Heures* belong to a kind of map that selected certain natural and architectural phenomena and combined placement of them in space with a description of their appearance.

Early maps of Rome, like medieval maps in general, reduce spatial complexities to simple, conventional patterns. Thus the map made in 1320 by the Franciscan friar Paolino da Venezia, following of course an earlier model, presents Rome as an ellipse (Fig. 730).[537] Two-dimensional representations of the facades of buildings, statues, and even hills lie flat along principal lines of the plan. A seal made in 1328 for the Emperor Louis the Bavarian contains a remarkable view of a few of the principal monuments of the city (Fig. 733).[538] The representation, clearly the work of a major artist, reflects the profound change that had occurred in pictorial representation beginning with Cavallini, Giotto, and Duccio. The buildings are seen from a high point of sight in a spatial relationship within the walls that greatly condenses, but still approximates, actuality.

This seal of 1328 is based on principles that were developed in later fourteenth-century and early fifteenth-century maps or views. It is fascinating to observe that just as basic aspects of late antique and early Christian painting are revived in Italy *ca.* 1300, so the real predecessors of the Trecento map are Roman maps of the fourth and fifth centuries, if we can trust the later copies of them (Fig. 736). These late antique maps combine a bird's-eye view of buildings placed oblique to the picture plane with an essentially flat, diagrammatic representation of the terrain.[539] The churches, castles and towns, for example, on a globe held by Prudence in a beautiful but little-known fresco of about 1380 in a private dwelling in Ferrara are similarly conceived (Fig. 732).[540] The ground, however, now began to be similarly seen. It undulates, and since this manifestly is a sphere three buildings, like the hand of Prudence, are partially seen over the edge!

The wide intervals between the buildings in this *mappa mundi* recall *Rome* in the *Très Riches Heures* (Fig. 580). Perhaps it is significant that the blue rivers, pale yellow-green ground, and pink buildings of the fresco likewise resemble the miniature, not because the Limbourgs knew this very work but because of the general similarity of color between North Italian painting of the late fourteenth century and French painting of the early fifteenth century, especially the Limbourgs.

This fresco in Ferrara gives us a good notion of the appearance of the map of Rome that the Limbourgs used as a model. It was, in our opinion, made in Italy, probably in Rome, in the third quarter of the century, and thus not long before the Ferrarese fresco. The miniature in the *Très Riches Heures* is very similar to a well-known frescoed map of Rome by Taddeo di Bartolo in his fresco cycle in the Palazzo Pubblico, Siena, finished in 1413–1414 (Fig. 731).[541] To this group, which shows South at the top, belongs a less well-known but beautiful map in a manuscript of the Catiline and Jugurtha of Sallust, preserved in a private collection (Fig. 4). This map has been hitherto described briefly as of the early fifteenth century,[542] but it is, in our opinion, definitely French. Indeed it as well as numerous initials and miniatures and two additional maps of different kinds in the manuscript were painted by the Orosius Master and his workshop *ca.* 1418 (Figs. 734, 737).[543]

The problem of Taddeo's model and of the relationship of his map to the one by the Limbourgs has been discussed for a long time. Historians have usually maintained that Taddeo copied a map made during the third quarter of the fourteenth century, and that the Limbourgs used a model of the same kind.[544] The evidence for this view has never, however, been adequately presented, and it has been possible for an eminent scholar to insist not long ago that the Limbourgs copied Taddeo's fresco, and that therefore one or more of them must have been in Italy *ca.* 1413.[545] The problem is obviously important, and we shall therefore examine these relationships more closely.

To facilitate this discussion we have numbered most of the monuments on the map in the *Très Riches Heures* (Fig. 721). Wishing to show, furthermore, approximately what these maps communicated we have suggested identifications for most of the buildings.[546] These proposals, listed in the key to the map printed opposite Figure 721, are based on a variety of sources, written as well as visual; only the principal ones are indicated in the key. The identifications are presented, furthermore, with two important qualifications. First, the degree of certainty varies greatly, from, say, the Castel Sant'Angelo or the Colosseum about which there can be no question, to churches such as S. Marcello or S. Susanna, where our uncertainty is so considerable that we have inserted question marks. In the second place no building in the *Très Riches Heures*, nor for that matter in Taddeo's fresco, bears a name. We may ask what the Limbourgs or Jean de Berry made of them. Certainly the man who produced the model knew far more. By proposing identifications we wish to show that these very early maps of Rome conveyed information, more or less precise, about the location and the character of the principal secular and religious monuments of the city.

Since the maps both in Siena and the *Très Riches Heures* lack inscriptions were they absent too from the model? We cannot be sure, because in the map by the Orosius Master a few buildings are identified: Capitolium, Sanctus Petrus, Castellum Sancti Angeli (Fig. 4).

In Taddeo's map the ground plane within the walls is dark brown and outside it becomes dark blue. Such uniform tones, often without any color at all, are characteristic of medieval maps, and they are still preserved in Italian maps of the entire fifteenth century (Figs. 732, 740), although a few hills are differentiated in some (Fig. 738). Paul and his brothers, seeking as always to tell more about the color and texture of the world, transformed the uniform plane into a pavement of large, more or less round stones. Thus what had been abstract, a neutral zone of space, acquires the same quality and degree of reality as the buildings. Like them the pavement is graded from light in the foreground to dark in the distance, and it is similarly subject to the laws of perspective, so that the stones grow increasingly smaller.

The Limbourgs had employed this same kind of pavement before 1404 in a street scene in the *Bible moralisée* (Fig. 322), and afterwards in numerous miniatures in the *Belles Heures* and the *Très Riches Heures* (Figs. 487, 583–586). On the other hand an Italian map of Constantinople as late as 1424, which resembles the Limbourgs' *Rome* in many respects, characterizes the water but still retains the abstract plane for the city itself (Fig. 739). The change to a pavement in *Rome* in the *Très Riches Heures* was accompanied by an increase in the intervals between the buildings, so that we are less impressed by the clutter of monuments and much more by the orderly expansion of the open space. The buildings are differentiated in color so as to promote this effect.

The introduction of the pavement, not we believe hitherto discussed, indicates strikingly the difference between the Limbourgs and their Italian predecessors or even contemporaries. It gives *Rome* in the *Très Riches Heures* a more advanced scenographic character. This is enhanced by the contrast between the gray pavement within the walls and the green country outside them. Above the distant walls, furthermore, there is a bright blue sky. The Orosius Master developed further this aspect of the Limbourg miniature, extending the landscape and adding trees and rural buildings (Fig. 4). Within the walls his speckled ground seems to be a reduction of the pavement of the *Très Riches Heures*. Since he was working in Paris while the Limbourgs were painting the *Très Riches Heures* he might readily have seen the map there.

We cannot yet be certain that the Orosius Master actually knew the map in the *Très Riches Heures* but he utilized beyond any doubt the same model. He needed it, for one thing, to compose the statues of the Dioscuri, which the Limbourgs left blank. His Colosseum has three stories, as compared to four in the *Très Riches Heures* and three plus an attic in Siena. His buildings are less attenuated and more massive than those of the *Très Riches Heures*, and in this respect they are closer to those of Taddeo and the Italian model. He even included such prominent features as the goose on the Capitol and the gigantic statue of a nude female near the Colosseum that neither the Limbourgs nor Taddeo represented but which may have appeared in the model. The *Mirabilia urbis Romae* speaks of a nude statue of Roma near this place,[547] but the gesture of the right hand suggests that in origin the figure was a *Venus pudica*. There was on this site, in fact, a temple dedicated to Venus and to Roma.[548]

Of the three plans, Taddeo's is much the closest to the model (Fig. 731). He alone, for instance, gives the columns their spiral friezes (32, 40). The upper stories of his Colosseum (64), Theatrum Marcelli (52), and Amphitheatrum (78) do not have a diminished circumference. He, but not the Limbourgs, shows the Fontana di Trevi below the Dioscuri (42). The Orosius Master represents the Fontana also. Whereas, furthermore, the Limbourgs misunderstood the pyramid known as the Sepulchrum Romuli (71) and conceived it to be a flat triangle of large stones somehow attached to the wall, the Orosius Master correctly restored its pyramidal character.[549] We can therefore be certain he did not depend only upon the *Très Riches Heures*; as we have already observed, he had access to the model, probably in Paris.

The Limbourgs represented fewer buildings than either Taddeo or the Orosius Master, preferring wider spaces between them. Despite this fact, Paul and his brothers included a few structures that are only partially or not at all visible in the fresco in Siena. The area outside the walls is larger in the miniature, and we see the entire Pons salarius (4). Taddeo squeezed in only the top of the tower of this bridge and the end of the walls; if the Limbourgs had been guided only by this fresco they, probably unfamiliar with the city itself, would surely not have bothered to reconstruct an entire bridge. Indeed, unless Taddeo himself were following a model he would not have inserted so fragmentary a form at the margin.

There are some structures in both the *Très Riches Heures* and in the Sallust which do not appear in Taddeo's map and which are so unusual that the French painters would not have conceived of them. One is the strange cage or *gabbia* on the Capitoline hill (49), left only in outline in the *Très Riches Heures* but fully painted by the Orosius Master. A single column is so close to the equestrian statue of Marcus Aurelius (65) that the Limbourgs apparently interpreted it as part of the base and left it as well as the statue unpainted. Taddeo represented a single column far away, below the Colosseum, and in the Sallust map too it is quite independent of the statue. Surely the Limbourgs took these unfamiliar forms from an Italian model. Where the Tiber flows through the southwestern wall of the city a large battlemented tower rises along the river in the Sallust and the *Très Riches Heures* but not in the Siena fresco. Though the Capitol (48) is generally similar on all three plans, the Limbourgs and the Orosius Master have provided it with a proper door at the head of the exterior stair and a porch over the entrance on the ground floor. Whereas some physical features included by Taddeo were not painted by the Limbourgs,[550] they did represent two roads not in the Siena plan (nor indeed in the Sallust), one leading from the Porta S. Paolo (12) to the church outside the walls, the other running from the foot of the Palatine to the entrance of the "Palacium maius" (60).[551]

Admittedly the Limbourgs might well have added a road or two for decorative or practical reasons, just as they gave the Porta Nomentana (6) one of their fine, functional drawbridges. They transformed secular buildings or groups of buildings into elaborate fortified Gothic castles, such as those of the Orsini in Monte Giordano (22), the Cenci? (37), or the Savelli in the Theatre of Marcellus (52). Most elaborate is the "Palacium maius" (60), with its flying buttresses. The Limbourgs did not admire or did not understand (usually the same thing) colonnaded buildings and porticoes. They either closed the spaces between the columns or eliminated them entirely, as in 25, 34, 53, 66, 81, 82. The illuminators attenuated almost all buildings and enhanced their lightness by multiplying slits and windows. Although it is risky to associate the map with one particular brother on stylistic grounds, its architecture seems more Gothic than Paul's and suggests Jean.

From all this we may answer confidently the question we put at the outset. The map in the *Très Riches Heures* was not based on Taddeo's but on an example of the same map he used for his fresco. Possibly the Limbourgs possessed the same copy—it could have traveled north in 1414—but more likely they had another example.[552] Since the Orosius Master consulted it also this map was undoubtedly in Paris, where he was established and the Limbourgs were frequent visitors at least. An *ante quem* date for the original, which we have already referred to the third quarter of the fourteenth century, may be gauged from one fact. The statue of St. Michael on the tower of Castel Sant'Angelo, represented by Taddeo di Bartolo, was destroyed in 1379.[553]

The two maps of Rome similar to the one by the Limbourgs do not help us decide its function in the manuscript. On the basis of its place before the Passion cycle and the representation in it of more than forty churches, we have already suggested that the miniature was intended to refer to the Roman Station Churches.

The meaning of Taddeo's *Roma*, painted on the intrados of an arch leading from the antechapel to the Sala del Mappamondo, is not entirely clear. The Sienese liked to believe, of course, that their city had been founded by Romulus and Remus. Taddeo's map belongs to a cycle illustrating civic virtue by worthies of Republican Rome.[554] The map, which contains many buildings of the Imperial period, appears above four Roman gods who refer to civic issues, whereas on the wall above presides the personification of Religio.[555]

In addition to the Sallust already described there is a record of another manuscript of the early fifteenth century dealing with Roman history that was provided with a map of Rome. An inventory of the manuscripts of Alfonso of Aragon made in Barcelona in 1412 lists a text in French "on the Romans and Carthaginians" which had at the beginning a map of Rome.[556]

Manuscripts of Sallust did not usually contain a map of Rome but, in accordance with a tradition that may go back to antiquity, they were embellished with a map of the world, in other words of the three known continents.[557] It illustrates chapter 17 of the *War with Jugurtha*, which refers to the continents (Fig. 734).[558] The map by the Orosius Master conforms to the type that appears most often in the Sallust manuscripts. It is the so-called T map, oriented with the East and Asia above, Europe and Africa below (Fig. 735). The provinces and cities that are named in the map by the Orosius Master prove its antiquity and its place of origin. In the West the only cities are Rome and Naples. Alexandria is there but not Jerusalem, and the crude cross in the Holy Land was probably added later. The corners of the square are filled with heroes, three of them (Nebuchadnezzar, Alexander, Augustus) pagan, one (Charlemagne) Christian. These figures were painted by the late fifteenth-century French illuminator who completed the illumination, and it is interesting that though three of the names are in the original script of *ca.* 1418, "Karolus magnus" was written later and represents a change of program. Unlike most of the earlier Sallust T maps the one by the Orosius Master is not flat but in relief, and the whole has the form of a curving disk or section of a globe. The illuminator has enhanced its scenic character by painting the Red Sea not blue but red, just as the Josephus Master did in his *Antiquités judaïques* and the Limbourgs in the *Belles Heures* (Figs. 170, 478). Actually the influence of the style of the Josephus Master is apparent in several miniatures in the Sallust.

Whereas the T map normally illustrates the Jugurtha of Sallust the third map in the manuscript, which immediately precedes the beginning of this text, is rare (Fig. 737).[559] It makes one quite dizzy, because of the disproportions in scale and because it is a map of the Mediterranean in which the Italian peninsula runs parallel to the coast of North Africa. It belongs to the kind of scenic map we have been considering, and if this aspect of the miniature is derivative the model would scarcely be older than the second quarter of the fourteenth century. The figures here, as in the T map, were drawn and only partially colored. The illuminator who was to do this special work did not complete it, and what he had done was respected by his successor in the late fifteenth century. The Romans (presumably) sail to Numidia. Kneeling men pay homage to the ruler of this country (Jugurtha?) and of Mauretania. Soldiers ride on camels near Gaetulia. Castel Sant' Angelo, on the correct side of the Tiber, clearly identifies Rome. The city beyond it is probably

Naples. Carthage and another city are shown in ruins—not partly broken in the medieval manner but irregularly leveled to the ground.

Descriptions of this kind and the increasing number of depictions of continents, regions and cities are related to the rising tide of travel on land and sea. Accounts of voyages to the Near and Far East were eagerly read, occasionally in illustrated manuscripts such as the *Merveilles du monde* or *Fleurs des histoires*.[560] Ambrogio Lorenzetti's large map of the world for the Council Chamber of the Town Hall of Siena, described in the eighteenth century as demonstrating what everyone wants to see, may have been a panoramic map of our type.[561] So too may have been the famous map of the world painted by Jan van Eyck, where, according to a later fifteenth-century description, "not only the places and locations of regions but also the measurable distances between the places could be recognized."[562]

Panoramic plans of Rome of the kind painted by the Limbourgs continued to be produced in the fifteenth century. Indeed the next important plan of the city, made probably during the 'forties, belongs to the same type, though it represents the monuments, especially the ancient ones, far more accurately.[563] We know it only in copies, first in a reduced version of 1453 or 1456 by Pietro del Massaio (Fig. 738). It appears among other plans designed according to a methodical principle in an ancient cartographical text, Ptolemy's *Geography*, which had been translated into Latin in 1406 and was studied with rapidly growing interest.[564] The best version of the drawing of the 'forties was made by Alessandro Strozzi in 1474 (Fig. 740), and it is this map which has served as the principal key to our identification of monuments in the miniature in the *Très Riches Heures* and the related paintings.

Panoramic plans, particularly in Italy, were increasingly influenced by the diffusion of systematic focus perspective. As a type they were distinct from another kind of representation that likewise was gradually altered by perspective—views of cities or parts of cities without a cartographic purpose. From a high point of view we see a conglomeration of Roman buildings in a little-known fresco painted as early as *ca.* 1300 in the Cappella Minutolo of the Cathedral of Naples (Fig. 741).[565] *Ca.* 1342 Florence, with its Baptistry and rising Cathedral façade, was similarly portrayed in the famous fresco in the Loggia del Bigallo (Fig. 742). A century later, about 1435, Masolino painted a broad view of Rome and its surrounding hills in the Baptistry at Castiglione d'Olona (Fig. 743). Though the perspective is far more systematic the Pantheon rises as a preternaturally large symbol of the city. Unlike the cartographic views these inevitably conceal the space between the buildings and part or all of many monuments themselves.

10 · THE BOAR AND THE HOUNDS

For a long time historians have been aware of the extraordinary similarity between the group of the boar and the hounds in the miniature of *December* (Fig. 549) and a drawing in a famous pattern-book in Bergamo, all or part of which is ascribed to Giovannino de'Grassi (Fig. 714). His authorship is, indeed, proclaimed in an inscription of the fifteenth century on folio 4v: Johaninus de Grassis designavit. The subjects of the drawing on folio 17 and the miniature are so unusual and the relationship so close that scholars have concluded, rightly beyond doubt, that one must depend upon the other, or both on a common prototype. Until the last few years historians based their choice between these alternatives less upon the qualities of the two works than upon their general conception of the direction of the flow of influence between Lombardy and France.[566] The two compositions must, therefore, be studied more closely.

The miniature, to begin with, contains not only three hunters lacking in the drawing but two more hounds. One of the men blows a horn to signal the *Hallali* or moment of the final attack of the hounds just before the death of their prey.[567] Perhaps the rather conspicuous stones lying on the ground are the ones which the hunter, in accordance with the tradition of the hunt, will throw at the boar before finally driving his spear into its neck. Though the design seems to leave the bugler rather loosely related to the animals the other two hunters are much more involved, and the approximately hemispherical shape of the group is repeated by the curving wood behind. The composition is therefore unified in shape though not equally in color.

The case of the drawing is very different. It appears on folio 17 of the *taccuino*, which with folio 20 composes a folded sheet of parchment. The composition is too wide for the folio, and the tail of the dog at the left is therefore incomplete. Nor does it appear on folio 20v, which, when the sheet is spread flat, faces 17. The draftsman therefore utilized this folio after the sheet had been folded. Certainly the very different artist (much closer I believe to Belbello da Pavia) who drew the nest of eagles on the verso must have worked after the folio was contained in a gathering, for his drawing continues on the facing folio, which belongs to another sheet (Fig. 717). We may with good reason suspect, then, that the two dogs present in the miniature but not in the drawing were omitted for lack of space. One of them would have extended still farther to the left, and the other, just over the head of the boar, would have widened the composition also. All the hounds in the drawing, furthermore, plunge onto the boar except one. His restraint, unexplained in the drawing, is due in the miniature to the intervention of the hunter who holds him by the ears.[568] Just below this hound where, we suspect, the draftsman has compressed the composition of the miniature, the outline of the boar is lower than in the miniature; in fact, it dips strangely. The chest of the hound contains an odd patch of a different tone, and it is impossible here to distinguish the surface of the hound from that of the boar. The anatomy of the muzzle of the boar—the common *sus scrofa*—is, moreover, much inferior in the drawing. The lower jaw is too short, the tooth quite the wrong shape, and the upper lip curls around it as though it were an obstacle.

We must conclude, then, that the drawing might well be a copy of the miniature but that the reverse is extremely improbable. The drawing is exceptional in the *taccuino*; no other shows so numerous a group of animals involved in a common action. The possibility that both it and the miniature derived from a lost model is somewhat reduced by the fact, not hitherto observed, that the three brown dogs in the miniature who reappear in the drawing have there been given a more or less conspicuous brown tint. The open mouth of one dog is red, as in the miniature.[569] The model, in other words, would have had to possess the color of the miniature, and, as the requirements increase, the probability of a lost model decreases.

So far I have said nothing about the stylistic qualities of the two works. A few historians—with whom I agree—maintain that the drawings in the Bergamo manuscript were the work of several hands. I recently became quite certain, after close study of the *Uffiziolo visconteo* illuminated by Giovannino de'Grassi and associates, that the drawing was not made by him or in his immediate circle. It is much more linear than the drawings in folios 1 through 7 of the pattern-book, which are the only folios attributable to Giovannino, as Cadei has now convincingly argued.[570] The following folios are clearly by several hands, and even the cheetah below the *Hallali* on folio 17 is by still another, inferior artist. The hounds and the boar seem much further from "life" than Giovannino's own drawings or the December miniature. The draftsman has lost sight of the implications of the high point of sight, so that he has tended to complete the upper edges of the hounds in profile instead of describing, as Paul did, the upper surfaces of their bodies.

Surely, then, the boar and hounds in Bergamo were copied from a model. Was not this model, however, as some scholars have suggested, an earlier Lombard design rather than *December* in the *Très Riches Heures*? A miniature of the Temptation of St. Anthony in a Lombard manuscript illuminated about 1380 demonstrates quite clearly that in this region a composition somewhat related to the *Hallali* was known earlier than either the Bergamo drawing or the Limbourg miniature (Fig. 716). The *Temptation of St. Anthony* seems to demonstrate clearly also, however, that a radial composition like the one under consideration would not have been understood, much less created, at this early date. The painter of the miniature placed his animals almost parallel to the picture-plane, and when, as in the instance of the lion, he tried a more oblique position, he got into real trouble.

It seems probable that the radial composition of the *Hallali* was first conceived in the early fifteenth century. Did it not then originate in the December miniature, as our observations hitherto would indicate? The hypothesis confronts a difficulty: neither Paul nor his brothers designed a similarly compact, not to mention radial group. Perhaps the closest analogies are the *Lamentation* and *Entombment* in the *Belles Heures* (Figs. 343, 455). The *Annunciation to the Shepherds* in the *Belles Heures* shows us, however, that some seven or eight years before painting *December*, and before making his second trip to Italy, Paul painted a white dog very much like the corresponding ones in the *Très Riches Heures* (Fig. 411). The subject of the Hallali, too, was long established in France. We may see hounds attacking a stag and the hunter blowing his horn in a *bas-de-page* of a *Bible historiale* illuminated in the circle of Jean Pucelle (Fig. 715). The plastic sophistication, however, and the rhetoric of the boar and hounds seem to indicate that the original design was Lombard. The composition, moreover, persisted in Italy, as a Florentine engraving of about 1470 in the Fine Manner shows (Fig. 718).[571]

11 · THE EXALTATION OF THE CROSS

Many miniatures of the *Très Riches Heures* contain exceptional forms or actions that clearly imply contributions by learned clerics and scholars. With help of this kind Herman produced in the painting of the Exaltation of the Cross an entirely novel representation, so novel, indeed, that its meaning has entirely escaped all modern scholars, not to mention fifteenth-century copyists (Fig. 596).

The text of the Mass for the Exaltation of the Cross, which appeared in the same form near the end of the *Belles Heures*, was illustrated in that earlier manuscript by a much simpler and more traditional miniature (Fig. 486). A woman and a man kneel at an altar, at the center of which stands a cross bearing scourges and the crown of thorns. A second miniature in the *Belles Heures* approaches much more closely the one in the *Très Riches Heures*. Appearing within the Suffrages and following immediately the story of Heraclius (Figs. 487, 488) it shows four men, one of them perhaps the emperor, adoring the cross (Fig. 485).[572] The men, differentiated especially with regard to headgear, kneel before an altar on which stands an enormous golden cross. Its double traverse is a form that was commonly employed for a relic of the cross,[573] of which Jean de Berry possessed some specimens, one of them a splinter cut from the famous relic in the Ste-Chapelle, Paris, and given to him by his brother, King Charles V. The shape of the reliquary in the Ste-Chapelle belonged to the same type.[574]

The same kind of cross, the lamps (reduced from eleven to five), and the exotic kneeling figures reappear in the *Très Riches Heures*, but differently characterized and among other mysterious figures and objects that have intrigued historians for nearly a century. Durrieu long ago asserted that the golden cross represents the "croix au serpent" described in the inventory of 1413.[575] In important respects the painted crucifix is different, but like the "croix au serpent" it is supported by a rock, silver however instead of enameled, and on the rock rests a yellow, green and gold (rather than simply gold) lizard.[576] Like the serpents of earlier, especially Carolingian, crucifixes, the tail of the lizard entwines the cross. Durrieu suggested that the king and queen kneeling in adoration might be an imperial couple important in the history of the cross, Constantine and Helena.[577] Longnon and Cazelles suggested the couple might be Heraclius and his second wife, Martine.[578] These interpretations confront the immediate difficulty that the ruler clearly wears not an imperial but a royal crown.

A key to the identity of these figures and to the meaning of the scene as a whole is provided by the golden statues that stand on the tabernacle. At the center appears Moses, distinguished absolutely by his horns and the tablets of the law. He has a justifiable prominence in an illustration of the Exaltation of the Cross, because the lessons for Matins of this Office are drawn from his story. In the wilderness after leaving Egypt the Israelites, bitten by poisonous serpents, upbraided Moses, and on command of the Lord he put a serpent of brass upon a pole.[579] Whoever looked upon this brazen serpent would be protected from the mortal consequences of the bite of the real reptiles. The Fathers of the Church saw in this miraculous image a symbol of the crucifix and of redemption. "The brazen serpent," St. Ambrose said, "is a representation of the Cross." Christ himself prophesied: "As Moses lifted up the serpent in the wilderness, even so must the Son of Man be lifted up: That whosoever believeth in Him should not perish but have eternal life."[580]

In the same sense in which the principal form on the altar is the brazen serpent as well as the cross, the ciborium on which Moses stands, crowned by a dome, is both the Temple and the Church. Similarly the cloth that covers the porphyry altar bears crosses as well as exotic script that may refer to Hebrew. Because the crucifix on the altar is embedded in a very conspicuous rock we naturally think of a specific church—the one built by Constantine (and subsequently rebuilt) on the site of Calvary.[581] The church was described by a pilgrim as early as the sixth century; in it the altar in the chapel of the Crucifixion was apparently covered by a ciborium.[582] One of the most precious objects owned by Jean de Berry was a "joyau du Mont de Calvaire," in which a relic of the Cross appeared below a vault supported, as in the miniature, by six columns.[583]

The statue of Moses is accompanied by two others. Are these figures, male, bearded and wearing peaked hats, really Old Testament prophets, as Durrieu said? What prophets carry hammers and long timbers perforated by dowel holes, as each of these men does? Since Moses with the tablets indicates that the structure is the Temple, the men would seem to be its builders. They are, in fact, carpenters holding beams cut, according to the legend of the cross, from the tree that grew from the little branch planted by Seth on Adam's grave. The beams, hewn upon Solomon's orders from the tree, kept changing length miraculously so that they could not be fitted into his temple. Discarded and used to span a stream and later thrown, according to the *Golden Legend*, into the pool of Bethesda, as we shall see (Fig. 805), they were later used for the cross.

The kneeling king and queen do not look at the altar in front of them but up at the ciborium and its statues. If our interpretations are developing in the right direction the king should be the builder of the Temple, Solomon. As an ante-type of Christ, Solomon was earlier represented in prayer before a crucifix on an altar.[584] For the presence of this king of the Old Testament in the miniature we find compelling evidence in the identity of his female companion, who is surely the Queen of Sheba. The ruler of southern Arabia, the territory of the legendary Prester John, wears the wimple and the wide-brimmed hat borrowed from the Byzantines in which we customarily find her in fifteenth-century paintings, especially Italian (Fig. 726). Decisive is the negro servant, who commonly accompanies her, and whom we may see in for example the sculpture of the north portal of the Cathedral of Chartres[585] as well as in a miniature in the *Hours of Catherine of Cleves* (Fig. 727).[586] The miniature represents the famous episode when the Queen, refusing to put foot on the bridge because she recognizes in it the wood destined for the cross, hikes up her skirts and wades across the pond. According to one version of the story the action proved not unimportant in another respect also because it cured her of her one blemish—duck feet.[587] Is the very oddly tucked-up blue mantle of the queen in the miniature, so unexpected on a formal occasion, an allusion to this event?

The composition of the *Exaltation* is symmetrical, and the three figures, one standing, two kneeling, on one side of the altar are matched on the other. Here, however, not one but all three are black—unique and mysterious figures, although we have observed the prominence of black people in other miniatures of the *Très Riches Heures* (Figs. 556, 563, 592).[588] The three men hold silvery metal crosses, which, however, they do not touch because their hands are covered with a white cloth. They must be Christians, and they are striking in their rich brown robes over blue tunics, blue hoods and leather belts. Despite all these attributes they have never been recognized, but they are surely the black Christians who officiated in the Chapel of Calvary to which the crucifix on its silver rock has seemed to refer. In the fourteenth and fifteenth centuries pilgrims gained only limited knowledge of the Near East and they remained generally ignorant about Africa, so that they classified these Christians somewhat differently, especially with regard to their origins, but there can be no doubt of their presence in the Chapel. Fra Jacopo da Verona, who made a pilgrimage to the Holy Land in 1335, wrote that Nubians or black Ethiopians of Prester John, the land of the Queen of Sheba, were officiating in the chapel day and night. Each of them, he said, carried a cross in his hand.[589]

In his *Songe du vieil pelerin*, completed in 1393, Philippe de Mézières wrote that because the Nubians threatened to divert the waters of the Nile the Egyptians and the "Babilonians" gave them passage free of toll through their lands; they traveled carrying "en leurs mains une belle croix de fer bien taillee."[590] Friar Felix Fabri of Ulm, visiting the Holy Places about 1480, wrote about the Nubians as follows:

> The Georgians, who are also called Nubians, and who are most generally known as Christians of the Cincture, come from parts very far distant from the Holy Land. . . . In the Church of the Holy Sepulchre they own Mount Calvary, and they always have a guardian of the holy rock shut up in the church. . . . They also own the chapel beneath Mount Calvary. . . .[591]

Fabri tells us that the Nubians, whom Fra Jacopo associates with the kingdom of Prester John (a descendent of the Magus Melchior), were generally known as Christians of the Cincture. These Christians were identified with others who wore leather belts, particularly the followers of St. Thomas, a group in the Near East and supposedly in India (Fig. 563) which, in turn, was often confused with the Jacobites of Syria.[592] A French pilgrim of 1395–1396, Ogier d'Anglure, wrote that the "Chrestiens de la saincture" wore a blue hood.[593] Indeed the three chief religious groups in the Holy Land distinguished themselves by the color of their headdress: the Christians blue, the Moslems white, and the Jews yellow.[594] The five lamps over the altar in the miniature might refer to the major Christian churches which had rights in the chapel: the Latins, Greeks, Armenians, Jacobites and Copts.

As we have observed in a contemporary map (Fig. 734), the Nile River was believed to divide Africa from Asia, so that the Queen of Sheba and the Nubians could be considered Asians and even Indians. Our travelers, furthermore, did not always distinguish consistently between the several Christian sects they encountered in the Holy Land,[595] but it seems quite clear from their accounts that black Christians bearing crosses and wearing a leather girdle as well as a blue hood officiated in the Chapel of Calvary.[596] Information of this kind was available in the circle of Jean de Berry not only from the written accounts but from the oral reports of the travelers. Ogier d'Anglure was well known at the French courts; furthermore Jean de Berry once sent an emissary to the King of Ethiopia,[597] and on another occasion he gave alms to two Dutch pilgrims returning from the Holy Sepulchre.[598]

We have said nothing so far about the two principal figures, the men behind the altar, because their identity depends to a large extent upon the context. Their attributes, long staffs, do not appear unequivocal, but the heavily bearded man in a high conical hat with yellow lappets and a richly decorated white, red, and gold mantle looks like an Old Testament priest.[599] Near the front of the altar his left hand rests on a reliquary, probably containing a piece of the cross. If our interpretation of the scene is correct up to this stage it is interesting to learn from Brother Fabri, who said the Nubians owned the Chapel of Calvary, that "the Eastern Christians say in this place was buried Melchisedech, the first priest of Jerusalem, of whom we read in the fourteenth chapter of Genesis, and in the hundred and tenth Psalm. But this is not received by the Latin and Western Church. . . ."[600] Melchisedek appears only twice, and then briefly, in the Old Testament. Psalm 110 (109) contains the phrase: "Thou art a priest for ever after the order of Melchisedek." In Genesis Melchisedek, King of Salem (Jerusalem) and a priest, comes forward with bread and wine to meet Abraham, who is returning with booty after a successful battle.[601] Abraham, says the Epistle to the Hebrews, gave Melchisedek "the tithes of all," an action often illustrated in medieval Bibles (Fig. 722).[602] St. Paul singles out the mysterious priest, emphasizing that he was without father, mother, or children, and that his life had neither a beginning nor an end. He prefigured, Paul said, the priesthood of Christ, and Abraham's payment foretold the rendering of tithes to the Church. Following St. Paul this interpretation was accepted by later Christianity. In the fourteenth century in France the *Ovide moralisé* said:

> Lors Abraham au cuer loial
> S'en retorna, par Val Roial,
> Droit a Solyme ou a Salem,
> Mes puis ot non Jherusalem:
> "La citez en Jherosolime".
> Là donna Abraham la disme
> De quanqu'il avoit conqueste
> Au grant prestre de la cite.
>
> Li donna Abraham la disme.
> De la sont li disme venu
> Que Sainte Yglise a puis tenu,
> ou elle ou li sien avoe.[603]

As a consequence of these interpretations the altar of Abraham and Melchisedek on Golgotha was venerated throughout the Middle Ages.[604] The silver coins on the crucifix in the miniature, quite similar to Abraham's on the altar, may be another reference to the relation between redemption and ecclesiastical tithes.

In the miniature, then, Abraham counts out the tenth part of his possessions for the Church. He pays not only for himself but as the father of all humanity—"if ye be Christ's, then are ye Abraham's seed," said St. Paul.[605] The priest Melchisedek receives, and the cross in the reliquary probably refers to his offering of bread and wine.[606] In the Canon of the Mass the gifts of Abraham and Melchisedek prefigure the sacrifice of Christ on the cross (Fig. 723).

The concordance in this miniature between the two parts of the Bible is therefore complete. Forms and figures of the Old Testament foretell, indeed in a mystical sense already *are*, essential forms and figures of the New. Moses gives the law, and the brazen serpent prefigures the crucifix that stands on the altar. The Queen of Sheba, who has recognized in the footbridge the wood that linked Adam with the cross, venerates the miraculous beams of the carpenters and the temple that her host, Solomon, has built. This temple is both the Chapel of Calvary and, generically, the Church. In it worship also its particular keepers, the Nubians, who remind us, as did the miniature of the Preaching of the Apostles (Fig. 563), that Christianity embraces all mankind. Abraham, as its father, pays the tithes of the church to the priest Melchisedek, the ante-type of Christ.

Although the counselors of the Duke and all three brothers may have participated in the planning of this miniature it was executed by Herman. Signs of his presence are the strong contrasts of color within the tabernacle and the dense olive green of its rear wall. Melchisedek has Herman's frequent large features and surly, aggressive countenance, and the surfaces are less luminous than those of his brothers.

Whereas the building in the miniature of the *Exaltation* represents the Temple and the Church it refers also to a single monument—the altar and the ciborium over it in the chapel of the Crucifixion in the church on Calvary. Like the Duke's own "joyau du Mont de Calvaire" the structure is hexagonal and rests on six columns or piers; apparently the ciborium existing in the church at that time was believed to be of this design. As often in medieval architecture the inclusion of one such characteristic element sufficed to "re-present" a sacred building.[607] Certainly neither the Duke of Berry nor his scholars or painters sought a complete copy of the altar of Calvary. Half a century later, however, Giovanni Rucellai, wishing a "Holy Sepulchre" in his own church of S. Pancrazio in Florence, sent an engineer and craftsmen to the Holy Land to measure the existing tomb and to make a copy of it. In the end, however, his architect, Leone Battista Alberti, provided him not with a replica of the monument that had been measured but, as Heydenreich proposed, a reconstruction of the supposed form of the original Sepulchre—Early Christian, and thus more antique.[608]

In their depiction of the monastery of St. Catherine in the *Belles Heures* (Fig. 448) the Limbourgs achieved the kind of replica that corresponds more closely to what seems to have been Rucellai's initial intention. In the *Exaltation*, on the other hand, they reproduced actuality not in the architecture, of which they probably did not possess very exact knowledge, but in the occupants of the chapel, whom the pilgrims described in detail. The Limbourgs were, as we have seen, fascinated by exotic costume and ethnic diversity, and their wish for accuracy in these respects is not unrelated to the concern of contemporary philologists, French as well as Italian, with the establishment of correct texts. The achievement by the Limbourgs of a new kind of historical truth is an important aspect of their modernity.

The unprecedented illustration of the Exaltation of the Cross provided special opportunities for the painter in the realm of form. The Nubians offered areas of those dark browns that so subtly extend their pattern of color (Figs. 563, 571). Paul had already employed brown to rich effect in the *Belles Heures* (Figs. 451, 641). The brothers liked to describe tools and craftmanship, so that Herman must have enjoyed the depiction of the carpenters of the temple, with their hammers and beams full of carefully spaced dowel holes. He and Jean, trained as goldsmiths, delighted in the depiction of *orfèvrerie*, and he transformed the necessary crucifix on the altar into a magnificent *joyau* of gold, silver, enamel and precious stones. It is bedecked with a chain of medals or coins, silver glazed in blue like Abraham's money. One can readily imagine that these are some of the forms the illuminators suggested as they discussed with their advisers the design of this extraordinary painting. The silver in the dress of the Queen's servant was chosen partly to set off the rich chocolate brown of her face. The reddish brown, reddish blue, and light blue of the Nubians, their bluish silver crosses and tan leather girdles, all enriched by the exquisite luminous white of the handkerchiefs, constitute one of the most beautiful passages in the manuscript.

Perhaps it was in part this setting, so full of rich materials and precious metals, that led Herman to represent Moses and the carpenters in gold. Thus they gain, too, in prominence and distinctiveness. Conceivably they repeat similar golden statuettes on the *Joyau du Mont de Calvaire*. When choosing gold for his three figures, however, Herman ignored a convention observed in other miniatures of the *Très Riches Heures*. The statues of prophets and Old Testament personages are invariably of unpainted stone, as we may see in the *Annunciation*, *Purification*, the *Healing of the Possessed*, and probably also the *Flagellation*, where stone or marble statues apparently of Adam and Eve stand in canopies on the building (Figs. 559, 573, 584, 591). It is normally the pagan idols that are golden, as in the *Entry*, *Christ led to the praetorium*, the *Meeting of the Magi*, and the *Raising of Lazarus* (Figs. 571, 583, 593, 594). Although gold usually connoted the divine the Limbourgs presumably associated it with nude idols as another aspect of their seductiveness. The *Exaltation* is not, however, the only miniature in which these broad distinctions were ignored for special reasons. In the obscurity of *Hell* the devils gleam with gold, even when not directly lighted by the flames (Fig. 581), and in the miniature on folio 29 the Ark of the Covenant in the form of a medieval shrine is surmounted by a golden prophet (Fig. 564).

Only a limited number of contemporaries of Jean de Berry would have understood the full significance of the miniature of the Exaltation. Because of the interest of a patron or an illuminator it was copied twice in Paris within thirty years of its execution, and in both instances crucial elements, such as the statues and the rock of Calvary, were omitted. In a miniature in a Missal painted *ca.* 1440 Solomon and Sheba, transformed into emperor and empress, still gaze at the now bare top of the ciborium, and the Nubians have given place to the episcopal patron and his acolytes (Fig. 724).[609] More of the original composition is preserved in a miniature in the *Dunois Hours*, illuminated about 1435–1440, but the important statues are again missing (Fig. 725).[610]

The *Exaltation* has a density of meaning that may be exceptional in the *Très Riches Heures*, but we have seen signs of the kind of thought that shaped it everywhere in the manuscript, in the statues standing on other buildings, in the unique illustrations of the Psalter, in the *Fall of the Rebel Angels* (Fig. 577) and in the unprecedented astronomical calculations and the *Zodiacal Man* (Fig. 550). The *Exaltation of the Cross* confirms our assumption—if confirmation still be needed—that the miniatures of the *Très Riches Heures* and the details in them may have more than one level of meaning, and that the entire manuscript is the consequence of a collaboration with clerics and scholars such as Gontier Col, Martin Gouge, Jean Gerson, and their own brother, Roger, who was a canon of the Cathedral of Bourges. In this respect the intellectual environment in which the *Très Riches Heures* was produced resembles, let us say, Mantegna's at the court of Lodovico Gonzaga, though of course the specific values of the later Quattrocento were different.

12 · THE RESURRECTION OF LAZARUS

A depth of meaning similar to that in the *Exaltation of the Cross* may be observed in the *Resurrection of Lazarus* (Figs. 647, 593). The scene is unprecedented. The enactment of the miracle follows the Northern tradition, to be sure, with Lazarus rising from his tomb.[611] Behind the figures, however, the greensward extends to the horizon, marked by four gravestones that indicate a cemetery, as in the *Burial of Diocrès* in the *Belles Heures* (Fig. 468). Out of this grassy plain a large pale green ecclesiastical structure rises before the blue background. It is the most spectacular ruin in the art of the first half of the fifteenth century. Only its west facade and part of its north nave wall still stand. Of the strange arches that carried across the nave only the springing remains. The edges of all the broken members are jagged, the facade is threatened by a long crack, and the silvery clerestory windows are shattered.

What is this surprising and hauntingly beautiful building? Its arches are round below, pointed above. In general the architecture resembles that used by the Limbourgs for the Temple (Figs. 591, 573).[612] In the Gospel of John (12, 13), the only one which describes the raising of Lazarus, the miracle is said to be a decisive event. It won so many believers that the priests and Pharisees, deeply shaken, decided to bring about Christ's death. And his death, Christ prophesied at other times, would lead to the destruction of the Temple. The contrast in the miniature between the miracle, the ruin and the cemetery gives visual form to the content of the Gospel of St. Matthew, which at this point stresses the difference between the light and the dark, between the seers of the new truth and the blind. It is the blind who lead to the death of Christ and to the destruction of Jerusalem and the Temple.[613]

There is one form, however, that might seem not to conform. Over the main door there is a golden statue, its gleaming surface repeated in the arabesques behind. This male figure stands under a Gothic tabernacle, but it is nude, with a scepter in its left hand and an elaborate crown on its head. It must be a pagan idol, and indeed it resembles the one standing over the door of Pilate's praetorium (Fig. 583). Probably the fact that the Romans had put idols in the Temple was well known from a widely read text, the *Antiquités judaïques* by Josephus (Fig. 170).[614] The era of Grace, in any event, surpassed the era *before* the Law as well as the era under the Law.

The ruined Temple in the *Très Riches Heures* is not only unprecedented but without clear successors, a unique form among the many representations of the subject.[615] It obviously is not based on any familiar text or idea. The proposal to show the Temple was no doubt made to the painters by one of the learned men in the Duke's circle, but the great scale and prominence of the building should probably be ascribed to the Limbourgs, or to Herman, the painter of the miniature. He certainly knew in the library of Jean de Berry three splendid manuscripts—the *Bréviaire de Belleville*, the *Petites Heures*, and the *Grandes Heures*—that showed the progressive demolition of the Temple, stone by stone, through twelve stages, one for each month.[616]

The cycle of the destruction of the Temple in the *Bréviaire* was planned by Pucelle *ca.* 1325. Shortly afterward, in a fresco in S. Croce, Florence, Maso di Banco portrayed a ruinous Roman Forum as a setting for a miracle of St. Sylvester. *Ca.* 1360, in the murals of the castle of Karlstejn, a city shaken by an earthquake illustrated *Revelations*, XI, 19,[617] and we have seen Carthage in a much more advanced stage of destruction in a miniature of *ca.* 1418 in the Sallust (Fig. 737). It is after the *Très Riches Heures*, however, that ruined buildings become prominent in episodes of the chief Christian cycles, such as the Nativity and the Adoration of the Magi. The shed in these scenes, which in the fourteenth century and in the *Belles Heures* itself (Fig. 333) showed a dilapidated roof, became a building with a broken wall in a miniature *ca.* 1420 by the Egerton Master (Fig. 719) or in the famous predella of 1423 by Gentile da Fabriano.[618] In scenes of the Adoration of the Magi later in the century, by such painters as Ghirlandaio and Botticelli, Gentile's simple broken building became a great ruinous structure in "modern" style, full of associations with antiquity.

In these works, with their allusion to the decay of an earlier era, we recognize a similarity with the *Raising of Lazarus* painted half a century earlier. What underlies all these paintings is not simply a broad conception of religious progress but a more vivid sense of history and of time. This sense we have recognized in other aspects of the *Très Riches Heures*—in historical reconstruction as well as in description of the seasons and of the time of day—and it is ultimately responsible for the passionate depiction of a great ruin behind a revivified Lazarus.

VII

The Limbourgs: Conclusion

1 · THE LIMBOURGS AND PANEL PAINTING

During the ten or eleven years that the Limbourgs worked for Jean de Berry they were chiefly occupied with the illumination of two exceptional Books of Hours and a few additions to manuscripts of this kind already in the ducal collection. The inventories identify them as the authors of only one other object—the simulated book they gave their patron for New Year 1411,[619] which contained "neither pages nor any text," and which was painted on wood. This is the only certain indication we possess of painting by the Limbourgs outside the book. If the "peintre allemand" working for the Duke in 1408 at the Château de Bicêtre was, as seems very probable, Paul,[620] he might have been painting murals or panels, as has often been inferred; possibly he was adding to the large cycle of historical portraits for which Bicêtre was famous.[621] He might just as well, however, have been working on a manuscript, perhaps indeed finishing his share in the *Belles Heures*. His brothers would not have been mentioned in the document because it concerns only Paul's marital problem.

Apart from the fake book, the one other indication of painting by the Limbourgs not in manuscripts is provided by a copy of a portrait of Jean de Berry made for the antiquarian Roger de Gaignières before his death in 1715 (Fig. 604). This drawing, which I have discussed at length elsewhere,[622] is inscribed "pris sur un pastel original." The same phrase appears below a copy, made also for Gaignières, of a portrait of Louis II d'Anjou, the original of which still exists (Figs. 885, 886). Since that portrait was painted in watercolor on paper, the original of the Duke of Berry might have been the same. In any event the figure resembles the Duke as we see him in the copy of the illustration of the Itinerary added by the Limbourgs to the *Très Belles Heures de Notre-Dame* (Fig. 404); in both portraits he seems to wear the same magnificent golden *escharpe*, rendered in yellow in the Gaignières drawing. Such *bandes*, perhaps an Armagnac emblem, are usually worn over the left shoulder, as in the *Itinerary*, so that the drawing may be reversed, as a copy might well be. *Bandes* of this kind are described in the Duke's inventories, and an especially splendid one, which he wore after the lifting of the siege of Bourges in 1412, was described by Monstrelet as "toute semée de marguerites."[623] In the drawing "marguerites," or pearls, cover the surface of the *escharpe* around the larger stones. In both representations the great collector gently and affectionately touches the splendid *joyau*.

Despite the similarity of the two images the independent portrait was not copied by the draftsman of Gaignières from the figure in the scene. To the reasons I have already given for this conclusion—changes in the iconography of the Duke and in the placing of the hands—should be added the fact that in the drawing the Duke appears not *en buste* but in more than half-length. This is a design for portraits and Madonnas that, though rare elsewhere, was favored in France in the first half of the fifteenth century—a fact that the draftsman would surely not have known (Fig. 603).[624]

Whatever the original medium of the portrait of Jean de Berry the Limbourgs would not have been exceptional in metropolitan France for work outside the book. We know that the Parement Master was active as a painter as well as an illuminator, and there are, as we have observed, good reasons for supposing a similar career for Jacquemart de Hesdin. The principal sources of Jacquemart's style, in any event, were the sculpture of Beauneveu and the panels of the Sienese. The Rohan Master, as we shall see, worked on large as well as small scale, and we suspect that the Medallion Master practiced similarly. One of the most striking aspects of the painting of this time was the close relation between illumination and monumental painting. The greatest patron of illumination, Jean de Berry, transformed the book by bringing into it artists such as the Parement Master, Beauneveu, and Jacquemart. If the Boucicaut Master was, as seems possible, Jacques Coene, he was equally well known as a painter. The Limbourgs themselves conform with this situation, because major sources of their style were the panels of Jean de Beaumetz and the early work of their uncle and sponsor Jean Malouel (Figs. 356, 368, 380).

Because the *historieurs* learned so much at this time from the *peintres*, and because the two often exchanged hats, this account of French painting has included both—and stained glass, too, when it seemed closely related. The *Parement* and the half-dozen surviving panels executed in metropolitan France—as well as a few, such as Broederlam's, executed outside it (Figs. 338, 360, 368, 373, 377, 378, 380, 608, 642)—have been introduced at appropriate places in the story.[625] These extant panels probably do not represent adequately the range of panel painting in their time. The most impressive of them were executed for and in Dijon (Figs. 377, 378, 380). Three of the others—the *Man of Sorrows* at Troyes, the *Entombment* and the *Lamentation* in the Louvre (Figs. 338, 373, 484)—are remarkably homogeneous, compared at least with the diversity of contemporary illumination.

The most distinctive of the panels is the *Coronation of the Virgin* in Berlin (Fig. 605). The iconography, to be sure, including the angel holding the Virgin's long mantle, is familiar in French illumination, although the angel peeking at the event from behind a curtain is unusual in this scene. It is a motive that shortly began to enliven representations of the Annunciation.[626] All the figures in the *Coronation* are exceptionally youthful; the angels are children and Christ a very young man. They as well as the Virgin have the small features and the demure look of figures in Upper Rhenish painting, and Italian components seem conspicuously lacking.

The laws of chance would not have led one to expect that the rather exceptional *Coronation* would be approximated by a new addition to the small group of extant panels. The *Madonna* discovered quite recently does, however, precisely that (Fig. 603).[627] It has a similar delicate, flowery beauty. Figures, ornament, and tooling of the gold are all related. The Virgin, like the sitters in portraits that we have just considered, conforms with the French convention of rising more than half-length above the lower frame. A cloth of honor enriches the setting of the tall, slender, majestic figure. In that respect the new panel anticipates the *Madonna* in the Walters Art Gallery, painted, as Miss Miner has shown, towards 1420 in a style that has strong Netherlandish as well as French qualities (Fig. 720).[628] In this tondo the angels hold the cloth behind a Madonna of Humility seated on a crescent moon.

The cloth of honor, a traditional medieval form, was revived for novel purposes in French painting of the late fourteenth and early fifteenth centuries. Spread across the lowest part of the pictorial field in representations of the Madonna and of the Man of Sorrows, it normally appeared in front of, rather than behind, the principal figures, as in a miniature by the Boucicaut workshop of *ca.* 1415 (Fig. 602).[629] The drapery along the lower edge of the painting serves as a base or ledge for the figure; it also bridges the real and the pictorial space, and suggests that a curtain has been dropped to disclose the image. The "entrance curtain" has become an even more explicit bridge in the recently discovered *Madonna and Angels* in Berlin, where folds of her blue mantle fall in front of the curving white, red, black and gold cloth (Fig. 642).[630] The curtain has some of the functions of the "entrance arch," which we have seen in some miniatures by the Limbourgs in the *Bible moralisée* (Figs. 306, 309), and which was to be employed frequently in Flemish panels by Petrus Christus, Dierck Bouts, and Roger van der Weyden.[631]

A similar ornamented curtain curves along the lower edge of only one of the numerous extant copies of lost early fifteenth-century portraits, a drawing of the early eighteenth century of Jean sans Peur (Fig. 376). The figure of the Duke, furthermore, like the *Madonna* in Berlin, has a relatively small head at the apex of a towering pyramidal body, and the prince, too, is wrapped in the voluminous folds of his mantle.[632] Even the long tapering fingers of the hand and the folds falling from the arm are similar. The representation of the Duke cannot have been independent because his hands are raised in prayer. The similarities of this portrait and the *Madonna* are so extensive that they almost certainly formed a diptych of the kind familiar later in Netherlandish painting, as Colin Eisler and I proposed some time ago.[633] Reversal of the portrait, as in the illustration (Fig. 376), produces a plausible, indeed an impressive ensemble.[634] Both halves gain strength. The glance of the Madonna toward the left, and still more, the lunge of the Child in the same direction, not adequately motivated by the cherry, require some sort of balancing or opposing form. It is notable too that the composition of the *Madonna* is much more firmly closed at the right than at the left, where the Virgin's shoulder is deeper in space, her arm creates a path of movement upward toward the Child, and the angels press in upon her with a less restrained fervor than is proper to the prayerful Duke.

If this reconstruction is correct it has important consequences. About 1410, when the Madonna and presumably its pendant were painted, Jean Malouel was serving as the painter of Jean sans Peur and he would naturally have been the most likely candidate for a portrait of the Duke—indeed, he is known to have made one.[635] We have, therefore, a painting that can with some assurance be connected with Malouel. The identification cannot be decided, however, without considering the relation to the *Trinity* in the Louvre, because it too was made for a Burgundian duke—Jean's father Philippe le Hardi—about 1400, after Malouel had entered his service (Fig. 380).[636] The similarity between the two paintings, which Eisler and I have discussed in detail elsewhere,[637] is so deep and pervasive that the equally apparent differences might be explained by the development of Malouel's style. Study of the sculpture of Sluter could have induced him to transform the more exquisite, tender, Simonesque forms of the *Trinity* into the bolder, more animated, and more physical art of the Madonna. The Child, so eager for the cherry, even puts his tongue between his lips.[638]

A definitive solution of the problem of the relation of the two paintings is rendered more difficult by differences of technique. The *Madonna*, which measures 107 x 81 cm, is painted on cloth, the only work of this kind that has come down to us from the early fifteenth century in France.[639] It of course lacks the smooth enamel of painting on wood; the texture of the cloth dulls the colors. They are, nevertheless, saturated and strong and surprisingly well preserved. The rendering of the filmy tunic of Christ is breathtaking, and in very few images of the Madonna has the blue preserved an equal transparency and depth, so that the full richness of the convolutions of the mantle may still be enjoyed.

In many respects the miniatures of the Limbourgs belong to the world of these paintings. The Zodiacal Man resembles Christ as Man of Sorrows (Figs. 380, 550), the sensuous flesh of the Madonna in Berlin recalls Paul's Virgin in the *Adoration of the Magi* or the *Visitation* (Figs. 567, 572, 642). In the *Visitation* moths and butterflies, like those in the painting in Berlin, appear in the border. The haloes, with rays darting over and beyond disks, are similar, and the cascading folds of the Virgin's mantle resemble those of the painting in Berlin. Whereas the Limbourgs continued, no doubt, throughout their career to study Malouel's figures, we have no reason to believe, on the basis of surviving works, that they could have learned anything from him or from other panel painters about spatial composition. Although the Berlin *Madonna* was painted perhaps a decade later than the *Trinity* a planar design still persisted.

That this mode was characteristic of Malouel's larger paintings, too, is perhaps indicated by the altarpiece executed in 1416 by his successor at the Burgundian court, Henri Bellechose (Figs. 607, 608). The flat design and the tiered figures would have seemed old-fashioned already to Jacquemart de Hesdin in 1400—so advanced were the illuminators in this respect. It is true, to be sure, that the *Martyrdom of St. Denis* departs from the principles of Malouel and moves in a new direction. The composition is more compact. Its effect depends to a greater extent upon salient, pulsating outlines and tense, twisting movements (Fig. 608). It is much less Italianate. In these respects it differs profoundly from the last phase of Paul de Limbourg, and it belongs to a general trend that gathers momentum toward the end of the second decade of the century. In illumination this trend is exemplified by the Rohan Master and other artists who will be considered below. We may thus find signs of it in panel painting also.

The new values guided the design of the portrait of Louis II d'Anjou, which must have been painted shortly before he died in 1417 (Fig. 886). They are more evident in the portrait of a woman in the National Gallery, Washington (Fig. 606). The painting, executed about 1420, still contains reminiscences of Malouel and the Limbourgs, but volume is now compressed and sacrificed for fluctuating outline.[640] The design unfolds in a series of ellipses. These qualities are only one aspect, however, of the new phase. Together with a diminished mass and space there appeared a new realism of "surface." The portrait in Washington was once, curiously enough, ascribed to Pisanello,[641] who did indeed study French painting and particularly the Limbourgs, as we shall see, but the searching description of the flesh, the revelation of the distended nostrils and the sensual mouth, are remote from the generalizing sculptural idiom of that master and of all Italian painting until the later fifteenth century. Related qualities may be found in a portrait of the same period by the Rohan Master that we shall consider shortly (Fig. 806).

2 · THE PROBLEM OF THE LIMBOURGS AND THE ANTIQUE

The probability of the imitation of ancient statuary by the Limbourgs has been maintained by numerous historians since 1885, when F. von Duhn claimed that Adam in *Paradise* in the *Très Riches Heures* was based on the Roman statue of a kneeling Persian in the museum at Aix (Figs. 558, 657).[642] The resemblance between the two figures is so striking that the thesis of a dependence was accepted by Schlosser, Durrieu, Adhémar, Porcher, and, most recently, Brendel.[643] Other scholars have been skeptical of the relation, some because of the troublesome fact that the statue in Aix proved to have been discovered only in 1514. Professor Brendel, however, has now pointed to the existence of other versions, Roman or Etruscan, of the entire group of Pergamene originals, one of which is reflected in the statue in Aix. Though other scholars did not specify the source of their doubt about the origin of the figure of Adam it was, we believe, their sense that a study by the Limbourgs of a Roman figure was inconsistent with the prevailing conception of French pictorial style of the time as exclusively "courtly" and "international Gothic," in other words remote from antiquity.[644]

The problem needs to be reconsidered, first of all, in the light of the fascination of contemporary French humanists and scholars with ancient literature, history, and mythology. Like their fellow-humanists in Italy, they communicated their enthusiasm to their patrons, as we have observed in the first section of this book. Gontier Col, secretary of Jean de Berry, Pierre de Montreuil, an occasional counselor, and Christine de Pisan had a significant influence upon the great collector as well as upon Louis d'Orléans. It is true that the early French humanists, like their Italian counterparts, had little, if any, understanding of the visual arts of antiquity. Petrarch, to be sure, collected Roman coins, but he valued them as symbols of a great vanished civilization. When, however, Jean de Limbourg painted *Paradise* he was surrounded by, or at least had access to, a collection that contained many ancient cameos and coins as well as numerous Early Christian and Byzantine objects that preserved antique types and motifs.[645] The Duke of Berry's group of carved ancient gems and cameos was so large and important that, as I have remarked elsewhere, it would seem to presuppose an appreciation that transcended the common medieval interest in them as talismans and as seals.

Neither the Duke of Berry nor any member of his entourage had formed a clear notion of Greco-Roman art. The Duke's inventories, so rich in classifications of different kinds, had no term for them.[646] Yet such objects represented for him the remote ancient world. Their subject, therefore, was essential; as for the form, the vaguely conceived "ancienne façon" sufficed. Neither artists nor scholars seem yet to have begun to do with artifacts what contemporary philologists, such as Montreuil and Clamanges, had done for literature: recognize the difference between ancient texts and "corrupt" post-antique versions of them. With respect to the correct identification of ancient art, however, the gap between Italy and France was not as wide as has often been assumed. Jean de Berry's medals of Constantine and Heraclius were believed to be antique in Italy itself until the late sixteenth century.

There is no need to recount here the signs of the Duke's fascination with antiquity. His interest in it was compounded of various motives—historical, dynastic, moral, and religious. His manuscripts of the *Epître d'Othéa* and of the *Ovide moralisé* exemplify this mixture. For him, as for his contemporaries in France and in Florence itself, antique forms were charged with Christian meanings.[647]

It does not therefore seem improbable that Jean de Limbourg should have been attracted by an old, vaguely classified statue, statuette, or figure in a relief, understood as a warrior, perhaps a militant Christian, in distress (Fig. 657). Such a conclusion, however, only suggests a possibility; what does the visual evidence tell us? First of all, the complexity of Adam is not only exceptional in the work of the Limbourgs but entirely unprecedented in the scene of the Temptation. In the cycle of St. Catherine and of the Litany in the *Belles Heures* Paul introduced some daring figures, boldly foreshortened (Figs. 441, 444, 452, 641) but neither he nor his brothers were greatly concerned with the study of pantomime or the design of elaborate postures. The figure of Adam, with its turning torso supported by an arm and a firmly planted hand, while the upper arm fends off Eve and the foreshortened face is turned anxiously toward her, involves an understanding of the structure of the body and a tension in its functioning that cannot be paralleled in any other Limbourg painting. How could it have been achieved without a complete model? Sources have been suggested that provide only part of the posture, such as Isaac in Brunelleschi's competitive relief,[648] but they clearly do not suffice. Indeed, the loss of an arm makes even the statue in Aix inadequate. The marble of another figure of the group now in the Vatican preserves its upper arm and folded fingers, precisely as in Adam (Fig. 656).

The rhetoric of Adam isolates him in the Garden. He is alien to the kind of action that occurs there. The movement of his upper arm, too, seems somewhat misdirected, as though the posture were not devised for this particular composition. So involved a resistance is not needed by Eve's gentle approach, holding the apple in one hand and touching his shoulder with the other. The figure, in other words, betrays its origin in a desperate defense against a greater force. The model is apparently seen from a rather low point of sight.[649] As a result the genitals of Adam are conspicuous. Although not inappropriate to the story at this point they had always earlier, it seems, been covered. In the *Bible moralisée* the devils have genitals whereas in the *Très Riches Heures* they appear not only on Adam and again on devils but, significantly, on the "ancient" male statues that stand on buildings.[650] Thus we may have one more sign that the model of Adam was antique.

It is instructive that the Limbourgs depicted the figure once again in the *Très Riches Heures*, but reversed and seen from a different point of view (Fig. 565). Here, with genitals concealed, it serves as one of the resurrected in a small miniature of the *Last Judgment*. In this somewhat different form the figure resembles closely the Vatican copy of a Pergamene, who moreover is nude (Fig. 656).[651] The resurrected man, furthermore, expresses some of the pathos present in the ancient statues but largely lacking in Adam. Surprisingly Jean de Limbourg had already tried to deal with the model in his miniature of the *Temptation* in the *Bible moralisée*, painted in 1402 at the very beginning of his career as an illuminator (Fig. 655). Here the posture is less meaningful than in the *Très Riches Heures* because Adam does not attempt to fend off Eve. With his upper hand he holds the apple he has already accepted—indeed he has bitten into it—and with his other arm and hand he does not support his inclined body but clutches, it seems, his throat, as in somewhat earlier representations of the Temptation we have cited above (Fig. 803). His genitals are already just visible, but the drawing of the limbs and the understanding of the body are so weak that we cannot suppose that Jean himself had invented the figure for this occasion. It is even astonishing that at this moment he should have elected to copy so complex and difficult a model. He was then working for the brother of Jean de Berry, Philippe le Hardi, but since, as we have seen, the two men were intimate friends in Paris, where both of them lived, Jean probably had seen Berry's collection and we cannot exclude the possibility that the model was in it. There is no definite evidence to show that at this early date the brothers had already been in southern France and Italy. On the other hand we do not know that Jean de Berry possessed Roman statues, although if he did they probably would not have been included in the inventories.

The Limbourgs were fascinated by the contraposto involved in this type. Paul gave his *St. John* a related posture (Fig. 551), and Herman introduced a simpler version in his *Crucifixion* in the *Belles Heures* (Fig. 497). One of the resurrected in a *Last Judgment* in a Breviary illuminated in Rouen in 1412 resembles Adam in the Bible, though the one leg still in the earth is like that of the resurrected in the *Last Judgment* in the *Très Riches Heures* (Figs. 565, 654, 655).[652] Although the miniatures in the Breviary are not generally related to the Limbourgs or to Paris the composition of the *Last Judgment* is, as Miss Miner observed, generally Italianate,[653] and the illuminator might have known the work of the Limbourgs.

For the simpler versions of this figure a Trecento model is certainly conceivable, although it has not yet been found. For Adam in the *Bible moralisée* and the resurrected man in the *Très Riches Heures* such a source seems less likely, and for Adam in the *Très Riches Heures* this explanation will not do. The beautiful delineation of the body and the synchronization of its movement make the hypothesis of an ancient model more plausible. It would also allow for the low point of sight and offer the possibility of a second view, useful for the resurrected man. The Limbourgs might have come into possession of drawings of ancient statuary by a Trecento painter; but then we must retreat in time to the period of Ambrogio Lorenzetti, and even he apparently undertook nothing so complex. Here, then, we leave the problem, puzzled about questions of transmission but confronted with impressive suggestions of a relation between the Limbourgs and the antique.

Other proposals for the use by the Limbourgs of ancient models seem much less persuasive. Neither the relation of the figures back to back in the zodiacal miniature with the Three Graces nor the bound thief in the *Exit from the Praetorium* with a Roman statue seem to call for serious discussion (Figs. 550, 585).[654] It is true, on the other hand, that the structure of the figure of Lazarus has deeper resemblances, the shroud notwithstanding, with an ancient river god than with a resurrected man in the *Last Judgment* at Reims with whom he has been compared (Figs. 593, 658, 659).[655] The Limbourgs were probably familiar with ancient coins representing river gods in Jean de Berry's collection—indeed, they may even have received one from him in the group of 21 coins he gave them.[656] It seems possible, however, that Herman de Limbourg had in mind an Italian Trecento figure in a posture closer than the river god to the resurrected Lazarus he wished to paint. Jean de Limbourg used this posture, with the further arm crossed over the body, for one of the resurrected in the same *Last Judgment* in the *Très Riches Heures* that contains a version of

Adam (Fig. 565) and again in the *Crucifixion* (Fig. 587). He adumbrated it already in the *Bible moralisée* (Fig. 292).

One figure in the *Très Riches Heures*—or rather one series of figures—that has not been mentioned in discussions of the relationship with ancient models is the chariot of the sun in the twelve calendar pictures (Figs. 539–549, 562). The beautifully drawn horses vary from miniature to miniature, but they all race ahead above the clouds, their legs extended foreward and back almost into horizontal positions. Even the most advanced Trecento representations of the sun are far from comparable (Fig. 653), and Pegasus or the horses of quadrigas on Roman coins seem very much closer (Figs. 660, 661). A similar winged horse, indeed, appears in an initial in the text for Christ giving up the Ghost (folio 156), and Pegasus is probably intended, because Bersuire compares the mythical horse to the soul ascending to Paradise.[657]

These horses and the astonishing Adam in the *Garden of Eden* prove that we must seriously entertain the thought of a relationship of the Limbourgs with the antique. They had, after all, learned as much about the human body as the best Trecento painters, and they could therefore do what a few of those *Trecentisti* occasionally did—turn to antique models. Current French interest in the ancient world, shared by their patron, would certainly not have hindered their study. At best, however, they took advantage of only a few forms and figures, and the borrowings were marginal to their art. We must remember, nonetheless, that it was not the founders of Renaissance painting who can be proved to have copied the antique but Pisanello (Fig. 662), a student at the same time of the Limbourgs themselves.

3 · THE BREVIARY MASTER AND THE FOLLOWERS OF THE LIMBOURGS

The chief illuminator of the Breviary of Jean sans Peur, an impressive painter, is also in certain respects the most mysterious master of the first two decades of the fifteenth century (Figs. 610, 611, 618–622, 648). In 1911 Friedrich Winkler identified him with Paul de Limbourg,[658] and accounted for the differences from the *Belles Heures* and the *Très Riches Heures* by placing the Breviary shortly after 1400. This attribution or this date, or both, have won adherents for half a century.[659] In 1922, however, Paul Durrieu called attention to a relationship that eventually spelled trouble.[660] He pointed to the similarity of the *Martyrdom of St. Mark* in the Breviary with the same subject in the *Très Riches Heures*, both, he believed, painted by the Limbourg brothers (Figs. 559, 619). The miniature in the Breviary is only by an assistant, but even the best work in the manuscript differs in fundamental respects from the *miniatures* in the *Belles Heures* and *Très Riches Heures*—a difference we have already emphasized in the discussion of the illuminator's contribution to the *Très Riches Heures*. Many forms common to the two paintings of St. Mark are characteristic of the Limbourgs and not of the Master of the Breviary of Jean sans Peur. For these reasons, and also because the subject was rarely represented, the miniature in the Breviary probably derives from the composition created for the *Très Riches Heures*.

There are many other indications in the Breviary of a similar derivation. The unusual shape of the miniature below the *Crucifixion*, for instance, with its projection up between the columns of text, derives from the design of the folio of the *Miracle of Diocrès* in the *Très Riches Heures* (Figs. 578, 611). The flowers, birds, and foliage on these two folios, both executed by the workshop of the master, are very similar. The patterns in the backgrounds of many miniatures are identical with diapers in the *Très Riches Heures* and the *Belles Heures*.[661] Relationships like this, and others to be discussed shortly, lead us to conclude that the Breviary was not painted at the beginning of the century but later, between about 1413 and 1419, when Jean sans Peur was murdered. It is tempting to connect the manuscript with a gift by the Duke to the Duchess of 300 francs in May 1412 for a Breviary and other books.[662] In that event the Breviary Master, not long after that date, would have begun the illumination of the manuscript for the Duchess just after abandoning his work on the *Très Riches Heures*.

Of the surprisingly few paintings by the Breviary Master that have come down to us one can be dated as early as 1406 (Fig. 366). It is the *Crucifixion* in a manuscript given to Marie de Berry in that year, which we have related above to the representation of the same subject by Paul de Limbourg in the *Bible moralisée* (Fig. 367). The composition by the Breviary Master is even closer to a miniature in a Book of Hours painted by a follower of the Limbourgs after *ca.* 1414 (Fig. 365). The figure of the Virgin, in fact, is almost identical, and since the Breviary Master normally depended upon the Limbourgs for his repertory of figures and his compositions we may probably infer that the model for the seated Virgin had been created by Paul before 1406.

The golden ivy around the miniature by the Breviary Master was painted by the Luçon workshop. When the Breviary Master took over, he painted not only the miniature but also the initial and the acanthus in it—an important innovation at this date.[663] He added, too, the curling vines in the border. Their rounded, flowing leaves are given an exceptional luminosity by punches in the gold and by rays that appear to issue from them. The painter tooled similar forms into the haloes and the gold background.

This transformation of the sheen of smooth burnished gold into a more lively, irregular sparkle is accompanied by a corresponding change in the painted areas. The spots and strokes of shade, for one thing, are spaced so widely on the lighter ground that they produce an effect of vibration. The painter, abandoning line, created forms in color and light to a greater degree than any of his contemporaries except the Boucicaut Master when painting landscapes. The luminous hues of the Breviary Master are already visible in this early *Crucifixion*—uncommon and exquisite combinations, too, such as the reddish blue mantle of the Virgin and the pink mantle of John shaded in gray-blue over a mustard yellow tunic shaded in orange-brown.

The early style of the Breviary Master, but probably not his own hand, may be seen again in several miniatures in a manuscript of *Privileges* of the city of Avignon (Figs. 613, 614). The text seems to indicate that these paintings, not hitherto mentioned as far as we know, were executed before 1412. Some of the miniatures show an admixture of South French elements, and we may therefore infer that the illuminators worked in Avignon. The art of the Breviary Master, however, has nothing whatever in common with the painting of the region.

The Breviary Master took figures and compositions from the Limbourgs not only in his miniature of 1406 and in his *Martyrdom of St. Mark* but in many other paintings. He seems to have been familiar with all their work. Thus two of the miniatures they added to the *Très Belles Heures de Notre-Dame* are reflected in the Breviary. David in the miniature at the beginning of the Psalter is an almost exact replica of a man in prayer in the *Très Belles Heures de Notre-Dame*; the Breviary Master adapted the Lord and the angels to his circular rather than rectangular frame (Figs. 500, 648). The quatrefoils of the borders, on the other hand, resemble the *Grandes Heures* or the *Brussels Hours*, which, as we shall see presently, the Breviary Master certainly knew. One of the quatrefoils in the Breviary is overlapped by the frame, and in this respect it resembles one of the medallions similarly filled with angels around *St. Michael* in the *Très Riches Heures* (Fig. 597).[664]

In character, however, the illumination of the Breviary is very different from any of these models. Where else would one see God the Father rendered in brown-mauve on dull gold, enveloped by a gorgeous cloth of honor? Who else gave the mantle of the Virgin so delicate and luminous a violet? Unmistakable touches of the Breviary Master, moreover, are the punching of the gold units in the background and the shield of Goliath in the lower right quatrefoil. Even the small crown of David is finely tooled. A flower rises between the two columns of text, and in the margins below there are remarkable studies of three violets. A finch, a crane, a hoopoe, a parakeet and a pheasant perch on the leaves or fly among them. Most of these forms we have seen in the borders of the *Très Riches Heures*, and on folio 44 of that manuscript there is a Madonna embracing a small Child similar to the one in the initial.

The *Itinerary* in the *Très Belles Heures de Notre-Dame* provided the setting in the Breviary for the journey of Christ to heaven (Figs. 404, 610). The building and the landscape, though reversed, correspond in almost every detail. The composition of the illustration of the prayer for travel, which shows clerics welcoming the Duke of Berry upon his arrival at the gate of a town, very probably prompted the novel iconography of the Ascension. It is not only the apostles with the Virgin who witness the miraculous event but a group of laymen also, who, like the clerics in the *Itinerary*, emerge from a gate.

The Breviary contains many quotations from the *Belles Heures*, as Jean Porcher observed.[665] One example may suffice to illustrate the nature of the dependence and, more important, the degree of individuality of the result. Though the figures of the Breviary Master in the *Baptism* are arranged differently, they owe much to the miniature in the *Belles Heures*, or to a drawing by the Limbourgs for it (Figs. 431, 620). The Baptist, however, pours with his usual right hand, not his left. Moreover, in the Breviary the colors and the sumptuous textures are entirely different. The sparkle of the tooled gold, including the *situla*, is matched by the pointillism of the painted surface. The unusual blue of Christ's robe reappears in the lower sky, in the pond, where it is mixed with green, and in the shadows on the dull gilt robe of the Baptist. Even the water spilled on Christ has become a cool blue. Warm orange is reserved for the luminous wings of the angel and for God the Father, who as a supernatural figure has much less substance than the others. Even in this very small miniature the illuminator has rendered with skill and pleasure the transparency of Christ's loincloth. The colors and the lustrous textures of this miniature recall examples of the highly developed contemporary French technique of gold enamel.

When painting single figures the Breviary Master frequently followed Limbourg models quite closely. Thus the drapery that gives impressive stature to St. Philip, winding around the broad body and cascading from a hand (Fig. 622), was inspired by such figures as Nebuchadnezzar in the *Très Riches Heures* (Fig. 566), or St. Paul in the *Belles Heures* (folio 159v). The remarkable breadth of John the Evangelist in the Breviary as well as the pattern of drapery folds cannot really be matched in the paintings of the Limbourgs and they reflect, directly or indirectly, the figures of Claus Sluter (Fig. 621).

In the largest miniature in the Breviary the chief illuminator copied the miniature of the Crucifixion by Jacquemart de Hesdin in the *Brussels Hours*, at that time in the possession of Jean sans Peur (Figs. 611, 612). The Breviary Master once again made a number of small compositional changes, adding the sponge and showing the arms of the thieves, which in the model had been rather ambiguously concealed by the cross-bars. The arched upper frame permitted a more elevated and detached Christ. His distinctiveness is increased by the long rays that issue from his head and by a very unusual cross, golden but still preserving the grain of wood. The Breviary Master has given the large shield the effect of metal glazed in red by skillfully spotting red and black on a silvery gray. It is indeed in the realm of color that the illuminator discloses most fully his individuality and his imaginative gift. For the rather light colors of the Brussels *Crucifixion*—pale green, rose, yellow, and vermillion—he has substituted cool tones, using blues among the figures and gray in the landscape, all displayed in a diffused light. His desire for maximum luminosity is evident also in his transformation of Jacquemart's border. He gave the vertical stem patches of brightly burnished gold. The flowers and the greatly varied birds, though probably executed by an assistant, are freshly studied and seen in an unusual, soft light.

The Breviary Master and his assistants worked on the similar borders in the *Très Riches Heures* a short time earlier. The borders of Jean de Berry's manuscript that were painted by the Breviary Master himself (Figs. 551, 556, 592) are superior to those in the Breviary, in which his role was much more limited. The circumstances, too, were quite different. Paul de Limbourg, for one thing, surely supervised the work on the *Très Riches Heures*, and we have seen that more often than not the borders match the miniatures in color. There is, furthermore, a real difference between collaboration with a great painter for a unique patron and less inspired work, including greater reliance on assistants, for a prince who had no special enthusiasm for the arts.[666]

Apart from the Breviary and the *Très Riches Heures* very little by the Breviary Master has come down to us. His style, if not actually his hand, may be found in one small and damaged miniature of the Annunciation in a Book of Hours in Vienna.[667] The two other styles in the manuscript point to Besançon and to eastern France.[668] By him or his workshop also are two miniatures in a minute Book of Hours in Palermo, the rest of which was painted by the Boucicaut workshop.[669] Much more important are some miniatures in another Horae now in the Walters Art Gallery. The chief illuminator of the manuscript was the interesting Master of Walters 219.[670] Near the end of the text he inserted four miniatures by the Breviary Master, pasting them into blank frames.[671] How he obtained these miniatures is a matter for speculation; he himself was probably active in Besançon, so that, as in the instance of the Vienna Book of Hours, we are drawn eastward. The follower of the Boucicaut Master, however, who collaborated in the Palermo manuscript presumably—but not necessarily—worked in Paris. One of the collaborators in the illumination of the Breviary of Jean sans Peur, the Egerton Master, was established in the metropolis.[672] The other recalls a minor but interesting illuminator, the Master of the Madonnas of Humility, who worked on occasion in Paris or Bourges. Thus the associates of the Breviary Master point to northeast France, to Paris, and perhaps to Bourges.

The miniatures by the Breviary Master in Walters 219 vary in quality. One of the best, the *Martyrdom of St. Denis and his Companions*, is very similar to the miniature of the same subject in the Breviary (Fig. 624).[673] The choice of colors for the *Baptist* reveals at once an exceptional artist (Fig. 623). The Saint, wearing a delicate violet mantle over his hair-shirt, stands in a pale green and buff landscape. The painter's fascination with the play of light on color in an atmospheric space has led him to develop still further the technique of stippling we have observed in the Breviary. Stippling, which was restrained in the painted surfaces of the borders of the *Très Riches Heures* to maintain a harmony with the smooth enamel of the adjacent miniatures, reached its highest development in Walters 219 (Fig. 623).

This remarkable pointillism had its roots in the fourteenth century, when it began to be developed in the miniatures of the Bible of Charles V of 1371, illuminated by masters of Netherlandish training or inclination.[674] The Breviary Master did not limit his very advanced pointillism to his painted surfaces; he treated the gold similarly. He was, indeed, probably influenced by the *opus punctorium* of the goldsmiths (Fig. 617), though in metal the stippling usually created the lights and in his paintings the darks. Goldsmiths transferred the technique, furthermore, from metals to enamels. The earliest extant example, a small medallion of the Aracoeli in the Walters Art Gallery, datable about 1425, is in style somewhat related to the Limbourgs (Fig. 615). It has even been very tentatively connected with the youngest of the brothers, Arnold, who inherited part of the property of his three famous brothers upon their death in 1416, and who became a goldsmith's apprentice in Nijmegen in 1417.[675]

A pictorial technique similar to that of the Breviary Master may be seen in one of the most beautiful miniatures of the first quarter of the fifteenth century (Fig. 609). It represents the *Madonna Nursing* on a crescent moon. Golden rays descend upon her from a stellated crown held by two seraphim. The folio, about ten inches high, was inserted into a prayer book that belonged to the dukes of Burgundy. The exceptional veneration of the image, which may originally have been an independent painting, damaged its surface. Ex-votos, now removed, were attached to it, and dark stains were produced by frequent touching and perhaps kissing. Despite the losses and discoloration it remains the most ethereal Madonna of its time.

The painting has been ascribed to the Limbourgs,[676] and indeed the design of the Virgin resembles that of the Madonna on the crescent in the *Très Riches Heures* (Fig. 557). The seraphim with the crown are equally similar to corresponding figures in the *Coronation of the Virgin* of that manuscript, but—and the difference is significant—they are light orange-red, not dense vermilion (Fig. 574). The Child, curiously, is cast in a very different mold. The figure belongs to the tradition created by Ambrogio Lorenzetti's S. Francesco Madonna, but the head, with its foreshortened eye, derives from the suckling Child in the much earlier first *Madonna* in the *Brussels Hours*, then in Burgundian possession.[677] The motive for this imitation may have been in part religious, but the composite nature of the image as a whole, and its resemblances with the Limbourgs, clearly conform with what we know of the Breviary Master.

Like the figures of the Breviary Master the Madonna is voluminous but not heavy. The folds of her mantle are as soft and pliant as those of *St. Philip* and *St. John* in the Breviary (Figs. 621, 622), and the fold falling from her head is not unlike that of *St. James* (Fig. 618). The painter's touch is as sure and delicate as that of the Breviary Master at his best. The face of the Madonna is evoked by touches of rose on the cheeks, eyes, brows, and mouth—laid, as in all flesh areas, on the bare vellum. Her eyes are clear, light blue, her hair pale yellow. Parallel lines of blue, rather widely spaced, give vibrancy to the crown, and the entire mantle of the Madonna is composed of small, parallel blue strokes. Though the figures are much larger than any others by the Breviary Master, and for this reason alone somewhat different, he very probably painted them.

The Breviary Master brought to a culmination in his time one method of depicting form and color affected by atmosphere and light. His taste, shaped by *orfèvrerie*, seems somewhat related also to such Netherlandish paintings as the *Somme le roi* of 1415 in Brussels or the triptych, probably Mosan, now in the Boymans Museum, Rotterdam.[678] It is worth noting that in the triptych the haloes show similar tooling, to obtain the same effects of luminosity. At a time when the major painters of cosmopolitan France were learning pantomime and geometrical composition from the Italians, the Breviary Master, like later Dutch artists such as Geertgen and the Virgo Master, remained steadfastly "Netherlandish." For his figures and his compositions he was normally quite content to depend, as we have seen, on the Limbourgs, and occasionally on Jacquemart de Hesdin. Like Paul de Limbourg he observed highlights, as on the brooch of his remarkable *Baptist* (Fig. 623), but he did not exploit them consistently. Though he failed to understand the Boucicaut Master's epoch-making perception of the principle of diminished color on distant objects, he rendered more effectively than that master the effect of atmosphere on forms and figures nearby. He widened the range of value, but he preserved his pattern of color from obfuscation by deep shadow. It seems clear that the Breviary Master, who was patronized by Jean sans Peur, was a not insignificant artist in the milieu from which emerged Jan van Eyck and the Master of Flémalle.

* * * *

Whereas the Breviary Master retained a quite distinctive style despite his close relationship with the Limbourgs during a decade or more, including a major project of collaboration, another illuminator whom we cannot prove to have worked with the three brothers owed his art entirely to them. The miniatures by him in the beautiful Book of Hours belonging to Count Seilern have the refinement, the clear color, and the elegance of Jean's work in the *Très Riches Heures* (Figs. 424, 425, 469, 625–633). The illuminator, whom we may call, after this manuscript, the Seilern Master, produced a pretty version of Jean's paintings, using soft rose, mauve, blue and green, and surrounding the miniatures with wide borders full of waving plumes of acanthus and charming violets (Figs. 626). The flowers and leaves recall those by the Breviary Master in the *Très Riches Heures*, and they suggest to us what that manuscript might have looked like if the Breviary Master had been in charge. Even the snails which play so prominent a part in the borders of the *Feeding of the Five Thousand* glide over (or near) the acanthus on the folio of the *Nativity* and the vines in other miniatures of the Seilern manuscript (Figs. 592, 627).[679] The miniatures are full-page, as in the second plan of the *Très Riches Heures*.

Whereas the Seilern Master usually employed his borrowed forms more for decorative purposes—his snails, for example, do not always rest on foliage—he sometimes varied his color or his objects to communicate the mood or the meaning of a miniature. Thus the leaves in the border of the *Flagellation* are darker—olive-green and mauve—and the landscape behind the figures in the *Betrayal* is a very deep green (Fig. 628). In the borders around the *Entombment* there are owls, the birds of night and of evil, and birds of prey—brown predators with their catch in their talons (Fig. 632). Symbolism of this kind, however, is not consistently employed. The *Betrayal*, menacing and nocturnal, is celebrated, surprisingly enough, in the borders by four angels sounding musical instruments (Fig. 628). To describe them as celebrants is not misleading; three of the four figures are identical with angels in the border of the *Annunciation* in the *Très Riches Heures* (Fig. 559).[680]

Musical angels are at home in the Annunciation and not in the Betrayal, so that this relation would at once cast doubt on the older opinion that the *Seilern Hours* was painted in the first years of the century and that it anticipated in several respects the *Très Riches Heures*.[681] This view is weakened further by the fact that the composition of the *Annunciation* itself (Fig. 625) is remarkably similar to that of the miniature in the *Très Riches Heures* (Fig. 559). If there should be any doubt about the nature of this relation the wider, more open space of the Seilern miniature, characteristic of all the miniatures in this manuscript, points to its later date. In 1953 and 1955 Jean Porcher said that "certain compositions" of the *Seilern Hours* derived from the *Très Riches Heures* as well as from the *Belles Heures*, and consequently he dated the manuscript *ca.* 1416–1420, ascribing it to the first of the three painters who, he believed, painted in succession the three gatherings of the *Bible moralisée*.[682] A date not before *ca.* 1415 seems to us abundantly proved by the evidence, but in 1959 Porcher revised his view and concluded, for reasons not specified, that the *Seilern Hours* was painted somewhat earlier, and that the miniatures resembling those in the *Très Riches Heures* do not follow but foreshadow them.[683]

A comparison of the *Nativity* in the *Seilern Hours* and in the *Très Riches Heures* confirms the relationship indicated by the *Annunciation* (Figs. 569, 627). Although the figures in the foreground are quite similar to those in the *Très Riches Heures*, which represent the early work of Paul in this manuscript, the deep landscape behind reflects the later miniatures. The two angels in the borders, deriving from the *Annunciation* of the *Très Riches Heures* (Fig. 559), repeat those in the borders of the *Betrayal* (Fig. 628)—a kind of repetition that is foreign to the principal miniatures of the *Belles Heures* and the *Très Riches Heures*. The Seilern Master, following the corresponding miniature in the *Très Riches Heures*, introduced a deep landscape and a distant city into the *Annunciation to the Shepherds*, and he certainly drew the averted shepherd from the same miniature (Figs. 570, 626). The three angels, however, repeat those in the miniature of this scene in the *Belles Heures* (Fig. 411). The Seilern *Last Judgment* is based upon the same scene in two Psalm illustrations in the *Très Riches Heures*, on folios 34 and 34v (Figs. 555, 565, 633).

It is, indeed, one of the peculiarities of the Seilern Master that, although he was familiar with at least a few miniatures of the *Très Riches Heures*, he much more frequently employed figures and designs of the earlier *Belles Heures*. From this manuscript he took the figures in, for example, the *Betrayal*, the *Adoration of the Magi*, the *Entombment*, and, with more modifications, the *Agony in the Garden* (Figs. 343, 631, 632, 496).[684] The frightened monk, anachronistic in the *Entombment*, is a copy of an equally startled monk in the *Miracle of Diocrès* in the *Belles Heures* (Figs. 632, 467).

We observed above that St. Luke in the *Seilern Hours* reverses a figure in the scene of Diocrès teaching, with the result that his inkwell appears on the left side (Figs. 423, 424).

The most unexpected source for a miniature in the *Seilern Hours* is the *Brussels Hours*, from which the illuminator took the entire composition of the *Flight into Egypt* (Fig. 630).[685] He could not resist, however, transforming all Jacquemart's bare trees into leafy ones. The Limbourgs had not painted the miniature of this subject in the *Très Riches Heures*, and Paul's composition in the *Belles Heures* probably seemed too voluminous and too monumental (Fig. 415). The use in the *Seilern Hours* of the earlier miniature by Jacquemart is a testimony to its beauty and its advanced landscape. The illuminator must have had access to the manuscript, which was then in the collection of Jean sans Peur. It is all the more significant, therefore, that a Flemish illuminator added four miniatures to the *Seilern Hours*, and that the calendar is Flemish.[686] The Seilern manuscript may well have been produced for, and perhaps at, the Burgundian court.

The Seilern Master must have acquired his command of the Limbourg style and technique by working for a time with one or more of the three brothers. Other painters who exploited the work of the Limbourgs could have learned simply by imitation of their miniatures. One of these minor illuminators executed most of the miniatures in a Book of Hours in the Spitz Collection in Chicago, including a *Nativity* which discloses the illuminator's debt to the *Très Riches Heures* (Figs. 569, 634).[687] The deep marine view in the *St. Christopher* ends at a horizon above which rise spires and towers, implying a clear understanding of the curvature of the surface of the earth (Fig. 636). This illuminator curiously resembles the Seilern Master, because he joins a few compositions of the *Très Riches Heures* with many more taken from the *Belles Heures*,[688] and he likewise seems to have been familiar with the *Brussels Hours*. The prostrate shepherd in the *Annunciation to the Shepherds* in that manuscript seems to have been the source of the similar, more unexpected figure in the *Spitz Hours* (Fig. 635).[689] The manuscript should be dated *ca.* 1422.

At an earlier date the chief illuminator of the Spitz manuscript executed another Book of Hours, use of Paris, now at Chantilly.[690] This manuscript has simpler borders, but it too was probably painted later than the *Très Riches Heures*, or later at least than Paul's *Nativity* in it, which once again served as a model. The *Annunciation to the Shepherds*, on the other hand, repeats the *Belles Heures*, and the figures in the *Crucifixion* resemble closely, as we have observed, those in the same subject in the miniature painted by the Breviary Master in 1406 (Figs. 365, 366).

Here, and probably in other instances still to be discovered, the miniatures of these illuminators from the circle of the Limbourgs extend our knowledge of the paintings by the three brothers themselves. They prove that the Limbourgs did not remain isolated, as has sometimes been supposed.[691] To the tributes of these followers should be joined the very numerous copies of compositions in the *Belles Heures* and the *Très Riches Heures* made by French illuminators of diverse styles during the lifetime of the Limbourgs or within fifteen years of their death.[692] And of course the exchanges with the Boucicaut Master were vital to the growth of his—and their—art.

4 · THE LIMBOURGS AND EUROPEAN PAINTING

Though the leading painter of the *Bible moralisée*, whom we take to be Paul, had come from a sculptor's family in Nijmegen, his miniatures reflect chiefly the art of the Burgundian panel painter, Jean de Beaumetz, and the early work of Jean Malouel. Before 1400 Jean and Herman were apprenticed to a goldsmith in Paris and Jean's pictorial style in the *Bible moralisée* does in fact show some resemblances with *orfèvrerie.* A few of Paul's miniatures in the Bible are related to the *Brussels Hours* of Jacquemart, and others imply study of Italian panels. Shortly afterward, in his first miniatures in the *Belles Heures*, Paul shows a deeper understanding of Lorenzettian and Giottesque painting—so deep, in fact, that he quite probably had visited Tuscany. There he, like Masaccio later, responded more to Trecento painting than to leading contemporary masters such as Lorenzo Monaco (Fig. 471). He doubtless admired Ghiberti's drawings for his North Door or some reliefs if they were visible, but even Ghiberti's sculpture surely seemed to him linear and too committed to abstract compositional rhythms. These qualities would have suited Jean much better.

If indeed the border of the *Annunciation* in the *Belles Heures* was inspired by the *Porta della Mandorla* Paul must have been in Florence *ca.* 1405 (Figs. 408, 410). So far as we can see, however, he did not—in either the *Belles Heures* or the *Très Riches Heures*—disclose a similar interest in any other equally advanced Italian work. There is no instance in his painting like the apparent dependence of the Boucicaut Master's *St. Paul* upon an Italian model. That figure has a *standbein* and a *spielbein*, and the sense of balance maintained through internal, organic effort is remarkable (Fig. 747). The head inclines toward the heavy book that St. Paul braces against his chest while the firmly planted opposing shoulder is felt through the mantle flung deliberately across it. The earliest extant Florentine figure with a similar *déhanchement* is, as Professor Janson has observed, Nanni di Banco's *Isaiah* in the Cathedral of Florence, dated 1408 (Fig. 746).[693] This relationship would seem to indicate a date for the *Boucicaut Hours* after 1408, but then it would fall into the period of manuscripts in a different style, and an earlier Florentine figure of this type, perhaps by Nanni, may have been lost. Indeed, one would envisage a model that showed not only the functional differentiation of the two legs but also the motif of the open book, tilted head and concentrated glance over the *standbein* balanced by the long diagonals of the *spielbein* and the sword. All of this is not likely to have been invented by the Boucicaut Master himself.

In their generation in Italy as well as France the Limbourgs were the major students of early Trecento painting and of the art of Altichiero. Although the growth of the style of the Boucicaut Master too was guided by the figural articulation and geometric designs of Trecento painting the Limbourgs alone transferred to their miniatures figures and entire compositions they had copied from Italian models. Nothing illuminates the monumental character of their small paintings more than the fact that many—perhaps most—of the Italian works they borrowed were in frescoes. In the *Très Riches Heures* the composition of the *Purification* is a copy of the fresco by Taddeo Gaddi in S. Croce or possibly of a drawing related to it (Figs. 573, 668). Jean's Virgin in the *Deposition* surely derives directly from the Virgin by Andrea da Firenze in the Spanish Chapel (Figs. 588,

649), and the remarkably close approximation to the model suggests study in Florence at an advanced moment in the development of Jean's command of the figure, after the completion of the *Belles Heures*, in which he showed no such accomplishment. The journey probably included Padua, because the frescoes by Giotto and by Altichiero and his followers in the Santo and the Cappella di S. Giorgio, which earlier provided motifs (Fig. 475) and served to increase the figural repertory of the brothers, now no doubt impressed them for their populous narratives, their spectacular settings, and their scale. Thus the fresco of *St. James* in the Santo, from which the Limbourgs early adopted a type of gate, moat, and bridge (Figs. 345, 404), in *February* probably influenced the entire landscape and the man driving a donkey (Fig. 540). Foreshortened figures in unusual positions in Paul's miniatures in the *Belles Heures* seem to reflect the damned in Giotto's *Hell* (Figs. 452, 453, 641), whereas miniatures in the *Très Riches Heures* such as the *Raising of Lazarus* show not only single gestures of Giotto but his compositional principles themselves (Figs. 593, 670).

The study of Lombard illumination implied by the *Très Riches Heures*, especially of miniatures by Giovannino and Michelino, might well have brought the brothers to Milan and Pavia, although examples of this school were surely available in the collections of Louis and Valentina d'Orléans and Jean de Berry; we know that the latter, in fact, possessed an illustrated treatise on the medicinal value of plants and animals that was probably a Lombard *Tacuinum sanitatis*.[694] The model for the boar and the hounds in *December* was Lombard, and the realistic rendering of plants and animals in the miniatures of this school no doubt proved suggestive to the Limbourgs, as Otto Pächt proposed. The most important contributions of Giovannino and Michelino were, however, their novel, blonder colors, juxtaposed in unprecedented combinations and shimmering in a soft, pervasive light.

The interest of the Limbourgs in North Italian manuscripts and frescoes did not diminish their central commitment to the principles of Tuscan painting. Below their surfaces partly *alla lombarda* lay the structure of Tuscan design. It is notable that when in the *Très Riches Heures* the brothers wanted to paint a spectacle they copied in its entirety, not a composition by Altichiero, but Taddeo's *Presentation of the Virgin*, probably the most scenographic painting produced in Tuscany before their time. Ambrogio Lorenzetti remained their major source for the representation of landscape, and the exquisite modulations and linear beauty of Simone Martini's paintings still exerted their spell, especially upon Jean. Herman was more attracted by the solid forms and robust figures of Giotto and his followers.

From these diverse sources the Limbourgs created a highly distinctive art, which has little relation to the chief French representatives of the International Style such as the Luçon Master (Figs. 69, 513). The *Belles Heures* already was absolutely unique in European painting, and the time has passed when historians can or should hesitate over the regional classification of works of this kind. Nothing could be less "International" than Paul's last phase. Sweeping curvilinear rhythms, so characteristic of the art of the early fifteenth century, had in the first decade already become less prominent in the miniatures of Parisian illuminators such as the Roman Texts Master (Figs. 7, 59, 190). They virtually disappeared from Paul's latest paintings of 1415–1416, replaced by a rhythm of solids and voids, of dense form and light-filled space. Taking advantage in the calendar pictures of a freedom from conventional religious imagery Paul moved into a new style more decisively than any painter in Europe—except Campin and Jan van Eyck, to whom we shall turn shortly. We do not know how consistently Paul would have applied his new principles to traditional religious representations; certainly in them the Boucicaut Master, his superior in aerial perspective, did not equal his new realistic figure (Figs. 548, 640, 677).[695] In the Boucicaut miniatures figure and environment remained more distinct, belonging to different modes of visualization.

Paul's last works resemble the incunabula of the new Flemish art as much as they do the paintings that preceded them. With Campin, who was described as a master in Tournai in 1406,[696] there may even have been some kind of exchange. Paul might have become familiar with him and his work on a trip to Nijmegen at the beginning of 1415.[697] He could then have seen something like his earliest surviving painting, the Seilern triptych probably executed just around that time (Figs. 758–760).[698] Although the landscapes of the two painters seem related,[699] the figures of Campin have a greater plastic and emotional force, derived partly from sculpture. They show a more sophisticated use of highlights and transparent cast shadows and a deepening of tones to provide a greater range of value. In other respects, however—especially the primacy of the tightly woven vertical pattern—the design of Campin is less advanced than Paul's latest miniatures (Fig. 548). The religious subject of Flémalle's triptych partly accounts for its more conservative aspects, but *October*, too, was affected, and in a sense limited, by requirements of iconography and the patron's interest. Since one of the two subjects in the miniature is a portrait of the Louvre Paul gave the castle and its wall greater definition than the scarecrow far less deep in space.

Until the problem of the date of the Eyckian miniatures in the Milan-Turin Hours is finally resolved one cannot speak confidently about the relation of Paul's last work and Jan's first (Figs. 644, 645). These miniatures and the closely related panels in the Metropolitan Museum are the only known Eyckian paintings that can be placed before *ca.* 1427, the approximate date of the *Madonna in the Church*, although this panel too has sometimes been relegated, wrongly and for wrong reasons I believe, to a much later period.[700] This is not the place for one more discussion of the relative advantages and disadvantages of classifying the miniatures as imitative paintings executed toward 1440 or as works executed by Jan himself early in his career, around 1422, when we first hear of him, as Charles Sterling, the most recent student of the stylistic aspect of the entire problem, agrees.[701] The proponents of the late date must suppose the existence of a superb follower of Jan van Eyck of whom nothing else is known, and who, despite his exceptional gifts, was still in the late thirties employing—or indeed reviving—figures characteristic of the late second or early third decade of the century.

The women in the *Birth of the Baptist* and God the Father in the initial have the rippling lines, the thin drapery folds, and the delicacy of the earlier period (Fig. 645); their shape and their relation to the space is fundamentally different from that of Jan's little but voluminous figures of 1437, as we see them in the background of his *St. Barbara* (Fig. 755). It is true that the river in the *Baptism* moves straight into a low horizon and thus may seem more advanced than the landscape of the *Adoration of the Lamb* in the Ghent altarpiece, but flat landscapes, not unrelated, appeared several years earlier than the Eyckian miniature in the late work of the Boucicaut Master and in Paul's *October*—if the castle is subtracted (Figs. 548, 752).

I have not been able to hold one view about the "Hand G" miniatures consistently,[702] but I am inclined to believe they were painted shortly after 1422, when Jan was serving as painter and *valet de chambre* of John of Holland.[703] If this view is correct the miniatures show, six to eight years after Paul's last work, an art that shared his central purpose and carried his mode of vision to an astonishing new stage. Form rendered by light acting on color, highlights and texture, in short *lustro* and *lume*—to use Leonardo's terms instructively applied by Gombrich[704]—are developed to an almost magical result in the *Birth of the Baptist* and the *Baptism of Christ* or the *Requiem Mass* (Fig. 645).

The advance beyond Paul's work may be exemplified by the castle near the horizon in the *Baptism*. Jan, lacking to be sure Paul's wish to achieve a portrait, held his castle to a dull gray tone so that, by contrast, the sky becomes luminous and infinitely deep. Patches of strong color, such as red, remain small and overlapped by other objects so that they are held back in their proper places. These miniatures, as Panofsky said, "convey an experience of space in all its aspects—expanse and limitation, unity and multiplicity, color and light."[705] The richness of detail, especially in the landscape of the *Baptism*, is breathtaking. Still, we may observe that the painter has not maintained Paul's pervasive sense of formal order and geometric design. This kind of elevating order, so fundamental even to a nocturne such as *Ego sum*, has yielded in the related Turin *Betrayal* to encyclopaedic diversity (Figs. 582, 753). Even in the black and white photograph of the destroyed miniature one can recognize a wider range of color and of value than in Paul's nocturne, which is realized only in gray, brown, green, silver, and gold.[706] Range and variety are attained at the sacrifice of Mediterranean monumentality.

Paul's last miniatures, together with the late paintings of the Boucicaut Master and the first panels of the Master of Flémalle, are the major precedents of Eyckian style. It is Paul's plowman in *March* rather than Jan van Eyck's Adam who first has face and hands roughened by the weather. What, then, might such similarities actually signify? How would Jan van Eyck have become familiar with Paul's last phase? Although several excellent Boucicaut manuscripts existed, and one, such as Mazarine 469, could have gone to the Burgundian court, there was only one *Très Riches Heures*, and the subtle pictorial innovations of the calendar pictures were certainly not preserved in copies. Did Jan, a youthful painter around 1415, journey at that time to Paris, the great artistic center? Perhaps the two masters met when Paul traveled to Nijmegen in 1415. Possibilities of communication exist, and the manuscript seems to us to have remained in northern or central France for at least a couple of decades after the death of Jean de Berry.

Compositional ideas and motifs, unlike style, are readily transmitted by copies, and here we may feel absolutely certain about the significance of French illumination for Netherlandish painting. Specific precedents have been cited by Panofsky, Baldass, the writer and other scholars: the *Requiem Mass* by the Boucicaut Master, for example, for Jan's miniature of this subject;[707] the same master's Madonna on a balcony and the *Rolin Madonna*,[708] or his representation of the Annunciation in a church, adopted by the Flémallesque painter of the panel in the Prado;[709] the Boucicaut Master's *St. George* and the panel (by Campin or Roger?) in Washington (Fig. 754); the angel with crossed hands, holding a lily, in the *Annunciation* of the *Belles Heures* and the Ghent altarpiece, or the *Annunciation* of the *Très Riches Heures* in relation to the panel—by Petrus Christus?—in the Metropolitan Museum.[710] The apostles in the *Last Judgment* probably by Jan van Eyck in the same museum resemble the Elders enthroned in heaven in *St. John* in the *Très Riches Heures*, and some of the damned in the panel fall like the Rebel Angels in the manuscript (Figs. 551, 577).

One interesting instance of the transmission of these motifs seems to have passed unnoticed. The averted Child in Jan's *Madonna* in Antwerp (Fig. 750) is a late member of a series of such representations which, although developing out of the *Glikophilousa* or the *Madonna del latte*, are basically unmedieval because they present the back of the principal figure. The radically new form appeared in Paris in the early fifteenth century in a miniature by the Brussels Initials Master and, a little later, in the medallion that bore, on its reverse, a portrait of Jean de Berry.[711] Jean de Limbourg partially averted the Child in his enthroned Madonna in the *Belles Heures* (Fig. 751), and the motif then appeared in the Netherlands in the prayer book of Mary of Guelders, illuminated in Utrecht in 1415 (Fig. 748).[712]

What is true of Netherlandish panel painting applies also to illumination of the region. Observations during the course of our own investigation have pointed to the central role of metropolitan France in transmitting to the Netherlands the extraordinary innovations of Italian pantomime and iconography. It was French illumination of the time of Jean de Berry rather than, as has been said, Netherlandish illumination of the late second and third decades that adopted and diffused the Madonna of Humility and the various aspects of the Brigittine Nativity.[713]

The reputation of the *Très Riches Heures* survived until the early sixteenth century, when it provided the stimulus in the Southern Netherlands for well-known cycles of full-page calendar illustrations. In the *Grimani Breviary*, probably the earliest of these, the illuminator decided that in *February* the peasants needed more visible protection against the cold than they have in the *Très Riches Heures*, and he proceeded to close partially the front wall of the house, although all but a few flaming sticks of Paul's great fire are thereby excluded (Figs. 540, 757).[714] Then, to compensate for the greater separation of the room from the icy world, the illuminator introduced at the entrance a boy who pisses out onto the snow—a curious innovation, perhaps suggested by the display of genitals in his model which he decided to conceal. The Grimani *October*, like other miniatures in the calendar, still clearly discloses its origins, despite all the bustling activity of muscular men and horses; labor has become so central a theme that even the scarecrow has been pressed into service as a live archer (Figs. 548, 756). The harrow now moves, surprisingly, *across* the plowed furrows. One group from the calendar of the *Très Riches Heures*—Paul's plowman with his oxen and plow—has even escaped from a miniature into the middleground of a large panel by Patinir.[715]

All these copies were drawn from the calendar of the *Très Riches Heures* and from no other part of the manuscript. They may therefore have been based on a set of drawings; but, even though we have argued against the usual assumption of documentary evidence for the presence of the manuscript in the collection of Margaret of Austria,[716] it may nevertheless have somehow been accessible to the Flemish painters. After their tribute to the manuscript it disappeared from history, both written and painted, until its discovery in Genoa in 1855.

At several points in the preceding account we have referred to the interest of French illuminators in the Lombard book. Before 1400 the Epître Master had contemplated at length the miniatures of Giovannino and the manuscripts of the *Tacuinum sanitatis*. Lombard studies of fauna and flora—semi-scientific illustrations (Fig. 745)—proved meaningful to the Boucicaut Master, and still more, to the Limbourgs and the Breviary Master. Giovannino's style, on the other hand, contained Northern ingredients. He had studied Bohemian painting as well as French, learning to rival its pale luminous colors and its rich, varied textures. In the scene of Joachim in his sheepfold in the *Visconti Hours* the landscape is not the usual bare Trecento rock but a green meadow, as in some miniatures of the Boqueteaux illuminators.[717] French borders of ivy were the point of departure for Lombard illuminators.[718] The superb linear fluency of Michelino was probably enhanced by French models of the late fourteenth century, such as the early Luçon Master (Figs. 513, 744). Lombardy was linked with France by intermarriages as well as by common political interests, and French art, music, and culture were highly esteemed at the Visconti court. French romances, which remained popular throughout Italy during the Quattrocento,[719] were beautifully illuminated in Lombardy already before 1400.[720] In the newly discovered murals in the Palazzo Ducale in Mantua Pisanello illustrated, in a style related to the Limbourgs, episodes of the Arthurian cycle.

About 1410 the Boucicaut Master and his workshop illuminated a Book of Hours for the Visconti.[721] Ten years or so earlier the master was no doubt in Milan—precisely in 1399 if he was identical with Jacques Coene—and then or a few years later he seems to have visited Florence, as we have observed above.[722] Around 1415 he and his assistants illuminated a splendid Missal for Lorenzo Trenta, who probably took it or sent it to Lucca shortly afterwards.[723]

We know only one modest work by the Limbourgs that was probably painted in Italy, *Valerius Maximus in his study* in the manuscript in the Vatican (Fig. 429). Perhaps this miniature was painted during a first journey in 1404–1405, before they undertook the *Belles Heures*. They seem to have returned to the peninsula *ca.* 1410–1411, and, as we have suggested above, they may have left behind some examples of their work. Otherwise Italian painters could not have seen their work without going to France.

Although historians of art always emphasize the internationalism of this period and assume an exceptional degree of artistic exchange between the major centers, it is striking that good French illuminators seem to have painted abroad only two or three manuscripts, and remarkably few important French manuscripts of this period left the country in which they were produced. In addition to the two examples by the Boucicaut workshop already mentioned the only others we know are the Vitruvius with a modest frontispiece by the Virgil Master, which was in Florence at least by the time of Francesco Sassetti (Fig. 58), and the Bible containing beautiful additions by Jacquemart and the Trinity Master, given by Jean de Berry to Pope Clement VII in Avignon, but later taken to Rome and inventoried in the papal library in 1455.[724] Surely numerous more ordinary manuscripts, especially Books of Hours, passed from Paris to the Italian centers, representatives of the more perfunctory production of the capital and giving only hints of the innovations of the great masters.[725] No French panel is known to have gone to Italy, and no Italian painter (except the Master of the Brussels Initials) to France.[726]

Against this background claims of French influence on Italian painting of the first three decades of the fifteenth century must be advanced with more than usual caution. There is no lack, as has often been said, of stylistic similarities. The pliant figures of Lorenzo Monaco have the rhythmical dash of those of the Luçon Master. Lorenzo, like the Limbourgs, was fond of night scenes, and he ventured, though more tentatively than they, into the exploration of color modified by light. Such similarities might imply an exchange, easily effected if the Limbourgs were, as we have suggested, in Florence about 1405. They might, however, be the consequences of independent though related innovations, because both Lorenzo and his French contemporaries drew from a common source, Trecento painting.

In general it is much easier to identify and to formulate French borrowings from Italian painting than the reverse. Typically the Northerners copied figures and compositions whereas the Italians were impressed primarily by less definable qualities—color, light, and texture.[727] Occasionally, however, a specifically French motif appeared in central Italy. The Man of Sorrows held by an angel was represented at the center of the predella of an altarpiece in the Cathedral of Florence, as we know from a Filippinesque copy as well as a written description.[728] This type might have been brought to Italy by the Boucicaut manuscript now in the Ambrosiana (Fig. 749), but it surely was by the Master of the Bambino Vispo, who no doubt saw it in Valencia before going to Florence (Fig. 766).[729]

Many aspects of the paintings of Gentile da Fabriano and his Venetian followers in the third and fourth decades of the century recall the miniatures of the *Très Riches Heures*: the nocturnes with starry skies, the processions and spectacles, the richly textured dress, and the landscapes admitting, between the usual Italian bare hills, rows of trees and patches of green. Perhaps during his early years in Venice or his stay in Brescia (1414–1419) Gentile saw something the Limbourgs had left in Italy or copies of their work now lost (Fig. 763).

Certainly those Tuscan paintings of the second quarter of the century that have rightly been connected with the Limbourgs look, when compared, like a mathematical demonstration (Fig. 762). Sassetta's panels equal the exquisite miniatures of Jean in linear beauty but his surfaces are relatively dry and his landscapes largely bare, offering less distraction from the volumes and the complete geometry that are the most eloquent aspects of his work. It is only by moving later in time, to a Venetian painter active in Florence, that one finds a kind of elevated sensuousness like that of Paul de Limbourg (Fig. 761). Domenico Veneziano's *Adoration of the Magi* has not merely all the obvious qualities of Paul's spectacle of the same subject but a beautiful light that produces similar soft and richly varied textures. Both paintings include a green, productive, geometrically structured landscape. The hats and mantles of Domenico's figures as well as the harnesses of their horses bear mottoes, following a fashion which had appeared in the early fifteenth century in France.[730]

Domenico's panel, indeed, pays tribute to French painting and civilization in general, of which the *Très Riches Heures* had been a high peak. Though we have no reason to believe he had seen this manuscript or the *Belles Heures*, Paul's fresh and marvellously subtle color, especially in the miniatures of the Great Litany (Fig. 641), anticipated his own in a remarkable way. The precedent for the background of roses in Domenico's *Madonna* in Washington is very likely a French painting like Malouel's in Berlin (Figs. 642, 764).

Butterflies along with flowers provide a kind of bower behind the woman (probably Ginevra d'Este) portrayed by Pisanello in his panel in the Louvre (Fig. 765). When we stressed the telling differences between this painting and the portrait of a woman in Washington, which is clearly not his,[731] we did not consider the undeniable similarities (Fig. 606). They include even elliptical patterns, which are basic to the design of the French portrait. Pisanello might have seen French manuscripts or even a French panel when in 1424 he worked for Filippo Maria Visconti in the Castello at Pavia. As late as 1448–1449 he still gave a medal a stellated sky, not to mention conical hills that are reminiscent of French art of the early fifteenth century (Fig. 772). Some of his paintings are anthologies of forms he found visually interesting, and he never approximated Paul's intensive analysis of the contents of a single view.

In his panel in London Pisanello set in the sky the kind of visually complete, half-length Madonna that was first created by the Limbourgs in the *Belles Heures* (Figs. 389, 768).[732] His sporty St. George, with enormous straw hat and two steeds, proves that Italian painters and courtiers could outdo, in elegance and fancy, the dress of their predecessors in France.[733] The dense wood rising behind a ground strewn at first with rocks and then deeper in space with leaves creates a setting remarkably similar to Paul's *December* (Fig. 549). Behind St. Anthony, furthermore, lies not his usual small pig but an animal that, except for the absence of tusks, resembles strikingly the boar in Paul's miniature.

All these similarities pique our curiosity, especially when we recall that the Madonna in glory is a Limbourg type. Curt Glaser observed, furthermore, that a drawing from the circle of Pisanello—probably a copy of a drawing by the master himself—closely resembles the Virgin in the *Cour celeste* in the *Belles Heures* (Figs. 389, 767),[734] and Otto Pächt remarked that where the drawing differs conspicuously, as in Mary's crossed hands, it approximates French rather than Italian conventions. The model was, therefore, another, lost Madonna by the Limbourgs.[735] Pisanello evidently made a drawing of this Madonna, which resembled one in the *Belles Heures* (Fig. 397), before undertaking the panel, which is usually dated late in his career.

There can, then, be no doubt of the interest of Pisanello in the painting of the Limbourgs. He seems to have been familiar with certain forms in the *Belles Heures*, the *Très Riches Heures*, and in a lost work. Perhaps he knew in Italy a manuscript like the *Seilern Hours* that contained copies of both the *Belles Heures* and the *Très Riches Heures*. No manuscript exists, however, that contains so much of the character of the art of the brothers as Pisanello apparently saw, and we therefore wonder what one or more of the Limbourgs painted in Italy during visits there *ca.* 1405 and again *ca.* 1410. During the second trip they might have executed the model for the *St. Jerome* in the *Bible moralisée*, which we have discussed above (Fig. 357).[736] If the two Italian drawings that copy different parts of this composition are not, as has been maintained, from the immediate circle of Pisanello but by one or two Lombard draughtsmen *ca.* 1450 (Figs. 770, 771), we must infer that the Limbourgs had left a drawing in Milan or Pavia. This or another, practically identical, version must however have been available in France to the Master of St. Jerome (Fig. 357).

Motivengeschichte is often intricate and inconclusive, but the evidence it provides in the instance of the celestial half-length Madonna is decisive. We may well wonder whether the most plausible practical explanation of this proven borrowing and of the other signs of Pisanello's familiarity with the work of the Limbourgs is not simply a trip to Paris. There too he would have seen, or at least heard about, the Duke of Berry's medals; they would have given him the impetus to produce similar medals for his princely patrons in Italy (Figs. 267, 268, 482, 483, 772). A visit to Paris would readily have provided the French example that has often been inferred for Pisanello's medallic art.

The fact that at least one design by the Limbourgs proved interesting in Italy in the second quarter of the Quattrocento adds some substance to our speculation about the effect of the more elusive but historically more important qualities of color, light, and texture.

The Boucicaut style, represented by many more manuscripts than that of the Limbourgs, was far more widely diffused in Northern Europe; and because of its character one would expect a greater response to it there. To be sure, a few of the iconographic innovations of "Pol et ses frères," such as the shepherds and the radiant Child in the Nativity, soon were adopted everywhere.[737] Only occasionally, however, does a painting seem to reflect their style or their compositions; one of the panels of the Tiefenbronn altarpiece by Lukas Moser may be, as Charles Sterling has now suggested, an example.[738] In France the illuminators who rose to leading positions towards the end of the second decade, the Rohan and Bedford Masters, both exploited the art of the three brothers for their own different purposes. The style of Jean Bapteur in Savoy is related, but we are not convinced he knew any manuscripts by the Limbourgs.[739]

Although the premises of the art of the Limbourgs and the Boucicaut Master were challenged and denied in the years after their disappearance, two or three great painters of the third quarter of the century returned to them. Fouquet and the René Master created such profoundly similar works that the language of Paul and his brothers seems to have survived, as it were, without being spoken for a generation. In his *Coronation* of 1454, moreover, Enguerrand Quarton manifested a similar sympathy. It was Jean Fouquet, however, who understood best what Paul de Limbourg and the Boucicaut Master were saying.

Like them Fouquet went to Italy, and during the years 1444 to 1448 or slightly later he studied the new painting that had not yet appeared when Paul was there. The innovations of the leading masters, especially of Fra Angelico, transformed Fouquet's art. Nevertheless Fouquet's *Descent of the Holy Ghost upon the Faithful*, painted after his Italian sojourn, manifests a conception of style that resembles Paul's as much as Angelico's (Fig. 774). Large circles and triangles do not preclude singular forms or rich variety. Even the quality of the light resembles Paul's. The Cathedral of Notre-Dame, an architectural portrait without parallel in Italy, rises above the Seine and the Ile de la Cité, associating the Faithful with Paris. The Cathedral and its setting have the same formal and iconographic meaning as the view of Paris in the *Meeting of the Magi* in the *Très Riches Heures* (Fig. 571). In another miniature by Fouquet Job lies on his dung heap near the Château de Vincennes (Fig. 704). The castle, like Paul's Louvre or Saumur in the *Très Riches Heures* (Figs. 547, 548), is set oblique to the picture plane, with nearly horizontal orthogonals, and it is evident that both painters liked this design in plan as well as in elevation. The basic plan of many of Fouquet's miniatures is, indeed, a parallelogram, with an angle nearest the picture plane.[740] His representation of the court of Charles VII resembles in this respect Paul's *July* (Figs. 545, 773).

For his shimmering light Fouquet was more indebted to the Boucicaut Master than to the Limbourgs.[741] To increase the role of atmosphere and of space he muted the color of the figures to a degree that his predecessors would have found unacceptable. He tended, in fact, toward painting in tone. When depicting nocturnes, however, such as the *Nativity* and the *Betrayal* in the *Hours of Etienne Chevalier*, he compromised and admitted brighter colors than Paul did in *Ego Sum* (Fig. 582).

The Master of King René, too, preserved many of the pictorial values of Paul de Limbourg. In a miniature painted after 1457 and showing Cuer reading an inscription at sunrise, the illuminator held the planar and spatial aspects of the design in equilibrium, as Paul had done in *October* (Figs. 548, 775). Now even the shadows become essential elements of the geometry of the composition.

Paintings of this kind prove that although the movement led by Paul and by the Boucicaut Master was suddenly cut short, it gave significant definition to the future course of French pictorial art. It was, *pace* Johan Huizinga, less a waning than a waxing; no autumn but a spring. It must be recognized as a major phase of a movement that, initiated by Jean Pucelle, began decisively with Jacquemart de Hesdin. The movement is not adequately characterized by the terms which are commonly applied to it, Late Gothic, Courtly, or International. More appropriate would be *ars nova*, a historical concept first introduced in France in the time of Pucelle to define novel contemporary polyphonic music and still employed for this purpose by musicologists today.[742] The concept has, however, been pre-empted for Flemish panel painting.[743]

A new art, however, certainly appeared. Just as the French humanists of the early fifteenth century cared more about the style of ancient writers than their content—and hence reserved their highest admiration for Cicero—painters and illuminators became concerned in a new way with color and design, in other words with the rhetoric of painting. The range of styles in Paris was surely greater than ever before, and to a striking degree commissions were matched with individual talent and experience. Thus the Luçon Master, the Parisian illuminator who conforms best with current notions of the International Style (Fig. 513), specialized in Books of Hours, not produced apparently for the most cultivated patrons. The fiery Apocalypse and Medallion Masters illuminated the two manuscripts of *Revelations* undertaken at this time, and in them produced their best work (Figs. 804, 808). Since Italian art seemed, quite rightly, closer than any other to antiquity, Italianate painters—the Josephus, Orosius and Roman Texts Masters—undertook the illustration of Terence, Virgil, and of the other ancient authors after whom they are named.

The Limbourgs matched style and subject in an especially subtle way. If our hypotheses are correct their choices showed an extraordinary awareness of their own gifts and inclinations. In the *Belles Heures* and still more in the *Très Riches Heures* Paul avoided tasks that would normally have been his so as to continue more freely his explorations of form and of realistic reconstruction. The speed of his stylistic growth, particularly in his last years, reflected the same unprecedented self-awareness. His development was stimulated by the high esteem of a rare patron, who gave him a special security and freedom, not to mention friendship, and who made possible a new mode of life for a painter. He and his brothers presumably had the time and funds to visit Italy for study, not once but twice. They were preceded in this journey by other French painters and illuminators, chief among them Jean Pucelle and Jacquemart. These artists traveled not to learn a new technique nor to visit a specific master—as Dürer still did for Schongauer—but to see an entirely new art created over a period of decades in a distant country.

When designing their novel Books of Hours the Limbourgs surely consulted learned clerics in Jean de Berry's circle such as Martin Gouge, Jean de Montreuil, or Jean Gerson. Although Paul and his brothers illustrated only religious books these scholars, together with Nicolas de Clamanges and a non-ecclesiastical humanist such as Gontier Col, Berry's secretary, awakened the interest of the Duke, of Louis d'Orléans and other princes in the world of antiquity. Jean de Berry collected ancient coins and cameos, and medals "de la façon ancienne" (Figs. 265, 266). He had numerous Early Christian or Byzantine objects that were not clearly distinguished from ancient ones. He and other princes commissioned, bought or were given illustrated manuscripts of Terence and Virgil as well as cycles of ancient history and mythology.

The influence of ancient art upon painting of the time remained, as we have seen, marginal, but all these cultural events represented nevertheless an approach to the ancient world that was novel in scope and intensity. During the first decades of the Early Renaissance, painters in Italy likewise do not seem to have been influenced by ancient models, but their contemporaries in sculpture, whom they studied closely, were. For this and other reasons the great renewal in France was somewhat different from the one in Italy. We do, however, assert once again that the course of pictorial development in France up to 1420 resembled remarkably what was happening in Italy. The degree of likeness is far greater than the usual antithesis between medieval or Gothic and Renaissance implies.

In our consideration of painting in France we have often pointed to the greater prominence and independence of aesthetic values. These values emerged in the realm of religious as well as secular art, and they proved to be the principal stimulus to collecting. The major painters became aware of their creative power, and Paul de Limbourg sensed his own unique gifts as well as his capacity to form a new style. His insights into the color and texture of nature were not matched in Italy until the middle of the century. He and his colleagues gained new knowledge not only of the surrounding natural world but of lands distant in space and remote in time. Geography and history became especially significant to illuminators, who were enlightened by both the content of their texts and by the words of their scholarly and humanist advisers. They therefore introduced such remarkable representations as the monastery of St. Catherine at Sinai (Fig. 448) or the Nubians in the Chapel of Calvary (Fig. 596). Historical reconstruction and the representation of the exotic, which have often been associated with the early Renaissance in Italy, were in fact developed equally, or indeed more extensively, in France. The portrait, long regarded as the most striking manifestation of a new Italian individualism, became popular first at the north European, and especially French, courts. No Italian work of art was as pervaded by the interests of a patron as the *Très Riches Heures* was by the Duke of Berry.

If the rendering of light was one of the great themes of fifteenth-century painting, that theme was most boldly and beautifully announced soon after 1400 in France. There the Boucicaut Master discovered aerial perspective, and Paul de Limbourg opened the new world of highlights and cast shadows. The equilibrium between planar and spatial design achieved in Paul's late works anticipated strikingly the paintings of Uccello, Domenico Veneziano, and Piero della Francesca. Paul anticipated these painters also in his concentration on problems of form; indeed this is the least recognized, but surely the deepest, level of relationship between his art and that of his Italian successors. Although his glorious adventures in color, especially in the *Belles Heures*, may have remained unknown in Italy, the state of mind which produced them probably was communicated somehow to Florence and Venice.

The eclipse of the new French pictorial art must be attributed in large measure to the English conquest and the fall of Paris as well as to the shift of the Burgundian capital from Dijon (and in a real sense, with regard to the arts, from Paris) to Bruges and Lille. The turmoil in France lay behind the ascendancy of a painter with so different an outlook as the Rohan Master. After these events, from about 1420 on, European painting was polarized, as Panofsky observed, in Italy and the Netherlands.[744] Without the historical accidents, however, there might have been a third major pole. If Paris and Dijon had remained great centers of patronage and creativity Jan van Eyck might well have worked for the Duke of Burgundy there instead of in Lille and Bruges, with results that may probably be surmised.

Quite apart, however, from the disasters, the deaths and the decline of patronage there were circumstances in France that might have slowed the exceptionally venturesome course of painting. Although unique in northern Europe it was not as broadly based as the related movement in Italy. Sculpture and architecture remained impervious to the fundamental Italian innovations. The advanced French painters from 1380 to 1420 seem to have been unsupported by critical thought or literary acclaim, from which their contemporaries in Italy benefited. Their achievement remains, however, impressive and momentous. They stood midway between the Netherlands, whence most of them came, and Italy, to which they went. In the art of painting they ended, and permanently, the divorce of France from the Mediterranean. The Limbourgs and the Boucicaut Master brought into a rich new synthesis the seemingly irreconcilable values of Italy and the Low Countries. They blended naturalism with the more intellectual and elevated Italian tradition, giving a distinctive stylistic mode to the one Northern people that speaks a language of Mediterranean descent. This mode was still maintained by Poussin (Fig. 776), and, it is not too much to say, Seurat.

Although the Limbourgs and their contemporaries worked for a society that was still largely feudal, they based their style upon forms created in Italian, early bourgeois, republican city-states and in the rather similar Netherlandish cities. Neither the new naturalism nor the new Italianism can be associated exclusively with one social structure; they are part of the changing values of European civilization as a whole.

Having offered this and other equally general observations I should add that I would not wish to go quite as far as the historian of art who, writing about a problematic painter of this period, said: "Wir kennen mit Sicherheit kein einziges Werk, aber das Gesamtbild ist klar."

VIII

Epilogue: Expressionism

1 · THE APOCALYPSE AND MEDALLION MASTERS

At few times in the long and glorious artistic history of Paris was there a larger number of gifted painters than in the first years of the fifteenth century. Among them two not hitherto discussed shared especially similar aims, and their work is notable not only for its artistic strength but for what it portended for the future. Both artists appeared toward the end of the first decade of the century. One, the Master of the Duke of Berry's Apocalypse, reconstructed independently and at the same time nearly twenty years ago by both Carl Nordenfalk and the writer,[1] has begun to be generally appreciated. The other, the Medallion Master, is rare and almost unknown. His mature style is discernible, it seems, in only one manuscript; but that one, an Apocalypse and an abbreviated story of the Bible painted in medallions, is an extensively illustrated and superb work.

These two masters have in common not only their stylistic direction but also their specialized role in Parisian illumination. We know, to be sure, only two manuscripts by the Medallion Master, but many more by the Berry Apocalypse workshop, and there is not a single Book of Hours among them. These illuminators normally undertook manuscripts with a larger cycle of miniatures, and they developed a technique to suit their practice. They painted in washes, rapidly laid, and their drawing has more openly the character of improvisation. Their stories gain thereby in animation if not in subtlety. They employed a limited number of colors, and they did not attempt a fine, careful graduation of plane. The colors are, however, distinctive and beautifully blended. They are usually pale, and the vellum itself serves for the high values, so that the entire folio—miniature, text, and vellum—acquires an impressive unity.

Although the miniatures by these masters are more colorful, their brushwork resembles that of the grisaille painters of the fourteenth century.[2] Neither master retained, of course, the diapered background, although a follower of the Apocalypse Master, the Boethius illuminator, tended to preserve it.[3]

The Apocalypse Master, and the Medallion Master to the extent to which we know him, collaborated less than usual with other Parisian workshops.[4] What practical implications this fact might have are not clear. We are informed about the seller of only one of their manuscripts. In 1413 Jean de Berry purchased a historical treatise, *Le brut d'Angleterre*, from Jean Colin, qualified as "escolier."[5] Curiously, both the Apocalypse Master and the Medallion Master illustrated texts for which the Virgil Master painted a frontispiece. This is true of two manuscripts by the Medallion Master, which we shall discuss shortly, and of one by the Apocalypse Master, a *Cité de Dieu*, fr. 25, which we believe to be his earliest work, painted *ca.* 1408–1410 (Figs. 51, 782).[6]

Inasmuch as the Virgil Master was an older illuminator who was active already in the 'nineties, the unique association of the Apocalypse Master with him in the *Cité de Dieu* tends to confirm its early date. Apart from the frontispiece the style of the miniatures in this manuscript derives principally, however, from the Boucicaut Master. That master's art is the source of the settings, the perspective platforms, and the basic mold of the figures, though they are more impulsive in their movement (Fig. 782). In this *Cité de Dieu* the Apocalypse Master possesses already, however, his distinctive palette—delicate green, brown, and beige with chalky white highlights sometimes touched with gold.

Miniatures not much later than those in the *Cité de Dieu* appear in a *Testament* of the author of the second part of the *Roman de la rose*, Jean de Meun (Fig. 780), and in a manuscript of the travel books of Hayton and Marco Polo, M. 723 in the Morgan Library. The silken figures in the *Testament* imply execution by the master himself, whereas the workshop produced the sketchier, quickly realized miniatures in the Morgan *Merveilles*.

The *Brut d'Angleterre* purchased by Jean de Berry in 1413 contains lively although rather mediocre illustrations by the workshop, but some of the powerful figures in a slightly later *Roman de la rose* in Stuttgart, though crudely executed, clearly reveal the master's imagination (Figs. 784, 785). This manuscript, after the magnificent but still unclassified Morgan M. 245, is the outstanding illustrated copy of this text in the first half of the fifteenth century. The Apocalypse Master himself closely supervised also the illustrations of a *Manuel d'histoire* written in 1416, and a few of the miniatures he surely executed himself.[7] One of these, representing Aristotle as teacher brandishing the rod over Alexander and two princely youths, shows the wide spaces, attenuated figures, and stronger rhythmical flourishes of the master's late style (Fig. 786).

This style may be seen at its best in the Morgan Apocalypse—excellent, no doubt, because it was probably made for, and certainly acquired by, Jean de Berry (Figs. 787, 788, 790, 792, 808, 811). The artist, furthermore, found the text of the Apocalypse especially congenial; St. John's vivid, exciting images roused his spirit. He decided to pitch his color at a more strident level, painting all the skies a strong red (Fig. 808)—a stronger red than in the related, earlier Apocalypse tapestries in Angers designed by Jean Bondol.[8] The ground is pale green, with olive shades and bright areas often consisting of the bare vellum. In one of the most beautiful miniatures, entirely by the master himself, a superb angel, poised yet rhythmically alive to the last lock of hair, presents the book, with a fine flourish, to St. John (Fig. 808). The burning eyes of the passionately eager saint are entranced by the writing on the open pages. Behind him the hills heave and the tree sputters. The Woman of the twelfth chapter, identified by an inscription with Mary and the Church, stands majestically on the moon, confronted by a long, seven-headed dragon that curls around her (Fig. 787). In another miniature, given verve by the streaking ground, the flaming trees and the fluttering drapery, St. John points to an abnormally tall Baptist—whose presence is not mentioned by the text and who was, in fact, dead when the Evangelist wrote (Fig. 788).[9]

St. John's apocalyptic text did not arouse nearly as much interest around 1400 as it had a century earlier. One well-known, scintillating but I think rather showy and monotonous example was painted in the Netherlands.[10] It may be significant that the two French manuscripts to which we have referred were produced about 1415, that is at a time of intensified civil conflict and of an alarming English invasion. These two manuscripts bear witness to that extraordinary matching of illuminators and commissions to which we have often referred as one of the signs of the sophistication of the Parisian scene.

Like the Apocalypse Master, the author of the manuscript in Chantilly, the Medallion Master, realized his gifts fully in the illustration of Revelation (Figs. 789, 791, 794–797, 802, 812). He painted with exceptional freedom. His brush dashes across the surface, leaving *taches* of color and fluid, flickering shapes. Inanimate forms, such as the towering rocks alongside the gate to Hell, come alive, moving with a more obvious vitality than the figures (Fig. 789). The illuminator surpassed all painters of the time in the portrayal of fire and fumes. Thus Revelation 8, 3–5, gave him an opportunity to show an angel taking the fire of the altar into a censer and then throwing it down on the world, while smoke rises toward the Lord (Fig. 791). The workshop of the Apocalypse Master illustrated merely a part of the text: the censing of the altar (Fig. 792). This workshop normally chose only one section of the text and abbreviated the representation.

The relationship of the two manuscripts, especially with regard to iconography, is discussed in some detail in the Catalogue of Manuscripts. For many miniatures the two illuminators employed the same model. What it looked like we can judge quite well by considering the illustration of Revelation 7, 1:

> And after these things I saw four angels standing on the four corners of the earth, holding the four winds of the earth, that the wind should not blow on the earth, nor on the sea, nor on any tree.

In the Chantilly miniature four angels hold the heads of the winds around a medallion enclosing the world (Fig. 794), and the illuminator surely knew the representation in the Apocalypse now in Cambrai or a similar manuscript (Fig. 793). The Cambrai miniature even contains a circle within a rectangle, the basic design of all the Chantilly miniatures. No known Apocalypse contains illustrations in medallions, but they appear in other texts and other arts of the Romanesque and early Gothic period.[11] The Apocalypse Master, choosing an entirely different composition, showed only one angel, but this one more decisively deflects the wind from the earth by tilting the head upward and closing its eyes and its mouth (Fig. 790).

Instead of reducing the complexity of his text the Medallion Master sometimes expanded upon it. Thus in the *Crucifixion*, which appears not in Revelation but in the *Histoire de la Bible*, Christ is accompanied not only by the two usual condemned men but by five (Fig. 804). The cross of one is cracking, and a fifth cross has already broken, throwing the body to the ground. All of this occurs in front of strangely shaped, dune-like hills painted in various shades of tan and warm or cool brown. These same hues, more saturated, appear on the figures, alongside blue and much gray-white or, as in the Morgan Apocalypse, bare vellum. The terrain behind them is light green. This beautiful and highly distinctive pattern is framed by the brick-red medallion and the "spandrels"—light green above, blue below, both filled by fine curling leaves tinted with orange.

Although the bosky garden in the *Temptation* is rendered entirely in tan and green, the painter modulates his hues so subtly as to produce an effect of great coloristic richness (Fig. 803). This effect is enhanced by the liveliness of the patches of color; they merge in a design that overlies the objects with which, in another sense, they are associated. The verve and assurance of the painter's brush are unmatched anywhere at this time.

All, however, is not delicate and gay in this leafy garden. Eve, to be sure, is dainty and sensuous, but as she offers the fruit her mate clutches his Adam's apple. A large dark corpse, furthermore, lies between them, symbolizing sin and death and transforming the idyll into tragedy. This iconography is not new; it appeared *ca.* 1405 in a miniature in a *Cité de Dieu* by the Virgil Master,[12] who painted the frontispieces of the Chantilly manuscript. The Medallion Master, however, made it more startling and dramatic by transforming a normal, supine body into a brown, skeletonized corpse.

Throughout the Chantilly manuscript the Medallion Master proved capable of representing effectively scenes of very different kinds. The Great Whore of the Apocalypse was never so seductively conceived (Fig. 795). Rolling her flirtatious eyes, she wears a dark dress, décolleté, and a magnificent broad hat with bells around its brim. Because of a startling, and certainly erroneous conflation she has the attributes—sun and moon—of the Woman of the twelfth chapter of *Revelation*, whom the commentator introduced again at this point and who alone is in fact represented in the Morgan Apocalypse. Many miniatures by the Medallion Master, very different in content from the *Great Whore*, convey powerfully the destruction described by the text. When an imposing, mitred Antichrist, in a blasphemous gesture, touches the Church, it wilts instantly like a flower (Fig. 797). In the metaphor in Revelation 14, a kind of farmer's nightmare describing the "harvest of the earth," angels toss sharp sickles out of the sky, striking down men and animals in a universal carnage (Fig. 796).[13]

This miniature, like many others in the Chantilly manuscript (Figs. 789, 798), depicts a wide, deep space; the painter prefers to design boldly, on a large scale. These qualities suggest he might normally have worked on panel or even on the wall, and this hypothesis would have the advantage of accounting for the rarity of paintings by him in the book. We know, in fact, only two other manuscripts with miniatures in his style, a *Légende dorée* of about 1407, and a *Roman de la rose*, executed by his workshop two or three years later (Figs. 437, 809, 810).

The hypothesis that the Medallion Master was a painter rather than an illuminator encounters, however, an obstacle. The larger miniatures in Chantilly—the two frontispieces—were not painted by him but by the Virgil Master. Furthermore, about seven or eight years earlier the Medallion Master illuminated, with assistants, a *Légende dorée*, fr. 414, and again the frontispiece was entrusted to the Virgil Master, as we have observed above (Figs. 388, 437, 809).[14] Since the Virgil Master was almost certainly an illuminator his execution of the frontispieces does not suggest that his collaborator in the smaller miniatures that follow was a painter of large-scale works.

These earlier miniatures of *ca.* 1407 already show the subtle blending of color that is so impressive an aspect of the Chantilly manuscript. Shades of brown, from tan to chocolate, are already prominent, together with pale blue-green, gray, and white. As we have seen, the Medallion Master, like the Virgil Master, adopted compositions from the *Belles Heures*, which was then perhaps not yet quite completed (Figs. 388, 437). To the two compositions already discussed, *All Saints* and *St. Catherine with the Doctors*, a third will be added shortly.[15] The later Apocalypse in Chantilly also quite definitely reflects the *Belles Heures*. The Virgil Master's Emperor Domitian listening to a counselor who holds up his cap repeats the group of Nero and a similar adviser in the *Martyrdom of Sts. Peter and Paul* in the *Belles Heures* (Figs. 799, 800). A proposal by Jean Porcher that a miniature in Chantilly 28 depended upon *January* in the *Très Riches Heures* seems inconclusive,[16] but a relation is possible because the two manuscripts were being illuminated at the same time. The Duke of Berry's Apocalypse was definitely completed before his death in June 1416. The similarity of its style to the Apocalypse Master's *Manuel d'histoire* of 1416 indicates that it was illuminated *ca.* 1415. Chantilly 28, as we have observed, should be dated at the same time.[17]

2 · THE ROHAN MASTER AND THE TWENTIES

When we contemplate the miniatures of the mature Rohan Master we enter a world similar to that of the Apocalypse and Medallion Masters. His paintings, like theirs, are charged with strong feeling, created by clamorous color, dashing brushwork, powerful rhythms, and impulsive gestures. These fundamental similarities are not, however, clearly the consequence of the influence of the two older masters upon the younger—if, indeed, he really was younger. Here we have already struck the difficult problem of the chronology of the manuscripts in the Rohan style, about which we hold opinions different from those hitherto maintained. We are aware, however, that much remains to be learned, especially by identifying the associates of the master and then undertaking the subtle task of tracing the development of each. External evidence for the dates of the manuscripts is exceptionally scanty, and we possess no facts about the painter at all.

The best works in the Rohan style, such as the *Lamentation* in the *Rohan Hours* (Fig. 888), are now widely admired; everyone agrees that he was an extraordinary artist. His full stature can be recognized, however, only if the paintings for which he was entirely responsible are distinguished from those to which he made a partial contribution—a contribution that ranged from the provision of compositional drawings to merely setting an example to followers. The peculiarities of his practice make such distinctions very difficult, as earlier students of his work recognized. The power and subtlety of his art, however, tend to rescue us from insoluble intricacies. We shall concentrate on those paintings for which he was, in our opinion, largely, if not exclusively, responsible. These major paintings can be arranged in sequence with the help of the evidence provided by his response to the work of better documented masters. Without a scaffold of works firmly fixed in time, however, the actual dates of most of the paintings must remain approximate.

The *Rohan Hours*, after which the painter was named, is obviously a very advanced work. It reveals a knowledge of the late miniatures in the *Très Riches Heures*, painted in 1415–1416 (Figs. 539–549), and it has been variously dated from *ca.* 1418 to, according to Durrieu, the late 'thirties at least.[18] The painter most responsible for a Book of Hours normally executed the miniature of the Annunciation at the beginning of the principal office, Matins of the Hours of the Virgin. In the *Rohan Hours* the best master departed from this practice in a most unusual way (Fig. 868). The composition, to be sure, is strong, and he no doubt designed it. He adopted a kind of building favored by the Limbourgs as a solid, spacious setting for their saints or sacred events. In the *Rohan*

Hours it still retains suggestions of enclosure and of depth; indeed the floor is composed not of flat tiles but of strongly plastic cubes. They rise, however, almost vertically, carrying the head of the Virgin close to the vaults. Similarly, the spindly columns as well as the red vaults edged in gold function less as architectural elements than as shapes in an exciting linear pattern. Though the angel and to a lesser degree the Virgin are rounded figures it is their outlines that are most telling, and the heads of both are in perfect profile. So active and compelling is the pattern that it readily assimilates, even as a normal and necessary element, the bust of the prophet Isaiah, for which there would certainly be no place in any rational tri-dimensional space.

Throughout the composition vestiges of naturalistic and rational canons serve to create surprise and tension when they are denied. The building itself does not even rest on the ground. Below it, as on the three other sides, angels flutter and declaim in a blue sky. The entire environment of the large structure, indeed, is celestial and supernatural. Possibly the painter intended to allude to the miracle of the house of the Annunciation in Nazareth, which angels later carried across the Mediterranean to Loreto.

For the first time, to my knowledge, in an Annunciation the chair is turned inward, whereas Mary, who is averted but not clearly seated in it, appears largely in profile. Gabriel, too, is represented in profile—and how magnificently! Just ending his flight, his locks and mantle still streaming, he lifts his eager face, the strain of bearing the message released as he parts his lips at the beginning of speech. The designs of the Rohan Master always culminate in the face and the gesture. The dour countenance of Isaiah turns almost into full profile, and his pointing hand is emphasized by the deep blue of his mantle. Both the Boucicaut Master and the Limbourgs, concerned with volume and space, tended to avoid profile; furthermore, they usually represented forms and figures within one space on a similar scale, subject only to the diminution of perspective. Even the sacred figures, when appearing at a distance, are frequently smaller in size. The Rohan Master, however, reduced the scale of Isaiah, compared to the two principal figures, even though he is nearer the beholder. On the other hand God the Father is represented on the largest scale in the painting. Such conspicuous differences, associated in earlier medieval painting with the varying religious significance of the figures, acquire in this more naturalistic context a peculiar expressive value.

At this moment the Virgin is, of course, the principal person, but with her relatively flat mantle, long neck, small head, and enigmatic face she is far less interesting than Gabriel, who is surely one of the most beautiful messengers ever conceived. His tunic and mantle still preserve some of the textural richness and subtly modulated planes of the Limbourgs and the Boucicaut Master. The reader may already have wondered about the qualitative difference between the two principal figures, and there can really be no doubt that the Rohan Master himself painted Gabriel while leaving the Virgin to an assistant—a surprising conclusion, which has however already been approximated by an earlier critic.[19] The Rohan Master, who no doubt designed the entire composition, was, it seems clear, responsible for the execution of only one other figure, the Deity. His workshop painted the rest. Of the hundreds of miniatures in this Book of Hours the master executed only three almost entirely with his own brush.

This exceptional kind of collaboration can be more readily identified in the late work of the master, when he had established his own idiom and painted with greater assurance. It can be discerned in preceding miniatures also, as we shall see, but when we consider the earliest works the difficulties of identification increase. I agree with Adelheid Heimann that the small Book of Hours now in the Royal Ontario Museum in Toronto contains the earliest work we know in the Rohan style—although not of 1400 or earlier, as she maintained for stylistic and textual reasons,[20] but towards 1410.[21] The folio of the *Annunciation* bears the arms of Louis de Giac impaling those of his wife Jeanne du Peschin (Fig. 813).[22] Louis was cup-bearer to the king and chamberlain to the Dukes of Berry and Burgundy. He went off on the crusade of 1396 and failed to return, and since the prayers almost always imply a feminine donor, and since this "pecheresse" repeatedly pleads for protection for "ton serf,"[23] Miss Heimann inferred that the text was written for Jeanne soon after Louis failed to return. There are, however, no such narrow chronological constraints, because in 1407 the codicil of the will of Louis' father refers to him as still in the hands of the infidel.[24] Precisely how long Jeanne believed her husband was still alive we do not know; by 1418, however, when she had become intimate with Jean sans Peur, she was described as a widow.[25]

The figures in the *Annunciation* in the *Giac Hours* scarcely conform with Parisian canons, but the scale of the Virgin implies familiarity with the painting of the Boucicaut Master, who, with the Limbourgs, soon proved to be the chief source of the growth of the Rohan Master. Already at this early moment the Rohan Master—if this is, as we believe, he—radically transformed his models, multiplying the twisting folds of the Virgin's mantle and employing the tiled floor more for its sparkle than as an index of depth. It is significant that the highly peculiar forms of the throne appear in an *Annunciation* in the *Ranshaw Hours* painted about 1410 by the Troyes workshop (Fig. 814).[26] The Rohan Master liked the exceptional height of the structure so much that he allowed it to project far beyond the frame. The unique placement of the Virgin's crown at the top of both thrones proves that the two representations are linked. The *Annunciation* by the Troyes Master probably was the Rohan Master's model. Even the arabesque tooled in the gold of the Troyes *Annunciation* is repeated in paint by the Rohan Master. In other miniatures of the *Giac Hours* he, like the Troyes Master, tooled the same bold arabesques in the gold (Fig. 825).

There may be another sign of the familiarity of the Rohan Master with the work of the Troyes Master. In the *Giac Hours* and in his later painting up to the *Rohan Hours* itself he employed the unusual kind of cruciform halo of the Troyes workshop in which the cross seems composed of bands that widen as they fold around the disk (Figs. 819, 820, 829). Perhaps, too, it was the revival by the Troyes Master of an earlier type of Trinity in which the second person is a child that stimulated the Rohan Master to develop, as always in his own way, representations of this kind (Figs. 829, 830). About 1415, furthermore, for the illustration of the Office of the Dead the Troyes Master adopted neither the traditional service around the bier nor the newer subject of a burial service; he introduced instead the starker theme of a sorrowful contemplation of the naked corpse (Fig. 846). It was in similar miniatures for this Office that the Rohan Master, fascinated by bodily decay and death, introduced his famous innovations. In the Princeton manuscript the corpse is not mourned by the usual monks and *pleureurs* but only by the family, it seems, of the deceased (Fig. 847). In one eerie scene supernatural light seems to draw from their graves three grinning corpses which dangle and dance like ghostly puppets (Fig. 849).

The relationship of the Rohan Master with the modest painter we have just considered throws some light on the highly controversial problem of his origins. The Troyes Master was a conservative illuminator who appeared about 1395 and who, though aware of developments in Paris, illuminated manuscripts for Châlons, Sens and, most frequently, nearby Troyes; hence the name I have given him.[27] It is an important fact that although the use of the *Giac Hours* is Rome, the texts of two Books of Hours by the Rohan Master and associates, Ste. Geneviève 1278 and Harley 2934, painted soon after the *Giac Hours*, are connected with Troyes. No less than seven later Books of Hours by assistants and followers of the Rohan Master are use of Troyes also.[28] Apparently there, in the Champagne, the young painter worked, making occasional visits to Paris.

In the *Giac Hours* the Rohan Master and his assistants linealized, flattened, and animated the compositions of his contemporaries. His fantasy was sometimes playful: the little angel diving down to hold the Virgin's mantle in the *Visitation*, for instance (Fig. 825), or the aged shepherd behind the fence in the *Nativity*, his white beard alone hanging down in front of it, like Lytton Strachey's, as he said, over his blankets (Fig. 816). The iconography of this *Nativity* recalls in several respects that of the *Belles Heures* (Fig. 329): the adoration of the Child by a kneeling Virgin and a standing Joseph, the shed, the rays issuing from the Child, and the presence of a "shepherd." There seem to be other indications of a study of miniatures by the Limbourgs. In the *Deposition* one hat looks like a fanciful version of the leaf or blade crowns used by the Limbourgs and occasionally by the Boucicaut Master (Figs. 571, 826). The starry blue sky, employed again in other miniatures (Fig. 822), suggests awareness of the work of the Boucicaut Master. A similar source seems to be implied by the *repoussoir* in *St. George*, from which the horse emerges (Fig. 818).

The *Deposition*, like the *Nativity* and many other miniatures in the *Giac Hours*, shows exceptionally wide spaces between the figures, so that the lively design they compose can become peculiarly slender and tenuous (Fig. 826). In the *Deposition* John, while he supports the swooning Mary, looks back up at Christ. This is a group which the Rohan Master will employ more dramatically in later works (Figs. 834, 888). The colors of the miniatures in the *Giac Hours* are distinctive, yet recognizably related to later works in the Rohan style: gray, blue, rust, rose, and white (Fig. 816). The play of light over the rose mantle of Elizabeth in the *Visitation* anticipates the subtle modulation of planes in later paintings by the master (Figs. 825, 862, 867). All these similarities with later miniatures indicate that the *Giac Hours*, despite differences, represents the early style of the Rohan Master. If indeed the genial chief illuminator of this manuscript is not that master who could he possibly be? We know no other great painter in this circle, and it is always unwise to multiply geniuses.

In miniatures such as the *Baptist* and *St. Silvanus* the illuminator, like Hieronymus Bosch, produced eerie effects by animating the inanimate (Figs. 815, 817). These saints compose powerful, staccato patterns in front of the painter's favorite wide backgrounds, their apparent size increased by the use of small varicolored diapers. The Rohan workshop continued to employ this kind of foil for the figures. In the Boccaccio of about 1415 it acquires an unstable, raking character, as though it were part of a pavement in perspective turned into a vertical plane (Fig. 828).

Although the *Giac Hours* and later miniatures of the Rohan workshop were influenced by the Troyes Master, and the Rohan Master seems to have been active in the same town, he clearly kept his distance, partly perhaps because he felt the painting of his colleague uncongenial and unexciting. The representations of the Coronation of the Virgin by the two artists, for example, are similar—and the Giac miniature still *ca.* 1410 adheres to the type of the Virgin seated alongside Christ[29]—but the difference of style strikes deep (Figs. 819, 820). The Rohan Master had already learned many of the subtleties of late fourteenth-century Parisian painting that the Troyes Master could not comprehend.

There are other puzzling qualities in the *Giac Hours* that lead one to speculate about a prior sojourn of the painter in Provence. South French illumination showed a similar realism, for example, in the *Annunciation to the Shepherds*, or lively, puppet-like animals in the *Nativity* (Figs. 821, 827). Many figures, such as the Virgin in *Pentecost*, have a Provençal cast (Figs. 823, 824). The problem, which touches the origins of the Rohan Master's art, is difficult, and my observations are intended not as conclusions but suggestions for further study.

Jean Porcher ascribed numerous manuscripts, in whole or in part, to the Rohan workshop between about 1400, when he believed the *Giac Hours* was painted, and about 1414. We do not share his view of any of these manuscripts; some seem to us later in date, others not products of associates or of any relationship that could be defined as a workshop.[30] After the *Giac Hours*, painted towards 1410, the workshop in our opinion undertook two small Books of Hours of the use of Troyes, Harley 2934 and Ste. Geneviève 1278 (Figs. 831–838).[31] In both manuscripts the dense ivy borders of the *Giac Hours* were abandoned for arabesques and flowers that came into favor after 1410. On some folios of Harley 2934 large figures closely related to the subject of the miniature appeared in the lower and outer borders (Fig. 837); they are a kind of equivalent of the historiated roundels that began to be used at this time by the Boucicaut and Bedford workshops. The Rohan workshop shortly enclosed such figures in frames, not, however, round or irregular (except in the Fitzwilliam Hours) but rectangular; they became characteristic of all later works of the atelier. The blazing sun in the *Visitation* of the Harley manuscript is another sign of Boucicaut influence (Fig. 831), and the landscapes of this manuscript as well as the deeper, more variegated ones of the later Ste. Geneviève Hours derive from the same source (Figs. 831, 836).

The theme of the protective St. John turning from the Virgin to Christ, which had appeared in the Giac *Descent from the Cross* (Fig. 826), was introduced in the Harley manuscript in its more usual context, the *Crucifixion* (Fig. 834). Just as these impressive figures, executed no doubt on designs by the master, anticipate a miniature in the *Rohan Hours* (Fig. 888), the *Flight into Egypt* in the Harley horae predicts the entire composition of this subject in the later manuscript (Figs. 832, 870). The miracle of the grain is represented below while the Holy Family flees high in the landscape, the Virgin's head close to, or touching, the upper frame. In the *Rohan Hours* the flight is, contrary to convention, from left to right, possibly to permit, on a recto, a flow of movement toward the center of the book.

The unusual setting of the Harley *Adoration of the Magi* consists of a vaulted chamber that supports an arcaded dome, a tower, a half-timber house, and other architectural elements (Fig. 833). This conglomeration recalls the miniatures of the Brussels Initials Master, whereas the half-timber structure derives rather from the work of the Boucicaut Master (Fig. 859).[32] The prominent dome, although crowned by a nude statue, may refer to the Synagogue, and indeed it was frequently employed with that specific connotation in both the *Boucicaut Hours* and in later Rohan representations of the Presentation in the Temple.[33] In these later Rohan miniatures, such as the one in the *De Buz Hours* at Harvard (Fig. 842), the drum of the dome has become greatly stretched, as part of a process of attenuation that affected all forms. This tendency increased throughout the activity of the workshop. The high drum of the dome over the Marriage of the Virgin in the Fitzwilliam Hours, painted about 1417–1418, is marked by very strong vertical members (Fig. 863).

Unlike the domed chamber of the Marriage of the Virgin in the Fitzwilliam manuscript the Virgin's room alongside is entirely Gothic. It is an attenuated version of a structure designed by the Limbourgs about 1411, which we know through a copy by the Master of St. Jerome (Fig. 357).[34] Some elements of this structure had been used *ca.* 1414, and in more robust form, by the Rohan workshop in the *Annunciation* in the Ste. Geneviève Hours (Fig. 835). As in the prototype two of the statues under canopies raise their hands high under their mantles. The building behind the chapel of the Annunciation is domed, indicating the world *ante* Christ. A nude statue kneels near it but also, probably by error, over the Virgin. The latest and most airy version of this structure was designed by the Rohan Master for the *Annunciation* in the *Rohan Hours* (Fig. 868).

In several of the borders of the Ste. Geneviève Hours violets with their own proper leaves curl freely into space like those painted by the Breviary Master in the *Très Riches Heures* (Figs. 556, 836, 838). More perfunctory versions of these flowers appear in some borders of the Harley manuscript (Fig. 834). They might, of course, have been accessible to the Rohan workshop in an earlier work by the Breviary Master, and the Ste. Geneviève Hours is otherwise not related to the Limbourgs and their circle. At this time the Rohan workshop looked rather to the Boucicaut Master, who provided models for the landscapes and for the *Coronation of the Virgin*.[35] Indeed, not far from the time of execution of the Ste. Geneviève Hours the Rohan workshop collaborated with the Boucicaut illuminators, painting the calendar for a Book of Hours in the Boucicaut style (Figs. 839, 841).[36] The text of the manuscript is not for Troyes but Paris, and since the Boucicaut workshop was established in the metropolis part at least of the Rohan workshop apparently moved there at this time. This transfer is confirmed by two other manuscripts. The workshop collaborated with illuminators of the Bedford trend, active in Paris, on a *Livre de la chasse* now in Dresden and largely ruined in the last world war (Fig. 840). The arms in the manuscript may be those of the Dauphin, Louis duc de Guyenne, who died in 1415.[37] The miniatures adhere generally to the iconography of hunting books represented by fr. 616 (Fig. 260).

In a *Cas des nobles hommes et femmes* (fr. 226) the Rohan workshop again collaborated with illuminators of the Bedford trend, and also with the Cité des Dames workshop—all painters established in Paris (Figs. 848, 850, 851). For this cycle the recently completed illustrations in the *Boccace de Jean sans Peur* (Arsenal 5193) seem to have served generally as a model.[38] The dedication of the manuscript to Jean de Berry is preceded by a portrait of the prince that includes the characteristic attributes of the last years of his life, even a little dog,[39] so that though the manuscript does not bear the Duke's arms or ex libris and cannot be identified in the inventories it was probably illuminated for him before 1416.[40] The several styles of the illustrations support this date. Illuminators of the Bedford trend painted the dedication miniature and numerous others, including the outlandish episode of Joan, a transvestite who had been elected pope, suddenly giving birth to a child during a procession moving from the Colosseum to S. Clemente, on the way to the Lateran (Fig. 850).

The Rohan workshop, with its dynamic designs of contrasting diagonals and its dashing brushwork, could readily give Hercules the wild force described by Boccaccio and maintained in the version of Laurent de Premierfait (Fig. 851):[41]

> Hercules . . . avoit le visaige hideux, barbe noire mal agencee. . . . une robe faicte de la peau d'un leon lequel il prist et tua en une forest de Grece appellee Nemea, et portoit en sa main dextre une massue.

In another miniature King Laius of Thebes goes to the temple of Apollo, which has become a strikingly un-antique building with a retable of the Crucifixion on the altar and a Gothic superstructure reminiscent of the elaborate throne of the Virgin in the Giac *Annunciation* (Figs. 813, 848).

Whereas a part of the Rohan group was working in Paris *ca.* 1414–1416, other associates of the master seem to have remained in Troyes—or, at the least, produced in Paris several Books of Hours for the use of Troyes.[42] An impressive example, divided between the Arsenal and Princeton,[43] may be readily distinguished from the early manuscripts by the greater vehemence of the figures and the increased attenuation, which produced spidery patterns against the lively diapered backgrounds (Figs. 847, 855, 856). The principal miniature is accompanied by a smaller one in each lateral border, which compose a kind of triptych above a free-standing rectangular "predella." The *Crucifixion* contains a group of the swooning Virgin and St. John like that in the Harley Hours (Figs. 834, 855), and a similar group occupies a side panel of the *Deposition* (Fig. 856).

Many of the figures in the *De Buz Hours* at Harvard move with the extreme impulsiveness of those in the *Arsenal-Princeton Hours.* In the dazzling *Reception of the Virgin in Heaven* a Christ much larger than his mother leans over her in an almost frightening manner (Fig. 843). He wears, as usual in Rohan miniatures, the white hair and beard of God the Father. In representations by other artists of this moment of joyous reunion choirs of angels sing; in the subordinate fields here they zealously cense. The Rohan aged Christ, alone with his youthful, diminutive mother, exhibits a very large cross.

In the *De Buz Hours* the colors are more delicately modulated and more subtly blended than in the group of manuscripts we have just discussed; in the *Burial Service* the hues become even lustrous (Fig. 844). This miniature implies a closer study of Parisian painting, especially of the Boucicaut Master and the Limbourgs. It is not surprising to learn that the use of this Book of Hours is not Troyes but Paris.

Some figures in the *De Buz Hours*, such as a standing *Madonna* for the prayer *Obsecro te*, are broad and wrapped in voluminous drapery (Fig. 854). As a counterpart to the beautiful sway of the massive Virgin the Child moves away from her, revolving in the opposite direction from her supporting arm. This cantilevered Child, adumbrated in the St. Geneviève Hours,[44] exhibits a boldness and a mastery of dynamic design that can be equalled only in much later art. No less original is a second Madonna nearby, illustrating another prayer, which reads near the beginning: "Je te salue Maria a qui dieu son fils maria a humaine fragilite Dieux quel mariage si a povrete riche mari a lymon est joint a deite. Immortel a mortalite." In the illustration the Madonna is revealed behind a cloth of honor held by two angels—a design that, as we have seen, was popular in France for the Man of Sorrows and, a little later, for the Madonna (Figs. 373, 602, 642, 852). She bends down to kiss the very large, heavy Child who lies asleep in her arms. This is the first image of the sleeping Child in French and perhaps all Northern painting. It was probably inspired by an Italian panel, most likely from Venice where the subject was introduced in the late fourteenth century. The Duke of Berry, in fact, possessed a Venetian example.[45]

Both the prayer and the small miniatures in the margins throw light on the content of the image. In Italian representations the meanings range from the "dolcezza e grazia" of the sleep of the new-born Child or invocations to wake him so that the process of redemption can proceed, to allusions to the death that lies ahead. The prayer refers to Christ become man, and one of the miniatures shows the Virgin, as in a Nativity, adoring the Infant lying naked on the ground, whereas in the other miniature he takes his first steps. The painter thus explicitly tells us that an important aspect of the image of the sleeping Child is, as I have often remarked, joyful and lyric. Although neither of these subsidiary miniatures contain any proleptic allusions, "humaine fragilite" in the prayer implies the subjection of Christ to the human condition, and the limp, fallen arm in the miniature, touched by an angel, probably refers to it.[46] Thus the joy of birth is already pervaded by premonitions of death. The Rohan Master attained his greatest heights in the portrayal of sorrow, and he created here the most moving of all the early paintings of the sleeping Christ, rarely equaled, indeed, at any period.

These two impressive paintings of the Madonna may not have been painted by the Rohan Master himself, but he certainly designed them. Apart from their exceptional beauty, who else in his circle would have struck out in a new direction, creating the swelling volumes of the *Madonna with the Sleeping Child*? They were surely inspired by the figures of Paul de Limbourg in the *Belles Heures* (Figs. 398, 455). The familiarity of the Rohan Master with the style of the three brothers, suggested already by his earlier work,[47] is proved by the *De Buz Hours*. The *Annunciation to the Shepherds* in this manuscript is in large part a copy of the corresponding miniature in the *Belles Heures* (Figs. 411, 853). The averted Virgin on the ass in the *Flight into Egypt* probably was suggested likewise by the *Flight* in the same manuscript (Fig. 415, 845).[48]

Of the three major Books of Hours by the Rohan workshop that remain to be considered two are for the use of Paris and one for Angers. All of them are extensively illuminated. They are all more or less definitely connected with the Anjou family, and the Parisian use, as we shall see, may not indicate that they were produced in the metropolis. The earliest of these manuscripts is Fitzwilliam 62; certainly the *Rohan Hours* and the Hours for the use of Angers in a private collection are considerably later, whereas the place in this series of lat. 1156A remains less clear. A clue to the date of the Fitzwilliam Hours is given by the similarity of the *Annunciation* to representations of the same subject by the Boucicaut workshop *ca.* 1415–1417 (Figs. 863, 864).[49] The kind of church with projecting dome partly unsupported, dormer windows in the roof, and a turret alongside was not used by the Boucicaut workshop before this period. In the Fitzwilliam *Annunciation* the illuminator took from the same source the turning posture of the Virgin. Even the flowers in the border are similar, and it seems certain that if the Rohan illuminator did not know this very Book of Hours, now in a private collection, he was familiar with another that was quite similar. The small miniatures in the borders of the Fitzwilliam manuscript, moreover, are not rectangular, as in most Rohan manuscripts, but rounded and inserted into the foliage, as in Boucicaut manuscripts of *ca.* 1415 such as the Mazarine Hours[50] and on the folio of *Diocrès* in the *Très Riches Heures* (Fig. 578). Indeed the violets and delphinium in the borders of the Boucicaut manuscript (Fig. 864) probably reflect examples by the Breviary Master.

It is not necessary to describe again the transformation of the Boucicaut forms in the Rohan miniature, especially because this *Annunciation*, though in the most prominent place in the manuscript, was executed by an assistant. The full force of the concept "assistant" is disclosed by turning to the miniature illustrating the *Sept requêtes* (Fig. 862). Even without awareness of what the scene represents, the beauty of Christ's mantle, with its luminous, undulating, richly textured folds, demonstrates a mastery far beyond anything in the *Annunciation* (Fig. 863). This gaunt figure, swaying uncertainly and indeed too tall to stand upright within the frame, was surely painted by the Rohan Master himself. He left everything else in the miniature, and of course the border also, to an assistant.[51]

The *Sept requêtes* are prayers in which the pious ask God to remember man on seven occasions, beginning with the incarnation and ending, in the seventh request, with Christ's consideration of the good thief on his cross.[52] The unusual—perhaps unique—subject in the miniature, however, was no doubt inspired by the less common prologue to the Prayers, which gives assurance to the reader of the *requêtes* that he will not die on that very day without confession and "ne mourra villainement . . ." Christ is present to assure this latter promise, because he appears as Man of Sorrows and he shows the wounds that are the signs of redemption to two men who rise on the day of judgment from their tombs. In accordance with a concept basic to contemporary nominalist theology, he demonstrates that the promise of salvation will be fulfilled.

The standing Man of Sorrows, often bearing a cross, began to be widely diffused in Germany and Italy from the early fifteenth century on.[53] In the Fitzwilliam miniature, however, Christ also addresses two souls, and in the border he judges in the conventional way. Perhaps it is merely fortuitous that precisely the same kind of Christ in two roles, though with a cross, may be seen in a group of thirteenth-century Flemish Psalters (Fig. 860).[54] Here the image illustrates the first Psalm; the two rising figures are presumably the Blessed, whereas the group remaining immobile underground are the "ungodly" who, as the Psalm says, "shall not stand in the judgment."

Only a few figures in two other miniatures in the Fitzwilliam Hours equal *Christ as Man of Sorrows and Judge*. One such group is the Madonna between Peter and Paul on a large crescent (Fig. 865). They are all more or less half-length but self-sufficient figures in the Limbourg manner, although Peter does need to cling to the end of the moon. The Madonna and Child are unusually gentle for the Rohan Master, painted in light colors and swathed in luxuriously soft stuffs. Peter and Paul have the same exquisite and luminous surfaces, but they are lean, drawn, and anxious—imbued with a religious fervor as rare in contemporary French painting as it was common in German. Perhaps Peter, who gesticulates, asks the Madonna to intercede for the poor and wretched represented in the small miniature near him. The angels and the Trinity above—the prayer illustrated is Creator coeli—were again painted by assistants.

The third miniature partly executed by the Rohan Master is the best known (Fig. 867). It is the only full-page miniature in the manuscript, so large in fact that it is framed simply by a narrow gold band, outside of which there is a little bare vellum. Only the large standing Madonna and Child, until 1953 often ascribed to the Limbourgs,[55] approximates the art of the master—approximates, one must say, because the design of the Virgin is unexpected and unique in several respects. Unsupported on the left side she is kept from toppling only by the triangular, ascending floor and the architectural elements that frame her head. Her head and neck are relatively unarticulated, and the Infant is unformed compared to, for example, the Limbourgian Christ in the *De Buz Hours* (Fig. 852). Yet the group shows the same sensuous surfaces, delicately rendered, as the miniatures in the manuscript that are clearly by the master. The Virgin wears an unusual and very beautiful buff tunic, patterned and unlaced at the center. This is wrapped in a fine gray mantle. Both figures have warm yellow hair, from which issue golden rays. There is no other painter in the Rohan workshop capable of so impressive and exceptional an image and we are therefore strongly inclined to accept it as entirely his work. But of what date? It lacks the voluminous forms of the Madonnas in the *De Buz Hours* (Figs. 852, 854). and preserves, on the other hand, many qualities of the earliest miniatures in the Giac and Harley Hours (Figs. 813, 831). Indeed, the style of the assistant who painted the rest of the miniature is still that of these early manuscripts. He even employs the unusual friezes of curling acanthus leaves that were used frequently in the *Giac Hours*.[56] The extreme attenuation of the forms in most of the other miniatures in the Fitzwilliam Hours proves, however, that it cannot be early (Fig. 866),[57] and thus confirms the date of *ca.* 1417–1418 indicated by the composition of the *Annunciation* (Fig. 863).

The miniature of the Madonna serves as frontispiece to the *Fifteen Joys of the Virgin*, and two of them are represented at the sides. At the left is her marriage, which occurs in a chamber surmounted, as we have observed, by the dome as well as the towers and half-timber structure that designate the Temple in the *Presentation* in the *De Buz Hours* (Fig. 842). The Rohan Master used these elements later in the scene of the *Presentation* in the *Rohan Hours*—not however for the central space, which is a Gothic cathedral, but for the exterior structure at the left (Fig. 869). At the right in the Fitzwilliam miniature the Virgin mounts the stairs of the Temple to the waiting high priest. Below at the left the well probably signifies the "living waters" in the closed garden described by the Song of Songs.[58] The principal building, adapted, as we have seen, from the Limbourgs, and perhaps originally used by them for St. Jerome's study (Fig. 357), here definitely serves as the Church. Its walls are covered with stars, and a statue of a defeated Synagogue stands over a niche. The blue and gold floor, the red books and varicolored prophets make the Church the brightest zone of the miniature, but the Temple at the left shines, too, with golden moldings.

What the Rohan Master chose from the iconographic repertory of his predecessors and contemporaries gives us insight, of course, into his own artistic purposes. In some of his miniatures the evangelists, normally represented writing the Gospels, gaze toward heaven in an ectasy of creative inspiration, almost as though the painter had seen Carolingian models.[59] St. John in the Fitzwilliam Hours composes more quietly, so absorbed in his work that he does not perceive the mischief of the devil, who plunges forth from the saint's bench, it seems, and with a long hook overturns his inkwell (Fig. 857). The devil's attempt to prevent in this way the composition of the Gospel of St. John, normally on Patmos, is a late medieval invention. The earliest representation we know is in a Bible of *ca.* 1400 that belonged to Jean de Berry, which he gave to a friend in 1410 (Fig. 858).[60] No textual source connected with the Evangelist has been found but Jan van Gelder has now discovered the same story in the legend of St. John Chrysostom.[61]

The Fitzwilliam Hours bears the arms of Isabella Stuart, daughter of James I of Scotland (Figs. 857, 862, 863).[62] She became the second wife of Francis I of Brittany, and it has been inferred that she received the manuscript as a consequence of this marriage, because the first wife of Francis was Yolande d'Anjou, the daughter of the Yolande who seems to have been, as we shall see, the patron of the Rohan Master. For this history of the manuscript there is no proof.[63] Another Book of Hours, however, was indubitably made for a member of the Anjou family—indeed, it bears more signs of its original patron and early history than most manuscripts of the time. If these signs pointed unambiguously at one person we would have the only precise date available for any of the later Rohan manuscripts. It is therefore especially frustrating that the problem remains unsolved, despite the efforts of Durrieu, of interested colleagues, and our own inexpert explorations.[64]

The manuscript is often described as the *Hours of René d'Anjou*, and there is no doubt whatever that this prince possessed it when he succeeded his older brother Louis III as Duke of Anjou and King of Sicily in 1434. Not long after that date René commissioned a painter to add a full-page portrait of himself as well as two of his favorite images, angels holding a large Host and a crowned skeleton, which bears his arms as they were then.[65] The same painter also retouched the miniature by the Rohan workshop for the Office of the Dead—a miniature copied from the *Belles Heures*.[66] The entire manuscript was formerly dated late in the 'thirties, but—and now we revert to style—the Rohan workshop, which was responsible for the original illumination, borders as well as miniatures, could not have produced the work at that date.

Throughout the manuscript each of the outer and lower borders contains one of two emblems: an eagle with a patriarchal cross and a crown, or a sail with the motto *en dieu en soit* (Figs. 878, 883, 884). These emblems and the motto were used by René in 1434 and later; earlier examples have not yet been found. The emblems were, however, painted in the original campaign. The vigorous, twisting, aggressive eagles bear the stamp of the Rohan workshop, and at many places one can ascertain that spaces were reserved for them and for the sails in the bars or vines of the border. The Book of Hours would seem, therefore, to have been commissioned for the youthful René—he was born in 1409—probably by his mother, Yolande. On the other hand, the initials at the beginning of the Offices bear arms, apparently original, of Jerusalem, *Anjou ancien*, and *Anjou moderne, tiercé en pal* (Fig. 884). These all pertain, of course, to Anjou, but they cannot yet be connected with a particular prince. Durrieu suggested they might belong to Louis II, who died in April 1417, or to his oldest son Louis III,[67] but then they seem to conflict with the emblems.[68]

To compound the difficulty, the illustration of a prayer to St. René shows the saint confronted by a relatively large portrait bust, which was painted by a better hand than the rest of the miniature. It is a copy of an extant watercolor of Louis II or of a practically identical portrait (Figs. 881, 886).[69] The bust in the miniature appears above a ledge; at the right it is framed by a crude black band, which overlaps part of the *houppelande* but not the turban. The watercolor now shows more of the sitter than the miniature, but only because strips were added on all sides. A portrait of approximately the present form appears in a copy made in the seventeenth century for Gaignières, which includes a parapet below the sitter (Fig. 885). Inasmuch as the bust in the miniature has puzzling elements it is difficult to understand the interrelationship of these portraits. Probably the *original* watercolor resembled the portrait in the miniature, and the latter then prompted the patching out of the surviving fragment, which was given still larger dimensions. A comparison of watercolor and miniature would inevitably have been made by the perceptive collector Roger de Gaignières, who owned both of them.[70]

The illuminator intended this unique effigy to appear within a kind of window or conceivably as a painted relief. In the late Middle Ages it was quite possible to pray by effigy. People who could afford them placed sculptures, often busts, in chapels near their patron saints.[71] The transfer of an "easel" portrait into a miniature for this purpose, however, unmodified by the addition of a praying gesture, is highly exceptional. We know that Louis II venerated St. René; in his will he asked to be buried at the altar of this saint in the Cathedral of St. Maurice in Angers.[72] Inasmuch as the emblems and the motto (though not the arms) indicate that the manuscript was made for René the portrait was apparently designed as a tribute to his father.

The illumination of the manuscript lacks artistic distinction; the Rohan Master took practically no part in the painting. Even the best miniature, the *Man of Sorrows*, often attributed to him,[73] does not quite qualify, although he probably designed the composition (Fig. 882). The surface is much drier, and the figure of Christ more spidery, than the *Man of Sorrows* in the Fitzwilliam Hours (Fig. 862)—an indication not only of inferior execution but of later date. The near identity of the *Madonna on the Crescent* in lat. 1156A with the *Madonna* in the Fitzwilliam Hours serves to prove more readily how inferior the former really is (Figs. 865, 878).

Lat. 1156A is later, then, than the Fitzwilliam Hours. Once again, as in that manuscript, the dependence of the *Annunciation* (Fig. 883) upon a Boucicaut design gives us at least a *post quem* date. As Miss Heimann observed,[74] the model for lat. 1156A was the Corsini Hours of *ca.* 1416[75] or another, similar Boucicaut manuscript of this approximate date. Lat. 1156A is considerably later, too, than the *De Buz Hours*. The *Flight into Egypt* generally repeats the corresponding composition of that manuscript (Figs. 845, 884) but the surfaces are less luminous and the scale of the figures is decisively increased, precisely as in the latest major manuscript of the workshop, the *Rohan Hours*.

Like the Fitzwilliam manuscript the *Rohan Hours* bears the arms only of a later owner, in this instance a member of the Rohan family, for whom they were added at some time before 1516.[76] The prayers are in the masculine form, and the use, like that of the Fitzwilliam Hours and lat. 1156A, is Paris—but of course the owners might have been attached to the capital by tradition or sentiment, without actually residing there. We must therefore turn to the illumination for ideas about the date and place of execution. The work was surely done after about 1415–1416, because some figures derive from miniatures in the *Très Riches Heures* which were painted at that time. It has long been recognized that the horsemen in the *Flight into Egypt*—soldiers witnessing miraculously grown grain—are copies of a Magus and a member of his retinue in the *Meeting of the Magi* in the *Très Riches Heures* (Figs. 571, 870). Of course the kind of white mane curving out from the hat of the aged soldier as well as the dense red, blue and green of the figures are modifications of the Rohan workshop. In the *Annunciation to the Shepherds* the woman calmly milking a sheep with (to judge from the size of her jug) rather surprising expectations—an unprecedented rural chore performed at this important moment—was probably inspired by the woman shearing sheep in *July* in the *Très Riches Heures* (Figs. 545, 874). Absorbed in her work, she seems entirely unaware of the message read by the angels, and her relatively enormous companion, sounding his pipe, jigs with a kind of melancholy glee. His strange movement was anticipated by a shepherd running to Bethlehem in the *De Buz Hours* (Fig. 853), but we cannot be sure what his action signifies here. Even the behavior of the dog with the red spiked collar seems ambiguous. Is this the only creature who attends to the angels, as has been said? Or is he merely howling, perhaps in response to the pipe?[77]

From such adaptations we learn that the Rohan Master had seen the *Très Riches Heures*—where and when is unclear, because the Fitzwilliam Hours of *ca.* 1418 shows little, if any awareness of it, and the Duke's great manuscript perhaps left Paris in late 1418. It may have been this manuscript that suggested to him the use for his principal miniatures of very narrow frames and empty, undecorated borders. The Rohan Master did not adopt these for their original purpose of enhancing the spatial illusion; indeed, he preserved the script the Limbourgs had banished entirely, inserting it, in a novel way, on a small rectangle reserved from the miniature.[78] He sought only to increase the size of the pictorial field almost to the dimensions of the folio. Thus his strong rhythms and bold color attained a maximum effect.

Although reflecting the *Très Riches Heures*, the *Rohan Hours* depends far more upon the earlier Book of Hours of the Limbourgs. The heavenly host, for example, painted by his workshop on folio 29v is a copy, with the familiar distortions (see the Magdalene!), of a miniature in the *Belles Heures* painted by Paul de Limbourg for *All Saints* (Figs. 389, 390). The composition of the *Flight into Egypt* is an intensified (and reversed) version of the *Flight* in the early Harley Hours (Figs. 832, 870), but the Rohan Master inserted into it not only the Magus from the *Très Riches Heures* but the peasant binding a sheaf of grain in *July* in the *Belles Heures* (Fig. 861). He now lies on the bundles, a diminutive figure compared to his companion, not to mention the huge figures and the ass deepest in the space. The sower of the *Belles Heures* stalks the land of *September* in the *Rohan Hours* like an uncouth giant (Figs. 687, 876). These and numerous other borrowings, pointed out by Porcher, provide an important clue.[79]

At an earlier date, when painting the *De Buz Hours*, the Rohan Master and his workshop had already been aware of the *Belles Heures*, as we have observed. They borrowed a composition and a motif (Figs. 845, 853), and the master emulated Paul's voluminous figures (Fig. 852). Later manuscripts by the Rohan workshop, including the Fitzwilliam Hours and lat. 1156A, seem unrelated to the *Belles Heures*, and the *Rohan Hours* itself shows no similarity of *style*. A deep relationship of that kind was precluded by the very different character of the Master's late phase. He and his associates, however, did adapt from the *Belles Heures* numerous figures and compositions. By good luck we happen to know in whose possession it then was. A few months after the death of the Duke of Berry in June, 1416 the Duchess Yolande of Anjou, the wife of his nephew, Duke Louis II, borrowed it and soon, before April 29, 1417, bought it. This is a very interesting fact, because lat. 1156A was made for Louis or one of his sons.

Long ago scholars observed that the *Rohan Hours* is related in another way with the Anjou. Two miniatures and the long sequence of marginal illustrations were based on a *Bible moralisée* that was illuminated in Naples, capital of the kingdom which Duke Louis II spent much of his life in a vain effort to reclaim.[80] Although the Duke of Berry possessed an outstanding Neapolitan manuscript,[81] this Bible was not listed in his inventories, and the most likely owner in metropolitan France was a Duke of Anjou. The *Crucifixion* in the *Rohan Hours*, not painted by the master himself, transformed the sculptural figures and spatial order of the Neapolitan model into a flat but exciting design (Figs. 871, 872). The Bible very probably inspired also the unusual *Vesperbild* in the *Rohan Hours*; the group in the *Massacre of the Innocents* of a mother, her hands raised in despair mourning her dead child, resembles strikingly the Rohan Madonna and Christ.[82]

Still another manuscript relates the Rohan Master to Anjou. It is a Book of Hours for the use of Angers, formerly in the possession of Martin le Roy and now in a private collection. In style it closely resembles the *Rohan Hours*, and must be of approximately the same date. Unlike that manuscript, however, only one miniature was painted by the master himself, as Durrieu recognized long ago.[83] Indeed, the Rohan Master did not even paint all of this single miniature (Fig. 807). He executed a dramatic and altogether superb St. Peter, then left everything else—the architecture, the angels, the background, and the drapery—to an assistant. The saint looks up to heaven while pointing to his open book in which is legible "Omnipotens sempiterne deus qui creavit. . . ." St. Peter appears at the beginning of a series of the twelve apostles, exceptional in a Book of Hours. All the following apostles stand; he alone is revealed by a lowered cloth, like the Madonna or the Man of Sorrows (Figs. 852, 882).

Nearly thirty years ago Jean Porcher took account of the relations with Anjou of the late manuscripts of the Rohan Master and his workshop, and he proposed that Yolande of Anjou, becoming acquainted in Paris with manuscripts illuminated by the Rohan workshop, invited the master to Angers, where, far from the turmoil of the capital at that time and assured of the support of a powerful and discriminating patron, he produced his best work. Part of this attractive hypothesis is probably correct, but some facts not hitherto considered open new perspectives. When in 1416 Yolande acquired the *Belles Heures* she was indeed spending much of her time in or near Angers, the capital of Anjou, where her husband, Duke Louis II, died on April 29, 1417. During the next two very troubled years, however, Yolande moved about from Anjou (including her own chateau of Saumur), to the Touraine, and to Mehun-sur-Yèvre near Bourges, the famous chateau of the late Jean Duke of Berry (Fig. 590).[84] This chateau became at that time the residence of her daughter Marie, fiancée of Charles, son of King Charles VI. Young Charles, who was Dauphin of France from April 5, 1417, had a month later become Duke of Berry.

Since 1413, when Charles and Marie engaged to marry, Yolande acted as the boy's principal protectress and counselor. When in 1418 Paris was convulsed yet again by the conflict between the Burgundians and the Armagnacs, Charles fled to Bourges. Yolande soon followed him and her daughter there and to the chateau of Mehun, his newly acquired possession in Berry.[85] In 1420 the English occupied Paris, in 1422 King Charles VI died, and the Dauphin became Charles VII—the King of Bourges, he was derisively called. In the same year he and Marie d'Anjou were married in Bourges. Yolande had departed in 1419 with her son Duke Louis III for Provence, a possession of the Anjou. There they raised funds for another of those vain Angevin campaigns to recover the kingdom of Naples—a campaign from which Louis returned only in 1426. Yolande remained as administrator of Provence until 1423. Coming north in that year she again became deeply involved in affairs of state and she often lived with the court at Mehun or at Bourges until 1427.[86]

Between 1419 and 1427, then, Yolande was either continuously in Provence or frequently in Berry, and these are the years when the evidence of style indicates that the *Rohan Hours* and the manuscripts most closely related to it were illuminated. Thus the number of possible centers of activity of the master increases, but it is premature to speculate about the most likely. Perhaps he worked in Angers and for a time between 1423 and 1427 in Bourges. It is droll, in any event, to imagine him not only building his style upon the achievements of Jean de Berry's painters and then denying their basic values but even perhaps doing some of this within the Duke's own buildings, on the very site of the great artistic triumphs that he was vehemently criticizing.

Dauphin Charles became the Duke of Berry a few months after Yolande acquired the *Belles Heures*, one of the most beautiful manuscripts of the great Jean. The reasons for her interest in this Book of Hours certainly became more than purely artistic. Possibly she even gave it to Jean de Berry's young successor. Later fifteenth-century copies of its miniatures in manuscripts produced in the west and northwest of France seem to indicate that it was for a time in that region, most likely Angers.[87] Since the prayers in the *Rohan Hours* are in masculine form it might have been made, on Yolande's order, for this very youth, her protegé and her daughter's fiancé. The importance for this young couple of illuminated prayer books is shown by the fact that in 1418 Marie herself received a large sum from King Charles VI to purchase one.[88] This acquisition might have been the fine Book of Hours by the Rohan Master and his workshop now in the Fitzwilliam Museum, which I would in any event date *ca.* 1418.

In the absence of facts about the ownership of the Rohan manuscripts it seems justifiable to speculate a little on the basis of the evidence we possess.[89] If the *Grandes Heures de Rohan* was made for Charles, Duke of Berry (and from October 1422 King of France), the abundance of quotations from the *Belles Heures*, altogether exceptional in the manuscripts of the Rohan workshop, probably reflected the political and cultural circumstances of the patron. The same concerns perhaps affected another unusual aspect of the *Rohan Hours*—the long cycle copied from a Neapolitan Bible, which therefore alluded to the Angevin past, artistic and religious as well as dynastic. The universally recognized intelligence and political acumen of Duchess Yolande justify such speculation. The relationship with the Bible (but not with the *Belles Heures*) would have retained its special meaning if the Rohan Hours had been produced, on the other hand, for Yolande's oldest son, Duke Louis III. He might have received it in Italy, where he remained from 1420 to 1426.

Scholars are agreed that the Rohan Master himself painted only a small number of the miniatures in the *Grandes Heures*, though there have been differences of opinion about the precise number.[90] Entirely his, in my opinion, are only the *Madonna* (Fig. 877), the *Lamentation* (Fig. 888), and the *Dying Man before Christ* (Fig. 889). He painted, as we have seen, Gabriel and God the Father in the *Annunciation* (Fig. 868), and also the shepherds in the *Annunciation to the Shepherds* (Fig. 874), as well as the High Priest in the *Presentation in the Temple* (Fig. 869), some apostles in *Pentecost* (Fig. 873), and Christ in the *Last Judgment* (Fig. 898). He certainly designed these miniatures and others in which he likewise did little, if any, painting. In this group I would include *St. John* (fol. 19) and *St. Matthew* (Fig. 875), with their soaring, tangled buildings, as exciting as Piranesi's *Carceri*; the *Visitation* (fol. 70), in which the angel is a duplicate of the one by the master in the *Annunciation*; *November*; and the *Flight into Egypt* (Fig. 870). The judgment that the Rohan Master was responsible for these designs is of course based upon their similarity to the compositions that he also clearly executed. It is not easy to determine whether—or how much of—the underdrawings partially visible in many miniatures are his. Certainly conformity of the final painted surface with the drawing is no criterion. The folds of the drapery of the Virgin and God in the *Lamentation* (Fig. 888) or of God when he appears to the dying man (Fig. 889), all painted by the Rohan Master himself, are different from the underdrawing.

It cannot be an accident that two of only three miniatures in the manuscript the Rohan Master chose to execute entirely with his own brush are concerned with death. In them he gave an unforgettable form to two central and related themes: the death of Christ and the death of man. One of these miniatures adopts for the Office of the Dead a form of illustration that had been developed by the Boucicaut Master in the second decade of the century (Figs. 879, 889).[91] In this iconography, which replaced both the older funeral ceremony around the bier and the newer burial service in a cemetery, the dying man lies naked and alone on the ground while angels and devils fight for his soul under the eyes of the distant Deity. Here man, as in the burial service and in many contemporary poems, leaves the world naked as he entered it.

All these elements the Rohan Master brought together into an unprecedented confrontation. The body, reminiscent of the emaciated *transi* that appeared at this time on French tombs (Fig. 880), lies on a rich blue cloth surrounded by skulls and bones—a contrast between the earthly past, with its sensuous pleasures, and the lifeless present. The red stripes on the cloth look like blood. The man still clings to the beautiful shroud with pitiful spidery fingers at the end of a shrunken arm. The body seems thrust upward for a closer colloquy with Christ, whose name is inscribed in his halo. He is an enormous old man, white-haired like God the Father, who emerges from a swarm of angels. Occasionally in Trecento painting, as in Maso's fresco in the Capella di S. Silvestro, S. Croce, Christ as Judge appeared in the sky at the resurrection of a single person, but he never approached so closely as in the Rohan miniature. Christ's personal solicitude is reassuring, and the probable victory of Michael and his aides over the blood-stained devil gives man reason for ultimate hope.

This is confirmed by the content of the unprecedented dialogue. The man addresses Christ, committing to him his spirit in the words of the Psalm that are part of the Last Sacraments for the Dying. Christ replies that, after penance for sins, "On the Day of Judgment you will be with me."

The corpse:	In manus tuas Domine commendo spiritum meum.
	Reddemisti me Domine. . . .
The Deity:	Pour tes pechiez penitence feras.
	Au jour du jugement avecque moy seras.

We cannot fail to marvel at the fact that the corpse speaks the language of the Church and of all well-educated Europeans, Latin, whereas the Deity replies in French. The use of the vernacular localizes Christ's words, and thus gives another sign of his intimate relation with the dying Frenchman. His words also award a privileged position to the French language.

Man's prayer, Christ says, is heard, and his trust will not prove vain. In the view of Nominalist theologians God was committed by his very nature—*de potentia ordinata*—to redeem the man who has done what he could. For the followers of Occam such as Jean Gerson and others who chose the *via moderna*, the trustworthiness of God—a fascinating and beautiful conception—is the foundation of redemption. The painting by the Rohan Master seems to demonstrate what was understood to be the covenant of salvation.[92]

In the miniature representing the *Last Judgment*, the moment to which Christ's words refer, the Judge, now spattered with blood from his wounds, is again relatively close to the resurrected bodies (Fig. 898). Most of them do not, in conformity with tradition, rise in the prime of life; two of them are even aged, with white hair and beards. The most striking of these figures struggles mightily to raise himself from the ground. Since he alone is clothed and does not emerge from the earth, and since he is larger and also overlaps the frame, he might represent those who are still alive on the Day of Judgment.[93] We shall, however, find him in another, probably earlier context shortly.

The entirely novel composition with which the Rohan Master chose to illustrate the Hours of the Cross shows, like the Office of the Dead, a corpse stretched on the ground (Fig. 888). Now, however, blood streams from many wounds, and the oversize celestial figure is God the Father, hailing the sacrifice undertaken by his son for the redemption of man. Mary nevertheless wilts under the unbearable impact of her loss, and John, holding her tightly, turns his plain, strange, querulous countenance toward the originator of the entire plan. Like Gabriel and the annunciate Mary, the two principal figures are in perfect profile, but the heads here are turned in opposing directions to heighten the strain that is central to the design. The body of the Virgin is as limp as that of Christ is rigid. In this miniature the Rohan Master has created one of the most memorable of all images of sorrow and death.

Under the brush of this extraordinary painter even a subject such as the Madonna nursing her Child, normally expressive of tender and joyous maternal feelings, is permeated by a strange disquiet and melancholy (Fig. 877). Mary, far from conforming with the contemporary ideal of a perfect woman, has unnaturally short, spindly arms and a greatly swollen head. Indeed, we recognize here that the Rohan Master works not only with differences in scale between several figures in a composition, as we have observed earlier, but also with disproportions in a *single* figure. Unlike his predecessors and contemporaries he was more interested in faces than in bodies. He cared less about what people do than what they feel. Like other artists at all times who seek enhanced expressiveness, he employed the kind of surprising disproportion and deformation that, before the twentieth century, was most familiar in caricature. For the painter's contemporaries, as for us, the full impact of his distortions depends on an awareness of the conventions he disregarded. In his search for the unexpected he even made a formal zodiacal sign of the calendar serve as a wild animal in the desert: the lion of July, for example, struts across the landscape of the *Flight into Egypt* (Fig. 870).

The role of the Rohan Master in the design and execution of the miniatures in the *Rohan Hours* is larger than in any other manuscript except his earliest ones. Still, even if we include supervision of the entire work, his own contribution was not very great. Why was this so, especially in a manuscript obviously made for a great patron? Why did he even turn over to assistants miniatures he had himself partly painted (Figs. 807, 868)? These questions, which have never been asked, are not easy to answer. Perhaps he was overseeing the production of several manuscripts at the same time. This would be an adequate explanation for the years before *ca.* 1416 when he was apparently acting as the head of a workshop, like that of the Boucicaut Master, in Paris. Even the Boucicaut Master, however, undertook to paint most of three Books of Hours and numerous miniatures in other manuscripts. When, moreover, the Rohan Master succeeded in finding important patrons, apparently the Anjou, one would have expected him to become far more personally involved.

The nature of the relation of the Rohan Master to the production of the *Rohan Hours* is, we have seen, not peculiar to this book. His participation in other manuscripts, such as the Fitzwilliam Hours and the *Heures d'Angers*, ranged equally from the execution of the principal figures in a few miniatures to varying degrees of supervision of the rest. He worked closely with certain assistants, who even completed his own miniatures. Other followers, such as the one in the *Rohan Hours* responsible for most of the Suffrages, went ahead on their own, although they drew on a common stock of patterns. Collaboration of this kind, though not common at the time, did occur in the Boucicaut and other workshops. Even a surviving panel which was, as we shall see, in part painted by the Rohan Master shows a related kind of collaboration. It can also be discerned in the earliest works in the Rohan manner, the Giac and Harley Hours, where the style of the master himself, still undergoing rapid change, is more difficult to disengage. There is, however, only one great painter involved in these works and he provided the impetus for the new style.[93a]

Two objects indicate that the peculiar practice of the Rohan Master may be explained in another way. They prove that his activity was not limited to the illumination of books; he worked on a larger scale. A panel by his workshop, over three feet long, survives in the Museum at Laon, as Grete Ring first observed (Figs. 806, 887).[94] It is painted on both sides, and one of them bears the marks of hardware at the left (Fig. 806).[95] These indications as well as the iconography of both faces prove that the panel was the right wing of a larger work. Gabriel bearing the message of the Annunciation implies the Virgin, and the six apostles on the opposite face must have been accompanied by the other six, so that the entire work was at least twofold.[96] The red background and the lack of the usual gesso preparation suggest that the painting was not used as an altarpiece. Since the angel Gabriel looks up, the Virgin or more probably the Deity was represented at a higher level. The appearance of the angel, the saint (the Magdalene?), and the donor on a grassy knoll, amidst wild flowers, is unusual. The panel was painted more broadly and with less preparation and refinement than other extant French panels, only one of which, to be sure, the *Martyrdom of St. Denis*, is large but, unlike the Laon panel, surely served on the altar.

Abrasion, losses, and retouching have reduced the effect of the painting at Laon;[97] perhaps that is why it has received so little attention. The apostles and busts of prophets on the exterior, not very close in style to the Rohan Master, must have been painted by an associate. The powerful rhythms of the inner face, however, surely imply a design not simply by the workshop, as Miss Ring said, but by the Rohan Master himself. The large figure of Gabriel, dressed in white shaded in delicate, bluish gray, has remarkably small, delicate, and gentle hands. As he alights, his tunic is flung beautifully onto the ground. Perhaps damage alone does not account for the less than excellent execution, especially apparent in the head, the hair, the sleeves, and the wings. As so often, an assistant may have taken over. The beauty of the painting of the abbot or canon supports this hypothesis. In his white and gold cope, lined in rose, and his pale olive-green tunic he is a superb figure. The searching, relentless description of his bald head, pug nose and sagging skin, which surrounds bright, fervid eyes, makes this the most memorable of all early French portraits.

The second object that connects the Rohan Master with monumental art is a drawing on vellum in the Herzog Anton Ulrich-Museum at Braunschweig. It is a magnificent work, equal in artistic strength to the portrait of the bishop and to the few miniatures we have ascribed to the mature master.[98] It is similar to most of them in tragic mood also. It represents a story described by St. John:

> Now there is at Jerusalem by the sheep market a pool, which is called in the Hebrew tongue Bethesda, having five porches. In these lay a great multitude of impotent folk, of blind, halt, withered, waiting for the moving of the water. For an angel went down at a certain season into the pool, and troubled the water: whosoever then first after the troubling of the water stepped in was made whole of whatsoever disease he had. And a certain man was there, which had an infirmity thirty and eight years. When Jesus saw him lie, and knew that he had been now a long time in that case, he saith unto him, Wilt thou be made whole? The impotent man answered him, Sir, I have no man, when the water is troubled, to put me into the pool: but while I am coming, another steppeth down before me. Jesus saith unto him, Rise, take up thy bed, and walk. And immediately the man was made whole, and took up his bed, and walked. . . . (St. John 5:2–9)

In medieval painting the two miracles—the stirring of the pool and the man carrying his bed—were sometimes represented in sequence and occasionally in the same space, as in a miniature in the Neapolitan *Bible moralisée* which was the source of many compositions in the *Rohan Hours* (Fig. 896).[99] Unlike the miniature and other illustrations of the story the drawing by the Rohan Master makes far more vivid the frightful disease and deformity of the poor creatures gathered around the pool than the healing which is the point of the story. The despairing figure held over the water by a kind helper recalls the deposition of Christ from the cross, the angel holding the Man of Sorrows, or even St. John and the Virgin (Figs. 826, 882, 888); indeed, it constitutes the master's most characteristic and expressive group. Quick notations of posts behind the figures refer to the five porches described by the Gospel, but the significance of the imposing man who comes onto the scene from the left remains unclear. Tall, bearded and dressed in a cope, he would be identifiable as Christ (with the attributes of God the Father) if he had a halo—which he definitely lacks. Possibly, as we shall see, he is Solomon.

The drawing is large—about 6 x 10 inches[100]—and it has been considerably reduced at the right as well as a little on the other three sides. This size and the high finish of the figures indicate that it was a study not for a miniature but for a work on a larger scale—a scene, perhaps, in the story of the cross for a mural cycle, for stained glass, or a large altarpiece. Probably then it was not in a book but in a monumental work that the Master of Catherine of Cleves saw the *Miracle of Bethesda* by the Rohan Master which he utilized for a miniature in the *Hours of Catherine of Cleves* now in the Morgan Library (Fig. 895).[101] The Cleves Master owed to his model not simply the design and the postures but the feelings of pain and grief that they convey. It is fascinating to see that the great Dutch painter was unable, however, either to make the old man's body hang from the arms of his helper or to cast his pathetic head forward and down. Lacking the French and ultimately Italian culture of the Rohan Master he could not communicate an equally deep emotion through tension in bodily structure. He compensated for this inability by more agitated postures and more extreme facial expressions.

The tree-trunk that floats in the pond is the sacred wood which, according to the legend of the cross, gave the water its therapeutic properties.[102] Solomon, having found the wood unusable for his temple, ordered that it be thrown into the pond. In some representations of the Miracle of Bethesda, in which the floating wood frequently appears, Solomon stands nearby,[103] so that the mysterious figure at the left in the Braunschweig drawing might be the king. Since the principal model of the Cleves Master was probably not the drawing but the subsequent large-scale work by the Rohan Master it might have included the wood. I would not, furthermore, exclude the possibility that other scenes in the legend of the cross in the *Hours of Catherine of Cleves*, especially the chopping of the tree and the measuring of the timber, reflect compositions of the same lost Rohan cycle.[104]

The Master of Catherine of Cleves was not the only later illuminator who was impressed by the Rohan *Miracle of Bethesda*. Two of the figures were chosen for a miniature in the *Hours of Marguerite d'Orléans* that represents the apostles healing the sick (Fig. 894). The manuscript was illuminated after 1426, and it is interesting that in addition to this copy of the *Miracle of Bethesda*, four miniatures derive from the manuscript that attracted the Rohan Master himself, the *Belles Heures*,[105] then probably in the possession of Yolande d'Anjou in or near Angers.

In 1912, long before the Laon panel or the Braunschweig drawing had been connected with the Rohan Master, the extraordinary Paul Durrieu suggested that the character of the artist's miniatures implied that he worked on larger scale.[106] Other painters of this period in metropolitan France—the Parement Master, for example, and probably Jacquemart de Hesdin and Paul de Limbourg—worked both in the book and on panel or the wall, and they too depended to an unusual degree on assistants. The Rohan Master could rely on them still more because the effect of his painting derived less from subtleties of shape, color, or finish. Although he modulated his own surfaces with great refinement he was willing to allow his associates to present broad, flat areas of strident, even raw color. Indeed, such surfaces clearly had their own emotional impact.

In the lower right corner of the Braunschweig drawing a pathetic man with a clubfoot struggles to rise from the ground with the aid of a stick. A similar figure appears in the *Last Judgment* in the *Rohan Hours* (Fig. 898). He is the most prominent of the resurrected, and he too struggles to rise, although without the aid of a pole. Despite his deformed foot he may, we infer, succeed, whereas the less tense man in the drawing seems doomed to fail. This figure the Rohan Master had probably first seen in a manuscript that, from the time of the *De Buz Hours*, had greatly interested him —the *Belles Heures*. In any event, the figure has an interesting and informative earlier history.[107]

In the scene of the ill and the crippled at the bier of St. Jerome in the *Belles Heures* a similar figure lies on the ground (Fig. 891). He leans back, supporting his weight on a stick and on his right hand, which is flattened on the ground. His further leg is bent, his nearer one, lacking a foot, is stretched out on the ground. This cripple was adopted by the Medallion Master for a miniature in the *Légende dorée*, normally dated 1405 but dependent in two other instances, as we have shown above, on the *Belles Heures*.[108] The miniature represents St. Bartholomew in India, visiting the temple of the idol Astaroth, which was supposed to cure the ill (Fig. 892). The cripple differs from the one in the *Belles Heures* insofar as the body is turned inward and the nearer leg is bent. In this respect, and also in its intensity, the figure resembles those by the Rohan Master, who might have known this manuscript or this painter in Paris. In the same form as in the *Légende dorée* and in the Rohan drawing the cripple was represented again in the *Bréviaire de Jean sans Peur*, in the scene of Sts. Peter and John healing a lame man at the gate of the Temple (Fig. 893). In this composition the figure faces left, as in the Rohan drawing, with which, indeed, it shares numerous details. This relation is unusual in the Breviary, which depends so extensively upon the *Belles Heures*.

The cripple in the *Belles Heures* was anticipated by Jean Pucelle nearly a century earlier in a manuscript which had entered the collection of Jean de Berry before the Limbourgs began to work for him (Fig. 890).[109] The relation is clear, although of course Pucelle's shepherd does not possess the articulation and the functional movement of the wounded man in the *Belles Heures*, and he merely rises slightly from his reclining posture upon the appearance of the angel. This miniature by Pucelle proves once again the significance of the collection of Jean de Berry to the artists of his time—a significance that has been demonstrated throughout this account of the history of French painting.

Since the expressive miniatures of the Apocalypse Master and the Medallion Master, which we have discussed above, are not well known, the Rohan Master has seemed to be more of a maverick in and around Paris than he actually was. Still, his singularity cannot be denied, and it is attested by the universal belief that he came from Spain or Germany or the Netherlands—almost anywhere but France. No specific origins for his style in those countries, however, have yet been cited. Indeed the foreign character has not been discerned in his early work, where it would normally appear more clearly, but in late paintings, especially in the *Rohan Hours*, as though some native propensity were emerging late in his career. This is a difficult hypothesis, and objectionable insofar as it assumes a hereditary character. The art of El Greco, for example, does indeed have the passionate intensity of the Rohan Master, but this "Spanish painter par excellence" was born in Crete and formed in—of all places—Venice! Some artists, moreover, who were born in France, such as Jean Duvet, created a highly emotional style.

Better knowledge of early fifteenth-century illumination throughout Europe might provide the decisive evidence we now lack about the origins of the Rohan Master's early style. His first known works show certain similarities with the illumination of Provence, and it may be significant that Yolande d'Anjou resided there frequently.[110] More substantial are the connections of the Rohan Master with Troyes. These links permit a tentative hypothesis that he began in Provence and then worked in Troyes (with visits to Paris) from about 1410 to 1414. By the latter date he had moved to the capital and, as we have seen, collaborated with ateliers established there, such as that of the Boucicaut Master or the like-minded Apocalypse Master and painters of the Bedford trend.[111]

It was only through study of the painting of the great metropolitan French masters that the art of the Rohan Master attained the strength we recognize in the *Grandes Heures de Rohan*. If he was, as Panofsky said, a "magnificent barbarian,"[112] he certainly learned fast. Although he remained one of the most inventive of painters his imagination was, paradoxically, stimulated to an exceptional degree by the work of others. He continually found in their forms elements with which to create new combinations of his own. One instance of such an adoption is exceptionally meaningful; it concerns the master's miniature of the Lamentation, which we have already discussed (Fig. 888). He had earlier introduced the group of St. John embracing the Virgin protectively and gazing back at Christ on the cross in the Giac *Deposition* and in the Harley *Crucifixion* (Figs. 826, 834). It had appeared still earlier, in the fourteenth century, in a number of representations of the Crucifixion. The half-dozen examples hitherto cited are German,[113] but the Rohan Master was probably most impressed by the version of an earlier French illuminator, the Passion Master, who employed the group in the *Crucifixion* in his superb Passion cycle in the *Petites Heures* of Jean de Berry (Fig. 897). Since Robinet d'Estampes, whose wife had received the *Petites Heures* from the Duke, resided in Bourges the manuscript was visible there.[114] The Rohan Master would surely have been attracted by this highly congenial art, similarly emotional, mercurial, and querulous. There he would have found an equally impish St. John and dozens of ugly roguish faces of the kind he himself introduced in *Pentecost* (Fig. 873). Equally significant is the fact that the Rohan Master revived the background filled with angels (Figs. 888, 889), which was common in the paintings of the Passion Master and related illuminators of his period but outmoded in the early fifteenth century—except in the work of a provincial illuminator such as the Troyes Master.

It is a striking fact that the ugly, often irreverent saints of the Rohan Master, his insistent color and wild pathos should have found favor with a great princely house. Art produced for courts was not always what is called Court Art—it was not necessarily elegant, decorous and restrained. Perhaps the turmoil in France not only influenced the Rohan Master's work but also created an audience for it. Looking at his miniatures we might even be tempted to accept the view of a historian that "in the long anarchy which we call the reign of Charles VI, all bonds had been loosened, all well-being blighted, all order overwhelmed."[115]

The Rohan Master proved that the long, flowing lines of the lyric, more Gothic trend in early fifteenth-century painting could be utilized for sombre moods and intense emotions. Reversing the current strong predilection for youth, he found special values in age. Always verging toward extremes, he chose to represent Christ either as an aged man or a very small child (Figs. 829, 889). Whereas his great predecessors, the Boucicaut Master and the Limbourgs, discovered unseen beauty in the natural world, he explored the realm of human feeling. They are most memorable for luminous color, monumental designs and narrative spectacles, he for the depiction of pain, grief, and death. Their art led directly to the first great Flemish panel painters, the Master of Flémalle and Jan van Eyck. His had only minor echoes, but diagrams of equally profound emotion appeared shortly in the painting of Roger van der Weyden.

IX

Catalogue of Panels

Basel

ÖFFENTLICHE KUNSTSAMMLUNG, KUPFERSTICHKABINETT (Fig. 356)
Jean de Beaumetz, *Madonnas*. 116×210 mm. Silverpoint heightened in white on pale green ground. Vellum.

This excellent drawing is a series of studies of three different types of Madonnas. It has been referred to two diverse stylistic trends, Broederlam (Burckhardt and Wescher) and Jacquemart (Pächt) or Paris (Ring). These different estimates are significant, for the drawing does reflect diverse styles, the Flemish and the Italo-French. The oscillation between these two stylistic poles reappears in the panels of Jean de Beaumetz and his workshop in Cleveland and in the Louvre, and Beaumetz is, as the writer has argued (1967), the author of this important drawing.

BIBLIOGRAPHY: Burckhardt, 1906, p. 184; Wescher, 1937, p. 16; Ring, *French Painting* [1949], p. 193 f., pl. 15; Pächt, *Gaz. B.-A.*, 1963, p. 111; Troescher, *Burgundische Malerei* [1966], pp. 231, 293, fig. 361; Meiss, *Late XIV Century*, 1967, p. 279 f., fig. 830.

Berlin-Dahlem

STAATLICHE MUSEEN (Fig. 642)
Jean Malouel (?) and assistant, *ca.* 1412. *Madonna and Angels*. 107×81 cm. Tempera on cloth (see Meiss and Eisler, especially p. 489; not transferred to cloth, as Winkler and later Troescher maintained).

The *Madonna* in Berlin was published by Winkler (1959—appeared in 1960), who ascribed it to the circle of the Limbourgs, Malouel, and Bellechose, and a couple of months later by Meiss and Eisler, who regarded it tentatively as a late work of Malouel, on the grounds of its similarity to the Louvre *Trinity* and the strong probability that a lost portrait of Jean sans Peur known from a drawing originally formed a diptych with it (Fig. 376). Pächt, 1963, accepted the attribution and Laclotte, 1966, and Castelnuovo regarded it as probable.

The superb figure of the Madonna—the most monumental in French painting of the time—has some of the grandeur of Sluter's sculpture. As in the paintings of Beaumetz there are variations in mode and in quality. The six angels in the Berlin *Madonna* would seem to have been executed by an assistant.

BIBLIOGRAPHY: Winkler, 1959 (1960), p. 179 ff.; Meiss and Eisler, 1960, p. 233 ff., fig. 1; *ibid.*, p. 489; Pächt, *Gaz.B.-A.*, 1963, p. 117; Laclotte, *Primitifs français* [1966], p. 13; Troescher, *Burgundische Malerei*, 1966, pp. 77 f., 83, 160, fig. 55; Meiss, *Late XIV Century*, 1967, pp. 63, 280; Castelnuovo, *Gotico internazionale*, n.d.

Berlin-Dahlem

STAATLICHE MUSEEN (Fig. 605)
French, *ca.* 1405. *Coronation of the Virgin*. Circular panel, diameter 20,5 cm. Tooled gold ground.

This panel is less Simonesque and less Italianate than most of the extant French panels. It is also exceptional for the deep space behind the figures created by the canopy. This, the rendering of the flowers strewn on the tessellated floor, and other qualities lead us to infer, tentatively, a date of *ca.* 1405.

A canopy is introduced into the *Coronation* in the approximately contemporary *Boucicaut Hours*. In the *Visitation* in that manuscript angels hold the Virgin's train, as in this panel. The motif of the angel withdrawing a curtain to look at a sacred event appeared in the *Annunciation* in the *De Lévis Hours* by the Bedford workship, *ca.* 1417.

BIBLIOGRAPHY: Durrieu, *Monuments*, XXIII, 1918–1919, p. 80 ff.; [Sterling] *Peintres du moyen âge*, 1942, catalogue p. 7 no. 30, pl. 32; Ring, *French Painting* [1949], p. 197 no. 49, pl. 6; Panofsky, *Netherlandish Painting*, 1953, p. 81; Vienna, Kunsthist. Mus., *Katalog*, 1962, p. 89 f. no. 16, pl. 81; Troescher, *Burgundische Malerei*, 1966, pp. 162 ff., 195, fig. 164.

Brussels

MUSEE DES BEAUX-ARTS
French. *Lamentation with a Cistercian*. 21,5×18,5 cm. Tooled gold ground.

This painting is obviously related to the small panels in the Louvre and at Troyes, but the tooling is cruder and so much of the surface has been damaged that a more precise estimate of the work is impossible, as Grete Ring observed.

BIBLIOGRAPHY: [Sterling] *Peintres du moyen âge*, 1942, catalogue p. 9 no. 27, pl. 30; Ring, *French Painting* [1949], p. 192 no. 10, fig. 25; Meiss and Eisler, 1960, p. 234 n. 12; Troescher, *Burgundische Malerei* [1966], p. 62, fig. 26.

Cleveland

MUSEUM OF ART (Fig. 368)

Jean de Beaumetz and assistant. *Calvary with a Carthusian.* 56,5×45,5 cm. Tooled gold ground.

One of two extant panels identified by Sterling with a series of 26 executed between 1390 and *ca.* 1395 by Beaumetz and his workshop for the monastic cells of the Chartreuse de Champmol. For the other panel see Paris, Louvre. The style of Beaumetz was compounded of Netherlandish and Italo-French qualities. In this beautiful panel the figure of Christ resembles more the latter tradition whereas the figures below derive to a greater extent from the former.

BIBLIOGRAPHY: Sterling, 1955, p. 57 ff., fig. 2; Francis, 1966, p. 329 ff.; Cleveland, Mus. of Art (Wixom), 1967, pp. 238, 374 f.; Meiss, *Late XIV Century*, 1967, p. 279 f., fig. 831.

Laon

MUSEE (Figs. 806, 887)

See Catalogue of Workshops, Rohan Master

New York

FRICK COLL.

Madonna and Child. Ca. 1395. 21.9×14.3 cm. 30.8×23.5 cm. including the carved frame, which is part of the same piece of wood as the panel. Tooled gold ground. In the nimbus of the Madonna is the inscription AVE MARIA GRACIA.

Although some miniatures, especially South Netherlandish, are surrounded by cove moldings filled with decorative units, this panel, with its naturalistic branches, is exceptional. In style the painting resembles more than anything else the small French panels in the Louvre and the *Man of Sorrows* at Troyes (Figs. 338, 373, 484). Its art, however, is simpler, less sophisticated, and perhaps also earlier. The crossed wrists of the Virgin are rather common in French illumination from the 'eighties (Jacquemart, *Petites Heures*, fol. 22). According to the catalogue of the Frick Collection Otto Pächt in 1966 suggested that the painting is Burgundian. He compared it to the *Annunciation* in the Walters Art Gallery, which seems to us from the Netherlands (Guelders?).

BIBLIOGRAPHY: [Sterling], *Peintres du moyen âge*, 1942, catalogue p. 12 no. 45, pl. 41; Ring, *French Painting* [1949], p. 199 no. 62; Meiss, *Late XIV Century*, 1967, p. 170, fig. 633; New York, Frick Coll., *Illustrated Catalogue*, II, 1968, p. 121 f., plate opp. p. 122.

Paris

BIBL. NAT., CABINET DES ESTAMPES (Fig. 886)

French, *ca.* 1415. *Portrait of Louis II, Duke of Anjou.* Pen and water-color on paper. The original part measures 22×17 cm.; later additions bring it to 30,7×21,5 cm. The inscription "Louis d'Anjou R. de Naples et Sicile" is on the part which has been added.

For a discussion of this portrait in relation with other versions see the chapter on the Rohan Master.

BIBLIOGRAPHY: Bouchot, 1886; Paris, Louvre, *Exposition*, 1904, p. 11 no. 26; Ring, *French Painting* [1949], p. 199 no. 63, pl. 26; Porcher, 1961; Meiss, *Late XIV Century*, 1967, pp. 68, 75 f., fig. 505.

Paris

MUSEE DU LOUVRE (Fig. 360)

Jean de Beaumetz and assistant. *Calvary with a Carthusian.* 60,1×48,2 cm. Tooled gold ground.

One of two extant panels identified by Sterling with a series of 26 executed between 1390 and *ca.* 1395 by Beaumetz and his workshop for the monastic cells of the Chartreuse de Champmol. For the other panel see Cleveland. In the painting in the Louvre the Italianate aspect of the style of Beaumetz is much less evident than in the Cleveland panel. Such differences may partly be ascribed to the participation of assistants, of whom we know Beaumetz had several.

BIBLIOGRAPHY: Demonts, 1937, p. 248; [Sterling] *Peintres du moyen âge*, 1942, p. 25, catalogue p. 8 no. 34, pl. 37; Ring, *French Painting* [1949], p. 197 no. 50; Sterling, 1955, p. 57 ff., fig. 1; Meiss, *Late XIV Century*, 1967, p. 279 f.

Paris

MUSEE DU LOUVRE (Figs. 607, 608)

Henri Bellechose. *Martyrdom of St. Denis.* 162×211 cm. Transferred from wood to canvas in 1852. Gold ground.

According to Burgundian accounts this panel was finished by Bellechose by May, 1416, for the church of the Chartreuse de Champmol. After the death of Malouel in 1415 Bellechose had become the painter of Jean sans Peur. Until the correct reading of the documents by Reynaud in 1961 the painting was usually believed to have been begun by Malouel and completed by Bellechose (but already in 1960, p. 236, Meiss and Eisler observed the uniformity of style and therefore ascribed the work to Bellechose alone).

This painting, the largest extant French "primitive" and the only altarpiece, shows a tendency towards a more animated and expressive art like that we have observed in some contemporary illumination.

BIBLIOGRAPHY: Paris, Louvre, *Exposition*, 1904, p. 8 no. 16; [Sterling] *Peintres du moyen âge*, 1942, catalogue p. 7 f., no. 31, pls. 35, 36; Ring, *French Painting* [1949], p. 198 no. 54, pl. 20; Panofsky, *Netherlandish Painting*, 1953, pp. 83–85, fig. 100; Meiss and Eisler, 1960, p. 236, fig. 2; Reynaud, 1961, p. 175 f.; Vienna, Kunsthist. Mus., *Katalog*, 1962, p. 81 f. no. 4, pl. 84; Paris, Louvre (Sterling and Adhémar), 1965, p. 5 no. 11, pls. 28–38; Laclotte, *Primitifs français* [1966], p. 13, pls. V, VI; Troescher, *Burgundische Malerei*, 1966, pp. 56, 113 ff., 121, figs. 109, 110.

Paris

MUSEE DU LOUVRE (Fig. 380)

Jean Malouel (?). *Trinity with Man of Sorrows.* Tondo: 64,5 cm. in diameter including frame. Painted surface 52 cm. Gold ground. On the reverse: the arms of Philippe le Hardi.

The subject is unusual: a Trinity which includes a Man of Sorrows who is mourned by the Virgin and St. John. The most exquisite of extant French panels, this famous tondo has often been associated with Malouel because it bears the arms of his first Burgundian patron. Since Philippe le Hardi died in April, 1404, the painting was surely executed earlier, and *ca.* 1400 is the date generally accepted. If the *Trinity*, which is more Simonesque and less Sluteresque than the Berlin *Madonna*, is actually a work painted 10 years earlier by the same master the identification with Malouel becomes much more compelling. For this problem see Berlin, *Madonna*.

BIBLIOGRAPHY: Paris, Louvre, *Exposition*, 1904, p. 7 f. no. 15; [Sterling] *Peintres du moyen âge*, 1942, catalogue p. 8 no. 32, pl. 34; Ring, *French Painting* [1949], p. 198 no. 53, pl. 18; Panofsky, *Netherlandish Painting*, 1953, p. 84 f., fig. 101; Meiss and Eisler, 1960; Vienna, Kunsthist. Mus., *Katalog*, 1962, p. 92 f. no. 19, pl. 82; Paris, Louvre (Sterling and Adhémar) 1965, p. 4 no. 8, pls. 21–25; Laclotte, *Primitifs français* [1966], p. 13, pl. IV; Troescher, *Burgundische Malerei*, 1966, pp. 75, 78, 80, figs. 50, 53A; Meiss, *Late XIV Century*, 1967, p. 279 f., fig. 832.

Paris

MUSEE DU LOUVRE (Fig. 484)

French, *ca.* 1408. *Lamentation.* Roundel. 22,8 cm. in diameter, including frame. Painted surface 17 cm. Gold ground. On the reverse, on red: the three nails of the Crucifixion in a crown of thorns.

Although this roundel together with the *Entombment* in the Louvre and the *Man of Sorrows* in Troyes has usually been dated *ca.* 1400 or in the preceding decade, it bears signs of a somewhat later execution. The design contains more movement, the figures are more animated though flatter, and the planes twist. In these respects the *Lamentation* anticipates the much later (1416) altarpiece by Bellechose.

The tentative connection of the panel by Troescher with Arnoul Picornet does not seem substantial.

BIBLIOGRAPHY: Durrieu, *Monuments*, XXIII, 1918–1919, p. 63 ff.; [Sterling] *Peintres du moyen âge*, 1942, catalogue p. 7 no. 29, pl. 33; Ring, *French Painting* [1949], p. 192 no. 8, pls. 4, 175; Vienna, Kunsthist. Mus., *Katalog*, 1962, p. 91 f. no. 18, pl. 80; Paris, Louvre (Sterling and Adhémar), 1965, p. 4 no. 7, pls. 18–20; Troescher, *Burgundische Malerei*, 1966, p. 62, figs. 25, 53B.

Paris

MUSEE DU LOUVRE (Fig. 338)

French, *ca.* 1405. *Entombment.* 32,8×21,3 cm. Tooled gold ground.

This beautiful painting, like other French panels of its time, is deeply imbued with the art of Simone Martini, but its color is more delicate and luminous. Remarkable at this date is the steeply tilted ground plane and the painter's uncertainty about spatial relations, particularly in the placing of Nicodemus (?), who holds the feet of Christ, in front of the sarcophagus.

BIBLIOGRAPHY: Paris, Louvre, *Exposition*, 1904, p. 4 no. 4; [Sterling] *Peintres du moyen âge*, 1942, catalogue p. 7 no. 28, pl. 31; Ring, *French Painting* [1949], p. 192 no. 9, pl. 5; Paris, Louvre (Sterling and Adhémar), 1965, p. 3 f. no. 6, pls. 15–17; Laclotte, *Primitifs français* [1966], p. 14; Troescher, *Burgundische Malerei*, 1966, pp. 62 ff., fig. 27; Meiss, *Late XIV Century*, 1967, p. 94, fig. 695.

Paris

MUSEE DU LOUVRE, COLL. C. DE BEISTEGUI

French, *ca.* 1410. *Madonna and Child.* 21,4×15 cm. Gold ground. Traces of paint and of a halo in the upper right suggest the presence of another figure.

The style of this fragmentary but beautiful painting is by common consent a French version of Broederlam.

BIBLIOGRAPHY: Paris, Louvre, *Exposition*, 1904, p. 7 no. 13; [Sterling] *Peintres du moyen âge*, 1942, catalogue p. 8 no. 35, pl. 38; Ring, *French Painting* [1949], p. 197 no. 51, pl. 25; Panofsky, *Netherlandish Painting*, 1953, pp. 95, 297; Paris, Louvre (Sterling and Adhémar) 1965, p. 5 no. 10, pl. 27; Laclotte, *Primitifs français* [1966], p. 14, pl. VII; Troescher, *Burgundische Malerei*, 1966, pp. 76 f., 80, 232, fig. 54.

Paris

COLL. VITALE BLOCH (Fig. 603)

Master of the Berlin Coronation (?), *ca.* 1410. *Madonna and Child with two Angels.* 19×15,2 cm., including the frame which is an integral part of the picture. Tooled gold ground. In places the film of paint is abraded.

In general the identification of a master's second painting is more risky than any thereafter, especially within a context of few similar extant works. In style this very delicate and lyrical little picture closely resembles the not much larger roundel in Berlin, and might well be a slightly later work by the same master (Fig. 605).

BIBLIOGRAPHY: Vegas, 1972, p. 396 f., fig. 1.

Troyes

MUSEE DES BEAUX-ARTS (Fig. 373)

French, *ca.* 1390–1400. *Man of Sorrows.* 39×26 cm. Gold ground.

This badly damaged but still very impressive painting resembles to a degree the *Lamentation* and the *Entombment* in the Louvre. The iconography of the Man of Sorrows with the Virgin and St. John derives from Trecento art, and so does the motif of the crossed arms of Christ. The angels, on the other hand, holding a shroud, are a characteristic French addition.

BIBLIOGRAPHY: Paris, Louvre, *Exposition*, 1904, p. 7 no. 14; [Sterling] *Peintres du moyen âge*, 1942, catalogue p. 8 no. 33; Ring, *French Painting* [1949], p. 197 no. 52, fig. 28; Laclotte, *Primitifs français* [1966], p. 13; Troescher, *Burgundische Malerei*, 1966, pp. 65 f., 78, fig. 53; Meiss, *Late XIV Century*, 1967, pp. 63, 218, fig. 694.

Washington

NATIONAL GALLERY (Fig. 606)

French, *ca.* 1420. *Portrait of a Lady in Profile.* 52×37 cm.

This panel, recognized as French by Richter and Degenhart, was previously ascribed to Pisanello—an attribution still occasionally maintained in publications on this Veronese painter. The erroneous attribution is significant in view of our awareness of Pisanello's study of the painting of the Limbourgs, to which the portrait shows a certain relation.

The portrait is not perfectly preserved. The ornaments on the robe seem to have been reworked and the jewel at the end of the links suspended from the collar has been lost.

BIBLIOGRAPHY: Richter, 1929, p. 139; Degenhart, *Pisanello* [1945], p. 39, fig. 4; Ring, *French Painting* [1949], p. 199 no. 64, pl. 27; Panofsky, *Netherlandish Painting*, 1953, pp. 82, 171, fig. 92; Laclotte, *Primitifs français* [1966], p. 23 pl. XI; Troescher, *Burgundische Malerei*, 1966, p. 82 ff., figs. 71, 72; Meiss, *Boucicaut Master*, 1968, p. 153 n. 29; Sterling in Białostocki et al., *Spätmittelalter*, 1972, p. 189.

X

Catalogue of Single Manuscripts

Manuscripts are ordered topographically except when classified according to text. The names of the illuminators appear in the lists of miniatures, either in groups at the beginning of each list or after the subject of a single folio.

BOCCACCIO, DES CAS DES NOBLES HOMMES ET FEMMES

Geneva

BIBL. PUBLIQUE ET UNIVERSITAIRE, fr. 190 (Figs. 69, 507, 509, 512)

Boccaccio, *Des cas des nobles hommes et femmes*, translation by Laurent de Premierfait. Two volumes. 179 and 189 fols.; 405×290, 400×290 mm. There are frames for miniatures which were left unexecuted on fols. 46v and 55v. A gathering between fols. 64 and 65 is missing.

EARLY HISTORY: Martin Gouge, Archbishop of Chartres, gave this manuscript to Jean de Berry for New Year, 1411. The Duke's ex libris appears at the end of the second volume. The scholar Laurent de Premierfait translated Boccaccio's *De casibus virorum illustrium* first in 1400. Laurent states in the prologue to his second version that his earlier translation was not well received, and there remain no illuminated copies of it. His second version, freer than the first and containing more historical allusions, was finished on April 15, 1409. In the dedication to Jean de Berry which precedes the prologue Laurent says that he undertook the translation on the "especial mandemant" of the Duke, whom he was then serving as secretary. It was not the first time that the initial illustrated copy of a translation the Duke had commissioned was given to him by one of his counselors. In 1401 Nicholas de Gonesse finished a translation of Valerius Maximus for Berry, who then received an illustrated copy as a New Year's gift from his treasurer Jacques Courau (Bibl. nat., fr. 282).

Paris

BIBL. DE L'ARSENAL, ms. 5193 (Figs. 66, 159, 508, 510)

Boccaccio, *Des cas des nobles hommes et femmes*, translation by Laurent de Premierfait. 405 fols.; 402×298 mm. There are sketches for miniatures in the margins of fols. 107, 130v, 133v, 212, 213. Frames for miniatures were left unexecuted on fols. 48v, 59, 128, 135v, 138v, and 143v.

EARLY HISTORY: The manuscript was recorded in the inventory of the library of Jean sans Peur made in 1420.

STYLE AND DATE OF THE TWO MANUSCRIPTS: The cycle of miniatures in these two early copies of Laurent's translation is almost identical. A single workshop, that of the Luçon Master, illuminated the Geneva Boccaccio immediately after the completion of the text in April, 1409. The miniatures in the Arsenal copy were executed a couple of years later, most of them by the workshop of the Cité des Dames Master. The chief illuminator reserved for himself several folios, such as 224, 229 and 403v. A small group of miniatures was executed by an illuminator related to the Adelphi Master and another artist likewise connected with the Bedford trend (fols. 30, 107, 127–141v, 208, 213, 305, 378, 385, 389v and 393v).

With a few exceptions, such as the miniatures for Book V, Chapter II, the compositions by the Cité des Dames workshop in the Arsenal Boccaccio are the same as the corresponding miniatures in the Geneva copy (Figs. 507–510), whereas the illuminators belonging to the Bedford trend did not follow the same model. In general the Geneva Boccaccio served as a model for the Arsenal copy. The Cité des Dames workshop adopted aspects of the Luçon style, such as tooled gold decoration and twisted crags (Fig. 508). The representation of death and torture is always more telling in the Luçon miniatures. Hercules in the miniature by the Cité des Dames workshop, for example, does not wince from the pain of wearing the fiery shirt of Nessus, which causes him to uproot trees and hurl rocks. Occasionally a miniature in the Geneva manuscript represents aspects of the text that are lacking in the Arsenal copy. In the scene by the Luçon Master and his workshop in which Pope John XII orders the torture of two cardinals, the Pope is accompanied by a huntsman and four hounds (Fig. 512). The text states that the Pope kept dogs and birds and that he lived the life of a secular person. "Il discutoit du droit des choses divines entre les hommes darmes entre les braconniers et chasseurs tandiz quil voloit aux oyseaulx et quil chassoit les bestes a cours de chiens en la compaigne des chasseurs et des varlets crians apres les bestes et entre les ribauldelles suivans la court papale." (Arsenal, ms. 5193, fol. 374.) In the corresponding miniature in the Arsenal Boccaccio the Cité des Dames workshop omitted the hunter and hounds (see Martin, *Boccace*, 1911, pl. CXXXV).

The Cité des Dames Master himself took more initiative than his workshop in changing the axis of a composition in the Geneva manuscript and in elaborating a setting. The illuminator related to the Adelphi Master in the Arsenal manuscript deviated much more from Geneva even though he was given directions for most of his scenes in small sketches in the lower margins. His version of Hannibal drinking poison shows that he understood neither the text nor his model, for he clothed the dead Hannibal differently from the live figure (Fig. 159).

The miniatures by this illuminator as well as those by the Cité des Dames Master and workshop indicate a date towards 1412.

BIBLIOGRAPHY

Geneva, Bibl. publique et universitaire, fr. 190: Reinach, 1907, p. 172; Durrieu, *Boccace*, 1909, p. 23 f.; Aubert, 1911, pp. 581–586; *idem*, 1912, pp. 70–73, pl. XXXIV; Paris, Bibl. nat., Couderc, 1927, p. 84; Martens, *Meister Francke*, 1929, pp. 196, 241 n. 222, 243 n. 227, 245 n. 245, 265 n. 470; Meiss, *Art Bull.*, 1956, p. 193, fig. 4; Gagnebin, 1957, pp. 129–148; Meiss, *Late XIV Century*, 1967, index; *idem*, *Boucicaut Master*, 1968, index, figs. 380, 384, 389, 397, 399.

Paris, Bibl. de l'Arsenal, ms. 5193: Paris, Arsenal, Martin, V, 1889, p. 116 f. no. 5193; Champeaux and Gauchery, *Travaux*, 1894, p. 156; Martin, *Comptes rendus*, 1904, p. 124; *idem*, *Rev. archéol.*, 1904, pp. 28, 43, figs. 5, 6; Doutrepont, *Inventaire*, 1906, p. 44 no. 82; Durrieu, *Boccace*, 1909, p. 24; *idem*, Bibl. *Ecole des Chartes*, 1910, pp. 65–67, pl. opp. p. 66; Martin, *Boccace*, 1911; Durrieu, *Rev. de l'art chrét.*, 1913, p. 313; Martens, *Meister Francke*, 1929, p. 62; Paris, Bibl. nat. (Porcher), 1955, p. 83 no. 170; Meiss, *Art Bull.*, 1956, p. 193; *idem*, *Late XIV Century*, 1967, pp. 357, 359, 363 n. 45; *idem*, "*Decameron*," 1967, p. 60 f.; *idem*, *Boucicaut Master*, 1968, pp. 35, 47, 50 ff., 102, figs. 381, 385, 393, 395, relationship to Arsenal 5077, p. 54; Bozzolo, 1968, pp. 4–6.

BOOK	CHAP.	Geneva fr. 190 Vol. I *Folio*	Arsenal 5193 *Folio*	
I	1	7v	8v	Adam and Eve in the Garden of Eden
	3	10	11v	Nimrod supervises construction of Tower of Babylon
	5	11v	13	Saturn devours one of his children
	6	14v	16v	Cadmus receives plan of Thebes from architect; workers build city
	8	18	19v	Shepherd suspends infant Oedipus from tree
	9	20	22	Atreus orders sons of Thyestes served to their father as food
	10	22	24	Theseus slays bull in Marathon
	12	28	27v	Hercules, wearing shirt of Nessus, destroys rocks and trees
		—	30	Hercules, wearing shirt of Nessus, destroys rocks and trees
	13	31v	33v	Priam murdered at altar by Pyrrhus
	14	—	37	Hecuba witnesses murder of one of her children (Heads chap. 14, which does not treat this subject)
	15	35v	37v	Agamemnon murdered by Aegisthus
	16	—	40	Diogenes in barrel observes boy drinking from hands
	17	39	41	Samson destroys temple
	18	—	43	A queen caresses a king
	19	44v	46v	Pyrrhus stabbed by priest of Apollo
II	Prologue	46v	48v	Frame for a miniature left blank
	2	47	49	Samuel anoints Saul
	3	49	51	Saul, discovering his three sons dead, stabs himself
	4	49v	51v	Vanquished kings Hadar-Ezer and Hadad trample their crowns and break their scepters
	5	50	52	King Rehoboam holds court
	6	51	53v	King of Egypt imposes conditions of peace on Rehoboam
		52v	54v	Mucius Scaevola burns his right hand to punish himself
	7	53v	55v	Besieged usurper Zambri destroys himself by fire
	8	—	56v	Commanded by high priest, executioners drag Queen Athaliah by her hair
	9	55	58v	Beheading of Athaliah
	10	55v	59	Frame for a miniature left blank
	11	56	59v	Dido sees her husband murdered by her brother
	12	59v	63v	Suicide of Dido

BOOK	CHAP.	Geneva fr. 190 Vol. I *Folio*	Arsenal 5193 *Folio*	
	13	60	64	Soldier tells Sardanapalus IV, surrounded by his wives, that enemy are at the gates of Nineveh
	14	63	66v	Suicide of Sardanapalus
	15	64v	68v	King Uzziah, sacrificing sacrilegiously, becomes leprous
	16	66v	70	Zedekiah blinded at command of Nebuchadnezzar
	17	68v	72v	Zedekiah dies in prison
	18	69	73	Shepherd observes Cyrus nursed by wild dog
	19	72v	76v	Dream of Simonides
	20	74v	78v	Candaules shows off nude wife
	21	75v	80	Servant mistakenly kills Croesus
	22	77	81v	Thomyris has Cyrus's head placed in barrel of blood
	23	80v	85	Preparation for execution of Mettius Fufetius
	24	82	86v	The author (or translator) speaks
III	1	83	88	Struggle between Poverty and Fortune (Misfortune tied to a stake in Ars. 5193)
	2	86	90v	Tullus Hostilius struck by fire
	3	88v	93v	Murder of Tarquin
		89v	94v	Suicide of Lucretia
	4	—	96v	A king addresses a woman
	5	95v	102	Cambyses stabs himself
	6	100	107	Xerxes I and his army cross bridge
	7	102v	109v	Xerxes I dismembered by Artabanus, commander of his body guard
	8	104v	111v	Artabanus killed by Artaxerxes
	9	106v	113v	Verginius beheading Verginia
	10	109	116v	Suicide of Appius Claudius
	11	110v	118	Cyclopes driven out of Sicily
	12	111v	119	Expedition of Alcibiades sailing to Sicily
	13	114	122	Bed of Alcibiades set afire
	14	115v	123v	The poet and the knight
	15	117	125v	Carthalo hanged by order of his father
	16	118v	127	Execution of Hanno, Duke of Carthage
	18	121v	130v	Three unfortunate princes
	19	124	133v	Artaxerxes observes the massacre of his sons (and their wives in fr. 190)
IV	2	126v	136v	Manlius Capitolinus routs a Gaul from Capitol
	4	130	140v	Assassination of Clearchus
	5	131	141v	Betrayal of women of Locri by Dionysius II, tyrant of Syracuse
	7	133	144	Polycrates throws ring into river; Polycrates hanged
	8	134v	145v	Callisthenes tortured at command of Alexander
	9	137v	149	Alexander of Epirus murdered in river Acheron
	10	139	151	Dying Darius III addresses Persian soldier
	11	142v	154v	Death of Leosthenes
	12	145	157	Eumenes dying in prison
	13	146v	159	Murder of Olympias, mother of Alexander the Great
	14	150	162v	Dying Agathocles tells wife and sons to flee to Sicily
	15	153	166	Barsine tries to protect her son from assassin
	16	157v	171	Sons of Arsinoë murdered
	17	159v	173	Ptolemy Ceraunus killed in battle
	18	163	177	Death of Pyrrhus of Epirus
	19	164v	179	Murder of Aristodemus of Epirus
V	1	169	184	Murder of Antiochus III, King of Syria
	2	171	186v	Laodamia murdered in temple of Diana
	3	173	188v	Death by torture of Marcus Attilius Regulus
	5	177v	194	Murder of Ptolemy IV of Egypt; his concubine and her daughter hanged
	6	1	196v	Masinissa in the wilderness
	7	2v	198	Soldiers leading prisoners
	8	6	202v	Antiochus III of Syria massacred after pillaging temple
	9	8v	205	Corpses of Hieronymus of Syracuse, his wife and his daughter
	10	11	208	Hannibal drinks poison
	11	14v	212	Ars. 5193: Prusias II, King of Bithynia, begging Fr. 190: Prusias killed by his son
	12	15v	213	Ars. 5193: Perseus and two sons led as prisoners by Aemilius Paulus

BOOK	CHAP.	Geneva fr. 190 Vol. I *Folio*	Arsenal 5193 *Folio*	
				Fr. 190: King Philip of Macedonia has his son Demetrius killed by placing huge stone slabs on his head and body
	13	17	214v	Massacre of Ammonius, ruler of Antioch, disguised as woman
	14	18	215v	False Philip of Macedonia in stocks
	15	19	217	Head of Alexander Balas of Syria brought to Ptolemy VI Philometor
	16	20v	218	Wife of Hasdrubal, General of the Carthaginians, throws herself and two sons onto fire
	17	22v	220v	Demetrius II Nicator beheaded as he tries to land at Tyre
	18	25	223	Alexander Zebinas murdered before Antiochus Gryphus
	19	26	224	Dismembered body of her son served to Cleopatra at table
	20	27v	226	Jugurtha thrown into Tiber
VI	1	30v	229	Boccaccio and Fortune
	2	37	235v	Slave completes murder of Caius Marius; head of Telesinus displayed on pole
	4	42	—	Cleopatra's hand cut off as she seeks refuge in a temple
	5	43	241v	Mithridates victorious in jousting
	6	49	247	Animals devour body of murdered Eucratides
	7	49v	247v	Orodes I crowning his son
	8	51v	250	Consul Posthumius Albinus stoned by his soldiers
	9	53v	251v	Murder of Pompey
	11	61v	260	Julius Caesar swims holding a letter
	12	—	264v	Execution of Cicero
	14	—	271	Two dead soldiers mourned by companions
	15	66	272v	Anthony and Cleopatra in their tomb
VII	2	71	278v	Massacre of the Innocents
	3	76	283v	Debate between Tiberius, Messalina and Caligula
	4	82	290v	Nero drinking over the corpse of his mother
	5	89	—	Galba's head sacrificed to the gods of hell by Patrobolus
	6	90v	298v	Corpse of Aulus Vitellius dragged to the Tiber
	8	96v	305	Destruction of Jerusalem; Titus receives tribute money; Jews driven into captivity
	9	101	309v	Famished Jewess devours her child
VIII	1	102v	311	Boccaccio and Petrarch
	2	105v	314	Emperor Commodius strangled by Marcia
	4	109v	318v	Sapor stepping on Valerian to mount horse
	5	112v	321v	Emperor Carus struck by lightning
	6	114	323v	Emperor Aurelian leads Queen Zenobia captive
	7	115v	325	Diocletian gives crown to Constantius; Diocletian dead after drinking poison
	8	117v	327	Emperor Maximian surrenders crown; Maximian killed
	9	119	329	Emperor Galerius on his deathbed
	10	121	331	Suicide of the tyrant Magnentius and of his brother Decentius Magnus
	11	123	333	Julian the Apostate killed by enemy soldier
	13	126v	337	Heretic Emperor Valens orders massacre of orthodox Christians
	14	130v	341	Stilicho and lieutenants feast before starving army of Radagaisus
	15	132v	343	Assassination of Rufinus
	16	134v	345	Murder of Odoacer, King of Italy
	18	137	348	Decapitation of Symmachus and Boethius
	19	139	349v	King Arthur and Knights of the Round Table
	21	143	353v	Strangling of Sindual
	22	143v	354v	Helmechis forces Rosamund to drink poison
IX	1	147	357v	Mohammed preaching
	2	153v	364v	Assassination of Emperor Constans II Pogonatus
	3	155	366	Romilde of Friuli impaled
	4	156v	368	Torture of Justinian II and of Philippicus of Constantinople

BOOK	CHAP.	Geneva fr. 190 Vol. I *Folio*	Arsenal 5193 *Folio*	
	5	158v	370	Imprisonment of Desiderius, King of the Lombards, and his family
	6	159v	371	Pope Joan giving birth
	7	161v	373	Pope John XII orders torture of two cardinals
	8	163v	375	Assassination of Ernest, Duke of Swabia
	9	164v	376	Blinding of Emperor Romanus IV Diogenes
	10	165	377	Henry I captures his brother at the Battle of Tinchebrai
	11	166	378	Humiliation and torture of Emperor Andronicus I Comnenus (In Ars. 5193 Andronicus, riding sideways on a donkey, is blinded in one eye. In fr. 190 Andronicus is hung and tortured by populace)
	13	168v	380v	Torture of Emperor Isaac II Angelus
	14	169	381	Torture of William III, King of Sicily
	15	170	382v	Guy de Lusignan, embarking for Cyprus, pursued by Saladin
	16	170v	383	Suicide of Henry, son of Emperor Frederick II, before his father
	18	172	385	Imprisonment of Enzio, son of Frederick II
	19	173	386	Coronation of Charles d'Anjou by Pope Clement IV
	20	175v	—	Pope Boniface VIII on deathbed
	21	176	389v	Templars about to be burned before Philippe le Bel
	23	180	393v	Philippe le Bel killed by a wild boar
	24	—	395v	Gautier de Brienne struck down at Battle of Poitiers
	26	185v	401	Torture of Filippa of Catania and her family
	27	188	403v	Jean II le Bon taken into captivity

BOCCACCIO, DES CLERES ET NOBLES FEMMES

Paris

BIBL. NAT., fr. 598 and 12420

(Figs. 6, 73 and 3, 46, 74, 200)

Fr. 598: 2+161 fols.; 365×260 mm. Fr. 12420: 167 fols.; 352×243 mm.

EARLY HISTORY: Laurent de Premierfait finished his translation of *De mulieribus claris* in September, 1401. An illustrated manuscript (fr. 12420) was given to Philippe le Hardi for New Year 1403 by Jacques Raponde. A year later, in February 1404, the Duke of Berry received a copy (fr. 598) from Jean de la Barre, *receveur general des finances* in Languedoc and Guyenne.

STYLE AND DATE: The similarity of corresponding compositions in the two manuscripts indicates that one was based on the other or both on the same model. The styles, too, are related; indeed Bella Martens, and after her other scholars, concluded that both manuscripts were illuminated by a so-called Master of 1402 and his assistants. As I observed in 1967, however, the differences between the two manuscripts are scarcely less significant than their similarities. Each was supervised and executed in part by a distinctive and important illuminator, the Cleres Femmes Master, named from Berry's manuscript, and the Coronation Master. Both illuminators seem to have been first trained in the Netherlands. A Dutch inscription in fr. 598 on the scroll of Cassandra on fol. 48v—"hort het wort"—is early but not original.

In fr. 12420 an assistant of the Cité des Dames Master painted two miniatures on folios 46 and 46v. Certain other folios, for instance 42v and 43, are by a weak artist influenced by both the Coronation and Cité des Dames styles.

The two manuscripts were probably illuminated at about the same time. Details, such as the occupations of the "children" of the deities (Figs. 73, 74, 200), are given more attention in the Boccaccio of Philippe le Hardi than in Berry's copy. Philippe's manuscript, of which we hear a year earlier, may have served as a model for Berry's. Many scenes, too, which are appropriately indoors in fr. 12420, have been moved outdoors in fr. 598. An exception, however, is *Caritas*

Romana, represented outside in fr. 12420 but more correctly in prison in fr. 598. The Cleres Femmes Master, less interested in Italianate French traditions, abandoned tessellated floors, which appear frequently in fr. 12420. Unlike the Coronation Master he often combined two episodes in one space. In a few landscapes he replaced the patterned backgrounds in fr. 12420 with modulated skies, which are a more advanced form.

BIBLIOGRAPHY

Paris, Bibl. nat., fr. 598: Durrieu, 1895, p. 178 f.; Martens, *Meister Francke*, 1929, p. 193, figs. 42, 48–50, 52, 53, 80; Panofsky, *Netherlandish Painting*, 1953, I, pp. 52 f., 76, 381 nn. 52[6,7], 53[1,2], II, figs. 53, 55, 56; Porcher, *Belles Heures*, 1953, p. 13 f., fig. 7; Paris, Bibl. nat. (Porcher), 1955, p. 78 f. no. 158; Meiss, *Art Bull.*, 1956, p. 194; Porcher, *Enluminure*, 1959, p. 55 f., fig. 60; Vienna, Kunsthist. Mus., *Katalog*, 1962, p. 180 no. 125; Meiss, *Late XIV Century*, 1967, index, figs. 289, 291, 294, 561; *idem*, *Boucicaut Master*, 1968, index, figs. 369, 373; Bozzolo, 1968, p. 42 f.

Paris, Bibl. nat., fr. 12420: Peignot, *Bibl. ducs de Bourgogne*, 1841, p. 31; Durrieu, 1895, p. 167 f., figs. pp. 161, 165; Paris, Louvre, *Exposition*, 1904, p. 36 no. 98; Martin, *Miniature française*, 1923, pp. 72 f., 101, figs. CXI–CXIII; Paris, Bibl. nat. (Couderc), 1927, p. 83 f., pl. LIII; Martens, *Meister Francke*, 1929, pp. 192 f., 241 n. 221, figs. 7, 43, 59; Pächt, 1940–1941, p. 88 no. 1; Baldass, *Jan van Eyck* [1952], p. 6 n. 2; Panofsky, *Netherlandish Painting*, 1953, I, pp. 52 f., 150, 171, 381 nn. 52[6,8], 391 n. 80[5], 424 n. 171[2], II, fig. 54; Porcher, *Belles Heures*, 1953, pp. 13, 17, fig. 6; Paris, Bibl. nat. (Porcher), 1955, p. 78 no. 157; Meiss, *Art Bull.*, 1956, p. 194; *idem*, *Late XIV Century*, 1967, pp. 4 f., 47, 252, 355; *idem*, *Boucicaut Master*, 1968, index, figs. 368, 372; Bozzolo, 1968, pp. 46–48.

BIBL. NAT.,

fr. 12420	fr. 598	
3	—	Boccaccio seated with a manuscript before three auditors
4v	3	Boccaccio presents his manuscript to Andrée, contesse de Haulteville
—	4v	Boccaccio consults his manuscript
6v	6v	Serpent tempts Eve; avenging angel stands behind
8	8	Semiramis with her soldiers and her son Ninus
10v	10v	Opis in a temple
11	12	Juno in heaven above her children including a woman in childbirth
12	11	Ceres presides over plowing, sowing and reaping; Triptolemus obeisant
13v	13	Minerva instructs men in making armor, preparing wool, and in flute playing
15	15v	Venus honored with incense in the presence of her worshippers
16	16v	Isis, on board a ship, arrives in Egypt
17v	18	Europa lands in Crete
18v[a]	19[a]	Libya and her subjects
18v[b]	19[b]	Martesia and Lampedo, Queens of the Amazons
20	20v	Thisbe finds the body of Pyramus and stabs herself
22	22v	Hypermnestra sends away Lynceus to protect him from her father Danaus
24	24v	Niobe among the bodies of her dead children and as a statue
25	26	Hypsipyle, who helps her father and children escape by sea to Chios, attacked by Lemnians
26v	27v	Medea has her brother Sbsyrtus killed and prepares to flee with Jason
28	29	Arachne hangs herself before her loom
29	30v	Hercules fights the Amazons
30	31	Erythraea writes down a prediction
31	32	Perseus arrives in a ship to abduct Medusa
32	33	Hercules seated among Iole's women, spinning
34v	35v	Hercules shoots at Nessus as he abducts Deianira
35	36	Jocasta kills herself; Oedipus puts out his eyes; Polynices and Eteocles kill each other
36	37	Amalthea writing
37	38	Nicostrata gives the alphabet to the Latins
39v	40v	Cephalus shoots Procris and offers her jewels
41	41v	Argia discovers the dead body of her husband Polynices
42v	43	Manto foretells the future from fire and the entrails of animals
43v	44	The wives of the Minyans rescue their husbands
46	46	Penthesilea and the Amazons go to the aid of Hector
46v	47	Neoptolemus sacrifices Polyxena at the tomb of Achilles
47v	47v	Hecuba watches the slaughter of Priam and her children
48v	48v	Death of Cassandra, Agamemnon watching

fr. 12420	fr. 598	
49	49v	Clytaemnestra holds Agamemnon, entangled in his robes, as Aegisthus clubs him and an attendant prepares to kill him
50v	51	Helen and Paris watch the Greeks besiege Troy
54	54v	Circe receives Ulysses' companions
56	56	Camilla, Queen of the Volscians, hunting
58	58	Penelope weaves as Ulysses, Sybotes and Telemachus slaughter her suitors
60v	60	Ascanius presents to Lavinia the crown of Laurentum
61v	61v	Death of Dido (in 598 embraced by a man)
67v	67v	Nicaula (Sheba), accompanied by some of her Ethiopian countrymen, offers Solomon a balsam fir
69	68v	Pamphile collects cotton bolls and prepares cotton thread for weaving
69v	69	Rhea Ilia, men digging her grave; her sons Romulus and Remus suckling a wolf
71	70v	Gaia before her loom and women spinning
71v	71v	Sappho reads her poems to other authors
73	72v	Lucretia stabs herself in the presence of her husband and relatives
74v	74v	Thamyris, Queen of the Scythians, kills Cyrus
76v	76	Leaena in the hands of her torturers
78	78	Athaliah orders the slaughter of the princes of Judah (and in 598 is stoned)
81	81	Cloelia on horseback crosses the Tiber
82	83	Hippo drowns herself from a ship
83	83v	Megullia Dotata collecting her dowry
83v	82v	Veturia, Volumnia and her children meet Coriolanus (in 12420 Volumnia absent)
86	86	Thamyris paints a Madonna
87	86v	Artemisia defeats the Rhodians
90	90	Death of Verginia
92v	92	The paintress Irene
93	92v	Leontium embraced by a man while reading philosophy
93v	93v	Death of Olympias
95	95	Claudia defends Appius Claudius in his triumphal chariot
96[a]	96	Verginia, wife of Lucius Volumnius, cast out of the temple of Pudicitia
96[b]		Verginia worships in her own temple of Pudicitia
98v	97	Festival of the goddess Flora
100	99	*Caritas Romana*
101v	100v	Marcia paints her portrait
102v	101v	Sulpicia swings a censer in the temple of Venus Verticordia (Venus on altar in fr. 598)
103v	102v	Harmonia observes the death of a girl disguised as herself
104v	103v	Busa distributes money and clothes to Romans after Cannae
106	105	Sophonisba takes poison
108	107	Theoxena and her family, fleeing in a ship, take poison in order not to be captured
110	109v	Berenice avenges the murder of her sons
111	110v	Drigiagon's wife presents to her husband the head of her ravisher
113	112	Tertia Aemilia
114	113v	Dripetrua waits on her father Mithridates
114v	114	Sempronia refuses the embrace of Equitius
116	115	Claudia Quinta pulls the ship bearing Cybele
117	116	Mithridates and Hypsicratea in armor
119	118	Sempronia, among her musical instruments, embraces an admirer
120v	120	The wives of the Cimbrians hang themselves
122	121v	Death of Julia
123	122	Portia eats hot coals
124	123v	Turia hides her husband
125	124v	Hortensia pleads with the Triumvirs
126	125	Sulpicia accompanied by her servants prepares to follow her husband into exile
127	126	Cornificia, poetess
127v	127	Death of Mariamne, wife of Herod
129v	128v	Cleopatra dying at the side of Anthony
134	132v	Antonia, widow of Drusus, refuses her suitors
134v	133v	Agrippina in prison refuses food
136	134v	In the temple of Isis Paulina is seduced by Mundus
137v	136	Death of Agrippina observed by Nero
139v	138v	Epicharis, tortured, strangles herself
142	139v	Pompeia Paulina saved from bleeding to death in a bath in which Seneca is dying
143v	141	Sabina Poppaea carried in a funeral litter
146	142v	Triaria in battle
147	143v	Proba writes *Cento*
148v[a]	145	Faustina Augusta worshipped at an altar
148v[b]		Faustina with her lovers
150	146	Semiamira among the Roman senators

fr. 12420	fr. 598	
152v	148^{a}	Zenobia hunting
	148^{b}	Zenobia with her soldiers
155v	151	Pope Joan in procession gives birth to an infant
157	152	Irene disposed by Constantine
158v	153v	Engeldruda given in marriage to Guido by the Emperor Otho IV
$159v^{a}$	154v	Constance promised to Henry VI
$159v^{b}$		Constance discards her nun's habit to marry him
161	155v	Camiola delivers Roland from prison
165	159	Jeanne, Queen of Sicily and Jerusalem, receives gifts from her subjects

CHRISTINE DE PISAN, CITE DES DAMES

The Cité des Dames Master made the model for these manuscripts. For the character of his illustrations as well as for the interrelations of these manuscripts see the chapter "The Cité des Dames."

Christine finished her text by Easter 1405. Shortly afterward she presented copies to the Dukes of Berry (fr. 607) and Burgundy (Brussels). About the same time the Cité des Dames workshop illustrated two other copies, fr. 1178 and 1179, and a third was included in a collection of Christine's works which the poet presented to Queen Isabeau about 1410 (Harley 4431).

PARIS Bibl. nat. 607 (Figs. 36, 39, 43)	BRUSSELS Bibl. roy. 9393 (Figs. 37, 40, 44)	PARIS Bibl. nat. 1178 (Fig. 41)	PARIS Bibl. nat. 1179 (Fig. 35)	LONDON Brit. Mus. Harley 4431 (Figs. 38, 42, 45, 114, 136, 137, 142, 148, 151, 154, 155)	
2	3	3	3	290	*Raison*, *Droiture* and *Justice* appear to Christine; *Raison* helps the poet build the *Cité*
31v	35v	64v	—	323	*Droiture* welcomes Christine and companions to the *Cité*
67v	74v	135	—	361	*Justice*, Christine and other ladies welcome the Virgin and saints
79 fols. 346×255 mm.	86 fols. 363×264 mm.	159 fols. 300×211 mm.	134 fols. 305×215 mm.		

BIBLIOGRAPHY

Brussels, Bibl. royale, ms. 9393: Doutrepont, *Inventaire*, 1906, p. 69 no. 109; Brussels, Bibl. roy., Gaspar and Lyna, I, 1937, p. 412 f. no. 170, pl. XCVIa; Schaefer, 1937, pp. 184–187, figs. 115, 117, 119; Meiss, *Art Bull.*, 1956, p. 193; Brussels, Bibl. roy. (Dogaer and Debae), 1967, p. 102 f. no. 150; Meiss, *Late XIV Century*, 1967, p. 356; *idem*, *Boucicaut Master*, 1968, p. 149 n. 44.

Paris, Bibl. nat., fr. 607: Paris, *Manuscrits françois*, V, 1842, p. 183; Couderc, *Portraits* [1910], p. 24, pl. LV; Brussels, Bibl. roy., Gaspar and Lyna, I, 1937, p. 412 no. 170; Schaefer, 1937, pp. 184–187, figs. 116, 118, 120; Paris, Bibl. nat. (Porcher), 1955, p. 80 no. 162; Meiss, *Art Bull.*, 1956, p. 193; *idem*, *Late XIV Century*, 1967, pp. 299, 312, 356.

Paris, Bibl. nat., fr. 1178: Meiss, *Late XIV Century*, 1967, p. 356; *idem*, *Boucicaut Master*, 1968, pp. 49, 149 n. 44.

Paris, Bibl. nat., fr. 1179: Schaefer, 1937, pp. 183–187, fig. 114; Meiss, *Art Bull.*, 1956, p. 193; *idem*, *Late XIV Century*, 1967, p. 356; *idem*, *Boucicaut Master*, 1968, pp. 49, 149 n. 144.

London, Brit. Mus. Harley 4431. See Christine de Pisan, Collected Writings.

CHRISTINE DE PISAN, MUTACION DE FORTUNE

Christine de Pisan finished the composition of the *Mutacion* late in 1403. Immediately she engaged the Epître Master and his assistants to illuminate four copies. She presented one (Brussels) to Philippe le Hardi in January, 1404. Jean de Berry received his (The Hague) later that year in March. All four manuscripts share the same program of illustration.

Several years later the Cité des Dames Master developed his own program for two copies of the text now in Paris and Munich. The Paris *Mutacion*, which includes the poet's *Livre des faits d'armes*, was illustrated by the workshop about 1410; the Munich *Mutacion* followed shortly afterwards.

For the cycles of illustrations by the two workshops see the chapter "La Mutacion de Fortune."

THE HAGUE Kon. Bibl. 78 D 42 (Figs. 14, 19, 23)	CHANTILLY Musée Condé 494 (Figs. 1, 20, 24, 30, 32)	BRUSSELS Bibl. roy. 9508 (Figs. 12, 21, 25, 29, 33)	Formerly PARIS Pierre Berès (Figs. 2, 22, 26, 34)	CHANTILLY Musée Condé 493	
1	1	2	—	232	Christine writing her manuscript
13	13	14	—	244v	Richesse seated before a portal of the Château de Fortune; Eur welcomes newcomers
16v	16	17v	16	248v	Fortune and her two brothers Eur and Meseur
34v	34	36v	33v	267v	Pope and Antipope enthroned in the Château de Fortune
54v	54	58	54	290v	Paintings in the Salle de Fortune: Liberal Arts and a siege
70	70	75	70	308	A siege (Babylon and the army of Ninus?)
—	—	—	—	346v	Assault on Troy
171 fols.	177 fols.	190 fols.	178 fols.	429 fols.	
330×261 mm.	333×255 mm.	349×251 mm.	345×253 mm.	290×240 mm.	

PARIS, Bibl. nat. ms. fr. 603 (Figs. 11, 15, 27)		MUNICH, Bayerische Staatsbibl. ms. gall. 11 (Figs. 13, 16, 28, 31)	
81v		2	Christine writing her manuscript
91		13	Richesse seated before a portal of the Château de Fortune; Eur welcomes newcomers; chains support château
109		33	Pope and Antipope enthroned in the Château de Fortune
127v		53	Christine beholding the paintings in the Salle de Fortune
143v	Council of Ninus before attacking Babylon	69	Ninus and his army
174	Amazons fighting the Greeks	103v	Penthesilea and other Amazons fight Pyrrhus and the Greeks
206v	Construction of a city, probably of Rome		
242 fols.		140 fols.	
370×275 mm.		350×255 mm.	

BIBLIOGRAPHY

Brussels, Bibl. roy., ms. 9508: Brussels, Bibl. roy., Gaspar and Lyna, I, 1937, p. 436 f., pl. CIIa; Solente, *Mutacion*, I, 1959, pp. XCIX–CIX; Brussels, Bibl. roy. (Dogaer and Debae), 1967, p. 105; Meiss, *Late XIV Century*, 1967, pp. 300, 358.

Chantilly, Musée Condé, ms. 493: Chantilly, Musée Condé, *Cabinet*, II, 1900, pp. 84–86; Solente, *Mutacion*,

I, 1959, p. CXXVII f.; Mombello, 1967, pp. 106–116; Meiss, *Late XIV Century*, 1967, p. 356.

Chantilly, Musée Condé, ms. 494: Chantilly, Musée Condé, *Cabinet*, II, 1900, p. 87 f.; Solente, *Mutacion*, I, 1959, pp. CIX–CXIII; Meiss, *Late XIV Century*, 1967, pp. 300, 358, figs. 835, 836.

The Hague, Kon. Bibl., ms. 78 D 42: Netherlands. Byvanck, 1931, p. 45 f.; Schaefer, 1937, pp. 166 f., 190 f., figs. 51, 143–145; Solente, *Mutacion*, I, 1959, pp. CXXII–CXXVII; Meiss, *Late XIV Century*, 1967, index.

Munich, Bayerische Staatsbibl., ms. gall. 11: Solente, *Mutacion*, I, 1959, pp. CXIII–CXIX; Meiss, *Late XIV Century*, 1967, p. 356.

Paris, Bibl. nat., fr. 603: Couderc, *Portraits* [1910], p. 24 f., pl. LVI; Schaefer, 1937, pp. 191–193, 195, figs. 49, 151–156, 164, 177, 178; Meiss, *Art Bull.*, 1956, p. 193; Solente, *Mutacion*, I, 1959, pp. CXXII, CXIX–CXXII; Meiss, *Late XIV Century*, 1967, p. 356.

Whereabouts unknown (formerly Paris, M. Pierre Berès): London, Sotheby, July 1, 1946, lot 21, p. 19; Solente, *Mutacion*, I, 1959, pp. CXXXIII–CXXXV, CXLII; Berès, Pierre, *Manuscrits et livres*, Cat. 60, n.d. (1963); Meiss, *Late XIV Century*, 1967, p. 358.

CHRISTINE DE PISAN, COLLECTED WRITINGS

After commissioning illustrated copies of *La Mutacion* Christine decided to prepare a manuscript containing several of her works. This extensively illustrated manuscript, now in Paris, was followed by a second, similar collection, now in the British Museum. The latest text in the first collection is of October, 1405. The three parts of this manuscript, fr. 606, 835–836, were probably destined for Louis d'Orléans; some of the texts contain dedications to that prince. Jean de Berry acquired it after the assassination of Louis in 1407. The place of the item describing the manuscript in the Duke's inventory of 1413 indicates that it was accessioned in 1408. Both manuscripts include Christine's first major work, the *Epître d'Othéa*, which contains an important cycle of illustrations of ancient myths. An impressive illuminator, who was a close student of Lombard painting, was in charge of the illustration of Jean de Berry's copy, from which he takes his name. The Epître Master was aided by an assistant and two other distinctive illuminators—the Egerton and Saffron Masters.

About 1410 Christine prepared the second copy for Queen Isabeau de Bavière (Harley 4431). This collection includes two additional texts—the *Cité des Dames* and *Cent ballades d'amant et de dame*. This time Christine chose the Cité des Dames Master to supervise the illustration. The master himself painted the famous frontispiece, which represents the poet presenting her manuscript to the Queen (Fig. 151). The miniatures in the *Epître d'Othéa* are copies of the cycle by the Epître Master. The Cité des Dames workshop followed the miniatures of the other texts in Berry's manuscript less closely. An illuminator in the Bedford trend painted a few miniatures in Isabeau's copy.

For the iconography and relationship of these two manuscripts see the chapter "Epître d'Othéa."

BIBLIOGRAPHY

Paris, Bibl. nat., fr. 606: Couderc, *Portraits* [1910], p. 23 f., pl. LIII; Campbell, *L'Epître d'Othéa*, 1924; Becker, 1931, p. 148 f.; Panofsky, 1932–1933, p. 246; Schaefer, 1937, pp. 163 ff., 199, figs. 61–82; Porcher, *Belles Heures*, 1953, pp. 19, 39; Saxl and Meier, *Verzeichnis*, 1953, III, pt. 1, pp. 173–187, pt. 2, pls. XXXIX, XL, XLVII; Paris, Bibl. nat. (Porcher), 1955, p. 74 f. no. 149, pl. XIX; Meiss, *Art Bull.*, 1956, p. 193; Milan, Palazzo Reale, *Arte Lombarda* [1958], p. 38 no. 86, pl. LVI; Porcher, *Enluminure*, 1959, p. 56, fig. 62, pl. LXI; Vienna, Kunsthist. Mus., *Katalog*, 1962, p. 174 no. 115, pl. 138; Mombello, 1964; *idem*, 1967; Meiss, *Late XIV Century*, 1967, index, figs. 817, 833, 834; *idem*, *Boucicaut Master*, 1968, index, fig. 478; Meiss with Off, 1971, pp. 228, 233.

Paris, Bibl. nat., fr. 835–836: Paris, Louvre, *Exposition*, 1904, p. 36 f. no. 102; Couderc, *Portraits* [1910], p. 24, pls. LIII, 2, LIV, 1, 2; Campbell, *Epître d'Othéa*, 1924, p. 9 ff.; Paris, Bibl. nat. (Martin), 1928, pp. 66, 110, figs. LXXXIV, LXXXV; Meiss, *Art Bull.*, 1956, p. 193; *idem*, *Late XIV Century*, 1967, index, fig. 324, see also Paris, Bibl. nat., ms. fr. 606; *idem*, *Boucicaut Master*, 1968, pp. 142, 152 n. 26.

London, Brit. Mus., Harley 4431: Delisle, *Charles V*, 1907, I, p. 134 f.; Martin, *Miniature française*, 1923, pp. 75 f., 101 f., fig. CXIV; London, Brit. Mus., *Reproductions*, IV, 1928, p. 14, pl. XXXV; London, Brit. Mus., Millar, 1933, p. 31 f. no. 40, pl. XL; Schaefer, 1937, pp. 119–208, figs. 1–40; Porcher, *Belles Heures*, 1953, pp. 7 n. 10, 20 n. 38, 25 f., 45 f.; Saxl and Meier, *Verzeichnis*, III, 1953, pt. 1, pp. 173–187; Meiss, *Art Bull.*, 1956, p. 193; *idem*, *Late XIV Century*, 1967, index; *idem*, *Boucicaut Master*, 1968, index.

MINIATURES:

Français 835, 606, 836:
All miniatures are by the Epître Master and his workshop unless otherwise indicated.

Harley 4431:
All miniatures are by the Master of the Cité des Dames and his workshop unless otherwise indicated.

Paris, BIBL. NAT., fr. 835
(Figs. 139, 145)
103 fols.; 350×260 mm.

London, BRIT. MUS., Harley 4431
(Figs. 38, 42, 45, 114, 136, 137, 142, 148, 151, 154, 155)
398 fols.; 368×285 mm.

MINIATURES:

PARIS Folio	LONDON Folio	
	3	Christine presents her manuscript to Isabeau de Bavière (*Epître à la Reine Isabelle*)
1	4	Christine writing *Cent Ballades* (*Cent Ballades*)
50	48	A duke presents his complaint to a noble lady (*Complainte amoureuse*)
45	51	A messenger delivers a letter to Cupid (*Epître au dieu d'Amours*)
	56v (Bedford trend)	The lover presents his complaint to his lady (*Une autre complainte amoureuse*)
52	58v	Christine presents the two lovers to Louis d'Orléans (*Le Débat de deux Amants*)
64	71v	Christine presents the three pairs of lovers to Jean de Werchin, Seneschal of Hainaut (*Le Dit des trois Jugements amoureux*)
74 (Egerton workshop)	81	Christine and courtiers journey to Poissy (*Le Dit de Poissy*)

Paris, BIBL. NAT., fr. 606
(Figs. 61, 62, 75, 76, 85, 87, 91, 102, 105, 106, 108, 122, 127, 133, 134, 138, 141, 146, 149)
103 fols.; 346×260 mm.

London, BRIT. MUS., Harley 4431 (continued)

MINIATURES:

PARIS Folio	LONDON Folio	*L'Epître d'Othéa*
1	95	Christine presents her manuscript to Louis d'Orléans
1v	95v	Othéa gives a letter to Hector
2v	96v	Temperance holds a clock; below, five women sit on the ground
3	97	Hercules, having killed the dragon, fights two lions
4	98	King Minos condemns two nude men
4v	98v	Perseus rescues Andromeda
5v	99v	Jupiter pours a sweet liquid on men standing below
6	100	Venus holds in her lap the hearts of her devotees who, standing below, raise their hearts to her
6v	100v	Saturn, holding a sickle, in sky above wise men
7[a]	101[a]	Apollo plays his lyre next to a white raven; below, the enlightened discourse
7[b]	101[b]	Phoebe shoots arrows, striking people with frenzy and melancholy
7v	101v	Mars excites men to war
8	102	Mercury, holding a flower as symbol of eloquence, influences the speech of the learned men
8v	102v	Minerva, inventor of armor, gives it to soldiers
9	103	Minerva holds a sword and Pallas a book; below, groups of warriors and learned women
9v	103v	Penthesilea, Queen of the Amazons, rides through a forest to aid the Trojans
10[a]	104[a]	Narcissus looks at his reflection in a fountain
10[b]	104[b]	The Fury Tesiphone induces King Athamas to kill his wife Ino and his two children
10v	104v	Mercury turns Aglauros into a stone statue
11	105	Ulysses blinds the Cyclops
11v	105v	Latona turns four bathers into frogs for muddying the water she wishes to drink
12	106	Bacchus and his "children" drink wine
12v	106v	Pygmalion kneels before Venus and begs her to bring life to his statue

PARIS *Folio*	LONDON *Folio*	
13	107	Diana, guardian of chastity, with maidens and nuns, all reading
13v[a]	107v[a]	Ceres sows a field
13v[b]	107v[b]	Isis grafts a tree
14	108	Midas, with donkey's ears, judges the contest between Pan and Apollo
14v	108v	In Tartarus Theseus and Pirithoüs kill devils as Hercules confronts Cerberus
15[a]	109[a]	Cadmus kills the serpent at the fountain; behind, the construction of Thebes
15[b]	109[b]	Io and her disciples writing
15v	109v	Mercury playing his flute puts Argus to sleep and steals Io, transformed into a cow
16	110	Pyrrhus avenges the death of his father, Achilles, in battle against the Trojans
16v[a]	110v[a]	Cassandra kneels before an altar in a temple
16v[b]	110v[b]	Neptune guides a ship in a storm
17	111	Atropos hovers over popes, kings and noblemen with her arrows of death
17v	111v	In a palace chamber Bellerophon rejects his stepmother
18	112	Memnon prepares to fight Achilles; in the background, Achilles kills Hector
18v[a]	112v[a]	Laomedon, King of Troy, threatens Hercules, Jason and their companions who have landed in a boat
18v[b] (Saffron Master)	112v[b]	Thisbe stabs herself on finding Pyramus dead; in the background, the lion vomits on Thisbe's kerchief
19v (Saffron Master)	113v	Aesculapius makes a diagnosis; in the foreground, Circe spears frogs for a potion
20[a] (Saffron Master)	114[a]	Paris and his companions kill Achilles who kneels before an altar in the temple of Apollo; Hecuba stands on the left
20[b] (Saffron Master)	114[b]	King Busiris offers to the gods the heads of three decapitated men
20v (Saffron Master)	114v	Hero dives into the sea after Leander
21 (Saffron Master)	115	Greek messengers demand that Priam return Helen
21v (Saffron Master)	115v	Aurora brings dawn; below, a peasant stands before his hen house
22 (Saffron Master)	116	Pasiphaë embraces a bull; in the foreground, four cows
22v (Saffron Master)	116v	Thydeus and Polinices fight in the palace of King Adrastus who sleeps in his bedroom above
23 (Saffron Master)	117	Cupid takes the hand of a young knight
23v	117v	Apollo shoots an arrow at Coronis because the white raven had reported her unfaithfulness
24	118	Juno, goddess of wealth, holds a purse; below, five misers with their coins
24v[a] (Saffron Master)	118v[a]	King Adrastus rides with his army to attack Thebes
24v[b]	118v[b]	Saturn places his fingers on his mouth and counsels those below not to speak too much
25	119	A white raven and a black crow are perched in two trees
25v	119v	Apollo kills Ganymede in a contest when an iron bar, which he threw into the air, falls striking Ganymede in the eye
26	120	Jason fights a dragon which guards the golden ram on Colchis
26v	120v	Perseus kills the gorgon
27	121	Apollo, at a window, surprises Mars and Venus in bed; Vulcan enchains the lovers in the presence of other gods
27v	121v	Before Thamyris, Queen of the Amazons, and three Amazons, an executioner has beheaded several men and has placed the head of Cyrus in a vat
28[a]	122[a]	Medea, who sits on her bed, hands a casket to Jason who kneels before her
28[b]	122[b]	Polyphemus surprises Acis and Galatea
28v	122v	At the wedding feast of Peleus and Thetis, Discord brings the golden apple to Juno, Pallas and Venus sitting at the foremost of three tables
29	123	The Greeks, who have landed in their boats, kill Laomedon, King of Troy
29v	123v	Juno, an old woman, gives bad advice to Semele who is loved by Jupiter
30[a]	124[a]	Diana, assisted in the hunt by her maidens, shoots an arrow at a stag
30[b]	124[b]	Arachne stands at her loom and boasts of her skill to Pallas who will change her into the spider shown above
30v	124v	Adonis killed by a boar in a forest
31	125	As the army of King Laomedon of the first Troy comes out to oppose the army of Hercules and finds their ships empty, the ambushed army of Telamon enters the undefended city from the rear

PARIS *Folio*	LONDON *Folio*	
31v[a]	125v[a]	Orpheus plays his lyre among birds and animals
31v[b]	125v[b]	Mercury brings the golden apple to Paris who sleeps, resting on a fountain; behind, stand Juno, Venus and Minerva
32	126	Actaeon surprises Diana bathing; behind, the stag into which Diana changed Actaeon
32v	126v	Orpheus, playing his lyre, looks back at Eurydice whom he leads out of hades
33v	127v	Ulysses discovers Achilles disguised among nuns in a convent when the latter chooses a sword as his gift
34	128	Atalante races Hippomenes who holds a golden apple
34v	128v	Judgment of Paris
35[a]	129[a]	Fortune turns her wheel
35[b]	129[b]	Paris embraces Helen
35v	129v	Cephalus kills Procris in a forest
36	130	Helenus warns Paris not to go to Greece to abduct Helen
36v	130v	Morpheus brings sleep to a man in bed
37	131	King Ceyx takes leave of his family
37v	131v	King Priam, ignoring the advice of four elders, listens to Troilus who advocates that Paris abduct Helen
38	132	Calchas tells Achilles the outcome of the Trojan war in the Temple of Delphi
38v	132v	Hermaphroditus and the nymph Salmacis bathe in a spring
39	133	Ulysses plays chess before his tent
39v	133v	Briseis and Diomedes; Cupid above
40[a]	134[a]	Hector kills Patroclus in battle
40[b]	134[b]	Narcissus turns away from Echo at a spring
40v	134v	Apollo gathers leaves from Daphne changed into a laurel tree
41	135	Hector's family begs him not to go into battle
41v	135v	King Ninus besieges Babylon
42	136	Priam seizes the bridle of Hector's horse and begs his son not to fight; behind Hector are his knights
42v[a]	136v	Death of Hector in battle
42v[b]	137	Achilles spears Hector in the seat of his armor as the latter, on horseback, leans forward to grasp Polybetes' armor
43	137v	Funeral of Hector
43v	138	Ajax, his face and arm uncovered, is shot by an enemy arrow in battle
44	138v	Antenor betrays Troy by indicating the open gate of Troy to Greeks carrying olive branches
44v	139	The Trojan gate is enlarged to permit entrance to the Trojan horse which has a castle on its back
45[a]	139v	The fortress of Ilion in Troy burns, and an army enters Tunis (Thunne, Carthage?)
45[b]	140	Circe changes Ulysses and his companions into boars
45v	140v	Ino has one peasant boil corn and another sow this unfertile grain
46 (Egerton Master?)	141	Legend of Aracoeli

Paris, BIBL. NAT., fr. 836

(Figs. 135, 140, 144, 147)

98 fols.; 350×255 mm.

London, BRIT. MUS., Harley 4431

MINIATURES:

PARIS *Folio*	LONDON *Folio*	
		Le Duc des vrais amants
65 (Egerton workshop)	143	Christine and the duke
65v (Egerton workshop)	144	The duke rides to the hunt with his companions
66v (Egerton workshop)	145	The duke and his companions entertain ladies in a garden
71v (Egerton workshop)	150	In a joust before ladies, the duke and his cousin fight two knights
74v (Egerton workshop)	153	The lady returns home
76 (Egerton workshop)	154v	The duke, resting on his bed, laments to his cousin
		Le Chemin de long estude
1	178	Christine presents her manuscript to Charles VI
3v	180v	Christine in bed dreams of the Cumaean Sibyl who sits next to the bed
5v	183	The Sibyl shows Christine the nine muses bathing in the *fontaine de Sapience*; Pegasus rears above the fountain
10v	188	The Sibyl leads Christine to the ladder of Speculation which is held in place by an old man in a cloud above

PARIS *Folio*	LONDON *Folio*	
12	189v	Christine and the Sibyl in the fifth heaven which is the firmament
15	192v	The Sibyl shows Christine *Sagesse*, *Noblesse*, *Chevalerie* and *Richesse* enthroned around the empty throne of *Raison*
19	196v	The Sibyl indicates to Christine *Raison*, holding a sword and an olive branch, enthroned in her court of four queens; aiding *Raison* is *Droiture*
40v	218v	The Sibyl presents Christine to *Raison*, enthroned in her court
48 (Egerton workshop)	221 (Bedford trend)	A shepherdess watches her sheep (*Le Dit de la Pastoure*)
63 (Egerton workshop)	257	Man of Sorrows with the emblems of the passion (*Oraison Notre Seigneur*)
	259v (Bedford trend)	Christine instructs four men (*Les Proverbes moraux*)
42	261v (Bedford trend)	Christine instructs her son Jean de Castel (*Les Enseignements moraux*)
45v	265 (Bedford trend)	Christine kneels before the Virgin and Child (*Oraison Notre Dame*)
	290	On the left, Christine before *Droiture*, *Raison* and *Justice* in her study; on the right, the construction of the *Cité des Dames* (*Cité des Dames*)
	323	*Justice* leads the queens into the *Cité*
	361	The female saints enter the *Cité*
	376	Lovers in conversation (*Cent ballades d'amant et de dame*)

ST. JOHN, APOCALYPSE

CHANTILLY 28 AND MORGAN 133

Chantilly 28 and Morgan 133 have certain textual and iconographic similarities which indicate either the use of the same model or the dependence of one on the other. To begin with, the same abridged version in French of a commentary written by Berengaudus accompanies both Apocalypses. As far as we know, the only other Apocalypse with this particular version of the Berengaudus commentary is an earlier fourteenth-century manuscript in Paris, fr. 1768. These three manuscripts contain the same textual inconsistencies. For example, Revelation II precedes Revelation I, 12–20, and at Revelation II, 8, "And to the angel of the Church of Smyrna write," the copyist omitted what pertains to Smyrna and substituted what belongs to Pergamos. Also Revelation V, 1–5 was mistakenly copied between Revelation IV, 1–8 and Revelation IV, 10–11. Despite, however, the textual similarity of fr. 1768 to the two early fifteenth-century Apocalypses, it certainly was not the pictorial model. Its mediocre miniatures are different in composition and iconography.

In the Chantilly and Morgan Apocalypses the eighty-five miniatures, which begin with the Martyrdom of St. John by the Emperor Domitian, often illustrate the commentary rather than Revelations itself. Most of the miniatures in the two cycles resemble each other iconographically, but in Chantilly 28, as in the earlier thirteenth-century Apocalypses, St. John is usually present as a witness to the event. The illuminators of Morgan 133 usually omitted not only him but other figures as well (Figs. 791, 792). When there are striking differences between the two cycles they are usually due to the choice by the Berry Apocalypse Master of a more traditional Biblical scene in the commentary rather than an image in Revelations itself. To illustrate Revelation XIV, 19, for example, the Medallion Master shows two angels dropping sickles onto vines and wheat (Fig. 796). Dead men and animals lie scattered on the ground. For the corresponding miniature in Morgan 133, folio 56v, the Apocalypse Master, drawing from the commentary which states that on the day of judgment devils and evil doers will perish, depicted a Last Judgment.

The Chantilly Medallion Master clearly had a pictorial model which he did not always understand, so that his miniatures differ from the text. According to the text for Revelation VII, 1–3, the angels prevented the winds from blowing upon earth by averting their heads, and earlier illustrations of this passage, such as the one in the Cambrai Apocalypse (Fig. 793), convey this image clearly. The Medallion Master, utilizing a miniature of this kind, failed to avert the heads sufficiently (Fig. 794). In the Chantilly manuscript the miniature does not clearly illustrate this passage. In Morgan 133, the Apocalypse

Master reduced the scene to one angel who quite properly covers the mouth of a single wind (Fig. 790). In this miniature, unlike that in Chantilly 28 and in earlier Apocalypses, the earth is a normal landscape, not contained in a round medallion. In the illustration by the Medallion Master for Revelation X, 1–7 on folio 63v, the angel below the rainbow stands with his right foot on land and his left foot in water (Fig. 802). According to the text and to earlier cycles, the position of his feet should be reversed. Furthermore, the angel's drapery is caught up strangely over his left knee, recalling earlier cycles in which the angel gathers his robe up over his arm (Fig. 801).

No Apocalypses with scenes in medallions survive, but a late thirteenth-century type might have existed. Illustrations in medallions within squares with leaves in the corners appear in, for example, a psalter illuminated towards 1260 for the Abbey of Evreux (Brit. Mus. Add. 16975).

Scholars have recognized the relationship of the miniatures in Chantilly 28 and Morgan 133 with some thirteenth-century Apocalypses represented by a beautiful manuscript which, destroyed in World War II, was formerly in the Bibl. de la Ville in Metz, ms. Salis 38. A copy of this manuscript is preserved in the Bibl. de la Ville in Cambrai, ms. 422. The Apocalypse tapestries in Angers designed by Bondol in 1378 for Louis d'Anjou also depend upon an early manuscript of this type. However, the Angers tapestries are more faithful to the Metz Apocalypse than are the Chantilly and Morgan miniatures.

One of the main differences of the Chantilly and Morgan Apocalypses from the Metz version is that the two-horned beast becomes the ecclesiastical figure of Antichrist as described in Revelation XIII–XVI (Fig. 797). The Chantilly and Morgan Apocalypses have in common, moreover, another feature which is unique among manuscripts of this text. In the miniatures for Revelation XII, 17–18 (Fig. 811), the dragon that fights the family of the woman does not have the seven heads usually given to it, in accordance with a description in a preceding verse (XII, 3). It has instead the head of a man, and this is precisely the attribute mentioned in a unique description on the folio opposite the miniature in Morgan 133. This addition to the commentary was made by the original scribe. It reads:

> En listoire et pourtraiture de ce chapitre est paint et figure saint Jehan qui regarde plusieurs gens lesquelx sont sur le ruiage de la mer et en y a de tous estas et dautrepart un dragon a teste humaine qui se combat a eulx. Et plusieurs deables sont la voletans par dessus ces gens lesquelx deables fierent et frappent ces gens et hurent.

Curiously, it is not the facing miniature that resembles most this description. The miniature in Chantilly includes the river and the devils attacking the people; of all the elements only St. John is lacking. Apparently, then, the scribe of the Morgan manuscript had before his eyes a representation of the same kind that served the Medallion Master as a model. The Apocalypse Master remained less interested, even though the description lay in front of him.

The dragon preserves its human head with long beard in the following scene in Chantilly 28, from Revelation XIII, 1–3 (Fig. 812), but in the corresponding miniature in the Morgan Apocalypse the creature is no longer anthropomorphic. In both miniatures the dragon and the beast exchange a document as a symbol of power, whereas earlier manuscripts, as well as the Angers tapestry, show the dragon giving the beast a scepter. Numerous similarities such as this prove that the Chantilly and Morgan Apocalypses were based upon the same lost model. They were also probably painted about the same time, very possibly *ca.* 1415.

Chantilly

MUSEE CONDE, ms. 28 (1378)

(Figs. 789, 791, 794–798, 800, 802–804, 812)

Histoire extraite de la Bible and *Apocalypse* in French with an abridged version of the commentary by Berengaudus. 121 fols.; 313×220 mm.

EARLY HISTORY: There are no indications of original ownership.

STYLE AND DATE: The miniatures are exceptional in so far as they are contained in roundels within square frames; acanthus normally fills the corners. The Virgil Master painted the frontispiece of the Apocalypse, leaving the first miniature in the Bible to a follower. The Medallion Master, originally trained it seems by the Virgil Master but a much superior artist, painted all the remaining miniatures. From them we have given him his name. His bold, vigorous designs qualified him especially for the illustration of the text of Revelation. His brushwork was exceptionally deft and open, and he laid his color in *taches*. He employed a limited number of pale hues, especially browns, grays, and blues, but blended them with exceptional sensibility.

The two styles in the manuscript all point towards a date about 1415.

BIBLIOGRAPHY: Delisle and Meyer, *L'Apocalypse en français*, 1901, pp. XCI–XCIV no. 14; Chantilly (Meurgey), 1930, I, pp. 85–89; Porcher, *Enluminure*, 1959, p. 64, fig. 69; Meiss, *Late XIV Century*, 1967, p. 360.

New York

PIERPONT MORGAN LIBRARY, M. 133

(Figs. 787, 788, 790, 792, 808, 811)

Apocalypse in French with an abridged version of the commentary by Berengaudus. 87 fols.; 300×209 mm.

EARLY HISTORY: This Apocalypse belonged to Jean de Berry, who wrote his ex libris on fol. 86v. The manuscript was not, however, listed in any of the Duke's inventories. He did own another, unidentified, Apocalypse in French, which was inventoried in 1402, as well as a tapestry with illustrations of the same text (Guiffrey, *Inventaires*, I, 1894, p. 233 no. 895; II, p. 207).

STYLE AND DATE: This manuscript, from which the Master of the Berry Apocalypse takes his name, is his major extant work. He painted powerful figures in grisaille against a red background, chosen to express the dramatic, visionary character of the text. Assistants, who executed many of the miniatures, closely approximated the master's style. They worked from written instructions, such as "couleur," visible under the red of the background. Though other phrases were erased, some are still faintly legible under ultraviolet light.

The manuscript was probably illuminated a year or two before the Duke of Berry's death in 1416 and around the same time as another Apocalypse in Chantilly, which has essentially the same text and a related pictorial cycle.

BIBLIOGRAPHY: James, *Apocalypse*, 1931, p. 4; New York, Pierpont Morgan Library [1934], p. 53 f., pl. 81; Nordenfalk, *Kung praktiks*, 1955, p. 61, fig. 64; Meiss, *Art Bull.*, 1956, p. 196, figs. 11, 12; *idem*, *Late XIV Century*, 1967, pp. 277, 300, 311, 354, fig. 843.

Chantilly, MUSEE CONDE, ms. 28 (ex 1378)

Histoire extraite de la Bible and *Apocalypse*

MINIATURES:

Folio	
1	Creation of animals, fish and birds
1v	Creation of angels
2	Fall of the rebel angels
2v	Creation of Eve
3	Adam and Eve in Paradise
3v	Temptation with death as a cadaver at the foot of the tree
4v	Expulsion from Paradise
5	An angel brings clothing to Adam and Eve outside of Paradise
5v	Adam cultivates the soil while Eve spins
7v	Noah's ark
8v	Tower of Babel
9	Temple of Ninus "King of Surie"
10v	Sacrifice of Abraham
14v	Crossing the Red Sea
15	Construction of Troy
17	King David playing his harp
17 bis	Temple of Solomon
20	Destruction of the temple and city of Jerusalem by Nebuchadnezzar
21	Siege of Samaria
22	Conquest of Babylon by Cyrus
22v	City and Temple of Jerusalem
23	Temple of Garisim
24v	Poisoning of Alexander
31	Adoration of the Magi
33	Crucifixion

Apocalypse

CHANTILLY 28 *Rev.*	*Folio*		MORGAN M. 133 *Folio*	
	36	Martyrdom of St. John	1	Martyrdom of St. John by the Emperor Domitian
I, 1	37v	St. John on Patmos; apparition of the angel	2v	The angel appears to St. John on Patmos
11	38v	The seven angels and the seven churches	3v	Seven angels representing the seven churches in one church
I, 12–17	39v	The Lord holds seven stars in his right hand with a sword in his mouth and sits between seven candlesticks; St. John prostrate before the Lord	4v	The Lord, holding seven stars in his left hand, with a double-edged sword in his mouth, enthroned between seven candlesticks

Rev.	CHANTILLY 28 Folio	MORGAN M. 133 Folio
IV, 1–8	40v The Lord with seven lamps enthroned in a mandorla rimmed by the symbols of the four Evangelists and the twenty-four elders	5v Lord in heaven with the seven lamps surrounded by the twenty-four elders and the symbols of the four Evangelists
V, 1–5	41v St. John between an angel and an elder	6v St. John, an elder and the strong angel
IV, 10–11	42v The twenty-four elders worship the Lord casting their crowns before the throne	7v The twenty-four elders worship the Lord casting their crowns before the throne
V, 6	43v The Lamb, the symbols of the Evangelists and the twenty-four elders	8v The Lamb, having seven horns and seven eyes, on the altar
V, 7–8	44v The Lord enthroned in a mandorla with the Lamb and the Book with seven seals, surrounded by the symbols of the Evangelists and the twenty-four elders	9v The Lamb takes the Book of Seven Seals from the Lord
VI, 1–2	45v Opening of the first seal: St. John, the angel of St. Matthew and a crowned archer on a horse	10v A crowned archer on a white horse and the angel of St. Matthew
VI, 3–4	46v Opening of the second seal: a knight with a sword on horseback, St. John, and a winged lion in the sky	11v A rider bearing a sword on a red horse and the lion of St. Mark
VI, 5	47v Opening of the third seal: St. John, a rider holding scales, and a winged ox in the sky	12v A rider holding scales and the ox of St. Luke
VI, 7–8	48v Opening of the fourth seal: St. John, an eagle in the sky and Death galloping out of Hell	13v Death galloping out of Hell; above, the eagle of St. John
VI, 9–11	49v Opening of the fifth seal: an angel brings stoles to souls under an altar	14v An angel gives a stole to one of the souls under the altar
VI, 12–16	50v Opening of the sixth seal: an earthquake below the sun and moon	15v An earthquake below the sun and moon
VII, 1	51v Circular earth, with a landscape, encircled by four angels holding the four winds and an angel with a *buisine*	16v An angel holding one of the four winds
VII, 9–11	52v The Lord holding the Lamb and Book in a mandorla encircled by the symbols of the Evangelists. Below, the multitude of all nations	17v The multitude, with palms in their hands, worship the Lord and the Lamb in heaven
VIII, 2	53v The Lord in a mandorla above the seven angels with their *buisines*	18v Seven angels sounding trumpets before the Lord
VIII, 3–5	54v The Lord in a mandorla above two angels censing an altar and pouring fire on earth	19v An angel burns incense before the altar
VIII, 6–7	55v The seven angels with their *buisines* and the rain of hail, blood and fire	20v Sounding of the seven angels
VIII, 8–9	56v The second angel blows his *buisine*, producing a mountain of fire on the sea, sinking ships, and killing men	21v A mountain cast into a ship-filled sea
VIII, 10–11	57v The third angel blows his *buisine*; fall of the star Wormwood into the water, death of those who drink the bitter water	22v The star from heaven falling upon the water
VIII, 12	58v The fourth angel sounds his trumpet below the moon, sun and stars	23v A third part of the sun, moon and stars darkened and the fourth angel, blowing a trumpet, flying over earth

Rev.	CHANTILLY 28 Folio	MORGAN M. 133 Folio
VIII, 13	59v St. John seated below the eagle bearing a banderole inscribed *douleur* three times	24v An eagle flying over earth with a banner on which is written *douleur, douleur*
IX, 1–3	60v The fifth angel sounds his trumpet; fall of the star with the key to the bottomless pit; figures swallowed by the pit from which smoke rises; St. John and a locust as a man on a winged horse	25v A rider on a winged horse before the star from heaven and the key to the abyss (a well)
IX, 13–15	61v The sixth angel sounds his trumpet; St. John observes four angels ordered to kill the third part of men	26v Two angels, one with a spear and the other with a sword, before the golden altar
IX, 17–18	62v Knights mounted on horses with lion heads, the dead extended before them; St. John grieves	27v Vision of knights mounted on horses with lion heads
X, 1–4	63v Under a rainbow, the angel with the face of the sun has one foot on the earth and the other in the sea; an angel closes St. John's book	28v An angel comes to close St. John's book
X, 8–9	64v An angel tells St. John to take the open book from the angel which stands on the sea	29v St. John takes the book from an angel in a cloud
XI, 1–2	65v St. John receives a reed from the angel; St. John measures the church and its worshippers	30v St. John standing before an altar and a reed
XI, 3–6	66v Two candelabra support the two witnesses; an angel holds two candles	31v Elijah carried up to heaven in a cart drawn by a horse; Enoch floating behind him
XI, 7	67v St. John observes the destruction of the two witnesses by the beast and by Antichrist on horseback	32v The beast bites the shoulder of one witness; Antichrist on horseback
XI, 9	68v St. John sits beside a town where Enoch and Elijah are observed by the multitude	33v Enoch and Elijah viewed by the multitude
XI, 11–12	69v Ascension of Enoch and Elijah	34v Ascension of Enoch and Elijah
XI, 15–16	70v The seventh angel sounds his trumpet. The Lord encircled by twenty-four elders in prayer above St. John	35v Four elders before the Lord
XII, 1–4	71v St. John observes the Woman clothed with the sun confronted by the dragon; two angels carry a crib (?)	36v The Woman, holding a palm branch and a book, standing on the moon; the seven-headed dragon with stars on his tail
XII, 7–9	72v St. John; St. Michael and his angels kill the dragon and other reptiles	37v St. Michael fights devils
XII, 14	73v The Woman winged, her child in her arms, flees from the dragon; two angels before a church	38v The Woman, with eagle's wings, flying from the dragon
XII, 15	74v The Woman, carrying her child and riding a donkey led by a man (Joseph?), flees from the dragon; above, an angel holds two crowns for the Woman and her child	39v The Woman, with her child in her arms, fleeing from the dragon
XII, 17	75v The dragon, with a human head, makes war on the family of the Woman	40v The dragon with a human head fights the family of the Woman
XIII, 1–2	76v St. John; the dragon, with a human head, gives a document to the beast, with seven heads and ten horns, emerging from the sea	41v The beast and the dragon

Rev.	CHANTILLY 28 Folio		MORGAN M. 133 Folio	
XIII, 4	77v	Men worship the beast and Antichrist, a hooded rider on horseback; St. John	42v	Men worship the dragon and Antichrist; a rider on horseback
XIII, 6	78v	Antichrist, as a bishop with a devil on his back, blasphemes the Church and the saints who are being slaughtered in the foreground	43v	Antichrist, as a bishop with a devil on his back, blasphemes the Church
XIII, 7	79v	St. John; Antichrist on horseback; men devoured by the beast (an ass with long horns with snakes wrapped around them)	44v	Antichrist, a horse crowned by three horns bearing heads, tramples on three nude saints
XIII, 11–13	80v	The two-horned beast commands worship of the first beast; St. John	45v	The two-horned beast causes fire to descend on three men
XIII, 15	81v	The two-horned beast, as a horned friar, speaks to his followers in a chapel and causes fire to descend on those without; St. John	46v	The two-horned beast, a man labeled Antichrist, threatening those unwilling to worship the image of the beast
XIII, 16	82v	St. John; Antichrist distributes effigies of the beast which he takes from a plate carried by the horned friar	47v	The worshippers of the beast receive his mark
XIV, 1–2	83v	The Lamb on Mt. Sion adored by the faithful and observed by an angel playing a *cythole* and St. John	48v	The Lamb and three saints; above, an angel playing a *cythole*
XIV, 2–3	84v	The Lord and the symbols of the Evangelists with angels playing instruments; below, St. John sleeps resting on two books	49v	The Lord and four angels playing instruments
XIV, 6	85v	St. John asleep; above the multitude an angel flies holding the Gospels	50v	An angel holding the Gospels flies over five men
XIV, 8	86v	St. John, standing with other figures, contemplates the ruins of Babylon shown to him by an angel	51v	An angel points to Babylon
XIV, 9–10	87v	St. John; a group of men contemplate two angels holding a ciborium and burettes	52v	Those who worshipped the beast led into hell by the devil
XIV, 13	88v	An angel before St. John asleep; above, the celestial court	53v	The faithful at the gate of Paradise met by St. Peter
XIV, 14–15	89v	St. John; an angel at the portal of a temple tells a crowned angel who holds a sickle and who sits on a cloud to reap the earth	54v	An angel tells a crowned angel who holds a sickle and who sits on a cloud to reap the earth
XIV, 18	90v	Before the temple an angel tells an angel with a sickle to gather grapes below; St. John	55v	An angel cutting clusters of grapes from a vine with a sickle
XIV, 19	91v	Two angels drop sickles onto the earth causing the death of men and animals; St. John	56v	Last Judgment
XV, 1	92v	The Lord in a mandorla above seven female figures standing on the sea of glass mingled with fire; St. John	57v	The seven plagues personified as sins
XV, 7	93v	The Lord worshipped; St. John asleep below (This miniature does not illustrate the text and belongs properly on fol. 104v)	58v	The seven angels with their seven vials received from the lion of St. Mark
XVI, 1–2	94v	Seven angels pour the contents of their vials on the cadavers of men and animals below; an angel blows a *buisine* as St. John sleeps	59v	The first angel pours the plague of sores upon five men

CHANTILLY 28 *Rev.*	*Folio*		MORGAN M. 133 *Folio*	
XVI, 3	95v	St. John and some men watch the second angel pour the contents of his vial into the sea	60v	The second angel pours his vial on the sea
XVI, 8–9	96v	The fourth angel throws flames on the figures seeking refuge under trees and rocks; St. John	61v	The fourth angel pours his vial to scorch the men and animals attempting to hide below
XVI, 10	97v	The fifth angel pours the contents of his vial on different figures among which are some ecclesiastical personages; St. John	62v	The fifth angel pours his vial upon five heretic ecclesiastics
XVI, 13	98v	Black spirits issue from the mouths of the beast, the dragon and the false prophet; St. John	63v	The seven-headed dragon emits unclean spirits (devils)
XVI, 17–18	99v	The seventh angel destroys houses and temples; St. John	64v	The seventh angel pours his vial causing an earthquake
XVII, 1–2	100v	One of the seven angels speaks to St. John; the great whore, who by confusion has the sun on her head and the moon at her feet, with two men (partly from commentary)	65v	The Woman clothed with the sun enthroned, her feet on a round moon and her head crowned by the sun (from commentary)
XVII, 3–4	101v	An angel shows St. John the whore, crowned and holding a chalice. She rides a beast with six serpent heads and a lion's head with ten horns	66v	The great whore holding a cup and riding the seven-headed beast
XVIII, 1–2	102v	St. John and the angel; the ruins of Babylon become the dwelling of devils	67v	An angel announces the fall of Babylon which has become the habitation of devils
XVIII, 21	103v	The angel who throws the millstone into the sea is watched by the multitude of disloyal persons; St. John	68v	An angel casts a stone like a millstone into the sea
XIX, 1	104v	The winged lion gives the seven angels the seven vials; St. John (This miniature does not illustrate the text and belongs on fol. 93v)	69v	The Lord and four angels, playing instruments, rejoice over the destruction of the great whore
XIX, 6–8	105v	St. John hears the voice of many waters (figures stand around a spring); the bride of the Lamb encircled by a group of figures	70v	St. John sleeps; two men sit with open books before water
XIX, 9	106v	The celestial court prays before St. John the Baptist who holds the Lamb above the angel and St. John	71v	St. John writing and the Baptist holding the Lamb
XIX, 11–15	107v	The angel shows St. John the Faithful One on a white horse and his army	72v	The Faithful One, crowned, a sword in his mouth and riding a white horse, accompanied by four horsemen of his army
XIX, 17–18	108v	An angel, standing in the sun, calls the birds to feast on the men and animals below; St. John	73v	An angel calling the birds to feast on the men and animals below
XIX, 19	109v	The Woman mounted on the beast with kings on horseback; the Lamb on a horse accompanied by saints; St. John	74v	The Woman mounted on the beast, labeled Antichrist, ready for combat
XIX, 20	110v	The beast enchained; the damned thrown into hell; St. John	75v	An angel enchains the beast
XX, 1–3	111v	The dragon enchained by an angel who holds the key to the abyss; St. John	76v	An angel with the key to the abyss casts the devil into the abyss

CHANTILLY 28 *Rev.*	*Folio*		MORGAN M. 133 *Folio*	
XX, 4	112v	The Lord enthroned in a mandorla, the celestial court, and below the dead with their souls issuing from them; an angel takes St. John's soul	77v	The Lord, with four saints, judges three nude bodies below
XX, 7–8	113v	Satan at the entrance to the abyss; St. John	78v	Satan at the entrance to the abyss
XX, 10	114v	St. John watches devils plunged by angels into the lake of fire where is the beast	79v	The devil is cast into the mouth of hell
XX, 11–12	115v	The Lord reads the Book of Life, supported by an angel, in a mandorla between the Virgin and St. John the Baptist; below the blessed, and the damned enchained	80v	An angel, holding the Book of Life, before the Lord; below, the resurrection of the dead
XXI, 2	116v	Jerusalem represented as a church in which the Lord marries Adam and Eve; St. John with the angel, writes in the foreground	81v	The Lord marrying Adam and Eve; above, a vision of the new Jerusalem
XXI, 9–10	117v	The angel shows the soul of St. John a vision of the Bride of the Lamb kneeling before Jerusalem	82v	The bride kneeling before the Lamb outside of Jerusalem
XXII, 1–2	118v	The angel shows the soul of St. John a vision in heaven of the Lamb from whose seat flows the water of life onto an arbor below	83v	The river, proceeding from the Lamb, and the tree of life
XXII, 8–9	119v	The Lord with the symbols of the Evangelists and twenty-four elders; below, the Lamb shows a book to St. John	84v	St. John kneels before the angel who shows him a book
XXII, 18	120v	On the left, the Lord shows a book to St. John who kneels before him; on the right, St. John shows the book to a group of figures	85v	St. John testifies to the prophecy of the book before several men

VIRGIL, ECLOGUES AND GEORGICS

The copies of Virgil in Lyon and in Holkham Hall have the same program of illustration for the *Eclogues* and *Georgics*. The cycle in Lyon, illustrated by the Master of the Roman Texts and an assistant, may have been the model for the copy in Holkham Hall, which was illustrated by the Luçon workshop. Both copies were illuminated about 1411.

For these two manuscripts see the chapter "Virgil."

Lyon

BIBLIOTHEQUE, ms. 27
(Figs. 226, 228, 232–236, 239, 241, 243, 245, 247, 250, 251)

Virgil, *Eclogues*, *Georgics* and *Aeneid*. 248 fols.; 248 × 170 mm.

EARLY HISTORY: There are no marks of original ownership. The manuscript may have been intended, however, for the unknown patron of a Terence now in Paris (lat. 8193), which was likewise illustrated by the Roman Texts Master. The manuscript was part of a gift made in 1769 by Pierre Adamoli, a collector in Lyon, to the Academy of Lyon.

STYLE AND DATE: Although the text was completed in the first decade of the fifteenth century, the illustrations were executed in three campaigns. About 1411 the Roman Texts Master and an assistant painted the miniatures through the *Georgics*. In the mid-fifteenth century an indifferent illuminator executed those on fols. 66–108 in the *Aeneid*. Fols. 121–232 were finished only in the late fifteenth century. No vines or other decoration was intended in the borders.

BIBLIOGRAPHY: Lyon, Bibl., *Cat. général des mss.*, XXX, 1898, p. 9 f.; Lyon, Bibl. (Leroquais), 1920, p. 25 no. 30, pl. XXXI; Cotton, 1965, pp. 266, 289, figs. 48a, 48b.

Holkham Hall (Norfolk)

COLL. OF THE EARL OF LEICESTER, ms. 307 (Figs. 227, 229, 237, 238, 240, 242, 244, 246)

Virgil, *Eclogues* and *Georgics* with the commentary of Servius. 129 fols.; 278 ×200 mm.

EARLY HISTORY: At the end of the manuscript a name, partially erased, is followed by "scripsit." Dorez reconstructed R[aphaël de Marca]tellis from the letters which he could still distinguish and suggested that the manuscript belonged to Raphaël de Marcatel, a natural son of Philippe le Bon. But Raphael surely could not have written the manuscript; he died in 1508. Although not illuminated in Lyon, the manuscript found its way there; it was described in an inventory of the Augustinians. Thomas Coke, builder of the existing Holkham Hall, acquired the Virgil in Lyon in 1713.

STYLE AND DATE: A miniature illustrates each book as well as the beginning of the commentary of Servius on fol. 54. There is also an illustration of the zones of the earth in the middle of the first book of the *Georgics*. The Luçon workshop illuminated the text *ca.* 1411–1412, using as a model the Lyon Virgil or a lost manuscript with a similar cycle of miniatures.

BIBLIOGRAPHY: Holkham Hall (Dorez), 1908, p. 61 f., pls. XL–XLI; Meiss, *Art Bull.*, 1956, p. 193 n. 23; *idem*, *Late XIV Century*, 1967, p. 358.

	LYON	HOLKHAM	
Eclogue	*Folio*	*Folio*	
I	1v	1	Tityrus and Meliboeus
II	3v	6v	Corydon courts Alexis
III	5	11	Palaemon judges a musical contest between Damoetas and Menalcas
IV	8	17	Virgil, writing, celebrates the birth of Pollio's son
V	9	20	Mopsus and Menalcas mourn the death of Daphnis
VI	11	23v	Chromis, Mnasylos and Aegle, a nymph, find Silenus asleep
VII	13	28	Meliboeus or Daphnis judges a musical contest between Thyrsis and Corydon
VIII	14v	31	Damon mourns the loss of his mistress who departs with Mopsus; a witch casts a spell to obtain Daphnis' love
IX	17	35v	Lycidas and Moeris, Virgil's bailiff
X	18v	38v	Virgil consoles Gallus at the loss of his mistress

Georgic	*Folio*	*Folio*	
I	20v	43	Virgil honors Augustus and invokes the earth goddess
		54	Commentary of Servius (added later)
II	30	67v	Bacchus oversees planting and pruning
III	40	88v	Breeding and care of cows and horses
IV	51	109v	Beekeeping

CATALOGUE OF SINGLE MANUSCRIPTS IN TOPOGRAPHICAL ORDER

Baltimore

WALTERS ART GALLERY, ms. 219
(Figs. 522, 523, 528, 623, 624)

Book of Hours, Paris calendar. 265 fols.; 135×99 mm.

EARLY HISTORY: No evidence of the original owner. Unidentified arms of the late fifteenth century on the foredges and in the margins.

STYLE AND DATE: This Book of Hours has a very unusual cycle of illustrations, which has been described by Dorothy Miner as follows: "The Lessons are illustrated not by the usual representations of the Evangelists themselves, but by some incident drawn from their Gospels. The miniatures of the Hours of the Virgin select their themes from the contents of the Psalms for the respective office, sometimes representing Old Testament subjects such as the victory of David over Goliath at Lauds or the Crossing of the Red Sea at Vespers, at other times allegorically rendering some verse in the contingent Psalms, such as Mercy and Truth meeting each other, and Peace and Justice kissing (Psalm 84:11), at Prime. To clarify the significance of such scenes a little historiated initial, introducing the text below, often encloses a prophet with a banderoll inscribed with the pertinent words." (*International Style*, 1962, p. 62 f.)

The style of the illumination is as unusual as its iconography. The artist responsible for all the work except four miniatures by the Breviary Master is so profoundly Italian that he probably was, in our opinion, a painter first trained in Lombardy who had settled in eastern France. In Lombard prayer books of the late fourteenth century, such as Paris, Bibl. nat., Smith-Lesouëf 22, prophets appear in initials at the beginning of the Offices. In the manner of Lombard illuminators the Walters Master laid out his leaves, flowers, and plants in the borders as if they were specimens on display.

The four miniatures on fols. 249v–255 in the style of the Breviary Master (see the chapter on this illuminator) were pasted into rectangular frames prepared for them (as L. M. J. Delaissé observed). The frames of all preceding miniatures are arched. The Walters Master gave his final miniature, on fol. 257, a rectangular shape also. He sought conformity, too, by abandoning on this last folio the more traditional acanthus that he had introduced into all the borders up to 249v, the first folio designed to contain a miniature by the Breviary Master.

The illumination is more easily dated by the miniatures in the Breviary style than by those of the Master of Walters 219. The *Baptist* and the *Martyrdom of St. Denis and his companions*, with their very advanced pointillism, probably are the latest works we have by the Breviary Master. They were not painted, therefore, before *ca.* 1418.

BIBLIOGRAPHY: De Ricci, *Census*, I, 1935, p. 791 no. 215; Baltimore, Walters (Miner), 1949, p. 33 no. 87, pl. XXXVIII; Meiss, *Art Bull.*, 1956, p. 195, figs. 8, 9; Baltimore, Walters, *International Style* (Miner), 1962, pp. 62–64 no. 58, pl. LVI; Meiss, *Late XIV Century*, 1967, pp. 355, 360; *idem*, *Boucicaut Master*, 1968, pp. 25, 101, fig. 479; *idem*, "Breviary Master," 1970, p. 11, pl. XIIa.

MINIATURES:

Folio
16 Creation of Eve (Lection from John)
18v Marriage of the Virgin (Lection from Luke)
21 Massacre of the Innocents (Lection from Matthew)
23v St. John the Evangelist revives two men (Lection from Mark)

Hours of the Virgin
26 Virgin embroiders the veil with stars and moon (Matins)
55 David cuts off the tongue of the slain Goliath (Lauds)
74 Justice and Peace kiss; three men aid a poor cripple (Prime)
80v Battle of St. Michael and Devil for soul of a dying man (Terce)
86v Garden party surprised by Death riding in on an ox (Sext)
92 God gives Adam and Eve the spade and spindle; Eve nurses Cain and Abel (None)
98 Pharoah's army pursues Moses and the Israelites (Vespers)
109v Flagellation (Compline)

Penitential Psalms
130 Last Judgment

Hours of the Cross
158 Crucifixion

Hours of the Holy Ghost

165	Trinity

Office of the Dead

171v	Raising of Lazarus

Prayer to the Virgin

234	Bishop saint presents donor to the Virgin and Child

Suffrages

240v	Mass of St. Gregory
245	St. Nicholas saves a ship in a storm
246v	St. Anthony tempted by demons
248	St. Catherine before the Doctors
249v	St. John the Baptist
251	St. Christopher
253	Martyrdom of St. Denis and his companions
255	Martyrdom of St. Sebastian
257	St. Margaret

Barcelona

BIBL. CENTRAL, ms. 1850

Book of Hours (in Latin and French). 202 fols.; 157×113 mm.

EARLY HISTORY: The original owner was probably the lady before St. Anne and the Virgin on fol. 181, but there are no clues to her identity.

STYLE AND DATE: The Cité des Dames Master painted the miniatures on fols. 1v and 2 and, with an assistant, the last six miniatures from fol. 181. The Luçon Master painted all the other miniatures. This manuscript has a peculiar importance because it bears a date. An inscription on fol. 25v reads: "L'an de grace mil quatre cens et un furent faitez ces heures p Colin le besc." Colin may be identical with Jean Colin from whom Jean de Berry acquired manuscripts (Guiffrey, *Inventaires*, I, 1894, p. 254 no. 962 and II, 1896, p. 338). This inscription was written in the section illuminated by the Luçon Master. Although the first two miniatures are on a separate sheet and fol. 181 begins a new gathering, there is no reason to believe that the illustrations on these folios by the Cité des Dames workshop are not contemporary with the Luçon miniatures. These last miniatures, furthermore, illustrate the Suffrages, an important part of a Book of Hours, and they were therefore doubtless executed at the same time.

BIBLIOGRAPHY: *Inventario de la colección de libros donada per D. Santiago España y Brunet*, 1960, no. 5; Bohigas, 1964, pp. 48–57, pls. 9, 9 bis; Kreuter-Eggemann, *Daliwe*, 1964, I, fig. 11; Meiss, *Late XIV Century*, 1967, index, figs. 334, 705, 706, 810; *idem*, "*Decameron*," 1967, p. 60, fig. 9.

MINIATURES:

Folio

1v	St. Gregory kneels before Man of Sorrows
2	Assumption of the Virgin
3–14v	Calendar
23	Madonna and Child
26v	Four Evangelists

Hours of the Virgin

32	Annunciation
53v	Visitation
64	Nativity
70	Annunciation to the Shepherds
74v	Adoration of the Magi
78v	Presentation in the Temple
83	Flight into Egypt
90	Coronation of the Virgin

Penitential Psalms

96	David prays

Hours of the Cross

114v	Two angels hold the Cross and instruments of the Passion

Hours of the Holy Ghost

122v	Pentecost

Office of the Dead

129	Last Judgment
172	*Fons Vitae*
177v	Man of Sorrows (Doulz dieu)

Suffrages

181	Female donor before St. Anne and the Virgin
183	Three Marys
184	St. Michael
187	St. Sebastian
188v	St. Christopher
195v	St. Claude
197	St. Genevieve

Brussels

BIBL. ROYALE, ms. 9393

See Christine de Pisan, *Cité des Dames*

Brussels

BIBL. ROYALE, ms. 9508

See Christine de Pisan, *Mutacion*

Cambridge, England

FITZWILLIAM MUSEUM, ms. 62 (Figs. 857, 862, 863, 865–867)

Book of Hours, Use of Paris. 234 fols.; 248×178 mm.

EARLY HISTORY: The original owner can at best be inferred. The manuscript shows the arms of Isabel Stuart, daughter of James I of Scotland, after her marriage in 1442 to Francis I Duke of Brittany. It is presumably her portrait that appears on folio 20. The first wife of Francis I was Yolande d'Anjou, whom he married in 1431 and who died in 1440. She was the daughter of Louis II of Anjou and of Yolande d'Aragon, who probably was a patron of the Rohan Master.

STYLE AND DATE: Although all of this extensively illustrated Book of Hours is in the Rohan style the master himself painted only a few figures—the superb Christ as Man of Sorrows, the Madonna and Child between Peter and Paul, and the standing Madonna and Child.

Borrowings from the Boucicaut workshop indicate a date towards 1417–1418. The *Annunciation* is remarkably close to a late Boucicaut composition of this scene, particularly the one in a Book of Hours, executed *ca.* 1415–1417, in a private collection. Boucicaut designs of about 1415, such as those in the Mazarine Hours, are reflected in the scenes in the borders framed by vines and flowers which form roundels. The ecclesiastical structure sheltering the standing Madonna and Child was adapted from a Limbourg composition of *ca.* 1411 reflected in the frontispiece to fr. 166 by the Master of St. Jerome.

BIBLIOGRAPHY: Cambridge, Fitzwilliam Museum (James), 1895, pp. 156–174; Fry, 1905, pp. 435–443; Durrieu, *Rev. de l'art a. et m.*, 1912, pp. 167–170; Heimann, 1932, pp. 5–10, figs. 6–9; Wescher, 1946, p. 33 f., fig. 3; Toynbee, 1946; Ring, *French Painting* [1949], p. 203 f.; Panofsky, 1949, pp. 167 n. 9, 171 n. 14, 180–182; *idem, Netherlandish Painting*, 1953, p. 262 n. 262[6]; Porcher, *Belles Heures*, 1953, p. 27 n. 52; Meiss, *Gaz. B.-A.*, 1963, pp. 147 f., 152 f., fig. 4; Cambridge, Fitzwilliam Museum (Wormald and Giles), 1966, p. 30 no. 68, pl. 19; Meiss, *Boucicaut Master*, 1968, p. 71, fig. 483.

MINIATURES:

Folio

1–12v Calendar
13 St. John the Evangelist
14v St. Luke
16v St. Matthew
18v St. Mark
20 St. Catherine presents a donor to the Virgin and Child (Obsecro te)
24 Virgin and Child (O Intemerata)

Hours of the Virgin

29 Annunciation
53 Visitation
65 Adoration of the Child at the Nativity
71 Annunciation to the Shepherds
76 Adoration of the Magi
81 Presentation in the Temple
86 Flight into Egypt
93 Coronation of the Virgin by the Trinity

Penitential Psalms

99 Trinity

Hours of the Cross

119 Nailing of Christ to the Cross and Crucifixion

Hours of the Holy Ghost

127 Pentecost

134 Deposition (Passio sec. Johannem)
136v Virgin and Child between Peter and Paul, all half-figures on a crescent. The Trinity above (Creator coeli)
141v Virgin and Child (Quinque gaudia B.M.V.)

Office of the Dead

147 Funeral service

192 Virgin and Child (Doulce dame de misericorde)
199 Man of Sorrows (Sept requêtes)

Each folio has a small oblong miniature in the border. These miniatures form continuous illustrations of Guillaume de Deguilleville's *Pèlerinage de Jhesucrist*, the *Pèlerinage de vie humaine* and the *Pèlerinage de l'âme*, and the *Apocalypse* of St. John. On the remaining folios miniatures in the border illustrate subjects suggested by the text or various legends.

Cambridge, U. S. A.

HARVARD COLLEGE (HOUGHTON) LIBRARY, Richardson ms. 42

(Figs. 842–845, 852–854)

Book of Hours (*De Buz Hours*), Use of Paris. 197 fols.; 232×165 mm.

EARLY HISTORY: There are no indications of original ownership, but in the second quarter of the sixteenth century the manuscript was in the possession of Antoine de Buz, Seigneur de Villemareule, and his wife Barbe de Loan (or Louen).

STYLE AND DATE: The strongest miniatures in this beautiful manuscript—the Virgin with the sleeping Child, for example—are unusual in the Rohan group because of their stylistic resemblances to the *Belles Heures*. One composition, furthermore—the *Annunciation to the Shepherds*—is largely based on the corresponding miniature in that manuscript. The averted Virgin in the *Flight into Egypt* was probably inspired by the *Belles Heures* also. Whether or not the Rohan

Master himself painted a few figures in the best miniatures, he certainly designed them and supervised the execution closely. Like most of the Rohan manuscripts this is difficult to date precisely, but we suggest *ca.* 1415.

BIBLIOGRAPHY: Panofsky, 1949; Baltimore, Walters (Miner), 1949, p. 36 no. 96, pl. XLIII; Panofsky, *Netherlandish Painting*, 1953, I, nn. 61[1], 133[1], 137[6], 287[3], II, fig. 96; Cambridge, Harvard University, 1955, p. 21 no. 64, pl. 29; Baltimore, Walters, *International Style* [Miner], 1962, pp. 60–62 no. 57, pl. LXI; Cleveland, Mus. of Art (Wixom), 1967, pp. 284, 381; Meiss, *Boucicaut Master*, 1968, p. 147 n. 30.

MINIATURES:

Folio	
1–11	Calendar (January missing)
12	St. John
14	St. Luke
16	St. Matthew
18	St. Mark
Hours of the Virgin	
20	Annunciation
32	Visitation
45	Adoration of the Child at the Nativity
52	Annunciation to the Shepherds
57	Adoration of the Magi
62	Presentation in the Temple
67	Flight into Egypt
75	Coronation of the Virgin
Hours of the Cross	
82	Descent from the Cross and Lamentation
Hours of the Holy Ghost	
86	Pentecost
Penitential Psalms	
90	Last Judgment (David prays in lower border)
108	Virgin and Child (Fifteen Joys of the Virgin)
114	Trinity (*Sept requêtes*)
Office of the Dead	
118	Burial service in a cemetery
151	Virgin and Child (*Obsecro te*)
155	Virgin and Child (*Je te salue, Maria*)

Chantilly

MUSEE CONDE, ms. 28

See St. John, *Apocalypse*

Chantilly

MUSEE CONDE, ms. 65 (Figs. 536–597, 643, 644, 646, 647, 721)

Très Riches Heures. Book of Hours, Use of Paris. 206 fols.; 290×210 mm. *Ca.* 1411–1416.

The manuscript, still unfinished and unbound, is described in the inventory drawn up after the Duke's death in June, 1416 as "plusieurs cayers d'une tres Riches Heures que faisoit Pol et ses freres."

Subjects of the Parts of this Entry:

MEASUREMENTS OF MINIATURES AND MARGINS
GATHERINGS AND DESCRIPTION
ESTIMATE OF THE MISSING TEXT, HOURS OF THE PASSION
OBSERVATIONS ON THE HISTORY OF THE TRES RICHES HEURES
BIBLIOGRAPHY

MEASUREMENTS OF MINIATURES AND MARGINS

Dimension in parenthesis records highest or widest point

	Folio	Dimensions of min. (dimensions include frames) *Height*	*Width*	Outer margin	Top margin	Bottom margin (from text where it exists)
Miniature in first plan		132–144 mm.	112–115 mm.	69–74 mm.	36–47 mm.	80–90 mm.
Miniature in first plan plus four lines of text		161–171 mm.	112–115 mm.	69–74 mm.	36–47 mm.	80–90 mm.
January	1v	241	153	38	5	42
February	2v	223	136	45	5	61
March	3v	217	137	48	9	62
April	4v	217	139	44	12	62

	Folio	Dimensions of min. *Height*	*Width*	Outer margin	Top margin	Bottom margin
May	5v	217	138	44	11	62
June	6v	225	137	43	7	59
July	7v	224	136	44	7	59
August	8v	225	137	43	7	60
September	9v	224	138	43	10	59
October	10v	223	135	48	8	60
November	11v	226	134	48	7	55
December	12v	223	134	48	11	58
Zodiacal Man	14v	249	194			
St. John on Patmos	17	141 (171)	113	71	40 (10)	87
St. Mark dragged to martyrdom	19v	142 (168)	112	72	40 (12)	90
The Fall of Man	25v					
The Annunciation	26	132 (159)	115	70	47 (19)	81
The Visitation	38v	134 (163)	112	70	43 (15)	82
The Nativity	44v	133 (160)	112	73	45 (19)	83
Annunciation to the Shepherds	48	133 (162)	112	68	47 (19)	83
Meeting of the Magi near Paris	51v	188 (217)	147	26	44 (20)	57
Adoration of the Magi	52	184 (212)	147	27	45 (19)	57
Purification of the Virgin	54v	180 (205)	145	45	31 (7)	77
Coronation of the Virgin	60v	134 (157)	116 (165)	41 (67)	46 (23)	79
Fall of the Rebel Angels	64v	198 (223)	143	39	39 (14)	50
Procession of St. Gregory	71v	225 (251)	196	10	46 (19)	18
Procession of St. Gregory	72	228	194	15	44	18
Funeral of Diocrès	86v	133 (168)	112	31	10	35
Hell	108	187 (210)	153	34	45 (22)	56
Plan of Rome	141v	190 diameter		7	52	47
Christ in Gethsemane	142v	177	126	59	39	74
Christ led to the Praetorium	143	176 (210)	132	43	22 (10)	70
Flagellation	144	166 (183)	116	67	45 (27)	78
Christ leaving the Praetorium	146v	188	131 (153)	64 (53)	23	78
Christ bearing the Cross	147	188	122 (147)	67 (42)	24	77
Death of Christ	153	168 (194)	115 (144)	70 (38)	40 (17)	81 (48)
Deposition	156v	171 (190)	117	69	41 (23)	77
Christmas Mass	158	133 (164)	110	71	46 (15)	81
The Devil tempting Christ	161v	136 (169)	114	68	44 (11)	80
Healing of the Dumb-Possessed	166	135 (164)	113	71	40 (11)	85
Feeding of the Five Thousand	168v	135 (160)	114	69	46 (21)	81
Raising of Lazarus	171	137 (168)	113	74	43 (12)	83
Entry into Jerusalem	173v	144 (162)	115	72	37 (17)	80
Exaltation of the Cross	193	134 (173)	114	70	42 (4)	85
St. Michael slaying the dragon above Mont-Saint-Michel	195	133 (164)	113 (130)	69 (51)	44 (12)	85

GATHERINGS AND DESCRIPTION

A miniature described as first plan closely approximates the dimensions given at the head of the preceding table; the four lines of text beneath are laid out in double columns. A second plan miniature is much larger and has no text beneath. Departures from the norm with respect to shape, borders, etc., all discussed in the text, are classified here simply as variants or modifications. Unless otherwise stated all script, all small initials, and all line endings are from the period of the Limbourgs. Only those line endings are noted that may possibly be associated with the work of certain decorators. No distinction is made between the work of Colombe and of his assistants. It was necessary to analyze the present makeup of the manuscript in a *bound* book, which of course had to be treated with the greatest care. I studied the upper and lower edges of the vellum under magnification. I would be more skeptical of my observations if they had not agreed in essential points with those of Durrieu.

TABLE OF VARIATIONS WITHIN CALENDAR TEXT

	Folio (and conjugate folio)	Feasts in gold not filled in	Latin Headings	Pale Red Ink	Painters of Initials: Spindly Master	Painters of Initials: Dry Master	Painters of Initials: Plush Master	Calendrical Data in Miniature on verso missing	Painter of Miniature on verso
Gathering 1									
Blank	1 (8)							x	Jean (Jan.)
January	2 (7)	x			x				Paul (Feb.)
February	3 (6)				x				Paul & Colombe (Mar.)
March	4 (5)	x	x	x		x		x	Jean (April)
April	5 (4)	x	x	x		x		x	Jean (May)
May	6 (3)				x				Paul & Jean or Herman, & Colombe (?) (June)
June	7 (2)	x			x				Paul (July)
July	8 (1)	x	x	x	x			x	Jean (Aug.)
Gathering 2									
August	9 (12)						x		Paul & Colombe (Sept.)
September	10 (11)						x		Paul & Colombe (?) (Oct.)
October	11 (10)						x		Colombe (Nov.)
November	12 (9)						x		Paul (Dec.)
Gathering 3									
December	13 (16)						x		

GATHERING 1

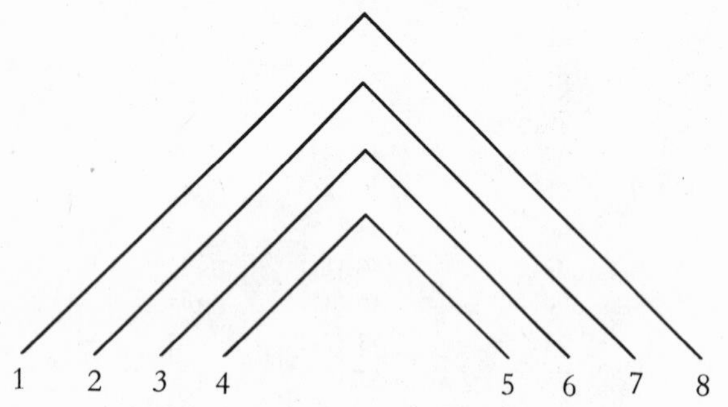

GATHERING 3

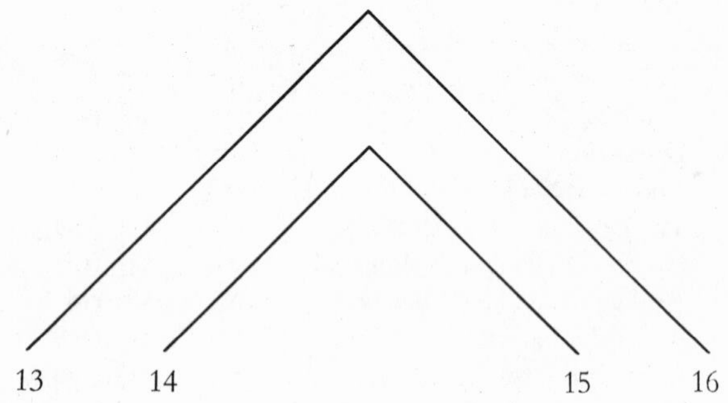

GATHERING 2

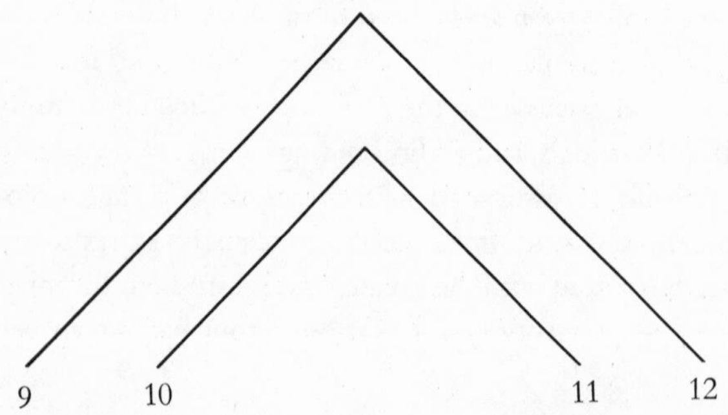

TEXT: 13 December calendar.
Blank folios: 13v, 16 ruled rectangles; 14, 15, 15v unruled; 16v two horizontal lines ruled.

MINIATURE: 14v *Zodiacal Man*. Paul and Jean.

DECORATION: 14v Limbourgs.

GATHERING 4

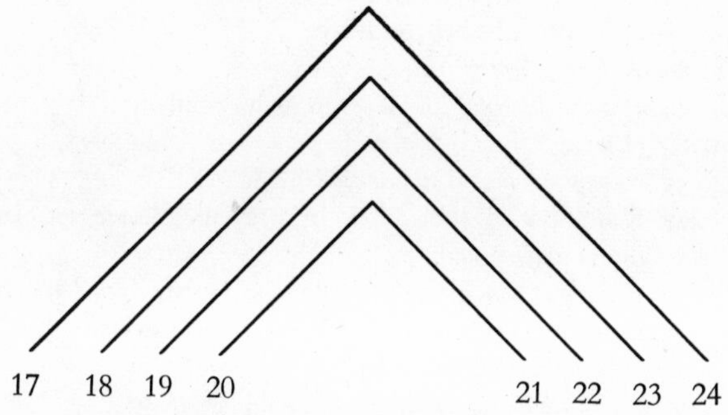

TEXT: Gospel readings

17, 17v John 1, 1–14 and rubric for Luke.
18, 18v Luke 1, 26–38.
18v, 19 Matthew 2, 1–12.
19v, 20 Mark 16, 14–20.
Prayers to the Virgin
20–21v *Obsecro te.*
22–23v O *Intemerata.*
24, 24v blank, ruled for two text columns.

MINIATURES:

17 *St. John.* Paul and collaborator, tooled haloes by Breviary Master. 1st plan but only 3 lines of text.
18 *St. Luke,* with symbol of Matthew.
18v *St. Matthew,* with symbol of Luke.
19v *St. Mark.* Jean and Herman (?). Tooled halo and chasuble of Mark, chalice and gold border of altar by Breviary Master. 1st plan but only 3 lines of text.
22 *Aracoeli.* Madonna by Paul. Augustus and Sibyl by Herman (?). Tooled haloes and crescent by Breviary Master.

INITIALS AND DECORATION:

17–18v, 19v, 20, 22 by Breviary Master and assistant.
18, 18v symbols of Matthew and Luke and associated foliage by Limbourgs.

LINE ENDINGS:

17v, 23v foliate.

GATHERING 5

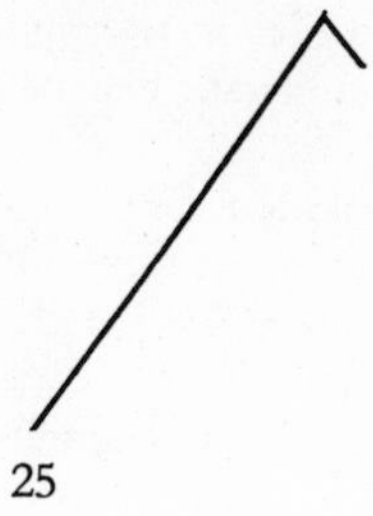

Single leaf, conjugate stub passes round gathering 6.
Much heavier parchment.
25 Blank. Unruled.

MINIATURE:

25v *Fall of Man.* Jean. Unruled.

GATHERING 6

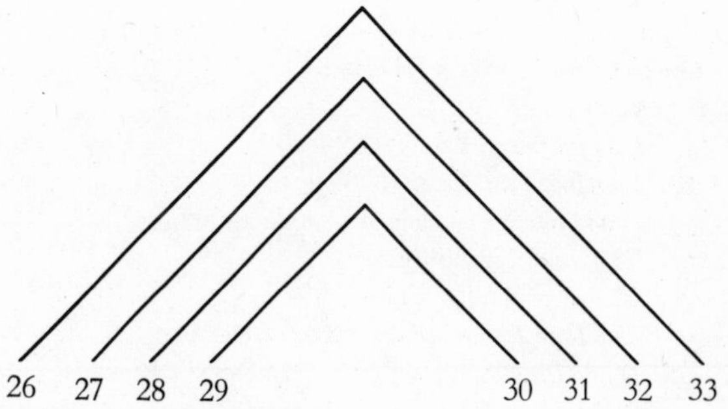

TEXT: Hours of the Virgin

26v–33v Matins.
All seven psalms along with *tituli* in alternate lines of blue and gold. Correct catchword on fol. 33v.

MINIATURES:

26 *Annunciation* by Jean on design of Paul, haloes and Gabriel's dalmatic by Breviary Master. 1st plan.
26v *David contemplates Christ Child,* Ps. 94 (95). Herman.
27v *David praises God,* Ps. 8. Herman.
28 *Apostles preaching,* Ps. 18 (19). Herman (?).
29 *Ark entering Temple,* Ps. 23 (24). Herman.
31 *Christ and the Church,* Ps. 44 (45). Jean.
32 *Korah and his sons,* Ps. 45 (46). Limbourgs.
32v *David and the Church,* Ps. 86 (87). Limbourgs.

INITIALS AND DECORATION:

26 border by Jean (?), but two lower shields, bears, and swans by Breviary Master, who also painted the two large initials.
26v initial and decoration prepared by Breviary Master, head in initial by Colombe, drawing of iris in pot by Limbourgs (Paul?).
27, 27v, 28, 29, 30, 30v, 31, 32, 32v all initials and decoration by Breviary Master and assistant.
33, 33v incomplete decoration; three initials prepared by Breviary Master, heads only by Colombe.

LINE ENDINGS:

26, 26v, 27, 28, 28v, 29, 29v, 31, 31v, 32, 32v, all include foliate endings.

GATHERING 7

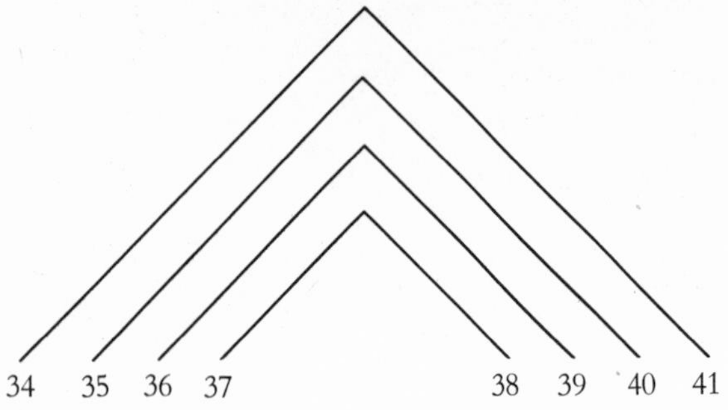

TEXT: Hours of the Virgin
34–37 Matins continued.
37v, 38 *Te Deum*, rubric for Lauds.
38v–41v Lauds.
Blank spaces for *tituli* of all eight psalm miniatures.
Correct catchword on fol. 41v.

MINIATURES:
34 *Last Judgment*, Ps. 95 (96). Jean(?).
34v *Last Judgment*, Ps. 96 (97). Jean.
35v *David foresees building of Temple*, Ps. 97 (98).
37v *Te Deum*. Limbourgs.
38v *Visitation*. Paul. 1st plan.
39 *The Lord Enthroned*, Ps. 92 (93). Herman (?).
39v *David Praying*, Ps. 99 (100) and *David's Vision of Resurrection*, Ps. 62 (63). Herman (?).
40v *Fiery Furnace*, Canticle.
41v *Christ in Majesty*, Ps. 148 (149). Jean (?).

INITIALS AND DECORATION:
34, 34v, 35v, 36, 36v, 37v, all by Breviary Master himself.
38v all by Paul, but initial and tooled gold around it by Breviary Master.
39, 39v all, and tooled gold in miniatures, by Breviary Master.
40, 40v by Breviary Master.
41v all, and tooled gold in miniature, by Breviary Master.

LINE ENDINGS:
No foliates.

GATHERING 8

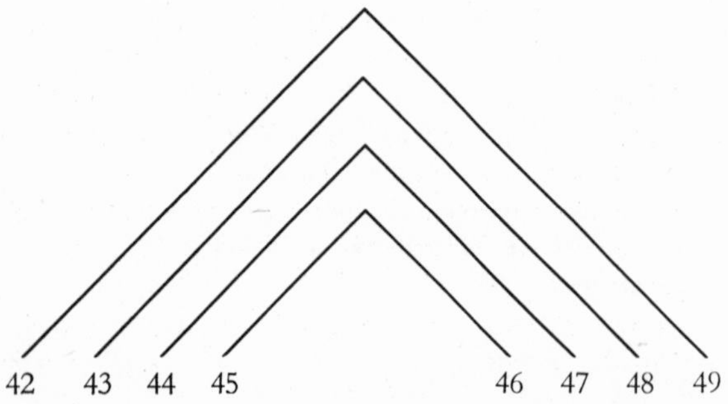

TEXT: Hours of the Virgin
42–44 Lauds continued. Rubric for Prime.
44v–47v Prime. Rubric for Terce.
48–49v Terce.
Blank spaces for *tituli* of all seven psalm miniatures.

MINIATURES:
43v *Annunciation to Zachariah*, Canticle. Jean.
44v *Nativity*. Paul, tooled halo by Breviary Master. 1st plan.
45 *David playing harp*, Ps. 1.
45v *Victorious King*, Ps. 2. Tooled halo by Breviary Master.
46v *David beseeching the Lord*, Ps. 5. Tooled halo by Breviary Master.
48 *Annunciation to the Shepherds*. Paul. 1st plan.
48v *David in Prayer*, Ps. 119 (120).
49 *David and captives released*, Ps. 120 (121). Herman.
49v *David before Temple in construction*, Ps. 121 (122).
Limbourg psalm miniatures end.
Large 1st plan miniatures lack borders.

INITIALS AND BORDERS:
42–45v, 46v–49v by Breviary Master and assistant.

GATHERING 9

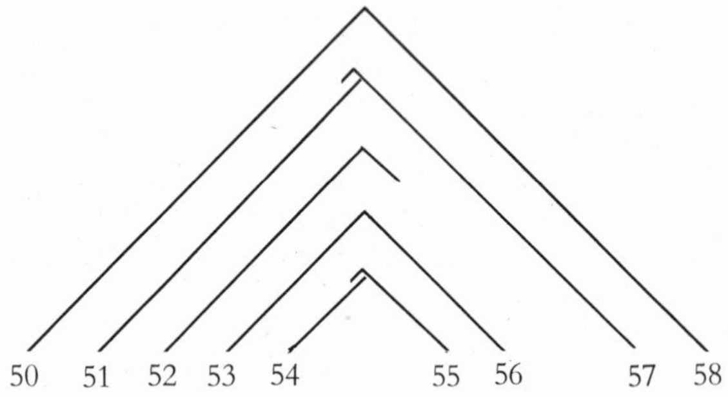

As the diagram shows, fol. 51 is pasted to conjugate stub of 57; fol. 52 is attached to small stub passing around 56; fol. 54 is pasted to conjugate stub of 55.

TEXT: Hours of the Virgin
50, 50v Terce continued. Rubric for Sext.
51 Blank, unruled.
52v–54 Sext. Rubric for None.
52v Beginning of Office and hymn *Veni Creator Spiritus* considerably contracted to 22 column lines (identical text in Terce 30 column lines). Script in brown ink by scribe of Colombe. Ruled at this time.
53 Unusually many contractions in 1st column, *Gloria* omitted, script heavier and bolder than preceding Limbourg scribe; ink black.
53v Script similar to 53 but ink faded.
54 Brown ink, Colombe scribe, including rubric in red, *Ad nonam*. No line endings. Single leaf glued to stub of 55.
55–56v None.
55 Lacks those lines of text at beginning of Office that appeared below 1st plan miniatures in preceding Hours.
55v, 56 No unusual contractions.

56v Concluding prayer for None, *Ecclesiam tuam* . . . , here reduced to *Eccamt'*, normally occupies a minimum of 9 column lines. No room for Vespers rubric.

57–58v Vespers

57 Rubric *Ad vesperam* precedes text below miniature. Certainly original; followed by Limbourg line ending.

57v–58v Text normal but no spaces left for miniatures for the 5 psalms.

MINIATURES:

51v *Meeting of the Magi.* 2nd plan. Herman (?). Unruled.
52 *Adoration of the Magi.* 2nd plan. Paul. Unruled.
52v Psalm miniature. Colombe.
53 Psalm miniature. Colombe.
53v Psalm miniature. Colombe.
54v *Purification of the Virgin.* Herman. 2nd plan.
55 Psalm miniature. Colombe.
55v Psalm miniature. Colombe.
56 Psalm miniature. Colombe.
57 *Rest on the Flight into Egypt.* Prepared for 1st plan, including ruling, but painted by Colombe.

INITIALS AND DECORATION:

Entire gathering by Colombe.

LINE ENDINGS:

All Limbourg period, except 52v by Colombe (54 has none).
Foliate endings: 50, 55v, 57v, 58, 58v.
Row of pots: 55v, 56.

GATHERING 10

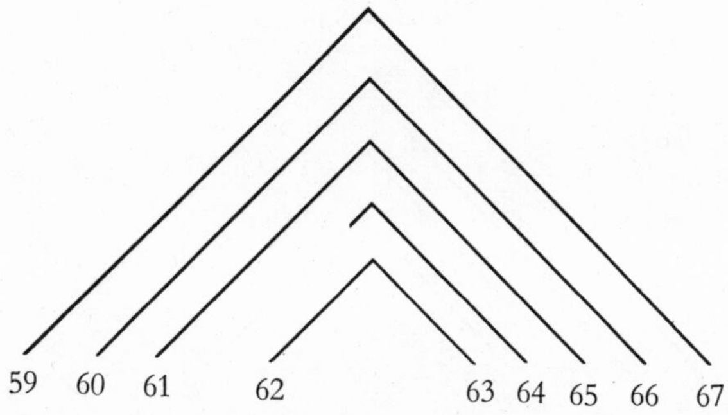

TEXT: Hours of the Virgin

59–60 Vespers continued. Rubric for Compline.

60v–63v Compline. No rubric for Penitential Psalms although 3 empty lines.

64 Blank and unruled. Conjugate stub passes around bifolio 62, 63. Marks of stitching are visible near the present outer edge indicating that the miniature on 64v was at one time inserted as a recto.

65–67v Penitential Psalms. Correct catchword.

MINIATURES:

59v *Virgin in the house of St. Elizabeth, Magnificat.* Colombe.
60v *Coronation of the Virgin.* Jean. Modified 1st plan (frame has 2 lateral lobes).
61 Psalm miniature. Colombe.
61v Psalm miniature. Colombe.
62 Psalm miniature. Colombe.
63 Psalm miniature. Colombe.
64v *Fall of the Rebel Angels.* Paul. 2nd plan.
65 Psalm miniature. Colombe.
65v Psalm miniature. Colombe.
66v Psalm miniature. Colombe.
67v Psalm miniature. Colombe.

INITIALS AND DECORATION:

59–63v, 65, 65v, 66v, 67v by Dry Master and assistant.

LINE ENDINGS:

59, 59v, 60v, 61, 65v, 67 rows of pots. No foliates.

GATHERING 11

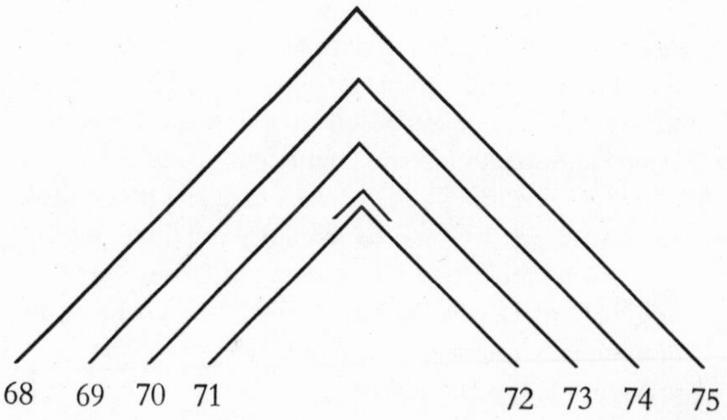

71 and 72 form a bifolio not sewn in but pasted to an added stub.

TEXT:

68–71v Penitential Psalms continued.

72–74v Litany. Rubric for Hours of the Holy Cross. The following petitions do not appear in the *Belles Heures*: Ss. Bernarde, Hilari, Guill(aum)e, Maure, Maria Cleophe, Maria Salomee, Felicitas, Perpetua, Petronilla, Scolastica, Appolonia, Iuliana. *A damynaciones perpetua libera nos domine, A furore tuo* . . . , *A morbo malo* . . . , *Ab inimicis n(ost)ris* . . . , *A peste et clade et fame* . . . , *A pericolo inferni*. . . .

75, 75v Hours of the Holy Cross, Matins and Prime. Correct catchword.

MINIATURES:

68v Psalm miniature. Colombe.
70 Psalm miniature. Colombe.
70v Psalm miniature. Colombe.
71v, 72 *Great Litany Procession.* Begun by Paul and completed by Colombe.
75 *Man of Sorrows.* Prepared for 1st plan (including ruling) but painted by Colombe.

INITIALS AND DECORATION:

68v, 70, 70v Colombe. But frames of initials on 70, 70v prepared early.
72 Spindly Master; initial tooled.
75, 75v Colombe.

LINE ENDINGS:

72v row of pots of a different, squat type.

GATHERING 12

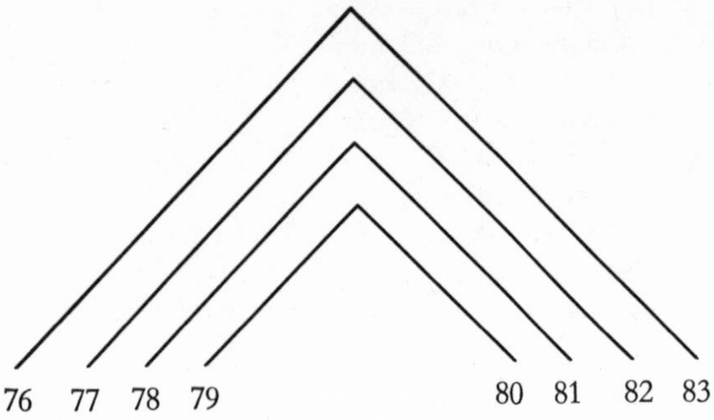

TEXT:

76–78v Hours of the Holy Cross continued. Rubric for Hours of the Holy Ghost.

79–81v Hours of the Holy Ghost. Beginning of Office incomplete. Four lines of original text on fol. 79 obliterated by Colombe miniature and replaced by first seven words only. ". . . annunciabit laudem tuam. Deus in adiutorium meum intende" omitted.

82–83v Office of the Dead, Vespers. Original text on fol. 82 obliterated by Colombe and last word "orat(ionis)" incomplete. Since text is too short to fill four lines of original script a small departure from first plan may have been intended, perhaps with three lines only as in gathering 4, fols. 17 and 19.

MINIATURES:

79 *Pentecost*. Colombe. Folio, including ruling, originally prepared for variant of 1st plan.

82 *Job exhorted by his friends*. Colombe. Folio, including ruling, originally prepared for a variant of 1st plan (see under TEXT).

INITIALS AND DECORATION:

Colombe.

LINE ENDINGS:

77v row of pots.

GATHERING 13

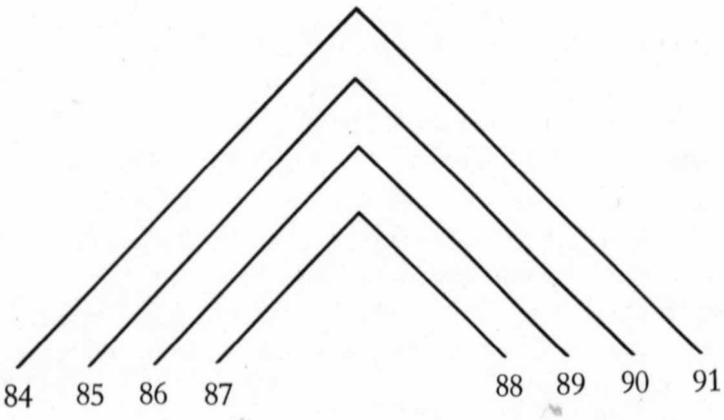

TEXT:

84–86 Office of the Dead, Vespers continued. Rubric for 1st nocturn of Matins.

86v–90 Matins, 1st nocturn. Original text below miniature on 86v.

90v–91v Matins, 2nd nocturn. Original text on 90v obliterated by Colombe's miniature and last syllable of *loco* repeated on 91.Text again too short to have filled four lines of original script. Correct catchword (on 91v).

MINIATURES:

84 Psalm miniature by Colombe.

85 Psalm miniature by Colombe.

86v *Funeral of Diocrès*, the *Three Living and Three Dead*, and scenes in the roundels illustrating the life of St. Bruno and founding of the Carthusian Order. All Colombe but prepared for modified 1st plan (wide surmounting arch, arabesque border). A drawing by the Limbourgs underlies the funeral scene, and they probably planned foliate decoration in the lower border, or even a miniature extending up between the columns of text, as on fol. 71v.

88 Psalm miniature. Colombe.

90v *Horseman of Death*. Colombe. Folio originally prepared for variant of 1st plan.

INITIALS AND DECORATION:

84–85v, 87v, 88, 90, 91v by Colombe.

86, 86v (border but not scenes in roundels; initial but not skeleton), 89, 89v by Spindly Master.

GATHERING 14

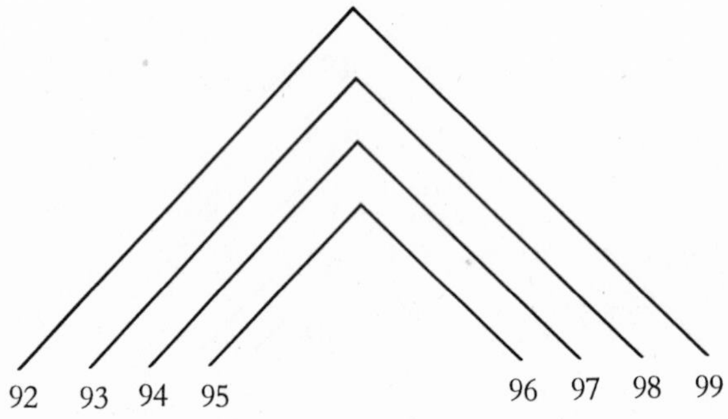

TEXT:

92–94v Office of the Dead, Matins, 2nd nocturn continued. Rubric for 3rd nocturn.

95–99v Matins, 3rd nocturn. Original text obliterated by Colombe's miniature on 95 but again too short to have filled four lines of original script. Correct catchword on 99v.

MINIATURES:

92v Psalm miniature. Colombe.

95 *David triumphs over his enemies*. Colombe. Folio probably prepared for variant of 1st plan.

96 Psalm miniature. Colombe.

97v Psalm miniature. Colombe.

INITIALS AND DECORATION:

92v, 93v–94v, 96, 97v, 98v–99v by Colombe.

GATHERING 15

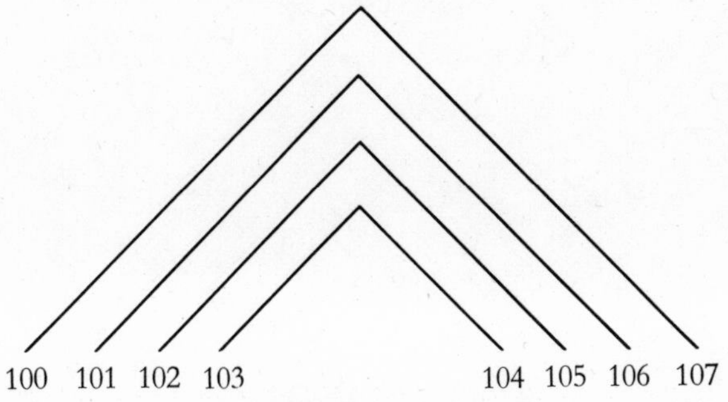

TEXT:

100 Office of the Dead, Matins, 3rd nocturn concluded. Rubric for Lauds.

100v–107v Lauds. No catchword on 107v.

MINIATURES:

100v *David calling on the Lord* and *Battle Scenes*. Colombe. Original 1st plan text and ruling preserved.

101v Psalm miniature. Colombe.

103v Psalm miniature. Colombe.

INITIALS AND DECORATION:

100v, 101v, 102v–103v, 104v–105v, 106v, 107, by Colombe.

LINE ENDINGS:

100v by Colombe.

GATHERING 16

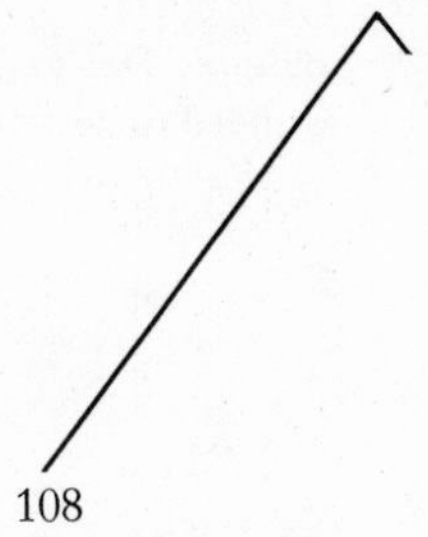

Single leaf. Conjugate stub passes around gathering 17.

MINIATURE:

108 *Hell*. Jean. 2nd plan.

108v Blank, unruled.

GATHERING 17

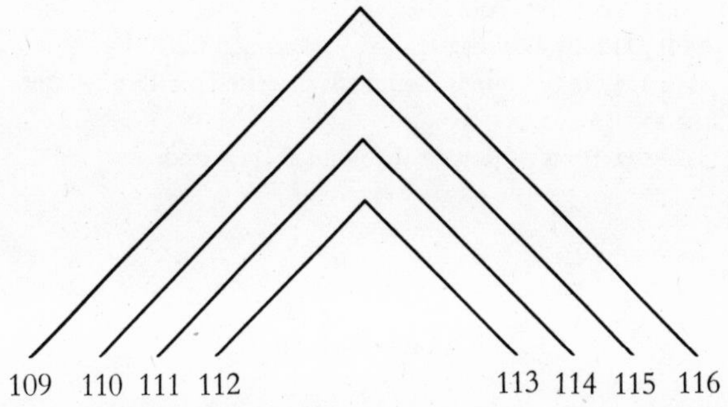

TEXT: Short Offices for days of the week.

110–113 Office of the Trinity. Sunday. 109 blank except for *nihil hic* in center and rubric for Office. Text begins correctly on 110. Rubric for following Office on 113.

114–116v Short Office of the Dead, Monday. Text begins correctly on 114. Correct catchword on 116v.

Script throughout this gathering bolder and more widely spaced. Since fols. 109v and 113v were prepared for full-page miniatures it is probable that the text was rewritten for 2nd plan.

MINIATURES:

109v *Baptism of Christ*. Colombe. Prepared for 2nd plan.

113v *Purgatory*. Colombe. Prepared for 2nd plan.

INITIALS AND DECORATION:

110–111v, 114–115v by Colombe.

112–113, 116, 116v by Dry Master, who worked only on bifolios designed to bear a full-page miniature on one face.

LINE ENDINGS:

112–113, 116v rows of pots and of diamond shaped studs.

GATHERING 18

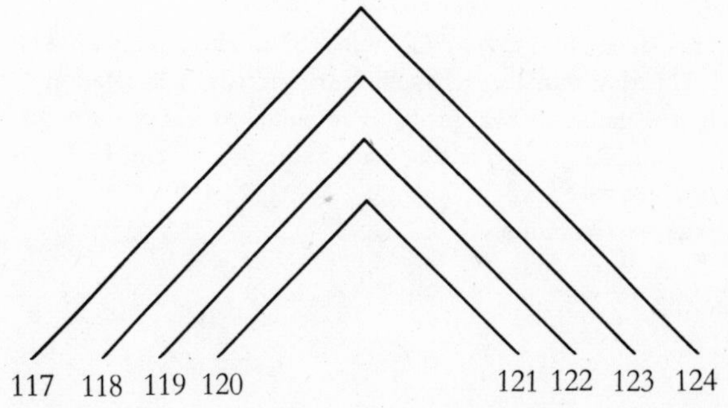

TEXT:

117–122 Short Office of the Dead continued. Rubric for following Office on 122.

122v–124v Short Office of the Holy Ghost, Tuesday. Text begins correctly on 123. Correct catchword on 124v.

MINIATURES:

122v *Apostles going forth to preach*. Colombe. Prepared for 2nd plan.

INITIALS AND DECORATION:

117–118v, 123–124v decoration, heads within initials 120, 121, 121v by Colombe.

119v, 122 by Dry Master (see gathering 17).

120, 121, 121v frames for initials prepared for Dry Master.

LINE ENDINGS:

119–122 rows of pots or diamond shaped studs.

GATHERING 19

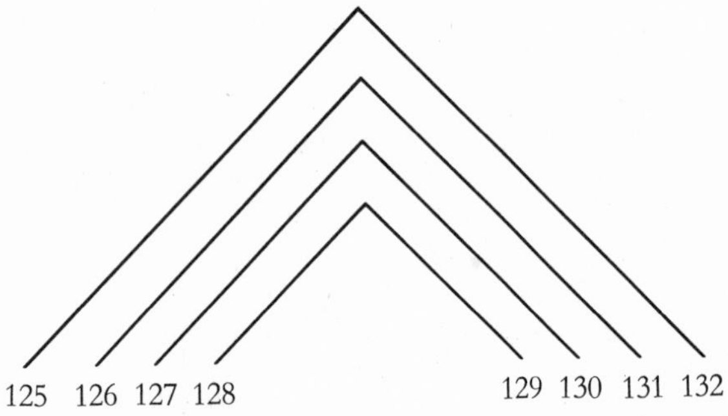

TEXT:

125, 125v Short Office of the Holy Ghost continued. Rubric for following Office on 125v.

126–129 Short Office of All Saints, Wednesday. Text continues correctly on 126v. Rubric for following Office on 129.

129v–132v Short Office of the Sacrament, Thursday. Four lines of original text on fol. 129v, identical to All Saints (126), obliterated by Colombe miniature. Colombe inscription omits "——*torium meum intende.*"

MINIATURES:

126 *All Saints.* Colombe. Prepared for 1st plan.

129v *The Sacrament.* Colombe. Prepared for 1st plan but modified by Colombe.

INITIALS AND DECORATION:

125–129, 130–132v by Colombe. Since even the bifolios bearing miniatures have no early initials or decoration the gathering was probably intended to be rewritten for 2nd plan, in accordance with gatherings 17 and 18.

LINE ENDING:

126 by Colombe.

GATHERING 20

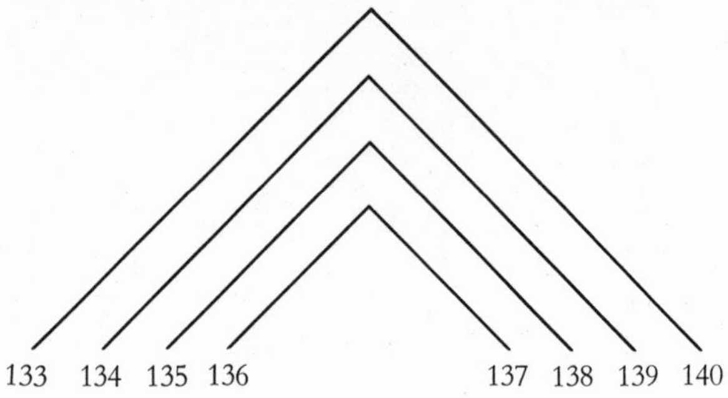

TEXT:

133 Short Office of the Sacrament continued. Text abbreviated and no rubric for following Office.

133v–136v Short Office of the Cross, Friday. Original text on 133v obliterated by Colombe miniature but on the analogy of 126 it evidently occupied less than four lines, since 134 begins *meum intende.* However 134 omits the response *Domine ad adiuvandum me festina* and proceeds directly to the *Gloria* so there may have been an error on the part of the scribe. Colombe text on scroll of 133v omits *Deus in adiutorium.* Rubric for following Office on 136v.

137–140v Short Office of the Blessed Virgin Mary, Saturday. Original four lines of text on 137 obliterated by Colombe miniature. Colombe omitted ——*us in adiutorium meum intende.* No rubric for Hours of the Passion on 140v.

MINIATURES:

133v *Finding of the Cross.* Colombe. Prepared for variant of 1st plan (?). Ruling original.

137 *Presentation of the Virgin.* Colombe. Prepared for 1st plan.

INITIALS AND DECORATION:

133, 134–136v, 137–140v by Colombe. This gathering, like gathering 19, was probably intended to be rewritten for 2nd plan.

GATHERING 21

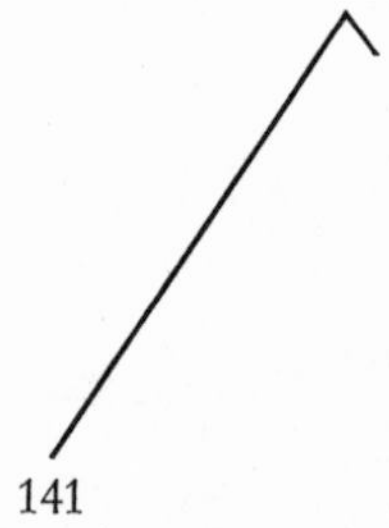

Single leaf held by stub.

TEXT:

141 Blank.

MINIATURE:

141v *Rome*. Jean (?). Unruled.

GATHERING 22

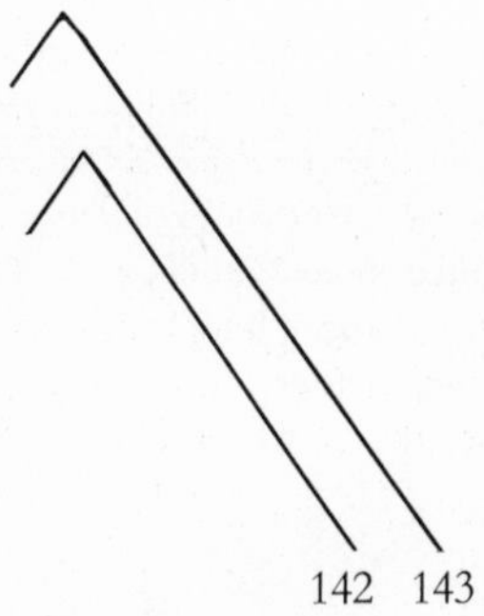

TEXT:

Hours of the Passion, Matins and Lauds missing (they were to be rewritten for 2nd plan?).

142, 143v Blank, unruled.

MINIATURES:

142v *Gethsemane* by Paul. 2nd plan. Unruled.

143 *Christ led to the Praetorium*. Jean. 2nd plan. Unruled.

GATHERING 23

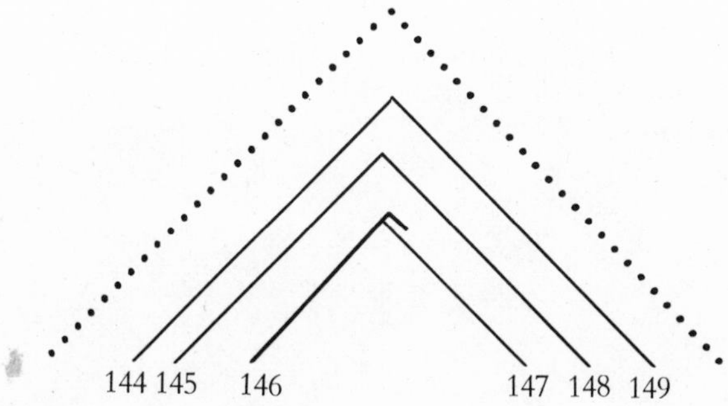

TEXT:

144v–146 Hours of the Passion, Prime. Text starts correctly on 144v and continues without omissions or unusual contractions (therefore written or rewritten for 2nd plan). Last five lines and rubric *ad terciam* on 146.

147v–149v Terce. Text starts on 147v, on verso of miniature, as in Prime. Rubric *ad sextam* on 149v.

MINIATURES:

144 *Flagellation*. Paul. 2nd plan. Miniature within rulings except for projections and a fraction along right edge.

146v *Christ led from the Praetorium*. Paul and Jean. 2nd plan. Exceeds ruling of 1st plan on all sides.

147 *Way to Calvary*. Paul. 2nd plan. Exceeds ruling of 1st plan on all sides.

147v Psalm miniature. Colombe.

INITIALS AND DECORATION:

144v (large initial tooled), 147v (large initial tooled), 149v (swan in initial bears Berry arms) by Dry Master. All large initials composed of foliage.

145v by Colombe.

LINE ENDINGS:

145 diamond shaped studs and circles. 145: circles.

GATHERING 24

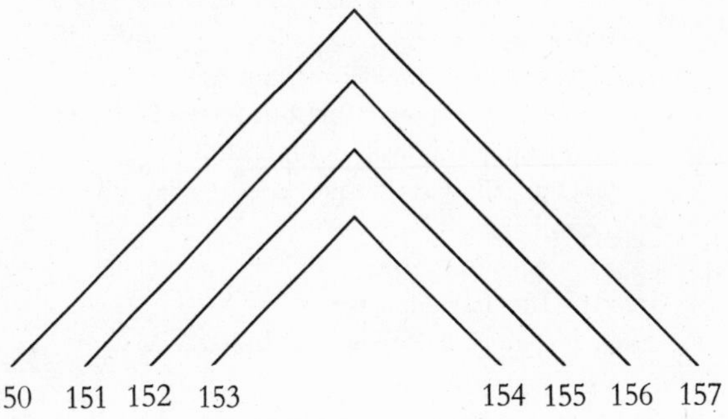

TEXT:

150–152 Sext. Text. Rubric *ad nonam* on 152.

153v–156 None. Text starts on 153v. Rubric *ad vesperas* on 156.

157v Vespers. Text starts on 157v, on verso of miniature as in Prime and Terce. Catchword on 157v does not conform with text on 158.

MINIATURES:

150 Psalm miniature. Colombe.

152v *Crucifixion*. Colombe. Prepared for 2nd plan.

153 *Darkness at Noon*. Jean. 2nd plan, but ruled for 1st.

153v Psalm miniature. Colombe.

156v *Deposition*. Jean. 2nd plan, but ruled for 1st.

157 *Entombment*. Colombe. Ruled for 1st plan.

157v Psalm miniature. Colombe.

INITIALS AND DECORATION:

150 (one initial with Jean de Berry's arms), 152 (one initial with Jean de Berry's swan), 153v, 155v, 156, 157v by Dry Master.

153 border by Spindly Master (?).

152v arabesques copied from 158 by Colombe.

LINE ENDINGS:

154 row of squat pots.

GATHERING 25

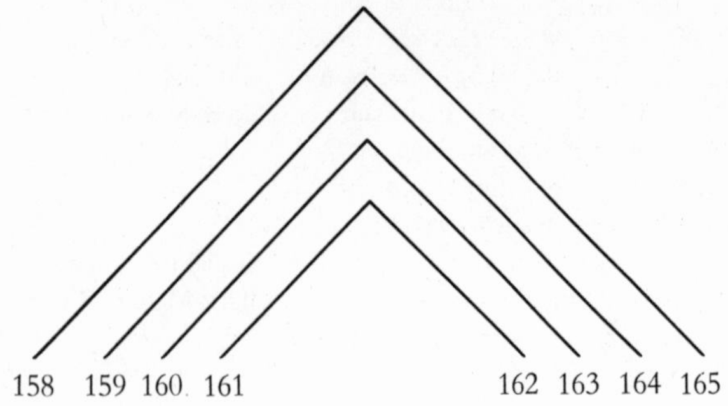

TEXT: Masses for the Liturgical Year.

158–161 Christmas Day, 3rd Mass. Folio and text designed for modified 1st plan.

161v–163v 1st Sunday of Lent (rubric). Text 1st plan.

164–165v 2nd Sunday of Lent, rubric on 163v. Text and presumably original design of folio 1st plan. Catchword.

MINIATURES:

158 *Christmas High Mass.* Begun by Limbourgs, completed by Colombe, who also executed figures in arabesque border. Modified 1st plan (wide surmounting arch, arabesque border).

161v *Temptations of Christ.* Herman. 1st plan.

164 *The Canaanite Woman.* Colombe. Prepared for 1st plan (ruling original), but modified by Colombe. Does not illustrate the gospel of the day (the Transfiguration).

INITIALS AND DECORATION:

161–162v by Breviary Master.

158, 158v, 165, 165v by follower of Breviary Master (Spindly).

158 (initial completed), 159, 160, 160v, 163, 163v, 164, 164v by Colombe.

GATHERING 26

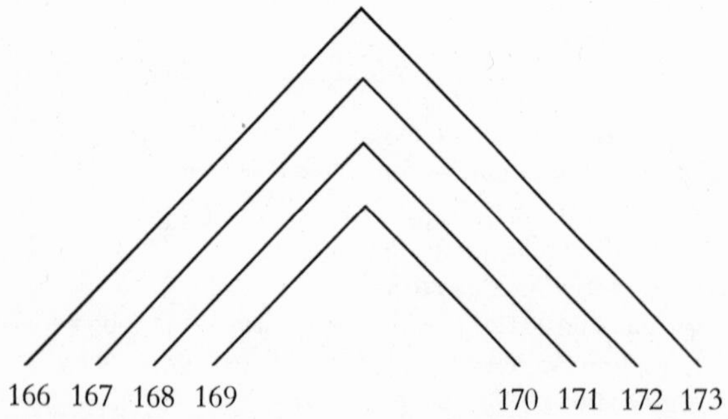

TEXT: Masses for the Liturgical Year continued.

166–168 3rd Sunday of Lent, including rubric. Text 1st plan. Rubric for following Mass on 168.

168v–170v 4th Sunday of Lent. Text 1st plan. Rubric for following Mass on 170v.

171–173 Passion Sunday (5th of Lent). Text 1st plan. Rubric for following Mass on 166v.

173v Palm Sunday. Text 1st plan. Correct catchword.

MINIATURES:

(166, 171, and 173v conform with 1st plan except for rectangular projections above)

166 *Healing of the Dumb Possessed.* Herman. 1st plan.

168v *Feeding of the Five Thousand.* Herman. Modified 1st plan, but exceptional border.

171 *Raising of Lazarus.* Herman. Modified 1st plan. Does not illustrate gospel of the day (the Jews disputing with Christ in the Temple, John 8, 46–59).

173v *Entry into Jerusalem.* Herman. 1st plan.

INITIALS AND DECORATION:

166 (initial tooled), 166v, 168, 168v (initial tooled), 171, 171v, 173 (both initials tooled), 173v (initial tooled) by Breviary Master and assistant.

167, 169, 169v, 170v, 172 by Colombe.

GATHERING 27

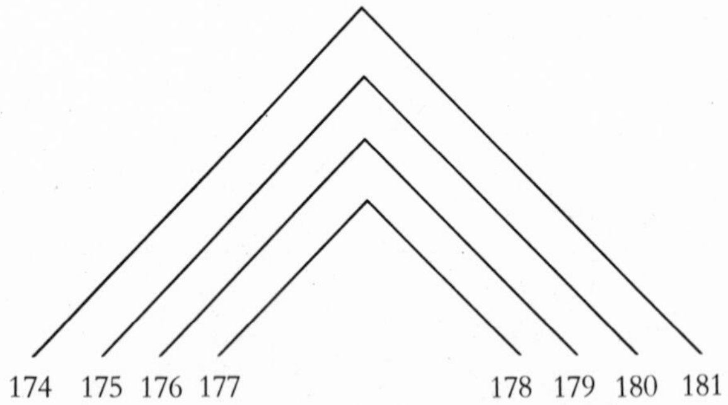

TEXT:

174–181v Mass for Palm Sunday continued. Rubric for following Mass on 181v.

MINIATURES:

None.

INITIALS AND DECORATION:

174, 174v, 181v by Colombe.

GATHERING 28

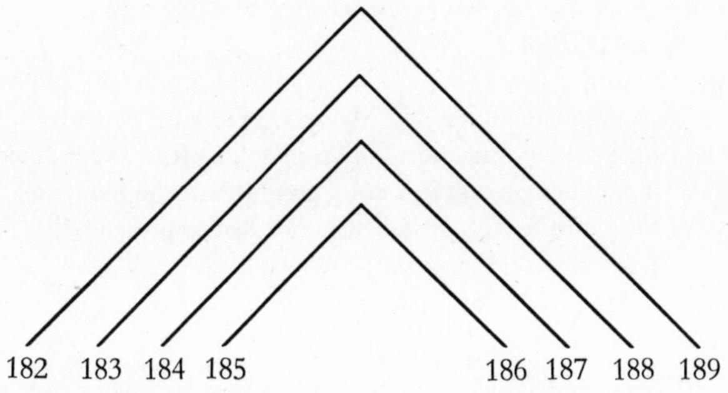

TEXT: Masses for the Liturgical Year continued.

182–183v Easter Sunday. Text 1st plan. Rubric for following Sunday on 183v.

184–186 Ascension, text 1st plan. Rubric for following Mass on 186.

186–188 Pentecost, text allows for small single column miniature. Rubric for following Mass on 188.

188–189v Trinity Sunday, as above. Rubric on 189v.

189v Corpus Christi, as above. Catchword for continuation on next gathering (missing).

MINIATURES:

182 *Resurrection*. Colombe, perhaps in part on Limbourg design. Modified 1st plan (wide surmounting arch, arabesque border). Colombe added figures in arabesques.

184 *Ascension*. Colombe. Prepared for 1st plan.

186 *Pentecost*. Colombe, within original dimensions.

188 *Christ blessing the World*. Colombe, within original dimensions.

189v *Communion of the Apostles*. Colombe, within original dimensions.

INITIALS AND DECORATION:

182 arabesques and foliage by assistant of Breviary Master (Spindly?); 182v and 189v by Spindly Master. 182 (initial completed), 183–188v, 189v (large initial) by Colombe.

LINE ENDINGS:

182v row of squat pots.

GATHERING 29

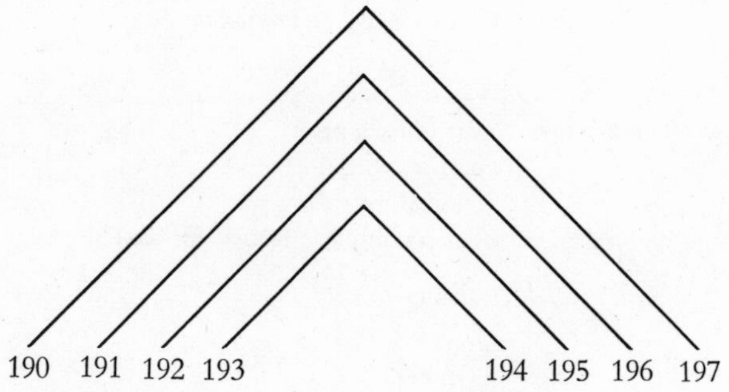

TEXT: Masses for Liturgical Year continued.

190–191 Assumption of the Virgin; beginning of *Introit* and miniature missing. Rubric for following Mass on 191.

191v–192v Common of the Mass of the Virgin, text allows for single column miniature. Rubric for following Mass on 192v.

193–194v Exaltation of the Cross. Text 1st plan. Rubric for following Mass on 194v.

195–197 St. Michael. Text 1st plan. Rubric for following Mass on 197.

197–197v All Saints, text allows for single column miniature. Correct catchword on 197v.

MINIATURES:

191v *Madonna and Child*. Colombe, within original dimensions.

193 *Exaltation of the Cross*. Herman. 1st plan, modified as in gathering 26.

195 *St. Michael killing the Dragon* and medallions. Jean. Modified 1st plan (rectangular lateral extension).

197 *The Pope blessing*. Colombe, within original dimensions.

INITIALS AND DECORATION:

192–195v by Breviary Master and assistant.

190–191v, 196–197v by Colombe.

GATHERING 30

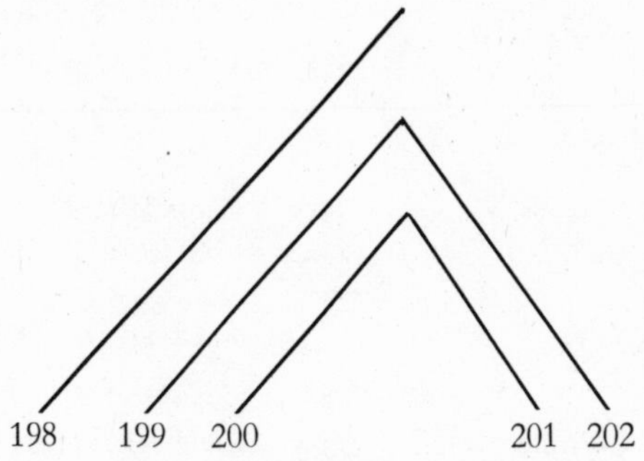

TEXT: Masses for the Liturgical Year continued.

198–199 All Saints continued. Rubric for following Mass on 199.

199v–200v All Souls. Text allows for single column miniature. Rubric for following Mass on 200v.

201–202v St. Andrew. Text and ruling 1st plan. No rubric or catchword on 202v.

MINIATURES:

199v *Mass for the Dead*. Colombe, within original dimensions.

201 *Martyrdom of St. Andrew*. Colombe. Prepared for 1st plan.

INITIALS AND DECORATION:

198v by Breviary Master.

199–202v by Colombe.

Since the catchword on 197v is picked up correctly on 198, and there is an original rubric on 200v for the Mass of St. Andrew, this gathering was planned as a gathering of six and not of eight folios. The conjugate folio of 198 was obviously prepared for a large miniature, which is now missing. Perhaps it was the *Purification* now on 54v (see gathering 31).

GATHERING 31

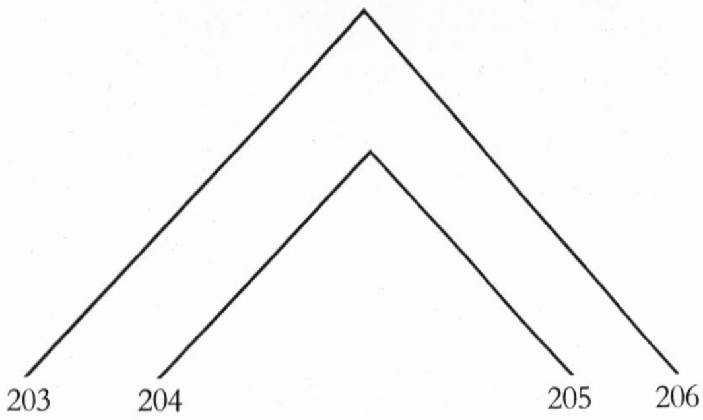

TEXT: Masses of the Liturgical Year continued.
203–204v Purification of the Virgin, including rubric.
205–206v Blank.

MINIATURES:
None. All of the foregoing Masses are preceded either by single column miniatures or large miniatures of a modified 1st plan design, and it is quite possible that the miniature of the Purification on 54v was intended to precede this Mass.

INITIALS AND DECORATION:
203–204v by Colombe.

ESTIMATE OF MISSING TEXT—HOURS OF THE PASSION

	Belles Heures Folio		Folio	*Très Riches Heures*
Matins	123	*Agony in the Garden* + 8 lines of text	141	*Plan of Rome*
	123v	*Betrayal* + 8 lines of text	142v	*Ego Sum*
	124	*Christ before Caiaphas* + 8 lines of text		(*Betrayal*?)
	124v–131	Text (*ca.* $13\frac{2}{3}$ pp.)		Entire text missing
		TEXT TOTAL: *ca.* $14\frac{1}{4}$ pp.		Est. total (incl. probably four psalm miniatures): 14–15 pp.[1]
Lauds	131v	*Christ Mocked* + 8 lines of text		(*Christ before Caiaphas*?)
	132	*Flagellation* + 8 lines of text	143	*Christ led to the Praetorium*
	132v–135	Text (*ca.* $5\frac{1}{2}$ pp.)		Entire text missing
		TEXT TOTAL: *ca.* $5\frac{7}{8}$ pp.		Est. total (incl. two psalm miniatures): *ca.* 7 pages.[2]
Prime	135v	*Christ before Pilate* + 8 lines of text		(*Release of Barabbas* or *Christ mocked before Herod*?)
	136	*Pilate ordering deliverance of Barabbas* (?) + 8 lines of text	144	*Flagellation*
	136v–137v	Text (*ca.* $2\frac{5}{8}$ pp.)	144v–146	Text (*ca.* 3 pp.)
		TEXT TOTAL: 3 pp.		TEXT TOTAL (psalm miniature was omitted): *ca.* $3\frac{1}{10}$ pp.[3] Text complete. Rubric for Terce.
Terce	138	*Pilate washing his Hands* + 8 lines of text	146v	*Christ leaving the Praetorium*
	138v	*Way to Calvary* + 8 lines of text	147	*Way to Calvary*
	139–141	Text (*ca.* $4\frac{1}{2}$ pp.)	147v–149v	Text (*ca.* $4\frac{3}{4}$ pp.)
		TEXT TOTAL: *ca.* $4\frac{7}{8}$ pp.		TEXT TOTAL (incl. one psalm miniature): 5 pp. Text complete. Rubric for Sext.
Sext	141v	*Christ nailed to the Cross* + 8 lines of text		(missing)
	142	*Christ offered the Sop* + 8 lines of text		(missing)
	142v–144v	Text (*ca.* $4\frac{2}{3}$ pp.)	150–152	Text (*ca.* $4\frac{2}{3}$ pp.)
		TEXT TOTAL: *ca.* 5 pp.		TEXT TOTAL (incl. 1 psalm miniature): 5 pp. Text complete. Rubric for None.

	Belles Heures Folio		Très Riches Heures Folio	
None	145	*Christ pierced with a Lance* + 8 lines of text	152v	*Crucifixion* (Colombe)
	145v	*Death of Christ* + 8 lines of text	153	*Death of Christ*
	146–148v	Text (*ca.* 5¾ pp.)	153v–156	
		TEXT TOTAL: *ca.* 6⅒ pp.		TEXT TOTAL (incl. 1 psalm miniature): 6 pp. Text complete. Rubric for Vespers.
Vespers	149	*Deposition* + 8 lines of text	156v	*Deposition*
	149v	*Lamentation* + 8 lines of text	157	*Lamentation* (Colombe)
	150–151v	Text (*ca.* 3¾ pp.)	157	Only this folio of text survives.
		TEXT TOTAL: *ca.* 4⅒ pp.		Est. total (incl. 1 psalm miniature + 1 canticle): *ca.* 5 pp. 157 ends "in oppro——" and bears a catchword.
Compline	152	*Entombment* + 8 lines of text		(missing)
	152v	*Sleeping Soldiers beside the Tomb* + 8 lines of text		(missing)
	153–154v	Text (3½ pp.)		Text missing.
		TEXT TOTAL: *ca.* 4 pp.		Est. total (incl. 1 psalm miniature): *ca.* 4 pp.

[1] If the verso of the hypothetical third miniature was left blank, Matins, incl. miniatures, could have fitted on ten folios (20 sides).

[2] As fol. 143v is blank, Lauds, incl. miniatures, would have fitted on five folios (10 sides).

[3] Possibly the psalm miniature was omitted with the intention of condensing the text in three pages and leaving the recto of fol. 146 blank. It bears only the last five lines of the Office and the rubric *Ad terciam*.

OBSERVATIONS ON THE HISTORY OF THE TRES RICHES HEURES

The manuscript gives us no assistance in identifying any owner after Jean de Berry until late in the fifteenth century. The arms and portraits of Charles I of Savoy and of his wife Blanche of Montferrat appear below a miniature added by Jean Colombe (fol. 75). Since Charles was Duke of Savoy from 1482 to 1489, and he married Blanche in 1485, we know within narrow limits the date of the completion of the manuscript.

It has generally been assumed that Jean de Berry's daughter, Bonne d'Armagnac, was instrumental in transmitting the Book of Hours. Both Charles I and his wife Blanche were in direct line of descent from children of her first marriage, Amadeus VIII of Savoy or his sister Jeanne, married to the Marquis of Montferrat. If this were so the manuscript, as we shall see, would have been sent to Bonne in the Auvergne, to Rodez or Carlat, before August 1417; and at her death in 1435 it would have left France for Savoy or Montferrat. Documentary evidence, however, indicates that this was not the case.

A study of the will of Jean de Berry and of the documents on the disposal of his estate gives us some facts not hitherto presented—mostly about what did *not* happen to the manuscript. An *aide-mémoire*, drawn up, as we shall see, after the Burgundians entered Paris in May 1418, provides a useful summary of the course of events after the Duke's death on June 15th 1416 in the Hôtel de Nesle.[1] At the insistence of the executors his possessions in the Hôtel were removed to the residence of one of their number, his son-in-law Bernard d'Armagnac, and by June 29th the household had been dissolved.[2] An inventory of the contents of the Duke's other residences of Mehun-sur-Yévre and Bourges was prepared, and everything was brought to Bernard's house. At the request of the creditors and the heirs the King placed a stay on the execution of the will. He also ordered that nothing should be disposed of until the Duke's younger daughter, Marie de Bourbon, had received a sum still outstanding on her dowry. Eventually all parties reached an accommodation and both daughters were permitted to take goods to an agreed value. No manuscript remotely resembling the *Très Riches Heures* appears in the early posthumous inventory. Furthermore, the items chosen by Bonne or Marie, or set aside to satisfy certain specific bequests, are always identified.

The *aide-mémoire* states that the residue was moved, under the supervision of representatives of the creditors, the executors and the King, to the *hôtel* of Etienne de Bonpuis. The transfer was effected before August 24th 1417, and two notaries were instructed to draw up an inventory for the benefit of the creditors. They seem to have proceeded slowly for they had not completed the work by May of the following year, when the Burgundians entered Paris. Porteclef, the responsible notary, fled and subsequently died. Guillaume Agotin, author of the *mémoire*, describes himself as heir to Jehan Lebourne, who was responsible for the accounts of the liquidation.[3] Agotin came to Paris and found the unfinished document in the possession of the widow of the second notary. This he now completed, though he disclaims responsibility for the goods placed in safekeeping with Bonpuis.

These lists completed by Agotin consist largely of objects included in inventories drawn up during the Duke's lifetime, but certain items, including the *Très Riches Heures*, are new. Unlike the earlier lists presented to the daughters for their choice, there is no indication as to whether the goods were previously in Mehun, Bourges or the Hôtel de Nesle. Probably the collection did not remain complete while Agotin was working, because between October 1417 and April 1418 the King instructed Bonpuis to hand over items to the value of 20,000 *livres* "pour le fait de sa guerre."[4]

The residue cannot have been very satisfying to the creditors; 53 tapestries, hangings and other furnishings, 249 items of jewelry, etc., and 64 manuscripts, all inventoried in groups, are valued collectively at only 13,908 *livres*.[5] There follows a small, oddly assorted, list of 19 tapestries, etc., 17 lots of jewels, and five books, reaching the much more impressive total value of just over 24,825 *livres*.[6] Among these items we find a tapestry appraised at a uniquely high price, the unfinished and still unbound *Très Riches Heures*, and the *Grandes Heures*, which with its precious covers was valued at the imposing sum of 4,000 *livres*. Since we know that the *Grandes Heures* was rebound for Charles VIII in 1488, possibly it entered royal possession at this time, together with some or all of the valuable accompanying lots.[7]

This evidence that the Duke's unfinished manuscript did not pass to Bonne d'Armagnac seems conclusive, but if more were needed documents can be cited to show precisely which items from her father's estate she gave or willed to her children. Under a deed of gift of 1427 her son Amadeus VIII was to receive on her death:

> Et primo quamdam cameram de paramento de cyrico, auro, et argento, operatam, de Tapisseria ad altam liciam, factam ad personagia, et munitam suis tentis, videlicet Caelo capite, coportura [*sic*], et tribus cortinis currentibus a lateribus et pedibus. Nec non sex tapissis mixtum operatis de cirico, auro, et argento ac lana, ac [*sic*] personagia similia camerae predictae. Nec non sex oriellieriis, sive carrellis, factis ad decorationem dictae camerae. Item plus, unum aliud tapissum operatum mixtum lana, cirico, auro et argento, in quo sunt operatae et depictae septem virtutes et septem vicia, et quod tapissum est de alta licia, et factum ad decorationem unius magnae aulae. Item plus unum tapissum vellutum magnum diversorum colorum, in quo sunt figurata diversa animalia grossa, et quod tapissum est factum pro ponendo et tenendo in aliqua camera, super terram, pro deambulando desuper, et hoc ad decorationem dictae camerae. Item plus, unam bibliam in pargameno, et gallico scriptam, istoriatam, et copertam de Cameloto albo, et quae biblia est voluminis ad modum unius missalis communis, vel quasi. Item, quemdam alium librum pergameneum, istoriatum, continentem in Gallico facta nobilium hominum. Et quae camera, tapissia, et ornamenta, ut supra proxime declarata, et data dicto domino duci donatario, fuerunt predictae dominae donatrici legata, data, et concessa, per praefatum dominum de Biturio ducem, eiusdem dominae donatricis genitorem, in uno ultimo et nuncupativo testamento . . .[8]

In her will drawn in 1430 Bonne leaves Amadeus only a golden St. Michael with no indication of its provenance. Her daughters, Bonne and Jeanne de Savoie, were only to receive certain sums of money.[9]

Although the manuscript did not enter the family of Savoy at the time of Bonne's death, they had ample opportunities to acquire it by gift or purchase at a later date. Relations between the ducal family and the French court were at all times close, though not always entirely amicable. Yolande of France, mother of Philibert I and Charles I, was betrothed to Amadeus IX at an early age, and in 1452 her brother, Louis XI, married Charlotte of Savoy. Caught in the rivalry between France and Burgundy the duchy fell under French domination. Following the death of his mother Yolande in 1478, the young Duke Philibert I was summoned by Louis XI to Tours with his sisters and his brother, Charles. Charles returned to his own duchy only after the death of the King in 1483, a year after he had succeeded his brother as duke.[10] It is not only his decision to complete the *Très Riches Heures* that informs us of his interest in his library. Bayard, his page from 1485, tells us: "Il estoit plaisant et de belle humeur, et malgré ce il estoit point de vieil autheur grec ou latin qu'il ne sceut expliquer secundum cathedram."[11]

At her husband's death in 1489 the Duchess Blanche of Savoy became regent for Charles II, her infant son. He too died in 1496, and her regency ended with the succession of her late husband's uncle, Philippe II. His reign lasted only a year, and an inventory made in Turin at the accession of Philibert II lists objects of value still in the possession of the Duchess Blanche. Among her books we find: "Unes belles grandes heures escriptes a la main en parchemin couvertes de cramoysi et les fermeaulx d'or."[12] This could be an abbreviated description of the *Très Riches Heures*. It is in any event through Blanche and her successors that the Book of Hours may have gone to Turin—a city near Genoa, where the manuscript appeared in the eighteenth century.

In the discussion above of the *Très Riches Heures* and of the followers of the Limbourgs we have cited numerous copies of the miniatures painted during the course of the execution of the book or, in most instances, after the cessation of work on it in 1416. The copyists had been, or still were, active in the Parisian region. It is difficult to be certain whether they saw the *Très Riches Heures* or worked from drawings. We suspect that the manuscript remained in metropolitan France for a decade after the death of the Duke.

Seeking to explain the influence of the calendar miniatures of the *Très Riches Heures* on such later manuscripts as the *Grimani Breviary* and the *Hennessy Hours*, Durrieu tried to prove that Margaret of Austria had taken it to Flanders after the death in 1504 of her husband Philibert le Beau.[12] He proposed to identify it with an item listed among the appointments of her chapel in Malines: "Une grande heure escripte a la main lesquelles n'ont point de couverte ne fermeilletz (Depuis couverte de velours et y mis ung fermilet d'argent)."[13] As evidence for the identification Durrieu pointed to the fact that the manuscript was unbound and without clasps. Surely, however, Charles and Blanche, having completed the *Très Riches Heures*, would have provided it with a cover. Moreover, prayerbooks kept in a chapel were presumably for daily use, and one would expect that a manuscript of such artistic value as to have served as a model would have found a place not in the chapel but on the library shelves, beside Margaret's other more precious Books of Hours. She might, of course, have possessed the *Très Riches Heures*, as Durrieu argued. The late Flemish copies prove the accessibility either of the manuscript or of drawings of the calendar. The relationship of Savoyard painting and illumination from *ca.* 1430 with the *Très Riches Heures* (Edmunds, 1970, p. 231) does not, however, seem to us so considerable as to require the presence of the manuscript in Savoy.

The copies of motifs or entire compositions of the *Très Riches Heures* in French illumination up to about 1435—copies which are discussed in the preceding text, especially in the consideration of the influence of the manuscript—seem to indicate that it remained during this period in metropolitan France. The *Très Riches Heures* was exploited in this way by followers of the Limbourgs as well as by the Harvard Hannibal Master, the Master of St. Jerome, and the Bedford workshop.

The present eighteenth-century covers of the manuscript are impressed with the arms of the Genoese family of Spinola. Subsequently the arms of the Serra family, also of Genoa, were superimposed on one cover. From these last owners it passed by inheritance to the Barone Felix de Margherita. Finally, in 1855, it was purchased by the Duc d'Aumale.

NOTES

1. Guiffrey, II, pp. 256–259.
2. *Ibid.*, pp. 205, 256, 297.
3. *Ibid.*, p. 205.
4. *Ibid.*, p. 344.
5. *Ibid.*, pp. 275, 278.
6. *Ibid.*, p. 281.
7. For the *Grandes Heures* see Meiss, *Late XIV Century*, p. 266.
8. Paris, Bibliothèque nationale, Fonds Doat, vol. 215, fol. 46. Transcription of *vidimus* inscribed in Geneva May 11th 1436. The document was drawn up at Carlat in the presence of Bonne, counsellors and notaries from the Auvergne, Savoy and the Dauphiné.
9. Paris, Archives nationales, P 1363, fol. 18: "quoddam nostrum jocale sive oratorium aureum factum ad ymaginem sancti michaelis cum pede argenti deaurato, sive locum quo

posita est dicta ymago aurea facta ad similitudinem unius castri." Bonne died at Carlat in 1435. Apart from specific bequests she appointed as heir general her second son Bernard d'Armagnac, comte de Pardiac. A generation later Louis XI in a letter to his treasurer (Paris, Bibl. nat., ms. fr. 10988, fol. 228) quotes Bernard's son Jacques, duc de Nemours, as claiming to be "heritier pour le pluspart de feu prince de bonne mémoire Jehan, premier duc de Berry. . . ." (See B. de Mandrot, "Jacques d'Armagnac, duc de Nemours," *Revue historique*, XLIII, 1890, p. 299 n. 3).

10. V. de Saint-Genis, *Histoire de Savoie*, Chambéry, I, 1868, p. 477 ff.

11. *Ibid.*, p. 480 f.

12. P. Vayra, *Le lettere e le arti alla corte di Savoia nel secolo XV, inventari dei castelli di Ciamberì, di Torino e di Ponte d'Ain 1497–98* (*Miscellanea di storia Italiana*, XXII), [Turin, 1883], p. 178, no. 1265. Blanche died in 1519 at her usual residence at Carignano, near Turin (Litta, *Famiglie celebri italiane*, [Milan], VIII [1839], table XI).

13. P. Durrieu, *Bibl. Ecole des Chartes*, 1903, pp. 321–328.

14. M. Michelant, "Inventaires des vaisselles, joyaux, tapisseries, peintures, manuscrits, etc., de Marguerite d'Autriche, regénte et gouvernante des Pays-Bas, dressés en son palais de Malines, le 9 juillet 1523," *Comte rendu des séances de la commission royale d'histoire ou recueil de ses bulletins* (Bruxelles, *Académie royale des sciences*), 3rd ser., XII, 1871, pp. 5–78, 83–136.

For the Book of Hours cited by Durrieu see p. 15; for those on the library shelves see p. 31 f.; for detailed descriptions of three Books of Hours in a small room near the chapel see p. 91 f.

BIBLIOGRAPHY: Waagen, *Galleries*, 1857, pp. 248–259; Hulin de Loo, 1903, pp. 178 ff.; Durrieu, *Très Riches Heures*, 1904; Hulin de Loo, 1908, p. 183 ff.; Winkler, 1911, pp. 536–543; Martin, *Miniature française*, 1923, p. 103, figs. CXIX, CXX; Chantilly (Meurgey), 1930, pp. 59–71 no. 30, pls. XXXIX–XLV; Winkler, 1930, p. 95; [Sterling] *Peintres du moyen âge* [1941], p. 22 f., pls. 19–21; Malo, *Très Riches Heures*, 1945; Porcher, *Très Riches Heures*, 1950; Panofsky, *Netherlandish Painting*, 1953, I, pp. 34, 63–66, II, figs. 80–84, 87–91, 93, 95; E. Morand, 1954, pp. 1–5; Porcher, *Belles Heures*, 1953; Gorissen, 1954, pp. 153–221; Meiss, *Art Bull.*, 1956, p. 195; Porcher, *Enluminure*, 1959, pp. 62–64, figs. 67, 68, pl. LXXI; Brendel, 1967, pp. 62–70; Meiss, *Late XIV Century*, 1967, index, figs. 419–424, 442, 489, 844; *idem*, *Boucicaut Master*, 1968, index, figs. 378, 477; Longnon, Cazelles and Meiss, *Très Riches Heures*, 1969; Meiss, "Breviary Master," 1970.

Chantilly

MUSEE CONDE, ms. 493

See Christine de Pisan, *Mutacion*

Chantilly

MUSEE CONDE, ms. 494

See Christine de Pisan, *Mutacion*

Florence

BIBL. LAURENZIANA, Med. Pal. 69 (Figs. 223, 264)

Virgil, *Eclogues*, *Georgics* and *Aeneid*. 265 fols.; 400 × 291 mm.

EARLY HISTORY: As he stated in the colophon on folio 265v, Pierre de l'Ormel, a licensed bookdealer of the University of Paris, finished this manuscript in July, 1403, for Jacques Courau. Courau, who was the treasurer and *maître d'hôtel* of Jean de Berry, commissioned several manuscripts for the Duke, including a copy of Valerius Maximus by the same workshop which illuminated the Virgil.

STYLE AND DATE: The verses of Virgil are accompanied by extensive glosses, and scholia have been carefully copied between the lines of text. The illuminator responsible for the charming frontispiece to *Georgics*, which shows the activities of peasants in their fields, takes his name, the Virgil Master, from this manuscript. The other miniature is by an assistant in his workshop.

BIBLIOGRAPHY: Meiss, *Late XIV Century*, 1967, pp. 189, 298, 360, fig. 841.

MINIATURES:

Folio	
	Eclogues: Frontispiece cut out
18	*Georgics*: Plowing, sowing, beekeeping and pruning
64v	*Aeneid*: Building of Troy and an army at sea

Geneva

BIBL. PUBLIQUE ET UNIVERSITAIRE, ms. 190

See Boccaccio, *Cas des nobles hommes et femmes*

The Hague

BIBL. ROY., ms. 78 D 42

See Christine de Pisan, *Mutacion*

Holkham Hall (Norfolk)

COLL. EARL OF LEICESTER, ms. 307

See Virgil

London

BRIT. MUS., Add. 32454 (Figs. 165, 166)

Book of Hours, Use of Rome; French (Paris?) calendar. 118 fols.; 255×180 mm.

STYLE AND DATE: This Book of Hours was painted about 1415, probably in Paris. It shows a surprisingly large number of diverse styles, the rarest of which are those of the Josephus Master and an assistant.

BIBLIOGRAPHY: Durrieu in Michel, *Histoire*, 1907, p. 168, fig. 96; London, Brit. Mus., *Reproductions*, II, 1910, p. 11 f., pl. XXV; Winkler, 1911, p. 453; London, Brit. Mus., *Schools of Illumination*, VI, 1930, p. 9, pl. 7b; London, Brit. Mus., Millar, 1933, p. 36, pl. L; Porcher, *Belles Heures*, 1953, pp. 7 n. 10, 28; Meiss, *Art Bull.*, 1956, p. 192; Pächt, *Burl. Mag.*, 1956, p. 150, fig. 13, p. 148; London, Brit. Mus., *Grenville Library* (Turner), 1967, p. 45 f.; Meiss, *Late XIV Century*, 1967, pp. 265, 357, figs. 257, 258.

MINIATURES:

Folio

2–7v Calendar (workshop of Egerton Master)
8 Crucifixion (Josephus Master)
9 St. John on Patmos (workshop of Pseudo-Jacquemart)
9v St. Luke (workshop of Pseudo-Jacquemart)
10v St. Matthew (workshop of Pseudo-Jacquemart)
11 St. Mark (workshop of Pseudo-Jacquemart)
12 Virgin and Child on Crescent
14v Mourning Virgin Mary and St. John (workshop of Pseudo-Jacquemart)

Hours of the Virgin

22 Visitation (Pseudo-Jacquemart)
29 Nativity (Bedford trend)
32 Annunciation to Shepherds (Pseudo-Jacquemart)
35 Adoration of Magi (Bedford trend)
38 Presentation in Temple (Bedford trend)
41 Flight into Egypt (workshop of Josephus Master)
46 Coronation of Virgin (workshop of Josephus Master)

Penitential Psalms

59 David at Prayer (workshop of Josephus Master)

London

BRIT. MUS., Add. 35311 and Harley 2897
(Figs. 611, 620, 648 and 610, 618, 619, 621, 622, 893)

EARLY HISTORY: Add. 35311 is the first half of a Breviary originally designed as a single volume but subsequently divided in two. The missing sections, together with a copy of the Calendar, Psalter and Ordinarium, are contained in Harley 2897. Since Harley 2897 bears the arms of Jean sans Peur of Burgundy and of his Duchess Margaret of Bavaria, held by a young woman below the miniature of the Ascension (fol. 188v), the Breviary was certainly made either for the Duke or for his wife. However, no Breviary listed in the 1420 inventory made after the Duke's death or in Margaret's inventory of 1423 can be identified with these manuscripts. It has been erroneously stated that the Calendar and use are Parisian (Leroquais, *Un livre d'heures de Jean sans Peur*, 1939, p. 71), and it was thus assumed that the volumes were identical with the Paris Breviary the Duke had with him when he was murdered in 1419 at Montereau (Doutrepont, *Littérature française*, 1909, p. 202). The Calendar and use have also been described as Franciscan (London, Brit. Mus., Warner, 1903; London, Brit. Mus., Millar, 1933), but only two of the Franciscan feasts in the Calendar (19 July and 28 September) would not be expected in the Roman use, and neither is in gold. Several important Franciscan feasts that appear in the Calendar are missing in the Sanctoral (e.g. Stigmata, St. Louis of Toulouse, Translation of St. Anthony). However, St. Clare appears in the Litany (fol. 2), and certain rubrics indicate a Franciscan connection (e.g. Harley 2897, fols. 276v, 277v, 310). Both Jean sans Peur and his Duchess were connected with the Franciscans. The Duke was defended by a Franciscan, Jean Petit, after the murder of Louis d'Orléans in 1407 (Petit, *Itinéraires*, 1888, p. 591), and the Duchess had a close relationship with Colette de Corbie, the spirited Franciscan reformer (1381–1447). See E. Sainte-Marie Perrin, *La belle vie de Sainte Colette de Corbie*, Paris, 1921, p. 108 ff. Rubrics in French and the presence in the Litany of St. Margaret and St. Agatha (twice) may also point to a Breviary for the personal use of the Duchess rather than for her husband. It is noteworthy that on May 22, 1412 Jean sans Peur gave his wife 300 francs "pour la façon d'un Bréviaire et autres livres qu'elle fait faire" (Doutrepont, *Littérature française*, 1909, p. 200 f.). On the evidence of the Burgundian inventories the ducal chapel habitually used a Parisian Breviary (Doutrepont, *Inventaire*, 1906, p. 18). The only specifically Parisian reference in our Calendar is to the exposition of St. Clement's head (November 24), preserved in the Sainte-Chapelle (S. Morand, *Histoire de la Sainte-Chapelle*, Paris, 1790, p. 43).

STYLE AND DATE: Painted between 1413 and 1419 by the Breviary Master, his assistants, and minor illuminators. See the chapter on the Breviary Master.

BIBLIOGRAPHY: Peignot, *Bibl. ducs de Bourgogne*, 1841, p. 80; London, Brit. Mus., Warner, 1903, text and pls. 45, 46; London, Brit. Mus., *Reproductions*, I, 1907, p. 11, pl. XXVII, III, 1910, p. 13 f., pls. XXIX–XXXI; Herbert, *Illuminated Manuscripts*, 1911, p. 270 f.; Winkler, 1911, pp. 536–542; Durrieu, *Très Belles Heures de Notre-Dame*, 1922, p. 74; London, Brit. Mus., *Schools of Illumination*, VI, 1930, p. 7 f., pl. 6; London, Brit. Mus., Millar, 1933, p. 29 f., pls. XXXVI–XXXVII; Wescher, 1946, p. 34; Panofsky, *Netherlandish Painting*, 1953, I, notes 62[6], 76[4], 82[3], 237[7]; Meiss, *Art Bull.*, 1956, p. 195; London, Brit. Mus., *Grenville Library* (Turner), 1967, p. 45; Meiss, *Late XIV Century*, 1967, index, figs. 323, 678; *idem*, "*Decameron*," 1967, p. 58; *idem*, *Boucicaut Master*, 1968, p. 93; *idem*, "Breviary Master," 1970.

BRIT. MUS., Add. 35311

Breviary, Use of Rome, 1st Part (Nov. 29–April 22). 438 fols.; 244 × 178 mm. All miniatures are by the Master of the Breviary of Jean sans Peur and his assistants unless otherwise indicated. The small initials, all by assistants, are not stylistically classified.

MINIATURES:

Folio

Psalter

8 David in prayer and dictating (Ps. 1)
26v David in prayer (Ps. 26 [27])
37 David pointing to his tongue, the devil behind him (Ps. 38 [39])
45v David in prayer and a Fool (Ps. 52 [53])
53v David in the water (Ps. 68 [69])
64v David playing carillon (Ps. 80 [81])
74 David with singers (Ps. 97 [98])
85 Trinity (Ps. 109 [110])

Temporale

158v Nativity
180v Martyrdom of St. Thomas à Becket
190 St. Sylvestre baptizing Constantine
193 St. Leo the Great dictating
199 Adoration of the Magi
208 Annunciation to the Shepherds
216 Baptism of Christ
221v St. Paul handing his epistles to a kneeling man
238v St. Paul preaching
279 Temptation of Christ (Circle of the Humilities Master)
286 Isaac blessing Jacob (Circle of the Humilities Master)
294 Joseph sold by his brothers
302 Moses and the burning bush (Circle of the Humilities Master)
310v Bishop blessing (?) people (Circle of the Humilities Master)
322v Entry into Jerusalem (Egerton workshop)
327 Judas receiving silver (Egerton workshop)
329 Jeremiah lamenting (Egerton workshop)
333v Crucifixion, flagellation below
337 Entombment (Egerton workshop)

Sanctorale

341 Martyrdom of Sts. Saturninus and Sisinus (initial)
342 St. Andrew
345 St. Nicholas, miracle of the three children
346 St. Ambrose (initial)
348v Helsinus saved from drowning by the Virgin
351 St. Melciadus (initial)
351v St. Damasus performing a miracle (initial)
352 Martyrdom of St. Lucy
354 St. Thomas casting down idols
355v St. Felix of Nola casting down an idol (initial)
357v St. Anthony abbot
360 Martyrdom of St. Fabian
360v Martyrdom of St. Sebastian
362 St. Agnes and the virgins appearing to her family at her tomb
364v St. Vincent
367v Conversion of St. Paul
371 Purification of the Virgin
374v Martyrdom of St. Agatha
377v St. Peter as pope (*Cathedra Petri*)
379 St. Matthias
381v St. Gregory (initial)
382 St. Benedict (initial)
384 Annunciation
388 Martyrdom of St. Anicetus (initial)

Common of the Feasts of the Virgin

419 Visitation (initial)
422v Nativity (initial)
424 Annunciation to the Shepherds (initial)
425 Adoration of the Magi (initial)
426v Presentation (initial)
427v Flight into Egypt (initial)
430 Coronation (initial)

Office of the Dead

435 Job on the dung heap exhorted by his wife and friends

London

BRIT. MUS., Harley 2897

Breviary, Use of Rome, 2nd Part (April 22–Nov. 25). 452 pp.; 250×132 mm. All miniatures are by the Master of the Breviary of Jean sans Peur and his assistants unless otherwise indicated. The small initials, all by assistants, are not stylistically classified.

MINIATURES:

Folio
Psalter
23v David in prayer (Master of Guillebert de Metz)
33v David pointing to his tongue, the Devil behind him (Master of Guillebert de Metz)
42v David in prayer, Fool (Master of Guillebert de Metz)
50v David in the water (Master of Guillebert de Metz)
62 David playing carillon (Master of Guillebert de Metz)
72v David with five singers (Master of Guillebert de Metz)
84 Trinity (Master of Guillebert de Metz)

Temporale
156 Risen Christ with two disciples on road to Emmaus (Circle of the Humilities Master)
157v Bishop (St. Augustine?) preaching (Circle of the Humilities Master)
158v Miraculous draught of fishes (Circle of the Humilities Master)
159 Angel appears to Holy Women at the empty sepulchre (Egerton Master and workshop)
160 Saint Bishop (St. Ambrose?) preaching (Circle of the Humilities Master)
161 Mary Magdalene finds the tomb empty (Circle of the Humilities Master)
164v Risen Christ appears to the disciples (Circle of the Humilities Master)
170 St. John on Patmos, the Devil behind him (Circle of the Humilities Master)
179v St. James the Greater preaching (Circle of the Humilities Master)
182 St. Peter preaching (Circle of the Humilities Master, strongly influenced by Breviary Master)
184 St. John preaching (Circle of the Humilities Master, on miniature begun by Breviary Master)
186v St. Jude writing (Circle of the Humilities Master)
188v Ascension
211v Elevation of the Host (St. Thomas Aquinas?) (Circle of the Humilities Master)
220 Anna before the priest Eli (Circle of the Humilities Master)
225v David mourning Saul and Jonathan (Circle of the Humilities Master)
228 Abisag placed in David's bed (Circle of the Humilities Master)
229v Ahaziah ill in bed, Elijah threatens the messenger, the altar of Beelzebub (Circle of the Humilities Master)
249 Job's city in the Land of Uz (Egerton Master and workshop)
252v Tobias the Elder greets Tobias the Younger and Sarah at the gate (Egerton Master and workshop)
254v The city of Ekbatana attacked (Egerton Master and workshop)
258 Battle of Darius and Philip of Macedon (Egerton Master and workshop)

Sanctorale
282 St. George and the dragon
282v Martyrdom of St. Mark
283v Martyrdom of St. Cletus or St. Marcellus (initial)
284 St. Vitale (initial)
285 St. Philip
285v St. James the Less
288v Invention of the Cross, angels with Passion symbols
290 St. John (before the Latin Gate)
302 St. Barnabas (initial)
303v St. Anthony of Padua (initial)
315 Birth of St. John the Baptist
321v St. Leo the Great (initial)
323 St. Peter and St. John healing the cripple before the temple
326 Christ giving the keys to St. Peter
328v Martyrdom of Sts. Processus and Martianus (initial)
333 Martyrdom of the Seven Brothers (initial)
336 Mary Magdalene
338 Martyrdom of St. Christine (initial)
338v St. James the Greater
339v St. Christopher
340v St. Anne teaching the Virgin to read
347v Sts. Abdon and Sennen in prison (initial)
349 Angel appearing to St. Peter in prison (Circle of the Humilities Master)
350v Beheading of St. Stephen, pope (initial)
351v Finding of the body of St. Stephen (initial)
353 St. Dominic (initial)
358 Martyrdom of St. Lawrence (Circle of the Humilities Master)
366v Death of the Virgin (Circle of the Humilities Master)
379 Martyrdom of St. Bartholomew
380 St. Augustine (Circle of the Humilities Master)
381v Beheading of St. John the Baptist
385 Birth of the Virgin (Egerton Master and workshop)
390v Heraclius carrying Cross (Circle of the Humilities Master)
394v Martyrdom of St. Lucy (Circle of the Humilities Master)
396 St. Maurice carrying his head (Circle of the Humilities Master)
399v Sts. Cosmas and Damian (initial)
401 St. Michael fighting the Devil (Circle of the Humilities Master)
404v St. Jerome (Circle of the Humilities Master)

Folio	
406	St. Remigius (initial)
407v	St. Francis receiving stigmata (Circle of the Humilities Master)
421	Martyrdom of Sts. Dionysus, Rusticus and Eleutherius
422v	St. Luke
426	St. Simon with Cross
426v	St. Jude
435	St. Martin and the beggar
440v	Angel, Sts. Cecilia and Valerian (Circle of the Humilities Master)
444v	Martyrdom of St. Clement (Circle of the Humilities Master)
447v	St. Catherine of Alexandria (Circle of the Humilities Master)
449v	Christ (?) attended by angels blessing a church (Circle of the Humilities Master)

London

BRIT. MUS., Egerton 1070 (Fig. 334)

Book of Hours, Use of Paris. 154 fols.; 220×162 mm.

HISTORY: The original owner is unknown. René d'Anjou acquired it, and for him an illuminator added a sail with the motto "En Dieu en soit" in the lower border of the folios at the beginning of each Office. This device appears in the margins of another manuscript, lat. 1156 A, perhaps René's also. His additions in Egerton 1070 include also: on fol. 4v his arms, which indicate a date after 1435, when the death of Jeanne de Naples gave him Hungary, Jerusalem and Sicily; the *City of Jerusalem* on fol. 5; a *Skeleton holding René's arms* on fol. 53; *Angels holding the host* on fol. 110, and *King David receiving homage* on fol. 139. Prayers written in a humanist script were added on fols. 14–14v, 23v, 43v–44.

STYLE AND DATE: With his workshop the Egerton Master painted all of the full-page miniatures of the Hours of the Virgin, the Penitential Psalms and the Office of the Dead. These large miniatures, always on a verso, are faced by historiated initials, some with delicate landscapes painted in a pointillist technique. Since this illumination is the most important we possess by the Egerton Master, Mrs. Schilling has appropriately named the illuminator after it.

The Egerton Master worked with assistants of the Boucicaut Master (see *Boucicaut Master*, p. 95 f.), with a follower of the Parement Master and a follower of Jacquemart de Hesdin. The manuscript may probably be dated about 1410.

BIBLIOGRAPHY: Durrieu, *Rev. de l'art a. et m.*, XX, 1906, p. 24 f.; Durrieu, in *Florilegium Melchior de Vogüé*, 1909, pp. 197–207; London, Brit. Mus., *Reproductions*, II, 1910, p. 14, pls. XXXVI, XXXVII; Durrieu, *Rev. de l'art chrét.*, 1913, p. 310; London, Brit. Mus., Millar, 1933, p. 34 f., pl. XLVII; Schilling, 1954, p. 272 ff.; Meiss, *Art Bull.*, 1956, p. 190; Pächt, *Cahiers*, 1956, p. 41 ff.; Meiss, *Late XIV Century*, 1967, pp. 357, 381 n. 64; *idem*, *Boucicaut Master*, 1968, index, figs. 148, 205–209.

CLASSIFICATION OF MINIATURES:

Egerton Master and workshop: fols. 6v–45, 54v–90v, 95–96v, 98–103v, 105–109v.

Boucicaut workshop: fols. 91–94v, 111–134, 140.

Follower of the Parement Master: fols. 97, 97v.

Follower of Jacquemart de Hesdin: fols. 104, 104v.

MINIATURES:

Folio	
4v	Arms of René d'Anjou (between 1435–1453)
5	City of Jerusalem
6–11v	Calendar
12	St. John the Evangelist (medallion)
12v	St. Luke (medallion)
13	St. Matthew (medallion)
13v	St. Mark (medallion)
Hours of the Virgin	
15v	Annunciation
16	Virgin weaving (initial)
24v	Nativity
25	Virgin standing (initial)
29v	Visitation
30	Virgin before *prie dieu* (initial)
32v	Annunciation to the Shepherds
33	Shepherd leaning on staff gazes upward (initial)
34v	Adoration of the Magi
35	Three Magi (initial)
36v	Presentation in the Temple
37	Side of a building (initial)
38v	Flight into Egypt
39	Cornfield (initial)
41v	Coronation of the Virgin
42	Gold stars in a blue sky (initial)
Penitential Psalms	
44v	David praying
45	Landscape (initial)
Office of the Dead	
53	Skeleton and arms of René d'Anjou
54v	Funeral service
55	Tomb in a landscape (initial)

Folio

Hours abridged for each day

70v	Trinity. Prophet in initial (Sunday)
72	Procession of two monks and two mourners (Monday)
73v	Male saints. Angel censing in initial (Tuesday)
74v	Pentecost (Wednesday)
75	Holy Ghost (initial)
76	Sacrament: Altar with the host; Angel with chalice in initial (Thursday)
77v	Crucifixion. Three crosses in initial (Friday)
79	Madonna holding Christ Child. Angel with basket in initial (Saturday)
80v–109v	Saints, and the following scenes: 81v Conception of the Virgin; 82 Nativity; 83 Massacre of the Innocents; 83v Adoration of the Magi; 87 Presentation of the Christ Child; 89 Annunciation; 90 Resurrection; 91v Finding of the True Cross; 92v Ascension; 93 Pentecost; 93v Trinity and Mass; 99 Ascension of the Virgin; 101v Birth of the Virgin and Exaltation of the Cross; 103 Instruments of the Passion; 106 Mass for the Dead
110	Two Angels hold Host
111v	Madonna and Child and St. John the Evangelist (O Intemerata)
112	Trinity (Office of the Holy Ghost)
113	Last Supper (Office of the Holy Sacrament)
115	Madonna and Child enthroned (Office of the Virgin)
116	Crucifixion (Office of the Cross)
117	Funeral Service (Office of the Dead)
118v	Betrayal
124v	Way to Calvary
129v	Flagellation
134v	Crucifixion
139	King David receives homage
140	Creation of Adam, Creation of Eve, Cain kills Abel

London

BRITISH MUSEUM, Harley 2934

(Figs. 831–834, 837)

Book of Hours, Use of Troyes. 195 fols.; 157×107 mm.

EARLY HISTORY: There are no signs of original ownership. The arms in the borders were added later.

STYLE AND DATE: All the miniatures and borders were painted by the Rohan workshop. Figures related to the subject of the miniature, included in secondary framed miniatures in later manuscripts, appear here in the borders. They stand on the vines or on patches of ground between the acanthus and strawberries. Though the style of the master does not seem to have been formed in Paris, he had clearly begun to study Parisian illumination. The influence of the Boucicaut Master is seen in the landscapes, particularly in the blazing sun in the *Visitation*. The arcaded dome, half-timber house and tower above the chamber in which the Magi adore the Christ Child recall the combination of edifices in the miniatures by the Boucicaut Master and the Brussels Initials Master.

The manuscript contains compositions and motifs used later by the workshop. The motif of a St. John who supports the Virgin but turns his head to look up at Christ, introduced earlier in the *Deposition* in the *Giac Hours*, appears here in the *Crucifixion* and later in the famous *Lamentation* in the *Rohan Hours*. The composition of another miniature in the *Rohan Hours*, the *Flight into Egypt*, was first introduced here.

This manuscript was probably painted at an early date, towards 1412.

BIBLIOGRAPHY: Porcher, *Rohan Hours*, 1959, p. 32 n. 11; Meiss, *Late XIV Century*, 1967, p. 398 n. 98; *idem*, *Boucicaut Master*, 1968, p. 147 n. 35.

MINIATURES:

Folio

3–14v	Calendar
Gospel Readings	
15	St. Luke
17	St. John
19	St. Mark
21	St. Matthew
Hours of the Virgin	
34	Visitation
46	Nativity
52	Annunciation to the Shepherds
57	Adoration of the Magi
61v	Presentation in the Temple
66v	Flight into Egypt
74	Coronation of the Virgin
Penitential Psalms	
82	David praying
Office of the Dead	
106	Cadaver lies on the ground next to coffin
154	Crucifixion
160	Pentecost

London

BRIT. MUS., Harley ms. 4431

See Christine de Pisan, *Collected Writings*

London

COLL. OF COUNT ANTOINE SEILERN

(Figs. 424, 425, 469, 625–633)

Book of Hours, Use of Rome. 153 fols.; 229×178 mm.

EARLY HISTORY: The early history of this manuscript is unknown.

STYLE AND DATE: This beautiful Book of Hours, with its soft colors and unusually rich borders, is by far the best manuscript painted by a follower of the Limbourgs. Jean Porcher, in fact, ascribed the illumination to one of the brothers, but, apart from the stylistic differences, the fact that several miniatures repeat more or less closely compositions of the *Belles Heures* and the *Très Riches Heures* discloses an attitude unlike that of the Limbourgs themselves.

For a fuller discussion of this manuscript see the chapter on the followers of the Limbourgs.

BIBLIOGRAPHY: London, Sotheby, October 13–15, 1942, lot 117; Schilling, 1942, pp. 194–197; Pächt, *Mary of Burgundy* [1948], p. 53 n. 20; *idem*, 1950, p. 40 n. 2; Panofsky, *Netherlandish Painting*, 1953, I, p. 62, n. 62[6]; Porcher, *Belles Heures*, 1953, pp. 7, 23 f., 42 f., figs. 13, 14; Paris, Bibl. nat. (Porcher), 1955, p. 93 f. no. 191; Porcher, *Enluminure*, 1959, p. 64, fig. 70; *idem*, in *Enciclopedia dell' arte*, VIII, p. 619 ff.; Meiss, *Boucicaut Master*, 1968, p. 32, fig. 144.

MINIATURES:

(Manuscript is not foliated)

Gospel Readings

St. John
St. Luke
St. Matthew
St. Mark

Passion according to St. John

Man of Sorrows

Hours of the Virgin

Annunciation
Visitation
Nativity
Annunciation to the Shepherds
Adoration of the Magi
Presentation (Flemish artist)
Flight into Egypt
Coronation of the Virgin (Flemish artist)

Penitential Psalms

Last Judgment

Office of the Dead

Mass for the Dead

Hours of the Passion

Agony in the Garden
Betrayal
Pilate washes his hands
Flagellation
Mockery. The Crowning with Thorns
Crucifixion
Descent from the Cross
Deposition (Flemish artist)
Entombment

Lyon

BIBL., ms. 27

See Virgil

Munich

BAYERISCHE STAATSBIBL., ms. gall. 11

See Christine de Pisan, *Mutacion*

New Haven

YALE UNIVERSITY, BEINECKE LIBRARY, ms. 400

(Fig. 262)

De Lévis Hours, Book of Hours, Use of Paris. 189 fols. (others missing); 216×165 mm.

EARLY HISTORY: Phrases such as "michi famulo tuo" indicate that the manuscript was executed for a man. Armorial shields and a motto (fol. 93: or three chevrons sable and the motto "A James"; fol. 77: the same, but impaling or five piles issuant from the dexter side sable) perhaps indicate an owner of about the seventeenth century belonging to the French De Lévis family.

STYLE AND DATE: This very interesting manuscript was illuminated by masters from two quite different workshops. The Luçon Master himself painted the miniature on fol. 93, and assistants executed those on fols. 51, 62, 77, and 169. These are manifestly the latest works we know in the Luçon style, and they may be dated *ca.* 1417. The remaining miniatures in the manuscript, painted by two illuminators in the Bedford workshop, can likewise be dated about the same time.

The *De Lévis Hours* makes a basic contribution to our understanding of the illuminators associated in the

Bedford group because it presents an earlier version of many compositions familiar from the well-known Books of Hours of the 'twenties.

BIBLIOGRAPHY: New York, Grolier Club, *Catalogue*, 1892, no. 41; Hoe, *Catalogue*, 1909, p. 33 f.; London, Sotheby, May 9, 1933; Schilling, 1954, p. 278 n. 20; Meiss, *De Lévis Hours*, 1972.

MINIATURES:

Calendar		
1		
Gospel Lessons		
13		
Hours of the Virgin		
23	Annunciation	*Matins*
42	Visitation	*Lauds*
51	Nativity	*Prime*
56	Annunciation to the Shepherds	*Terce*
	(Adoration of the Magi	*Sext)*
62	Presentation in the Temple	*None*
66	Flight into Egypt	*Vespers*
72	Coronation of the Virgin	*Compline*
Penitential Psalms		
77	David	
Hours of the Passion		
93	Betrayal	*Matins*
98v	Christ before Pilate	*Lauds*
104	Flagellation	*Prime*
107	Way to Calvary	*Terce*
		(Sext)
		(None)
		(Vespers)
119	Entombment	*Compline*
Hours of the Holy Ghost		
126	Pentecost	
Office of the Dead		
130		
Five Wounds		
169	Last Judgment	

Note: Miniatures in parentheses are missing.

New York

METROPOLITAN MUS: OF ART, THE CLOISTERS

(Figs. 329, 333, 341, 343, 363, 364, 371, 385, 386, 389, 397, 398, 402, 403, 406, 407, 409–411, 415–418, 420–423, 426–428, 430, 431, 434–436, 438, 439, 441, 442, 444, 445, 448, 451, 452, 454, 455, 463, 466–468, 470, 472–474, 476–479, 485–488, 492, 493, 496–499, 503, 637, 638, 641, 687, 693, 751, 799, 861, 891)

Belles Heures de Jean de Berry. Use of Paris. 225 fols.; 238×170 mm.

EARLY HISTORY: The description of this manuscript in the inventory of 1413 does not specify the names of the illuminators (see above, Limbourgs, Documents). The position of the item in the inventory indicates that the Duke received the completed work in 1408 or early in 1409, and this date coincides with the evidence of style. Soon after the death of the Duke in 1416 the Book of Hours was acquired by Yolande d'Anjou, wife of Duke Louis II.

STYLE: All three brothers appear to have worked on the manuscript, and their respective contributions are usually indicated in the following list of miniatures. These brief indications need to be supplemented by the foregoing text, which attempts to deal more fully and more precisely with the complexity of a collaborative work of this kind. When no author is listed the writer has not succeeded in identifying the brother who was chiefly responsible for the miniature.

BIBLIOGRAPHY: Delisle, *Mélanges*, 1880, pp. 283–293; *idem*, *Cabinet*, III, 1881, pp. 179 no. 100, 340; Guiffrey, *Inventaires*, I, 1894, pp. CLXVI no. 26, 253 no. 960; II, 1896, pp. 238 no. 507, 319; Durrieu, *Gaz. B.-A.*, 1906, pp. 265–292; Delisle, *Charles V*, II, 1907, pp. 239 no. 100, 290; Winkler, 1930, p. 95 f.; Panofsky, *Netherlandish Painting*, 1953, I, p. 62 f., n. 249[3]; Porcher, *Belles Heures*, 1953; Freeman, 1956, pp. 93–104; New York, The Cloisters, Rorimer and Freeman, *Belles Heures*, 1958; Porcher, *French Miniatures*, 1959, pp. 62, 64, fig. 66; pl. LXVIII; *idem*, in *Enciclopedia dell' arte*, VIII, p. 619 ff.; Meiss, *Gaz. B.-A.*, 1963, pp. 148, 150 f., 156 f., 159 f., 162, figs. 5, 8, 10, 12, 13; Pächt, *Gaz. B.-A.*, 1963, pp. 109–122; Meiss, *Late XIV Century*, 1967, index, figs. 261, 495, 496, 518, 746, 779, 785; *idem*, *Boucicaut Master*, 1968, index, figs. 126, 145, 146, 155, 157, 487; *idem*, "Breviary Master," 1970, pp. 2 f., 7–9, 18, pls. IIIa, VIIIb; Meiss with Off, 1971, pp. 228, 233; April, 1971.

COLLATION:

Gathering	*Folios*	*No. of Folios*	
1	A–1	2	Guard, plus folio with inscription of Flamel
2	2–13	12	
3	14–20	6+1	14 blank on both sides; attached to small stub, around 20. 20v has a gold frame for miniature and a border but no text.

Gathering	*Folios*	*No. of Folios*	
4	21–29	7+2	21 and 29 compose a sheet of whiter vellum added around gathering 4 long ago (color of 30 transferred to 29v but not to 28v). The last four lines of text of St. John appear at the beginning of 22; the preceding text and the miniature are lost. 28, now a single leaf, was no doubt originally part of a sheet that contained much of the missing text.
5	30–37	8	Ends with catchword
6	38–45	8	Ends with catchword
7	46–53	8	Ends with catchword
8	54–61	8	Ends with catchword
9	62–69	8	Ends with catchword
10	70–79	10	78–79v merely ruled in red on one side. 73–74 and 75–76 are both bifolios placed at the center of this gathering.
11	80–87	8	
12	88–93	6	93v is only ruled.
13	94–98	4+1	98, an inserted leaf, blank on both sides.
14	99–106	8	Ends with catchword
15	107–114	8	Ends with catchword
16	115–122	8	122 merely ruled on both sides. On verso an informal catchword: dne labia+
17	123–130	8	Ends with catchword
18	131–138	8	Ends with catchword
19	139–146	8	Ends with catchword
20	147–154	8	
21	155–162	8	Ends with catchword
22	163–170	8	Ends with catchword
23	171–178	8	Ends with catchword
24	179–182	4	
25	183–189 +190	6+1	No 188. 190, an inserted leaf, blank on both sides.
26	191–194	4	
27	195–202	8	Ends with catchword
28	203–210	8	Ends with catchword
29	211–218	8	Ends with catchword
30	219–222	4	
31	223–225	2+1	223 a single, inserted leaf, blank.

GATHERING 4

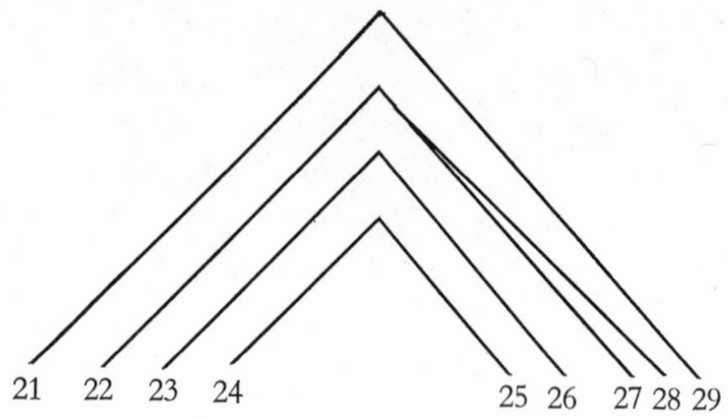

GATHERING 10

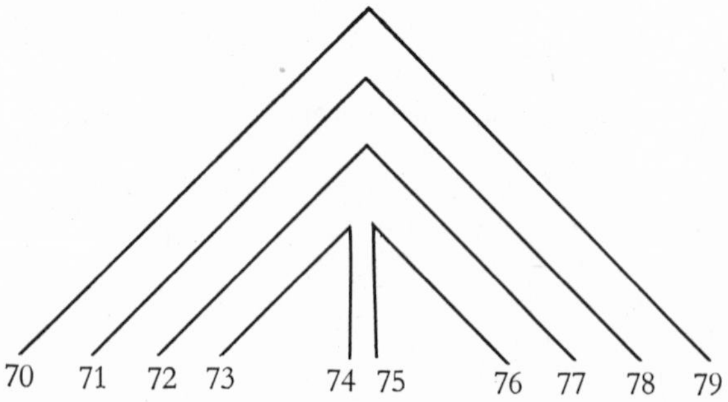

This collation is similar to, but by no means identical with, the one published by Porcher, *Belles Heures*, 1953, p. 34 f. It is also more complete. Contrary to his statement there was never a miniature for the prayer *Obsecro te*. The empty frame on 20v was not, as he says, intended for a miniature of St. John. Comparison with the *Très Riches Heures* shows that the amount of text of St. John on the missing folio would have left room also for a miniature. The empty frame is the same size as the miniatures in the Catherine cycle.
The one rubric that refers to the picture cycles was not written in the minium of the original scribe but in the blue and red of the titles and at a later moment in the production of the book. This rubric, on folio 182v, reads in full:

> Secuntur misse. Et primo de nativitate domini n(ost)ri ih(es)u xr(ist)i. Et primo ponitur vita beati ieronimi tota ystoriata.

The repetition of "Et primo" is odd, and suggests that the rubric is itself composite, reflecting two stages of thought.

MINIATURES:

Folio

2 January. Two men drinking, back to back (Janus); Water Bearer (Paul)
3 February. A man before a fire; Fishes (Paul)
4 March. Two men tending trees; Ram (Paul)
5 April. A man with flowers; Bull (Jean or Herman?)
6 May. Hawking; Twins (Jean or Herman?)
7 June. Scything; Crab (Paul?)
8 July. Binding sheaves; Lion (Paul)
9 August. Threshing grain; Virgin (Paul: upper)
10 September. Treading grapes; Balance (Paul: upper)
11 October. Sowing; Scorpion (Paul and Herman)
12 November. Beating down acorns for pigs; Archer
13 December. Slaughtering a pig; Capricorn (Paul)

Story of St. Catherine

15 St. Catherine studying (Jean?)
15v St. Catherine before Maxentius refuses to worship an idol (Paul and Jean)
16 St. Catherine confounding the doctors (Paul)
16v St. Catherine cast into prison (Paul and Jean)
17 St. Catherine bound to a column (Paul)
17v St. Catherine tended by angels and visited by the Queen (Paul)
18 The converted Queen beheaded before Maxentius (Paul and Jean)
18v Angels destroying the wheel (Paul)
19 Beheading of the converts, Porphyrius and his companions (Paul and Jean)
19v St. Catherine beheaded (Paul)
20 Angels carry St. Catherine's body to Mount Sinai (Paul)

Gospel Readings

St. John is missing
22 St. Matthew (Herman)
23 St. Luke (Herman?)
24 St. Mark

Prayers to the Virgin

26v Ara Coeli. *O Intemerata* (Jean and Herman?)

Hours of the Virgin

30 Annunciation. *Matins* (Paul)
41 St. Ambrose and St. Augustine. *Te Deum*
42v Visitation. *Lauds* (Paul and Jean)
48v Nativity. *Prime* (Paul)
52 Annunciation to the shepherds. *Terce* (Paul)
54v Adoration of the Magi. *Sext* (Paul)
57 Presentation in the Temple. *None* (Paul)
59v Massacre of the Innocents. *Vespers* (Herman?)
63 Flight into Egypt. *Compline* (Paul)

Penitential Psalms

66 David calling upon the Lord; an angel strikes down his enemies. Psalm 6 (Herman)
66v David in prayer. Psalm 31 (32)
67v David pierced by arrows. Psalm 37 (38)
68v David reproached by Nathan. Psalm 50 (51)
70 Two men in a cave call upon the Lord. Psalm 101 (102)
71v Two men in a cave, their jailer sleeping, call upon the Lord. Psalm 129 (130)
72 David on horseback pursued by Absalom (?). Psalm 142 (143) (Herman)

The Litany

73 Institution of the Great Litany by St. Gregory in time of Plague (Paul)
73v St. Gregory's procession (Paul)
74 Archangel Michael sheathes his sword (Paul)
74v Procession of Flagellants (Paul)

Hours of the Cross

80 Descent from the Cross (Paul assisted)

Hours of the Holy Spirit

84 Pentecost (Paul)

Fifteen Joys of the Virgin

88 A king and followers pray to the ascending Virgin
91 Jean de Berry in prayer

Seven Prayers invoking the Incarnation and Passion

91v Jeanne de Boulogne prays to the Trinity
93 Two men venerating the Cross. *Prayer to the Holy Cross*

Story of St. Bruno

94 Diocrès teaching
94v Diocrès declares himself justly accused by God
95 Burial of Diocrès (Paul)
95v St. Bruno and his students leaving Paris
96 The Bishop of Grenoble dreaming
96v St. Bruno and his companions before the bishop
97 They enter the Grande Chartreuse near Grenoble (Paul)
97v The Grande Chartreuse
99 Office of the Dead (design by Paul)

Office of the Passion

123 Agony in the Garden. *Matins* (Jean and Paul)
123v Betrayal. *Matins* (Herman and Paul)
124 Christ before Caiaphas. *Matins* (Herman)
131v Christ mocked. *Lauds* (Herman)
132 Flagellation. *Lauds* (Herman)
135v Christ before Pilate. *Prime* (Herman)
136 Pilate ordering the deliverance of Barabbas (?). *Prime* (Herman)
138 Pilate washing his hands. *Terce* (Herman)
138v Way to Calvary. *Terce* (Herman)
141v Christ nailed to the Cross. *Sext* (Herman)
142 Christ offered the sop. *Sext* (Herman and Paul)
145 Christ pierced with a lance. *None* (Herman)
145v Death of Christ. *None* (Herman)
149 Deposition. *Vespers* (Jean)
149v Lamentation. *Vespers* (Paul)
152 Entombment. *Compline* (Paul assisted)
152v Sleeping soldiers beside the tomb. *Compline* (Herman)

Suffrages to the Saints

155 Pentecost and Trinity

Story of Heraclius and the Cross

156 Heraclius in his *carpentum* returning the Cross to Jerusalem. (Jean and Herman?)
156v Heraclius on foot bearing the Cross (Herman with Paul)

Folio

157 Heraclius (?) and three others venerating the Cross
157v Enthroned Virgin with Child. *Commemoration of the Virgin* (Jean)
158 Archangel Michael trampling the chained devil
158v St. John the Baptist (Jean)
159 St. John the Evangelist (Jean)
159v St. Peter and St. Paul (Jean)
160 St. Andrew
160v St. James Major (Jean)
161 Martyrdom of St. Bartholomew (Paul and Jean)
162 Martyrdom of St. Stephen (Paul and Herman?)
162v Martyrdom of St. Lawrence (Jean)
163 Martyrdom of St. Vincent (Jean)
163v Martyrdom of St. Clement (Herman?)
164v St. Eustace (Jean)
165 St. Christopher (Jean)
165v St. Sebastian transfixed by arrows (Jean)
166v Martyrdom of St. Denis (Jean)
167 St. George killing the dragon (Jean)
168 St. Nicholas saving seafarers in a storm (Herman?)
169 St. Martin with a beggar (Jean with Paul)
170 St. Anthony of Padua preaching, and exorcising a devil (Jean)
171 St. Francis receiving the Stigmata (Jean)
172 St. Ambrose baptizing (Jean or Herman?)
172v St. Augustine recording his vision of the Trinity (Jean)
173 St. Louis approaching the Holy Land (Herman?)
174 St. Charlemagne
174v St. Maurus
175 St. Benedict
175v St. Bernard
176v St. Mary Magdalene wiping Christ's foot with her hair (Jean)
177 St. Margaret (Jean)
178 St. Agnes miraculously clothed in her hair
178v Martyrdom of the eleven thousand virgins (Herman?)
179 Martyrdom of St. Agatha (Jean)
179v Martyrdom of St. Lucy (Jean)
180 Martyrdom of St. Cecilia (Jean)
181 St. Geneviève (Jean)

Story of St. Jerome

183 St. Jerome following a course in pagan philosophy (Jean or Herman?)
183v St. Jerome dreams he is scourged before God for reading pagan authors (Jean)
184 St. Jerome ordained presbyter and cardinal (Jean or Herman?)
184v St. Jerome appears at Matins dressed as a woman (Jean)
185 St. Jerome leaves Constantinople (Jean)
185v St. Jerome in prayer contemplating the tomb of Christ (?) (Jean)
186 St. Jerome tempted by a vision of two women (Jean)
186v St. Jerome extracting the thorn from the lion's paw (Jean)
187 The lion, having found the missing ass, chases a caravan towards the monastery (Jean)
187v St. Jerome translating the Bible (Jean or Herman?)
189 Death of St. Jerome (Jean)
189v The ill at St. Jerome's bier during burial procession (Jean)

Story of St. Anthony Abbot and St. Paul the Hermit

191 St. Paul the Hermit and a companion watch a Christian spit his tongue in the face of a seductress (Jean)
191v St. Anthony seeking St. Paul's hermitage
192 St. Anthony guided by a centaur
192v St. Anthony and St. Paul fed by a dove (Jean)
193 St. Anthony sees St. Paul's soul carried to heaven by angels (Jean)
193v St. Anthony, helped by two lions, buries St. Paul (Jean)
194 St. Anthony attacked by demons (Jean)
194v Death of St. Anthony

Masses

195 Nativity. *Christmas* (Jean)
198 Resurrection. *Easter* (Jean)
199v Ascension. *Ascension* (Jean)
202 Celebration of Pentecost Mass. *Whitsunday* (Jean)
204 The Trinity. *Trinity Sunday* (Jean)
205v Elevation of the Host. *Corpus Domini* (Herman)
207v Man and a woman kneeling before an altar with the Cross. *Exaltation of the Cross* (Herman)
209 Virgin and Child with two angels. *Mass of the Virgin* (Paul)

Story of St. John the Baptist

211 The Baptist in the desert (Paul)
211v Baptism of Christ (Paul)
212 Decollation of the Baptist
212v Salome presenting the Baptist's head to Herod. *Nativity of St. John the Baptist* (Jean)
215 Death of Simon the Magician. *St. Peter and St. Paul*
215v Martyrdom of Sts. Peter and Paul (Herman)
218 Virgin and Child in Glory, surrounded by Saints. *All Saints* (Paul)
221 Funeral Service. *All Souls* (Paul)
223v Jean de Berry on a journey. *Prayer for travelers* (Paul and Jean)

A SUMMARY OF OBSERVATIONS ON THE MAKEUP AND DECORATION BY JOHN PLUMMER

As the collation above makes clear, the original scribal plan was laid out in gatherings of eight leaves, except for 10 with an extra bifolio with miniatures; 12 with six leaves; 24 and 30, each with a half gathering of four leaves to complete the texts of the Suffrages and the Masses; and 31 with three leaves that appear to be an addition to the original plan. On the contrary, all of the pictorial gatherings (3, 13, 25, and 26) consist of four or six leaves and do not appear to have been part of the scribal plan.

Among the blank leaves, those without rulings appear to be guard leaves inserted to protect various miniatures, while those with rulings are unused pages at the ends of sections of text. Ruled blanks, including some ruled on only one side, occur at the end of the Litany (fols. 78–79v), of gathering 12 with the Fifteen Joys (fol. 93v), and of the Office of the Dead (fols. 121v–122v). Gathering 12, with its six leaves and blank final page, was an afterthought. The other unused pages and the two "terminal" gatherings of four leaves indicate that the manuscript was written in the following units: gatherings 5–10, 14–16, 21–24, 27–30. These units, with some refinements, are also indicated by the original scribal catchwords written in a *bâtarde* script, which link together the following gatherings: 5–10, 14–16, 17–20, 21–24, 27–28, 29–30. A second kind of catchword written in a Gothic minuscule has been erased and trimmed in binding, but two examples are still legible under ultraviolet light. On folio 87v one can still read the word "placebo," though it has been badly trimmed. It proves that gathering 11 was to have been followed by gathering 14, and that gatherings 12 (Fifteen Joys) and 13 (Diocrès-Bruno cycle) were later intrusions. It also proves that these catchwords reflect an early, probably the original, plan of the manuscript and suggest that they may have been the work of the original editor. The second example of this kind of catchword occurs at the end of gathering 20 (fol. 154v) and reads "dn̄e labia." It indicates that the Office of the Passion was originally followed by the Hours of the Cross (gathering 11) or by some other Office or Hours that is now missing. Neither solution is entirely satisfactory, nor is either clearly preferable, but the catchword does show that the present manuscript does not conform to the original plan. A third kind of catchword, also written in a Gothic minuscule, but by a different hand and not erased, occurs on folios 122v and 210v. Both examples reflect the present order of gatherings and were added after many, if not all, of the miniatures were executed. They may have been added by the binder.

Besides the original rubrics written in minium, there are some later ones written in the same purplish red used in the legends of the pictorial cycles. These are employed exclusively in gatherings 4 and 12 and thus lend support to the other evidence showing that both gatherings were additions to the original plan. The purplish red is also used on three other pages: on folio 131 for the rubric for Lauds of the Office of the Passion, which had been presumably omitted by the original rubricator; on folio 154v for the rubric of the Suffrages, which gives further evidence that the Suffrages did not originally follow directly after the Office of the Passion; and on folio 182v for the rubric of the Masses and, as an afterthought, of the Jerome cycle, which connects the purplish red ink with the stage at which the miniature cycles were being added.

A study of the decoration in the manuscript makes abundantly clear that the illumination of the borders began with either gathering 4 or 5 and proceeded in roughly three stages from there to the end of the manuscript. The first stage runs from gathering 5 through 10, although gathering 7 was probably decorated later, in the third stage, and the bifolio with the Gregory cycle was surely done in that stage. The second stage of gatherings 12 through 20, including the Diocrès-Bruno cycle, shows the introduction of some new motifs, of which at least one is peculiar to this stage. Gathering 11 was apparently decorated out of sequence, since it has several third-stage motifs. This may be the result of changing its location from after the Office of the Passion to its present position. The third stage, gatherings 21 through 30, introduces many new motifs, which are also found in the Catherine cycle (gathering 3) and the Gregory cycle (fols. 73–74v) and thus argue that both cycles were done late and inserted into the earlier part of the manuscript. The calendar and gathering 31 were done last, since they share motifs not found in the rest of the manuscript, and the calendar with many unique motifs was probably done after gathering 31.

From the evidence cited above it is apparent that the *Belles Heures* was originally conceived as a rather modest manuscript with fewer texts and miniatures. Before the writing of the Office of the Passion, the plan included only single miniatures at the beginning of various texts and omitted the Gospel selections and Fifteen Joys (gatherings 4 and 12), as well as the preceding picture cycles of Catherine, Gregory, and Diocrès-Bruno. With the Office of the Passion, the scribes left space for multiple miniatures, and with the Suffrages for picture cycles with their own special legends. This revised and augmented plan, according to the evidence of the gatherings, catchwords, rubrics, and decoration, included the insertion into the earlier part of the manuscript of gatherings 3, 4, 12, and 13 and the bifolio with the Gregory cycle. These results agree with the conclusions presented by Millard Meiss in the text above. The new plan surely reveals the desire of the Limbourgs, in concert with the Duke de Berry, to continually enlarge their ambitions and to surpass their own achievements.

(This is a shortened version of an article that will be published elsewhere with fuller documentation.)

New York

PIERPONT MORGAN LIBRARY, M. 133

See St. John, *Apocalypse*

New York

PIERPONT MORGAN LIBRARY, M. 515

(Fig. 412)

Book of Hours, Use of Nantes. 216 fols.; 140 × 100 mm.

EARLY HISTORY: In the colophon on fol. 216v the scribe Yvo Luce states that the manuscript was written and illuminated at Nantes in 1402: "L'an mil IIII (C) et II furent escriptes et enlumines cestes matines a la ville de Nantes." Yvo signed his name in several other places as well. At the end of the Hours of the Virgin, on fol. 94, an inscription contemporary with the text but now erased gives the name of the original owner, Guillaume Mauléon. "Ceste matine sont a Guileume Mauleon." In the seventeenth century the manuscript belonged to the Mazerie family, which was related to the Mauléon through intermarriage.

STYLE: All the miniatures are in the style of the Coronation Master, and the *chef* himself probably painted the *Crucifixion* and the imposing *Man of Sorrows*. If the colophon is to be believed the illumination would be the only work in this style known to have been executed outside of Paris, and it seems highly improbable, in any event, that the illuminators remained in Nantes for any significant length of time.

BIBLIOGRAPHY: De Ricci, *Census*, II, 1937, p. 1464 no. 515; Panofsky, *Netherlandish Painting*, 1953, I, pp. 383 n. 58², 453 n. 237⁸; Meiss, *Late XIV Century*, 1967, pp. 355, 399 n. 28, fig. 823; *idem*, *Boucicaut Master*, 1968, index.

MINIATURES:

Folio	
35	Visitation
50v	Nativity
58v	Annunciation to the Shepherds
64v	Adoration of the Magi
70	Presentation in the Temple
76	Flight into Egypt
95	Christ in Majesty
125	Crucifixion
130v	Man of Sorrows
135	Trinity
153	Funeral Service

Paris

BIBL. DE L'ARSENAL, ms. 664

(Figs. 63, 160, 161, 164, 176, 178, 182, 188, 193, 194, 199, 204, 210, 230)

Terence, *Comedies* (in Latin). 237 fols. 335 × 240 mm.

EARLY HISTORY: The inventory of Jean de Berry tells us that the Duke acquired this manuscript after the death in 1415 of the Dauphin Louis, duc de Guyenne, through the latter's confessor, Jean d'Arsonval. When Berry died the executors of the Dauphin's estate demanded its return. The manuscript has therefore been named the *Térence des ducs*.

One cannot be certain that the Dauphin Louis was the original owner even though he collected manuscripts and a dolphin appears on the sign of an inn on fol. 36v (Fig. 161). In the margin of the frontispiece an angel holds a banner decorated with the royal arms, *France ancien*. There is, however, no additional evidence to show that the manuscript was executed for King Charles VI; it did not appear in the inventories of his library in 1411 or 1413. Putti hold scrolls with a motto "De bien en mieux" that neither we nor any of the specialists we have consulted have been able to identify. Evidence not hitherto cited for the Dauphin Louis as the original owner is his connection with Martin Gouge, discussed above. It was Gouge who had given an illustrated Terence to Jean de Berry for New Year, 1408.

The subsequent history of the manuscript is unknown until it appeared in the mid-eighteenth century in the library of the comte d'Argenson, minister of war of Louis XV. The Marquis de Paulmy, founder of the Arsenal library, acquired the Terence as well as many other manuscripts from the Argenson library after the latter's death. Some time before the early nineteenth century six folios were cut from the manuscript, which originally had thirty gatherings of eight leaves each. Missing from the existing manuscript are folios 33 and 40 (the first and last folios of the fifth gathering), folio 110 (the sixth folio of the fourteenth gathering), folio 149 (the fifth folio of the nineteenth gathering) and the third and sixth folios of the last gathering. Miniatures belonging to two of these folios were acquired in 1814 by the city of Nantes for the local Museum, where they are framed as little pictures (Fig. 203). They had belonged to Pierre-Nicolas Fournier, the *inspecteur voyer de la ville de Nantes*. They were cut from the original fol. 40, Act V, scene 3 of the *Lady of Andros*, and from the third folio of the last gathering, Act V, scene 2 of the *Mother-in-law*. The two miniatures have been damaged and reworked, but the restorer preserved the original forms so that the Luçon and Orosius styles are still recognizable.

Of the three copies of the *Comedies* illustrated in the early fifteenth century the *Térence des ducs* has the best text, complete with scholia. A prologue in large script heads each play. Each scene begins with a description of the action, the *argumentum*. The miniature falls between the *argumentum* and the names of the characters, which are written in red. The order of the plays, however, is unlike the one that was traditional from the Carolingian period on and which was preserved in the other two early fifteenth-century French Terences.

STYLE AND DATE: Four workshops collaborated on the illumination of this Terence. The Luçon Master was no doubt in charge, and he imposed an exceptional degree of uniformity on his collaborators, who normally worked in diverse manners. He and his assistants painted the miniatures in the first two plays through fol. 85v, as well as fols. 169–204v in *Phormio*. The master himself painted the frontispiece, but the border was executed by an artist belonging to the Bedford trend. The Cité des Dames workshop took up the illumination in the *Self-Tormentor*, fols. 90–125, imitating the style of the Luçon workshop. *The Adelphoe* and the first miniature in *Phormio*, which ends a gathering (fols. 128–168), were illustrated by a readily distinguishable illuminator in the Bedford trend who also worked in the famous *Livre de la chasse*, fr. 616. The Orosius Master and his workshop painted the *Mother-in-law*, fols. 209v–235v, giving the manuscript some of its finest miniatures. The manuscript is famous for its clear, transparent color and its exquisite finish.

The illuminators of the *Térence des ducs* certainly knew Jean de Berry's Terence. The Luçon Master copied its frontispiece. The costumes of the two manuscripts are similar, especially in the *Lady of Andros*. These relations are readily understood if it was Martin Gouge, the donor of Berry's Terence, who also ordered the *Térence des ducs*.

All evidence, especially the styles of the participating workshops, indicates that the Arsenal Terence was completed around 1412.

BIBLIOGRAPHY: Paris, Arsenal, Martin, II, 1886, p. 1 f. no. 664; Guiffrey, *Inventaires*, I, 1894, p. 335, II, 1896, p. 301; Martin, *Comptes rendus*, 1904, pp. 124, 131; *idem*, *Rev. archéol.*, 1904, pp. 28, 45; *idem*, *Térence*, 1907; Holkham Hall (Dorez), 1908, p. 62; Martin, *Miniature française*, 1923, pp. 78, 102 f., fig. CXVIII, color pl. 4; Martens, *Meister Francke*, 1929, p. 61; Panofsky, *Netherlandish Painting*, 1953, I, pp. 61, 76, 383 n. 58[2]; Paris, Bibl. nat. (Porcher), 1955, p. 81 no. 165; Meiss, *Art Bull.*, 1956, p. 193; Thomas, 1958, p. 114 f.; Porcher, *Enluminure*, 1959, p. 65; Vienna, Kunsthist. Mus., *Katalog*, 1962, p. 180 f., no. 127; Meiss, *Late XIV Century*, 1967, index; *idem*, *Boucicaut Master*, 1968, pp. 35, 62, 82; *idem*, "*Decameron*," 1967, p. 60 f.; Meiss and Off, 1972; Meiss, *De Lévis Hours*, 1972, pp. 15, 23.

MINIATURES:

Folio

1v Frontispiece Above, Calliopius reads in a Roman theatre; below, Terence, seated, points to his manuscript

Andria (The Lady of Andros)

4v Simo confides in Sosia; Simo's two slaves carry provisions to the kitchen

8v Simo approaches Davus; Simo warns Davus

10 Davus sees Mysis leave her house

11 Archilis attends to Glycerium; Mysis, on leaving the house, sees Pamphilus

12 Pamphilus reflects, his back to Mysis; on the right they discuss

14v Charinus speaks to Byrria; Charinus speaks to Pamphilus

16v Davus brings good news to Pamphilus and Charinus

19 Davus advises Pamphilus; on the right, Simo approaches

20 Byrria overhears Pamphilus, who stands with Davus, tell Simo that he agrees to be married

21 Simo questions his servant Davus

Folio	
22	Simo and Davus overhear Mysis tell Lesbia that Pamphilus will educate Glycerium's child
23	Within the house, Lesbia gives directions to Archilis; Simo and Davus listen outside
25	Simo meets Chremes
27	Simo informs Davus that Pamphilus' marriage is settled; Davus despairs at the arrival of Pamphilus
28v	Pamphilus and Davus
29v	Charinus reproves Pamphilus
31v	Mysis invites Pamphilus into Glycerium's house; Charinus and Davus stand aside
34v	Chremes overhears Davus and Mysis discussing the plight of the child at Simo's door
36v	Crito greets Mysis before an inn with a sign bearing a blue dolphin
37v	Chremes informs Simo of the new-born child
38v	Davus speaks to Simo and Chremes; Dromo leads Davus away
	Pamphilus confronts Simo and Chremes; Crito stands aside (miniature in Nantes)
41v	Chremes learns from Crito that Glycerium is his daughter; Davus released from the stocks
43v	Pamphilus tells Davus and Charinus that he may marry Glycerium
Eunuchus	(The Eunuch)
47	Parmeno counsels his master, Phaedria; Thais leaves her house
48v	Thais asks Phaedria to visit the country
51v	Phaedria asks Parmeno to send two slaves—Dorus, the eunuch, and an Ethiopian maid—to Thais
52v	Gnatho speaks to Parmeno; Gnatho presents Pamphila to Thais
54v	Chaerea meets Archidemides; Chaerea asks Parmeno about Pamphila
57v	Parmeno eavesdrops on Thraso and Gnatho
59v	Thais and Pythias greet Thraso and Gnatho; Parmeno presents the Ethiopian and Chaerea, disguised as the eunuch Dorus, to Thais
61v	Chremes addresses Pythias; Dorias leads Chremes to Thraso's house
62v	Antipho looks for Chaerea
63v	Chaerea, as the eunuch, tells Antipho about Pamphila
66	Dorias carries Thais' jewels
67	Phaedria encounters Pythias
68	Dorias and Pythias tell Phaedria that the eunuch has raped Pamphila
69	Phaedria, Dorias and Pythias confront Dorus, the eunuch
71	Chremes speaks with Pythias; Thais approaches
72	Pythias brings the casket containing proof that Pamphila is Chremes' sister to Thais and Chremes
73v	Thraso and his soldiers are repulsed by the reply of Thais and Chremes at the windows of Thais' house
75v	Pythias informs Thais that Chaerea has raped Pamphila
76v	Chaerea, in the eunuch's costume, avoids his father and mother but is accosted by Pythias and Thais
78v	Chremes returns with Sophrona
79v	Pythias tells Parmeno that Chaerea will be punished; arrival of Laches
81	Parmeno tells all to Laches; Pythias listens in the doorway
82v	Pythias tells Parmeno that she has made a fool out of him
83v	Thraso and Gnatho; Chaerea leaves Thais' house
84v	Chaerea tells Parmeno of his coming marriage to Pamphila; Thraso and Gnatho listen
85v	Gnatho contrives that Phaedria and Chaerea admit Thraso into their household
Heautontimorumenos	(The Self-Tormentor)
90	Chremes reproves Menedemus for working too hard
93	Within his house Clitipho speaks in turn to Clinia and to Chremes
95	Clitipho and Clinia; Syrus and Dromo approach with Bacchis and Antiphila
96v	Syrus, with Dromo standing next to him, counsels Clitipho and Clinia
100	Clinia and Antiphila are reunited
101v	Menedemus tells Chremes that Clinia has returned
104	Syrus speaks with Chremes; Clitipho stands aside
105v	Chremes observes Clitipho's attentions to Bacchis; Syrus reveals his plot to Chremes
107v	Sostrata tells Chremes that Antiphila possesses the ring which identifies her as their daughter
111v	Syrus persuades Bacchis to move to the house of Menedemus; Dromo conducts them to the house
113	Syrus wheedles money out of Chremes
115	Clitipho rests; Syrus tells Clitipho how he has tricked Chremes into promising him money
116	Chremes gives Clitipho the money
117	Chremes tells Menedemus that he will marry his daughter to Clinia
118v	Chremes speaks to his wife; Menedemus informs Chremes that Bacchis is Clitipho's mistress
121	Clitipho's plea to Chremes is without avail; Syrus suggests to Clitipho that he is not Chremes' son
123	Sostrata chides Chremes for having treated Clitipho so harshly; Clitipho approaches them
124	Clitipho repents before his parents
125	Clitipho is pardoned through the intercession of Menedemus
Adelphoe	(The Brothers)
128	Micio, Storax and Demea
129v	Demea rebukes Micio for his indulgence of Aeschinus
131v	Sannio is frustrated in his attempt to regain Callidia from Aeschinus and Ctesipho
133v	Syrus bargains with Sannio
135	Ctesipho meets Syrus on his way to thank Aeschinus
136	Aeschinus receives Ctesipho's thanks; Syrus stands with Sannio
137v	Sostrata worries about Pamphila who is in labor

Folio

138v Geta informs Sostrata that Aeschinus has carried off Callidia
140v Syrus tells Demea that Ctesipho had nothing to do with Callidia's abduction
141v Hegio and Geta complain to Demea of Aeschinus' conduct
144 Demea tells Hegio and Geta that he will speak to Micio; Hegio consoles Sostrata
146 Demea approaches Ctesipho and Syrus; Ctesipho enters his house
147 While Ctesipho listens in the doorway, Syrus praises him to Demea
150 Aeschinus goes to clear himself to Sostrata
151v Micio reassures Sostrata; Micio promises Aeschinus that he may marry Pamphila
154 Micio tells Demea that Aeschinus will marry Pamphila and that Callidia will remain in his house
156 Demea upbraids Syrus for his trickery
157 Dromo asks Syrus the whereabouts of Ctesipho; Demea goes to look for Ctesipho in Micio's house
158 Micio tells Sostrata that all has been prepared for the wedding; Demea arrives
160 Demea praises Syrus
161v Geta speaks to Sostrata; Demea praises Geta
162v Demea gives orders to Geta, Syrus and Aeschinus; Micio arrives
163v All the characters are united in marriage

Phormio (Phormio)

168 Davus comes to Geta to repay a loan
169 Davus speaks to Geta; a servant brings a scroll?
171v Antipho and Phaedria lament over their tribulations while Geta approaches
173 Geta announces the arrival of Demipho
175 Phaedria pleads the case of Antipho before Demipho
177v Phormio promises Geta to defend Antipho's marriage; Demipho arrives
179 Demipho complains that he has been badly treated while Geta and Phormio speak together; Demipho speaks with Phormio and Geta
181v Demipho and his three friends; Geta leaves in search of Antipho
182v Geta speaks with Antipho; Phaedria approaches
183v Dorio threatens to sell the music girl, Pamphila, unless Phaedria buys her that day
185v Geta, Antipho and Phaedria plan how to raise money to buy Pamphila
187 Demipho meets Chremes
188 Geta approaches Demipho and Chremes
189 Antipho eavesdrops on Geta, Demipho and Chremes
191 Geta explains his plan to Antipho; Chremes approaches
192v Demipho, Geta and Chremes discuss paying Phormio
193v Sophrona tells Chremes that Antipho's wife is his Lemnian daughter, Phanium
195 Demipho sends Geta to announce his arrival to Nausistrata
196 Chremes informs Demipho that Phanium is his daughter in the presence of Nausistrata
198 Antipho considers his plight
199 Phormio tells Antipho that Pamphila has been purchased; Geta approaches
200 Geta tells Antipho and Phormio that Chremes is Phanium's father
202 Chremes and Demipho ask Phormio to return their money
204v Phormio tells Nausistrata of Chremes' secret marriage

Hecyra (The Mother-in-Law)

209v Syra, the procuress, warns Philotis against liberality
210v Parmeno tells Philotis what has passed in his master's house
213v Laches accuses Sostrata of having offended Philumena
215 Phidippus announces that Philumena does not wish to return to Laches' house; Laches and Phidippus leave for the Forum
216v Sostrata reflects that she has been judged harshly
217 Parmeno informs Pamphilus that his wife is with her mother
218v Pamphilus discovers that Philumena is pregnant
219v Pamphilus tells Sostrata that Philumena has a fever
220v Pamphilus reflects, sitting under a tree, as Parmeno, Sosia and two other servants arrive
222v Pamphilus sends Parmeno to the Citadel; Phidippus and Laches approach
224 Pamphilus informs Phidippus and Laches that he will not live with his wife Philumena
226 Phidippus censures his wife, Myrrina
228 Sostrata tells Pamphilus that she will go to the country; Laches listens outside
229v Laches and Sostrata prepare to move to the country
230v Phidippus reproaches Philumena in her bedroom; outside Laches, Phidippus and Pamphilus discuss Philumena's fate
233v Sosia takes Bacchis to Laches
235v Bacchis shows the ring to Myrrina
Phidippus speaks to a nurse; Laches introduces Bacchis to Phidippus (miniature in Nantes)

Paris

BIBL. DE L'ARSENAL, ms. 5057–58 (Fig. 521)

Guiart des Moulins, *Bible historiale*. 571 fols.; 450×322 mm.

EARLY HISTORY: The ex libris of Jean de Berry was at one time legible on fol. 571v, and the manuscript appears in the Duke's inventory of 1413 with a group of undated manuscripts. Formerly a single volume, the second folio begins, "Des generacions Caym." Fol. 3, which may have contained a half-page miniature, was cut from the manuscript.

STYLE AND DATE: The workshop of the Master of Berry's Cleres Femmes executed a majority of the miniatures in the Bible. The master himself painted, among other folios, the Solomon page, which comes close in its vigorous naturalism to the Flemish illustrations of the astrological manuscript given to Berry by Abbot Hautschild in 1403 (Morgan 785). In several of the creation scenes God the Father has a red halo with gold rays, as do some of the pagan deities in another manuscript by the workshop which also belonged to Berry, *Des cleres et nobles femmes* (fr. 598). The Master of Berry's Cleres Femmes and his associates painted the strongest miniatures in the manuscript, rich and original in color and telling in narrative. This workshop collaborated with the workshops of the Virgil Master and the Cité des Dames Master. The Virgil Master himself painted a charming Virgin and Child in the *Tree of Jesse* (Fig. 521). A weak illuminator with a dry and stringy style and a predilection for striped robes painted a few miniatures. The styles of the workshops point to a date towards 1405. The subjects of the miniatures generally follow those of earlier Parisian copies of the text. However, the artists lost the meaning of some of the scenes. In *Solomon's Judgment of the Two Mothers* only the living child is shown. In the *Judgment of the Three Sons* who are told to shoot at their father's corpse, only one son is represented. As in some other contemporary copies of the *Bible historiale* the miniature for *Dixit insipiens*, which traditionally showed a fool holding a club and eating a loaf of bread, has become a fool biting a dog's tail.

BIBLIOGRAPHY: Berger, *Bible française*, 1884, pp. 206, 216, 366 f.; Paris, Arsenal, Martin, v, 1889, p. 28 f. nos. 5057–58; Paris, Louvre, *Exposition*, 1904, p. 71 no. 218; Delisle, *Charles V*, 1907, II, pp. 225 no. 8, 272; Martin, *Miniature française*, 1923, pp. 68 f., 99, fig. C; Martens, *Meister Francke*, 1929, pp. 118, 239 n. 212, 241 n. 221, 243 n. 227; Paris, Arsenal, Martin and Lauer, 1929, p. 31 f., pl. XXXVIII; Panofsky, *Netherlandish Painting*, 1953, I, pp. 53, 108, 381 n. 53[3,4], II, figs. 57, 58; Schilling, 1954, pp. 277–281, pls. 30[d], 31[b]; Paris, Bibl. nat. (Porcher), 1955, p. 79 no. 159; Meiss, *Art Bull.*, 1956, p. 193 f.; *idem*, *Late XIV Century*, 1967, index, fig. 829.

CLASSIFICATION OF MINIATURES:

Berry's Cleres Femmes Workshop: Fols. 1–8, 11–15, 17v–75v, 84–87v, 108v, 109v, 123, 132, 133v, 141, 157–168, 187, 209v–238, 250–264, 290, 300–316, 339v–420, 427–441v

Virgil Workshop: Fols. 77, 111, 111v, 145v, 155, 173v–183v, 247, 248v, 322, 421–423v, 451–568

Cité des Dames Workshop: Fols. 114, 119v, 121, 128v, 138, 196v, 272–276v, 283v, 285v

Minor illuminator: Fols. 9, 16, 81, 93v, 107, 120v, 125, 131v, 150, 245v, 267v, 279

MINIATURES:

MS. 5057

Folio	
1	A monk preaches (preface of Guiart des Moulins)
1v	A scholar seated in a cathedra consults a book
2v	Petrus Comestor presents manuscript to the Archbishop of Sens
4	Lord separates darkness and light
4v	Lord creates the firmament
5	Lord separates land from water
5v	Lord places the sun and the moon
6v	Lord creates fishes
7	Creation of Adam
8(a)	Rest on the seventh day
8(b)	Lord carries Adam into Paradise
9	Creation of Eve
11	Offerings of Cain and Abel
11v	Cain kills Abel with a donkey's jawbone; Lord receives Abel's soul
13v	Building of the ark overseen by Noah and the Lord
15	Noah brings his family into the ark
16	Noah's sacrifice
17v	Nimrod oversees building of the tower of Babel
22	Sodom destroyed by fire
24v	Sacrifice of Isaac
29	Isaac blesses Jacob in the presence of Rebekah
35	Joseph is thrown into a well
38	Joseph sells corn to his brothers
44	Counselors of Pharaoh advise him to oppress the Israelites
67v	Offerings at the altar
75v	Lord tells Moses to count the Israelites
77	The Tabernacle
81	Israelites leave the desert of Sinai
84	Man who collected wood on the Sabbath being strangled and stabbed
85	Lord tells Moses to take a rod from each tribe
87v	Balaam is stopped by an angel
93v	Moses proclaims the Law to the Israelites
107	Joshua leads the Israelites
108v	Fall of the walls of Jericho

MS. 5057
Folio

109v	Achan is stoned
111	Hanging of the five kings of the Amorites
111v	Kings killed in battle by Joshua and the Israelites
114	Judah leads Israelites in battle against the Canaanites
119v	Samson kills the lion
120v	Samson kills Philistines with a jawbone
121	Delilah cuts Samson's hair
123	Ruth gathers wheat while Boaz gives orders to two reapers
125	Prayer of Hannah and Elkannah
128v	Coronation of Saul
131v	Coronation of David in the presence of his brothers
132	David defies Goliath
133v	Michal lets David down in a basket to escape the city
138	The Amalekite brings David news of Saul's death
141	The Ark of the Covenant is carried in procession to Jerusalem
145v	Absalom, hanging from a branch by his hair, is pierced by Joab
150	Coronation of Solomon
155	Solomon orders the carving of two gold cherubim
157	Two priests receive a sacrificial lamb at an altar
160	Visit of the Queen of Sheba
164v	Jezebel sends a messenger to warn Elijah
168	Elijah taken up into heaven in the presence of Elisha
173v	Jehu sends letters to the lords of Samaria; letter is given to the notables of Samaria
179	Hezekiah reopens the Temple
183v	Jehoiakim, King of Judah, kills Urijah
187	Tree of Jesse (Chronicles I)
196v	Solomon offers vessels of gold in the Temple
209v	Cyrus, King of Persia, listens to the Lord
212	Nehemiah speaks to Hanani
216	Josiah offers a lamb to priests at an altar
221	Lord permits the devil to tempt Job
231v	Job sits next his three friends, his wife stands before them
232v	Tobit gives money to cripples and beggars
234	Tobias takes his father's letter addressed to Gabael
234v	Tobias seizes a huge fish
235	Tobias and Sarah pray in their bedroom
236	Tobias sprinkles some gall on the eyes of his father in presence of Raphael
236v	Raphael reveals his identity. He appears as an elegant young man and above as an angel on a rock
238	Jeremiah tells the remnant of Judah not to flee to Egypt
245v	Daniel frees Susanna from the accusations of the two elders
247	The idol Bel
248v	Jews return to Jerusalem
250	Nebuchadnezzar sends Holofernes to war
253v	Judith kills Holofernes
254	Achior shows Holofernes' head above the walls
258v	Ester kneels before Ahasuerus
264	King Ochus receives one of his officials
267v	David playing the harp
272	Dominus illuminatio: David points to his eye
274v	Dixi custodiam: David points to his mouth
276v	Dixit insipiens: fool with cudgel biting a dog's tail
279	Salvum me fac: David in the water prays to the Lord
283v	Exultate deo: David plays on bells
285v	Cantate domino: clerics singing; David seated, the Lord above
290	Dixit dominus: the Lord and Christ

MS. 5058
Folio

300	Judgment of the mothers; judgment of the sons; visit of the Queen of Sheba; Solomon as a teacher with his pupils
311	Solomon declaring that all is vanity before a peasant with a spade (Ecclesiastes)
316	Wisdom: a queen, holding a sword, enthroned before three noblemen (Wisdom)
322	Wisdom personified as a queen and her courtiers (Ecclesiasticus)
339v	Isaiah speaks to three men in the temple
360	Prophet sawn in two (text for Jeremiah, but pictorial tradition for Isaiah)
381	Jeremiah lamenting city of Jerusalem
383v	Baruch reads the Law to three Israelites
386v	Ezekiel's vision of the four wheels
403	Daniel receives an open book from the Lord
410v	Birth of Jezreel
413v	Joel orders several men to blow their trumpets
414v	Amos stands near Jerusalem and is inspired by the Lord
417	Obadiah
417v	Jonah emerges praying from the mouth of the whale
418v	Micah and the falling city of Samaria
420	Nahum and his friends regard the Lord
421	Habakkuk regards the Lord
422	An angel shows Zephaniah the host of heaven upon the housetops
423	Haggai brings the word of the Lord to Zerubbabel and Joshua, the high priest
423v	Zechariah looks at a book; the Lord above
427	Malachi looks up at the Lord
428	Mattathias about to strike the renegade Jew
441v	A messenger brings a letter from the Jews of Jerusalem to those of Egypt
451	Tree of Jesse (St. Matthew)
466	St. Mark
476v	St. Luke
494	St. John the Evangelist
507v	St. Paul's epistle to the Romans
513v	St. Paul gives his letter to the Corinthians to a messenger
518v	St. Paul speaks to a small crowd (II Corinthians)
522v	St. Paul indicates a city to a small crowd (Galatians)
524v	St. Paul speaks to children (Ephesians)
527v	St. Paul talks to a small group of men praying to the Lord (Colossians)

MS. 5058

Folio	
529	St. Paul addresses kneeling men, indicating the Lord (I Thessalonians)
531	St. Paul gives a book to a child (I Timothy)
533v	St. Paul speaking to a group of men (Titus)
535	Nativity in a cave; St. Paul kneeling (Hebrews)
539	Pentecost
552	St. James gives his epistle to a messenger
553v	St. Peter speaks to a small group
556	On an island St. John writes, observed by group of men
557v	St. Jude gives a letter to a messenger
558	St. John on Patmos next to the seven-headed beast; above the Lord between two angels, one holding a jar and the other a candlestick
560v	Two angels blow trumpets and locusts attack men
563	An angel shows St. John the Lamb on Mount Sion adored by a crowd of men
565v	An angel shows St. John the great whore riding the scarlet beast and holding a cup
568	An angel shows St. John the rider on the white horse and his heavenly army; to the left, the kings of the earth and their armies in a flaming pit

Paris

BIBL. DE L'ARSENAL, ms. 5193

See Boccaccio, *Cas des nobles hommes et femmes*

Paris

BIBL. NAT., fr. 25 (Figs. 51, 782)

Saint Augustine, *La Cité de Dieu* (translation and commentary by Raoul de Praelles). First Volume, Books I–X. 306 fols.; 455×310 mm.

EARLY HISTORY: The original owner is unknown. In the mid-fifteenth century, however, the manuscript belonged to Jacques d'Armagnac, Duke of Nemours, whose device, "Fortune d'amis," appears in a mixed combination of letters on the book edge. His ex libris, no longer legible, appeared on folio 306. The manuscript subsequently passed into the possession of an advisor to Louis XI, Tanneguy Du Châtel, who added his arms on the book edge.

STYLE AND DATE: The Virgil Master illuminated the frontispiece, which was copied by his workshop a few years later in a *Cité de Dieu* in Paris, fr. 6272. The Berry Apocalypse Master and his workshop painted the remaining miniatures, with the exception of an initial in grisaille on the first folio by a Netherlandish illuminator. The Apocalypse Master himself painted the miniatures on folios 128, 161, 196 and 267v, which show an exceptionally free and assured brushwork. He placed his figures, dressed in pale grey or brown robes, in chocolate colored interiors or in olive green landscapes. Touches of gold emulsion or of bright red brighten the restricted color scheme. The styles of the miniatures by the Apocalypse and Virgil Masters indicate a date towards 1408–1410.

BIBLIOGRAPHY: Laborde, *Cité de Dieu*, 1909, II, pp. 314–318, pl. XXII d; Paris, Bibl. nat. (Porcher), 1955, p. 80; Meiss, *Art Bull.*, 1956, p. 196; Porcher, *Enluminure*, 1959, p. 56, pl. LIX; Meiss, *Late XIV Century*, 1967, pp. 354, 360.

MINIATURES:

Folio		
1	Prologue	Raoul de Praelles presents his translation to Charles V (initial)
5	Book I	The two cities: on the right, the Goths take Rome; on the left, St. Augustine presents his treatise to the Lord
29v	Book II	In an open temple three pagans worship three idols on columns
68v	Book III	Three pagans worship an idol on a pedestal while two philosophers discuss theology
128	Book IV	St. Augustine speaks to three philosophers
161	Book V	A king topples from his throne losing his globe; above, Fortune holds her wheel on the left, and on the right, the Lord. Two philosophers debate the nature of Fortune
196	Book VI	On the left, three pagans worship three idols; on the right, three Christians implore Christ
213v	Book VII	On the left, three pagans worship two idols; on the right, four Christians implore the Lord
239v	Book VIII	Three Christians kneel before the Lord; three pagans in discussion behind them
267v	Book IX	St. Augustine, inspired by two angels above, speaks with four pagans who are inspired by demons
282v	Book X	St. Augustine and three Christians adore the Trinity

Paris

BIBL. NAT., fr. 166

(Figs. 278–325, 327, 328, 332, 337, 346, 348, 357, 367, 655)

Bible moralisée. 169 fols.; 415×290 mm.

This manuscript is, we believe, the Bible for which Philippe le Hardi paid Paul and Jean de Limbourg from February, 1402 until January, 1404. The two brothers completed the first three gatherings of the manuscript, fols. 1–24v, and they designed and partially painted much of the fourth gathering, fols. 25–32v.

See the chapter devoted to this manuscript in the preceding text.

BIBLIOGRAPHY: Camus [1800], pp. 112–124, pls. I–III; Paris, *Manuscrits françois*, II, 1838, pp. 18–33; Bouchot, 1890, pp. 276–278, pl. opp. p. 278; Delisle, 1893, pp. 241–243; Champeaux and Gauchery, *Travaux*, 1894, pp. 138, 149–151; Durrieu, *Le manuscrit*, 1895, pp. 120–122, 130, figs. in text; Paris, Louvre, *Exposition*, 1904, p. 33 no. 88; Bouchot, 1905, pp. 23–26, 30, fig. p. 22; Durrieu, *Gaz. B.-A.*, 1906, p. 280; Delisle, *Charles V*, 1907, I, p. 174; Mâle, *Fin du moyen âge*, 1908, pp. 240–242, fig. 110; Martin, *Miniature française*, 1923, pp. 80 f., 103, figs. CXXII, CXXIII; Laborde, *Bible moralisée*, V, 1927, pp. 94, 97 f., 102–114; IV, 1921, pls. 739–750; Paris, Bibl. nat. (Martin), 1928, pp. 63 f., 109 f., figs. LXXXII, LXXXIII; Paris, Bibl. nat., 1937, p. 65 no. 132; Ring, *French Painting* [1949], pp. 200 nos. 67, 68, 203 f. no. 88, fig. 13; Bourges, Musées [1951], pp. 34–36 no. 12, pls. X–XI; Panofsky, *Netherlandish Painting*, 1953, I, p. 125 (and see index); Porcher, *Belles Heures*, 1953, pp. 6 f., 22 f., 48, 51, figs. 11, 12; Paris, Bibl. nat. (Porcher), 1955, p. 91 f. no. 188, pl. XXIII; Porcher, in *Enciclopedia dell'arte*, VIII, p. 619 ff.; Vienna, Kunsthist. Mus., *Katalog*, 1962, p. 168 f. no. 105; Meiss, *Gaz. B.-A.*, 1963, p. 149 ff.; *idem*, *Late XIV Century*, 1967, index, fig. 781; *idem*, *Boucicaut Master*, 1968, pp. 3, 13, 61, 131, figs. 471, 472; *idem*, *Breviary Master*, 1970, pp. 5–8, 17, pls. IIa, IVa; Avril, in *Encyclopaedia Universalis*, IX, 1971, p. 1024 f.

Paris

BIBL. NAT., fr. 247 (Figs. 167, 170)

Flavius Josephus, *Les antiquités judaïques*. 312 fols. 400 × 295 mm. (The second volume is Nouv. acq. fr. 21013)

EARLY HISTORY: Jean de Berry, whose ex libris is found at the end of the second volume, was the first owner. Undoubtedly the manuscript was not listed in the Duke's inventories because the illuminators had only begun the work before his death in 1416. The next possessor was probably Bernard VIII d'Armagnac, the son of Bonne de Berry, who added a miniature to the manuscript *ca.* 1420. In the margin a lady holds his crest, a helmet with a sheaf of corn. Eventually Bernard's son, Jacques d'Armagnac (1433–1477), inherited the manuscript and completed the illumination. He added an inscription of ownership under Berry's. Pierre de Bourbon acquired the manuscript after he arrested Jacques d'Armagnac in 1476.

STYLE AND DATE: On folio 311v, François Robertet, Pierre de Bourbon's secretary, wrote after 1488 that the first three miniatures were by an illuminator of Jean de Berry and that Fouquet painted the others. In fact, only two miniatures on folios 25 and 49 were completed for the Duke, probably shortly before his death in 1416. They were painted by a remarkable artist whom we have named the Josephus Master after this work. The miniature on folio 3, however, was painted about 1420 for Bernard d'Armagnac by the Harvard Hannibal Master. This illuminator also executed the woman holding the Armagnac emblem in the margin. When Jacques d'Armagnac acquired the manuscript, he added his arms held by two sirens to this lower margin, and he commissioned Fouquet to paint the remaining miniatures.

BIBLIOGRAPHY: Paris, Louvre, *Exposition*, 1904, p. 45 no. 128; Martin, *Miniaturistes*, 1906, pp. 92, 211 f.; Paris, Bibl. nat., *Antiquités* (Omont) [1906]; Durrieu, *Fouquet*, 1908; Martin, *Miniature française*, 1923, pp. 81 f., 104, fig. CXXIV; Paris, Bibl. nat., *Catalogue*, 1926, pp. 47–49 no. 61, pl. opp. p. 41 (Fouquet); Paris, Bibl. nat. (Couderc), 1927, pp. 91–93, pl. LXIV (Fouquet); Paris, Bibl. nat. (Martin), 1928, p. 109, figs. LXXX, XCVIII, XCIX; Wescher, *Fouquet*, 1945, p. 46, pl. 29; Bourges, Musées [1951], p. 39 no. 21; Paris, Bibl. nat. (Porcher), 1955, p. 95 no. 196; Porcher, *Enluminure*, 1959, p. 64, pl. LX; Meiss, *Late XIV Century*, 1967, index, fig. 683.

MINIATURES:

(Only the three early miniatures are described here. There are eleven large miniatures by Fouquet, not nine as recorded by Robertet)

Folio

3 Marriage of Adam and Eve
25 History of Joseph
49 Hebrews in the desert

Paris

BIBL. NAT., fr. 598

See Boccaccio, *Des cleres femmes*

Paris

BIBL. NAT., fr. 603

See Christine de Pisan, *Mutacion*

Paris

BIBL. NAT., fr. 606, 835, 836

See Christine de Pisan, *Collected Writings*

Paris

BIBL. NAT., fr. 607

See Christine de Pisan, *Cité des Dames*

Paris

BIBL. NAT., fr. 926 (Figs. 131, 366)

Saint Bonaventura, *L'aiguillon d'amour divin*, John of Swabia, *L'horloge de sapience* and other treatises. 334 fols.; 297×215 mm.

EARLY HISTORY: Marie de Berry, daughter of Jean, received this manuscript from her confessor Simon de Courcy. A statement on the verso of the first folio tells us that Courcy commissioned the manuscript and that it was finished in May, 1406.

STYLE: The workshop of the Luçon Master illuminated all but one of the miniatures, including the initial miniature in which Marie is shown kneeling before the Madonna and the writing Christ Child. This Madonna, which may have been painted by the master himself, is a copy of an earlier representation of the same subject in the initial diptych of the *Brussels Hours*.

The Master of the *Breviary of Jean sans Peur* painted the exquisite *Crucifixion* on fol. 52 as well as the initial below it.

BIBLIOGRAPHY: Paris, *Manuscrits françois*, VII, 1848, pp. 256–268; Couderc, *Portraits* [1910], p. 22, pl. L; Aubert, 1912, p. 66 n. 1; Heimann, 1932, p. 22 n. 47; Parkhurst, 1941, p. 302, fig. 35; Porcher, *Belles Heures*, 1953, p. 10 f., fig. 3; *idem*, 1953, pp. 121–123; Paris, Bibl. nat. (Porcher), 1955, p. 90 no. 185; Meiss, *Art Bull.*, 1956, p. 193; Porcher, *French Miniatures* [1959], p. 62, fig. 64; *idem*, in *Enciclopedia dell'arte*, VIII, p. 619 ff.; Meiss, *Late XIV Century*, 1967, index, figs. 667, 780; *idem*, "Breviary Master," 1970, pp. 4–8, 12 f., pl. IIa.

MINIATURES:

Folio	
2	Madonna with Marie de Berry and an attendant
52	Crucifixion
113	Sapience-Attrempance demonstrates a clock to Suso
216v	A student sees a vision of a gold wheel containing the masters of the seven sciences

Paris

BIBL. NAT., fr. 1023 (Fig. 671)

Jacques le Grand, *Le livre des bonnes moeurs*. 88 fols.; 280×195 mm.

EARLY HISTORY: Jacques le Grand, an Augustinian friar, gave this copy of his interesting treatise on good conduct and morals, especially princely, to Jean de Berry on March 4, 1410. The Duke's secretary, Flamel, recorded the gift on the verso of the guard folio, and Berry's ex libris appears at the end.

STYLE AND DATE: The workshop of the Luçon Master was responsible for the illumination of the manuscript. The master himself painted *Death stalking a Nobleman*, but he curiously left the presentation miniature with a portrait of the Duke to an assistant. The style of the miniatures is close to that in the illustrations of a Boccaccio, now in Geneva, executed by the atelier in 1410. In both manuscripts the backgrounds are diapered and the figures lack the volume they acquired in later miniatures by the workshop. The *Livre des bonnes moeurs* was undoubtedly painted just before its presentation to the Duke in 1410.

BIBLIOGRAPHY: Guiffrey, *Inventaires*, I, 1894, pp. CLXVIII no. 34, 264 no. 991; II, 1896, p. 238 no. 522; Delisle, *Charles V*, 1907, II, p. 245 no. 134; Couderc, *Portraits* [1910], p. 29, pl. LXIV; Durrieu, *Très Belles Heures de Notre-Dame*, 1922, p. 77; Bourges, Musées [1951], p. 38 no. 19; Porcher, *Belles Heures*, 1953, p. 14; Paris, Bibl. nat. (Porcher), 1955, p. 95 no. 195; Meiss, *Art Bull.*, 1956, p. 193; *idem*, *Late XIV Century*, 1967, index, figs. 486, 643.

MINIATURES:

Folio	
2	Jacques le Grand presents his manuscript to Jean de Berry
5	Fall of the Rebel Angels
8v	Jonah, emerging from the whale, prays to the Lord; the Ninevites pray to the shore
16v	Job prays on a dung hill while his house burns and his family departs
18	Lucretia commits suicide in the presence of her father and husband
20v	Moses receives the Tables of Law
23v	St. John, the Virgin and St. Catherine
25v	Sons of Jacob murder Sichem as he embraces Dina; Absalom kills Amon
27	Cain kills Abel
29	Isboseth assaulted while asleep; his assailant runs away
31v	Alexander conquers kingdoms by his liberality rather than by force
37	A pope blesses three kings and three bishops; three cardinals stand aside
43	A king pardons four prisoners
55	A rich man thanks the Lord for his wealth
56v	Diogenes meditates in the entrance of a barrel; Demetrius throws his wealth into the sea
57v	An old man gives advice to two young men
59	An old man gives advice on governing to five young men
60v	Marriage ceremony
74	Death, holding a spear, approaches a nobleman

Paris

BIBL. NAT., fr. 1178

See Christine de Pisan, *Cité des Dames*

Paris

BIBL. NAT., fr. 1179

See Christine de Pisan, *Cité des Dames*

Paris

BIBL. NAT., fr. 12201

Hayton, *Fleur des histoires de la terre d'Orient, Liber Provinciarum, Livre fait d'un Tartar qui se nomme Themirbey que aucuns autres appellent la Tamurlan*. 97 fols.; 307×216 mm.

EARLY HISTORY: One of the three copies of the work which Philippe le Hardi bought in 1403 from Jacques Raponde and presented to Jean de Berry on March 22, 1403 in Paris. The manuscript was recorded in Berry's inventory of 1413.

STYLE AND DATE: The workshop of the Coronation Master probably finished this manuscript just before the Duke of Burgundy acquired it from Raponde in 1403. None of the miniatures was painted by the master himself. All of them, even those with landscapes, have the diapered grounds characteristic of this workshop.

BIBLIOGRAPHY: Guiffrey, *Inventaires*, I, 1894, p. 244 no. 933; Durrieu, 1895, p. 179 f., fig. p. 177; Delisle, *Charles V*, 1907, II, pp. 264, no. 256, 313; Martens, *Meister Francke*, 1929, pp. 197, 266 n. 509, 511; Panofsky, *Netherlandish Painting*, 1953, I, pp. 52, 76, 87, 150, 381 nn. 52^{3-5}, II, fig. 51; Porcher, *Belles Heures*, 1953, p. 13; Paris, Bibl. nat. (Porcher), 1955, p. 77 f. no. 156; Vienna, Kunsthist. Mus., *Katalog*, 1962, p. 179 f. no. 124, pl. 136; Meiss, *Late XIV Century*, 1967, index, fig. 438; *idem*, *Boucicaut Master*, 1968, index.

MINIATURES:

Folio	
1	Hayton presents his manuscript to Pope Clement V
10v	Caesar Augustus and the empress served at table by two kings
17v	In a dream a knight informs Canguis that he will be crowned emperor of the Tartars
49	Pope Clement V speaks with Hayton and others about a crusade to the Holy Land
84	Tamerlane and his soldiers lay siege to a rich city

Paris

BIBL. NAT., fr. 12420

See Boccaccio, *Des cleres femmes*

Paris

BIBL. NAT., nouv. acq. fr. 14285 (Fig. 786)

Trésor des histoires. 33 fols.; 320×230 mm.

EARLY HISTORY: 33 fols. detached from a copy of the text called the *Trésor des histoires* expanded from a history written for Baudouin d'Avesnes in the thirteenth century. According to a passage on fol. 24, this manuscript was written in 1416 in Paris: "... car aussi comme jadis la cité d'Athenes estoit en Grece la mere des sept arts et des sciences et nourrice des philozophes, aussi Paris maintenant aourne et eslieve toute France et toute Crestiente en science, en meurs et en honneurs. Si fu escript ce present livre en l'an de l'in-

carnation de nostre seigneur Jhesu Crist Dieu mil quatre cens et seize . . ."
There are no marks of original ownership.

STYLE AND DATE: Each folio has a half-page miniature. Most of them were painted by the Master of the Berry Apocalypse and his workshop. The Boethius illuminator, a follower of the Apocalypse Master, painted the frontispiece on fol. 1. A third and rather weak illuminator illustrated fols. 6, 7, 9v, 10v, 12v, 13v, 15v, 24v, 25v, 31, 32, and 33. The manuscript was probably illuminated just after the text was written in 1416.

BIBLIOGRAPHY: Rosset, 1913, pp. 123–126; Nordenfalk, *Kung praktiks*, 1955, p. 61, fig. 68; Meiss, *Art Bull.*, 1956, p. 196 n. 35; Paris, Hotel Drouot, June 17, 1960, *Précieux manuscrits à peintures du XIIIe au XVIIe siècle*, no. 6, pls. II, XV; Meiss, *Late XIV Century*, 1967, p. 354; Ross, 1969, p. 177 ff., pls. 51–53.

MINIATURES:

Folio	
1	Creation of Eve
2	Finding of Moses
3	Death of Abimelech
4	Rehoboam, King of Judah, with his counselors
5v	Socrates in prison
6	Combat between King Cambyses of Persia and Arphasat of Medea
7	King Denis, before the idols of Jupiter, Esculapius and Apollo, steals from Jupiter his gold robe and from Esculapius his gold beard
8	Aristotle teaches Alexander
9v	Alexander accepts tribute from the Romans
10v	Alexander fights wild animals
11	Zoroaster at his desk with three devils before him
12v	Hyrcanus, the Hebrew, cultivates the earth; Hyroan presents his family to the King and Queen of Egypt
13v	Death of Hasdrubal, whose head is presented to Hannibal
14v	Death of Jonathan and his two sons
15v	Roman commissaries divide the kingdom of Numidia between Jugurtha and Adherbal
16v	Battle between Jugurtha and the four dukes of Mauretania
17v	Sylla receives tribute from the subjects of Scipio; Hadrian thrown into the fire before Utica
18v	Aristobulus surrenders Jerusalem to Pompey
19v	Caesar, Cicero and Decius Selanus judge prisoners; Cato speaks
20v	Julius Caesar sends a message to King Ariovistus
21v	Caesar and the Romans besiege Soissons
22v	Battle of Caesar and the Romans against the French
23v	Caesar enters Armenia
24v	The camp of Caesar in Thessaly; Pompey addresses his followers at Dyrrhachium
25v	Coronation of Cleopatra; battle between Caesar and King Pharnaces
26v	Birth of the son of Xerxes
27v	Ghent and Bruges
28v	Animals of Mauritania
29v	View of Rome with the Capitol and the Pantheon
30v	Chess game between Jeremodath and Xerxes
31	The mother of Brutus dies after his birth; Brutus shoots an arrow into his father's breast
32	Story of Robert le Fuselier
33	Story of the fair judge

Paris

BIBL. NAT., lat. 1156A (Figs. 878, 881–884)

Book of Hours, Use of Paris. *Heures de René d'Anjou.* 1–1v+148 fols.; 260×185 mm.

EARLY HISTORY: Notes, added later to the calendar, give the dates of birth and death of members of the Anjou family until 1446, when a child was born to King René's oldest daughter. The arms of Jerusalem, *Anjou ancien*, and *Anjou moderne* appear in the initials on folios 18v, 23, 39, 48, 52, 55, 58, 62, 68, 82, 87v, 92, 97, 100 and 114. In this form, *tiercé en pal*, they cannot yet be connected definitely with any member of the family. They might belong to Louis II, who died on April 29, 1417. His portrait, placed before an image of St. René, appears in a miniature on folio 61, at the beginning of a prayer to this saint. Conceivably the manuscript was illuminated after the death of Louis II, as its style seems to indicate, for his oldest son Louis III, but in honor, so to speak, of his father. We can, however, cite no analogous work. Furthermore, the eagles with patriarchal crosses and the sails bearing the motto "en dieu en soit," which must, we believe, belong to the original campaign, are emblems known to be used by René alone, on existing evidence from 1434 on. These emblems occur in the borders of all the original folios, even where there is neither text nor miniature. Despite the puzzling arms the manuscript was, therefore, probably commissioned for the youthful René—he was born in 1409—by his mother Yolande. The Book of Hours definitely belonged to him later, and after 1434 he added miniatures on three folios, 22, 81v and 113v, including his portrait and a skeleton holding his arms. The illuminator who painted these miniatures also touched up the miniature and initial on folio 114, which face his own work on folio 113v.

In the seventeenth century the manuscript was in the collection of Roger de Gaignières.

STYLE AND DATE: The Rohan workshop executed all of the miniatures with the exception of those added by René and a small miniature depicting the *Stoning of St. Stephen* on folio 79v. The Rohan Master may have designed the *Man of Sorrows* on folio 82, but he probably had little to do with the execution, and the workshop was responsible for all the other miniatures. The *Annunciation* derives from a composition introduced by the Boucicaut Master about 1416. The dependence of the *Office of the Dead* upon the corresponding miniature in the *Belles Heures* suggests a similar *post quem*, because that manuscript was acquired by Yolande d'Anjou in 1416.

BIBLIOGRAPHY: Couderc, *Portraits* [1910], pl. LXVIII; Durrieu, *Rev. de l'art a. et. m.*, 1912, pp. 164–167, 176–178, figs. 11, 13; Leroquais, *Livres d'heures*, 1927, I, pp. 64–67 no. 20, pls. XLIII–XLV; Paris, Bibl. nat. (Martin), 1928, pp. 65 f., 111, fig. LXXXIX; Panofsky, in *Studies Porter*, 1939, II, p. 488 n. 33, fig. 14; Ring, *French Painting* [1949], p. 203 no. 87, fig. 5; Panofsky, *Netherlandish Painting*, 1953, I, pp. 171, 410 n. 127[5], 424 n. 171[3]; Porcher, *Belles Heures*, 1953, pp. 24, 29, 40; Paris, Bibl. nat. (Porcher), 1955, p. 108 no. 231; Meiss, *Late XIV Century*, 1967, p. 18, fig. 332; *idem*, *Boucicaut Master*, 1968, p. 32.

MINIATURES:

Folio

1–12	Calendar
13	St. John the Evangelist
14v	St. Luke
16	St. Mark
17	St. Matthew
18v	Madonna and Child on a crescent (*Obsecro te*)
22	Four angels holding the Host
Hours of the Virgin	
23	Annunciation; *bas de page*: Virgin at the loom
39	Visitation
48	Nativity
52	Annunciation to the Shepherds
55	Adoration of the Magi
58	Presentation in the Temple
61	St. René, Bishop of Angers; portrait of Louis II d'Anjou on the left
62	Flight into Egypt
68	Coronation of the Virgin
Suffrages	
71v	Crucifixion
72v	St. Christopher
73	St. Sebastian
73v	St. Nicholas
74	St. Anthony
74v	St. Mary Magdalene
75	St. Catherine
75v	St. Anne and the Virgin
76	St. John the Baptist
76v	St. John the Evangelist
77	St. Michael
77v	St. George
79v	St. Stephen
81v	Portrait of René d'Anjou
82	Man of Sorrows (Hours of the Cross)
87v	Pentecost (Hours of the Holy Ghost)
92	Madonna and Child (15 Joys)
97	Christ in Majesty (*Sept requêtes*)
100	Trinity (Penitential Psalms)
Office of the Dead	
113v	Death: a crowned skeleton
114	Monk praying in a cemetery near two skeletons

Paris

BIBL. NAT., lat. 7907 A

(Figs. 64, 163, 174, 177, 180, 183, 185, 189, 191, 195, 197, 202, 209)

Terence, *Comedies* (in Latin). 159 fols. 290×205 mm.

EARLY HISTORY: Jean de Berry received this manuscript from his treasurer Martin Gouge as a New Year's gift in 1408. Three years later Gouge, a learned man, gave Berry the earliest illuminated manuscript of the French version of Boccaccio's *De casibus* (see Catalogue of MSS, Geneva, fr. 190). The extensive cycles of illustrations in both the Terence and the Boccaccio served as models for two other famous manuscripts, the *Térence des ducs* and the *Boccacce de Jean sans Peur*.

The text, unlike that in the *Térence des ducs*, does not contain scholia. The names of the characters and their roles, which usually head each scene in red, appear here only from fol. 22. There is an ivy border in the margin of the frontispiece, but none around the remaining miniatures, which have only simple gold frames.

STYLE AND DATE: Inasmuch as the *Comedies* were not illustrated in the thirteenth and fourteenth centuries, the illuminators of Berry's Terence looked to earlier manuscripts, among them probably the Carolingian manuscript lat. 7899, which was in St. Denis at that time (Figs. 172, 186). The order of the plays is the same as in the Carolingian Terences, and there is a miniature at the beginning of each scene as well. Likewise the names of the characters are written above their heads, and in one miniature, on fol. 26v, the role of the figure is specified also, as was customary in the Carolingian miniatures.

With the exception of Thraso's assault on the house of Thais in the *Eunuch*, fol. 43, and the abduction of Callidia on fol. 77v (Fig. 185), there is little overt action in the *Comedies*. The illuminators of Berry's Terence retained the shallow ground plane of the early medieval manuscripts and their confronted, regularly aligned figures. They departed from the Carolingian tradition, however, by introducing successive episodes and by repeating characters within a frame.

For his associates the artist in charge wrote brief directions, still partially legible under ultraviolet light, as Marcel Thomas first observed. Most of these directions can still be seen in the *Brothers* from fol. 76 through fol. 82v. A full description of the scene remains above the miniature on fol. 77v. In other miniatures inscriptions, such as "la mere" or "maison," appear above the figures and buildings. In the *Brothers* Micio is called "ladvocat" and Demea "le paisant," although both are gentlemen, one living in the city, the other in the country. An inscription on fol. 39, read earlier by Henry Martin as "Hainbert" and judged to be the signature of Imbert Stanier, is actually the word "chamberie[re]," an inscription indicating the servant Dorias, as Marcel Thomas pointed out. As in lat. 8193, a contemporary Terence, the *chef* may have originally made drawings within the frames. Illuminators working in two different styles painted the miniatures, probably not long before Martin Gouge gave the manuscript to Berry. An excellent colorist and follower of Jacquemart de Hesdin, author of two miniatures in Berry's *Antiquités judaïques*, fr. 247 and therefore called the Josephus Master, painted the frontispiece (Fig. 209). His assistant illustrated the miniatures in the first play, the *Lady from Andros*. A closely related illuminator painted the miniatures in the next play, the *Eunuch*, through fol. 42. The Orosius Master and his workshop finished the manuscript.

BIBLIOGRAPHY: Martin, *Térence*, 1907, pp. 18 f., 38–40; Bourges, Musées [1951], p. 38 no. 18; Paris, Bibl. nat. (Porcher), 1955, p. 81 f. no. 166; Thomas, 1958, p. 114 f.; Meiss, *Late XIV Century*, 1967, index, fig. 440; *idem*, *Boucicaut Master*, 1968, p. 151 n. 19.

MINIATURES:

Folio	
2v	Frontispiece. Above, Calliopius reads in a Roman theatre; below, Terence, seated, points to his manuscript
Andria	(The Lady of Andros)
3v	Simo confides in Sosia; Simo's two slaves carry provisions to the kitchen
6v	Simo approaches Davus; Simo warns Davus
7v	Archilis attends to Glycerium; Mysis, on leaving the house, sees Pamphilus
8	Pamphilus reflects, his back to Mysis; on the right they talk
9	Charinus speaks to Byrria; Charinus speaks to Pamphilus
10	Davus brings good news to Pamphilus and Charinus
11v[a]	Simo approaches; on the right, Davus advises Pamphilus
11v[b]	Byrria overhears Pamphilus, who stands with Davus, tell Simo that he agrees to the marriage
12	Davus chides Simo for his parsimonious wedding preparations
13	Davus and Simo overhear Mysis tell Lesbia that Pamphilus will educate Glycerium's child
13v	Within the house, Lesbia gives directions to Archilis; Davus and Simo listen outside
14v	Simo meets Chremes
15v	Simo informs Davus that Pamphilus' marriage is settled; Chremes leaves on the right
16	Davus and Pamphilus
16v	Charinus reproves Pamphilus
18	Mysis invites Pamphilus into Glycerium's house; Charinus and Davus stand aside
18v	Davus gives the child to Mysis; Davus tells Mysis to place the child on Simo's doorstep
19	Chremes overhears Davus and Mysis discussing the plight of the child at Simo's door
20v	Crito greets Mysis; Davus stands behind the house on the left
21	Chremes informs Simo of the new-born child
21v	Davus speaks to Simo and Chremes; Dromo leads Davus away
22v	Pamphilus speaks to Simo; Chremes stands behind Simo
23	Chremes, in the presence of Simo and Pamphilus, learns from Crito that Glycerium is his daughter
24v	Pamphilus, with Charinus, seeks his benefactor Davus
25	Pamphilus tells Davus that he may marry Glycerium and promises Charinus to help him win Philumena
Eunuchus	(The Eunuch)
26v	Parmeno counsels his master, Phaedria
27v	Thais asks Phaedria to visit the country; Parmeno stands on the right
30	Phaedria asks Parmeno to send two slaves—Dorus, the eunuch, and an Ethiopian maid—to Thais

Folio

30v On the left, Parmeno leads Dorus and the Ethiopian to Thais' house; on the right, Gnatho brings Pamphila

32 Parmeno, followed by Dorus and the Ethiopian, encounters Chaerea who inquires about Pamphila

34 Parmeno, followed by Dorus and the Ethiopian, eavesdrops on Thraso and Gnatho

35 Thais greets Thraso and Gnatho; Parmeno presents the Ethiopian and Chaerea disguised as the eunuch Dorus

36 Chremes addresses Pythias; Dorias leads Chremes to Thraso's house

37 Antipho looks for Chaerea

37v Chaerea, as the eunuch, tells Antipho about Pamphila

39 Dorias sits in Thais' house

39v Phaedria returns from the country

40 Dorias and Pythias tell Phaedria that the eunuch has raped Pamphila

40v Phaedria, Dorias and Pythias confront Dorus, the eunuch

42 Chremes speaks with Pythias

42v Pythias and Chremes before Thais who proves that Pamphila is his sister

43 Thraso and his soldiers are repulsed by the reply of Thais and Chremes at the windows of Thais' house

44 Pythias informs Thais that Chaerea has raped Pamphila

44v Chaerea, in the eunuch's costume, is accosted by Pythias and Thais

46 Chremes returns with Sophrona

46v Pythias approaches Parmeno from behind

47 Pythias tells Parmeno that Chaerea will be punished

47v Laches speaks with Parmeno

48v Pythias tells Parmeno that she has made a fool out of him

49[a] Thraso and Gnatho

49[b] Chaerea announces his coming marriage to Pamphila; Thraso and Gnatho listen

49v Gnatho contrives that Phaedria and Chaerea admit Thraso into their household

Heautontimorumenos (The Self-Tormentor)

52 Chremes reproves Menedemus for working too hard

54v Within his house Clitipho speaks in turn to Clinia and to Chremes

55v Clitipho reflects on the extravagance of his mistress Bacchis

56[a] Clitipho tries to allay Clinia's fears concerning Antiphila

56[b] Clitipho and Clinia within a house; Syrus and Dromo approach with Bacchis, Antiphila and their servants

58v Antiphila and Bacchis approach the house in which stand Clinia and Syrus

59v Chremes and Menedemus discuss the return of Clinia

61 Syrus and Chremes

62 Chremes, seconded by Syrus, scolds Clitipho for his attentions to Bacchis

63v Sostrata, holding the ring which identifies Antiphila as her daughter, speaks to the nurse; Chremes and Syrus stand in the next room

64v Syrus

65 Syrus persuades Clinia to take Bacchis to the house of Menedemus

66 Clinia conducts Bacchis and her retinue to the house of his father

66v Syrus wheedles money out of Chremes

67v Syrus informs Clitipho how he has tricked Chremes into promising him money

68v[a] Chremes gives Clitipho the money, Syrus stands between them

68v[b] Chremes tells Menedemus that he will marry his daughter to Clinia

69v Chremes speaks to his wife; Menedemus informs Chremes that Bacchis is Clitipho's mistress

71 Menedemus informs Clitipho that his father has disinherited him; Syrus suggests to Clitipho that he is not Chremes' son

72 Sostrata chides Chremes for having treated Clitipho so harshly

72v Clitipho repents before his parents

73 Clitipho is pardoned through the intercession of Menedemus

Adelphoe (The Brothers)

74v Micio calls out to his servant Storax who enters his house

76 Demea rebukes Micio for his indulgence of Aeschinus

77v Sannio is frustrated in his attempt to regain Callidia from Aeschinus and Ctesipho (?)

78v Syrus bargains with Sannio

79v Ctesipho meets Syrus on his way to thank Aeschinus

80 Sannio; Ctesipho thanks Aeschinus; Syrus

81 Sostrata talks anxiously with the nurse Cantara about Pamphila who is about to have a child

81v Geta informs Sostrata, who stands with Cantara, that Aeschinus has carried off Callidia

82v Demea; Syrus enters the house

83 Syrus informs Demea that Ctesipho had nothing to do with Callidia's abduction while he also gives orders to a servant cleaning fish

84v Hegio and Geta complain to Demea of Aeschinus' conduct

86 Demea approaches Ctesipho and Syrus

86v While Ctesipho listens, Syrus praises him to Demea and sends the latter off on a wild-goose chase in search of Micio

88 Micio and Hegio on their way to visit Sostrata

88v Aeschinus goes to clear himself to Sostrata

89 Micio reassures Sostrata; Aeschinus knocks on their door

90v Demea returns from his vain search for Micio

91 Micio tells Demea that Aeschinus will marry Pamphila and that Callidia will remain in his house

Folio	
92	Demea upbraids Syrus for his trickery
92v[a]	Syrus tries to prevent Demea from entering Micio's house; Dromo stands at the side
92v[b]	Micio tells Sostrata that all has been prepared for the wedding; Demea arrives and greets Micio
94	Demea praises Syrus
95[a]	Sostrata remains alone in the house; Demea praises Geta
95[b]	Demea gives orders to Aeschinus, Geta and Syrus
96	Demea, with Aeschinus, prevails upon Micio to marry Sostrata
96v	Demea induces Micio to grant Syrus his freedom
Hecyra	(The Mother-in-Law)
99v	Syra, the procuress, advises Philotis the courtesan
100	Parmeno tells Philotis, who stands with Syra, what has passed in his master's house
102	Laches accuses Sostrata of having offended Philumena
103	Phidippus announces that Philumena does not wish to return to Laches' house; Laches and Phidippus leave for the Forum; Sostrata stands in the doorway
104	Sostrata reflects that she has been judged harshly
104v	Parmeno informs Pamphilus that his wife is with her mother
105v	Sostrata speaks with Parmeno; Pamphilus enters the house
106	Pamphilus reflects as Parmeno, Sosia and another servant arrive
107v	Pamphilus sends Parmeno to the Citadel
108	Pamphilus informs Phidippus and Laches that he will not live with his wife, Philumena
109v	Phidippus censures his wife, Myrrina
111	Sostrata tells Pamphilus that she will go to the country
111v	Laches accepts Sostrata's decision to move to the country
112	Laches, Phidippus and Pamphilus discuss Philumena's fate
114	Bacchis tells Laches that she has not admitted Pamphilus to her favors
115	Phidippus with the nurse for Philumena's child; Laches, Bacchis and her two maids
115v	Bacchis sends Parmeno on an errand
116v	Parmeno informs Pamphilus that Bacchis' ring belonged to Philumena
Phormio	(Phormio)
119	Davus comes to Geta to repay a loan
119v	Geta speaks with Davus
121v	Antipho and Phaedria lament over their tribulations
122	Geta approaches Antipho and Phaedria
123	Geta announces to Phaedria the arrival of Demipho
125	Phormio promises Geta to defend Antipho's marriage; Demipho arrives
125v	Demipho complains to Hegio, Cratinus and Crito that he has been badly treated while Geta and Phormio speak together
127v	Demipho with Hegio, Cratinus and Crito; Geta leaves in search of Antipho
128	Geta speaks with Antipho
128v	Dorio threatens Phaedria that he will sell the music girl, Pamphila, unless she is bought that day; Geta and Antipho stand on the right
129v	Phaedria, Antipho and Geta plan how to raise money to buy Pamphila
130v	Demipho meets Chremes
131	Geta approaches Demipho and Chremes
131v	Antipho eavesdrops on Geta, Chremes and Demipho
133	Geta explains his plan to Antipho; Chremes approaches from a doorway
133v	Geta, Demipho and Chremes prepare to pay Phormio
134	Sophrona tells Chremes that Antipho's wife is his Lemnian daughter, Phanium
135	Demipho sends Geta to announce his arrival to Nausistrata
135v	Chremes comes to inform Demipho that Phanium is his daughter in the presence of Nausistrata
136v[a]	Antipho considers his plight
136v[b]	Phormio tells Antipho that Pamphila has been purchased
137	Geta tells Antipho and Phormio that Chremes is Phanium's father
138	Chremes and Demipho ask Phormio to return their money
140	Phormio, held by Chremes and Demipho, tells Nausistrata of Chremes' secret marriage

Paris

BIBL. NAT., lat. 8193
(Figs. 7, 59, 181, 187, 190, 192, 196, 198, 205)

Terence, *Comedies* (in Latin). 185 fols.; 225 × 160 mm.

HISTORY: There seems to be no clue to the identity of the original owner of this manuscript. The manuscript begins with the life of Terence, *De Terencii vita in antiquis libris*, folios 1–2v, which is followed after two blank folios by a prologue on folio 5. In addition to the usual miniature at the beginning of each scene four unfilled gold frames show that exceptional miniatures were planned on folios 9v (I,2), folio 161v (II,1), folio 176v (V,3), and folio 182v (V,8). Both the illumination and the text remained incomplete. Descriptions of the scenes, the *argumenta*, were written in the margins only through folio 123, the end of a gathering. Scholia were inserted between the lines only through folio 46. The writing of the text seems not to have been closely supervised by a scholar familiar with classical manuscripts because the traditional names of the characters and their roles were omitted at the beginning of each scene. The order of the plays, however—the *Andria*, *Eunuchus*, *Heautontimorumenos*, *Adelphoe*, *Hecyra* and *Phormio*—is the same as in Berry's Terence and in the Carolingian copies.

STYLE AND DATE: This Terence was illuminated by a master who appears in only one other manuscript, a Virgil in Lyon; we have therefore called him the Roman Texts Master. He himself painted the first miniature in each play except for the *Eunuchus* and the *Phormio* (which was not illustrated). He also executed the second miniature in the *Adelphoe*, folio 99. He gave instructions to his assistants in the form of drawings with inscriptions, such as "vallet," "mere," "frere," "l'autre." These inscriptions still appear faintly over the figures in the miniatures in the *Adelphoe*. They may also be seen over drawings not yet painted on folios 107v, 111v, 112v, 114, 114v, 115v, 118.

As a model for his illustrations the Roman Texts Master used the Terence presented to Jean de Berry on January 1, 1408 (lat. 7907A). The miniatures heading the *Andria* and *Heautontimorumenos* in both manuscripts are similar (Figs. 189, 190, 191, 192). Syra in the frontispiece for *Hecyra* has the same features, the same strained neck muscles, and a headdress similar to that of the procuress in Berry's Terence (Figs. 59, 163). In the series of illustrations in the *Adelphoe* some of the figures are in the same positions as in Berry's Terence, although the composition as a whole is not the same. Furthermore, one of the more complete drawings in lat. 8193, on folio 112v, resembles the same scene in lat. 7907 A, folio 86v. We believe that lat. 8193 was painted at approximately the same time as Berry's Terence, and at most a short period later.

BIBLIOGRAPHY: Martin, *Térence*, 1907, p. 19 f.; Meiss, *Late XIV Century*, 1967, pp. 10 f., 363 n. 51, figs. 299, 300.

MINIATURES:

Folio

Andria (The Lady of Andros)

5v Simo confides in Sosia; Simo's two slaves carry provisions to the kitchen

Eunuchus (The Eunuch)

36v Parmeno counsels his master Phaedria, who has just left Thais' house

Heautontimorumenos (The Self-Tormentor)

68 Chremes reproves Menedemus for working too hard

Adelphoe (The Brothers)

98 Micio beckons to Storax

99 Demea rebukes Micio for his indulgence of Aeschinus

100v Sannio is frustrated in his attempt to regain Callidia from Aeschinus and Parmeno

102v Syrus bargains with Sannio

103v Ctesipho meets Syrus on his way to thank Aeschinus

104 Sannio; Aeschinus receives Ctesipho's thanks; Ctesipho stands with Syrus

105 Pamphila lies on her bed; Sostrata gives directions to Canthara

105v Geta informs Sostrata that Aeschinus has carried off Callidia

107v Syrus tells Demea that Ctesipho had nothing to do with Callidia's abduction

109v Hegio and Geta complain to Demea of Aeschinus' conduct

Hecyra (The Mother-in-Law)

128v Syra, the procuress, warns Philotis against liberality

Drawings for miniatures on folios 112v, 114, 114v, 115v, 118

Paris

BIBL. NAT., lat. 8886 (Figs. 511, 513)
Missal and Pontifical, Use of Luçon. 486 fols.; 395 × 300 mm.

EARLY HISTORY: Notes as well as phrases in the text, giving the use of Luçon and the date (fol. 296v) of the consecration of "Stephanus Lucionensis episcopus" on March 15, 1387 (o.s.), indicate that the manuscript was made for Etienne Loypeau, Bishop of Luçon. The manuscript, including in part the notes relative to the Bishop of Luçon, was copied, however, from an earlier Missal-Pontifical now in the Chapter Library of the Cathedral of Bayeux, ms. 61. Apparently Etienne Loypeau commissioned the second manuscript for Jean de Berry, whose arms, held by two angels, appear on the first folio. Etienne Loypeau was a protégé of the Duke and lived for a time in the latter's house as a keeper of his reliquaries.

The manuscript has been erroneously identified with a Pontifical "escript de très grosse lettre" owned by the Duke in 1402 and given to the Sainte-Chapelle in Bourges. This Pontifical was furthermore connected with a payment made in 1400 to a friar Goureau of Luçon, who executed a Pontifical intended for the Sainte-Chapelle in Bourges. However, lat. 8886 does not fit the description in the Duke's inventory. The incipit of the fourth folio and the last words of the text do not coincide, and the entry states that the Duke's arms are held not by angels but by two bears.

STYLE AND DATE: The manuscript contains some of the most beautiful miniatures by the Luçon Master and his workshop. Many of them have a long format to include complex architectural structures, which sometimes serve as the frame of the miniature itself. The manuscript was painted in the period 1405–1407, shortly before the death of Loypeau in 1407. The arms of the Duke, which were carefully tooled in the Luçon manner, are part of the original campaign.

BIBLIOGRAPHY: Delisle, 1856, pp. 152–154; Hiver de Beauvoir, 1857, p. 99 no. 21; Delisle, *Cabinet*, I, 1868, p. 66; III, 1881, p. 178 no. 90; *idem*, 1887, pp. 527–534; Bourloton, 1895, pp. 145–161; Guiffrey, *Inventaires*, I, 1894, p. 229 no. 874; II, 1896, pp. 169 no. 156, 236 no. 466; Bouchot, *Primitifs*, 1904, pp. 73 n. 2, 157–161; Paris, Louvre, *Exposition*, 1904, p. 29 no. 73; Delisle, *Charles V*, 1907, II, pp. 236 no. 90, 281; Martin, *Miniature française*, 1923, pp. 69, 99 f., fig. CIII; Leroquais, *Sacramentaires*, 1924, II, pp. 373–377, pls. LXXVI–LXXIX; Martens, *Meister Francke*, 1929, pp. 88–90, 179, 193 f., 237 n. 196, 245 n. 238, 248 n. 285, 257 n. 392, figs. 33, 103; Leroquais, *Pontificaux*, 1937, II, pp. 148–154, pls. LXXXIII–XCIV; Paris, Bibl. nat. (Porcher), 1955, p. 94 no. 192; Meiss, *Art Bull.*, 1956, p. 193; *idem*, *Late XIV Century*, index, figs. 268, 483; *idem*, *Boucicaut Master*, 1968, p. 15; *idem*, *De Lévis Hours*, 1972, p. 15 f., fig. 24.

MINIATURES:

Note: The folio numbers in parentheses include the missing folios.

Folio		
1		Tiara placed on the new pope. Jean de Berry's arms below
2		Bishop of Albano recites the first prayer
5	(6)	Prelate anointing the pope
8	(10)	Prelate returns the Gospels to the pope
16	(18)	New pope reenters the Lateran
38	(40)	Madonna enthroned
46	(49)	Emperor taking oath before the Roman people; emperor received by the clergy
47v	(50v)	Emperor taking oath before the pope
51	(54)	Delivery of the sword
58	(65)	Coronation of the King
61	(68)	Crowning of the Queen: the archbishop returns the scepter
88	(95)	Bishop prepares to celebrate pontifical mass
94	(101)	"Ad te levavi"
98	(105)	St. Luke writing his Gospel
123v	(130v)	Nativity
128	(135)	Epiphany
206v	(213v)	Entry into Jerusalem
256	(263)	Resurrection
276	(283)	Ascension
284v	(291v)	Pentecost
290v	(297v)	Benediction of an abbot
293v	(300v)	Kiss of peace given to a new abbot
318v	(325v)	Procession of Corpus Christi
355	(362)	Bishop dedicates a church
386	(393)	Stoning of St. Stephen
390	(397)	St. Hilary reading at a desk
393v	(400v)	Charlemagne
395v	(402v)	Presentation of the Christ Child in the Temple
401	(408)	Annunciation
413	(420)	Birth of St. John the Baptist
414v	(421v)	Translation of St. Hilary
421v	(428v)	St. Mary Magdalene
428	(435)	Transfiguration
432	(439)	St. Radegunde in prayer
435v	(442v)	St. Louis, King of France
439v	(446v)	Birth of the Virgin
440v	(447v)	Exaltation of the Holy Cross
444v	(451v)	St. Michael fighting the dragon
447	(454)	Martyrdom of St. Denis and his companions
451	(458)	St. Martin sharing his cloak
452v	(459v)	St. Catherine of Alexandria
456v	(463v)	Twelve apostles

Paris

BIBL. NAT., lat. 9471

(Figs. 390, 829, 868–870, 872–877, 888, 889, 898)

Book of Hours (*Grandes Heures de Rohan*), Use of Paris. 239 fols.; 290×208 mm.

EARLY HISTORY: The original owner is not known, but for speculation about the possibilities see the chapter on the Rohan Master. The arms now in the book were added later, before 1516, by a member of the Rohan family, after whom the manuscript takes its name.

STYLE AND DATE: The contribution of the Rohan Master to this extensively illustrated Book of Hours is greater than to any other manuscript. He completed, in our opinion, three large miniatures: the *Lamentation*, the *Madonna* (33v), and the *Dying Man before Christ*. He painted Gabriel and God the Father in the *Annunciation*, the shepherds when the angel brings the message to them, the High Priest in the *Presentation in the Temple*, some apostles in *Pentecost*, and Christ in the *Last Judgment*. He assumed responsibility as well for the design of other compositions and figures. He seems, on the other hand, to have had little if anything to do with numerous miniatures, particularly the long cycle of marginal illustrations based on a Neapolitan *Bible moralisée*, fr. 9561. Whereas in this model, as in all illustrated manuscripts of this text, the biblical scene and the allegorical interpretation of it are juxtaposed, the two miniatures are separated in the *Rohan Hours*, one appearing on the recto and the other on the verso.

Along with a figure of St. Peter in the *Heures d'Angers*, the miniatures by the Rohan Master in this manuscript represent the latest known stage of his art. With all the tentativeness needed at the present time when assigning actual dates to manuscripts in the Rohan style, we suggest for this Book of Hours the early 'twenties.

See the chapter on the Rohan Master in the preceding text.

BIBLIOGRAPHY: Delisle, 1893, p. 252 f.; Mâle, 1904, p. 52 f.; Durrieu, *Rev. de l'art a. et m.*, 1912, pp. 93–98, 170 f., figs. 1, 2, 4–10, 16, 17; Laborde, *Bible moralisée*, V, 1927, pp. 117–122; IV, 1921, pls. 768–781; Leroquais, *Livres d'heures*, 1927, I, pp. 281–290, pls. XXXVIII–XLII; Paris, Bibl. nat. (Martin), 1928, pp. 65, 110, fig. LXXXVI; Heimann, 1932, pp. 1–61, figs. 15–26, 32; Panofsky, in *Studies Porter*, 1939, II, pp. 479, 490 n. 39, 491 n. 42, fig. 18; [Sterling] *Peintres du moyen âge* [1941], p. 21, pl. 17; Porcher, 1945, pp. 1–6; Ring, *French Painting* [1949], p. 202 f. no. 86, pls. 37–40; "Meister der *Grandes Heures de Rohan*," in Thieme-Becker, XXXVII, 1950, pp. 124–126; Panofsky, *Netherlandish Painting*, 1953, I, pp. 74, 106, 376 n. 43[1], 389 f. nn. 74[4–6], II, figs. 97, 98; Porcher, *Belles Heures*, 1953, pp. 20, 24, 36 f., 42–46; *idem*, *Rohan Hours*, 1959; Vienna, Kunsthist. Mus., *Katalog*, 1962, p. 176, pls. 140, 141; Laclotte, *Primitifs français* [1966], p. 20, pl. XII; Meiss, *Late XIV Century*, 1967, pp. 8, 17, 268, fig. 327; Cleveland, Mus. of Art (Wixom), 1967, pp. 282, 380 f.; Meiss, *Boucicaut Master*, 1968, pp. 33, 40, fig. 166.

MINIATURES:

Folio	
1–18	Calendar
19	St. John the Evangelist
21	St. Matthew
23	St. Mark
25	St. Luke
26v	Angels holding banners
27	Crucifixion
29v	*Cour céleste* (*Obsecro te*)
33v	Virgin nursing the Child (*O Intemerata*)
38	Virgin holding the Child on a crescent
41	*Vesperbild* (Five sorrows of Mary)
Hours of the Virgin	
45	Annunciation
70	Visitation
	(Nativity—lost)
85v	Annunciation to the Shepherds
	(Adoration of Magi—lost)
90	Herod consulting the high priests and the scribes
94v	Presentation in the Temple
99	Flight into Egypt
106v	Coronation of the Virgin
135	Lamentation (Hours of Cross)
143v	Pentecost (Hours of Holy Ghost)
154	Last Judgment (*Sept requêtes*)
Office of the Dead	
159	Office of the Dead
167	Cadaver raising the cover of his coffin
173	Funeral procession
176	Funeral service
182	Two burials
185	Monks pray for the dead who await burial
192	Funeral service; grave-diggers
196	Dying Man
Suffrages	
210	Trinity
211	St. Peter
212	St. Paul
213	St. Bartholomew
214	St. John Baptist
215	St. John Evangelist
216	St. James
217	St. Andrew
218	St. Anthony
219	St. Lawrence
220	St. Christopher
221	St. Sebastian
222	St. Ivo
223	St. George
224	St. Nicholas
225	St. Martin
226	Group of Saints
227	Virgin and Child
230v	St. Anne and the Virgin
231v	St. Catherine
232v	St. Margaret
233v	St. Mary Magdalene
234v	St. Apollonia
236	Virgin saints
237	Christ on the Cross between the Virgin and St. John

Marginal decoration taken from a Neapolitan *Bible moralisée*, Paris, Bibl. nationale, fr. 9561. Scenes begin on folio 1 with the Creation of the World and end on folio 239v with the Death of the Ancient Law and its Interment by the Church.

Paris

BIBL. SAINTE-GENEVIEVE, ms. 1278
(Figs. 835, 836, 838)

Book of Hours, Use of Troyes. 225 fols.; 195×145 mm.

EARLY HISTORY: The identity of the original owner is unknown. The manuscript may, however, have been commissioned by the female donor represented on folio 201.

STYLE AND DATE: The Rohan workshop painted all the miniatures and initials. The use of saffron yellow suggests familiarity with the work of the Troyes Master. Although the vines in the borders are conventional some of them contain acanthus leaves and very well painted violets. The landscapes derive from the Boucicaut manuscripts, which provided also the model for the *Coronation of the Virgin*. The borders and compositions indicate a relatively early date, *ca.* 1413–1415.

BIBLIOGRAPHY: Durrieu, *Rev. de l'art a. et m.*, 1912, p. 171 f., fig. 19; Heimann, 1932, pp. 3–5, figs. 3, 5; Panofsky, in *Studies Porter*, 1939, II, pp. 479 n. 2, 490, figs. 11, 15; Paris, Bibl. nat. (Porcher), 1955, p. 107 no. 229.

MINIATURES:

Folio

1–12v Calendar
13 St. John the Evangelist
15v St. Luke
17v St. Matthew
19v St. Mark

Hours of the Trinity
21v Trinity (three persons) in initial

Prayer to God the Father
25v God the Father, the points of two swords in his mouth (initial)

Hours of the Dead (Monday)
29 Burial (initial)

Hours of All Saints (Tuesday)
33 All saints (initial)

Hours of the Holy Ghost (Wednesday)
37 Pentecost

Hours of the Sacrament (Thursday)
41 Last Supper (initial)

Hours of the Cross (Friday)
45 Deposition and Lamentation

Hours of the Virgin (Saturday)
49 Virgin spinning (initial)

Prayer to Trinity (Sunday)
53 Trinity (initial)

Hours of the Virgin
77 Annunciation
89 Visitation
101 Nativity
106v Annunciation to the Shepherds
111 Adoration of the Magi
115 Presentation in the Temple
120 Flight
127 Coronation of the Virgin

Penitential Psalms
133 Trinity

Office of the Dead
153 Two nude cadavers lying on the ground next to their coffins

Fifteen Joys
201 Female donor presented by a pilgrim saint (St. James?) to a standing Madonna and Child

Seven Requests
206v Last Judgment

Obsecro te
210 Virgin and Child (initial)

Philadelphia

MUSEUM OF ART, ms. 45-65-1
(Figs. 218, 277, 665)

Saint Augustine, *La Cité de Dieu* (translation and commentary by Raoul de Praelles). First Volume, Books I–V. 173 fols.; 435×312 mm.

EARLY HISTORY: The text ends abruptly near the end of the commentary in Chapter 26, Book V; possibly the manuscript was never finished. Within the miniatures on fols. 12 through 24, which have narrower frames than those following, a strip of parchment was left bare of paint below the upper frame; an ornamental frieze or conceivably an inscription was planned but never added. The program of illustration was changed during the course of the work. Books I and II are extensively illustrated, whereas each of Books III through V have only a half-page miniature at the beginning. There are no marks of original ownership; the armorial shield on fol. 5 is blank. Though Miss Scott suggested that the manuscript might be identified with a *Cité de Dieu* owned by Jean de Berry (Guiffrey, *Inventaires*, I, p. 241 f., no. 927), the phrase "pluseurs ont usurpé" cited in the inventory for folio 2 appears only on folio 6 in the Philadelphia *Cité de Dieu*.

STYLE AND DATE: The Orosius Master and his workshop painted all the miniatures, which show the characteristic palette: burnt orange, olive green, blue, violet and pink, which are sometimes set off by gold. The illustrations reflect the Terence on which the Orosius workshop collaborated—the manuscript given to Berry on New Year's Day, 1408 (lat. 7907 A). The Roman theater in the *Cité de Dieu* seems to derive from the frontispiece of this Terence (Figs. 209, 218). Furthermore, many of the figures, like those in the Terence, are inscribed with their names. The *Cité de Dieu* was probably painted, therefore, about 1408–10.

The cycle of illustrations is unique. No contemporary copy of the text was as extensively illustrated. The Orosius Master took great delight in presenting his conception of the Greeks and Romans, their deities as well as their daily lives.

BIBLIOGRAPHY: Philadelphia, *Museum Bulletin*, 1962, p. 16 f., illustrations on p. 15 f.; Scott, *Cité de Dieu*, 1967; Meiss, *Boucicaut Master*, 1968, pp. 45, 142, fig. 488.

MINIATURES:

Folio

1 Dedication. Raoul de Praelles presents his translation to Charles V
2v Prologue. Raoul de Praelles writing
3v Preface. St. Augustine writing
5 Book I. City of God; Pagan City; God the Father and the Fall of the Rebel Angels
6 Alaric invades Rome
6v Aeneas sails from Troy. Aeolus tries to send him a favorable wind but is restrained by Juno
7v Troy in flames; Panthus, with his grandson, hands Aeneas the city's idols for safe keeping
8 Temple of Juno in Troy containing the city's treasure held by Ulysses and Phoenix
8v Marcus Marcellus at the siege of Syracuse
9 Fabius, conqueror of Taranto, gives orders regarding the city's treasures
11 Paulinus, Bishop of Nola, offers a purse to free prisoners
12 Paulinus, Bishop of Nola, offers himself as a prisoner to free the son of a widow
12v King Lysimachus threatens to crucify Theodorus of Cyrene
13 A dying man gives his children instructions for burial
13v Arion, playing his harp, carried to safety on the back of a dolphin
14 Son of Regulus, in reprisal, condemns the Carthaginian prisoners to death
15v Marcus Regulus is put to death
Suicide of Hasdrubal's wife at the fall of Carthage
16v Collatinus proud to find his wife Lucretia at home
17 Rape of Lucretia
18 Suicide of Lucretia
18v Jephthah slays his daughter in fulfillment of a vow
19 Theobertus commits suicide after reading Plato's "Immortality of the Soul"
19v Suicide of Cato in Utica
20v Manlius Torquatus orders the execution of his son
21v Suicide of Sempronia
22 Ypo throws herself into the sea to escape from abductors
23 Death of Empedocles on Etna
23v Roman senators entrust the care of idols to Scipio Nasica
24 The Phrygian idol of Cybele brought to Rome by sea
25 Romans supplicate gods to avert plague
26 Roman theater
26v Sacrifice of "Black Beasts" as part of ritual of "Lectisternium"
27 Romulus and Remus within their sanctuary
28v Book II. St. Augustine witnesses the Roman feast called "Lectisternium"
29 St. Augustine with a disciple
30 Ruse of Hercules and flight of the shepherd Faunus
31v Self-emasculation of Athis before idol of Berecynthia
33 Jupiter and Ganymede
34v Two lovers in a garden
35v Plautus turning the mill
37 Nævius in prison writes his retractions
Aeschines offers himself to Socrates
38 Labeo talks to the Roman Emperor
38v Dispute on the theater between the Greeks and Romans
39v Romulus and Remus consult the oracle of the birds
42 The priest Flamen Dialis in the Temple of Mars
43 Three Roman ambassadors journey to Athens to copy Solon's laws
45 Rape of the Sabines
46v Insurrection of the Roman populace against nobles
49 Nævius Agrippa calming the Roman populace
49v Suicide of Sardanapalus when conquered by Arbaces
50v Tiberius Gracchus is slain by the Roman nobles
53 Siege of the Roman capitol by the Gauls; a goose gives alarm
56v Silla makes Gaius Marius a prisoner
58v During sacrifice for Silla a crown of gold is discovered in entrails of victim
60v Battle of the gods
62 St. Augustine witnesses lewd rites performed at the altar of goddess of chastity
63 Cicero presides at the rites of Flora
64 The Christian church
Contrast between the pagan and Christian church
66v Book III. The founding and destruction of Troy
115v Book IV. Varieties of scourges: earthquake, rain of fire, city swallowed in a chasm
143v Book V. Hippocrates in the presence of Posidonius ministers to twins in bed; Nigidius proves the fallacy of horoscopes by means of a trick on the potter's wheel

Rome

BIBL. VATICANA, Pal. lat. 1989

(Figs. 8, 9, 689)

Boccaccio, *Décaméron* (translation by Laurent de Premierfait). 327 fols.; 298×225 mm.

EARLY HISTORY: The manuscript belonged to Jean sans Peur. Although there are no marks of ownership, the first two words on the second folio and the last words of the text identify the manuscript with an entry in the inventory compiled after the Duke's assassination in 1419. Philippe le Bon inherited the manuscript.

STYLE AND DATE: The illustrations were no doubt painted soon after Laurent de Premierfait completed the translation of the text on June 15, 1414. The Vatican manuscript, prepared for the Duke of Burgundy, Jean sans Peur, contains the earliest full cycle of illustrations for the *Decameron*. No preceding Italian copy approximated the hundred miniatures in the Vatican manuscript; the Italian manuscripts contained a miniature for each day, not each story. The illuminators of the Vatican manuscript proceeded, therefore, without pictorial models. How they fared the writer discussed in an article of 1967.

All the miniatures were painted by the Cité des Dames Master and his workshop. The Master himself was entirely responsible for a few, the first miniatures in certain gatherings (fols. 11, 34v, and 105v). The miniatures were executed in the free, wash technique employed by these illuminators in their latest phase.

BIBLIOGRAPHY: Doutrepont, *Inventaire*, 1906, p. 160 f. no. 238; Durrieu, *Comptes rendus* (Décaméron), 1909, pp. 342–350; *idem*, *Bibl. École des Chartes*, 1910, pp. 64–69; *idem*, *Comptes rendus*, 1910, pp. 342, 350; *idem*, *Bulletin*, 1911, p. 89 f.; Purkis, 1955, pp. 1, 8, 9; Meiss, *Late XIV Century*, 1967, index, figs. 318, 319, 321; *idem*, "*Decameron*," 1967, pp. 56–61.

MINIATURES:

Folio			
11	First Day.	1st	*nouvelle.*
16		2nd	*nouvelle.*
18		3rd	*nouvelle.*
20		4th	*nouvelle.*
22		5th	*nouvelle.*
23v		6th	*nouvelle.*
25v		7th	*nouvelle.*
27v		8th	*nouvelle.*
29v		9th	*nouvelle.*
31v		10th	*nouvelle.*
34v	Second Day.	11th	*nouvelle.*
37		12th	*nouvelle.*
40		13th	*nouvelle.*
43v		14th	*nouvelle.*
46		15th	*nouvelle.*
51v		16th	*nouvelle.*
57		17th	*nouvelle.*
65		18th	*nouvelle.*
71v		19th	*nouvelle.*
77		20th	*nouvelle.*
82	Third Day.	21st	*nouvelle.*
85		22nd	*nouvelle.*
87v		23rd	*nouvelle.*
91		24th	*nouvelle.*
93v		25th	*nouvelle.*
97		26th	*nouvelle.*
100		27th	*nouvelle.*
105v		28th	*nouvelle.*
110		29th	*nouvelle.*
114		30th	*nouvelle.*
120	Fourth Day.	31st	*nouvelle.*
124v		32nd	*nouvelle.*
128v		33rd	*nouvelle.*
131v		34th	*nouvelle.*
134		35th	*nouvelle.*
136		36th	*nouvelle.*
139		37th	*nouvelle.*
141		38th	*nouvelle.*
143v		39th	*nouvelle.*
145v	Fifth Day.	40th	*nouvelle.*
150v		41st	*nouvelle.*
155v		42nd	*nouvelle.*
158		43rd	*nouvelle.*
161		44th	*nouvelle.*
163v		45th	*nouvelle.*
166		46th	*nouvelle.*
168v		47th	*nouvelle.*
171v		48th	*nouvelle.*
174v		49th	*nouvelle.*
177v		50th	*nouvelle.*
183	Sixth Day.	51st	*nouvelle.*
184		52nd	*nouvelle.*
185v		53rd	*nouvelle.*
186v		54th	*nouvelle.*
188v		55th	*nouvelle.*
189v		56th	*nouvelle.*
191		57th	*nouvelle.*
192v		58th	*nouvelle.*
193v		59th	*nouvelle.*
195		60th	*nouvelle.*
201	Seventh Day.	61st	*nouvelle.*
203v		62nd	*nouvelle.*
205		63rd	*nouvelle.*
207v		64th	*nouvelle.*
210		65th	*nouvelle.*
213		66th	*nouvelle.*
215		67th	*nouvelle.*

Folio			
217v		68th	*nouvelle.*
221		69th	*nouvelle.*
226		70th	*nouvelle.*
229	Eighth Day.	71st	*nouvelle.*
230v		72nd	*nouvelle.*
232v		73rd	*nouvelle.*
236		74th	*nouvelle.*
238		75th	*nouvelle.*
239v		76th	*nouvelle.*
242v		77th	*nouvelle.*
251v		78th	*nouvelle.*
253v		79th	*nouvelle.*
259v		80th	*nouvelle.*
265v	Ninth Day.	81st	*nouvelle.*
268v		82nd	*nouvelle.*
271		83rd	*nouvelle.*
273		84th	*nouvelle.*
275		85th	*nouvelle.*
278v		86th	*nouvelle.*
280v		87th	*nouvelle.*
282		88th	*nouvelle.*
284		89th	*nouvelle.*
287		90th	*nouvelle.*
289v	Tenth Day.	91st	*nouvelle.*
291v		92nd	*nouvelle.*
293v		93rd	*nouvelle.*
296v		94th	*nouvelle.*
299v		95th	*nouvelle.*
301v		96th	*nouvelle.*
304		97th	*nouvelle.*
307		98th	*nouvelle.*
313v		99th	*nouvelle.*
320		100th	*nouvelle.*

Rome

BIBL. VATICANA, Reg. lat. 939 (Fig. 429)

Valerius Maximus, *De dictis factisque mirabilibus.* 331 × 240 mm.

EARLY HISTORY: The original ownership is undetermined. On folio 100, in the lower right column, there is a trace of an inscription, perhaps of the owner. It is not legible, however, even in ultraviolet light. A subsequent owner added his name in ink to a later shield on folio 1.

STYLE AND DATE: The single miniature, a frontispiece showing the author in his study, is very close to the work of Jean de Limbourg in the *Belles Heures* and it was doubtless painted by him. Since the script of the manuscript is Italian he may well have executed the miniature during one of the trips which took him to Florence and Padua and elsewhere in Italy.

BIBLIOGRAPHY: Durrieu, *Bulletin*, 1911, p. 90 f. no. VI; Porcher, *Belles Heures*, 1953, pp. 7 n. 10, 51; Meiss, *Gaz. B.-A.*, 1963, p. 162; Pächt, *Pantheon*, 1963, p. 139 n. 12, fig. 8.

Toronto

ROYAL ONTARIO MUSEUM, University of Toronto (Lee of Fareham Collection)
(Figs. 813, 815–818, 820, 822, 824–826)

Book of Hours, Use of Rome. Hours of Jeanne du Peschin, wife of Louis de Giac. 216 fols.; 197 × 146 mm.

EARLY HISTORY: The arms below the *Annunciation* on folio 17 are those of Louis de Giac impaled by those of his wife Jeanne du Peschin. She is represented before the Madonna on fol. 131v, and the prayers are in feminine form. Louis de Giac was chancellor of France during the minority of Charles VI as well as chamberlain to both Philippe le Hardi and Jean de Berry. In 1396 he went to Hungary on an expedition to support King Sigismond against Sultan Bajazet and never returned. His wife, who commissioned the manuscript, repeatedly asked for the protection of "ton serf," presumably her husband, in a prayer on folio 151v.

STYLE AND DATE: This Book of Hours seems to be the earliest manuscript known to us illuminated by the Rohan Master and his workshop. Miss Heimann, who first published it, thought that it might be dated even before 1400, and Porcher was inclined to accept this view, which seemed strongly supported by the supposed death of Louis de Giac in 1396 or shortly afterwards. The codicil of 1407 to the will of his father-in-law, however, proves that he was then still believed to be alive, a prisoner of the Turks. The manuscript can then be dated *ca.* 1410, where its style, in our opinion, would place it. The miniatures imply a knowledge of the work of the Limbourgs and the Boucicaut Master. The *Annunciation* is related to a composition painted towards 1410, by the Troyes Master, who was active in Troyes (or at least Champagne), and the Rohan Master himself was probably then working in the same city.

BIBLIOGRAPHY: Anselme, *Histoire généalogique*, VI, 1730, p. 343 ff.; London, Sotheby, June 4, 1934, lot 10; Heimann, 1937, p. 83 f.; Porcher, *Rohan Hours*, 1959, p. 32 n. 11.

MINIATURES:

Hours of the Virgin

Folio

17	Annunciation
26	Visitation
35v	Nativity
39v	Annunciation to the Shepherds
43v	Adoration of the Magi
47	Presentation in the Temple
50v	Flight into Egypt
57	Coronation of the Virgin
73	Last Judgment
87	Crucifixion
90	Pentecost

Office of the Dead

95	Mass for the Dead

Prayer to the Virgin

131v	Jeanne du Peschin before Madonna and Child
135	Deposition

Suffrages

171	Three Archangels
173v	Annunciation
174	St. Anne and the Virgin
175	St. Mary Magdalene
175v	St. Margaret
176v	St. Catherine of Alexandria
177	St. Susanna
177v	St. Claude de Besançon
178v	St. Silvanus
179	St. Blaise
180	St. Leonard
180v	St. Anthony
181	St. John on Patmos
181v	St. Benedict
182v	St. Fiacrius
183	St. Christopher
183v	St. John the Baptist
184	St. Peter and St. Paul
185	St. James the Great
185v	St. Sebastian
186	St. Francis
186v	St. Bartholomew
187v	Nativity
188	Stoning of St. Stephen
188v	Massacre of the Innocents
189v	St. Agnes
190	Presentation in the Temple
190v	St. Agatha
191	St. Matthew
192	Adoration of the Cross
192v	Resurrection
193	St. George
193v	St. Mark
194v	St. Philip and St. James the Less
195	Invention of the Holy Cross
195v	Ascension
196	Pentecost
196v	St. Barnabas
197v	St. Lawrence
198	Assumption of the Virgin
198v	St. Luke
199	St. Simon and St. Jude
200	Birth of the Virgin
200v	All Saints
201	St. Martin of Tours
202	St. Andrew
202v	St. Nicholas
203	St. Thomas
204	St. Eutropius
204v	St. Yves de Treguier

Private Collection
(formerly Paris, Pierre Berès)

See Christine de Pisan, *Mutacion*

Private Collection
(formerly Paris, Martin Le Roy) (Fig. 807)

Book of Hours, Use of Angers. 196 fols.; 220×157 mm.

EARLY HISTORY: There are no indications of the identity of the original owner.

STYLE AND DATE: The Rohan Master painted only the figure of St. Peter (not the entire miniature) on fol. 160. His workshop painted all the other miniatures. In style the manuscript is exceptionally close to the *Rohan Hours.*

BIBLIOGRAPHY: Durrieu, *Heures à l'usage d'Angers*, 1912; Heimann, 1932, pp. 38 ff.; Paris, Bibl. nat. (Porcher), 1955, p. 110 no. 235; Porcher, *Medieval French Miniatures*, 1959, p. 69.

MINIATURES:

Folio

2–13	Calendar
14	St. John the Evangelist
16	St. Luke
18	St. Matthew
20	St. Mark

Hours of the Virgin

31	Annunciation
42	Visitation
54	Pentecost
56	Nativity
63	Annunciation to the Shepherds
68v	Adoration of the Magi
74	Presentation in the Temple
80	Flight into Egypt
88	Coronation of the Virgin

Folio

Penitential Psalms

95	Christ on the Cross intercedes before God the Father

Office of the Dead

113	Prayer for the souls of the dead

Prayers to the Apostles

160	St. Peter
161	St. Paul
162	St. Andrew
163	St. James Major
164	St. John the Evangelist
165	St. Thomas
166	St. James Minor
167	St. Philip
168	St. Bartholomew
169	St. Matthew
170	St. Simon
171	St. Jude
172	Virgin and Child blessed by God the Father (Doulce Dame de Misericorde)
177	Last Judgment (Doulx Dieux)

Suffrages

182	Virgin and Child enthroned below the Trinity
184	St. Michael; St. Mary Magdalene
186	St. Stephen; St. Radegunde
188	St. Martin; St. Anthony abbot
190	St. Sebastian; St. Barbara
192	St. Christopher; St. Margaret
194	St. Lawrence; St. Catherine
196	St. Nicholas; All Saints

Private Collection

(formerly Alexandrine Rothschild)

(Figs. 514, 517, 518)

Book of Hours, Use of Paris. 201 fols.; 230×160 mm.

EARLY HISTORY: Although there are no indications of original ownership, a list of births on folio 172v informs us that the manuscript belonged in the mid-fifteenth century to Jean d'Angennes II, Seigneur de Rambouillet.

STYLE AND DATE: All but one of the miniatures, which are in a remarkably fresh condition, are in the late style of Pseudo-Jacquemart. The single exception, the *Betrayal*, was painted by the Egerton Master. Two compositions by Pseudo-Jacquemart, who collaborated on several manuscripts illuminated for Jean de Berry, derive from miniatures in major manuscripts of the Duke. The *Adoration of the Christ Child at the Nativity* (fig. 518) is an almost literal copy of Jacquemart de Hesdin's *Nativity* in the *Brussels Hours*. The *Virgin on a Crescent* is based on Paul de Limbourg's *Virgin and Child in Glory* for All Saints in the *Belles Heures* (figs. 389, 514). On the other hand the composition of the miniature of *David in prayer* is repeated in the miniature by the Luçon workshop in the *De Lévis Hours* about 1417 (Meiss, *De Lévis Hours*, 1972, fig. 4). For these and other reasons our Book of Hours should be dated between 1410 and 1415.

BIBLIOGRAPHY: Paris, Palais Galliera, June 24, 1968, lot 4; Meiss, *Boucicaut Master*, 1968, p. 142.

MINIATURES:

Folio	
17v	Coronation of the Virgin who rests on a crescent
25	Annunciation
43	Visitation
52	Nativity
57	Annunciation to the Shepherds
61	Adoration of the Magi
65	Presentation in the Temple
69	Flight into Egypt
75	Coronation of the Virgin
80	David prays before God
94	Crucifixion
99	Pentecost
104	Betrayal
136	Illustration of Office of the Dead
173	Virgin and Child
178	Last Judgment

There are seven small miniatures in the Hours of the Passion which represent *Christ before Pilate*, *Mockery of Christ*, *Flagellation*, *Way to Calvary*, *Crucifixion*, *Descent from the Cross* and the *Entombment*.

XI

Reintegrated French Workshops 1380-1420

This catalogue subsumes its predecessors in the *Late XIV Century* and in the *Boucicaut Master*. It differs from them in several respects. Changes of classification have been made, especially in the category of "related manuscripts," but none of them affects significantly the reintegration of the workshops published earlier. The number of manuscripts has increased. Many have been added to the workshop lists, and a few illuminators appear here for the first time. In the preceding catalogues only the signature of a manuscript and the title of its text were cited; here the folios bearing miniatures by the workshop are specified. This catalogue is therefore fuller and more precise. It includes also bibliographical references for each workshop and each manuscript.

The lists of the works of illuminators such as Jacquemart and the Brussels Initials Master who were discussed at some length in the text of the preceding volumes appear in briefer form here. When the reader encounters such brief lists consisting only of the signature and title of a manuscript he will find full information in the *Late XIV Century*; the illuminator in whom he is interested can be readily found in both the table of contents and the index of that volume. The miniatures in the Boucicaut style, to which an entire volume has already been devoted, are omitted from this catalogue.

ANDRE BEAUNEVEU

Paris, Bibliothèque nationale	fr. 13091	Psalter of Jean de Berry
Paris, Musée du Louvre, Cabinet des Dessins, drawing, Inv. 9832		*Death, Assumption and Coronation of the Virgin* (copy of Beauneveu)

BIBLIOGRAPHY: for Beauneveu as illuminator see Hulin de Loo, 1925, p. 123 ff.; Panofsky, *Netherlandish Painting*, 1953, p. 40 f.; Meiss, *Late XIV Century*, 1967, pp. 113, 135 ff., 147 ff., 331 f.

JACQUEMART DE HESDIN

Barcelona, S. María del Mar		*Madonna*, after Jacquemart (destroyed)
Brussels, Bibliothèque royale	ms. 11060–1	*Brussels Hours*
London, British Museum	Yates Thompson 37	Book of Hours
New York, Pierpont Morgan Library	M.346	Pattern Book
Oxford, Bodleian Library	Rawl. C. 538	*Secret des secrez*
Paris, Bibliothèque nationale	fr. 13091	Psalter of Jean de Berry
	lat. 18014	*Petites Heures* of Jean de Berry
Paris, Musée du Louvre		*Way to Calvary*
Rome, Biblioteca Vaticana	lat. 50–51	Bible

RELATED MANUSCRIPTS

Baltimore, Walters Art Gallery	ms. 96	Book of Hours
London, British Museum	Harley 4381–2	*Bible historiale*
London, British Museum	Egerton 1070	Book of Hours
Paris, Bibliothèque nationale	fr. 380	*Roman de la rose*
Parma, Biblioteca Palatina	lat. 159	Book of Hours

BIBLIOGRAPHY: Panofsky, *Netherlandish Painting*, 1953, pp. 42–49, 56; Meiss, *Art Bull.*, 1956, p. 191 ff.; Pächt, *Rev. des arts*, 1956, pp. 149–160; Meiss, *Late XIV Century*, 1967, pp. 169 ff., 194 ff., 209 ff., 256 f., 270 ff.

THE LIMBOURG BROTHERS

See the chapters on these masters.

BIBLIOGRAPHY: Hulin de Loo, 1903, pp. 178 ff.; Durrieu, *Très Riches Heures*, 1904; Hulin de Loo, 1908, p. 183 ff.; Winkler, "Limbourgs," in Thieme-Becker, XXIII, 1929, pp. 227–229; *idem*, 1930, p. 95 ff.; Pächt, 1950, pp. 37–47; Baldass, *Van Eyck* [1952], p. 9; Panofsky, *Netherlandish Painting*, 1953, pp. 61–66; Porcher, *Belles Heures*, 1953; Gorissen, 1954, pp. 153–221; Porcher, *French Miniatures* [1959], pp. 62–67; *idem*, in *Enciclopedia dell'arte*, VIII, p. 619 ff.; Pächt, *Gaz. B.-A.*, 1963, pp. 109–122; Avril, in *Encyclopaedia Universalis*, IX, 1971, p. 1024 f.

Bourges, Charter of Ste-Chapelle (lost) (Fig. 387)
Jean de Berry investing a canon of the Ste-Chapelle.
Charter dated April 18, 1405.
Copy by Bastard of the Limbourgs.
BIBLIOGRAPHY: Bastard, *Peintures*, 1832–1869; Porcher, *Belles Heures*, 1953, p. 7 n. 10; Meiss, *Burl. Mag.*, 1963, p. 51; Meiss, *Late XIV Century*, 1967, pp. 79, 84 f., 246, fig. 481; *idem*, "Breviary Master," 1970, p. 6.

Chantilly, MUSEE CONDE, ms. 65
Très Riches Heures de Jean de Berry. Ca. 1411–1416.
See Catalogue of Manuscripts.

New York, METROPOLITAN MUS. OF ART, THE CLOISTERS
Belles Heures de Jean de Berry. Between 1405 and 1409.
See Catalogue of Manuscripts.

Paris, BIBL. NAT., fr. 166
Bible moralisée. 1402–1404. Paul and Jean de Limbourg.
See Catalogue of Manuscripts.

Paris, BIBL. NAT., lat. 18014 (Fig. 405)
Book of Hours (*Petites Heures of Jean de Berry*), Use of Paris. 292 fols.; 215 × 145 mm.
Belonged to Jean de Berry before 1402 (Inventory of 1402). Given by the Duke to the wife of Robinet d'Estampes in 1416.
Fol. 288v added by Jean de Limbourg *ca.* 1412.
For miniatures by Jacquemart de Hesdin, Pseudo-Jacquemart, and the Passion and Trinity Masters see Meiss, *Late XIV Century*, 1967, pp. 334–337 (Catalogue).
BIBLIOGRAPHY: For earlier bibliography see Meiss, *Late XIV Century*, 1967, p. 335. For the Limbourg miniature see *ibid.*, pp. 71 f., 92 f., 334 ff., fig. 498.

Paris, BIBL. NAT., nouv. acq. lat. 3093 (Figs. 500, 501)
Très Belles Heures de Notre-Dame of Jean de Berry. 240 pages; 279 × 199 mm.
Begun very probably for Jean de Berry, no later than around 1384. In 1412 the Duke gave the manuscript to Robinet d'Estampes (Inventory of 1413).
Pages 225 and 240 added by Jean and Paul de Limbourg *ca.* 1410. Furthermore a miniature representing the Itinerary of the Duke, reproduced by Bastard d'Estang, was probably added to this manuscript by the Limbourgs.
For miniatures by the workshops of the Baptist Master, the Holy Ghost Master and the Parement Master see Meiss, *Late XIV Century*, 1967, pp. 337–340 (Catalogue).
BIBLIOGRAPHY: For bibliography on the earlier campaigns in this manuscript see Meiss, *Late XIV Century*, 1967, p. 338; Paris, Bibl. nat. (Avril and Lafaurie), 1968, p. 100 f. no. 175; Meiss with Off, 1971, pp. 229 f., 233. For the participation of the Limbourgs see Meiss, *Late XIV Century*, 1967, pp. 71 f., 92, 112, 134, fig. 497.

Paris, BIBL. NAT., Cabinet des Estampes, (Fig. 604)
Gaignières Coll., Oa 13 Rés., fol. 15.
Portrait of Jean de Berry. Copy *ca.* 1700.
BIBLIOGRAPHY: Meiss, *Burl. Mag.*, 1963, pp. 51–53, fig. 4; *idem*, *Late XIV Century*, 1967, pp. 75 ff., 80, 86, fig. 490.

Rome, BIBL. VATICANA, ms. Reg. lat. 939
Valerius Maximus, *De dictis factisque mirabilibus.*
See Catalogue of Manuscripts.

RELATED MANUSCRIPTS

Chantilly, MUSEE CONDE, ms. 66 (1383) (Fig. 365)
Book of Hours, Use of Paris. 154 fols.; 200 × 140 mm.
All miniatures by a follower of the Limbourgs who also illuminated the *Spitz Hours.*
BIBLIOGRAPHY: Chantilly (Meurgey), 1930, p. 71 f. no. 31, pl. XLVI; Porcher, *Enluminure*, 1959, p. 64, fig. 71.

Chicago (Glencoe), MRS. J. SPITZ COLL. (Figs. 391, 634–636)
Book of Hours, Use of Paris. 245 fols.; 204 × 146 mm.
All miniatures except the *Visitation* and *Presentation* by a follower of the Limbourgs. *Ca.* 1422.
For the miniatures by the Harvard Hannibal workshop see this Catalogue.
BIBLIOGRAPHY: see Harvard Hannibal.

Fort Worth (Texas),
ARTHUR HADDAWAY COLL.
Book of Hours, Use of Paris. 174 fols.; 219 × 155 mm.
Belonged to Louis XI, while he was still Dauphin, and Charlotte of Savoy, whose arms were added in the borders of the folios with large miniatures.
Fols. 7, 9, 10, 13v by Limbourg follower who illuminated much of the *Spitz Hours. Ca.* 1420.
For the miniatures by the workshops of the Bedford and Guise Masters see this Catalogue.
BIBLIOGRAPHY: see Bedford.

London, COUNT ANTOINE SEILERN COLL.
Book of Hours.
See Catalogue of Manuscripts.

Washington, D.C., NATIONAL GALLERY OF ART, Rosenwald Collection, B–13, 520
Saint Christopher carrying the Christ Child. A leaf from a Book of Hours. 205 × 150 mm.
In 1956 I ascribed this miniature, abraded in places but still impressive, to the "atelier of the Limbourgs"—a classification that still seems correct as indicative of closeness to the work of the three brothers. The figures in the miniature resemble the *St. Christopher and the Christ Child* in the *Belles Heures*, fol. 164v. On the other hand the Washington *St. Christopher* has a much deeper landscape, which, with its mountains set at intervals in the receding space, cannot be matched in the *Belles Heures*. The character of the border of the Washington folio, however, which recalls the borders of the *Belles Heures*, is characteristic of the first decade of the century. The leaf should be dated *ca.* 1409.
BIBLIOGRAPHY: Baltimore, Walters (Miner), 1949, p. 30 no. 78; Meiss, *Art Bull.*, 1956, p. 195, fig. 10; Baltimore, Walters, *International Style* (Miner), 1962, p. 60 no. 56, pl. XLI; Köllner, 1970.

MASTER OF THE ANDRIA

The Andria Master is known only for his miniatures in the *Lady from Andros* in a copy of the *Comedies* of Terence which Martin Gouge gave to Jean de Berry in 1408 (Figs. 64, 177, 189). With this master a close associate painted the miniatures in the subsequent play, the *Eunuch*, through folio 42 (Figs. 180, 195). His Italianate style, deriving from Jacquemart, closely resembles that of the Josephus Master, who painted the frontispiece of this manuscript.

For the discussion of this illuminator see the chapter on Terence.

Paris, BIBL. NAT., lat. 7907 A
Terence, *Comedies*. Just before 1408.
See Catalogue of Manuscripts.

MASTER OF THE BAPTIST

London, British Museum	Yates Thompson 37	Book of Hours
Paris, Bibliothèque nationale	nouv.acq.lat. 3093	*Très Belles Heures de Notre-Dame*
Paris, Musée du Louvre, Cabinet des Dessins		2 folios from the *Très Belles Heures de Notre-Dame*
Turin, Biblioteca nazionale (formerly)	"*Heures de Turin*"	*Très Belles Heures de Notre-Dame*
Turin, Museo Civico	"*Heures de Milan*"	*Très Belles Heures de Notre-Dame*

BIBLIOGRAPHY: Hulin de Loo, *Heures de Milan*, 1911, pp. 17–19; Durrieu, *Très Belles Heures de Notre-Dame*, 1922, p. 69 f.; Meiss, *Late XIV Century*, 1967, p. 248 ff.

THE MASTER OF THE BEDFORD HOURS AND THE BEDFORD TREND

The classification of the miniatures and manuscripts that follow presents unusual difficulties, of nomenclature as well as of style. Long ago the Bedford Master was named after his work in the *Bedford Hours* in the British Museum, datable *ca.* 1422, and the still later *Bedford Breviary* in Paris. Miniatures in many earlier manuscripts were ascribed, more or less tentatively, to the same illuminator and his associates; they include the *Grandes Heures* of 1409, the *Boccace de Jean sans Peur* about 1410, the *Livre de la chasse*, the *Missal of St. Magloire* of 1412, the *Adelphoe* in the *Térence des ducs*, and the *Merveilles du monde* before 1412. Certain of these paintings, for example in the *Livre de la chasse* (Fig. 255), the *Adelphoe* of the Terence (Figs. 199, 204), and the Boccaccio, are especially close to one another. In some paintings soon after 1412 we may clearly recognize, we believe, the style of the principal illuminator of the later Hours in the British Museum (Fig. 777) and of the Breviary in Paris. These works include miniatures as well as initials in the Breviary at Châteauroux before 1415. These paintings show greater artistic strength than any of those before 1412. On the other hand they do not show an equal measure of originality, and we may therefore ask whether the Master of the Bedford Hours simply emerged as a better illuminator from the earlier trend or whether he had also taken a part in shaping it.

Both the earlier and the later miniatures combine stocky, bulbous-nosed figures derived from Netherlandish painting with the elegant, sinuously draped figures of the Simonesque tradition. Curving mounds or flamboyant crags rise behind complex buildings and nimble, restless figures. The bent and twisted figures gesticulate emphatically, but the gestures seldom convey any specific meaning. The "Bedford illuminators" abhor the poise, moderation, and propriety that are norms of the Boucicaut Master; they prefer an intense though generalized vitality and expressiveness. The stylistic trend, then, is quite distinctive, although we have not attempted to identify the individual contributions to it. Small stylistic groups emerge clearly but their limits are difficult to define and we leave this task to others. Inasmuch as the name of the Bedford Master has frequently been attached to the entire group it seems right at present not to abandon it entirely. Already in 1968 I therefore employed the term "trend to Bedford" or, briefly, "Bedford trend" for all paintings of the group earlier than the Châteauroux Breviary, in which the chief master of the Bedford Hours seems to Professor Spencer and to me indubitably identifiable.

The repetition of forms and figures in this long series of paintings implies that the illuminators were in actuality associated and employed common models. The constitution of the group was not constant over its entire history from 1409 or earlier into the late 'thirties; occasionally one illuminator dropped out or another came in. Each of these masters developed somewhat differently, but the continuous mutual exchange resulted in a collective evolution of the entire group. Thus the best miniatures painted during the second decade of the century are comparatively luminous and spatial, whereas a more linear, elaborate, and intense style is characteristic of the 'twenties—the period of the well-known Books of Hours in London, Vienna, and Lisbon. In the Breviary illuminated for the Duke of Bedford in the years preceding his death in 1435 the masters revived to a degree their forms of the second decade and they responded to the new world of the Flemish panel painters.

Since this publication includes only in special instances paintings of the 'twenties none of the Bedford manuscripts of this or the following decade is included in the following catalogue.

BIBLIOGRAPHY: Martens, *Meister Francke*, 1929, p. 241 n. 222; Panofsky, *Netherlandish Painting*, 1953, p. 61; Meiss, *Art Bull.*, 1956, p. 194; Porcher, *Medieval French Miniatures* [1959], pp. 67–69; Spencer, 1965, pp. 495–502; *idem*, 1966, pp. 607–612; Meiss, *Boucicaut Master*, 1968, p. 35 f.; *idem*, *De Lévis Hours*, 1972.

THE MASTER OF THE BEDFORD HOURS

Châteauroux, BIBL. MUNICIPALE, ms. 2
Breviary, Use of Paris (Summer section only). 454 fols.; 280×195 mm.
On fol. 430 arms of the Dauphin: very probably Louis, duc de Guyenne, who died in 1415.
Fols. 8–76v, 98, 100v, 106–215, 226v–230, 249, 254v, 258v, 261v, 280–296, 340v, 357v–360, 372v, 373v, 376, 379v, 382v, 387v and some miniatures in the calendar by the Bedford Master and workshop *ca.* 1414.
For miniatures by the Orosius workshop see this Catalogue. For the Boucicaut miniatures see Meiss, *Boucicaut Master*, 1968, pp. 81–85 (Catalogue).
BIBLIOGRAPHY: *Ibid.*, p. 82, index, figs. 101–117; *idem*, *De Lévis Hours*, 1972, p. 22, fig. 46.

Fort Worth (Texas), COLL. OF ARTHUR HADDAWAY
Book of Hours, Use of Paris. 174 fols.; 219×155 mm.
Belonged to Louis XI, while he was still Dauphin, and Charlotte of Savoy, whose arms were added in the borders of the folios with large miniatures.
Fols. 17, 63v. *Ca.* 1420.
For miniatures by the workshop of the Guise Master and by a follower of the Limbourgs see this Catalogue.
BIBLIOGRAPHY: London, Sotheby, June 24, 1969, no. 59; Austin, University of Texas, *Manuscripts*, 1971, pp. 33–35; Meiss, *De Lévis Hours*, 1972, pp. 11 f., fig. 17.

Lisbon, GULBENKIAN FOUNDATION
Book of Hours (*Lamoignon Hours* or the *Hours of Isabelle of Brittany*), Use of Paris. 291 fols.; 263×193 mm.
Belonged to Isabelle of Brittany who, between 1430 and 1442, added her arms impaled by those of her husband Guy de Laval on fols. 202v and 286v.
All miniatures. *Ca.* 1419–1423.
BIBLIOGRAPHY: London, Brit. Mus., Millar, 1933, p. 31 no. 39, pl. XXXIX; London, Sotheby & Co., June 21, 1937, lot 1; Spencer, 1965, pp. 497, 501; *idem*, 1966, p. 612; Meiss, *De Lévis Hours*, 1972, pp. 12 f., 18, 21–23, 25, figs. 18, 33, 43, 44.

London, BRIT. MUS., Add. 16997
Book of Hours, Use of Paris. 226 fols.; 159×114 mm.
Belonged to Etienne Chevalier.
Fol. 72v by Master. *Ca.* 1418.
For the Boucicaut miniatures see Meiss, *Boucicaut Master*, 1968, p. 92 (Catalogue).
BIBLIOGRAPHY: *Ibid.*, p. 92, index, figs. 134, 172, 174, 283–295, 299.

London, BRIT. MUS., Add. 18850 (Fig. 777)
Book of Hours (*Bedford Hours*), Use of Paris. 289 fols.; 260×182 mm.
Painted about 1422, when John of Bedford contracted to marry Anne of Burgundy, or slightly later. At Christmas 1430 Anne gave the manuscript to her nephew, Henry VI. Arms, mottoes and portraits of the Duke and Duchess.
All miniatures by Bedford Master and workshop except those on fols. 15v, 16v, 17v, 288v, which were added in 1429–1430.
BIBLIOGRAPHY: Gough, *Illuminated Missal*, 1794; Vallet de Viriville, 1866, pp. 275–285; London, Brit. Mus., Warner, 1903, text and pl. 47; London, Brit. Mus., *Reproductions*, III, 1910, p. 14, pls. XXXII–XXXIV; Herbert, *Illuminated Manuscripts*, 1911, pp. 273–275; London, Brit. Mus., *Schools of Illumination*, VI, 1930, p. 96, pls. 8, 9; London, Brit. Mus., Millar, 1933, p. 30 no. 38, pl. XXXVIII; Spencer, 1965, pp. 495–502; *idem*, 1966, p. 612; London, Brit. Mus. (Turner), 1967, p. 46 no. 58, pl. 14; Meiss, *Late XIV Century*, 1967, p. 389 n. 58; *idem*, *Boucicaut Master*, 1968, pp. 31, 35, 70, figs. 150, 160, 482; Munby, 1968, p. 404 f.; Meiss, *De Lévis Hours*, 1972, pp. 13–15, 17–25, figs. 20, 23, 31, 35, 38, 39, 45, 56; Munby, *Connoisseurs*, 1972, pp. 2–13.

London, BRIT. MUS., Add. 18856–57
Guiart des Moulins, *Bible historiale*. 296 and 251 fols.; 460×330 mm. and 460×325 mm.
Add. 18856: 1–207, 216, 226–233v, 238–255, 269–287;
Add. 18857: 1, 14, 21v, 57v, 138v–162, 188, 204, 214–

218, 222–224, 239v–243 by workshop and associated illuminators. *Ca.* 1420.
For miniatures by the Cité des Dames workshop see this Catalogue.
BIBLIOGRAPHY: Berger, *Bible française*, 1884, pp. 219, 406 f.; Schilling, 1954, p. 279 n. 24; Meiss, *De Lévis Hours*, 1972, pp. 22–24, figs. 51, 57, 58.

New Haven, YALE UNIVERSITY, BEINECKE LIBRARY, ms. 400
Book of Hours (*De Lévis Hours*). *Ca.* 1417.
See Catalogue of Manuscripts.

Paris, BIBL. DE L'ARSENAL, ms. 623
Missal of Saint-Magloire. A–H+410 fols.+fols. 213A and 213B; 335×255 mm. Presented to Saint-Magloire, Paris in 1412 by Jean de la Croix and his wife Jeanne la Coquatrixe.
Fols. 213 A, 213 B and initial on fol. 1: Bedford Trend.
BIBLIOGRAPHY: Paris, Bibl. de l'Arsenal, Martin, *Catalogue*, I, 1885, p. 470 ff. no. 623; Champeaux and Gauchery, *Travaux*, 1894, p. 204; Durrieu, *Rev. de l'art a. et m.*, 1904, p. 258; Martin, *Miniature française*, 1923, pp. 69 f., 100; Leroquais, *Sacramentaires*, 1924, III, p. 5 f.; Paris, Bibl. de l'Arsenal, *SFRMP*, Martin and Lauer, 1929, p. 34; Martens, *Meister Francke*, 1929, pp. 183, 196, 222, 227; Panofsky, *Netherlandish Painting*, 1953, p. 61; Paris, Bibl. nat. (Porcher), 1955, p. 83 no. 171; Meiss, *Art Bull.*, 1956, p. 194; *idem*, *Boucicaut Master*, 1968, pp. 35, 39, 69, 99, 134, 147 f. n. 6.

Paris, BIBL. NAT., fr. 9
Guiart des Moulins, *Bible historiale*. 317 fols.; 450×310 mm.
Fol. 283. *Ca.* 1412. Bedford Trend.
For miniatures by the Cité des Dames, Egerton and Guise workshops see this Catalogue. For the Boucicaut miniatures see Meiss, *Boucicaut Master*, 1968, p. 114 f. (Catalogue).
BIBLIOGRAPHY: see Cité des Dames.

Paris, BIBL. NAT., lat. 919
Book of Hours (*Grandes Heures of Jean de Berry*), Use of Paris. 126 fols.; 400×300 mm.
Made for Jean de Berry and completed in 1409 (inscription).
Fol. 96. Bedford Trend. This important miniature, which had been ascribed to the Boucicaut Master (Panofsky 1953, Porcher 1955), I gave to the Bedford Master in 1956, then uncertainly to him or his shop in 1967, and finally in 1968 to the Trend.
For miniatures by the Egerton workshop see this Catalogue. For miniatures by the Boucicaut workshop, Pseudo-Jacquemart and Jacquemart de Hesdin (Louvre, *Way to Calvary*) see Meiss, *Late XIV Century*, 1967, pp. 332–334 (Catalogue); *idem*, *Boucicaut Master*, 1968, p. 125 f. (Catalogue).
BIBLIOGRAPHY: For earlier bibliography see Meiss, *Late XIV Century*, 1967, p. 333, index, figs. 216–244, 249, 251; *idem*, *Boucicaut Master*, 1968, index, figs. 61, 62; see also Thomas, *Grandes Heures*, 1971.

Paris, BIBL. NAT., lat. 17294
Breviary, Use of Salisbury. 712 fols.; 255×173 mm.
Executed for John, Duke of Bedford, between 1424 and 1435. Left unfinished.
BIBLIOGRAPHY: Leroquais, *Bréviaires*, 1934, III, pp. 271–348, pls. LIV–LXV; Paris, Bibl. nat. (Porcher), 1955, p. 103 f. no. 217; Spencer, 1966; Meiss, *Boucicaut Master*, 1968, p. 35; *idem*, *De Lévis Hours*, 1972, pp. 14, 25, fig. 52.

Vienna, NATIONALBIBL., ms. 1855 (Fig. 375)
Book of Hours, Use of Paris. 261 fols.; 265×190 mm.
All miniatures. *Ca.* 1420–1422.
For drolleries by the Cité des Dames workshop see this Catalogue.
BIBLIOGRAPHY: Delisle, *Livres royaux*, 1902; Winkler, 1911, p. 536 f.; Vienna, Nationalbibl., Beer, 1912, pp. 15–19, pls. V–VIII; Winkler, 1914, pp. 114–116, pls. XVII, XVIII, figs. 1–3, 5; Vienna, Nationalbibl. (Hermann), 1938, pp. 142–185, pls. XLI–XIV; Parkhurst, 1941, p. 298, fig. 24; Vienna, Nationalbibl., Trenkler, 1947–1948, pp. 7–38; Trenkler, *Livre d'heures* [1948]; Panofsky, *Netherlandish Painting*, 1953, I, pp. 373 n. 34[2], 409 n. 127[1]; Vienna, Nationalbibl. (Unterkircher), 1957, p. 53; Vienna, Kunsthist. Mus., *Katalog*, 1962, p. 170 no. 109; Meiss, *Late XIV Century*, 1967, index; *idem*, *Boucicaut Master*, 1968, pp. 25, 31, 70; *idem*, *De Lévis Hours*, 1972, pp. 13–15, 17–19, 21–23, 25, figs. 19, 22, 30, 34, 36.

RELATED MANUSCRIPTS

Baltimore, WALTERS ART GALLERY, ms. 281
Book of Hours. 242 fols.; 202×140 mm.
Belonged to Thomas Malet de Berlettes and his wife Jeanne de Lannoy.
All miniatures.
BIBLIOGRAPHY: De Ricci, *Census*, I, 1935, p. 797 no. 261; Baltimore, Walters (Miner), 1949, p. 37 no. 99,

pl. XL; Baltimore, Walters, *International Style* (Miner), 1962, p. 64 f. no. 60, pl. LVIII; Meiss, *Late XIV Century*, 1967, p. 389 n. 58.

Dresden, SÄCHSISCHE LANDESBIBL. (formerly), ms. Oc 61
Gaston Phébus, *Livre de la chasse*; Jean de Vignay, *Jeu des échecs moralisé*; *Ordre de chevalerie*. 152 fols. Arms of the dauphin in the lower border of the frontispiece may indicate ownership of Louis, duc de Guyenne, who married Marguerite de Bourgogne. Burgundian inventory of 1420.
Fol. 134 and perhaps others.
For miniatures by the Rohan workshop see this Catalogue.
BIBLIOGRAPHY: see Rohan.

Paris, BIBL. NAT., fr. 20087–88
Guiart des Moulins, *Bible historiale*. 583 fols.; 455×320 mm.
Ca. 1417–1420.
BIBLIOGRAPHY: Paris, Bibl. nat. (Porcher), 1955, p. 101 f. no. 214.

BEDFORD TREND

Brooklyn, BROOKLYN MUSEUM, ms. 19.78
Book of Hours. 194×138 mm. Manuscript not foliated. *Ca.* 1418.
Belonged to Marie de Bretagne, Abbess of the Convent of La Magdalene des Orléans. She died in October, 1477.
BIBLIOGRAPHY: Comstock, 1926, pp. 44–48.

Cambridge, TRINITY COLLEGE, ms. B. 11. 31
Book of Hours, Use of Paris. 234 fols.; 219×178 mm. Calendar and fols. 59v–103. *Ca.* 1415.
For miniatures by the Virgil workshop see this Catalogue.
BIBLIOGRAPHY: see Virgil.

Chantilly, MUSEE CONDE, ms. 878 (1197)
Jean Petit, *La justification du duc de Bourgogne, Jean sans Peur*. 47 fols.; 194×142 mm.
Written in March, 1408.
Manuscript has frontispiece only.
BIBLIOGRAPHY: Chantilly, Musée Condé, *Cabinet*, III, 1901, p. 143 f. no. 878.

Cleveland, CLEVELAND MUSEUM OF ART, ms. 51.120
Book of Hours. 209 fols.; 188×127 mm.
BIBLIOGRAPHY: Cleveland, Museum (Wixom), 1963, p. 202 no. 15; Meiss, *De Lévis Hours*, 1972, p. 22 n. 54.

Geneva, BIBL. PUBLIQUE ET UNIVERSITAIRE, lat. 54
Sallust, *Catilinarius*, *De Jugurtino*. 78 fols.; 318×222 mm.
BIBLIOGRAPHY: Aubert, 1909, p. 279 f.; Porcher, *Jean Lebègue*, 1962, pp. 13, 15 and illustrations.

Lisbon, GULBENKIAN FOUNDATION, ms. L.A. 141
Book of Hours. Not foliated. *Ca.* 1412–1415.

Lisbon, GULBENKIAN FOUNDATION, ms. L.A. 143 (formerly Yates Thompson)
Boccaccio, *Des cleres et nobles femmes*. 190 fols. (originally 270 fols.); 409×292 mm.
Belonged to Prigent de Coëtivy. Manuscript damaged by a flood in 1967.
Fols. 5, 34–37. Between 1410 and 1415.
For miniatures by the Cité des Dames and Harvard Hannibal workshops see this Catalogue. For the Boucicaut miniatures see Meiss, *Boucicaut Master*, 1968, pp. 88–91 (Catalogue).
BIBLIOGRAPHY: see Cité des Dames.

London, BRIT. MUS., Add. 30899
Fragment of a Book of Hours. 6 fols.; 200×140 mm. Fols. 1, 4. *Ca.* 1410.
For miniatures by the Egerton workshop see this Catalogue.
BIBLIOGRAPHY: see Egerton.

London, BRIT. MUS., Add. 32454
Book of Hours. *Ca.* 1415.
See Catalogue of Manuscripts.

London, BRIT. MUS., Harley 4431
Christine de Pisan, *Œuvres*. *Ca.* 1410.
See Catalogue of Manuscripts.

New York, COLL. OF CLARA PECK (Fig. 258)
Gaston Phébus, *Livre de la chasse*. 125 fols.; 386×285 mm.
All miniatures by Bedford Trend and associated illuminators. *Ca.* 1410.
BIBLIOGRAPHY: New York, Pierpont Morgan Library, *Sports and Pastimes*, 1946, p. 9; New York, Metropolitan Museum, The Cloisters (Gómez-Moreno), 1968, no. 4.

Orange (Texas), STARK COLL.
Book of Hours, Use of Paris. 192 fols.; 175×125 mm. Fols. 13–29, 66–86v, 100, 115, 184v. *Ca.* 1410–1415.

For miniature by the Egerton workshop see this Catalogue. For miniatures by a follower of the Boucicaut Master see Meiss, *Boucicaut Master*, 1968, p. 105 (Catalogue).
BIBLIOGRAPHY: see Egerton.

Oxford, BODLEIAN LIBRARY, Douce 144
Book of Hours, Use of Paris. 144 fols.; 215×160 mm.
An inscription on fol. 27 states that the manuscript was completed in 1407.
Fol. 5v.
For the miniatures by the Master of St. Jerome see this Catalogue. For the Boucicaut miniatures see Meiss, *Boucicaut Master*, 1968, pp. 106–108 (Catalogue).
BIBLIOGRAPHY: For earlier bibliography see Meiss, *Boucicaut Master*, 1968, p. 107, index, figs. 49–60.

Paris, BIBL. DE L'ARSENAL, ms. 664
Térence des ducs. Ca. 1412.
See Catalogue of Manuscripts.

Paris, BIBL. DE L'ARSENAL, ms. 5193
Boccaccio, *Cas des nobles hommes et femmes. Ca.* 1410–1412.
See Catalogue of Manuscripts.

Paris, BIBL. NAT., fr. 226 (Fig. 850)
Boccaccio, *Cas des nobles hommes et femmes* (trans. by Laurent de Premierfait). 275 fols.; 430×308 mm.
Frontispiece on fol. 1 shows arms of Berry.
Fols. 1–8, 12v, 143–274. *Ca.* 1415.
For miniatures by the Cité des Dames and Rohan workshops see this Catalogue.
BIBLIOGRAPHY: Guiffrey, *Inventaires*, I, 1894, p. CLXXIX f. no. 30; Durrieu, *Rev. de l'art a. et m.*, 1912, p. 172 f., fig. 15; Heimann, 1932, p. 2 f., fig. 1; Paris, Bibl. nat. (Porcher), 1955, p. 85 no. 176; Meiss, *Art Bull.*, 1956, p. 193 n. 25; Porcher, *Rohan Hours*, 1959, p. 9; Meiss, *Late XIV Century*, 1967, index, fig. 503; *idem*, *Boucicaut Master*, 1968, p. 148 n. 6 (Ch. III); Bozzolo, 1968, p. 14 f.

Paris, BIBL. NAT., fr. 616 (Figs. 253, 260)
Gaston Phébus, *Livre de la chasse*, *Oraisons*; Gace de La Bigne, *Déduits de la chasse.* 215 fols.; 357×270 mm.
Belonged to Aymar de Poitiers.
All miniatures by Bedford Trend and associated illuminators. *Ca.* 1410.
BIBLIOGRAPHY: Paris, *Manuscrits françois*, V, 1842, pp. 213–215; Delisle, *Cabinet*, II, 1874, p. 299 f.; Champeaux and Gauchery, *Travaux*, 1894, p. 152 f.; Paris, Louvre, *Exposition*, 1904, p. 34 no. 92; Paris, Bibl. nat. (Couderc), 1909; *idem*, *Portraits* [1910], pp. 20–22, pls. XLVIII–XLIX; Martin, *Miniature française*, 1923, pp. 71, 101, figs. CIX, CX; Paris, Bibl. nat., *Catalogue*, 1926, pp. 36–38 no. 45; Paris, Bibl. nat. (Couderc), 1927, pp. 77–80; Paris, Bibl. nat. (Martin), 1928, pp. 55, 107, figs. LXXI, LXXII; Martens, *Meister Francke*, 1929, pp. 171, 197, 255 n. 375, 266 nn. 505–507, figs. 78, 79; Panofsky, *Netherlandish Painting*, 1953, I, pp. 51 f., 380 n. 51², fig. 50; Paris, Bibl. nat. (Porcher), 1955, p. 101 no. 212, pl. XXVIII; Porcher, *Enluminure*, 1959, p. 65, pl. LXXIV; Vienna, Kunsthist. Mus., *Katalog*, 1962, p. 173 no. 113, pl. 137; Wilhelm, *Das Jagdbuch* [1965]; Spencer, 1966, p. 612; Meiss, *Late XIV Century*, 1967, pp. 59, 218, 363 n. 39, fig. 439; *idem*, *Boucicaut Master*, 1968, pp. 35, 131.

Paris, BIBL. NAT., fr. 2810
Le livre des merveilles. 297 fols.; 420×298 mm.
Inscription on a guard folio at the beginning of the book by the Duke of Berry's secretary, Flamel, states that it was given to Jean de Berry by his nephew, John, Duke of Burgundy. Berry's inventory of 1413 gives the date of the gift as January, 1413. The Burgundian shield was replaced by the Berry arms on fols. 1, 97, 136v, and 226 and by the arms of the next owner, Jacques d'Armagnac on fols. 116, 141 and 268.
Fols. 17, 19v, 22v, 24–42, 44–78, 142v–147, 182–197, 227–266. Shortly before January, 1413.
For miniatures by the Boucicaut workshop see Meiss, *Boucicaut Master*, 1968, pp. 116–122 (Catalogue).
BIBLIOGRAPHY: For earlier bibliography see Meiss, *Boucicaut Master*, 1968, p. 117. See also *idem*, *Late XIV Century*, 1967, index; *idem*, *Boucicaut Master*, 1968, index, figs. 80–100.

Paris, BIBL. NAT., fr. 20320
Valerius Maximus, *Faits et dits mémorables* (trans. by Simon de Hesdin and Nicolas de Gonesse). 377 fols.; 420×320 mm.
Fols. 21–25v.
For miniatures by the Rohan workshop and those related to the Berry Apocalypse Master see this Catalogue.
BIBLIOGRAPHY: see Rohan.

Paris, BIBL. NAT., lat. 5762
Sallust, *Catilinarius, De Jugurtino.* 110 fols.; 245×175 mm.
Arms of the King of France.
Fols. 3, 38v.
BIBLIOGRAPHY: Paris, Bibl. nat. (Porcher), 1955, p. 100 no. 210; Porcher, *Jean Lebègue*, 1962, pp. 13, 15 plus illustrations; Paris, Bibl. nat., *Livre*, 1972, p. 86 f. no. 256.

Paris, BIBL. NAT., lat. 9684
Sallust, *Catilinarius.* A–D+42 fols.; 260×183 mm.
Fol. 1. Orléans arms in initial.
Probably before 1407 when Louis d'Orléans died.
BIBLIOGRAPHY: Paris, Bibl. nat. (Porcher), 1955, p. 100 no. 209; Porcher, *Jean Lebègue*, 1962, pp. 13, 15.

Philadelphia, MUSEUM OF ART, ms. 45-65-5
Book of Hours. 298 fols.; 205×137 mm.
Manuscript is paginated.
Pages 25–37, 349, 352–376, 380 following. *Ca.* 1412.
For miniatures by the Luçon workshop see this Catalogue.
BIBLIOGRAPHY: Meiss, *Art Bull.*, 1956, p. 193 n. 23; Philadelphia Mus., *Bulletin*, 1962, p. 19, pp. 29, 147, 155, 363 reproduced on p. 18 f.; Meiss, *Late XIV Century*, 1967, p. 359; *idem*, *De Lévis Hours*, 1972, pp. 15, 22, figs. 25, 26, 47.

Vienna, NATIONALBIBL., ms. 1840
Book of Hours. 238 fols.; 250×173 mm.
Written by Johannes Parvi.
Fol. 27. *Ca.* 1415. Other miniatures date towards 1470.
BIBLIOGRAPHY: Vienna, Nationalbibl., Beer, 1912, p. 18 f., pls. IX–XI; Vienna, Nationalbibl. (Hermann), 1938, pp. 129–137, pl. XXXIX; Vienna, Kunsthist. Mus., *Katalog*, 1962, p. 171 f. no. 110.

Vienna, NATIONALBIBL., ms. 2657
Jean Petit, *Justification du duc de Bourgogne, Jean sans Peur, sur le fait de la mort du duc Louis d'Orléans.* 71 fols.; 193×140 mm.
Written in March, 1408.
Fol. 1v the only miniature.
BIBLIOGRAPHY: Vienna, Nationalbibl. (Hermann), 1938, pp. 27–29 no. 2657, pl. VII; Meiss, *Boucicaut Master*, 1968, p. 147 f. n. 6.

MASTER OF THE BERRY APOCALYPSE

Active from about 1407 to 1418–1420. The Berry Apocalypse style was formed chiefly by that of the Boucicaut Master. Whereas Boucicaut's monumental figures, however, are balanced in the Italian manner, those of the Apocalypse Master, charged with sweeping folds, are more lively and expressive. He employed washes of pale grey, brown or magenta, touched by an opaque white and irregularly accented by heavy outlines. He usually painted skies streaked in pale blue strokes and simple landscapes, devoid of peasants in the fields or cities on the horizon. This aspect of his style was not appreciated by all of his followers, especially the Boethius illuminator, who continued to use tesselated grounds. Continuing in later years to experiment with the effect of a restricted palette, the Apocalypse workshop limited its colors to black, brown and gold (*Histoire ancienne*, Egerton 912, Fig. 783).

In a later manuscript, an *Apocalypse* which belonged to Jean de Berry and from which the artist takes his name, he revised his pattern of color to communicate the vivid, wild images of the text. He used a broad expanse of red for the sky and bright green for the ground.

The Master's earliest known work is the illustration of a French translation of St. Augustine's *City of God*, ca. 1410 (fr. 25). The frontispiece, however, was painted by the older and more conservative Virgil Master. Unlike the Virgil Master, the Apocalypse Master did not exploit the narrative possibilities of the text. Most of his illustrations are simple variations on the theme of pagan and Christian worship, with a few confronted figures (Fig. 782). The Master's preference for compositions of this kind manifests itself in the *Apocalypse* (Morgan 133) which belonged to Berry and which was painted probably a year or so before the Duke's death in 1416 (Figs. 787, 792, 808).

The *Apocalypse* was not the only manuscript by the workshop owned by Jean de Berry. In 1413 he bought a copy of the *Brut d'Angleterre* (fr. 1454). Another patron, Pierre de Fontenoy, who was financial minister of Charles VI, ordered two manuscripts from the workshop and related illuminators, fr. 1134 and Morgan M. 804. The second important dated manuscript by the workshop is a chronicle which was written in 1416 (Nouv. acq. fr. 14285) (Fig. 786).

Unlike most chefs-d'atelier in the first two decades of the fifteenth century the Berry Apocalypse Master did not closely supervise the illuminators who adopted his style; perhaps they became independent. Consequently the style often appears in modified and diminished form. While a few of these followers are readily distinguishable, it does not seem profitable at the present time to single out their work from within the group of manuscripts classified as "related to the style of the Apocalypse Master."

One such painter, whom we call the Boethius illuminator because he illustrated a Boethius (fr. 12459) in 1414, executed about the same time a Boccaccio (Royal 20 C V) and a copy of the French translation of St. Augustine's *City of God.* His predilection for bright primary colors flattened his forms, and his work was in general inferior. The Boethius illuminator had assistants, and together they participated in the illustration of over a dozen manuscripts between approximately 1414 and 1418–1420. They joined forces with the workshop and followers of the Rohan Master to produce several manuscripts, including a Froissart (fr. 2663–2664), a Valerius Maximus (fr. 20320), and a *Propriété des choses* (fr. 22531). They aided the Boucicaut workshop in the illumination of the *Trésor des histoires* (Arsenal 5077). Even the frontispieces in two manuscripts by the Apocalypse workshop (Egerton 912 and Nouv. acq. fr. 14285) were painted by the Boethius illuminator and his assistants.

BIBLIOGRAPHY: Nordenfalk, *Kung praktiks*, 1955, p. 61; Meiss, *Art Bull.*, 1956, p. 196; *idem, Late XIV Century*, 1967, pp. 300, 354.

Leningrad, STATE LIBRARY, ms. Fr. Q. v. 111 4
Alars de Cambrai, *Les dis moraux des philosophes* (trans. by Guillaume de Tignonville). 90 fols.; 270×195 mm.
Fol. 2 (other miniatures not seen).
BIBLIOGRAPHY: Leningrad (Saint-Pétersbourg), Bertrand, 1873, p. 468 f.; Leningrad (Saint-Pétersbourg), Laborde, 1936, pp. 26–28, pl. XIX; Nordenfalk, *Kung praktiks*, 1955, p. 61; Meiss, *Art Bull.*, 1956, p. 196 n. 35; *idem, Late XIV Century*, 1967, p. 354; *idem, Boucicaut Master*, 1968, p. 71, fig. 480.

London, BRIT. MUS., Egerton 912 (Fig. 783)
Paulus Orosius, *Histoire ancienne.* 397 fols.; 440×295 mm.
All miniatures with exception of frontispieces on fols. 10 and 202. *Ca.* 1418.

New York, PIERPONT MORGAN LIBRARY, M. 133
Apocalypse. Before 1416.
See Catalogue of Manuscripts.

New York, PIERPONT MORGAN LIBRARY, M. 723
Hayton, *Fleur des histoires d'Orient* and Marco Polo, *Livre des merveilles d'Asie.* 266 fols.; 315×220 mm.
All miniatures. *Ca.* 1412.
BIBLIOGRAPHY: New York, Pierpont Morgan Library [1934], p. 39 no. 75; Nordenfalk, *Kung praktiks*, 1955, p. 61, fig. 65; Meiss, *Art Bull.*, 1956, p. 196 n. 35; *idem, Late XIV Century*, 1967, p. 354.

Paris, BIBL. NAT., fr. 25
St. Augustine, *La Cité de Dieu.* Vol. I. *Ca.* 1408–1410.
See Catalogue of Manuscripts.

Paris, BIBL. NAT., fr. 953
Jacques le Grand, *Livre des bonnes moeurs.* 65 fols.; 320×232 mm.
All miniatures. *Ca.* 1410–1412.

Paris, BIBL. NAT., fr. 964
Jean de Blois, Commentary on Psalms and other texts. 163 fols.; 290×215 mm.
All miniatures. *Ca.* 1417.
BIBLIOGRAPHY: Meiss, *Art Bull.*, 1956, p. 196; *idem, Late XIV Century*, 1967, p. 354.

Paris, BIBL. NAT., fr. 1454
Le brut d'Angleterre. 105 fols.; 300×225 mm.
Purchased by Jean de Berry from Jean Colin, September 3, 1413 (ex libris and inventory of 1413).
All miniatures. *Ca.* 1410.
BIBLIOGRAPHY: Guiffrey, *Inventaires*, I, 1894, pp. CLXXIV no. 59, 330 no. 1231; II, 1896, p. 239 no. 527, 338; Delisle, *Charles V*, 1907, II, p. 266 no. 271; Meiss, *Late XIV Century*, 1967, pp. 314, 354.

Paris, BIBL. NAT., fr. 17183
Honoré Bonet, *Arbre des batailles.* 105 fols.; 295×225 mm.
All miniatures. *Ca.* 1415.
BIBLIOGRAPHY: Coopland, *The Tree of Battles of Honoré Bonet*, 1949, pl. 1; Meiss, *Late XIV Century*, 1967, p. 354.

Paris, BIBL. NAT., nouv. acq. fr. 14285
Trèsor des histoires. Written in 1416.
See Catalogue of Manuscripts.

Stuttgart, WÜRTTEMBERGISCHE LANDESBIBL., ms. poet. 6 (Figs. 784, 785)
Guillaume de Lorris and Jean de Meun, *Roman de la rose.* 196 fols.; 335×240 mm.
All miniatures. *Ca.* 1416.
BIBLIOGRAPHY: Kuhn, 1912, p. 48 f., fig. 31; Germany, *Manuscrits français* (Olschki), 1932, p. 51 f., pls. LXI, LXII;

Meiss, *Art Bull.*, 1956, p. 196 n. 35; *idem*, *Late XIV Century*, 1967, p. 354.

WHEREABOUTS UNKNOWN (formerly London, Robinson Trust, ms. Phillipps 832) (Fig. 780)
Jean de Meun *Œuvres*. 82 fols.; 293×211 mm.
All miniatures. *Ca.* 1410.
BIBLIOGRAPHY: Durrieu, 1889, p. 392 no. XXIV; Meiss, *Late XIV Century*, 1967, pp. 317, 354; London, Sotheby, November 30, 1971, lot 505, pls. D, 14.

RELATED MANUSCRIPTS

Besançon, BIBL. MUNICIPALE, ms. 865
Froissart, *Chroniques*. Vol. II. 460 fols.; 360×270 mm.
BIBLIOGRAPHY: Castan, 1865, pp. 114–148; Valenciennes, *Froissart*, 1937, pp. 38–41 nos. XXVI–XXVIII, pls. XIX–XXI, XXIII; Meiss, *Late XIV Century*, 1967, p. 354.

Brussels, BIBL. ROYALE, ms. 9475
Thomas Aquinas (Pseudo), *Livre de l'informacion des roys et des princes*. 104 fols.; 303×208 mm.
Executed for Jean sans Peur (Burgundian Inventory of 1420).
BIBLIOGRAPHY: Doutrepont, *Inventaire*, 1906, p. 72 no. 115; Brussels, Bibl. roy., Gaspar and Lyna, I, 1937, p. 442 f. no. 186, pl. CIV; Nordenfalk, *Kung praktiks*, 1955, p. 61, fig. 77; Brussels, Bibl. roy., 1970, p. 69 f., pl. 25.

Ghent, BIBL. DE L'UNIVERSITE, ms. 141
Bible. 196 fols.; 370×263 mm.
BIBLIOGRAPHY: Nordenfalk, *Kung praktiks*, 1955, pp. 61, 94, fig. 66; Meiss, *Late XIV Century*, 1967, p. 354.

Grenoble, BIBL. PUBLIQUE, ms. 870
Livre de l'information des princes. 156 fols.; 303×224 mm.
Armorials of the Maréchal de Boucicaut.
Ca. 1410.
BIBLIOGRAPHY: Grenoble, Bibl. publique, *Catalogue général des manuscrits*, VII, 1889, p. 261 f. no. 870; Meiss, *Boucicaut Master*, 1968, p. 143 n. 18.

The Hague, KON. BIBL., ms. 133 A 2
Les traités dits de Sidrac et Lucidaire. 211 fols.; 405×290 mm.
Written by Guillebert de Metz for Jean sans Peur (Burgundian Inventory of 1420).
Fol. 17 by follower.
BIBLIOGRAPHY: The Hague, Kon. Bibl., Byvanck, 1924, pp. 41–43 no. 15, pl. XVIII.

London, BRIT. MUS., Add. 21602
Boethius, *Consolacion de la philosophie* (trans. by Jean de Meun). 119 fols.; 253×188 mm.
BIBLIOGRAPHY: Stone, 1937, p. 23.

London, BRIT. MUS., Harley 4385
Gilles de Rome, *Le gouvernement des roys et des princes* (trans. by Henri de Ganchy). 168 fols.; 283×220 mm.
All miniatures. *Ca.* 1410–1412.

London, BRIT. MUS., Royal 19 D VI, VII
Guiart des Moulins, *Bible historiale*. 287 and 255 fols.; 450×325 mm.
All miniatures. *Ca.* 1418–1420.
BIBLIOGRAPHY: Berger, *Bible française*, 1884, pp. 290 f., 394.

London, BRIT. MUS., Roy. 20 C V
Boccaccio, *Des cleres et nobles femmes*. 168 fols.; 385×275 mm.
The initial on fol. 1 contains the Beaufort badge, a portcullis and chains surmounted by a coronet.
All miniatures by Boethius illuminator and his assistants. *Ca.* 1414.
BIBLIOGRAPHY: London, British Museum, Warner and Gilson, 1921, II, p. 372; Saxl and Meier, *Verzeichnis*, III, 1953, pt. 1, p. 222 f., pt. 2, pl. XLI; Branca, *Decameron*, 1966, II, illustrations on pp. 447, 586, 605, 643; III, pp. 709, 761, 796, 811, 831, 871, 915.

Manchester, JOHN RYLANDS LIBRARY, French ms. 2
Guillaume de Deguilleville, *Pèlerinage de Jhesucrist*.

Munich, BAYERISCHE STAATSBIBL., ms. gall. 26
Jeu des échecs (trans. by Jean de Vignay). 75 fols.
BIBLIOGRAPHY: Germany, *Manuscrits français* (Olschki), 1932, p. 9, pl. III; Meiss, *Art Bull.*, 1956, p. 196 n. 35; *idem*, *Late XIV Century*, 1967, p. 354.

New Haven, YALE UNIVERSITY, BEINECKE LIBRARY
St. Augustine, *La Cité de Dieu* (trans. by Raoul de Praelles). 209, 187, 146 and 211 fols. in four vols. (two vols. originally).
Manuscript not foliated. 341×252 mm.
BIBLIOGRAPHY: Durrieu, 1889, p. 392; Laborde, *Cité de Dieu*, I, 1909, pp. 301–305 no. 25; Anonymous, "Eight Medieval Manuscripts," *Yale University Library Gazette*, XXIX, 1955, pp. 105, 109.

New York, PIERPONT MORGAN LIBRARY, M. 804
Froissart, *Chroniques*. 363 fols.; 365×270 mm.
Commissioned by Pierre de Fontenay.
Fols. 265–315 by Boethius illuminator. Other miniatures by an associate. *Ca.* 1412.
BIBLIOGRAPHY: Mirot, 1922, pp. 297–330; New York, Pierpont Morgan Library, *Catalogue*, 1939, p. 13 no. 40; New York, Pierpont Morgan Library, 1941, pp. 41–46, pls. VI, VII; New York, Pierpont Morgan Library, 1949, p. 38 no. 60, pl. 26; Nordenfalk, *Kung praktiks*, 1955, p. 61, fig. 67; Meiss, *Art Bull.*, 1956, p. 196 n. 35; *idem*, *Late XIV Century*, 1967, p. 354.

Oxford, BODLEIAN LIBRARY, Douce 202–3
Valerius Maximus, *Faits et dits mémorables* (trans. by Simon de Hesdin and Nicolas de Gonesse). 193 and 263 fols.; 375×285 mm.
202: 1, 4–64. *Ca.* 1420.
For miniatures by the Rohan workshop see this Catalogue.
BIBLIOGRAPHY: see Rohan.

Oxford, BODLEIAN LIBRARY, ms. Rawl. Liturg. f. 17
Book of Hours, Use of Paris. 176 fols.; 170×117 mm.
All miniatures by Boethius illuminator and assistant. *Ca.* 1412.
BIBLIOGRAPHY: Pächt and Alexander, *Bodleian Manuscripts*, 1966, p. 52 no. 662, pl. LI.

Paris, ARCHIVES NATIONALES, MM 8982
Abrégé de l'histoire universelle. Roll. 11×0,56 meters.
First miniature.
For miniatures by the Cité des Dames workshop see this Catalogue.
BIBLIOGRAPHY: see Cité des Dames Master.

Paris, BIBL. DE L'ARSENAL, ms. 5076
Trésor de sapience. 262 fols.; 390×280 mm.
BIBLIOGRAPHY: Paris, Arsenal, Martin, V, 1889, p. 40 no. 5076.

Paris, BIBL. DE L'ARSENAL, ms. 5077
Trésor des histoires. 391 fols.; 386×280 mm.
Belonged to Prigent de Coëtivy.
Fols. 57–70, 80v–131v, 150–164, 214v–220, 246–251v. *Ca.* 1415.
For the Boucicaut miniatures see Meiss, *Boucicaut Master*, 1968, pp. 108–113 (Catalogue).
BIBLIOGRAPHY: For earlier bibliography see Meiss, *Boucicaut Master*, 1968, p. 109 and pp. 38, 53 f., 68, 88, 108 ff., figs. 405–418.

Paris, BIBL. NAT., fr. 3
Guiart des Moulins, *Bible historiale*. Vol. I. 302 fols.; 465×337 mm.
Fols. 1, 3v–117v, 122, 130–149, 179–206, 221v–237v. *Ca.* 1420.
BIBLIOGRAPHY: Berger, *Bible française*, 1884, pp. 197, 219, 326; Meiss, *Late XIV Century*, 1967, p. 354.

Paris, BIBL. NAT., fr. 20–21
St. Augustine, *La Cité de Dieu*. 274 and 266 fols.; 460×325 and 460×325 mm. *Ca.* 1414.
BIBLIOGRAPHY: Laborde, *Cité de Dieu*, 1909, I, pp. 290–295 no. 23, pl. XVIII c; Meiss, *Art Bull.*, 1956, p. 196 n. 35; *idem*, *Late XIV Century*, 1967, p. 354.

Paris, BIBL. NAT., fr. 828
Guillaume de Deguilleville, *Pèlerinage de vie humaine. Pèlerinage de l'âme. Pèlerinage de Jhesucrist*. 215 fols.; 335×247 mm.
Fols. 146–214v by follower.

Paris, BIBL. NAT., fr. 1134
Collection of texts, including *La somme des vices et des vertus*. 207 fols.; 270×185 mm.
Executed for Pierre de Fontenoy.
All miniatures. *Ca.* 1415–1420.

Paris, BIBL. NAT., fr. 2649
Froissart, *Chroniques*. 417 fols.; 395×290 mm.
Fols. 36–318. *Ca.* 1415–1417.
BIBLIOGRAPHY: Valenciennes, *Froissart*, 1937, p. 24 no. VII; Meiss, *Late XIV Century*, 1967, p. 354.

Paris, BIBL. NAT., fr. 2663
Froissart, *Chroniques*. Vol. I (Vol. II is fr. 2664). 406 fols.; 367×280 mm.
Given to Jean de Derval by Tanneguy Du Châtel.
All miniatures with the exception of fol. 6.
For miniature by the Harvard Hannibal workshop see this Catalogue.
BIBLIOGRAPHY: Heimann, 1932, p. 3; Valenciennes, *Froissart*, 1937, pp. 27 f. nos. XII, XIII, pls. XX, XXI, XXII; Paris, Bibl. nat. (Porcher), 1955, p. 85 no. 175; Meiss, *Art Bull.*, 1956, p. 196; *idem*, *Late XIV Century*, 1967, p. 354.

Paris, BIBL. NAT., fr. 12459
Boethius, *Consolacion de la philosophie*. 142 fols.; 300×220 mm.
Manuscript completed April, 1414.
All miniatures by Boethius illuminator and assistant. *Ca.* 1414.
BIBLIOGRAPHY: Delisle, 1873, p. 28.

Paris, BIBL. NAT., fr. 15393–94
Guiart des Moulins, *Bible historiale.* 533 fols.; 445×326 mm.
Fr. 15393: 161, 190v–243, and fr. 15394: 244–264v, 441v–533, by close follower of the Berry Apocalypse Master. Fols. 1–148 in fr. 15393 by an assistant of the Boethius illuminator.
For miniatures by the Rohan workshop see this Catalogue.
BIBLIOGRAPHY: Berger, *Bible française*, 1884, pp. 197, 219, 257, 356 f.; Paris, Bibl. nat. (Porcher), 1955, p. 84 no. 172; Porcher, *Rohan Hours*, 1959, p. 8 f.

Paris, BIBL. NAT., fr. 20320
Valerius Maximus, *Faits et dits mémorables* (trans. by Simon de Hesdin and Nicolas de Gonesse). 377 fols.; 420×320 mm.
Fols. 5v, 43v, 53v by Boethius illuminator.
For miniatures by the Bedford Trend and Rohan workshop see this Catalogue.
BIBLIOGRAPHY: see Rohan Master.

Paris, BIBL. NAT., fr. 22531
Bartholomaeus Anglicus, *Le livre de la propriété des choses* (trans. by Jean Corbechon). 400 fols.; 370×295 mm.
Fols. 20v–33v, 99v–216, 257v–324 by Boethius illuminator and assistants. *Ca.* 1418.
For miniatures by the Rohan workshop see this Catalogue.
BIBLIOGRAPHY: see Rohan.

Paris, BIBL. NAT., lat. 1108
Missal of Saint-Denis de la Chartre. 72 fols.; 200×145 mm.
Fol. 19v, the only miniature, by follower. (Called to our attention, with correct attribution, by François Avril.)
BIBLIOGRAPHY: Leroquais, *Sacramentaires*, 1924, II, p. 358 no. 531.

Paris, BIBL. NAT., lat. 13287
Missal and book of private devotion. 181 fols.; 132×95 mm.
Fol. 1 the only miniature. (Called to our attention, with correct attribution, by François Avril.)

Paris, BIBL. NAT., lat. 14245, fols. 157–196
Jacques le Grand, *Traité des vices et des vertus.* 388×282 mm.
Made for the abbey of St. Victor in Paris.
Fol. 191v by an assistant of the Boethius illuminator.
For miniature by the Rohan workshop see this Catalogue.
BIBLIOGRAPHY: see Rohan.

Prague, LIBRARY OF THE CASTLE OF KYNŽVARTĚ, ms. 23 A 12
Grandes Chroniques de France. 244 fols.; 415×305 mm.
BIBLIOGRAPHY: Čáda, *Rukopisy Knihovny Státního Zámku v Kynžvartě*, 1965, p. 131 f. no. 85, fig. 5.

San Marino, HUNTINGTON LIBRARY, H.M. 1142
Book of Hours. 131 fols.
All miniatures by Boethius illuminator. *Ca.* 1414.
BIBLIOGRAPHY: Meiss, *Late XIV Century*, 1967, p. 354.

Waddesdon Manor (Bucks.), COLL. OF JAMES A. DE ROTHSCHILD, ms. 63
Miniatures cut from a *Bible historiale.*

WHEREABOUTS UNKNOWN
(London, Sotheby & Co., January 2, 1960, lot 312)
Chroniques de Normandie. 146 fols.; 289×190 mm.
BIBLIOGRAPHY: London, Sotheby, January 2, 1960, lot 312; Meiss, *Late XIV Century*, 1967, p. 354.

MASTER OF BERRY'S CLERES FEMMES

Active during at least the first decade of the fifteenth century, apparently in Paris. Named after a beautiful manuscript of Boccaccio's *Cleres et nobles femmes* received by Jean de Berry in February 1404. Originally trained in Flanders, because his luminous forms, narrative vivacity, and physiognomic expressiveness recall manuscripts such as the astrological treatise Morgan 785, illuminated before 1403 in Bruges. A Dutch inscription on a scroll in a miniature on fol. 48v of the Boccaccio is early, but not original (see *Boucicaut Master*, p. 152 n. 17).

The miniatures in Berry's *Cleres Femmes* were identified with those of Philippe le Hardi's copy of the same text and with other manuscripts by Bella Martens, who called the author the "Master of 1402." This classification was rather widely accepted. The two copies of the *Cleres Femmes* are certainly related and were painted at about the same time, but two quite distinctive masters are, as I proposed in 1967, involved. Both may be identified in other manuscripts also. For the other illuminator see the Coronation Master.

In addition to the Boccaccio, Jean de Berry acquired three manuscripts by the Cleres Femmes workshop, a Livy in Geneva (fr. 77) (Fig. 272), a *Lancelot du Lac* (fr. 117–120) and a *Bible historiale* (Arsenal 5057–58), as well as a *Cité de Dieu* (fr. 172) in a related style. All of these manuscripts were completed by 1407.

The *Lancelot* bought by Berry from the dealer Regnault du Montet in 1405 is identical in its text and program of illustration (but not script) to another copy in the Bibliothèque de l'Arsenal (Arsenal 3479–80) (Fig. 5). This second copy may be the *Lancelot* which Jean sans Peur bought from Jacques Raponde in February, 1406. Here the Cleres Femmes workshop collaborated with the atelier of the Cité des Dames Master. About the same time these two workshops joined forces also for Jean de Berry's *Bible historiale*, mentioned above.

The career of the Cleres Femmes Master becomes unclear towards 1410. Versions of his style may be found until 1415 or even later, but his own hand cannot be recognized with any assurance. Followers painted another copy of Boccaccio's *Cleres Femmes*, now in Brussels, approximately five years later. Other illuminators trained in his style continued to work into the third lustrum of the century. One of them painted the frontispieces of a *Bible historiale* acquired by Jean sans Peur in 1415 (Brussels 9024–25) (Fig. 664). Much earlier, related illuminators illustrated a Book of Hours, Walters 209, and the early miniatures in a Psalter, Cotton Domitian A XVII.

BIBLIOGRAPHY: Martens, *Meister Francke*, 1929, p. 241 n. 221; Meiss, *Late XIV Century*, 1967, pp. 252 f., 354 f.

Berlin, STAATSBIBL., Theol. lat. qu. 7
(lost during World War II)
Book of Hours. 170 fols.; 130/160×110 mm.
Fols. 25, 92, 99, 105, 132v, 141v, 157v, 162v, 163v. *Ca.* 1410–1412.
For miniatures by the Luçon workshop see this Catalogue.
BIBLIOGRAPHY: see Luçon.

Brussels, BIBL. ROYALE, ms. 9509
Boccaccio, *Des cleres et nobles femmes.* 165 fols.; 345×247 mm.
All miniatures. *Ca.* 1410–1415.
BIBLIOGRAPHY: Brussels, Bibl. roy., Gaspar and Lyna, I, 1937, pp. 459–461, pl. CXIIb; Branca, *Decameron*, 1966, illustrations on pp. I, 131, 162, 167, 182, 222, 243, 254, 308; II, 416, 421, 480, 511; III, 649, 733, 842, 872, 914.

Geneva, BIBL. PUBLIQUE ET UNIVERSITAIRE, fr. 77 (Fig. 272)
Titus Livius, *Histoire romaine* (trans. by Pierre Bersuire). 450 fols.; 450×315 mm.
Belonged to Jean de Berry (signature of Berry and inscription of Flamel).
Fols. 68–439. *Ca.* 1405.
For miniature by Orosius workshop see this Catalogue.
BIBLIOGRAPHY: Delisle, *Charles V*, 1907, II, pp. 261 no. 236 bis, 311 f.; Aubert, 1909, pp. 498–504; *idem*, 1912, pp. 65–70, pls. XXXII, XXXIII; Gagnebin, 1959, pp. 193–214, figs. 26, 28–30, 32, 34, 35, 37; Meiss, *Late XIV Century*, 1967, index, fig. 825; *idem*, *Boucicaut Master*, 1968, pp. 56, 142, figs. 438, 440.

Paris, BIBL. DE L'ARSENAL, ms. 3479–80 (Fig. 5)
Lancelot du Lac. 624 and 678 pages. 460×318 mm. and 455×310 mm.
3479: pages 339–442. 3480: pages 101, 125, 130, 483–495. *Ca.* 1405. Perhaps the *Lancelot* that Jean sans Peur bought from Jacques Raponde in February, 1406.
For miniatures by the *Cité des Dames* workshop see this Catalogue.

BIBLIOGRAPHY: Loomis, *Arthurian Legends*, 1938, pp. 105–107, figs. 279, 281–285; Thomas, 1952, pp. 81–89; Meiss, *Late XIV Century*, 1967, pp. 356, 371 n. 137, 399 n. 26.

Paris, BIBL. DE L'ARSENAL, ms. 5057–58
Guiart des Moulins, *Bible historiale. Ca.* 1405.
See Catalogue of Manuscripts.

Paris, BIBL. NATIONALE, fr. 117–120
Lancelot du Lac. 602 fols. in 4 vols.; 490×340 mm.
Manuscript illuminated shortly before purchase by Jean de Berry from Regnault du Montet in January, 1405. Inscription of Berry erased on fol. 602v. Later the manuscript belonged to Jacques d'Armagnac, who had most of the miniatures repainted.
All miniatures.
BIBLIOGRAPHY: Guiffrey, *Inventaires*, I, 1894, p. 239 no. 920; Delisle, *Charles V*, 1907, II, p. 266 no. 270; Loomis, *Arthurian Legends*, 1938, pp. 105 ff., 109, 111, figs. 280, 286, 287; Thomas, 1952, pp. 81–89; Porcher, *Belles Heures*, 1953, p. 13 f. n. 24; Meiss, *Late XIV Century*, 1967, index, fig. 824.

Paris, BIBL. NAT., fr. 598
Boccaccio, *Des cleres et nobles femmes.* Just before 1404.
See Catalogue of Manuscripts.

RELATED MANUSCRIPTS

Baltimore, WALTERS ART GALLERY, ms. 209
Book of Hours, Use of Paris. 272 fols.; 140×90 mm.
All miniatures. *Ca.* 1407.
BIBLIOGRAPHY: De Ricci, *Census*, I, 1935, p. 789 n. 207; Baltimore, Walters (Miner), 1949, p. 31 n. 81, pl. XXXV; Baltimore, Walters, *International Style* (Miner), 1962, p. 54 f. no. 50, pl. LI; Cleveland, Mus. of Art (Wixom), 1967, pp. 268, 378 f.

Baltimore, WALTERS ART GALLERY, ms. 232
Book of Hours, Use of Paris. 198 fols.; 170×135 mm.
Fols. 59v, 80, 93, 139, 191, 196v.
For miniatures by the Luçon workshop see this Catalogue.
BIBLIOGRAPHY: see Luçon.

Baltimore, WALTERS ART GALLERY, ms. 265
Book of Hours, Use of Paris. 247 fols.; 185×125 mm.
BIBLIOGRAPHY: De Ricci, *Census*, I, 1935, p. 790 no. 213; Baltimore, Walters (Miner), 1949, p. 33 no. 88, pl. XXXV; Panofsky, *Netherlandish Painting*, 1953, pp. 48 n. 4, 112 n. 5; Baltimore, Walters, *International Style* (Miner), 1962, p. 55 no. 51, pl. LIV.

Brussels, BIBL. ROYALE, ms. 9001–02 (Fig. 663)
Guiart des Moulins, *Bible historiale.* 435 and 385 fols.; 456×330 mm. Petrus Gilberti executed line endings.
9001: 19–24v. 9002: 3, 61, 223 (fol. 223 similar to miniatures in Bedford Trend). *Ca.* 1414–1415.
For miniatures by the Cité des Dames and Virgil workshops see this Catalogue.
BIBLIOGRAPHY: Berger, *Bible française*, 1884, pp. 206, 216, 287 f., 421; Durrieu, 1895, pp. 82 f., 98–100, 142, fig. p. 85; Leroquais, *Bréviaire Philippe le Bon*, 1929, p. 113 f., pl. 97; Brussels, Bibl. roy., Gaspar and Lyna, I, 1937, pp. 445–450 no. 189, pls. CVI–CVIII; Schilling, 1954, p. 277 ff.; Delaissé, *Miniatures médiévales*, 1959, pp. 96–99 no. 21, pl. p. 97; Brussels, Bibl. roy. (Dogaer and Debae), 1967, p. 12 f. no. 6; Meiss, *Late XIV Century*, 1967, p. 13; *idem*, *Boucicaut Master*, 1968, pp. 97, 142; *idem*, *De Lévis Hours*, 1972, p. 9 n. 8.

Brussels, BIBL. ROYALE, ms. 9024–25 (Fig. 664)
Guiart des Moulins, *Bible historiale.* 294 and 263 fols.; 395×294 mm.
Bought by Jean sans Peur in 1415 from Jean Chousat.
9024: 1–13v, 106v, 109v, 120, 135v, 147–151, 158v, 172v, 177.
9025: 1, 145.
For miniatures by the Cité des Dames workshop and related to the Virgil workshop see this Catalogue.
BIBLIOGRAPHY: Berger, *Bible française*, 1884, pp. 217, 295, 422; Durrieu, 1895, pp. 82–87; Brussels, Bibl. roy., Gaspar and Lyna, II, 1947, pp. 1–6 no. 199, pls. CXIV–CXVa–c; Schilling, 1954, p. 279 f., pl. 30b; Brussels, Bibl. roy. (Dogaer and Debae), 1967, p. 12 no. 5, pl. 24; Meiss, *Late XIV Century*, 1967, p. 356; *idem*, *Boucicaut Master*, 1968, p. 148 n. 9 (Ch. IV).

Brussels, BIBL. ROYALE, ms. 9049–50
Titus Livius, *Histoire romaine* (trans. by Pierre Bersuire). 256 and 359 fols.; 440×330 mm.
Burgundian inventory of 1420.
9049: 9, 64v, 114v. 9050: 31v, 266–330v by follower. *Ca.* 1410.
For miniatures by the Cité des Dames workshop see this Catalogue.
BIBLIOGRAPHY: Doutrepont, *Inventaire*, 1906, p. 164 f.

nos. 241, 242; Brussels, Bibl. roy., Gaspar and Lyna, I, 1937, pp. 430–433, pl. C; Brussels, Bibl. roy. (Dogaer and Debae), 1967, p. 144 f. no. 224; Meiss, *Late XIV Century*, 1967, p. 355.

Brussels, BIBL. ROYALE, ms. 10230
Cuvelier, *Livre de Messire Bertrant du Guesclin*. 144 fols.; 280×220 mm.
Burgundian inventory of 1420.
Fol. 3 (the only miniature). Frames for miniatures never executed. *Ca.* 1410.
BIBLIOGRAPHY: Doutrepont, *Inventaire*, 1906, p. 159 no. 235; Brussels, Bibl. roy., Gaspar and Lyna, I, 1937, p. 458 f., pl. CXIIa; Brussels, Bibl. roy. (Dogaer and Debae), 1967, p. 128 no. 194; Meiss, *Late XIV Century*, 1967, p. 355.

Cleveland, MUSEUM OF ART, ms. 64.40
Book of Hours (*Hours of Charles le Noble*), Use of Paris. 668 pages; 200×140 mm.
Arms of Charles III of Navarre beneath each half-page miniature.
Pages 287, 355 by follower. *Ca.* 1405.
For miniatures by the Brussels Initials Master see Meiss, *Late XVI Century*, 1967, p. 323 f. (Catalogue). For miniatures by the Egerton workshop see this Catalogue.
BIBLIOGRAPHY: see Egerton.

London, BRIT. MUS., Cotton Domitian A.XVII
Psalter. 288 fols.; 193×137 mm.
Belonged to Henry VI, whose arms were added on the clothing of a prince.
Fols. 13, 50, 75, 98, 123, 151, 178, 207.
For miniatures by the Master of St. Jerome see this Catalogue.
BIBLIOGRAPHY: London, Brit. Mus., *Schools of Illumination*, VI, 1930, p. 10, pl. 10a; London, Brit. Mus., Millar, 1933, p. 35 f., pl. XLIX; Evans, 1948, p. 4, pl. III; Panofsky, *Netherlandish Painting*, 1953, p. 405 n. 118[5]; Porcher, *Belles Heures*, 1953, pp. 26 f., 42 f., 48, fig. 16; Meiss, *Gaz. B.-A.*, 1963, pp. 149–152, 163, figs. 7, 9; Spencer, 1966, p. 612; London, Brit. Mus., *Grenville Library* (Turner), 1967, p. 44 no. 54; Meiss, *Late XIV Century*, 1967, p. 355; *idem*, *Boucicaut Master*, 1968, p. 148 n. 6 (Ch. III).

Milan, BIBL. TRIVULZIANA, ms. 693 (Fig. 57)
Cicero, *Pro Marcello et de Senectute* (also a trans. of the second treatise into French, made by Laurent de Premierfait for Louis II de Bourbon in 1405). 105 fols.; 269×198 mm.
All miniatures. *Ca.* 1410.
Borders added *ca.* 1420.
BIBLIOGRAPHY: Milan, Bibl. Trivulziana (Santoro), *I codici miniati*, 1958, p. 108 f. no. 113, pls. LXXXVI–LXXXVIII.

Paris, BIBL. NAT., fr. 172–173
St. Augustine, *La Cité de Dieu* (trans. by Raoul de Praelles). 311 and 304 fols.; 425×315 and 435×315 mm.
Given to Jean de Berry by Pierre Salmon *ca.* 1407.
Signature of Berry in fr. 173, fol. 304.
Inventory of 1413.
BIBLIOGRAPHY: Guiffrey, *Inventaires*, I, 1894, pp. 255 no. 964, 341; II, 1896, pp. 238, 301; Laborde, *Cité de Dieu*, 1909, I, pp. 284–288, pl. XVIII; Paris, Bibl. nat. (Porcher), 1955, p. 100 f. no. 211; Meiss, *Late XIV Century*, 1967, pp. 50, 312, 371 n. 117; Meiss with Off, 1971, pp. 229, 233.

Paris, BIBL. NAT., lat. 10528
Hours of Marguerite de Clisson. 325 fols.; 215×157 mm.
Fol. 29v. *Ca.* 1405.
BIBLIOGRAPHY: Couderc, *Portraits* [1910], p. 17, pl. XXXVIII; Leroquais, *Livre d'heures*, 1927, I, pp. 322–326.

Vienna, NATIONALBIBL., ms. 2537
Tristan, *Romans de la table ronde et de la quête du Saint Graal*. 492 fols.; 477×335 mm.
BIBLIOGRAPHY: Vienna, Nationalbibl. (Hermann), 1938, pp. 44–64 no. 11, pls. XIII–XVII; Vienna, Kunsthist. Mus., *Katalog*, 1962, p. 181 no. 129; Unterkircher, 1962, p. 260; *idem*, *European Illuminated Manuscripts* [1967], pp. 188–191.

WHEREABOUTS UNKNOWN
(London, Sotheby and Co. Dec. 3, 1968 lot 23)
Book of Hours (five folios). *Ca.* 1407.
BIBLIOGRAPHY: London, Sotheby, Dec. 3, 1968, p. 72 f. lot 23, pls. D, 29, 30.

MASTER OF THE BREVIARY OF JEAN SANS PEUR

See the chapter on this master.
BIBLIOGRAPHY: Meiss, *Art Bull.*, 1956, p. 195; *idem*, *Late XIV Century*, 1967, pp. 202, 355; *idem*, "Breviary Master," 1970.

Baltimore, WALTERS ART GALLERY, ms. 219
Book of Hours.
See Catalogue of Manuscripts.

Brussels, BIBL. ROYALE, ms. 11035–37 (Fig. 609)
Prayer Book of Philippe le Hardi and his successors. 144 fols.; 255×178 mm.
Fol. 6v *Madonna and Child on a Crescent* added *ca.* 1415.
BIBLIOGRAPHY: Lyna in *Mélanges Hulin de Loo*, 1931, pp. 249–259; Brussels, Bibl. roy., Gaspar and Lyna, I, 1937, pp. 419–423 no. 175, pl. XCVIII; Porcher, *Belles Heures*, 1953, p. 11 f.; Delaissé, *Miniatures médiévales*, 1959, pp. 100–103 no. 22, illustration facing p. 100; Meiss, *Late XIV Century*, 1967, pp. 202, 207, 321, fig. 668.

Chantilly, MUSEE CONDE, ms. 65
Très Riches Heures of Jean de Berry. *Ca.* 1411–1416.
See Catalogue of Manuscripts.

London, BRIT. MUS., Add. 35311, Harley 2897
Breviary of Jean sans Peur. *Ca.* 1413–1417.
See Catalogue of Manuscripts.

Palermo, BIBL. NAZIONALE, ms. 1.A.15
Book of Hours. 102×76 mm.
Fols. 93, 165.
Other miniatures by the Boucicaut workshop.
BIBLIOGRAPHY: Meiss, *Late XIV Century*, 1967, p. 355; *idem*, *Boucicaut Master*, 1968, pp. 70, 114; *idem*, "Breviary Master," 1970, p. 11.

Paris, BIBL. NAT., fr. 926
St. Bonaventura, *L'aiguillon d'amour divin*. Written in 1406.
See Catalogue of Manuscripts.

Paris, BIBL. NAT., lat. 5221 (Fig. 613, 614)
Privileges granted to Clement VI and other popes and to those who strike the coins in the city of Avignon and in the county of Vaucluse. 93 fols.; 295×223 mm. (Called to our attention by François Avril.)
Fols. 12v and perhaps 12 by an illuminator who had been in the workshop. Fols. 3, 3v, 5v, 7v, 8v, 9v, 11, 13v, 14v influenced by the style of the Breviary Master. Before 1412.

Vienna, NATIONALBIBL., ms. Ser. nov. 2613
Book of Hours, Use of Châlons-sur-Marne. 219 fols.; 185×127 mm.
Fol. 14.
For miniatures by the workshops of the Troyes Master and the Master of Walters 219 see this Catalogue.
BIBLIOGRAPHY: see Troyes.

RELATED MANUSCRIPTS

Besançon, BIBL. MUNICIPALE, ms. 863
Chroniques de Saint-Denis. 463 fols.; 420×313 mm.
Miniatures by follower.
BIBLIOGRAPHY: Besançon, Bibl. mun., *Catalogue général des manuscrits*, XXXII, 1897, p. 546 f. no. 863.

London, BRIT. MUS., Royal 15 D III
Guiart des Moulins, *Bible historiale*. 532 fols.; 460×330 mm.
Fols. 256v, 403v, 406, 494–500 by followers. *Ca.* 1415.
For miniatures by the Egerton and Virgil workshops see this Catalogue. For the Boucicaut miniatures see Meiss, *Boucicaut Master*, 1968, pp. 96–99 (Catalogue).
BIBLIOGRAPHY: see Egerton.

Paris, BIBL. MAZARINE, ms. 469
Book of Hours, Use of Paris. 209 fols. + 7; 250×175 mm.
Medallions in border on fol. 83 by a close follower. *Ca.* 1415.
For the Boucicaut miniatures see Meiss, *Boucicaut Master*, 1968, p. 113 f. (Catalogue).
BIBLIOGRAPHY: For early bibliography see Meiss, *Boucicaut Master*, 1968, p. 114. See also Cleveland, Mus. of Art (Wixom), 1967, pp. 280, 380. For the medallions by a follower of the Breviary Master see Meiss, *Late XIV Century*, 1967, p. 355; *idem*, *Boucicaut Master*, 1968, pp. 70, 113 f., fig. 269.

MASTER OF THE BRUSSELS INITIALS

Amsterdam, Rijksmuseum, Prentenkabinet	37.1	A prophet (from the same ms. as Cini and Maggs cuttings)
Baltimore, Walters Art Gallery	ms. 326	Book of Hours
Bologna, Biblioteca del Archiginnasio		*Statuti della compagnia dello Spedale di S. Maria della Vita*
Brussels, Bibliothèque royale	ms. 11060–1	*Brussels Hours*
Cleveland Museum of Art		*Heures de Charles le Noble*
Djursholm (Stockholm), Mittag-Leffler Foundation		*Livre des problemes d'Aristote*
Holkham Hall	ms. 120	Lactantius
London, British Museum	Add. 29433	Book of Hours
	(?) Add. 34247	Book of Hours
Madrid, Biblioteca del Palacio	ms. 2099	Book of Hours
Modena, Biblioteca Estense	ms. 1021	St. Catherine, added to a Gradual, fol. 195
Oxford, Bodleian Library	Douce 62	Book of Hours
	e Mus. 43	*Songe du Vergier*
Parma, Biblioteca Palatina	lat. 159	Book of Hours
Venice, Fondazione Cini		A prophet
Warsaw, Biblioteka Narodowa	lat. Q.v.1.111	Paris calendar
Whereabouts unknown (formerly London, Maggs Bros.)		St. Dominic

BIBLIOGRAPHY: Pächt, *Mary of Burgundy* [1948], p. 52 n. 19; Meiss, *Art Bull.*, 1956, p. 194; *idem*, *Late XIV Century*, 1967, p. 229 ff.; *idem*, *Boucicaut Master*, 1968, p. 142.

MASTER OF THE CITE DES DAMES

This master formed one of the largest and most prolific associations of illuminators in Paris during the first two decades of the fifteenth century. They specialized in secular texts, and they contributed to only two Books of Hours, both at the beginning of their career. The impressive miniatures in the *Barcelona Hours*, painted in 1401, are so exceptionally close to the work of Jacquemart in the *Brussels Hours* that their attribution to the Cité des Dames Master might seem questionable. Miniatures definitely painted by the master and his workshop in the following years prove, however, that Jacquemart was a principal stylistic source. The Cité des Dames Master adopted not only Jacquemart's figures and compositional geometry but also his technique, Italian in origin, of a green underpainting in the flesh areas.

These qualities appear in the earlier copy—about 1404—of two manuscripts of the *Cité de Dieu* illustrated by the workshop. They are less prominent in a little Book of Hours in the Ecole des Beaux-Arts, in which the master himself was less involved (Fig. 504), but conspicuous in a cycle of illustrations of *Le chevalier errant*, remarkable for their spatial advances and colorful variety (Figs. 18, 47–49, 56). The Cité des Dames Master himself shared Jacquemart's enthusiasm for Trecento painting. He preferred the Italian to the French type of Man of Sorrows, and he based several illustrations of

Genesis in a Bible (fr. 9) painted about 1412 on frescoes by Bartolo di Fredi in the Collegiata at S. Gimignano (Figs. 534, 535).

Perhaps it was the Italianate aspect of the art of the Cité des Dames Master that led Christine de Pisan to engage him about 1405. Under the poet's supervision he seems to have designed a model for her *Cité des Dames*; four copies by his workshop remain, two painted for the Dukes of Berry and Burgundy (Figs. 36, 37). A fifth cycle of this text was included in a collection of Christine's writing (Harley 4431) which was almost entirely illustrated by the workshop, and which the author gave to Queen Isabeau de Bavière about 1410 (Figs. 38, 42, 45). The miniatures for the *Epître d'Othéa* in this manuscript are copies of the illustrations of 1405–1408 by the Epître Master (Figs. 62, 91, 114, 154). In the Queen's copy the Cité des Dames Master himself painted the frontispiece (Fig. 151). His workshop illustrated other texts of Christine, the *Livre des trois vertus* (Boston 1528), the *Mutacion de Fortune* (fr. 603 and Munich), and about 1410 the *Livre des faits d'armes* (Brussels 10476), in which the miniature seems influenced by the *Itinerary* of the *Belles Heures*.

While working for Christine de Pisan the atelier collaborated with Berry's Cleres Femmes Master on a Bible (Arsenal) and a *Lancelot* (Arsenal). With the Boucicaut workshop, which had painted one miniature in the early Book of Hours in Paris, the Cité des Dames atelier worked in 1409 on the *Dialogues de Pierre Salmon* (fr. 23279), *ca.* 1412 on a Bible (fr. 9–10) and on a *Cleres Femmes* in Lisbon. The workshop specialized, in fact, in the illustration of the French translations of Boccaccio. About 1410 the master and his assistants had already illuminated much of a *Cas des nobles hommes et femmes* (Arsenal 5193) (Figs. 66, 508, 510), and about 1415 they worked on three additional copies of this text (Royal 20 C IV, fr. 226 and 16994). At very nearly the same time they undertook the first cycle of illustrations of the *Decameron*, the translation of which was completed in June 1414 (Vatican—Figs. 8, 9, 689).

Several scenes in the splendid *Decameron* show two interiors set side by side—a device that offers narrative advantages, and which had been employed a couple of years earlier in the famous *Térence des ducs*, on which the Cité des Dames workshop collaborated. This workshop introduced street scenes, in which only the lower sections of distant houses are visible below the upper frame (Fig. 519)—a very advanced spatial conception that appeared only a decade later in Italy. The extraordinary, extensive flat landscapes of the Cité des Dames Master in the *Dialogues* of 1409 anticipate the late compositions of his collaborator, the Boucicaut Master.

BIBLIOGRAPHY: Schaefer, 1937, pp. 119–208; Meiss, *Art Bull.*, 1956, p. 193; *idem*, "*Decameron*," 1967; *idem*, *Late XIV Century*, 1967, pp. 299 f., 356 f.

Barcelona, BIBL. CENTRAL, ms. 1850
Book of Hours. Written in 1401.
See Catalogue of Manuscripts.

Berlin, STAATSBIBL., Phillipps 1917
Grandes Chroniques de France. 528 fols.; 412×295 mm.
Arms of Rolin family in the initial on fol. 1v.
BIBLIOGRAPHY: Berlin, Staatsbibl. (Kirchner), 1926, pp. 100–106, figs. 107–108; Berlin, Staatliche Museen (Wescher), 1931, pp. 143–145; Berlin, Staatsbibl., *Schöne Handschriften*, 1931, pp. 112–114; Germany, *Manuscrits français* (Olschki), 1932, p. 36, pl. XLI; Meiss, *Art Bull.*, 1956, p. 193 n. 25; *idem*, *Late XIV Century*, 1967, p. 356.

Boston, PUBLIC LIBRARY, ms. 1528
Christine de Pisan, *Livre des trois vertus*. 98 fols.; 290×190 mm.
Manuscript has only a frontispiece.
BIBLIOGRAPHY: Willard, 1950, p. 291 ff.; Meiss, *Late XIV Century*, 1967, p. 356; Kansas, University of Kansas Museum of Art, Schrader, 1969, p. 14 no. 8.

Brussels, BIBL. ROYALE, ms. 9001
Guiart des Moulins, *Bible historiale*. 435 fols.; 456×330 mm.
Petrus Gilberti executed line endings.
Fol. 132. *Ca.* 1414–1415.
For miniatures by the workshop of the Virgil Master and related to the Cleres Femmes workshop see this Catalogue.
BIBLIOGRAPHY: see Berry's Cleres Femmes: Related manuscripts.

Brussels, BIBL. ROYALE, ms. 9024–25 (Fig. 70)
Guiart des Moulins, *Bible historiale*. 294 and 263 fols.; 395×294 mm.
Bought by Jean sans Peur in 1415 from Jean Chousat.
9024: 26v–103, 123–128, 144, 162v, 167v, 190v, 209, 226–242, 247–252.
For miniatures related to the Virgil and Berry's Cleres Femmes workshops see this Catalogue.
BIBLIOGRAPHY: see Berry's Cleres Femmes.

Brussels, BIBL. ROYALE, ms. 9049–50
Titus Livius, *Histoire romaine* (trans. by Pierre Bersuire). 256 and 359 fols.; 440×330 mm.
Burgundian inventory of 1420.

9049: 172. 9050: 54v–201, 236v, 249. *Ca.* 1410.
For miniatures related to the Berry's Cleres Femmes workshop see this Catalogue.
BIBLIOGRAPHY: see Berry's Cleres Femmes.

Brussels, BIBL. ROYALE, ms. 9393
Christine de Pisan, *Cité des Dames*. Shortly after completion of the text in 1405.
See Catalogue of Manuscripts.

Brussels, BIBL. ROYALE, ms. 10476
Christine de Pisan, *Livre des faits d'armes*. 132 fols.; 297×212 mm.
Manuscript has only a frontispiece. *Ca.* 1410.
BIBLIOGRAPHY: Brussels, Bibl. roy., Gaspar and Lyna, I, 1937, p. 457 f. no. 194; pl. CXIb; Schaefer, 1937, p. 195 f., fig. 179; Brussels, Bibl. roy. (Dogaer and Debae), 1967, p. 83 no. 117; Meiss, *Late XIV Century*, 1967, p. 356.

The Hague, ROYAL LIBRARY, ms. 72 A 24 (Fig. 688)
Vincent of Beauvais, *Miroir historial* (trans. by Jean de Vignay). 401 fols.; 425×322 mm.
All miniatures. *Ca.* 1410–1412.
BIBLIOGRAPHY: Netherlands, Byvanck, 1931, p. 46; Meiss, *Art Bull.*, 1956, p. 193 n. 24; *idem*, *Late XIV Century*, 1967, p. 356.

Lisbon, GULBENKIAN FOUNDATION, ms. L.A. 143
Boccaccio, *Des cleres et nobles femmes*. 190 fols.; 409×292 mm.
Belonged to Prigent de Coëtivy.
Fols. 44–89, 122–138. Between about 1410 and 1415.
For miniatures by the Bedford circle and the Harvard Hannibal workshop see this Catalogue. For the Boucicaut miniatures see Meiss, *Boucicaut Master*, 1968, pp. 88–91 (Catalogue).
BIBLIOGRAPHY: London, Sotheby, March 23, 1920, lot 56, p. 119 f.; Meiss, *Late XIV Century*, 1967, p. 356; *idem*, *Boucicaut Master*, 1968, index, figs. 366, 367, 370, 371, 374–377.

London, BRIT. MUS., Add. 18856–57
Guiart des Moulins, *Bible historiale*. 296 and 251 fols.; 460×330 and 460×325 mm.
Add. 18856: 211, 222, 235, 265. Add. 18857: 15v, 38v, 80v, 83, 102, 110, 112v, 113v, 117, 118v, 120v, 122, 126, 172, 200, 209, 212, 219, 219v, 221, 227v, 244v, 245. *Ca.* 1420.
For miniatures by the Bedford workshop see this Catalogue.
BIBLIOGRAPHY: see Bedford.

London, BRIT. MUS., Burney 257
Statius, *Thebais et Achilleis*. 248 fols.; 285×192 mm.
Fols. 137v–144v, 162v–168. *Ca.* 1405.
For miniatures by the Virgil workshop and related to the Orosius workshop see this Catalogue.
BIBLIOGRAPHY: Saxl and Meier, *Verzeichnis*, III, 1953, pt. 1, pp. 98–114; pt. 2, pl. XXII, figs. 57–60.

London, BRIT. MUS., Egerton 2709
Conquête et les conquérants des Iles Canaries. 36 fols.; 268×180 mm.
Burgundian inventory of 1420.
Manuscript has only one miniature. *Ca.* 1405.
BIBLIOGRAPHY: (Anonymous), *Bibl. École des Chartes*, 1890, p. 208 f.; Delisle, *Journal des Savants*, 1896, pp. 644–659; Margry, *La Conquête et les conquérants des Iles Canaries*, 1896; Doutrepont, *Inventaire*, 1906, pp. 96–98 no. 146; Meiss, *Art Bull.*, 1956, p. 193 n. 25; *idem*, *Late XIV Century*, 1967, p. 356.

London, BRIT. MUS., Harley 4431
Christine de Pisan, *Œuvres*. *Ca.* 1410.
See Catalogue of Manuscripts.

London, BRIT. MUS., Royal 19 E VI
Gonzalo de Hinojosa, Bishop of Burgos, *Croniques de Burgues* (trans. by Jean Golein). 457 fols.; 443×335 mm.
Bought by Jean de Berry in 1407. Ex libris. (Inventory of 1413.)
All miniatures. *Ca.* 1405–1407.
BIBLIOGRAPHY: Delisle, *Charles V*, 1907, I, p. 101 f., II, p. 264 no. 254; London, Brit. Mus., Warner and Gilson, 1921, II, p. 349; Meiss, *Art Bull.*, 1956, p. 193; *idem*, *Late XIV Century*, 1967, pp. 311, 356, 405 n. 106.

London, BRIT. MUS., Royal 20 C IV (Fig. 71)
Boccaccio, *Cas des nobles hommes et femmes* (trans. by Laurent de Premierfait). 348 fols.; 390×285 mm.
All miniatures.
BIBLIOGRAPHY: London, Brit. Mus., Warner and Gilson, 1921, II, p. 371 f.; Saxl and Meier, *Verzeichnis*, 1953, III, pt. 1, p. 222; Branca, *Decameron*, 1966, I, illustration on p. 147.

London, MR. MARTIN BRESLAUER
Valerius Maximus, *Faits et dits mémorables* (trans. by Simon de Hesdin and Nicholas de Gonesse). 419 fols.; 375×260 mm.
Fol. 1. *Ca.* 1405–1407.

Other miniatures added later by a Flemish illuminator.
BIBLIOGRAPHY: Warner, *Library Perrins*, 1920, I, p. 110 f. no. 39, II, pl. XLV; London, Sotheby, December 1, 1959, lot 68, p. 50 f., pls. 18, 19; London, Martin Breslauer, *Valerius Maximus*, 1965; Meiss, *Late XIV Century*, 1967, p. 356.

Melbourne, NATIONAL GALLERY OF VICTORIA, ms. Felton 3
Titus Livius, *Histoire romaine* (trans. by Pierre Bersuire). 510 fols.; 440×325 mm. Manuscript belonged to Jean sans Peur, Philippe le Bon and Antoine, Grand Bastard of Burgundy.
Fols. 1–137, 188, 377. *Ca.* 1400–1403.
Other miniatures by a minor Parisian illuminator who worked mostly in the 1390's. The scribe Gillequin Gressier signed his name.
BIBLIOGRAPHY: London, Sotheby, June 23, 1931; Sinclair, 1959; Meiss, *Late XIV Century*, 1967, p. 356; Melbourne, Nat. Gall. of Victoria, Hoff and Plant, 1968, p. 24, pl. on p. 25.

Munich, BAYERISCHE STAATSBIBL., ms. gall. 11
Christine de Pisan, *Mutacion de Fortune*.
See Catalogue of Manuscripts.

New York, PIERPONT MORGAN LIBRARY, M. 536
Grandes Chroniques de France. 376 fols.; 420×320 mm.
All miniatures. *Ca.* 1410–1412.
BIBLIOGRAPHY: Meiss, *Art Bull.*, 1956, p. 193 n. 25; *idem*, *Late XIV Century*, 1967, p. 356.

New York, PIERPONT MORGAN LIBRARY, M. 537
Bartholomaeus Anglicus, *Le livre de la propriété des choses* (trans. by Jean Corbechon). 429 fols.; 394×280 mm.
Fol. 50. *Ca.* 1415.

Paris, ARCH. NAT., ms. MM 8982
Abrégé de l'histoire universelle. Roll, 11×0.56 meters.
All roundels. *Ca.* 1415.
For miniatures related to the Berry Apocalypse workshop see this Catalogue.
BIBLIOGRAPHY: Meiss, *Late XIV Century*, 1967, p. 356.

Paris, BIBL. DE L'ARSENAL, ms. 664
Térence des ducs. *Ca.* 1412.
See Catalogue of Manuscripts.

Paris, BIBL. DE L'ARSENAL, ms. 3479–80
Lancelot du Lac. 624 and 678 pp.; 460×318 mm. and 455×310 mm.
Ms. 3479: 1, 155, 478. Ms. 3480: 351, 442–481, 499, 522–541, 559, 629. *Ca.* 1405. Perhaps the *Lancelot* that Jean sans Peur bought from Jacques Raponde in February, 1406.
For miniatures by the workshop of the Master of Berry's Cleres Femmes see this Catalogue.
BIBLIOGRAPHY: see Berry's Cleres Femmes.

Paris, BIBL. DE L'ARSENAL, ms. 5057–58
Guiart des Moulins, *Bible historiale*. *Ca.* 1405.
See Catalogue of Manuscripts.

Paris, BIBL. DE L'ARSENAL, ms. 5193
Boccaccio, *Cas des nobles hommes et femmes*. *Ca.* 1410–1412.
See Catalogue of Manuscripts.

Paris, BIBL. DE L'ECOLE DES BEAUX-ARTS, Fond le Soufaché 483 (Fig. 504)
Book of Hours. 214 fols.; 167×120 mm.
All miniatures by the workshop with the exception of fol. 111 by the Boucicaut workshop. *Ca.* 1402.
For the Boucicaut miniature see Meiss, *Boucicaut Master*, 1968, p. 140.
BIBLIOGRAPHY: Paris, Ecole des Beaux-Arts, Bengy-Puyvallée, 1908, p. 83 f. no. 483; Meiss, *Boucicaut Master*, 1968, p. 140.

Paris, BIBL. MAZARINE, ms. 2028 (Fig. 153)
Grandes Chroniques de France. 464 fols.; 440×335 mm.
Fols. 2–31, 124–427v. *Ca.* 1410–1412.
For miniatures by the Epître workshop see this Catalogue.
BIBLIOGRAPHY: see Epître.

Paris, BIBL. NAT., fr. 9–10 (Fig. 534)
Guiart des Moulins, *Bible historiale*. 599 fols.; 450×310 mm.
Fr. 9: 1–16v, 28v–32v, 63–113, 168v–184v, 229, 232, 253v–273v. Fr. 10: 416–572. *Ca.* 1412.
For miniatures by the Bedford, Egerton and Guise workshops see this Catalogue. For the Boucicaut miniatures see Meiss, *Boucicaut Master*, 1968, p. 114 f. (Catalogue).
BIBLIOGRAPHY: Berger, *Bible française*, 1884, pp. 197, 329; Durrieu, *Rev. de l'art a. et m.*, XX, 1906, p. 22; *idem*, *Rev. de l'art chrét.*, 1913, p. 312; Martens, *Meister Francke*, 1929, p. 241 n. 222; Schilling, 1954, pp. 274, 276, pls. 28, 29; Paris, Bibl. nat. (Porcher), 1955, p. 99 no. 204; Meiss, *Art Bull.*, 1956, pp. 193 n. 24, 194 n. 29, fig. 5; *idem*, *Late XIV Century*, 1967, index, figs. 325, 393; *idem*, *Boucicaut Master*, 1968, index, fig. 343; *idem*, *De Lévis Hours*, 1972, p. 22 f., figs. 50, 55.

Paris, BIBL. NAT., fr. 23–24
St. Augustine, *La Cité de Dieu* (trans. by Raoul de Praelles). 294 and 288 fols.; 460×340 mm. and 467×346 mm.
All miniatures. *Ca.* 1405–1407.
BIBLIOGRAPHY: Laborde, *Cité de Dieu*, 1909, I, pp. 277–281; III, pl. XVIII a, b; Meiss, *Art Bull.*, 1956, p. 193 n. 24; *idem*, *Late XIV Century*, 1967, p. 356.

Paris, BIBL. NAT., fr. 131
Boccaccio, *Cas des nobles hommes et femmes* (trans. by Laurent de Premierfait). 312 fols.; 430×310 mm.
Belonged to Gontier Col.
Fols. 1, 176. *Ca.* 1415.
BIBLIOGRAPHY: Laborde, *Cité de Dieu*, 1909, I, p. 278 n. 4; Meiss, *Late XIV Century*, 1967, pp. 79 f., 93, 318, 356, fig. 500; Bozzolo, 1968, p. 12 f.

Paris, BIBL. NAT., fr. 174
St. Augustine, *La Cité de Dieu* (trans. by Raoul de Praelles). Vol. II. 374 fols.; 395×285 mm.
Belonged to Jean de Montaigu († 1409).
All miniatures. *Ca.* 1403–1405.
BIBLIOGRAPHY: Laborde, *Cité de Dieu*, 1909, I, 260–265 no. 14, III, pl. XVI b; Meiss, *Art Bull.*, 1956, p. 193; *idem*, *Late XIV Century*, 1967, p. 356; *idem*, *Boucicaut Master*, 1968, p. 62.

Paris, BIBL. NAT., fr. 226
Boccaccio, *Cas des nobles hommes et femmes* (trans. by Laurent de Premierfait). 275 fols.; 430×308 mm.
Fols. 8v–11v. *Ca.* 1415.
For miniatures by the Bedford Trend and Rohan workshop see this Catalogue.
BIBLIOGRAPHY: see Bedford.

Paris, BIBL. NAT., fr. 260–262
Titus Livius, *Histoire romaine* (trans. by Pierre Bersuire). 270, 204 and 161 fols.; 385×280, 393×290, 397×290 mm.
3 vols.
All miniatures. *Ca.* 1405–1408.

Paris, BIBL. NAT., fr. 264
Titus Livius, *Histoire romaine* (trans. by Pierre Bersuire). 280 fols.; 376×305 mm. The illumination of fr. 265 and 266, which contain the Second and Third Decades, remained unfinished. The scribe Raoul Taingui signed his name in fr. 265, fol. 7 and on fol. 208 in fr. 266 where his name also appears in verses.
Fols. 13, 72, 106, 135v, 208, 229v, 256v. *Ca.* 1410. These miniatures show strong influence of the Luçon style.
For miniatures by the Luçon workshop see this Catalogue.

Paris, BIBL. NAT., fr. 603
Christine de Pisan, *Livre des faits d'armes* and *Mutacion de Fortune.*
See Catalogue of Manuscripts.

Paris, BIBL. NAT., fr. 607
Christine de Pisan, *Cité des Dames.* Shortly after the completion of the text in 1405.
See Catalogue of Manuscripts.

Paris, BIBL. NAT., fr. 1178
Christine de Pisan, *Cité des Dames.* Shortly after completion of the text in 1405.
See Catalogue of Manuscripts.

Paris, BIBL. NAT., fr. 1179
Christine de Pisan, *Cité des Dames.* Shortly after completion of the text in 1405.
See Catalogue of Manuscripts.

Paris, BIBL. NAT., fr. 6446 (Fig. 169)
Josephus, *Antiquités judaïques.* 414 fols.; 433×315 mm.
Belonged to Jean de Berry (inscription).
All miniatures. *Ca.* 1410.
BIBLIOGRAPHY: Guiffrey, *Inventaires*, I, 1894, p. CLXIX no. 38; Delisle, *Journal des savants*, 1903, p. 269 f.; *idem*, *Charles V*, 1907, II, p. 257 no. 210 bis; Durrieu, *Fouquet*, 1908, p. 9; Meiss, *Late XIV Century*, 1967, pp. 314, 356, 405 n. 106.

Paris, BIBL. NAT., fr. 12559 (Figs. 18, 47–49, 56)
Thomas de Saluces, *Chevalier errant.* 209 fols.; 343×263 mm.
Manuscript belonged to the Saluces family.
All miniatures. The arms of Philippe le Hardi, who died in 1404, appear on the last tent to the right in the miniature on fol. 161v (Fig. 18), as M. Jean-Bernard de Vaivre has kindly called to my attention. The style also indicates a date *ca.* 1404.
BIBLIOGRAPHY: Champollion-Figeac, *Documents*, 1868, p. 423 f.; Manfreni, *Il cavaliere errante*, 1890; Gorra, 1892, p. 82; Jorga, *Thomas de Saluces*, 1893; Pellegrin, 1964, p. 409; Meiss, *Late XIV Century*, 1967, p. 356.

Paris, BIBL. NAT., fr. 16994 (Figs. 54, 72, 519)
Boccaccio, *Cas des nobles et femmes* (trans. by Laurent de Premierfait). 345 fols.; 390×278 mm.
All miniatures. *Ca.* 1415.

BIBLIOGRAPHY: Meiss, *Art Bull.*, 1956, p. 193 n. 25; *idem, Late XIV Century*, 1967, p. 356; Bozzolo, 1968, p. 27 f.

Paris, BIBL. NAT., fr. 23279
Pierre Salmon, *Réponses à Charles VI et lamentation au roi sur son état*. 121 fols.; 280×205 mm.
Manuscript illuminated shortly before it was given in 1410 to Charles VI by Pierre Salmon.
Fols. 5, 9, 19, 54, 59v, 64v, 65, 81.
For the miniatures by the Boucicaut workshop see Meiss, *Boucicaut Master*, 1968, pp. 124 f. (Catalogue).
BIBLIOGRAPHY: Couderc, *Portraits* [1910], p. 25 f., pls. LVII–LXI; Aubert, 1912, p. 74 f.; Martin, *Miniature française*, 1923, pp. 76 f., 102, figs. CXV, CXVI; Bourges, Musées [1951], p. 38 f. no. 20; Panofsky, *Netherlandish Painting*, 1953, I, pp. 55, 59, 382 n. 55[3], II, fig. 68; Paris, Bibl. nat. (Porcher), 1955, p. 96 no. 197, pl. XXV; Meiss, *Art Bull.*, 1956, p. 193; *idem, Late XIV Century*, 1967, index, fig. 487; *idem, Boucicaut Master*, 1968, index, figs. 67, 68, 70, 71.

Pavia, MUSEO CIVICO
Six miniatures cut out of a Boccaccio, *Cas des nobles hommes et femmes*.
All miniatures.
BIBLIOGRAPHY: Meiss, *Art Bull.*, 1956, p. 193 n. 25; *idem, Late XIV Century*, 1967, p. 357.

Rome, BIBL. VATICANA, Pal. lat. 1989
Boccaccio, *Décaméron*. Between 1414 and 1419.
See Catalogue of Manuscripts.

Turin, BIBL. NAZIONALE, R. 1680
Thomas de Saluces, *Chevalier errant*.
All miniatures. Damaged.
BIBLIOGRAPHY: Meiss, *Late XIV Century*, 1967, p. 357.

Vienna, NATIONALBIBL., ms. 311–48
Boccaccio, *Cas des nobles hommes et femmes* (trans. by Laurent de Premierfait). 368 fols.; 300×240 mm.
All miniatures. *Ca.* 1415–20.
BIBLIOGRAPHY: Vienna, Nationalbibl., Trenkler, *SFRMP*, 1938, p. 21 no. 11; pl. II.

Vienna, NATIONALBIBL., ms. 1855
Book of Hours, Use of Paris. 267 fols.; 265×190 mm.
Workshop executed drolleries. *Ca.* 1422.
For miniatures by the Bedford workshop see this Catalogue.
BIBLIOGRAPHY: see Bedford.

Vienna, NATIONALBIBL., ms. 2569
Chroniques de Normandie. 107 fols.; 330×250 mm.
All miniatures.
BIBLIOGRAPHY: Vienna, Nationalbibl. (Hermann), 1938, pp. 41–43, pls. X, XI; Meiss, *Late XIV Century*, 1967, p. 357; *idem*, "*Decameron*," 1967, p. 61, fig. 13.

Vienna, NATIONALBIBL., ms. 2615
Geoffroy de la Tour, *Le livre du Chevalier de la Tour*. 117 fols.; 267×197 mm.
Manuscript has only a frontispiece.
BIBLIOGRAPHY: Vienna, Nationalbibl. (Hermann), 1938, p. 43 f. no. 10, pl. XII; Meiss, *Late XIV Century*, 1967, p. 357.

Waddesdon Manor (Bucks.), COLL. OF JAMES A. DE ROTHSCHILD, ms. 54
Hours of Guillebert de Lannoy, Use of Tournai. 117 fols.; 196×135 mm.
Arms and motto of Guillebert de Lannoy.
Fol. 17. *Ca.* 1420–1425.
For miniatures by the workshops of the Harvard Hannibal and Guise Masters see this Catalogue.
BIBLIOGRAPHY: see Harvard Hannibal.

RELATED MANUSCRIPTS

Chantilly, MUSEE CONDE, ms. 493
Christine de Pisan. *Œuvres*.
See Catalogue of Manuscripts.

Paris, BIBL. NAT., fr. 2675
Froissart, *Chroniques*.
Fol. 1 by follower *ca.* 1430.
BIBLIOGRAPHY: Meiss, *Late XIV Century*, 1967, p. 356.

MASTER OF THE CORONATION OF THE VIRGIN

The career of this illuminator, so far as can be ascertained now, was surprisingly brief. He appeared in Paris shortly before 1400 and cannot be found after 1405, though his style lingers on for a time. Like the Master of Berry's Cleres Femmes he seems to have been first trained in the Netherlands. His origins may be related to those of the Boucicaut Master; his miniatures in the period 1400–1403 almost—but not quite—look like early works by that master. He is one of the two principal artists classified by Bella Martens and subsequent historians as the "Master of 1402." I gave him his name in 1967 after a beautiful *Coronation of the Virgin*, a frontispiece to fr. 242. I have called the other illuminator in the "1402 group" the Master of Berry's Cleres Femmes. In Paris the art of the Coronation Master became very refined. To a greater degree than the Master of Berry's Cleres Femmes he assimilated Parisian and Italian pantomime and concepts of space.

In his earliest works, a *Bible historiale* completed before 1402, and a *Légende dorée* of 1402–1403, he collaborated with conservative and inferior French illuminators. The *Cleres Femmes* given to Philippe le Hardi for New Year 1403, however, was illuminated almost entirely by the master and assistants he had trained. How he and an assistant contributed to a Book of Hours illuminated, according to an original inscription, in Nantes in 1402, is not clear (Fig. 412).

If the Boucicaut Master was Jacques Coene, as seems possible, the two masters would have worked for the same patron at the same time. Through Jacques Raponde, Philippe le Hardi commissioned a Bible in which Coene painted some miniatures in 1404. On New Year's Day, 1403, Raponde gave the Duke of Burgundy a copy of Boccaccio's *Cleres et nobles femmes* (fr. 12420) illuminated by the Coronation Master and his workshop (Figs. 3, 46, 74, 200). In the same year Burgundy ordered three copies of the *Fleur des histoires* from Raponde, giving one, which is by assistants of the Coronation Master, to Jean de Berry (fr. 12201).

BIBLIOGRAPHY: Martens, *Meister Francke*, 1929, p. 241 n. 221; Meiss, *Late XIV Century*, 1967, pp. 252 f., 355; *idem*, *Boucicaut Master*, 1968, pp. 63–65.

Colorado Springs (Colorado), COLL. OF MARK LANSBURGH

Book of Hours (formerly Lathrop Harper), Use of Paris. 218 fols.; 184×130 mm.
All miniatures. *Ca.* 1402.
Fols. 21, 53, 63 and 156v have been retouched.
BIBLIOGRAPHY: New York, Lathrop C. Harper, Cat. 10 [1960], p. 1 f., no. 1, 2 figs.; Meiss, *Late XIV Century*, 1967, p. 355; *idem*, *Boucicaut Master*, 1968, p. 65, fig. 464; Lansburgh, 1968, p. 64, fig. 5; Feldman, *Seventy One*, 1971, no. 32.

Leningrad, STATE LIBRARY, ms. fr. Q.v. XIV, 4
Alexandre de Bernai, *Roman d'Athis et Prophilias*. 133 fols.; 290×210 mm. For the identification of the second part of this manuscript see this Catalogue, Luçon Master, Leningrad, State Library, fr. Q.v.XIV, 3.
Burgundian inventory of 1420.
Fol. 17v (other miniatures not seen).
BIBLIOGRAPHY: Doutrepont, *Inventaire*, 1906, p. 67 no. 107; Leningrad (Saint-Pétersbourg), Laborde, 1936, p. 55 f. no. 55, pl. XXVI, 3; Meiss, *Late XIV Century*, 1967, p. 355.

New York, PIERPONT MORGAN LIBRARY, M. 515
Book of Hours, Use of Nantes. Written and illuminated in 1402.
See Catalogue of Manuscripts.

Paris, BIBL. NAT., fr. 159
Guiart des Moulins, *Bible historiale*. 545 fols.; 401×292 mm.
Manuscript illuminated a few years before 1402, when it was given to Jean de Berry by Raoulet d'Auquetonville. (Inscription by Flamel and ex libris of Berry on fol. B. Inventory of 1402.)
Fols. 10–256v, 266v–542. *Ca.* 1400. An artisan illustrated fols. 9v, 260–264.
BIBLIOGRAPHY: Paris, *Manuscrits françois*, II, 1838, pp. 10–12; Berger, *Bible française*, 1884, p. 333 f.; Guiffrey, *Inventaires*, I, 1894, pp. CLXI no. 6, 225 no. 854; II, 1896, p. 236 no. 456; Durrieu, *Le manuscrit*, 1895, p. 178 f.; Paris, Louvre, *Exposition*, 1904, p. 24; Delisle, *Charles V*, 1907, II, pp. 225 no. 9, 272; Paris, Bibl. nat. (Martin), 1928, pp. 54, 106, fig. LXVIII; Panofsky, *Netherlandish Painting*, 1953, I, pp. 53, 381 n. 53[3]; Porcher, *Belles Heures*, 1953, pp. 13, 14 n. 25, fig. 4; *idem*, *Enluminure*, 1959, p. 55, pl. LVIII; Meiss, *Late XIV Century*, 1967,

index, fig. 822; *idem*, *Boucicaut Master*, 1968, pp. 63 f., 101, figs. 459–463.

Paris, BIBL. NAT., fr. 242
Jacobus de Voragine, *Légende dorée* (trans. by Jean de Vignay). 336 fols.; 392×287 mm.
Text 1402 or later.
Fol. A (*Coronation of the Virgin*). *Ca.* 1403.
BIBLIOGRAPHY: Porcher, *Belles Heures*, 1953, pp. 9 f., 51, fig. 1; *idem*, in *Enciclopedia dell' arte*, VIII, p. 619 ff.; Meiss, *Late XIV Century*, 1967, index; *idem*, *Boucicaut Master*, 1968, index.

Paris, BIBL. NAT., fr. 12201
Hayton, *Fleur des histoires de la terre d'Orient*. Just before 1403.
See Catalogue of Manuscripts.

Paris, BIBL. NAT., fr. 12420
Boccaccio, *Des cleres et nobles femmes*. Shortly before 1404.
See Catalogue of Manuscripts.

RELATED MANUSCRIPTS

Brussels, BIBL. ROYALE, ms. 11140
Livre du trésor amoureux. 144 fols.; 270×195 mm.
Burgundian inventory of 1420.
All miniatures by follower. *Ca.* 1410.
BIBLIOGRAPHY: Doutrepont, *Inventaire*, 1906, p. 80 f. no. 125; Brussels, Bibl. roy., Gaspar and Lyna, I, 1937, p. 453 f. no. 191, pl. CXa; Brussels, Bibl. roy., 1967, p. 102 no. 149, pls. v & 26; Brussels, Bibl. roy. (Dogaer and Debae), 1967, p. 22 no. 10.; Meiss, *Late XIV Century*, 1967, p. 355; *idem*, *Boucicaut Master*, 1968, p. 139.

Cleveland, MUSEUM OF ART, ms. 62.287
Missal (*Gotha Missal*), Use of Paris. 164 fols.; 272×196 mm.
Fol. 1
BIBLIOGRAPHY: New York, H. P. Kraus, *Catalogue 100* [1962], pp. 32–39, pls. XXIV–XXVII; Wixom, 1963, pp. 158–173, 186 f.; Cleveland, Mus. of Art (Wixom), 1967, pp. 220, 371 f.; Meiss, *Late XIV Century*, 1967, pp. 80, 102, 355, 390 n. 82, fig. 519.

Oxford, BODLEIAN LIBRARY,
Canon. Liturg. 75
Book of Hours, Use of Paris. 193 fols.; 183×131 mm.
Fols. 50, 62, 78 by follower.
For miniatures by the Egerton workshop see this Catalogue.
For the Boucicaut miniatures see Meiss, *Boucicaut Master*, 1968, p. 105 f. (Catalogue).
BIBLIOGRAPHY: see Egerton.

Vienna, NATIONALBIBL., ms. 2656
Book of Hours. 43 fols.; 138×196 mm.
BIBLIOGRAPHY: Vienna, Nationalbibl. (Hermann), 1938, pp. 137–141, pl. XL; Vienna, Nationalbibl., Trenkler, 1938, p. 28 f., pl. va; Vienna, Kunsthist. Mus., *Katalog*, 1962, no. 111; Meiss, *Late XIV Century*, 1967, p. 355.

MASTER OF EGERTON 1070

The early works of minor artists are difficult to identify, and those of the Egerton Master are no exception. His style seems to appear at approximately the same time, but in somewhat differing versions, in two Books of Hours, one in Cleveland and the other in Madrid. His three miniatures in the manuscript in Cleveland show more vibrant luminosity and a more pungent narrative than the drier, more composed scenes in the Madrid manuscript (Fig. 339). These early works define a range that becomes characteristic of the later paintings. Since both the collaborators in the two Books of Hours, the Brussels Initials Master in Cleveland and the Boucicaut workshop in Madrid, were apparently established in Paris the Egerton Master was presumably already working there, too. His style, however, suggests a Netherlandish origin, and indeed an illuminator who emerged from the same milieu, a follower of the Cleres Femmes Master, painted two miniatures in the Cleveland manuscript.

The Egerton Master began to learn rapidly from his Parisian co-workers. His later borders owe much to the rich acanthus arabesques and scampering putti of the Brussels Initials Master. Between 1405 and 1408 the Egerton Master, certainly established in Paris, painted a few miniatures in the famous first illustrated collection of the writings of Christine de Pisan, for which the Epître Master had the primary responsibility (Figs. 135, 139, 140, 400). The Egerton Master made some of his miniatures conform with those of his colleague by adopting his subtle pale palette. In 1409 Christine then asked the Egerton Master to paint the frontispiece in three copies of her *Sept psaumes*, which she completed in that year.

The Egerton Master and his assistants worked mostly with the atelier of the Boucicaut Master, with which they had begun. Together they completed over half a dozen Books of Hours, two Bibles and a copy of the *Grandes Chroniques*. This group includes the most important work by the Egerton Master, Egerton 1070, after which Rosy Schilling, who first identified some of his works, gave him his name (Fig. 334). About 1409–1410 he and his workshop painted in it all of the full-page miniatures, and in a few of them, such as the *Nativity*, the illuminator shows an awareness of the work of the Limbourgs. His association with the Boucicaut workshop continued until about 1420, in the *Heures de Guise* at Chantilly, which contains the latest miniatures of both workshops.

To extend his effects of shimmering atmosphere into the sky the Egerton Master exploited the technique of glazed metal, preferring particularly a stippled blue on silver. For water he used green on the same metal. It was probably his pointillism that induced the Breviary Master, who had developed the same technique, to invite him, in the period *ca.* 1413–1417, to participate in the execution of the Breviary of Jean sans Peur. His vibrant miniatures, some of them unfinished, are painted in his favorite colors, violet, blue-green, and yellow-brown. Altogether his delight in light-filled space, impulsive movement and surprisingly bold ornament make him a minor spiritual ancestor of the Virgo Master.

BIBLIOGRAPHY: Schilling, 1954, pp. 272 ff.; Meiss, *Art Bull.*, 1956, p. 194 f.; *idem*, *Late XIV Century*, 1967, pp. 242, 357 f.

Besançon, BIBL. MUNICIPALE, ms. 550

Bible in verse by Herman de Valenciennes. 97 fols.; 285 × 188 mm.

BIBLIOGRAPHY: Besançon, Bibl. municipale, *Catalogue général des manuscrits*, XXXII, 1897, p. 317 f. no. 550.

Brussels, BIBL. ROYALE, ms. 10987

Christine de Pisan, *Sept psaumes de pénitence*. 87 fols.; 223 × 158 mm.

Burgundian inventory of 1420.

Illuminated just after 1409, when text was written. Manuscript has only a frontispiece.

BIBLIOGRAPHY: Doutrepont, *Inventaire*, 1906, p. 6 f. no. 8; Brussels, Bibl. roy., Gaspar and Lyna, I, 1937, p. 429 f. no. 178, pl. XCIX.

Chantilly, MUSEE CONDE, ms. 64 (1671)

Hours of François de Guise. 204 fols.; 240 × 175 mm.

Fol. 103. *Ca.* 1420.

For miniatures by the Guise Master see this Catalogue. For the miniature by a follower of the Boucicaut Master see Meiss, *Boucicaut Master*, 1968, p. 81 (Catalogue).

BIBLIOGRAPHY: see Guise.

Cleveland, MUSEUM OF ART, ms. 64.40 (Fig. 339)

Book of Hours (*Hours of Charles le Noble*), Use of Paris. 668 pages; 200 × 140 mm.

Arms of Charles III of Navarre beneath each half-page miniature.

Pages 367, 395, 405. *Ca.* 1405.

For miniatures by the Brussels Initials Master see Meiss, *Late XIV Century*, 1967, p. 323 f. (Catalogue). For miniatures by a painter influenced by the Master of Berry's Cleres Femmes see this Catalogue.

BIBLIOGRAPHY: Meiss, *Art Bull.*, 1956, p. 195, fig. 7; Pächt, *Burl. Mag.*, 1956, p. 115 n. 24; Porcher, *Enluminure*, 1959, p. 56, fig. 61; Meiss, *Gaz. B.-A.*, 1963, p. 159 and fig. 17; Wixom, 1965, pp. 50–83; Cleveland, Mus. of Art (Wixom), 1967, pp. 264, 377 f.; Meiss, *Late XIV Century*, 1967, p. 357, index, figs. 729–731, 734, 745, 749, 758, 759, 761, 764, 772, 789, 804, 805, 809, 812, 813; *idem*, *Boucicaut Master*, 1968, index, fig. 467.

Florence, COLL. PRINCE TOMMASO CORSINI (Fig. 719)

Book of Hours. Not foliated; 220 × 160 mm.

For list of miniatures including those by the Boucicaut workshop see Meiss, *Boucicaut Master*, 1968, p. 86 f. (Catalogue).

BIBLIOGRAPHY: Toesca, 1917, pp. 118–126, figs. 2–4, 6, 7; Heimann, 1932, p. 15, fig. 13; Panofsky, *Netherlandish Painting*, 1953, I, pp. 59, 384 n. 59[3], 433 n. 193[4]; Schilling, 1954, p. 274; Meiss, *Art Bull.*, 1956, p. 194 n. 29; *idem*, *Late XIV Century*, 1967, p. 357; *idem*, *Boucicaut Master*, 1968, index, figs. 128, 167–170, 278–282.

Langres, MUSEE DU BREUIL

Book of Hours.

(Microfilm in the Bibliothèque nationale.)

London, BRIT. MUS., Add. 30899

Leaves from a Book of Hours. 6 fols.; 200 × 140 mm.

Fols. 2, 3, 5, 6. *Ca.* 1410.

For miniatures by Bedford Trend see this Catalogue.

BIBLIOGRAPHY: Meiss, *Art Bull.*, 1956, p. 195; *idem*, *Late XIV Century*, 1967, p. 357; *idem*, *Boucicaut Master*, 1968, p. 152 n. 26.

London, BRIT. MUS., Add. 32454
Book of Hours. *Ca.* 1415.
See Catalogue of Manuscripts.

London, BRIT. MUS., Add. 35311, Harley 2897
Breviary of Jean sans Peur. *Ca.* 1413–1417.
See Catalogue of Manuscripts.

London, BRIT. MUS., Cotton Nero E. II
Grandes Chroniques de France. 487 fols.; 395×251 mm.
Vol. I: 172v–174v. Vol. II: 115, 124v. *Ca.* 1415.
For the Boucicaut miniatures see Meiss, *Boucicaut Master*, 1968, pp. 92–95 (Catalogue).
BIBLIOGRAPHY: Meiss, *Art Bull.*, 1956, p. 195; *idem*, *Late XIV Century*, 1967, pp. 11 f., 357, figs. 304–311, 314, 315; *idem*, *Boucicaut Master*, 1968, index, figs. 419–429.

London, BRIT. MUS., Egerton 1070
Book of Hours, Use of Paris. *Ca.* 1410.
See Catalogue of Manuscripts.

London, BRIT. MUS., Royal 15 D III
Guiart des Moulins, *Bible historiale.* 532 fols.; 460×330 mm.
Petrus Gilberti signed his name in a line ending on fol. 15v.
Fols. 1–6, 62–180, 285–402v, 405, 432, 520v–532. *Ca.* 1415.
For miniatures by the Virgil Master and by a follower of the Breviary Master see this Catalogue. For the Boucicaut miniatures see Meiss, *Boucicaut Master*, 1968, pp. 96–99 (Catalogue).
BIBLIOGRAPHY: Berger, *Bible française*, 1884, p. 387; Durrieu, *Rev. de l'art a. et m.*, XX, 1906, p. 22; *idem*, *Rev. de l'art chrét.*, 1913, p. 310; London, Brit. Mus., Warner and Gilson, 1921, II, p. 172 f., IV, pl. 95; Schilling, 1954, pp. 274 ff., pls. 26, 28, 29; Meiss, *Art Bull.*, 1956, pp. 193 n. 24, 194 n. 29, 195; *idem*, *Late XIV Century*, 1967, index, fig. 317; *idem*, *Boucicaut Master*, 1968, index, figs. 344–354.

Madrid, BIBL. NACIONAL, Vit. 25 no. 1
Book of Hours. 240×168 mm.
Fols. 3–312v. *Ca.* 1405.
For miniature by the Boucicaut workshop see Meiss, *Boucicaut Master*, 1968, p. 101 (Catalogue).
BIBLIOGRAPHY: Durrieu, *Rev. de l'art chrét.*, 1913, p. 311; Domínguez Bordona, *Manuscritos*, 1933, I, p. 418 no. 979, fig. 356; Meiss, *Art Bull.*, 1956, p. 194 f.; *idem*, *Late XIV Century*, 1967, p. 357; *idem*, *Boucicaut Master*, 1968, index, figs. 141, 176, 178.

New York, PIERPONT MORGAN LIBRARY, M. 919
Book of Hours. 248 fols.; 200×137 mm.
Fol. 13. *Ca.* 1418.

Orange (Texas), STARK COLL.
Book of Hours, Use of Paris. 192 fols.; 175×125 mm.
Fol. 94. *Ca.* 1410–1415.
For miniatures in the Bedford Trend see this Catalogue. For miniatures by a follower of the Boucicaut Master see Meiss, *Boucicaut Master*, 1968, p. 105 (Catalogue).
BIBLIOGRAPHY: New York, Harper Catalogue No. 10, 1960, p. 1 no. 1; Meiss, *Boucicaut Master*, 1968, p. 105, figs. 163, 222–226.

Oxford, BODLEIAN LIBRARY, Canon. Liturg. 75
Book of Hours, Use of Paris. 193 fols.; 183×131 mm.
Fols. 68v, 82v, 97, 131–140v. *Ca.* 1410.
For miniatures by a follower of the Master of the Coronation see this Catalogue. For the Boucicaut miniatures see Meiss, *Boucicaut Master*, 1968, p. 105 f. (Catalogue).
BIBLIOGRAPHY: Pächt and Alexander, *Bodleian Manuscripts*, 1966, p. 50 no. 642; Meiss, *Boucicaut Master*, 1968, p. 105 f., figs. 227–229.

Paris, BIBL. DE L'ARSENAL, ms. 650
Book of Hours. 173 fols.; 195×137 mm.
Probably corresponds with a Book of Hours purchased by Jean de Berry in 1415.
Fols. 15, 25v, 71, 89. Other miniatures related in style to the Boucicaut Master.
BIBLIOGRAPHY: Paris, Arsenal, Martin, I, 1885, p. 491 f. no. 650; Guiffrey, *Inventaires*, I, 1894, p. 330 no. 1232; Delisle, *Charles V*, 1907, II, pp. 241 no. 110, 299; Meiss, *Late XIV Century*, 1967, pp. 311, 357.

Paris, BIBL. NAT., fr. 9–10
Guiart des Moulins, *Bible historiale.* 599 fols.; 450×310 mm.
Fr. 9: 19–25v. Fr. 10: 334–387. *Ca.* 1412.
For miniatures by the Bedford, Cité des Dames and Guise workshops see this Catalogue. For the Boucicaut miniatures see Meiss, *Boucicaut Master*, 1968, p. 114 f. (Catalogue).
BIBLIOGRAPHY: see Cité des Dames.

Paris, BIBL. NAT., fr. 340
Livre du roy Méliadus. 207 fols.; 418×305 mm.
Belonged to Prigent de Coëtivy.

Fols. 121v–205v, *ca.* 1406–1407, by workshop, completing a cycle begun by a mediocre painter of *ca.* 1400.
BIBLIOGRAPHY: Meiss, *Late XIV Century*, 1967, pp. 357, 363 n. 51.

Paris, BIBL. NAT., fr. 606, 835–836
Christine de Pisan, *Œuvres*. Between 1405 and 1408.
See Catalogue of Manuscripts.

Paris, BIBL. NAT., nouv. acq. fr. 4792
Christine de Pisan, *Sept psaumes de pénitence*. 88 fols.; 180×135 mm.
Illuminated just after 1409, when text was written.
Manuscript has only a frontispiece.
BIBLIOGRAPHY: Meiss, *Late XIV Century*, 1967, p. 357.

Paris, BIBL. NAT., lat. 919
Book of Hours (*Grandes Heures of Jean de Berry*), Use of Paris. 126 fols.; 400×300 mm.
Made for Jean de Berry and completed in 1409 (inscription).
Fol. 1 tree by Egerton workshop; fol. 6v December scene and tree at lower left in Egerton style.
For miniature by the Bedford Trend see this Catalogue.
For miniatures by the Boucicaut workshop, Pseudo-Jacquemart and Jacquemart de Hesdin (Louvre, *Way to Calvary*) see Meiss, *Late XIV Century*, 1967, pp. 332–334 (Catalogue); *idem*, *Boucicaut Master*, 1968, p. 125 f. (Catalogue).
BIBLIOGRAPHY: see Bedford.

Paris, LIBRAIRIE COULET ET FAURE
Christine de Pisan, *Sept psaumes de pénitence*. 87 fols.; 200×140 mm.
Illuminated shortly after 1409, when text was written.
Manuscript has only a frontispiece.

Paris, MUSEE DE CLUNY, ms. 11314
Leaves from a Book of Hours, Use of Paris. 12 fols. of a calendar; 220×153 mm.
All miniatures.
BIBLIOGRAPHY: Paris, Chambre des Députés, Boinet, 1922, p. 12 f., pl. IV; Warsaw, Sawicka, 1938, p. 65; Meiss, *Art Bull.*, 1956, p. 195; *idem*, *Late XIV Century*, 1967, p. 357.

Paris, COLL. OF COUNT JEAN DURRIEU
Book of Prayers. 107 fols. but manuscript is not foliated; 180×130 mm.
For list of miniatures see Meiss, *Late XIV Century*, 1967, p. 341 (Catalogue).
BIBLIOGRAPHY: Meiss, *Late XIV Century*, 1967, pp. 264, 275, 341, 357, figs. 245–247.

Seville, BIBL. COLOMBINA, ms. 1717
Book of Hours. 168 fols.; 165×120 mm.
Fols. 13–42, 67v, 80, 105v, 167v. Fols. 161v–166v by follower. *Ca.* 1410.
For the Boucicaut miniatures see Meiss, *Boucicaut Master*, 1968, p. 135 f. (Catalogue).
BIBLIOGRAPHY: Durrieu, *Rev. de l'art chrét.*, 1913, p. 314; Domínguez Bordona, *Manuscritos*, 1933, II, p. 143 f., no. 1717; Meiss, *Late XIV Century*, 1967, p. 357; *idem*, *Boucicaut Master*, 1968, index, fig. 230.

WHEREABOUTS UNKNOWN (formerly Alexandrine Rothschild)
Book of Hours, Use of Paris. *Ca.* 1410–1415.
See Catalogue of Manuscripts.

RELATED MANUSCRIPTS

London, BRIT. MUS., Royal 19 D III
Guiart des Moulins, *Bible historiale*. 606 fols.; 445×340 mm. and 450×335 mm.
Written in 1411 for Thomas du Val, canon of Notre Dame de Clerefontaine in the diocese of Chartres.
BIBLIOGRAPHY: Berger, *Bible française*, 1884, p. 392 f.; London, Brit. Mus., Warner and Gilson, 1921, II, pp. 342–345, IV, pl. 112; London, Brit. Mus., Millar, 1933, p. 33 f. nos. 43, 44, pls. XLIII, XLIV; Schilling, 1954, pp. 278 n. 23, 280; Meiss, *Art Bull.*, 1956, p. 195 no. 30; *idem*, *Late XIV Century*, 1967, index, figs. 312, 313.

London, VICTORIA AND ALBERT MUSEUM, ms. A.L. 1646–1902 (Reid ms. 4)
Book of Hours, Use of Paris. 190 fols.; 179×130 mm.
Fol. 16 by follower. *Ca.* 1415.
For Boucicaut miniatures see Meiss, *Boucicaut Master*, 1968, p. 99 (Catalogue).
BIBLIOGRAPHY: (Anonymous), *Burl. Mag.*, I, 1903, p. 389, fig. p. 388; Schilling, 1952, p. 169; *idem*, 1954, p. 274, pl. 27 d; Meiss, *Art Bull.*, 1956, p. 194 n. 29; *idem*, *Late XIV Century*, 1967, p. 358; *idem*, *Boucicaut Master*, 1968, index, figs. 276, 277.

Munich, BAYERISCHE STAATSBIBL., ms. gall. 3
Jacobus de Voragine, *Légende dorée* (trans. by Jean de Vignay). 317 fols.
BIBLIOGRAPHY: Munich, Bayerische Staatsbibl., Leidinger, 1912, p. 26 no. 150; Germany, *Manuscrits français* (Olschki), 1932, p. 10 f., pl. VI; Meiss, *Art Bull.*, 1956, p. 195 n. 30; *idem*, *Late XIV Century*, 1967, p. 358.

Paris, BIBL. NAT., fr. 30
Titus Livius, *Histoire romaine* (trans. by Pierre Bersuire). 511 fols.; 455×325 mm.
All miniatures. *Ca.* 1414.
BIBLIOGRAPHY: Porcher, *Belles Heures*, 1953, p. 17 n. 31; Paris, Bibl. nat. (Porcher), 1955, p. 76 no. 153; Meiss, *Late XIV Century*, 1967, p. 358.

Paris, COLL. OF MADAME LA BARONNE DE CHARNACÉ (formerly Paul Durrieu)
Book of Hours, Use of Paris. Not paginated; 184×135 mm.
Calendar and small miniatures. *Ca.* 1415–1420.
For the Boucicaut miniatures see Meiss, *Boucicaut Master*, 1968, p. 133 f. (Catalogue).
BIBLIOGRAPHY: Durrieu, 1914, p. 28, figs. 15, 16, pl. opp. p. 28; Paris, Bibl. nat. (Porcher), 1955, p. 99 no. 206; Meiss, *Late XIV Century*, 1967, p. 358; *idem*, *Boucicaut Master*, 1968, pp. 29, 99, 133 f., figs. 131, 272–275.

Paris, COLL. OF COUNT JEAN DURRIEU (formerly Paul Durrieu)
Book of Hours. Not paginated; 190×135 mm. *Ca.* 1415.
For the Boucicaut miniatures see Meiss, *Boucicaut Master*, 1968, p. 134 (Catalogue).
BIBLIOGRAPHY: Durrieu, *Rev. de l'art a. et m.*, XX, 1906, p. 24, fig. p. 29; *idem*, 1914, p. 28, fig. 17; Paris, Bibl. nat. (Porcher), 1955, p. 99 no. 207; Meiss, *Late XIV Century*, 1967, p. 358; *idem*, *Boucicaut Master*, 1968, index, figs. 251–252.

Philadelphia, FREE LIBRARY, Widener no. 4
Book of Hours. 206 fols.; 210×150 mm.
Calendar scenes by follower.
For miniatures by the Luçon workshop see this Catalogue.
BIBLIOGRAPHY: see Luçon.

Philadelphia, FREE LIBRARY, Widener no. 6
Book of Hours. 252 fols.; 218×160 mm.
Fols. 147v–155 by follower.
BIBLIOGRAPHY: De Ricci, *Census*, II, 1937, p. 2116 no. 6; Meiss, *Late XIV Century*, 1967, p. 358; *idem*, *Boucicaut Master*, 1968, index.

Wolfenbüttel, LANDESBIBL., ms. 1. 5. 3. 1 Aug. fol.
Bartholomaeus Anglicus, *Le livre de la propriété des choses* (trans. by Jean Corbechon). 323 fols.; 402×320 mm.
BIBLIOGRAPHY: Wolfenbüttel, Landesbibl. (Heinemann), I, 1890, p. 27 f. no. 1591; Germany, *Manuscrits français* (Olschki), 1932, p. 43 f., pl. LI; Meiss, *Art Bull.*, 1956, p. 195 n. 30; *idem*, *Late XIV Century*, 1967, p. 358.

WHEREABOUTS UNKNOWN (formerly New York, H. P. Kraus)
Book of Hours, Use of Paris. 197 fols.; 189×140 mm.
For miniatures by a follower of the Boucicaut Master see Meiss, *Boucicaut Master*, 1968, p. 137 f. (Catalogue).
BIBLIOGRAPHY: London, Sotheby, December 7, 1953 lot 52; New York, Kraus, *Catalogue 100* [1962], p. 49 no. 23; Meiss, *Late XIV Century*, 1967, p. 358; *idem*, *Boucicaut Master*, 1968, p. 137 f., figs. 235, 236.

MASTER OF THE EPITRE D'OTHEA

This rare illuminator is known only in copies of two poems of Christine de Pisan. He and his assistants illuminated for her four manuscripts of the *Mutacion de Fortune* (Fig. 2), the text of which she finished in November 1403, and, more important, the beautiful *Epître d'Othéa* of 1405–1408 (Figs. 61, 62). The miniatures painted a few years later in a *Grandes chroniques* are uninspired and were probably executed by assistants (Fig. 152). The brevity of the career of this remarkable master is puzzling, and his origins are similarly not clear, though he had certainly studied Lombard illumination.

For the work of the Epître Master see the chapters on the *Mutacion* and the *Epître d'Othéa*.
BIBLIOGRAPHY: Paris, Bibl. nat. (Porcher), 1955, pp. 74–76 nos. 149–151; Meiss, *Late XIV Century*, 1967, pp. 299 f., 358.

Brussels, BIBL. ROYALE, ms. 9508
Christine de Pisan, *Mutacion de Fortune*. After November, 1403, and before January, 1404.
See Catalogue of Manuscripts.

Chantilly, MUSEE CONDE, ms. 494
Christine de Pisan, *Mutacion de Fortune*. Shortly after November, 1403.
See Catalogue of Manuscripts.

The Hague, KON. BIBL., ms. 78 D 42
Christine de Pisan, *Mutacion de Fortune*. After November, 1403 and before March, 1404.
See Catalogue of Manuscripts.

Paris, BIBL. MAZARINE, ms. 2028 (Fig. 152)
Grandes chroniques de France. 464 fols.; 440×335 mm.
Fols. 52v–115. *Ca.* 1410–1412.
For miniatures by the Cité des Dames workshop see this Catalogue.
BIBLIOGRAPHY: Paris, Mazarine, Molinier, II, 1886, p. 328 no. 2028; Paris, Bibl. nat. (Porcher), 1955, p. 76 no. 151; Meiss, *Art Bull.*, 1956, p. 193 n. 24; *idem, Late XIV Century*, 1967, p. 357 f.

Paris, BIBL. NAT., fr. 606, 835–836
Christine de Pisan, *Œuvres*. Between 1405 and 1408.
See Catalogue of Manuscripts.

WHEREABOUTS UNKNOWN (formerly Paris, Pierre Berès)
Christine de Pisan, *Mutacion de Fortune*. Shortly after November, 1403.
See Catalogue of Manuscripts.

MASTER OF THE GUISE HOURS

The Guise Master, named after his miniatures in the *Hours of François de Guise* in Chantilly, collaborated with the Boucicaut, Cité des Dames and Egerton Masters in the second decade of the fifteenth century. He continued to work into the third decade. His style derived chiefly from that of the Boucicaut Master (Fig. 533). His colors, however—rather stark red, blue and green—resemble those used by the Cité des Dames workshop, with which he collaborated *ca.* 1412 on a *Bible historiale* now in Paris (fr. 9–10). Both workshops painted red skies streaked by gold clouds.

Baltimore, WALTERS ART GALLERY, ms. 276
Book of Hours, Use of Paris. 158 fols.; 205×148 mm.
Fols. 155, 156.

Chantilly, MUSEE CONDE, ms. 64 (1671)
Hours of François de Guise. 204 fols.; 240×175 mm.
Fols. 47–67, 178v, 180v–193. *Ca.* 1420.
For the miniature by the Egerton workshop see this Catalogue.
For the miniature by a follower of the Boucicaut Master see Meiss, *Boucicaut Master*, 1968, p. 18 (Catalogue).
BIBLIOGRAPHY: Durrieu, *Rev. de l'art a. et m.*, XX, 1906, p. 24 f.; *idem, Rev. de l'art chrét.*, 1913, p. 309; Chantilly (Meurgey), 1930, pp. 52–54 no. 25, pl. XXXIVb; Schilling, 1954, p. 274; Meiss, *Art Bull.*, 1956, p. 194 n. 29; *idem, Late XIV Century*, 1967, p. 357; *idem, Boucicaut Master*, 1968, index, fig. 132.

Cleveland, MUSEUM OF ART, ms. 42.169
Book of Hours. 193 fols.; 202×146 mm.
Fol. 93v.
BIBLIOGRAPHY: Oberlin, Oberlin College (Delaissé), 1960, p. 97 f.; Cleveland, Museum of Art, *Gothic Art 1360–1440* (Wixom), 1963, p. 202 no. 14; Meiss, *Boucicaut Master*, 1968, p. 139, fig. 320.

Fort Worth (Texas), COLL. OF ARTHUR HADDAWAY (Fig. 533)
Book of Hours, Use of Paris. 174 fols.; 219×155 mm.
Belonged to Louis XI, while he was still Dauphin, and Charlotte of Savoy, whose arms were added in the borders of the folios with large miniatures.
Fols. 51, 54, 95. *Ca.* 1420.
For miniatures by the workshop of the Bedford Master and by a follower of the Limbourgs see this Catalogue.
BIBLIOGRAPHY: see Bedford.

Paris, BIBL. NAT., fr. 9–10
Guiart des Moulins, *Bible historiale*. 599 fols.; 450×310 mm.
Fr. 9: 35v–49v, 119v–159v, 188v–225v, 237–249, 275–278, 288–306. Fr. 10: 410–412v, 585v–598v. *Ca.* 1412.
For the miniatures by the Bedford, Cité des Dames and Egerton workshops see this Catalogue. For the Bouci-

caut miniatures see Meiss, *Boucicaut Master*, 1968, p. 114 f. (Catalogue).
BIBLIOGRAPHY: see Cité des Dames.

Vienna, NATIONALBIBL., ms. 2561
Boccaccio, *Décaméron* (trans. by Laurent de Premierfait). 391 fols.; 258×355 mm.
Fols. 27, 31v, 35 and a few others. *Ca.* 1425–1430.
BIBLIOGRAPHY: Vienna, Nationalbibl. (Hermann), 1938, pp. 64–86, pl. XVIII; Branca, *Decameron*, 1966, I, illustration on p. 46.

Waddesdon Manor (Bucks.), COLL. OF JAMES A. DE ROTHSCHILD, ms. 54
Hours of Guillebert de Lannoy, Use of Tournai. 117 fols.; 196×135 mm. Arms and motto of Guillebert de Lannoy.
Fols. 61, 75, 115. *Ca.* 1425.
For miniatures by the Cité des Dames and Harvard Hannibal workshops see this Catalogue.
BIBLIOGRAPHY: see Harvard Hannibal.

MASTER OF THE HARVARD HANNIBAL

The reconstruction of this illuminator was begun recently. In 1966 Pächt and Alexander grouped three manuscripts. In 1968 the writer, before he had seen this initial grouping, brought together three different manuscripts, and named the artist after a large *Coronation of Hannibal* in a Livy belonging to Harvard University.

The style of this illuminator was clearly formed in the circle of the Boucicaut Master. Indeed he collaborated with the Boucicaut workshop between 1410 and 1415 on the Harvard Livy and on a copy of Boccaccio's *Des cleres et nobles femmes* in Lisbon. His early miniatures contain such motifs as barrel vaults, large gold-rayed suns and star-filled skies. Occasionally he borrowed entire compositions. His *Visitation* and *St. George and the Dragon* in a Book of Hours in the Walters Art Gallery (W. 287, fols. 46, 144) are reversed versions of the same subjects in the *Boucicaut Hours*.

Although he normally preferred bright reds, greens, blues and yellow, he did on occasion choose a different palette. In a *Cité de Dieu* (Boulogne-sur-Mer), which is perhaps his earliest work, he used the colors of the miniatures by the Boucicaut workshop in the *Livre des merveilles* (fr. 2810) (Fig. 520). Areas of polished white are combined with clear blue, pink, lavender and persimmon. Later, *ca.* 1422, he and an assistant worked in grisaille in a *Méditations de la vie de Christ*.

A veritable sponge, the Harvard Hannibal Master sometimes copied entire cycles of miniatures. He took his compositions in the *Cité de Dieu* at Boulogne from a model by the Virgil Master (fr. 6272; The Hague, Museum Meermanno-Westreenianum, ms. 10 A 12). A *Cas des nobles hommes et femmes* (fr. 131), illuminated by the workshop of the Cité des Dames Master, served as a model for his own illustrations in a copy of this text (Bodleian 265).

The Harvard Hannibal Master collaborated with a follower of the Limbourgs in the Spitz Hours, and he became almost as familiar with the work of the three brothers as he had been with that of the Boucicaut Master. In the Waddesdon Book of Hours he freely copied the *Martyrdom of St. Catherine* in the *Belles Heures*. He knew even unfinished compositions by the Limbourgs themselves in the *Très Riches Heures*. Indeed we owe to two of his miniatures, as we have said above, knowledge of the main architectural elements and the figures in the *Christmas Mass* drawn by the Limbourgs but painted in a somewhat different form by Colombe (Figs. 589, 599, 601).
BIBLIOGRAPHY: Pächt and Alexander, *Illuminated Manuscripts*, I, 1966, p. 52 no. 663; Meiss, *Boucicaut Master*, 1968, pp. 57, 142.

Baltimore, WALTERS ART GALLERY, ms. 259
Book of Hours. 168 fols.; 195×145 mm.

Baltimore, WALTERS ART GALLERY, ms. 287 (Fig. 599)
Book of Hours. Paris calendar. 200 fols.; 203×168 mm.
All miniatures. *Ca.* 1420.
BIBLIOGRAPHY: Baltimore, Walters (Miner), 1949, p. 37 f. no. 100; Baltimore, Walters, *International Style* (Miner), 1962, p. 64 no. 59, pl. LXIII; Meiss, *Late XIV Century*, 1967, p. 265, fig. 262.

Boulogne-sur-Mer, BIBL. MUNICIPALE, ms. 55 (Fig. 520)
St. Augustine, *La Cité de Dieu*. Vol. II. 352 fols.; 390×275 mm.
Ca. 1412.
BIBLIOGRAPHY: Laborde, *Cité de Dieu*, 1909, I, pp. 296–301 no. 24, pl. XX; Paris, Bibl. nat. (Porcher), 1955, p. 79 no. 160.

Cambridge, Mass., HARVARD COLLEGE, HOUGHTON LIBRARY, Richardson ms. 32
Titus Livius, *Histoire romaine, deuxième décade* (trans. by Pierre Bersuire). Vol. II. 192 fols.; 417×316 mm.
Fol. 263. *Ca.* 1415.
For the Boucicaut miniatures see Meiss, *Boucicaut Master*, 1968, p. 80 f.
BIBLIOGRAPHY: New York, American Art Association—Anderson Galleries, *Lothian*, 1932, lot 12; Baltimore, Walters (Miner), 1949, p. 35 no. 93; Cambridge, Harvard University, 1955, p. 22 no. 65; De Ricci, *Census, Supplement*, 1962, p. 247; Meiss, *Boucicaut Master*, 1968, pp. 56 ff., 70, 80 f., 89, 142, figs. 433, 437.

Cambridge, Mass., HARVARD COLLEGE, HOUGHTON LIBRARY, ms. Typ 207 H
Guillaume de Tignonville, *Les dis moraux des philosophes*. 29 fols.; 301×225 mm.
All miniatures by workshop. *Ca.* 1418–1420.
First miniatures abraded and retouched.
BIBLIOGRAPHY: Cambridge, Harvard University, 1955, p. 20 no. 55, pl. 33.

Chicago (Glencoe), COLL. OF MRS. J. SPITZ
Book of Hours, Use of Paris. 245 fols.; 204×146 mm.
Visitation and *Presentation*. *Ca.* 1418–1420.
For miniatures by a follower of the Limbourgs see this Catalogue.
BIBLIOGRAPHY: Meiss, *Boucicaut Master*, 1968, p. 147 n. 30, fig. 154; *idem*, *De Lévis Hours*, 1972, p. 71 n. 53.

Detroit, INSTITUTE OF ARTS,
Gift of Mrs. James Couzins Fund, 27.162
Pentecost
Round (760 mm. diam.) miniature which formerly decorated the reverse of a polychromed wax medallion.
BIBLIOGRAPHY: Panofsky in *Beiträge G. Swarzenski*, 1951, pp. 70–84; Kansas, University of Kansas Museum of Art, Schrader, 1969, p. 11 f. no. 6, pl. XII.

Lisbon, GULBENKIAN FOUNDATION, ms. L. A. 143
Boccaccio, *Des cleres et nobles femmes*. 190 fols.; 409×292 mm.
Belonged to Prigent de Coëtivy. Damaged in a flood, 1967.
Fols. 101–119, 141–180v. Between about 1410 and 1415.
For miniatures by the Bedford circle and the Cité des Dames workshop see this Catalogue. For the Boucicaut miniatures see Meiss, *Boucicaut Master*, 1968, pp. 88–91 (Catalogue).
BIBLIOGRAPHY: see Cité des Dames.

London, BRIT. MUS., Cotton Vesp. A. XIX
Work of the Bishop Adelwol.
Folios with miniatures added on 1v, 28, 103v, 104. *Ca.* 1420.

London, BRIT. MUS., Royal 20 B IV
St. Bonaventura, *Méditations de la vie de Christ* (trans. by Jean Galopes dit le Galoys). 169 fols.; 255×190 mm.
All miniatures. *Ca.* 1422.
BIBLIOGRAPHY: London, Brit. Mus., Warner and Gilson, 1921, II, p. 360 f., IV, pl. 114; Lyna, 1946–1947, p. 113; Meiss, *Art Bull.*, 1956, p. 196 n. 35; *idem*, *Late XIV Century*, 1967, pp. 12, 354, fig. 316.

London, BRIT. MUS., Royal 20 B XX
Le livre et la vraye hystoire du bon roy Alixandre. 97 fols.; 285×197 mm.
All miniatures except fols. 21, 24, 56, 57, 73, 73v, 80, 80v. *Ca.* 1420–1425.
BIBLIOGRAPHY: London, Brit. Mus., Warner and Gilson, II, 1921, p. 369 f.; Pächt and Alexander, *Bodleian Manuscripts*, 1966, p. 52 no. 663.

London, LAMBETH PALACE, ms. 326
Liber peregrinacionis anime (Latin prose trans. by Jean Galopes dit le Galoys). 145 fols.; 272×211 mm. Probably the copy of the text written for John, Duke of Bedford, in 1427 by the scribe Jean Thomas.
All miniatures.
BIBLIOGRAPHY: London, Lambeth Palace, Millar, *Bull. SFRMP*, 1925, pp. 13–15, pl. XLII; London, Lambeth Palace, James, 1932, pp. 427–431 no. 326.

New York, PIERPONT MORGAN LIBRARY, M. 455
Book of Hours, Use of Paris. 194 fols.; 215×154 mm.
Fols. 23, 59–69v, 84v–109, 121v–170. *Ca.* 1417.
BIBLIOGRAPHY: New York, Pierpont Morgan Library [1934], p. 53 no. 114, pl. 80; Meiss, *Boucicaut Master*, 1968, pp. 139, 142, 146 f. n. 30, figs. 324, 325.

Oxford, BODLEIAN LIBRARY, ms. Bodley 265

Boccaccio, *Cas des nobles hommes et femmes* (trans. by Laurent de Premierfait). 328 fols.; 422×315 mm.
All miniatures. *Ca.* 1420.
BIBLIOGRAPHY: Pächt and Alexander, *Bodleian Manuscripts*, 1966, p. 51 f. no. 658, pl. LI; Meiss, *Late XIV Century*, 1967, p. 357.

Oxford, BODLEIAN LIBRARY, ms. Liturg. 100 (Fig. 601)
Book of Hours, Use of Paris.
All miniatures. *Ca.* 1420.
BIBLIOGRAPHY: Pächt and Alexander, *Bodleian Manuscripts*, 1966, p. 52 no. 663, pl. LII.

Paris, BIBL. NAT., fr. 247
Josephus, *Antiquités judaïques*.
See Catalogue of Manuscripts.

Paris, BIBL. NAT., fr. 2663
Froissart, *Chroniques*. 406 fols.; 367×280 mm.
Given to Jean de Derval by Tanneguy Du Châtel.
Fol. 6. *Ca.* 1415.
For miniatures related to the Berry Apocalypse Master see this Catalogue.
BIBLIOGRAPHY: see Berry Apocalypse: Related manuscripts.

Paris, BIBL. NAT., nouv. acq. lat. 3109
Book of Hours, Use of Paris. 145 fols.; 175×125 mm.
All miniatures. *Ca.* 1420.
BIBLIOGRAPHY: Paris, Bibl. nat., Porcher, *Boisrouvray*, 1961, p. 69 f. no. 14, pls. 39–44.

STONYHURST COLLEGE, Lancs., ms. 33
Book of Hours, Use of Paris.
All miniatures.
BIBLIOGRAPHY: Pächt and Alexander, *Bodleian Manuscripts*, 1966, p. 52 no. 663.

Waddesdon Manor (Bucks.), COLL. OF JAMES A. DE ROTHSCHILD, ms. 54
Hours of Guillebert de Lannoy, Use of Tournai. 117 fols.; 196×135 mm.
Arms and motto of Guillebert de Lannoy.
Fols. 13, 15, 19–29, 113v, 114 and all historiated initials. *Ca.* 1425.
For miniatures by the Cité des Dames and Guise workshops see this Catalogue.
BIBLIOGRAPHY: Waddesdon Manor, Delaissé and Morrow, in press.

WHEREABOUTS UNKNOWN (London, Sotheby & Co., February 9, 1948, lot 225)
Book of Hours, Use of Arras. 237 fols.; 200×140 mm.
Some miniatures. *Ca.* 1420.
BIBLIOGRAPHY: London, Sotheby, February 9, 1948, lot 225.

MASTER OF THE HOLY GHOST

Paris, Bibliothèque nationale — nouv. acq. lat. 3093 — *Très Belles Heures de Notre-Dame*

BIBLIOGRAPHY: Hulin de Loo, *Heures de Milan*, 1911, p. 20 f.; Durrieu, *Très Belles Heures de Notre-Dame*, 1922, p. 79 ff.; Kreuter-Eggemann, *Daliwe*, 1964, pp. 61–72; Meiss, *Late XIV Century*, 1967, p. 253 ff.

MASTER OF THE HUMILITY MADONNAS

London, British Museum	Add. 35311 and Harley 2897	Breviary of Jean sans Peur
	Harley 2952	Book of Hours
	Yates Thompson 37	Book of Hours

RELATED MANUSCRIPTS

Oxford, Bodleian Library	Douce 102	Book of Hours

BIBLIOGRAPHY: Meiss, *Late XIV Century*, 1967, p. 276 f.

MASTER OF JOSEPHUS, ANTIQUITES JUDAIQUES

About 1415 this master painted two large miniatures in a manuscript of Josephus, *Antiquités judaïques*, which belonged to Jean de Berry (Fig. 170). Just before 1408 he painted the frontispiece to the *Comedies* of Terence which the Duke received from his counsellor Martin Gouge. The painter also probably supervised the execution of the entire cycle of illustrations; the miniatures in the *Andria* resemble his style most closely. He was a follower of Jacquemart de Hesdin, and he may normally have practiced as a *peintre* rather than an *enlumineur* or *historieur*.

For this master see the chapter on the manuscripts of Terence, and also Meiss, *Late XIV Century*, 1967, p. 227.

Paris, BIBL. NAT., fr. 247
Flavius Josephus, *Les antiquités judaïques*.
See Catalogue of Manuscripts.

Paris, BIBL. NAT., lat. 7907 A
Terence, *Comedies*. Just before 1408.
See Catalogue of Manuscripts.

RELATED MANUSCRIPTS

London, BRIT. MUS., Add. 32454
Book of Hours.
See Catalogue of Manuscripts.

MASTER OF LUÇON

For this prolific illuminator we happen to possess an early dated work—the Barcelona Hours of 1401. In it his style seems already fully developed so that his career had no doubt begun even earlier, in the 'nineties. The Barcelona manuscript shows his characteristic, attenuated figures echoed in their ambiance by long, curling lines. He had not yet, however, added to the drapery those bands of burnished and delicately tooled gold that are the hallmark of his later work. In a period distinguished by subtlety of color and value and an exquisite finish his painting was surpassed only by that of Jean de Limbourg for elegance and refinement. Apart from Jean in certain phases the Luçon Master may be described as the principal representative in Paris of what is generally called the International Style.

The Luçon Master and his workshop painted an unusually large number of Books of Hours. For the miniatures he established designs which he tended to preserve with little alteration throughout his career. He paid almost no attention to the accomplishments of his greater contemporaries. Although the Luçon Master was not normally an innovator, he occasionally introduced new compositions, two of which appear in the Barcelona Hours of 1401 as well as in Walters 231. Christ as Man of Sorrows supported by angels emerges from clouds, and the Virgin bathing the Christ Child is separated from the scene of the *Nativity*. In the Barcelona Hours the bath represents in a homely way the phrase of the prayer, "fontaine de tous biens." In Fitzwilliam McClean 80 soaring angels bear the cross.

In 1406, or shortly before, the Luçon Master and an assistant painted all but one of the miniatures in a collection of moral treatises which Marie de Berry received from her confessor Symon de Courcy (fr. 926) (Fig. 131). The illuminator took his composition of the Madonna and Child from the first frontispiece in the *Brussels Hours*, and the Virgin kneeling on the bed in the *Nativity* of that manuscript served him for two compositions of the same subject (Morgan 743 and Walters 231). Shortly before his death in 1407 Etienne Loypeau, Bishop of Luçon and a protégé of Jean de Berry, commissioned the workshop to paint a missal and pontifical for the Duke, whose arms appear on the first folio. In 1956 I gave the illuminator his name from the extensive and exquisite cycle of miniatures in this manuscript (Figs. 511, 513).

As in the instance of other illuminators, the manuscripts of the Luçon workshop acquired by the Duke of Berry provide a chronological scaffold. In 1410 Jacques le Grand gave the Duke a copy of his *Livre des bonnes moeurs* (Fig. 671). As a New Year's gift the following year the Duke received the earliest illustrated copy of Boccaccio's *Cas des nobles hommes et femmes* (Figs. 69, 507, 509, 512). Around the same time the Luçon workshop illustrated other secular texts, including Virgil's *Eclogues* and *Georgics* (Holkham Hall ms. 307) (Figs. 227, 229, 237) and, *ca.* 1412, the *Térence des ducs* (Figs. 193, 210). Several workshops collaborated on the *Térence des ducs*, but the Luçon Master, who painted the frontispiece, was undoubtedly in charge. His workshop painted over half of the miniatures and other illuminators tried to conform to his style. Borrowings by the Luçon Master, on the other hand, give us valuable information about his models. Thus his workshop took a conical tree shaded on the underside from the Roman Texts Master, whose Virgil probably served as the model for the copy by the Luçon atelier (Figs. 226, 227, 230).

The latest miniatures by the master and his workshop are in the *De Lévis Hours* in Yale, illuminated *ca.* 1417 in collaboration with the Bedford workshop.

BIBLIOGRAPHY: Meiss, *Art Bull.*, 1956, p. 193; *idem*, *Late XIV Century*, 1967, pp. 298, 358 f.; *idem*, *De Lévis Hours*, 1972, pp. 15–17.

Baltimore, WALTERS ART GALLERY, ms. 231
Book of Hours, Use of Paris. 167 fols.; 180×130 mm.
All miniatures. *Ca.* 1405.

BIBLIOGRAPHY: De Ricci, *Census*, I, 1935, p. 791 no. 214; Baltimore, Walters (Miner), 1949, p. 32 no. 84, pl. XXXVII; Panofsky, *Netherlandish Painting*, 1953, I, p. 380 n. 484; Meiss, *Art Bull.*, 1956, p. 193 n. 23; Baltimore, Walters, *International Style* (Miner), 1962, p. 50 f., pl. LV; Meiss, *Late XIV Century*, 1967, pp. 358, 394 n. 66; Cleveland, Mus. of Art (Wixom), 1967, pp. 260, 377; Meiss, *De Lévis Hours*, 1972, p. 16, fig. 28.

Baltimore, WALTERS ART GALLERY, ms. 232
Book of Hours, Use of Paris. 198 fols.; 170×135 mm.
Fols. 68v, 73, 85v, 105, 124v, 132v. *Ca.* 1407.
For miniatures related to the Berry's Cleres Femmes workshop see this Catalogue.

BIBLIOGRAPHY: De Ricci, *Census*, I, 1935, p. 786 n. 181; Baltimore, Walters (Miner), 1949, p. 32 no. 85, pl. XXXVII; Meiss, *Art Bull.*, 1956, p. 193 n. 23; Baltimore, Walters, *International Style* (Miner), 1962, p. 52 no. 48, pl. LV; Meiss, *Late XIV Century*, 1967, pp. 355, 358.

Barcelona, BIBL. CENTRAL, ms. 1850
Book of Hours. Written in 1401.
See Catalogue of Manuscripts.

Berlin, STAATSBIBL., Theol. lat. qu. 7
(lost during World War II)
Book of Hours. 170 fols.; 130/160×110 mm.
Fols. 35v, 46v, 52v, 56v, 60v, 64v, 70v, 76. *Ca.* 1410–1412.
For miniatures by the workshop of the Master of Berry's Cleres Femmes see this Catalogue.

BIBLIOGRAPHY: Berlin, Staatsbibl., Rose, *Lateinischen Handschriften*, XIII, 1903, p. 737 f. no. 729; Berlin, Staatsbibl., *Schöne Handschriften*, 1931, p. 114 f. no. 66, pl. opp. p. 112; Meiss, *Art Bull.*, 1956, p. 193 n. 23; *idem*, *Late XIV Century*, 1967, p. 358.

Bern, COLL. L. V. RANDALL
Miniature of the *Coronation of the Virgin*.

BIBLIOGRAPHY: Vienna, Kunsthist. Mus., *Katalog*, 1962, p. 180 no. 126; Meiss, *Late XIV Century*, 1967, p. 359.

Brussels, BIBL. ROYALE, ms. 9089–9090
Aristotle, *Politiques* and *Ethiques* (trans. by Nicole Oresme). 479 fols.; 375×290 mm.
Burgundian inventory of 1420.
All miniatures. *Ca.* 1400–1402.
BIBLIOGRAPHY: Doutrepont, *Inventaire*, 1906, p. 150 f. no. 223; Brussels, Bibl. roy., Gaspar and Lyna, I, 1937, pp. 440–442 no. 185, pl. CIII; Meiss, *Art Bull.*, 1956, p. 193; *idem, Late XIV Century*, 1967, p. 358.

Cambridge, England, FITZWILLIAM MUSEUM, Founders 59
Book of Hours, Use of Paris. 238 fols.; 140×96 mm.
All miniatures. *Ca.* 1405–1410.
BIBLIOGRAPHY: Cambridge, Fitzwilliam Museum (Wormald and Giles), 1966, no. 69, pl. 18; Meiss, *Late XIV Century*, 1967, p. 358.

Cambridge, England, FITZWILLIAM MUSEUM, McClean 80
Book of Hours, Use of Paris. 200 fols.; 201×139 mm.
All miniatures. *Ca.* 1410–1412.
BIBLIOGRAPHY: Cambridge, Fitzwilliam Museum (James), 1912, pp. 164–166; Cambridge, Fitzwilliam Museum (Wormald and Giles), 1966, no. 71; Meiss, *Late XIV Century*, 1967, p. 358; *idem, De Lévis Hours*, 1972, p. 15 n. 31.

Cambridge, Mass., HARVARD UNIVERSITY, HOUGHTON LIBRARY, Richardson 45
Book of Hours. 169 fols.; 191×136 mm.
All miniatures. *Ca.* 1405.
BIBLIOGRAPHY: London, Sotheby, Dec. 6, 1937, lot 959; Baltimore, Walters (Miner), 1949, p. 32 no. 84; Cambridge, Harvard University, 1955, p. 17 no. 42, pl. 28; Meiss, *Art Bull.*, 1956, p. 193 n. 23; *idem, Late XIV Century*, 1967, p. 358.

Frankfurt-am-Main, MUSEUM FÜR KUNSTHANDWERK, Linel, L. M. 19
Book of Hours, Use of Paris. 131 fols.; 211×152 mm.
All miniatures.
BIBLIOGRAPHY: Swarzenski and Schilling, *Handschriften*, 1929, p. 119, pls. 51, 52; Meiss, *Late XIV Century*, 1967, p. 358.

Geneva, BIBL. PUBLIQUE ET UNIVERSITAIRE, fr. 190
Boccaccio, *Cas des nobles hommes et femmes*. Shortly before January, 1411.
See Catalogue of Manuscripts.

Holkham Hall (Norfolk), COLL. OF THE EARL OF LEICESTER, ms. 307
Virgil, *Eclogues* and *Georgics*.
See Catalogue of Manuscripts.

Leningrad, STATE LIBRARY, Fr. Q.v.XIV, 3
Gerbert de Montreuil, *Roman de la violette* and Nicole de Margival, *Dit de la Panthère d'amors*. 65 fols.; 290×210 mm.
Burgundian inventory of 1420.
This manuscript together with the *Roman d'Athis et Prophilias* (Leningrad, State Library, ms. fr. Q.v.XIV, 4) belonged to Jean sans Peur. Both manuscripts are the same size. Their identity with an item in the Burgundian inventory of 1420 (Doutrepont, *Inventaire*, 1906, p. 67 no. 107) has not been recognized because the librarian who recorded the manuscripts confused the order of the texts. According to the incipits cited in the inventory for the second and last folios the order should have been *Violette*, *Panthère*, and *Athis and Prophilias*. The first words on the second folio of the Leningrad *Violette* are "A lez bellemāt." The beginning of the last folio of the Leningrad *Athis* is "Puis que mort est." For the *Athis* in Leningrad see the Catalogue, Master of the Coronation of the Virgin, Leningrad.
BIBLIOGRAPHY: Leningrad (Saint-Pétersbourg), Bertrand, 1873, p. 547 n. 3D; Doutrepont, *Inventaire*, 1906, p. 67 no. 107; Delisle, *Charles V*, 1907, II, p. 315 f.; Leningrad (Saint-Pétersbourg), Laborde, 1936, pp. 53–55 no. 54, pl. XXVI; Meiss, *Art Bull.*, 1956, p. 193 n. 23; *idem, Late XIV Century*, 1967, pp. 317, 358.

London, BRIT. MUS., Add. 29433
Book of Hours, Use of Paris. 219 fols.; 223×160 mm.
Fols. 202v, 205, 211v, 212. *Ca.* 1406–1407.
BIBLIOGRAPHY: London, Brit. Mus., *Reproductions*, I, 1907, p. 11, pl. XXVI; London, Brit. Mus., *Schools of Illumination*, VI, 1930, p. 8, pl. VIIa; London, Brit. Mus., Millar, 1933, p. 34 no. 46, pl. XLVI; Pächt, *Mary of Burgundy* [1948], p. 52 n. 19; Meiss, *Art Bull.*, 1956, pp. 193 n. 23, 194; *idem, Late XIV Century*, 1967, index.

London, BRIT. MUS., Yates Thompson 37
Book of Hours, Use of Bourges. 198 fols.; 190×140 mm.
Fols. 53v–62. Fols. 66, 72. *Ca.* 1405–1410.
BIBLIOGRAPHY: London, Thompson Collection (Thompson), 1912, pp. 141–145 no. CVI; London, Thompson Collection, *Illustrations*, VII, 1918, p. 5 f., pls. XVI–XX; Meiss, *Florence and Siena*, 1951, p. 142, fig. 150; *idem, Art Bull.*, 1956, pp. 192, 193 n. 23; Pächt, *Burl.*

Mag., 1956, p. 150 n. 18; Meiss, *Late XIV Century*, 1967, index, figs. 263–267, 269, 271, 272, 276; *idem, Boucicaut Master*, 1968, p. 15.

Montecassino, ABBEY
Book of Hours.
Photographs in London, Courtauld Institute, library.

New Haven, YALE UNIVERSITY, BEINECKE LIBRARY, ms. 400
Book of Hours (*De Lévis Hours*). *Ca.* 1417.
See Catalogue of Manuscripts.

New York, PIERPONT MORGAN LIBRARY, M. 743
Book of Hours, Use of Poitiers. 172 fols.; 180×120 mm.
All miniatures except those on fols. 17v and 20. *Ca.* 1410–1415.
BIBLIOGRAPHY: New York, Pierpont Morgan Library, 1930, p. 64 f.; De Ricci, *Census*, II, 1937, p. 1494 no. 743; New York, Pierpont Morgan Library, *Catalogue*, 1939, p. 13 no. 41; Panofsky, *Netherlandish Painting*, 1953, I, p. 380 n. 48[4]; Meiss, *Art Bull.*, 1956, p. 193 n. 23; *idem, Late XIV Century*, 1967, pp. 359, 394 n. 66.

Paris, BIBL. DE L'ARSENAL, ms. 664
Térence des ducs. Ca. 1412.
See Catalogue of Manuscripts.

Paris, BIBL. MAZARINE, ms. 491
Book of Hours. 261 fols.; 137×95 mm.
All miniatures.
BIBLIOGRAPHY: Paris, Mazarine, Molinier, I, 1885, p. 188 f. no. 491; Mâle, 1904, p. 53; Panofsky, *Netherlandish Painting*, 1953, I, p. 411 n. 131[4]; Meiss, *Art Bull.*, 1956, p. 193; *idem, Late XIV Century*, 1967, p. 359.

Paris, BIBL. NAT., fr. 208
Aristotle, *Politiques* and *Ethiques* (trans. by Nicole Oresme). 383 fols.; 346×272 mm.
All miniatures. *Ca.* 1408–1410.
BIBLIOGRAPHY: Meiss, *Art Bull.*, 1956, p. 193 n. 23; Menut, 1957, p. 803 f.; Meiss, *Late XIV Century*, 1967, p. 359.

Paris, BIBL. NAT., fr. 264
Titus Livius, *Histoire romaine* (trans. by Pierre Bersuire). 280 fols.; 376×305 mm. The illumination of fr. 265 and fr. 266, the Second and Third Decades, remained unfinished. The scribe Raoul Taingui signed his name in fr. 265, fol. 7 and on fol. 208 in fr. 266, where his name also appears in verses.
Fols. 42, 91v, 162v, 185v. *Ca.* 1410.
For miniatures by the Cité des Dames workshop see this Catalogue.

Paris, BIBL. NAT., fr. 926
St. Bonaventura, *L'aiguillon d'amour divin.* Written in 1406.
See Catalogue of Manuscripts.

Paris, BIBL. NAT., fr. 1023
Jacques Le Grand, *Le livre des bonnes moeurs.* Shortly before 1410.
See Catalogue of Manuscripts.

Paris, BIBL. NAT., lat. 1082
Psalter and Hours, Use of Ste-Chapelle, Paris. 141 fols.; 220×155 mm.
All miniatures. *Ca.* 1400.
BIBLIOGRAPHY: Leroquais, *Livres d'heures*, 1927, I, p. 61 f. no. 18; Paris, Bibl. nat. (Porcher), 1955, p. 63 no. 129; Meiss, *Art Bull.*, 1956, p. 193; *idem, Late XIV Century*, 1967, p. 359.

Paris, BIBL. NAT., lat. 6147
Valerius Maximus, *Facta et dicta memorabilia.* 238 fols.; 220×160 mm.
Only one miniature in manuscript (fol. 2). *Ca.* 1408. (Called to our attention with correct attribution by François Avril.)

Paris, BIBL. NAT., lat. 8886
Missal and Pontifical of Etienne Loypeau. *Ca.* 1405–1407.
See Catalogue of Manuscripts.

Paris, BIBL. NAT., lat. 16785
Bersuire, *Reductorium morale.* Vol. I. 292 fols.; 440×304 mm.
Ms. has frontispiece only. *Ca.* 1405–1410. (Called to our attention with correct attribution by François Avril.)

Philadelphia, FREE LIBRARY, Widener no. 4
Book of Hours. 206 fols.; 210×150 mm.
All miniatures except calendar scenes.
For miniatures related to the Egerton workshop see this Catalogue.
BIBLIOGRAPHY: Quaile, *Illuminated Manuscripts*, 1897, pp. 135–139, pls. II, III; De Ricci, *Census*, II, 1937, p. 2116 no. 4; Baltimore, Walters, *International Style* (Miner), 1962, p. 51; Meiss, *Late XIV Century*, 1967, p. 358 f.; *idem, De Lévis Hours*, 1972, p. 16, fig. 29.

Philadelphia, MUS. OF ART, ms. 45–65–5
Book of Hours. 298 fols.; 205×137 mm. Manuscript is paginated.
Pages 116–265. *Ca.* 1412.
For miniatures by the Bedford Trend see this Catalogue.
BIBLIOGRAPHY: see Bedford.

Vienna, NATIONALBIBL., ms. Inc. 4 B 17
Initials, probably from a Book of Hours, pasted into Nicolò dei Manerbi's *Le leggende de' santi.*
Fols. 4, 113v, 116, 134v, 154v.
BIBLIOGRAPHY: Vienna, Nationalbibl. (Hermann), 1938, pp. 18–20 no. 2, pl. II.

WHEREABOUTS UNKNOWN (London, Sotheby & Co., Northwick Sale, May 21, 1928, lot 17)
Book of Hours, Use of Paris. 190×133 mm.
BIBLIOGRAPHY: London, Sotheby, May 21, 1928, lot 17, p. 18, pl. opp. p. 18; Meiss, *Late XIV Century*, 1967, p. 358.

WHEREABOUTS UNKNOWN (London, Sotheby & Co., Springel Sale, June 28, 1962, lot 49)
Pentecost. Single miniature. 185×135 mm.
BIBLIOGRAPHY: London, Sotheby, June 28, 1962, lot 49; Meiss, *Late XIV Century*, 1967, p. 358.

WHEREABOUTS UNKNOWN (formerly New York, Mr. Jacob Hirsch)
Miniature of the *Ark of the Covenant.*
BIBLIOGRAPHY: Meiss, *Late XIV Century*, 1967, p. 359.

WHEREABOUTS UNKNOWN
Book of Hours (Delaissé, 1950). 193 fols.; 190×135 mm.
Fol. 25. *Ca.* 1405.
For miniatures by the Virgil workshop see this Catalogue.
BIBLIOGRAPHY: see Virgil.

RELATED MANUSCRIPTS

Baltimore, WALTERS ART GALLERY, ms. 100
Book of Hours, Use of Paris. 234 fols.; 172×125 mm.
BIBLIOGRAPHY: Meiss, *Art Bull.*, 1956, p. 193 n. 23; Baltimore, Walters, *International Style* (Miner), 1962, p. 49 f. no. 46, pl. L; Meiss, *Late XIV Century*, 1967, pp. 184, 186, 359, fig. 650.

Baltimore, WALTERS ART GALLERY, ms. 103
Book of Hours. 148 fols.; 197×140 mm. *Ca.* 1405.
BIBLIOGRAPHY: De Ricci, *Census*, I, 1935, p. 785 no. 178; Baltimore, Walters (Miner), 1949, p. 34 no. 91; Meiss, *Art Bull.*, 1956, p. 192 n. 18; *idem, Late XIV Century*, 1967, p. 359.

Bourges, MUSEE DE BERRY
Hours of Anne de Mathefelon. 166 fols.; 207×151 mm. *Ca.* 1415.
BIBLIOGRAPHY: Mater, 1902, pp. 145–159; Meiss, *Art Bull.*, 1956, p. 193 n. 23; *idem, Late XIV Century*, 1967, p. 359.

Brussels, BIBL. ROYALE, ms. 9226
Jacobus de Voragine, *Légende dorée* (trans. by Jean de Vignay). 312 fols.; 396×298 mm.
BIBLIOGRAPHY: Brussels, Bibl. roy., Gaspar and Lyna, II, 1947, pp. 15–18 no. 205, pl. CXVIII; Meiss, *Art Bull.*, 1956, p. 193 n. 23; *idem, Late XIV Century*, 1967, p. 359.

Cambrai, BIBL. MUNICIPALE, ms. 97 (98)
Breviary, Use of Cambrai. 375 fols.; 220×156 mm.
Written between 1400 and 1402 by Jean Petit de Bretagne for Raoul Leprêtre, canon of Cambrai and archdeacon of Hainaut. Leprêtre gave the manuscript to Pierre d'Ailly.
BIBLIOGRAPHY: Leroquais, *Bréviaires*, I, 1934, pp. 186–189; Meiss, *Late XIV Century*, 1967, p. 359.

Milan, BIBL. AMBROSIANA, I. 7. Sup.
Book of Hours. 191 fols.; 187×130 mm.
Some miniatures.
For miniatures by the Troyes workshop see this Catalogue.
BIBLIOGRAPHY: Meiss, *Late XIV Century*, 1967, p. 359; Milan, Bibl. Ambrosiana, Cipriani, 1968, p. 71, pl. XVI.

Milan, BIBL. AMBROSIANA, L. 58. Sup.
Book of Hours.
BIBLIOGRAPHY: Meiss, *Late XIV Century*, 1967, p. 359.

Paris, BIBL. NAT., nouv. acq. lat. 3108
Book of Hours, Use of Paris. 168 fols.; 195×140 mm.
All miniatures by follower. *Ca.* 1405. Some repainting, especially in the faces, on fols. 19, 52v, 107, 151.
BIBLIOGRAPHY: Paris, Bibl. nat., Porcher, *Boisrouvray*, 1961, p. 65 f. no. 13, pls. 37, 38; Meiss, *Late XIV Century*, 1967, p. 359.

MASTER OF THE CHANTILLY MEDALLIONS

See the section on this illuminator in the text.

Chantilly, MUSEE CONDE, ms. 28 (1378)
Histoire extraite de la Bible and *Apocalypse*. *Ca.* 1415.
See Catalogue of Manuscripts.

Paris, BIBL. NAT., fr. 414
(Figs. 437, 809, 892)
Jacobus de Voragine, *Légende dorée* (trans. by Jean de Vignay). 419 fols.; 347×275 mm. Colophon gives date of September, 1404 for the text.
All miniatures except fol. 1. *Ca.* 1407.
For the miniature by the Virgil Master see this Catalogue.
BIBLIOGRAPHY: Bourges, Musées [1951], p. 34 no. 11, pl. IX; Porcher, *Belles Heures*, 1953, pp. 8–10, 50, fig. 2; Paris, Bibl. nat. (Porcher), 1955, p. 91 no. 187; Porcher, *Enluminure*, 1959, p. 61, fig. 65; *idem*, in *Enciclopedia dell' arte*, VIII, p. 619 ff.; Meiss, *Burl. Mag.*, 1963, p. 51; *idem*, *Late XIV Century*, 1967, p. 360; Cleveland, Mus. of Art (Wixom), 1967, p. 379.

RELATED MANUSCRIPTS

Oxford, BODLEIAN LIBRARY, Douce 371
(Fig. 810)
Guillaume de Lorris and Jean de Meun, *Roman de la rose*. 142 fols.; 400×300 mm.
All miniatures. *Ca.* 1410.
BIBLIOGRAPHY: Saxl and Meier, *Verzeichnis*, III, 1953, pt. 1, pp. 380–382, pt. 2, pl. L; Pächt and Alexander, *Bodleian Manuscripts*, 1966, p. 49 no. 632, pl. XLVIII.

THE OROSIUS MASTER

The Orosius Master was named in 1968 after his important miniatures in a *Histoire ancienne*, based in part on the history of Orosius and sometimes entitled *Histoires d'Orose*. His earliest work appears to be the series of historiated initials in a Breviary produced for Pope Benedict XIII, 1394–1409 (Fig. 515). The script is Italian and the manuscript may have been written and illuminated in Avignon. The style of the initials, which indicates a date immediately after the election of the pope in 1394, is so deeply Bohemian that the illuminator must have been trained in Prague, and he may actually have been a Bohemian artist who went to Avignon and then to Paris, where he was certainly established from about 1400 to 1418. The sources of his very plastic, curling acanthus leaves and his squat, rounded figures are not the new Bohemian styles of the later 'eighties and 'nineties that appeared in the *Willehalm* (Schmidt in *Gotik in Böhmen*, 1969, figs. 170, 172, 174) or in the Bible of King Wenzel (*ibid.*, figs. 173, 175, 176, 177), but the older art of the famous manuscripts of Johann von Neumarkt (*Late XIV Century*, fig. 551, *Boucicaut Master*, fig. 465), elements of which may still be seen in the Morgan Bible dated 1391 (Fig. 516).

The *Histoire ancienne* or Orosius was bought by Jean de Berry in 1402 from Bureau de Dampmartin (Fig. 274). The vivid cubic spaces, stocky figures, doughy drapery and rocks *soufflés* are still reminiscent of Bohemian painting, but the illuminator has developed a distinctive color: violet, pale yellow, blue and blue-green, and burnt orange. Value variations are very subtly graduated, and the planes turn with exceptional smoothness. The illuminator's usual enthusiasm for volume and space has in this instance been increased by the fact that he and his assistants were copying Neapolitan illustrations of the same text made for the Anjou, perhaps King Robert (died 1343) (Fig. 275). This manuscript, too, now Brit. Mus. Royal 20 D I, was acquired by Jean de Berry *ca.* 1402, in other words, about the same time he bought the French copy of it.

The Duke of Berry continued to collect other manuscripts illuminated by the Orosius Master. In 1404 Nicolas Viaut gave him a Boethius (lat. 9321), probably illustrated towards 1400, which the Duke in turn presented to the Ste-Chapelle. The Orosius Master specialized in classical texts and works on ancient history and he was evidently favored by scholars with humanist interests. Martin Gouge asked him to undertake a novel enterprise: an extensive pictorial cycle for a Roman text that was neither translated into French nor glossed. The workshop painted the majority of the miniatures in the *Comedies* of Terence that Gouge gave to Berry as a present at New Year 1408 (Figs. 163, 183, 185, 191, 197, 202). Shortly afterwards the Orosius Master and his assistants illustrated the first five books of St. Augustine's *Cité de Dieu* (Figs. 218, 277, 665). About 1412 the workshop participated in the illustration of a second Terence, collaborating with other illuminators from the Luçon and Cité des Dames workshops and in the Bedford Trend (Figs. 63, 164). This Terence, which belonged to the Dauphin Louis, Duke of Guyenne, passed to Berry after the Dauphin's death in 1415.

A splendid Breviary was illuminated for the Dauphin Louis about 1414 by the Orosius Master with the Bedford Master and the Boucicaut Master. Influenced by these and other painters the Orosius Master strove in his late work for a more vibrant luminosity, abandoning his finely graded planes for an open, *pointilliste* brushwork.

The latest work by the master we know, of about 1418, was left unfinished. It may be found in a little-known Sallust in a private collection. The miniatures include three fascinating maps (Figs. 4, 734, 737, 781).
BIBLIOGRAPHY: Meiss, *Boucicaut Master*, 1968, p. 142.

Châteauroux, BIBL. MUNICIPALE, ms. 2
Breviary, Use of Paris (summer section only). 454 fols.; 280×195 mm.
On fol. 430 arms of the Dauphin: very probably Louis, duc de Guyenne, who died in 1415 at the age of 18.
Fols. 91, 91v, 103, 218v, 223v, 242–246, 250v, 255–257, 259, 260, 266v–269v, 298v–313v, 318v–321v, 330v–337v, 342v–343v, 361, 363, 363v, 370, 378v, 381, 384, 385, 395v–401, 410–452v plus some miniatures in the calendar. *Ca.* 1414.
For miniatures by the Bedford workshop see this Catalogue. For the Boucicaut miniatures see Meiss, *Boucicaut Master*, 1968, pp. 81–85 (Catalogue).
BIBLIOGRAPHY: see Bedford.

Geneva, BIBL. PUBLIQUE ET UNIVERSITAIRE, fr. 77
Titus Livius, *Histoire romaine* (trans. by Pierre Bersuire). 450 fols.; 450×315 mm. Belonged to Jean de Berry (signature of Berry and inscription of Flamel).
Fol. 46v. *Ca.* 1405.
For miniatures by the workshop of the Master of Berry's Cleres Femmes see this Catalogue.
BIBLIOGRAPHY: see Berry's Cleres Femmes.

Paris, BIBL. DE L'ARSENAL, ms. 664
Térence des ducs. Ca. 1412.
See Catalogue of Manuscripts.

Paris, BIBL. NAT., fr. 301 (Fig. 274)
Paulus Orosius, *Histoire ancienne*. 294 fols.; 375×290 mm.
Manuscript illuminated shortly before purchase by Jean de Berry from Bureau de Dampmartin in April, 1402 (Inventory of 1413, no. 912; see Avril, 1969 (1970), p. 308). The miniatures are based on a cycle in a Neapolitan manuscript of the same text, Brit. Mus., Royal 20 D I, likewise acquired by Jean de Berry.
Fols. 90v–96v, 97v, 104v, 145–160v, 170v–176v, 185v–192v, 202v–208v.
BIBLIOGRAPHY: Meyer, 1885, pp. 63, 67; Paris, Bibl. nat. (Porcher), 1955, p. 74 no. 148; Meiss, *Late XIV Century*, 1967, p. 318; *idem*, *Boucicaut Master*, 1968, pp. 82, 142; Avril, 1969 (1970), pp. 305–309, pl. x.

Paris, BIBL. NAT., lat. 7907 A
Terence, *Comedies*. Just before 1408.
See Catalogue of Manuscripts.

Paris, BIBL. NAT., lat. 9321
Boethius, *De Consolatione*. 250 fols.; 392×280 mm.
Presented to Jean de Berry in 1404 by Nicolas Viaut and then given by the Duke to his Ste-Chapelle (list of 1404 and ex libris).
One miniature remaining (fol. 157) and diagrams. *Ca.* 1400.
BIBLIOGRAPHY: Guiffrey, *Inventaires*, I, 1894, p. CLXVII no. 32; Delisle, *Charles V*, 1907, II, p. 249 no. 158; Meiss, *Late XIV Century*, 1967, p. 316; *idem*, *Boucicaut Master*, 1968, p. 142.

Philadelphia, MUSEUM OF ART, ms. 45-65-1
St. Augustine, *La Cité de Dieu*. *Ca.* 1408–1410.
See Catalogue of Manuscripts.

Vienna, NATIONALBIBL., ms. 1254 (Fig. 515)
Breviary of Benedict XIII (Pedro de Luna). 704 fols.; 260×177 mm.
All illumination. *Ca.* 1395 (certainly after 1394, when Benedict XIII was elected).

BIBLIOGRAPHY: Vienna, Nationalbibl. (Hermann), 1938, pp. 1–18 no. 1, pls. I, II; Vienna, Kunsthist. Mus., *Katalog*, 1962, p. 183 no. 132; Meiss, *Boucicaut Master*, 1968, p. 142.

PRIVATE COLLECTION

(Figs. 4, 734, 737, 781)

Sallust, *Catilinarius*, *De Jugurtino*. Manuscript not foliated; 320×230 mm.

Miniatures begun but left unfinished *ca.* 1418. Workshop of Colombe executed remaining miniatures.

BIBLIOGRAPHY: Gnoli, *Piante inedite*, 1941, pp. 3–7, pls. 1, 4; Frutaz, *Piante*, 1962, pl. 150.

RELATED MANUSCRIPTS

The Hague, KON. BIBL., ms. 72 A 22

St. Augustine, *La Cité de Dieu* (trans. by Raoul de Praelles). Vol. I. 338 fols.; 425×325 mm.

Fols. 1–76v, 176, 234, 294v, 312 by follower and his assistant.

BIBLIOGRAPHY: Laborde, *Cité de Dieu*, 1909, I, pp. 271–274 no. 17, pl. XV; The Hague, Kon. Bibl., Byvanck, 1924, p. 30 f. no. 10, pls. XIII–XIV; Meiss, *Art Bull.*, 1956, p. 195 n. 30; *idem*, *Late XIV Century*, 1967, p. 357.

London, BRIT. MUS., Burney 257

Statius, *Thebais et Achilleis*. 248 fols.; 285×192 mm.

Fols. 226v–239v. *Ca.* 1405.

For miniatures by the Cité des Dames and Virgil workshops see this Catalogue.

BIBLIOGRAPHY: see Cité des Dames.

MASTER OF THE PAREMENT DE NARBONNE

Paris, Bibliothèque nationale	nouv. acq. lat. 3093	*Très Belles Heures de Notre-Dame*
Paris, Musée du Louvre		*Parement de Narbonne*
Paris, Musée du Louvre, Cabinet des Dessins		2 folios from the *Très Belles Heures de Notre-Dame*
Turin, Biblioteca nazionale (formerly)	"*Heures de Turin*"	*Très Belles Heures de Notre-Dame*
Turin, Museo Civico	"*Heures de Milan*"	*TBHND*

RELATED MANUSCRIPT

London, British Museum	Egerton 1070	Book of Hours

BIBLIOGRAPHY: Hulin de Loo, *Heures de Milan*, 1911, pp. 11–16; Durrieu, *Très Belles Heures de Notre-Dame*, 1922, pp. 59–67; Panofsky, *Netherlandish Painting*, 1953, pp. 41 f., 44–46; Meiss, *Art Bull.*, 1956, p. 190; Paris, Louvre (Sterling and Adhémar), 1965, p. 1 no. 2; Meiss, *Late XIV Century*, 1967, pp. 100 ff., 113 ff.

PASSION MASTER

London, British Museum	Yates Thompson 27	*Heures de Yolande de Flandre*
Paris, Bibliothèque nationale	lat. 1052	*Bréviaire de Charles V*
	lat. 18014	*Petites Heures* of Jean de Berry

ADDITIONS PROPOSED BY FRANÇOIS AVRIL

London, British Museum	Yates Thompson 34	Epistolary
Lyon, Bibliothèque	ms. 5122	Missal
New York, Metropolitan Museum of Art, the Cloisters		Psalter of Bonne de Luxembourg
Paris, Bibliothèque de l'Arsenal	ms. 161	Evangeliary
	ms. 5212	*Bible historiale*
Paris, Bibliothèque nationale	nouv. acq. lat. 3145	*Heures de Jeanne de Navarre*

ATTRIBUTIONS BY PÄCHT AND ALEXANDER

Cleveland, Museum of Art	Gotha Missal	Canon pages
Oxford, Bodleian Library	Auct. 7Q2.13	Canon pages from a Missal

BIBLIOGRAPHY: Panofsky, *Netherlandish Painting*, 1953, p. 44; Meiss, *Art Bull.*, 1956, p. 191; Morand, *Pucelle*, 1962, pp. 27, 41; Pächt and Alexander, *Bodleian Manuscripts*, 1966, p. 47 no. 608; Meiss, *Late XIV Century*, 1967, p. 159 ff.; Avril, *Revue de l'Art*, 1970, pp. 37–48; *idem*, *Jahrbuch der Hamburger Kunstsammlungen*, 1970, pp. 45–76.

MASTER OF THE ROHAN HOURS

See the chapter on this painter and his workshop.

BIBLIOGRAPHY: Mâle, 1904, p. 52 f.; Durrieu, *Rev. de l'art a. et m.*, 1912, pp. 81–98, 161–183; Heimann, 1932, p. 1 ff.; Meiss, 1935, pp. 65–75; Heimann, 1937, p. 83 f.; Panofsky, in *Studies Porter*, 1939, II, pp. 479–499; Porcher, 1945, pp. 1–6; Panofsky, 1949, pp. 163–182; Ring, *French Painting* [1949], pp. 202–204 nos. 86–90; "Meister der *Grandes Heures de Rohan*," in Thieme-Becker, XXXVII, 1950, pp. 124–126; Paris, Bibl. nat. (Porcher), 1955, pp. 82 no. 168, 84 f. nos. 172–176, 106–112 nos. 225–240; Porcher, *Rohan Hours*, 1959.

Amiens, BIBL. MUNICIPALE, ms. Lescalopier 17
Book of Hours, Use of Troyes. 255 fols.; 100×70 mm.
All miniatures by workshop.
BIBLIOGRAPHY: Paris, Bibl. nat. (Porcher), 1955, p. 107 f. no. 230.

Baltimore, WALTERS ART GALLERY, ms. 741
Book of Hours, Use of Troyes. 169 fols.; 180×130 mm.
All miniatures by workshop.
BIBLIOGRAPHY: De Ricci, *Supplement*, 1962, p. 197 f. no. 563; Meiss, *Boucicaut Master*, 1968, p. 32, fig. 159; Miner, 1968–1969, pp. 78–81, figs. 27, 28.

Braunschweig, HERZOG ANTON ULRICH MUSEUM (Fig. 805)
Drawing on vellum. *Miracle of Bethesda.* 150×220 mm.
BIBLIOGRAPHY: Meiss, 1935, pp. 65–75; Panofsky, in *Studies Porter*, 1939, II, p. 479 n. 2; Ring, *French Painting* [1949], p. 204 no. 90, pl. 36; Meiss, *Late XIV Century*, 1967, p. 279; *idem*, *Boucicaut Master*, 1968, p. 40, fig. 485.

Cambridge, FITZWILLIAM MUSEUM, ms. 62
Book of Hours, Use of Paris. *Ca.* 1417–1418.
See Catalogue of Manuscripts.

Cambridge, U.S.A., HARVARD COLLEGE, HOUGHTON LIBRARY, Richardson ms. 42
Book of Hours (*De Buz Hours*), Use of Paris.
See Catalogue of Manuscripts.

Chantilly, MUSEE CONDE, ms. 67 (1371)
Book of Hours, Use of Troyes. 172 fols.; 220×153 mm.
All miniatures by workshop.
BIBLIOGRAPHY: Chantilly, Musée Condé, *Cabinet*, I, 1900, p. 72 f. no. 67; Chantilly (Meurgey), 1930, pp. 58 f. no. 29, pl. XXXVIII; Heimann, 1932, p. 60, fig. 41; Porcher, *Rohan Hours*, 1959, p. 32 n. 11.

Chicago (Glencoe), COLL. OF MRS. J. SPITZ
Book of Hours, Use of Troyes.
All miniatures by workshop.

Chillicothe (Ohio),
ROSS COUNTY ART MUSEUM
Book of Hours (formerly McKell Collection), Use of Troyes.
All miniatures by workshop.
BIBLIOGRAPHY: Porcher, *Rohan Hours*, 1959, p. 32 n. 11.

Dresden, SÄCHSISCHE LANDESBIBL., ms. Oc. 61 (Fig. 840)
Gaston Phébus, *Livre de la chasse*; Jean de Vignay, *Jeu des échecs moralisé*; *Ordre de chevalerie*. 152 fols.; 340×270 mm.
Arms of the dauphin in the lower border of the frontispiece may indicate ownership of Louis, duc de Guyenne who married Marguerite de Bourgogne. Burgundian inventory of 1420.
Badly damaged during World War II.
Fol. 1 and others by workshop.
For miniatures in the Bedford Trend see this Catalogue.
BIBLIOGRAPHY: Werth, *Jagdlehrbücher*, 1889, pp. 71–74; Dresden, Sächsische Landesbibl., Schmidt, III, 1906, p. 124 f.; Doutrepont, *Inventaire*, 1906, p. 163 f. no. 240; *idem*, *Littérature française*, 1909, p. 269; Paris, Bibl. nat. (Couderc) [1909], p. 20 f.; Germany, *Manuscrits français* (Olschki), 1932, pp. 17–19, pl. XVI, XVII; Porcher, *Rohan Hours*, 1959, p. 9.

Laon, MUSEE DE LAON (Figs. 806, 887)
The Angel of the Annunciation with Donor (inside face of hinged wing of an altarpiece). *Apostles and Prophets* (outside face). 95×103.5 cm.
The inside surface by the Rohan Master, the outside by the workshop.
BIBLIOGRAPHY: Ring, *French Painting* [1949], p. 204, no. 89, pls. 41–42; Panofsky, *Netherlandish Painting*, 1953, I, p. 389 f. n. 74[4]; Vienna, Kunsthist. Mus., *Katalog*, 1962, p. 118 no. 52.

London, BRIT. MUS., Harley 2934
Book of Hours, Use of Troyes. *Ca.* 1412.
See Catalogue of Manuscripts.

London, BRIT. MUS., Harley 2940
Book of Hours, Use of Paris. 183 fols.; 192×137 mm.
Fol. 175 by workshop. *Ca.* 1420.
For miniatures by the Boucicaut workshop see Meiss, *Boucicaut Master*, 1968, p. 96 (Catalogue).
BIBLIOGRAPHY: London, Brit. Mus., *Harleian Manuscripts*, II, 1808, p. 721 no. 2940; Durrieu, *Arts anciens de Flandre*, II [1906?], p. 18; *idem*, *Rev. de l'art a. et m.*, XX, 1906, p. 24; *idem*, *Rev. de l'art chrét.*, 1913, p. 310; London, Brit. Mus., *French Horae*, 1927; Meiss, *Boucicaut Master*, 1968, pp. 96, 147 n. 39, figs. 322, 323.

London, VICTORIA AND ALBERT MUSEUM, ms. A.L. 1647–1902 (Reid 5)
Book of Hours, Use of Troyes. 217 fols.; 178×128 mm.
All miniatures by workshop. Some repainting of the flesh.
BIBLIOGRAPHY: Panofsky, in *Studies Porter*, 1939, II, p. 479 n. 3; Ker, *British Libraries*, I, 1969, p. 379.

London, COLL. OF D. AND J. ZWEMMER (Figs. 839, 841)
Book of Hours, Use of Paris. 281 fols.; 210×153 mm.
Calendar scenes by workshop. *Ca.* 1415.
For the Boucicaut miniatures see Meiss, *Boucicaut Master*, 1968, pp. 99 f. (Catalogue).
BIBLIOGRAPHY: London, National Book League, *A Thousand Years of French Books*, London, 1948, p. 12 f.; Meiss, *Boucicaut Master*, 1968, pp. 28, 96, 99 f., 144 n. 33, 152 n. 9, figs. 120, 138, 239–244.

Lyon, BIBL., ms. 5140
Book of Hours, Use of Paris. 180 fols.; 250×175 mm.
Calendar by workshop. Other miniatures less closely related. *Ca.* 1425–1430.
BIBLIOGRAPHY: Porcher, *Belles Heures*, 1953, p. 25; Paris, Bibl. nat. (Porcher), 1955, p. 110 no. 234; Porcher, *Rohan Hours*, 1959, pp. 11, 32 n. 11; Cotton, 1965, p. 297 no. 68, fig. 60.

Oxford, BODLEIAN LIBRARY, Douce 202–3
Valerius Maximus. *Faits et dits mémorables* (trans. by Simon de Hesdin and Nicolas de Gonesse). 193 and 263 fols.; 375×285 mm.
202: 2, 118–189. 203: all miniatures by workshop. *Ca.* 1420.
For miniatures related to the Master of the Berry Apocalypse see this Catalogue.
BIBLIOGRAPHY: Pächt and Alexander, *Bodleian Manuscripts*, 1966, p. 50 no. 640; pl. L.

Paris, BIBL. DE L'ARSENAL, ms. 647
Second part in Princeton, University Library, Garrett ms. 48
Book of Hours, Use of Troyes. 121 fols.; 220×160 mm.
All miniatures by workshop.
BIBLIOGRAPHY: Mâle, 1904, p. 52 n. 2; Paris, Arsenal, Martin, I, 1885, p. 489 f. no. 647; Durrieu, *Rev. de l'art a. et m.*, 1912, p. 171 f., fig. 29; Heimann, 1932, pp. 10–12, fig. 11; Panofsky, in *Studies Porter*, 1939, II, pp. 479–499,

figs. 1–4; *idem*, *Netherlandish Painting*, 1953, I, pp. 380 n. 48[4], 408 n. 125[2].

Paris, BIBL. NAT., fr. 226 (Figs. 65, 828, 848, 851)
Boccaccio, *Cas des nobles hommes et femmes* (trans. by Laurent de Premierfait). 275 fols.; 430×308 mm.
Frontispiece on fol. 1 shows arms of Jean de Berry.
Fols. 14–140v by workshop. *Ca.* 1415.
For miniatures by the Bedford Trend and the Cité des Dames workshop see this Catalogue.
BIBLIOGRAPHY: see Bedford.

Paris, BIBL. NAT., fr. 2664
Froissart, *Chroniques*. Vol. II (fr. 2663 is Vol. I). 209 fols.; 370×285 mm. Given by Tanneguy Du Châtel to Jean de Derval.
All miniatures by workshop.
BIBLIOGRAPHY: see Berry Apocalypse: Related manuscripts, Paris, Bibl. nat., fr. 2663.

Paris, BIBL. NAT., fr. 15393–94
Guiart des Moulins, *Bible historiale*. 533 fols.; 445×326 mm.
Fr. 15393: 180; fr. 15394: 275–427v by workshop.
For miniatures related to the Berry Apocalypse workshop see this Catalogue.
BIBLIOGRAPHY: see Berry Apocalypse: Related manuscripts.

Paris, BIBL. NAT., fr. 16995
Boccaccio, *Cas des nobles hommes et femmes* (trans. by Laurent de Premierfait). 360 fols.; 375×282 mm.
Executed for Béraud III, count of Clermont and dauphin of Auvergne; chevalier from 1401–1426.
All miniatures by workshop.
BIBLIOGRAPHY: Paris, Bibl. nat. (Porcher), 1955, p. 107 no. 228; Porcher, *Rohan Hours*, 1959, p. 9; Bozzolo, 1968, p. 28 f.; Meiss, *Boucicaut Master*, 1968, p. 123.

Paris, BIBL. NAT., fr. 20320
Valerius Maximus, *Faits et dits mémorables* (trans. by Simon de Hesdin and Nicolas de Gonesse). 377 fols.; 420×320 mm.
Fols. 3, 14, 31v, 33, 67–374v by workshop.
For miniatures by the Bedford Trend and related to the Berry Apocalypse Master see this Catalogue.
BIBLIOGRAPHY: Durrieu, *Rev. de l'art a. et m.*, 1912, p. 172 f.; Heimann, 1932, pp. 1–3, fig. 2; Paris, Bibl. nat. (Porcher), 1955, pp. 84 f. no. 174; Porcher, *Rohan Hours*, 1959, p. 9.

Paris, BIBL. NAT., fr. 22531
Bartholomaeus Anglicus, *Le livre de la propriété des choses* (trans. by Jean Corbechon). 400 fols.; 370×295 mm.
Fols. 12, 14, 47v, 58v, 227v, 372, 393 by workshop.
For miniatures related to the Berry Apocalypse Master see this Catalogue.
BIBLIOGRAPHY: Mâle, 1904, p. 52 n. 2; Durrieu, *Rev. de l'art a. et m.*, 1912, p. 172 f.; Heimann, 1932, p. 1 n. 4; Paris, Bibl. nat. (Porcher), 1955, p. 84 no. 173; Porcher, *Rohan Hours*, 1959, p. 9.

Paris, BIBL. NAT., lat. 1156 A
Book of Hours, Use of Paris.
See Catalogue of Manuscripts.

Paris, BIBL. NAT., lat. 9471
Book of Hours, Use of Paris.
See Catalogue of Manuscripts.

Paris, BIBL. NAT., lat. 13262 (Fig. 849)
Book of Hours, Use of Paris. 184 fols.; 130×95 mm.
All miniatures by workshop except fols. 153 and 154, which were painted in the second quarter of the 15th century.
BIBLIOGRAPHY: Mâle, 1904, p. 52 n. 2; Durrieu, *Rev. de l'art a. et m.*, 1912, p. 172; Heimann, 1932, p. 16; Leroquais, *Livres d'heures*, 1927, II, pp. 47–49 no. 190; Paris, Bibl. nat. (Porcher), 1955, p. 109 no. 232.

Paris, BIBL. NAT., lat. 14245, fols. 157–196
Jacques le Grand, *Traité des vices et des vertus*. 388×282 mm.
Made for the abbey of St. Victor in Paris.
Fol. 158 by workshop.
For miniature related to the Berry Apocalypse Master see this Catalogue.
BIBLIOGRAPHY: Paris, Bibl. nat. (Porcher), 1955, p. 106 no. 225; Porcher, *Rohan Hours*, 1959, p. 9; Meiss, *Late XIV Century*, 1967, p. 354.

Paris, BIBL. SAINTE-GENEVIEVE, ms. 1278
Book of Hours, Use of Troyes. *Ca.* 1413–1415.
See Catalogue of Manuscripts.

Paris, MUSEE DES ARTS DECORATIFS, ms. Mosticker 40342
Book of Hours. 210×145 mm. Ms. not foliated.
All miniatures by workshop. (Called to our attention with correct attribution by Eleanor Spencer.)

Princeton, UNIVERSITY LIBRARY, Garrett ms. 48 (Figs. 847, 855, 856)
Book of Hours, Use of Troyes. Second part in Paris, Bibl. de l'Arsenal ms. 647. 105 fols.; 215×160 mm.

All miniatures by workshop.

BIBLIOGRAPHY: Panofsky, in *Studies Porter*, 1939, II, pp. 480–491; Baltimore, Walters (Miner), 1949, p. 36 f. no. 97, pl. XLII; Meiss, *Boucicaut Master*, 1968, p. 147 n. 35.

Stockholm, NATIONALMUSEUM, NMB 1906
Visitation. 178×120 mm.

Toronto, ROYAL ONTARIO MUSEUM,
Lee of Fareham Collection, University of Toronto
Book of Hours, Use of Rome.
See Catalogue of Manuscripts.

PRIVATE COLLECTION (formerly Martin le Roy Collection)
Book of Hours, Use of Angers.
See Catalogue of Manuscripts.

RELATED MANUSCRIPTS

Dublin, TRINITY COLLEGE, ms. K 4.27
Book of Hours.

Paris, BIBL. NAT., fr. 812
Boethius, *Consolacion de la philosophie; Jeu des échecs* (trans. by Jean de Vignay); Guillaume de Lorris and Jean de Meun, *Roman de la rose*; *Les dis moraux des philosophes* (trans. by Guillaume de Tignonville). 320 fols.; 300×255 mm.
Fols. 1, 76v by a mediocre illuminator, perhaps provincial, influenced by the Rohan workshop.
BIBLIOGRAPHY: Porcher, *Rohan Hours*, 1959, p. 9.

Paris, BIBL. NAT., fr. 2662
Froissart, *Chroniques*. 413 fols.; 363×285 mm.
BIBLIOGRAPHY: Paris, Bibl. nat. (Porcher), 1955, p. 106 f. no. 226.

Paris, BIBL. NAT., lat. 18026
Book of Hours. 249 fols.; 244×170 mm.
Belonged to Jean de Montauban after his marriage in 1432.
Miniatures by provincial follower.
BIBLIOGRAPHY: Leroquais, *Livres d'heures*, 1927, II, pp. 206–213; Heimann, 1932, p. 30, fig. 27; Porcher, *Belles Heures*, 1953, p. 25; Paris, Bibl. nat. (Porcher), 1955, p. 110 f. no. 236.

Toulouse, BIBL. MUNICIPALE, ms. 511
Froissart, *Chroniques*. 268 fols.; 420×300 mm.
BIBLIOGRAPHY: Valenciennes, *Froissart*, 1937, p. 41 f. no. 29, pl. XXII.

Vienna, NATIONALBIBL., ms. 2573
Livre du Roi Modus et de la Reine Ratio. 181 fols.; 310×217 mm.
Some miniatures including fol. 2v.
BIBLIOGRAPHY: Vienna, Nationalbibl. (Hermann), 1938, pp. 100–111, pls. XXVII–XXX; Nordenfalk, *Kung praktiks*, 1955, p. 93 f., figs. 6, 14, 22, 38–39; Porcher, *Rohan Hours*, 1959, p. 9; Vienna, Kunsthist. Mus., *Katalog*, 1962, p. 185 no. 137.

MANUSCRIPTS ERRONEOUSLY ASSOCIATED WITH THE ROHAN STYLE

Brussels, Bibl. royale, ms. 9004, fol. 1, *Bible historiale* (Panofsky, in *Studies Porter*, 1939, II, p. 479 no. 3); Paris, Bibl. nat., fr. 958, *Somme le roi* (Porcher in Paris, Bibl. nat., 1955, p. 112 no. 240); Paris, Bibl. nat., fr. 1302, *Livre du roi Modus* (Porcher in Paris, Bibl. nat., 1955, p. 82 no. 168); Paris, Bibl. nat., fr. 2675–76, Froissart, *Chroniques* (Porcher, *Rohan Hours*, 1959, p. 32 n. 4); Paris, Bibl. nat., lat. 1159, *Heures de Pierre II, duc de Bretagne* (Porcher in Paris, Bibl. nat., 1955, p. 111 no. 237); Paris, Bibl. nat. lat. 1369, *Heures d'Isabelle Stuart* (Porcher in Paris, Bibl. nat., 1955, p. 112 no. 239).

We have not seen the following manuscripts ascribed to the Rohan workshop by Porcher: Brussels, Bibl. royale, ms. II, 88; two Books of Hours in Cat. Boerner, November 28, 1912, London, Sotheby, June 28, 1948 lot 219; two copies of Froissart's *Chroniques* sold at London, Sotheby, December 6, 1954, lot 43 and Paris, Pierre Berès, Cat. 57, no. 8; Rennes, Bibl. municipale, ms. 34; Stonyhurst College, ms. 1.

MASTER OF THE ROMAN TEXTS

With assistants this interesting and rare painter illustrated manuscripts of two Roman texts, a Terence *ca.* 1408–1410, and a Virgil *ca.* 1411. For these cycles see the chapters on the manuscripts of these two authors.

Lyon, BIBL., ms. 27
Virgil, *Eclogues*, *Georgics* and *Aeneid*. *Ca.* 1411.
See Catalogue of Manuscripts.

Paris, BIBL. NAT., lat. 8193
Terence, *Comedies*. *Ca.* 1408–1410.
See Catalogue of Manuscripts.

THE MASTER OF ST. JEROME

Named by the writer after the large drawing of St. Jerome in his study, added later as a frontispiece to the *Bible moralisée* begun by Paul and Jean de Limbourg (Fig. 357). This drawing seems to have been based on a composition by the Limbourgs of *ca.* 1411–1413. The Master of St. Jerome exploited similarly compositions of the *Belles Heures* and the *Très Riches Heures*, although, active chiefly in the 'twenties, he transformed his models into more dramatic designs, especially in the instance of the spectacular miniatures he added to the Psalter in London. His work is discussed in the chapters on the *Belles Heures* and the *Très Riches Heures*.
BIBLIOGRAPHY: Porcher, *Belles Heures*, 1953, p. 26 f.; Pächt, *Pantheon*, 1963, pp. 131–142; Meiss, *Gaz. B.-A.*, 1963, pp. 147–170.

London, BRIT. MUS., Cotton Domitian A.XVII (Figs. 526, 600)
Psalter. 288 fols.; 193 × 137 mm. Belonged to Henry VI, whose arms were added on the robe of a prince.
Fols. 12v, 49v, 74v, 122v, 150v, 177v, 206v added by Master to original manuscript *ca.* 1421.
For miniatures related to the Master of Berry's Cleres Femmes see this Catalogue.
BIBLIOGRAPHY: see Berry's Cleres Femmes.

Oxford, BODLEIAN LIBRARY, Douce 144 (Figs. 458–461)
Book of Hours, Use of Paris. 144 fols.; 215 × 160 mm.
Manuscript dated 1407 on fol. 27.
Drawings added in borders of folios 105–110 *ca.* 1417.
For miniature by the Bedford Trend see this Catalogue.
For the Boucicaut miniatures see Meiss, *Boucicaut Master*, 1968, pp. 106–108 (Catalogue).
BIBLIOGRAPHY: see Bedford.

Paris, BIBL. NAT., fr. 166
Bible moralisée. Frontispiece, drawing.
See Catalogue of Manuscripts.

RELATED MANUSCRIPTS

Baltimore, WALTERS ART GALLERY, no. 44.462 (Fig. 615)
Medallion in grisaille enamel highlighted in gold, *Ara Coeli*. Obverse: *Madonna and Child in glory*. Reverse: *Emperor Augustus*. 50 mm. in diameter. *Ca.* 1425.
BIBLIOGRAPHY: Verdier, 1961, pp. 9 ff.; Meiss, "Breviary Master," 1970, p. 18, pl. XVII.

MASTER OF THE TRINITY

Paris, Bibliothèque nationale	lat. 18014	*Petites Heures* of Jean de Berry
London, British Museum	Yates Thompson 37	Book of Hours
Rome, Biblioteca Vaticana	lat. 51	Bible

BIBLIOGRAPHY: Meiss, *Art Bull.*, 1956, p. 191; *idem*, *Late XIV Century*, 1967, p. 176 ff.

MASTER OF TROYES

A minor master, who illuminated manuscripts for Troyes and two other towns nearby in the Champagne, Sens and Châlons-sur-Marne. He seems to have been active, with assistants, from about 1390 to 1415. He influenced the Master of Walters 219. His best miniatures are in a Missal, Morgan 331, and in an extensively illustrated Book of Hours, use of Troyes (lat. 924).
BIBLIOGRAPHY: Meiss, *Late XIV Century*, 1967, p. 359.

Brussels, BIBL. ROYALE, ms. 9125
Missal of Sainte-Chapelle, Paris. 525 fols.; 400×285 mm. Burgundian inventory of 1420.
Initial on fol. 7. *Ca.* 1405.
BIBLIOGRAPHY: Doutrepont, *Inventaire*, 1906, p. 23 f. no. 51; Delisle, *Charles V*, 1907, I, p. 158 f. no. XIII bis; II, p. 31 no. 165 bis; Brussels, Bibl. roy., Gaspar and Lyna, I, 1937, pp. 396–399 no. 166, pls. XCI–XCII; Panofsky, *Netherlandish Painting*, 1953, I, pp. 51 f., 380 n. 51[3]; II, fig. 52; Delaissé, *Miniatures médiévales*, 1959, pp. 82–85 no. 17, pl. p. 83; Brussels, Bibl. roy., 1967 (Dogaer and Debae), p. 18 f. no. 13, pls. 10–11; Meiss, *Late XIV Century*, 1967, p. 359.

Chicago, COLL. FIELDING MARSHALL (Fig. 814)
Miniatures from a Book of Hours ("Ranshaw Hours") including the *Annunciation*, *Visitation* and *St. Christopher*. *Ca.* 1410. Other miniatures from this Book of Hours by a second painter, who was probably East French and distantly related to the Master of the Breviary of Jean sans Peur, are in the Los Angeles County Museum (*Nativity* 47. 19. 1) and in the Boston Museum of Fine Arts (43. 212–215). In Boston are the *Annunciation to the Shepherds*, *Betrayal*, *Descent from the Cross* and *Entombment*.
BIBLIOGRAPHY: Schilling, 1944, pp. 20–24, figs. A–F; Swarzenski, 1944, pp. 28–33, figs. 1, 2, 4, 5; Panofsky, *Netherlandish Painting*, 1953, I, p. 56; London, Sotheby, June 28, 1962, lot 48; Meiss, *Late XIV Century*, 1967, p. 359; Kansas, University of Kansas Museum of Art, Schrader, 1969, p. 10 f. no. 5, pl. XII.

Edinburgh, UNIVERSITY LIBRARY, ms. 44
Book of Hours, Use of Sens. 196 fols.; 178×121 mm.
All miniatures.
BIBLIOGRAPHY: Edinburgh, University Library, Borland, 1916, pp. 78–81 no. 44, pl. XII.

Hamburg, KUNSTHALLE, ms. fr. 2
(formerly Mrs. J. Möring Huth)
Book of Hours, Use of Châlons-sur-Marne. 189 fols.; 195×141 mm.
All miniatures.
BIBLIOGRAPHY: Meiss, *Late XIV Century*, 1967, p. 359.

Milan, BIBL. AMBROSIANA, I. 7. Sup.
Book of Hours. 191 fols.; 187×130 mm.
Some miniatures.
For miniatures related to the style of the Luçon Master see this Catalogue.
BIBLIOGRAPHY: see Luçon: Related manuscripts.

New York, PIERPONT MORGAN LIBRARY, M. 331 (Fig. 830)
Missal, Use of the Cathedral of St. Stephen at Châlons-sur-Marne. 312 fols.; 300×209 mm.
All miniatures. *Ca.* 1400.
BIBLIOGRAPHY: New York, Pierpont Morgan Library [1934], p. 40 no. 79, pl. 66; De Ricci, *Census*, II, 1937, p. 1428 no. 331; Panofsky, *Netherlandish Painting*, 1953, I, p. 380 n. 51[1]; Baltimore, Walters, *International*

Style (Miner), 1962, p. 47 f. no. 44, pl. XLV; Meiss, *Late XIV Century*, 1967, pp. 5, 359, fig. 297.

Paris, BIBL. NAT., lat. 864
Missal, Use of the Church of Ervy-le-Châtel near Troyes, in the diocese of Sens. 200 and 215 fols.; 415×277 and 425×295 mm. 2 vols.
All miniatures. (Called to our attention, with correct attribution, by François Avril.)
BIBLIOGRAPHY: Leroquais, *Sacramentaires*, 1924, III, p. 27 f. no 581.

Paris, BIBL. NAT., lat. 924 (Fig. 819)
Book of Hours, Use of Troyes. 312 fols.; 250×180 mm. Arms of a member of the Berthier family of Troyes on fol. 17.
All miniatures. *Ca.* 1400.
BIBLIOGRAPHY: Couderc, *Portraits* [1910], p. 23, pl. LII; Leroquais, *Livres d'heures*, 1927, I, pp. 39–42 no. 10, pls. XX–XXII; Panofsky, *Netherlandish Painting*, 1953, I, pp. 52, 381 n. 52[2], 410 n. 129[3]; Paris, Bibl. nat. (Porcher), 1955, p. 147 no. 311; Meiss, *Late XIV Century*, 1967, index, fig. 533.

Paris, BIBL. NAT., lat. 962
Pontifical of Sens. 275 fols. and A–G; 307×224 mm.
Leroquais identified the arms (Montaigu and Saint-Pierre-le-Vif) on fol. 1 as those of Odon de Montaigu, abbot of Saint-Pierre-le-Vif of Sens between 1385 and 1390. However, the miniatures, which include so advanced a spatial design as fol. 264, seem to indicate a date between 1400 and 1405.
BIBLIOGRAPHY: Leroquais, *Pontificaux*, 1937, II, pp. 76–82, III, pls. LXIX–LXXVIII.

San Marino, HUNTINGTON LIBRARY, HM 1179
Book of Hours, Use of Troyes (according to Delaissé). 166 fols.; 194×135 mm.
All miniatures.
BIBLIOGRAPHY: Meiss, *Late XIV Century*, 1967, p. 359.

Vienna, NATIONALBIBL., ms. Ser. nov. 2613
Book of Hours, Use of Châlons-sur-Marne. 219 fols.; 185×127 mm.
All miniatures except the first on fol. 14 and the *Trinity*. For miniatures by the workshops of the Breviary Master and the Master of Walters 219 see this Catalogue.
BIBLIOGRAPHY: Vienna, Nationalbibl., Trenkler, 1938, p. 27 f., pl. vb; Meiss, *Late XIV Century*, 1967, pp. 355, 359; *idem*, "Breviary Master," 1970, p. 10.

WHEREABOUTS UNKNOWN (London, Sotheby & Co., July 8, 1970, lot 120)
Book of Hours. 251 fols.; 239×173 mm.
All miniatures. *Ca.* 1415.
BIBLIOGRAPHY: London, Sotheby, July 8, 1970, lot 120, with attribution to Troyes Master by Meiss.

RELATED MANUSCRIPTS

Chicago, UNIVERSITY OF CHICAGO LIBRARY, ms. 26–250961
Book of Hours, Use of Châlons-sur-Marne. 126 fols.; 120×90 mm.
BIBLIOGRAPHY: Meiss, *Late XIV Century*, 1967, p. 359; Farquhar, 1968, pp. 243–249, pls. 22–24.

Oxford, BODLEIAN LIBRARY, Douce 102
Book of Hours, Use of Troyes.
All miniatures with the exception of fol. 54, which is related to the Master of the Humility Madonnas.
BIBLIOGRAPHY: Pächt and Alexander, *Bodleian Manuscripts*, 1966, p. 51 no. 646, pl. LI; Meiss, *Late XIV Century*, 1967, p. 359.

Toulouse, BIBL. MUNICIPALE, ms. 512
Grandes Chroniques de France. 467 fols.
BIBLIOGRAPHY: Toulouse, Bibl. municipale, *Catalogue*, VII, 1885, p. 316 f. no. 512; Meiss, *Late XIV Century*, 1967, p. 359.

THE VIRGIL MASTER

As far as we can now see the career of the Virgil Master began in the 'nineties and extended into the second decade of the fifteenth century. A limited artist, his style remained more constant than that of the better Parisian illuminators and it would therefore be difficult to arrange his manuscripts in a series on stylistic grounds alone. Many, however, are datable by other means.

Fortunately Jean de Berry acquired more than a half dozen manuscripts, chiefly by gift, and his inventories yield, as usual, chronological information. The interest of the Virgil Master in narrative apparently made his illustrations of Bibles, chronicles and other historical texts especially attractive. The Duke owned a Livy already in 1402 (fr. 263). On his order his treasurer and *maître d'hôtel*, Jacques Courau, commissioned Nicholas de Gonesse to finish a French translation of *Facta et dicta memorabilia* by Valerius Maximus that had been initiated by Charles V. Courau presented a copy to his patron as a New Year's gift in 1402 (fr. 282) (Figs. 271, 413, 414). For himself Courau acquired in 1403 a good copy of Virgil's *Bucolics* and *Aeneid* (Bibl. Laurenziana, Med. Pal. 69) (Figs. 223, 264). This is the manuscript that gives the master his name. Two copies of the *Cité de Dieu* illuminated by the atelier are extant: Brussels 9294–95, about 1405, and fr. 6272 (Vol. I) with The Hague, Museum Meermanno-Westreenianum, ms. 10 A 12 (Vol. II), about 1410–1412. Around 1408–1410 the Virgil Master painted the frontispiece of a third copy, fr. 25, the rest of which was illuminated by the Apocalypse workshop. The Virgil workshop illuminated a lively chronicle of Richard II's campaign in Ireland which Jean de Montaigu gave to Jean de Berry about 1405 (Harley 1319).

The Duke also owned two Bibles illustrated in part by the Virgil workshop. The atelier illuminated most of the miniatures, but not the frontispieces, in Harley 4381–82 towards 1403, and it collaborated with two other workshops about 1405 to produce Arsenal 5057–58. In this latter Bible the Master himself painted the *Tree of Jesse* (Fig. 521). Finally the Duke acquired a collection of the works of Durand de Champagne illuminated by the workshop about 1410 (Brussels 9555–58).

The Virgil Master worked with a much bolder painter, the Medallion Master. They collaborated on a version of the *Légende dorée* (fr. 414), datable about 1407 because of reflections of the *Belles Heures*. The Virgil Master, in fact, took his frontispiece from Paul de Limbourg's composition for All Saints in this manuscript (Figs. 388, 389). Later, about 1412–1415, the two masters collaborated again on a remarkable *Histoire extraite de la Bible* and *Apocalypse* (Chantilly 28). Here as in fr. 414 the Virgil Master with an assistant illustrated the two frontispieces while his associate painted the rest. Still under the influence of the Limbourgs, the Virgil Master in his frontispiece to the Apocalypse quoted from the *Belles Heures* an enthroned figure listening to a man holding a hood (Figs. 799, 800).

About 1411 the Virgil workshop collaborated with the Boucicaut workshop in a Book of Hours (Nouv. acq. lat. 3107). The Master painted some of his most beautiful miniatures in a *Bible historiale* (Royal 15 D III) illustrated about 1415 in association with the Boucicaut and Egerton workshops. At about the same time, when he felt the strength of the Boucicaut style, he worked with illuminators in the Bedford Trend on a Book of Hours in Cambridge (Trinity B. 11. 31).

The forms of the Virgil Master show a distinctive pliancy. Landscapes and figures seem continuously to flow and undulate. He often applied his colors—slate, pale rose, light green, violet—in a thin film which left visible the drawing underneath.

BIBLIOGRAPHY: Meiss, *Late XIV Century*, 1967, pp. 298, 360.

Brussels, BIBL. ROYALE, ms. 9001

Guiart des Moulins, *Bible historiale*. 435 fols.; 456×330 mm.

Petrus Gilberti executed line endings.

Fols. 192v, 225. *Ca.* 1414–1415.

For miniatures by the Cité des Dames workshop and related to the Cleres Femmes workshop see this Catalogue.

BIBLIOGRAPHY: see Berry's Cleres Femmes: Related manuscripts.

Brussels, BIBL. ROYALE, ms. 9294–95

St. Augustine, *La Cité de Dieu*. 418 and 382 fols.; 352×270 and 357×273 mm. *Ca.* 1405.

BIBLIOGRAPHY: Laborde, *Cité de Dieu*, 1909, I, pp. 176 f., 196, 268–270, pl. XVI; Brussels, Bibl. roy., Gaspar and Lyna, I, 1937, pp. 413–415 no. 171, pl. XCVI.

Brussels, BIBL. ROYALE, ms. 9555–9558
Durand de Champagne, *Le mirouer des dames*. 179 fols.; 313×228 mm.
Ex libris of Jean de Berry.
All miniatures. *Ca.* 1410.
BIBLIOGRAPHY: Guiffrey, *Inventaires*, I, 1894, p. CLXXVI no. 65; II, 1896, p. 318; Delisle, *Charles V*, 1907, II, pp. 269 no. 285 bis, 316; Brussels, Bibl. roy., Gaspar and Lyna, I, 1937, pp. 454–456, pl. CX; Meiss, *Late XIV Century*, 1967, pp. 298, 309, 359.

Cambridge, FITZWILLIAM MUSEUM, McClean 79
Book of Hours, Use of Paris and Rome. 146 fols.; 232×162 mm.
Written for a member of the Order of St. Anthony.
All miniatures. *Ca.* 1400–1405.
BIBLIOGRAPHY: Cambridge, Fitzwilliam Museum (James), 1912, p. 163 f.; Meiss, *Late XIV Century*, 1967, p. 360.

Cambridge, TRINITY COLLEGE, ms. B.11.31
Book of Hours, Use of Paris. 234 fols.; 219×178 mm. Fols. 13–54. *Ca.* 1415.
For miniatures by the Bedford Trend see this Catalogue.
BIBLIOGRAPHY: Cambridge, Trinity College, James, I, 1900, pp. 379–382 no. 269; Meiss, *Boucicaut Master*, 1968, p. 142.

Chantilly, MUSEE CONDE, ms. 28 (1378)
Histoire extraite de la Bible and *Apocalypse*. *Ca.* 1412–1415.
See Catalogue of Manuscripts.

Chantilly, MUSEE CONDE, ms. 867 (324)
Grandes Chroniques de France. 490 fols.; 420×284 mm.
All miniatures. *Ca.* 1400–1405.
BIBLIOGRAPHY: Chantilly, Musée Condé, *Cabinet*, III, 1901, p. 134, pl. opp. p. 134; Meiss, *Late XIV Century*, 1967, p. 360.

Florence, BIBL. LAURENZIANA, Med. Pal. 69
Virgil, *Eclogues*, *Georgics* and *Aeneid*. Written in 1403.
See Catalogue of Manuscripts.

Florence, BIBL. LAURENZIANA, Plut. XXX.10 (Fig. 58)
Vitruvius, *De architectura*; Cato, *De re rustica*; Varro, *De re rustica*. 116 fols.; 385×285 mm.
This manuscript is the copy that Jean de Montreuil said (in a letter) he would make of a manuscript of these three texts that he had acquired in Italy. He himself wrote the rubrics in the Laurenziana copy (G. Ouy, verbal communication). Later this manuscript belonged to Francesco Sassetti.
Manuscript has only a frontispiece. *Ca.* 1400–1405.
BIBLIOGRAPHY: Fontana, in *Miscellanea Supino*, 1933, p. 320, fig. 1; Florence, Bibl. Mediceo-Laurenziana, *Mostra*, 1949, p. 41 n. 124; Rome, Palazzo Venezia, *Mostra* [1953], p. 286 n. 454, pl. XCVII; Billanovich, 1964, p. 345 f.; Krinsky, 1967, p. 54 f.; Meiss, *Late XIV Century*, 1967, p. 360; Sabbadini, *Scoperte*, ed. 1967, p. 165.

The Hague, MUSEUM MEERMANNO-WESTREENIANUM, ms. 10 A 12
St. Augustine, *La Cité de Dieu*. Vol. II (Vol. I is Paris, Bibl. nat., fr. 6272). 285 fols.; 420×310 mm. *Ca.* 1410–1412.
BIBLIOGRAPHY: Laborde, *Cité de Dieu*, 1909, II, pp. 309–311 no. 27; Meiss, *Late XIV Century*, 1967, p. 360.

The Hague, KON. BIBL., ms. 72 A 25
Froissart, *Chroniques*. 372 fols.; 385×288 mm.
All miniatures.
BIBLIOGRAPHY: Netherlands, Byvanck, 1931, p. 45; Valenciennes, *Froissart*, 1937, pp. 43–45, pls. XXII–XXIV; Meiss, *Late XIV Century*, 1967, p. 360.

London, BRIT. MUS., Add. 29986
Durand de Champagne, *Le mirouer des dames*. 175 fols.; 312×236 mm.
Belonged to Jean de Berry (Inventory of 1413).
Both miniatures. *Ca.* 1407–1410.
BIBLIOGRAPHY: Guiffrey, *Inventaires*, I, 1894, pp. CLXXV no. 64, 262 no. 983; Delisle, *Charles V*, 1907, II, p. 268 no. 285; Meiss, *Late XIV Century*, 1967, p. 310.

London, BRIT. MUS., Burney 257
Statius, *Thebais et Achilleis*. 248 fols.; 285×192 mm. Fols. 10v, 11. *Ca.* 1405.
For miniatures by the Cité des Dames workshop and related to the Orosius workshop see this Catalogue.
BIBLIOGRAPHY: see Cité des Dames.

London, BRIT. MUS., Harley 1319
Fall of Richard II. 78 fols.; 285×208 mm.
Given to Jean de Berry by Jean de Montaigu *ca.* 1405. (Inventory of 1413.)
All miniatures. Between 1401–1405.
BIBLIOGRAPHY: London, Brit. Mus., *Harleian Manuscripts*, II, 1808, p. 3; Webb, 1824, pp. 1–423; Thompson, 1904, pp. 160–172, pls. I–IV, pp. 267–270, pls. V–VIII; London, Brit. Mus., *Reproductions*, IV, 1928, p. 13 f., pl. XXXIII; Meiss, *Late XIV Century*, 1967, p. 360; Meiss with Off, 1971, pp. 228 f., 233.

London, BRIT. MUS., Harley 4381–82
Guiart des Moulins, *Bible historiale*. 284 and 267 fols.; 415×305 and 415×300 mm.
Belonged to Jean de Berry (inscription).
All miniatures by workshop except fols. 3, 6v, 9, 9v in 4381 and fol. 1 in 4382 by a follower of Pseudo-Jacquemart; and fols. 1, 3v–5v, 7–8, 10–16 in 4381 and fols. 159–199 in 4382 by a follower of Jacquemart de Hesdin. *Ca.* 1403–1404.
BIBLIOGRAPHY: Berger, *Bible française*, 1884, pp. 216 f., 293, 401; Guiffrey, *Inventaires*, I, 1894, p. CLXII no. 7; II, 1896, p. 317 no. 12 bis; London, Brit. Mus., Warner, 1903, pl. 44; Delisle, *Charles V*, 1907, II, pp. 225 no. 11 bis, 273; London, Brit. Mus., *Schools of Illumination*, VI, 1930, pl. 5; London, Brit. Mus., Millar, 1933, p. 32 f., pl. XLII; Schilling, 1954, p. 277 n. 19; Evans, 1967, pp. 394–398, pl. 45d; Meiss, *Late XIV Century*, 1967, index, figs. 617, 622.

London, BRIT. MUS., Royal 15 D III
Guiart des Moulins, *Bible historiale*. 532 fols.; 460×330 mm.
Fols. 209, 220v, 236, 481v–491, 503–509. *Ca.* 1415.
For miniatures by the Egerton workshop and by a follower of the Breviary Master see this Catalogue. For the Boucicaut miniatures see Meiss, *Boucicaut Master*, 1968, pp. 96–99 (Catalogue).
BIBLIOGRAPHY: see Egerton.

London, COLL. OF COUNT ANTOINE SEILERN
Alchandreus, *De astrologia*; Boethius, *De arithmetica* and *De musica*. 118 fols.; 403×312 mm.
All miniatures. *Ca.* 1410–1415.
BIBLIOGRAPHY: London, Sotheby, July 1, 1946, p. 11 no. 11, pls. XVI, XVII; Meiss, *Late XIV Century*, 1967, p. 360.

Miami (Florida), COLL. OF MRS. JEAN M. KANE
Book of Hours. 154 fols.; 165×120 mm.
Fols. 79, 85v. *Ca.* 1400.

Oxford, BODLEIAN LIBRARY, Douce d. 13, fol. 30a
Single miniature taken from a *Bible historiale*.
BIBLIOGRAPHY: Pächt and Alexander, *Bodleian Manuscripts*, 1966, p. 51 no. 655.

Paris, BIBL. DE L'ARSENAL, ms. 5057–58
Guiart des Moulins, *Bible historiale*. *Ca.* 1405.
See Catalogue of Manuscripts.

Paris, BIBL. DE LA CHAMBRE DES DEPUTES, ms. 3
Guiart des Moulins, *Bible historiale*. 346 fols.; 423×315 mm.
All miniatures. *Ca.* 1395–1400.
BIBLIOGRAPHY: Berger, *Bible française*, 1884, pp. 203, 218, 369; Paris, Bibl. de la Chambre des Députés, *Catalogue*, 1907, pp. 6–9; Paris, Bibl. de la Chambre des Députés, Boinet, 1922, pp. 40–46, pl. X; Schilling, 1954, p. 277 f. n. 19, pl. 31 c; Meiss, *Late XIV Century*, 1967, p. 360.

Paris, BIBL. DE L'INSTITUT, ms. 264
Boethius, *De Consolatione*. 94 fols.; 290×200 mm.
All miniatures. *Ca.* 1403–1405.
BIBLIOGRAPHY: Delisle, 1873, p. 21; Paris, *Bibliothèque de l'Institut* (M. Bouteron and J. Tremblot), 1928, p. 36 no. 264; Courcelle, *Consolation*, 1967, pls. 32, 72, 101, 108, 112.

Paris, BIBL. NAT., fr. 25
St. Augustine, *La Cité de Dieu*. Vol. I. *Ca.* 1408–1410.
See Catalogue of Manuscripts.

Paris, BIBL. NAT., fr. 45–46
Valerius Maximus, *Faits et dits mémorables* (trans. by Simon de Hesdin and Nicolas de Gonesse). 270 and 156 fols.; 420×320 and 430×310 mm.
All miniatures. *Ca.* 1405–1410.

Paris, BIBL. NAT., fr. 263
Titus Livius, *Histoire romaine* (trans. by Pierre Bersuire). 480 fols.; 420×320 mm.
Belonged to Jean de Berry (Inscription. Inventory of 1402).
All miniatures. *Ca.* 1400.
BIBLIOGRAPHY: Guiffrey, *Inventaires*, I, 1894, pp. CLXIX no. 40, 226 no. 856; Delisle, *Charles V*, 1907, II, pp. 261 no. 233, 310; Meiss, *Late XIV Century*, 1967, pp. 298, 313, 360.

Paris, BIBL. NAT., fr. 282 (Figs. 271, 413, 414)
Valerius Maximus, *Faits et dits mémorables* (trans. by Simon de Hesdin and Nicolas de Gonesse). 411 fols.; 386×280 mm.
Given to Jean de Berry by Jacques Courau in 1402. Inventory of 1402.
All miniatures. Shortly before 1402.
BIBLIOGRAPHY: Guiffrey, *Inventaires*, I, 1894, pp. CLXIX no. 39, 236 no. 911; Delisle, *Charles V*, 1907, II, p. 256 no. 206; Meiss, *Late XIV Century*, 1967, index.

Paris, BIBL. NAT., fr. 414 (Fig. 388)
Jacobus de Voragine, *Légende dorée* (trans. by Jean de Vignay). 419 fols.; 347×275 mm.
Colophon gives date of 1404 for text.
Fol. 1. *Ca.* 1407.
For miniatures by the Medallion workshop see this Catalogue.
BIBLIOGRAPHY: see Medallion Master and the discussion in the text of this volume.

Paris, BIBL. NAT., fr. 819–820
Miracles de Notre-Dame. 2 + 262 and 2 + 298 fols.; 330×235 mm.
Fr. 820: 139–280. Other miniatures in fr. 820 and all miniatures in fr. 819 by illuminators working in an older style and influenced by the style of the Virgil Master. *Ca.* 1395.
BIBLIOGRAPHY: Laborde, *Miracles de Nostre Dame*, 1929, p. 15; Meiss, *Late XIV Century*, 1967, p. 360.

Paris, BIBL. NAT., fr. 823
Guillaume de Deguilleville, *Pèlerinage de vie humaine. Pèlerinage de l'âme. Pèlerinage de Jhesucrist.* 3 + 246 fols.; 315×220 mm. The scribe Oudin de Carvanay signed his name in acrostic. The manuscript is dated at the end of the second part, on folio 168v, April 29, 1393.
Fols. 105v, 126v, 137, 151v, 152 very probably by Virgil Master.
BIBLIOGRAPHY: Delisle, *Charles V*, 1907, I, p. 80; Martin, *Miniature française*, 1923, p. 67; Paris, Bibl. nat. (Porcher), 1955, p. 72 n. 143.

Paris, BIBL. NAT., fr. 6272 (Figs. 50, 212, 248)
St. Augustine, *La Cité de Dieu*. Vol. I (Vol. II is the Hague, Museum Meermanno-Westreenianum, ms. 10 A 12). 318 fols.; 425×305 mm.
Ca. 1410–1412.
BIBLIOGRAPHY: Laborde, *Cité de Dieu*, 1909, I, pp. 305–308 no. 26, pls. XXII a, b; Paris, Bibl. nat. (Porcher), 1955, p. 80 f. no. 164; Meiss, *Late XIV Century*, 1967, p. 360.

Paris, BIBL. NAT., fr. 6445 (Fig. 52)
Valerius Maximus, *Faits et dits mémorables* (trans. by Simon de Hesdin and Nicholas de Gonesse).
304 fols.; 398×300 mm.
All miniatures. *Ca.* 1410.
BIBLIOGRAPHY: Meiss, *Late XIV Century*, 1967, p. 360 (text wrongly listed as Livy).

Paris, BIBL. NAT., nouv. acq. lat. 3107
Book of Hours, Use of Rome. 251 fols.; 220×165 mm.
Fols. 68, 72v, 86. *Ca.* 1411.
For the miniatures by the Boucicaut workshop see Meiss, *Boucicaut Master*, 1968, pp. 128 f. (Catalogue).
BIBLIOGRAPHY: Paris, Bibl. nat. (Porcher), 1955, p. 98 no. 203; Paris, Bibl. nat., Porcher, *Boisrouvray*, 1961, pp. 59–62 no. 12, pls. VI, 29–36; Meiss, *Boucicaut Master*, 1968, p. 142, index, figs. 127, 142, 147, 151, 210–221.

Soissons, BIBL. DE SOISSONS, ms. 210–212
Guiart des Moulins, *Bible historiale*. 217 numbered 225, 202 numbered 226–435, and 111 numbered 437–548 fols. in three vols.; 430×313 mm.
Ms. 210: 1, 73v, 74v. Ms. 211: 309, 351v, 374v, 391. *Ca.* 1405.
BIBLIOGRAPHY: *Catalogue général des manuscrits*, III, 1885, p. 135 f. no. 210–212.

WHEREABOUTS UNKNOWN
Book of Hours (Delaissé, 1950). 193 fols.; 190×135 mm.
Fols. 62, 68v, 96, 115. *Ca.* 1405.
For miniatures by the Luçon workshop see this Catalogue.
BIBLIOGRAPHY: Delaissé, 1950; Meiss, *Late XIV Century*, 1967, p. 359 f.

RELATED MANUSCRIPTS

Brussels, BIBL. ROYALE, ms. 9024–25
Guiart des Moulins, *Bible historiale*. 294 and 263 fols.; 395×294 mm.
Bought by Jean sans Peur in 1415 from Jean Chousat.
9025: 135v, 159v–259v.
For miniatures by the Cité des Dames workshop and related to the Berry's Cleres Femmes workshop see this Catalogue.
BIBLIOGRAPHY: see Berry's Cleres Femmes.

Brussels, BIBL. ROYALE, ms. 9554
Gilles de Rome, *Le livre du gouvernement des roys et des princes*. 140 fols.; 320×235 mm.
Fol. 1. *Ca.* 1407.
BIBLIOGRAPHY: Brussels, Bibl. roy., Gaspar and Lyna, I, 1937, p. 439 f. no. 184, pl. CIIC; Meiss, *Late XIV Century*, 1967, p. 360.

WHEREABOUTS UNKNOWN (London, Christie, Manson and Woods, July 16, 1969, lot 140)
Book of Hours, Use of Paris. 157 fols.; 185×138 mm.
Ca. 1400.

BIBLIOGRAPHY: London, Christie, Manson and Woods, July 16, 1969, lot 140.

WHEREABOUTS UNKNOWN (London, Sotheby & Co., December 3, 1968, lot 24)

The Armagnac Breviary, Use of Rome. 336 fols.; 207 × 140 mm. 2 vols. Manuscript belonged to Jean d'Armagnac, Bishop of Castres (1440–1493).

Vol. I: fol. 1.

BIBLIOGRAPHY: London, Thompson Coll. (formerly), James, *Fifty Manuscripts*, 1898, pp. 179–183; London, Sotheby, December 3, 1968, lot 24.

THE MASTER OF WALTERS 219

This master is the most interesting of the illuminators who remained in the provinces. Probably the time of his appearance—*ca.* 1417 as far as we now know—accounts for his failure to move into the capital, because at that time patronage declined greatly. The manuscript that contains his most extensive extant cycle of miniatures is the Book of Hours, Walters 219 (Figs. 522, 523, 528). It is one of two manuscripts that have a Paris calendar (the other is the former Beatty horae) but they were surely produced elsewhere. A Book of Hours at Ripon has the use of Châlons-sur-Marne, whereas two other manuscripts of the same kind have the use of Besançon. One of these Books of Hours, by the master himself, was sold at Sotheby in 1962, and a second, by a close follower, is in the library of that city. It seems probable that there, in the capital of Franche-Comté, the Master of Walters 219 was established. This conclusion is supported by a relationship of his work to that of the Troyes Master, who was active not far away in the Champagne.

Walters 219 is perhaps the earliest of these manuscripts. The four miniatures by the Breviary Master and an assistant that were pasted into the manuscript near the end may be dated *ca.* 1418 or shortly thereafter (Figs. 623, 624). Most of the borders contain the ivy and acanthus that were commonly used in the second decade of the century. The same forms fill the borders of the Hours for Besançon, mixed, as in Walters 219, with a few large specimens of flowers and leaves. The Besançon Hours, which is larger than the Walters manuscript, has one miniature, a *Raising of Lazarus*, that shows a remarkably deep and complex landscape. In it there are scenes of daily life, which began to appear behind the religious representations in landscapes painted in the circle of the late Jacquemart (Yates Thompson 37), but which did not become frequent until the third decade of the century.

The latest borders of Walters 219 abandoned acanthus (though not ivy) for more prominent leaves, flowers, and plants. In the borders of the Books of Hours in the Rau Collection and formerly Beatty the ivy, too, has disappeared, leaving the field to large and exquisitely painted botanical specimens (Figs. 529, 531). These plants are described with such pale tones of blue, violet, rose, and straw yellow that they are difficult to reproduce in black and white. Interspersed among the plants are a few insects, animals, and drolleries. Neither of these two manuscripts would have been painted, we believe, much before 1420.

The illuminator's manner of laying out the plants as specimens in the border derives, as Otto Pächt observed, from Lombard illumination. It was Lombard illumination, too, that provided the plan, adopted in Walters 219, of introducing prophets into initials at the beginning of the Offices (see Bibl. nat., Smith-Lesouëf 22). In the *Beatty Hours* he combined the Magi adoring the Child with their journey (Fig. 531)—a combination that first appeared in a Sienese painting by Bartolo di Fredi. In his scene in the Walters manuscript of Death entering a *locus amoenus* he was one of the first artists to show the skeleton riding a bull—an animal that became characteristic of illustrations of Petrarch's *Trionfo della morte*. The Master of Walters 219 shared with Italian Trecento painting a primary concern with solid form rather than with color or light. Even when his space is deep he gave priority to dense, voluminous figures, buildings and terraced rocks. His Italianism is so profound that he seems —as the writer has suggested earlier—a painter first trained in Italy who was working in France rather than, as Otto Pächt proposed, a deeply Italianate French illuminator.

Professor Pächt has pointed to the special importance of one aspect of the Book of Hours formerly in the

Beatty collection: it contains a series of twelve miniatures in the calendar, full-page, at least within their wide, decorated borders. The scenes, executed by the Master of Walters 219 and an assistant, show activities characteristic of the months, some of them occurring in the fields before a chateau (Fig. 524). In these respects they resemble the calendar pictures in the *Très Riches Heures*, and even some figures, such as the broad-hatted mowers in *June*, recall the corresponding miniatures of the Limbourgs (Figs. 525, 544). These similarities might be fortuitous, and the Beatty calendar may reflect a cycle like that in the Torre dell' Aquila at Trent (Fig. 694). It is important to recall, however, that *ca.* 1417 the Master of Walters 219 utilized miniatures of an illuminator who had worked on the *Très Riches Heures*, and he probably obtained them directly from their author, the Breviary Master. It might well have been he who gave the Master of Walters 219 the idea of designing *ca.* 1420 a cycle of relatively large calendar pictures.

BIBLIOGRAPHY: Cockerell, in London, Burlington Fine Arts Club, *Exhibition*, 1908, nos. 204, 205; Pächt, 1950, p. 44 n. 1; Meiss, *Art Bull.*, 1956, p. 195; *idem*, *Late XIV Century*, 1967, p. 360; *idem*, "Breviary Master," 1970, p. 11.

Baltimore, WALTERS ART GALLERY, ms. 219
Book of Hours.
See Catalogue of Manuscripts.

Ripon (Yorkshire), COLL. OF ARTHUR RAU (Figs. 530, 531)
Book of Hours, Use of Châlons-sur-Marne. 121 fols.; 167×114 mm. The motto *pour son vouloir* appears in the margins.
All miniatures.

BIBLIOGRAPHY: London, Burl. Fine Arts Club, *Exhibition* (Cockerell), 1908, no. 205; Pächt, 1950, p. 44 n. 1; Meiss, *Art Bull.*, 1956, p. 195; London, Sotheby, December 9, 1958, lot 17; Meiss, *Late XIV Century*, 1967, p. 360.

Vienna, NATIONALBIBL., ms. Ser. nov. 2613
Book of Hours, Use of Châlons-sur-Marne. 219 fols.; 185×127 mm.
Trinity.

For miniatures by the workshops of the Troyes Master and the Master of the Breviary of Jean sans Peur see this Catalogue.

BIBLIOGRAPHY: see Troyes.

WHEREABOUTS UNKNOWN (formerly Chester Beatty coll., ms. 84) (Figs. 524, 525, 529)
Book of Hours, Paris calendar. 246 fols. (originally 273 fols.); 197×146 mm.
Arms (three girouettes) of the Giroux or Girouas family. Motto: *sans plus*.

BIBLIOGRAPHY: London, Burl. Fine Arts Club, *Exhibition* (Cockerell), 1908, p. 99 no. 204, pl. 131; Pächt, 1950, p. 44 f., pls. 6d, 13 b, c; Meiss, *Art Bull.*, 1956, p. 195; *idem*, *Late XIV Century*, 1967, p. 360.

WHEREABOUTS UNKNOWN (London, Sotheby & Co., June 18, 1962, lot 122) (Fig. 527)
Book of Hours, Use of Besançon. 140 fols.; 179×130 mm.
Manuscript probably executed for a member of the family of Fauquier of Franche-Comté, whose arms appear in an initial on fol. 22v.
Fols. 16, 91 (these two folios have been reproduced. We have not seen the manuscript).

BIBLIOGRAPHY: London, Sotheby, July 1, 1946, lot 20; Pächt, 1950, p. 44 n. 1; London, Sotheby, June 16, 1952, lot 35; Meiss, *Art Bull.*, 1956, p. 195 n. 32; London, Sotheby, June 18, 1962, lot 122, pl. 9; Meiss, *Late XIV Century*, 1967, p. 360.

RELATED MANUSCRIPTS

Baltimore, WALTERS ART GALLERY, ms. 290
Book of Hours, Use of Rome. 205 fols.; 257×162 mm.

BIBLIOGRAPHY: Meiss, *Art Bull.*, 1956, p. 195; *idem*, *Late XIV Century*, 1967, p. 360.

Besançon, BIBL. MUNICIPALE, ms. 123
Book of Hours, Use of Besançon. 111 fols.; 150×111 mm.

BIBLIOGRAPHY: Besançon, Bibl. mun., *Catalogue général des manuscrits*, XXXII, 1897, p. 81 no. 123; Meiss, *Late XIV Century*, 1967, p. 360.

PSEUDO-JACQUEMART

Bourges, Bibliothèque municipale	ms. 16	Breviary
	ms. 33–35	Lectionary of the Sainte-Chapelle, Bourges
	ms. 48	Evangeliary
Leningrad, State Library	ms. Q.v.1.8	Book of Hours
London, British Museum	Add. 32454	Book of Hours
	Harley 4947	Lactantius
	Royal 19 B XVII	*Légende dorée*
	Yates Thompson 37	Book of Hours
Paris, Bibliothèque nationale	fr. 170	*Cité de Dieu*
	fr. 13091	Psalter of Jean de Berry
	lat. 919	*Grandes Heures de Jean de Berry*
	lat. 18014	*Petites Heures de Jean de Berry*
Paris, Collection Comte Jean Durrieu		Prayer Book
Paris, formerly Alexandrine Rothschild		Book of Hours

RELATED MANUSCRIPTS

Baltimore, Walters Art Gallery	ms. 94	Book of Hours
	ms. 103	Book of Hours
London, British Museum	Harley 4381–82	*Bible historiale*
Lyon, Bibliothèque	ms. 5994	Book of Hours
Oxford, Bodleian Library	Laud. lat. 56	Vegetius, *De re militari* (Pächt and Alexander, *Bodleian Manuscripts*, 1966, no. 660)

BIBLIOGRAPHY: Meiss, *Art Bull.*, 1956, p. 191 f.; *idem*, *Late XIV Century*, 1967, p. 179 ff.; *idem*, *Boucicaut Master*, 1968, p. 142; Thomas, *Grandes Heures*, 1971.

APPENDIX A

THE BOOKKEEPING OF ROBINET D'ESTAMPES AND THE CHRONOLOGY OF JEAN DE BERRY'S MANUSCRIPTS

THE following tables reproduce the findings about the Duke's manuscripts that were obtained by an analysis of the structure of Robinet's inventories of the entire collection. The complete analysis, which we published in the *Art Bulletin*, 1971, pp. 225–235, yielded much more precise chronological information about numerous illuminated manuscripts, notably the *Belles Heures*, the *Très Belles Heures de Notre-Dame*, and the most important copy of the collected works of Christine de Pisan.

Fourth Account of Robinet

Compiled from February 1, 1412, through January 31, 1413

DATED ITEMS

(Undated surviving manuscripts inserted in italics. Starred items are not in chronological sequence)

Les Livres des Inventoires

(850–909 Manuscripts in inventory of 1402; no item dated)

Les autres livres que mondit Seigneur a euz depuis ledit inventoire, tant par achat comme par don, et autrement

Et premièrement s'ensuivent les livres declairez en deux chapitres, l'un commançant ou IIe XXXVIIe et l'autre ou IIe XXXVIIIe feuillez du livre des comptes precedens

	Item	*Date of accession*	
	910	*Before 1402*	*London, Brit. Mus. Roy. 19 D I*
Acquired 1402–05, mostly by purchase	911	Jan. 1, 1402	Bibl. nat. fr. 282
	912	April, 1402	Bibl. nat. fr. 301
	913	Feb., 1403	
	917	Jan., 1404	
	918	Feb., 1404	Bibl. nat. fr. 425
	919	May, 1404	
	920	Jan., 1405	Bibl. nat. fr. 117–120
	921	Jan. 21, 1405	
	922	Dec. 16, 1405	
	923	Dec. 16, 1405	
	924	Dec. 16, 1405	
	925	Dec. 16, 1405	Bibl. nat. fr. 256
	928	*ca. 1405*	*Bibl. nat. fr. 829*
(on folio 242)	*929	Aug. 27, 1405	
(on folio 243)	*931*	*1405–1406*	*Très Belles Heures de Notre-Dame*

Autres livres declairez ou chapitre commançant ou IIe XLVe feuillet dudit livre

	Item	*Date of accession*	
Given to Berry between 1402 and 1406	932	March 20, 1403	
	933	March 22, 1403	Bibl. nat. fr. 12201
	934	April 25, 1403	Bibl. de l'Arsenal MS 5212
	935	June 7, 1403	Morgan Library M 785
	936	July 7, 1403	Bibl. nat. fr. 380
	937	July 7, 1403	
	938	Jan. 1, 1404	
	939	Jan. 1, 1404	
	940	Feb., 1404	Bibl. nat. fr. 598
	941	May, 1404	
	942	June 20, 1404	
	943	Jan. 1, 1405	
	944	Sept., 1405	
	946	*1405*	*Bibl. nat. nouv. acq. fr. 24541*
	947	*1405*	*Chantilly, Musée Condé MS 277; Bibl. nat. fr. 9106*
	948	*1405*	*London, Brit. Mus. Harley 1319*
	950	Jan. 1, 1406	
	951	Jan. 1, 1406	
	*952	March, 1404	The Hague, Royal Library, MS 78 D. 42

Autres livres declairez ou chapitre commançant ou IIIe XXXIe feuillet dudit livre desdiz comptes precedens

	Item	*Date of accession*	
Acquired 1407–1409, mostly by purchase or commission	955	Oct. 29, 1407	London, Brit. Mus. Roy. 19 E VI
	957	*1408*	Recovery o *Brit. Mus. Burney 275* from Louis d'Orleans (died Nov. 23, 1407)
	959	*1408*	*Bibl. nat. fr. 606, 835–836*
	960	*1408–09*	*New York, Cloisters, Belles Heures*
	961	1409	Bibl. nat. lat. 919 (MS dated 1409)
	962	July 9, 1409	

Autres livres declairez ou chapitre commançant ou IIIe XXXVe feuillet du livre desdiz comptes precedens

	Item	*Date of accession*	
Given to Berry between 1407–1410	*963*	*ca. 1407*	First volume of *Bréviaire de Belleville* charged out
	964	*ca. 1407*	*Bibl. nat. fr. 172–173*
	965	Aug. 18, 1407	Malines, Bibl. du séminaire, MS 1
	966	Aug., 1407	Bibl. nat. fr. 5707
	967	Nov. 8, 1407	
	*968	Oct. 23, 1407	
	969	Jan., 1408	Bibl. nat. lat. 7907 A
	970	April, 1408	
	971	*1409*	Recovery of *Bibl. nat. lat. 1052* after death of Duchess of Orléans (Dec. 4, 1408)
	972	*1409*	Recovery of *Bibl. nat. nouv. acq. fr.* 15939–44 after death of Jean de Montaigu (Oct. 17, 1409)
	973	Nov., 1409	
	974	Nov. 17, 1409	
	*975	Oct. 25, 1409	
	976	Jan. 1, 1410	
	977	Jan. 1, 1410	

Autres livres declairez ou chapitre commançant ou IIIe XLIIIIe feuillet dudit livre
978–988 No dated items and only one source

Autres livres declairez ou chapitre commançant ou IIIe LXVe feuillet dudit livre

	Item	*Date of accession*	
Bought in 1410	989	Feb., 1410	Bibl. nat. fr. 1210
	990	March, 1410	

Autres livres declairez ou chapitre commançant ou IIIe LXVIe feuillet ensuivant

	Item	*Date of accession*	
Given to Berry between 1410–11	991	March 4, 1410	Bibl. nat. fr. 1023
	992	Nov. 8, 1410	
	993	Jan. 1, 1411	Geneva, Bibl. publique et universitaire, fr. 190
	994	Jan. 1, 1411	

Autres livres qui sont avenuz a mondit Seigneur le duc depuis lesdiz comptes precedens et ne sont point declairez oudit livre

	Item	*Date of accession*
Bought and given 1412–13	995	May, 1412
	996	May, 1412
	998	Nov., 1412
	999	Nov., —
	1000	Oct., 1412
	1001	Oct., 1412
	1002	Jan., 1413

	Item	*Date of accession*	
	1003	Jan. 1, 1413	
	1004	Jan. 1, 1413	
	1005	Jan., 1413	Bibl. nat. fr. 2810
	*1006	July, 1412	

End of dated items of Fourth Account.

Fifth Account of Robinet

Compiled from February 1, 1413 to June 15, 1416

Dated Manuscripts (other objects omitted)
(Undated surviving manuscripts inserted in italics. Starred items are not in chronological sequence)

	Item	*Date of accession*	
bought	1228	Feb., 1413	
	1229	Feb., 1413	
	1230	Sept., 1413	
	1231	[documented Sept. 3, 1413]	Bibl. nat. fr. 1454
	1232	Dec. 11, 1415	
	1234	March 2, 1416	
	1235	March 2, 1416	
	1236	March 2, 1416	
given	1238	Jan. 1, 1414	
	1239	Jan. 1, 1414	
	1240	Jan. 1, 1414	
	*1241	Sept. 19, 1413	
	1242	Sept., 1414	Bibl. nat. lat. 10426
	1243	Jan. 1, 1415	
	1244	Jan. 1, 1415	
	1245	Jan. 1, 1416	
	1247	March, 1416	
	1248	*1416*	*Bibl. de l'Arsenal,* MS *664*
	*1251	Jan., 1416	

RECONSTRUCTION OF ROBINET'S LOST ACCOUNTS FOR THE PERIOD BETWEEN 1402 AND 1412

Manuscripts only

Presumed First Account 1402–1406

Folio No. in lost book of accounts	*Item in Fourth Account*	*Object*	*Date*	*Given or bought*
237–238ff.	*910–928*	*livres*	*1402–05*	*bought*
242	*929*	*livres*	*Aug. 27, 1405*	*bought*
243	*931*	*livre*	*1405–06*	—
245ff.	*932–952*	*livres*	*1402–Jan., 1406*	*given*

Presumed Second Account Feb. 1406–1410

Folio No. in lost book of accounts	*Item in Fourth Account*	*Object*	*Date*	*Given or bought*
331ff.	*953–962*	*livres*	*1407–09*	*bought*
335ff.	*963–977*	*livres*	*1407–Jan. 1, 1410*	*given*
344ff.	*978–988*	*livres*	—	—

Presumed Third Account Feb. 1, 1410–Jan. 31, 1412

Folio No. in lost book of accounts	*Item in Fourth Account*	*Object*	*Date*	*Given or bought*
365	*989–990*	*livres*	*Feb. and March 1410*	*bought*
366	*991–94*	*livres*	*March, 1410–Jan., 1411*	*given*

APPENDIX B

PRINCIPAL COLLECTIONS OF ILLUMINATED MANUSCRIPTS
SELECTIVE LISTS

Philippe le Hardi

Brussels 9049–50	*Livy*. Cleres femmes workshop. Burgundian inventory of 1420. See Catalogue of Workshops.
Brussels 9094	*Propriété des choses*, bought in 1403. Late "Boqueteaux" style (Gaspar and Lyna, *Principaux manuscrits*, no. 151).
Brussels 9157	Bible in Latin. Flemish, *ca.* 1340. Inventory of 1404. Arms of Philippe le Hardi (Gaspar and Lyna, *Principaux manuscrits*, no. 126).
Brussels 9505–6	*Ethiques*. "Boqueteaux" style. Made for Charles V. Taken by Louis d'Anjou. Inventory of 1404 (Gaspar and Lyna, *Principaux manuscrits*, no. 148). See Meiss, *Late XIV Century*, fig. 517.
Brussels 9508	Christine de Pisan, *Mutacion de Fortune*. Epître Master, 1404. Figs. 12, 21. See Chapter on this manuscript and Catalogue of Manuscripts.
Brussels 10197–98	*Les trois pèlerinages*. Artois or Flemish. Inventory of 1404 (Gaspar and Lyna, *Principaux manuscrits*, no. 164).
Brussels 10392	*Horae*. "Boqueteaux" style (Gaspar and Lyna, *Principaux manuscrits*, no. 145).
Brussels 11035–37	Prayerbook (Gaspar and Lyna, *Principaux manuscrits*, no. 175). Fig. 609. See Catalogue of Workshops, Breviary Master.
Brussels 11042	Théodore Paléologue, *Enseignemens et ordenances pour un seigneur qui a guerres*. "Boqueteaux" style. Executed for Philippe le Hardi (Gaspar and Lyna, *Principaux manuscrits*, no. 154).
Brussels 11053–54	Victor de Capoue, *Diatessaron*. Inventory of 1405 (Gaspar and Lyna, *Principaux manuscrits*, no. 117).
Brussels 11060–61	*Brussels Hours*. Jacquemart de Hesdin. Given by Jean de Berry to Philippe le Hardi (Meiss, *Late XIV Century*, p. 321 ff.). Figs. 340, 342, 369, 399, 456, 495, 612.
Brussels 11140	*Le trésor amoureux*. Related to the Coronation Master. Inventory of 1405 (Gaspar and Lyna, *Principaux manuscrits*, no. 191). See the Catalogue of Workshops.
Cambridge, Fitzwilliam 3–1954	*Horae*. "Boqueteaux" style. See Meiss, *Late XIV Century*, figs. 564, 608, 609.
Paris, fr. 166	*Bible moralisée*. Paul and Jean de Limbourg, 1402–1404. Figs. 278–325, 327, 328, 332, 337, 346, 348, 357, 367, 655. See the Catalogue of Manuscripts.
Paris, fr. 167	*Bible moralisée*. *Ca.* 1370. Inventory of 1420. Figs. 326, 331.
Paris, fr. 12201	*Fleur des histoires*. Workshop of Coronation Master. Given to Jean de Berry, 1403 (Berry inventory of 1413). See Catalogue of Manuscripts.
Paris, fr. 12420	*Des cleres femmes*. Coronation Master and workshop, 1403. Figs. 3, 46, 74, 200. See Catalogue of Manuscripts.

Jean sans Peur

Brussels 9024–25	*Bible historiale*. Bought by Jean sans Peur in 1415 for his wife (Gaspar and Lyna, *Principaux manuscrits*, no. 199). Figs. 70, 664. See the Catalogue of Workshops, Master of Berry's Cleres Femmes, related manuscripts.
Brussels 9089–90	Aristotle, *Ethiques et Politiques*. Luçon workshop. Inventory of 1420 (Gaspar and Lyna, *Principaux manuscrits*, no. 185). See the Catalogue of Workshops.

Brussels 9125 — Missal of Paris, Ste.-Chapelle (Gaspar and Lyna, *Principaux manuscrits*, no. 166).

Brussels 9393 — Christine de Pisan, *Cité des Dames*. Cité des Dames workshop. Inventory of 1420 (Gaspar and Lyna, *Principaux manuscrits*, no. 170). Figs. 37, 40, 44. See the Catalogue of Manuscripts.

Brussels 9394–6 — *Le nouveau testament. Ca.* 1400. Belonged to Marie de Berry. Inventory 1420 (Gaspar and Lyna, *Principaux manuscrits*, no. 172).

Brussels 9427 — Bréviaire de Louis de Mâle. Inventory of 1420. Manuscript probably belonged to Philippe le Hardi who married the daughter of Louis de Mâle (Gaspar and Lyna, *Principaux manuscrits*, no. 144).

Brussels 9475 — St. Thomas Aquinas, *Livre de l'informacion des roys et des princes*. Follower of the Apocalypse Master. Made for Jean sans Peur (Gaspar and Lyna, *Principaux manuscrits*, no. 186). See Catalogue of Manuscripts.

Brussels 9509 — Boccaccio, *Des cleres femmes*. Cleres femmes workshop (Gaspar and Lyna, *Principaux manuscrits*, no. 196). See Catalogue of Workshops.

Brussels 9542 — Geoffroy de la Tour-Landry, *Livre pour l'enseignement de ses filles*. Late fourteenth century. Belonged to Berry. Inventory of 1420 (Gaspar and Lyna, *Principaux manuscrits*, no. 138).

Brussels 9553 — *Dialogues de Saint Grégoire*. Late fourteenth century. Given to Jean sans Peur by Jean de Berry (Gaspar and Lyna, *Principaux manuscrits*, no. 137).

Brussels 9634–35 — *Bible historiale*, vol. II, dated 1355. Inventory of 1420 (Gaspar and Lyna, *Principaux manuscrits*, no. 133).

Brussels 10230 — Cuvelier, *Livre de Messire Bertrant du Guesclin*. Related in style to Cleres Femmes Master. Inventory of 1420 (Gaspar and Lyna, *Principaux manuscrits*, no. 195). See Catalogue of Workshops.

Brussels 10309 — Christine de Pisan, *Livre de l'avision. Ca.* 1405. Inventory of 1420 (Gaspar and Lyna, *Principaux manuscrits*, no. 183).

Brussels 10987 — Christine de Pisan, *Les sept psaumes*. Egerton workshop. Inventory of 1420 (Gaspar and Lyna, *Principaux manuscrits*, no. 178). See Catalogue of Workshops.

Brussels 10993 — *Les Quatre Evangiles*. French, third quarter of fourteenth century. Inventory of 1420 (Gaspar and Lyna, *Principaux manuscrits*, no. 146).

Dresden, Sächsische Landesbibliothek, ms. Oc. 61 — *Livre de la chasse*, Rohan workshop and Bedford trend. Inventory 1420. Fig. 840. See Catalogue of Workshops.

The Hague, Bibl. royale, ms. 133 A 2 — *Les traités dits de Sidrac et Lucidaire*, written by Guillebert de Metz. Follower of the Berry Apocalypse Master. See Catalogue of Workshops.

Leningrad, State Library, fr. Q.v.XIV, 3 and fr. Q.v.XIV, 4 — *Roman de la violette, Dit de la violette, Dit de la Panthère d'amors, Roman d'Athis et Prophilias*. Luçon and Coronation workshops. Inventory of 1420. See Catalogue of Workshops.

London, Brit. Mus., Add. 35311, Harley 2897 — *Breviary of Jean sans Peur*. Breviary Master and associates. Arms. Figs. 610, 611, 618–622, 648, 893. See Catalogue of Manuscripts.

London, Brit. Mus., Egerton 2709 — *La conquête et les conquérants des Iles Canaries*. Cité des Dames workshop. Inventory of 1420. See Catalogue of Workshops.

Paris, Bibl. de l'Arsenal, ms. 5193 — *Boccaccio, Cas des nobles hommes et femmes*. Cité des Dames Master and workshop, and Bedford trend. Inventory of 1420. Figs. 66, 159. See Catalogue of Manuscripts.

Paris, Bibl. nat., fr. 2810 — *Livre des merveilles*. Boucicaut Master and workshop, and Bedford trend. According to inscription given to Jean de Berry, January 1413. See Meiss, *Boucicaut Master*, p. 116 ff., figs. 80–100.

Paris, Bibl. nat., fr. 6446 — *Antiquités judaïques*. Belonged to Jean de Berry. Cité des Dames workshop. Inventory of 1420. Fig. 169. See Catalogue of Workshops.

Paris, Bibl. nat., lat. nouv. acq. 3055	*Horae*. Master of Guillebert de Metz. Made for Jean sans Peur.
Rome, Vatican Library, Pal. lat. 1989	*Decameron*. Cité des Dames Master and workshop. Inventory of 1420. Figs. 8, 9, 689. See Catalogue of Manuscripts.

Louis d'Orléans

London, Burney 275	*Priscian*. Early fourteenth century. Clement VII gave manuscript in 1387 to Jean de Berry, who in turn gave it to Louis d'Orléans, and then recovered it after the death of the latter. See *Late XIV Century*, p. 310.
Paris, fr. 312–314	*Miroir historial*. Late "Boqueteaux." Ordered from Etienne l'Angevin in 1395. Arms of Louis d'Orléans, supported by two wolves.
Paris, fr. 9106 and Chantilly 277	*Politiques, Economiques, Ethiques*. Late "Boqueteaux." Ordered from Etienne l'Angevin in 1397. Arms of Louis d'Orléans, supported by two wolves.
Paris, lat. 1052	Breviary. Passion Master. Given by Charles VI. After his death Valentine gave it to Jean de Berry. See Meiss, *Late XIV Century*, figs. 351, 359, 362, 367–371, 839.
Paris, lat. 9684	Sallust. *Catalina*. Related to the Bedford trend. Arms. See Catalogue of Workshops.

ADDENDA

LIST OF BERRY'S EXTANT ILLUMINATED MANUSCRIPTS

LONDON, Brit. Mus., Harley 1319.
Jean Creton, *Fall of Richard II*. Virgil workshop.
The *incipit* on fol. 3, which is the second folio of the text, is, as in the inventory item, "qu'il eust."
Guiffrey, *Inventaires*, I, 1894, p. 249 no. 948; Delisle, *Charles V*, 1907, II, p. 263 no. 252; Meiss with Off, 1971, p. 228 f. See the Catalogue of Workshops.

LONDON, Brit. Mus., Royal 20 D I (Fig. 275).
Histoire ancienne. Neapolitan.
The *incipit* on the second folio identifies the manuscript with an item in Berry's inventory of 1413.
Guiffrey, *Inventaires*, I, 1894, p. 236 no. 910; Delisle, *Charles V*, 1907, II, p. 260 no. 226; Avril, "Trois manuscrits napolitains," 1969 (1970), p. 309 f.

PARIS, Bibl. nat., fr. 301 (Fig. 274).
Histoire ancienne. Orosius workshop.
Bought by Berry in April, 1402 from Bureau de Dampmartin.
The *incipit* on the second folio is the same as an item in Berry's inventory of 1413.
Guiffrey, *Inventaires*, I, 1894, p. 237 no. 912; Delisle, *Charles V*, 1907, II, pp. 260 no. 227, 310; Avril, "Trois manuscrits napolitains," 1969 (1970), p. 308 f. See the Catalogue of Workshops.

PARIS, Bibl. nat., nouv. acq. fr. 15939–15944 (formerly Dublin, Coll. A. C. Beatty, ms. 75).
Vincent de Beauvais, *Mirouer historial*. "Boqueteaux" style. See *Late XIV Century*, 1967, p. 310.

ROME, Bibl. Casanatense. Missal (Adorisio, in *Miscellanea*, 1973; in press).

SCOTLAND, Coll. of the Marquess of Bute.
Grandes Chroniques de France. "Boqueteaux" style.
The arms of Berry appear in the central space between the first four miniatures. Several damaged folios of this manuscript are in the British Museum, Cotton Vitellius E. II.
Delisle, *Charles V*, 1907, I, pp. 314–317; London, Burlington Fine Arts Club, *Exhibition*, 1908, no. 145, pl. 100; Paris, Bibl. nat. (Avril and Lafaurie), 1968, p. 113 no. 196.

APPENDIX C

ASTRONOMICAL AND CALENDRICAL DATA IN THE TRES RICHES HEURES

Notes by O. Neugebauer

It is not surprising that a work of the artistic excellence displayed in the *Très Riches Heures* also shows competence on the part of the makers of the calendar which precedes in traditional fashion the devotional sections. What "competent" means in this line of work in the early 15th century is perhaps not obvious to historians of art. We therefore hope to contribute a little to the appreciation of the *Très Riches Heures* when we draw attention to some aspects of medieval astronomy embedded in the tables and miniatures which open the book.

We begin with two strictly astronomical topics: the variation of the length of daylight during the year and the motion of the sun through the ecliptic. We then turn to the calendaric treatment of the lunar motion, both in its traditional ecclesiastic form and "nouvel." Finally we touch upon the "dies aegyptiaci" and the figure of the Zodiac Man, inserted after the calendar. That many questions remain unanswered may be taken as proof that it is worth while looking into these matters.

In the center of the following discussion always lie the *Très Riches Heures*. Occasionally, however, a comparison with the calendars in one of the other Books of Hours of the Duke of Berry is of interest. I refer to all these calendars by the conventional names:[1]

Petites Heures (*ca.* 1385)
Très Belles Heures de Notre Dame (*ca.* 1404/5)
Belles Heures (1406–1408)
Grandes Heures (1407–1409)
Très Riches Heures (1413–1416).

1. Length of Daylight

Following the list of saint- and feast-days the calendar pages of the *Très Riches Heures* show a column headed "Quantitas dierum" or "la quantite des jours" which gives day by day, in "hore" and "minuta," the length of daylight. The lowest value (m) is 8^h, listed for December 11 to 15, the highest (M) of 16^h is found for June 13 to 16.

Before going to the details of this table we can draw an immediate conclusion from the data mentioned. Since early Greek astronomy the ratio of longest to shortest daylight served to characterize a location on the terrestrial sphere. With the advancement of spherical trigonometry the correct relation of this ratio to the terrestrial latitude ϕ was established and hence we find, e.g. in the Almagest, tables which relate M to ϕ. There we see[2] that $M=16^h$ corresponds to $\phi=48;32°$, a latitude which fits Paris (48;52°) better than Bourges (47;5°). Of course we should not assume that the Almagest was used by the calendar makers at the end of the 14th century; but the Alfonsine Tables (epoch 1252), among many other tables in circulation at the time, contain also a "Tabula Quantitatis Dierum" which gives the length of daylight for each degree of latitude between 36° and 55°. Here we find[3]

for $\phi = 47°$ $\quad M = 15;42^h$
for $\phi = 49°$ $\quad M = 16;0^h$.

Again Paris is clearly preferable to Bourges.

The bulk of the table for the "Quantitas Dierum" shows the effects of sloppiness common in mediaeval tables, in each copy increased by some new scribal errors.[4] At several occasions whole groups of numbers are out of place; for example the same value $9;45^h$ is given for January 31 and February 1 although the daily increment in that region is 3 minutes. Consequently all numbers until February 8 are 3 minutes too low. At that point the error was detected and the numbers change abruptly from $10;9^h$ to $10;15^h$ (which is correct for February 9). The whole correct sequence in inverse order is found between October 16 ($10;15^h$) and October 25 ($9;45^h$).

Errors of this type abound throughout the calendar tables. In order to reconstruct the correct table from which our calendar was ultimately derived one can make use of the symmetry which must exist in schemes of this type: the same sequence of numbers between winter solstice and summer solstice should appear in inverse order for the other half of the year. Inspection of the actual numbers shows furthermore for long stretches the use of constant increments, e.g., 4, 3, or 2 minutes for many days. Using this experience in combination with the principle of symmetry one can reconstruct the whole original table for the length of daylight. The result is shown in Fig. 1; the numbers written beside the graph show the constant increment (in minutes) valid in the corresponding section.

How a table of this kind had been computed is in principle well known. Again following ancient and medieval (Islamic and Byzantine) tradition astronomical tables usually contain a table of oblique ascensions for given geographical latitudes. The length of daylight for a given solar longitude is then the total of the oblique ascensions for a semicircle of the ecliptic from the position of the sun to its diametrically opposite point.[5] Since one can compute with the traditional methods the longitude of the sun for every day of the year one can also tabulate the length of daylight day by day.

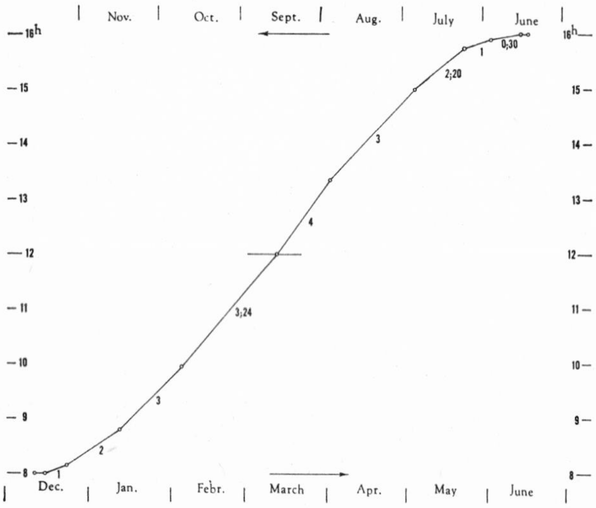

FIGURE 1

It is clear, however, that the table in our text was based only on a few accurately computed values whereas linear interpolation was used otherwise. Most of the constant differences had been chosen as convenient round numbers, a procedure which implies some doctoring of the few originally computed numbers. Where nevertheless fractions of minutes could not be avoided for the increments the results were given by truncation of the seconds.

It is of course impossible to say how far back this process of tabulation reaches. Most likely the table in the calendar of the *Très Riches Heures* was simply copied from some contemporary set of astronomical tables, adjusted for the latitude of Paris.[6]

In contrast to the astronomically meaningful scheme that describes in the *Très Riches Heures* the variation of the length of daylight one should remember that the *Petites Heures* as well as the *Belles Heures* display a much more primitive and utterly useless pattern. There we find at the beginning of each calendar table a statement "la nuit a . . . heurs le iour . . . " The numbers (always totalling 24) vary with the constant difference of 2 hours from month to month, the shortest daylight of 6 hours listed for December, the longest of 18 hours for June. Not only does the abrupt change at the solstices from increase to decrease and vice versa contradict all direct experiences but the ratio 3:1 for the extrema would only be correct at a geographical latitude of about 58° (almost the latitude of Stockholm). Linear schemes for the length of daylight go back to the early hellenistic period when Babylonian arithmetical methods made their influence felt on nascent Greek astronomy. At the fringes of the ancient world these primitive arithmetical methods survived for many centuries, often step by step modified into totally meaningless rules of procedure. Mediaeval astronomy, in India, in Ethiopia, and in western Europe provides us with many examples of this process.

2. Solar Motion

The table for the length of daylight provides us also with the dates assumed for the solstices and equinoxes. The entries for 12^h are found at March 12 and September 15. The shortest daylight is listed for the five days from December 11 to 15, the longest for June 13 to 16; hence we can accept December 13 and June 14/15 for the solstices.

The calendar tables, however, are not the only source for this information. The calendar miniatures which face the tables contain in the crowning semicircular field a host of astronomical information. The two outermost circles give degrees and zodiacal signs of the solar travel during the month in question. The innermost circle gives the consecutive days of the month; a radial line which separates the pictures of the zodiacal signs allows us to read off the date at which the sun transgresses from one sign into the next. In this way we find once more the dates for the cardinal points: entry into Aries and Libra on March 12 and September 15 respectively and December 12/13 and June 13/14 for the solstices in reasonably good agreement with the data derived from the calendar.[7]

Looking back to our graph for the length of daylight (Fig. 1, p. 422) we observe that the curve is not symmetric to the equinoxes. The reason for this phenomenon lies in the fact that our table uses days as independent variable and not solar longitudes. For equidistant solar longitudes the curve for the corresponding

MONTH	BOUNDARY		TEXT	DEGREE	
	BETWEEN	DAY		FIRST	LAST
I	♑ ♒	11 | 12	———	♑ 20	♒ 20
II	♒ ♓	10	Finis. graduum|aquarii|Initium|piscium|gradus.|19.	♒ 22	♓ 19
III	♓ ♈	12	finis.|. graduum.|piscium.|. Initium.|arietis.|. gradus.|.20.	♓ 20	♈ 19
IV	♈ ♉	12	———	♈ 20	♉ 18
V	♉ ♊	13	———	♉ 19	♊ 17
VI	♊ ♋	13 | 14	finis.|graduum.|.cancri.| Inicium.|.Leonis.|gradus.|.16.	♊ 19	♋ 16
VII	♋ ♌	15	Finis|graduum|Cancri.|Inicium|Leonis.|gradus. 16.	♋ 17	♌ 16
VIII	♌ ♍	15 | 16	———	♌ 17	♍ 16
IX	♍ ♎	15 | 16	Finis.|graduum|virginis.|Inicium.|Libre.|gradus. 15.	♍ 17	♎ 15
X	♎ ♏	15	Finis|graduum.|Libre|Initium.|Scorpionis.|gradus.|16	♎ 16	♏ 17
XI	♏ ♐	14	Finis|graduum|Scorpionis.|Inicium.|sagittarii.|gradus.|17.	♏ 17	♐ 17
XII	♐ ♑	12 | 13	Finis.|graduum.|sagittarii.|Initium.|capricorni.|gradus.|18.	♐ 18	♑ 19

TABLE I

NOTES TO TABLE I

I. ♑ 20: not a full space for 20; ♒ 20: should be 21; cf. next month

II. ♒ 22: preceded by a little blank space

III. gradus 20: should be gradus 19; ♓ 20: preceded by a little blank space; ♈ 19: followed by a little blank space

IV. ♉ 18: followed by a little blank space

V. ♊ 17: followed by about half a space, left blank; cf. next month

VI. ♊ 19: preceded by about half a space, left blank; one could assume that ♊ 18 was divided between the months V and VI. The text "finis graduum cancri, inicium leonis" belongs to the next month; the pictures give correctly Gemini and Cancer

VIII. ♍ 16: not quite a full space

IX. ♍ 17: preceded by one space left blank; nothing missing. ♎ 15: followed by a little space left blank

X. ♎ 16: space for 16 left blank. ♏ 17: 17 written into the last small space; actually 16 should be the final degree; cf. the text and the next month

XI. ♐ 17: followed by a little blank space

XII. ♐ 18: space for 18 left blank. The text "capricorni gradus 18" should be emended to gradus 19; cf. last degree in month XII and first degree in month I.

lengths of daylight would have been symmetric with respect to the equinoxes. The variation in the solar velocity, however, relates different intervals of solar longitudes to equidistant days and thus produces a deviation from the symmetric pattern.[8] Hence, as it had to be expected, the solar anomaly had been taken into account for the computation of the table of the length of daylight.

Again the calendar miniatures provide corroborating information about the anomalistic solar motion. We can determine the variable solar velocity in two ways: first, the dates of the entry into the consecutive signs tells us how many days are required to cover 30°; secondly we obtain from the outermost circle the number of degrees travelled by the sun in the number of days contained in each month.

Table I shows the data which we obtain from the miniatures. If two consecutive days are mentioned for the crossing of a boundary between signs the separating radius separates also the two day numbers of the innermost ring. Otherwise the radius leads (more or less accurately) into the middle of the space for one day. Similarly, in the outermost ring, we are shown the first and last degree for the sun in the given month; the last degree is also mentioned in the text of the second ring. Unfortunately the spaces are not drawn accurately enough that one could operate with fractions of degrees or days. This restriction to integers explains the irregularities in the solar motion deduced from these pictorial presentations.

Table II shows what we can conclude from Table I by using the time intervals Δt between entering of the sun into consecutive signs. Since each such interval corresponds to a travel of 30° in longitude the solar velocity during that sign is given by $30/\Delta t$.

Table III is based on the extremal points reached by the sun in each month. Hence we can determine the longitudinal travel $\Delta\lambda$ and find the velocity during this month by dividing Δλ by the number of days in the corresponding month.

The two results are schematically represented in Fig. 2. The solid line corresponds to Table III, the dotted line (for the sake of clarity set one half space to the right) gives the values from Table II.[9] It is clear that both tables are based on true solar longitudes which lead to a maximum velocity of about $1;2^{\circ/d}$, a minimum of about $0;57^{\circ/d}$.[10] No doubt the data in the *Très Riches Heures* were compiled by people who could competently handle the contemporary astronomical tables.

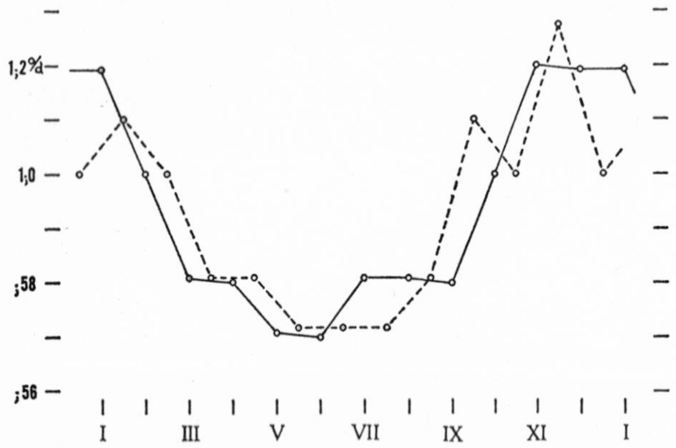

FIGURE 2

ENTERING SIGN	DATE	Δt	30/Δt
♒	I 11/12		
		29;30[d]	1;1,1°/d
♓	II 10		
		30	1;0
♈	III 12		
		31	0;58,4
♉	IV 12		
		31	0;58,4
♊	V 13		
		31;30	0;57,8
♋	VI 13/14		
		31;30	0;57,8
♌	VII 15		
		31;30	0;57,8
♍	VIII 15/16		
		31	0;58,4
♎	IX 15/16		
		29;30	1;1,1
♏	X 15		
		30	1;0
♐	XI 14		
		28;30	1;3,9
♑	XII 12/13		
		30	1;0
♒	I 11/12		

TABLE II

MONTH	Δt	DEGREE FIRST	DEGREE LAST	Δλ	Δλ/Δt
I	31[d]	♑ 20	♒ 21	32°	1;1,56°/d
II	28	♒ 22	♓ 19	28	1;0
III	31	♓ 20	♈ 19	30	0;58,4
IV	30	♈ 20	♉ 18	29	0;58
V	31	♉ 19	♊ 18?	29;30?	0;57,6
VI	30	♊ 18?	♋ 16	28;30?	0;57
VII	31	♋ 17	♌ 16	30	0;58,4
VIII	31	♌ 17	♍ 16	30	0;58,4
IX	30	♍ 17	♎ 15	29	0;58
X	31	♎ 16	♏ 16	31	1;0
XI	30	♏ 17	♐ 17	31	1;2
XII	31	♐ 18	♑ 19	32	1;1,56

TABLE III

3. Golden Number

In the *Très Riches Heures* the "Golden Numbers" occur three times: in two different versions in the calendar tables and once more in the calendar miniatures. In the left column of the calendar tables we find Golden Numbers in the arrangement which is traditional in the late Middle Ages; the right column is headed "numerus aureus nouus" or "nombre dor nouuel." As will be shown presently the miniatures display also the "new" variety.

We begin our discussion with the traditional scheme because in it one can easiest follow the basic idea upon which is built the "perpetual" luni-solar calendar which regulated the dates for the movable feasts of the church.

THE 19-YEAR CYCLE

Let us assume that a new moon[11] falls on December 24, that is to say that we assume that December 25, the first day of the ecclesiastical year, coincides with the first day of a lunar month. Let us furthermore assume that this first lunar month is a full month, i.e., 30 days in length. Then the next conjunction will take place on January 23. A year of this type, i.e. a year for which the

XII 1														
2 2/13	I 1 3	31 3	2	IV 1	V 1 11	31 11	30	30 19	29 19	28	28 8	27 8	27	26
3	2	II 1	3 11	2 11	2	VI 1	VII 1 19	31	30 8	29 8	29	28	28 16	27 17
4 10	3 11	2 11	4	3	3 19	2 19	2 8	VIII 1 8	31	30	30 16	29 16	29 5	28 6
5	4	3 19	5 19	4 19	4 8	3 8	3	2 16	IX 1 16	X 1 16	31 5	30 5	30	29
6 18	5 19	4 8	6 8	5 8	5	4 16	4 16	3 5	2 5	2 5	XI 1	XII 1	31 13	30 14
7 7	6 8	5	7	6 16	6 16	5 5	5 5	4	3	3 13	2 13	2 13/2	I 1 3	31 3
8	7	6 16	8 16	7 5	7 5	6	6	5 13	4 13	4 2	3 2	3	2	
9 15	8 16	7 5	9 5	8	8	7 13	7 13	6 2	5 2	5	4	4 10	3 11	
10 4	9 5	8	10	9 13	9 13	8 2	8 2	7	6	6 10	5 10	5	4	
11	10	9 13	11 13	10 2	10 2	9	9	8 10	7 10	7	6	6 18	5 19	
12 12	11 13	10 2	12 2	11	11	10 10	10 10	9	8	8 18	7 18	7 7	6 8	
13 1	12 2	11	13	12 10	12 10	11	11	10 18	9 18	9 7	8 7	8	7	
14	13	12 10	14 10	13	13	12 18	12 18	11 7	10 7	10	9	9 15	8 16	
15 9	14 10	13	15	14 18	14 18	13 7	13 7	12	11	11 15	10 15	10 4	9 5	
16	15	14 18	16 18	15 7	15 7	14	14	13 15	12 15	12 4	11 4	11	10	
17 17	16 18	15 7	17 7	16	16	15 15	15 15	14 4	13 4	13	12	12 12	11 13	
18 6	17 7	16	18	17 15	17 15	16 4	16 4	15	14	14 12	13 12	13 1	12 2	
19	18	17 15	19 15	18 4	18 4	17	17	16 12	15 12	15 1	14 1	14	13	
20 14	19 15	18 4	20 4	19	19	18 12	18 12	17 1	16 1	16	15	15 9	14 10	
21 3	20 4	19	21	20 12	20 12	19 1	19 1	18	17	17 9	16 9	16	15	
22	21	20 12	22 12	21 1	21 1	20	20	19 9	18 9	18	17	17 17	16 18	
23 11	22 12	21 1	23 1	22	22	21 9	21 9	20	19	19 17	18 17	18 6	17 7	
24 19	23 1	22	24	23 9	23 9	22	22	21 17	20 17	20 6	19 6	19	18	
25	24	23 9	25 9	24	24	23 17	23 17	22 6	21 6	21	20	20 14	19 15	
26 8	25 9	24	26	25 17	25 17	24 6	24 6	23	22	22 14	21 14	21 3	20 4	
27	26	25 17	27 17	26 6	26 6	25	25	24 14	23 14	23 3	22 3	22	21	
28 16	27 17	26 6	28 6	27	27	26 14	26 14	25 3	24 3	24	23	23 11	22 12	
29 5	28 6	27	29	28 14	28 14	27 3	27 3	26	25	25 11	24 11	24 19	23 1	
30	29	28 14	30 14	29 3	29 3	28	28	27 11	26 11	26	25 19	25	24	
31 13	30 14	III 1 3	31 3	30	30	29 11	29 11	28	27 19	27 19	26	26 8	25 9	

TABLE IV

"January Lunation" extends from the preceding December 24 to January 23, is given the Golden Number 1 thus being made the first year in a cycle of 19.

Continuing in this first year we make the second lunar month "hollow," i.e. 29 days long, and thus continue with alternating full and hollow months since we know that consecutive conjunctions are in the mean about $29\frac{1}{2}$ days apart. Our Table IV shows the new moon dates obtained in this way for a year with the golden number 1:

Jan. 23	May 21	Sept. 16
Febr. 21	June 19	Oct. 15
March 23	July 19	Nov. 14
Apr. 21	Aug. 17	Dec. 13

The arrangement of Table IV in columns of always 30 days length, regardless of the number of days in a julian month, makes it easy to distinguish between full and hollow months: if the golden number remains in the same line the lunation is full, if it moves one line up, it is hollow.

After the last lunation of the first year which is hollow and ends on December 13 we place again a full lunation which thus ends on January 12 of the second year. Thus we find the Golden Number 2 associated with January 12 and then, operating as before with alternating full and hollow months, with February 10, March 12, etc. This procedure cannot be continued indefinitely since the length of the mean lunation is a little more than $29\frac{1}{2}$ days. We therefore find in 19 years 7 cases in which a full month is inserted after a full month (cf. Fig. 3). This is done in all those years in which 13 conjunctions take place, i.e. in the years No. 3, 5, 8, 11, 13, 16, and 19 of the cycle. In the last year, however, we find not only a duplication of a full month but also twice a pair of hollow months.[12] This brings us back from No. 19 Dec. 24 to No. 1 Jan. 23 of the next 19-year cycle.

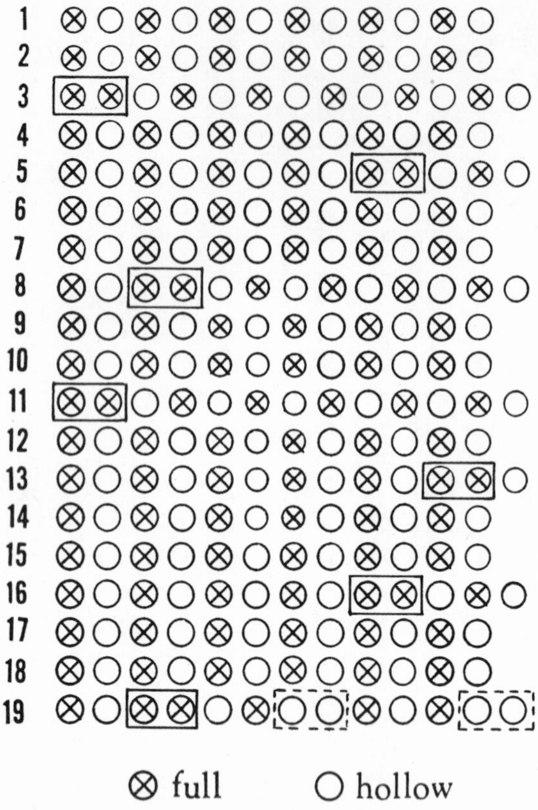

FIGURE 3

Fig. 3 allows us to rapidly determine the numerical basis of this cycle. The number of lunations in the whole cycle is obviously

$$19 \cdot 12 + 7 = 235 \text{ months.}$$

The number of days can be found as follows: each pair of full plus hollow months represents 59 days and we have 6 of such pairs in each year, hence

$$19 \cdot 6 \cdot 59 = 6726 \text{ days.}$$

To this we must add seven full months, i.e., 210 days. In year 19, however, one full month was replaced by a hollow one (cf. Fig. 3); hence we have to subtract one day. This gives the total

$$6726 + 210 - 1 = 6935 \text{ days.}$$

Since $6935 = 19 \cdot 365$ we can say that the cycle as represented in Table IV would exactly fit the length of 19 Egyptian years. Our calendars assume, of course, Julian years which assign every fourth year 29 days to February. By simply deciding that the golden numbers remain the same also for Julian leap years we add implicitly 19/4 days to the above total for a cycle of 19 Julian years. One can express this rule also in the form that four cycles, i.e. 76 Julian years, contain

$$4 \cdot 6935 + 19 = 27759 \text{ days.}$$

We shall come back presently to this 76-year cycle (p. 429).

VARIANTS

There are more variants among the five calendars of the Duke than one should *a priori* expect. As far as simple scribal errors are concerned the two closely related calendars of the Petites and the Grandes Heures are by far the worst[13] whereas the Très Belles Heures de Notre Dame and the Belles Heures both show only few scribal errors[14] and agree very closely with the Très Riches Heures.

There exist, however, also variants which are not evidently copyist mistakes. The Belles Heures and the Très Riches Heures agree in assigning to December 2 two cycle numbers, 2 as well as 13. The Petites and the Grandes Heures change this to 13 for Dec. 1 and 2 for December 2; the Heures of Notre Dame assign 13 to December 2 and 2 to December 3. These changes influence the sequence of full and hollow months as shown in Fig. 3. The Heures of Notre Dame would make the last month in line 2 full and therefore the first in line 3 hollow. Similarly the last pair in line 13 interchanges full and hollow in the arrangement of the Petites and the Grandes Heures. I do not know what motivated these changes.

More variants exist for the cycle year 19. In this case we know that the mediaeval computists were puzzled by the above-mentioned necessity (p. 426) to subtract 1 day from the 235 lunar months which constitute the 19-year cycle. A simple solution consists, of course, in making one of the seven intercalary months hollow. Where such a reduction, the "saltus lunae," should be localized within the cycle is a question on which the mediaeval calendar makers did not reach a final agreement. Consequently we find even among our five calendars variants in the placing of the golden number 19, a fact which also increased the chance for errors, again exemplified in our material.

Obvious errors are found in the Belles Heures where 19 is associated with August 28—September 28—October 26 and in the Grandes Heures which give 19 to August 28—September 28—October 27. In the first instance a lunar month of 31 days would be followed by 28 days, in the second case at least the second interval of 29 days would be permissible. A simple emendation of the first case would be the replacement of September 28 by September 27, the date found in the four remaining calendars.[15] The second case can also be repaired by the same correction. Finally a plausible correction can be made in the Petites Heures where all entries from February 4 to 13 are one day too late in comparison with the remaining calendars. If we therefore move the golden number 19 from February 4 to 3 we obtain the customary beginning: full—hollow (instead of full—full).

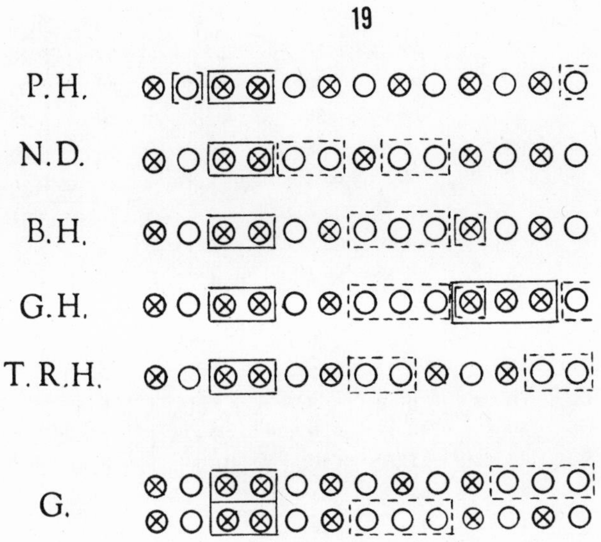

FIGURE 4

Fig. 4 illustrates the different ways in which our five calendars distribute the last golden number of the cycle. Not two of these patterns are identical. Only one of the two patterns (G) which Ginzel considers to be standard is represented here (Belles Heures).

APPLICATIONS

What we have obtained so far is a pattern for a sequence of 235 full and hollow months which repeats itself every 19 Julian years. Each year in the cycle is assigned a number between 1 and 19, the "Golden Number," which characterizes the position of the year in the cycle. Because of the strict periodicity of this pattern one speaks of an "eternal" Julian calendar which furnishes the dates of all new moons: if one knows, e.g., that the current year has the golden number 5 we see from Table IV that January 9 should be a new moon, followed by February 7, March 9, etc. In the next year January 28, February 26, etc. should be new moons.

To apply this scheme one has to know, however, the Golden Number (g) of the year (N) in question. One of the several equivalent rules for the determination of g is the following one: g is the residue of the division of N—531 by 19.[16]

According to this rule A.D. 532 has the Golden Number $g = 1$; consequently January 23 should be a new moon—as is indeed the case.[17] This year is the first year of the Easter Tables of Dionysius Exiguus; hence the counting of A.D. 532 as a year 1 of the cycle.

According to our rule also the year A.D. 1387 receives the Golden Number 1 because $1387 - 531 = 856 = 45 \cdot 19 + 1$. Checking again the astronomical facts one finds, however, that not January 23 but January 20 was a new moon. This is not surprising because 19 Julian years are only approximately the equivalent of 235 mean synodic months while the cyclic determination of the Golden Numbers assumes exact equality. In spite of the slowly accumulating error the liturgical calendar remained based on the strict application of the cyclic computation long after it had become clear that the cyclically computed new moons would more and more deviate from the observable facts.

NOMBRE D'OR NOUVEL

The last column of the calendar pages of the *Très Riches Heures* gives a set of numbers under the heading "numerus nouus" or "nombre dor nouuel." The numbers, shown in our Table V, form again a pattern with a 19-year period.

The calendar miniatures give under the title "primaciones lune" in the innermost ring a sequence of letters which can be easily transposed into numbers by their alphabetical order:

a	b	c	d	e	f	g	h	i	k	l	m	n	o	p	q	r	s	t
1	2	3	4	5	6	7	8	9	10	11	12	13	14	15	16	17	18	19

Wherever the calendar miniatures are completed[18] the resulting numbers agree exactly with the nombres d'or nouvelles in the tables.

In the same way as before one can derive from Table

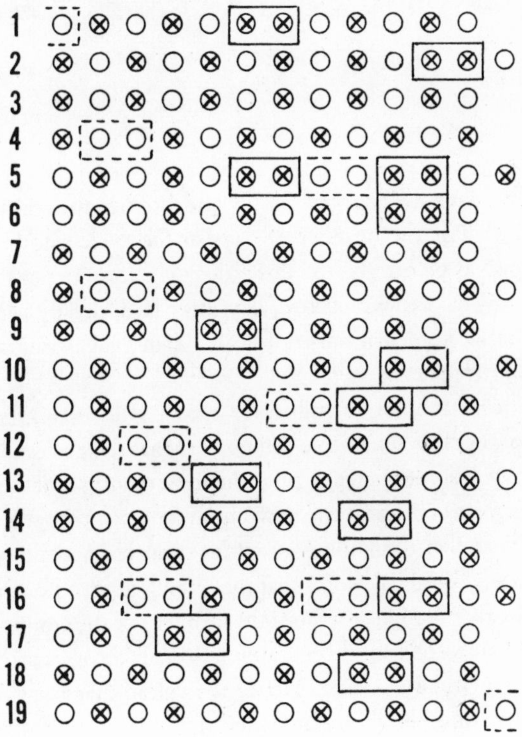

FIGURE 5

XII 1 10														
2	I 1 19	31 19	2 8	IV 1 8	V 1	31 16	30 16	30	29 5	28 5	28 5	27	27 13	26 14
3 18	2	II 1 8	3	2 16	2 16	VI 1	VII 1	31 5	30	29	29 13	28 13	28	27
4 7	3 8	2	4 16	3	3 5	2 5	2 5	VIII 1	31 13	30 13	30	29	29 2	28 3
5	4 16	3 16	5 5	4 5	4	3	3 13	2 13	IX 1	X 1 2	31 2	30 2	30	29 11
6 15	5 5	4 5	6	5 13	5 13	4 13	4	3 2	2 2	2	XI 1	XII 1 10	31 10	30
7 4	6	5 13	7 13	6	6	5 2	5 2	4	3 10	3 10	2 10	2	I 1 19	31 19
8 12	7 13	6	8	7 2	7 2	6	6 10	5 10	4	4	3 18	3 18	2	
9	8	7 2	9 2	8	8 10	7 10	7	6 18	5 18	5 18	4	4 7	3 8	
10 1	9 2	8	10 10	9 10	9	8 18	8 18	7	6	6 7	5 7	5	4 16	
11	10 10	9 10	11	10 18	10 18	9	9	8 7	7 7	7	6 15	6 15	5 5	
12 9	11	10 18	12 18	11	11	10 7	10 7	9	8 15	8 15	7 4	7 4	6	
13 17	12 18	11	13	12 7	12 7	11	11 15	10 15	9 4	9 4	8	8 12	7 13	
14	13	12 7	14 7	13	13 15	12 15	12 4	11 4	10	10 12	9 12	9	8	
15 6	14 7	13	15 15	14 15	14 4	13 4	13	12 12	11 12	11	10	10 1	9 2	
16	15 15	14 15	16 4	15 4	15	14 12	14 12	13	12	12 1	11 1	11	10 10	
17 14	16	15 4	17	16 12	16 12	15	15	14 1	13 1	13	12 9	12 9	11	
18 3	17 4	16	18 12	17	17 1	16 1	16 1	15	14 9	14 9	13	13 17	12 18	
19	18 12	17 12	19 1	18 1	18	17	17 9	16 9	15	15 17	14 17	14	13	
20 11	19 1	18 1	20	19 9	19 9	18 9	18	17 17	16 17	16	15	15 6	14 7	
21 19	20	19 9	21 9	20	20	19 17	19 17	18	17 6	17 6	16 6	16	15 15	
22 8	21 9	20	22 17	21 17	21 17	20	20 6	19 6	18	18	17 14	17 14	16	
23	22 17	21 17	23	22	22 6	21 6	21	20 14	19 14	19 14	18	18 3	17 4	
24 16	23	22	24 6	23 6	23	22 14	22 14	21	20	20 3	19 3	19	18 12	
25	24 6	23 6	25	24 14	24 14	23	23	22 3	21 3	21	20 11	20 11	19 1	
26 5	25	24 14	26 14	25	25	24 3	24 3	23 11	22 11	22 11	21	21 19	20	
27 13	26 14	25	27	26 3	26 3	25	25 11	24	23	23 19	22 19	22 8	21 9	
28	27	26 3	28 3	27	27 11	26 11	26	25 19	24 19	24 8	23 8	23	22 17	
29 2	28 3	27	29 11	28 11	28	27 19	27 19	26 8	25 8	25	24 16	24 16	23	
30	29 11	28 11	30	29 19	29 19	28 8	28 8	27 16	26 16	26 16	25	25	24 6	
31 10	30	III 1 19	31 19	30 8	30 8	29	29 16	28	27	27	26 5	26 5	25	

TABLE V

V the sequence adopted for full and hollow months (cf. Fig. 5). For the number of days in the cycle one finds exactly as before the total of $19 \cdot 354 + 209 = 6935 = 19 \cdot 365$ days to which 19/4 days may be added by using the same golden numbers for all Julian years, ordinary and intercalary.

The reason for introducing "new" golden numbers becomes clear when one remembers that the ecclesiastic scheme assumes January 23 as the new moon's date for a cycle year 1 whereas the new moon in A.D. 1387 (which is a year 1 in the Dionysian cycle) occurred actually on Jan. 20.[19] Table V shows that the "new" golden number 1 was given to Jan. 19. Since the moment of the conjunction had to be found by computation an error of a few hours is not surprising. Hence it is clear that the new golden numbers were introduced in order to restore better agreement with observable facts.

Rather senseless, however, is the change in the distribution of hollow and full months (cf. Fig. 5). It lies in the very nature of any perpetual scheme for lunations that one must operate with mean synodic months, i.e. for the main part with simple alternations between full and hollow months as shown in Fig. 3 (p. 426). Hence one could have simply copied the pattern of Fig. 3 with the only difference that it should start with 1 at January 19 instead of at January 23.

Our reformer introduced, however, many pairs of full and of hollow months which in most cases cancel each other out (cf., e.g., in Fig. 5 the years 5, 11, 16). There exist, of course, in reality sequences of two hollow or two full months but no 19-year cycle can reproduce periodically such sequences of true lunations by the simple reason that the variation in the lunar velocity has not a period of 19 years. The complicated pattern of the nombres d'or nouvelles is therefore a valueless and arbitrary modification of the canonical scheme.

HISTORICAL REMARKS

The nombres d'or nouvelles of the *Très Riches Heures* do not represent the only available evidence for attempts to restore to the 19-year cycle agreement with the actual course of the moon, though none of the other Books of Hours of the Duke of Berry contains more than the traditional golden numbers in its calendar.

Best known is the reform suggested by Grosseteste, Bishop of Lincoln.[20] In order to distinguish his golden numbers from the traditional ones he introduced letters in alphabetical order in the same fashion as we have seen them used in the calendar miniatures of the Très Riches Heures. Nevertheless the nombres d'or nouvelles do not follow the system of Grosseteste which is based on a 76-year cycle, not on a simple 19-year cycle as in the Très Riches Heures. As we have seen (above p. 426), the 19-year cycle implicitly assumes that 235 lunar months contain $6935 + 19/4 = 6939^3/_4$ days. In order to avoid fractions of days Grosseteste operated with a cycle of $4 \cdot 19 = 76$ years $= 27759$ days and correspondingly 940 lunations[21]—repeating the shift from the Metonic to the Callippic cycle suggested in the fourth century B.C.

Grosseteste furthermore refined his system by determining the dates of the conjunctions not by simple alternation between full and hollow months (and occasional additions of one day) but by operating with hours. This increase in numerical accuracy requires a four column table of golden numbers, one column for each year in a julian quadruple of years. The adjustment to the real new moons seems to consist in assigning the number 1 to September 12 of 1208, indeed the date of a new moon. Our Table V shows that the nombres d'or nouvelles of the Très Riches Heures associate 1 with September 13, this time a little later than in reality.[22] But it is again clear that our text does not follow accurately the Lincolnian scheme. It is interesting to see that attempts to correct the position of the golden numbers within the traditional 19-year cycle begin so soon after the invention of this device around 1200.[23]

A few remarks may be added on the 19-year cycle itself on which the concept of the golden number ultimately rests. The fact that 235 lunar months correspond closely to 19 solar years was established by Babylonian astronomers in the fifth century B.C. Hence a definite system of intercalations was adopted in which 7 times in 19 years a 13th lunar month was added to the ordinary 12, thus bringing the beginning of the year (Nisan) again near to the vernal equinox. This rule of intercalation prevailed in Mesopotamia not only during the late Persian period but also under Seleucid and Parthian rule. Naturally this calendaric system had also its influence on the date of the Jewish Passah Feast and then on its Christian version.

The Babylonian astronomers of the last four centuries B.C. were fully aware of the approximate character of the 19-year cycle; for the determination of the true lunations they used very refined, and of course non-cyclic, methods. Only for the civil calendar the 19-year cycle remained a very convenient arrangement. Greek mathematical astronomy from Hipparchus in the second century B.C. to Ptolemy in the second century A.D., and to Pappus and Theon in the fourth, completely ignored the problems of the lunar calendar. The Fathers of the Church, however, in their desire to maintain the lunar definition of Easter without copying exactly the Jewish rules argued violently, and without real understanding of the underlying astronomical facts, about the theological implications of various rules of thumb until one accepted eventually the cycles proposed by Dionysius exiguus and other Computists of the early Middle Ages. The fact that the spacing of the seven intercalary years in the scheme for the golden numbers in the early 15th century is still exactly the same as in the Mesopotamian calendar is one of several cases which testify to the influence Babylonian astronomy had on later ages.

The 19-year cycle and its Golden Numbers are not the only residue of reckoning by lunar months in our calendars. Each one of the five calendars begins each month with a sentence of the type "Feurier a 28 jours Et la lune 29." The first number is always the number of days corresponding to the Julian calendar. The second, however, obviously concerns lunar months, either full or hollow.

Astronomically it is utterly meaningless to associate a lunar month with each Julian month since any such direct correlation would rapidly become invalid since 12 lunar months add up only to about 354 days. If one should, however, give for some antiquarian reason a sequence of lunar months the only reasonable arrangement would be alternation between full and hollow months. Fig. 6 shows that traces of such alternating lengths are visible in all calendars but most of the time the scribes gave simply arbitrary numbers with the effect that no two calendars agree and that even the total of 354 days is nowhere obtained. Obviously there is no calendaric topic that could make use of these "lunar months."

	P.H.	N.D.	B.H.	G.H.	T.R.H.
I	⊗	⊗	O	⊗	⊗
II	O	O	⊗	O	O
III	⊗	⊗	⊗	⊗	⊗
IV	O	⊗	O	O	O
V	⊗	⊗	⊗	⊗	⊗
VI	O	⊗	O	O	O
VII	O	⊗	O	⊗	O
VIII	O	⊗	⊗	⊗	⊗
IX	O	⊗	⊗	⊗	⊗
X	⊗	⊗	⊗	⊗	⊗
XI	O	⊗	⊗	⊗	⊗
XII	O	⊗	O	⊗	⊗
total	352	359	355	357	356 days

FIGURE 6

	N.D.	B.H.	G.H.	T.R.H.
I	1, 25	1	—	—
II	4 VIII hora, 26	5, 26	—	—
III	1, 28	1, 28	—	1, 28
IV	10 XX h., 20 XI h.	10, 20	—	10, 19
V	3	3, 25	—	—
VI	—	10, 16	—	—
VII	13, 22	13	—	13, 22
VIII	1, 30	1, 30	—	—
IX	3, 21	3, 21	3, 21	—
X	3	4, 22	—	—
XI	5, 28	5, 28	—	—
XII	7	7, 22	7	—

TABLE VI

4. Dies Aegyptiaci

With a few days we find in the calendar tables the letter *D* after the saint's name, indicating a "dies aegyptiacus,"[24] i.e., a day unfavorable for actions and, e.g., for bleeding.[25] Concept and terminology go back to late Roman antiquity[26] but the principle of selection is not clear. The fact that one usually has 25 Egyptian days in a year, two each month with one third one in January, looks like some lunar scheme of new and full moons (and epagomenal days?) but no clear pattern can be deduced even from the earliest extant sources.

The "dies aegyptiaci" were noted only for three months in the Très Riches Heures: March 1 and 28, April 10 and 19, July 13 and 22. These are precisely the months which use Latin terminology: "quantitas dierum," "numerus aureus," ". . habet dies . . . , luna habet dies . . ." Obviously the Latin copy had *D*-s, the French not.

By the end of the Middle Ages there existed already many variants for the dates of the Egyptian days. As far as one can tell from the published sources the *Belles Heures* agree with the *Très Riches Heures*, though all headings are in French.

This pattern, however, is not valid for the other calendars. The *Belles Heures* are all in French, the *Heures of Notre Dame* all in Latin and both calendars give a rather complete list of Dies Aegyptiaci. On the other hand the *Petites Heures* and the *Grandes Heures* are both in French, the calendar of the first has no *D*'s, the second only for September and December. Table VI gives a concordance of the dates which show a *D*, obviously based on a common pattern if one ignores a few omissions and copyist errors.

An unusual feature is found in the *Heures of Notre Dame*. For February 4 and April 10 and 20 hours are added to the *D*-dates. These hours must be equinoctial hours since April 10 gives "XX hora." The epoch of these hours is probably midnight since VIII, XI, and XX after midnight seem to be more reasonable than hours after noon which would bring XI deep into the night.

5. Melothesia

The last calendar table, for December, occupies the first page of the third signature, fol. 13^{r}. After two blank pages follows on fol. 14^{v} a beautiful miniature of a "Zodiac Man." The remaining pages of the quire, fol. 15^{r} to 16^{v}, are again blank; with fol. 17^{r} begins the main part of the Book of Hours.[27]

The Zodiac Man in the center of the miniature on fol. 14^{v} presents the well known pattern of medieval iatromathematical diagrams which illustrate the association between the signs of the zodiac and the parts of the body.[28] The second figure, however, seen from the back, raises many problems. Harry Bober in his excellent study of this miniature[29] thinks of another figure from the iatromathematical literature, the "Vein Man." At least to my knowledge this is the only interpretation proposed so far which connects also this part of the miniature with otherwise attested iconographical features. What speaks against it is the absence of a text which describes the location of the veins.

From the astronomical or astrological point of view the figure of the Zodiac Man poses no problems. Its origin lies in the theory of "Melothesia" of Hellenistic-

Roman astrology,[30] handed down, practically unaltered, through the Middle Ages. Another conventional astrological element are the short textual sections in the four corners of the present miniature, reading as follows:

Aries. leo. sagittarius. sunt calida et sicca collerica masculina. Orientalia.

Taurus. uirgo. capricornus. sunt frigida et sicca melancolica feminina. Occidentalia.

Gemini. aquarius. libra. sunt calida et humida masculina sanguinea. meridionalia.

Cancer. scorpius. pisces. sunt frigida et humida flemmatica feminina. Septentrionalia.

These are traditional descriptions of the qualities of the triplicities, again going back to classical astrology.[31] It is not clear, however, why these data were given here with the Zodiac Man. According to astrological lore the trigona are of vital importance in connection with planetary positions. This could indicate that also a planetary melothesia was contemplated to be represented in a second pair of figures but this time showing the planets on the body of the man facing the reader.[32]

The zodiac which in the shape of a mandorla surrounds the Zodiac Man has an outermost ring divided into 12 signs of 30 degrees each. The signs themselves are arranged in counterclockwise order, Aries to Virgo on the left side, Libra to Pisces on the right. An inner ring shows the days of the twelve months, each full space representing two days, with half spaces at the end of the months of 31 days. In spite of this apparent accuracy of the divisions the relation between ecliptic degrees and days is purely schematic: the boundaries between signs are always lined up with the midpoints of the months. This implies that equinoxes and solstices are simply taken to fall on the 15th of their respective months, in contrast to the astronomical accuracy underlying the calendar miniatures (cf. above p. 423).

The zodiacal figures here and in the calendar miniatures show some peculiarities worth notice, though they are not without parallels in other medieval sources.[33] For example, the Gemini are represented as man and woman, thus unrelated to the Dioscuri; Virgo is holding two ears of corn though only one would be needed for Spica. Capricorn has gone a long way from its Mesopotamian prototype, the "Goat-Fish." The twisted tail of late ancient and most medieval pictures has become a snail's house (twice in the Melothesia and in the December miniature) or a conch from which the goat emerges in the January miniature.[34] Aquarius is pouring water from a jar on his shoulder in the January miniature while he holds the vessel at his hip in the Melothesia and in the February miniature. The lack of a systematic study of the iconography of the zodiacal constellations makes it impossible to say which branch of the medieval tradition inspired the artists who designed these subsidiary elements in the Books of Hours for the Duke of Berry.

6. Summary

Even the most superficial comparison of the five calendars which preface, as it were, the Books of Hours of the Duke of Berry must recognize that the *Très Riches Heures* strive for a definite advance beyond the traditional calendars. Not only is the primitive and totally valueless linear scheme for the length of daylight (in the *Petites* and *Belles Heures*) replaced by an astronomically meaningful table, adjusted for the latitude of Paris, but also to the traditional set of "golden numbers" is added another set of "nombres d'or nouvelles" and this not only in the calendar tables but also prominently displayed on the rings of the calendar miniatures. The tendency to be "modern" is unmistakable.

That modernization need not be a factual progress holds for the Middle Ages as well as for our times. The column for the length of daylight could be handled by any user of the calendar to tell him with reasonable accuracy the time of sunrise or sunset for the day in question. The nombres d'or nouvelles, however, are nothing but a display of empty learning. Even supposing that these new golden numbers are in better agreement with the actual lunations (which is true only in a very limited sense) they serve no purpose. The only place where the schematic lunar calendar, inherited from antiquity, is of any interest is the liturgical calendar; and here no attention was paid to the corrections suggested by the new golden numbers.

In fact the inclusion of traditional as well as of new golden numbers in a calendar for a layman's use could hardly ever have been of practical value. Even assuming the knowledge of the position of the current year within the 19-year cycle one has very little gain from then knowing in principle the dates of the new- or full-moons. One may rightly doubt that a non-professional user ever could determine from it the dates of Easter and other movable festivals. And of course the days of the lunar months (cf. Fig. 6, p. 430) are without relation to any real lunar phase.

The assembly of unrelated and often meaningless material is in no way an otherwise unknown feature of mediaeval astronomical tables. Tables which display trigonometric functions computed with high accuracy (of Islamic origin) and for small increments of the argument are perfectly able to give also one of the primitive Indian "Kardaga" tables which proceed in steps of 15°. Huge solar, lunar, and planetary tables can be assembled in the same work without realizing that contradictory elements had been used in different tables. It is not before the Renaissance (Peuerbach, Regiomontanus, Copernicus) that one felt the need to understand the astronomical reason and the empirical basis for technical tables of any kind. For many centuries it was enough in the West (and often also in Muslim circles or in Byzantium) to follow the computational rules which would, *deo volente*, produce a numerical answer in some relation to the question proposed.

How little our calendars were meant for serious use is drastically demonstrated by the "dies aegyptiaci." We have seen (p. 430) that the scribe who followed a Latin archetype included these days, omitted in the French version. Table VI makes it abundantly clear that the total disregard in the Petites Heures, the complete listing in the Heures of Notre Dame and the Belles Heures, and the arbitrary scattering of Egyptian Days over the calendars of the *Grandes* and *Très Riches Heures* has absolutely nothing to do with a changing evaluation of these critical days. We may be sure that the Duke was bled not on the consultation of his calendars but under the careful supervision of his physician who had certainly a rule book of his own.

As far as we know the assumption of inherent danger at specific days has no astrological basis but is simply one of the many manifestations of a belief in lucky and unlucky days, existing among all the ancient civilizations. But even if the Egyptian Days had any connections with astrology it would not have been considered improper to have the name of a Saint followed by a warning *D*. Miniatures of zodiacal signs are most common in calendars, associated naturally with the seasons and the labors of the months. To us the melothesia miniature at the end of the calendar in the *Très Riches Heures* seems purest astrological doctrine. To the Middle Ages these relations between parts of the body and solar or planetary positions were probably not much more than to us considerations of "environment" in the widest sense on human nature and health. In every aspect it is well-established tradition, sometimes rational and perhaps more often purely conventional, which dictated the choice of astronomical and calendaric matters which were combined with superb artistic skill in the illuminated calendars of the late Middle Ages.

NOTES TO THE TEXT

NOTES TO INTRODUCTION

1. Courajod, *Leçons . . . Origines*, 1901, p. 94 ff. Courajod based his case primarily upon sculpture. He was quite unaware of the deep influence of Trecento painting upon painting in France already in the fourteenth century.
2. Paris, Louvre (Sterling and Adhémar), 1965, p. 5.
3. *Galleries and Cabinets of Art in Great Britain, Supplement*, London, 1857, pp. 248–259. Waagen even made an attempt to distinguish the styles of the miniatures, which he ascribed to four illuminators.
4. Philobiblon Society, *Miscellanies*, London, I, 1854, pp. 1–11.
5. Munby, *Connoisseurs*, 1972, p. 156. Although, as Munby remarks, Seroux d'Agincourt was much interested in medieval illumination Waagen seems to have been the first to propose a study of its entire history in relation to panel painting.
6. Delisle, *Gaz. B.-A.*, 1884, p. 401 f.
7. These publications, which may readily be found under the names of these authors in the bibliography of the *Late XIV Century*, include Delisle's *Recherches sur la librairie de Charles V*, Durrieu's articles on the Boucicaut and Rohan Masters, Couderc's *Portraits*, Mâle's *Fin du Moyen âge*, and the *Cité de Dieu* as well as the *Bible moralisée* by Laborde.
8. Hulin de Loo, 1903, p. 189 f.
9. See, for example, Henderson, *Gothic*, 1967, p. 139 ff. Białostocki et al., *Spätmittelalter und Beginnende Neuzeit*, 1972, pls. 38, 39, illustrate from the *Très Riches Heures August* and *Paradise*, both late works in the same "courtly" style, and in our opinion by Jean de Limbourg. The *Temptation* is reproduced (pl. 74) for its architectural portrait.
10. Paris, Musée du Louvre, *Exposition*, 1904.
11. Paris, Bibl. nat. (Porcher), 1955.
12. Paris, Musée du Louvre, *Exposition*, 1904.
13. Courajod, *Leçons*, 1901, pp. 158, 271.
14. Published in 1919 in Dutch; English trans. London, 1924.
15. *Waning*, ed. 1924, pp. 241, 256 f.
16. *Ibid.*, p. 273. Trying to characterize a period Huizinga often clutches at straws, and his book (see, for example, the discussion of passion and violence on p. 40) contains more nonsense than any good historical book I know.

NOTES TO CHAPTER II

1. See now for the latter Buchthal, *Historia Troiana*, 1971.
2. See, for example, the *Epître d'Othéa*, fig. 120.
3. For the illustration of travel books see *Boucicaut Master*, p. 42 ff.
4. *Late XIV Century*, p. 32.
5. See Buchthal, *op. cit.*, p. 16 ff., and Bologna, *I pittori*, 1969, p. 139 f.
6. For this manuscript, fr. 301, see Catalogue of Workshops. Avril, "Trois manuscrits," 1969 (1970), demonstrated that both manuscripts were acquired by Jean de Berry.
7. Brit. Mus., Stowe 54. Wormald (1956) identified the arms as those of Louis de Sancerre, Constable of France, who died in 1403, but they do not conform with those in fr. 12399, which belonged to him, nor with those on his effigy in St. Denis (Michel, *Histoire*, III, 1907, part 1, p. 379).
8. *Late XIV Century*, p. 287 f.; *Boucicaut Master*, p. 56.
9. *Boucicaut Master*, p. 46 ff.
10. Meiss, "*Decameron*," 1967.
11. Valencia, University Library 1327 is a beautiful manuscript but not clearly French and probably after 1420. The splendid Morgan Library M. 245 is not French either.
12. The best general work on Christine de Pisan remains Pinet, *Christine de Pisan*, 1927. The basic studies of her writings will be cited at the appropriate places.
13. According to Willard, 1965, Christine was active also for many years as a scribe.
14. Of the enormous literature on this subject it may suffice to cite Richardson, *Forerunners*, 1929, and Lehmann, *Rôle de la femme*, 1952.
15. Pinet, *op. cit.*, p. XXI.
16. "Hélas Dieux, pourquoy ne me faiz tu naistre au monde en masculin sexe." *Cité des Dames*, Bk. I, chap. 1.
17. Guiffrey, *Inventaires*, I, p. 243 no. 932. Another copy

of this text, Brussels 10982–3, is also in grisaille, but it seems to me later (cf. Schaefer, 1937, figs. 96–105).

18. See *Late XIV Century*, pp. 299 f., 358; *Boucicaut Master*, p. 142.

19. Christine gives us this information in her life of Charles V mentioned above.

20. Solente, *Mutacion*, I, 1959, p. CXLI. For the receipt of the manuscript in the Hague by Jean de Berry in March, 1404, see *Late XIV Century*, p. 310.

21. *Idem*, 1929, p. 357.

22. See Solente, *Mutacion*, I, p. CXXI. The miniature in another manuscript of the *Livre des fais*, Brussels 10476, was painted by a different, less advanced hand in the same workshop. Schaefer, 1937, p. 195 f., fig. 179, and Brussels, Bibliothèque Royale (Gaspar and Lyna), I, 1937, p. 457 f., said fr. 603 derived from it.

23. Solente, *op. cit.*, I, p. CXLI.

24. Schaefer, 1937, p. 192, dated this manuscript close to Harley 4431, without recognizing that it was made in the same workshop, several years later in my opinion.

25. For the relevant verses see Solente, *op. cit.*, I, pp. 69–76. Christine probably took the personifications of Eur and Meseur from the late thirteenth-century *Panthère d'Amours* by Nicole de Margival.

26. Instead of the sword ("glaive") described by the texts.

27. Courcelle, *Consolation*, 1967, figs. 87–92.

28. The illuminators of the manuscripts in the Hague and in the Berès collection differentiate the crown but depict the ugly side less clearly.

29. Schaefer, *op. cit.*, p. 190 f.

30. Here Christine was no doubt influenced by the didactic paintings or reliefs introduced in earlier mediaeval poems, such as the *Roman de la rose* (*Verger de déduit*) or *Divina Commedia* (*Purgatorio*).

31. All five of the earlier surviving manuscripts of the *Cité des Dames* are by one or another hand in the workshop—Paris, Bibl. nat. fr. 1179, which has only one miniature, at the beginning of the text (Fig. 35), fr. 607, which bears the signature of Jean de Berry (Figs. 36, 39, 43), Brussels 9393, acquired by Jean sans Peur of Burgundy (Figs. 37, 40, 44), and two later cycles, fr. 1178 (Fig. 41) and Harley 4431 (Figs. 38, 42, 45). The miniatures in these manuscripts, particularly the first three, resemble each other very closely.

32. Brussels, Bibl. roy. 10987; Paris, Bibl. nat. n.a. fr. 4792; Messrs. Coulet and Faure, 5 rue Drouot, Paris (in 1970).

33. For these observations about the dress I wish to thank Prof. Maureen Curnow, who is preparing the first modern edition of the *Cité des Dames*.

34. For example, his *Maestà* at Massa Marittima.

35. See *Late XIV Century*, p. 3 and n. 3, where the French passage is given.

36. For my reasons see *ibid*. The word has not been carefully studied, and the dictionaries of early French by Greimas, Godefroy, or W. von Wartburg (*Französisches etymologisches Wörterbuch*, Berlin, II, 1940, p. 152) offer little help. J. Dupont, *Gothic Painting* [1954], p. 157, follows H. Martin's reading of "landscapes," whereas Mombello, 1967, p. 15 n. 3 describes Anastaise as a decorator, not a miniature painter.

37. *Late XIV Century*, p. 168.

38. *The Craftsman's Handbook*, trans. D. V. Thompson, Jr., New Haven, 1933, p. 16.

39. A woodcut in *Von Etlichen Frauen*, Ulm, 1473. See *Late XIV Century*, fig. 288.

40. Pinet, *op. cit.*, p. 413. Louis d'Orléans, Christine's first important patron, had them represented alongside the *preux* in 1400 in his Château de Coucy. See Le Roux de Lincy, *Paris*, 1867, p. 515 ff.

41. Gorra, *Studi*, 1892; Jorga, *Thomas III*, 1893.

42. From left to right the *Preuses* are labelled Deyphille, Synoppe, Hyppolite, Menalyppe, Semiramis, Lampheto, Thamaris, Thenea, Penthezille.

43. H. Pepwell, *Cyte of Ladies*, London, 1521.

44. In addition to the famous figures of the period there are numerous less well-known women such as Cassandra Fidelis, Laura Cereto, and Alessandra Scala, to whom Paul O. Kristeller has kindly drawn my attention. See also E. P. Rodocanichi, *La femme italienne à l'époque de la Renaissance*, Paris, 1907; C. Seltman, *Women in Antiquity*, London, 1956; P. Monnier, *Le Quattrocento*, Paris, 1901, I, p. 68 ff.

45. For the representation of Fortuna in antiquity see Roscher, *Lexikon*; for the later history Patch, *Goddess Fortuna*, 1927, and Doren, in *Vorträge*, 1924.

46. Raoul de Praelles, however, in his commentary on Book IV, Chapter 18, describes the "ydole ou ymage de fortune" with her wheel. She has a divided, light and dark face, as in the *Mutacion de Fortune*.

47. The miniature was first published by Courcelle, *Consolation*, 1967, p. 148, fig. 76, 2.

48. The face of Philosophy has been retouched.

49. For an example see Fleming, *Roman*, 1969, fig. 30.

50. See the chapter *Mutacion de Fortune*.

51. Gorra, in *Studi*, 1892, pp. 44–48; Jorga, *Thomas III*, 1893, pp. 115–117.

52. See p. 14 f.

53. *Boucicaut Master*, fig. 71.
54. *Roman de la rose*, lines 5921–6182. See Fleming, *op. cit.*, p. 125 f.
55. Valencia, University Library, ms. 387. For other miniatures see Fleming, *op. cit.*, pls. 7, 22, 27, 31, 33, 38, 41, 42.
56. Patch, *op. cit.*, p. 21; A. Barbeu du Rocher, "Ambassade de Pétrarque auprès du roi Jean le Bon," *Mémoires de l'Académie des inscriptions et belles-lettres de l'Institut de France*, 2nd ser., III, 1854, pp. 172–228.
57. The last miniatures in the earliest manuscripts of the French translation show the capture of King John by the English (Geneva, Bibl. publique et universitaire, ms. fr. 190, vol. II, fol. 188, and Paris, Arsenal 5193, fol. 403v; see Catalogue of Manuscripts).
58. See *Boucicaut Master*, p. 46 ff.
59. In the second sentence of the Introduction.
60. Bk. III.
61. In fr. 131, another *Cas des nobles hommes et femmes* illustrated by the Cité des Dames workshop, Misfortune tied to the column is mistakenly represented with a crown, and seems to have been confused with Fortune (fol. 71v). As we shall observe in the chapter on humanism, this manuscript bears the signature of the humanist, Gontier Col. The error is repeated in another manuscript of the text by the Harvard Hannibal workshop, which utilized fr. 131 as a model for the entire cycle (Oxford, Bodl. 265, fol. 73v). Bodl. 265 has the same unusual frontispiece as fr. 131.
62. The noun in the French title is "debat," which signifies debate as well as struggle.
63. Baxandall, *Painting and Experience*, 1972, p. 42.
64. See *Boucicaut Master*, p. 51 f.

NOTES TO CHAPTER III

1. *Late XIV Century*, p. 302 f.
2. Sabbadini, *Scoperte*, 1914, pp. 64–87; Simone, *Coscienza*, 1949, and, among numerous later works, *Rinascimento francese*, 1961; Eng. ed. *The French Renaissance*, 1969.
3. These scholars are more or less closely associated with an international group that has been meeting since 1963, and in 1968 became the *Equipe de Recherche sur l'Humanisme français des XIVe et XVe siècles* of the Centre National de la Recherche Scientifique, under the direction of M. Gilbert Ouy.
4. Cecchetti, in *Miscellanea*, 1967.
5. Simone, *French Renaissance*, 1969, p. 78 ff.
6. Berchorius, *De formis*, ed. 1966.
7. Lowinsky, 1954, p. 510; Reese, *Music in the Middle Ages*, 1940, p. 331 ff.
8. Ornato, *Muret*, 1969.
9. Ouy, 1970, p. 86. For Col see Lehoux, *Berri*, II, 1966, pp. 180 n. 3, 204 n. 1, 288 n. 4, and Coville, *Col*, 1934, p. 15 ff.; for Montreuil *ibid.*, Ornato, *op. cit.*, p. 189 f., and M. Wilmotte, "Montreuil," in *Biographie nationale publiée par l'académie royale des sciences, des lettres et des beaux-arts de Belgique, XV*, Brussels, 1899.
10. Coville, *loc. cit.*
11. Prologue, in the earliest manuscript, Vatican, pal. lat. 1989; see Catalogue of Manuscripts. For Laurent see Hauvette, *De Laurentio*, 1903.
12. The idea of the *translatio* was advanced in 1385 by Pierre d'Ailly and in 1389 by Gerson (Cecchetti, *op. cit.*, p. 40 f.; Simone, *Rinascimento*, 1961, p. 47).
13. Gauthier, *Emaux*, 1972, p. 287. The scepter of Charles V, which survives, is crowned with a figure of Charlemagne (Krautheimer, *Ghiberti*, 1956, fig. 17).
14. E. Martène and U. Durand, *Veterum scriptorum et monumentorum historicorum, dogmaticorum, moralium, amplissima collectio*, Paris, II, 1724, *ep.* XXII (cols. 1352–1354), *ep.* XLV (cols. 1406–1409).
15. *Late XIV Century*, p. 302. Clamanges voiced this idea in a letter to Gontier Col. See Simone, *Coscienza*, 1949, p. 37; Ullman, *Studies*, 1955, p. 23; Ouy, 1970, p. 88.
16. Ouy, *op. cit.*, p. 95 f.
17. *Ibid.*, p. 97.
18. *Ibid.*
19. Cecchetti, *op. cit.*, p. 33 ff. The sheep symbolize the faithful in the Church and the poem refers to the papal schism.
20. Billanovich, 1964, p. 337 ff. On Salutati and the French humanists see Donovan, in *Studies in the Renaissance*, 1967, p. 185 ff.
21. *Ibid.* M. Ouy has kindly told me the rubrics in the manuscript were written by Jean de Montreuil. For the entire letter see Montreuil, *Opera*, ed. Ornato, I, 1963, p. 224.
22. Ornato, *Muret*, 1969, p. 233.

23. *Ibid.*
24. Ouy, 1970, p. 94.
25. Ornato, *Muret*, 1969, p. 189 f.
26. In one sermon, for example, Gerson quoted fifteen ancient authors (*Œuvres*, v, 1963, p. 584 ff.).
27. Di Stefano, 1965.
28. Ornato, *op. cit.*, p. 233.
29. Ouy, 1970, p. 91 f.
30. Simone, *Coscienza*, 1949, p. 36.
31. Gerson, *Œuvres*, II, 1960, p. 212 f.
32. Zarebski, Bibl. Jagielloński, *Biuletyn*, 1964, pp. 39–48.
33. Fr. 131 (*Late XIV Century*, p. 79, fig. 500, and Bozzolo, 1968). See Catalogue of Workshops, Master of the Cité des Dames. The *De casibus* is Florence, Bibl. Laurenziana, pal. 228.
34. Di Stefano, 1963, 1965.
35. Di Stefano, 1965. For the Duke's manuscript, fr. 282, given to him in 1402 by his treasurer Jacques Courau, see Figs. 271, 413, 414 and *Late XIV Century*, p. 313. For the Duke of Berry Courtecuisse translated the *Quatre vertus* ascribed to Seneca (Guiffrey, *Inventaires*, II, p. 317). Di Stefano, 1967.
36. Santoro in Milan, Bibl. Trivulziana, *I codici*, 1958, p. 108, believed this copy was destined for Louis of Bourbon because of the arms; however, they are not Bourbon and apparently not original. A manuscript of the same texts and with miniatures in a similar style (but cruder) is Bibl. nat., lat. 7789. This manuscript bears no armorials.
37. Though Petrarch was greatly admired by the humanists his *De viris illustribus* was not translated. The *De remediis* was turned into French by Nicolas de Gonesse, using Salutati's text (Di Stefano, 1965).
38. For the earliest manuscript see Catalogue of Manuscripts, Rome, Vatican, pal. lat. 1989.
39. Panofsky, *Renaissance and Renascences*, 1960, p. 260 ff., said that this kind of nostalgia, lacking in the North, differentiated it from Italy.
40. Simone, *Coscienza*, 1949, p. 36.
41. The dates given in the *Late XIV Century*, p. 307, for the death of Col and of Montreuil are slightly inaccurate and for Clamanges (1420) very incorrect.
42. Cecchetti, in *Miscellanea*, 1967, p. 44 f.
43. For the early Italian humanists and the visual arts see Krautheimer, *Ghiberti*, 1956, p. 294 ff. and Gombrich, *Norm*, 1966, p. 19 f.
44. I must thank M. Gilbert Ouy for his observation about this matter.
45. P. 52.
46. Coville, *Col*, 1934, p. 110. *Late XIV Century*, p. 303.
47. Focillon, *Art of the West* [1963], p. 142 f.
48. Panofsky, *Renaissance and Renascences*, 1960, p. 206 ff.
49. Panofsky, *op. cit.*, p. 170 ff., has stressed the use of contemporary dress in Italian mythological painting. See also Gombrich, *op. cit.*, p. 20.
50. Mombello, 1964, p. 401 ff. The French text has not been published in modern times but we now have the English translation of the later fifteenth century; see Christine de Pisan, *The Epistle of Othea*, ed. Bühler, 1970.
51. *Ibid.*, p. XII. The design of the woodcuts in the first French edition, Pigouchet, Paris, implies a model similar to Bibl. nat., fr. 606 or Brit. Mus., Harley 4431.
52. Boccaccio's *De mulieribus claris* was in fact one of Christine's sources for the *Epître* (see Campbell, *Epître*, 1924, p. 184 f.).
53. For the sources of the *Othéa* see Campbell, *op. cit.*, and *Epistle*, ed. Bühler, 1970, p. XXVIII.
54. See especially Tuve, *Allegorical Imagery*, 1966, p. 286 ff.
55. The poem has been published by De Boer *et al.*, 1915–1938, and an abridged prose version made in 1466 for René d'Anjou has been edited by C. de Boer, *Ovide moralisé en prose*, 1954. The most succinct account of the intricate history of mythological and mythographical texts in the late Middle Ages may be found in Panofsky, *Renaissance and Renascences*, 1960, pp. 78–81.
56. Preface to P. Berchorius, *De formis*, 1966.
57. *Late XIV Century*, pp. 288, 311.
58. Panofsky's date of 1380 (*Renaissance and Renascences*, *cit.*) seems to me too early; see *Late XIV Century*, pp. 288, 313.
59. The passage on Saturn may be found in the printed text of Berchorius cited above in note 56, p. 4 f. It reads: "Saturnus ergo pingebatur & supponebatur esse homo senex, curvus, tristis & pallidus, qui una manu falcem tenebat & in eadem drachonis portabat ymaginem qui dentibus caudam propriam commordebat, altera vero filium parvulum ad os applicabat & eum propriis dentibus devorabat. Quatuor iuxta se habebat liberos s. Iovem, Iunonem, Neptunum & Plutonem, quorum Iupiter patris virilia amputabat. Mare eciam ante eum pictum erat in quo vid. dicta Saturni scissa virilia proiecta videbantur, de quibus Venus puella pulcherrima nascebatur."

   For Saturn in the verse *Ovide moralisé* see Bk. I, l. 513 ff.
60. See *Late XIV Century*, pp. 250–253; *Boucicaut Mas-*

ter, p. 65 f., and below, chapter on Jean de Berry and the antique.

61. The style is related to that of the astrological manuscript (now Morgan Library 785) probably illuminated in Bruges and given by the Abbot of Eeckhout near Bruges to Jean de Berry in 1403 (Figs. 361, 362). See also *Late XIV Century*, p. 250 f., figs. 826, 827.

62. Avril, 1969 (1970), p. 306 n. 1, referring to a verbal opinion of Otto Pächt, has ascribed the miniatures in these two manuscripts to the same illuminator, an opinion that I had formed independently. The borders in the manuscripts, with small naturalistic leaves, are also very similar.

63. Her first gloss states, in the words of her early English translator Scrope: "And as thei (the ancients) hadde a custom to wurship all thing, the which above the comune course of thinges hadde prerogatif of some grace, many wise ladies in their tyme were called goddesses." (*Epistle*, ed. Bühler, 1970, p. 6.)

64. Preserved in certain branches of the medieval mythographic tradition, such as manuscripts of Hrabanus Maurus (Panofsky, 1933, p. 258).

65. For this manuscript see Van den Gheyn, *Epître*, 1913; Winkler, *Flämische Buchmalerei*, 1925, p. 166; *La librairie de Philippe le Bon*, Brussels, 1967, p. 85.

66. For a full account of the myth and representation of the god see Klibansky, Panofsky, and Saxl, *Saturn and Melancholy*, 1964, esp. p. 207 ff.

67. "Mercurius est planette qui donne influence de beau lengage . . . il a la bourse pleine, car par bel lengage souvent vient on a grant richece."

68. Seznec, *Pagan Gods*, 1953, p. 70 ff.

69. Panofsky and Saxl, 1933, p. 246.

70. *Ibid.*

71. Jupiter is shown here, according to the text, dispensing fire.

72. Courcelle, *Consolation*, 1967, p. 69. This miniature was incorrectly identified as Pentecost by Panofsky and Saxl, *ibid.*, fig. 32.

73. Since this rubric has not to my knowledge been published (none of the special rubrics for the planets were included in the printed edition of 1499 or in Scrope's English translation) I give the text: ". . . les VII planettes ou ciel sont tournans autour des cercles que on nomme zodiaques. Sont les ymages des VII planettes . . . figurees assises sur cercles et pour ce que elles sont ou firmament assises au dessus des nues sont elles cy pourtraites ou ciel estoile . . ." (Harley 4431, fol. 99).

74. "Chi vole vivere felice ghuardi chostei cheglie sugieto amore egli altri idei MCCCCXXI."

75. Meiss, *Art in America*, 1936, pp. 137–143.

76. J. Pope-Hennessy, *Giovanni di Paolo*, London, 1937, p. 23; C. Brandi, *Giovanni di Paolo*, Florence, 1947, p. 10.

77. See *Boucicaut Master*, figs. 1, 4, 5, 36.

78. Bk. IV, 665 ff.

79. See also the paintings from the Casa dei Dioscuri, Museo nazionale, Naples and another in A. Maiuri, *Roman Painting*, Geneva, 1953, pl. 79.

80. See also the painting from Boscotrecase, Metropolitan Museum, New York.

81. Of all ancient writers only Lucian (*Dialogues of the Sea-Gods*, 14) describes her as "largely uncovered from the breasts down." For descriptions of Andromeda in bridal robes see L. Séchan, *Etudes sur la tragédie grecque dans ses rapports avec la céramique*, Paris, 1926, pp. 253–273, and Achilles Tatius of Alexandria, *Adventures of Leucippe and Clitophon*, Bk. III, 7. In Ovid's *Metamorphoses* (IV, 676) Perseus envisages Andromeda as a marble statue (and thus either dressed or nude). Phillips, 1968, pp. 9, 13, referred to a Campanian vase and an Etruscan bronze in which Andromeda is represented nude—unusually, he said.

82. Bk. IV, lines 6618, 6643, 6650.

83. She is completely naked in an early twelfth-century manuscript in Durham, Cathedral Library, Hunter ms. 100, fol. 62, but in another manuscript of the same century she wears bridal robes (Brit. Mus. Roy. 13 A XI, fol. 106v).

One of the pairs of ringlets on the arms of the nude Andromeda is vestigial fetters.

84. See Woodward, *Perseus*, 1937, pp. 88–92 and figs. 31–33 (for the clothed Andromeda). For other classical sources on the winged feet of Perseus (Hyginus, LXIV, and the Mythographers) see also Campbell, *Epître*, 1924, p. 123 f.

85. Berchorius, *Reductorium*, 1962, p. 85: ". . . Perseus cum equo suo ascendit aera . . . quoddam in Aethiopia venisset volando vidit in littore maris Andromeda. . . ." For a recent account of Bersuire's text see Samaran, *Bersuire*, 1962, p. 336 ff.

86. Bk. XII, 24. After associating Pegasus with Perseus Boccaccio immediately describes the journey to Andromeda, "remeans in patriam cum exelso vidisset in syrio littore. . . ." In the 5th cent. B. C. Melian reliefs Perseus rides a wingless horse (Pegasus?) in the battle with Medusa, and Bellerophon is on Pegasus when attacking the Chimera (P. Jacobsthal, *Die Melischen*

Reliefs, Berlin, 1931, pls. 28, 29, 63). Similar conceptions are maintained in the verse *Ovide moralisé*, Bk. IV, lines 5702 (Medusa) and 5896 (Bellerophon), and Boccaccio, Bersuire and Christine may have confused them with the story of Perseus and Andromeda.

87. Berchorius, *Reductorium*, 1962, pp. 85, l. 12 f.; 86, l. 7 f.; 87, l. 19 f.

88. Ed. De Boer, 1954, p. 166.

89. The block by Bernard Salomon was first used in *La metamorphose d'Ovide figurée*, Lyon, 1557. The text does not explicitly put Perseus on Pegasus when he battles for Andromeda.

90. See also the seventeenth-century painting by Turchi in Cassel (A. Pigler, *Barockthemen*, Budapest, 1956, II, p. 23).

91. Perseus flies on winged feet already in Piero di Cosimo's painting in the Uffizi (Fig. 98). See also Panofsky, *Problems in Titian*, 1969, pp. 166–168—but he does not discuss Andromeda's nudity.

92. See also Benvenuto Cellini, Bargello, Florence; Tintoretto, private collection, Venice (E. von den Bercken, *Die Gemälde des Jacopo Tintoretto*, Munich, 1942, pl. 9); woodcut in the edition of the Metamorphoses, Venice, 1509, Georgius de Rusconibus.

93. Stechow, *Apollo und Daphne*, 1932, pp. 14–16.

94. *Ibid.*

95. See the woodcut in the first printed edition, Paris, 1499–1500, reproduced by Stechow, *op, cit.*, fig. 8.

96. Winkler, *Flämische Buchmalerei*, 1925, p. 75; *La librairie de Philippe le Bon*, Brussels, 1967, p. 85.

97. See, for instance, Statius, *Thebaid*, VIII, 376, quoted by Dobbert, 1881, p. 27 f.

98. M. Meiss, *Florence and Siena*, 1951, fig. 85.

99. For some examples see, for instance, E. Panofsky, "Mors Vitae Testimonium," in *Studien zur Toskanischen Kunst* (Festschrift L. H. Heydenreich), Munich, 1964, p. 221 ff.

For the Neapolitan relief, which is an ex-voto of Franceschino di Brignale, see G. Doria, *Il Museo e la Certosa di S. Martino* (Naples, 1964), p. 97.

100. For the fresco in Assisi see B. Kleinschmidt, *Die Basilika San Francesco in Assisi*, Berlin, 1926, II, fig. 128. For equestrian skeletons see Meiss, 1933, p. 169 f.; Van Marle, *Iconographie de l'art profane*, II, 1932, figs. 402, 405; Guerry, "*Triomphe de la Mort*," 1950.

When in these compositions Death is equestrian there may be an allusion to the rider of the Apocalypse.

101. Meiss, *Late XIV Century*, fig. 643.

102. The finger-nails, as well as other parts of the figure, are repainted, but the feet and the toe-nails are original.

Death was represented as a blindfolded, mounted woman in Apocalyptic cycles beginning with the sculptures at Paris, Amiens and Reims (Panofsky, *Iconology*, 1939, p. 111 f. and Sauerländer, *Gotische Skulptur*, 1970, pl. 150).

103. Faral, 1962, p. 10 ff.

104. Quant en l'enfermerie fu
Et une piece y oi ieu
Soutainement et en seursant
Une vieille qui estoit haut
Montee sur mon lit. . . .
Une faus en sa main tenoit.
Et i sarclis de fust portoit. . . .

105. See the cups reproduced by M. I. Rostovtsev, *Social and Economic History of the Roman Empire*, 2nd ed. rev. by P. M. Fraser, Oxford, 1957, I, pl. VII. For this reference I am indebted to James F. Gilliam.

106. Horace, *Satirae*, II, 1, 57. For this passage, and similar ones in Greek and Roman literature see Dobbert, 1881, p. 26 ff., and Roscher, *Lexikon*, s.v. *Mors*. An ivory of the fourth century in the British Museum represents both Death and Sleep as winged women (O. Dalton, *Catalogue of the Ivory Carvings of the Christian Era . . . in the British Museum*, London, 1909, no. 1).

107. Bk. I, s.v. *Mors*.

108. Copies of the *Genealogiae* were available in the Parisian region. Nicolas de Gonesse used one for his defense of poetry (G. di Stefano, 1963, p. 406). Gontier Col possessed a copy, now in Cracow (see *Humanism*, note 32) and there was another in the papal library at Avignon (Mombello, "I manoscritti," 1971, p. 99). Campbell, *Epître*, 1924, p. 124, who did not know of these copies, is not certain that Christine knew the *Genealogiae*. In two respects, however, her account of Perseus accords with his and not with the verse *Ovide*, her common source. Perseus rides Pegasus when delivering Andromeda and Persia is said to be named after him.

109. "And a woman shrouded in a dress of black,
With fury such as had perchance been seen
When giants raged in the Phlegraean vale,
Came near . . ." (trans. by E. H. Wilkins, *The Triumphs of Petrarch*, Chicago, 1962, p. 54). It should be added that E. Pellegrin (see n. 121) has not been able to identify a copy of Petrarch's text in French libraries around 1400.

110. The fresco in Pisa is not precisely dated by external evidence (cf. Meiss, in *Atti del Congresso giottesco 1967*, 1971, p. 401 ff., with references to other opinions ranging from ca. 1330–1370) and *idem*, *Burl. Mag.*, 1971, p. 182 ff. Petrarch and Boccaccio were at work on their respective texts during the third quarter of the century.

Death in British Museum, Cotton Tiberius C.VI, fol. 6v, of the eleventh century has sometimes been described as a woman but the figure is bearded (F. Wormald, "An English Eleventh-Century Psalter with Pictures. British Museum, Cotton MS Tiberius C.VI," *Walpole Society*, XXXVIII, 1960–1962, pl. 2).

111. (C.) A. Rosenberg, *Der Erynien*, 1874; Pauly-Wissowa, *Real-Enzyclopädie der classischen Altertumswissenschaft*, supp. vol. VIII, 1956, p. 13 ff.

112. Brieger, Meiss and Singleton, *Illuminated Manuscripts*, 1969, pls. 127 ff.

113. See lines 19805 ff. (*Roman de la rose*, ed. E. Langlois, V, 1924, p. 17). The image of Atropos suckling Cerberus is described as "inventive, frightful, and frightening" by Tuve, *Allegorical Imagery*, 1966, p. 271.

114. British Museum, Harley 4431, fol. 111.

115. In addition to the examples reproduced see Erlangen, ms. 2361, *ca.* 1460; the late fifteenth-century miniature, Oxford, Bodl. 421, fol. 29v (Saxl and Meier, *Verzeichnis*, III, pt. 1, 1953, p. 301).

116. For the representation of an emaciated woman in the third quarter of the fifteenth century see Essling and Müntz, *Pétrarque*, 1902, pp. 1, 139, 173, 189, 191.

117. For examples of the substitution of the skeleton for Petrarch's woman in black see *ibid.*, p. 118 ff. Also Van Marle, *Iconographie*, II, 1932, pp. 124 ff., 361 ff., 397, figs. 135, 138, 153; G. Carandente, *I Trionfi nel Primo Rinascimento*, Turin, 1963, fig. 31; Schubring, *Cassoni*, 1923, pp. 357, 407, figs. 215, 578, 582; Essling and Müntz, *op. cit.*, pp. 151, 165 f., 187, 197, 201, 227.

118. New York, Morgan Library, M. 132, fol. 140v. A skeleton, riding a horse, again illustrates the same passage in the *Roman de la rose* in Bodleian Library, Douce ms. 195, fol. 141v, datable about 1470 (cf. Saxl and Meier, *op. cit.*, III, p. 355).

119. E. Mâle, *L'art religieux après le Concile de Trente*, Paris, 1932, p. 204 ff., esp. p. 225. Also Panofsky, "Mors Vitae Testimonium," *cit.*

120. *Op. cit.*, pp. 118, 209, 211.

121. *Ibid.*, pp. 202 ff., 271, and Pellegrin, 1964, p. 422 f.

122. Tuve, 1963, p. 282.

123. See his brilliant essay, 1969, p. 206 ff.

124. K. Steinweg, *Andrea Orcagna*, Strassburg, 1929, pl. 19.

125. Van Marle, *Development*, II, 1924, fig. 268.

126. White, *Medieval Technology*, 1962, p. 124.

127. Bedini and Maddison, 1966, p. 20.

128. Panofsky, *Renaissance and Renascences*, 1960, p. 208.

129. Bedini and Maddison, 1966, p. 20.

130. Meiss, 1945.

131. White, *op. cit.*, p. 125.

132. Mombello, 1967, p. 29. It is true that in this manuscript the design of the folios, which has been regarded as a sign of an early date, does not economically use the vellum, but the arrangement of *glose*, *texte*, and *allegorie* seems quite logical. The manuscript has four miniatures, two of them showing two subjects each. Mrs. Charity Willard kindly informs me that she believes this manuscript was written by Christine herself.

133. Also Brit. Mus. Harley 4431, which will be discussed shortly.

134. "Attrempance estoit aussi appellee deese et pour ce que nostre corps humain est compose de diverses choses et doit estre attrempe selon raison, peut estre figure a l'orge ou a plusieurs roes et mesures, et toutefois ne vault riens l'orloge s'il n'est attrempe; semblablement non fait nostre corps humain se attrempance ne l'ordonne." (Fr. 606, fol. 2v.)

135. Two extensively illustrated manuscripts of the *Epître* earlier than fr. 606 are lost. One was given to Jean de Berry by Christine apparently very late in 1405 or on New Year's Day 1406 (Guiffrey, *Inventaires*, I, p. 249 no. 949). The manuscript was entered in the Duke's inventory at about this date (see Appendix A). Though the inventory describes the manuscript as "très bien historié" it was appraised at a low price (50 *sous*) after the Duke's death in 1416. It seems probable, therefore, that this manuscript, like others prepared by Christine during the first years of the century (Brussels 10983 and Bibl. nat. fr. 848, for instance), was illustrated with drawings (perhaps tinted) only. The manuscript carried the dedication to the Duke of Berry that we know only from later copies (Mombello, 1967, pp. 329, 345). Fr. 606 bears the dedication to Louis d'Orléans.

A copy of the *Epître* sold at Sotheby in 1825 and since not identified (*ibid.*, p. 221) was described as containing "115 miniatures executed for Philip the Hardy." This description might be based only on a dedication to the Duke copied in a manuscript of a later date. The dedication to Philippe le Hardi was originally written late in 1403 or, in any event, before his death April 27, 1404 (Mombello, 1969, p. 307).

There are two other copies of the *Epître*, each with a few mediocre illustrations, that may be dated in the first decade of the century, probably after 1405–1406 (Chantilly 492 and fr. 12779—see Mombello, 1967, pp. 63 ff., 106 ff.).

136. Fr. 926, fol. 113. This manuscript, given to Marie de Berry in 1406, is discussed in several chapters of this book, especially VII, The Breviary Master.

137. White, 1969, p. 211; Suso, ed. Bihlmeyer, 1907, p. 45 ff.; Spencer, 1963, p. 282. The illustrations of Suso have not yet, however, been collected.

138. The Hague, Kon. Bibl., Byvanck, 1924, p. 35, pl. 16. The manuscript is 76 E 19.

139. "Tu ne dois belles raisons rendre
a qui bien ne les scet entendre."

140. One painted fol. 1, a second, notable for very pale colors and smooth surfaces, began on fol. 27.

141. See *Late XIV Century*, p. 235.

142. Bibl. de l'Arsenal 5057, fols. 15, 35, 67v, 75v, 85, 155, 216, 234, 234v, 238, 250, 290.

143. Just about 1405 clouds began to float in the skies of Parisian miniatures by the Boucicaut Master and from the circle of Jacquemart. See *Late XIV Century*, p. 275; *Boucicaut Master*, p. 15 and n. 61, with a reference to the textual source of the clouds in one miniature.

144. Christine confuses Memnon (or Mennon, in the *Ovide moralisé*) with Cygnus, son of Neptune, who was changed into a swan (*Ovide moralisé, poème*, pp. 88, 308 f., 322).

145. "Por la mort de son fil ocis
Ot la mere au cuer tel dolour
Que cele vermeille colour
Pali, par cui la matinee
Sielt jadis estre enluminee.
En signe de sa grant tristesce
Fu li cieulz couvers de nublesce." (Bk. XIII, 2338 ff.)

Based on Ovid, *Metamorphoses*, XIII, 576 ff. For Cycnus, *ibid.*, II, 367; VII, 371; XII, 72, 581.

146. Roy, *Œuvres poétiques*, I, 1886, p. v ff.; Lecoy, in *Mélanges Guiette*, 1961, and the recent summary by Mombello, 1967, p. 16 ff.

147. Meiss, with Off, 1971, p. 228.

148. Lecoy, *loc. cit.* Christine composed the *Epître à la Reine*, which is included, in October, 1405. *Ballades* addressed to Jean de Bourbon in 1410 are not included; they had provided Lecoy with an *ante quem*, now not needed. Porcher, in Paris, Bibl. nat., 1955, p. 74, dated the manuscript 1400–1402.

149. For a contrary view see Schaefer, 1937, p. 198 f.

150. Lecoy, in *Mélanges Guiette*, 1961, suggested that the first 40 folios of fr. 835 were written as early as the end of 1403 or the beginning of 1404. That may be, but the Epître workshop scarcely painted the first folio of this manuscript earlier than 1405.

151. Other miniatures in this group are fr. 836, fols. 65, 65v, 66v.

152. *Late XIV Century*, pp. 36, 91 f.; Schlosser, 1899, p. 220.

153. Other miniatures in this group are fr. 606, fol. 46 (*Late XIV Century*, fig. 817), fr. 836, fols. 48, 63, 71v.

154. This text, written in 1399, initiated the defense of women against the strictures of the *Roman de la rose*. See Pinet, *op. cit.*, p. 67.

155. For the story see the fifteenth-century French prose version of the *Ovide moralisé*, ed. De Boer, 1954, p. 174 f. See the *Metamorphoses*, V, 256 ff.

156. See Catalogue of Manuscripts, *Epître d'Othéa*. For a discussion of this manuscript see Mombello, 1967, p. 199 ff.; Becker, 1930, p. 148 ff. On fol. 100 of Harley 4431, one of the "children" of Venus wears the broom, emblem of Charles VI.

157. See *Boucicaut Master*, fig. 67.

158. Fr. 23279, fol. 53; *Boucicaut Master*, fig. 67.

159. A few miniatures, on fols. 56v, 221, 259, 261v, 265, were painted by an illuminator who belonged to that large group I designate as the Bedford Trend. Schaefer, 1937, p. 153 ff., identified this illuminator as the Boucicaut Master, and the rest of the miniatures in the manuscript likewise appeared to her to be close to this master.

160. Lecoy, in *Mélanges Guiette*, 1961; Mombello, *loc. cit.*

161. Campbell, *Epître*, 1924, p. 23.

162. Especially fols. 103v, 105v.

163. Harley 4431, fol. 183; fr. 836, fol. 5v (Fig. 144). On fol. 101 of the Harley manuscript the arrows of Phoebe do not fly against the stricken figures as they do in fr. 606, fol. 7.

164. It is conceivable that the swan was deliberately suppressed to correct Christine's confusion of Cygnus and Memnon (see n. 144).

165. Cephalus lacks a spear in fr. 606, and Lavin, 1954, p. 264 n. 2, finds his pose more meaningful in Harley 4431, where he holds it. Since the spear already pierces Procris in this miniature it appears *twice*.

166. See Catalogue of Workshops; *Late XIV Century*, p. 24; *De Lévis Hours*, 1972, p. 23 f.

167. Fr. 1176, fol. 1 (*Livre de la vision*, written 1405–

1406); Arsenal 2681, fol. 4 (*Corps de policie*, written 1406–1407—see Schaefer, 1937, fig. 53).

168. The relationship of a few miniatures with fr. 606 was first recognized by Porcher (Paris, Bibl. nat., 1955, p. 76 no. 151). He ascribed to the atelier of the *Térence des ducs* the remaining miniatures here given to the Cité des Dames workshop.

169. *Medieval French Miniatures*, New York [1959], p. 59.

170. For the *Tacuinum* in Vienna see *Miniature lombarde*, 1970, figs. 413–416, and *Tacuinum sanitatis*, 1967. See also Toesca, *Lombardia*, 1912, pp. 366–368.

171. The *livre de medecine*, probably Lombard, in the collection of Jean de Berry was accessioned only in 1412 (Guiffrey, *Inventaires*, I, p. 269 no. 1003).

172. Martin, *Térence des ducs*, 1907. See the Catalogue of Manuscripts.

173. See the Catalogue of Manuscripts. The banners in the borders of the frontispiece, which bear *France ancien*, seem to have been painted over the completed border, but there must originally have been a banner on each of the staffs. For the arms of the Dauphin at this time see the Breviary of Châteauroux, ms. 2, fol. 430 (*Boucicaut Master*, p. 81 f.).

174. See the Catalogue of Manuscripts, Boccaccio, *Des cas des nobles hommes et femmes*.

175. See the Catalogue of Manuscripts. Specimens of the miniatures and the preliminary sketches were discussed and reproduced for the first time in *Late XIV Century*, p. 10 f., figs. 299, 300. See also Martin, *op. cit.*, p. 19 f.

176. Through the use of infrared and ultraviolet light Marcel Thomas (1958, p. 114 ff.) found numerous brief inscriptions classifying the figures for the illuminator. Thus on folio 39 he was able to identify *chamberiere*. These instructions, which are not in Arsenal 664, led M. Thomas to conclude that its cycle depends upon lat. 7907A.

Martin (*Térence des ducs*, 1907, pp. 19, 38 f.) suggested that Arsenal 664 may have preceded lat. 7907A. Panofsky (*Netherlandish Painting*, 1953, I, p. 61, note 58[2]) and Porcher, (*Enluminure française*, 1959, p. 65) dated the Arsenal Terence around the time of Berry's copy, or earlier. In *Renaissance and Renascences*, 1960, p. 104, Panofsky described the Arsenal ms. as the earliest Terence of its period. This view was held earlier by Herrmann, *Forschungen*, 1914, and Borcherdt, *Europäische Theater*, 1935.

177. He painted fols. 30, 107, 127, 130v, 133v, 305, *etc.*, in Arsenal 5193. See also Martin, *op. cit.*, p. 36.

178. See *Boucicaut Master*, pp. 17 f., 54.

179. Both the Virgil and the Terence have penwork by the same Italian calligrapher. Since both manuscripts were left unfinished (the remaining miniatures in the Virgil were painted later in the fifteenth century), they were perhaps ordered for the same collector. It is not inconceivable that this patron was Louis d'Orléans, who died in 1407. His secretary and the tutor to his children, Nicholas Garbet, owned a Terence, lat. 7917. The inventory drawn up in 1417 of the manuscripts of Charles d'Orléans, most of which were inherited from his father, contained several copies of Virgil and Terence. See Delisle, *Cabinet*, I, 1868, pp. 105–107; Le Roux de Lincy, *Bibliothèque de Charles d'Orléans*, 1843, pp. 17, 23 f.

180. Brit. Mus., Add. 32454, fols. 8, 12, 41, 46, 59. See Catalogue of Manuscripts.

181. By an unknown translator. See also Durrieu, *Antiquités judaïques*, 1908, p. 6. A Latin copy of the text was in the 1402 Inventory of Berry (Delisle, *Charles V*, 1907, II, pp. 257, 308).

182. Durrieu, *op. cit.*, p. 46, erroneously said that the miniature was retouched.

183. See *Boucicaut Master*, pp. 57, 80, 89, 142.

184. See *Late XIV Century*, p. 314.

185. *Antiquités*, III, 1, 2, 6. For the first miniature in the story of Joseph on fol. 25 see *Late XIV Century*, fig. 683.

186. For a camel in the possession of Jean de Berry see *Late XIV Century*, p. 32.

187. *Ibid.*, pp. 253–255, figs. 16–21.

188. The *Comedies* were read also, of course, for their content, for the moral significance of examples of human frailties in the great capital of the past.

189. For lat. 7899 see Jones and Morey, *Manuscripts of Terence* [1930–1931], p. 53 ff.; Paris, Bibl. nat., 1954, p. 41 f. no. 99. For Vat. lat. 3868 see Köhler, *Karolingische Miniaturen*, 1971, p. 36. For lat. 7900 see Paris, Bibl. nat., 1954, p. 43 no. 104.

190. See Martin, *Térence des ducs*, 1907, p. 18 f. Panofsky, *Dürer*, 1943, I, p. 28, wrote that "Neither the *Térence des Ducs* of 1407/08 nor the *Térence* of Martin Gouge . . . show any trace of classical influence."

191. Jones and Morey, *op. cit.*, p. 203 f.

192. The first encounter occurred, according to the *Andria*, outside a house, not in a landscape. In their desire to vary the scenes, the illuminators of Arsenal 664 placed figures alternatively in the street or in the countryside although the play called for an urban setting. The artists of lat. 7907A complied with the early me-

dieval model by introducing only necessary stage properties, such as buildings, and by otherwise placing the figures on a nondescript plane.

193. Loeb ed., II, p. 257.
194. *Ibid.*, II, p. 231 ff.
195. See above note 176.
196. See also the Catalogue of Manuscripts.
197. Loeb ed., I, p. 123.
198. See Jones and Morey, *op. cit.*, II, figs. 455–457.
199. See also the tree type peculiar to the Roman Texts Master which was adopted by the Luçon workshop (Figs. 59, 230).
200. Nicoll, *Masks*, 1931, p. 200.
201. "Scena autem erat locus infra theatrum in modum domus instructa cum pulpito, qui pulpitus orchestra vocabatur; ubi cantabant comici, tragici, atque saltabant histriones et mimi. Ibi poetæ comœdi et tragœdi ad certamen conscendebant, hisque canentibus alii gestus edebant." Here and in the following passages we give the translation of Nicoll, *op. cit.*, p. 208. For Isidore and his successors see also Herrmann, *Forschungen*, 1914, p. 286 f.; Borcherdt, *Europäische Theater*, 1935, p. 69 ff.; and Marshall, 1950, pp. 471–482. Herrmann and Borcherdt believed the *Térence des ducs* to be the original and more important manuscript.
202. Nicoll, *op. cit.*, p. 208.
203. *Ibid.*
204. . . . car lors les theatres estoient fais par maniere de sieges en montant ainsi comme par degrez par telle maniere que chascun pouoit tout veoir sans empeschement sicomme il peut encores apparoir par la disposicion des anciens theatres. Et pour ce que ces jeux sceniques vindrent de grece les apele il la luxure ou superfluite de grece. Mais pour ce que nous avons parle de tragedie et comedie tu dois savoir que sicomme dit Ysidore oudit XVIII liure de ses ethimologies tragedie est faicte de faiz enormes des grans roys et des grans princes et de leurs cruaultez et mauvaistiez. Comedie est faicte des fais des personnes privees de puterie de femmes et des hommes et des conchiements quilz faisoient en telles ribaudies . . . Et encores dois tu savoir la difference du theatre et de lamphiteatre car lamphiteatre estoit tout rond et y faisoit len tous jeux qui appartenoient a excercite darmes et de personnes et y donnoit le pris au mieulx faisant. Et le theatre estoit fait en la forme de la moytie de lamphiteatre. Et la se faisoient les jeux sceniques les baleries et danseries et les personnaiges de tragedies et comedies. (Bk. I, Ch. 31.)

   . . . asena . . est une petite maison ou milieu du theatre en laquelle avoit ung letrin ou len lisoit les tragedies et comedies des poetes et y avoit gens desguisez qui faisoient les contenances de ceulx pour lesquelz len chantoit et faisoit ces jeux ainsi comme tu vois que len fait encores au jour duy les jeux de personnaiges et charivalis. Et y avoit joueurs de divers instrumens et autres qui se desguisoient et contrefaisoient les personnes de qui la tragedie ou comedie parloit. Et dit titus livius que ces jeux proufiterent peu et si nuisirent a plente car ilz corrumpirent les meurs des rommains. Et encores dit il que au commencement quilz furent ordonnez ilz furent assez attrempez et dassez petit coust mais depuis il y eut tant de superfluitez et de coustages et si grans appareillemens que a peines les peussent soustenir ne tollerer les grans princes et les grans roys et furent commencies par deux censeurs de rome desquelz lun estoit apele messala et lautre casius. . . . (Bk. I, Ch. 31.)
205. Florence, Bibl. Laurenziana, Ashb. 361. See R. Klein, *La forme et l'intelligible*, Paris, 1970, p. 306 f., pl. 17 (this section with H. Zerner).
206. Nicoll, *op. cit.*, pp. 157 ff., 164 f. See also Kindermann, *Theatergeschichte Europas*, I, 1957, p. 412.
207. Nicoll, *op. cit.*, pp. 60–90.
208. *City of God*, Bk. I, Ch. 31.
209. Nicoll, *loc. cit.*, and Barasch, 1967, pp. 79–81.
210. Named after the miniatures in the French translation of Valerius Maximus, fr. 286. His workshop illuminated a second copy of Valerius Maximus in the Bibl. Mazarine, ms. 1595. The miniature in the Arsenal ms. is an illustration for Book II.
211. For the interpretation of these figures simply as statues see Laborde, *Cité de Dieu*, 1909, I, p. 276. In the first miniature in another *Cité de Dieu*, French *ca.* 1375 (Brit. Mus., Add. 15244, fol. 3) an idol holds a shield that takes the form of a mask.
212. Nicoll, *op. cit.*, p. 165.
213. *Ibid.*, p. 190 f.
214. Kernodle, *From Art to Theatre*, 1944, p. 160 ff.
215. Leombruno, *Calumny*, Brera, Milan; Bronzino, *Exposure of Luxury*, National Gallery, London.
216. The miniature is a repetition in Book III of a subject which properly belongs to Book II. See Catalogue of Manuscripts, *Cité de Dieu*.
217. Herrmann, *op. cit.*, p. 322, connects this much debated structure with the occasional medieval practice of erecting buildings for distinguished spectators when plays were performed in a square or other open area. Panofsky, on the other hand, found its source in the *circumspectaculum*, a round structure for the audience

described by Isidore (letter of 1955 printed in Williamstown, *Terence* (Richmond), 1955, p. 28).

218. A German translation of the *Eunuch* alone was printed earlier in 1486 in Ulm. For reproductions see Williamstown, *Terence* (Richmond), 1955, p. 15.

219. Panofsky, *Dürer*, 1943, I, p. 27 f.; Römer, 1927.

220. See the discussion above of the mythological representations in the *Epître d'Othéa*.

221. Kernodle, *op. cit.*, p. 162.

222. Paris, Bibl. de l'Arsenal, ms. 1135.

223. See Lawton, *Térence en France au XVIe siècle*, 1926.

224. Weitzmann, *Ancient Book Illumination*, 1959, pp. 59 f., 89 f.

225. See Weitzmann, *loc. cit.*, p. 91. Berlin, ms. germ. fol. 282 has 136 illustrations executed about 1200 (Boeckler, *Eneide*, Leipzig, 1939). A tenth-century manuscript in Naples, Bibl. naz. lat. 6, has five scenes (P. Courcelle, 1939, pp. 249–279). Recently F. Avril has found a twelfth-century manuscript with numerous historiated initials (each of which contains one or two figures). An illustration of the *Eclogue* in a relief on the ninth-century *Flabellum of Tournus* in the Bargello implies some continuity with late antiquity (L. E. A. Eitner, *Flabellum of Tournus*, New York, 1944, fig. 31).

226. See the chapter on Humanism.

227. *Late XIV Century*, p. 288; Delisle, *Charles V*, 1907, II, p. 265 no. 263. The manuscript, in the inventory of 1402, passed to the Ste.-Chapelle in Bourges.

228. *Late XIV Century*, p. 303. For the texts in the library of Philippe le Hardi and Jean sans Peur see Doutrepont, *Littérature*, 1909, and Appendix B.

229. See J. Rowlands, "Simone Martini and Petrarch," *Apollo*, LXXXI, 1965, p. 264 ff.

230. See the chapter on Humanism and the Catalogue of Workshops, Virgil Master.

231. The illustration of the *Aeneid* on fol. 64v, by an assistant in the workshop, represents the building of Troy and an army at sea.

232. See the Catalogue of Manuscripts.

233. *Late XIV Century*, fig. 199.

234. A similar crown, shaded by dark spots of varying density, may be seen in Byzantine painting (cf. Bibl. nat. gr. 1208—A. Grabar, *Byzantine Painting*, New York [n.d.], p. 180) but the resemblance is perhaps fortuitous.

235. *The Works of Virgil*, Dryden transl., Oxford, 1961, p. 3.

236. D. Comparetti, *Virgilio nel medio evo*, Florence, 1896, 2 vols.; J. W. Spargo, *Virgil the Necromancer*, Cambridge (Mass.), 1934.

237. Brieger, Meiss, and Singleton, *Dante Manuscripts*, 1969, figs. 46, 47, 114b, 121, 122c, 127b, 138b. In the miniature for the first *Eclogue* in the tenth-century manuscript in Naples (see n. 225) it is Meliboeus who wears a conical hat or *pilleus*. For Botticelli's Dante illustrations see A. Venturi, *Botticelli*, London, 1927, pls. CXLIV–CLIX.

238. See V. Zabughin, *Vergilio nel Rinascimento italiano*, Bologna, II, n.d., p. 387 f.

239. See the Catalogue of Manuscripts, Virgil.

240. *Ibid.*

241. See also fols. 85v, 173, 185v and Terence chapter, p. 43.

242. Loeb ed., I, p. 29.

243. *The Works of Virgil*, *cit.*, p. 19.

244. The double pipe of Menalcas, used in antiquity, was also employed in the Middle Ages; see, for example, Simone Martini, *The Knighting of St. Martin*, S. Francesco, Assisi.

245. Loeb ed., I, p. 43.

246. *Ibid.*, p. 61.

247. *De Civitate Dei*, Book VIII, Ch. 24.

248. "muliebri et delicato corpore . . . frons eius pampino cingitur. . . . coronam viteam et cornu habet." (Isidore, VIII, 11, 43–44.) See Saxl, *Lectures*, I, p. 237.

249. *De formis*, ed. 1966, p. 42. For Hrabanus see Migne, *Pal. lat.*, 111, col. 429, and for the horned Bacchus in the famous manuscript of his text of 1023 see Seznec, *Pagan Gods*, 1953, fig. 65.

250. See the horses and other animals in the *Merveilles du monde* (*Boucicaut Master*, figs. 89, 90).

251. Fr. 616 was painted by the Adelphoe Master and his assistants towards 1410. This illuminator, who belongs to the stylistic trend from which the Bedford Master emerged (see Catalogue of Workshops), takes his name from the miniatures of the *Adelphoe* in the *Térence des ducs*. Panofsky (*Netherlandish Painting*, 1953, I, p. 51 f.) dated fr. 616 in the first years of the fifteenth century and attributed the miniatures to the workshop responsible for fr. 12201. Porcher (Paris, Bibl. nat., 1955, p. 101 no. 212; *Enluminure française*, 1959, p. 65) attributed the manuscript to the atelier of the Bedford Master and dated it between 1405 and 1410.

Towards the end of the fifteenth century the manuscript belonged to Aymar de Poitiers who added his arms to the lower margin of folio 13.

252. Miss Peck's copy of the *Livre de la chasse* was exe-

cuted by the workshop responsible for fr. 616 about the same time. See the Catalogue of Workshops, Bedford Trend.

253. Although fr. 619 is the earliest known example and bears the arms of Foix and Béarn, we do not think, as we suggest above, that the manuscript is the original illuminated copy of the text furnished by Gaston Phébus in 1387. The devise *J'ay belle dame* in the ex-libris on folio 112v shows that the ms. belonged early in the fifteenth century to Jean I, comte de Foix. See Paris, Musée du Louvre, 1904, p. 34; Paris, Bibl. nat. (Couderc), 1909, p. 15 f.

Two other interesting copies date from the second and third decades of the fifteenth century. For the earlier of these manuscripts, which is in Dresden, ms. Oc 61, see Catalogue of Workshops, Rohan Master. The other ms. is in Leningrad, Publīchnaiâ bībl., fr. F.v.X, 1. See Leningrad, Publīchnaiâ bībl., Laborde, I, 1936, p. 48 f. no. 50, pl. XXIII.

254. *Georgics*, IV, 64.

255. Poirion, *Guillaume de Machaut à Charles d'Orléans*, 1965.

256. Curtius, *European Literature*, ed. 1963, p. 195. However Pächt, 1950, p. 46 f., finds that an aesthetic appreciation of landscape may first be found in Italian poetry of the fourteenth century (Folgore da San Gimignano).

257. Drouot, 1942; David, *Sluter*, 1951, pp. 138–140.

258. *Golden Legend.* Monget, *Chartreuse*, I, 1898, pp. 251 ff., 408.

259. Drouot, 1942, p. 11 f.

260. For evidence of similar scenes in, for instance, Berry see *ibid.*, p. 9.

261. Possibly the miniature represents Ptolemaeus Physcon, who married his sister-in-law and then their daughter (fr. 282, fols. 352, 353), and Mithridates, who ordered the murder of 80,000 Roman merchants (fol. 363).

262. Avril, "Trois manuscrits napolitains," 1969 (1970), pp. 300–314.

263. See Meyer, 1855, and Monfrin, 1964.

264. Royal 20 D I belonged to Charles V before passing to Jean de Berry. Guiffrey, *Inventaires*, I, p. 236 f. nos. 910, 912; see Bologna, *Pittori*, 1969, p. 139 f.; Saxl, *Lectures*, 1957, I, p. 135 f., and especially Buchthal, *Historia Troiana*, 1971, pp. 16–19.

265. Brit. Mus., Burney 257. See Catalogue of Workshops and Saxl and Meier, *Catalogue*, III, pt. 1, 1953, pp. 98–114.

266. *Thebaid*, I, 46–48.

267. *Ibid.*, I, 75–78.

268. *Late XIV Century*, p. 31 ff.; Lehoux, *Berri*, passim.

269. M. Longnon, who referred to this phrase in his commentary on the *Très Riches Heures*, 1969, pl. no. 2, generously communicated to me his exact reading. The identical phrase for Troy was used in a *balade* by Deschamps, *Oeuvres*, I, 1878, p. 137. See also *Late XIV Century*, p. 59, with remarks that are superseded by the present text.

270. Guiffrey, *Inventaires*, I, p. 237 no. 912. Also *ibid.*, pp. 236 no. 910, 239 no. 919, 228 no. 866, 235 no. 903 (a number of gatherings, not bound). See also the next note.

On the story of Troy in the Middle Ages see Buchthal (*Historia Troiana*, 1971), who has brilliantly demonstrated that the legend was utilized in the fourteenth century by the Doge of Venice, Andrea Dandolo, in the interest of his own political theories and ambitions.

271. Guiffrey, *op. cit.*, p. 245 no. 937.

A contemporary chronicler may give us still one more example of Jean de Berry's interest in subjects of this kind. In 1389 the French and the English held an important conference in search of peace. When describing this meeting in a chapel at Lelinghen the chronicler said that Jean de Berry arranged to cover the worn old walls with a series of tapestries representing ancient battles, which might have been Trojan ("antiqua et varia prelia"). See Religieux de Saint-Denys, *Chronique*, II, 1890, pp. 77, 79.

272. *Late XIV Century*, p. 43.

273. *Ibid.*, pp. 302–306.

274. *Ibid.*, p. 55 f.

275. For other, similar occurrences see the capitulum for Terce; First Vespers, fourth Antienne; and the *responsum* given in the text.

276. In a letter to Paola St. Jerome referred similarly to this marble statue of Venus: ". . . in crucis rupe statua ex marmore Veneris a gentibus posita colebatur, existimantibus persecutionis auctoribus, quod tollerent nobis fidem resurrectionis et crucis. . . ."

NOTES TO CHAPTERS IV, V, VI, VII

1. The alternate reading of Bonne for Bolure is cited in the Documents, Chapter IV.
2. For the earlier family records in Nijmegen see the important article by Gorissen, 1954, esp. p. 168 f. The father of the Limbourgs had come from Aachen.
3. See Lespinasse, *Métiers*, II, 1892, p. 20.
4. See Godefroy, *Dictionnaire*, s.v. In the contemporary biography of the Maréchal de Boucicaut he was described as "si jeune enfant" at the age of 15 (*Livre des faits*, 1850, p. 389). Gorissen, 1954, p. 168, estimates the older boy was 14.
5. See below, p. 100.
6. Because of the lack of comparable documents of this period for outstanding illuminators we may observe that in 1397 and 1399 Malouel was paid 8 gros a day, equivalent to about 13 sous (Gorissen, 1954, nos. 46, 52, 58). In 1386 the Duke of Berry's sculptor Jean de Cambrai received exactly the same wages—300 sous a month—as each of the Limbourgs (Champeaux and Gauchery, *Travaux*, 1894, p. 38). In 1383 Philippe le Hardi paid Dreue de Dampmartin 8 sous a day as "maistre général de ses oeuvres de maconnerie pour tous ses pays" (Monget, *Chartreuse*, I, 1898, p. 24).
7. Monget, *Chartreuse*, I, 1898, p. 336.
8. *Boucicaut Master*, 1968, p. 60.
9. See Meiss with Off, 1971, pp. 228, 233; *Late XIV Century*, pp. 44, 270, 297, and Appendix A.
10. *Late XIV Century*, p. 37; Monstrelet, *Chroniques*, ed. 1836, p. 215.
11. Champeaux and Gauchery, *Travaux*, 1894, pp. 140 f., 203; Gorissen, 1954, p. 170.
12. See Paris, Arch. nat. J 187, B h° 48, which was called to my attention by M. Jean-Yves Ribault. This document invalidates in one detail or another the statements of Lehoux, *Jean de Berri*, II, 1966, p. 102 n. 5; Champeaux and Gauchery, *op. cit.*, p. 140; Durrieu, *Très Belles Heures de Notre-Dame*, 1922, p. 74.
13. Monget, *Chartreuse*, I, 1898, p. 180.
14. Paul died in 1416, and we know from a record kindly communicated by M. Ribault that his widow Gilette married, before July 1422, André Le Roy, who in the document of 1434 possessed the house.
15. *Late XIV Century*, p. 32.
16. These gifts were said to coincide with the termination of the *Belles Heures* according to an earlier view, which we believe cannot be maintained.
17. Historians have simply concluded that he settled in Bourges and remained there (see, for example, Gorissen, 1954, p. 175). Gorissen even states, without any justification whatever, that the document of 1434 indicates that Paul died in this house.
18. See Documents, 1416, and Gorissen, 1954, p. 216.
19. See below. Also see Meiss, *Gaz. B.-A.*, 1963, and Catalogue of Workshops.
20. This date I owe to M. Ribault. For 1416–1417 and 1435 see Champeaux and Gauchery, *Travaux*, 1894, p. 142; Gorissen, 1954, pp. 215, 220.
21. Le Roux de Lincy, *Paris et ses historiens*, 1867, p. 233.
22. *Late XIV Century*, p. 294 f.
23. Furthermore, as M. Ribault has pointed out to me, when the Duke decided in 1409–1410 to add some manuscripts to those he had given to the Ste.-Chapelle, the additional manuscripts were taken from the library at Mehun (Archives du Cher, 8 G 1636, fol. 57). Of course during this period the Duke occasionally visited Bourges, whereas after 1412 never.
24. Guiffrey, *Inventaires*, II, p. 239 f.
25. See Catalogue of Manuscripts, Observations on the History of the *Très Riches Heures*.
26. For manuscripts in the chapel of the Hôtel de Nesle, inventoried on May 26, 1416 shortly before the Duke's death, see Archives du Cher, 8 G 1452, very kindly photocopied for me by M. Ribault. The manuscripts are a Pontifical, Gradual, and four Breviaries. The list was published by Guiffrey, *Inventaires*, II, p. 313 ff. but without the statement that the manuscripts came from the Hôtel de Nesle. For the general *déménagement* of the Hôtel de Nesle, which required four days, see Archives du Cher, 8 G 1455.
27. *Late XIV Century*, p. 291 f.
28. *Ibid.*, p. 34.
29. Meiss, *Gaz. B.-A.*, 1963, pp. 147–170. Two drawings discussed in this article, in the Louvre and the Boymans Museum, which had both been attributed to Pisanello by Degenhart and others, and about which I expressed some hesitation (p. 155), have since been classified as Lombard, *ca.* 1450, by Fossi Todorow, *Disegni*, 1966, pp. 133, 199, and by Bean, in Musée Bonnat, *Dessins*, 1960, no. 223.
30. See especially Delisle, *Livres d'images*, 1893, p. 239; Durrieu, 1895, pp. 103, 114, 130. The dependence of

fr. 166 upon fr. 167 was already stressed by Prost, 1890–1891, p. 344.

31. For miniatures in related styles and with similar architectural frames, see Morgan Library M 772 (*Pèlerinages*). They are the subject of a forthcoming study by François Avril.

32. Durrieu, 1895, p. 121.

33. *Late XIV Century*, pp. 17, 122 f. and figs. 325, 326, 572.

34. In the twelfth-century murals in the Chapter House at Sigena, by English painters, Adam holds a spade while an angel, similarly equipped, gives him a lesson in its use. In the *St. Swithin Psalter* (Brit. Mus., Cotton Nero C. IV, fol. 2), likewise English and of the same century, an angel gives Adam a spade.

The key has a theological overtone: Christ as the new Adam unlocks Paradise through his sacrifice.

35. See 1v no. 6; 2 no. 6; 4 nos. 1, 3; 4v no. 3; 6 no. 1; 9 no. 2. The tools are not represented in the corresponding miniatures of fr. 167.

36. For the significance of the cross and the heap of stones behind the pilgrims see Chap. VI, notes 339, 340.

37. Panofsky, *Netherlandish Painting*, 1953, p. 170 f. Panofsky introduced his own psychological and sociological inferences to account for the interest in peasants, craftsmen, and St. Joseph.

38. Mgr. Glorieux in Gerson, *Œuvres*, I [1961], p. 113 ff.

39. Oberman, *Harvest*, 1963, p. 332 ff.

40. In a letter written November 23, 1413, which begins "En considerant moult et souvent et en escripvant de lexcellence et dignite de saint Joseph" Gerson asks Jean de Berry to help establish the feast of his marriage to Mary. Gerson praises the Duke for his gifts to Notre-Dame of "fondacions et dotacions," of reliquaries, organs, vestments, and precious liturgical objects. *Œuvres*, II [1961], p. 155 ff.

41. Leviticus 11, 15; Bersuire, *Dictionarii*, 1583, p. 5 (raven feeds on human bodies). See also Brit. Mus., Royal 2 B VII (Queen Mary's Psalter), fol. 7; Bibl. nat., lat. 10525 (St. Louis Psalter), fol. 3v.

42. The chief contrary opinions were expressed by Porcher, Paris, Bibl. nat., 1955, p. 91 f., and in *Enciclopedia universale dell'arte*, s.v. Limbourgs, n.d. See also Longnon and Cazelles, *Très Riches Heures*, 1969, p. 19. Durrieu, 1895, pp. 115–122, said that he could not resolve the problem of the identification, and Panofsky (*Netherlandish Painting*, 1953, p. 125) refrained from judgment.

In view of Philippe le Hardi's devotion to the Carthusian Order it is interesting that in fr. 166 the "devote ame q(ui) recoit ihesu crist et se trait hors du monde" is not the crowned woman of fr. 167 but a Carthusian (fol. 19, no. 6). The only identifiable saint in the first three gatherings of fr. 166 is Catherine (fol. 20), patron of the Duchess of Burgundy but of other ladies of high station as well.

43. It is puzzling that they apparently designed even the miniature on 31v (Fig. 332), which contains a building that seems to imply knowledge—as the *Purification of the Virgin* in the *Très Riches Heures* certainly does—of the temple in Taddeo Gaddi's fresco of the Presentation of the Virgin (Fig. 668). Had the Limbourgs already seen in Paris a drawing of this composition such as the one now in the Louvre? This drawing in the Louvre, however, belonged to Baldinucci in the seventeenth century and then was acquired by the museum. The architectural elements of the temple on 31v—high flight of stairs, flying buttresses—reappear in an illustration of a Psalm in the *Très Riches Heures* (Fig. 561).

44. *Gaz. B.-A.*, 1963, p. 162; *Late XIV Century*, pp. 44, 270, 297.

45. See *ibid.*, p. 102 f.

46. *Late XIV Century*, p. 289.

47. *Vie de Nostre Sauveur*, p. 19 f.

48. See Panofsky, *Netherlandish Painting*, 1953, p. 46.

49. Guiffrey, *Inventaires*, I, no. 879; Avril, "Trois manuscrits napolitains," 1969 (1970), p. 328 n. 1.

50. *Late XIV Century*, figs. 6, 11.

51. As Stejskal, 1970, p. 52, pointed out. In addition to the *Annunciation ca.* 1360 in the Emmaus Monastery, Prague, which he cited, see also John in a *Crucifixion* in a Missal dated 1409 in the Nationalbibliothek, Vienna, reproduced in *Gotik in Böhmen*, 1969, fig. 186. See also Jan van Eyck's *Annunciation* in the National Gallery, Washington.

52. For the Cleveland panel see The Cleveland Museum of Art, *Gothic Art 1360–1440*, 1963, p. 203.

53. *Late XIV Century*, p. 130 ff. The connection of the panel in Cleveland with Bohemian painting is supported by the fact that Gabriel's scroll is equally prominent in the fresco in the Emmaus Monastery cited in n. 51 and seems to have the same significance.

54. See the end of the chapter on Virgil.

55. Panofsky, *Netherlandish Painting*, 1953, p. 63 and n. 3. See also *Late XIV Century*, fig. 652.

56. Meiss and Kirsch, *Visconti Hours*, 1972, LF f. 11. See also the Lombard Missal of 1395, Bibl. capitolare of S. Ambrogio, Milan (Gengaro, *Miniature lombarde*,

1970, fig. 350). For slightly later Tuscan examples see the Pisan panel, *ca.* 1400, Museo nazionale, Pisa, and intarsia by Domenico di Niccolo, Palazzo Pubblico, Siena, *ca.* 1415 (*Late XIV Century*, figs. 553, 630).

57. In his account of the Brigittine Nativity in France Panofsky (*op. cit.*, pp. 46, 125) overlooked this miniature. Consequently he overstated the rarity and strangeness of the composition, and he interpreted its significance in the Bible somewhat differently from the text above. Here in the *Belles Heures*, it must be stressed, the new composition, somewhat altered, is employed for the Mass of the Nativity, and it therefore has the same meaning as in Italian art.

58. See *Boucicaut Master*, p. 95.

59. See earlier examples, such as the *Nativity* by Pseudo-Jacquemart *ca.* 1385 in the *Petites Heures* (*Late XIV Century*, fig. 131).

60. *Boucicaut Master*, fig. 26, and Nordenfalk, "St. Bridget," 1961, p. 389 ff., who first dealt with the representation. No textual source for the miracle has yet been found.

61. *Late XIV Century*, p. 236 and figs. 752, 755, 756. For St. Joseph and the candle see Meiss, 1945, p. 176 n. 2, and, fully, Panofsky, *Netherlandish Painting*, 1953, p. 126.

The lack of early French representations of St. Bridget is probably connected with the fact that France did not recognize her canonization in 1391 by P. Boniface IX. The canonization was, however, confirmed at the Council of Basel in 1415 despite the continued opposition of Jean Gerson (*Œuvres*, I [1961], p. 38).

62. Many of the elements of this composition (but not the figure in front of the tomb) may be seen in an *Entombment* by the Egerton Master in the *Heures de Charles le Noble* in the Cleveland Museum (Fig. 339), which I have dated *ca.* 1405 (*Late XIV Century*, p. 242, fig. 805). This illuminator was, as I have said, influenced early in his career by the Limbourgs.

63. See Catalogue of Panels. Also Louvre, *Peintures, école française* (Sterling and Adhémar), 1965, p. 3 f. Troescher, *Burgundische Malerei*, 1966, p. 62 ff., incorrectly, we believe, connects this panel with Beaumetz and ascribes it tentatively to his pupil Picornet. For Troescher's thesis that Beaumetz brought the concept of a diagonal composition from the Netherlands see the valid objection to Pešina (1971, p. 176 n. 37) that this kind of design had already appeared in the third quarter of the fourteenth century in Parisian illumination, and that Beaumetz was in Paris as early as 1371.

64. This gesture, Prof. Moshe Barasch will point out in his forthcoming book, seems first to appear in Giotto's *Last Judgment* in the Arena Chapel.

65. Durrieu, 1895, pp. 121 f., 130. Durrieu was curiously noncommittal about his reasons for doubting the identification. Throughout his career he held to this negative view. He did not include the Bible in his account of the Limbourgs in Michel, *Histoire*, III, 1, 1907, p. 166 ff. In 1923, in the *Très Belles Heures de Notre-Dame*, p. 79 ff., he ascribed the miniatures in the third gathering to Paul and the preceding ones to "less able collaborators."

66. Paris, Bibl. nat. (Porcher), 1955, p. 91 f.

67. Later Jean used it occasionally for his quatrefoils; see fol. 14v, no. 3.

68. Folio 12.

69. *Late XIV Century*, p. 206, fig. 280.

70. *Boucicaut Master*, figs. 1, 25. In a review of this book in *Revue de l'art*, 1970, no. 8, p. 82 f., A. Châtelet suggested that the main body of the *Boucicaut Hours* was painted between 1410 and 1415, and then the four folios of the second gathering were added after the battle of Azincourt in 1415, when the Marshal was taken prisoner. He is represented, Châtelet believes, on the left hand of St. Leonard, patron of prisoners (fol. 9v). While, as I noted in my book, this figure does show some resemblance to the Marshal, the ear is not as pointed and the nose as bulbous as in the certain portraits on fols. 26v and 38v. In these portraits, furthermore, Boucicaut has brown hair and no beard; the man in 9v has white hair and a beard. If this man were the Marshal, why should he as the donor be on the saint's *left* rather than the right?

The second gathering is, indeed, unusual, and for more reasons than Châtelet gives. It consists of only four leaves instead of the normal eight. In the second place, five of the eight faces are blank (8, 8v, 9, 10v, 11). It seems highly probable, however, that at least the sheet containing folios 8 and 11 belonged to the original plan. The first fol. (12) of the third gathering, which is an integral part of the gathering and of the manuscript, contains the beginning of the prayer to St. Michael. The prayer definitely presupposes a miniature of the saint, and that does appear on the last fol. (11v) of gathering two, which probably therefore existed originally. This miniature of Michael is, furthermore, one of the less advanced paintings, as Panofsky had already observed, and for this reason, too, it was not added later.

It is certainly possible that the sheet comprising

fols. 9 and 10 was not present at the beginning. Fol. 10, containing the prayer to St. Leonard (which is very short), shows one small peculiarity. Folios at the beginning of a prayer normally have a border decorated along the inner margin and partway across the top. Fol. 10 lacks the decoration at the top. As I observed in the *Boucicaut Master* (p. 21), *St. Leonard* does seem more impressive than some miniatures in the manuscript, but it is not more advanced than fols. 17v, 24v, 29v, 32v, and many others. It contains, furthermore, the same pigments in the same degree of saturation as the rest of the miniatures. The halo is identical also. If therefore the miniature was not in the original plan it was, I believe, added during the later course of the work.

Professor Châtelet does not deal at all with the fundamental problem of inserting the *Boucicaut Hours* and its supposed addition among the manuscripts dated from 1410 on. He claims only that the landscapes in the *Visitation* and the *Flight* are exceptional in the manuscript because of their aerial perspective, and that the Boucicaut Master was here influenced by the *July* and *October* pictures in the *Très Riches Heures*, painted about 1415. Does the Boucicaut Master, however, not demonstrate his knowledge of aerial perspective also in the miniatures of the *Annunciation to the Shepherds* and *David before the Lord*? What in my opinion resemble the miniatures in the *Très Riches Heures* much more are the late, flat landscapes painted by the Boucicaut Master just before 1415 in the Breviary at Châteauroux and a little later in Add. 16997. Observations on relations between the *Boucicaut Hours*, the Limbourgs, and other painters of this time appear throughout the following text, and they all are significant for the date of the masterpiece by the Boucicaut Master.

71. She describes the removal of the garment just before the whipping and the search for it immediately afterward. "Deinde iubente lictore, seipsum vestibus exuit, columnam sponte amplecte[n]s, reste ligatur, et flagellis aculeatis, infixus aculeis, et retractis, non evellendo, sed fulcando totum corpus eius laceratur. . . . Et iam solutus filius meus a columna, primum ad vestimenta sua se co[n]vertit, nec tamen spatium induendi se ei conceditur. Sed adhuc dum traheretur, brachia sua manicis inseruit. Vestigiaque eius, in quibus ad columnam stetit, plena erat sanguine, taliter, quod ego bene potera[m] omnia vestigia eius, quae ivit, signo sanguinis agnoscere, qui tunc vultu[m] suum manarte sanguine tunica detersit. . . ." *Revelationes*, 1628, I, p. 413 (Bk. IV, Ch. 70).
72. *Late XIV Century*, p. 217.
73. *Meditations*, ed. Ragusa and Green, 1961, p. 328 f. Also Ludolph of Saxony, *Vita Christi*, 1519, Ch. 62: "Sicut remossus fuerat ab herode cu[m] alba veste: sic remansit in eadem veste usq[e] ad horam flagellationis. . . ." This white garment is represented in the bas-de-page of Christ before Herod in the *Très Belles Heures de Notre-Dame* (*Late XIV Century*, fig. 25). All three garments are mentioned in the Gospels: Luke 23, 11 ("veste alba"); Matt. 27, 28 ("chlamydem coccineam"); Mark 15, 17 ("veste purpurea"); Matt. 27, 31 ("vestimentis eius"). When Christ was sent out from the praetorium he was dressed in his own blue tunic so that the populace would recognize him.
74. Follower of the Boucicaut Master, Cracow, Muzeum Narodowe, ms. Czart. 2032, p. 449 (*Boucicaut Master*, fig. 317); Bedford workshop, Vienna ms. 1855, fol. 21v (Trenkler, *Livre d'heures* [1948], pl. 5); panel, school of Cologne, formerly Renders Coll., Bruges (illustrated in *Early Flemish Paintings in the Renders Collection at Bruges, shown in the Belgian Exhibition, Burlington House, January 1927*, London, 1927, p. 16).
75. See Gauthier, *Emaux*, 1972, p. 288.
76. *Late XIV Century*, fig. 239. This subject, though uncommon, was represented occasionally; see, for example, Naples, Church of S. Maria di Donna Regina, Cavallinesque fresco; London, Victoria & Albert Museum, Ivory diptych, 14th century, inv. no. 5623. 1859.
77. Guiffrey, *Inventaires*, II, 1896, p. 93 no. 712.
78. The *Brussels Hours* includes also, in the *Deposition*, an unprecedented doffed mantle of the Virgin.
79. For instance, Memling, Altarpiece, Galleria Sabauda, Turin. In later painting see, for example, Le Sueur, *Christ at the Column*, Paris, Louvre (P. Doncoeur, *Le Christ dans l'art français*, Paris [1939], I, p. 129).
80. Meiss, *Master of the Breviary*, 1971, p. 7 f.
81. *Late XIV Century*, p. 199 ff.
82. *Ibid.*, pp. 291–293.
83. For the remarkably full records of the life of Philippe le Hardi see Petit, *Itinéraires*, pp. 320–338 (1402–1404). For Jean de Berry see Lehoux, *Jean de Berri*, III, 1967, p. 497.
84. *Late XIV Century*, pp. 199, 315. While the two Limbourg brothers worked on the *Bible moralisée* in the house of Jean Durand, Jacques Coene, Ymbert Stanier

and Haincelin de Haguenau illuminated a second Bible in Latin and French for Philippe le Hardi. Jean sans Peur gave this Bible to Jean de Berry. See *Boucicaut Master*, pp. 61, 141. An illuminated early fifteenth-century French *Bible moralisée* that might seem identifiable with Philippe's Bible (Vat. reg. lat. 25) was produced by four painters, not three, and mediocre ones at that. For Philippe's manuscripts see Appendix B.

85. The white pigment has, as often (see the *Boucicaut Hours*), adhered less well than other colors, and its loss, together with the brown or gray lines on it that model the planes, has seriously diminished the effect of numerous miniatures.

86. See Bouvy, D.P.R.A., *Middeleeuwsche Beeldhouwkunst in de noordelijke Nederlanden*, Amsterdam, 1947.

87. Delaissé, *Dutch Illumination*, 1968, pp. 13–15, frontispiece and fig. 1. Gaspar and Lyna, Bibl. royale, I, 1937, p. 372 ff., also seem to prefer an early date, which is based on identification of the Emperor as Charles IV. However, Gorissen, 1954 (legend opposite his pl. 3), points out that the folio on which *Charles IV and the Electors* is drawn originally had a different format and was cut to fit into the *Wapenboek* (this observation not cited by Delaissé). The altarpiece in Kranenburg that Gorissen dates about 1400 (pl. 2) must be much later.

88. De Coo, 1965. For the panel of the Nativity see *Late XIV Century*, fig. 629.

89. See Panofsky, *Netherlandish Painting*, 1953, p. 98 f., fig. 114.

90. They are not at all, however, rigid and wooden, like the figure of Christ in a *Vesperbild* on fol. 191v of a second copy of Dirk van Delft, produced it seems immediately after Walters 171 and now Add. 22288 in the British Museum. This entire *Vesperbild*, which Delaissé singled out for enthusiastic discussion at the beginning of his book (*Dutch Illumination*, 1968, p. 17, fig. 7) and described as "one of the most moving Pietàs of the Middle Ages," is a much later and very crude repainting, which leaves visible only a minute trace of the early fifteenth-century miniature.

91. See Byvanck, *Miniature*, 1937, p. 51 f., figs. 89–94; London, Sotheby, Dec. 1, 1970, Library of Major J. R. Abbey, pp. 39–41, pls. 16, 17. The second illuminator in the manuscript had a large share in the Prayer Book of Mary of Guelders, dated 1415.

92. *Late XIV Century*, figs. 94, 130, 245, 618.

93. This relationship has not, we believe, previously been observed.

94. Pseudo-Jacquemart, Brit. Mus. Yates Thompson 37, fol. 19 (*Late XIV Century*, fig. 276). In the *Flight into Egypt* in the Utrecht ms. the Virgin rides side-saddle and averted, as in the *Belles Heures*.

95. Berlin, Staatsbibliothek, cod. germ. 42, 4°.

96. A colophon reads: "Das buch ist der hochgeborne frow e frow Margreta geboren von Cleve. Sol behalte werden von de couvent zu Schonensteinbach zu ewe' gedachtnis." The manuscript is LA 148 in the Gulbenkian Collection. I can find no reference to this important manuscript in the comprehensive work of Hoogewerff nor in the recent book of Delaissé, *Dutch Illumination*, 1968.

97. Néerlandais 3. Tentatively ascribed to Liège and highly praised by Panofsky, *Netherlandish Painting*, 1953, p. 111 f., figs. 150–152.

98. *Late XIV Century*, p. 250 f.; Panofsky, *op. cit.*, p. 106 f., figs. 135–137.

99. *Late XIV Century*, pp. 252, 354 f.

100. *Op. cit.*, p. 131 ff. See also my discussion of the symbolism of the rays and the glass (1945).

101. Whereas Broederlam does seem here to have intended a juxtaposition of the Old Testament and the New, the continuation of such a contrast in immediately subsequent French painting does not seem quite as clear as Panofsky proposed (*op. cit.*, p. 132 f.). Thus whereas the *Annunciation* by the Boucicaut workshop in lat. 1161 (*Boucicaut Master*, fig. 125) does indeed show Gothic pinnacles at the left and three small domes at the right the object on the altar with a round arch does not appear to be the Tablets of the Law, as Panofsky said. If that were the case the two tablets would be set at the left edge of the altar (we must infer from the shape of the altar that no more than half of it is visible). The object was much more likely a triptych. Similarly the "tower" in lat. 10538 (*Boucicaut Master*, fig. 129) seems, unlike Broederlam's, a normal Gothic element of the period.

102. *Late XIV Century*, pp. 24, 100. For the *Crucifixion* in Antwerp by Simone Martini see *ibid.*, fig. 674.

103. For Beaumetz see the fundamental article by Sterling, 1955; *Late XIV Century*, pp. 7, 38, 100, 293; Catalogue of Panels. Sterling identified the panels of the Crucifixion in Cleveland and the Louvre with the commission Beaumetz received in 1388 and executed, with his workshop, from 1390 to about 1395.

104. *Late XIV Century*, p. 8; Monget, *Chartreuse*, I, 1898, p. 133.

105. The connection of the panels in Cleveland and the

Louvre with Beaumetz depends, of course, upon the fact that they were painted for the Chartreuse at Champmol, and the only (non-stylistic) evidence for this is the presence of a Carthusian monk in both panels. From the time of the appearance of the panels all historians have assumed that the monks are members of this Order. It is true that both men are tonsured and wear a white outer garment over a white tunic. In the panel in the Louvre this outer garment conforms with Carthusian convention. It is a broad scapular, the front and back parts of which are connected on both sides by a band which, despite some damage, is still visible. This band appears clearly in fol. 97 of the *Belles Heures* (Fig. 416) and in other approximately contemporary representations of Carthusians (Sterling, 1955, figs. 7, 8). Since the outer garment in the Cleveland panel did not seem to conform clearly with this design I appealed to William Wixom of the Cleveland Museum, who very kindly examined the surface in the laboratory. The line that seems to define the lower boundary of the left part of a band is, he reports, original and carries, faintly but properly, towards the right. The tunic, which is a grayer white than the scapular, appears below this band, as it should. The visible area of the tunic is triangular because of the fall of the garments. There can thus be no doubt that the habit is Carthusian.

106. *Late XIV Century*, p. 279 f.; Catalogue of Panels.

107. For an account of this gesture see Meiss, *Gaz. B.-A.*, 1961, p. 286 f. At Strasbourg the gesture appeared in the relief of the Death of the Virgin, *ca.* 1235. For the *Crucifixion* in the Douce Missal see *Late XIV Century*, fig. 536.

108. Gorissen, 1954, pp. 164–167; Monget, *op. cit.*, I, pp. 21 ff., 336, 346; *Late XIV Century*, p. 293.

109. For other examples of the angel supporting Christ see *Late XIV Century*, figs. 15, 326, 572, 622, 806. For the Louvre tondo see Catalogue of Panels.

110. Meiss and Eisler, 1960; Sterling in Vienna, Kunsthistorisches Museum, *Europäische Kunst*, 1962, p. 70 and Paris, Musée du Louvre, *Peintures*, 1965, p. 4 no. 8; Pächt, *Gaz. B.-A.*, 1963, p. 117; Laclotte, *Primitifs* [1966], p. 13; Castelnuovo, *Gotico internazionale*, II (n.d.). See Catalogue of Panels. Sterling, in Białostocki et al., *Spätmittelalter*, 1972, p. 188 now doubts that the *Madonna* and the Louvre tondo are by the same painter.

111. For a discussion of paintings on cloth see Meiss and Eisler, *op. cit.*, p. 234 f.

112. Monget, *op. cit.*, I, p. 346.

113. Bastard, *Peintures*, 1832–1869. See *Late XIV Century*, p. 84, n. 10.

114. *Burl. Mag.*, p. 51. Also *Late XIV Century*, 1967, p. 84, where this copy is fully discussed.

115. Two other copies of the charter have survived which contain initial letters nearly identical with those in the document copied by Bastard. One, bearing the same date, Easter (April 19) 1405, is in French (Arch. du Cher 8 G 1452, titre scellé 195). Another was dated December 1404 at Bicêtre (Arch. du Cher 8 G 1447). Only in the charter of Bastard is the name of the Duke not aligned with the rest of the line; and only in it, furthermore, does the first letter J crowd the first letter of the second line. The charter of Bastard alone has a miniature and acanthus twisting around the first letter.

116. Porcher, *Belles Heures*, 1953, p. 7 n. 10, preferred a later date, partly because of an erroneous belief that the Duke did not employ *France moderne* in 1405. Troescher, *Burgundische Malerei*, 1966, p. 143, says that Michelet Saumon probably painted the charter.

117. *Late XIV Century*, fig. 482.

118. *Ibid.*, figs. 474–502.

119. See Appendix A.

120. Fols. 2, 13, 30, 181, 215.

121. Meiss with Off, 1971, p. 228 and passim. See Appendix A.

122. *Ibid.*, pp. 233, 235.

123. *Late XIV Century*, p. 44.

124. *Ibid.*, p. 147 f.

125. *Belles Heures*, fols. 59v, 66, 80, 123, 171, 202. The fine ivy leaves on triple stems in the inner border of fr. 282, fol. 1, reappear on fols. 174, 174v of the *Belles Heures* (Fig. 407).

126. He put his name, in one form or another, on fols. 12v, 94, 150v, and in the colophon on 216v.

127. "Y. Lucas. l'an mil IIII C et II furent escriptes et enlumines cestes matines a la ville de Nantes. . . ."

128. Bibl. nat., fr. 242. See also *Late XIV Century*, pp. 252, 355, 399 n. 28, figs. 822, 823; *Boucicaut Master*, p. 63 ff., fig. 458, and Catalogue of Workshops.

129. On the acanthus and the Bodleian Horae, Douce 144, see *Boucicaut Master*, pp. 36, 107.

130. For borders by the Brussels Initials Master see *Late XIV Century*, figs. 752–755, 771, 772, 789, 790. Similar borders of acanthus on wide gold bands were adopted by the Boucicaut workshop *ca.* 1410 (*Boucicaut Master*, p. 106, figs. 123, 227, 232–235).

131. 1930, p. 94 ff.

132. Within narrower limits there is more than one "style" in the ivy borders. Compare, for example,

those on the folios with miniatures 42v–66 with those on 163–170. Fol. 223v resembles this second group, but it is still less dense, and it was apparently produced more independently of the others. On numerous folios small flowers appear in openings or gaps in the ivy border or they were added on the inner side of the ivy. See especially gatherings 11 and 24, described in the Catalogue of Manuscripts, and the observations there by John Plummer.

133. See, for example, the miniatures in a Lombard *Giron le Courtois* in Paris, Bibl. nat., nouv. acq. fr. 5243; *Late XIV Century*, p. 144, fig. 585.

134. The small miniatures in the manuscript that have arched upper frames are all in the last section also: fols. 155, 158, 158v, 159v, 160v, 162v, 195, 202.

135. Meiss with Off, 1971, p. 229 f., and Appendix A.

136. *Late XIV Century*, p. 247 ff.

137. *Ibid.*, p. 212.

138. *Ibid.*, p. 259, figs. 83–85, 217, 218.

139. *Ibid.*, p. 256 f.

140. For what follows see *ibid.*, pp. 265–269.

141. *Ibid.*, p. 226 ff.

142. The following pages, which have miniatures on the verso, are blank: 9, 12, 13, 17, 53, 117, 129, 163, 181, 185, 189, 193, 197. Folios containing text on the verso of the miniature include page 72 *Nativity*, p. 82 *Annunciation to Shepherds*, p. 90 *Adoration of Magi*, p. 98 *Presentation*, p. 106 *Flight*, p. 168 *Christ before Pilate*, p. 202 *Office of the Dead*; see also Calkins, 1970, pp. 23–26.

143. *Late XIV Century*, pp. 265–269, 285.

144. This practice of inserting single folios was described by Delaissé, *Dutch Illumination*, 1967, pp. 19, 71, as characteristic of Holland, and particularly Utrecht. He cited for the first quarter of the century only one possible example of 1409, but he referred to a document implying the establishment of the practice in Utrecht. He overlooked the *Grandes Heures* and the *Très Riches Heures*.

145. *Late XIV Century*, p. 117, figs. 6–50.

146. *Ibid.*, p. 160, figs. 94–176.

147. *Ibid.*, p. 68 f., fig. 231.

148. For the mid-thirteenth-century miniature of the reception of King Edward the Confessor in heaven, the similar reception of Giangaleazzo Visconti painted by Michelino da Besozzó in 1403, and the Wilton diptych, which perhaps shows Richard II at a comparable moment, see Wormald, 1954, p. 201 f. Levey, *Painting at Court*, 1971, p. 21 f., compares the miniature in the *Grandes Heures* with the Wilton diptych and the miniature of Edward without pointing out that only Jean de Berry was still alive.

Stejskal, 1970, pp. 52–54, proposed that the miniature in the *Grandes Heures* was related to the fresco in the Emmaus Monastery, Prague, painted *ca.* 1360, which shows God the Father receiving Enoch in heaven (Dvořáková *et al.*, *Gothic Mural Painting*, 1964, fig. 89). He observed that the compositions of the Emmaus cycle were copied in manuscripts, and could in this form have been transmitted to Paris. Stejskal refers to a painting ordered by the chancellor John of Streda during the lifetime of Emperor Charles IV that showed him "in regnum coelorum." This painting, now lost, seems to have come closer to the miniature in the *Grandes Heures*.

149. We should cite, in connection with this miniature, a pendant that the Duke was accustomed to wear at least near the end of his life. It is described in the inventory drawn up after his death in 1416. "Un fermail d'or en maniere d'un reliquiaire, garny de 6 rubiz, 6 grosses perles, et ou millieu un saphir taille d'un image de Dieu, pendant a un tessu noir que ledit feu Monseigneur de Berry souloit porter au col . . ." (Guiffrey, *Inventaires*, II, p. 342 f.). The miniature does indeed show six pearls but not one of the six rubies nor the black ribbon or any evidence of carving on the sapphire.

Jean de Berry might have known of the talisman believed to be Charlemagne's; it consisted of two sapphires in a jewelled setting that originally contained a hair of the Virgin between them, and it was said to have been around the Emperor's neck when his tomb was opened.

150. *Late XIV Century*, fig. 219. The Duke is represented at prayer in three initials (*ibid.*, figs. 234, 243, 244).

151. *Ibid.*, p. 92.

152. The coronet is different from those he wears in the few instances when artists thus refer to his ducal position. *Ibid.*, figs. 94, 486, 491, 502.

153. Possibly a turban of the kind worn by Louis II d'Anjou (Fig. 886) but not known in any of the numerous extant portraits of Jean de Berry. Despite the extension of the dark zone in the miniature down over the forehead the original headgear might have been the kind of fur hat he liked to wear from about 1405 on. See *Late XIV Century*, pp. 85, 93, figs. 487, 489, 490, 497–500. Originally the entire figure was turned slightly more to the beholder, and the head a little downward.

In my study of the portraits of Jean de Berry (*Late XIV Century*, 1967, esp. p. 79 ff.) I concluded that the Duke was clean-shaven until 1405, that he sprouted a goatee or a beard from 1406 until 1409–1410, and thereafter removed it. One important portrait that I then dated before 1409—the portrait by the Baptist Master in the *Heures de Turin* (*ibid.*, fig. 488)—did not fit this scheme because the Duke is clean-shaven. This miniature, however, belongs to a group that can now probably be dated 1404–1405 (Meiss, with Off, 1971), and thus the difficulty is eliminated. The fact that the Duke is clean-shaven in the portrait in the *Belles Heures* would indicate a date in 1405 or early 1406.

154. The drapery over the prie-dieu, however, displays simply the fleur-de-lys, without any particular emblem of Berry.

155. For the acquisition of the *Belles Heures* by the Duchess of Anjou see Limbourg Documents (p. 80).

156. *Late XIV Century*, p. 71 f.

157. Durrieu, *Très Belles Heures de Notre-Dame*, 1922, pp. 45, 121.

158. Whereas Bastard's copies of the miniatures themselves are reliable they are sometimes surrounded by the wrong borders, owing to a fire and confusion in the workshop. See *Late XIV Century*, pp. 92, 379 n. 88.

159. On what follows see *ibid.*, pp. 71 f., 92 f.

160. "Le 5 janvier 1407 (1408), se tint une journée à Hypre, laquelle dura quatorze jours, ou estoient le roy de Sicile, le duc de Berry et autres du conseil du roy, qui vinrent trouver monseigneur le duc" (fol. 194, 2nd account of Jean de Pressy, Bibl. nat., Coll. Bourg., LXV). See Petit, *Itinéraires*, 1888, p. 588. After the two weeks at Ypres they apparently removed to Amiens, where they met on January 19, 1408 (Lehoux, *Berri*, III, 1967, pp. 114–117). Also *Chronique de la Pucelle*, ed. Vallet de Viriville, Paris, n.d., p. 100 f.

161. Barker, *Manuel II*, 1969, p. 397.

162. For this "escharpe" see below, p. 225. If it is an Armagnac emblem the miniature may, like the *Itinerary* in the *Belles Heures*, refer to a political event.

163. The mace-bearer wears the same indented collar as the figure in the initial of the Charter of Ste.-Chapelle who holds the canon's hood (Fig. 387).

164. *Late XIV Century*, p. 92.

165. The angel repeats the one by Paul in the *Flight* in the *Belles Heures* (Fig. 415).

166. *Breviary Master*, 1971.

167. See below, n. 371, 373.

168. See *Boucicaut Master*, p. 17 f. and figs. 4, 42.

169. *Late XIV Century*, p. 84, fig. 482.

170. *Ibid.*, p. 334.

171. *Ibid.*, pp. 48, 291. Lehoux, *Berri*, III, 1967, p. 142 n. 9, refers to a meeting at Mehun in 1409. They were together in Bourges during the siege of 1412 because Monstrelet (II, p. 289) mentions her presence at a banquet. She was in the Auvergne when the Duke died in Paris (Lehoux, *op. cit.*, III, p. 407 n. 6), and she received very little in his will.

172. Of course the Duke could have commissioned the manuscript for her and then changed his mind.

173. Guiffrey, *Inventaires*, I, 1894, p. 56 no. 139; II, 1896, p. 91 no. 703. St. Catherine, herself a princess, was chosen as patron by many royal ladies.

174. St. Catherine was represented on the seal of the university (*Vie des saints*, ed. Bénédictins de Paris, Paris, XI, 1954, p. 863). For the royal foundation of St. Catherine-Val-des-Ecoliers see Le Roux de Lincy, *Paris et ses historiens*, 1867, p. 190.

175. Meiss, *Painting in Florence and Siena*, 1951, pp. 107–109.

176. This idea is stated in the first sentence of the long life of St. Catherine in the *Golden Legend*, which is the major source of her legend in the late Middle Ages and of the titles in the *Belles Heures*.

177. Philippe de Mézières, *Songe du vieil pelerin*, 1393, quoted in *Late XIV Century*, p. 69 f. See also Bell, *Le songe*, 1955, and Coopland, *Le songe*, 1969.

A prayer in the Collect of the Mass for the feast of St. Catherine, which first appeared during the fourteenth century in a Missal of the Curia, begins by associating Moses with her (*Vie des saints*, ed. Bénédictins de Paris, XI, 1954, p. 859). This prayer is in the suffrage for Catherine in the *Belles Heures*.

178. These relationships were observed by Porcher, *Belles Heures*, 1953, p. 42. He noticed that compositions more or less related appear in a Missal for the use of Troyes, lat. 865 A, fol. 1; in a Book of Hours in the Bibl. municipale, Lyon, ms. 5140, fol. 18; and in the *Rohan Hours*, lat. 9471, fol. 21.

179. The *Golden Legend* here draws from a letter Jerome sent to Eustochium. See especially the fourteenth-century Tuscan version, *Leggenda aurea*, ed. A. Levasti, Florence, 1926, III, p. 1237 f.

180. See, for example, the apostles preaching in the *Très Riches Heures* (Fig. 563), or St. Paul in the *Grandes Heures* (*Late XIV Century*, figs. 217, 218).

181. See, for example, V. Rossi, *Il Quattrocento*, 1938, p. 56 ff.

182. Particularly the Hieronymites of Fiesole. See Meiss,

"Scholarship and Penitence," in the press. For another Italian representation of the flagellation of Jerome see Bisogni, 1972, p. 69 ff.

183. Meiss, *Gaz. B.-A.*, 1963, p. 157 ff.

184. This miniature in Bibl. nat., lat. 757, fol. 370, comes closer to the description of the *joyau* than any painting I was able to cite earlier (Meiss, *ibid.*, p. 169 f., in reply to Pächt, *Pantheon*, 1963).

185. Meiss, *Gaz. B.-A.*, 1963, p. 160 ff.

186. *Ibid.*, and Documents on the Limbourgs.

187. *Late XIV Century*, p. 288 and chapter on Berry and the antique.

188. As Durrieu, *Bulletin*, 1911, p. 90 ff., suggested. Porcher, *Belles Heures*, 1953, p. 7 n. 10, following Durrieu rightly pointed to the similarity of the composition with *St. Luke* in the *Belles Heures*, but inferred, questionably I believe, that the miniature in Rome was a copy. It shows a far clearer organization of the space and a more advanced perspective of the tiled floor.

189. See, for example, Andrea da Bologna, 1368, fresco in the chapel of St. Catherine, Lower Church, S. Francesco, Assisi; Altichiero, *ca.* 1380, Oratorio di S. Giorgio, Padua (G. L. Mellini, *Altichiero e Jacopo Avanzi*, Milan, 1965, fig. 179); Spinello Aretino, *ca.* 1387, fresco in Oratorio di S. Caterina, Antella; Boucicaut follower, Chantilly ms. 1671, fol. 192v; Masolino, S. Clemente, Rome.

190. See Ambrogio's fresco of the Pope and St. Louis, in S. Francesco, Siena.

191. *Boucicaut Master*, figs. 81, 93.

192. Porphirius often attends Faustina outside, as in Andrea da Bologna's cycle of 1368 in S. Francesco, Assisi.

193. The removal of her breasts, ordered by the Emperor before her decapitation and represented by Andrea da Bologna, is omitted in the *Belles Heures*.

194. See, for example, Spinello Aretino's fresco at Antella, and Andrea da Bologna's in S. Francesco, Assisi.

195. See also the corresponding scenes by Spinello and Andrea da Bologna.

196. Perhaps for the illuminator the monastery was not distinct from the hermitage higher on the mountain.

197. *Boucicaut Master*, p. 7. *The Miracles of Madame Saint Katherine of Fierbois*, translated from the ed. of the Abbé J. J. Bourassé, Tours, 1858 by A. Lang, London, 1897, p. 14 f.

198. Labib, *Pèlerins*, 1961, p. 42, pl. IV. Charles V had a stone from the tomb of Catherine set in a ring (J. Ebersolt, *Orient et Occident*, Paris, 2nd ed. 1954, p. 102). Jean de Berry himself possessed a similar stone (Guiffrey, *Inventaires*, II, p. 114).

199. *Boucicaut Master*, p. 119 f.

200. See *ibid.*, fig. 92.

201. *Œuvres de Ghillebert de Lannoy*, 1878, p. 69. The author uses here the word "esglise," but the context indicates he intended the compound!

202. *Saint voyage de Jherusalem*, ed. Bonnardot and Longnon, 1878, p. 46.

203. Religieux de Saint-Denis, *Chronique*, II, 1840, p. 692 f. (Latin text and later French trans.).

204. The English text of the *Golden Legend* is taken throughout this book from the translation by G. Ryan and H. Ripperger, London, 1941.

205. For Spinello's fresco see Berenson, *Italian Pictures, Florentine School*, 1963, I, fig. 403; the badly damaged fresco in the Duomo of Siena has not, to my knowledge, been photographed or reproduced. The Giovanni di Paolo is RF 672 in the Louvre.

206. St. Luke's portrait of the Madonna was painted on panel and inserted into the fresco in the sacristy of the Duomo of Siena, a most unusual device intended perhaps, as in the instance of God the Father in the Arena Chapel, to give the image a special iconic character.

The subject is represented in two scenes, one above the other. Between the two appears the inscription: E IDIO LIBERA ROMA DE LA PISTOLENCIA PER LI MERITI E INTERCESSIONE DI SCO GREGORIO PAPA ED EL SUE CHERICI. . . . St. Michael stands on a rectangular tower that emerges from a circular drum. The lower scene, most of it lost, is not high enough to show the buildings of Rome that appear in the upper scene. There are only figures, of whom a bishop and some kneeling clerics are visible. As usual in Italian representations no figures fall stricken to the ground.

207. For the flagellants in Rome see *Le compagnie de' Battuti in Roma nell'anno MCCCLXXXXVIIII*, Bologna, 1862 (Scelta di curiosità letterarie inedite o rare). For Verona see n. 209.

208. Froissart, *Œuvres*, V, 1868, p. 275 f. Guillaume de Machaut, observing that the church opposed the flagellants, said they violated Nature herself (*Œuvres*, I, 1908, p. 145 f.)

209. Ogier d'Anglure, visiting Verona in 1396, described flagellants dressed in the same way (see *Saint voyage de Jherusalem*, ed. Bonnardot and Longnon, 1878, p. 99).

210. See *Gilles le Muisit, chronique et annales*, ed. H. Lemaître, Paris, 1906, p. 238 ff., esp. 249.

211. Froissart, *Œuvres*, V, 1868, p. 276: ". . . portoient

sus lors chief lons capiaus de feutre, casqune compagnie de une colour. . . ."

212. This derivation was observed by Porcher, *Belles Heures*, 1953, p. 41. The use and symbolism of the straw dragon in the Litany procession were described earlier by Sicardus of Cremona (died 1215): see Migne, *Pat. lat.*, vol. 213, col. 368. Such dragons were still carried in procession in France in the nineteenth century (M. Vloberg, *Les fêtes de France*, Grenoble [1936], p. 132 ff.).

213. Recently Longnon and Cazelles, *Très Riches Heures*, 1969, nos. 73–74, recognized Colombe only in the faces on fol. 72.

214. *Très Riches Heures*, 1904, p. 215 f.

215. See, for example, the miniatures in a *Giron le Courtois* in Paris, Bibl. nat., nouv. acq. fr. 5243. *Late XIV Century*, fig. 585.

216. See, for example, Salmi, *Miniatura* [1955], pl. LIX b.

217. For Bodleian, Douce 144 see *Boucicaut Master*, p. 106 f.

218. See discussion of *St. Jerome* in the *Bible moralisée*, Catalogue of Workshops, and Meiss, *Gaz. B.-A.*, 1963. Durrieu, *Très Riches Heures*, 1904, p. 216, attributed the drawings to one of the Limbourgs.

219. See Meiss, *Gaz. B.-A.*, 1963, p. 151, and for the document Gorissen, 1954, p. 216 n. 154.

220. See the life of Bruno in the *Acta Sanctorum*, Oct. 6, p. 703 f., which recounts the story of Diocrès. It was included in the Office for St. Bruno until the reform of the Breviary by Urban VIII.

221. There are only four representations of St. Bruno in the Index of Christian Art in Princeton.

222. A.-L. Millin, *Antiquités nationales ou receuil de monumens*, Paris, 1790–[1799], V, pp. 7–68, VI, pls. no. LII, 1–12; *History of the Great Chartreuse*, 1934, p. 170.

223. We happen to possess a record of a visit to the Chartreuse of Paris in 1398 by Jean de Berry in the company of Philippe le Hardi (L. Douët-d'Arcq, *Comtes*, 1865, p. 312).

224. The Order admitted many nobles and wealthy merchants, who left the world for it especially in times of trouble. The Duke of Berry added a codicil to his will in 1391 in favor of the Chartreuse of Vauvert, leaving them land, 20,000 francs and a reliquary. See Lehoux, *Berri*, II, 1966, p. 273.

225. See the anonymous article in *Bulletin de la Société Académique de Laon*, XXIV, 1882, p. 52 f.

226. See Porcher, *Belles Heures*, 1953, p. 42. The principal figure is repeated also in the *Rohan Hours*, fol. 167.

227. The title on fol. 95v is relevant to the miniature on 95, the title on 96 to the miniature on 95v.

228. Painting in the Louvre, Paris.

229. See Bruno also on fol. 96v (Meiss and Beatson, *Belles Heures*, 1974).

230. *History of the Great Chartreuse*, 1934, p. 199 ff.

231. Grenoble was in the Dauphiné, which had become part of the royal domain in 1349.

232. For a donation of Philippe le Hardi see Prost, *Inventaires des ducs de Bourgogne*, I, 1902, p. 453.

233. *History of the Great Chartreuse*, 1934, p. 228 f.

234. See n. 240 for references to frescoes in St. Antoine-le-viennois.

235. This is the first extensive cycle of the life of St. Jerome that we know, so that once again the illuminators of the *Belles Heures* probably had no pictorial models. The three scenes in two Carolingian Bibles (Venturi, *San Girolamo*, 1924, figs. 1, 2) and the four in a mid-fourteenth-century Passional (Vat. lat. 8541) are unrelated.

236. Porcher (*Belles Heures*, 1953, p. 47) offered the puzzling proposal that the painter followed a passage of the *Golden Legend* in which Jerome compares his hermitage to a prison.

237. According to the *Golden Legend* these subjects on fols. 186v, 187 should follow rather than precede Jerome's work in Bethlehem (fol. 187v).

238. Guiffrey, *Inventaires*, II, 1896, p. 128 no. 1001; I, 1894, p. 263 no. 990. The first *Vie des pères* was given to Abbot Hautschild of Eeckhout not long after 1402. The second manuscript was acquired in March, 1409 or 1410.

239. Jean de Berry possessed relics of the saint (Guiffrey, *op. cit.*, I, pp. 56, 63), and also a small golden representation of him (*ibid.*, pp. 46, 283). Another "ymage" was a present from Philippe le Hardi (*op. cit.*, II, pp. 13, 460).

240. Roques, *Peintures murales*, 1961, pp. 206 ff. The chapel of the Holy Arm, founded by Giangaleazzo Visconti, was frescoed in 1383, the chapel of St. Paul 1389–1405. A hanging with a cycle of scenes was copied in a manuscript of 1426 at Valletta (*A Picture Book of the Life of St. Anthony*, ed. R. Graham, 1937).

241. Haloes of this kind appeared first, perhaps, in Sienese painting: see the *Annunciation* by Simone Martini. An early, and unusual, French example is the halo of Christ when he appears before Caiaphas in the *Heures de Jeanne de Navarre*, fol. 110. See *Late XIV Century*, fig. 348.

242. For the antlered man, perhaps a confusion with the satyr mentioned by the *Golden Legend* (without horns), see also the fourteenth-century Bible, Vat. lat. 8541, p. 99.

243. The arcaded sarcophagus of St. Anthony is similar to that of Christ in the *Bible moralisée* (Fig. 301).

244. For all the medals see *Late XIV Century*, pp. 53–58. Although the Fourth Account of Robinet d'Estampes gives no date for the purchase of the Heraclius medal it was acquired in 1402 or 1403, because it appears at that date in the first account of Robinet d'Estampes, fols. 151–152 of his lost book (see Meiss with Off, 1971, p. 235, and Appendix A). The Duke had a copy in gold made of it. Presumably the original was given to Jean de Montaigu, and after his death in 1409 the Duke recovered it. At his death in 1416 the Duke ordered that the medal be returned to Montaigu's heirs (Guiffrey, II, p. 282 no. 1191).

245. *Ibid.*, p. 74.

246. *Ibid.*, p. 57 f., and R. Weiss, 1963. Weiss showed that the title of the emperor on the medal assumed a form not employed in the West but characteristic of the Byzantine chancery.

247. As I suggested in 1963, p. 52.

248. The Latin inscription around the perimeter refers to the defeat by Christ of symbols of evil: the basilisk, asp, lion, and dragon.

249. W. Treue, *Achse Rad und Wagen. Fünftausend Jahre Kultur- und Technikgeschichte*, Munich [1965], pp. 150–152, fig. p. 151.

250. In addition to the representation by Agnolo Gaddi see the copy of it by Cenni di Ser Francesco Cenni, 1410, S. Francesco, Volterra. Also Benedetto di Bindo, 1412, Opera del Duomo, Siena (Fig. 489), and Masolino, 1424, Collegiata, Empoli.

251. See the informative discussion of this point by C. Gilbert, *Change in Piero della Francesca*, New York, 1968, p. 80. For an earlier representation of this episode see the fresco in S. Francesco, Pistoia in the style of the follower of Maso who is probably identical with Bonaccorso di Cino, not Alesso (Meiss, "Alesso di Andrea," 1971, fig. 40, and "Notable Disturbances in the Classification of Tuscan Trecento Paintings," *Burl. Mag.*, CXIII, 1971, p. 182 ff.).

252. It has apparently not been observed that the Latin inscription on the recto of the medal is the verse used for the Introit of the Mass of both the Exaltation and Invention of the Cross: "Illumina vultum tuum Deus super tenebras nostras militabor in gentibus." Vespers of the Office of the Exaltation contains a hymn of triumph relevant to the scene on the medal.

253. Panofsky (*op. cit.*, p. 65) pointed to this connection when discussing *Gethsemane* in the *Très Riches Heures*.

254. Matt. 26, 40; Mark 14, 37. The contemporary pilgrim, Ogier, said that here the wood of the Cross had once bridged the brook, and indeed Paul put a cross on the bridge in his miniature of this subject in the Bible (Fig. 319).

255. Panofsky, *Netherlandish Painting*, 1953, pl. 176.

256. Except for the angels, who are replaced by standing figures, the composition was copied in the *Seilern Hours*.

257. Jean Porcher (*Belles Heures*, 1953, p. 35) proposed that three of the cycles: the Great Litany, Diocrès and Bruno, and Paul and Anthony were not planned at the beginning of the production of the manuscript. He believed, however, that they resemble the other cycles to such a degree that they were not produced much later.

258. For a reproduction of the *Decapitation of St. Lucy* see Meiss and Beatson, *Belles Heures*, 1974, fol. 179v. Whereas most of the composition derives from fol. 19v the raised sword of the executioner was drawn from 19.

259. Paris, Ecole des Beaux-Arts, Fond Le Soufaché 483, fol. 79. Panofsky (1949, p. 174 n. 17), unaware of the instance in fr. 823, cited the Antwerp panel as the earliest example. For the *Flight* in the Antwerp quadriptych see Panofsky, *Netherlandish Painting*, 1953, pl. 56.

260. Fol. 419: "Cy fenist la vie des sains nommee la legende doree le samedi apres la nativite notre dame lan mil quatre cens et quatre." The royal arms below the miniature are a later addition. For Porcher's view see the following note.

261. Porcher in Bourges, *Musées* [1951], p. 34 no. 11; *idem*, *Belles Heures*, 1953, pp. 8–10, 50; *idem*, Paris, Bibl. nat., 1955, p. 91 no. 187; *idem*, *Enluminure*, 1959, p. 61. Verdier, 1968, p. 103, also thought the miniature was probably an early work of Paul de Limbourg, and the model for the *Cour celeste* in the *Belles Heures*.

262. A *dependence* of the miniature upon the Limbourgs was proposed by the writer in *Burl. Mag.*, 1963, p. 51.

263. Pächt, *Gaz. B.-A.*, 1963, p. 118. Pächt, who first called attention to this kind of design, thought it probably originated in a lost work of the Limbourgs, with some elements derived from Malouel. Since Pächt dated the *Belles Heures* toward 1413 the miniature in

it seemed too late to be the original, and he did not adduce the Madonnas in fr. 414 (Fig. 388) and on fol. 209 of the *Belles Heures* (Fig. 398).

264. The Limbourgs met the problem of celestial figures not only by the use of concealing drapery but also by such devices as a disproportionately large book that serves as a sort of airship (see fol. 155).

265. *Boucicaut Master*, p. 21.

266. Meiss with Off, 1971, p. 228. See Appendix A.

267. *Late XIV Century*, p. 235. The connection of the miniature in the *Boucicaut Hours* with the composition of Aracoeli was suggested in *Boucicaut Master*, pp. 21, 146 n. 71.

268. *Late XIV Century*, p. 233 ff.

269. I thank Philippe Verdier for calling these interesting reliefs to my attention and for giving me photographs of them.

270. Meiss, *Painting in Florence and Siena*, p. 141 f.; *Late XIV Century*, p. 126.

271. For an account of the history of the image see *ibid.* To the examples in Trecento painting there given should be added one by Giovannino dei Grassi in the *Visconti Hours* (Meiss and Kirsch, *The Visconti Hours*, 1972, pl. BR150v). Like the other Madonnas in Italian representations of this period this one is half-length.

272. P. 85.

273. The fresco has been described by V. Lusini, *Il Duomo di Siena*, Siena, 1911, p. 291. Lusini also published the documents of payment to three painters for work in the three chapels of the sacristy (p. 344), but they do not seem to identify the author of the chapel at the left, the Cappella degli Arliqui. Berenson, *Central and North Italian Schools*, ed. L. Vertova, London, 1968, I, p. 38, lists the frescoes as the work of Benedetto di Bindo. Neither author understood the subject of the painting.

The Child carrying a cross represents a transposition —unprecedented as far as I know—into this subject of a motif common in Sienese painting from the third quarter of the fourteenth century (see Meiss, 1946, p. 6 f., figs. 2, 7, 9).

Another, somewhat earlier Sienese fresco of the Aracoeli in the Spedale, Siena, has, so far as I know, remained unpublished. Again the Madonna appears as a half-length figure within a round mandorla. The Child holds a scroll.

274. The composition of the *Cour celeste* was more carefully, but dryly, copied by a follower of the Limbourgs in a Book of Hours in the Spitz Collection, Chicago (Fig. 391). This miniature resembles fr. 414 more than the *Belles Heures* in certain details: St. Peter wears the pallium, Catherine's wheel has spikes, and Margaret is bare-headed. Perhaps the Spitz Master used a Limbourg drawing.

275. *Late XIV Century*, p. 337 f. In both miniatures a narrow red-brown band was added *inside* the gold frame on three sides, and *outside* the lower frame.

276. Durrieu, *op. cit.*, p. 108, erroneously described the text as a prayer to the angels. The clasps of the book on the ground on page 225 were drawn but not painted. The peeling of the brown paint from the gray hill has disclosed the drawing of vegetation and a small man.

277. See *Late XIV Century*, p. 235.

278. Meiss with Off, 1971, p. 229.

279. For Delisle's opinion see his *Cabinet*, III, 1881, p. 179 no. 101; *Gaz. B.-A.*, 1884, p. 403; also Longnon and Cazelles, *Très Riches Heures*, 1969, p. 26, quoting a letter of 1881.

280. Bouchot, 1905, p. 18 ff. Bouchot argued that the *Très Riches Heures* was painted by the same masters as fr. 166 and that manuscript was in his opinion the work of Jacques Coene and his associates.

281. Discrepancies of one or two details have led some recent historians to insist that the *Brussels Hours* is not the manuscript in an item in the Duke's inventory of 1402 with which most scholars, beginning with Delisle in 1868, identified it. See especially Delisle, *Gaz. B.-A.*, 1884; Durrieu, *Très Belles Heures de Notre-Dame*, 1922, p. 4 f. One of the numerous kinds of evidence, stylistic as well as documentary, that I educed in 1967 for the identification was the fact, already pointed out by Fierens-Gevaert, that the *Brussels Hours* was covered in old black satin when it appeared in 1840, and the third and last description in a Burgundian inventory (1424) of the manuscript I and others take to be the *Brussels Hours* referred to a black satin cover (*Late XIV Century*, p. 198 ff.). Calkins, 1970, rightly remarks that the notice of 1424 reads "couvertes d'une chemise de satin noir," and thus refers not to a cover (which curiously is not mentioned in this third Burgundian notice) but to a slip-cover or bag of the kind then employed. Calkins supposes that the removal of this one bit of evidence greatly weakens the case as a whole, but his procedure is not serious. He again misrepresents my views (as he does Panofsky's) in his discussion of the differences between the preliminary drawings for the miniatures and the paintings themselves. He stated (p. 8) that I interpret "these irregularities as evidence of the participation of

assistants. . . ." On page 211 of the *Late XIV Century*, when first referring to these changes, I said on the contrary that "Jacquemart made some small changes in his design as he passed from the drawing to the painting" in the miniature of the Duke before the Madonna, and, on a larger scale, in the *Annunciation*. On page 223 I wrote that "the changes in the course of work . . . are clear signs of the painter's constant searching study."

282. For a discussion of this problem see *Late XIV Century*, pp. 198–202, and the present text, p. 94.

283. The description of the *Brussels Hours*, of the manuscript itself apart from its cover, is brief because it was written before 1402, when the more complete form of notice of Robinet d'Estampes was developed. When Robinet referred to the *Très Belles Heures de Notre-Dame* in his Fourth Account the manuscript had already been given away and he presumably condensed the description in his earlier account (see Appendix A, and Meiss with Off, 1971, p. 229).

284. The miniatures for the Offices are $6\frac{1}{4}\times4\frac{1}{4}$ inches or larger, compared with $4\times3\frac{1}{4}$ inches in the *Belles Heures*. For the exact dimensions of all the miniatures by the Limbourgs see the table in the Catalogue of Manuscripts.

285. All the text, for example, of Matins and Lauds of the Hours of the Passion. Towards the end of this Office, between fols. 157 and 158, an entire gathering is missing. For a full description of the text and illumination of the *Très Riches Heures* see the Catalogue of Manuscripts.

286. See the essay by Prof. Neugebauer in the Catalogue of Manuscripts.

287. Most notes for illuminators were written in French. For example in a *Pèlerinage* (fr. 823, fol. 18v) the following note to an illuminator occurs: "Remiet ne faites rien cy car je y ferai une figure qui y doit estre."

All the prayers and the rubrics of the *Très Riches Heures* are in Latin.

288. In subsequent gatherings Colombe and his assistants either left blank the spaces provided by the scribe for titles or extended the psalm miniature upward to cover them.

289. Pächt, 1950, p. 45, pointed to the only Book of Hours that is similar in this respect, formerly in the Chester Beatty collection. Pächt thought the Beatty manuscript was earlier, but we think the opposite is much more likely (see Catalogue and Figs. 524, 525, 529). See also Catalogue of Workshops, Master of Walters 219.

290. On this figure see the fundamental article by Bober, 1948, and the comments by O. Neugebauer in his essay. We shall mention here, as Professor Neugebauer also does below, that the frontal figure does not represent "the feminine character," as claimed by Longnon and Cazelles, *Très Riches Heures*, 1969, no. 14. It lacks the long hair and well defined breasts of the women on this folio (Virgo and Gemini).

291. Saxl, *Lectures*, I, 1957, p. 67, and Van Wijk, *Nombre d'or*, 1936, p. 37.

292. *Late XIV Century*, p. 31.

293. The boat in the scene of St. John on Patmos in the Apocalypse appears in the miniatures of a group of Apocalypse manuscripts of which Bibl. nat. néerl. 3, fol. 2, perhaps Liège *ca.* 1400 (see above, p. 253, n. 10), is one example (Hontoy, 1946–47, pl. 28).

294. Laclotte, 1969, pp. 3–14. The *Fall of the Angels* has been transferred from panel to cloth, a treatment that was undergone also by the curious painting of St. Martin and the beggar that was painted on its opposite face. Professor Mojmír Frinta kindly informs me that the decorative punches in the border of the *Fall of the Angels* confirms a date in the second quarter of the fourteenth century. The evidence of the tooling on the opposite side of the panel is less clear.

Although the painting was discovered in Bourges it was said to have been acquired earlier in Italy.

295. The Duke's accounts for 1398–1399 include a payment "A Thomas du Sault jardinier de Monceaux qui avoit apporte de la violete a Monseigneur . . ." (Douët-d'Arcq, *Comtes*, 1865, p. 301).

296. Koch, 1964, p. 70 ff.; Behling, *Pflanze*, 1957, p. 52; Fritz, 1952, pp. 99–110.

297. Koch, *op. cit.*, p. 74 n. 31.

298. For the fly and evil see Friedman, *Symbolic Goldfinch* [1946], p. 26 f.

299. Deschamps, *Œuvres*, IX, 1878, p. 158.

300. *Master of the Breviary*, 1971.

301. Some of the calendar miniatures in the *Belles Heures* have gold backgrounds finely tooled in the manner of the Breviary Master (fols. 2, 4, 12). In this manuscript the Limbourgs also used haloes painted to simulate tooling (e.g., Figs. 398, 406, 474, 493). Jean again gave Christ such a halo here in his *Christ led to the Praetorium* (Fig. 583).

302. Mark, 16, 15. An important relic of the evangelist was in the church of Limours near Jean de Berry's chateau of Dourdan (H. Martin, *Les quatre évangelistes*, Paris, 1927, p. 57).

303. It seems possible that the right frame of the *An-*

nunciation originally coincided with the ruling or, in other words, the right edge of the script, and that during the course of execution the miniature was extended a few mm. at the right.

304. White, *Birth and Rebirth*, 1957, p. 230 f., observed that the oblique setting, used by Giotto and the Lorenzetti, was abandoned in the later Trecento, and he asked whether the reappearance of it in the painting of the Limbourgs should be understood as an independent development or the consequence of familiarity with early Trecento painting. The oblique setting, which is common already in fr. 166, is only one aspect of a pervasive relationship of the Limbourgs to early Trecento painting.

305. New York, The Cloisters, *Heures de Jeanne d'Evreux*, fol. 16. See *Late XIV Century*, fig. 335.

306. *Ibid.*, pp. 120, 165 f.; *Boucicaut Master*, p. 28.

307. See *Mandeville's Travels*, 1919, I, p. 75; Johannes of Hildesheim, *La légende des rois mages* (trans. M. Elissagaray, Paris [1965], p. 148).

308. See for this and what follows Meiss, 1945, pp. 175–181.

309. The image appears also in Dante, *Paradiso*, XXIX.

310. *Netherlandish Painting*, 1953, p. 174.

311. Ceste noble incarnacion nous fut figuree en la bible que aron estoit dessouls ung tabernacle et tenoit une verge blanche toute peslee laquelle florit et porta amandres blanches Cestoit signiffiance que une vierge floriroit et concevroit sans pechie et porteroit amandres ce fust le precieux corps ihesus crist (*Vie de nostre sauveur*, 1380, p. 10 f.).

312. See Ludolph of Saxony, *Vita Christi*, 1519, Bk. I, ch. 5; Lutz and Perdrizet, *Speculum*, I, 1907, p. 17.

313. Haloes of this kind were employed earlier by the Limbourgs in the *Bible moralisée*, in the *Belles Heures* (fol. 187v), and in the manuscript of Boccaccio's *Cleres Femmes* that Jean de Berry received in 1404 (Fr. 598—see Fig. 73).

314. When representing the Nativity (see above, p. 86) the Limbourgs began in the Bible with a cave (Fig. 327), an old Byzantine form revived by St. Bridget, then they "regressed" to the shed in the Hours of the Virgin in the *Belles Heures* (Fig. 333). In the illustration of the Nativity Mass in the *Belles Heures* the Adoration of the Child is combined with the shed and bed (Fig. 329). In the *Très Riches Heures* the bed is suppressed, and the Virgin's garment, which had been white in fr. 166 and the *Belles Heures* fol. 195, becomes blue.

315. See above, p. 86. An early instance of rays around the Child in Tuscan Nativities is the intarsia by Domenico di Niccolo in the Cappella del Popolo, Palazzo Pubblico, Siena. Domenico may previously have visited the court of Jean de Berry (*Late XIV Century*, p. 46 f.).

316. My strong doubt that the cherubim who hold the Child with their hands in the *Nativity* of the *Très Riches Heures* derived from the seraphim who enfold the Virgin with their wings in the *Assumption* by Taddeo di Bartolo in the Palazzo Pubblico Siena (1413–1414) was already expressed in 1963, p. 169 n. 48. For the contrary view see Durrieu, *Mémoires*, 1911, p. 365 ff. and Pächt, 1950, p. 41 n. 1.

317. *Late XIV Century*, figs. 185, 188.

318. *Vie de Nostre Seigneur*, p. 22.

319. Because of a rare lapse Panofsky said that a miniature for the Annunciation to the Shepherds did not appear in French Books of Hours until the end of the fourteenth century (*Netherlandish Painting*, 1953, p. 70).

320. Longnon and Cazelles, *Très Riches Heures*, 1969, fol. 48, have unconvincingly identified this figure as a woman.

321. *Très Riches Heures*, 1904, p. 201, pl. 35. L. Magne, however, is very skeptical of the identification, especially of the Tour Maubergeon (*Palais de Poitiers*, 1904, p. 14).

322. Breviary in Châteauroux. A very deep landscape appears also in a miniature by the Boucicaut workshop of the *Flight into Egypt* now in the Gallery in Birmingham (Fig. 532). This folio belonged to a Book of Hours dated 1408. Several miniatures in this manuscript are repainted, and the entire background of the *Flight* is reworked and untrustworthy. The Book of Hours, already dismembered, appeared as lot 58 in the Chester Beatty Sale, Sotheby, June 24, 1969. The miniatures show a combination of styles similar to the one in a Book of Hours dated one year earlier, Oxford, Bodleian Douce 144 (See *Boucicaut Master*, p. 106 ff., figs. 49–60).

323. See, for example, Pächt, *Mary of Burgundy*, 1948, p. 29, who says that most of the miniatures were left "without decorative framework" because the Duke of Berry died before the work on the manuscript was completed.

324. *Late XIV Century*, p. 52 ff.

325. "Et exinde venit in conswetudinem in partibus illis quod nullus vacuis manibus et absque terre osculacione ante pedes. Soldani vel alicuius regis in Oriente ipsis loqui possit; vnde fratres mendicantes ibidem offerunt eis poma vel pira, allegantes quod eis aurum vel

argentum non licet possidere; que ab eis cum magna reuerencia suscipiuntur." (Johannes of Hildesheim, *Historia trium regum*, chap. 20, ed. 1886, p. 236.)

326. See note 377.

327. In our opinion *Zodiacal Man* was probably part of the original plan. Otherwise it would be difficult to explain why the text of December was written on the first folio of gathering 3 instead of on a folio in a second gathering that would have consisted of 6 rather than the existing 4 folios. Throughout the calendar both miniatures on a bifolio were executed by the same *frère* and since Paul and Jean collaborated on *Zodiacal Man* the decision to place it on an independent folio was probably dictated by the need to exchange it freely without interrupting work on a conjoint miniature. There was also more to be done by the scribes than on any calendar illustration. To have cut away the conjoint leaf would have left a visible and unsightly stub at the center of the gathering. Possibly the intention was to insert folio 13 (December calendar) with a stub, leaving only one blank leaf (instead of the present two) between *Zodiacal Man* and the Gospel readings.

328. Durrieu is silent on these questions. Longnon and Cazelles, *Très Riches Heures*, 1969, p. 24, say that the reason the artists *or the Duke* added them remains unexplained. Sterling in Białostocki *et al.*, *Spätmittelalter*, 1972, p. 181, reflects current opinion when he says that the miniature of *Paradise* (the only miniature of this kind with which he was concerned) was not intended for the *Très Riches Heures*.

329. *Late XIV Century*, p. 269.

330. For Delaissé's view that this practice began later in Holland see Chapter *Belles Heures*, n. 144.

331. This point is crucial. Durrieu, *Très Riches Heures*, 1904, p. 122, simply said that a full-page miniature of the Adoration, as well as of the Meeting and the Presentation in the Temple, were found by Colombe and set into the book because the Limbourgs had not painted miniatures of these subjects before the death of the Duke.

332. In his analysis of the manuscript Durrieu paid insufficient attention to the rubrics, so that he described the *Adoration* and the *Meeting of the Magi* as occurring *between* Terce and Sext (*Très Riches Heures*, 1904, p. 122). The rubric, however, puts them *in* Sext.

333. Folio 57. Although Durrieu (*op. cit.*, pp. 205–207) proposed the *Meeting* was designed to face the *Adoration* he said that they were inserted *by Colombe* at Sext in the Hours of the Virgin.

334. Kehrer, *Heiligen drei Könige*, I, 1908, p. 63; Panofsky, *Netherlandish Painting*, 1953, pp. 64, 83 n. 1. For the Latin text and the Early English translation see C. Horstmann, *The Three Kings of Cologne*, London, 1886 (Early English Text Society, vol. 85). The *Meeting* was represented behind the *Adoration* in the small diptych in the Bargello.

335. Although the King of France would not normally have a black banner-bearer. This difficulty is not mentioned by Marinesco, *Soc. des Ant.*, 1958, p. 38 f., who proposed the identification. The corresponding king in the *Adoration of the Magi* does not have a black banner-bearer.

336. *Late XIV Century*, p. 57 f. Marinesco, *Acad. des Inscr. 1957*, 1958, p. 23 ff., identified this Magus with Heraclius because his companion was copied from the medal of Constantine. R. Weiss, 1963, preferred Manuel II. Panofsky, *Netherlandish Painting*, 1953, p. 64, proposed that this figure was taken from the Duke's medal of Augustus or Tiberius, but the obverse of these showed only a "visaige" (Meiss, *Late XIV Century*, p. 54 f.).

337. In addition to the portraits reproduced herewith see *Late XIV Century*, figs. 487 (1409), 499 (*ca.* 1410), 500, 503.

A chronicler described the hat of Manuel II as a "pileus imperiale" (*Religieux de Saint-Denis*, II, p. 756).

338. See the discussion above of Aracoeli, p. 139 ff.

339. According to the *Vie de Nostre Seigneur* (p. 29 f.) the junction of the three roads was marked by an "oratoyre selon leur loy comme nous faysons auiourduy les croix es parties des chemins." Mandeville (*Travels*, p. 62) describes the point from which the pilgrims had their first view of the city as Montjoie "for it geveth ioye to pilgrims hertes because that men seen first Jerusalem." The three kings arrived separately in a fog and it was only when they met at the shrine that the mist cleared and they were able to see the city (*Historium trium regum*, p. 231). The erection of a Montjoie on the spot where a place of pilgrimage first came into sight may have originated from the custom of each pilgrim adding a stone to a heap (see Du Cange, *Glossarium*, *s.v. Mons gaudii*). For a Limbourg miniature in the *Bible moralisée* (fr. 166) showing pilgrims to Jerusalem kneeling beside a heap of stones and a stepped cross see fig. 307. See also note 334, and M. Roblin, "L'origine du mot montjoie," *Bulletin de la Société nationale des antiquaires de France*, 1945–47, p. 45 ff.

340. See note 339. Also Durrieu, *Très Riches Heures*,

1904, p. 205; Evans, 1949, p. 96 ff.; Oursel, *Les pèlerins*, 1963, pp. 60 ff., 94; Branner, "The Montjoies of Saint Louis," 1967, pp. 13–16. Similar monuments are represented at crossroads in *March* and *September* (Figs. 541, 547).

341. *Late XIV Century*, p. 32. Queen Isabeau de Bavière possessed a "guépard." Among the officers of Jean de Berry in 1401–1402 was "Henry Bar, garde du dromedaire." Bibl. nat., ms. Clairambault 834, p. 1427.

342. New York, Metropolitan Museum, The Cloisters, *Hours of Jeanne d'Evreux*, 1957, nos. 14, 15.

343. For example, the two pages behind the Queen of Sheba when she kneels at the bridge, S. Francesco, Arezzo.

344. A fifteenth-century *Notitia dignitatum* (Paris, Bibl. nat., lat. 9961), derived from a Roman fourth-century manuscript transmitted through a now lost ninth-century copy, shows Roma crowned with rather similar blades (Fig. 778).

345. As we have noted above (n. 43) the drawing now in the Louvre did not reach France until *ca.* 1800, so that it does not seem probable that it was the specific model for the Limbourgs, as Keller, *Italien*, 1967, p. 101 f., proposed. His argument about the steps overlooks the fact that in the fresco they were, until the cleaning in 1961, repainted in incorrect perspective (the repainted section has been removed in Fig. 668). The damaged drawing, furthermore, can be proved to have been made not by the Rinuccini Master but by Taddeo or his workshop (see Tintori and Meiss, *The Painting*, 1962, pp. 21–25, figs. 7, 8, 74).

346. Curiously, in the presentation of *Mary* in the Temple described by Philippe de Mézières in his play performed in Avignon in 1382 Mary carries a candle and two doves. See Young, *Drama*, II, 1962, p. 233. The usual fifteen steps, present in Taddeo's representation, are reduced to fourteen in the *Très Riches Heures*.

347. Support for this hypothesis may be derived from the fact that near the end of the manuscript the Breviary Master illuminated only the bifolios designed to bear a miniature; he did not succeed in carrying his work beyond this stage. Fol. 198, a single leaf by this illuminator, may well have been the conjoint leaf of the *Purification*. The gathering immediately after this large miniature beginning with fol. 203 starts with the proper rubric and the text of the Mass of the Purification, leaving no room for a small miniature such as appears at the beginning of other Masses. The large miniature of the Purification, unlike the other miniatures inserted in the Hours of the Virgin, is ruled in red for the first plan.

348. In the *Boucicaut Master*, p. 64, I cited a Lorenzettian fresco of 1368 at Paganico as a source for the angels holding the mantle of the Virgin. In an Austrian altarpiece of about the same date at Wilten a flying angel holds the Virgin's train (Oberhammer, *Altar vom Schloss Tirol*, 1948, pl. 33). The most likely source for the Limbourgs was the beautiful relief of the *Coronation* at La Ferté-Milon, in which the similarly long train of the Virgin is held by angels (see *Boucicaut Master*, fig. 470, where the date *ca.* 1410 should be corrected to before 1407. No work would have been carried forward at this chateau of Louis d'Orléans after his assassination in that year).

349. See, for example, a Madonna by a follower of the Cioni in the Accademia in Florence. Meiss, 1936, fig. 13.

350. Hulin de Loo, 1903, p. 189 f.; Durrieu, *Très Riches Heures*, 1904, pp. 58–60.

351. See *Boucicaut Master*, figs. 53, 54, 262–268.

352. *Late XIV Century*, p. 37 f.

353. *Ibid.*, figs. 430, 435. The river may represent the Yèvre, which was alive with boats in the early fifteenth century. The enormous multi-oared craft is a repetition of the one in the miniature of St. Jerome leaving Constantinople in the *Belles Heures* (Meiss and Beatson, *Belles Heures*, fol. 185).

354. Matthew 4, 1–11; Mark 1, 12–13; Luke 4, 1–13.

355. Verdier, *L'Oeil*, 1968, p. 15, is inclined in fact to conclude that the miniature represents primarily this second temptation. However, the Gospel for the day describes all three temptations.

356. See also Duccio's *Temptation* from the *Maestà*, now in the Frick Collection, New York.

357. Meiss, 1946, p. 11 f., fig. 19.

358. Lehoux, *Berri*, 1967, III, p. 372; Monstrelet (ed. Douët-d'Arcq), III, 1859, p. 53. Jean de Berry did not, however, remove many, at least, of his possessions, as the post-mortem inventory proves. In 1419 the Dauphin, who was also Duke of Berry and the future Charles VII, took up residence there.

359. In the *Speculum humanae salvationis*, cap. XIII, l. 89 f., the lion and the bear were associated with the third temptation, because it is prefigured by David killing these two animals. See Lutz and Perdrizet, *Speculum*, I, 1907, p. 29.

360. Luke 11, 14; see also Matthew 9, 32–34. Neither Gospel specifies the location.

361. They may be found in a few other combined Books of Hours and Missals, such as lat. 757, Lombard, *ca.* 1380 (Leroquais, *Livres d'Heures*, 1927, I, p. 5).

With regard to the *Feeding*, John 6, 5–10, refers to the grass upon which the throng sits.

362. Guiffrey, *Inventaires*, II, 1896, p. 17.

363. Many of the arabesques and diapers in the backgrounds of the *Très Riches Heures* resemble those in the *Belles Heures*.

364. One man removes the lid in a scene in the thirteenth-century glass of Bourges Cathedral (A. Martin and C. Cahier, *Monographie de la Cathédrale de Bourges*, I, *Vitraux du XIII*[e] *siècle*, Paris, 1841–44, pl. XI). See E. Mâle, "La résurrection de Lazare," *Revue des arts*, 1951, pp. 45–52.

365. In the *Entry* by Pietro Lorenzetti and his *équipe* at Assisi the two stone idols on the gate appear in front of a gilt panel.

366. See Jacquemart's *Christ Carrying the Cross* in the *Brussels Hours* (*Late XIV Century*, fig. 194).

367. "Et quand lanesse fut venue avecques son poulai(n) les disciples despoullerent leurs robes et e(n) courire(n)t premiereme(n)t le poulai(n) Et quant n(ot)re seigneur fust dessus il commenca a ruer et a giguer Lors nostre seigneur descendit hastiveme(n)t car il navoit mie acoustume de chevaucher poulains Et apres il monta sus lanesse Ceste anesse signifioit le viel testament et le poulai(n) signifioit le nouveau et cestoit aussi signifia(n)ce que ai(n)si co(mm)e lasne et le poulai(n) avoit sostenu ihesus crist quil soustiendroyt et porteroyt la peine des pechiez du viel testame(n)t et du nouveau le seigneur de tout le monde en un nouveau estat se(n) alloit en iherusale(m) chevauchant une anesse couverte de povres robes et avoit bride de cordes aussi avoit este prophetise pour abaisier lorgueil des seigneurs mondai(n)s qui chevauchent a gros chevaux pares de beaux arnois Mais le roy des roys chevauche asne a bride de corde dont gra(n)t peuple le suyvoyent sur les arbres et lui gectans les fleurs et les rameaux de la verdure sus les chemins." (*Vie de nostre sauveur*, 1380, p. 130 f.) Palm Sunday was known in France as *Pâques fleuries*.

368. Only the Gospel of Matthew mentions the foal. It is represented in a window of Bourges Cathedral (Martin and Cahier, *op. cit.*, pl. 5) and in paintings by, for example, Guido da Siena in the Pinacoteca, Siena, and Duccio in the *Maestà*.

369. See the pilgrimage of Jacopo da Verona in 1335: "Ante illam portam ad duos jactus lapidis, est locus, ubi Cristus invenit ficulneam viridem et maledixit ei et statim arefacta est." ("Liber peregrinationis Frater Jacobus de Verona," *Revue de l'orient latin*, III, 1895, p. 203.)

370. St. Michael wears his tunic of mail over a blue alb or dalmatic, so that he is both the militant conqueror of *Revelation*, XII, 7–8 and the liturgically clothed "archangel standing at the right hand of the altar of incense" of the Mass. The angels in the roundels wear copes over white albs as if they were sub-ministers.

371. Hulin de Loo, 1903.

372. His example, *September*, was not well chosen. From the fact that the lower part was left unfinished one would prefer to infer that one master was working from the top down.

373. *Netherlandish Painting*, 1953, p. 64 f.

374. *Ibid.*, fig. 94; *Late XIV Century*, p. 76, fig. 506. Sterling and Adhémar (in Louvre, *Peintures*, 1965, p. 4) are inclined to date the original in 1404, because Jean sans Peur, who became Duke in that year, holds the ring of investiture. In a miniature of *ca.* 1412, which may reflect this or a similar portrait, he seems to hold the ring also (Meiss, *Boucicaut Master*, 1968, p. 39).

375. *Très Riches Heures*, 1904, p. 118 ff.

376. The positions these miniatures were intended to occupy should be considered together with the problem of the missing text for Matins, Lauds, Vespers (apart from the first page), and Compline (see Catalogue, gatherings 22–24). Because of the change of plan eliminating the four lines beneath both miniatures for each Hour the entire Office would have had to be largely, if not entirely, rewritten and decorated. Miniatures on rectos for Prime, Terce, None, and Vespers (both miniatures for Sext are missing) all bear second-plan text on the versos with initials and decoration by the Dry Master. Since Matins and Lauds are almost as long as all the other Hours combined (see Catalogue, Hours of the Passion), the painters could have gone ahead quicker if the rewriting started at Prime, leaving Matins and Lauds to the last. While waiting they could immediately have painted folios that required no text: the *Plan of Rome* and two miniatures on single leaves to be inserted with stubs as versos for Matins and Lauds. If this was the plan it would confirm the present position of *Ego sum* as a verso for Matins, but *Christ led to the Praetorium* would have been meant not as a facing recto but as a verso

for Lauds with the blank recto facing the end of the previous Hour. There was evidently not time to complete the rewriting of the new text.

377. Durrieu lists 8 miniatures as "peintures hors texte"; *Zodiacal Man* (fol. 14v), *Fall of Man* (fol. 25v), *Meeting of the Magi* (fol. 51v), *Adoration of the Magi* (fol. 52), *Purification of the Virgin* (fol. 54v), *Fall of the Rebel Angels* (fol. 64v), *Hell* (fol. 108), *Plan of Rome* (fol. 141v). See *Très Riches Heures*, 1904, I, pp. 28 ff., 116 f.

378. Whereas the proof of the existence of this panel now in the Louvre (and others originally in the series) at Dijon at this time does not seem to us entirely convincing, French painters were apparently familiar with it. For remarks on this question, and for the relation of Jacquemart to Simone's *Way to Calvary* see *Late XIV Century*, pp. 215 f., 272 f.

379. John 18, 4–6.

380. The stars are small bits of gold laid on the blue sky.

381. *Late XIV Century*, p. 27 ff., figs. 408–412. The manuscript is there ascribed to Naples and dated in the third quarter of the fourteenth century. In his comprehensive study of Neapolitan painting Bologna, *Pittori di Napoli*, 1969, p. 314 ff., dates the manuscript *ca.* 1350–1355, and proposes, rightly we believe, that the principal artist of the large miniatures painted frescoes of the legend of the Magdalen in the Cappella Pipino, S. Pietro a Majella. The best illuminator of the text of the *Bible moralisée* itself, whom I had earlier identified with the illuminator of a Neapolitan Missal (Avignon, Musée Calvet ms. 138), has been shown by Bologna to be the author also of a cycle of frescoes in the Cappella Leonessa of the same church.

382. Conway, 1916, p. 45.

383. *Très Riches Heures*, 1904, p. 30. The relationship of Jean de Berry and of France to the papacy during the final years of the Great Schism was complex. The claimant supported by France, John XXIII, entered Rome in 1411, and French representatives, including Jean de Montreuil, attended the Council of Rome in 1412–1413 (Valois, *France et le Schisme*, IV, 1902, pp. 138, 205 ff., and passim).

384. On the verso of this miniature the text of Matins would presumably have begun. The miniatures in the Spitz and Seilern Books of Hours, however, by close followers of the Limbourgs both contain a representation of the Betrayal that was based on the *Belles Heures*. They give no indication that such a scene existed in the *Très Riches Heures*.

385. P. Ugoni, *Historia delle stationi di Roma che si celebrano la Quadragesima*, Rome, 1588.

386. Apocalypse 12, 7–9. It must be noted that there is no rubric for the Penitential Psalms on fol. 63v (where one would expect it) even though there is ample room for it. Possibly a full-page miniature of David in prayer was planned for 64v (with a rubric on 64) but never executed. See for the subject in general K.-A. Wirth, s.v. Engelsturz, in *Reallexikon zur deutschen Kunstgeschichte*, Stuttgart, V, 1967.

387. The only other possible explanation of the arrangement would seem to be that the text of the Psalms was *rewritten* so as to include on fol. 65 the first four lines which would have appeared below the miniature originally planned for 64v.

Near the left edge of the folio are holes and marks indicating that the miniature of the Fall was at one time stitched into the book in the opposite way. The left margin, however, is the larger and the proper width for an *outer* margin, but it is true that the present inner margin could have been significantly wider because the folio is inserted with its own stub.

388. For this manuscript, Brussels 9024–25, see Durrieu, *Le Manuscrit*, II, 1895, pp. 81–87; Gaspar and Lyna, II, 1947, pp. 1–6 no. 199, pls. CXIV–CXV; Brussels, Bibl. royale, 1967, p. 12 no. 5, pl. 24.

389. Metamorphosis of the angels is occasionally represented from the High Middle Ages on (see, for example, Herrade de Landesberg, *Hortus deliciarum*, ed. A. Straub and G. Keller, Strasbourg, 1901, pl. 2).

390. For this *Livre des bonnes moeurs* see *Late XIV Century*, pp. 314, 359.

391. The sparks, flames, and smoke are painted over the other colors, especially the blue of the angels' tunics.

392. The scene includes angels and devils or beasts in two manuscripts of the Apocalypse of *ca.* 1414–1415, Morgan Library M. 133, fol. 37v, by the Master of the Berry Apocalypse, and Chantilly ms. 28, fol. 72v, by the Medallion Master. See the Catalogue of Manuscripts and the chapter Expressionism.

393. *Cité de Dieu*, Baltimore, Walters Art Gallery, ms. 770, fol. 16v. See *Boucicaut Master*, 1968, fig. 334. The two lowest angels have bats' wings.

394. The painting by Meister Bertram belongs to a cycle of Creation scenes.

395. One famous opening into Hell was on an Irish island venerated as St. Patrick's Purgatory. The saint was believed to have closed it with a stone. See *Œuvres de Ghillebert de Lannoy*, 1878, p. 171.

396. The three tiers of thrones appear again in a contemporary miniature of the Fall, which illustrates the Biblical section of the text in Chantilly ms. 28, by the

Medallion Master. See above, note 392. Other miniatures in this manuscript reflect one specific motif in the *Belles Heures* (see p. 255), and it might thus be related to the *Très Riches Heures* also.

397. Could it perhaps have been intended to fall between fols. 113–114, at the beginning of the Monday Office of the Dead?

398. See *Late XIV Century*, p. 241.

399. *Très Riches Heures*, 1969, no. 91. The accompanying color plate is one of the very few in the volume that alters the general effect of the miniature. The gray rocks should be much darker.

400. The text was translated into French and other languages. For the description of Satan in a fifteenth-century version in Languedoc see *Voyage au Purgatoire*, ed. Jeanroy and Vignaux, 1903, p. 93 f. For early Italian: ed. F. Corazzini, in *Curiosità letterarie*, CXXVIII, 1872, p. 72 f. See Mâle, *Fin du moyen âge*, 1908, pp. 508–510.

401. *Voyage au Purgatoire*, cit., p. 37 f.

402. Small hand-bellows appear in earlier representations of Hell, in the *Bible moralisée*, fol. 2v no. 5 (Fig. 283) and in the one by the Brussels Initials Master cited above. See *Late XIV Century*, fig. 790.

403. The sky shows the usual extraordinary subtlety of the brushwork of the Limbourgs. The strokes of blue are vertical, those of the gray clouds horizontal.

404. See, for example, the *Three Tower Reliquary* of *ca.* 1375 in the Treasury of Aachen (Lasko, 1962, p. 260, and E. Grimme, *Aachener Goldschmiedekunst im Mittelalter von Karl den Grossen bis zu Karl V*, Cologne [1957], p. 80 ff., pls. 40, 44).

405. Cambridge, Fitzwilliam Museum, ms. 251, fol. 16; see *Boucicaut Master*, fig. 457.

406. New York, Coll. Kettaneh, *Cas des nobles hommes et femmes* (*ibid.*, fig. 379).

407. Eve has gilt in her hair before the Fall likewise in the *Cas des nobles hommes et femmes*, Arsenal 5193, fol. 8v, painted by the Cité des Dames workshop shortly before the miniature in the *Très Riches Heures* (*Boucicaut Master*, 1968, fig. 381).

408. See the diagrams in the Catalogue.

409. *Très Riches Heures*, 1969, folio 11v.

410. These miniatures are the only ones that represent specific persons. (The astronomical content, however, would not, as Professor Neugebauer shows, be related to specific events.) Other indications of the peculiarities of these folios are the Latin headings on their rectos (see the table in the Catalogue), which support the conclusion that these sheets were prepared for one painter.

411. See the complete table in the Catalogue. In all the miniatures of the first gathering except *January* the vertical lines coincide with the vertical frames. *January*, which is uniquely large in both dimensions, overlaps the ruled lines. The outer vertical line in all three miniatures in the second gathering falls within the miniature and more or less at the springing of the outer gold frame defining the starry arch of the sky.

412. It is true, however, that a scribe would have needed to complete the calendaric data above four miniatures and to write the feasts in gold on some folios of the text (see the Catalogue). Folio 26v, furthermore, constitutes a partial exception, because the miniature, a small Psalm illustration, was completed and even the title was written but the initial and border were painted only in part (Fig. 560). The other half of this exceptional sheet, fol. 33, likewise was left incomplete by the Breviary Master, but there is no miniature on either face. Numerous folios on the other hand, show borders completed in the time of Jean de Berry but the miniatures not: 59v, 61, 61v, 62, 62v, 63, 65, 65v, 66v, 67v, 71v, 72, 86v, 147v, 150, 153v, 157v, 158, 189v.

The only logical reason for postponing the decorative work would be the wish of the miniaturist to defer until the moment of execution his decision about the size and shape of his painting. We have seen, however, that except for the somewhat larger dimensions of *January* all the other calendar miniatures conform with the ruling and one norm.

413. Pächt, *Master of Mary of Burgundy* [1948], p. 29.

414. See, for example, the Lombard Missal of the third quarter of the fourteenth century, Vat. pal. lat. 506, fols. 114b and c (Gengaro and Cogliati Arano, *Miniature lombarde*, 1970, figs. 117, 118).

415. The upper tips of some forms of Colombe have been cut (fols. 75, 109v, 184, 201).

416. See *Late XIV Century*, p. 340 f. Marcel Thomas, *Grandes Heures*, 1971, pl. 110, suggests that one of the difficulties of connecting this miniature with the Passion cycle in the *Grandes Heures* could be met by identifying the two girls in the foreground not as donors but as children of the "Daughters of Israel" whom Christ at this moment, according to Luke (23, 28), addressed. We still must account, however, for the perfect profile of both figures, and for the diadem worn by one as well as for the two dogs, emblematically confronted.

417. For the relationship of miniature, border, and script see *Late XIV Century*, p. 203 f., fig. 659.

418. See, for example Delaissé, *Miniature flamande*, 1959, pls. 18, 38–40, 47–49.

419. See, for instance, Brit. Mus. Add. 16997 (*Boucicaut Master*, figs. 134, 283–295).

420. On 152v the workshop of Colombe copied the border of fol. 182.

421. They were first introduced by the Brussels Initials Master (*Late XIV Century*, p. 246), and then appeared in Bodl. Douce 144, dated 1407 (*Boucicaut Master*, p. 107), in part by the Boucicaut workshop, and on a large scale in a manuscript of about 1415 by the Boucicaut Master and his workshop, Mazarine 469 (*ibid.*, p. 113 f.).

422. This flower has often been confused with the flower that appears on fol. 17 on the *Très Riches Heures*, that is, columbine (Pächt, *Master of Mary of Burgundy* [1948], p. 30; Longnon and Cazelles, *Très Riches Heures*, 1969, no. 124).

423. Meiss, *Master of the Breviary*, 1971, p. 14 f. Charles V possessed a *joyau* (a *nef*) "ou sont plusieurs lymassons yssans de grosses perles et audessus est Nostre Seigneur en yssant du sepulchre . . ." (Labarte, *Inventaire*, 1879, no. 2290). I owe this reference to Mme. Marie-Madeleine Gauthier.

424. *Ibid.*, pl. XIIIb.

425. Emblematic significance here would not be precluded by the fact that the snail reappeared in the borders of manuscripts painted by followers of the Limbourgs, but not for Jean de Berry. See the *Nativity*, *Agony in the Garden*, and *Pilate Washing his Hands* in the *Seilern Hours* (Figs. 627, 631), and the *Agony in the Garden* in the Spitz Hours (see below, pp. 237–239, n. 688). Among the creatures of the wilderness around the Baptist, the Duke's saint, in the *Petites Heures* (*Late XIV Century*, fig. 167) three snails are close by and prominent.

426. Meiss, *Master of the Breviary*, 1971, p. 15.

427. Deschamps, *Œuvres*, v, 1887, p. 115 f.

428. Trans. in *Penguin Book of French Verse*, ed. B. Woledge, I, Harmondsworth, 1961, pp. 238–240.

429. Pp. 152, 165.

430. *Late XIV Century*, fig. 344.

431. *Ibid.*, fig. 178.

432. 1950, p. 30 f.

433. Bibl. palatina, pal. 56.

Such floreate borders (not to mention the *Très Riches Heures*) antedate by many years the borders of this type in Dutch manuscripts, where Delaissé repeatedly has stated the type began (*Dutch Illumination*, 1968, p. 82). The manuscripts he cited are from the twenties!

434. Meiss and Kirsch, *Visconti Hours*, 1972, pl. BR 128 (workshop of Giovannino).

435. Gengaro and Cogliati Arano, *Miniature lombarde*, 1970, fig. 362.

436. Pächt, *Master of Mary of Burgundy* [1948], pp. 29 f., 52 n. 19.

437. See Plummer, *Catherine of Cleves* [n.d.], nos. 119, 129.

438. See above, pp. 67, 72.

439. A Book of Hours formerly in the Chester Beatty collection that Pächt, 1950, p. 45, considered a model for the *Très Riches Heures* can be shown, we believe, to be later in date and probably influenced by it. See Master of Walters 219, Catalogue of Workshops, and chapter on the Breviary Master.

440. See the Catalogue.

441. There is a four-wheeled wagon in a miniature on fol. 14 of fr. 166 (Fig. 306) that somewhat resembles the wagon of the sun (see H. Bouchot, 1905), but it has round staves and is otherwise dissimilar.

442. Saxl and Meier, *Verzeichnis*, III, 1953, fig. 8.

443. As observed by Schlosser, 1897, p. 78, and Durrieu, *Très Riches Heures*, 1904, p. 39.

444. Toesca, *Lombardia*, 1912, p. 419 n. 1 and fig. 271; Pächt, 1950, p. 42.

445. For observations on the relationship of French and Italian cycles at this period see *Late XIV Century*, p. 231 f., and the bibliography there cited.

446. Panofsky, *Netherlandish Painting*, 1953, p. 66, however, tends to view this combination as an innovation of the early fifteenth century.

447. Meiss with Off, 1971, p. 233. See Appendix A.

448. Panofsky, *op. cit.*, pp. 372 f. n. 3, 373 n. 1, 2.

449. Avril, *Rev. de l'art*, 1970, p. 48 n. 51 attributes the *Psalter of Bonne de Luxembourg* to the Passion Master. I had earlier pointed to the close relationship to his style (*Late XIV Century*, p. 20).

450. *Netherlandish Painting*, 1953, p. 33 f.

451. See *Late XIV Century*, fig. 83 and Thomas, *Grandes Heures*, 1971, pl. 3.

452. *Late XIV Century*, pp. 172, 214, figs. 184, 185.

453. Rasmo, *Frescoes at Torre Aquila*, 1962; *idem*, 1957. See also Kurth, 1911; Pächt, 1950, p. 38 f.; Keller, *Italien*, 1967, p. 150.

454. *Late XIV Century*, pp. 219–221, figs. 197, 264, 537. See also Meiss, *Gaz. B.-A.*, 1961.

455. Smoke issues from the chimney in *February* already

in a miniature of the early fifteenth century by the Troyes Master in lat. 924, fol. 2. See Leroquais, *Livres d'heures*, 1927, pl. XX. See also Warner, *Queen Mary's Psalter*, 1912, pl. 125.

456. Book 26, chapter 18. For this manuscript see the Catalogue of Workshops.

457. Though Boccaccio does speak of Régnier's movement around the court.

458. See the Catalogue of Manuscripts. Also Meiss, "Decameron," in *Essays for Wittkower*, 1967, p. 56.

459. 1903, p. 189.

460. *French Verse*, ed. Woledge, 1961, p. 244. For the two final stanzas, see *ibid.*, p. 245.

461. On the difficulty of identifying this vessel with the "salière du pavillon" described in the ducal inventories see *Late XIV Century*, p. 51.

462. See *ibid.*, p. 72 f.

463. As Panofsky, *Netherlandish Painting*, 1953, p. 65, and Hulin de Loo, p. 182, thought.

464. See the chapter Jean de Berry and the Antique.

465. *Très Riches Heures*, 1904, p. 131.

466. This possibility was suggested by Jacques Thuillier, whom I wish to thank for mentioning it to me.

467. Meiss and Kirsch, *Visconti Hours*, 1972, pl. BR 115.

468. It is composed of bold strokes of deep blue against lighter blue, but the technique here adds no depth or transparency.

469. For the identification of the buildings see below, p. 203 f.

470. For a somewhat related group of noble riders see the *Cleres femmes* given to Jean de Berry in 1404, fr. 598, fol. 46.

471. Douët d'Arcq, *Choix*, I, 1863, p. 163 ff., referring to gifts of May 1, 1400; Durrieu, *Très Riches Heures*, 1904, p. 140; M. Vloberg, *Les fêtes de France*, Grenoble, 1936, pp. 105, 111; Laborde, *Ducs de Bourgogne*, III, 1852, p. 470 f.

472. Morand, 1954, pp. 54–61; Lehoux, *Berri*, 1966, II, p. 433 n. 1.

473. Morand, *loc. cit.* Morand incorrectly states the marriage took place in late May. The most probable date, June 24, is given by the Religieux de Saint-Denys, *Chronique*, II, 1840, p. 758 (quoted by Lehoux, *op. cit.*, II, p. 435).

474. See Montfaucon, *Monumens*, III, 1731, pp. 49 f., 67, pls. XI, XVI. The letters on the harness of the gray horse, no doubt meaningful also, have not been identified. Though in the drawing by Gaignières of Louis II de Bourbon the other courtiers wear similar ornaments, they all have more than seven studs (Fig. 779).

475. The Dauphin Louis duc de Guyenne was heir presumptive to the Duchy of Berry—the Duke gave him the Chateau of Mehun in 1414—but in 1400 he was only three years old.

476. The rider of the white horse is described by Longnon & Cazelles (*Très Riches Heures*, 1969, no. 9) as a man. However, the white hood and side-saddle identify her as a woman.

477. Reaping is normally represented for July; it appears in the *Belles Heures*. Shearing however is rare.

478. *Late XIV Century*, p. 218, fig. 385; *Boucicaut Master*, p. 24, figs. 71, 299.

479. This retouching is often overlooked, or at least not mentioned. See Castelnuovo, *Il gotico internazionale, II*, n.d. I have considered at length the possibility of retouching on the face and scarf of the plowman. The white lines that compose his beard, for example, are of a higher value than those used by Colombe; they are more knowingly laid than Colombe's to create a fluffy, luminous beard. The red scarf is rigid—but deliberately?

480. Or perhaps an *imitation* silver, because there seems to be no trace of oxidation.

481. For Ambrogio's plowman see Rowley, *Ambrogio Lorenzetti*, 1958, II, fig. 230. Similar oxen had appeared in fr. 166, fol. 13 no. 11.

482. Porcher, *Belles Heures*, 1953, pl. 4. The sower in *October* is bearded, but not old (Fig. 687).

483. Meiss, 1968, p. 116 f.; Maginnis, 1971, p. 63 f.

484. Tintori and Meiss, *Painting of St. Francis*, 1962, pp. 124, 140 ff.; Meiss, *Great Age of Fresco*, 1970, p. 45; Maginnis, 1971, p. 63 f.

485. Maginnis, *loc. cit.*; Meiss, *Great Age of Fresco*, 1970, p. 70. The cleaning of the frescoes by Taddeo Gaddi in the Baroncelli Chapel a few years ago seems to me to have proved what I suspected earlier: that what have been described as shadows cast by objects in his simulated cupboards are only dark areas produced by dirt and by variations of the surface due to accidents of preservation. For the view that Taddeo painted shadows see Sterling, *Still Life Painting*, 1959, pp. 18, 136 n. 21, with reference to C. de Tolnay, 1952, p. 151 f.

486. On the introduction of highlights in the fifteenth century see the valuable article by Gombrich, 1964 (without specific reference, however, to the Limbourgs). I am inclined to doubt that the Byzantine and medieval convention of lighted ridges, a residue to a degree of reflected light in ancient painting, played a significant role in the introduction of highlights by the Limbourgs, Flémalle and Jan van Eyck.

487. Hulin, 1903, p. 184, said that Colombe worked on a drawing by the Limbourgs but we cannot find it, apart from the color mentioned above.

488. See White, *Birth*, 1957, p. 224.

489. One of the actions in *November* in the *Torre dell' Aquila* is a bear hunt. See Rasmo, *Frescoes at Torre Aquila*, 1962, pl. 11.

490. The sleeve, too, appears to have been retouched.

491. The small areas of red in the roofs are ground color exposed by the loss of patches of blue.

The gift by the Limbourgs in 1411 of the fake book suggests to us the excitement aroused at the time by the artists' new power to simulate reality, to achieve, in other words, trompe l'oeil. The cover, however, was not painted but was actual velvet.

492. Panofsky, *Netherlandish Painting*, p. 61 f.

493. See the fundamental study by H. Landais, 1964, pp. 523–578, esp. p. 550. Also Ritter, *Châteaux*, 1953, pl. XXXVIII; Enaud, *Châteaux forts* [1958], p. 155.

494. Some details of Saumur, particularly of the entrance portico, resemble Jean de Berry's château de Mehun-sur-Yèvre. See Landais, *op. cit.*, p. 552.

495. Champeaux and Gauchery, *Travaux*, 1894, p. 33; Beauchamp, 1904, p. 135; Lehoux, *Berri*, II, 1966, p. 416; Meiss, *Late XIV Century*, p. 37, fig. 423 (tentatively). The correct identification was made by L. Magne (*Palais de Poitiers*, 1904, p. 12 f.) and accepted by Durrieu, *Très Riches Heures*, 1904, p. 149 f. Some historians describe the building as Saumur but state it belonged to Jean de Berry (C. Hohler in *Flowering of the Middle Ages*, London, 1966, p. 134) or even that he built it (Verdier, 1968, p. 15).

496. See the chronicler Jean Juvénal des Ursins, in *Histoire de Charles VI*, ed. 1850, p. 470, ". . . une moult belle maison, richement et notablement edifiée, et peinte, qui estoit au duc de Berry. Et y bouterent le feu, et fut arse, si bien qu'il ne demeura que les parois. Et avant ladite demolition, le peuple ostoit les beaux huis, et les beaux chassis de verres, et les emportoient."

497. K. Conant, *Carolingian and Romanesque Architecture*, Harmondsworth, 1959, pl. 99A.

498. Chastillon, *Topographie françoise*, 1648, no. 97. See also Champeaux and Gauchery, *op. cit.*, pp. 57–60; Robuchon, *Paysages*, II, p. 138. Since this text was written Crozet (1971) compared this engraving with *July* and concluded that the latter, too, represented the *château*.

499. Magne, *Palais de Poitiers*, 1904, pp. 6–8.

500. Sterling and Adhémar, Louvre, *Peintures, école française*, 1965, p. 17.

501. *Ibid.*, p. 19.

502. For a recent account see Paris, Bibl. nat., *La librairie de Charles V*, ed. F. Avril and J. Lafaurie, 1968, p. 45 f.

503. See Hoffbauer, *Paris*, 1885, pls. I, IV, V, fig. 8.

504. Durrieu, *Très Riches Heures*, 1904, p. 142; Morand, 1954, p. 57 f.; Lehoux, *Berri*, II, 1966, p. 433 n. 1. Following these authors I very tentatively suggested Riom in *Late XIV Century*, p. 37.

505. P. 52. This identification was accepted by Longnon and Cazelles, *Très Riches Heures*, 1969, no. 6. We do not agree with M. Papertiant that Riom appears in the background of Fouquet's miniature of St. Anne in the *Heures d'Etienne Chevalier*.

506. Finó, *Forteresses*, 1967, p. 343 ff.

507. *Ibid.*, p. 346 f.; Enaud, *Châteaux forts*, 1958, p. 115; Lefèvre-Pontalis, *Congrès archéologique*, 1919, p. 3 ff.; Lefèvre, 1908, pp. 17–20.

508. Monstrelet, *Chronique*, II, 1858, p. 222 f.; Fleureau, *Antiquitez d'Estampes*, 1683, p. 175 f.

509. Champeaux and Gauchery, *Travaux*, 1894, p. 61 f.

510. See *Late XIV Century*, p. 37; Champeaux and Gauchery, *op. cit.*, p. 17; Longnon and Cazelles, *Très Riches Heures*, 1969, no. 4; Wylie, *Henry the Fifth*, II, 1919, p. 438 ff.

511. *Les plus excellents bastiments de France*, I, 1576, pp. 3, 47 ff.

512. Baldass, *Jan van Eyck* [1952], p. 12 n. 2.

513. Vallery-Radot, 1965. See also Bazin, *Mont Saint-Michel*, 1933, I, p. 47.

514. See above, p. 156.

515. See n. 339.

516. For the close correspondence of the miniature and old engravings of the chateau see *Late XIV Century*, figs. 424, 425.

517. Raynal, *Histoire du Berry*, II, 1884, p. 496; Monstrelet, *Chronique*, ed. Douët-d'Arcq, III, 1859, p. 53.

518. The first scene in the cycle: St. Francis honored by a simple man.

519. Berenson, *Italian Pictures, Florentine School* [1963], I, fig. 233.

520. Meiss, *Painting in Florence and Siena*, p. 97, fig. 94.

521. See Metman, 1968, pp. 159–166.

522. Rasmo, *Die Fresken im Adlerturm*, 1962, p. 13.

523. See Coffin, in *Scritti*, 1966, who observed that the Italian tradition began in the Villa Belvedere of Pope Innocent VIII, which included views of cities, described by Vasari "alla maniera de'Fiamminghi" (*Vite*, ed. 1906, III, p. 498). Coffin suggested a connection with the *Très Riches Heures*.

524. See M. Fenaille, *Etat général des tapisseries de la*

manufacture des gobelins, 1600–1900, Paris, 1903, p. 160.

525. See also *Pentecost* (fol. 84), the *Cross* (fol. 93), and *Salome before Herod* (fol. 212v).

526. *Boucicaut Master*, p. 13 f.; Panofsky, *Netherlandish Painting*, 1953, p. 58. Inasmuch as the monograph on the little known *Belles Heures* had not been published when Panofsky wrote about the diaphragm arch in *Netherlandish Painting* he somewhat overestimated the role of the Boucicaut Master.

527. *Boucicaut Hours*, fol. 142, *Funeral Service*. On fol. 24 (*St. Thomas*) of the *Boucicaut Hours* he employed the same color, and on fol. 38 (*St. Catherine*) he gave the arch a slightly higher value.

528. Durrieu, *Très Riches Heures*, 1904, pp. 107, 219, 243 f.; Longnon and Cazelles, *Très Riches Heures*, 1969, fols. 86v, 158.

529. The conjugate leaf, 89, was also decorated in this style, which is otherwise not present in the gathering. See the Description of the manuscript in the Catalogue.

530. See above, p. 82 and the Catalogue of Workshops.

531. *Très Riches Heures*, 1904, p. 143. He said the vaults, the statues, and the window-shafts were drawn by the Limbourgs. See also Longnon and Cazelles, *Très Riches Heures*, 1969, fol. 158.

532. The upward glance of the cleric in the foreground in the *Très Riches Heures* is motivated by the angels who hover high above the altar, and the similar (though less decisive) upward tilt of the cleric's head in the Bodleian miniature suggests that the angels were included in the design by the Limbourgs. This conclusion is proved by the singer who looks up in both the *Très Riches Heures* and the Walters manuscript.

Though the dragons at the base of the two gray arches in the *Très Riches Heures* now show only the surface of Colombe they are favorite motifs of the Limbourgs and were often copied by the Master of St. Jerome (Fig. 600).

533. See *Late XIV Century*, p. 38.

534. He copied this kind of border for his *Crucifixion* on fol. 152v.

535. A long sarcophagus was employed also in the *Resurrection* in the *Belles Heures* (see Meiss and Beatson, *Belles Heures*, 1974, fol. 198).

536. For the similarity of *January* and the *Dance of Salome* see White, *Birth*, 1957, p. 224. For Eyck's *Madonna in the Church* see *Boucicaut Master*, p. 72, fig. 497. The recent argument of Philip, *Ghent Altarpiece*, 1971, p. 136 f., for a much later date for this painting seems to me unconvincing for many reasons. Suffice it to comment here on her first major point. The two patches of sunlight on the floor near the Madonna indicate a date later than the *Annunciation* in the Ghent altarpiece, she says, because it, with its somewhat similar patches, must be the source of this metaphor. "It is utterly improbable," Prof. Philip says, that this motif was invented for the painting in Berlin because the symbolism of light was traditional in representations of the Annunciation but not of the Virgin and Child. On the border of the Virgin's tunic in the Berlin panel, however, near the patches of sunlight, is still visible part of the phrase "Hec est speciosior sole"—"she is more beautiful than the sun" (see my article in the *Art Bulletin*, 1945, not cited by the author). If, furthermore, the two patches of light refer to the twofold nature of Christ, the allusion would be perfectly appropriate to the Berlin Madonna, the lost frame of which bore an inscription referring to the incarnation of Christ ("Deus homo natus. . . ;" see my same article). Prof. Philip's argument seems especially surprising in view of her announced intention of giving more weight to iconography when dating Jan van Eyck's paintings.

537. Of the three known copies of this plan the one reproduced is in Venice, Bibl. Marciana, lat. Zan. 399, fol. 98. Frutaz, *Piante*, 1962, I, p. 115 f.

538. Frutaz, *op. cit.*, I, p. 119 f. For what follows see the similar but fuller account—the only good one I know—by Schulz, in *Saggi*, 1970 (appeared late 1972), p. 17 f., which reached me after the above text was written.

539. See Paris, Bibl. nat., *Notitia dignitatum*, n.d., pls. 44–57, 85–102. A similar kind of representation was used in the fourth century also by the Roman land surveyors. See Dilke, 1961, pls. 1–9.

540. Ragghianti, *Affreschi Minerbi*, n.d., p. 14.

541. Gnoli, *Piante*, 1941, p. 3 f.; Frutaz, *op. cit.*, I, p. 126 f.

542. Frutaz, *op. cit.*, I, p. 126 f.

543. The manuscript measures 32×23, and the map of Rome 14.7×13.8 cm. (For these dimensions and help of various kinds I am much indebted to Prof. Irving Lavin.) Many of the margins contain brief Latin instructions for the illuminators. The manuscript is not foliated. See the Catalogue of Workshops.

Many miniatures are divided into two compartments (Fig. 781), a kind of design that the Orosius Master adopted *ca.* 1412 when working on the *Térence des ducs* (see for example, Martin, *Térence*, figs. 122, 127, 129). The attenuated, linealized figures also point to a late date—*ca.* 1418, so that the miniatures in this manuscript are the latest we know of the workshop. Some miniatures were left incomplete, others probably not even begun, and the illumination was completed late in the century by a master influenced by Colombe (Fig. 734). Often this later master added the figures to a setting painted by the Orosius workshop. The latter painted the handsome initials throughout the book.

544. Müntz, 1885, and *Les antiquités de la ville de Rome*, Paris, 1886, p. 4 ff.; Gnoli, *op. cit.*, p. 4 ff.; Frutaz, *op. cit.*, I, p. 123 f.

545. Pächt, 1950, p. 40 f.

546. Gnoli, *op. cit.*, pl. IV, identified some sixty buildings.

547. Frutaz, *loc .cit.*

548. See J. Gagé, "Le 'Templum Urbis' et les origines de l'idée de 'Renovatio,' " in *Mélanges Franz Cumont*, Brussels, 1936, I, pp. 51–187.

549. The Limbourg pyramid bears a remarkable resemblance, with regard to two-dimensionality and the large size of the stones, to the pyramids in a map of Egypt in a fifteenth-century copy of (ultimately) a fourth-century Roman manuscript of the *Notitia dignitatum imperii romani* (Paris, Bibl. nat., lat. 9661). See *Paris, Bibliothèque nationale, Notitia dignitatum*, n.d., pl. 44.

550. See the stream entering the city from the south and flowing into the Tiber near the Pons S. Maria (17), and another stream running from the Mausoleum of Augustus (26) to a point near the Ponte S. Angelo (21).

551. The dome on the tower of the Therme Antoniane (72) is lacking in Taddeo's plan but does appear in the plan of Pietro del Massaio (Fig. 738).

552. Both Pierre d'Ailly and Jean de Montreuil returned to Paris from the Council of Rome early in 1413. See Valois, *La France et le grand Schisme*, IV, 1902, p. 213 f.

553. The marble veneer on the base of Castel Sant'Angelo, which seems to be represented by Taddeo, was torn off in 1379. At this time a chapel on the tower was destroyed also.

554. Rubinstein, 1958, p. 195 and passim.

555. S. Symeonides, *Taddeo di Bartolo*, Siena, 1965, pl. 69.

556. "libre . . . en frances qui tracta dels romans e cartegenosos e al principi es piantada la ciutat de Roma. . . ." See T. de Marinis, *Biblioteca dei re d'Aragona*, I, 1947, p. 219.

557. *Mappemondes, A. D. 1200–1500*, ed. M. Destombes, 1964, pp. 65–73. This recent, exhaustive list of *mappae mundi* in the Sallust manuscripts does not include the one we reproduce (Fig. 734). No reference is made, on principle, to the presence of maps of other kinds in these manuscripts. See also Beazley, *Modern Geography*, 1901, II, p. 578 ff.

558. *Sallust*, ed. J. C. Rolfe, Cambridge (Mass.), 1960 (Loeb ed.), p. 171.

559. I have found no reproduction of a similar map, but I have not examined the sixty manuscripts of Sallust of the 13th–15th centuries that bear a *mappa mundi*.

560. *Boucicaut Master*, 1968, pp. 42 ff., 61.

561. Rowley, *Ambrogio Lorenzetti*, 1958, p. 98.

562. Panofsky, *Netherlandish Painting*, 1953, pp. 3, 361.

563. Scaglia, 1964.

564. Quite similar maps of Rome by Massaio appear in copies of the *Geography* dated 1469 (Vat. lat. 5699) and 1472 (Vat. urb. lat. 277).

565. The view of Rome was probably influenced by Cimabue's in the vault of the Upper Church, Assisi (see Bologna, *Pittori di Napoli*, 1969, p. II–4).

566. The first scholar to discuss the relationship, Conway in 1910, thought the miniature derived from the drawing. This was the view also of Panofsky, *Netherlandish Painting*, 1953, p. 64 and of Porcher, in *Enciclopedia*, VIII, p. 619 ff. Pächt, 1950, p. 42, also believed that the model was Lombard, either the Bergamo drawing or a similar one. The scholars who concluded there was an earlier, Lombard model for both include Van Schendel, *Dessin en Lombardie*, 1938, pp. 60–63. The dependence of the drawing on the miniature was upheld by Kurth, 1911, p. 98; Baldass, *Conrad Laib*, Vienna, 1946, p. 161. Cadei, 1970, p. 35 n. 15, suggested that the drawing is later than the miniature.

567. See Thiébaux, 1967, p. 271 f., depending upon Gaston Phébus, *Livre de la chasse* and *Roy Modus et royne Ratio*.

568. The adjoining brown hound in the miniature is restrained either by fear of the handler or because he is partly pinned down by the boar. His forelegs are visible.

569. There are, on the other hand, details in the drawing that do not appear in the miniature: blood on the hindquarters of the boar, two rings on the collar of the dog second from left, and a collar on the dog at the extreme right, but these differences do not seem to be equally telling.

570. The last three folios of this first gathering (7v, 8, 8v) are by a very different and inferior hand. See Cadei, 1970.

571. See Hind, *Early Italian Engraving*, part I, I, 1938, p. 70.

572. The man at the left wears on his belt a drum-like object that is worn in other miniatures by a soldier accompanying an emperor (fols. 15v, 156, 161).

The two men adoring the cross in a third miniature of the subject in the *Belles Heures* (fol. 93) are likewise not identifiable.

573. Jean de Berry himself owned a golden cross within which there was "une croix à double croisée qui est du fust de la vraie croix . . ." (Guiffrey, *Inventaires*, I, p. 14 no. 9). For this form see P. Thoby, *Le crucifix* [Paris], 1959, pl. LXVI no. 151.

574. The certificate of authenticity of the relic survives. See *Late XIV Century*, p. 82 f., fig. 475. For the reliquary in the Ste.-Chapelle in Paris see *op. cit.*, fig. 428.

575. *Très Riches Heures*, 1904, p. 37.

576. Guiffrey, *op. cit.*, I, p. 12 no. 7 "ladicte croix sur un pie d'or esmaillie en maniere d'une roche ou il a par dessus un lezart d'or de haute maille [taille]; . . ." I pointed to some of the differences in *Late XIV Century*, p. 51. The "croix au serpent" was small, it showed on the reverse a Virgin on the crescent moon, and it did not contain the string of coins or medals that is visible in the *Très Riches Heures*. The lizard in the miniature has in its mouth what seems to be a green fruit with red seams. Is this a pomegranate or perhaps an apple? See Eve and the serpent at Reims (Sauerländer, *Gotische Skulptur*, 1970, pl. 259). The lizard in the *Très Riches Heures* resembles St. Margaret's dragon in the *Belles Heures*, fol. 177.

577. *Très Riches Heures*, 1904, p. 37.

578. *Très Riches Heures*, 1969, no. 133.

579. Numbers 21, especially 8 and 9.

580. St. John 3, 14–15, contains the prophecy of Christ. For St. Ambrose: "Imago enim crucis aereus serpens est . . ." *De Spiritu Sancto*, Bk. III, ch. 8, 50, trans. by R. J. Deferrari, *St. Ambrose, Theological and Dogmatic Works*, Washington, 1963, p. 170 (The Fathers of the Church, vol. 44).

581. K. Conant, *Carolingian and Romanesque Architecture*, Harmondsworth, 1959, pp. 207–209.

582. "Et est ibi mons Calvariae ad quem montem per gradus callis est. Ibi Dominus crucifixus est et ibi est altare grande, sub uno tecto est." *Theodori liber de situ Terrae Sanctae* in *Itinera hierosolymitana et descriptiones Terrae Sancte*, ed. T. Tobler and A. Moliner, Geneva, I, 1879.

583. Guiffrey, *Inventaires*, I, p. 292 f., no. 1111.

584. Solomon's prayer illustrates the Wisdom of Solomon. See for example Princeton, University Library, Garrett 28, fol. 158 (English Bible, thirteenth century).

585. See Sauerländer, *Gotische Skulptur*, 1970, pl. 92. The Queen has black followers in Italian painting of the fifteenth century (Schubring, *Cassoni*, 1915, no. 197).

586. See Plummer, *Hours of Catherine of Cleves* [n.d.], no. 85.

587. The Queen of Sheba was represented with a duck's foot in, for example, the sculpture of the cathedrals (Sauerländer, *op. cit.*, figs. 8, 9, 45). In the portal of Angers it may be the Queen who holds up her overskirt (*ibid.*, pl. 33).

588. See Longnon and Cazelles, *Très Riches Heures*, 1969, nos. 18, 23, 24, 124.

589. ". . . una capella parva, que habet unum hostium usque plateam sepulchri; et in illa dicunt et cantant et officium faciunt Nubiani calogeri, valde spirituales homines, qui sunt Ethiopes nigri de gente presbyteri Johannis. . . . semper portant crucem unam in manu, vocantur cristiani Sancti Thome. . . ." *Liber peregrinationis Fratris Jacobi de Verona, 1335*, p. 190. A similar description was given *ca.* 1350 by Ludolph von Suchem, *Description of the Holy Land*, 1895, p. 103.

590. *Songe*, ed. Coopland, 1969, I, p. 221 f.

591. *The Book of the Wanderings of Brother Felix Fabri*, 1896, II, pp. 373, 435. Fabri said this chapel had only recently passed to the Nubians, and at another point (p. 387) he observed that it belonged to the Christians of India.

592. A German pilgrim of 1346–1347 said that the Christians of St. Thomas, who always hold a cross in their hands, officiated in the Church of the Holy Sepulchre (*Deutsche Pilgerreisen*, 1880, p. 56 f.).

593. ". . . un faissel de touaille taincte en collour perse." Ogier points out that the hood of the Saracens was white, of the Jews yellow. *Saint Voyage de Jherusalem*, 1873, p. 43. Ogier was a prominent person, known at the courts of the king, Berry and Burgundy. He was, in fact, with the king and Jean sans Peur at the siege of Bourges in 1412.

594. In addition to Ogier cited in the preceding note see *Mandeville's Travels*, 1919, p. 72 f.

595. See Janin, *Eglises orientales et les rites orientaux*, 1955.

596. Jacopo da Verona said that the blue hood was worn by "cristiani de centura" known as the "Jacobini" (Jacobites). *Liber peregrinationis Fratris Jacobi de Verona, 1335*, p. 217.

597. Jorga, *Voyageurs français dans l'Orient européen* [1928], p. 20.
598. Douët d'Arcq, *Comptes de l'hôtel des rois*, 1865, p. 312.
599. See the priest in the temple in the *Purification of the Virgin* (Fig. 573). Bersuire, *Dictionarii seu repertorii moralis*, part III, bk. I, describes the hat of the high priest as "ad modum pyramidis."
600. *The Book of the Wanderings of Brother Felix Fabri*, 1896, II, p. 371. Ludolph von Suchem, *ca.* 1350, reports the same fact (*Description of the Holy Land*, 1895, p. 103).
601. Genesis 14, 18–20.
602. Hebrews, 7, 1–11.
603. *Ovide moralisé*, 1915, p. 116 f.
604. See Antoninus Placentinus, late sixth century (Migne, *Pat. lat.*, LXXII, col. 906); Felix Fabri of Ulm, 1480 (*Book of the Wanderings*, 1896, p. 366 ff.). Fabri says that Melchizedek blessed Abraham here, and that on Golgotha the brazen serpent was set up.
605. Galatians, 3, 29; Romans 4.
606. For a similar small reliquary in the collection of the Duke see Guiffrey, *Inventaires*, I, p. 289 no. 1101.
607. Krautheimer, 1942.
608. "Cappella Rucellai," in *De artibus*, 1961, p. 291 ff.
609. The arms in this miniature are those of Denis du Moulin, bishop of Paris 1439–1447 (Paris, Bibl. de l'Arsenal (Martin and Lauer), 1929, p. 39 f.).
610. Brit. Mus. Yates Thompson ms. 3. Here the miniature is accompanied in the border by the scene of St. Helena and the finding of the cross. Other miniatures in this manuscript derive from the *Très Riches Heures* (see n. 692).
611. See above, p. 164.
612. See also the scenes of the Old Testament on fols. 29, 35v, 45, 49v, 54v (Figs. 564, 561, 573). The building on fol. 29 has a round-arched portal, a rose window, and slender columns supporting a vault. A triangular pediment appears in the *Healing* (Fig. 591). This building, which may be the temple, also has similar clerestory windows.
613. See Matthew 24, and *Meditations on the Life of Christ*, ed. Ragusa and Green, 1961, p. 306 f.
614. See Book II, chap. 10, Book VI, chap. 6.
615. This generalization has been facilitated by the careful study of Dorsch, *Raising of Lazarus*, 1966. In numerous representations of the subject in the sixteenth and seventeenth centuries ruinous buildings appear in the distance; while they cannot be identified with the Temple they may convey a related idea.
616. *Late XIV Century*, p. 139, figs. 83–85, 217, 218, 249.
617. Dvořáková *et al.*, *Gothic Mural Painting in Bohemia*, 1964, fig. 140.
618. The building that was described as poor and delapidated in many texts, including the *Meditations*, is connected with the Old Testament by John of Hildesheim, *Historia trium regum*, who said that the Nativity took place in the cellar of the ruined house of David (Panofsky, *Netherlandish Painting*, 1953, p. 136 n. 1).
619. P. 69, and for the full inventory notice, the documents in Chapter IV, 1.
620. See the documents in Chapter IV, 1.
621. *Late XIV Century*, pp. 37, 74.
622. *Ibid.*, pp. 75–77, 86, and *Burl. Mag.*, 1963. A virtually identical engraving was printed a little later in Montfaucon, *Monumens*, III, 1731, p. 181, pl. XXVIII, 1.
623. Monstrelet, *Chroniques*, ed. 1836, p. 245.
624. See Schwager, in *Argo*, 1970, p. 210 ff. See also the portrait of Jean sans Peur in the Louvre (*Late XIV Century*, fig. 506).
625. For these paintings see the Catalogue of Panels and the indices in the *Late XIV Century* and *Boucicaut Master*, especially for: French, *Portrait of Jean le Bon*; French, *Portrait of Jean sans Peur* (copy); Parement Master, *Parement de Narbonne*; the drawing of Madonnas by Beaumetz in Basel, Kupferstichkabinett, and the copy of a drawing by Beauneveu (?) of the *Death, Assumption, and Coronation of the Virgin* in the Louvre, Cabinet des Dessins.
626. Meiss, *De Lévis Hours*, 1972, p. 11 ff.
627. Vegas, who first published the painting (1972, p. 399), already spoke of a special relation between the two panels.
628. Miner, 1966.
629. For the Man of Sorrows see for example the Parement Master (*Late XIV Century*, fig. 15); Jacquemart (*ibid.*, fig. 94); and the panel at Troyes, where, however, the cloth is actually the shroud held by angels (*ibid.*, fig. 694). In the *Beistegui Madonna* in the Louvre a curved drapery is tooled into the gold behind the figure. See Paris, Louvre (Sterling and Adhémar), 1965, p. 5, pl. 27.
630. Meiss and Eisler, 1960, p. 235.
631. Birkmeyer, 1961.
632. The *houppelande* is decorated with the notorious *rabot* of Jean sans Peur.
633. Meiss and Eisler, 1960, p. 239 f.
634. For the one difficulty in this reconstruction—the fact that the Duke faces right—see *ibid.*
635. Sterling, 1959, p. 302 f. Malouel worked on this portrait in the period 1411–1413.
636. The identification of the *Madonna* with Malouel

was considered probable by Sterling in Vienna, Kunsthist. Mus., *Katalog*, 1962, p. 70 f. Sterling and Adhémar in Paris, Louvre, 1965, p. 4 no. 8 describe the identification as hypothetical to the same degree as the *Trinity with Man of Sorrows*. Pächt, *Gaz. B.-A.*, 1963, p. 117 f. accepted the attribution of the Berlin *Madonna* to Malouel, and Laclotte, *Primitifs* [1966], p. 13, regarded both the *Madonna* and the Trinity in Louvre as probable works of this painter.

637. Meiss and Eisler, 1960, p. 236 f.

638. In the *Beistegui Madonna* in the Louvre, painted under the influence of Broederlam, probably at Dijon, the Child puts his finger on his lips.

639. For this aspect of the painting cf. Meiss and Eisler, 1960, p. 234 f. Our conclusion (unlike Winkler's) that the painting was originally on cloth and not transferred from panel, reached by the study of the character of its present surface, was subsequently confirmed by Dr. Müller Hofstede in the laboratory of the Berlin Museum (see Meiss and Eisler, 1960, p. 489).

640. The painting is somewhat damaged and reworked. The ornamental motif on the blue robe was originally composed of three leaves: the pattern visible now is modern. The pendant jewel supported by the two links attached to the collar has been lost.

641. By Adolfo and Lionello Venturi, Berenson, and still in the recent large monograph of Sindona, *Pisanello*, New York [1961], pp. 39, 127, pl. 137, with full bibliography.

642. For the history of this problem see the excellent account by Brendel, in *Wittkower Essays*, 1967, p. 63 f.

643. Schlosser, 1897, p. 95; Durrieu, *Très Riches Heures*, 1904, p. 38 f.; Winkler, 1930, p. 95 f.; Adhémar, *Influences antiques*, 1939, p. 301 f.; Porcher in *Enciclopedia dell'arte*, VIII, p. 619 f.

644. See Chapter 1.

645. *Late XIV Century*, pp. 303–305.

646. *Ibid.*, p. 42 f.

647. See the penetrating study by Ettlinger, 1972.

648. Proposed by Panofsky, *Netherlandish Painting*, 1953, p. 64.

649. I owe this observation to Willibald Sauerländer.

650. It should be added that they are partly visible, too, on the nude good thief in the *Exit from the Praetorium* (Fig. 585), but when this figure is near Christ in the *Way to Calvary* and turned toward the observer he wears a loincloth.

651. Brendel, *op. cit.*, fig. 2.

652. Miner, in Baltimore, Walters, *International Style*, 1962, p. 68, connects the figure of the resurrected with Adam in *Paradise* in the *Très Riches Heures*. She rightly remarks that the posture seems more suitable to the *Last Judgment* than to the *Temptation*.

653. *Ibid.*

654. The connection with the *Three Graces*, proposed by F. de Mély, 1912, p. 195 ff., was approved by Adhémar, *op. cit.*, p. 301 n. 1, who rejected, however, the hypothesis about the thief advanced by Durrieu (*Très Riches Heures*, 1904, p. 38 f.).

655. Durrieu, *loc. cit.*

656. See Documents, "after 1404–1405."

657. Berchorius, *Ovidius moralizatus*, ed. 1962, p. 85: "Tandem vero super pegasum id est corpus glorificatum per resurrectionem ascendit cum quo in ascensione in paradisum volavit." A Roman example of Pegasus was visible at the same time in the Sainte-Chapelle, Paris, where the larger *Cameo of France* was then preserved.

658. Winkler, 1911, pp. 536–543. He reaffirmed the attribution and dated the manuscript between 1404–1410 in *Kunstchronik*, VIII, 1955, p. 11. See the Catalogue of Manuscripts.

659. See for example Wescher, 1946, p. 34; Panofsky, *Netherlandish Painting*, 1953, pp. 62 n. 6, 82 n. 3. Martens, *Meister Francke*, 1929, p. 194, dated the Breviary *ca.* 1400 and associated it with the painter of lat. 8886 in the Bibliothèque nationale, Paris (in my view, the Luçon Master).

660. *Très Belles Heures de Notre-Dame*, 1922, p. 74. Whereas Durrieu believed the Limbourgs worked on the Breviary Hulin de Loo thought it was only closely related ("Traces de Hubrecht van Eyck; Empreintes contemporaines en Suisse et Allemagne," *Annuaire des Musées Royaux de Belgique*, IV, 1943–1944, p. 20 f.).

661. Cf., for example, the blue lozenges set in a gold filigree of *St. Mark* (Fig. 619) with *Très Riches Heures* fols. 26v, 46v. Also *David before the Lord* (Fig. 648) with *Très Riches Heures* fols. 27v, 43v.

662. See the Catalogue of Manuscripts.

663. Meiss, *Late XIV Century*, p. 246.

664. Many of the initials in the Breviary, like those in the *Très Riches Heures*, are composed of pseudo-acanthus leaves, which had already appeared in the initial of 1406 by the Breviary Master (Fig. 366).

665. *Belles Heures*, 1953, p. 25 f. Porcher said that only the *Martyrdom of St. Mark* in the Breviary could be ascribed to the Limbourgs. *St. Martin* on fol. 435 of the Breviary comes from the *Belles Heures*, fol. 169, of which it is a truncated copy minus the second beggar and part of the horse. It does not fit into the narrower field. The *Flaying of Bartholomew* on fol. 379 is likewise taken from the *Belles Heures*, fol. 161.

666. Jean sans Peur did commission a superb manuscript by the Boucicaut Master, Bibl. nat., fr. 2810, which he gave, however, to his uncle, Jean de Berry, and the Breviary is beautiful, but his Book of Hours is mediocre. For a list of manuscripts owned by Jean sans Peur see Appendix B.

667. Nationalbibliothek, Ser. nov. 2613, fol. 14; see *Late XIV Century*, p. 355 and Trenkler, 1938, p. 27 f. Trenkler already remarked on a relation of the manuscript to the Breviary of Jean sans Peur.

668. The *Trinity* on fol. 124 is close in style to the Master of Walters 219, whereas the *Visitation* (28), *Nativity* (49v), *Adoration of the Magi* (55v), and *Funeral Service* (128) resemble the Troyes Master.

669. Bibl. nazionale, I. A. 15; see *Late XIV Century*, p. 355; *Boucicaut Master*, pp. 70, 114.

670. See the Catalogue of Workshops. Also Meiss, *Art Bull.*, 1956, p. 195 and *Late XIV Century*, p. 360.

671. The observation that the miniatures are neatly pasted in, made originally by L. M. J. Delaissé, was kindly communicated to me by Miss Dorothy Miner.

672. See Catalogue of Manuscripts and of Workshops.

673. Harley 2897, fol. 421.

674. *Late XIV Century*, figs. 382, 386.

675. Verdier, 1961, p. 9 ff.; Meiss, *Gaz. B.-A.*, 1963, p. 151.

676. Pächt, for example, ascribed it to Paul ("The Avignon Diptych," 1961, p. 402, n. 4).

677. *Late XIV Century*, fig. 180. Lyna in, *Mélanges*, 1931, even believed that the painter of the Madonna in the *Brussels Hours* also actually executed the Child in the *Madonna on the crescent*.

678. For the *Somme le roi*, Brussels ms. 11044, see Panofsky, *Netherlandish Painting*, 1953, figs. 140, 141, and for the Rotterdam triptych, *ibid.*, fig. 107.

679. Pächt, *Mary of Burgundy* [1948], p. 53 n. 20, said that the scrolls and tendrils in these borders were not painted by the authors of the miniatures, in his view the Limbourgs, but were added by a contemporary or later illuminator.

680. The fourth angel (lower right) derives from one in the balcony of the *Annunciation*, and even the brown bear in the border of that folio reappears in the Seilern border. Two of the angels are in the borders of the Seilern *Visitation* also.

681. Schilling, 1942, p. 194 ff.

682. *Belles Heures*, 1953, pp. 7, 23 f.; Paris, Bibl. nat., 1955, p. 93 no. 91. For Porcher's conclusions about fr. 166 see the chapter on this manuscript. At this time Porcher considered the *Seilern Hours* to be the latest of the works of the Limbourgs, and asked whether it too was made for Jean de Berry.

683. *L'enluminure*, 1959, p. 64.

684. Most of these similar designs were pointed out by Schilling, 1942, and Porcher, *Belles Heures*, 1953, pp. 23 f., 42 f. The group of copies includes also *Pilate washing his hands*, *St. John*, *Office of the Dead*, *Flagellation*, and *Mockery*.

685. For the Brussels *Flight* see *Late XIV Century*, fig. 188.

686. Schilling, *op. cit.* Pächt, *Mary of Burgundy* [1948], p. 53 n. 20, pointed out that the Flemish illuminator who worked on the *Seilern Hours* employed the composition of the *Annunciation to the Shepherds* in another of his manuscripts.

687. See the Catalogue of Workshops. The *Annunciation* and the *Flagellation* also derive from the *Très Riches Heures*—the latter is, indeed, a full copy.

688. Closely related to the corresponding miniatures in the *Belles Heures* are *St. Catherine in Prison*, the *Annunciation*, *Betrayal*, *Way to Calvary*, *Deposition*, *Cour celeste*, and *Office of the Dead* (*Boucicaut Master*, fig. 154). The *Agony in the Garden* is especially close to the miniature in the Seilern Book of Hours.

689. For the *Annunciation to the Shepherds* in the *Brussels Hours* see *Late XIV Century*, fig. 185.

690. See Catalogue of Workshops. We cannot accept Porcher's opinion (*L'enluminure*, 1959, p. 64) that this illuminator painted the *Seilern Hours* also, as well as the first gathering of fr. 166.

691. Delaissé, *Dutch Manuscript Illumination*, 1968, p. 70, has asserted that their "Dutch" art was not understood in France.

692. In addition to the numerous copies discussed in the foregoing text many others are cited in the chapters on interior space in the *Très Riches Heures*, on the Exaltation of the Cross, and on the Rohan Master. The Breton Book of Hours, Morgan 865, has copies of five miniatures of the *Belles Heures*: *Annunciation*, *Visitation*, *Nativity*, *Annunciation to the Shepherds*, and *Adoration of the Magi*. The *Hours of Marguerite d'Orléans*, lat. 1156 B, perhaps Breton also, contains several copies (see p. 275). The *Annunciation* in Ste. Geneviève 2713 is based on the *Belles Heures*.

The *Dunois Hours*, Brit. Mus., Yates, Thompson ms. 3, contains the following miniatures related to the *Très Riches Heures*: *January*, *May*, *Nativity*, *Presentation in the Temple*, *Flagellation*, *Way to Calvary*, and *Exaltation of the Cross* (Fig. 725).

693. Janson, review of Wundram, *Donatello und Nanni*

di Banco, in *Art Bull.*, LIV, 1972, p. 548. Janson speculates about the possibility of a model outside Florence, in Venice or North Italy, but nothing that seems to me adequate for the Boucicaut Master has yet come to light.

694. Guiffrey, *Inventaires*, I, p. 269 no. 1003.
695. See also *Boucicaut Master*, figs. 115, 116, 174, 299.
696. Panofsky, *Netherlandish Painting*, 1953, p. 154.
697. See Documents.
698. The Seilern triptych has been dated 1410–1415 by Van Gelder, 1967, p. 2, and Sterling, 1972, p. 27, whereas Panofsky, *op. cit.*, p. 160, proposed 1415–1420.
699. Van Gelder, 1967, p. 4, points rather to the Boucicaut Master.
700. Lotte Philip (*Ghent Altarpiece*, 1971, p. 136). See n. 536.
701. Sterling, "Christus," 1971, p. 11 ff. The difficulties inherent in this view, and recognized for some time, have now been increased by the observations of Marrow in two important papers, 1966 and 1968. Lotte Philip (*op. cit.*, pp. 140, 223 f.) stresses all the problems without recognizing the strength of the miniatures nor the severe difficulties presented by a *late* date. See, for example, the *Prayer on the Beach* reproduced near a detail of Jan's *St. Barbara* of 1437 (her figs. 132, 133).
702. In 1945, n. 47, I pointed to the very large highlights in the *Birth of the Baptist* as indications of an imitator rather than an innovating genius, but the extraordinary beauty of the miniatures and the undeniably early character of the figures are difficult to account for in the 'thirties.
703. Panofsky, *Netherlandish Painting*, 1953, p. 178. Panofsky stated that Jan was decorating the castle but, as Sterling, 1971, p. 11 n. 47, recently stressed, he might equally well have been painting miniatures; no specific task is described or implied by the document.
704. Gombrich, 1964.
705. *Netherlandish Painting*, 1953, p. 236.
706. Not "no color," as Panofsky said (*ibid.*, pp. 65, 236).
707. *Boucicaut Master*, p. 72, figs. 173, 174.
708. Panofsky, *op. cit.*, p. 192.
709. Baldass, *Jan van Eyck* [1952], fig. 23.
710. Panofsky, *Netherlandish Painting*, 1953, p. 231 f., fig. 284, but without reference to the *Très Riches Heures*.
711. *Late XIV Century*, figs. 466, 784.
712. Panofsky, *op. cit.*, p. 100 ff.
713. Our investigations have confirmed and further substantiated the critique by Pächt (*Burl. Mag.*, 1956, p. 115) of Panofsky's thesis of the importance in this respect of Netherlandish illumination (*Netherlandish Painting*, 1953, p. 123 ff.). Kreuter-Eggemann, furthermore, has pointed out that Jacques Daliwe copied at least one figure from the *Flagellation* in the *Belles Heures* (*Skizzenbuch*, 1964, p. 14 ff.).
714. See *Bréviaire Grimani*, ed. De Vries and Morpurgo, 1904, I. For a second cycle, about a decade later and related in style and design see the *Heures d'Hennessy* in the Bibliothèque royale, Brussels (see Destrée, *Heures de Hennessy*, 1923).
715. Koch, *Patinir*, 1968, p. 27 f. and fig. 16. The group is reversed. Koch observes that the group, very close to the *Très Riches Heures*, cannot derive from the altered design in the *Grimani Breviary*.
716. See *Très Riches Heures*, Catalogue of Manuscripts.
717. See, for example, Bibl. nat., fr. 1584, *Late XIV Century*, fig. 385. For *Joachim in his sheepfold* in the *Visconti Hours* see Meiss and Kirsch, *Visconti Hours*, 1972, fol. BR 2V.
718. See, for example, the manuscript of Dante's *Commedia* written at Piacenza in 1387 and illuminated there or nearby (*Late XIV Century*, fig. 403) and the more imaginative development of French forms in manuscripts such as Bibl. nat., lat. 11727 (Gengaro et al., *Miniature lombarde*, 1970, fig. 410).
719. Rossi, *Quattrocento*, 1938, pp. 408 ff., 434 ff.
720. See the Giron, Bibl. nat., n.a. fr. 5243 (*Late XIV Century*, fig. 585) and the Lancelot, fr. 343 (Gengaro et al., *op. cit.*, figs. 287–294).
721. *Boucicaut Master*, pp. 68 f., 136 f. An early Book of Hours by the Boucicaut workshop is in the Ambrosiana Library (*ibid.*, pp. 72, 101 f.).
722. P. 240. For the relation of the Boucicaut style to Tuscan painting see *Boucicaut Master*, *passim*.
723. *Boucicaut Master*, pp. 62, 68, 100, figs. 356–365.
724. For the Vitruvius in Florence, Bibl. Laurenziana, plut. 30.10, see Virgil Master, Catalogue of Workshops; for the Bible see *Late XIV Century*, p. 342.
725. See, for example, the Books of Hours illuminated in a style related to that of the Luçon Master, now in the Ambrosiana, Milan (see Catalogue of Workshops); but we do not know where they were in the early fifteenth century.
726. If the Master of Walters 219 was Lombard he should be mentioned here also. See Catalogue of Workshops.
727. As Pächt, *Gaz. B.-A.*, 1963, p. 109, observed.

728. Meiss, 1954, p. 314 ff.

729. For a drawing in the Ambrosiana for (or after?) a predella by this master see Fossi Todorow, *Pisanello*, 1966, p. 173, pl. 127, who rightly rejects the frequent attribution to Pisanello, but she does not connect the drawing with this predella or with the Master of the Bambino Vispo. For the French type in Valencian painting of the early fifteenth century see a panel in the Provincial Museum, Valencia (Post, *Spanish Painting*, III, 1930, p. 104, fig. 290).

730. See Meiss, "*Decameron*," 1967, p. 59 f.

731. See above, p. 228. The black background of the panel in Washington is surprising, but x rays do not disclose any forms beneath it.

732. See p. 139 ff.

733. For Pisanello's famous studies of the fantastic dress of Italian nobles see, for example, Hill, *Pisanello*, 1905, pl. 45.

734. Paris, Louvre, Cabinet des dessins inv. no. 2623v. See Glaser, 1913–1914, p. 156.

735. Pächt, *Gaz. B.-A.*, 1963, p. 109 ff. Even with knowledge of this publication Fossi Todorow (*Pisanello*, 1966, p. 160 no. 285) maintained that the drawing in the Louvre is a copy of Pisanello's panel. Already in 1905 Hill (*Pisanello*, p. 158) rightly observed that the drawing reflected the painter's thought *before* he executed the panel.

736. See p. 82.

737. See, for example, for the Child in the *Nativity* by Meister Francke, Kunsthalle, Hamburg, and for the shepherds a *Nativity* by Hans Multscher, Berlin-Dahlem (Strange, *Deutsche Kunst*, 1923, pls. 42, 48).

738. Sterling, 1972, p. 27.

739. For a contrary view see Gardet, *Apocalypse*, 1969, p. XXI f., and Edmunds, 1970, p. 321 n. 10.

740. See, for example, the scenes in the *Antiquités judaïques* fr. 247, fol. 213v and in the *Hours of Etienne Chevalier, Sts. Martin* and *Apollonia* (ed. Sterling and Schaefer, 1971, nos. 36 and 45). The celestial throng in Fouquet's *Trinity* seems to be reminiscent of the choir of angels in Paul's *Fall of the Rebel Angels* (Fig. 577).

741. Although Sterling suggested (*Hours of Etienne Chevalier*, 1971, p. 8) that the *Boucicaut Hours* was in Tours in the possession of the Maréchal's family when Fouquet was forming his style, the historical circumstances seem to contradict this view (Meiss, *Das Stundenbuch des Maréchal de Boucicaut, Faksimile-Ausgabe*, Berlin, in press).

See Sterling, *loc. cit.*, p. 14, for illuminating comments on the relation of Fouquet to the Boucicaut Master and the Limbourgs.

742. Lowinsky, 1954, pp. 510, 543; Reese, *Middle Ages*, 1940, p. 331 ff.

743. Panofsky, *Netherlandish Painting*, 1953, p. 150, taking the term from the later (*ca.* 1475) treatise of Tinctoris, who reapplied the term to Dufay and Binchois and to the period beginning *ca.* 1425.

744. *Ibid.*, p. 1 ff.

NOTES TO CHAPTER VIII

1. Nordenfalk, *Kung praktiks*, 1955, pp. 61, 94, and Meiss, *Art Bull.*, 1956, p. 196. I believe all the six manuscripts in Nordenfalk's list belong to the group, but Ghent and Morgan 804 are inferior (see Catalogue of Workshops).

2. *Late XIV Century*, p. 141, figs. 335, 384, 385.

3. See, for example, his miniatures in Longon, Brit. Mus., Royal 20 C V or Paris, Bibl. nat., fr. 12459. For manuscripts by the Boethius illuminator see the Catalogue of Workshops, Apocalypse Master.

4. The Boethius illuminator, however, worked with the Boucicaut, Rohan and Bedford workshops. See Catalogue of Workshops.

5. Bibl. nat., fr. 1454. See bibliography of this manuscript in Catalogue of Workshops, and for a reference to another learned text that belonged to Colin see Guiffrey, *Inventaires*, II, 1896, p. 338.

6. See also Meiss, *Art Bull.*, 1956, fig. 12.

7. See Catalogue of Workshops.

8. *Late XIV Century*, figs. 380, 381, 387.

9. Could he have been added as the name-saint of Jean de Berry? Perhaps the Baptist refers to Christ as the Lamb, and is thus related to the Apocalypse.

10. Bibl. nat., néerl. 3. The text of this manuscript does not belong to the same group as the Morgan and Chantilly manuscripts. See Hontoy, 1946–47, p. 289 ff. and Panofsky, *Netherlandish Painting*, 1953, p. 110 f. I cannot share Panofsky's unbounded enthusiasm for this manuscript.

11. See, for example, the *Temptation* in a Psalter, late

thirteenth century, Brit. Mus., Add. 16975, fol. 13.

12. Brussels, Bibl. roy., ms. 9295, fol. 41v. See also Boulogne-sur-mer, Bibl. municipale, ms. 55, fol. 38v (Fig. 520). Both of these manuscripts are copies of the *Cité de Dieu*.

13. The corresponding miniature in Morgan 133, fol. 56v, does not illustrate the text but the commentary, and represents a Last Judgment.

14. See above, p. 138.

15. See below, p. 275 f.

16. *Belles Heures*, 1953, pp. 28, 64, with reference to *Alexander at Table* on fol. 24v. Porcher dated Chantilly 28 *ca.* 1420.

17. See also Catalogue of Manuscripts.

18. Durrieu, *Rev. de l'art a. et m.*, 1912, p. 22; *Heures d'Angers*, 1912, p. 21. Sterling, in Białostocki et al., *Spätmittelalter*, 1972, p. 181, dated the *Rohan Hours ca.* 1418 and thought that the manuscript was probably painted in Paris.

19. Miss Heimann (1932, p. 24) found that the Rohan Master participated in the painting of God the Father and Gabriel while an assistant executed the Virgin and prophet.

20. Heimann, 1937, p. 83 f. Miss Heimann believed that neither of the two painters she found in the manuscript was the Rohan Master, but only assistants. She saw one illuminator, to whom she ascribed most of the miniatures in the Hours of the Virgin, as close to the "Master of 1402"; the other, who painted the Suffrages, seemed to her closer to the Rohan Master.

21. Although costume in this period has not been sufficiently studied to provide dependable evidence, we note that Jeanne du Peschin wears *cornettes* (fol. 131v).

22. For arms of Peschin see La Chenaye-Desbois and Badier, *Dictionnaire de la noblesse*, XV, 1869, col. 730.

23. Fols. 151v–152v.

24. Anselme, *Histoire généalogique*, Paris, VI, 1730, p. 345.

25. Pocquet du Haut-Jussé, *La France*, 1959, p. 130 no. 293.

26. For the *Ranshaw Hours* see Catalogue of Workshops, Troyes Master, Chicago, coll. Fielding Marshall. The Troyes workshop painted only three of the known miniatures of this dismembered manuscript.

27. See Catalogue of Workshops.

28. These Books of Hours are: Amiens Lescalopier 17; Baltimore, Walters 741; Chantilly 67 (1371); Chicago, Spitz Coll.; Victoria & Albert Museum, ms. 1647–1902; Ohio, Chillicothe, Ross County Art Museum; Arsenal 647/Princeton, Garrett ms. 48. For all these manuscripts see the Catalogue of Workshops.

29. Already supplanted by the kneeling Virgin in the *Brussels Hours* by Jacquemart. For a discussion of this change see *Late XIV Century*, p. 215.

30. For the manuscripts incorrectly ascribed, in our opinion, to the Rohan workshop or to followers see the end of the section on this workshop in the Catalogue of Workshops.

The following manuscripts were dated between 1405 and 1415 by Porcher, *Rohan Hours*, 1959, p. 8 f. He listed them in what he judged to be their chronological order—an order which we preserve in the following list. None of these manuscripts seems to us before 1415.

Paris, Bibl. nat., fr. 15393–94; fr. 20320; fr. 2662; fr. 2664; Toulouse, Bibl. municipale, ms. 511; Vienna, Nationalbibl., ms. 2573; Dresden, Sächsische Landesbibl., ms. Oc 61; Paris, Bibl. nat., fr. 22531; fr. 226; fr. 16995; fr. 812; lat. 14245.

He ascribed the following Books of Hours to the Rohan atelier during the same period: Paris, Bibl. Sainte-Geneviève, ms. 1278; Paris, Bibl. de l'Arsenal, ms. 647 and Princeton, University Library, Garrett 48; Amiens, Bibl. municipale, ms. Lescalopier 17; Cambridge, Harvard College Library, Richardson ms. 42; Baltimore, Walters Art Gallery, ms. 741 (formerly Eisemann Coll.); Toronto, Royal Ontario Museum (Lee of Fareham Coll.); Chantilly, Musée Condé, ms. 67; Ohio, Chillicothe, Ross County Art Museum (formerly McKell Coll.); London, Brit. Mus., Harley 2934; Paris, Bibl. nat., lat. 13262.

We have not seen the following manuscripts ascribed by Porcher to this early period: Brussels, Bibl. royale, ms. II, 88; Cat. Boerner, November 28, 1912; London, Sotheby, June 28, 1948, lot 219; London, Sotheby, December 6, 1954, lot 43; Oxford, Bodleian Library, Buchanan e. 9; Paris, Pierre Berès, Cat. 57, no. 8; Stonyhurst College, ms. 1. Buchanan e. 9 is dated in the second quarter of the century by Pächt and Alexander, *Illuminated Manuscripts*, I, 1966, no. 678.

31. Heimann, 1932, pp. 3–5, judged the Ste. Geneviève Hours to be relatively early, whereas Panofsky, in *Studies Porter*, 1939, II, p. 490, thought the manuscript was later, after the Princeton-Arsenal Horae, partly because it combined in one miniature, "illogically," the Descent from the Cross and the Lamentation. Iconography, however, varies unpredictably in the Rohan manuscripts so that it is not a reliable guide to date. Neither of these authors knew both the *Giac Hours* and the Harley manuscript.

32. See the *Boucicaut Master*, fig. 29.

33. See the *Presentation* in Baltimore, Walters ms. 741, fol. 50; for the *Presentation* in the *Boucicaut Hours* see *ibid.*, fig. 34. For the Old Testament connotation of the dome in the *De Buz Hours* see Panofsky, 1949, p. 170 ff. The Muslim shrine, the Dome of the Rock, was built in the precinct of the Temple and was often later confused with it.

34. For the history of this structure see Meiss, *Gaz. B.-A.*, 1963.

35. For scenes of the *Coronation of the Virgin* by the Boucicaut workshop see Meiss, *Boucicaut Master*, figs. 36, 268, 289.

36. See the *Boucicaut Master*, pp. 96, 99 f.

37. See Catalogue of Workshops.

38. Prusias, for instance, on fol. 143 appears in Arsenal 5193 but not in Jean de Berry's Boccaccio in Geneva.

39. *Late XIV Century*, p. 93, fig. 503.

40. Heimann, 1932, p. 2 f., gave 1409–1416 as the range. Porcher in Bibl. nat., 1955, p. 85, dated the manuscript *ca.* 1415. See Guiffrey, *Inventaires*, I, p. CLXXIX.

41. This miniature of Hercules and the one of King Laius (Figs. 848, 851) were singled out by Durrieu, wrongly we believe, as works of the Rohan Master himself (*Rev. de l'art a. et m.*, 1912, p. 172 ff).

42. See above, n. 28.

43. Panofsky, in *Studies Porter*, 1939.

44. Fol. 201.

45. For the early history of the subject see Meiss, 1966, pp. 360–362, and *Late XIV Century*, p. 62.

46. As Panofsky, 1949, p. 177, has pointed out. He suggested the transparent loin cloth refers to death also.

47. In addition to the observations about this relation already made, the Trinity on a crescent in the Ste. Geneviève Hours, fol. 21v, may derive from the *Belles Heures*, fol. 155 (Meiss and Beatson, *Belles Heures*, 1974, fol. 155).

48. These relations were observed by D. Miner, Baltimore, Walters Art Gallery [1962], pp. 60–62. The averted Virgin in the Flight, however, was introduced in French illumination well before the *Belles Heures* (see Fig. 502). Historians have usually not proposed a precise date for the *De Buz Hours*. Sterling, in Białostocki et al., *Spätmittelalter*, 1972, p. 180, suggested *ca.* 1425, ten years later than the date we have inferred.

49. Heimann, 1932, p. 10, dated the Fitzwilliam manuscript *ca.* 1420; Porcher, *op. cit.*, inclined to *ca.* 1415.

50. *Boucicaut Master*, figs. 262, 265–267.

51. The armorials in the borders are a later addition. See the Catalogue of Manuscripts.

52. See Leroquais, *Livres d'heures*, 1927, I, p. XXVII f.

53. Panofsky, "Imago pietatis," 1927, p. 261 ff., and Eisler, 1969.

54. Haseloff, *Psalterillustration*, 1938, p. 66.

55. Porcher, *Belles Heures*, 1953, p. 27 n. 52; Fry, 1905, and Wescher, 1946.

56. See, for example, fol. 192.

57. See also, for example, fols. 20 and 24.

58. Panofsky, 1949, p. 171.

59. See especially *St. Mark*, fol. 18v of the Fitzwilliam Hours. St. Matthew in the *Rohan Hours*, however, reads (Fig. 875). His lectern derives from *Diocrès* in the *Belles Heures* (Fig. 423).

60. *Late XIV Century*, p. 309.

61. Van Gelder, "Der Teufel," 1972. Another early example, not yet cited, is in the *Legende dorée*, fr. 242, fol. 18v, just after 1402. It is, in fact, the earliest representation of the devil in the very act of upsetting the ink; in the Walters Bible he has already done so.

62. Toynbee, 1946.

63. See Catalogue of Manuscripts.

64. Durrieu, "Les armoiries," 1908, p. 102 ff. We wish to thank, for his extremely generous assistance, M. Jean-Bernard de Vaivre of the Institut d'histoire des textes, specialist in the heraldry of this period.

65. See Catalogue of Manuscripts.

66. *Boucicaut Master*, fig. 158. The same composition is used for the illustration of the Office of the Dead in the *Heures d'Angers*.

67. This was the latest view of Durrieu, *Heures d'Angers*, 1912, p. 17. The same arms, *tiercé en pal*, were, however, used by Louis I d'Anjou; see Anselme, *Histoire généalogique*, I, 1726, p. 227. For the arms of Louis II and Louis III, see *ibid.*, p. 129 ff.

68. Durrieu, "Les armoiries," 1908, pp. 102–114.

69. Ring, *French Painting* [1949], p. 199 no. 63; C. Jacques [Sterling], *Peintres du moyen âge* [1941], cat. p. 7 no. 16. Porcher, 1961, ascribed the water color to the Rohan Master—a tempting but not really convincing hypothesis.

Heimann, 1932, p. 13 f., and Panofsky, *Netherlandish Painting*, 1953, p. 171, incorrectly ascribed the portrait of Louis II in lat. 1156A to the period after 1434 when additions were made for René. The portrait may not, to be sure, have been planned originally, because the color of the background is visible beneath it, but the addition was made by the illuminators of the first campaign.

It is true that the script on this folio, as well as the first line of the verso, is somewhat smaller and browner, so that the miniature and the text may represent a second moment within the first campaign. The borders are the usual ones.

70. For the history of the water color see Bouchot, 1886; Ring, *op. cit.*, p. 199 no. 63; for lat. 1156A see Leroquais, *Livres d'heures*, 1927, I, pp. 64–67, and Catalogue of Manuscripts. For an Italian drawing that seems to be a portrait of Louis II see Degenhart, *Corpus*, 1968, no. 185, pl. 205b.

71. *Late XIV Century*, p. 74.

72. Will of 1417, April 27. Paris, Arch. nat. P 1334^{17}. Pièce 52, fol. XI.

73. Heimann, 1932, p. 16.

74. *Ibid.*, p. 15, figs. 12, 13.

75. *Boucicaut Master*, fig. 128.

76. On fol. 26v angels bear two banners. The dexter banner now shows gules, 7 mascles or. These are the arms of Rohan in their early form (the mascles were later increased to 9), last borne by Jean II, vicomte de Rohan from 1461–1516 (see Anselme, *Histoire généalogique*, 3rd ed., IV, 1728, p. 57 f., and Durrieu, *Rev. de l'art a. et m.*, 1912, p. 161). Because the incompleted sinister banner has a gold ground Durrieu suggested that it was being prepared for the arms of either the wife of Jean II's predecessor Alain IX (m. Marie de Lorraine after 1428) or of Yolande de Laval, wife of Alain's son, who predeceased him in 1449 (Durrieu, *op. cit.*, p. 161 f.). Durrieu, followed by Leroquais (*Livres d'heures*, 1927, I, p. 290), believed the arms to be original but Laborde (*Bible moralisée*, V, 1927, p. 118 f.) proved that they were added later.

77. Not infrequently animals respond to a supernatural apparition (see the dog in Taddeo Gaddi's *Annunciation to the Shepherds* in S. Croce, Florence), but normally the principal figures do also.

78. Fouquet, in *Heures d'Etienne Chevalier*, and later illuminators sometimes inserted armorials and script on a formal tablet in the field of the miniature.

79. Porcher, 1945, p. 1 ff. In addition to the examples cited in the text see n. 93a and, for instance, *St. George* fol. 223, *St. Martin* fol. 225, the *Burial* fol. 185 and the *Mass for the Dead* fol. 192. *St. Matthew* (Fig. 875) depends upon *Diocrès teaching* in the *Belles Heures* (Fig. 423). There are occasional copies of miniatures of the *Belles Heures* in late manuscripts by Rohan followers; see, for example, Lyon, Bibl. municipale 5140, fol. 67 (*Stoning of St. Stephen*).

For comments on another hypothesis of the relation of the *Belles Heures* to the *Rohan Hours* advanced after this book was in the press see below, n. 93a.

80. Paris, Bibl. nat., fr. 9561. See Meiss, *Late XIV Century*, pp. 27–29, and Bologna, *Pittori di Napoli*, 1969, pp. 311–320. Bologna convincingly identifies the chief illuminator of the Bible with the painter of a fresco cycle in S. Pietro a Maiella, Naples.

81. The *Histoire ancienne*, Brit. Mus., Royal 20 D 1. (Fig 275).

82. My observation of this relationship was published by Panofsky, 1939, p. 491 n. 42. See *Late XIV Century*, figs. 327, 328.

83. Durrieu, *Heures d'Angers*, 1912.

84. Beaucourt, *Charles VII*, I, 1881, pp. 15 ff., 39, 68. For the chateau see *Late XIV Century*, p. 37 f.

85. *Ibid.*, I, pp. 70 ff.

86. *Ibid.*, I, pp. 59, 118, 185, 194, 235; II, p. 61 ff.

87. See, for example, the *Heures de Marguerite d'Orléans*, lat. 1156 B, which is discussed on p. 275; a Book of Hours illustrated by a provincial follower of the Rohan Master for Jean de Montauban, lat. 18026; a Book of Hours for the use of Nantes, executed for a member of the Quirisec family of Brittany now in the Pierpont Morgan Library, M 63; and another Morgan horae connected with Brittany, M 865.

88. "1417–1418. Madame Marie d'Anjou dauphine de Viennois duchesse de Touraine et de Berry. Le roy luy donna 200 escus d'or pour emploier en lachapt d'un livre a la devotion de la ditte Dame." (Bibl. nat., ms. Bourgogne 100, p. 792.)

89. What negative evidence there is should be recorded also. Yolande's household accounts, kept by her treasurer Jean Porcher at Angers, contain no entries for the purchase of manuscripts or works of art and they record no payments to scribes or painters (Paris, Arch. nat. K.K. 243 and 244). However they are not complete. The accounts start in 1408, but Porcher explains that during the lifetime of Louis II the two households were combined when Yolande was with him, which explains certain gaps. After the death of Louis in April 1417 the accounts continue until 1427, with a break from June 1419 to June 1423 when Yolande was in the South; her accounts were then kept at Aix-en-Provence. Yolande's will of 12 November 1442 (Arch. nat. P. 1334^{17}, cote 52) does not mention books or valuables, apart from a single necklace and some tapestries,

including the famous Apocalypse hangings. She explains that the large number of *meubles*, gold, silver, vessels and jewels left by her husband were used either to pay his debts, for defense of the realm, or for the wars of her son Louis III in Italy (fol. XXXI).

90. Durrieu (*Rev. de l'art a. et m.*, 1912, p. 161 f.) ascribed the eleven full-page miniatures, the *Madonna*, the *Trinity*, and *St. Andrew* to the master. Heimann, 1932, p. 17 ff., reduced the group to the *Office of the Dead*, the *Virgin and St. John*, the *Last Judgment*, and the *Madonna* (in part). My own view is almost the same.

91. For the history of the illustration of the Office of the Dead see *Boucicaut Master*, pp. 30–33, figs. 135–174. In the miniature by the Rohan Master the figure of St. Michael resembles the uppermost angel at the right in the Sienese *Fall of the Rebel Angels* (Fig. 666), as Laclotte, 1969, p. 11, observed.

92. Oberman, *Harvest*, 1963, pp. 43 ff., 132 ff., 168 ff., 331 ff.; Courtenay, 1971, p. 116 ff.

93. For this interpretation see Thomas in Meiss and Thomas, *The Rohan Master, A Book of Hours*, fol. 154 (in press).

93a. In an essay available to me only after this book was in the press Marcel Thomas proposes that the Rohan Master was not the head of the workshop that produced the *Rohan Hours* but a well-known artist invited to contribute a few miniatures to it (see Meiss and Thomas, *The Rohan Master, A Book of Hours*, Introduction II, in press). For this hypothesis M. Thomas gives two reasons. Pointing to F. Avril's interesting identification in the manuscript of two scribes—one (A) wrote most of the text preceding the Hours of the Virgin and all of it after the Office of the Dead, the other (B) the remaining central part of the manuscript—M. Thomas says that the Rohan Master painted only in the sections written by B, whereas two other illuminators, working quite independently, painted the sections written by A. M. Thomas admits that there is one exception to this correlation of scribes and painters: the Suffrages by A include the miniature of St. Andrew, which he ascribes to the Rohan Master. Since in my opinion this miniature is not by the master, it presents no problem, but I find many others because my judgment of the contribution of the chief artist differs from that of M. Thomas (who follows the opinion of Durrieu expressed in 1912—see above, n. 90). As I have stated above *Sts. John* and *Matthew*, in A's section, seem to me designed by the Rohan Master. To this group I would add 4 (*March*), 5v (*April*), 7 (*May*), 16 (*November*), and 210 (*Trinity*), all in A's section and designed, in my opinion, by the Rohan Master. On the other hand B's section contains much by associates of the chief master. They not only completed miniatures he had designed or even in part painted but executed many miniatures more or less independently, such as fols. 38, 41, 90, 167, 173, 176, 182, 192, 196. The deep influence of the Rohan Master on these illuminators remains unexplained by the proposal of M. Thomas. Equally unexplained are the continuities from the earlier to the later manuscripts of the Rohan group, including miniatures by the Rohan Master himself.

Thus my first consideration of the hypothesis of M. Thomas leads me to doubt that the Rohan Master was as independent of the production of the book as he suggests. The second reason advanced by M. Thomas to support his hypothesis is equally interesting but not, I think, quite acceptable: the borrowings from the *Belles Heures*—a much earlier manuscript—never appear in the miniatures by the Rohan Master but only in those of the other illuminators. In accordance with his own sytlistic classification that is largely but not entirely correct: the recumbent peasant in the *Flight into Egypt* by the Rohan Master is taken from *July* in the *Belles Heures*. In the text above, where I pointed to this relation, the design of the composition is ascribed to the Rohan Master. As I said above he seems to me to have designed also *St. Matthew*, and the same may be said of *November*, and probably *March*, *April*, and *September*, all influenced by the *Belles Heures*. (These miniatures are all, too, in gatherings written by A.) I am not therefore convinced that independence of the *Belles Heures* is a reason for separating the Rohan Master completely from the production of most of the *Rohan Hours*. The text above, however, emphasizes the peculiarity of the practice of the later Rohan Master as an illuminator and I said at the beginning that much remains to be learned about it.

94. Ring, *French Painting* [1949], p. 204. The panel now measures $37\frac{1}{2} \times 40\frac{3}{4}$ in. Mme. A. N. Rollas, *conservateur* of the museum, has kindly informed us that the panel was found in Laon, Rue Fosse Saint-Julien. The haloes of the apostles and the decorative motifs in the gold background are raised in relief (Fig. 887), a technique used also in Campin's early panel (Figs. 758–760).

95. Since this hardware appears at the center of the panel it may have been a lock and perhaps a bolt rather than a hinge. The wood below the "lock" remained

unpainted. Panofsky, *Netherlandish Painting*, 1953, p. 74 n. 4, spoke of the painting as part of a diptych.

96. The design, especially the architecture, of the painting of the apostles proves that the panel was originally about as wide as it is now. It surely was cut, however, at the bottom and probably also at the top (I have not, however, been able to inspect the outer edges of the panel when removed from the present frame).

97. A long wedge of new wood has been inserted in the figures of the donor and the saint; it is more clearly visible on the side of the apostles. A smaller wedge was inserted in front of Gabriel.

98. Meiss, 1935. The attribution to the Rohan Master I proposed in that article has been generally accepted. See Panofsky in *Studies Porter*, 1939, p. 479; Ring, *French Painting* [1949], p. 204 no. 90; and Sterling, in Białostocki et al., *Spätmittelalter*, 1972, p. 181.

99. For an outline of the representational tradition see Meiss, 1935, p. 71 ff.

100. 23.4×15.4 cm.

101. To my astonishment I discovered this copy when studying the collection of the Baron Maurice de Rothschild in 1936, just after the appearance of my article on the drawing by the Rohan Master.

102. *Légende dorée*, ed. de Wyzewa, Paris, 1929, p. 260.

103. Meiss, 1935, p. 74.

104. Plummer, *Hours of Catherine of Cleves*, n.d., nos. 83, 84. Some of the costumes as well as the design of several figures suggest this possibility.

105. Paris, Bibl. nat. (Porcher), 1955, p. 113 no. 241. The miniatures in this manuscript copied from the *Belles Heures* are: fol. 89, *Adoration of Magi*; fol. 133, *Betrayal*; fol. 135, *Christ before Pilate*; fol. 175, *St. Catherine*.

106. Durrieu, *Heures d'Angers*, 1912, p. 17, spoke of his "caractère large de travail."

107. I traced this history in 1935, but I then accepted the current dating of *ca.* 1402 for the *Breviary of Jean sans Peur*, and I was unaware of the examples in the *Belles Heures*, in fr. 414 and in Pucelle's *Heures de Jeanne d'Evreux* (Figs. 890–892). In his *Belles Heures*, 1953, p. 19 f., Porcher linked with my group the miniatures in the *Belles Heures*, lat. 1156B, and the *Hours of Catherine of Cleves* (Figs. 894, 895). He suggested the origin of the figure might be Netherlandish.

This figure is rather similar in posture to the one in Lorenzo Ghiberti's north door, which Krautheimer connects with a Roman fallen hunter (*Ghiberti*, 1956, pl. 34 and fig. 105). The latter, however, takes us still further from our French examples.

108. See above, p. 138 f.

109. See *Late XIV Century*, p. 311.

110. Yolande was married at Arles in 1400, and thereafter occasionally joined her husband in Provence (Lecoy de la Marche, *René*, I, 1875, p. 25 ff.). Her daughter Yolande was born at Arles in 1412 (Anselme, *Histoire généalogique*, 3rd ed., I, 1726, p. 230).

111. See also the Catalogue of Workshops. Manuscripts in which the Rohan workshop collaborated with the Boucicaut workshop are: London, Brit. Mus., Harley 2940; London, Coll. D. and J. Zwemmer, Book of Hours. With the Cité des Dames workshop the Rohan workshop illuminated Paris, Bibl. nat., fr. 226. With illuminators of the Bedford Trend the Rohan workshop produced the following manuscripts: Dresden, Sächsische Landesbibl. ms. Oc 61; Paris, Bibl. nat., fr. 226, fr. 20320, fr. 22531, lat. 14245. The Rohan workshop collaborated with illuminators influenced by the Apocalypse Master in: Oxford, Bodleian Library, Douce 202–3; Paris, Bibl. nat., fr. 2664, fr. 15393–94, fr. 20320.

112. *Netherlandish Painting*, 1953, p. 74.

113. Heimann, 1932, p. 47 f. An example of *ca.* 1400, which is Flemish or from northeastern France, is found in the *Pèlerinage* in Brussels, Bibl. royale, ms. 10176–8, fol. 280v, with John, as in the Rohan miniatures, looking back and up.

114. For the gift of the *Petites Heures* to Robinet's wife see *Late XIV Century*, p. 156. For Robinet as a "serviteur" of Charles VII and as a donor to the King of a tapestry see Beaucourt, *Charles VII*, I, 1881, p. 93 n. 2.

115. S. Leathes, in *Cambridge Modern History*, New York, I, 1907, p. 384.

NOTES TO APPENDIX C

by O. Neugebauer

1. For the dates and arrangement cf. the text of this book and of the *Late XIV Century*.
2. Almagest II 13 (ed. Heiberg, I p. 186 f.)—Notation: a semicolon separates degrees or hours from minutes, or in general, integers from sexagesimal fractions.
3. I quote from a printed edition of the Alfonsine Tables (Venice, 1518) in my possession.
4. E.g. 8;46 instead of 8;47 (Jan. 11) or 50 instead of 40 in the entries for April 27 to 29.
5. Cf., e.g., my Exact Sciences in Antiquity(2) p. 158 f.
6. A table of this type is, e.g., preserved in the set of the "Alfonsine Tables" Bib. Nat. Lat. 7295 A (fol. 135/6) of which my colleague G. J. Toomer has a copy. The numerical details differ, however, for the majority of entries, in spite of the identity of the main parameters.
7. These dates are essentially correct; cf., e.g., Ginzel, Handbuch d. math. u. techn. Chronologie III, p. 114, who gives for A.D. 1400 for the equinoxes March 11 and September 14, December 13 and June 13 for the solstices.
8. Since the apsides of the solar orbit nearly coincide with the solstices no appreciable asymmetry is caused by the solar anomaly for the length of daylight with respect to the solstices; hence the same curve in Fig. 1 represents both halves of the year.
9. It would be easy to correct the obviously wrong data in Table II for the months IX to XII. The error is caused by the difficulties in the relative spacing of the divisions in the outermost and innermost ring.
10. The maximum equation in the Alfonsine tables is 2;10° (p. 59 b of the printed edition, Venice, 1518) and explains the slightly exaggerated variation in the solar velocity.
11. "New Moon" means here and in the following always conjunction, not first visibility as in most of the ancient lunar calendars.
12. We shall presently return to the specific situation prevailing in the last year of the cycle.
13. Examples: In the Petites Heures the entries for February 4 to 13 and for April 7 to 15 are all one line too low. The same holds in the Grandes Heures for April 7 to 13. Both calendars write 14, 3, 11 instead of 15, 4, 12 in September 12 to 15 and in November 10 to 13.
14. Scribal errors in Notre Dame: May 6 and 12; in the Belles Heures: Sept. 24 and Oct. 4.
15. This also agrees with the alternative pattern given in Ginzel, Hdb. III, p. 136.
16. A list of the Golden Numbers for all years from A.D. 300 to 1794 is given in Ginzel, Handb. d. mathem. u. techn. Chronologie vol. III p. 393–405.
17. Cf. H. H. Goldstine, New and Full Moons, 1001 B.C. to A.D. 1651. Amer. Philos. Soc., Memoirs 94 (1973).
18. Left blank in the miniatures for January, April, May, and August. A scribal error occurred for September 8 with f = 6 instead p = 15.
19. Around noon time in western Europe.
20. Cf. Van Wijk, Le nombre d'or, La Haye, 1936, p. 39 ff.
21. This leads to a mean synodic month of about 29.53 days which is quite accurate (sexagesimally: 29;31, 51,3, . . .).
22. Cf. above p. 428: January 19 instead January 20.
23. Neither the date of the invention of the "golden numbers" nor of the terminology is certain; cf. Van Wijk, pp. 29–33.
24. The "Belles Heures" write once (Jan. 1) "*D. eg.*".
25. Cf., e.g., Thorndike, History of Magic . . . I, pp. 685–688; p. 695 f.
26. There exist many references to "Egyptian Days"; cf. for the standard literature e.g., Degrassi, Fasti et Elogia (Inscriptiones Italiae, vol. 13, 1963), p. 362 f. Furthermore W. E. Van Wijk, Le nombre d'or (1936) pp. 96–98; R. Dozy-Ch. Pellat, Le Calendrier de Cordoue (1961), p. 26 note 2 and p. 34 note 3.
27. Cf. the diagram given by H. Bober, J. of the Warburg and Courtauld Institutes 11 (1948), p. 29.
28. In the *Très Riches Heures*, 1969, this figure is assumed to be female. This not only contradicts the whole iconographic tradition of the Zodiac Man but also the representation of women here and in the calendar miniatures where women are always shown with long hair (cf., e.g., Gemini and Virgo).
29. Cf. note 27.
30. Cf., e.g., papyri from the second century A.D. (P. Mich. 149; PSI 1289) or the commentary of Porphyri (3rd cent.) to the Tetrabiblos (CCAG 5, 4 p. 216 f.). For the Latin literature cf. e.g., J. de Vreese, Petron 39 und die Astrologie (Paris, 1927) pp. 198–202.
31. Cf. Bouché-Leclerq, L'astrologie grecque (Paris,

1899) p. 154, p. 169; Boll-Bezold-Gundel, Sternglaube und Sterndeutung[4] (Leipzig, 1931) p. 54; Ptolemy, Tetrabiblos I, 18 (Loeb Classical Library, 1940). I do not know, however, a treatise which enumerates the qualities of the triplicities exactly in the order adopted here.

32. Cf., e.g., the two figures shown in Bober's article Pl. 4, c and d.

33. Useful references not only to ancient but also to medieval representations are found in Boll-Gundel's article "Sternbilder . . . bei Griechen und Römern" in Roscher, Lexikon der griechischen und römischen Mythologie VI (1937), col. 867–1072.

34. Also in the Belles Heures for December.

BIBLIOGRAPHY

The principal entries for all catalogues of exhibitions and of permanent holdings of libraries and museums are listed topographically. For instance *Arte lombarda dai Visconti agli Sforza* appears under Milan, Palazzo Reale.

KEY TO ABBREVIATIONS

Bull. de Gand=*Bulletin de la Société d'histoire et d'archéologie de Gand.*

Bull. SFRMP=*Bulletin de la Société Française de Reproductions de Manuscrits à Peintures.*

Comptes rendus=*Paris, Académie des Inscriptions et Belles-lettres. Comptes rendus.*

Gaz. B.-A.=*Gazette des Beaux-Arts.*

Mémoires=*Paris, Académie des Inscriptions et Belles-lettres. Mémoires.*

Rev. belge=*Revue belge d'archéologie et d'histoire de l'art.*

Rev. de l'art a. et m.=*Revue de l'art ancien et moderne.*

Walters Journal=*Journal of the Walters Art Gallery.*

Warburg Journal=*Journal of the Warburg and Courtauld Institutes.*

Adhémar H., *see* Paris, Musée du Louvre.

Adhémar, J., *Influences antiques dans l'art du moyen âge français*, London, 1939.

Adorisio, A. M., "Un messale miniato donato a Jean de Berry ed oggi nella Biblioteca Casanatense di Roma," in *Miscellanea in memoria di Giorgio Cencetti*, Turin, in press.

Alexander, J. G., *see* Pächt and Alexander.

Amadei, E., *Le torri di Roma*, Rome, 1932.

Androuet du Cerceau, J., *Les plus excellents bastiments de France*, Paris, I, 1576; II, 1579.

Anselme, P., *Histoire généalogique et chronologique de la maison royale de France, des pairs, grands officiers de la couronne et de la maison du roy*, Paris, 3rd ed., 1726–1733. 9v.

Arano, L. C., *see* Gengaro.

Armellini, M., *Le chiese di Roma dal secolo IV al XIX*, Rome, 1941.

Armstrong, C. A. J., "The Language Question in the Low Countries: The Use of French and Dutch by the Dukes of Burgundy and Their Administration," in *Europe in the Late Middle Ages*, ed. J. R. Hale, J. R. L. Highfield, and B. Smalley, Evanston, 1965, pp. 386–409.

Aubert, H., "Notice sur les manuscrits Petau, conservés à la Bibliothèque de Genève," *Bibl. École des Chartes*, LXX, 1909, pp. 247–302, 471–522; LXXII, 1911, pp. 279–313, 556–599.

Aubert, H., "Les principaux manuscrits à peintures de la Bibliothèque publique et universitaire de Genève," *Bull. SFRMP*, II, 1912, pp. 55–107.

Augustinus Aurelius, *La cité de Dieu*, trans. and commentary by Raoul de Praelles, Abbeville, Jean Dupré and Pierre Gerard, 1486–1487. 2v.

Austin. University of Texas. *Gothic and Renaissance Illuminated Manuscripts from Texas Collections*, Austin, 1971.

Avril, F., "Trois manuscrits napolitains des collections de Charles V et de Jean de Berry," *Bibl. École des Chartes*, CXXVII, 1969 (1970), pp. 291–328.

Avril, F., "Une Bible historiale de Charles V," *Jahrbuch der Hamburger Kunstsammlungen*, XIV–XV, 1970, pp. 45–76.

Avril, F., "Trois manuscrits de l'entourage de Jean Pucelle," *Revue de l'art*, IX, 1970, pp. 37–48.

Avril, F., "Les Limbourg," in *Encyclopaedia universalis*, IX, 1971, p. 1024 f.

Avril, F., *see also* Paris, Bibliothèque nationale.

Badier, *see* La Chenaye-Desbois and Badier.

Baldass, L., *Jan van Eyck*, New York [1952].

Baltimore. Walters Art Gallery. *Illuminated Books of the Middle Ages and Renaissance . . .* (D. Miner), Baltimore, 1949.

Baltimore, Walters Art Gallery. *The International Style* (mss. ed. by D. Miner; much else by P. Verdier), [Baltimore, 1962].

Baltrušaitis, J., *Le moyen âge fantastique*, Paris, 1955.

Baltrušaitis, J., *Réveils et prodiges; le Gothique fantastique* [Paris, 1960].

Barasch, M., "Masks in Renaissance Art," in *Studies in the Drama*, ed. A. Sachs, Jerusalem, 1967.

Barker, J., *Manuel II Palaeologus (1391–1425); a Study in Late Byzantine Statesmanship*, New Brunswick [1969].

Bastard, Auguste comte de, *Peintures et ornements des manuscrits . . . depuis le iv*[e] *siècle jusqu'à la fin du xvi*[e], Paris, 1832–1869.

Baxandall, M., *Painting and Experience in Fifteenth-Century Italy*, Oxford, 1972.

Bayonne. Musée Bonnat. *Les dessins italiens de la collection Bonnat* (J. Bean), Paris, 1960.

Bazin, G., *Le Mont Saint-Michel*, Paris, 1933.

Bean, J., *see* Bayonne, Musée Bonnat.

Beauchamp, R. de, "Note sur le château de Bicêtre," *Bull. de la Société des Antiquaires de l'Ouest*, x, 1904, p. 135.

Beaucourt, G. du Fresne de, *Histoire de Charles VII*, Paris, 1881–1891. 6v.

Beazley, C. R., *The Dawn of Modern Geography*, London, 1897–1906. 3v.

Becker, P. A., "Christine de Pizan," *Zeitschrift für französische Sprache und Literatur*, LIV, 1930, pp. 9–164.

Bedini, S. A., and F. R. Maddison, "Mechanical Universe: The Astrarium of Giovanni de' Dondi," *Transactions of the American Philosophical Society*, N.S. LVI, 1966, pt. 5, pp. 3–69.

Beer, R., *see* Vienna, Nationalbibliothek.

Behling, L., *Die Pflanze in der mittelalterlichen Tafelmalerei*, Weimar, 1957.

Bell, D., *Le songe du vieil pèlerin de Philippe de Mézières*, Geneva, 1955.

Bellaguet, L., *see* Religieux de Saint-Denys.

The Belles Heures of Jean, Duke of Berry, New York (and other eds.), 1974, *see* Meiss and Beatson.

Belon, P., *Les observations de plusieurs singularitez et choses mémorables, trouvées en Grece, Asie, Judée, Egypte, Arabie, et autres pays estranges, redigées en trois livres*, Paris, 1554.

Bénédictins de Paris, *Vie des saints et des bienheureux selon l'ordre du calendrier avec l'historique des fêtes*, Paris, XI, 1954.

Berchorius, P., *Dictionarii seu repertorii moralis*, Venice, 1583.

Berchorius, P., *Reductorium morale, Liber XV, cap. ii–xv, "Ovidius moralizatus" naar de Parijse druk van 1509: Metamorphosis Ovidiana Moraliter a Magistro Thoma Walleys . . . explanata* (Instituut voor Laat Latijn der Rijksuniversiteit), Werkmateriaal (2), Utrecht, 1962.

Berchorius, P., *De formis figurisque deorum* (*Reductorium morale, Liber XV: Ovidius moralizatus*, ed. J. Engels), Utrecht, 1966.

Berenson, B., *Italian Pictures of the Renaissance, Florentine School*, London, 1963. 2v.

Berger, S., *La Bible française au moyen âge. Etude sur les plus anciennes versions de la Bible écrite en prose de langue d'oïl*, Paris, 1884.

Berlin. Staatliche Museen. Kupferstichkabinett. *Beschreibendes Verzeichnis der Miniaturen-Handschriften und Einzelblätter des Kupferstichkabinetts der Staatlichen Museen, Berlin* (P. Wescher), Leipzig, 1931.

Berlin. Staatsbibliothek. *Die Handschriftenverzeichnisse der Königlichen Bibliothek zu Berlin*, XII–XIII; Rose, V., *Verzeichnis der lateinischen Handschriften*, 1893–1905, Berlin.

Berlin. Staatsbibliothek. *Beschreibendes Verzeichnis der Miniaturen und des Initialschmuckes in den Phillipps-Handschriften* (J. Kirchner), Leipzig, 1926.

Berlin. Staatsbibliothek. *Schöne Handschriften aus dem Besitz der Preussischen Staatsbibliothek*, Berlin, 1931.

Bernard, O., "Der Sonnengott auf griechischen und römischen Münzen," *Revue suisse de numismatique*, XXV, 1933, pp. 245–298.

Bersuire, P., *see* Berchorius.

Bertrand, G., *see* Leningrad, Publīchnaīa bīblīoteka.

Besançon. Bibliothèque municipale. Castan, A., *Catalogue général des manuscrits des bibliothèques publiques de France*, Paris, XXXII, 1897.

Białostocki, J., et al., *Spätmittelalter und Beginnende Neuzeit* (Propyläen Kunstgeschichte), Berlin, 1972.

Białostocki, J., "Ars auro prior," in *Mélanges de littérature comparée et de philologie; offerts à Mieczyslaw Brahmer*, Warsaw [1967], pp. 55–63.

Białostocki, J., "The Eye and the Window," in *Festschrift für Gert von der Osten*, Cologne [1970], pp. 159–176.

Bihlmeyer, K., see *Heinrich Seuse, Deutsche Schriften*.

Billanovich, G., "La prima lettera del Salutati a Giovanni di Montreuil," *Italia medioevale e umanistica*, VII, 1964, pp. 337–350.

Birkmeyer, K. M., "The Arch Motif in Netherlandish Painting of the Fifteenth Century, Part One," *Art Bull.*, XLIII, 1961, pp. 1–20.

Bisogni, F., "Contributo per un problema ferrarese," *Paragone*, CCLXV, 1972, pp. 69–79.

Bober, H., "The Zodiacal Miniature of the 'Très Riches Heures' of the Duke of Berry—Its Sources and Meaning," *Warburg Journal*, XI, 1948, pp. 1–34.

Bober, H., *see also* Saxl and Meier.

Boccaccio, G., *Decameron* (Introd. Vittore Branca), Florence, 1966. 3v.

Boeckler, A., *Heinrich von Veldeke Eneide. Die Bilder der Berliner Handschrift*, Leipzig, 1939.

Boer, C. de, see *Ovide moralisé*.

Bohigas, P., "Les manuscrits à miniatures de la Biblioteca Central de Barcelona (ancienne Biblioteca de Catalunya)," *Librarium. Zeitschrift der schweizerischen Bibliophilen-Gesellschaft*, VII, 1964, pp. 39–58.

Bologna, F., *I pittori alla corte angioina di Napoli*, Rome, 1969.

Bonnardot, F., see *Ogier d'Anglure, Le saint voyage de Jherusalem.*

The Book of the Wanderings of Brother Felix Fabri, London, 1896 (Palestine Pilgrims Text Society, vols. 7 & 8).

Borcherdt, H. H., *Das europäische Theater im Mittelalter und in der Renaissance*, Leipzig, 1935.

Borland, C. R., *see* Edinburgh, University Library.

Bossuat, R., *Manuel bibliographique de la littérature française du moyen âge*, Melun, 1951.

Bottai, G., see *Roma nei suoi rioni.*

Bouchot, H., *Les Primitifs français, 1292–1500; complément documentaire au catalogue de l'exposition*, Paris, 1904.

Bouchot, H., "Le Portrait de Louis II d'Anjou à la Bibliothèque nationale," *Gazette archéologique*, XI, 1886, pp. 64–67, 128–131.

Bouchot, H., "Jean Fouquet," *Gaz. B.-A.*, IV, 1890, pp. 273–281, 416–426.

Bouchot, H., 'I primitivi francesi: "l'ouvraige de Lombardie," ' *L'Arte*, VIII, 1905, pp. 18–32.

Bouchot, H., *see also* Paris, Musée du Louvre.

Boucicaut, see *Le livre des faicts du bon messire Jean le Maingre, dit Boucicaut.*

Bourges. Musées. *Chefs-d'oeuvre des peintres-enlumineurs de Jean de Berry et de l'école de Bourges* [Bourges, 1951].

Bourloton (E.), "Le pontifical d'Etienne Loypeau, évêque de Luçon," *Revue du Bas-Poitou*, 1895, pp. 145–161.

Bouteron, M., *see* Paris, Bibliothèque de l'Institut.

Bozzolo, C., "Il 'Decameron' come fonte del 'Livre de la Cité des Dames' di Christine de Pisan," in *Miscellanea di studi e ricerche sul Quattrocento francese*, ed. F. Simone, Turin, 1967, pp. 3–24.

Bozzolo, C., "Manuscrits des traductions françaises d'œuvres de Boccace dans les bibliothèques de France," *Italia medioevale e umanistica*, XI, 1968, pp. 1–69.

Branca, V., *Decameron*, Florence, 1966. 3v.

Branner, R., "The Montjoies of Saint Louis," in *Essays in the History of Architecture Presented to Rudolf Wittkower*, London, 1967, pp. 13–16.

Breckenridge, J., " 'Et prima vidit:' The Iconography of the Appearance of Christ to his Mother," *Art Bulletin*, XXXIX, 1957, pp. 9–32.

Bréholles, H., "Paul, natif d'Allemaigne, peintre du duc de Berry, grand oncle de Charles VII," in *Archives de l'art français*, Paris, VI, 1858–1860, p. 216 ff.

Brendel, O., "A Kneeling Persian: Migrations of a Motif," in *Essays in the History of Art Presented to Rudolf Wittkower*, London, 1967, pp. 62–70.

Bréviaire Grimani de la Bibliothèque de S. Marco à Venise, ed. S. de Vries and S. Morpurgo, Leyden, 1904–1910. 12v.

Brieger, P., with M. Meiss and C. Singleton, *Illuminated Manuscripts of the Divine Comedy*, New York, 1969. 2v.

Brossolet, J., *see* Mollaret and Brossolet.

Brussels. Bibliothèque royale de Belgique. Christine de Pisan, *Epître d'Othéa, déese de la prudence, à Hector, chef des Troyens; reproduction des 100 miniatures du manuscrit 9392 de Jean Miélot* (J. van den Gheyn), Brussels, 1913.

Brussels. Bibliothèque royale de Belgique. Gaspar, C., and F. Lyna, *Les principaux manuscrits à peintures de la Bibliothèque royale de Belgique, Bull. SFRMP*, Paris, 1937–1947. 2 pts. in 3v.

Brussels. Bibliothèque royale de Belgique. *La librairie de Philippe le Bon* (G. Dogaer and M. Debae), Brussels, 1967.

Brussels. Bibliothèque royale de Belgique. *La librairie de Bourgogne et quelques acquisitions récentes de la Bibliothèque royale Albert 1er. Cinquante miniatures.* Brussels, 1970.

Brussels. Musées Royaux, *see* Cologne, Kunsthalle.

Brussels. Palais des Beaux-Arts. *La miniature flamande. Le mécénat de Philippe le Bon* (L. M. J. Delaissé), Brussels, 1959.

Buchon, J. A. C., *see* Monstrelet.

Buchthal, H., *Historia Troiana. Studies in the History of Medieval Secular Illustration*, London, 1971.

Bühler, C. F., "The Apostles and the Creed," *Speculum*, XXVIII, 1953, pp. 335–339.

Bühler, C. F., *see also* Christine de Pisan.

Burckhardt, D., "Studien zur Geschichte der altoberrheinischen Malerei," *Jahrbuch der Preussischen Kunstsammlungen*, XXVII, 1906, pp. 179–197.

Busquet, R., *Histoire de Provence des Origines à la Révolution française*, Monaco, 1954.

Butler, P., *Legenda Aurea—Légende Dorée—Golden Legend*, Baltimore, 1889.

Byvanck, A. W., *La miniature dans les Pays-Bas septentrionaux*, Paris, 1937.

Byvanck, A. W., *see also* The Hague, Koninklijke Bibliotheek.

Byvanck, A. W., *see also* Netherlands.

Čáda, F., *see* Kynžvartě.

Cadei, A., "Giovannino de Grassi nel taccuino di Bergamo," *Critica d'arte*, XVII, 1970, pp. 17–36.

Cahier, C., *see* Martin and Cahier.

Calcaterra, C., *see* Petrarch.

Calkins, R., "The *Brussels Hours* Reevaluated," *Scriptorium*, XXIV, 1970, pp. 3–26.

Camau, E., *La Provence à travers les siècles*, Paris, 1930.

Cambridge. Fitzwilliam Museum. *A Descriptive Catalogue of the Manuscripts in the Fitzwilliam Museum* (M. R. James), Cambridge, 1895.

Cambridge. Fitzwilliam Museum. *A Descriptive Catalogue of the McClean Collection of Manuscripts in the Fitzwilliam Museum* (M. R. James), Cambridge, 1912.

Cambridge. Fitzwilliam Museum. *Illuminated Manuscripts in the Fitzwilliam Museum* (F. Wormald and P. M. Giles), Cambridge, 1966.

Cambridge. Harvard University. *Illuminated and Calligraphic Manuscripts; an Exhibition Held at the Fogg Art Museum and Houghton Library, February 14–April 1, 1955*, Cambridge, 1955.

Cambridge Modern History, New York, I, 1907.

Cambridge. Trinity College. James, M. R., *The Western Manuscripts in the Library of Trinity College, Cambridge. A Descriptive Catalogue*, Cambridge, 1900–1904. 4v.

Campbell, P.-G.-C., *L'Epître d'Othéa. Etude sur les sources de Christine de Pisan*, Paris, 1924.

Camus, "Notice de deux manuscrits de la Bibliothèque nationale cotés aujourd'hui 6829 et 6829[2] parmi les manuscrits français; le premier coté ci-devant 250, le second 517 et 1085," *Notices et extraits*, VI [1800], pp. 106–124.

Castan, A., "Etude sur le Froissart de Saint-Vincent de Besançon," *Bibliothèque de l'École des Chartes*, XXVI, 1865, pp. 114–148.

Castan, A., *see also* Besançon, Bibliothèque municipale.

Castelnuovo, E., *Il gotico internazionale, II*, Milan, n.d.

Catalogue général des manuscrits des bibliothèques publiques de France, *see* France, Ministère de l'Education.

Cazelles, R., with J. Longnon and M. Meiss, *The "Très Riches Heures" of Jean, Duke of Berry*, New York, 1969.

Cecchetti, D., "Un' egloga inedita di Nicolas de Clamanges," in *Miscellanea di studi e ricerche sul Quattrocento francese*, ed. F. Simone, Turin, 1967, pp. 27–57.

Champeaux, A. de and P. Gauchery, *Les travaux d'art exécutés pour Jean de France, duc de Berry, avec une étude biographique sur les artistes employés par ce prince*, Paris, 1894.

Champfleury, J. F., *Histoire de la caricature du moyen âge*, Paris, 1875.

Champion, P., *Histoire poétique du quinzième siècle*, I, 1923.

Champollion-Figeac, A., *Louis et Charles Ducs d'Orléans*, Paris, 1844.

Chantilly. Musée Condé. *Le cabinet des livres: Manuscrits*, Paris, 1900–1901. 3v.

Chantilly. Musée Condé. *Les principaux manuscrits à peintures du Musée Condé* (J. Meurgey), *Bull. SFRMP*, Paris, 1930. 2v.

Chastillon, C., *Topographie françoise*, Paris, 1648.

Christine de Pisan, *Oeuvres poétiques de Christine de Pisan*, ed. M. Roy (Société des Anciens Textes Français), Paris, 1886–1896. 3v.

Christine de Pisan, *The Epistle of Othea to Hector*, ed. J. D. Gordon, Philadelphia, 1942.

Christine de Pisan, *Le livre de la mutacion de fortune* (Société des Anciens Textes Français), ed. S. Solente, 1959. 3v.

Christine de Pisan, *The Epistle of Othea, Translated from the French Text of Christine de Pisan by Stephen Scrope*, ed. C. F. Bühler, London, New York, Toronto, 1970.

Christine de Pisan, *see also* Brussels, Bibliothèque royale de Belgique.

Cipriani, R., *see* Milan, Biblioteca Ambrosiana.

Cleveland. Museum of Art. *Gothic Art 1360–1440* (W. D. Wixom), Cleveland, 1963.

Cleveland. Museum of Art. Wixom, W. D., *Treasures from Medieval France*, Cleveland, 1967.

Cockerell, S. C., *see* London, Burlington Fine Arts Club.

Cockshaw, P., "Mentions d'auteurs, de copistes, d'enlumineurs et de libraires dans les comptes généraux de l'état Bourguignon (1384–1419)," *Scriptorium*, XXIII, 1969, pp. 122–124.

Coffin, D., "Some Aspects of the Villa Lante at Bagnaia," in *Scritti di storia dell'arte in onore di Edoardo Arslan*, Milan, 1966, pp. 569–575.

Cogliati Arano, L., *see* Gengaro.

Cologne, Kunsthalle, and Brussels, Musées Royaux. *Rhin-Meuse, art et civilisation 800–1400*, 1972.

Combes, A., *Jean de Montreuil et le chancelier Gerson; contribution à l'histoire des rapports de l'humanisme et de la théologie en France au début du XVe siècle*, Paris, 1942.

Combes, A., "Gerson et la naissance de l'humanisme, note sur les rapports de l'histoire doctrinale et de l'histoire littéraire," *Revue du moyen âge latin*, I, 1945, pp. 259–284.

Comstock, H., "The Brooklyn Museum's Manuscripts," *International Studio*, LXXXV, November, 1926, pp. 44–48.

Conway, W. M., "Giovannino de' Grassi and the Brothers van Limburg," *Burl. Mag.*, XVIII, 1910, pp. 144–149.

Conway, W. M., "Jacquemart de Hesdin," *Burl. Mag.*, XXIX, 1916, pp. 45–49.

Coo, J. de, "In Josephs Hosen Jhesus ghewonden wert," *Aachener Kunstblätter*, 1965, pp. 144–184.

Coopland, G. W., *The Tree of Battles of Honoré Bonet*, Cambridge, Mass., 1949.

Coopland, G. W., *see also* Philippe de Mézières.

Cornell, H., *The Iconography of the Nativity of Christ*, Uppsala, 1924.

Cotton, F., "Les manuscrits à peintures de la bibliothèque de Lyon," *Gaz. B.-A.*, LXV, 1965, pp. 265–320.

Couderc, C., *Album de portraits d'après les collections du Département des manuscrits, Bibliothèque nationale*, Paris [1910].

Couderc, C., *see also* Paris, Bibliothèque nationale.

Courajod, L., *Leçons professées a l'Ecole du Louvre. Vol.* II: *Origines de la Renaissance*, Paris, 1901.

Courcelle, P., *La Consolation de philosophie dans la tradition littéraire: Antécédents et Postérité de Boèce*, Paris, 1967.

Courcelle, P., "La tradition antique dans les miniatures inédites d'un Virgile de Naples," Ecole française de Rome, *Mélanges d'archéologie et d'histoire*, fasc. I–IV, 1939, pp. 249–279.

Courtenay, W. J., "Covenant and Causality in Pierre d'Ailly," *Speculum*, XLVI, 1971, pp. 94–119.

Coville, A., *Gontier et Pierre Col et l'humanisme en France au temps de Charles VI*, Paris, 1934.

Coville, A., *La vie intellectuelle dans les domaines d'Anjou-Provence de 1380 à 1435*, Paris, 1941.

Coville, A., "Recherches sur Jean Courtecuisse et ses oeuvres oratoires," *Bibl. École des chartes*, LXV, 1904, pp. 469–529.

Coyecque, E., *see* Paris, Bibliothèque de la Chambre des Députés.

Crozet, R., "A propos du Château de Poitiers," *Bulletin de la Société des Antiquaires de l'Ouest et des Musées de Poitiers*, XI, 1971, p. 235 f.

Curtius, E. R., *European Literature and the Latin Middle Ages*, New York, 1963.

Cuttler, C. D., *Northern Painting from Pucelle to Bruegel / Fourteenth, Fifteenth, and Sixteenth Centuries*, New York [1968].

D'Amat, R., "Gontier Col" in *Dictionnaire de biographie française*, Paris, 1960, s.v.

David, H., *Philippe le Hardi*, Dijon, 1947.

David, H., *Claus Sluter*, Paris, 1951.

Debae, M., *see* Brussels, Bibliothèque royale de Belgique.

Debraye, H., *see* Paris, Bibliothèque de la Chambre des Députés.

Degenhart, B., *Pisanello* [Turin, 1945].

Degenhart, B., and A. Schmitt, *Corpus der italienischen Zeichnungen, 1300–1450*, Berlin, 1968. 4v.

Deguilleville, G. de, *Le pèlerinage de vie humaine*, ed. J. J. Stürzinger (Roxburghe Club), London, 1893.

Deguilleville, G. de, *Le pèlerinage de l'âme*, ed. J. J. Stürzinger (Roxburghe Club), London, 1895.

Dehaisnes, C., *Documents et extraits divers concernant l'histoire de l'art dans la Flandre, l'Artois et le Hainaut avant le XVe siècle*, Lille, 1886. 2v.

Delaissé, L. M. J., *Medieval Illuminations from the Library of Burgundy in the Department of Manuscripts of the Royal Library of Belgium*, Brussels, 1958. French ed., Geneva, 1959.

Delaissé, L. M. J., *A Century of Dutch Manuscript Illumination*, Los Angeles, 1968.

Delaissé, L. M. J., "Le livre d'heures d'Isabeau de Bavière," *Scriptorium*, IV, 1950, pp. 252–260.

Delaissé, L. M. J., "Les miniatures du 'Pèlerinage de la vie humaine' de Bruxelles et l'archéologie du livre," *Scriptorium*, X, 1956, pp. 233–250.

Delaissé, L. M. J., *see also* Brussels, Palais des Beaux-Arts.

Delaissé, L. M. J., *see also* Oberlin, Oberlin College.

Delaissé, L. M. J., *see also* Waddesdon Manor.

Delaruelle, E., E.-R. Labande, and P. Ourliac, *L'Eglise au temps du Grand Schisme et de la crise conciliaire (1378–1449)*, 1964.

Delisle, L., *Le cabinet des manuscrits de la Bibliothèque impériale*. Paris, 1868–1881. 3v. and atlas. In v. 2–3 and atlas Bibliothèque nationale is substituted for Bibliothèque impériale.

Delisle, L., *Mélanges de paléographie et de bibliographie*, Paris, 1880.

Delisle, L. et P. Meyer, *L'Apocalypse en français au XIIIe siècle*, Paris, 1901.

Delisle, L., *Notice de douze livres royaux du XIIIe et du XIVe siècle*, Paris, 1902.

Delisle, L., *Recherches sur la librairie de Charles V*, Paris 1907. 2v. and plates.

Delisle, L., "Notes sur la bibliothèque de la Sainte-Chapelle de Bourges," *Bibl. École des Chartes*, II, 1856, pp. 142–159.

Delisle, L., "Anciennes traductions françaises de la consolation de Boèce conservées à la Bibliothèque nationale," *Bibl. École des Chartes*, XXXIV, 1873, pp. 5–32.

Delisle, L., "Les livres d'Heures du duc de Berry," *Gaz. B.-A.*, XXIX, 1884, pp. 97–110, 281–292, 391–405.

Delisle, L., "Le missel et pontifical d'Etienne de Loypau

évêque de Luçon," *Bibl. École des Chartes*, XLVIII, 1887, pp. 527–534.

Delisle, L., "Livres d'images destinés à l'instruction religieuse et aux exercises de piété des laïques," in *Histoire littéraire de la France*, XXXI, 1893, pp. 213–285.

Delisle, L., rev. of P. Margry, *La conquête et les conquérants des îles Canaries . . .* , Paris, 1896, *Journal des savants*, 1896, pp. 644–659.

Demonts, L., "Dessins français des cabinets d'Allemagne," *Bulletin de la Société de l'histoire de l'art français*, 1909, pp. 259–280.

Demonts, L., "Une Collection française de Primitifs," *Rev. de l'art a. et m.*, LXX, 1937, p. 247 ff.

Deschamps, E., *Oeuvres complètes*, ed. Q. de Saint-Hilaire [and G. Raynaud], Paris, 1878–1903. 11 v.

Destombes, M., ed., *Mappemondes, A.D. 1200–1500* (Monumenta cartographica vetustioris aevi, I), Amsterdam, 1964.

Destrée, J., *Le livre d'heures de Notre-Dame, dites de Hennessy*, Brussels, 1923.

Deutsche Pilgerreisen nach dem Heiligen Land, ed. R. Röhricht and H. Meisner, Berlin, 1880.

Dienstfrey, D., *The Depiction of Peasants and Shepherds in French and Italian Art, 1320–1420*, M.A. thesis, New York Univ., 1963.

Dilke, O. A. W., "Maps in the Treatises of Roman Land Surveyors," *Geographical Journal*, CXXVII, 1961, pp. 417–426.

Dobbert, E., "Der Triumph des Todes im Camposanto zu Pisa," *Repertorium für Kunstwissenschaft*, IV, 1881, pp. 1–45.

Dogaer, G., *see* Brussels, Bibliothèque royale de Belgique.

Donovan, R. B., "Salutati's Opinion of Non-Italian Latin Writers," in *Studies in the Renaissance*, XIV, 1967, pp. 185–201.

Doren, A., "Fortuna im Mittelalter und in der Renaissance," *Vorträge der Bibliothek Warburg*, I, 1924, pp. 71–144.

Dorez, L., *see* Holkham Hall.

Dorsch, G. T., Jr. *The Raising of Lazarus in Late Medieval Northern European Art: A Study in Iconography*, M.A. thesis, New York Univ., 1966.

Douët-d'Arcq, L.-C., *Comptes de l'hôtel des rois de France aux XIVe et XVe siècles*, Paris, 1865.

Douët-d'Arcq, L.-C., *see also* Monstrelet.

Doutrepont, G., *Inventaire de la "librairie" de Philippe le Bon (1420) . . .* , Brussels, 1906.

Doutrepont, G., *La littérature française à la cour des ducs de Bourgogne* (Bibl. du XVe siècle, VIII), Paris, 1909.

Dresden. Sächsische Landesbibliothek. Schmidt, L., *Katalog der Handschriften der königlichen öffentlichen Bibliothek zu Dresden*, Paris, III, 1906.

Drouot, H., "Autour de la Pastorale de Claus Sluter," *Annales de Bourgogne*, XIV, 1942, pp. 7–24.

Dupont, J. and C. Gnudi, *Gothic Painting*, Geneva [1954].

Durrieu, P., *Les Très Riches Heures de Jean de France, duc de Berry*, Paris, 1904.

Durrieu, P., *Les antiquités judaïques et le peintre Jean Fouquet*, Paris, 1908.

Durrieu, P., *Le Boccace de Munich . . .* , Munich, 1909.

Durrieu, P., *Les heures à l'usage d'Angers de la collection Martin Le Roy*, Paris, 1912.

Durrieu, P., *Les Très Belles Heures de Notre-Dame du duc Jean de Berry*, Paris, 1922.

Durrieu, P., "Les manuscrits à peintures de la bibliothèque de Sir Thomas Phillipps à Cheltenham," *Bibl. École des Chartes*, L, 1889, pp. 381–432.

Durrieu, P., "Manuscrits de luxe exécutés pour des princes et des grands seigneurs français (notes et monographies)," *Le manuscrit*, II, 1895, pp. 1–5, 17–21, 34–35, 49–54, 65–66, 81–87, 97–103, 113–122, 129–135, 145–149, 162–168, 177–181.

Durrieu, P., "Les *Très Riches Heures* du duc de Berry conservées à Chantilly, au Musée Condé et le *Bréviaire Grimani*," *Bibl. École des Chartes*, LXIV, 1903, pp. 321–328.

Durrieu, P., "L'exposition des primitifs français. III. La peinture en France depuis le commencement du XIVe siècle jusqu'à la fin du règne de Charles VI," *Rev. de l'art a. et m.*, XV, 1904, pp. 241–262.

Durrieu, P., "Les 'Belles Heures' de Jean de France duc de Berry," *Gaz. B.-A.*, XXXV, 1906, pp. 265–292.

Durrieu, P., "Le maître des Heures du Maréchal de Boucicaut," *Rev. de l'art a. et m.*, XIX, 1906, pp. 401–415; XX, 1906, pp. 21–35.

Durrieu, P., "Jacques Coene," *Arts anciens de Flandre*, II [1906?], pp. 5–22.

Durrieu, P., "La peinture en France, le règne de Charles VI," in A. Michel, *Histoire de l'art*, Paris, III, pt. 1, 1907, pp. 137–169.

Durrieu, P., "Les Armoiries du Bon Roi René," *Comptes rendus*, 1908, pp. 102–114.

Durrieu, P., "Le plus ancien manuscrit de la traduction française du *Décaméron*," *Comptes rendus*, 1909, pp. 342–350.

Durrieu, P., "Une vue de l'église du Saint-Sépulcre vers 1436, provenant du bon roi René," in *Florilegium; . . . Melchior de Vogüé*, Paris, 1909, pp. 197–207.

Durrieu, P., "Découverte de deux importants manuscrits de la 'librairie' des ducs de Bourgogne," *Bibl. École des Chartes*, LXXI, 1910, pp. 58–71.

Durrieu, P., "Les aventures de deux splendides livres d'heures ayant appartenu au duc Jean de Berry," *Rev. de l'art a. et m.*, XXX, 1911, pp. 91–103.

Durrieu, P., "Michelino da Besozzo et les relations entre l'art italien et l'art français à l'époque du règne de Charles VI," *Mémoires de l'Institut National de France. Académie des Inscriptions et Belles-Lettres*, XXXVIII, pt. 2, 1911, pp. 365–393.

Durrieu, P., "Notes sur quelques manuscrits à peintures d'origine française ou flamande conservés en Italie," *Bull. SFRMP*, I, 1911, pp. 85–106.

Durrieu, P., "Le maître des 'Grandes Heures de Rohan' et les Lescuier d'Angers," *Rev. de l'art a. et m.*, XXXII, 1912, pp. 81–98, 161–183.

Durrieu, P., "Les Heures du Maréchal de Boucicaut du Musée Jacquemart-André," *Rev. de l'art chrét.*, LXIII, 1913, pp. 73–81, 145–164, 300–314; LXIV, 1914, pp. 28–35.

Durrieu, P., "Une 'Pitié de Notre-Seigneur'; tableau français de l'époque du règne de Charles VI donné au Musée du Louvre," *Monuments et mémoires*, XXIII, 1918–1919, pp. 63–111.

Dvořáková, V., J. Krása, A. Merhantová, and K. Stejskal, *Gothic Mural Painting in Bohemia and Moravia 1300–1378*, London, 1964.

Edinburgh. University Library. *A Descriptive Catalogue of the Western Mediaeval Manuscripts in Edinburgh University Library* (C. R. Borland), Edinburgh, 1916.

Edmunds, S., "The Medieval Library of Savoy," *Scriptorium*, XXIV, 1970, pp. 318–327.

Egbert, V. W., "Reliquary of Saint Germain," *Burlington Magazine*, CXII, 1970, pp. 359–364.

Eisler, C., "The Golden Christ of Cortona and the Man of Sorrows in Italy," *Art Bulletin*, LI, 1969, pp. 107–118, 233–246.

Eisler, C., *see also* Meiss and Eisler.

Elissagaray, M., *see* Johannes of Hildesheim.

Enaud, F., *Les châteaux forts en France* [Paris, 1958].

Engels, J., *see* Berchorius.

Enlart, C., *Manuel d'archéologie française depuis les temps mérovingiens jusqu'à la renaissance*, Paris, Part 2, II, 2nd ed., 1932.

Essling, V. Masséna, Prince de, and Müntz, E., *Pétrarque*, Paris, 1902.

Ettlinger, L., "Hercules Florentinus," *Mitteilungen des Kunsthistorischen Institutes in Florenz*, XVI, 1972, pp. 119–142.

Evans, J., *Art in Mediaeval France, 987–1498*, New York, 1948.

Evans, J., "A Prototype of the Eleanor Crosses," *Burl. Mag.*, XCI, 1949, pp. 96–99.

Evans, J., see also *The Flowering of the Middle Ages*.

Evans, M. W., "Boethius and an Illustration to the *Bible historiale*," *Warburg Journal*, XXX, 1967, pp. 394–398.

Fabri, F., see *The Book of the Wanderings of Brother Felix Fabri*.

Faral, E., "Guillaume de Digulleville," in *Histoire littéraire de la France*, XXXIX, 1962, pp. 1–132.

Farquhar, J., "A Book of Hours from Châlons-sur-Marne," *Scriptorium*, XXII, 1968, pp. 243–249.

Fasanelli, J. A., "Some Notes on Pisanello and the Council of Florence," *Master Drawings*, III, 1965, pp. 36–47.

Feldman, D., *Seventy-One: The World of Books, Arts and Letters circa 1170–1970*, New York, 1971.

Finó, J.-F., *Forteresses de la France médiévale*, Paris, 1967.

Fleming, J., *The Roman de la rose*, Princeton, 1969.

Fleureau, Dom, *Les antiquitez de la ville d'Estampes*, Paris, 1683.

Florence. Biblioteca Mediceo-Laurenziana. *Mostra di manoscritti medicei in occasione del V centenario di Lorenzo il Magnifico alla biblioteca Laurenziana di Firenze*, 1949.

The Flowering of the Middle Ages, ed. J. Evans, London, 1966.

Focillon, H., *Art d'Occident, le moyen âge roman et gothique*, Paris, 1938. English ed.: *The Art of the West in the Middle Ages*, London [1963]. 2v.

Fontana, P., "Osservazioni intorno ai rapporti di Vitruvio colla teorica dell'architettura del Rinascimento," in *Miscellanea di storia dell'arte in onore di Igino Benvenuto Supino*, Florence, 1933, pp. 305–322.

Fossi Todorow, M., *I disegni del Pisanello e della sua cerchia*, Florence, 1966.

Fournier, P., *see* Grenoble, Bibliothèque publique.

France. Ministère de l'Education. *Catalogue général des manuscrits des bibliothèques publiques de France. Départements . . .* Paris, 1885–1933. 48v.

Francis, H. S., "Jean de Beaumetz Calvary with a Carthusian Monk," *Bulletin of The Cleveland Museum of Art*, LIII, 1966, pp. 329–338.

Freeman, M. B., "A Book of Hours Made for the Duke of Berry," *Bull. Metropolitan Museum*, XV, 1956, pp. 93–104.

Freeman, M. B., *see also* New York, Metropolitan Museum, The Cloisters.

Freeman, M. B., *see also* Rorimer and Freeman.

French Verse, Penguin Book. I: To the Fifteenth Century, ed. B. Woledge, Harmondsworth, 1961.

Friedmann, H., *The Symbolic Goldfinch*, Washington, 1946.

Frinta, M., rev. of H. Kreuter-Eggemann, *Das Skizzenbuch des Jaques Daliwe*, Munich, 1964, in *Art Bulletin*, LII, 1970, pp. 100–102.

Fritz, R., "Die symbolische Bedeutung der Akelei," *Wallraf-Richartz Jahrbuch*, XIV, 1952, pp. 99–110.

Froissart, J., *Œuvres*, ed. K. de Lettenhove, Brussels, 1867–1877.

Frutaz, A. P., *Le piante di Roma*, Rome, 1962. 3v.

Fry, R. E., "French Painting in the Middle Ages," *The Quarterly Review*, CC, 1904, pp. 576–598.

Fry, R. E., "On Two Miniatures by de Limbourg," *Burl. Mag.*, VII, 1905, pp. 435–445.

Gagnebin, B., "Le Boccace du duc de Berry," *Genava*, V, 1957, pp. 129–148.

Gagnebin, B., "Le Tite-Live du duc de Berry," *Genava*, VII, 1959, pp. 193–214.

Gardet, C., *De la peinture du moyen âge en Savoie, III. L'Apocalypse figurée des ducs de Savoie*, Annecy, 1969.

Gaspar and Lyna, *see* Brussels, Bibliothéque royale de Belgique.

Gauchery, P., *see* Champeaux and Gauchery.

Gauthier, M.-M., *Emaux du Moyen âge occidental*, Fribourg, 1972.

Gelder, J. G. van, "An Early Work by Robert Campin," *Oud Holland*, LXXXII, 1967, pp. 1–17.

Gelder, J. G. van, "Der Teufel stiehlt das Tintenfass," in *Kunsthistorische Forschungen, Otto Pächt Festschrift*, ed. A. Rosenauer and G. Weber, Salzburg, 1972, pp. 173–188.

Gengaro, M. L., and L. Cogliati Arano, *Miniature lombarde*, Milan, 1970 (Cassa di Risparmio delle provincie lombarde).

Germany. *Manuscrits français à peintures des bibliothèques d'Allemagne* (L. Olschki), Geneva, 1932.

Gerson, J., *Œuvres complètes*, ed. Mgr. Glorieux, Paris [1961–]. 7v.

Gheyn, J. van den, *Christine de Pisan, Epître d'Othéa*, Brussels, 1913.

Gheyn, J. van den, *see also* Brussels, Bibliothèque royale de Belgique.

Giles, P. M., *see* Cambridge, Fitzwilliam Museum.

Gilson, J. P., *see* London, British Museum, Warner and Gilson.

Glaser, C., "Italienische Bildmotive in der altdeutschen Malerei," *Zeitschrift für bildende Kunst*, XXV, 1913–1914, pp. 145–158.

Glaser, C., "The Louvre *Coronation* and the Early Phase of Fra Angelico's Art," *Gaz. B.-A.*, XXII, 1942, pp. 149–164.

Gnoli, U., *Piante di Roma inedite*, Rome, 1941.

Gnudi, C., *see* Dupont and Gnudi.

The Golden Legend of Jacobus de Voragine, tr. and adapted G. Ryan and H. Ripperger, New York, 1941.

Gombrich, E. H., *Norm and Form, Studies in the Art of the Renaissance*, London, 1966.

Gombrich, E. H., "Light, Form and Texture in XVth-Century Painting," *Journal of the Royal Society of Arts*, CXII, 1964, pp. 826–849.

Gómez-Moreno, C., *see* New York, Metropolitan Museum, The Cloisters.

Gordon, J. D., *see* Christine de Pisan.

Gorissen, F., "Jan Maelwael und die Brüder Limburg," *Gelre*, LIV, 1954, pp. 153–221.

Gorra, E., "Il cavaliere errante," in *Studi di critica letteraria*, Bologna, 1892.

Gotik in Böhmen, ed. K. M. Swoboda, Munich, 1969.

Gough, R., *An Account of a Rich Illuminated Missal Executed for John, Duke of Bedford, Regent of France under Henry VI and Afterwards in the Possession of the Late Duchess of Portland*, London, 1794.

Graesse, Th., see *Jacobus a Voragine. Legenda Aurea.*

Graham, R., ed., *A Picture Book of the Life of Saint Anthony the Abbot Reproduced from a Manuscript of the Year 1426 in the Malta Public Library at Valletta*, Oxford, 1937.

Green, R. B., *see Meditations on the Life of Christ.*

Greene, B. da Costa, *see* New York, Pierpont Morgan Library.

Grenoble. Bibliothèque publique. Fournier, P., E. Maignien and A. Prudhomme, *Catalogue général des manuscrits des bibliothèques publiques de France*, Paris, VII, 1889.

Guerry, L., *Le thême du "Triomphe de la Mort" dans la peinture italienne*, Paris, 1950.

Guiffrey, J., *Inventaires de Jean duc de Berry (1401–1416)*, Paris, 1894–1896. 2v.

Guiffrey, J., "Peintres, ymagiers, verriers, maçons, enlumineurs, écrivains et libraires du XIVe et du XVe siècle," *Nouvelles archives de l'art français*, VI, 1878, pp. 157–232.

The Hague. Koninklijke Bibliotheek. Byvanck, A., *Les principaux manuscrits à peintures de la Bibliothèque royale des Pays-Bas et du Musée Meermanno-Westreenianum à la Haye*, *SFRMP*, Paris, 1924.

Hahnloser, H., "Les heures de Jean de Gingis," in *La Sarraz*, ed. G. Duplain and E. Manganel, Lausanne, 1972, pp. 60–73.

Hamburg. Kunsthalle. *Meister Francke und die Kunst um 1400*, Hamburg, 1969.

Hamelius, P., see *Mandeville's Travels*.

Haseloff, G., *Die Psalterillustration im 13. Jahrhundert; Studien zur Geschichte der Buchmalerei in England, Frankreich und den Niederlanden* [Kiel], 1938.

Haussherr, R., "Templum Salomonis und Ecclesia Christi. Zu einem Bildvergleich der *Bible moralisée*," *Zeitschrift für Kunstgeschichte*, 1968, pp. 101–121.

Hauvette, H., *De Laurentio de Primofato*, Paris, 1903.

Heimann, A., "Der Meister der 'Grandes Heures de Rohan' und seine Werkstatt," *Städel-Jahrbuch*, VII–VIII, 1932, pp. 1–61.

Heimann, A., "The Giac Book of Hours," *Burl. Mag.*, LXXI, 1937, p. 83 f.

Heinemann, O. von, *see* Wolfenbüttel, Herzog-August-Bibliothek.

Heinrich Seuse. Deutsche Schriften, ed. K. Bihlmeyer, Stuttgart, 1907.

Held, J., rev. of E. Panofsky, *Early Netherlandish Painting: Its Origins and Character*, Cambridge, Mass., 1953, in *Art Bulletin*, XXXVII, 1955, pp. 205–234.

Henderson, G., *Gothic* (Style and Civilization), 1967.

Herbert, J. A., *Illuminated Manuscripts*, New York, 1911.

Hermann, H. J., *see* Vienna, Nationalbibliothek.

Herrmann, M., *Forschungen zur deutschen Theatergeschichte des Mittelalters und der Renaissance*, Berlin, 1914, pp. 318–329.

Heydenreich, L., "Die Cappella Rucellai von San Pancrazio in Florenz," in *De artibus opuscula XL: Essays in Honor of Erwin Panofsky*, New York, 1961, I, pp. 219–229.

Hildesheim, *see* Johannes of Hildesheim.

Hill, G. F., *Pisanello*, London, 1905.

Hind, A., *Early Italian Engraving*, London, 1938–1948. 7v.

Hirschfeld, P., "Hat Meister Francke für Jean sans Peur von Burgund gearbeitet?" *Zeitschrift für Kunstgeschichte*, XXXIII, 1970, pp. 54–60.

Histoire littéraire de la France, Quatorzième Siècle, XXIV, 1862.

The History of the Great Chartreuse by a Carthusian Monk, London, 1934 (tr. from the 7th French ed. of 1929).

Hiver de Beauvoir, A., "Description . . . du trésor . . . donné par Jean, duc de Berry, à la Sainte-Chapelle de Bourges," *Mémoires de la Société Historique, Littéraire et Scientifique du Cher*, I, pt. 1, 1857, pp. 1–128; pt. 2, 1860, pp. 255–280.

Hoe, R., *Catalogue of Manuscripts*, New York, 1909.

Hoepffner, E., *see* Machaut, G. de.

Hoff, U., *see* Melbourne, National Gallery of Victoria.

Hoffbauer, F., *et al.*, *Paris à travers les âges. Aspects successifs des monuments et quartiers historiques de Paris depuis le XIII*[e] *siècle jusqu'à nos jours*, Paris, 1885.

Hoffman, E. W. "Simon Marmion Re-considered," *Scriptorium*, XXIII, 1969, pp. 243–271.

Holkham Hall. *Les manuscrits à peintures de la bibliothèque de Lord Leicester à Holkham Hall, Norfolk* (L. Dorez), Paris, 1908.

Hontoy, M., "Les miniatures de l'Apocalypse flamande de Paris (Bibl. nat. fonds néerl. no. 3)," *Scriptorium*, I, 1946–47, pp. 289–309.

Hornik, H., "Three Interpretations of the French Renaissance," *Studies in the Renaissance*, VII, 1960, pp. 43–66.

Horstmann, C., *The Three Kings of Cologne*, London, 1886 (Early English Text Society, vol. 85).

Houzeau, J.-C., see *Œuvres de Ghillebert de Lannoy*.

Huizinga, J., *The Waning of the Middle Ages*, London, 1924.

Hulin de Loo, G., *Heures de Milan; troisième partie des Très belles Heures de Notre-Dame, enluminées par les peintres de Jean de France, duc de Berry et par ceux du duc Guillaume de Bavière, Comte du Hainaut et de Hollande*, Brussels, 1911.

Hulin de Loo, G., "Les Très Riches Heures de Jean de France, duc de Berry, par Pol de Limbourc et ses frères," *Bull. de Gand*, XI, 1903, pp. 178 ff.

Hulin de Loo, G., "La Bible de Philippe le Hardi, historiée par les frères de Limbourc: manuscrit français 166 de la Bibliothèque nationale à Paris," *Bull. de Gand*, XVI, 1908, pp. 183–188.

Hulin de Loo, G., "Rapport," *Académie Royale de Belgique, Bulletins de la Classe des Beaux-Arts*, VII, 1925, pp. 117–127.

Hulin de Loo, G., "Traces de Hubrecht van Eyck; empreintes contemporaines en Suisse et Allemagne," *Annuaire des Musées Royaux des Beaux-Arts de Belgique*, IV, 1943–1944, pp. 3–26.

Hülsen, C., *Le chiese di Roma nel medio evo*, Florence, 1927.

Ibn Butlan, Abu al-Hasan al-Mukhtar ibn al-Hasan, *Tacuinum sanitatis in medicina*, Graz [1965]–1967. 2v.

Imhoof-Blumer, F., "Fluss- und Meergötter auf griechischen und römischen Münzen," *Revue Suisse de numismatique*, XXIII, 1924, pp. 173–492.

Jacob, E. F., "Huizinga and the Autumn of the Middle Ages," in *Essays in Later Medieval History*, Manchester and New York, 1968, pp. 141–153.

Jacobus de Verona. ed. R. Röhricht, "Le pèlerinage du moine Augustin Jacques de Verone (1335), *Liber peregrinationis Fratris Jacobi de Verona*," *Revue de l'orient latin*, III, 1895, pp. 163–302.

Jacobus de Voragine, *Legenda Aurea*, ed. T. Graesse, Breslau, 1890.

James, M. R., *Apocalypse in Art*, London, 1931.

James, M. R., *see also* Cambridge, Fitzwilliam Museum.

James, M. R., *see also* Cambridge, Trinity College.

James, M. R., *see also* London, Lambeth Palace.

James, M. R., *see also* London, Thompson Collection (formerly).

Janin, R., *Les églises orientales et les rites orientaux*, Paris, 1955.

Janson, H. W., "The Right Arm of Michelangelo's *Moses*," in *Festschrift Ulrich Middeldorf*, Berlin, 1968, pp. 241–247.

Jean de Montreuil Opera, ed. E. Ornato, Turin, I, 1963.

Johannes of Hildesheim, *La légende des rois mages* (tr. M. Elissagaray, Paris [1965]).

Johannes of Hildesheim, *Historia trium regum*, see also Horstmann.

Jones, L. W., and C. R. Morey, *The Miniatures of the Manuscripts of Terence prior to the thirteenth century*, Princeton [1930–1931].

Jorga, N., *Thomas III, Marquis de Saluces*, Paris, 1893.

Jorga, N., *Les voyageurs français dans l'Orient européen*, Paris [1928].

Juvénal, J., *Histoire de Charles VI, Roy de France*, in *Nouvelle collection des mémoires pour servir à l'histoire de France depuis le XIII*[e] *jusqu'à la fin du XVIII*[e], ed. [J. F.] Michaud and [J. J. F.] Poujoulat, ser. 1, II, 1850, pp. 333–569.

Kansas. The University of Kansas Museum of Art. *The Waning Middle Ages. An Exhibition of French and Netherlandish Art from 1350 to 1500* (J. L. Schrader), 1969.

Kehrer, H., *Die heiligen drei Könige in Literatur und Kunst*, Leipzig, 1908–1909. 2v.

Keller, H., *Italien und die Welt der höfischen Gotik*, Wiesbaden, 1967.

Ker, N. R., *Medieval Manuscripts in British Libraries. I, London*, Oxford, 1969.

Kernodle, G. R., *From Art to Theatre: Form and Convention in the Renaissance*, Chicago, 1944.

Kindermann, H., *Theatergeschichte Europas*, Salzburg, I, 1957, p. 412.

Kirchner, J., *see* Berlin, Staatsbibliothek.

Kirsch, E. W., *see* Meiss and Kirsch.

Kirsch, E. W., *see also* Meiss, *Boucicaut Master*.

Klein R., and H. Zerner, "Vitruve et le théâtre de la Renaissance italienne," in *Le lieu théâtral de la Renaissance*, Paris, 1964, pp. 49–60.

Klibansky, R., E. Panofsky, and F. Saxl, *Saturn and Melancholy*, New York, 1964.

Koch, R. A., *Joachim Patinir*, Princeton, 1968.

Koch, R. A., "Flower Symbolism in the Portinari Altar," *Art Bulletin*, XLVI, 1964, pp. 70–77.

Köhler, W., *Karolingische Miniaturen*, Berlin, 1971.

Köllner, H., rev. of Helga Kreuter-Eggemann: *Das Skizzenbuch des "Jacques Daliwe*," Munich, 1964, in *Zeitschrift für Kunstgeschichte*, 1970, pp. 68–75.

Krása, J., *Die Handschriften König Wenzels IV* (no place), 1971.

Krása, J., "Deux dessins du Louvre et la peinture de manuscrits en Bohême vers 1400," *Scriptorium*, XXIII, 1969, pp. 163–176.

Krása, J., *see also* Dvořáková, Krása, Merhantová, and Stejskal.

Krautheimer, R. (in collaboration with T. Krautheimer-Hess), *Lorenzo Ghiberti*, Princeton, 1956.

Krautheimer, R., "Introduction to an Iconography of Medieval Architecture," *Warburg Journal*, V, 1942, pp. 1–33.

Kreuter-Eggemann, H., *Das Skizzenbuch des Jaques Daliwe*, Munich, 1964. 2v.

Krinsky, C. H., "Seventy-eight Vitruvius Manuscripts," *Journal of the Warburg and Courtauld Institutes*, XXX, 1967, pp. 36–70.

Kuhn, A., "Die Illustration des Rosenromans," *Jahrbuch der kunsthistorischen Sammlungen des allerhöchsten Kaiserhauses*, XXXI, 1913/1914, pp. 1–66.

Kurth, B., "Ein Freskenzyklus im Adlerturm zu Trient," *Jahrb. des Kunsthistorisches Institutes der K. K. Zentralkommission für Denkmalpfluge*, V, 1911, pp. 9–104.

Kynžvartě. Čáda, F., *Rukopisy Knihovny Státního Zámku v Kynžvartě*, Prague, 1965.

Labande, E.-R., *see* Delaruelle, Labande, and Ourliac.

Labarte, J., ed., *Inventaire du mobilier de Charles V, roi de*

France (Collections des documents inédits), Paris, 1879.

Labib, M., *Pèlerins et voyageurs au Mont Sinaï*, Cairo, 1961.

Laborde, A. de, *Les manuscrits à peintures de la Cité de Dieu de Saint Augustin*, Paris, 1909. 3v.

Laborde, A. de, *La Bible moralisée illustrée, conservée à Oxford, Paris et Londres* . . . Paris, 1911–1927. 5v.

Laborde, A. de, *Les miracles de Nostre Dame compilés par Jehan Miélot*, Paris, 1929.

Laborde, A. de, *see also* Leningrad, Publīchnaīa bīblīoteka.

Laborde, L., *Les ducs de Bourgogne*, Paris, 1849–1852. 3v.

La Chenaye-Desbois, F. de, and Badier, *Dictionnaire de la noblesse*, 3rd ed., Paris, 1863–1877. 19v.

Laclotte, M., *Primitifs français*, Paris [1966].

Laclotte, M., "Tableaux de chevalet français vers 1400," *Art de France*, III, 1963, pp. 220–222.

Laclotte, M., "Le 'Maître des anges rebelles,'" *Paragone*, no. 237, 1969, pp. 3–14.

Lafaurie, J., *see* Paris, Bibliothèque nationale, Avril and Lafaurie.

Landais, H., "Le château de Saumur," in *Société française d'archéologie, Congrès archéologique de France*, Paris, 1964, pp. 523–578.

Langlois, E., see *Le Roman de la Rose*.

Lansburgh, M., "The Illuminated Manuscript Collection at Colorado College," *Art Journal*, XXVIII, 1968, pp. 61–70.

Lasko, P., "The Thorn Reliquary," *Apollo*, LXXVI, pt. 1, 1962, pp. 259–264.

Lauer, P., *see* Paris, Bibliothèque de l'Arsenal, Martin and Lauer.

La Vallière, L. C. de la Baume Le Blanc. Library. *Catalogue des livres de la bibliothèque de feu M. le duc de la Vallière*, Paris, 1783. 3v. in 6.

Lavin, I., "Cephalus and Procris, Transformations of an Ovidian Myth," *Journal of the Warburg and Courtauld Institutes*, XVII, 1954, pp. 260–287.

Lawton, H. W., *Térence en France au XVIe*, Paris, 1926.

Lecoy, F., "Note sur quelques ballades de Christine de Pisan," in *Fin du moyen âge et Renaissance. Mélanges de philologie française offerts à Robert Guiette*, Antwerp, 1961, pp. 107–114.

Lecoy de la Marche, A., *Le roi René*, Paris, I, 1875.

Lefèvre, L. E., "Quatre études archéologiques étampoises," in *Bulletin de la conférence des sociétés savantes de Seine et Oise, 4e réunion à Etampes, 1908*.

Lefèvre-Pontalis, E., "Première excursion: Etampes," *Congrès archéologique de France*, 82, 1919, pp. 3–49.

Lehmann, A., *Le rôle de la femme dans l'histoire de France au moyen âge*, Paris, 1952.

Lehoux, F., *Jean de France, duc de Berri. Sa vie. Son action politique. 1340–1416*, Paris, 1966–1968. 4v.

Leidinger, G., *see* Munich, Bayerische Staatsbibliothek.

Leningrad. Publīchnaīa bīblīoteka. "Catalogue des manuscrits français de la Bibliothèque de Saint-Petersbourg," (G. Bertrand), *Rev. soc. savantes*, VI, 1873, pp. 373–599.

Leningrad. Publīchnaīa bīblīoteka. Laborde, A. de, *Les principaux manuscrits à peintures conservés dans l'ancienne Bibliothèque impériale publique de Saint-Pétersbourg, SFRMP*, Paris, 1936–1938. 2v.

Leroquais, V., *Les sacramentaires et les missels manuscrits des bibliothèques publiques de France*, Paris, 1924. 3v. and Plates.

Leroquais, V., *Les livres d'heures; manuscrits de la Bibliothèque nationale*, Paris, 1927. 3v. Text and Plates; *Supplément*, 1943.

Leroquais, V., *Le Bréviaire de Philippe le Bon; bréviaire parisien du XVe siècle; étude du texte et des miniatures*, Brussels, 1929. Text and Plates.

Leroquais, V., *Les bréviaires manuscrits des bibliothèques publiques de France*, Paris, 1934. 5v. and Plates.

Leroquais, V., *Les pontificaux manuscrits des bibliothèques publiques de France*, Paris, 1937. 3v. and Plates.

Leroquais, V., *Un livre d'heures de Jean sans Peur*, Paris, 1939.

Leroquais, V., *see also* Lyons, Bibliothèque.

Le Roux de Lincy, A. J. V., *La bibliothèque de Charles d'Orléans à son château de Blois en 1427*, Paris, 1843.

Le Roux de Lincy, A. J. V., *Paris et ses historiens aux XIVe et XVe siècles*, Paris, 1867.

Lespinasse, R. de, *Histoire générale de Paris: Les métiers et corporations de la ville de Paris*, Paris, 1886–1897. 3v.

Lettenhove, K. de, *see* Froissart.

Levey, M., *Painting at Court*, New York, 1971.

Lewis, P. S., see *The Recovery of France in the Fifteenth Century*.

Liber peregrinationis Fratris Jacobi de Verona, see Jacobus de Verona.

La librairie de Philippe le Bon, see Brussels, Bibliothèque royale (Dogaer and Debae).

Liebeschütz, H., *Fulgentius Metaforalis*, Leipzig and Berlin, 1926.

Livre de la chasse, par Gaston Phébus, see Paris, Bibliothèque nationale.

Le livre des faicts du bon messire Jean le Maingre, dit Boucicaut, in *Nouvelle collection des mémoires pour servir à l'histoire de France depuis le XIIIe jusqu'à la fin du XVIIIe*, ed. [J. F.] Michaud and [J. J. F.] Poujoulat, ser. 1, II, 1850, pp. 203–332.

Livre du cuer d'amours espris, see Vienna, Nationalbibliothek.

Lockwood, L., "Music at Ferrara in the Period of Ercole I d'Este," *Studi musicali*, I, 1972, pp. 101–131.

London. Martin Breslauer. *A 15th-Century Manuscript of Valerius Maximus in French*, The Hague, 1965.

London. British Museum. *A Catalogue of the Harleian Manuscripts in the British Museum*, London, 1808–1812. 4v.

London. British Museum. Warner, G. F., *Illuminated Manuscripts in the British Museum*, Ser. I–IV, London, 1903.

London. British Museum. *Reproductions from Illuminated Manuscripts*, Ser. I–IV . . . , London, I, 1907 (2nd ed. 1910)–IV, 1928. 4v.

London. British Museum. *Schools of Illumination: Reproductions from Manuscripts in the British Museum*, London, 1914–1930. 6 pts. Part VI: French mid-14th to 16th centuries.

London. British Museum. Warner, G. F., and J. P. Gilson, *Catalogue of Western Manuscripts in the Old Royal and King's Collections* [London], 1921. 4v.

London. British Museum. *Miniatures from a French Horae, British Museum Add. Ms. 16997, Fifteenth Century. Reproduced in Honour of John Alexander Herbert* [London], 1927.

London. British Museum. Millar, E. G., *Souvenir de l'exposition de manuscrits français à peintures organisée à la Grenville Library (British Museum) en janvier–mars, 1932*, Paris, 1933.

London. British Museum. *Illuminated Manuscripts in the Grenville Library* (D. H. Turner), London, 1967.

London. Burlington Fine Arts Club. *Exhibition of Illuminated Manuscripts* (S. C. Cockerell et al.), London, 1908.

London. Christie, Manson and Woods. *Valuable Illuminated and other Manuscripts, Miniatures and Autograph Letters*, July 16, 1969.

London. Lambeth Palace. Millar, E. G., "Les principaux manuscrits à peintures du Lambeth Palace à Londres," *Bull. SFRMP*, VIII–IX, 1924–1925.

London. Lambeth Palace. James, M. R., and C. Jenkins, *A Descriptive Catalogue of the Manuscripts in the Library of Lambeth Palace*. Parts I–V. Cambridge, 1930–1932.

London. Sotheby & Co. *Catalogue of Twenty-Six Illuminated Manuscripts . . . the Property of Henry Yates Thompson*, March 23, 1920.

London. Sotheby & Co. *Catalogue of Superb Illuminations from the Collection of the Late John, Lord Northwick, . . .* May 21, 1928.

London. Sotheby & Co. *Catalogue of the Livy of the Bâtard de Bourgogne*, June 23, 1931.

London. Sotheby & Co. *Catalogue of the Renowned Collection of Western Manuscripts, the Property of A. Chester Beatty, Esq.*, II, May 9, 1933.

London. Sotheby & Co. *Catalogue of Fine Illuminated Manuscripts from the Twelfth to the Sixteenth Century*, June 4, 1934.

London. Sotheby & Co. *Catalogue of the Magnificent Library. The Property of the Late Seventh Duke of Newcastle Removed from Clumber*, June 21, 1937.

London. Sotheby & Co. *The Clumber Library. Property of the . . . Duke of Newcastle*, December 6, 1937.

London. Sotheby & Co. *Catalogue of the Manuscripts, Printed Books and Autograph Letters Presented to the Duke of Gloucester's Red Cross and St. John Fund*, October 13–15, 1942.

London. Sotheby & Co. *Bibliotheca Phillippica; Catalogue of a Further Portion of the Renowned Library Formed by the Late Sir Thomas Phillipps*, July 1, 1946.

London. Sotheby & Co. *The Dyson Perrins Collection*: Part I, December 9, 1958. Part II, December 1, 1959.

London. Sotheby & Co. *Catalogue of Western and Oriental Manuscripts and Miniatures*, June 18, 1962.

London. Sotheby & Co. *Catalogue of Important Old Master Drawings*, Springell Sale, June 28, 1962.

London. Sotheby & Co. *The Chester Beatty Western Manuscripts: Part I. Catalogue of Thirty-Seven Manuscripts of the 9th to the 16th Century*, December 3, 1968.

London. Sotheby & Co. *The Chester Beatty Western Manuscripts: Part II. Catalogue of Thirty-Eight Manuscripts of the 8th to the 17th Century*, June 24, 1969.

London. Sotheby & Co. *Catalogue of Important Western Manuscripts and Miniatures*, July 8, 1970.

London, Sotheby & Co. *Catalogue of the Celebrated Library of the Late Major J. R. Abbey*, December 1, 1970.

London. Sotheby & Co. *Bibliotheca Phillippica Medieval Manuscripts: New Series: Part VI*, November 30, 1971.

London. Thompson Collection (formerly). James, M. R., *A Descriptive Catalogue of Fifty Manuscripts from the Collection of Henry Yates Thompson*, Cambridge, 1898.

London. Thompson Collection (formerly). *Illustrations of One Hundred Manuscripts in the Library of Henry Yates Thompson* (H. Y. Thompson), London, 1907–1918. 7v. VII. *The Remaining Twenty-Two MSS.*, 1918.

Longnon, A., see *Ogier d'Anglure, Le saint voyage de Jherusalem.*

Longnon, J., with R. Cazelles and M. Meiss, *The "Très Riches Heures" of Jean, Duke of Berry*, New York, 1969.

Loomis, R. S., and L. Hibbard Loomis, *Arthurian Legends in Medieval Art*, London, 1938.

Louis de France et Jean sans Peur, Orléans et Bourgogne 1400–1409, Extraits (ed. B. Zeller), in *L'histoire de France racontée par les contemporains*, Paris, XXVI, 1886.

Lowinsky, E. E., "Music in the Culture of the Renaissance," *Journal of the History of Ideas*, XV, 1954, pp. 509–553.

Ludolph of Saxony, *Vita Jesu Christi redemptoris nostri ex medullis evangelicis*, Lyon, 1519.

Ludolph von Suchem's Description of the Holy Land and of the Way Thither written in the Year A.D. 1350, tr. A. Stewart (Palestine Pilgrims Text Society), London, 1895.

Lutz, J., and P. Perdrizet, *Speculum humanae salvationis*, Mülhausen, 1907–1909. 2v.

Luzzatto, G. L., "Il libro d'ore del Duca di Berry nel Museo di Chantilly," *Bibliofilia*, XXXIV, 1932, pp. 217–237, 437–455.

Lyna, F., "Un livre de prières inconnu de Philippe le Hardi (Bruxelles, ms. 11035–37)," in *Mélanges Hulin de Loo*, 1931, pp. 249–259.

Lyna, F., "Les miniatures d'un ms. du 'Ci nous dit' et le réalisme préeyckien," *Scriptorium*, I, 1946–1947, pp. 106–118.

Lyna, F., *see also* Brussels, Bibliothèque royale de Belgique, Gaspar and Lyna.

Lyon. Bibliothèque (J. Vaesen). *Catalogue général des manuscrits des bibliothèques publiques de France*, Paris, XXXI, 1898.

Lyon. Bibliothèque. *Exposition de manuscrits à peintures du VIe au XVIIe siècle* (V. Leroquais), Lyon, 1920.

Machaut, G. de, *Œuvres*, ed. E. Hoepffner, Paris, I, 1908.

Maginnis, H. B.-J., "Cast Shadow in the Passion Cycle at San Francesco, Assisi: A Note," *Gazette des Beaux-Arts*, LXXVII, 1971, p. 63 f.

Magne, L., *Le Palais de Justice de Poitiers*, Paris, 1904.

Maignien, E., *see* Grenoble, Bibliothèque publique.

Mâle, E., *L'art religieux de la fin du moyen âge en France; étude sur l'iconographie du moyen âge et sur ses sources d'inspiration*, Paris, 1908.

Mâle, E., *Les saints compagnons du Christ*, Paris [1958].

Mâle, E., "La miniature à l'exposition des primitifs français," *Gaz. B.-A.*, XXXII, 1904, pp. 41–60.

Malo, H., *Très Riches Heures*, Paris, 1945.

Mandeville's Travels, ed. P. Hamelius, London, 1919.

Manfreni, C., *Il cavaliere errante*, Leghorn, 1890.

Margry, P., *La conquête et les conquérants des îles Canaries*, Paris, 1896.

Marijnissen, R.-H., "Note sur l'enluminure eyckienne 'La naissance de Saint Jean-Baptiste' des *Heures de Milan-Turin*," *Scriptorium*, XXIII, 1969, p. 225 f.

Marinesco, C., "Deux empereurs byzantins en Occident: Manuel II et Jean VIII Paléologue," in *Comptes rendus*, 1957, pp. 23–25.

Marinesco, C., "Deux empereurs byzantins," *Bulletin de la Société Nationale des Antiquaires de France*, 1958, pp. 38–40.

Marinis, T. de, *La biblioteca napoletana dei re d'Aragona*, Milan, 1947–1952. 4v.

Marle, R. van, *The Development of the Italian Schools of Painting*, The Hague, 1923–1936. 18v.

Marle, R. van, *Iconographie de l'art profane au moyen âge et à la Renaissance et la décoration des demeures*, The Hague, 1931–1932. 2v.

Marrow, J., "Pictorial Reversals in the Turin-Milan Hours," *Scriptorium*, XX, 1966, pp. 67–69.

Marrow, J., rev. of *Heures de Turin. Quarante-cinq feuillets à peintures provenant des Très Belles Heures de Jean de France, duc de Berry*, Paris, 1902, and Turin, 1967, in *Art Bulletin*, L, 1968, pp. 203–209.

Marrow, J., *see also* Waddesdon Manor.

Marshall, M. H., "Boethius' Definition of *Persona* and Mediaeval Understanding of the Theatre," *Speculum*, XXV, 1950, pp. 471–482.

Martens, B., *Meister Francke*, Hamburg, 1929. 2v.

Martin, A., and C. Cahier, *Monographie de la cathédrale de Bourges*, Paris, I (*Vitraux du XIIIe siècle*), 1841–44.

Martin, H. M. R., *Les miniaturistes français*, Paris, 1906.

Martin, H. M. R., *Le Térence des ducs*, Paris, 1907.

Martin, H. M. R., *Le Boccace de Jean sans Peur. Des cas des nobles hommes et femmes*, Brussels, 1911.

Martin, H. M. R., *La miniature française du XIIIe siècle au XVe siècle*, Paris, 1923.

Martin, H. M. R., "Les esquisses des miniatures," *Rev. archéol.*, IV, 1904, pp. 17–45.

Martin, H. M. R., "L'illustration des livres au moyen âge," *Comptes rendus*, 1904, pp. 121–132.

Martin, H. M. R., *see also* Paris, Bibliothèque de l'Arsenal.

Martin, H. M. R., *see also* Paris, Bibliothèque nationale.

Mater, M. D., "Le livre d'heures d'Anne de Mathefelon," *Mémoires de la Societé des Antiquaires du Centre*, XXVI, 1902, pp. 145–159.

Mattingly, H., *Coins of the Roman Empire in the British Museum*, London, 1923–1950. 5v.

Meditations on the Life of Christ, ed. I. Ragusa and R. B. Green, Princeton, 1961.

Meier, H., *see* Saxl and Meier.

Meisner, H., see *Deutsche Pilgerreisen nach dem Heiligen Land.*

Meiss, M., *Painting in Florence and Siena after the Black Death*, Princeton, 1951; New York, 1964 (with revised index).

Meiss, M., *French Painting in the Time of Jean de Berry. The Late XIV Century and the Patronage of the Duke*, London and New York, 1967. 2v. 2nd ed. 1969.

Meiss, M. (with the assistance of K. Morand and E. W. Kirsch), *French Painting in the Time of Jean de Berry. The Boucicaut Master*, London and New York, 1968.

Meiss, M., with P. Brieger and C. Singleton, *Illuminated Manuscripts of the Divine Comedy*, New York, 1969. 2v.

Meiss, M., with J. Longnon and R. Cazelles, *The "Très Riches Heures" of Jean, Duke of Berry*, New York, 1969.

Meiss, M., *The Great Age of Fresco: Discoveries, Recoveries and Survivals*, New York and London, 1970. French ed.: Paris, 1970. German ed.: Munich, Vienna, and Zurich, 1971.

Meiss, M., *The "De Lévis Hours" and the Bedford Workshop* (Yale Lectures on Medieval Illumination), New Haven, 1972.

Meiss, M., and E. H. Beatson, *The Belles Heures of Jean, Duke of Berry*, New York (and other eds.) 1974 (in press).

Meiss, M., and E. W. Kirsch, *The Visconti Hours*, New York, 1972 and other eds.

Meiss, M., and M. Thomas, *The Rohan Master. A Book of Hours*, in the press.

Meiss, M., "The Problem of Francesco Traini," *Art Bull.*, XV, 1933, pp. 97–173.

Meiss, M., "Un dessin par le maître des Grandes Heures de Rohan," *Gaz. B.-A.*, LXXVII, pt. 1, 1935, pp. 65–75.

Meiss, M., "The Earliest Work of Giovanni di Paolo: Venus and the Three Graces," *Art in America*, XXIV, 1936, pp. 137–143.

Meiss, M., "Light as Form and Symbol in Some Fifteenth-Century Paintings," *Art Bull.*, XXVII, 1945, pp. 175–181. Reprinted with slight changes in *Renaissance Art*, ed. C. Gilbert, New York, 1970, pp. 43–68.

Meiss, M., "Italian Primitives at Konopiště," *Art Bull.*, XXVIII, 1946, pp. 1–16.

Meiss, M., "The Exhibition of French Manuscripts of the XIII–XVI Centuries at the Bibliothèque nationale," *Art Bull.*, XXXVIII, 1956, pp. 187–196.

Meiss, M., and C. Eisler, "A New French Primitive," *Burl. Mag.*, CII, 1960, pp. 233–240.

Meiss, M., and C. Eisler, "A New French Primitive," Letter to the Editor, *Burl. Mag.*, CII, 1960, p. 489.

Meiss, M., "An Early Lombard Altarpiece," *Arte antica e moderna*, 1961, no. 13–16, pp. 125–133.

Meiss, M., " 'Highlands' in the Lowlands; Jan van Eyck, the Master of Flémalle, and the Franco-Italian Tradition," *Gaz. B.-A.*, LVII, 1961, pp. 273–314.

Meiss, M., "French and Italian Variations on an Early Fifteenth-Century Theme: St. Jerome and His Study," *Gaz. B.-A.*, LXII, 1963, pp. 147–170.

Meiss, M., "A Lost Portrait of Jean de Berry by the Limbourgs," *Burl. Mag.*, CV, 1963, pp. 51–53.

Meiss, M., "Sleep in Venice. Ancient Myths and Renaissance Proclivities," *Proceedings of the American Philosophical Society*, CX, 1966, pp. 348–382.

Meiss, M., "The First Fully Illustrated Decameron," in *Essays in the History of Art Presented to Rudolf Wittkower*, London, 1967, pp. 56–61.

Meiss, M., "Some Remarkable Early Shadows in a Rare Type of Threnos," in *Festschrift Ulrich Middeldorf*, Berlin, 1968, pp. 112–118.

Meiss, M., "The Original Position of Uccello's *John Hawkwood*," *Art Bulletin*, LII, 1970, p. 231.

Meiss, M., "The Master of the Breviary of Jean sans Peur and the Limbourgs" (Lecture on Aspects of Art), *Proceedings of the British Academy*, LVI, 1970, pp. 111–129. Also published separately, London, Oxford University Press, 1971.

Meiss, M., "Alesso di Andrea," in *Giotto e il suo tempo. Atti del Congresso Internazionale per la celebrazione del VII centenario della nascita di Giotto, 1967*, Rome, 1971, pp. 401–418.

Meiss, M., with S. Off, "The Bookkeeping of Robinet d'Estampes and the Chronology of Jean de Berry's Manuscripts," *Art Bull.*, LIII, 1971, pp. 225–235.

Meiss, M., and S. Off, "Deux miniatures perdues du *Térence des ducs*," *Revue de l'art*, XV, 1972, p. 62 f.

Meiss, M., "Scholarship and Penitence in the Early Renaissance: The Image of St. Jerome," in the press.

Meiss, M., *see also* Tintori and Meiss.

Melbourne. National Gallery of Victoria. Hoff, U., and M. Plant, *National Gallery of Victoria: Painting, Drawing, Sculpture*, Melbourne, 1968.

Mély, F. de, "Les 'Très Riches Heures' du duc Jean de Berry et les 'Trois Grâces' de Sienne," *Gaz. B.-A.*, LIV, 1912, pp. 195–201.

Menut, A. D., "Maistre Nicole Oresme: *Le livre de yconomique d'Aristote*," *Transactions of the American Philosophical Society*, N.S., XLVII, 1957, pp. 785–852.

Merhantová, A., *see* Dvořáková, Krása, Merhantová, and Stejskal.

Metman, Y., "A la gloire de l'art gothique: le 'réalisme modéré' des tailleurs de sceaux," in Paris, Hôtel de la Monnaie, *Collectionneurs et Collections numismatiques, monnaies, medailles et jetons*, Paris, 1968, pp. 159–166.

Metzger, B. M., "Names for the Nameless in the New Testament," in *Kyriakon, Festschrift Johannes Quasten*, Münster, n.d., pp. 79–99.

Meurgey, J., *see* Chantilly, Musée Condé.

Meyer, P., "Les premières compilations françaises d'histoire ancienne," *Romania*, XIV, 1885, pp. 1–81.

Michaud [J. F.], see *Le livre des faicts du bon messire Jean le Maingre, dit Boucicaut.*

Michel, A., *Histoire de l'art*, Paris, 1905–1929. 8v. in 17.

Milan. Biblioteca Ambrosiana. Cipriani, R., *Codici miniati dell'Ambrosiana*, Milan, 1968.

Milan. Biblioteca Trivulziana. *I codici miniati della Biblioteca Trivulziana* (C. Santoro), Milan, 1958.

Milan. Palazzo Reale. *Arte lombarda dai Visconti agli Sforza*, Milan [1958]. 2nd ed., Milan, 1959.

Millar, E. G., *English Illuminated Manuscripts of the XIVth and XVth Centuries*, Paris, 1928.

Millar, E. G., *see also* London, Lambeth Palace.

Miner, D., "A Madonna with Child Writing," *Art News*, February 1966, pp. 41–43, 60–64.

Miner, D., "Since De Ricci. Western Illuminated Manuscripts Acquired since 1934," *Journal of the Walters Art Gallery*, XXXI–XXXII, 1968–1969, pp. 40–115.

Miner, D., *see also* Baltimore, Walters Art Gallery.

Miniature lombarde, see Gengaro.

Mirot, L., "Notes sur un manuscrit de Froissart et sur Pierre de Fontenay, seigneur de Rance, son premier possesseur," *Bibl. École des Chartes*, LXXXIII, 1922, pp. 297–326.

Molinier, A., *see* Paris, Bibliothèque Mazarine.

Molinier, A., *see also* Soissons, Bibliothèque municipale.

Mollaret, H. H., and J. Brossolet, *La procession de saint Grégoire et la peste à Rome en l'an 590* (Service de la Peste de l'Institut Pasteur de Paris), Paris, n.d.

Mombello, G., *La tradizione manoscritta dell' "Epistre Othea" di Christine de Pizan* (Memorie dell' Accademia delle Scienze di Torino), Turin, 1967.

Mombello, G., "Per un'edizione critica dell' *Epistre Othea* di Christine de Pizan," *Studi francesi*, VIII, 1964, pp. 401–417; IX, 1965, pp. 1–12.

Mombello, G., "I manoscritti delle opere di Dante, Petrarca e Boccaccio nelle principali librerie francesi del secolo XV," in *Atti del convegno di studi, L'opera del Boccaccio nella cultura francese, 1968*, Florence, 1971, pp. 81–209.

Monfrin, J., "Humanisme et traductions au moyen âge," *Journal des Savants*, July–Sept., 1963, pp. 161–190.

Monfrin, J., "Les traducteurs et leur public en France au moyen âge," *Journal des Savants*, Jan.–March, 1964, pp. 5–20.

Monget, C., *La Chartreuse de Dijon d'après les documents des archives de Bourgogne*, Montreuil-sur-Mer, 1898–1905. 3v.

Monstrelet, E. de, *Chroniques* (*Choix de chroniques et mémoires sur l'histoire de France*), ed. J. A. C. Buchon, Paris, 1836.

Monstrelet, E., *La Chronique d'Enguerran Monstrelet*, ed. L. Douët-d'Arcq, Paris, 1857–1862. 6 vols.

Montfaucon, Bernard de, *Les monumens de la monarchie françoise*, Paris, 1729–1733. 5v.

Montreuil, *see* Jean de Montreuil.

Morand, E., "La Ville de Riom et la fête de Mai dans les *Très Riches Heures* du duc de Berry," *Bulletin de l'Académie des Sciences, Belles-Lettres et Arts de Clermont-Ferrand*, 1954, pp. 54–61.

Morand, K., *Jean Pucelle*, Oxford, 1962.

Morand, K., *see also* Meiss, *Boucicaut Master.*

Moranvillé, H., see also *Le songe véritable; pamphlet politique d'un parisien du XVe siècle.*

Morey, C. R., *see* Jones and Morey.

Morpurgo, S., see *Bréviaire Grimani de la Bibliothèque de S. Marco à Venise.*

Munby, A. N. L., *Connoisseurs and Medieval Miniatures: 1750–1850*, Oxford, 1972.

Munby, A. N. L., "The Bedford Missal," *Times Literary Supplement* (London), April 18, 1968, p. 404 f.

Munich. Bayerische Staatsbibliothek. Leidinger, G., *Verzeichnis der wichtigsten Miniaturen-Handschriften der Königliche Hof und Staatsbibliothek München*, Munich, 1912.

Müntz, E., "Notice sur un plan inédit de Rome à la fin du XIVe siècle," *Gazette archéologique*, X, 1885, pp. 169–176.

Müntz, E., *see also* Essling and Müntz.

Netherlands. Byvanck, A., "Les principaux manuscrits à peintures conservés dans les collections publiques du royaume des Pays-Bas," *Bull. SFRMP*, XV, 1931. Text and Plates.

New York. American Art Association – Anderson Galleries. *Illuminated Manuscripts, Incunabula and Ameri-*

cana, from the Libraries of the Marquess of Lothian, Jan. 27, 1932.

New York. The Frick Collection. *An Illustrated Catalogue*, New York, 1968–1970. 4v.

New York. Grolier Club. *Catalogue of an Exhibition of Painted Manuscripts and Books*, New York, 1892.

New York. L. C. Harper. *Catalogue 10: Fine Books and Illuminated Manuscripts* [1960].

New York. H. P. Kraus. *Catalogue 100*. New York [1962].

New York. Metropolitan Museum. The Cloisters. *The Hours of Jeanne d'Evreux*, ed. J. J. Rorimer, New York, 1957.

New York. Metropolitan Museum. The Cloisters. *The Belles Heures of Jean, Duke of Berry Prince of France*, ed. J. J. Rorimer and M. B. Freeman, New York, 1958.

New York. Metropolitan Museum. The Cloisters. *Medieval Art from Private Collections* (C. Gómez-Moreno), New York, 1968.

New York. Pierpont Morgan Library. *The Pierpont Morgan Library: a Review of the Growth, Development and Activities of the Library . . .* (B. da Costa Greene), New York, 1930.

New York. Pierpont Morgan Library. *Exhibition of Illuminated Manuscripts Held at the New York Public Library*, November 1933 to April 1934, New York [1934].

New York. Pierpont Morgan Library. *Illustrated Catalogue of an Exhibition held on the Occasion of the New York World's Fair 1939*, New York, 1939.

New York. Pierpont Morgan Library. *Review of the Activities and Acquisitions of the Library from 1936 through 1940 . . .*, New York, 1941.

New York. Pierpont Morgan Library. *Sports and Pastimes from the Fourteenth through the Eighteenth Century*, New York, 1946.

New York. Pierpont Morgan Library. *The First Quarter Century of the Pierpont Morgan Library . . .*, New York, 1949.

Nicoll, A., *Masks, Mimes and Miracles. Studies in the Popular Theatre*, London, 1931.

Nordenfalk, C. A. J., *Kung praktiks och drottning teoris jaktbok. Le livre des deduis du roi Modus et de la reine Ratio*, Stockholm, 1955.

Nordenfalk, C. A. J., "Französische Buchmalerei 1200–1500," *Kunstchronik*, IX, 1956, pp. 179–189.

Nordenfalk, C. A. J., "Saint Bridget of Sweden As Represented in Illuminated Manuscripts," in *De Artibus Opuscula XL. Essays in Honor of Erwin Panofsky*, New York, 1961, I, pp. 371–393.

Nouvelle collection des mémoires pour servir à l'histoire de France, see *Le livre des faicts du . . . Boucicaut*, and Juvénal, *Histoire de Charles VI*.

Nys, E., *Christine de Pisan et ses principales oeuvres*, Brussels, 1914.

Oberhammer, V., *Der Altar vom Schloss Tirol*, Innsbruck and Vienna, 1948.

Oberlin. Oberlin College. "An Exhibition of Netherlandish Book Illumination" (L. M. J. Delaissé), *Allen Memorial Art Museum Bulletin*, XVII, 1960, pp. 94–113.

Oberman, H. A., *The Harvest of Medieval Technology*, Cambridge (Mass.), 1963.

Œuvres de Ghillebert de Lannoy, ed. Ch. Potvin and J.-C. Houzeau, Louvain, 1878.

Off, S., *see* Meiss and Off, 1971, 1972.

Ogier d'Anglure, Le saint voyage de Jherusalem, ed. F. Bonnardot and A. Longnon (Société des anciens textes français, x), Paris, 1878.

Olschki, L. S., *see* Germany.

Omont, H. A., *see* Paris, Bibliothèque nationale.

Ornato, E., *Jean Muret et ses amis: Nicolas de Clamanges et Jean de Montreuil. Contribution à l'étude des rapports entre les humanistes de Paris et ceux d'Avignon (1394–1420)*, Geneva, 1969.

Ornato, E., see also *Jean de Montreuil Opera*.

Os, H. W. van, "Giovanni di Paolo's Pizzicaiuolo Altarpiece," *Art Bulletin*, LIII, 1971, pp. 289–302.

Ourliac, P., *see* Delaruelle, Labande, and Ourliac.

Oursel, R., *Les pèlerins du moyen âge, les hommes, les chemins, les sanctuaires*, Paris, 1963.

Ouy, G., *Le recueil épistolaire autographe de Pierre d'Ailly et les notes d'Italie de Jean de Montreuil. Umbrae codicum occidentalium*, IX, Amsterdam, 1966.

Ouy, G., "La réponse de Jean de Montreuil au chancelier de Florence," *Italia medioevale e umanistica*, VII, 1964, pp. 351–372.

Ouy, G., "Le songe et les ambitions d'un jeune humaniste parisien vers 1935," in *Miscellanea di studi e ricerche sul Quattrocento francese*, Turin, 1966.

Ouy, G., "Paris: l'un des principaux foyers de l'humanisme en Europe au début du XVe siècle," in *Bulletin de la Société de l'Histoire de Paris et de l'Ile-de-France*, 1970, pp. 71–98.

Ovide moralisé, poème du commencement du quatorzième siècle, ed. C. de Boer (Verhandelingen der Koninklijke Nederlandse Akademie van Wetenschappen te

Amsterdam, Afd. Letterkunde), New series XV, 1915 (bk. I–III), XXI, 1920 (bk. IV–VI), XXX, 1931 (bk. VII–IX), XXXVI/XXXVII, 1936 (bk. X–XIII), XLIII, 1938 (bk. XIV–XV).

Ovide moralisé en prose, ed. C. de Boer (Verhandelingen der Koninklijke Nederlandse Akademie van Wetenschappen, Afd. Letterkunde, New Series, LXI), Amsterdam, 1954.

Oxford, Bodleian Library, *see* Pächt and Alexander.

Paccagnini, G., *Pisanello e il ciclo cavalleresco di Mantova* [1972].

Pächt, O., *The Master of Mary of Burgundy*, London [1948].

Pächt, O., and J. G. Alexander, *Illuminated Manuscripts in the Bodleian Library, Oxford. I. German, Dutch, Flemish, French and Spanish Schools*, Oxford, 1966.

Pächt, O., "Jean Fouquet: a Study of his Style," *Warburg Journal*, IV, 1940–41, pp. 85–102.

Pächt, O., "Early Italian Nature Studies and the Early Calendar Landscape," *Warburg Journal*, XIII, 1950, pp. 13–47.

Pächt, O., "Panofsky's 'Early Netherlandish Painting'—I," *Burl. Mag.*, XCVIII, 1956, pp. 110–116.

Pächt, O., "A Forgotten Manuscript from the Library of the Duc de Berry," *Burl. Mag.*, XCVIII, 1956, pp. 146–153.

Pächt, O., "René d'Anjou et les Van Eyck," *Cahiers de l'association internationale des études françaises*, VIII, 1956, pp. 41–67.

Pächt, O., "Un tableau de Jacquemart de Hesdin?," *Rev. des arts*, VI, 1956, pp. 149–160.

Pächt, O., "The 'Avignon Diptych' and Its Eastern Ancestry," in *De Artibus Opuscula XL: Essays in Honor of Erwin Panofsky*, New York, 1961, I, pp. 402–421.

Pächt, O., "Die Gotik der Zeit um 1400 als Gesamteuropäische Kunstsprache," in Vienna. Kunsthistorisches Museum. *Europäische Kunst um 1400*, Vienna, 1962, pp. 52–65.

Pächt, O., "Zur Entstehung des 'Hieronymus im Gehäus,' " *Pantheon*, XXI, 1963, pp. 131–142.

Pächt, O., "The Limbourgs and Pisanello," *Gaz. B.-A.*, LXII, 1963, pp. 109–122.

Panofsky, E., *Studies in Iconology*, New York, 1939.

Panofsky, E., *Albrecht Dürer*, Princeton, 1943. 2v.

Panofsky, E., *Early Netherlandish Painting: Its Origins and Character*, Cambridge, Mass., 1953. 2v.

Panofsky, E., *Renaissance and Renascences in Western Art*, Stockholm, 1960.

Panofsky, E., *Problems in Titian, Mostly Iconographic*, New York, 1969.

Panofsky, E., "Imago pietatis," in *Festschrift für Max J. Friedländer zum 60. Geburtstage*, Leipzig, 1927, pp. 261–308.

Panofsky, E., and F. Saxl, "Classical Mythology in Mediaeval Art," *Metropolitan Museum Studies*, IV, 1933, pp. 228–280.

Panofsky, E., "Reintegration of a Book of Hours Executed in the Workshop of the 'Maître des Grandes Heures de Rohan,' " in *Medieval Studies in Memory of A. Kingsley Porter*, Cambridge, 1939, II, pp. 479–499. 2v.

Panofsky, E., "The de Buz Book of Hours," *Harvard Lib. Bull.*, III, 1949, pp. 163–182.

Panofsky, E., "A Parisian Goldsmith's Model of the Early Fifteenth Century?" in *Beiträge für Georg Swarzenski*, Berlin, 1951, pp. 70–84.

Panofsky, E., *see also* Klibansky, Panofsky, and Saxl.

Papertiant, G., "Les Très Riches Heures du duc de Berry," *Revue des arts*, II, 1952, p. 52.

Paris, P., *Les manuscrits françois de la bibliothèque du roi . . .*, Paris, 1836–1846. 7v.

Paris. Pierre Berès. *Manuscrits et livres du quatorzième au seizième siècle. Catalogue 60*, Paris, n.d.

Paris. Bibliothèque de l'Arsenal. Martin, H. M. R., *Catalogue des manuscrits de la Bibliothèque de l'Arsenal*, Paris 1885–1899. 9v.

Paris. Bibliothèque de l'Arsenal. *Les principaux manuscrits à peintures de la Bibliothèque de l'Arsenal à Paris; ouvrage posthume de H. Martin, terminé par Ph. Lauer, SFRMP*, Paris, 1929.

Paris, Bibliothèque de la Chambre des Députés. Coyecque, E., and H. Debraye, *Catalogue général des manuscrits des bibliothèques publiques de France*, Paris, 1907.

Paris. Bibliothèque de la Chambre des Députés. Boinet, A., "Les principaux manuscrits à peintures de la Bibliothèque de la Chambre des Députés à Paris," *Bull. SFRMP*, VI, 1922, pp. 31–61.

Paris. Bibliothèque de l'Institut. Bouteron, M., and J. Tremblot, *Catalogue général des manuscrits des bibliothèques publiques de France*, Paris, 1928.

Paris. Bibliothèque Mazarine. Molinier, A., *Catalogue des manuscrits de la Bibliothèque Mazarine*, Paris, 1885–1892. 4v.

Paris. Bibliothèque nationale. *Antiquités et Guerre des Juifs de Josèphe; reproduction des 25 miniatures des manuscrits français 247 et nouv. acq. 21013 de la Bibliothèque nationale* (H. A. Omont), Paris [1906].

Paris. Bibliothèque nationale. *Livre de la chasse par Gaston Phébus; reproduction réduite des 87 miniatures du manuscrit fr. 616* (C. Couderc), Paris [1909].

Paris. Bibliothèque nationale. *Catalogue de l'exposition du moyen âge: manuscrits, estampes, médailles et objets d'art, imprimés . . .*, Paris, 1926.

Paris. Bibliothèque nationale. *Les enluminures des manuscrits du moyen âge (du VIe au XVe siècle) de la Bibliothèque nationale* (C. Couderc), Paris, 1927.

Paris. Bibliothèque nationale. *Les joyaux de l'enluminure à la Bibliothèque nationale* (H. M. R. Martin), Paris and Brussels, 1928.

Paris. Bibliothèque nationale. *Les plus beaux manuscrits français du VIIIe au XVIe siècle conservés dans les bibliothèques de Paris*, Paris, 1937.

Paris. Bibliothèque nationale. *Les manuscrits à peintures en France du VIIe au XIIe siècle*, Paris, 1954.

Paris. Bibliothèque nationale. *Les manuscrits à peintures en France du XIIIe au XVIe siècle* (J. Porcher), Paris, 1955.

Paris. Bibliothèque nationale. Exhibition of mss., 1955, *see* Meiss, 1956; Nordenfalk, 1956; Wormald, 1956.

Paris. Bibliothèque nationale. Porcher, J., *Manuscrits à peintures offerts à la Bibliothèque nationale par le comte Guy du Boisrouvray*, Paris, 1961.

Paris. Bibliothèque nationale. *La librairie de Charles V* (F. Avril and J. Lafaurie), Paris, 1968.

Paris. Bibliothèque nationale. *Le livre*, Paris. 1972.

Paris. Bibliothèque nationale. *Notitia dignitatum imperii romani* (ms. lat. 9661), ed. H. A. Omont, Paris, n.d.

Paris, Bibliothèque nationale, *see also* Leroquais.

Paris, Bibliothèque nationale, *see also* Paris, Musée du Louvre.

Paris. Ecole des Beaux-Arts. Bengy-Puyvallée, M. de, *Catalogue des manuscrits de la Bibliothèque de l'Ecole des Beaux-Arts*, Paris, 1908.

Paris. Musée du Louvre. *Exposition des primitifs français au palais du Louvre . . . et à la Bibliothèque nationale*, Paris, 1904.

Paris. Musée du Louvre and Bibliothèque nationale. Bouchot, H., *L'exposition des primitifs français; la peinture en France sous les Valois*, 2nd ed., Paris, 1905.

Paris. Musée du Louvre. *Peintures, école française, XIVe, XVe, et XVIe siècles* (C. Sterling and H. Adhémar), Paris, 1965.

Paris. Palais Galliera. *Manuscrits à peintures XIII, XIV, XV, XVI siècles*, June 24, 1968.

Parkhurst, C. P., "The Madonna of the Writing Christ Child," *Art Bull.*, XXIII, 1941, pp. 292–306.

Patch, H. R., *The Goddess Fortuna in Medieval Literature*, Cambridge, Mass., 1927.

Peignot, G., *Catalogue d'une partie des livres composant la bibliothèque des ducs de Bourgogne au XVe siècle*, 2nd ed., Dijon, 1841.

Pellegrin, E., "Les manuscrits de Pétrarque dans les bibliothèques de France," *Italia medioevale e umanistica*, VII, 1964, pp. 405–522.

Perdrizet, P., *see* Lutz and Perdrizet.

Perroy, E., *The Hundred Years War*, New York, 1965.

Pešina, J., "Zur Frage der Chronologie des 'Schönen Stils' in der Tafelmalerei Böhmens," *Studia Minora Facultatis Philosophicae Universitatis Brunensis*, XIV–XV, 1971, pp. 167–191.

Petit, E., *Itinéraires de Philippe le Hardi et de Jean sans Peur, ducs de Bourgogne (1363–1419)*, Paris, 1888.

Petrarch, F., *Trionfi*, ed. C. Calcaterra, Turin [1927].

Petrarch, F., *The Triumphs*, tr. E. W. Wilkins, Chicago, 1962.

Philadelphia. Philadelphia Museum of Art. "Catalogue of the Collins Mediaeval Manuscripts," *Philadelphia Museum of Art Bulletin*, LVIII, 1962, pp. 13–34.

Philip, L. B., *The Ghent Altarpiece and the Art of Jan van Eyck*, Princeton, 1971.

Philippe de Mézières, *Le songe du vieil pèlerin*, ed. G. W. Coopland, Cambridge, 1969. 2v.

Phillips, K., "Perseus and Andromeda," *American Journal of Archaeology*, LXXII, 1968, pp. 1–23.

A Picture Book of the Life of Saint Anthony the Abbot, see Graham.

Pinet, M. J., *Christine de Pisan, 1364–1430; étude biographique et littéraire*, Paris, 1927.

Plant, M., *see* Melbourne, National Gallery of Victoria.

Plummer, J., *The Hours of Catherine of Cleves*, New York [n.d.].

Pocquet du Haut-Jussé, B.-A., *La France gouvernée par Jean sans Peur. Les dépenses du receveur général du royaume*, Paris, 1959 (Mémoires et documents publiés par la société de l'École des Chartes, XIII).

Poirion, D., *Le poète et le prince: L'évolution du lyrisme courtois de Guillaume de Machaut à Charles d'Orléans*, Paris, 1965.

Porcher, J., *Les Grandes Heures de Rohan* (Les trésors de la peinture française, I, 7, XVI), Geneva, 1943.

Porcher, J., *Très Riches Heures*, Paris, 1950.

Porcher, J., *Les Belles Heures de Jean de France, duc de Berry*, Paris, 1953.

Porcher, J., *L'enluminure française*, Paris, 1959; *Medieval French Miniatures*, New York (1959).

Porcher, J., *Hours of Rohan*, London, 1959; New York [1959].

Porcher, J., *Jean Lebègue, Les histoires que l'on peut raisonnablement faire sur les livres de Salluste*, Paris, 1962.

Porcher, J., "Two Models for the 'Heures de Rohan,' " *Warburg Journal*, VIII, 1945, pp. 1–6.

Porcher, J., "Les Très Belles Heures de Jean de Berry et les ateliers parisiens," *Scriptorium*, VII, 1953, pp. 121–123.

Porcher, J., "Limbourg," in *Enciclopedia universale dell' arte*, VIII, n.d. (after 1959), p. 619 f.

Porcher, J., "Le portrait de Louis II d'Anjou," *Art de France*, I, 1961, pp. 290–292.

Porcher, J., *see also* Paris, Bibliothèque nationale.

Port, C., *Les artistes peintres angevins*, Paris, 1872.

Port, C., *Les artistes angevins*, Angers, 1881.

Post, C. R., *A History of Spanish Painting*, Cambridge, Mass., 1930–1966. 14v.

Potvin, Ch., see *Œuvres de Ghillebert de Lannoy*.

Poujoulat [J. J. F.], see *Le livre des faicts du bon messire Jean le Maingre, dit Boucicaut.*

Prost, B., *Inventaires mobiliers et extraits des comptes des ducs de Bourgogne de la maison de Valois (1363–1477)*, Paris, 1902–1913. 2v.

Prost, B., "Quelques acquisitions de manuscrits par les ducs de Bourgogne Philippe le Hardi et Jean Sans Peur (1396–1415)," *Archives historiques*, II, 1891, pp. 337–353.

Prudhomme, A., *see* Grenoble, Bibliothèque publique.

Purkis, G. S., "Laurent de Premierfait's Translation of the *Decameron*," *Medium Aevum*, XXIV, 1955, pp. 1–15.

Quaile, E., *Illuminated Manuscripts: their Origin, History and Characteristics . . .*, Liverpool, 1897.

Ragghianti, C. L., *Gli affreschi di casa Minerbi*, n.d. (Associazione fra le Casse di Risparmio Italiane).

Ragusa, I., see *Meditations on the Life of Christ.*

Rains, R. R., "*Les sept psaumes allégorisés*" *of Christine de Pisan*, Washington (D.C.), 1965.

Randall, L. M. C., *Images in the Margins of Gothic Manuscripts*, Berkeley, 1966.

Randall, L. M. C., "The Snail in Gothic Marginal Warfare," *Speculum*, XXXVII, 1962, pp. 358–367.

Rasmo, N., *The Frescoes at the Torre Aquila in Trento*, Rovereto, 1962. German ed.: *Die Fresken im Adlerturm zu Trient*, Rovereto, 1962.

Rasmo, N., "Venceslao da Trento e Venceslao da Merano," *Cultura atesina*, XI, 1957, p. 21 ff.

Raynal, L., *Histoire du Berry depuis les temps les plus anciens jusqu'en 1789*, Bourges, 1844–1847. 4v.

Raynaud de Lage, G., " 'L'histoire ancienne jusqu'à César' et les 'Faits des Romains,' " *Le Moyen Age*, LV, 1949, pp. 5–16.

Raynaud de Lage, G., "Les romans antiques et la représentation de l'antiquité," *Le Moyen Age*, LXVII, 1961, pp. 247–291.

The Recovery of France in the Fifteenth Century, ed. P. S. Lewis, London, 1971.

Reese, G., *Music in the Middle Ages*, New York, 1940.

Reese, G., *Music in the Renaissance*, New York, rev. ed., 1959.

Reinach, S., "Manuscrits à miniatures de Genève," *Rev. archéol.*, X, 1907, pp. 172 f.

Religieux de Saint-Denys, *Chronique contenant le règne de Charles VI, de 1380 à 1422*, tr. L. Bellaguet, Paris, 1839–1852. 6v.

Renan, E., "Discours sur l'état des beaux-arts en France au XIVe siècle," in *Histoire littéraire de la France*, XXIV, 1862, pp. 603–757.

Renouard, Y., *The Avignon Papacy, 1305–1403*, London, 1970 (Paris, 1954).

Revelationes Stae Brigittae olim a Card. Turrecremata recognitae et approbatae et a Consalvo Duranto Episcopo Ferettrano notis illustrate, Rome, 1628.

Reynaud, N., "A propos du martyre de Saint Denis," *Revue du Louvre*, XI, 1961, pp. 175 f.

Reynaud, N., rev. of *Maître Francke et l'art autour de 1400* in *Revue de l'art*, IX, 1970, pp. 89–91.

Ricci, S. de, ed., *Census of Medieval and Renaissance Manuscripts in the United States and Canada*, New York, 1935–1940. 3v. *Supplement*, 1962.

Richardson, L. M., *The Forerunners of Feminism in French Literature of the Renaissance from Christine of Pisa to Marie de Gournay*, Baltimore, 1929.

Richmond, M., *see* Williamstown, Mass.

Richter, G. M., "Pisanello Studies," *Burl. Mag.*, LV, 1929, pp. 58 ff., 128 ff.

Ring, G., *A Century of French Painting*, 1400–1500, London [1949].

Ritter, R., *Châteaux, donjons et places fortes*, Paris, 1953.

Robuchon, J., ed., *Paysages et monuments du Poitou photographiés par Jules Robuchon*, Paris, I and II, 1890.

Röhricht, R., see *Deutsche Pilgerreisen nach dem Heiligen Land.*

Röhricht, R., *see also* Jacobus de Verona.

Roma nei suoi rioni, ed. G. Bottai, Rome, 1936.

Roman d'Amat, "Gontier Col" in *Dictionnaire de biographie française*, Paris, 1960, *s.v.*

Le Roman de la Rose by Guillaume de Lorris and Jean de Meung, ed. E. Langlois (Société des anciens textes français), Paris, 1914–1924. 5v.

Rome. Palazzo Venezia. *Mostra storica nazionale della miniatura. Catalogo*, Florence [1953].

Römer, E., "Dürers ledige Wanderjahre," *Jahrbuch der preussischen Kunstsammlungen*, XLVII, 1926, p. 118 ff.; XLVIII, 1927, pp. 77 ff., 156 ff.

Rondot, N., "Les enlumineurs de Troyes aux XIVe, XVe et XVIe siècles," *Nouvelles archives de l'art français*, 1882, pp. 42–52.

Rondot, N., "Les peintres de Troyes du XIIIe au XVe siècle," *Nouvelles archives de l'art français*, 1887, pp. 97–114.

Roover, R. de, "La communauté des marchands lucquois à Bruges de 1377 à 1404," *Annales de la Société d'Emulation de Bruges* (*Bijdragen van het genootschap. Société d'Emulation te Brugge*), LXXXVI, 1948, pp. 25–89.

Roques, M., *Les peintures murales de sud-est de la France, XIIIe au XVIe siècle*, Paris, 1961.

Rorimer, J. J., and M. B. Freeman, "The Nine Heroes Tapestries at the Cloisters," *Bull. Metropolitan Museum*, VII, 1949, pp. 243–260.

Rorimer, J. J., *see also* New York, Metropolitan Museum, The Cloisters.

Roscher, W., *Ausführliches Lexikon der griechischen und römischen Mythologie*, Leipzig [1884–1937]. 6v.

Rose, V., *see* Berlin, Staatsbibliothek.

Rosenberg, (C.) A., *Der Erynien*, Berlin 1874.

Ross, D. J. A., "Some Geographical and Topographical Miniatures in a Fragmentary *Trésor des Histoires*," *Scriptorium*, XXIII, 1969, pp. 177–186.

Rosset, A., "Le manuel d'histoire de Philippe VI de Valois et ses enluminures," *Les arts anciens de Flandre*, VI, 1913, pp. 123–126.

Rossi, V., *Il Quattrocento* (Storia letteraria d'Italia), Milan, 1938.

Rothe, E., *Mediaeval Book Illumination in Europe*, London, 1968.

Rowley, G., *Ambrogio Lorenzetti*, Princeton, 1958. 2v.

Roy, M., *see* Christine de Pisan.

Rubinstein, N., "Political Ideas in Sienese Art: the Frescoes by Ambrogio Lorenzetti and Taddeo di Bartolo in the Palazzo Pubblico," *Warburg Journal*, XXI, 1958, pp. 179–207.

Sabbadini, R., *Le scoperte dei codici latini e greci ne' secoli XIV e XV* (Bibl. storica del Rinascimento, V), Florence, 1914.

Sachs, A., *see* Barasch.

Saint-Hilaire, Q. de, *see* Deschamps, E.

Le saint voyage de Jherusalem, see *Ogier d'Anglure*.

Salet, F., "La 'Croix du Serment' de l'Ordre de la Toison d'Or," *Comptes rendus*, 1965, p. 116 f.

Salmi, M., *La miniatura italiana*, Milan [1955].

Samaran, C., *La maison d'Armagnac au XVe siècle et les dernières luttes de la féodalité dans le midi de la France*, Paris, 1907.

Samaran, C., *Pierre Bersuire* in *Histoire littéraire de la France*, Paris, XXXIX, 1962, pp. 259–450.

Samek, L. S., *Alfabeto di Giovannino de Grassi*, Modena, 1958.

Santoro, C., *see* Milan, Biblioteca Trivulziana.

Sauerländer, W., *Gotische Skulptur in Frankreich, 1140–1270*, Munich, 1970.

Saxl, F., and H. Meier, *Verzeichnis astrologischer und mythologischer illustrierter Handschriften des lateinischen Mittelalters*. Vol. III: *Handschriften in englischen Bibliotheken* (ed. H. Bober), London, 1953. (The book has an English title page also.)

Saxl, F., *Lectures*, London, 1957. 2v.

Saxl, F., *see also* Klibansky, Panofsky, and Saxl.

Saxl, F., *see also* Panofsky and Saxl.

Scaglia, G., "The Origin of an Archaeological Plan of Rome by Alessandro Strozzi," *Warburg Journal*, XXVII, 1964, pp. 137–163.

Schaefer, C., *see* Sterling and Schaefer.

Schaefer, L., "Die Illustrationen zu den Handschriften der Christine de Pizan," *Marburger Jahrb.*, X, 1937, pp. 119–208.

Schendel, A. van, *Le dessin en Lombardie jusqu'à la fin du XVe siècle*, Brussels, 1938.

Schilling, R., "A Book of Hours from the Limbourg Atelier," *Burl. Mag.*, LXXX–LXXXI, 1942, pp. 194–197.

Schilling, R., "An Unknown French Book of Hours (c.1400)," *Burl. Mag.*, LXXXIV–LXXXV, 1944, pp. 20–24.

Schilling, R., "The Nativity and Adoration of the Child Christ in French Miniatures of the Early Fifteenth Century," *Connoisseur*, CXXX, 1952, pp. 167–169, 221.

Schilling, R., "The Master of Egerton 1070 (Hours of René d'Anjou)," *Scriptorium*, VIII, 1954, pp. 272–282.

Schilling, R., *see also* Swarzenski and Schilling.

Schlosser, J. von, "Die ältesten Medaillen und die Antike," *Jahrb. Kunsth. Slgn.*, XVIII, 1897, pp. 64–108.

Schlosser, J. von, "Die Werkstatt der Embriachi in Venedig," *Jahrb. Kunsth. Slgn.*, XX, 1899, pp. 220–282.

Schmidt, G., "Buchmalerei," in *Katalog der Ausstellung Gotik in Österreich*, Krems a.d. Donau, 1967.

Schmidt, L., *see* Dresden, Sächsische Landesbibliothek.

Schmitt, A., *see* Degenhart and Schmitt.

Schrader, J. L., *see* Kansas, The University of Kansas Museum of Art.

Schubring, P., *Cassoni; Truhen und Truhenbilder der italienischen Frührenaissance. Ein Beitrag zur Profanmalerei im Quattrocento*, Leipzig, 1915. Supplement 1923.

Schulte-Nordholt, H., "Die geistesgeschichtliche Situation der Zeit um 1400," in Vienna. Kunsthistorisches Museum. *Europäische Kunst um 1400*, Vienna, 1962, pp. 27–51.

Schulz, J., "The Printed Plans and Panoramic Views of Venice," in *Saggi e memorie di storia dell'arte*, VII, 1970 (1972), pp. 7–108.

Schwager, K., "Über Jean Fouquet in Italien und sein verlorenes Porträt Papst Eugens IV," in *Argo, Festschrift für Kurt Badt*, Cologne, 1970, pp. 206–234.

Schwarz, H., "The Mirror in Art," *Art Quarterly*, XV, 1952, p. 96.

Scott, C., *The French Cité de Dieu in the Philadelphia Museum of Art* (M.A. thesis, 1967). The University of Pennsylvania.

Seznec, J., *The Survival of the Pagan Gods*, New York, 1953 (*La survivance des dieux antiques*, London, 1940).

Sherman, C. R., *The Portraits of Charles V of France (1338–1380)*, New York, 1969.

Simone, F., *La coscienza della rinascità negli umanisti francesi*, Rome, 1949.

Simone, F., *Il rinascimento francese*, Turin, 1961. English ed.: *The French Renaissance: Medieval Tradition and Italian Influence in Shaping the Renaissance in France* (abridged, ed. and tr. H. Gaston Hall), London, 1969.

Simson, O. von, "Meister Francke und Jacquemart de Hesdin," *Jahrbuch der Hamburger Kunstsammlungen*, XIV–XV, 1970, pp. 79–82.

Sinclair, K. V., *Descriptive Catalogue of Medieval and Renaissance Western Manuscripts in Australia*, Sydney, 1969.

Sinclair, K. V., "The Miniaturists of the Livy Manuscript in the National Gallery Collection," *Annual Bulletin of the National Gallery of Victoria*, I, 1959.

Sindona, E., *Pisanello*, New York [1961].

Singleton, C., with P. Brieger and M. Meiss, *Illuminated Manuscripts of the Divine Comedy*, New York, 1969. 2v.

Smital, O., *see* Vienna, Nationalbibliothek.

Smith (Off), S., *see* Meiss, 1971, 1972.

Soissons. Bibliothèque municipale (A. Molinier). *Catalogue général des manuscrits des bibliothèques publiques de France*, Paris, III, 1885.

Solente, S., rev. of Pinet, *Christine de Pisan, 1364–1430; étude biographique et littéraire*, Paris, 1927, in *Rev. belge*, VIII, 1929, pp. 350–359.

Solente, S., "Christine de Pisan," in *Histoire littéraire de la France*, Paris, XL, 1969, pp. 1–88.

Solente, S., *see also* Christine de Pisan.

Le songe véritable; pamphlet politique d'un parisien du XVe siècle, ed. H. Moranvillé [Mémoires de la Société de l'Histoire de Paris et de l'Ile-de-France, XVII (1890)], Paris, 1891.

Speculum humanae salvationis, see Lutz and Perdrizet.

Spencer, E. P., "L'horloge de Sapience," *Scriptorium*, XVII, 1963, pp. 277–299.

Spencer, E. P., "The Master of the Duke of Bedford: The Bedford Hours," *Burl. Mag.*, CVII, 1965, pp. 495–502.

Spencer, E. P., "The Master of the Duke of Bedford: The Salisbury Breviary," *Burl. Mag.*, CVIII, 1966, pp. 607–612.

Spencer, E. P., "The First Patron of the *Très Belles Heures de Notre-Dame*," *Scriptorium*, XXIII, 1969, pp. 145–149.

Stange, A., *Deutsche Kunst um 1400*, Munich, 1923.

Statius, tr. J. Mozley (*Loeb Classical Library*), London, 1928. 2v.

Stechow, W., *Apollo und Daphne*, Leipzig, 1932.

Stefano, G. di, "Ricerche sulla cultura avignonese del secolo XIV," *Studi francesi*, VII, 1963, pp. 1–16.

Stefano, G. di, "Tradizione esegetica e traduzioni di Valerio Massimo nel primo Umanesimo Francese," *Studi francesi*, VII, 1963, pp. 401–417.

Stefano, G. di, "Ricerche su Nicolas de Gonesse traduttore di Valerio Massimo," *Studi francesi*, IX, 1965, pp. 201–221.

Stefano, G. di, "L'opera oratoria di Jean Courtecuisse e la letteratura parenetica del secolo XV," in *Miscellanea di studi e ricerche sul Quattrocento francese*, Turin, 1967, pp. 93–164.

Steingräber, E., "Nachträge und Marginalien zur französisch-niederländischen Goldschmiedekunst des frühen 15. Jahrhunderts, *Anzeiger des Germanischen Nationalmuseums*, 1969, pp. 29–39.

Stejskal, K., "Výstava 'La Librairie de Charles V' A Některé Otázky Českého Umění XIV. Století," *Umění*, XVIII, 1970, pp. 31–60.

Stejskal, K., *see also* Dvořáková, Krása, Merhantová, and Stejskal.

[Sterling, C.], *La peinture française: les peintres du moyen âge*, par Charles Jacques [pseud.], Paris [1941].

Tuetey, A., *Journal de Nicolas de Baye, Greffier du Parlement de Paris 1400–1417*, Paris, I, 1885.

Turner, D. H., *see* London, British Museum.

Tuve, R., *Allegorical Imagery, Some Medieval Books and their Posterity*, Princeton, 1966.

Tuve, R., "Notes on the Virtues and Vices," *Warburg Journal*, XXVI, 1963, pp. 264–303.

Uffiziolo di Valentina Visconti, ed. by L. Cortesi, G. Mandel, R. Pesenti (Monumenta Bergomensia, XV), Bergamo, 1965.

Ullman, B., *Studies in the Italian Renaissance*, Rome, 1955.

Unterkircher, F., *A Treasury of Illuminated Manuscripts; a Selection of Miniatures from Manuscripts in the Austrian National Library*, New York, 1967.

Unterkircher, F., "Die Buchmalerei in der europäischen Kunst um 1400," in *Philobiblon*, December, 1962.

Unterkircher, F., see also *Tacuinum sanitatis in medicina.*

Unterkircher, F., *see also* Vienna, Nationalbibliothek.

Vaesen, J., *see* Lyon, Bibliothèque.

Valenciennes. *Catalogues des expositions organisées par la ville de Valenciennes en l'honneur de Jehan Froissart, 1937, Manuscrits à peintures des Chroniques de Froissart*, Valenciennes (1937).

Vallery-Radot, J., "L'abbatiale du Mont St-Michel," *Bulletin de la Société Nationale des Antiquaires de France*, 1965, pp. 70–77.

Vallet de Viriville, M., *Histoire de Charles VII*, Paris, 1862–1865. 3v.

Vallet de Viriville, M., "Notice de quelques manuscrits précieux," *Gaz. B.-A.*, XXI, 1866, pp. 275–285.

Valois, N., *La France et le grand schisme d'occident*, Paris, 1896–1902. 4v.

Vasari, G., *Le vite de' più eccellenti pittori, scultori, et architettori*, ed. G. Milanesi, Florence, 1906. 9v.

Vegas, L. C., "A new French Madonna dating from about 1400," *Burl. Mag.*, CXIV, 1972, pp. 396–399.

Venturi, A., *L'arte a San Girolamo*, Milan, 1924.

Verdier, P., "A Medallion of the *Ara Coeli* and the Netherlandish Enamels of the Fifteenth Century," *Walters Art Journal*, XXIV, 1961, pp. 9–37.

Vie de nostre benoit sauveur Jesus Christ, Lyon, Guillaume Leroy before 1480.

Vie des saints et des bienheureux selon l'ordre du calendrier avec l'historique des fêtes, see Bénédictins de Paris.

Vienna. Kunsthistorisches Museum. *Europäische Kunst um 1400*, Vienna, 1962. *See* O. Pächt, H. Schulte-Nordholt, C. Sterling.

Vienna. Nationalbibliothek. Beer, R., "Les principaux manuscrits à peintures de la Bibliothèque impériale de Vienne," *Bull. SFRMP*, II, 1912, pp. 5–53; III, 1913, pp. 5–55.

Vienna. Nationalbibliothek. *Livre du cuer d'amours espris*, ed. O. Smital and E. Winkler, Vienna, 1926. 3v.

Vienna. Nationalbibliothek. *Beschreibendes Verzeichnis der illuminierten Handschriften in Österreich.* N.F. VII, pt. VII, 2: *Die westeuropäischen Handschriften und Inkunabeln der Gotik und der Renaissance. Englische und französische Handschriften des XIV. Jahrhunderts*, ed. H. J. Hermann, Leipzig, 1936. N.F. VII, pt. VII, 3: *Französische und iberische Handschriften der ersten Hälfte des XV. Jahrhunderts*, ed. H. J. Hermann, Leipzig, 1938.

Vienna. Nationalbibliothek. Trenkler, E., "Les principaux manuscrits à peintures de la Bibliothèque nationale de Vienne. Manuscrits français," *Bull SFRMP*, 1938.

Vienna. Nationalbibliothek. Trenkler, E., "Meisterwerke der französischen Buchmalerei in der Oesterreichischen Nationalbibliothek," *Nationalmusei Årsbok*, 1947–1948, pp. 7–38.

Vienna. Nationalbibliothek. *Inventar der illuminierten Handschriften, Inkunabeln und Frühdrucke der Österreichischen Nationalbibliothek*: I. *Die abendländischen Handschriften* (F. Unterkircher), Vienna, 1957.

Voyage au purgatoire de Saint Patrice, ed. A. Jeanroy and A. Vignaux, Toulouse, 1903.

Vries, S. de, see *Bréviaire Grimani de la Bibliothèque de S. Marco à Venise.*

Waagen, G. F., *Galleries and Cabinets of Art in Great Britain*, London, 1857.

Waagen, G. F., "On the importance of manuscripts with miniatures in the history of art," Philobiblon Society, *Bibliographical and Historical Miscellanies*, I, 1854, no. 13, pp. 1–11.

Waddesdon Manor. Delaissé, L. M. J., and J. Marrow, *The James A. de Rothschild Collection at Waddesdon Manor*, Freibourg, in the press.

Ward, C. F., *The Epistles on the Romance of the Rose and Other Documents in the Debate*, Chicago, 1911.

Warner, G. F., *Queen Mary's Psalter*, London, 1912.

Warner, G. F., *Descriptive Catalogue of Illuminated Manuscripts in the Library of C. W. Dyson Perrins*, Oxford, 1920. 2v.

Warner, G. F., *see also* London, British Museum.

Warsaw. Biblioteka Narodowa. Sawicka, S., "Les principaux manuscrits à peintures de la Bibliothèque nationale de Varsovie, du château royal et des bibliothèques: des Zamoyskie à Varsovie, du séminaire de

Sterling, C., *Still Life Painting*, Paris, 1959.

Sterling, C., and C. Schaefer, *The Hours of Etienne Chevalier, Jean Fouquet*, New York, 1971.

Sterling, C., "Oeuvres retrouvées de Jean de Beaumetz, peintre de Philippe le Hardi," *Bulletin, Musées Royaux des Beaux-Arts*, IV, 1955, pp. 57–81.

Sterling, C., "La peinture de portrait à la cour de Bourgogne au début du XVe siècle," *Critica d'arte*, VI, 1959, pp. 289–312.

Sterling, C., "Die Malerei in Europa um 1400," in Vienna. Kunsthistorisches Museum. *Europäische Kunst um 1400*, Vienna, 1962, pp. 66–78.

Sterling, C., "Etudes savoyardes I: au temps du duc Amédée," *L'Oeil*, CLXXVIII, 1969, pp. 2–13.

Sterling, C., "Etudes savoyardes I, supplément," *L'Oeil*, CXCV–CXCVI, 1971, pp. 14–19, 36.

Sterling, C., "Observations on Petrus Christus," *Art Bull.*, LIII, 1971, pp. 1–26.

Sterling, C., "Observations on Moser's Tiefenbronn Altarpiece," *Pantheon*, XXX, 1972, pp. 19–32.

Sterling, C., *see also* Białostocki et al., *Spätmittelalter und Beginnende Neuzeit.*

Sterling, C., *see also* Paris, Musée du Louvre.

Stevenson, E., "Di una pianta di Roma dipinta da Taddeo di Bartolo nella cappella interna del palazzo del Comune di Siena (a. 1413–1414)," *Bullettino della Commissione archeologica comunale di Roma*, IX, 1881, pp. 74–105.

Stewart, A., see *Ludolph von Suchem's Description of the Holy Land. . . .*

Stone, L. W., "Old French Translations of the *De consolatione philosophiae* of Boethius," *Medium Aevum*, VI, 1937, pp. 21–30.

Straeten, J. van der, "Manuscrits hagiographiques de Bourges," *Analecta Bollandiana*, LXXXV, 1967, pp. 75–112.

Suso, H., *see* Heinrich Seuse.

Swarzenski, G., and R. Schilling, *Die illuminierten Handschriften und Einzelminiaturen des Mittelalters und der Renaissance in Frankfurter Besitz*, Frankfurt-am-Main, 1929. 2v.

Swarzenski, G., "Miniatures from a Lost Manuscript," *Bull. Mus. Boston*, XLII, 1944, pp. 28–33; figs. 1, 2, 4, 5.

Swarzenski, G., "A German Primitive," *Bull. Mus. Boston*, XLII, 1944, pp. 41–50.

Swoboda, K. M., see *Gotik in Böhmen.*

Tacuinum sanitatis in medicina (Vienna 2644), ed. F. Unterkircher, Graz, 1967. 2v.

Terence, tr. J. Sargeant (*Loeb Classical Library*)
I, 1953; II, 1947. 2v.

Thiébaux, M., "The Medieval Chase," *Spec*
1967, pp. 260–274.

Thomas, M., *The Grandes Heures of Jean, Duk*
New York, 1971.

Thomas, M., "Une prétendue signature de pe
un manuscrit du début du XVe siècle," *Bu*
Société Nationale des Antiquaires de France, 195

Thomas, M., *see also* Meiss and Thomas.

Thompson, E. M., "A Contemporary Acco
Fall of Richard the Second," *Burl. Mag.*, V,
160–172, 267–270.

Thompson, H. Y., *see* London, Thompson
(formerly).

Thorndike, L., "Notes on some Astronomic
logical and Mathematical Manuscripts of t
thèque nationale, Paris," *Warburg Journal*,
pp. 112–172.

Tintori, L., and M. Meiss, *The Painting of the*
Francis in Assisi, New York, 1962; 1967.

Toesca, P., *La pittura e la miniatura nella Lombar*
antichi monumenti alla metà del Quattrocent
1912.

Toesca, P., "Manoscritti miniati della Bibli
Principe Corsini a Firenze," *Rassegna d'A*
1917, pp. 117–128.

Tolnay, C. de, "Zur Herkunft des Stiles der Va
Münchner Jahrbuch der Bildenolen Kunst, IX,
320–338.

Tolnay, C. de, "Les origines de la Nature
Revue des arts, 1952, p. 151 f.

Toynbee, M. R., "The Portraiture of Isabel
Duchess of Brittany," *Burl. Mag.*, LXXXVIII,
300–306.

Tremblot, J., *see* Paris, Bibliothèque de l'Instit

Trenkler, E., *Livre d'heures: Handschrift 1855*
reichischen Nationalbibliothek, Vienna [1948].

Trenkler, E., "Les principaux manuscrits à pei
la Bibliothèque nationale de Vienne," *Bull.*
Paris, 1938, pp. 5–55.

Trenkler, E., *see also* Vienna, Nationalbiblioth

The Très Riches Heures of Jean, Duke of Berry, N
(and other eds.). See Longnon or Meiss.

Troescher, G., *Burgundische Malerei Maler und*
um 1400 in Burgund, dem Berry mit der Auverg
Savoyen mit ihren Quellen und Ausstrahlunger
1966, 2v.

Płock et du chapitre de Gniezno," *Bull. SFRMP*, XIX, 1938.

Webb, J., "Translation of a French Metrical History of the Deposition of King Richard the Second," *Archaeologia*, XX, 1824, pp. 1–423.

Weiss, R., "The Medieval Medallions of Constantine and Heraclius," *Numismatic Chronicle*, III, 1963, pp. 129–144.

Weitzmann, K., *Ancient Book Illumination*, Cambridge, Mass., 1959.

Werth, H., *Altfranzösische Jagdlehrbücher*, Halle, 1889.

Wescher, P., *Jean Fouquet und seine Zeit*, Basel, 1945.

Wescher, P., "Two Burgundian Drawings of the Fifteenth Century," *Old Master Drawings*, XII, 1937, p. 16 f.

Wescher, P., "Eine Modellzeichnung des Paul von Limburg," *Phoebus*, I, 1946, p. 33 f.

Wescher, P., *see also* Berlin, Staatliche Museen, Kupferstichkabinett.

White, J., *The Birth and Rebirth of Pictorial Space*, London, 1957.

White, L., Jr., *Medieval Technology and Social Change*, Oxford, 1962.

White, L., Jr., "The Iconography of *Temperantia* and the Virtuousness of Technology," in *Action and Conviction in Early Modern Europe*, ed. T. K. Rabb and J. E. Seigel, Princeton, 1969, pp. 197–219.

Wickhoff, F., *see* Vienna, Nationalbibliothek.

Wijk, W. E. van, *Le nombre d'or*, The Hague, 1936.

Wilhelm, P., *Das Jagdbuch des Gaston Phoebus*, Hamburg [1965].

Willard, C. C., "Christine de Pisan's 'Clock of Temperance,' " *L'esprit créateur*, II, 1962, pp. 149–156.

Willard, C. C., "An Autograph Manuscript of Christine de Pizan?," *Studi francesi*, IX, 1965, pp. 452–457.

Willard, C. C., "The Manuscript Tradition of the *Livre des trois vertus* and Christine de Pizan's Audience," *Journal of the History of Ideas*, XXVII, 1966, pp. 433–444.

Williamstown, Mass. Williams College, Chapin Library. *Terence Illustrated. An Exhibition in Honor of Karl Ephraim Weston*, ed. M. Richmond, Williamstown, Mass., 1955.

Winkler, E., *see also* Vienna, Nationalbibliothek.

Winkler, F., *Die flämische Buchmalerei des XV. und XVI. Jahrhunderts*, Leipzig, 1925.

Winkler, F., "Ein neues Werk aus der Werkstatt Pauls von Limburg," *Repertorium für Kunstwissenschaft*, XXXIV, 1911, pp. 536–543.

Winkler, F., "Zur Pariser Miniaturmalerei im dritten und vierten Jahrzehnt des 15. Jahrhunderts," *Beiträge zur Forschung*, pts. IV–V, 1914, pp. 114–120.

Winkler, F., "Limbourgs," in Thieme-Becker, XXIII, 1929, pp. 227–229.

Winkler, F., "Paul de Limbourg in Florence," *Burl. Mag.*, LVI, 1930, pp. 95 f.

Winkler, F., rev. of Erwin Panofsky, "Early Netherlandish Painting; its Origins and Character," Cambridge, Mass., 1953, *Kunstchronik*, VIII, 1955, pp. 9–26.

Winkler, F., "Ein frühfranzösisches Marienbild," *Jahrb. Berliner Museen*, I, 1959, pp. 179–189.

Wixom, W. D., "A Missal for a King," *Bull. Cleveland Museum of Art*, L, 1963, pp. 158–173, 186 f.

Wixom, W. D., "The Hours of Charles the Noble," *Bull. Cleveland Museum of Art*, LII, 1965, pp. 50–81.

Wixom, W. D., "An Enthroned Madonna with the Writing Christ Child," *Bull. Cleveland Museum of Art*, LVII, 1970, pp. 287–302.

Wixom, W. D., *see also* Cleveland, Museum of Art.

Woledge, B., see *French Verse, Penguin Book.*

Wolfenbüttel, Herzog-August-Bibliothek. *Die Handschriften der Herzoglichen Bibliothek zu Wolfenbüttel* (O. von Heinemann), Wolfenbüttel, 1884–1913. 10v.

Woodward, J., *Perseus, a Study in Greek Art and Legend*, Cambridge, 1937.

Wormald, F., "The Wilton Diptych," *Warburg Journal*, XVII, 1954, pp. 191–203.

Wormald, F., "French Illuminated Manuscripts in Paris," *Burl. Mag.*, XCVIII, 1956, pp. 330 f., 333.

Wormald, F., *see also* Cambridge, Fitzwilliam Museum.

Wylie, J. H., *The Reign of Henry the Fifth*, Cambridge, 1914–1919. 3v.

Yates Thompson, H., *see* Thompson, H. Y.

Young, C., *The Drama of the Medieval Church*, Oxford, 1962. 2v.

Zerner, H., *see* Klein and Zerner.

INDEX

References to reproductions are indexed topographically.